THE ORIGINS OF THE WORLD WAR

THE MACMILLAN COMPANY
NEW YORK · BOSTON · CHICAGO · DALLAS
ATLANTA · SAN FRANCISCO

MACMILLAN & CO., LIMITED
LONDON · BOMBAY · CALCUTTA
MELBOURNE

THE MACMILLAN COMPANY
OF CANADA, LIMITED
TORONTO

SIR EDWARD GREY

THE ORIGINS OF THE WORLD WAR

BY

SIDNEY BRADSHAW FAY

PROFESSOR OF HISTORY IN HARVARD UNIVERSITY

Second Edition, Revised
Two Volumes in One

Illustrated

New York
THE MACMILLAN COMPANY
1938

Set up and electrotyped. Published October, 1928. Reissued January, 1929; February, 1929; June, 1929; February, 1930. Second Edition, Revised. Two Volumes in One, October, 1930.
Reprinted July 1931.
Reprinted May 1932.
Reprinted September 1935.
Reprinted October 1936.
Reprinted February 1938.

Printed in the United States of America by
J. J. LITTLE AND IVES COMPANY, NEW YORK

PREFACE TO THE SECOND EDITION REVISED

SINCE the publication of the first edition nearly two years ago, the stream of new documentary material on the origins of the war has continued to flow very freely. Dr. G. P. Gooch and Professor H. W. Temperley have pushed forward with energy their admirable collection of *British Documents,* so that the sixth volume carries the story of Anglo-German relations through the failure of the Haldane Mission in 1912. Austrian scholars took everyone by surprise last Christmas by presenting the world with eight closely packed volumes on *Oesterreich-Ungarns Aussenpolitik,* containing nearly 12,000 documents from their archives covering the years 1908 to 1914. This collection runs parallel to the German *Die Grosse Politik,* and is of especial value for the additional light that it throws on Balkan problems in general and on Austro-Serbian relations in particular. The French Government has published three initial volumes of *Documents Diplomatiques Français,* a monumental series which will eventually illuminate French foreign policy from 1871 to 1914 in the same detail as has been done for German policy in the same period by *Die Grosse Politik.*

In addition to these official publications there have also appeared many valuable private publications containing important new documents or based on unpublished first-hand material. Dr. Bogitchevitch's unofficial collection, *Die Auswärtige Politik Serbiens 1903-1914,* partly compensates for the Serbian Government's persistent failure to follow the example of other states in disclosing fully and frankly their secret pre-war archives. Interesting light on leading English personalities and their psychology is contained in charming biographies, like Lord Newton's *Lord Lansdowne,* Mr. Harold Nicolson's *Lord Carnock* (better known as Sir Arthur Nicolson), and in Lord Morley's remarkable *Memorandum on Resignation.* In *La Politique Russe d'avant Guerre* Baron Taube has stated in no uncertain terms what he knew of Izvolski and certain episodes in Russia's pre-war policy. The present writer has also been privileged to read the advance pages of the first volume of Professor B. E. Schmitt's scholarly and detailed forthcoming work, *The Coming of the War, 1914.*

These and many other recent publications of source material, as well as innumerable secondary monographic studies, can usefully be drawn upon to add an infinite amount of new detail to the story of the main outline of the origins of the war which I have tried to give within the compass of two volumes. But I do not find that they so essentially modify the chief thread of my narrative or my general conclusions that it is necessary in a revised edition to recast the whole form of the book. I have therefore mainly confined the revision to rewriting several passages, to calling attention in the footnotes to important new material, and to adding a few supplementary notes at the end of the first volume. This has made possible the retention of the paging of the first edition, which it is hoped will be a convenience to students. Many of these revisions have already been made in the German and French editions.

SIDNEY B. FAY

Harvard University,
June 28, 1930.

PREFACE

When the World War suddenly set Europe aflame and American public opinion, soon under the influence of propaganda and war prejudice, began to denounce Germany and the Kaiser as being guilty of causing it, the present writer refused to join in the chorus. His historical sense told him that in this present case, as in the past, no one country or no one man was solely, or probably even mainly, to blame. A little study of the documents in the Blue, Yellow and Orange Books which were early issued by the English, French and Russian Governments quickly convinced him that these documentary publications were by no means so complete and reliable (though more so than the White and Red Books, issued by Germany and Austria) that one could safely base sound and final conclusions upon them, as seemed to be believed by the millions of men and women who read such facile and superficial arguments as those of Mr. James M. Beck, and others who followed his cue. Therefore the present writer during the War remained silent, except for his discussions of the subject in college class rooms.

When, however, the new socialist governments of Germany and Austria published in 1919 a very complete collection of documents from the secret archives relating to the diplomatic crisis of July, 1914, this seemed to provide material for reaching at last some tentative opinion about the immediate causes of the War. These the present writer ventured to express in "New Light on the Origins of the War" published in the American Historical Review in

1920-1921. This called to the attention of scholars in this country the desirability of reconsidering opinions formed during the heat of the battle as to the immediate responsibility of causing it. With the publication of more documents, especially from the Russian sources, and with the refusal of the French and British Governments to issue any such convincingly complete documentary record of their conduct in July, 1914, there soon arose a group of writers who demanded a "revision" of that clause in the Treaty of Versailles declaring that Germany and her allies were solely responsible. With some of these writers—especially with some of the anti-Poincaré revisionists in France—the pendulum of opinion has been in danger of swinging nearly as far away from the golden mean of historical truth as in the case of those who formerly followed in the propagandist path of Mr. Beck.

The present writer is no more inclined to accept the arguments of the former than of the latter. In the pages which follow he has no political motive, either to justify the Treaty of Versailles or to demand its revision but simply to carry out what a great master has defined as the proper task of the historian—to tell how it really came about. He has written, he hopes, *sine ira ac studio*. If he has made infrequent citations from the mass of controversial literature which has grown up in regard to the origin of the war, this is not because he has not read a very considerable part of it, but because he wishes to avoid controversy and reach his conclusions as far as possible from documentary evidence. The mass of documentary and autobiographical material is now so great that it affords either of two possibilities. On the one hand, a writer by centering attention on the acts of any one man or country, and by picking out passages in the documents to support his contention, can easily make a seemingly convincing argument for the uninitiated, that this or that man or country was altogether angelic or devilish in motives and methods. On the other hand, a writer may conscientiously try to look fairly at all sides of the question, explain acts from the point of view of the actors themselves instead of from that of their champions or enemies, and try to reach an unbiassed judgment. Needless to say it is the latter possibility which is attempted in the present volume. With what success, the reader must judge.

In the troublesome matter of transliterating Slavic proper names the best practice of American libraries has been followed, so far as is possible, without the use of diacritical marks. But in the case of some Russian names of German origin, like Schilling for Shilling, and in a few Serbo-Croat names, such as Princip for Printsip, popular usage has been allowed to prevail over proper practice.

Quotations from the documents and foreign works are usually made from direct translations from the original, rather than from translations into English which have been made by others. This is because the latter are sometimes abridged, or because the present writer made his translation prior to the publication of other translations, or because he prefers his own rendering to that of others. If the quotations from the documents are often tediously long, it is because he wishes to avoid as far as possible picking out phrases or sentences which might give a *suggestio falsi* or *suppressio veri*. In some cases, for the sake of brevity, prolix phrases and titles have been curtailed or omitted; "Austria," for instance, has been commonly used in place of "Austria-Hungary."

No formal bibliography is included in these volumes, because reference to all the more important recent literature of the subject has been made either in the List of Abbreviations, in the text, or in the numerous bibliographical footnotes in connection with each topic in the text; most of those which contain several titles are cited in the Index under "Bibliography."

Among the various bibliographies which include references to the less recent literature, the most helpful are the following: G. W. Prothero, *Subject Index of the Books relating to the European War, 1914-1918, acquired by the British Museum, 1914-1920* (London, 1922); A. von Wegerer, *Literatur zur Kriegsschuldfrage* (Berlin, 1923, new ed., 1926); J. L. Kunz, *Bibliographie der Kriegsliteratur* (Berlin, 1920); *Die Kriegsschuldfrage: Ein Verzeichnis der Literatur des In- und Auslandes, hrsg. vom Börsenverein der Deutschen Buchhändler* (Leipzig, 1925); A. Lumbroso, *Bibliografia ragionata della guerra delle nazioni* (Roma, 1920); H. H. B. Meyer, *Check List of the Literature and Other Material in the Library of Congress on the European War* (Washington, 1918); and the valuable *Catalogues Méthodiques* (Paris, 1921 ff.), issued by the *Bibliothèque et Musée de la Guerre,* and edited by J. Dubois, C. Appuhn, C. Bloch, and others.

For keeping abreast with current literature on the origins of the War there are two excellent periodicals largely devoted to the subject: *Die Kriegsschuldfrage,* edited by A. von Wegerer (Berlin, 1923 ff.); and *Revue d'Histoire de la Guerre Mondiale* (Paris, 1923 ff.). Articles, critical reviews, and titles of new books may be found in the various historical and political journals, such as the *American Historical Review, English Historial Review, Slavonic Review, Historische Zeitschrift, Revue Historique, Krasnyi Arkhiv, Foreign Affairs,* the New York Times *Current History, Political Science Quarterly, European Economic and Political Survey, Archiv für Politik und Geschichte, Europäische Gespräche, L'Europe Nouvelle, Evolution,* the *Bulletin of the Central Commission for Neutral Investigation of the Causes of the World War,* and many others.

To those who have kindly permitted the reproduction of

many of the illustrations the writer wishes to express his gratitude—to Mr. Hamilton Fish Armstrong for the portrait of M. Pashitch and the facsimile of the Austrian Declaration of War; to Mr. R. H. Lutz of the Hoover War Library for the Minutes of the Russian Council of Ministers; to the editors of *Current History* for the portraits of MM. Sazonov and Sukhomlinov; to the Frederick A. Stokes Company for the portraits of MM. Benckendorff, Cambon, Metternich, and Lichnowsky, which appeared in Viscount Grey's *Twenty-Five Years;* and to Herr A. von Wegerer for several of the German and Austrian portraits and for the material for the maps which appeared in *Die Kriegsschuldfrage.*

Finally, the author takes pleasure in acknowledging his indebtedness to Professor J. F. Jameson and the late Professor Coolidge, who first encouraged him to undertake this study; to Professor B. E. Schmitt, who read parts of the manuscript; and to Professors W. L. Langer and L. B. Packard, who read the proofs. But they are in no way responsible for the errors or the views expressed.

S. B. F.

July 28, 1928.
Northampton, Mass.

ABBREVIATIONS

Citations from collections in which the documents antedate July, 1914 (like "Affaires Balkaniques," "G.P.," "Siebert-Schreiner," and "Stieve") are by *volume and page*, because the documents are often long despatches extending over many pages, and a page reference is therefore more precise. But documents of July, 1914 (like those in "A.R.B.," "B.D.," etc.) are mostly short telegrams, and are cited by *serial number* of the publication in which they appear.

Affaires Balkaniques: Ministère des Affaires Étrangères, Les Affaires Balkaniques, 1912-1914, 3 vols., Paris, 1922.

A.R.B.: [Austrian Red Book of 1919] Diplomatische Aktenstücke zur Vorgeschichte des Krieges, 1914, 3 vols., Wien, 1919. (Eng. trans., 1920.)

B.B.B.: [British Blue Book] Great Britain and the European Crisis, Correspondence, and Statements in Parliament, together with an Introductory Narrative of Events. London, 1914. (Cd. 7467).

B.D.: British Documents on the Origins of the War, 1898-1914. Edited by G. P. Gooch and Harold Temperley. Vols. I-VI, XI. London, 1926-1930. (Vol. XI, Foreign Office Documents, June 28th-August 4th, 1914, cited merely as "B.D." and by serial number).

Bogitchevitch: M. Boghitschewitsch, Kriegsursachen. Zurich, 1919. (Eng. trans., 1919; 2nd ed. in French, 1925.)

Bourgeois et Pagès: E. Bourgeois et G. Pagès, Les Origines et les Responsabilités de la Grande Guerre. Paris, 1921.

Brandenburg: E. Brandenburg, Von Bismarck zum Welkriege, Berlin, 1924. (Eng. trans. of 2nd ed., 1927.)

Conrad: Feldmarschall Conrad von Hötzendorf, Aus meiner Dienstzeit. 5 vols., Wien, 1921-25.

D.D.F.: Ministère des Affaires Étrangères, Documents Diplomatiques Français, 1871-1914. Paris, 1929 ff.

Deutschland Schuldig?: Deutsches Weissbuch über die Verantwortlichkeit der Urheber des Krieges. 3rd ed., Berlin, 1919. (Eng. trans., 1924.)

Dirr: Dr. P. Dirr, Bayerische Dokumente zum Kriegsausbruch und zum Versailler Schuldspruch. Dritte erweiterte Auflage. Munich and Berlin, 1925.

Dobrorolski: S. Dobrorolski, Die Mobilmachung der russischen Armee, 1914. Berlin, 1921.

Frantz: Gunther Frantz, Russlands Eintritt in den Weltkrieg. Berlin, 1924.

F.Y.B.: [French Yellow Book] Ministère des Affaires Étrangères, La Guerre Européenne, 1914. Paris, 1914.

Gooss: Dr. Roderich Gooss, Das Wiener Kabinette und die Entstehung des Weltkrieges, Wien, 1919.

G.P.: Die Grosse Politik der Europäischen Kabinette 1871-1914, Sammlung der Akten des Deutschen Auswärtigen Amts, 40 vols. Berlin, 1922-27.

Grey: Viscount Grey of Fallodon, Twenty-five Years, 1892-1916, 2 vols. New York, 1925.

Investigating Commission: Die Deutsch Nationalversammlung: Beilagen. . . . über die Oeffentliche Verhandlungen des [ersten] Untersuchungsausschusses; Heft I, Zur Vorgeschichte des Weltkrieges; Heft II, Militärische Rüstungen und Mobilmachungen. Berlin, 1920-21 (Eng. trans. of Heft I, 1923.)

Jevtitch: B. Jevtitch, Sarajevski Atentat. Sarajevo, 1922.

K.A.: Kasnyi Arkhiv, 34 vols. Moskva, 1923-30.

K.D.: [Kautsky Documents] Die deutschen Dokumente zum Kriegsausbruch, edited by Karl Kautsky, Graf Max Montgelas and Prof. Walter Schücking, 4 vols. Berlin, 1919; new enlarged edition, 1927. (Eng. trans., 1924.)

KSF.: Die Kriegsschuldfrage: Berliner Monatshefte für internationale Aufklärung, hrsg. von der Zentralstelle für Erforschung der Kriegsursachen; ed. by Alfred von Wegerer. 8 vols. Berlin, 1923 ff.

L.N.: Un Livre Noir: Diplomatie d'avant-Guerre d'après les Documents des Archives Russes, 1910-1914, ed. R. Marchand, 2 vols. Paris, 1922-23.

Montgelas, Leitfaden: Graf Max Montgelas, Leitfaden zur Kriegsschuldfrage, Berlin and Leipzig, 1923. (Eng. trans., 1925.)

M.F.R.: [Materials for the History of Franco-Russian Relations] Materialy po Istorii Franko-Russkikh Otnoshenii za 1910-1914. Moskva, 1922.

Nicolson: Harold Nicolson, Sir Arthur Nicolson, Bart., First Lord Carnock. London, 1930.

Oe.-U.A.: Oesterreich-Ungarns Aussenpolitik von der Bosnischen Krise 1908 bis zum Kriegsausbruch 1914. Edited by L. Bittner, A. F. Pribram, H. Srbik and H. Uebersberger. 9 vols. Vienna and Leipzig, 1930.

Paléologue: M. Paléologue, La Russie des Tsars pendant la Grande Guerre, 3 vols. Paris, 1922. (Eng. trans., 1924-1925.)

Pharos: Professor Pharos [pseud.], Der Prozess gegen die Attentäter von Sarajewo. Berlin, 1918.

Poincaré: R. Poincaré, Au Service de la France, 5 vols. Paris, 1926-28. (Abridged Eng. trans., 1927 f).

Pribram: A. F. Pribram, Die politischen Geheimverträge Oesterreich-Ungarns 1879-1914. Wien, 1920. (Eng. trans., 1920.)

Renouvin: P. Renouvin, Les Origines Immédiates de la Guerre. 2nd ed. Paris, 1927. (Eng. trans., 1928.)

R.O.B.: [Russian Orange Book] Ministère des Affaires Étrangères: Recueil des Documents Diplomatiques, Négociations ayant précédé la Guerre, 10/23 Juillet-24 Juillet/6 Aout 1914. Petrograde, 1914.

Romberg: G. von Romberg, Falsifications of the Russian Orange Book. New York, 1923.

Schilling's Diary: How the War Began in 1914: Being the Diary of the Russian Foreign Office . . . of July, 1914; translated from the original Russian by Major W. Cyprian Bridge. London, 1925.

Schwertfeger: Zur Europäischen Politik: Unveröffentlichte [Belgische] Dokumente, herausgegeben unter Leitung von Bernhard Schwertfeger, 5 vols. Berlin, 1919; 2nd ed., 6 vols., 1925.

Seton-Watson: R. W. Seton-Watson, Sarajevo: A study in the Origins of the Great War. London, 1925.

Siebert-Schreiner: G. A. Schreiner, Entente Diplomacy and the World. New York, 1921. (Eng. trans., rearranged with annotations of Diplomatische Aktenstücke zur Geschichte der Ententepolitik der Vorkriegsjahre, hrsg. B. von Siebert. Berlin and Leipzig, 1921. New enlarged ed., 3 vols. Berlin and Leipzig, 1928.)

S.B.B.: [Serbian Blue Book] Les Pourparlers Diplomatiques 16/29 Juin-3/16 Aout. Paris, 1914.

Stieve: F. Stieve, Der Diplomatische Schriftwechsel Iswolskis, 1911-1914, 4 vols. Berlin, 1924.

Taube: Baron M. de Taube, La Politique Russe d'Avant-Guerre et la Fin de l'Empire des Tsars, 1904-1917. Paris, 1928. (Enlarged German edition, Berlin, 1929.)

TABLE OF CONTENTS

VOLUME II

ILLUSTRATIONS

I

II

I

BEFORE SARAJEVO

UNDERLYING CAUSES OF THE WAR

THE ORIGINS OF THE WORLD WAR

CHAPTER 1

INTRODUCTION

The Greek historian Thucydides, in his history of that catastrophe to ancient civilization when Spartan militarism triumphed over Athenian democracy, makes the distinction between the more remote or underlying, and the immediate, causes of war. It is the distinction between the gradual accumulation of inflammable material which has been heaped up through a long period of years and the final spark which starts the conflagration. The distinction is a good one. It is equally applicable to the World War. Failure to observe it has often led to confusion of thought in regard to responsibility for the War, since responsibility for the underlying causes does not always coincide with responsibility for the immediate causes. One country may for years have been much to blame for creating a general situation dangerous to peace, but may have had relatively little to do with the final outbreak of war—or *vice versa*.

The question of the causes of the War may be said to have passed through three phases during the past dozen years, each phase being determined to some extent by the material available for judging the question. During the first two phases the discussion centered largely around the question of the immediate causes, that is, the rapid train of events from the assassination of the Austrian Archduke at Sarajevo on June 28, to the outbreak of war between Germany and England on August 4. In the third phase, however, scholars have begun to explore more fully and justly the remoter causes of the War. In each of these phases there has been a change in the angle from which the question has been approached. At first, during the War, writers sought to fix the "guilt" for having caused this unparalleled "crime" upon a few single individuals—chiefly the Kaiser, the Pan-Germanists, and the Austrian and German militarists. Then, with the publication of more complete documents which began in 1919, it was seen that the Entente thesis of the sole responsibility of Germany and her allies was no longer tenable, and writers who demanded a "revision" of the Treaty of Versailles tended to go to the other extreme of fixing the "guilt" upon Entente leaders—MM. Izvolski, Poincaré, Sazonov, and even upon Sir Edward Grey. Finally, with the growing realization that all the Powers were more or less responsible, and with the increased attention which came to be given to the underlying causes of the War, more judiciously and historically minded persons were less inclined to accept the easy solution of explaining the War on the scapegoat or personal devil theory—that is, of the "guilt" of this or that individual.[1] They fell back on the truer explanation that the War was caused by the system of international anarchy involved in alliances, armaments, and secret diplomacy.[2] But, after all, the "system" was worked by individuals; their personal acts built it up and caused it to explode in 1914. In the discussion of the future, it will be the work of the historian to explain the political, economic, and psychological motives which caused these individuals to act as they did. He will also cease to talk about "war guilt," since no person in authority was guilty of deliberately working to bring about

1 *Cf.* M. H. Cochran, "New Phase of War Guilt Controversy," in *Current History,* XXVI, 71-76, April, 1927.

2 Mr. G. Lowes Dickinson gives a scholarly, effective, and charmingly written exposition of this view: *The International Anarchy, 1904-1914,* London, 1926.

a general European War. But he will still continue to discuss the "responsibility" which each statesman must bear for acts which ultimately contributed to the catastrophe.[3] For this reason the present writer has always preferred the term "war responsibility" to "war guilt." The German phrase, *Kriegsschuldfrage,* is open to either interpretation.

Let us now look briefly at the various phases through which the discussion has passed, as determined to some extent by the material upon which it has been based.

1. THE DISCUSSION OF "RESPONSIBILITY," 1914-1919

During the War and the Versailles Peace Conference, the discussion concerning responsibility for the immediate outbreak of the War, so far as it rested on anything more than national prejudice, war hatred, and deliberate propagandist misrepresentation, was based on the public statements of leading officials, and on the collections of diplomatic documents published by each government soon after July, 1914. The first of these was the "Preliminary Memoir and Documents Concerning the Outbreak of War," commonly known as the *German White Book.* It was laid before the Reichstag on August 3, having been, in the words of the German Chancellor, "put together under the pressure of overwhelming events." Its purpose was to prove to the German people that Germany was fighting a war of self-defense against Russian aggression. It was a plausible statement. It was supported by 27 telegrams and letters which were neatly fitted into the argument, but were not given in their proper chronological sequence. To the German people, to whom the book was primarily addressed, the argument was

[3] *Cf.* G. P. Gooch, *Recent Revelations of European Diplomacy* (London, 1927), pp. 206-214. This volume, which he describes as "a *causerie,* not a bibliography", is an admirably fairminded and well informed summary review of some three hundred of the most important documentary publications and other first-hand material appearing since the outbreak of the War and dealing with the period 1890-1919.

convincing. They went through the War, honestly believing that they were fighting a war of self-defense forced upon them by Russia. Outside of Germany, however, the *White Book* made the worst possible impression. It was quickly noted that among the 27 telegrams there was not a single despatch between Berlin and Vienna; and yet everyone knew that during the July crisis there must have been a very active interchange of telegrams between the two Central Powers. Germany had asserted that she tried to exert pressure upon Austria to accept negotiations to preserve peace, but there was not a document in the *White Book* to prove the assertion. People naturally concluded that Germany did not dare to publish the truth. They distrusted the specious argument by which the German Chancellor persuaded the Reichstag to vote the war credits. In fact, the *White Book,* instead of convincing persons outside Germany of her innocence, had exactly the opposite effect. As we now know, however, the *German White Book* contained a great deal of truth, but not the whole truth. One reason for the inclusion of so few documents was the physical impossibility of printing within a few hours the great mass of telegrams which had been exchanged during the preceding weeks. Even could they have been published in time to be laid before the Reichstag, it would have been impossible to read and digest their contents in a short time. The Chancellor evidently had to make a selection, and he selected those few letters and telegrams which were of greatest significance and which supported his arguments. He also omitted so far as possible matters which would have offended England and France, with whom Germany was still at peace at the time the *White Book* was compiled —a fact often overlooked in judging it later.[4]

In contrast to the *German White Book* was the *British*

[4] *Cf.* A. Bach, "Das erste deutsche Weissbuch," in *Die Kriegsschuldfrage,* III, 768-776, Nov., 1925.

Blue Book, which was laid before Parliament on August 6, 1914. This contained 159 documents.[5] They were arranged in strict chronological order and left to tell their own story. Compared with the German publication, the British book seemed to be fairly complete, candid and convincing. At first sight it appeared that all documents of any importance were included. They gave the impression that Sir Edward Grey had striven honestly for the preservation of peace, but that he had been thwarted in his efforts by Germany's rejection of all peace proposals, and by Austria's precipitate action against Serbia. Outside Germany, therefore, a host of writers hastily jumped to the conclusion that Germany and Austria had deliberately plotted the War and were solely responsible for it. This conclusion was strengthened by the documentary publications put forth by the other Governments in the following months.

A *Russian Orange Book,* published August 7, with 79 documents emphasized Russia's efforts for peace. By falsification and suppression of documents (as we now know) it concealed the truth about Russia's mobilization and placed the war guilt on the Central Powers. In October, a *Belgian Gray Book,* with 79 numbers, gave the details of Germany's flagrant violation of international law in disregarding the neutrality of Belgium. The *Serbian Blue Book* of November 18, 1914, recounted in 52 documents what this little country had had to suffer at the hands of Austrian oppression. It gave no hint of Serbia's guilty responsibility for the Sarajevo assassination which has recently been revealed. On the contrary, it asserted Serbia's innocence and regret. It pointed out the criminal deceit by which the Austrian Government at first assured Europe of its moderation, then suddenly issued an ultimatum impos-

[5] Two other documents, Nos. 160 and 161, were added in a later edition. *Cf.,* B.D., pp. vi-xiii. Further bibliographical details concerning this, and the other documentary publications mentioned below, may be found in the list of abbreviations above.

sible of acceptance, and finally made a general conflagration inevitable by declaring war on Serbia.

Finally, on December 1, 1914, the French Government, after ample time for compiling a collection of documents, published its *Yellow Book.* This differed from the collections hitherto published in that it contained a selection of alleged telegrams dating back several months prior to the Archduke's murder. These set forth all Germany's bellicose tendencies and military preparations, and easily convinced readers, who had been hearing exaggerated stories of German atrocities in Belgium and France, that William II "had come to think that war with France was inevitable," and "believed in the crushing superiority of the German army and in its certain success." The rest of the *French Yellow Book,* like the *English Blue Book,* appeared to be a fairly complete, candid, and convincing set of documents chronologically arranged; they are full of suspicions of German and Austrian duplicity and warlike intentions, in contrast to assertions of French desire for peace, as evidenced, for instance, by the order for the withdrawal of French troops ten kilometres behind the frontier. It was not till many years later that it became evident that the *French Yellow Book* was neither so complete nor candid after all, since some important telegrams had been suppressed altogether and others had been altered.[6]

An *Austrian Red Book,* published on February 3, 1915, as a reply to the *Serbian Blue Book,* contained 69 documents, but the most important of these had already appeared in the daily press, and the remainder threw but little light on the secret relations between Berlin and Vienna in connection with Austria's ultimatum to Serbia and the

[6] The most complete and severe criticism of it is by G. Demartial, *L'Évangile du Quai D'Orsay,* Paris, 1926. The German edition, *Das französische Gelbbuch von 1914,* Berlin, 1926, prints conveniently such French documents as have been made public since 1914, and contains valuable footnotes on others.

failure of all peace proposals. The *Austrian Red Book* evidently had suppressed a large number of essential documents. By persons outside Austria and Germany, therefore, it was generally thought to be as unreliable and self-incriminatory as the *German White Book* itself.

As the life and death struggle of the nations went on from month to month and became ever more grim and bitter, war hatred, national prejudice, and poisonous propaganda wrought such devastating results that few persons cared, or were able, to study carefully and critically even such documentary evidence as was now at hand. Leading officials in all countries had made war speeches asserting the innocence of their own acts, and throwing the responsibility upon the enemy. The result was that, at the close of the War, a "Commission on the Responsibility of the Authors of the War," presided over by Mr. Lansing, solemnly reported to the Peace Conference:

> The War was premeditated by the Central Powers together with their allies, Turkey and Bulgaria, and was the result of acts deliberately committed in order to make it unavoidable. Germany, in agreement with Austria-Hungary, deliberately worked to defeat all the many conciliatory proposals made by the Entente Powers.

In the deliberations of this Commission, as one of its members, Mr. J. B. Scott, tardily recognized five years later, "Unfortunately no Germans were allowed to take part." A German delegation, to be sure, was officially allowed to present a *German White Book Concerning the Responsibility of the Authors of the War*,[7] drawn up by Professor Hans Delbrück, the well-known historian, Professor Mendelssohn-Bartholdy, Count Montgelas, and Dr. Max Weber.

[7] *Deutschland schuldig? Deutsches Weissbuch über die Verantwortlichkeit der Urheber des Krieges*, Berlin, 1919. (Eng. trans. published by the Carnegie Endowment for International Peace, 1924).

"It is an official document whose importance can neither be overlooked nor minimized," as Mr. Scott correctly observes in the English translation published by the Carnegie Endowment for International Peace in 1924. It contained valuable new evidence tending to prove that the accusation formulated by the Commission was historically incorrect, and morally unjustifiable. In spite of this, the Commission paid virtually no attention to it, and Germany was forced to accept the dictum of the victors in Article 231 of the Treaty of Versailles:

> The Allied and Associated Governments affirm, and Germany accepts, the responsibility of Germany and her allies for causing all the loss and damage to which the Allied and Associated Governments and their nationals have been subjected as a consequence of the war imposed upon them by the aggression of Germany and her allies.

2. THE DISCUSSION OF "RESPONSIBILITY" AFTER 1919

(*a*) New Documents on the Immediate Causes

A second phase of the question of the immediate causes of the War began with the publication of the *Kautsky Documents*. These, and other new documents and memoirs to be mentioned below, made it clear that Germany had not plotted or wanted a European war. Scholars in all countries gradually came to agree that, though Germany was responsible for having at first foolishly encouraged Austria to take action against Serbia, Germany supposed (wrongly, as it turned out) that the conflict could be "localized"; but when it began to appear that "localization" was doubtful and that Russia might intervene, Germany tried to restrain Austria and made genuine efforts to prevent the Austro-Serbian conflict from developing into a World War. What are these new documents and memoirs upon which this revised view rests?

The *Kautsky Documents,*[8] published in December, 1919, were a consequence of the German revolution at the close of the War. The new German republic made the veteran Socialist leader, Karl Kautsky, Assistant Secretary of State for Foreign Affairs. He was authorized to edit all the documents in the German Foreign Office which might throw light on the origins of the World War. He and his assistants carefully copied, arranged, and annotated a mass of papers in eighteen volumes in the archives containing the diplomatic correspondence during the July crisis of 1914. In contrast with the meager *German White Book* of 1914, with its 27 documents, the Kautsky publication comprises 1123 documents, of which 937 are given *in extenso* and the remainder in a sufficiently full summary. The letters and telegrams are arranged in strict chronological order, and allowed to speak for themselves. The editors have merely added convenient cross references, indexes, and data as to the exact day, hour and minute when each despatch was sent and received. This extraordinarily precise and unprecedentedly complete compilation, containing detailed information which was unfortunately lacking in documentary publications issued early in the War, now made it possible to determine with considerable nicety just how much a German official knew when he took any action. It enabled one for the first time to judge with knowledge and fairness of the motives, the honesty, and the ability of the men guiding the German ship of state in 1914. It laid the basis for the beginning of a scholarly study of the immediate responsibility for the War. It showed scholars that during the critical days before the War, Germany had made real efforts to avert it, but that she had been guilty of blunders

8 *Die deutschen Dokumente zum Kriegsausbruch,* ed. by Karl Kautsky, Graf Max Montgelas and Prof. Walter Schücking, 4 vols., Charlottenburg, 1919, new enlarged edition, 1927; Eng. ed., *Outbreak of the World War, German Documents Collected by Karl Kautsky,* New York, 1924 (Carnegie Endowment for International Peace).

and mistakes in judgment which contributed to set fire to the inflammable material heaped up in the course of years. It showed, moreover, that the notion that Germany had deliberately plotted the World War was a pure myth.

In Vienna, Dr. Roderich Gooss did for the Austrian Foreign Office what Kautsky had done for the German. In contrast with the 69 documents of the original *Austrian Red Book,* Dr. Gooss's three-volume *Austrian Red Book of 1919,*[9] contained 352 documents. They revealed the reckless diplomacy by which Austria dragged Germany into a World War which Austria did not want, but which she was willing to risk in her determination to put an end to the danger which menaced her from the side of Serbia.

In Moscow the Bolshevists had already taken advantage of their advent to power to publish in their newspaper, *Pravda,* in the winter of 1917-1918, a series of secret treaties and other papers which revealed the imperialist and militarist aims of the fallen Tsarist régime between 1881 and 1917.[10] To these the Soviet Government added in 1922 a massive and invaluable collection of *Materials for the History of Franco-Russian Relations from 1910 to 1914.* This contained, among other things, the complete exchange of telegrams between the Russian Foreign Office and the Russian Embassy in Paris between July 24 and August 2, 1914.[11] Baron von Romberg took this series of telegrams and printed them in conjunction with the telegrams between Paris and St. Petersburg which had appeared in the *Russian Orange Book* of 1914. By using red ink for the former and black ink for the latter, his *Falsifications of the Russian*

[9] *Diplomatische Aktenstücke zur Vorgeschichte des Krieges 1914: Ergänzungen und Nachträge zum Österreichisch-Ungarischen Rotbuch,* 3 vols., Vienna, 1919 (Eng. trans. 1920).

[10] Rearranged and translated, in *Dokumente aus den russischen Geheimarchiven soweit sie bis zum Juli 1918 eingegangen sind,* Berlin, 1918

[11] *Materialy po Istorii Franko-Russkikh Otnoshenii za 1910-1914* Moskva, 1922, pp. 513-526.

Orange Book[12] gave striking proof of the deceptions by which the Russian Government had sought in 1914 to hide its responsibility for the War. Not only had it completely suppressed half of the telegrams actually exchanged between Paris and St. Petersburg, including some of great importance, but, even in the telegrams which were published, important passages were omitted, and in some cases deliberately forged words were added. These Russian revelations began to shake the confidence of scholars in the completeness and reliability of the other Entente documentary publications which had been accepted outside the Central Powers as good evidence of Entente innocence and German guilt.

The incompleteness and unreliability of the Tsarist *Russian Orange Book* was further evidenced in 1922 by the publication in the Bolshevist historical journal, *Red Archives,*[13] of all the despatches exchanged between St. Petersburg and the Russian Embassy in Berlin during July, 1914. Accompanying these is a long memoir which Bronevski, the Russian Chargé d'Affaires at Berlin, wrote immediately upon his return to Russia at the outbreak of War, in which he recounted in detail the events of his last days in Berlin.

In 1923 Baron Schilling's *Diary of the Former Ministry of Foreign Affairs,* which had lain hidden away in a cupboard, was discovered and published by the Bolshevists.[14] It gave a new and vivid account of the doings and conversations of the Russian Foreign Minister, M. Sazonov, between July 16 and August 1, 1914. The diary is especially valuable because Schilling was M. Sazonov's confidential assistant (*Chef de Cabinet*) at the Foreign Office, and sum-

12 G. von Romberg, *Die Fälschungen des russischen Orangebuches, Der wahre Telegrammwechsel Paris-Petersburg bei Kriegsausbruch,* Berlin and Leipzig, 1922 (Eng. trans., 1923).

13 *Krasnyi Arkhiv,* I, 163 ff.

14 "Nachalo Voiny 1914: Podennaia Zapis b. Ministerstva Inostrannykh Del," in *Krasnyi Arkhiv,* IV, 1-62.

marized on the spot conversations which his chief reported to him, but of which no other Russian record exists. Baron Schilling also pasted into the diary the text or summaries of important telegrams which passed in and out of the Foreign Office, but which were suppressed from the *Russian Orange Book,* and had hitherto remained unknown. In the introduction to Major Bridge's English translation of the diary, Baron Schilling, who has been living in London, confirms its authenticity and high historical importance, and gives interesting details of the manner in which it was composed.[15]

From these various Bolshevist publications we now have a fairly complete record of the Russian diplomatic correspondence for the July crisis. It consists of more than 200 telegrams, instead of the misleading and partly falsified 79 documents in the *Russian Orange Book of 1914*.[16]

Some Entente sympathizers, like Grelling, Romieu, and Ex-President Poincaré, have sought to throw suspicion and doubt on the honesty and reliability of these new revelations from the German, Austrian and Russian archives.[17] This is

15 Major W. Cyprian Bridge, *How the War Began in 1914, Being the Diary of the Russian Foreign Office* (London, 1925), pp. 11-17; cited hereafter as "Schilling's Diary," but the present writer does not always follow the wording of the English translation which is sometimes inaccurate; for instance telegrams Nos. 1504-1509 (p. 36 f.) belong under July "26" instead of "25."

16 A convenient German edition of them has been published by A. von Wegerer, *Das Russische Orangebuch von 1914,* Berlin, 1925. There appear to be still lacking some of the despatches exchanged by the Russian Minister of Foreign Affairs with Russia's representatives in London, Vienna and the Balkan States; for his despatches to his representatives in Turkey, Bulgaria, Rumania, and Italy from July, 1914, until the entrance of these states into the war, see *Das Russische Orangebuch ueber den Kriegsausbruch mit der Türkei,* ed. F. Stieve (Berlin, 1926); and *Das Zaristische Russland im Weltkriege,* ed. M. Pokrovski (Berlin, 1927).

17 R. Grelling, *La Campagne "Innocentiste" en Allemagne et le Traité de Versailles,* Paris, 1925; J. Romieu, *The Bolshevist Publications and French Policy,* Paris, 1922; R. Poincaré, "The Responsibility for the War" in *Foreign Affairs* (N.Y.), October, 1925, pp. 10-11; *Au service de la France,* I, 186 f., 308, 310, 360, 374; II, 336; III, 92 ff.

because these new documents have led scholars to believe that Germany was much less responsible, and that Russia and France were much more to blame, than was at first supposed. But no one has ever satisfactorily proved that the documents just described are in any way fictitious or falsified. On the contrary, all the new material fits together like a mosaic, and one part confirms another. Furthermore, one of the best reasons for believing that these documents are genuine and fairly complete, and that the Socialist editors have made no effort to exculpate Germany, Austria, and Russia, is to be found in the fact that the editors have each tried to place the war guilt upon his own former government. It is curious to see how they have written pamphlets, based on the documents in their own archives, tending to prove that their own former imperialist rulers were mainly to blame for the World War.[18] According to Kautsky, Germany deliberately and willingly pushed a hesitating Austria into action against Serbia and so into a World War. According to Gooss, the unsuspecting Emperor William was the sacrificial lamb offered up on the altar of Berchtold's reckless perfidy and obstinacy. While according to Pokrovski, the Director of the Archives in Soviet Russia—who is much nearer the truth—the causes of the War are to be found in the century-old Russian imperialist ambition for the control of Constantinople, the influence of Grand Dukes and militarists, the desire of Izvolski for revenge on Austria, and the support to these malign influences which the Tsarist régime felt encouraged to expect from the capitalist governments of France and England. While the historian may take such partisan conceptions

[18] K. Kautsky, *Wie der Weltkrieg entstand,* Berlin, 1919; R. Gooss, *Das Wiener Kabinett und die Entstehung des Weltkrieges,* Wien, 1919; M. N. Pokrovski, *Drei Konferenzen,* Hamburg, 1920; and Pokrovski's articles in various Russian periodicals which are summarized by A. von Wegerer, "Aus Russischen Quellen." in *Die Kriegsschuldfrage,* III, 159-177, March, 1925.

with a grain of salt, he may at least be sure that none of these editors have consciously suppressed documents which would incriminate their former rulers, or have concocted material which would exculpate them.

On the basis of this new documentary evidence, no serious historians any longer accept the dictum of the Allied victors of 1919 that Germany and her allies were solely responsible. They are all agreed that the responsibility is a divided one; they differ merely as to the relative responsibility of each of the Great Powers. Some writers, indeed, not alone in Germany but in other countries, especially in France,[19] have been inclined to push the pendulum to the other extreme. For various reasons, they tend to relieve Germany and Austria of a large part of the responsibility, and place an increasing amount of the blame upon Russia, Serbia, France, and even England. One reason for this is that Serbia and France have never made the same complete and frank publication of archive material as Germany, Austria and Russia; and England did not do so until December 1, 1926.

Finally, however, the British Government, realizing the undesirability of preserving further silence, and yielding to the request of distinguished historians, has at last, after a dozen years, issued an admirable collection of all its diplomatic documents relating to the July crisis of 1914.[20] It

[19] *E.g.*, Pevet, Demartial, Dupin, Morhardt, Victor Margueritte, Lazare, and others; and in America, Judge Bausman, Mr. J. S. Ewart, and Mr. H. E. Barnes.

[20] *Foreign Office Documents, June 28th-August 4th, 1914,* collected and arranged with introduction and notes by J. W. Headlam-Morley, London, 1926 (forming vol. XI of *British Documents on the Origins of the War, 1898-1914,* edited by G. P. Gooch and Harold Temperley). Among the numerous criticisms and reviews of these British Documents the following are especially noteworthy: H. Lutz, *Lord Grey und der Weltkrieg* (Berlin, 1927), pp. 171-261, 346-408 (Eng. trans., 1928); Count Montgelas, in KSF, 97-140, 443-448 (Feb.-Mar., 1927); Count Montgelas, *British Foreign Policy under Sir Edward Grey* (N. Y., 1928); H. Delbrück, in *Zeitschrift f. Politik,* XVI, 561-570 (May, 1927); H. E. Barnes, in (N. Y.) *Nation,* CXXV, 161-163 (Aug. 17, 1927); B. E. Schmitt, in

contains some 500 new documents and many important passages which were omitted from the *British Blue Book* of 1914. These suppressed passages relate largely to England's relations with France and Russia, who were soon to become her allies, and show the close solidarity of the Triple Entente Powers. The addition of private letters of Sir Edward Grey, Sir Arthur Nicolson, and Sir Eyre Crowe, of the British Foreign Office, and their marginal "minutes" upon the documents, enables one to trace with the same accuracy the development of events in London, as was made possible by the *Kautsky Documents* for Germany.

(*b*) MEMOIRS AND RECOLLECTIONS

In addition to these diplomatic documents, there has come a flood of apologetic memoirs and pamphlets from the men who played a prominent part in 1914. Some of these deal only with the diplomatic crisis immediately preceding the War; most of them also reach back and touch upon the remoter underlying causes as well. As was to be expected, the stream began to flow from the defeated side. After the German collapse of 1918, just as after the French *débâcle* of 1871, the ex-Kaiser's former officials sought to throw the blame for the War on the late enemy or upon fellow officials. Austrian leaders soon followed German example. And more recently the stream has been swollen by Russians in exile, Frenchmen on the defensive, injudicious Serbians, and even by hitherto reticent Englishmen. A full account of this autobiographical material may be found in Mr. G. P. Gooch's *Recent Revelations of European Diplomacy*, pubished in 1927, with *Supplements*, 1928-29. A few of the more important names may be mentioned at this point.

Current History, XXV, 844-851 (Mar. 1927); and other American scholars in *The Saturday Review of Literature*, III, 729 f., 750 f., 781 f. (April 16-30, 1927). Vols. I-VI of these *British Documents*, covering the years 1898 to 1912 in part, and the new *Documents Diplomatiques Français* (3 vols., Paris, 1929-30) will form, when completed, together with the new Austrian Documents (9 vols., 1930), invaluable counterparts to *Die Grosse Politik* mentioned below in notes 63-64.

The *Reflections on the World War* [21] by the late German Chancellor, Herr von Bethmann-Hollweg, deserve more serious attention than they have received; but they were written before peace was signed, under the terrible strain of war, by a man already broken in spirit and health. Without the new documentary material at his disposal, Bethmann still clung to the misconception which overtook him early in the War, that England was chiefly to blame. Herr von Jagow, the German Secretary of State for Foreign Affairs, in his *Causes and Outbreak of the World War*,[22] does not produce an impression of equal sincerity, but is illuminating in regard to the attitude of the German Foreign Office. Count Pourtalès, the German Ambassador in St. Petersburg, gives a very straightforward and reliable account of his last days in the Russian capital, and of his honest efforts to carry out the instructions of his Government to keep Russia quiet and thus preserve the peace of Europe. His narrative, *At the Parting of the Ways*,[23] has the advantage of being based on notes which he made on his journey home in August, 1914, while the facts were still fresh in his mind, and on the Embassy telegrams which he appears to have taken with him. Baron von Schoen, as German Secretary of State from 1907-1910 and Ambassador at Paris from 1910-1914, has left *Memoirs* [24] which are distinguished for their frankness and breadth of view; he is one of the few German diplomats of whom M. Poincaré speaks with cordiality and praise. These writers defend and justify the policy of the German Foreign Office.

In contrast to them are other Germans who are wise

21 Th. v. Bethmann-Hollweg, *Betrachtungen zum Weltkriege*, 2 vols., Berlin, 1919-20 (Eng. trans., 1920).

22 G. v. Jagow, *Ursachen und Ausbruch des Weltkrieges*, Berlin, 1919.

23 Graf Pourtalès, *Am Scheidewege zwischen Krieg und Frieden*, Berlin, 1922. This is amplified in his more recent volume, *Meine letzten Verhandlungen in St. Petersburg Ende Juli 1914*, Berlin, 1927.

24 Freiherr von Schoen, *Erlebtes: Beiträge zur politischen Geschichte der neuesten Zeit*, Berlin, 1921 (Eng. trans., 1922).

after the event. Admiral von Tirpitz,[25] in *My Memoirs* and in his more recent and valuable *Political Documents,* takes Bethmann severely to task for his optimism in hoping for a friendly understanding with England during the years before the War, and for his diplomatic bungling in the final crisis of 1914. Prince Lichnowsky's bitter pamphlet, *My London Mission,*[26] which was written during the War under a feeling of failure and the fire of criticism at home, is often unjust in its criticism of the German Government and not always well informed. It has been relied on outside Germany to an extent far beyond what it deserves. The *Memoirs*[27] of the ex-Kaiser at Doorn, which ungenerously attempt to lay the blame on everyone else but himself, are full of inaccuracies and misconceptions. They are of little historical value except for the psychological light they throw upon their author, and tend to obscure rather than elucidate the truth as to the causes of the War. General von Moltke's posthumous *Recollections*[28] consist largely of letters to his wife covering the thirty years before the War. The brief chapter on the July Crisis, written after the Battle of the Marne and his removal from active com-

[25] A. v. Tirpitz, *Erinnerungen,* Leipzig, 1919 (Eng. trans., 1921); also *Politische Dokumente: Der Aufbau der deutschen Weltmacht; Deutsche Ohnmachts-politik im Weltkriege,* 2 vols., Hamburg and Berlin, 1924-26.

[26] Prince Lichnowsky, *Meine Londoner Mission, 1912-1914,* Eng. trans. edited with notes by Amer. Assoc., for International Conciliation, No. 127, June, 1917, pp. 227-404. For criticisms of Lichnowsky, see G. von Jagow, *Remarks, ibid.,* pp. 352-367; and M. Ritter, *Der Ausbruch des Weltkrieges nach den Behauptungen Lichnowskys und nach dem Zeugnis der Akten,* Munich and Berlin, 1918. Of much greater value is Prince Lichnowsky's large, more recent work, *Auf dem Wege zum Abgrund,* 2 vols., Dresden, 1927, covering the whole period of his London mission and containing unpublished documents (Eng. trans., *Heading for the Abyss,* 1928).

[27] Wilhelm II, *Ereignisse und Gestalten, 1878-1918,* Berlin, 1922 (Eng. trans., 1922). Equally unreliable are his "Comparative Tables," which were neatly dissected by Ch. Appuhn and P. Renouvin, *Introduction aux Tableaux d'Histoire de Guillaume II,* Paris, 1923. Much more trustworthy and informing is his most recent volume, *My Early Years,* London, 1926.

[28] Helmuth v. Moltke, *Erinnerungen, Briefe, Dokumente, 1887-1916* Stuttgart, 1922.

mand, reflects his consternation at England's entrance into the War, and his despair at the Kaiser's delay in deciding for War, which the German militarists believed "inevitable," but which Bethmann and the Kaiser hoped to avert.

The Austrians, and with very good reason, have made relatively little effort to exculpate themselves. Count Berchtold, who more than anyone else was responsible for the World War, has long kept silent, except for a few short and tardy exculpatory articles, but his memoirs are now announced for early publication. Count Czernin, Austrian Minister to Rumania in 1914, and Austrian Foreign Minister during the War, wrote an interesting volume, *In the World War.*[29] Though dealing mainly with diplomacy during the War, he gave an excellent picture of the Archduke Franz Ferdinand's character and views, and expressed the opinion that the German Ambassador at Vienna, Tschirschky, used his personal influence to encourage Austria in her action against Serbia. Dr. Fraknói[30] has told us something of Count Tisza's initial opposition to an Austrian war against Serbia, not explaining altogether satisfactorily why the powerful Hungarian Premier changed his attitude in the middle of July, 1914. Count Tisza himself, had he lived, might have been able to tell the truth fearlessly, but he lies in a bloody grave, assassinated on his own doorstep at the close of the War; his lips were sealed forever, and the recent edition of his papers by the Hungarian Academy contains virtually nothing on the immediate causes of the War. Baron Musulin, who drew up the text of the Austrian ultimatum to Serbia, has published a delightful volume covering the experiences of his diplomatic life and his activity at the Austrian Foreign Office.[31] He

29 Ottokar Czernin, *Im Weltkriege,* Berlin and Vienna, 1919 (Eng. trans., 1919).

30 W. Fraknói, *Die ungarische Regierung und die Entstehung des Weltkrieges,* Vienna, 1919.

31 Freiherr von Musulin, *Das Haus am Ballplatz,* Munich, 1924.

is convincing everywhere except precisely in those chapters which deal with his share in the events which precipitated the World War. Here he minimizes his own share of responsibility, and his narrative, perhaps through faulty memory, is often contradicted by the contemporary records.

Count Bilinski, whose position as Austro-Hungarian Joint Finance Minister from 1912 to 1914 gave him direct charge of the civil administration of Bosnia and Herzegovina, has much to say in his Polish *Recollections and Documents*[32] concerning his efforts to ameliorate conditions in these troubled and restless provinces. But concerning the preparations of the Archduke's journey thither, and the lack of police precautions at Sarajevo, the alleged "warning" from Serbia, and the preparation of the ultimatum, he tells less than one might have hoped. These were tragic matters in connection with which he has been severely criticized, and over which in later years he preferred to draw the veil of silence. A Galician Pole by birth, he joined the Polish cause during the War, and is often regarded as a traitor to his former fatherland, which—in retrospect—he holds largely responsible for the War. More generous in tone and more readable in form is the volume by his predecessor as Joint Finance Minister, Count Burián, *Austria in Dissolution*.[33] Count Burián, who also became Austrian Foreign Minister during the War, makes no effort to shift the blame for the War to other shoulders, but gives an admirable account of the desperate situation in which Austria-Hungary found herself, because of the growing restlessness of her subject nationalities.

The only Austrian diplomatic representatives abroad in 1914, beside Count Czernin, who have left memoirs of importance, were Baron Szilassy at Athens and Baron Giesl

[32] Leon Bilinski, *Wspomnienia i Dokumenty, 1846-1922,* 2 vols., Warsaw, 1924-1925.

[33] Stephan Graf Burián, *Drei Jahre aus der Zeit meiner Amtsführung im Kriege,* Berlin, 1923 (Eng. trans., 1925).

at Belgrade. A broad-minded and intelligent Magyar, with French and English sympathies, whose horizon had been further enlarged in subordinate diplomatic positions in Tokio, St. Petersburg, Constantinople and elsewhere, Szilassy gives the impression in his *Fall of the Danubian Monarchy*[34] that the appointment of Count Berchtold as Austrian Foreign Minister was a colossal blunder—it gave minor officials in the Foreign Office, and militarists in the General Staff, the chance to seize upon the Archduke's assassination as the pretext for the "inevitable" war with Serbia. Baron Giesl, the Austrian Minister at Belgrade in 1914 and formerly at Cettinje, was well acquainted with the Turkish and Slavic languages; his Memoirs throw interesting light on Balkan conditions before the War and add some details concerning the final diplomatic rupture between Austria and Serbia.[34a]

The most valuable to the historian of all the Austro-Hungarian memoirs is the voluminous work of the Austrian Chief of Staff, Baron Conrad von Hötzendorf.[35] It consists in large part of an undigested mass of important documents of all sorts, copies of which he evidently took from the official files and published in chronological order, with a commentary of his own. It also includes conversations in dialogue form which appear to be taken from a diary kept from day to day. With extraordinary frankness, he recounts the repeated efforts he made to have Austria make war on Italy or Serbia on what he regarded as numerous favorable occasions between 1906 and 1914. In July, 1914, it was probably he, more than anyone else, who galvanized the incompetent and hesitating Berchtold into an active advocate of war against Serbia. Conrad is the best—that

[34] Baron von Szilassy, *Der Untergang der Donaumonarchie: Diplomatische Erinnerungen,* Berlin, 1921.

[34a] Baron Wladimir Giesl, *Zwei Jahrzehnte im nahen Orient,* Berlin, 1927.

[35] *Aus meiner Dienstzeit,* 5 vols., Vienna, 1921-25.

is, the worst—example of the militarist mind, which believes that war is "inevitable," is ever eager to wage a "preventive" war, and throws all its weight in favor of hasty mobilization in a time of diplomatic crisis. Conrad's views have been severely criticized by two of his generals.[36]

Another Austrian writer, who was not in an official position, yet who deserves mention because of his caustic criticism of the civilian and military officials whom he observed at close range in Vienna, is Herr Heinrich Kanner,[37] formerly editor of the Vienna Socialist daily, *Die Zeit.*

The Russian autobiographical material is almost wholly from hands which had been more accustomed to wield the sword than the diplomatic pen. Sazonov's Memoirs, written in exile more than ten years after the events, without notes and documents at hand, have been riddled by the reviewers as wholly unreliable.[37a] Few Russian diplomatic representatives abroad, except Baron Rosen,[38] have left their record of the immediate causes of the War. But many Russian military officers have left important recollections. General Dobrorolski, who was Chief of the Mobilization Section of the Russian General Staff in 1914, has revealed in a very frank and reliable pamphlet,[39] how the Russian militarists, upon hearing of the Austrian ultimatum, at once jumped to the conclusion that war was "inevitable," began

36 A. Krauss, *Die Ursachen unserer Niederlage,* Vienna, 1920; Auffenberg-Komarów, *Aus Oesterreichs Höhe und Niedergang,* Munich, 1924.

37 Heinrich Kanner, *Kaiserliche Katastrophenpolitik,* Vienna, 1922; also *Der Schlüssel zur Kriegsschuldfrage,* Münich, 1926.

37a S. D. Sazonov, *Fateful Years* (N. Y., 1928), has been confuted in numberless passages by F. Stieve and M. Montgelas, *Russland und der Weltkonflikt* (Berlin, 1927), and by others in *Rings um Sazonoff* (Berlin, 1928).

38 Baron Rosen, *Forty Years of Diplomacy,* 2 vols., N.Y., 1922. His memoirs deal more with the period preceding July, 1914, as do also: A. Nekludoff, *Diplomatic Reminiscences* (1920), and A. Savinsky, *Recollections of a Russian Diplomat* (1927).

39 S. Dobrorolski, *Die Mobilmachung der russischen Armee, 1914,* Berlin, 1921.

secret military preparations, and urged "general mobilization" at as early a date as possible. From Dobrorolski's account, it is also clear that "partial mobilization" against Austria was a mere diplomatic "bluff" by the threat of which Sazonov hoped to make Austria back down in her demands on Serbia; but the Russian military authorities had made no technical preparations for such a "partial mobilization," and were therefore absolutely opposed to it and insistently urged "general mobilization." Dobrorolski thus helps to establish the true facts in regard to the final orders for Russian mobilization, and corrects the falsehoods which were told so freely by General Sukhomlinov, who was Russian Minister of War in 1914, and by others, at the famous Sukhomlinov trial in 1917. Sukhomlinov's *Recollections,*[40] which were published in German in 1924, reveal a man full of loyalty to the Tsar, but very cloudy in his mind as to his own share in the fatal events of July, 1914. His volume, however, as well as General Polivanov's *Diaries,*[41] and the first part of General Danilov's *Russia in the World War,*[42] describe authoritatively and fairly satisfactorily the great efforts for the reorganization and increase of the Russian army which they made with a view to an "inevitable" war with Germany and Austria. Perhaps the most reliable and accurate sources for precise information concerning the Russian military preparations actually made in July, 1914, are the Russian military telegrams which were sent out by the Russian General Staff. More than a hundred of these were later captured by the Germans in the course of the War, and were published in 1919 in Robert Hoeniger's *Russia's Preparation for the World War.*[43] Five years

40 W. A. Suchomlinow, *Erinnerungen,* Berlin, 1924.

41 Gunther Frantz, *Russland auf dem Wege zur Katastrophe: Tagebücher des Grossfürsten Andrej und des Kriegsministers Poliwanow; Briefe der Grossfürsten an den Zaren,* Berlin, 1926.

42 J. Daniloff, *Russland im Weltkriege, 1914-1915,* Jena, 1925.

43 R. Hoeniger, *Russlands Vorbereitung zum Weltkrieg,* Berlin, 1919.

later, the telegrams were edited in more complete form and with a more adequate commentary by Gunther Frantz, *Russia's Entry into the World War.*[44] Though primarily a technical study of secret military measures, this excellent volume helps to clear away the legends and misstatements which have long passed current as a result of the Franco-Russian suppression of the truth in 1914 and the false assertions at the Sukhomlinov trial in 1917.

Foremost among French *apologias* is ex-President Poincaré's *Origins of the War,*[45] containing six lectures delivered at the Sorbonne in 1921. This is a skilful lawyer's statement of the case for France and a personal defense of his own policy. By centering attention largely upon Austria and Germany, and by concealing much of the activity of France and Russia, M. Poincaré gives plausible support to the official Entente thesis of German war guilt as embodied in the Versailles Treaty. In a notable article four years later on "The Responsibility for the War," in *Foreign Affairs* (N. Y., Oct., 1925), he abandons, to be sure, some of the legends concerning German guilt which have been proved to be wholly without foundation. But in spite of these concessions to a truer view of history, his later article is open to much the same criticism as his Sorbonne lectures. It is doubtful whether his plausible arguments convinced others than those who need no convincing.[46] Far more valuable is his magisterial defense of his foreign and domestic policy in the first four volumes of his memoirs which have so far appeared.[47] These describe minutely, almost day by day, his activities from the beginning of 1912 to August 3, 1914. Thus they throw light on both the un-

[44] G. Frantz, *Russlands Eintritt in den Weltkrieg,* Berlin, 1924.

[45] R. Poincaré, *Les Origines de la Guerre,* Paris, 1921.

[46] *Cf.* the present writer's article, "M. Poincaré and War Responsibility," in *The New Republic,* Oct. 14, 1925.

[47] R. Poincaré, *Au Service de la France,* 4 vols., Paris, 1926-27. (abridged Eng. trans. of vols. I and II, 1926).

derlying and the immediate causes of the War. M. Poincaré writes with lawyer-like vigor and perfect confidence in the wisdom and righteousness of all his acts. He quotes at length from his innumerable speeches in defense of the power and dignity of France, her love of peace and her loyalty to Russia and England. He uses much unpublished material from the French archives, which makes his volumes of great value to the historian. But he frequently turns aside, with sarcasm and with overwhelming minutiae of detail, in attempts to confute his critics; this often makes his work an acrid polemic rather than a calm historical retrospect.

M. Poincaré's most severe critics have been his own countrymen—Pevet, Judet, Fabre-Luce, Converset, Morhardt, Victor Margueritte, Lazare, and a host of lesser lights. They have charged him with getting rid of cautious ambassadors like M. Georges Louis in St. Petersburg and M. Crozier in Vienna to make way for a chauvinist like M. Delcassé or puppets like M. Paléologue and M. Dumaine, in order that he might be more free to work with Izvolski in bringing about a war which should recover Alsace-Lorraine for France and secure Constantinople and the Straits for Russia. Many of his replies to their criticisms are sound. He manages to explain away some of the incriminating remarks that Izvolski attributes to him. But in many other cases he seems to take refuge in the practice of throwing dust in the reader's eye by diverting attention from the main point to minor matters.

On the general question of war responsibility, M. Poincaré tries to prove that as Premier and President he in no way deviated from the pacific policy of his predecessors. He attempts to show that he and M. Georges Louis were in complete agreement as to the nature and interpretation of the Franco-Russian alliance. To one who has read all the available documents, his arguments are not always convincing. There was a distinct change during 1912, when he was Premier and Minister of Foreign Affairs, in the direction of tightening the alliance and extending French support to Russian ambitions in the Balkans. This was not, however, as many of his critics assert, with the aim of bringing about a war by which France should recover Alsace-Lorraine. It was to establish greater solidarity in the Triple Entente. In so doing he tended to divide the Powers more and more into two armed and opposing camps, so that the Triple Entente could impose its will on the Triple Alliance; or, if a diplomatic crisis should arise, the former could safely defy the latter, and willingly risk war with superior forces rather than accept a diplomatic defeat. This is exactly what happened in 1914. He believed a European war "inevitable"; in tightening the Entente and in making promises to Russia he did in fact tend to make it inevitable. Herein lies his responsibility.

After M. Delcassé had occupied the French Embassy at St. Petersburg for a few weeks in 1913, it was handed over to one of President Poincaré's old school friends and most devoted followers, M. Maurice Paléologue. In the opening pages of *An Ambassador's Memoirs,*[48] M. Paléologue describes vividly the gala events and chauvinistic enthusiasm accompanying President Poincaré's visit to the Tsar, and the situation in Russia on the eve of the War. Though the facts related by the French Ambassador do not always have the accuracy and definiteness which one would expect if his charmingly written book were really based on a diary written day by day, it is, nevertheless, of much value to the historian. It reproduces with fidelity the exultant war spirit inspired in Russian ruling circles by President Poincaré's presence and speeches. It describes dramatically, for instance, the gala banquet of July 22 at which the two

48 M. Paléologue, *La Russie des Tsars pendant la Grande Guerre,* 3 vols., Paris, 1922 (Eng. trans., 1924-26).

Montenegrin princesses (one of whom was the wife of the Grand Duke Nicholas) joyously told Paléologue how their father had written them that there would be war within a month. It pictures their ecstasy at the prospect of the ruin of Austria, the French reconquest of Alsace-Lorraine, and the defeat and destruction of Germany. Three days later, before it was known that Austria had rejected the Serbian reply as unsatisfactory, Paléologue tells how he went to the railway station to speed M. Izvolski on his return to France: "It is very lively on the platform; the trains are crowded with officers and soldiers. This suggested mobilization already. We exchanged rapidly our impressions and came to the same conclusion: *Cette fois, c'est la guerre.*"[49] The impression that he sympathized with the war spirit in Russia, and encouraged it by his repeated assurances that France would stand firm in the support of her ally, is confirmed by passages suppressed from the *British Blue Book* of 1914, but now printed in the new edition of British Documents.

Drab in comparison with Paléologue's vividness is the colorless picture presented by his colleague, M. Dumaine, the French Ambassador in Vienna.[50] For a man in ambassadorial position, M. Dumaine seems to have been surprisingly lacking in information and influence. From that trio of most able French Ambassadors, M. Paul Cambon at London, his brother, M. Jules Cambon at Berlin, and M. Barrère at Rome, we have unfortunately no full memoirs. However, an enterprising French journalist, M. Raymond Recouly, had the happy idea of interviewing them, and others, while their memories were relatively fresh, and has recorded these interviews in an excellent volume.[51]

49 M. Paléologue, *La Russie des Tsars pendant la Grande Guerre*, I, 27.

50 Alfred Dumaine, *La Dernière Ambassade de France en Autriche* Paris, 1921.

51 Raymond Recouly, *Les Heures Tragiques d'Avant-Guerre*, Paris, 1923.

The Serbian Government always denied that it was in any way directly responsible for the assassination of the Austrian Archduke. But the celebration of the tenth anniversary of his assassination and the outbreak of the War, which resulted in the creation of the united nation of which Serbian Nationalists had dreamed, inspired some interesting reminiscences which cast doubt on the official Serbian attitude. Ljuba Jovanovitch, who was Minister of Education in the Pashitch Cabinet of 1914, without perhaps quite realizing the importance of his words, let the cat out of the bag in 1924. In the *Blood of Slavdom,*[52] he describes in a vivid but simple way how some of the Pashitch Cabinet were aware of the Sarajevo plot for nearly a month; and yet, in spite of this guilty knowledge, took no effective steps to arrest the conspirators or to warn the Austrian authorities of the impending danger. This amazing admission on the part of a leading Serbian official has given rise to other Serbian revelations and denials concerning the part in the Sarajevo plot taken by the secret Serbian military organization commonly known as the "Black Hand," and especially by Col. Dragutin Dimitrijevitch. This reckless, generous, idolized, childish hero, who seems to belong to the spirit of the sixteenth rather than of the twentieth century, was the head of the espionage department of the Serbian General Staff. As the founder and dominating figure in the Serbian "Black Hand," he was the most influential military officer in Serbia. These Serbian revelations place the Austro-Serbian conflict in a new light and, if true, greatly increase the burden of Serbia's share of responsibility. They tend to confirm what Austrian officials suspected, but could not prove, in 1914. They help to explain, though they do not justify, Austria's determination to deal energetically with what was regarded as the Serbian

[52] Ljuba Jovanovitch, "After Vidov-Dan, 1914," in *Krv Slovenstva,* Belgrade, 1924.

menace to the very existence of the Hapsburg Monarchy.[53]

With characteristic regard for what Mr. Asquith calls the British tradition of being "scrupulously niggardly in imparting information as to the proceedings in the Cabinet," British officials have long been relatively chary of revealing the part they played. However, Lord Haldane's *Before the War* (1920) described with dignity and authority the failure of his efforts to secure a better understanding with Germany in 1912, and his activity in preparing an English army to fight on the Continent. Lord Loreburn, in *How the War Came* (1920), charged Sir Edward Grey with grave responsibility for the War, because of the secret engagements which he had made with France and which virtually committed England to support France and Russia in a European war. These commitments, he thinks, encouraged France and Russia in aggressive ambitions, but were long kept secret from the British Cabinet, contrary to English constitutional practice. Mr. Asquith's *Genesis of the War* (1924) tells us little of the true origin of the War. The ex-Prime Minister was still content to write in 1924 as if we knew no more about the causes of the War after a decade than we did in 1914. To him Germany is still solely responsible. He writes as a politician making a case, not as a statesman seeking to reveal the truth. In certain chapters, however, he gives an illuminating account of the splendid preparations for war made by the Committee for Imperial Defense. He quotes the significant statement which Sir Edward Grey made behind closed doors to the Dominion Premiers in May, 1911: "What really determines the foreign policy of this country is the question of sea power." This dictum is amply confirmed in *The World Crisis, 1911-1914* (1923) by Mr. Winston Churchill, First Lord of the

53 Some of these Serbian revelations were discussed by the present writer in *Current History,* Oct., Nov., 1925.

Admiralty during this period. Mr. Churchill gives us much valuable new information as to his strengthening and increasing of the British navy after Germany's folly in refusing British proposals for the limitation of naval armaments.

The memoirs of Sir George Buchanan, British Ambassador to Russia, add little to our knowledge of the immediate causes of the War beyond what can be learned from the *British Blue Book*. But when he says that, with one exception, this "recorded all the communications which passed between me and that Department [the British Foreign Office] during those critical days," [54] he is guilty of serious misrepresentation; the new *British Documents* contain more than a score of such communications not printed in 1914, not even counting the important passages omitted from several telegrams and letters. Lord Bertie's *Diary,* though mainly concerned with events after the outbreak of the War, contains some significant passages on the pacific attitude of the French people until they were stirred up by their newspapers, and by Izvolski. Of the latter he writes, July 27: "Izvolski is expected back here today or tomorrow, and he is not an element of peace." And on July 28: "Izvolski told Granville that war is inevitable. . . . He will do a good deal of mischief in fomenting a war spirit here." And later, on November 10: "What a fool Izvolski is! . . . At the beginning of the war he claimed to be its author:—'*C'est ma guerre!*' " [55] This attitude is confirmed by several passages now printed for the first time in the new *British Documents,* in which we learn that Bertie told the French that "public opinion in England would not sanction a war in support of Russia if she, as protector of Slavs, picked a quarrel with Austria over Austro-Serbian

54 Sir George Buchanan, *My Mission to Russia and other Diplomatic Memories* (2 vols., London, 1923), I, 211.

55 *The Diary of Lord Bertie of Thame, 1914-1918* (2 vols., London, 1924), I, 2, 3, 66.

difficulty." He also at first denounced "the absurd and obsolete attitude of Russia being the protectress of all Slav States, whatever their conduct." [56]

Most valuable of all the recent memoirs is Viscount Grey's *Twenty-five Years, 1892-1916* (1925). By charm of style and absence of bitterness, by transparent honesty of intention and nobility of tone, and by the sweet reasonableness of his retrospective reflections, Grey's *apologia* is unique. Though writing ten years or more after the events, he appears to have a remarkably clear memory. Furthermore, he has had his friend, Mr. Spender, search the Foreign Office records to refresh his mind on all points where he feared his memory might play him tricks. His book is thus, in a sense, a history based on the archives; yet the clear flow of his narrative is unclogged by quotations and footnotes. Admitting, however, Sir Edward Grey's absolute sincerity in attempting to preserve the peace of Europe and his unquestionable honesty of intent in his memoirs, serious criticisms remain to be made of his conduct of British foreign policy to which we shall return in a later chapter. At this point it may be merely noted that his great fault was what has been regarded as the great virtue of British constitutional leaders—the preference for practical compromise for the present instead of theoretical perfection for the future. He did not look far ahead, work out a logical policy, and study all its possible consequences. He was content in foreign affairs, as the British have always been content in dealing with their constitutional development, to meet situations as they arose and deal with them according to the most practical and common sense needs of the moment. As Grey himself says, when alleging that Great Britain never pursued a "Balance of Power" policy: "I suppose that in this, as in most investigations of British foreign policy, the true reason is not to be found in far-

[56] B.D., 129, 192.

sighted views or large conceptions or great schemes. . . . If all secrets were known it would probably be found that British Foreign Ministers have been guided by what seemed to them to be the immediate interest of this country without making elaborate calculations for the future."[57] The result of this hand-to-mouth procedure of *solvitur ambulando* was that he became more and more enmeshed in his secret understandings with France, until he was morally bound by them in 1914. Though he had always been careful to state to the French that his hands were to remain free, and that it would always be for Parliament to decide whether England would support France in a European war, he had, nevertheless, become gradually so committed that, as he twice admits, he would have felt bound to resign his office if he had been unable to persuade the Cabinet and Parliament to enter the war against Germany.[58]

In his retrospect, Viscount Grey rightly has much to say of the poisonous effect of suspicion as a cause of war, but he also reveals in several passages his own deep-rooted suspicion of Germany. "It seemed at the time (1914), and still seems true to me, that the military power in Germany chose the time and precipitated the War."[59] He seems to have believed that the German militarists even selected the month as well as the year for making war, choosing July in 1914 as they had chosen July in 1870 and were ready to choose July in 1905 and 1911 had it not been that France yielded in the first Morocco crisis, and that England assumed a very firm tone after Agadir.[60] Though Germany's actions gave much ground for suspicion, as we shall see, this

57 Grey, I, 6. 58 Grey, I, 303, 316. 59 Grey, I, 90.

60 "Had the [Agadir] crisis led to war, this would have come at the very season that we know was favoured for the purpose by German military leaders in 1870, and that was selected for the menace to France in 1905, and that we believe was decided by the military authorities for war in 1914." Grey, I, 231. For other passages indicating Grey's suspicion that the German militarists had fixed upon war for 1914, see I, 313-314; II, 23-31, 56, 144, 278.

particular suspicion of Sir Edward Grey's was wholly incorrect. But the fact that he harbored it must be accounted one of the immediate causes of the War, because it contributed to the failure of Germany's eleventh hour efforts to prevent a general European conflagration. To be sure, Viscount Grey generously and correctly acquits the German civil authorities of planning or desiring war in 1914, but he thinks that Bethmann and Jagow were powerless in the face of the militarists.

Thus, there is at present a wealth of documentary and memoir material, unprecedented in quantity and quality, at the disposal of historians seeking to find the immediate causes of the War. Never before in history have archives been so quickly and freely thrown open by so many Great Powers; never before have so many statesmen hastened to tell at such length the part they played. In this respect, as in so many others, the World War has outstripped all precedents and surpassed all expectations. In the case of former wars, at least a generation or two passed before satisfactory accounts of their causes could be written. Today, only fourteen years after the outbreak of the War, it may safely be said that the materials are now at hand on which to base a fairly exact statement of the course of events between the murder of the Archduke at Sarajevo on June 28, and the advent of war between England and Germany on August 4. This is the main subject of my second volume.

3. THE UNDERLYING CAUSES OF THE WAR

Though it is now possible, in a single volume, to treat in detail and somewhat definitively the immediate causes of the War, this is by no means true in the case of the underlying causes. These are so complex and reach so far back into the past that any attempt to describe them adequately would involve nothing less than the writing of the whole diplomatic history of Europe since 1870, or rather from

1789; some questions go back to the age of Louis XIV, and even to that of Charlemagne. It would also involve the difficult technical study of the military and naval forces of the various countries, their plans of campaign, the relation of the military to the civilian authorities in each country, the psychology of fear, and all the other factors which go to make up the somewhat vague conceptions of "militarism" and "navalism" as causes of war. No less important would be the analysis of that complex force which first began to be a powerful, disruptive agency during the French Revolution, and which steadily gathered strength for a century and a quarter, which we call "nationalism." This in turn is closely bound up with psychological and political questions of race, religion, democracy, education, and popular prejudice. Still more important, in many minds, as underlying causes of the War are the intricate political and economic problems which have arisen from the transformation of society during the past hundred years by the modern industrial system which began in England and subsequently penetrated more or less all the great countries of the world—problems of excess population, food supply, foreign markets and raw materials, colonial possessions, and the accumulation of capital seeking investment abroad. Finally, the influence of the newspaper press is a factor much greater than commonly supposed in causing the World War. For decades it fed the constant undercurrents of irritation of one country against another, and by its clamor and misrepresentations often made difficult or impossible the peaceful settlement of sources of conflict. How far government officials controlled newspaper opinion, and how far they themselves were hampered in their freedom of action by it, is a subject which greatly needs further careful historical investigation. Obviously, no single volume can hope to deal thoroughly with all these complex and interrelated factors which constitute the underlying causes of the World War. They may be conveniently grouped under five heads: (a) the system of secret alliances; (b) militarism; (c) nationalism; (d) economic imperialism; and (e) the newspaper press.

(*a*) THE SYSTEM OF SECRET ALLIANCES

The greatest single underlying cause of the War was the system of secret alliances which developed after the Franco-Prussian War. It gradually divided Europe into two hostile groups of Powers who were increasingly suspicious of one another and who steadily built up greater and greater armies and navies. Though this system of alliances in one sense tended to preserve peace, inasmuch as the members within one group often held their friends or allies in restraint for fear of becoming involved in war themselves, the system also made it inevitable that if war did come, it would involve all the Great Powers of Europe. The members of each group felt bound to support each other, even in matters where they had no direct interest, because failure to give support would have weakened the solidarity of the group. Thus, Germany often felt bound to back up Austria-Hungary in her Balkan policies, because otherwise Germany feared to lose her only thoroughly dependable ally. Similarly, France had no direct political (only financial) interests in the Balkans, but felt bound to back up Russia, because otherwise the existence of the Dual Alliance would have been threatened, the balance of power destroyed, and the best guarantee of French safety from a German attack would have been lost. Likewise, the officials of the British Foreign Office became increasingly convinced that England must support France and Russia in order to preserve the solidarity of the Triple Entente as a check to the Triple Alliance. In the crisis of July, 1914, it was not merely a question of Austria, Serbia and the Balkans; it was a question of the solidarity and prestige of the two groups of Powers into which Europe had become divided

As one reads the new *British Documents,* one is struck by the emphasis on this necessity of preserving the solidarity of the Triple Entente. As Sir Eyre Crowe noted in a "minute" early in the crisis: "It is clear that France and Russia are decided to accept the challenge thrown out to them. Whatever we may think of the merits of the Austrian charges against Servia, France and Russia consider that these are the pretexts, and that the bigger cause of Triple Alliance versus Triple Entente is definitely engaged. I think it would be impolitic, not to say dangerous, for England to attempt to controvert this opinion, or to endeavour to obscure the plain issue, by any representation at St. Petersburg and Paris. . . . Our interests are tied up with those of France and Russia in this struggle, which is not for the possession of Servia, but one between Germany aiming at a political dictatorship in Europe and the Powers who desire to retain individual freedom."[61] It was stated more bluntly by Herr Zimmermann to the British Ambassador in Berlin on August 1, when he saw with excited regret that Germany, France, and perhaps England, would be drawn into a war which none of them wanted: "It all came from this d——d system of alliances, which was the curse of modern times."[62]

In view of the fatal consequences of this system of secret alliances in 1914, and of the fact that there has recently appeared much new material throwing light upon it, an attempt to sketch in outline its development will be made in the three following chapters. As indicated above, many of the documents and memoirs dealing with the immediate causes of the War contain also material on the earlier period. But the most important single contribution to our fuller knowledge of the growth of the system of secret alliances is the great set of new German diplomatic documents cover-

61 B.D., 101.
62 B.D., 510.

ing the years from 1871 to 1914.[63] This consists of the most secret instructions sent by Bismarck and his successors to the German Ambassadors abroad, their reports to the German Foreign Office, and the secret papers exchanged between the German Emperor and his Foreign Office officials. It includes exceedingly interesting marginal notes on documents from the hand of Bismarck, and later from that of William II. Bismarck's notes reveal the Iron Chancellor's innermost thoughts on foreign policy. They formed the basis of instructions sent by the German Foreign Office to the ambassadors abroad. William II's marginal notes, which are more numerous, more emotional, and often merely indicative of the mood of the moment, are interesting as a study of the psychology of the imperial mind, but exercised somewhat less directive influence upon the German Foreign Office than did Bismarck's masterly notes. From this collection of documents one sees that the German Foreign Office did not always completely inform William II on all matters and often made its will prevail over his preferences. So far as one can judge, *Die Grosse Politik* is fairly complete within the limits set by the editors, and aims at giving the basis for an honest and detailed picture of German foreign policy from the Franco-Prussian War to the World War.[64] But we still lack any equally compre-

63 *Die Grosse Politik der Europäischen Kabinette, 1871-1914: Sammlung der Diplomatischen Akten des Auswärtigen Amtes,* edited by Johannes Lepsius, Albrecht Mendelssohn-Bartholdy and Friedrich Thimme, 40 vols., Berlin, 1922-27; cited hereafter as "G.P."

64 A further account of *Die Grosse Politik* is given by the present writer in the *Amer. Hist. Rev.,* XXVIII, 543-548; XXX, 136-141; XXXI, 130-133; XXXIII, 126-134. *Cf.* also the appreciations by various scholars in KSF, IV, 900-946. Dec., 1926; the criticisms of M. Lhéritier in *Rev. d'Hist. de la Guerre Mondiale,* IV, 97-116, April, 1926, and of E. Bourgeois, in *Revue Historique,* CLV, 39-56, May-June, 1927; and the replies to these criticisms by Albrecht Mendelssohn-Bartholdy and by F. Thimme in *Europäische Gespräche,* IV, 377-390, July, 1926, and V, 461-479. Sept., 1927.

A French translation of *Die Grosse Politik,* under the editorship of A. Aulard, in which the documents are arranged chronologically instead

hensive publication from the archives of France, Russia, and the other countries, which may be used to check and balance these German documents. Very recently, however, similar admirable collections of documents have been, or are being, officially issued: *Austria-Hungary's Foreign Policy, 1908-1914; British Documents on the Origins of the War, 1898-1914;* and the *French Diplomatic Documents, 1871-1914.*[64a]

Professor Pribram's invaluable edition of *The Secret Treaties of Austria-Hungary, 1879-1914,*[65] made possible for the first time a satisfactory study of the Triple Alliance treaties and their evolution from a purely defensive system into one which was used for aggressive purposes by Italy and Austria.

The Bolshevist *Materials for the History of Franco-Russian Relations from 1910 to 1914,* mentioned above, contains much of the correspondence between the Russian Foreign Office and the Russian Embassy in Paris during the four years before the War. It enables one to see how Izvolski and Poincaré were transforming the Franco-Russian alliance from its originally defensive character into a potentially aggressive combination to support Russian ambitions in the Balkans. Much of this material has been made easily accessible to Western readers in Réné Marchand's *Livre Noir.*[66] It has been further completed by some five hundred additional letters and telegrams of Izvolski's correspondence, which have been published in

of topically and in which the German editorial notes are omitted, is now being published, and is discussed by F. Thimme in KSF, V, 897-907, Sept., 1927.

[64a] For the full titles of these recent documentary publications, see "Oe.—U.A.," "B.D." and "D.D.F." in the List of Abbreviations above.

[65] A. F. Pribram, *Die politischen Geheimverträge Oesterreich-Ungarns,* 1879-1914, Vienna and Leipzig, 1920 (Eng. trans., ed. by A. C. Coolidge, 2 vols., Cambridge, Mass., 1920-22).

[66] *Un Livre Noir: Diplomatie d'Avant-Guerre d'Après les Documents des Archives Russes,* ed. by R. Marchand, 2 vols., Paris, 1922-23.

German translation by Friedrich Stieve.[67] Parallel to this Paris-St. Petersburg correspondence, supplementing and confirming it, is the London-St. Petersburg correspondence of Count Benckendorff for the years 1908-1914. His letters and other secret papers were clandestinely copied by B. von Siebert, a counsellor in the Russian Embassy at London. They were apparently sold or conveyed to German authorities, and published by von Siebert in a German edition in 1921.[68] They have been conveniently rearranged and published in English translation by G. A. Schreiner, *Entente Diplomacy and the World* (1921). They show the efforts of Russia and France to strengthen the friendship with England and to tighten the bonds of the Triple Entente into a combination which should be firm and powerful enough to defy the Triple Alliance, if necessary.

From the French archives, a few documents were published by Professors Bourgeois and Pagès, as a French Senate Report on *Les Origines et Les Responsabilités de la Grande Guerre.*[69] But these French documents are few and meager as compared with the German, Austrian and Russian publications, and are selected to prove a case, rather than to furnish historians with material for study. More valuable are the French *Yellow Books* containing documents on such special subjects as the *Franco-Russian Alliance* and *Balkan Affairs, 1912-1914,* though these are clearly far from complete.

(*b*) MILITARISM

A second underlying cause of the War, closely connected with the system of secret alliances, was militarism. The word is often used vaguely. But usually it includes at least

67 F. Stieve, *Der Diplomatische Schriftwechsel Iswolskis, 1911-1914,* 4 vols., Berlin, 1924.

68 B. von Siebert, *Diplomatische Aktenstücke zur Geschichte der Ententepolitik der Vorkriegsjahre,* Berlin and Leipzig, 1921.

69 Published in the *Journal officiel,* Jan. 9, 1921; republished, in book form, with some material from the Kautsky Documents, Paris, 1921.

two definite conceptions. First, the dangerous and burdensome mechanism of great standing armies and large navies, with the attendant evils of espionage, suspicion, fear, and hatred. Second, the existence of a powerful class of military and naval officers, headed by the General Staff, who tend to dominate, especially at a time of political crisis, over the civilian authorities.

The system of great armies, embracing the larger part of the male population capable of bearing arms, began with the French during the Revolution and under Napoleon. It was extended and efficiently developed by the Prussians in the War of Liberation. As a result of its success in the victories of Moltke and Bismarck in the Wars of 1864, '66 and '70, it came to be esteemed and imitated in the rest of Continental Europe. From the Franco-Prussian War onwards the military and naval armaments of all the Great Powers tended to grow larger and larger, and the financial burden became heavier and heavier. Armaments were alleged to be for defense and in the interests of peace, according to the fallacious maxim, *si vis pacem, para bellum*. They were intended to produce a sense of security. That was the argument used in getting from legislatures the necessary grants of money. What they really did produce was universal suspicion, fear, and hatred between nations. If one country increased its army, built strategic railways, and constructed new battleships, its fearful neighbors were straightway frightened into doing likewise. So the mad competition in armaments went on in a vicious circle. This was especially the case during and after the Balkan Wars of 1912-1913, when it seemed that the Great Powers might be involved. It was also accentuated by the system of alliances. Germany and Austria, uncertain of Italy's loyalty, believed they must increase their armaments to secure their own safety. France urged Russia to increase her army and build strategic railways against Germany, and readily loaned her half a billion francs on condition that it be spent for these purposes. Russia urged France to extend the term of French military service from two to three years. "Russia is ready; France must be also," declared the Russian Minister of War in an alarming newspaper article early in 1914. So armaments were increased, not only to give security to an individual country, but also to strengthen the alliance to which it belonged.

Militarism implied also the existence of an influential body of military and naval officers, whose whole psychological outlook was naturally colored by the possibility, if not the "inevitability," of an early war. To these professional fighters war held out the prospect of quick promotion and great distinction. It would, however, be a grave injustice to them to imply that they urged war for selfish motives of personal advancement. Nevertheless, the opportunity to put into practice the results of the work of preparation for war to which their lives were devoted cannot have failed to have its psychological effect. Quite aside from any personal motives, the military officers in all countries had a high sense of national honor and patriotic duty, as they understood it. It was their supreme duty to be ready at any moment to protect the state by force of arms. It was the constant preoccupation, day and night, of the General Staff in every country to be ready to make or meet an attack in the shortest possible time. To this end every General Staff drew up or revised every year the most minute and complete plans for mobilization and march to the frontier to satisfy all possible contingent situations. Military officers generally held to the theory that it was advantageous to take the offensive. This meant striking the foe before his mobilization was complete—at the moment, therefore, when the enemy country was in the most vulnerable process of transforming itself from a peace to a war footing. It meant also that the war, with all its frightful economic devastation and demoralizing political and psychological effects, would be carried on in the enemy's country instead of within one's own frontiers. In a political crisis, therefore, the military leaders were always quick to conclude that war was "inevitable," and exerted all their influence to persuade the ruling civilian authorities to consent to an order for general mobilization at the earliest possible moment, in order to gain the advantage of the offensive. But a general mobilization, according to prevailing military opinion, actually did make war inevitable. It was a process virtually impossible to halt when once begun. This was one of the greatest evils of militarism. It is always at a crisis, precisely when it is most difficult for diplomats to keep their heads clear and their hands free, that militarist leaders exert their influence to hasten decisions for war, or get the upper hand altogether.

Another evil of militarism was the fact that the plans of the General Staff were technical and were worked out and guarded in such absolute secrecy. Not only were they unknown to Parliament and the public; they were often not even known to the Minister of Foreign Affairs, or at least their details and significance were not grasped by him. Sir Edward Grey says that between 1906 and 1911 he knew nothing of the plans which the English and French military authorities were working out for Anglo-French military cooperation in Northern France. As to the negotiations between the Anglo-Russian naval authorities in the spring of 1914, he likewise writes: "I never enquired at the Admiralty afterwards, but I imagine the practical result of the consultations between the two naval authorities was not great. . . . [In the Siebert documents they] are constantly referred to as 'conventions.' How the military and naval authorities themselves described them, I do not know."[70] Similarly, in Russia, it is clear that M. Sazonov did not at

[70] Grey, I, 91, 274-277.

first grasp the fact that the plans of the militarists made a "partial mobilization" against Austria a piece of folly, if not a downright impossibility. And in Germany Herr von Bethmann-Hollweg never envisaged clearly the implications of the Schlieffen-Moltke plan to attack France through Belgium, although he was probably aware of it, according to Ludendorff, as early as 1912.

This then was another evil of militarism. The General Staffs worked out in absolute secrecy the plans which they calculated to be best adapted to bring military victory, regardless of the political implications which they might thereby impose on the civilian authorities. And when war became "inevitable," there was tremendous pressure upon the civilians to accept the arrangements which the militarists had long planned in secret. The militarist mind was much the same in all the countries, but there was a difference as to the extent to which the military and civilian authorities exercised control. General Joffre, in 1912, precisely like the German strategists, urged the strategic necessity of disregarding Belgian neutrality; but while Moltke was allowed to build his whole plan of campaign upon this violation of a treaty which Bethmann was helpless to avert if war came, M. Poincaré was strong enough and shrewd enough to veto General Joffre's views. He realized the bad effect it would have on public opinion in England, and the danger that it might cause the British Government to make use of its stipulated freedom to withhold armed aid.

Closely akin to this influence of military and naval officers was the pressure exerted on civilian authorities by munition makers and "big business."

Some militarists believed in "preventive" war—the waging of a war upon a neighbor while he was still weak, in order to prevent him growing stronger later on. So it is often alleged that Germany wanted war in 1914, in order to have a final reckoning with Slavdom before Russia should have completed her "Great Program" of military reorganization in 1916 or 1917. M. Poincaré and his associates are alleged to have wanted war in 1914 before Germany grew any stronger by reason of her rapidly increasing population, wealth, and naval force, and also before French Socialists, revolting against the burden of French military expenditure, should repeal the recently voted three-year term of service. For the same reasons Russian militarists are said to have wanted war sooner rather than later. England even is often said to have been glad of the opportunity to crush the growing German navy before it should become a greater menace to that of England. Though here and there some individual military and naval officers in most countries may have held such views, the present writer does not think that the militarist doctrine of preventive war was a decisive factor in causing the World War. Only in Austria-Hungary did it exercise a strong influence on state policy; here it was generally felt that a conflict with Serbia must come sooner or later, and, as Baron Conrad repeatedly urged, the sooner the better. The murder of the Heir to the Throne was eagerly seized upon as a good excuse for trampling upon the Greater Serbia danger.

Nor is there any more substantial truth in the common assertion that the German authorities welcomed war as a means of crushing the rising tide of socialism, than there is in the similar assertion that Russia welcomed war as a good way of putting an end to workingmen's strikes and revolutionary unrest.

Generally speaking, it may be said that this aspect of militarism—the influence of the military upon the civilian authorities—was a serious matter in the three eastern monarchies of Germany, Austria, and Russia. It was much less in France, and virtually non-existent in England, where civilian ministers were ordinarily in charge of the army and navy.[71]

We shall have something more to say about militarism and navalism in connection with the system of alliances.

(*c*) NATIONALISM

Nationalism, whose essence and development have recently been so admirably analyzed by a distinguished American historian,[72] must be accounted one of the major underlying causes of the War. In its chronic form of Pan-Germanism, Pan-Slavism and *revanche,* it nourished hatred between Germany and her two neighbors on the East and West. It worked in curious and devious ways. It had contributed happily to the unification of Germany and Italy. On the other hand, it had disrupted the Ottoman Empire and threatened to disrupt the Hapsburg Monarchy. In its virulent form, it had contributed for a century to a series of wars for national liberation and unity in the Balkans. It was such an important factor in the Balkan situation and led so directly to the immediate occasion of the World War that some account of it in this corner of Europe will be given below in the chapter on Balkan Problems.

(*d*) ECONOMIC IMPERIALISM

Economic imperialism embraces a series of international rivalries which resulted in large part from the Industrial Revolution in England and its subsequent introduction into the other great countries of the world.[73] It led to quantity

71 On these aspects of militarism, *cf.* H. N. Brailsford, *The War of Steel and Gold,* London, 1914; Karl Liebknecht, *Militarism,* New York, 1917; Munroe Smith, *Militarism and Statecraft,* New York, 1918; [F. C. Endres], *Die Tragödie Deutschlands,* 3rd ed., with abundant bibliographies, Stuttgart, 1924; and the admirable volume of G. L. Dickinson, *The International Anarchy, 1904-1914,* London, 1926.

72 C. J. H. Hayes, *Essays on Nationalism,* New York, 1926; and "Contributions of Herder to the Doctrine of Nationalism," in *Am. Hist. Rev.,* XXXII, 719-736 (July, 1927).

73 For an excellent recent discussion of this whole subject, see Parker

production of goods which in turn involved the struggle for new markets and new sources of raw materials. It resulted in a great increase of population, part of which sought to emigrate to the still unoccupied regions of the world, thereby sharpening the colonial rivalry of the Great Powers. It brought about the accumulation of capital which sought investment abroad, thus leading to economic exploitation and political competition. In consequence of these and other factors, the Great Powers began to partition Africa among themselves, to secure territory or exclusive spheres of influence in China, and to build railroads in Turkey and elsewhere. This struggle for markets, raw materials, and colonies became more acute during the last quarter of the nineteenth and the beginning of the twentieth century, owing to the fact that Germany and Italy entered the competition. Hitherto politically weak and divided, they had now secured national unity and wished to come forward to share with the other Powers in the partitioning of the world. It can hardly be said that any one of the Great Powers was more responsible than another for the international jealousies and friction which arose out of this economic imperialism. By 1914, all the Great European Powers had secured slices of Africa. In China, Italy only had failed to gain something for herself. In the matter of railway construction, which was one of the most important forms of economic imperialism because it involved political as well as economic interests, one sees the English building the Cape-to-Cairo railway, the Russians the Trans-Siberian, and the Germans the so-called Bagdad Railway. The first of these came into conflict with German, Belgian and French ambitions; the second was partly responsible for the Russo-Japanese War; the third caused endless sus-

T. Moon, *Imperialism and World Politics,* New York, 1926; and A. Lumbroso, *Le origini economichi e diplomatichi della guerra mondiale,* Milano 1927.

picions and friction between Germany and the Triple Entente.

Protective tariffs which usually accompanied the modern industrial system, except in England, were another form of economic imperialism. "Tariff wars" and retaliatory measures caused irritation between countries, especially in the mind of the man in the street and in newspaper discussion. There was always the danger that great merchants and industrialists would use official government support to secure economic advantages for themselves. This tended to bring governments into conflict with one another.

Generally speaking, however, this economic imperialism is usually exaggerated as one of the underlying causes of the War. It is often said, for instance, that the industrial development of Germany, and the jealousy with which it was regarded by England, made a war between these two countries "inevitable" sooner or later. This, however, is an unsound view. It arises from the fact that economic rivalry tends to become exaggerated in the mind of the public, because it is a subject which touches the pockets of wide classes, and is more generally discussed and perhaps understood than other questions like secret treaties, militarism, or nationalism. It often happens that great merchants or industrialists own or control newspapers which are selfishly interested in contributing to the exaggeration of these economic questions. But if one reads the diplomatic correspondence of the years before the War, one is struck by the relatively slight importance which is given to these economic rivalries which haunt so largely the mind of the average business man and newspaper editor. It is not so much questions of economic rivalry as those of prestige, boundaries, armies and navies, the Balance of Power, and possible shiftings in the system of alliances, which provoke reams of diplomatic correspondence and raise the temperature in Foreign Offices to the danger point.

(*e*) THE NEWSPAPER PRESS

Another underlying cause of the War was the poisoning of public opinion by the newspaper press in all of the great countries. This is a subject which is only beginning to receive the careful investigation which it deserves.[74]

Too often newspapers in all lands were inclined to inflame nationalistic feelings, misrepresent the situation in foreign countries, and suppress factors in favor of peace. In the diplomatic correspondence of the forty years before the War there were innumerable cases in which Governments were eager to establish better relations and secure friendly arrangements, but were hampered by the jingoistic attitude of the newspapers in their respective countries. Ambassadors and Cabinet Ministers frequently admitted the senseless attitude of the leading newspapers in their own country, apologized for it and promised to exert themselves to restrain it, if only the other Government would do the same toward its press. These were often quite genuine efforts and may frequently be seen in Anglo-German relations in the quarter of a century before the War. At other times, however, Ministers sought to score an advantage or to defend their attitude by alleging that their freedom of action was restricted because of the press and public opinion—that if they yielded the point under dispute there would be such a howl from the newspapers and the public that they would be turned out of office. Such allegations are sometimes true, but more often they are not, particularly in the countries of Central and Eastern Europe, where

[74] *Cf.* E. M. Carroll, "French Public Opinion in the War of 1870," in *Amer. Hist. Rev.*, XXXI, 679-700, July, 1926; J. F. Scott, *Five Weeks: a Study of the Surge of Public Opinion on the Eve of the Great War*, New York, 1927; I. C. Willis, *How We Went into the War*, London, 1918; L. M. Salmon, *The Newspaper and Authority* (N. Y., 1923), chs. xii-xiv; F. R. Flournoy, *Parliament and War—The Relation of the British Parliament to the Administration of Foreign Policy in Connection with the Initiation of War*, London, 1927.

the Government was generally able to exercise a greater control over the press than in England. It is, nevertheless, true that the newspapers of two countries often took up some point of dispute, exaggerated it, and made attacks and counter-attacks, until a regular newspaper war was engendered, which thoroughly poisoned public opinion, and so offered a fertile soil in which the seeds of real war might easily germinate. A particularly good example of this is to be seen in the press feud carried on between Austria and Serbia in the weeks following the murder of the Archduke Ferdinand. Here was a case in which the Governments of both countries, instead of apologizing for their press or trying to restrain it, deliberately allowed the newspapers to incite public opinion and fire it to an indignation and enthusiasm for war. It would, perhaps, be too much to say that, had it not been for this Austro-Serbian newspaper feud, the War might have been averted. But it is true that the violence of the Serbian press was one of the determining factors which led Count Tisza to change his opinion and to accept war with Serbia, whereas at first he had been stubbornly opposed to it; and without his consent Count Berchtold and the militarists could not have made war on Serbia.

There is a vast literature on freedom of the press, censorship of the press, slander and libel, and the professional aspects of journalism, but there is very little sound writing on the relations of the press to governmental control and on its influence in fomenting national hatreds and war. Yet there is abundant material for the study of this in the newspapers themselves; in *Die Grosse Politik,* and other diplomatic documents; and in the writings and biographies of men like W. T. Stead, Wickham Steed, Spender, and Northcliffe; of Busch, Hammann, and Theodor Wolff; of Lauzanne, Gauvin, and Tardieu; of Blowitz and Suvorin; and of Godkin, Ogden, Villard, and Lippmann. It is to be hoped that some careful scholars will turn their attention to this problem of the influence of the newspaper press as one of the underlying causes of the War. Bismarck's oft-quoted remark is even more true for the generation immediately preceding the World War than for his own: "Every country is held at some time to account for the windows broken by its press; the bill is presented, some day or other, in the shape of hostile sentiment in the other country."

CHAPTER II

THE SYSTEM OF SECRET ALLIANCES, 1871-1890: DOMINATION OF THE EASTERN EMPIRES

THE CONSEQUENCES OF THE FRANCO-PRUSSIAN WAR

THE Franco-Prussian War reversed a situation which had existed for two hundred years. After the Thirty Years' War in the seventeenth century Germany remained weak. Economically she had been exhausted by that terrible conflict in which all Europe trampled on her soil. Politically she was weak by her division into an incongruous multitude of states differing in size and character, and by the increasing rivalry for leadership between the decaying power of the Hapsburgs and the growing vigor of the Hohenzollerns. Consequently she was continually subject to the French policy of Richelieu and Mazarin, which aimed to keep her weak and divided. Occasionally, also, she was subject to actual invasion and dismemberment by French armies, as in the time of Louis XIV and Napoleon. Early in the nineteenth century, to be sure, in a time of great danger and humiliation, Prussia and Austria had temporarily sunk their mutual rivalry; with English and Russian assistance they had united in the War of Liberation to expel and dethrone Napoleon. But Waterloo did not end Germany's internal weaknesses. The loose Confederation of 1815 and the continued jealousy of Austria and Prussia left Germany still comparatively impotent and unimportant as an international power. Finally, in the 1850's at the Frankfort Diet, Bismarck became convinced that Germany's weakness could only be cured by a fratricidal war in which

Austria should be forcibly expelled from the German body politic. At Paris and at Biarritz, he learned to gauge the weakness and ambition of Napoleon III which could be turned to Germany's advantage. So he annexed Schleswig-Holstein, expelled Austria by the Prussian victory at Sadowa, and established the North German Federation under Prussian leadership. In 1870-1871, by Sedan and Versailles, he at last transformed Germany into a strong unified Empire. The situation between France and Germany was now reversed: it was no longer Germany, but France, which was weak and in danger from an attack from across the Rhine.

Bismarck's unification of Germany was hailed at the time as a desirable, even glorious, accomplishment of the spirit of nationalism. But it was accompanied by the annexation of Alsace-Lorraine. The French have always regarded this as a crime—"the brutal dismemberment of a nation," "the tearing of children from their mother." History shows that it was worse than a crime, it was a blunder.

In Bismarck's defense it has been said that he was only "liberating" territory which had been wrested from Germany by Louis XIV at a time when Germany was weak and divided against herself. Victors had always seized territory from the vanquished if they could, and if it suited their purposes. Moltke and the Prussian military authorities insisted that the provinces between the Vosges and the Rhine must be in German hands to prevent a possible attack by a revengeful France upon the South German States, which were none too enthusiastically or securely incorporated into the new German Empire. Bismarck, it is argued, could not come back to Berlin and face a Reichstag and the popular German demand for French territory without laying himself open to the charge of having been weakly generous to the successors of Louis XIV and Napoleon. Moreover, the majority of the population in the annexed districts spoke German. There is some truth in this point of view.

On the other hand, there is much more truth in another point of view. There was a vast difference between the French annexations in the seventeenth century and Bismarck's annexation in 1871. Between these two periods lay the French Revolution and the forces to which it had given rise. Louis XIV in seizing the Alsatian districts did not dismember Germany, because there was at that time no united German body politic—nothing but a conglomeration of mutually jealous German territories. The so-called Holy Roman Empire was neither Holy, nor Roman, nor an Empire, but "an irregular sort of a body like a monster,"[1] incapable of feeling a wound. The French Revolution, however, had swept away provincial boundaries in France, and created a new self-conscious nation, "one and indivisible." France, including the annexed districts of Alsace and Lorraine, had become one body, powerfully conscious of its unity and nationality; if one of its members suffered, all suffered together. Bismarck had mutilated a living body and the wound would not heal; it was to remain an awful open sore, threatening the peace of Europe for forty years. Nor was Alsace-Lorraine necessary to Germany's safety from a military point of view; the Rhine was as good a boundary as the Vosges. And though the majority of the million and a half people in Alsace and Lorraine were German speaking, that did not mean that they were German thinking; on the contrary, the great majority were bitterly opposed to separation from France and protested vigorously, but in vain. Could Bismarck have peered into the future and seen how French pride and French bitterness over the loss of Alsace-Lorraine was to vitiate every effort

[1] "Irregulare aliquod corpus et monstro simile," wrote "Severin de Monzambano" [Pufendorf] in his famous tract, *De Statu Imperii Germanici* (1667), cap. VI, sec. 9.

at permanently satisfactory relations between Germany and France—could he have foreseen how, by its direct and still more its indirect consequences, it was to be one of the main underlying causes of the World War, perhaps then he would have acted otherwise in 1871. But though he was possessed of unusual political foresight, he can scarcely have expected that the French would never become reconciled to their loss; that, on the contrary, the desire for *revanche,* unspoken perhaps, but fixed in the heart, would persist and even grow in intensity in later years. In fact, Bismarck's policy in the decade 1875-1885 seems to indicate that he had hopes of winning the French to something like frank friendship and an acceptance of the *fait accompli.*[2] Nevertheless, whatever he may have hoped as to the future, he had no illusions about the present. He knew that for the years immediately following the war, French resentment would run high. He must therefore protect the new German Empire, the child of his creation, by making it strong of itself—strong by holding France weak and isolated, and strong by the establishment of close relations with the two other Great Powers bordering on Germany on the east and south, that is, with Russia and Austria.

THE LEAGUE OF THE THREE EMPERORS, 1872-1878

Between Russia and Prussia there had existed traditional bonds of friendship ever since their armies had fought side by side for the overthrow of Napoleon. These bonds had been further strengthened during the Crimean War and the Polish uprising of 1863. Both Powers had a common interest in preventing the reëstablishment of Polish independence, which would have deprived them of the spoils of the partitions of Poland. During the Franco-Prussian

[2] "Je désire en arriver à ce que vous pardonniez Sedan comme vous avez pardonné Waterloo," Bismarck said to the French ambassador in December, 1884; Bourgeois et Pagès, *Les Origines et les Responsabilités de la Grande Guerre,* Paris, 1921, p. 307.

War, Russia had done Bismarck the great service of maintaining an attitude of benevolent neutrality and of tending to restrain Austria from joining France and seeking *revanche* for Sadowa. The long months during the siege of Paris were for Bismarck a critical and difficult period, and Russia might, if she had chosen, have greatly embarrassed him. Bismarck therefore at once frankly recognized the service which Russia had done him in 1870-1871 by assenting to the Tsar's abrogation of the humiliating Black Sea Clauses, imposed on Russia after the Crimean War. A still stronger bond between the two countries was the close personal tie between old Emperor William and his nephew, Alexander II, a tie which was renewed by the visit which the Tsar paid to Berlin in the month following the signature of peace between Germany and France.

With Austria, Bismarck was especially anxious to establish firm and friendly relations. Having accomplished his purpose of establishing German unity under Prussian leadership, he believed that the natural relation of the two countries which contained such large German elements and which for centuries had formed part of the same Holy Roman Empire should be one of friendship. After Sadowa he had purposely refrained from humiliating Austria further by annexing Austrian territory or by allowing the victorious German army to enter the Austrian capital. He had also maintained close relations with the powerful Magyar elements in Hungary who had used Prussian victories to secure for themselves from Francis Joseph the favorable constitutional Compromise of 1867. Austria, on her part, was ready to recognize 1866 as a *fait accompli* and to give up any hope of changing the arrangements which Bismarck had established. Accordingly, Bismarck was able to bring about friendly personal meetings between Emperor William and Francis Joseph in the summer of 1871 on Austrian soil. In November, 1871, the good relations between the two Powers were greatly strengthened through a change in the Foreign Office at Vienna: Count Beust, a Saxon who had never liked Bismarck and was inclined to the side of France, was replaced by Count Julius Andrássy, a Magyar and an old friend of Bismarck's.

In April, 1872, Count Andrássy suggested that Emperor Francis Joseph should pay a return visit to Emperor William at Berlin. When Tsar Alexander II heard of the intended visit he asked the German Ambassador in St. Petersburg, "Have they not written to ask you whether they would like to have me there at the same time with the Emperor of Austria?" [3]

Alexander did not want to be left out in the cold while his two brother monarchs were conferring together. He suggested that such a meeting of the three Eastern monarchs would be the strongest guarantee for the peace of Europe and would strike a blow at the French desire for *revanche* which was the most permanent menace to this peace. But his suggestion was a little embarrassing to Bismarck. He did not quite know how Francis Joseph would take it. When, however, the Austrian Emperor's consent had been secured, it was finally arranged that the three monarchs, accompanied by their Foreign Ministers, should visit Berlin together in the second week of September, 1872. This interview of the three Emperors, accompanied by extraordinary gala festivities meant to impress the world, resulted in a still closer understanding between the three Eastern Powers. Though no written agreement was signed, and though the Foreign Ministers conferred in pairs and not all together, there was established a close "understanding" or *"Entente à trois,"*—the basis for the "League of the Three Emperors" a few months later. In a sense, this Entente was a renewal of the old Holy Alliance of 1815; as in the days of Alexander I and Metternich the

[3] G.P., I, 197.

three Eastern Powers had stood together in defense of conservatism and the *status quo,* so now they were to stand together in defense of monarchical solidarity against the rising danger of international socialism, and for the preservation of the peace and *status quo* of Europe against possible moves of France or others to disturb it. On the whole, the meeting was a triumph for Bismarck, though he was not without irritation at the Russian minister, Gorchakov, whose vanity and suspected intrigues were ever a trial to his nerves. Gorchakov, for instance, on this occasion had greatly embarrassed Emperor William by remarking to him in the presence of the French Ambassador, "Well, I have just been at Prince Bismarck's to discuss with him the points on which we are agreed, but nothing has been put in writing; promises suffice between sovereigns and ministers."[4] For the suspicion which this remark may easily have aroused in the mind of the French Ambassador there was absolutely no ground. Alexander had no thought of participating in any aggressive policy toward France.

The Entente of the Three Emperors was further strengthened in the following year when Emperor William, accompanied by Bismarck and Moltke, visited St. Petersburg. A secret military convention was soon signed by which Russia and Germany promised to each other the assistance of two hundred thousand men in case either was attacked by a European Power.[5] A few weeks later, when Tsar Alexander journeyed to Austria to attend the Vienna Exhibition of 1873, he and Francis Joseph signed an agreement that they would consult one another on any questions in which they might have divergent interests; in case of any aggression by a third Power menacing the peace of Europe, they promised to come to an understanding with one another, without seeking or contracting new alliances, in order to reach a common line of conduct; and if, as a result of this

[4] G.P., I, 202.

[5] G.P., I, 203.

understanding, military action should become necessary, it should be arranged for by a special military convention. This agreement was communicated to Emperor William who gave his adhesion to it on October 22, 1873. In this way came into being the so-called League of the Three Emperors.[6]

Germany, as a result of her recent victories and her large army, was the strongest of the three Powers. And of the three ministers—Gorchakov, Andrássy and Bismarck—the last was by far the ablest in grasping the European situation as a whole, in seeing what the political interests of his neighbors were, and in being willing to recognize and bargain on the basis of these interests. The natural result was that the guiding spirit of the League was the German Chancellor. He used its influence to preserve the peace of Europe, and incidentally to prevent France from forming any coalition or seeking revenge against Germany. This at first was not difficult. Italy followed the lead of the three Emperors. England was still holding to her traditional policy of splendid isolation. France was too exhausted and too occupied with domestic political problems to think of disturbing the peace.

But in 1875, the harmony of the League was seriously ruffled. Gorchakov's vanity made it difficult for him to play second fiddle to Bismarck. With personal inclinations toward France, which were not shared by the Tsar, he listened to anti-German reports of his representatives at Berlin, Belgrade and Constantinople. He came into conflict with Bismarck over a Montenegrin affair and over the question of the rank to be enjoyed by Rosen, the German Consul General at Belgrade. Bismarck feared, with reason, that Gorchakov might influence the Tsar against Germany and thus weaken the League of the Three Emperors. He therefore sent Radowitz to St. Petersburg to take the

6 G.P., I, 206-209.

place of the German Ambassador who was on indefinite sick leave. Radowitz was to represent Bismarck's views to Gorchakov energetically, and he did so successfully. But Gorchakov then circulated rumors which grew into the French legend that Radowitz had been sent to bribe Russia to give Germany a free hand against France in return for Germany's giving Russia a free hand in the Orient. This alarmed France and England and contributed to the so-called "war-scare of 1875." Bismarck was unjustly suspected of contemplating a "preventive war" against France. Whether Bismarck had any hand in inspiring the German newspaper articles which added to the scare, or whether they started with the irresponsible communications of a newspaper reporter in Vienna, as now seems likely, is not wholly clear. At any rate, it is quite probable that he was willing to make use of it as a means of frightening France out of completing her proposed army reorganization, and there is no doubt that the French felt they were menaced. The French Foreign Minister appealed to Tsar Alexander and Queen Victoria to use their influence to prevent Germany from any aggressive action. Gorchakov easily persuaded the Tsar, on his visit to Berlin, to make it clear that Russia could not allow France to be crushed.[7] Gorchakov's pompous announcement from Berlin, "Now peace is assured," flattered his own vanity, but made Bismarck very angry, because Gorchakov seemed to have implied that Germany had really intended a preventive war and that Russia had averted it—an implication the truth of which Bismarck always energetically denied, and for which he

[7] *Cf.* J. V. Fuller. "The War Scare of 1875," in *Amer. Hist. Rev.*, XXIV, 196-226 (Jan., 1919). The current French version of the war-scare of 1875 needs correction in the light of *Die Grosse Politik,* I, 245-300; Radowitz, *Aufzeichnungen und Erinnerungen,* Stuttgart, 1925, I, 302 ff.; Hajo Holborn, *Bismarck's Europäische Politik zu Beginn der siebziger Jahre und die Mission Radowitz,* Berlin, 1925; and K. Klingenfuss, "Beust und Andrássy und die Kriegsgefahr von 1875," in *Archiv. f. Pol. u. Gesch.* IV., 616-643 (1926).

never forgave the Russian foreign minister.[8] The incident led to cooler relations between Berlin and St. Petersburg, but cannot be said to have really destroyed the League of the Three Emperors, since Alexander II and William I still remained close personal friends.

THE NEAR EASTERN CRISIS, 1875-1878

Another event in 1875 which threatened the harmony of the League of the Three Emperors was the outbreak of a new and prolonged crisis in the Balkans. The progressive dissolution of the Sick Man of Europe and the outrages committed by his savage soldiers on his long-suffering Christian subjects led Russia again to consider the possibility of his demise. In Herzegovina the cruelty of the land-owning aristocracy, a large part of whom were of Serb blood but who had become converted to Mohammedanism in order to live on better terms with the Turkish rulers, caused an uprising of the unhappy Christian peasantry in July, 1875. The uprising spread rapidly into Bosnia. It awoke the fanatical sympathy of Serb brethren in Austria-Hungary and the neighboring principality of Serbia. On account of the mountainous nature of the region and the inefficiency of the Sultan's government, the Turks seemed powerless to suppress the revolt. Russia and Austria were at once brought face to face again in their old rivalry over Balkan interests. Bismarck now had the difficult task during the next fifteen years of preventing this rivalry from causing a rupture between the two Powers whom he wished to have as friends

[8] *Cf.* Bismarck, *Reflections and Reminiscences,* ch. xxvi: "I reproached Prince Gorchakov sharply. It was not, I said, a friendly part suddenly and unexpectedly to jump on the back of a trustful and unsuspecting friend, and get up a circus performance at his cost; proceedings of this kind between us, who were the directing ministers, could only injure the two monarchies and states. If he was anxious to be applauded in Paris, he need not on that account injure our relations with Russia; I was quite ready to assist him and have five-franc pieces struck at Berlin, with the inscription *Gorchakov protège la France.*"

and whom he wished to prevent from gravitating toward France.

Russia's ambitions in the Balkans were of long standing. With the remarkable rise and consolidation of the Russian state at Moscow, the Slav Empire had begun to push steadily southward toward the Black Sea and the Dardanelles. Peter the Great, in wars with Turkey, had acquired for a short time at Azov his coveted "window" on the Black Sea, and given that impetus to Russian progress toward the south which his successors came to regard as Russia's historic mission. Catherine the Great, taking up anew the war with Turkey, had secured the Crimea and the whole northern shore of the Black Sea. Conveniently for Russia's ambitions, the spirit of nationalism awakened by the French Revolution had stimulated in Greeks and Slavs of the Balkans the desire to throw off the Turkish yoke. Russia was ready, as usual, to support their desire in order to fish in troubled waters herself. Already she had waged eight wars against Turkey, either for her own territorial expansion or for the ostensible purpose of assisting the subject nationalities of Slavic blood and Orthodox Greek faith. In the last of these wars—the Crimean—she had been checked by England and France and by the hostile attitude which Austria had assumed. This attitude of Austria, during the war and at the Congress of Paris, had contributed to Russia's loss of part of Bessarabia and caused great bitterness in Russia. It was felt to be an unpardonable act of Hapsburg ingratitude, coming, as it did, so soon after Nicholas I had sent a Russian army to help the Hapsburgs crush the Hungarian revolt of 1849. Russia's bitterness of feeling had subsided after the establishment of the League of the Three Emperors, but now there was danger that it might revive. Russia was anxious to win back the part of Bessarabia lost in 1856 and was inclined to support a new revolt like that in Bosnia and Herzegovina, which promised further to break up the Turkish Empire. Though Gorchakov had at first been opposed to Austria's annexing Bosnia and Herzegovina,[9] he gradually came round to accept such an arrangement, provided Russia in turn could secure adequate compensations for herself.

Austria, on the other hand, had no ostensible ties of religion and blood with the oppressed Christian nationalities in the Balkans and no desire to see them achieve independence as clients of Russia. Austria-Hungary—especially Hungary—already included more Slav peoples than could be easily assimilated. With the growing spirit of nationalism, these Slav subjects were becoming more and more difficult to govern. The Austrian Minister of Foreign Affairs, Andrássy, a Magyar, was therefore at first opposed to the acquisition of Bosnia and Herzegovina, which he feared would aggravate the internal problem of the Dual Monarchy of ruling over a large number of Slavs.[10] He preferred to have the Great Powers act jointly by way of a Conference and enforce reforms upon Turkey for the benefit of the peasantry in Bosnia and Herzegovina, but he did not desire to begin the partition of the Ottoman Empire. His desire found expression in the "Andrássy Note" of December 30, 1875, which demanded an armistice, a series of reforms, and the appointment of a mixed Christian and Mohammedan commission to look after the carrying out of the reforms. The Turks, as usual, made a pretense of accepting the demands; but the insurgent Bosnians, fired with enthusiasm by their successes and by their hope of support from their brother Serbs in Serbia and Montenegro, refused to abide by the terms of the Andrássy Note. The crisis became more serious.

Bismarck's chief concern in the whole Eastern Question was to prevent it from disturbing the peace of Europe and

[9] Wertheimer, *Graf Julius Andrássy,* II, 118.
[10] Wertheimer, *Graf Julius Andrássy,* II, 259 ff.

the satisfactory relations between Austria and Russia which had been established by the League of the Three Emperors. In a conversation with Gorchakov at Berlin in December, 1875, he had already emphasized this.[11] Germany herself, as he repeatedly declared, had no selfish interests of her own in the Balkans. "The whole Eastern question was not worth the bones of a Pomeranian grenadier."[12] But the danger of a split between Russia and Austria, or of the formation of a European coalition in connection with the Bosnian crisis, were very serious matters to him. Andrássy's idea of a conference of the Powers he did not look upon with favor, because he feared that Austria would naturally side with England and that Russia consequently might draw closer to France. Gorchakov, he suspected, would not be averse to flirting with France. But such a division of Europe into an Anglo-Austrian and Franco-Russian grouping would place Germany in a delicate and dangerous position: she would have the thankless task either of acting as arbitrator between the two groups, or she would have to cast in her vote on the Anglo-Austrian side, thus laying Germany open to hostile Powers on two fronts. Such a grouping would also endanger the League of the Three Emperors and its safeguarding of the peace of Europe.[13]

Meanwhile, however, Tsar Alexander and Emperor Francis Joseph, accompanied by their Ministers, had come together at Reichstadt and on July 8, 1876, reached a secret but somewhat hazy "agreement" without Bismarck's knowledge. They agreed to refrain from intervention in Turkey for the present. But for the future, if the Turks should regain the upper hand over the insurgents, Russia and Austria would protect the Serbs from excessive violence and insist upon real reforms. If, on the other hand, the insur-

11 G.P., I, 207.
12 Bismarck's Reichstag speech of December 7, 1876.
13 G.P., II 31 ff.

gents continued their successful resistance and the Ottoman Empire in Europe should crumble to pieces, Austria was to annex part of Bosnia, Russia was to regain the part of Bessarabia lost in 1856 and territories on the eastern shore of the Black Sea [in which Austria had no interest]; Bulgaria and Rumelia were to be autonomous; additions of territory were to be given to Serbia, Montenegro and Greece; and Constantinople was to be erected into a free city.[14]

By this Reichstadt Agreement Gorchakov had secured Austria's agreement in principle to the partition of Turkey. The terms, as Andrássy conceived them, were exceedingly favorable for Austria. The agreement contemplated the development of a number of small, weak states in the Balkans, but expressly excluded the creation of a large, strong Slav state, whether Serbian or Bulgarian, which would have naturally affiliated itself with Russia on racial and religious grounds and have been a menace to Austria. Moreover, by the stipulation that Austria might annex Bosnia and Herzegovina, Austria would assure the safety of her outlying Dalmatian possessions, would check the danger from the growing nationalist aspirations of the Serbs, and would acquire territory which might be regarded as compensation for the loss of Venetia in 1866. Andrássy, who had originally been opposed to the break-up of the

[14] Reichstadt "agreement" is a misnomer, since there was a misunderstanding from the outset. No formal document was drawn up, "agreed upon," and signed at Reichstadt. After the meeting, the Austrian and Russian ministers each dictated his own recollection of the substance of the views exchanged. This explains many marked differences between the Austrian and Russian versions of the "agreement" as printed respectively by Wertheimer (*Graf Julius Andrássy,* II, 322 ff.) and by the Bolsheviks in *Krasnyi Arkhiv* (Moscow, 1922), I, 36. According to the Russian version, for instance, Montenegro was to annex Herzegovina, and Austria was merely to take Turkish Croatia and a small adjacent part of Bosnia contiguous to the Austrian frontier. According to Andrássy's version, Austria was to annex all of Bosnia and Herzegovina except certain "extensions" allotted to Serbia and Montenegro "to round them off." *Cf.* G. H. Rupp, "The Reichstadt Agreement," in *Amer. Hist. Rev.* XXX, 503-510 (April, 1925); and G.P., II, 34-37.

Ottoman Empire, was now well content with the agreement. The failure of his efforts to secure reforms in the region from the Turks during the past months had convinced him of the futility of attempting to preserve the *status quo* or to secure any permanent satisfactory settlement for the Christian peasantry so long as they remained under Turkish misgovernment. And if Austria was to annex Bosnia and Herzegovina it was much better to do it in friendly agreement with Russia than in opposition to her.

But the fortunes of war in the Balkans during the following weeks did not bear out the probable expectation of Gorchakov and Andrássy that Turkey was on the point of collapsing. On the contrary, the Turks showed an extraordinary revival of energy. They defeated the insurgents in one encounter after another, until finally on August 29, Prince Milan of Serbia called for help. Gorchakov and the Russian Pan-Slavs were not deaf to the call. They felt that they must intervene on behalf of the oppressed Orthodox Slav peasantry, in spite of the principle of non-intervention for the present, which had formed the first clause of the Reichstadt Agreement. This at once renewed the old hostility between Russia and Austria over Balkan affairs and led to a tense situation between the two Great Powers. Both accordingly turned to Bismarck.

On September 13, 1876, Andrássy informed the German Ambassador in Vienna of the Reichstadt Agreement, which hitherto, at Gorchakov's request, had been concealed from Bismarck.[15] Gorchakov on his part resorted to a stratagem which aroused Bismarck's indignation. Instead of communicating in the proper official way through the Russian Ambassador at Berlin, he was suspected by Bismarck of instigating the Tsar to make use of Baron Werder, Emperor William's personal representative to the Tsar. Werder, who was staying with Alexander at Livadia in the Crimea

[15] G.P., II, 45-47.

was suddenly asked the blunt question whether in case of war between Russia and Austria, Germany would observe benevolent neutrality as Russia had done in 1870. Werder telegraphed the embarrassing and indiscreet question to Berlin. But Bismarck evaded giving any answer to it, and would have recalled Werder except for Emperor William's fear that it would hurt the Tsar's feelings. But a few days later, employing the correct channel of communications by instructions to the German Ambassador at St. Petersburg, Bismarck again emphasized his aim of preserving peace in Europe and harmony in the League of the Three Emperors. If Russia decided to intervene and make war on Turkey, Bismarck would use his influence to prevent Austria from attacking Russia, and he hoped he could succeed in this. If not, and if war broke out between Russia and Austria in spite of all his efforts, Germany would not necessarily abandon neutrality. He would make no promises beforehand, but he would say that German interests could not allow a coalition of all Europe permanently to weaken Russia's position as a Great Power; nor could he, on the other hand, permit Austria to be endangered in her position as a European Power or in her independence, and so cease to be one of the factors on which Germany could reckon in the European balance of power.[16] "We could endure that our friends should lose or win battles against each other, but not that one of the two should be so severely wounded and injured that its position as an independent Great Power, taking its part in the councils of Europe, would be endangered."[17]

Bismarck's refusal to give Russia a free hand against Austria caused Gorchakov to moderate his attitude. It was arranged that the representatives of the Christian Powers should meet in conference at Constantinople and convince

[16] G.P., II, 72-79; *cf.* also II, 108, and VI, 356 f.
[17] Bismarck, *Reflections and Reminiscences,* II, 234.

Abdul Hamid of the need of making real reforms. But convincing the Turk was about as easy a matter as making a donkey gallop. Abdul Hamid thwarted the conference by a clever pretense of proclaiming a constitution for Turkey and by promising even more wide-reaching reforms than the Powers themselves had demanded. Gorchakov, however, rightly had no confidence in the honesty of the Sultan's promises. He therefore prevailed upon Austria to sign a new secret Budapest Convention of January 15, 1877, providing for the war which Russia contemplated waging against Turkey. Austria agreed not to threaten the Russian flank upon its advance south of the Danube, and in return Russia approved the idea of Austria's annexation of Bosnia and Herzegovina and the other provisions which Andrássy understood had been agreed upon at Reichstadt.[18]

In April, 1877, as soon as weather conditions permitted, Russia opened against Turkey the war which she had long desired. Though checked for months at Plevna, she eventually won a series of victories which brought her armies to the outskirts of Constantinople and forced Turkey to accept the Treaty of San Stefano on March 3, 1878. This provided for the creation of a great Bulgarian State, more or less comprising the predominantly Bulgarian parts of Turkey and embracing an extensive sea coast on the Aegean. The Treaty met with objections on every side: by Greece, Serbia, and Rumania because this "Greater Bulgaria" was to be so much more powerful than any one of themselves. It was objected to by Austria and England who feared the greatly enlarged Bulgaria would be virtually a vassal state under Russian control; Austria did not like to see such an increase of Russia's power near her border, and England feared for the safety of the Suez Canal. Both these Powers therefore insisted on a Congress for the revision of the Treaty of San Stefano. Bismarck at first had no great

[18] G.P., II. 111-115.

liking for this proposal, but finally consented to act as "Honest Broker," and invited the Powers to the Congress of Berlin.

In the various preliminary negotiations which settled almost all the essential points before the Congress met, so that the Congress merely had to register decisions which had already been arranged by Bismarck, the German Chancellor strove hard to satisfy both Austrian and Russian interests. In the end, Austria was again accorded by the Treaty of Berlin the right to occupy and administer Bosnia and Herzegovina and also, if military necessity required, to occupy the tongue of territory between Serbia and Montenegro known as the Sanjak of Novibazar. Russia acquired the part of Bessarabia lost in 1856 and valuable territories between the Black and Caspian Seas. These were important gains for Russia, but to Gorchakov they seemed but slight rewards after all Russia's military efforts and successes. He left the Congress with bitter feelings against Bismarck. He felt that Bismarck had betrayed Russian interests and been guilty of unpardonable ingratitude in view of Russia's benevolent neutrality during the Franco-Prussian War. In Russia there was a violent outburst in the Pan-Slav press against Germany which Bismarck regarded as altogether unjustifiable. Though he had supported Austria and England on many points, he had also done Russia a real service, getting far more for her at the Congress than she could have gotten for herself. He thought Russia ought to look with satisfaction at the real gains that she had made, instead of comparing the Treaty of Berlin with what she would have gained by the Treaty of San Stefano. The result of this personal bitterness between the two Ministers and of the violent newspaper attacks of one country against the other put an end for the time being to that harmony and coöperation which had been the object of the League of the Three Emperors.

THE AUSTRO-GERMAN ALLIANCE OF 1879

The hostility between Russia and Germany was not confined merely to personal bitterness between the Ministers or to the recriminations of newspapers. In the commissions established for executing the terms of the Treaty of Berlin, the German delegates sided regularly with Austria against Russia. In reply, Russia undertook a vigorous increase in armaments and pushed her troops westward into Poland toward the German frontier. "Russia must prepare for War," declared General Miliutin, and his declaration was reiterated by the Pan-Slavs. At last, in the summer of 1879, even Alexander himself, unable longer to restrain his feelings, poured out his grievances to the German Ambassador in St. Petersburg, and wrote a letter to Emperor William complaining of Bismarck's policy and warning him of "the disastrous consequences which might follow." [19]

At about the same time Bismarck heard that his friend Andrássy was soon to resign and was likely to be replaced by Baron Haymerle, on whose friendship he did not feel sure that he could count. In view of the danger from Russia he decided to seek at once a defensive alliance with Austria while Andrássy was still in office. He accordingly drew up with him the Treaty of October 7, 1879, which established the Austro-German Alliance. He would have liked a treaty in which Austria and Germany would promise to support each other in case either were attacked by a third Power, whether Russia, France, or Italy. But Austria was unwilling to expose her eastern frontier to a Russian attack by promising unconditionally to assist Germany in the West in case the French should undertake a war of revenge. Austria was mainly concerned with the danger from the side of Russia. Therefore the treaty provided that should Austria or Germany be attacked by Russia, the

[19] G.P., III, 16.

two Contracting Parties were bound to come to the assistance one of the other with their whole war strength; should either be attacked by a Power other than Russia [such as France or Italy], the other Contracting Party bound itself to observe a benevolent neutrality; should, however, the attacking Power be supported by Russia, then the other Contracting Party would come to the assistance of her ally with her whole strength. The treaty was to be for five years and renewable. It was also to be secret, though if the armaments of Russia really proved menacing, the Contracting Powers would consider it a duty of loyalty to let the Tsar know, at least confidentially, that they would consider an attack on either as an attack on both.[20]

The Austro-German Alliance consolidated the Central Empires and became henceforth, until their collapse in November, 1918, the very foundation rock of German policy. It indicated a political course from which neither Bismarck nor his successors ever seriously swerved. In its origin, and as long as Bismarck remained at the helm, it was essentially defensive in purpose and fact. Germany and Austria mutually protected each other against the rising tide of Pan-Slavism; and Germany, if attacked by an outbreak of French *revanche*, could count upon Austria's neutrality, just as Austria could count on that of Germany in case of an outbreak of Italian Irredentism.

Contemporary opinion regarded Bismarck's establishment of this Alliance as a master stroke. In the words of the French Ambassador at Berlin: "From the point of view of his prestige in Europe and of his popularity in Germany, Bismarck has never accomplished a work so considerable as that of the Alliance with Austria. . . . He has realized without wars, without conquests dearly bought, without

[20] Pribram, I, 6-9. For the detailed negotiations by which Bismarck arranged this treaty and overcame his own sovereign's strong objections to it, see G.P., III, 1-136.

burdensome or enfeebling annexations, the German political dream of union of all the States where the German race dominates in a common political system and a powerful solidarity." [21] This contemporary opinion has for the most part been endorsed by posterity.[22] Only here and there before the World War were there those who criticized it. But after 1914, when German support of Austria became one of the causes which involved all Europe in war, many voices, even in Germany, questioned Bismarck's wisdom. They alleged that Bismarck, by further alienating Russia through alliance with Austria, made inevitable the Franco-Russian Alliance; and that by taking sides with Austria against Russia in the Balkans, he prepared the way for the clash which came in 1914.

Such critics, however, are wrong in thinking that Russia was permanently alienated from Germany after 1879. They did not know of the very secret treaty which Bismarck made with Russia within two years (June 18, 1881) and which he renewed (with modifications) and kept effective as long as he remained in power. They are wrong in thinking that it made the Franco-Russian alliance inevitable. This was perhaps "inevitable" anyway, in view of the growth of Pan-Slavism in Russia and the persistence of Alsatian memories in France. And they are wrong in thinking that Bismarck's alliance of 1879 necessarily involved an Austro-Russian clash in the Balkans. True to the defensive aims with which he had established the Austro-German Alliance, Bismarck continually warned Austria in the following years that Germany would not fight to support Austrian expansion or aggression in the Balkans. He repeatedly took occasion to remind her that the alliance was defensive, not offensive.[23] In 1885, for instance, with prophetic vision, he warned

[21] St. Vallier to Freycinet, March 22, 1880; Bourgeois et Pagès, p. 370

[22] *Cf.* C. Grant Robertson, *Bismarck,* p. 363 f.

[23] G.P., IV, 338: V, 8, 26 ff., 35 f., 136 ff., 149 ff., 194 f.

Austria that in supporting Serbia too strongly she might so arouse Serbian ambitions that Serbia would some day "turn against Austria and talk of a Serbia Irredenta in the Banat" of Hungary.[24] It was not until many years after Bismarck's dismissal that Austria began to pursue the more aggressive and independent policy, which tended to pervert the Austro-German Alliance from one which was defensive in form to one which became offensive in fact. Criticism should not be directed against Bismarck, but against his later successors—especially Bülow and Bethmann—who failed to follow sufficiently closely his conservative policy of holding Austria in check.

It is also a mistake to imply, as so many writers do, that Bismarck's choice of Austria in preference to Russia in 1879 was final, and that the wire between Berlin and St. Petersburg was permanently broken down. It was not. Bismarck was only waiting for an opportunity to repair it. He had by no means permanently turned his back upon Russia. In allying with Austria he was only taking a step which prudence for the moment counselled, but this did not preclude another step later in the direction of Russia. The opportunity for this soon came.

THE ALLIANCE OF THE THREE EMPERORS, 1881-1887

Among Russia's diplomats there were two who did not allow themselves to be blinded by indignation against Bismarck over the outcome of the Congress of Berlin. One of these was Giers, who soon assumed virtual charge of Russian foreign affairs in place of Gorchakov. The other was Peter Saburov, who foresaw the probability of an Austro-German alliance even before it was signed.[25] In January, 1880, Saburov came as Ambassador to Berlin, where he had many

[24] G.P., V, 11 f.

[25] *Cf.* his interesting and friendly conversations with Bismarck at Kissingen in July, 1879, in *Krasnyi Arkhiv,* I, 68-84.

intimate interviews with Bismarck with a view to reknitting the close personal relations between Tsar Alexander II and Emperor William I, thus reviving the League of the Three Emperors.[26]

Saburov, like all Russian diplomats, always had one eye out for Russian control or influence at Constantinople. He had realized in 1878 how easy it was for an English fleet to threaten the Turkish capital and he feared for the future. He therefore laid before Bismarck his view of Russia's danger in a memorandum to the following effect. In 1833 Russia had aided Turkey against the victorious army of Mehemet Ali, and was rewarded for this service by the Treaty of Unkiar Skelessi, in which Turkey undertook to close the Dardanelles to all enemy fleets which sought to penetrate to the Black Sea. This stipulation, negotiated exclusively for Russia's benefit, protected her southern shores from hostile attack; but this stipulation was modified to her detriment by the Treaty of London of 1840 and the Straits Convention of 1841, in which the principle of the closure of the Straits, hitherto applied to entry into the Black Sea, was equally extended to exit from it. Russia was thus shut off from sending her navy into the Mediterranean. These principles were confirmed in the Treaty of Paris in 1856 which in addition forbade Russia and Turkey to have ships of war on the Black Sea; this treaty remained in force until the Treaty of London of 1871. The London agreement, resulting from Russia's attempt to abrogate the Black Sea Clauses while France and Germany had their hands tied by the Franco-Prussian War, annulled the provision of 1856 forbidding Russian or Turkish war vessels on the Black Sea, but admitted for the first time the principle that foreign navies might enter the Straits if the Sultan

26 G.P., III, 139-179. J. Y. Simpson, "Russo-German Relations and the Sabouroff Memoirs," in *The Nineteenth Century,* LXXXII, 1111-1123; LXXXIII, 60-75 (Dec., 1917; Jan., 1918).

judged it necessary for the safeguarding of the other clauses of the Treaty of Paris. This reversed completely to Russia's disadvantage the principle of the closure of the Straits, which in its origin had been intended to provide Russia with a lock and chain at the Dardanelles for the protection of her shores and her influence over Turkey. At the Congress of Berlin, England had declared that "her obligations, concerning the closure of the Straits, were limited to an engagement to the Sultan to respect in this matter only the *independent* decisions of the Sultan"; in other words, England was not obliged to respect the decision of the Sultan if the latter tried to close the Straits at Russia's demand, for such a decision would not be "independent." England, Saburov concluded, was reserving the right to enter the Straits and threaten Russian interests whenever she pleased. Russia's lock and chain were valueless therefore, unless she could get the support of Germany and Austria.[27] This is what Saburov wanted and what Bismarck was willing to give, in return for the restoration of friendly relations with Russia. A friendly agreement with Russia would mean a renewal of the League of the Three Emperors, and tend to guarantee the peace of Europe. Saburov had also been duly impressed by the Austro-German Alliance and began to realize Russia's diplomatic isolation. Russia was anxious again for German and Austrian support.

Bismarck, on his side, in spite of his relatively friendly relations at this time with France, could never wholly rid

[27] Russian Aide-Mémoire of Feb. 5, 1880, given by Saburov to Bismarck; G.P., III, 144f. For an excellent historical sketch of the Straits question to 1878, see J. T. Shotwell, "A Short History of Question of Constantinople and the Straits" in *International Conciliation,* No. 180, Nov., 1922, pp. 463-527; see also S. M. Goriainov, *Le Bosphore et les Dardanelles,* Paris, 1910; P. H. Mishev, *La mer noire et les détroits de Constantinople,* Paris, 1899; E. Driault, *La Question d'Orient,* Paris, 1905; N. Dascovici, *La Question du Bosphore et des Dardanelles,* Genève, 1915; N. E. Buxton and C. Phillipson, *The Question of the Bosphorus and the Dardanelles,* London, 1917; and below, ch. v. especially note 11.

himself of the nightmare that the French might make a coalition with Russia against him. To diminish the likelihood of this, he believed it would be highly desirable to restore the old harmony between the three Eastern Emperors, which had existed before the Congress of Berlin. Austria also would derive advantage from such a renewal of good relations with both her neighbors, because it would tend to safeguard the new position which she had acquired in Bosnia and Herzegovina, and would make more certain that any future changes in the *status quo* in the Balkans—which was still very unstable—would not be made single-handed by Russia to the sole benefit of the Slavs and to the detriment of Austria; such changes would only be made on the basis of a mutual understanding between the three Eastern Empires.

In view of the advantages to each of the three Powers, it was not difficult to reach the very secret agreement which was signed by Bismarck, Saburov, and Szechenyi on June 18, 1881. It was regarded as so secret that Bismarck did not entrust the drawing up of documents in regard to it to the chancery secretaries, but wrote them out with his own hand; and the diplomatic correspondence dealing with it was marked with special numbers and reserved for the eye of as few initiates as possible. The secret was so well preserved that the world knew nothing of it until part of it was published by Professor Goriainov in 1918.[28] It provided among other things (Art. I) that "in case one of the High Contracting Parties should find itself at war with a fourth Great Power, the other two will preserve a benevolent neutrality toward it and will devote their efforts to the localizing of the conflict." In other words, if Germany should be at war with France, or Austria at war with Italy,

28 S. Goriainov, "The End of the Alliance of the Emperors," *Amer. Hist. Rev.*, XXIII, 325 (Jan., 1918). The full text is printed by Pribram, p. 11, and, with the negotiations leading up to it, in G.P. III, 139-179.

or Russia at war with Turkey, the country at war need have no fear of an attack on its rear by either of the other two Eastern Empires. Austria's interest in the Balkans was safeguarded by the provision that this first clause in Art. I should apply to a war between Russia and Turkey, "but only in case a previous agreement has been reached between the three Courts relative to the results of that war."

In Art. II the three Signatory Powers agreed to respect the rights acquired by Austria in Bosnia and Herzegovina by the Treaty of Berlin, and to make no changes in the territorial *status quo* of "Turkey in Europe" except by common consent. By tacit implication this meant that Russia could still pursue her forward policy in the Caucasus where Austria and Germany were not particularly interested.

Saburov's fears of an English fleet in the Straits were quieted by Art. III:

> "The three Courts recognize the European and mutually obligatory character of the principle of the closure of the Straits of the Bosphorus and of the Dardanelles. . . . They will take care jointly that Turkey shall make no exception to this rule in favor of the interests of any Government whatsoever by lending to warlike operations of a belligerent Power the portion of its Empire constituted by the Straits. In case of infringement, or to prevent it if such infringement should be in prospect, the three Courts will inform Turkey that they would regard her, in that event, as putting herself in a state of war towards the injured Party, and as having deprived herself thenceforth of the benefits of the security assured to her territorial *status quo* by the Treaty of Berlin."

A supplementary protocol provided for friendly coöperation between the consular and other agents of the Signatory Powers in the Balkans, and for the possible reunion of Bulgaria and East Rumelia. Russia's concessions to Austria in the Reichstadt Agreement and Budapest Convention were reaffirmed by a clause agreeing that:

> "Austria reserves the right to annex the provinces of Bosnia and Herzegovina [already occupied in 1878] at whatever moment she shall deem opportune."

This treaty of 1881, which revived the League of the Three Emperors and converted it into an alliance, served Bismarck's great purpose of preserving peace in Europe, and especially of preventing a conflict between Russia and Austria in the Near East. It established by tacit consent a kind of line of demarcation between the two. Russia was to have unhampered and dominant influence in Bulgaria and the Eastern Balkans such as Austria was to have in Serbia and the Western Balkans. The establishment of the frontier between Bulgaria and Serbia as the demarcation line dividing Russian and Austrian interests, Bismarck rightly believed, was the surest and best way to avoid dangerous rivalries and suspicions in the Balkans. He was quite ready to use Germany's decisive influence in the balance to force each of his allies to keep behind the line of demarcation in their proper spheres. In contrast to the policy of his successors, he was ready to restrain Austria by timely warnings and pressure from taking aggressive action in the Balkans which would arouse dangerous Russian opposition. He did not care who ruled in Bulgaria nor what took place there. That was Russia's sphere and she could do as she liked in it. Russia had originally established Alexander of Battenberg as Prince of Bulgaria; but if Russia wanted to turn him out when he no longer proved the pliant tool which the Pan-Slavs had expected, that was Russia's affair and Austria ought not object. He warned Austria that she must keep hands off in Bulgaria, and that he would not allow anyone to throw a noose about his neck in this matter which would embroil Germany with Russia. His wise advice to Austria was: "The Eastern Question is a game of patience; he wins who waits." [29]

[29] G.P., V, 195.

Bismarck's policy of a demarcation of interests between Austria and Russia, and the pressure he put upon each, helped to preserve the peace of Europe even during the violent Balkan crisis that arose through the union of the two Bulgarias in September, 1885. Austria did nevertheless so encourage the Serbians against the Bulgarians that Alexander III refused to renew the Alliance of the Three Emperors when the Treaty ran out in 1887.

The Tsar had an ineradicable distrust of Austria. He had inherited it from his grandfather at the time of Austria's "astonishing ingratitude" during the Crimean War. It had been fostered and nourished by his tutors and advisers, who belonged to the Pan-Slav group represented by Miliutin and Katkov, and it had taken a deep hold on him during the long Bosnian crisis which ended so unsatisfactorily for Russia in the Congress of Berlin. Bismarck worked hard to bring about the renewal of the tripartite agreement of 1881. He did not want to see it "thrown behind the stove." [30] But when he found that the Tsar was unshakeable in his distrust of Austria, he had no mind to forfeit Russia's friendship because of Austria's unnecessarily aggressive support of Serbians against Bulgarians. Moreover, his relations with France had grown very much worse during recent months as Boulanger had come into prominence, and he had heard rumors in September, 1886, and in the spring of 1887, of secret negotiations for a Franco-Russian coalition.[31]

THE RUSSO-GERMAN "RE-INSURANCE TREATY," 1887-1890

Bismarck therefore accepted with alacrity a Russian proposal that in place of the existing tripartite agreement, Russia and Germany should make a defensive treaty of their own without Austria. With a characteristic directness of action, Bismarck drew out of his portfolio the text of the

[30] Instruction of Dec. 21, 1886; G.P., V, 211. [31] G. P., VI, 89 ff.

Alliance of 1879 and read it to Schuvalov, declaring that he sincerely regretted that Russia's attitude at that time had compelled Germany to protect herself by means of this treaty. Nevertheless it existed; Germany must and would remain loyal to its terms and to Austria, and therefore this fact must be taken into consideration in framing any treaty between Russia and Germany. After the discussion of a number of alternatives, this difficulty was finally overcome by the wording agreed upon in Art. I: "If one of the High Contracting Parties shall find itself at war with a third Great Power, the other will maintain towards it a benevolent neutrality and will devote its efforts to the localization of the conflict. This provision shall not apply to a war against Austria or France resulting from an attack made upon one of these two powers by one of the Contracting Parties." [32] This defensive arrangement was perfectly satisfactory to Bismarck as he had no intention of attacking France; and in case France should attack Germany he had been insured since 1879 against danger on his Southern frontier by Austria's promise of benevolent neutrality. Now, by the new treaty with Russia, he was re-insured against any danger on his Eastern frontier. Furthermore, if Russia should attack Austria, the new "Re-insurance Treaty" in no way conflicted with his obligation to protect Austria, in accordance with the Austro-German Alliance.

With his characteristic willingness to consider the aims and ambitions of other Powers and to bargain on the basis of them, Bismarck then further recognized Russia's Balkan interests and Saburov's desire to secure a Russian lock and chain against the English in the Straits. The Re-insurance Treaty accordingly recognized (Art. II) "the rights historically acquired by Russia in the Balkan Peninsula and particularly the legitimacy of a preponderating and decisive influence on her part in Bulgaria and East Rumelia"; and

[32] G.P., V, 253; Pribram, p. 305.

Art. III reaffirmed the principle already agreed upon in 1881 that Russia and Germany should support each other in putting pressure on the Sultan to keep the Bosphorus and the Dardanelles closed to the warships of foreign Powers. They also pledged themselves to permit no modification of the *status quo* in the Balkan Peninsula except by a previous mutual agreement. In a supplementary protocol Bismarck went even further in recognizing the Russian point of view by agreeing that "in case Russia finds it necessary to undertake herself the task of defending the entrance into the Black Sea in order to safeguard the interests of Russia, Germany engages to lend her benevolent neutrality and her moral and diplomatic support to the measures which Russia shall deem necessary to guarantee the key to her Empire." This meant that, so far as Germany was concerned, Russia might take possession of territory on the Straits and perhaps even of Constantinople. The possession of this "key," which Russia would virtually have acquired by the Treaty of San Stefano in 1878 and which Bismarck now promised in 1887, meant much more than the mere lock and chain against the English fleet for which Saburov had stipulated in 1881. Bismarck was willing to concede even this "key" in order to lessen the likelihood of a coalition between Russia and France. He may also, no doubt, have counted upon the fact that England would still have something to say if Russia tried to oust the Sultan from his capital. This so-called "Re-insurance Treaty" of June 18, 1887, was to be in force three years.[33] It outlasted Bismarck's own tenure of office, but was not renewed by his successor, Caprivi. During the three years it was in force it did not wholly prevent the beginning of a *rapprochement* between France and Russia which eventually devel-

[33] For the text of the treaty and the negotiations leading up to it see G.P., V, 211-268; and Goriainov, in *Amer. Hist. Rev.*, XXIII, 330-349 Jan., 1918). Taube, *La Politique Russe d'Avant-Guerre* (Paris, 1928), 74-84.

oped into an Alliance, but there is no doubt that it delayed this coalition which had been Bismarck's worst nightmare.

Such was the success of one set of alliances, establishing the domination of the Eastern Empires, by which Bismarck for nearly a score of years conjured away an open clash between Russia and Austria in the Balkans, preserved almost unbroken the good relations of Germany with her powerful neighbors to the south and east, and thereby lessened the danger from the west. The very existence of the Alliance of 1881 with Russia and Austria had been preserved with such perfect secrecy that it gave rise to no suspicions or alarm on the part of France or other Powers.

THE TRIPLE ALLIANCE OF 1882

The formation of the Triple Alliance is commonly attributed to Bismarck. He is pictured as encouraging France to seize Tunis with the calculation that this "would arouse such bitterness in Italy that Bismarck could undoubtedly secure the consent of the Italian Government to an alliance with Austria and Germany."[34] It is true that he encouraged France to "pluck the ripe Tunisian fruit" and to engage in other colonial adventures. But he did this mainly in the hope of winning the friendship of the French by supporting their ambitions, and also of interesting them in colonial activities which would help them to forget the defeat of 1870. He hoped they would expend their energies

[34] Seymour, *The Diplomatic Background of the War, 1870-1914,* p. 35. *Cf.* also Matter, *Bismarck et son Temps,* III, 445, 512 f.; Hanotaux, *Histoire de la France Contemporaine,* IV, 740; Coolidge, *The Origins of the Triple Alliance,* 197 ff. For accounts of the Triple Alliance based on the new material in *Die Grosse Politik,* and Pribram, see Becker, *Bismarcks Bündnispolitik* (Berlin, 1923); Rachfahl, *Deutschland und die Weltpolitik, 1871-1914,* I, *Die Bismarck'sche Aera* (Stuttgart 1923), pp. 371-398; Granfelt, *Das Dreibundsystem, 1879-1916* (Stockholm, 1924); Lenz, *Deutschland im Kreis der Grossmächte, 1871-1914* (Berlin, 1925). The best account of the Tunis Question is by W. L. Langer, "The European Powers and the French Occupation of Tunis, 1878-1881," in *Amer. Hist. Rev.,* XXXI, 55-78, 251-265 (Oct., 1925; Jan., 1926).

in North Africa and China instead of preparing to regain Alsace-Lorraine. He was quite willing that the French should antagonize the Italians, but he was not calculating to secure the alliance of the latter. It was not with Bismarck that the Triple Alliance originated, but with Italy.

Early in 1882, Italy asked for a treaty of alliance with Germany and Austria. Italy wanted to strengthen her position and to gain support for future ambitions. Italy had come away from the Congress of Berlin "with clean hands," which meant empty hands, though Bismarck had told her that, as far as Germany was concerned, she might take Tripoli any time. She had just received what she regarded as a humiliating slap in the face from the French who had occupied Tunis, the very territory which Italy had not unnaturally been coveting for herself. And she was still afraid "the Prisoner of the Vatican" might attempt to regain his temporal possessions. Italy had everything to gain and little to risk in an alliance with Germany and Austria. This Bismarck fully recognized, and he was not therefore especially eager to incur an Italian liability. Earlier, in 1880, when a treaty with Italy was first suggested to him, his comment was, "You don't need to run after Italy if you want something of her; moreover, her promise will have no value if it is not in her interest to keep it." [35] Of the value of the Italians themselves as Allies, he had no very high opinion. In his private notes, recently published, he refers to "their fickle character," "their childish egoism," and "the restless, arrogant character of Italy's policy, which might easily involve her friends in trouble." [36] He argued the instability of alliances with parliamentary monarchies like Italy and England:

> "Not all countries are able to offer the same guarantee that their obligations will be strictly executed, especially in countries in which the legislature exercises more influence

[35] G.P., III, 185. [36] G.P., III, 185, 198; *cf.* also Pribram, I, 128 ff.

than the dynasty. With England, for instance, there could be no permanent alliance, because in England domestic politics take precedence over foreign affairs. Political parties, which alternate in the government of a country, do not necessarily recognize the obligations of their predecessors, and the monarch is not strong enough by himself to uphold his foreign policy against the party momentarily in power. . . . With us, as in Austria, the case is different. In these two countries, although they also have parliamentary institutions, there exists a sufficiently strong monarchy to be able to carry out its treaty promises under all circumstances." [37]

Nevertheless, Bismarck gradually came to regard with favor Italy's application for an alliance, owing to certain advantages it would have for Germany. But as the German Empire did not touch Italian territory, and was not so directly interested as Austria in a number of troublesome points which would have to be settled, Bismarck suggested that Austria should negotiate the terms of the treaty with Italy. The Italian Ambassador at Berlin was told that "the key to the door which leads to us must be sought in Vienna." [38] Accordingly, the ensuing Austro-Italian negotiations, with occasional suggestions from Bismarck, ultimately resulted in the Triple Alliance Treaty signed at Vienna on May 20, 1882, by Kálnoky, Robilant, and Reuss.[39]

The general purposes of Austria, Italy, and Germany were, according to the preamble, "to augment the guarantees of peace in general, to strengthen the monarchical principle, and by this to insure intact the maintenance of the social and political order in their respective states by agreeing to conclude a treaty which by its essentially conservative and defensive character aimed only to protect them against the dangers which might menace the safety of their states

37 G.P., III, 207.

38 G.P. III, 208.

39 G.P., III, 245-7; Pribram, 24-26.

and the peace of Europe." Though the treaty did not specifically guarantee Alsace-Lorraine to Germany against France, nor Rome to Italy against the papal claims to temporal power, it was hoped by each Power that it would have this effect.

By Art. I, "The High Contracting Powers mutually promise peace and friendship, and will enter into no alliance or engagement directed against any one of their States. They engage to proceed to an exchange of ideas on political and economic questions of a general nature which may arise, and they further promise one another mutual support within the limits of their own interests."

At the negotiations of the Austro-German Alliance of 1879 Andrássy steadily refused to promise Austrian armed support in case of a French attack on Germany, unless France were also joined by Russia; his successor persisted in this refusal in 1882, and hence in Art. II, dealing with a possible French attack, Austria's obligation extended only to Italy, while Germany's and Italy's obligations were mutual: "In case Italy, without direct provocation on her part, should be attacked by France for any reason whatsoever, the two other contracting parties shall be bound to lend help and assistance with all their forces. This same obligation shall devolve upon Italy in case of any aggression without direct provocation by France against Germany."

Art. III provided for the danger of a Franco-Russian coalition: "If one, or two, of the High Contracting Parties, without direct provocation on their part, should chance to be attacked and to be engaged in a war with two or more Great Powers non-signatory to the present treaty, the *casus foederis* will arise simultaneously for all the High Contracting Parties." This virtually extended to Italy the principle agreed upon between Austria and Germany in 1879, except that the addition of the words "without direct provocation" gave the obligation a more restricted and purely defensive character.

According to Art. IV: "In case a Great Power, non-signatory to the present treaty, should threaten the security of the states of one of the High Contracting Parties, and the threatened Party should find itself forced on that account to make war against it, the two others bind themselves to observe towards their Ally a benevolent neutrality. Each of them reserves to itself, in this case, the right to take part in the war if it should see fit to make common cause with its Ally."

Art. V was calculated to secure solidarity of action: "If the peace of one of the High Contracting Parties should chance to be threatened under the circumstances foreseen by the preceding Articles, the High Contracting Parties shall take counsel together in ample time as to the military measures to be taken, with a view to eventual coöperation. They engage henceforth, in all cases of common participation in a war, to conclude neither armistice, nor peace, nor treaty, except by common consent among themselves."

The Treaty of Alliance was for five years, and its contents and its existence were to be kept secret.

The Triple Alliance was expected to bring considerable advantages to each of its members. Italy gained an increase in prestige and power by alliance with the powerful German Empire, and could now be accounted one of the Great Powers. Her royal government, which had shown some signs of tottering before revolutionary agitation, was much strengthened and less likely to be disturbed by papal or French attacks. Moreover, Italy would have less fear of trouble with Austria, who now became her ally instead of her enemy—at least as far as the governments, if not the populations, of the two countries were concerned. The obligations which Italy assumed in return were not heavy. She did not have to assist Austria in a war between Austria and Russia alone. In case of an attack by France upon either Germany or herself, Italy would have the powerful assistance of Germany, and might look forward to a victorious outcome which might give her some increase of territory in the direction of Nice and Savoy or Northern Africa.

Austria's chief benefit from the treaty lay in the hope that in case of an attack from Russia over Balkan questions, she would no longer have to leave a part of her army to guard her southern frontier against the danger of Italian Irredentism. She could throw the whole weight of her forces against Russia or into the Balkans.

Germany hoped the treaty would prevent Italy from allying with France and from thus giving encouragement to the *revanche* party at Paris. In case France should make war, however, the French forces available against the Rhine would be diminished by those which would have to be directed to the Alpine frontier against Italy. If Russia joined France, it would be of great importance to Germany that Austria, no longer in fear for her Italian frontier, would be able to launch the whole strength of the Dual Monarchy against Russia, and thereby relieve the pressure on Germany's eastern front. Even if Italy were unable to provide large fighting forces—both Kálnoky and Bismarck had a very low opinion of Italy's military strength at this time—it was still highly advantageous to Germany and Austria that Italian forces should face west against France, instead of north upon Austria's rear. "Sparing the Austrian forces, rather than winning those of Italy, is our aim," was Bismarck's comment.[40]

The Triple Alliance in its wording and in its origin was essentially defensive in character, and designed primarily to preserve the peace of Europe. This is now clear from the detailed negotiations concerning its formation, which

[40] G.P., III, 224-225.

have been revealed by Pribram from the Austrian archives, and by the extensive German documents in *Die Grosse Politik*. Its defensive character is now admitted even by French historians who are by no means friendly to Bismarck.[41] Bismarck himself, in a private despatch which he never expected would be made public, referred to it as "our League of Peace." [42] Its peaceful and defensive intent was especially marked in the case of Germany. But it became less so in the case of Italy and Austria, who later wished to use it to support their aggressive intentions. It was, in fact, not long before Italy sought to make use of her new alliance to promote her ambitions in North Africa and elsewhere. Her request for German protection against alleged interference with Italian interests by the French in Morocco caused Bismarck to reply sharply:

> I am not without just irritation over this request of Mancini's, and observe in it a dilettante—confidentially I would even say banausic—ignorance of what is possible and desirable in high diplomacy. There is again manifest in this incident, to put it mildly, that lack of unselfishness which has already so often betrayed the Italians into sending other people into the water for the sake of Italian interests, without wetting even a finger of their own . . . We are ready to stand by Italy's side if she is attacked or even seriously threatened by France. But we cannot hear with indifference the expectation that we should begin trouble with France or place Europe before the possibility of a war of great dimensions, because of vague anxieties about Italy's interests which are not immediate, but which represent hopes for the future in regard to Morocco, or the Red Sea, or Tunis, or Egypt, or other parts of the world.[43]

In 1885, Italy irritated her new allies by seizing Massowah on the Red Sea without notifying them beforehand

[41] *Cf.* Bourgeois et Pagès, p. 197.

[42] "Unsere Friedensliga"; G.P., III, 263; see below at note 45.

[43] Bismarck to Keudell, April 6, 1884; G.P., III. 410.

of her intentions. When the time approached for renewing the Triple Alliance, Italy complained that she had gained nothing as a result of the treaty. Bismarck replied bluntly, but truly, that the Alliance was made to secure the peace of Europe and not to win new conquests for its members. When Italy hinted that she wanted promises of wider support given her as the price of her renewal, Bismarck at first told her flatly that she could renew it as it stood without modifications, or she could leave it and drop out. But later, in 1887, when Franco-German relations were strained, and Italy intimated that she would shift to the side of France if her desires were not heeded, Bismarck changed his mind. He was willing to recognize Italian ambitions in North Africa and even put pressure upon Austria to accept the principle that Italy had the right to share with Austria in the decision of the future fate of the Balkans, the Ottoman coasts, and the islands in the Adriatic and Aegean Seas.[44]

Austrian policy in the Balkans, after 1906, similarly attempted to make use of the Alliance for aggressive rather than peaceful purposes. But the details of this later perversion of the originally defensive character of the Triple Alliance cannot be discussed here. They do not alter the fact that Bismarck in no sense intended to use the Triple Alliance for aggressive action by Germany against France. For him it always remained, as it had been in its origin, a defensive treaty. Unfortunately it was not easy to convince the French of this. As its terms were secret, the French not unnaturally suspected that it constituted a menace to themselves. This suspicion was strengthened by

[44] Arts. I-IV of the separate Italo-German renewal treaty of Feb. 20, 1887; and Art. I of the Austro-Italian renewal treaty of the same date, which was embodied as the famous "Art. VII" of the last renewal treaty of Dec. 5, 1912. *Cf.* Pribram I, 44 ff. 103, and *passim;* G.P., IV, 179-260. For the text of these articles and the other concessions eventually made to Italy, see Arts. VI-XI of the 1912 renewal treaty in the Appendix below.

the rapid increase in German and Italian armaments in the 1880's, and by Bismarck's rather defiant tone during the Boulanger period. It was this secrecy as to the terms of the Triple Alliance, and the exaggerated suspicions to which it gave rise, which contributed so much toward the embitterment of Franco-German relations and to the formation of the Franco-Russian Alliance in the early 1890's.

THE RUMANIAN ALLIANCE OF 1883

Even the Triple Alliance did not complete the circle of treaties by which Bismarck wished to assure the peace of Europe. In the summer of 1883 King Carol, the Hohenzollern ruler of Rumania, visited Germany. Bismarck took the occasion to sound Austria, "whether it would not be desirable and possible to extend our League of Peace [Friedensliga] with Italy to the East, and thereby lead in firm paths the policy of Rumania, and eventually also that of Serbia and the Porte. Except for Russia and France, there is no state in all Europe today which is not interested in the maintenance of peace. The firm pivot for the crystallization of any such scheme would always be our own permanent Dual Alliance."[45] As Austria responded favorably, Bismarck had two long interviews with the Rumanian premier, whom he found "more declamatory than businesslike." M. Bratianu was very eager for the kudos which would come from an alliance with the Great Powers. He was loud in his denunciation of Russian intrigues in Austria as well as in Rumania and Bulgaria. At the prospect of Austro-German backing, his chauvinistic imagination began to build castles in the air in which the Italian conquest of Nice, Savoy, and Corsica should be but the prelude to Rumania's acquisition of the Danubian Delta and Bessarabia. He had to be brought down to earth by energetic reminders from Bismarck and Kálnoky that the proposal

45 Bismarck to Prince Reuss at Vienna, Aug. 19, 1883; G.P., III, 263.

under discussion was to secure peace, not conquests; the Contracting Powers ought mutually to promise that they would refrain from all acts of provocation which might disturb the peace; if, contrary to their efforts, any war should break out, it would be time enough later to discuss the division of the spoils.

M. Bratianu thereupon bridled his imagination and on October 30, 1883, signed the purely defensive kind of an alliance which Bismarck had in mind. The Austro-Rumanian Treaty, which formed the basis of Rumania's adherence to the Triple Alliance "Treaty of Peace," provided in substance that if Rumania or Austria were attacked without provocation on their part [by Russia], the two Contracting Powers would mutually assist one another against the aggressor. Russia was not named in the text of the treaty owing to Emperor William's wish on this point, and to the danger of adding fuel to Pan-Slav agitation in case the Treaty should leak out later through some indiscretion. But the negotiations show clearly that Russia was the state which the Contracting Powers had in mind. Germany, by an agreement signed on the same day, undertook the same obligations respectively toward Austria and Rumania that they had taken toward one another. The treaty was to be secret and to endure for five years with an automatic extension for three years more if not denounced by any of the parties. In 1889 Italy, like Germany, adhered to the Austro-Rumanian treaty, and the Quadruple Agreement was usually renewed from time to time (with slight modifications). The last renewal took place on February 5, 1913, when it was extended to July 8, 1920.[46]

[46] G.P., III, 269-282; Pribram, I, 29-34, 69-77, 85-90, 107-111, 209, 245 f. In this connection it may be mentioned that Austria had signed a secret treaty with Serbia on June 28, 1881, which virtually placed Serbia under Austria's protection and domination during the reign of the pro-Austrian ruler, Milan Obrenovitch, i.e., until 1889, thus temporarily bringing still

THE BREAKDOWN OF THE WIRE TO RUSSIA IN 1890

Thus, in the period 1871-1890, the peace of Europe was secured by the domination of the Eastern Empires and by the system of genuinely defensive alliances which Bismarck had built up, though during the last three years the system was somewhat less secure. No Power cared to risk a war against Germany's overwhelming military force, supported and insured as it was by the secret alliances which had brought Austria, Russia, Italy, Rumania, and even England more or less into coöperation with Germany. France in her painful isolation did not dare to undertake a war of *revanche*. England, though ready to coöperate with the Triple Alliance in the Mediterranean, did not care to depart from her traditional no-alliance policy.[47] She still preferred to enjoy the Balance of Power between any European coalitions which might arise. No one yet threatened that proud supremacy of the seas, so vital to her commerce and her imperial relations with her colonies.

But the dismissal of Bismarck in March, 1890, brought a change, and opened the way for the formation of an alliance between Russia and France. Even during the three preceding years, in spite of the Re-insurance Treaty, friction had increased between Germany and Russia, owing to complications in Bulgaria, and to the German newspaper campaign against Russian securities. But until Bismarck's dismissal, the loyalty of M. Giers, the Russian Minister of Foreign Affairs, to the German alliance, and Tsar Alexander's antipathy to France had prevented a Franco-Russian

another state within the circle of the Triple Alliance Powers; Pribram, I, 18 ff.

47 For England's failure to respond to Bismarck's feelers for an Anglo-German understanding or alliance in 1887 and in 1889, see G.P., IV 376 ff. The importance of these feelers has been exaggerated by Hammann, *Der Missverstandne Bismarck*, pp. 20 f., 59, and by Eckardstein, *Lebenserinnerungen*, II, 282; III, 1 ff.

coalition which had always been Bismarck's greatest nightmare.[48]

In December, 1889, well in advance of its expiration, Giers considered whether the Re-insurance Treaty of 1887 ought to be renewed by Russia and, if so, in what form. On the whole, it seemed more useful for Russian interests in the Balkans and for the preservation of peace than an alliance with France. The latter would endanger peace by encouraging French chauvinists and by embittering relations between France and Germany. In accordance with this policy, Count Schuvalov had an intimate conversation with Bismarck on February 10, 1890, in which both favored the renewal of the treaty. "It is a document that defines clearly the policy which we are following and which, in my judgment, ought not to be changed," said Bismarck.[49]

But the conflict of temperament and policy which had been developing between the aged German Chancellor and his imperious young master was nearing the explosion which took place on March 17. With Bismarck out of office Schuvalov did not know what to do. He reported that what was passing at Berlin was more than strange, and that one was forced to ask oneself whether the young Emperor was in a normal state. On the night of March 21, the Ambassador was awakened by a messenger from Emperor William who requested him to come to His Majesty at eight o'clock in the morning. Scarcely had he arrived when the Emperor received him with great kindness and cordiality saying,

48 In December, 1886, Giers said to the German Chargé d'Affaires in St. Petersburg: "Il n'y a pas de politique raisonable à faire avec ces gens-là [en France]"; and a week later, "Comment peuvent-ils être assez bêtes, ces Français, pour se figurer que l'Empereur Alexandre marcherait avec les Clemenceaus contre son oncle! C'est une alliance qui ferait horreur à l'Empereur, qui n'ira pas tirer les marrons du feu pour le Commune"; and again on October 20, 1887, "Les Français sont le plus infecte des peuples, le gouvernement français est mauvais, bête; le gâchis à Paris est complet"; G.P., VI, 107, 108, 118.

49 Goriainov, p. 341; G.P., VII, 1 ff.

"Sit down and listen to me. You know how much I love and respect your sovereign. Your Emperor has been too good to me for me to do otherwise than to inform him personally of the situation created by the events which have just taken place. . . . I beg you to tell His Majesty that on my part I am entirely disposed to renew our agreement, that my foreign policy remains and will remain the same as it was in the time of my grandfather."[50] After having read Schuvalov's despatch the Tsar wrote on it, "Nothing more satisfactory could be looked for. We shall see by the sequel whether deeds correspond to words."[51]

But there then emerged the malign and super-suspicious influence of Baron Holstein. He and another counsellor in the German Foreign Office drew up a long memoir of fine-spun arguments against the renewal; with these they won over the Kaiser and the new Chancellor, Caprivi. It was decided at Berlin on March 27 to drop the negotiations for renewal, because the terms of the Re-insurance Treaty were regarded as contrary to the spirit, if not the letter, of the Triple Alliance, and also because, "if the treaty became known, either by a deliberate or accidental indiscretion, it would endanger the Triple Alliance and be calculated to turn England away from us." Schweinitz, the German Ambassador at St. Petersburg, was hastily summoned back to Berlin for a consultation. He did not think it likely that Russia would deliberately divulge the treaty; but he recognized the "possibility of indiscretions from some other source,"[52] by which probably he meant no other than Bismarck himself. When Schweinitz returned to St. Petersburg next day, and reported Germany's negative decision, the Tsar was content, but his Foreign Minister, Giers, was "in some consternation." Already old and feeble, Giers feared that under his successors the Russian militarists and

50 Goriainov, p. 343; *cf.* G.P., VII, 21. 51 Goriainov, p. 344.
52 G.P., VII, 11.

Pan-Slavs might get the upper hand and threaten peaceful relations between Germany and Russia. He hoped by a treaty to bind his successors. Six weeks later he again brought up the subject and urged the renewal of the treaty. He was willing to make any changes Germany wanted, or even to have merely an exchange of notes, or at any rate some kind of a written agreement between the two countries. Since a further refusal on Germany's part might tend to drive Russia into the arms of France, Schweinitz advised "some kind of a written agreement which, even if it became known, could not be used against us." Just after this advice reached Berlin, Bismarck gave an interview to a Russian journalist, which alarmed the German Foreign Office,[53] and made them fear that even if the Tsar were discreet, the irritated ex-Chancellor might let the dangerous cat out of the bag. The leading Foreign Office officials—Marschall, Holstein, Kiderlen, and Raschdau—all hastened to write memorials against a renewal of the Re-insurance Treaty or anything resembling it; and the Kaiser and Caprivi accepted their view. Schweinitz was told positively to drop the whole matter. Thus fell one of the main props of Bismarck's balance between Russia and Austria. Russia was left isolated and more ready to listen to the solicitous voice of the republican radicals on the Seine.

Historians have generally exaggerated the non-renewal of the Re-insurance Treaty as a factor in the formation of the Franco-Russian Alliance. This is due partly to Bismarck himself. Esteemed by the German people as a demigod, but neglected by the young Emperor and the new Court, the lonely and morose old man at Friedrichsruh filled the columns of the *Hamburger Nachrichten* with ill-natured articles justifying his own successful policies and bitterly criticizing anonymously those of his successor: "Least of all is it Germany's business to support Austria's

53 G.P., VII, 23, 35.

ambitions in the Balkans." [54] "By following the path upon which she has entered, Germany is in danger of gradually becoming dependent upon Austria, and in the end she may have to pay with her blood and treasure for the Balkan policy of Vienna." [55]

This was bad taste on Bismarck's part, and it was very embarrassing to William II and Caprivi. They winced at his criticisms and descended to his rancorous level by an act of petty-minded folly. When Bismarck made a triumphal progress to Vienna in 1892 to attend the marriage of his son, Count Herbert, to Countess Hoyos, Caprivi ordered the German Ambassador in Vienna not to attend the wedding and, if possible, to prevent Bismarck's reception by Emperor Francis Joseph. Bismarck in revenge reproached Caprivi in the *Neue Freie Presse* with having lost for Germany the friendship of Russia. "The wire which connected us with Russia is torn down." He implied that the Tsar was therefore turning toward France and that Caprivi was responsible for the danger to Germany of the new coalition which he himself had always skilfully averted. The implication was strengthened by Caprivi's apparently self-incriminating statement in the Reichstag six months later (November 23, 1892): "We exerted all our care to keep the wire up; only we did not want it to draw us out of those connections which bind us with Austria-Hungary and Italy." The implication was finally accepted as a certainty when Bismarck virtually revealed in the *Hamburger Nachrichten* (four years later) the existence of the Re-insurance Treaty of 1887, closing with the blunt statement, "So came Kronstadt with the Marseillaise and the first drawing together of the absolutist Tsardom and the French Republic, brought about, in our opinion, exclusively

54 *Hamburger Nachrichten,* April 26, 1890: Hofmann, *Fürst Bismarck,* 1890-1898, I, 256.

55 January 24, 1892; Hofmann, *Fürst Bismarck,* 1890-1898, II, 5

by the mistakes of the Caprivi policy." [56] The accuracy of Bismarck's charge seemed to be finally confirmed by a curt official note a few days later,[57] denouncing his revelation as a "violation of the most confidential secrets of state which constituted a blow at the grave interests of the Empire."

So the world accepted the idea that the Franco-Russian Alliance was the result of Caprivi's stupidity in not continuing Bismarck's juggling feat of "keeping five balls in the air at once." But if one looks more closely at the documents now in hand, one can see that historians have been misled by the apparent conjunction of events in 1890-1891 and by Bismarck's propaganda. The Franco-Russian Entente did not result simply from Caprivi's failure to renew the Re-insurance Treaty. It was due to a number of other factors. One of these was the growth of German industry, commerce, naval ambition, and colonial expansion which started Germany on "The New Course" to Constantinople and Bagdad, thereby antagonizing Russia. Emperor William's desire for a naval base led to the so-called Heligoland Treaty of July, 1890, which made Russia suspect—incorrectly—that Germany would draw closer to England. A second factor was the growth of Pan-Slavism and of Russia's determination to dominate the Balkans. This antagonized Austria and made it impossible for Berlin to continue Bismarck's policy of maintaining a delicate equipoise between Vienna and St. Petersburg. William II had eventually to choose between Russia and Austria, and he chose Austria; whether he chose rightly is another question; but the choice having been made, Russia became perforce the enemy of the Central Powers. Therefore, according to a well-informed German writer, the mistake of Bismarck's successors was not in letting down the wire between Berlin and St. Petersburg—that was perhaps inevitable anyway; the mistake was in failing to conciliate

[56] Hofmann, *Fürst Bismarck,* 1890-98, II, 373.
[57] *Reichsanzeiger,* Oct. 27, 1896.

and win England by playing off England against her natural Russian and French rivals, and by coming to a reasonable understanding with England in regard to naval and colonial questions.[58] A third factor which made for the Franco-Russian Alliance, was the persistence of the *revanche* idea and the slow consolidation of power in the French Republic which followed the bursting of the Boulanger bubble. France had at last sufficiently settled down so that the Tsar was willing to overcome his repugnance to an alliance with the Revolutionary Government which had never forgiven Germany for the cruel wound inflicted in 1871.

FRANCO-GERMAN RELATIONS, 1871-1890

In the bitter years after the Franco-Prussian War, France sat alone among the Powers of Europe, like a wall-flower at a dance, watching Germany revolve with many partners. France was condemned to isolation by her own military weakness after defeat, by the methods which Bismarck adopted to keep her friendless, and by the instability of her Republican form of government which was regarded askance by the old monarchs of Europe. She had to suffer the humiliation and the inevitable friction of German armies on her soil until the billion dollar indemnity was paid. It was not until the War Scare of 1875 that France found for the first time that she had honest neighbors who, if they did not take her to their hearts as partners, were at least not willing to sit idly by with hands crossed and see her menaced or crushed. Tsar Alexander II of Russia gallantly informed General Le Flô, the French Ambassador at St. Petersburg, that "the interests of our two countries are common; you would know this very quickly and you would know it from us if, as I refuse to believe, you should be some day seriously menaced."[59] Queen Victoria likewise

58 Hammann, *Der Missverstandne Bismarck, passim.*
59 Bourgeois et Pagès, p. 168.

let it be known that in this matter she was of one opinion with the Tsar. But neither of these two Great Powers was yet ready to enter into any closer relations with the French Republic. Alexander II, with a natural antipathy to republican institutions, preferred the monarchical solidarity represented by the League of the Three Emperors, and his attention was engaged in the Eastern Question where German friendship was of greater value than French support. Similarly, the English acquisition of the Suez Canal and the resulting occupation of Egypt gave rise to a situation which made close Anglo-French relations virtually impossible for a quarter of a century.

Bismarck, however, in the ten years 1875-1885, made many efforts to win French good-will and induce the French to accept without reserve the settlement of 1871. He wanted to make them forgive and forget the loss of Alsace-Lorraine, so that Germany would not have to fear a war of revenge. In the interests of better relations between the two countries he was willing to receive a visit from Gambetta, who was regarded as the chief exponent of *revanche* in France until his death in 1882.[60] When St. Vallier succeeded Gontaut-Biron as French Ambassador at Berlin early in 1878, Bismarck overwhelmed him with marks of attention and kindness, and there was talk of "a new era" in the relations of France and Germany. At the Congress of Berlin, and on many subsequent occasions, he assured France of his readiness to give her diplomatic support if she wished to protect her Algerian frontier by taking Tunis. As he said to St. Vallier:

> "The Tunisian pear is ripe and it is time for you to pick it. The insolence of the Bey has been like an August sun to this African fruit, which might easily spoil meanwhile, or be stolen by someone else, if you leave it longer upon the tree. I don't know whether this tempts you or what you wish

60 G.P., III, 387.

to do, but I want to repeat to you what I said in July to M. Waddington, 'It is my desire to give you evidences of goodwill in questions which touch you and where there are no German interests opposed to yours.' This is, in fact, only right, for I appreciate the efforts which you and he have made to calm the feelings and restore security and confidence between our two countries. . . . I believe that the French people, though they are now giving evidence of great good sense, need satisfactions for their pride, and I desire sincerely to see them obtain those which they can find in the Mediterranean basin which is their natural sphere of expansion. The more success they have in this direction, the less they will be inclined to indulge against us the complaints and sorrows whose legitimacy I will not discuss, but the removal of which is not in our power." [61]

On later occasions Bismarck encouraged the French in the same way to an extension of their colonial power in other parts of Africa and in China. The recent publication of his private memoranda leaves no doubt that he hoped that, if France would turn her attention to colonial activities outside Europe, she would be more likely to forget Alsace-Lorraine. In the Madrid Conference on the Morocco question, he instructed the German representative to "go hand in hand with France who, because of her neighboring Algerian possessions, has rightly founded interests in Morocco," and for this attitude he received the genuine thanks of the French Ambassador.[62] In his instructions for the German Ambassador at Paris on July 16, 1881, he wrote:

"There is a wide field in the Mediterranean in which we can leave to the French a wholly free hand. It is not out of the question to hope that French policy in the end will come to see that a friendly German Empire with 45,000,000 inhabitants is more desirable and a stronger figure among

61 St. Vallier to Waddington, Jan. 5, 1879; Bourgeois et Pagès, p. 365 f.
62 G.P., III, 396 ff.

French assets than a million Alsace-Lorrainers. France can be certain that we shall never oppose her justifiable policy of expansion in the Mediterranean and there is reason to believe that Russia also will take the same attitude as Germany."[63]

This instruction represents Bismarck's sincere purpose of trying to secure a genuine reconciliation with France in the half dozen years following the Congress of Berlin. Similarly he refused to give any support to the family of Abd-el-Kader, the heroic Algerian chieftain who had carried on such a troublesome war of self-defense against French efforts at conquest and colonization in North Africa.[64] He refused to take notice of ebullitions of French chauvinism. Some French newspapers, the League of Patriots, and fire-eaters like Paul Déroulède still kept up a violent agitation against Germany. But Bismarck ordered his Ambassadors and the German Press to ignore them as far as possible. "It is best that matters of this kind be left in dead silence."[65]

In his irritation at England's dilatory action in regard to Southwest Africa and in his desire for a sincere *rapprochement* with France, he was willing to coöperate with the French in a conference on Egypt and other African colonial questions. By the fall of 1884, there was even talk of Franco-German naval coöperation which might grow into an alliance. But the French were suspicious of Bismarck's "Machiavellian motives." They suspected that he wished to embroil them with England.[66] The acceptance of the loss of Alsace and Lorraine as final and unquestioned was just what the French Ambassador always expressly refused:

"A nation, as regards the dismemberments which it has suffered, unless it courts with indifference the fate of Poland,

[63] G.P., III, 401. [64] G.P., III, 406.
[65] Instruction of September 16, 1882; G.P., III, 404.
[66] G.P., III, 421 ff.; Bourgeois et Pagès, pp. 190-211.

ought never to pardon anything, never forget anything [*ne doit jamais rien pardonner, jamais rien oublier*]. I have never said a word to the German Chancellor which could encourage him in any illusions as to us. . . . To work for peace for the present and to reserve the future [*pacifier le présent, réserver l'avenir*], such is the program which I have always had before my eyes. . . . At the beginning of our discussions I specified with Count Hatzfeldt and with the Chancellor himself that neither Alsace nor Lorraine should ever be a question between us, that here was a domain reserved on both sides where we ought to be forbidden to penetrate, because we could never meet in good agreement on it. I shall never speak of Alsace, I have said; and on your part, if you sincerely desire an understanding with us on various points, avoid drawing the sword over our wound, because the French nation will not remain in control of her feelings." [67]

This attitude of proud irreconcilability, asserted by the French Ambassador in 1884, sums up admirably one of the fundamental reasons for the failure of the olive branches which Bismarck had been holding out. Another reason was the underlying suspicion and distrust with which each side received the suggestions of the other. The result was that the period of relative friendliness which had characterized Franco-German relations in the decade 1875-1885 came to an end and was succeeded by the tense relations of the Boulanger period.

General Boulanger, who became Minister of War in the Freycinet Cabinet in January, 1886, speedily became for the French masses the symbol of military revival and the hope of *revanche*. For fifteen long and bitter years they had borne their isolation and humiliation. Now they listened eagerly to the man on horseback who declared in chauvinistic speeches and in his organ *La France Militaire*:

67 Baron Courcel to Jules Ferry, December 3, 1884; Bourgeois et Pagès, p. 387; *cf.* also pp. 205 ff.

"We remember that they are waiting for us in Alsace and Lorraine."[68] For the next fifteen months French Cabinets rose and fell, but public opinion always demanded that Boulanger be included among the Ministers. During this period he aimed to increase and strengthen the French army by every means. Lumber was purchased for new barracks, increased quantities of picric acid were imported from Germany for the manufacture of explosives, and French regular troops were gradually brought back from China and Africa. The Cabinet, though divided, was finally persuaded by Boulanger to approve a trial mobilization of part of the army for the fall of 1887. When a more cool-headed and responsible French statesman, like Rouvier, had the courage to constitute a Cabinet without Boulanger, in May, 1887, this only increased still further the General's popularity, and with it the peril to the internal and external peace of the country. He appeared before the ecstatic crowds on the Paris boulevards. By repeatedly standing for election to the Chamber of Deputies in the provinces, he gradually began to secure a national plebiscite in his favor. There were thousands who looked forward to the overthrow of the Republic which had been too yielding and conciliatory toward Germany and who hoped for a strong dictatorship under *"le brav' général."* French chauvinism was further stirred by the fiery speeches of Paul Déroulède, by the activities of the League of Patriots, and by the intemperate editorials of the greater part of the French Press. All these manifestations of French nationalism were duly reported to Bismarck at length by the German Military Attaché in Paris.[69]

The German Ambassador, Count Münster, however, sent moderate and more quieting reports as to conditions in France, though he admitted that there was an extraordi-

[68] Report of the German Military Attaché in Paris; G.P., VI, 133.
[69] G.P., VI, 127 ff.

nary outburst of *revanche* feeling among the people. He believed, nevertheless, that it was artificially stimulated, and that at bottom the French people really did not want *la guerre sainte,* however much they might talk about it in the newspapers and public meetings. The republicans in the provinces, in contrast to Paris, were decidedly peaceful, and Boulanger was not nearly so dangerous as people believed. He could hardly establish a dictatorship on account of the jealousy of other generals and of the solidity of republican feeling. Whatever the masses thought, the French Government really wanted peace, because they were afraid of Germany. Financially also France was too poor to wage war, and military service was unpopular. The Ambassador was so convinced that there was no real danger of a Boulangist *coup d'état* or an attack upon Germany, that he took the unusual step of writing his views in a personal letter to Emperor William I.

Bismarck, however, was not at all convinced of the accuracy of Münster's diagnosis of the French situation. He covered Münster's reports with question marks and doubts. He scolded him for writing a letter direct to the Emperor, which Münster thereupon agreed should not be delivered. Bismarck's distrust of France rested partly on his knowledge of French history and of the events of the Second Empire when Napoleon III had talked peace and yet had entered upon one war after another. It arose also from his futile efforts to come to a better understanding with France during the half dozen years before the rise of Boulanger. Still another reason for his distrust of the French were the rumors in September, 1886, that Russian agents in Paris had been putting out feelers toward a Franco-Russian alliance.[70] He instantly made inquiries at St. Petersburg to learn if the rumors had any foundation. In the negotiations a little later for the Re-insurance Treaty with Russia,

[70] G.P., VI, 93 ff.

he made surprisingly large concessions to Russian ambitions toward Constantinople, with the hope of holding Tsar Alexander III away from France and in firm friendship with Germany.[71]

A further reason why Bismarck was unwilling to accept Münster's optimistic views on France was the fact that he was preparing to lay before the Reichstag the Army Bill of 1887, which would considerably increase the size of the German army. French chauvinism was one of the best vote-getters possible for the bill. If Münster was correct, half the argument for the increase of the German army was gone. So Bismarck took the view of the military attaché instead of the ambassador at Paris. The German armament bill passed and thereby increased the suspicion and distrust in France and Russia, which always accompanied the growth of German armaments. New military expenditures on a wide scale were then made in France and Russia, and a still further increase was proposed in Germany in the following year. So great was the suspense and war-talk on both sides of the Rhine that there developed in the spring of 1888 another war scare not unlike that of 1875. On January 11, 1888, Bismarck made the famous speech in the Reichstag in which, while increasing Germany's armaments, he still insisted that Germany had no intention of provoking a war with France or with Russia.

In spite of "incidents" like the German arrest of Schnaebele,[72] which sharpened bitter feelings in both coun-

[71] G.P., V, 211 ff.

[72] Schnaebele, who had been accused of complicity in an espionage case at Strasbourg, was a French police officer near the Alsatian border. On April 20, 1887 he was arrested upon German soil while at an interview with a German police agent concerning border questions. The French Press made a great outcry that he had been enticed over the border in order that he might be seized. There is no proof of this. When Bismarck was finally convinced that Schnaebele crossed the border for an official interview upon the invitation of a German customs officer, he at once ordered his release; G.P., VI, 182-192. C. Grant Robertson, *Bismarck,* p. 460, is incorrect in concluding that the Schnaebele incident was delib-

tries, cooler counsels prevailed at Paris. Boulanger's credit sank more rapidly than it had risen, and Franco-German tension became less strained. But it was during this period that the first steps took place which may be regarded as the beginnings of Franco-Russian *rapprochement,* which later was extended to include England and thus formed ultimately the Triple Entente. The domination of the Eastern Empires was coming to an end.

erately planned to provoke the French into a serious indiscretion in order to assist the passage of the German Army Bill by the Reichstag. The dates are conclusive. The Army Bill passed on March 11. Bismarck knew nothing about the Schnaebele espionage case until March 12. Schnaebele was not arrested until April 20, and was set free eight days later. For a French view, see Bourgeois et Pagès, pp. 225-229.

CHAPTER III

THE SYSTEM OF SECRET ALLIANCES, 1890-1907; FORMATION OF THE TRIPLE ENTENTE

FRANCO-RUSSIAN RAPPROCHEMENT, 1887-1891

THE Franco-Russian Entente of 1891, which ripened into the Alliance of 1894, was the natural result of the suspicions, the feeling of isolation, and the irritation against Germany which existed in both countries. A *rapprochement* between them, in spite of the fundamental contrast between the republican and absolutist forms of government at Paris and St. Petersburg, was the obvious counterbalance to the Triple Alliance.

Notwithstanding Bismarck's generous promises to Russia in the Alliance of the Three Emperors and the Reinsurance Treaty, Alexander III had been greatly irritated at the election of Ferdinand of Coburg as Prince of Bulgaria. Ferdinand had hesitated to accept the Bulgarian throne, or at least had pretended to hesitate, but had been secretly persuaded into final acceptance, so the Tsar believed, by a treacherous intrigue on Bismarck's part. Though Bismarck had alleged openly that Germany was not interested in Bulgaria and that Russia might have a free hand to do as she pleased there, the German Ambassador at Vienna was supposed to have written a letter to Ferdinand secretly assuring him of Germany's support against Russia in case he accepted the throne of Bulgaria. The letter came into French hands and was conveyed by the French to the Tsar. Though Bismarck assured the Tsar later that the letter was a forgery, there is no doubt that for a time Alexander III shared some of the French feeling of bitterness toward Bismarck.[1] He could not reconcile Bismarck's assurances of disinterestedness in Constantinople and the Balkans with the despatch of German officers to drill the Turkish army and with the enthusiastic reception at the German maneuvers given to the Turkish general, Muktar Pasha. Like the French, he was suspicious and irritated at the publicly announced renewal of the Triple Alliance in 1887. As its terms were secret, he not unnaturally suspected that it might contain offensive designs on the part of Austria and Italy detrimental to Russia's ambitions in the Eastern Mediterranean. Soon after the renewal of the Triple Alliance, Crispi, who had become Italian Premier in July, 1887, had ostentatiously visited Vienna, and then gone on to confer with Bismarck at Friedrichsruh. On his return journey he informed the *Frankfurter Zeitung* that Italy wished well to Bulgaria, but "there can be no doubt that Italy, like every other European state, has every reason to fear Russia's advances to Constantinople. We cannot allow the Mediterranean to become a Russian lake." [2]

To all these grievances was added another. In the summer of 1887, Russia suddenly found that the ruble was falling in value and that there seemed to be a systematic campaign in Berlin against Russian securities. This was partly due to a ukase in May which naturally shook German faith in Russian credit: it forbade the acquisition or inheritance of landed property by foreigners in Western Russia, or their employment as managers of estates. As Germans owned much land in Russia and were largely employed in the management of estates, the ukase looked like an unjustifiable expropriation of property. This not unnaturally led to

[1] On the so-called "Bulgarian Documents" and their alleged forgery, see G.P., V. 338-350, and J. V. Fuller, *Bismarck's Diplomacy at its Zenith*, pp. 205 ff.; 292 ff.

[2] Quoted in Robertson, *Bismarck*, p. 460.

a German newspaper campaign against Russian credit. Though Bismarck may not have inspired these newspaper attacks, he at least looked upon them with approval as tending to make the Russians realize how dependent they were upon German good-will.[3]

The Russians, however, suspected that Bismarck had inspired this press campaign and were therefore the more ready to yield to the Pan-Slav desire that Russia should borrow in Paris. France at the moment was looking for a field of investment, because commercial conflict with Italy had shut off the Italian market for French capital.[4] A group of French bankers was formed at Paris and began negotiations for a series of Russian loans to be floated in France. The first, amounting to 500,000,000 francs, was at last approved by the Governments on both sides and the bonds were listed on the Paris Bourse in December, 1888. Naturally Germany looked askance at this proceeding, which might have eventual political significance. German newspapers did their best to scare off buyers; but the loan proved a huge success. Though the sum was a relatively large one for those days, the 4% bonds issued at 86.45 offered attractive returns and were at once largely oversubscribed. The Russians were encouraged the next year to contract two more loans, one for 700,000,000, and the other for 1,200,000,000 francs. Both met with equal success. Thus France set out on the financial path which led further than she foresaw at the moment, and which inevitably made thousands of her citizens interested financially and politically in Russia's ambitions. Occasionally saner minds in France took alarm, and the loans did not succeed so well, but for the most part Frenchmen were ready to give up an apparently unlimited amount of savings to invest at good

[3] G.P., V, 330-337; Fuller, p. 202 ff.

[4] *Cf.* Debidour, *Histoire Diplomatique de l'Europe, 1878-1916* (2nd. ed., Paris, 1917-1918), I, 130 f.

profits in a country which might become an ally against the common enemy, and which might one day assist in the *revanche* which so many Frenchmen had in their hearts.[5]

On the financial ground thus prepared the next step was for France to supply Russia with guns. The Grand Duke Vladimir, Alexander III's brother, on a visit to Paris, was initiated into the reorganization of the army which Freycinet had been carrying out. He was greatly impressed with the new Lebel rifle. Upon request he was given a model of it. Negotiations followed, and ultimately a contract was arranged by which France was to manufacture for Russia half a million rifles similar to the Lebel weapon.[6]

Neither William II nor his Foreign Office advisers supposed that "dropping the Pilot" and abandoning the Reinsurance Treaty would be followed by a Franco-Russian Alliance. But to lessen such a possibility, the Kaiser, with exaggerated views of his own personal influence in diplomacy, proceeded to return to the conciliatory policy toward France which Bismarck had pursued during and after the Congress of Berlin. He attempted to win French good-will by innumerable well-intentioned courtesies, by telegrams of congratulation and condolence, by recognizing the French protectorate over Madagascar, and by diplomatic support

5 Debidour, I, 137, reckons the total borrowings in France by the Russian Government up to 1906 at the enormous sum of 7,903,000,000 francs. These Russian government bonds did not include other vast sums which French private capitalists invested in Russian cotton mills, lumber mills, factories, and other undertakings of all sorts.

6 *Livre Jaune: L'Alliance Franco-Russe*, p. 49. This French Yellow Book, published in 1918, is the authoritative source for the early history of the Franco-Russian Alliance, and renders antiquated the older accounts of Cyon, Hansen, Daudet, Albin, Debidour, Tardieu, and Welschinger. The best recent brief studies are by L. B. Packard, "Russia and the Dual Alliance," in *Amer. Hist. Rev.*, XXV, 391-410, April, 1920; and by W. L. Langer, "The Franco-Russian Alliance," in the *Slavonic Review*, III, 554-575; IV, 83-100, March-June, 1925. See also G.P., VI, 91-124; VII, 191-458; the Belgian documents edited under the direction of B. Schwertfeger by W. Köhler, *Revanche-Idee und Panslawismus*, Berlin, 1919; and, for the later history of the alliance, George Michon, *L'Alliance Franco-Russe, 1891-1917*, Paris. 1927.

in other colonial questions where no German interests were involved. He showed special courtesy to Jules Simon, the head of the French delegation at the Working Men's Conference in Berlin. He invited French artists to participate in a German art exhibition—an invitation which was at first accepted but later refused on account of an outcry in the French Press. He arranged for a visit of his mother, the Empress Frederick, to Paris. But this eventually led to such a hostile demonstration that a serious scandal was narrowly averted by the energy of the French Government and by her departure from Paris on an earlier train than had been intended.[7] It contributed to a new chauvinist outburst and a renewed desire for closer relations with Russia.[8]

With Russia also the Kaiser sought to remain on the old friendly terms. He was profuse in assurances that German policy should suffer no change as a result of Bismarck's dismissal. In August, 1890, he visited the Tsar at Narva and relations seemed cordial between the monarchs as well as between Caprivi and Giers, though the latter failed in his further attempt to get some kind of a written agreement which should replace the Re-insurance Treaty. But in fact the Russians were becoming suspicious that Germany was drawing closer to England. The Treaty of June 14, 1890, by which Germany had given up claims to a great strip of African territory near Zanzibar in return for Heligoland, seemed to point in this direction.[9] If Lord Salisbury had given away a suit of clothes in exchange for a suspender button, as Henry M. Stanley sarcastically de-

[7] G.P., VII, 263 ff; Debidour, I, 165-168.

[8] The Russians had at first been alarmed at the Kaiser's efforts at reconciliation with France, and were delighted with the outburst against the Empress Frederick, in which they were suspected by the German Ambassador in Paris of having had a hand. The Tsar took advantage of the favorable opportunity to flatter the French by conferring the Order of St. Andrew upon President Carnot, who returned the compliment by bestowing the Grand Cross of the Legion of Honor upon the Russian Ambassador in Paris. G.P., VII, 196-201.

[9] G.P., VIII, 3-25.

scribed this transaction, there must be a reason, so the Russians argued to themselves. The London *Morning Post* announced that "the period of England's isolation is over." The Kaiser's visit to England in the summer of 1890 seemed a further sign of the way the wind was blowing. His allusion to the Triple Alliance at the opening of the Reichstag May 6, 1890, even though he spoke of it as a guarantee of universal peace, and his new Army Law increasing the German forces by some 18,000 men, were no less disturbing to the Russians than to the French.[10]

THE FRANCO-RUSSIAN ALLIANCE OF 1894.

Such was the situation which at last led the Russians to listen seriously to French feelers for closer relations. In view of the form ultimately given to the Franco-Russian Alliance and later to the Anglo-French military and naval arrangements, it is interesting to note that these first definite negotiations were carried on by the French and Russian military authorities and not by the regular diplomatic representatives. General Boisdeffre, who attended the Russian maneuvers for a fortnight in 1890, talked almost daily with the Russian Minister of War and with Obruchev, the Russian Chief of Staff. The latter had married a French wife and had long been an eager advocate of a Franco-Russian Alliance. Boisdeffre and the Russian generals quickly came to an agreement on the principle that "the two armies would have to act simultaneously in case of an attack from which they both had to fear the consequences." [11] This was a first step toward an Entente Cordiale which, though no written agreements had as yet been signed, was soon regarded by the Russian Ambassador at Paris as being "as solid as granite." [12] It had been solidified

[10] *Cf.* Goriainov, pp. 348-349

[11] Laboulaye, the French Ambassador to Russia, to Ribot, August 24, 1890; *L'Alliance Franco-Russe*, p. 1.

[12] Ribot to Laboulaye, March 9, 1891; *L'Alliance Franco-Russe*, p. 3.

by the Empress Frederick incident and by the growing Franco-Russian suspicion that England was adhering to the Triple Alliance to thwart Russian ambitions in the Eastern Mediterranean. It was just at this time that the Triple Alliance was renewed, in spite of the efforts of the French to detach Italy and the hopes of both French and Russians that Bismarck's dismissal might cause it to weaken and lapse. It had not, however, been renewed without difficulty, owing to Italy's demands for promises of greater support in the maintenance of the *status quo* in North Africa. Austria and Germany had been forced to yield to some extent to Italy's wishes and even to agree to exert themselves to secure England's adhesion to this new stipulation.[13]

The fact that the Triple Alliance had been renewed was published to the world by the Italian Premier, Rudini, in a speech on June 29, 1891. At the same time he also took occasion to refer to Italy's existing agreements with England in such a way as to strengthen Franco-Russian suspicions that England had in some way joined the Triple Alliance. Such a quadruple coalition, even though ostensibly aiming merely at the preservation of the *status quo*, was most annoying to the Russians who wanted to open the Dardanelles, and to the French who had not completed the development of their African colonial empire in the Western Mediterranean.

A few weeks later the French fleet under Admiral Gervais accepted the Tsar's invitation to visit Kronstadt. In addition to their suspicions of the Triple Alliance, Alexander III and Giers had been alarmed by the stiff attitude which the French had adopted in regard to a dispute between Roman Catholic and Greek Orthodox clergy concerning the use of a door in the Church of the Nativity at Beth-

[13] Art. IX of the Triple Alliance Treaty of May 6, 1891. *Cf.* Pribram, pp. 66, 208-229; and G.P., VII, 53-106; VIII, 41-72.

lehem.[14] They realized also the importance of making sure of French friendship if they were to be successful in borrowing more money at Paris.[15] The Kronstadt visit was made the occasion, especially by the French, for an extraordinary demonstration of Franco-Russian solidarity. It was to appear to the world as a counter-stroke to the renewal of the Triple Alliance. The Tsar and Tsarina came aboard the French flagship, talked to the sailors, showed a thousand acts of politeness to Admiral Gervais and his officers, and invited them to Peterhof. Hitherto, in absolutist Russia, the playing of the Marseillaise had been strictly forbidden, not only in public places, but even on a piano which might be heard on the street. But now the prohibition was relaxed—only to be re-imposed again after the departure of the French fleet—and the news was trumpeted abroad that the Autocrat of All the Russias had stood bareheaded while the bands played the marching song of the Sans-culottes of 1793.[16] It was, however, a stirring moment. "Those of us who reached manhood in 1890," writes President Poincaré twenty years later, "cannot, even today, recall without emotion the prodigious effect produced at that time in France by the demonstration of friendliness by Emperor Alexander III. It was for Republicans not only a recognition of the Republic by a government whose traditions and form were furthest removed from us and our institutions; it was for France herself the end of a prolonged isolation and the outward sign of her revival." [17]

The Kronstadt demonstration was received in France with incredible joy and enthusiasm. The man in the street believed that an alliance was already assured, that the long period of isolation was now past, and that France could

14 *L'Alliance Franco-Russe*, p. 3.

15 *Cf.* Langer, pp. 14-17.

16 *Cf.* the sarcastic comments of the Belgian minister in St. Petersburg, Schwertfeger, V, 295-300.

17 *Les Origines de la Guerre*, p. 55; *cf.* also Tardieu, *France and the Alliances*, pp. 11-14.

now dare to take a stiffer tone toward Germany. It created a new Boulangism without Boulanger. But the French ministry knew that the enthusiasm of the Paris populace was premature. They knew that it takes two to make an alliance or even an entente, and that the ceremonial courtesies of Kronstadt still fell far short of a signed and binding agreement. They therefore hastened to propose an alliance: the two governments should agree to consult with one another in case of any danger, and to mobilize simultaneously the moment any one of the Triple Powers should mobilize; the conditions of their simultaneous mobilization could be worked out by an understanding to be reached by the Russian and French General Staffs.[18]

But Giers, fearful that the French might have aggressive designs for recovering Alsace-Lorraine, wished to make the agreement vague and to extend its application beyond Europe to such places as Africa and China where peace might be threatened. It was only after several weeks that the French were able to secure a written accord in the following form:

> "1. In order to define and consecrate the cordial understanding [Entente Cordiale] which unites them, and in their desire to contribute with one accord to the maintenance of peace, which is the object of their sincerest wishes, the two Governments declare that they will confer on every question of a nature to threaten the general peace.
>
> "2. In case this peace should actually be in danger, and especially in case one of the two parties should be threatened by aggression, the two parties agree to come to an understanding on the measures which the realization of that eventuality would make it necessary for both Governments to adopt immediately and simultaneously." [19]

The rather vague and very limited character of this

[18] Ribot to Laboulaye, July 24, 1891; *L'Alliance Franco-Russe*, p. 4.

[19] Russian formula, confirmed by Ribot, Aug. 27, 1891; *L'Alliance Franco-Russe*, p. 16.

agreement merely obligating the two Governments to take counsel with one another in case of danger, betrayed the divergence of views which still separated Paris and St. Petersburg. France, in constant dread of an attack from across the Rhine and with the secret hope of some day recovering the lost provinces, thought mainly of war with Germany. She did not at this time greatly desire Russian support in North Africa or China, because, as later events showed, she could always come to a compromise agreement with Italy and England in these regions. Nor did the French wish the Russians to open the Dardanelles and control Constantinople. Giers, on the other hand, felt no great hostility to Germany. He and Alexander III were still anxious to maintain the traditional friendship between the two countries. They did not want an alliance directed primarily against the Hohenzollerns and dreaded being drawn into a war against Germany in support of French *revanche.* For Russia the main enemy was England, who blocked the Russian colossus both at the Straits and in the Middle East. But France naturally had no desire to pull these distant chestnuts out of the fire to please her new Russian friends.

Owing to this divergence of interests, as well as to the sickness of Giers and the Tsar's persistent distrust of the French, it was many months before the French were able to give the Entente a more binding and practical form. Upon Giers' visit to Paris in November, 1891, Ribot pointed out to him the danger that Germany might make a sudden surprise attack, which would find Russia and France unprepared. They would not have time to take adequate measures of defense before an irrevocable disaster might overwhelm them, so long as they merely "agreed to come to an understanding." It would be far more valuable and practical to come to an understanding beforehand, in time of peace, as to all the military arrangements which should come into force instantly in case of sudden war. The Entente ought to be supplemented by a Military Convention providing that, in case of a sudden German aggression, Russia and France would instantly mobilize their whole forces and use them to secure the maximum mutual advantage in accordance with plans which would have been already agreed upon. Giers not enthusiastic, consented to lay the idea before the Tsar.[20] Accordingly General Miribel worked out the basis for such a Military Convention. He estimated in detail the total Triple Alliance forces (even including the Rumanian) at only 2,810,000 men as against 3,150,000 for the Franco-Russian coalition. France would throw five-sixths of her forces against Germany. Russia was likewise urged to concentrate her attack upon Germany rather than upon Austria:

> "The essential thing is to aim at the destruction of the principal enemy. The defeat of the others will follow inevitably. In a word, once Germany is vanquished, the Franco-Russian armies will impose their wills on Italy and Austria."[21]

General Miribel's draft project, after some modifications to meet the Russian desires, and after long delays caused by the sickness of Giers and the journeys of the Tsar, finally took form as the "Draft of a Military Convention." It was signed by the French and Russian Chiefs of Staff, Boisdeffre and Obruchev, and approved in principle by the Tsar on August 17, 1892. But it was not signed by the Ambassador or Foreign Minister of either country, and therefore could not yet be regarded as having binding force. There were two serious political difficulties in the way. The Tsar was very anxious that absolute secrecy should be preserved, and that the document should be known only to the President and Prime Minister of France. "I fear," he said, "that if they discuss it in the Cabinet, it will have the fatal result

21 *L'Alliance Franco-Russe*, p. 39. 21 *Ibid.*, p. 39.

of becoming public, and then, as far as I am concerned, the treaty is nullified." [22] Another difficulty was the fact that the French Constitution did not permit the President of the Republic to make secret treaties. There was recognized at the very beginning of the negotiations, the "defect of our [French] constitution, which, through fear lest the Executive shall be too strong, has deprived the Head of the State of the essential prerogative of concluding treaties, and consequently deprived our foreign policy of the advantages of secrecy." [23] These two difficulties, as well as the essential divergence of interests noted above, caused a further delay of a year and a half.

Meanwhile, certain events took place which tended to lessen the Tsar's scruples and his distrust of France, and to increase his readiness to accept at last a binding agreement. A new German Army Law of 1892 increased the German forces by 60,000 men but reduced the term of service in the infantry from three to two years. No settlement had been reached in regard to a Russo-German commercial treaty and a tariff war was being waged between the two countries.[24] The Siam crisis of July, 1893, which brought France and England closer to war than was realized at the time, showed that the French were ready to take a stiff tone toward England, even in Asia, in a way which Russia liked to see, especially as England seemed to be drawing closer to the Triple Alliance. As a result, Alexander III consented to return the Kronstadt compliments by having the Russian Navy visit Toulon in October, 1893. The Russian officers and men were fêted with extraordinary enthusiasm by the French both at Toulon and Paris. But the Paris Press, at a wise hint from the French Government, refrained from chauvinistic editorials and implica-

[22] *L'Alliance Franco-Russe,* p. 94; *cf.* also pp. 66, 72, 87, 91 ff., 103 ff., 112 ff.

[23] *L'Alliance Franco-Russe,* p. 2; *cf.* also pp. 50, 54, 69, 90 ff., 99 ff., 114.

[24] G.P., VII, 389-458.

tions that a Russian alliance would aid in regaining Alsace-Lorraine. The Tsar was favorably impressed with the moderation and strength of the French Government. He accordingly gave his approval to an exchange of official diplomatic notes which was completed on January 4, 1894, and gave binding effect to the Military Convention of August 17, 1892.[25]

As neither the exchange of notes nor the Military Convention signed only by military officers was a formal treaty, neither had to be submitted to the French Parliament for ratification. The terms of the Military Convention, known only to the supreme military officials, did not even have to be divulged to Cabinets which rose and fell so rapidly in France. The text of the Military Convention was kept in an envelope bearing an annotation in President Faure's hand: "The Military Convention is accepted by the letter of M. de Giers giving to the Convention the force of a treaty." M. Viviani carried it under his arm to the Chamber of Deputies when he mounted the tribune to ask for war credits on August 4, 1914. He was prepared to read it if it should be asked for. But as no one demanded it, he prudently kept it in his portfolio.[26] It was never made public until published in a French Yellow Book in 1918. Thus the two difficulties in regard to secrecy and French constitutional requirements were effectively met.

The Military Convention which was given the force of a treaty on January 4, 1894, and thus became the basis of

[25] Montebello to Giers, Dec. 23, 1893; Jan. 4, 1894; *ibid.*, p. 128. "I have received your letter . . . in which you advise me that . . . the draft of the Military Convention . . . may be considered henceforth definitely adopted. . . . The French Government likewise considers the aforesaid Military Convention, the text of which has been approved by both parties, as executory henceforth. In consequence of this agreement, the two Staffs shall have power immediately to deliberate at any time and to communicate to each other all the information which may be useful to them."

[26] Poincaré, *Les Origines de la Guerre*, p. 60.

the very secret Franco-Russian Alliance is so short, simple, and clear that it may be quoted in full:

"France and Russia, animated by a common desire to preserve the peace, and having no other aim than to prepare for the necessities of a defensive war, provoked against either of them by an attack by the forces of the Triple Alliance, have agreed upon the following provisions:

"1. If France is attacked by Germany, or by Italy supported by Germany, Russia shall employ all her available forces to fight Germany.

"If Russia is attacked by Germany, or by Austria supported by Germany, France shall employ all her available forces to fight Germany.

"2. In case the forces of the Triple Alliance or of one of the Powers which compose it should be mobilized, France and Russia, at the first indication of the event, and without a previous agreement being necessary, shall mobilize all their forces immediately and simultaneously, and shall transport them as near to the frontiers as possible.

"3. The forces available which must be employed against Germany shall be for France, 1,300,000 men; for Russia, from 700,000 to 800,000 men. These forces shall begin complete action with all speed, so that Germany will have to fight at the same time in the east and in the west.

"4. The Staffs of the armies of the two countries shall constantly plan in concert in order to prepare for and facilitate the execution of the above measures. They shall communicate to each other in time of peace all the information regarding the armies of the Triple Alliance which is in or shall come into their possession. The ways and means of corresponding in time of war shall be studied and arranged in advance.

"5. France and Russia shall not conclude peace separately.

"6. The present Convention shall have the same duration as the Triple Alliance.

"7. All the clauses enumerated above shall be kept absolutely secret."[27]

The Franco-Russian Alliance of 1894, like the Austro-German Alliance of 1879 and the Triple Alliance of 1882, was in its origin essentially defensive in purpose. This is clear from the preamble to the Treaty itself and from the full account which we now have of the negotiations by which it was concluded.[28] There was originally no intention among responsible authorities of either party that the Alliance should be used for an aggression against Germany or any other Power, or that it should be employed to support dangerous and ambitious policies which might involve a conflict with any of the Triple Alliance Powers or with England. Whatever may have been the hopes inspired by the Alliance in the hearts of Pan-Slavs for realizing Russia's "historic mission" in the Balkans and the Far East, or in French chauvinists for the recovery of Alsace-Lorraine and the extension of French colonial power, the responsible Russian and French Ministers knew better. The French Cabinet did not count upon Russian armed support at Fashoda or in Morocco, nor the Russians upon that of France in the Far East or the Balkans. It was not until much later, in the days of Delcassé, Izvolski, and Poincaré, that the Franco-Russian Alliance was essentially changed in spirit from a defensive to a potentially offensive combination.

To be sure, the Alliance embodied from the outset the militarist doctrine, prevalent since the Napoleonic Wars, that the best military defensive is to wage offensive war. Mobilization by Germany was to be followed by the instant

[27] *L'Alliance Franco-Russe,* p. 92.

[28] *L'Alliance Franco-Russe, passim.* At one point in the negotiations Alexander III wished to insert a clause that the treaty would be nullified if France provoked a war; but he renounced the idea when General Boisdeffre pointed out that "it was concluded for a defensive war"; *ibid.*, p. 91.

mobilization of the French and Russian armies. Mobilization was expressly understood as being equivalent to war—to the actual opening of hostilities. In the negotiations for the Military Convention in July, 1892,

> "General Obruchev emphasized finally the necessity of the immediate and simultaneous mobilization of the Russian and French armies at the first news received by either of the two countries of a mobilization of the forces of the Triple Alliance. He understands further that this mobilization of France and Russia would be followed immediately by positive results, by acts of war, in a word would be inseparable from an 'aggression.'" [29]

Similarly, General Boisdeffre, in talking with the Tsar the day after the Military Convention had been approved, remarked:

> "The mobilization is the declaration of war. To mobilize is to oblige one's neighbor to do the same. Mobilization involves the carrying out of strategic transportation and concentration. Otherwise, to leave a million men on one's frontier, without doing the same simultaneously, is to deprive oneself of all possibility of moving later; it is placing oneself in the situation of an individual who, with a pistol in his pocket, should let his neighbor put a weapon to his forehead without drawing his own." [To which Alexander III replied], "That is exactly the way I understand it." [30]

This "offensive-defensive" character of the Alliance is further seen in the technical arrangements which were worked out annually later in great detail by the French and Russian General Staffs.[31] On the generally accepted principle that the best form of defensive warfare is to take the

[29] *L'Alliance Franco-Russe*, p. 56. [30] *L'Alliance Franco-Russe*, p. 95 f.

[31] For some of the Franco-Russian military conversations and protocols for the years 1900-1907, see A. Zaiontchkovski, "Relations Franco-Russes avant la Guerre de 1914," in *Les Alliés contre la Russie*, Paris, 1926, pp. 8-43; for the years 1911-1913, M.F.R., 697-718; and L.N., II, 419-437.

offensive against the main enemy force, the French and Russian Staffs were "perfectly in accord on the point that the defeat of the German armies continues to be, whatever the circumstances, the first and principal objective of the allied armies. This is all the more so now [1913] than formerly, in view of the considerable increase of the relative military strength of Germany in the Triple Alliance." [32]

Though the Franco-Russian Alliance aimed primarily at crushing Germany in case the latter should attempt an aggression, it did not at first arouse serious suspicions or antagonism beyond the Rhine. This was partly because its existence was kept so secret that for months after its establishment the German Ambassador in Paris optimistically refused to believe in its existence.[33] Even after the open references to the "Alliance," in speeches in the French chamber in 1895, or during the visits of Nicholas II to Paris in 1896 and of President Faure to Russia in 1897, Germany was not alarmed, because she felt that the Triple Alliance was still equal in strength to the new combination. She also believed that England, holding the Balance of Power, would never join with such long-standing opponents as France or Russia. The existence of the Franco-Russian Alliance inspired, however, a new respect in Germany for her two neighbors, and made her more ready to seek to cooperate with them on innumerable international questions. In this sense the Franco-Russian Alliance at first tended to

32 Art. I of the ninth annual conference of French and Russian Staff officers, Aug., 1913; M.F.R., p. 712; L.N., II, 432.

33 *Cf.* G.P., VII, 261-343; IX, 335-425; even as late as December, 1895, Count Münster was still convinced that "Russia's love [for France] is only Platonic. Platonic love usually ends in hate"; G.P., IX, 423. Even as late as December, 1898, after the Fashoda Affair, Count Eulenburg, the German Ambassador at Vienna and an intimate friend of the Kaiser's, "felt sure there was no formal alliance", and was convinced that France could not count on Russia in any Egyptian or other African quarrel; Rumbold to Salisbury, Dec. 5, 1898; *British Documents on the Origins of the War, 1914-1918,* I, p. 102.

secure the peace of Europe; also in the sense of the proverb that "one sword holds another in its sheath."

The new Alliance served well its purpose of relieving France and Russia from their isolation. It enabled France to take a stiffer tone toward England, but it did not yet constitute a combination which was strong enough, or which desired, to measure arms with the Triple Alliance. This situation continued for some ten years. Between the putting into force of the Alliance in 1894 and the establishment of the Anglo-French Entente in 1904, the equilibrium between the Triple Alliance and Franco-Russian Alliance was sufficiently well balanced so that neither combination could dare to risk disturbing it by force.

This situation of more or less equilibrium on the Continent even led to a series of temporary diplomatic combinations in which Germany coöperated with Russia and France. In 1894, Germany and France joined hands in preventing England from acquiring a strip of Congo territory for the Cape-to-Cairo Railway.[34] In 1895, Germany coöperated with France and Russia to compel Japan to restore part of the conquests taken from China.[35] In 1900, Russia proposed that the same three Powers should try to mediate between England and the Boers. Germany did not wish to antagonize England by such a step, but consented to discuss it. Quite possibly the three Powers might have attempted it, had not France been unwilling to enter into an arrangement with Germany which would have involved a mutual guarantee of territories, and consequently a second renunciation of Alsace-Lorraine.[36] In this same year also

[34] See below at note 40.

[35] Bourgeois et Pagès, pp. 248-253; G.P., IX, 241-333.

[36] G.P., XV, 406 note, 499-550; XVII, 105, 222 f.; XXIV, 173; Bourgeois et Pagès, pp. 286-289; Sidney Lee, *King Edward VII*, I, 761-773. According to the current Anglo-French version, the Kaiser instigated the mediation proposal, and then sought to lay the odium of it on France and Russia; according to the documents in G.P., the reverse is the fact—Russia originated it, and the French and the Russians then sought to put

German, French, Russian and English troops marched side by side to suppress the Boxer revolt. When the Tsar's proposal for the First Hague Conference—well meant but naïve for those times—took Europe by surprise, Germany and France, and even many of Russia's own officials, joined efforts to restrict the scope of the Conference as much as possible without incurring the odium of seeming to sabotage the Tsar's proposals. Nothing sums up dozens of despatches on this topic better than the confidence which Delcassé is reported to have made to the German Ambassador in Paris:

> "Our [French] interests in regard to the Conference are exactly the same as yours. You do not want to limit your power of defense at this moment nor enter upon disarmament proposals; we are in exactly the same position. We both want to spare the Tsar and find a formula for sidestepping this question, but not let ourselves in for anything which would weaken our respective powers of defense. To prevent a complete fiasco, we might possibly make some concessions in regard to arbitration, but these must in no way limit the complete independence of the Great Powers. Besides the Tsar, we must also spare the public opinion of Europe, since this has been aroused by the senseless step of the Russians."[37]

the odium of the proposal on Germany. Certainly the formal proposals were first made to Germany by Russia. Whether Muraviev or the Kaiser was the original Machiavellian instigator of this business can hardly be determined with certainty until the Russian despatches referred to by Lee are published in more complete form and subjected to comparison with those in *Die Grosse Politik.* The recent *British Documents* (I, 235 ff., 247 f.) seem to confirm the German contention that Muraviev first initiated the mediation proposal.

[37] G.P., XV, 186. On this whole conference, where Germany's bluntness caused her to be somewhat unduly blamed for the thwarting of the Tsar's suggestions for the limitations of armaments, see *ibid.*, XV, 141-364; Andrew D. White, *Autobiography,* II, chs. 45-49; F. W. Holls, *The Peace Conference at the Hague,* N. Y., 1900; W. J. Hull, *The Two Hague Conferences,* Boston, 1908; P. Zorn, *Die beiden Haager Friedenskonferenzen,* Stuttgart, 1915; Ch. Meurer, *Die Haager Friedenskonferenz,* 2 vols., München, 1905-07; J. B. Scott, *The Hague Peace Conferences,* 2 vols. Baltimore, 1909; E. J. Dillon, *The Eclipse of Russia,* ch. 14.

Finally, as noted below, the Kaiser frequently mooted a proposal to merge the Triple Alliance and the Franco-Russian Alliance into a grand "Continental League." Such a combination of all five Great Powers, he thought, would not only assure the peace of Europe, but could put a check on England's overweening domination in all colonial matters.

Thus the first years of the Franco-Russian Alliance tended to strengthen rather than endanger the peace of Europe. It established a healthy counter-poise to the Triple Alliance. Neither group was so greatly superior as to be able safely to attack the other, or even to seek to dominate it by threats of force. But during the decade 1894 to 1904, two changes occurred which tended ultimately to destroy this equilibrium. They are of the greatest importance in the development of the system of secret alliances—England's exchange of splendid isolation for an Entente Cordiale with France, and Italy's dubious loyalty toward her Allies.

ENGLAND AT THE PARTING OF THE WAYS, 1890-1898

England's traditional policy, generally speaking, had for centuries been one of "splendid isolation." By keeping her "hands free," she could enjoy the Balance of Power in Europe between the Continental groups and make English influence in either scale decisive. It was only at times when some one Power sought to become overwhelmingly strong, or threatened to endanger British control of the Channel and her maritime supremacy, that England intervened actively and decisively in European politics. In the years following the Franco-Prussian War, England still adhered to her traditional policy. Three times Bismarck sounded her as to an alliance with Germany—in September, 1879, in November, 1887, and in January, 1889,—but in all cases Bismarck's "feelers" came to nothing, partly because Lord

Salisbury feared that he could not get Parliamentary approval for such a policy.[38] England would depart no further from her no-alliance policy than merely to make an entente with Italy and Austria in 1887, in which the three countries expressed their common desire to maintain the peace and *status quo* in the Eastern Mediterranean and Turkey.[39] This agreement did not bind England to any military obligations, but it did confirm her friendly relations with the Triple Alliance. After Bismarck's fall this friendship continued and seemed at first to be strengthened by the Heligoland-Zanzibar Treaty and by the young Kaiser's personal ties and visits to England.

But at about the time of the formation of the Franco-Russian Alliance England appeared to have come to the parting of the ways. Isolation, though splendid, was not always safe or comfortable. Though a match upon the seas for either of the allied groups on the Continent, England was in danger of meeting unpleasant diplomatic defeats, if Germany and France, or Germany and Russia, coalesced against her. Lord Rosebery, in his careless energetic policy, had already had several disagreeable experiences which left a bad taste in the mouth. Without consulting the signatories of the Treaty of 1884, fixing the boundaries of the Congo State, he had signed a treaty giving up to the Congo State territory in the Upper Nile basin in exchange for a strip of Congo territory in the Tanganyika region, across which it was planned to run the British Cape-to-Cairo Railway. France and Germany protested, the latter on the ground that it tended to encircle German East Africa and was contrary to a previous treaty. Rosebery had to

[38] G.P., IV, 1-14, 376-419; Lady Cecil, *Life of Robert, Marquis of Salisbury,* II, 364-369; *cf.* also M. Ritter, *Bismarcks Verhältnis zu England und die Politik des Neuen Kurses,* Berlin, 1924; H. Rothfels, *Bismarcks Englische Bündnispolitik,* Berlin, 1924; F. Frahm, "England und Russland in Bismarcks Bündnispolitik," in *Archiv f. Pol. u. Gesch.*, V, Heft 4, 365-431 (1927).

[39] G.P., IV, 261-376; Pribram, pp. 36-42.

withdraw the arrangement, explaining apologetically that he was acting on memoranda left by Lord Salisbury and was unaware of the difficulties.[40] Similarly, in the misunderstandings which arose over the Siamese troubles in 1893, Rosebery found the French assuming a stiff attitude. He bristled up himself, and, on a Sunday, without consulting the Cabinet, sent off a telegram to the English commander at Bangkok which gave Queen Victoria a bad fright. He himself admitted it might have resulted in England's waking up on Monday morning to find herself at war with France.[41]

By her dangerously weak position in Egypt, England was continually exposed to the more or less united opposition of all the Continental Powers. Egypt was like a noose around the British neck, which any Great Power could tighten when it wanted to squeeze a diplomatic concession from the Mistress of the Seas—as France threatened to do in connection with the Siam controversy, and as Germany was felt to have done in connection with railway concessions in Turkey.[42] Such incidents exposed the hollowness of the phrase "splendid isolation." As Lord Grey truly says, speaking of his first Foreign Office experiences in 1892-1895, there was "the constant friction, rising on the slightest provocation to quarrel and hostility, between Great Britain and France or Russia. The ground swell of ill-will never ceased. British interests touched those of France and Russia in many parts of the world; and where interests touch, an atmosphere of ill-will is always dangerous. The blackest suspicion thrives in it, like noxious growth under dark skies in murky air." [43]

40 G.P., VIII, 428-475; for a somewhat different version, see Viscount Grey, *Twenty-five Years, 1892-1916,* I, 21 f.

41 G.P., VIII, 103-112; Grey, I, 12-15.

42 Grey, I, 9-11; G.P., VIII, 143-235, especially 185 ff; and XIV, 451-464; E. M. Earle, *Turkey, the Great Powers, and the Bagdad Railway* (N. Y., 1923), ch. iii.

43 Grey, II, 11.

Some such considerations as these gradually led English statesmen to the decision that "splendid isolation" was no longer possible. In 1895, Lord Salisbury indicated the changed British attitude by hinting to Germany that the time had come to partition Turkey. Though England had formerly pursued the policy of bolstering up a decrepit Turkish Empire, Salisbury had now at last come to the conclusion that this was a hopeless task. He had been betting on the wrong horse. Turkey might as well be carved up, or at least the slices had better be provisionally assigned in case the Ottoman Empire should finally go to pieces.

The Sultan's misgovernment had steadily weakened Turkey; the Christian populations under Turkish oppression were becoming more and more restless; and the frightful massacres of Armenians, with the more or less tacit approval and connivance of Abdul Hamid, had shocked and roused Europe. Lord Salisbury's proposal was to the effect that in partitioning Turkey, Egypt should go to England, Tripoli to Italy, Salonica to Austria, and Constantinople or the control of the Straits to Russia. Such a partition, based on friendly agreement beforehand and securing a fair share to each of the three Great Powers, might conceivably have gone a long way toward solving the Near Eastern Question, if the great difficulties connected with it could have been overcome.

Unfortunately, Berlin failed to take up Salisbury's suggestion. Marschall and Holstein, who at this time largely determined German policy, were excessively suspicious. They foresaw that France and Italy would be difficult to satisfy. Moreover, what should Germany receive? They feared that an attempt to partition Turkey would give rise to more problems than it settled, and might even involve the Powers in war. They suspected that Salisbury's proposal was intended to sow discord between Russia and the Triple Alliance, so that England would have an opportunity to fish in troubled waters. Accordingly, when Salisbury renewed his suggestion directly to the Kaiser a month later at Cowes, where William was attending the English yachting races, the Kaiser gave a cool reply; he said he believed it was best to attempt to sustain Turkey, and to force proper reforms for the protection of the Sultan's Christian subjects. Thereupon Lord Salisbury let the matter drop.[44]

By 1898 the political situation made still more evident to the British Cabinet the advisability of abandoning the isolation policy. In Central Africa friction with France over the Niger boundary was acute; France also was extending her power eastward toward the Upper Nile; and Major Marchand, leading an exploring expedition toward the Sudan, had not yet been checked by Kitchener at Fashoda. In South Africa English friction with the Boers had been steadily increasing, and was to break out some months later in the most humiliating and costly war which England had ever fought. The Kruger Telegram had shown the lively interest which the Kaiser and his subjects took in the Boers, and the desirability therefore of putting an end to any possible support, either secret or open, which Germany might be inclined to give to the South African Republics. Finally, in the Far East, Germany had just secured the lease of a naval base at Kiauchau; Russia was getting an economic grasp on Manchuria through the extension of the Trans-Siberian Railway; and by the lease of Port Arthur she would have a foothold which would menace

44 G.P., X, 1-41, 76 f., 111-114. The German documents indicate the incorrectness of Sir Valentine Chirol's contention (*London Times,* Sept. 11, 13, 1920) that the partition proposal came first from the German and not from the English side; they also correct many of Eckardstein's legendary assertions in his *Erinnerungen* (I, 207 ff.; II, 284; III, 12 ff.) concerning the Cowes conversations of 1895. *Cf.* also R. J. Sontag, "The Cowes Interview and the Kruger Telegram", in *Political Science Quarterly,* XL, 217 ff. (June, 1925); and E. N. Johnson and J. D. Bickford, "The Contemplated Anglo-German Alliance, 1890-1901," in *Political Science Quarterly,* XLII, 10 ff. (March, 1927).

Peking and seriously jeopardize Britain's naval and commercial predominance in the Far East. The English Press was clamoring to know how the Cabinet would stop Russia.

MR. CHAMBERLAIN'S ALLIANCE PROPOSALS TO GERMANY, 1898-1901

Under these circumstances the British first turned to Russia. On January 19, 1898, they proposed to the Tsar an entente which should put an end to all the long-standing sources of friction between the Bear and the Lion. The idea was to harmonize British and Russian policy in the two decaying empires of China and Turkey, instead of being constantly opposed. What Lord Salisbury secretly suggested to Russia in regard to China and Turkey was "no partition of territory, but only a partition of preponderance" of political influence.[44a] But the Tsar and his shifty ambitious Ministers did not receive the proposal in a way to inspire confidence or to encourage the British to proceed with it. Instead, Russia secured the lease of Port Arthur, and the British made a counter-move by doing likewise in regard to Wei-hai-Wei. Thereupon Mr. Joseph Chamberlain, the British Colonial Secretary, was allowed to try his hand at making an alliance with Germany.

On March 29, 1898, while Lord Salisbury was absent in France for his health, Count Hatzfeldt, the German Ambassador in London, was asked to dinner with Mr. Chamberlain at Alfred Rothschild's house. Chamberlain there declared quite frankly that England had decided to abandon her isolation policy. England and Germany, he admitted, had many petty points of friction in colonial matters, but no great fundamentally opposing interests. He therefore

[44a] Salisbury to O'Conor, Jan. 25, 1898; *British Documents on the Origins of the War, 1914-1918* (London, 1927), I, p. 8. The story of this British offer to Russia was first revealed in detail, *ibid.*, pp. 5-41, though the Kaiser got an inkling of it from the Tsar (see below, at note 50).

suggested an Anglo-German defensive alliance.[45] To satisfy Germany's fears that later British Cabinets might not keep the agreement, he was ready to get the treaty publicly approved by Parliament; this, however, "would not prevent the inclusion in the treaty of one or more secret articles," as he remarked confidentially three days later.[46] Finally he hinted that if England did not succeed in making an alliance with Germany, which was the more natural for her, she might turn toward France and Russia. This was said as a hint but not as a threat.

There was no reason to doubt that Chamberlain was sincerely seeking to open negotiations which should lead to an alliance. To have succeeded would have been a great feather in his cap. But other members of the Cabinet, like Lord Salisbury and Balfour, not to mention the Prince of Wales, who were all more Francophil, were less enthusiastic. They were not unwilling to see his efforts fail.

Chamberlain's offer was received in Berlin with the same suspiciousness as the proposed partition of Turkey three years earlier. Count Bülow, who had replaced Marschall as Secretary of State for Foreign Affairs, feared that a publicly announced alliance with England might involve Germany in the risk of being attacked on two fronts—the Russian and the French—where the British navy would be of

45 G.P., XIV, 193-199, 212-216; Eckardstein, I, 292 ff. At a shooting party in January, 1898, the Kaiser had already suggested to the British Military Attaché the desirability of such an alliance, which he said he had been striving after for eight years but had met with no response. At a luncheon at Friedrichshof in August he repeated the suggestion to the British Ambassador. But at a dinner in December he concurred with the Ambassador that "there was certainly no necessity for a formal alliance", because if it became advisable for them to act in common the arrangements could be made in twenty-four hours; *British Documents*, I, pp. 69, 100-105. The editors of the *British Documents* state (p. 101) that these are the only references to the proposals of 1898 for an Anglo-German alliance which they have been able to find in the Foreign Office Archives. This extraordinary fact that the British archives contain no mention of the Chamberlain proposal suggests that this was his own personal venture rather than any official move on the part of the British Cabinet.

46 G.P., XIV, 202.

little assistance to Germany. Moreover, he doubted whether the English Parliament, in view of the bitter public feeling in England since the Kruger Telegram, would ever ratify an Anglo-German alliance. German public opinion would also be against it. He therefore directed Hatzfeldt neither to accept nor reject Chamberlain's offer, but to deal with it in a dilatory fashion. By this means he believed that Germany and England might come to an agreement on some of their outstanding colonial problems, without going so far as to risk a definite alliance.[47]

In this connection the Kaiser took a step which reveals the lack of honesty which he sometimes displayed in his attempts to manage German foreign policy. Without consulting his Ministers, and in spite of the fact that the Chamberlain proposals had been strictly confidential, he wrote to the Tsar on May 30, 1898, saying that England had thrice within the last few weeks asked for an alliance, making enormous offers which opened a brilliant future for Germany, and begging for a quick reply. Before answering the British, the Kaiser added, he wanted to tell "Nicky" of this, since it was a life and death matter. Such an alliance would evidently be directed against Russia. "Now I ask you, as my old and trusted friend, to tell me what you can offer me, and what you will do for me if I refuse the British offers." [48]

This letter was a gross exaggeration, because no "enormous offers" had been made by England. The Kaiser was deliberately attempting by his exaggeration to bid Russia and England up against one another, and to use Chamberlain's offer to sow discord between Russia and England. What he wanted to secure from Nicky was Russian cooperation for bringing France into a Continental League,

[47] G.P., XIV, 199-249; see also pp. 337-344.

[48] M. Semenoff, *Correspondance entre Guillaume II et Nicolas II, 1894-1914* (Paris, 1924), pp. 38-42; *Briefe Wilhelm II an den Zaren 1894-1914* (ed. W. Goetz), Berlin, 1920, p. 309 ff.

which should draw together the Triple and Dual Alliance, and thus make a strong group of the five great European Powers. This idea of a Continental League continually hovered before his imagination for years. By it he hoped to secure the peace of Europe. If Russia could bring the French into such a combination, France would be expected to give up the thought of revenge and the hope of recovering Alsace-Lorraine. This would remove one of the fundamental sources of danger to the peace of Europe. Furthermore, such a Continental League could be effectively used to check England's excessive colonial pretensions in Africa and Asia, and eventually, perhaps, after the growth of the German navy, to place a check on England's supremacy on the seas.[49]

The Tsar, however, did not allow himself to be fooled by the Kaiser into making any commitments. But he replied at once on June 3, 1898:

> Dearest Willy,
>
> . . . Three months ago, in the midst of our negotiations with China, England handed us over a memorandum containing many *tempting* proposals trying to induce us to come to a full agreement upon *all the points* in which our interests collided with her's. These proposals were of such a new character, that I must say, we were quite amazed and yet—their very nature seemed suspicious to us; never before had England made such offers to Russia. That showed us clearly that England needed our friendship at that time, to be able to check our development, in a masked way, in the Far East. Without thinking twice over it, their proposals were refused. . . .
>
> It is very difficult for me, if not quite impossible, to answer your question whether *it is* useful *or not* for Germany to accept these often repeated English proposals, as I have not got the slightest knowledge of their value.

49 G.P., XI, 67-92, XIII, 63, 89; XIV, XIX-XXI, *passim;* and *Willy-Nicky Correspondence, passim.*

You must of course decide what is best and most necessary for your country.

Germany and Russia have lived in peace since old times, as good neighbours, and God grant! that they may continue so, *in close and loyal friendship*. . . .

I thank you once more for writing to me at such a grave moment for you!

God bless you my dearest Willy.

Believe me ever your loving cousin and trusting friend,

Nicky.[50]

This news of "amazing" British offers to Russia, made just before Chamberlain's proposals, made the Kaiser naturally suspect that "perfidious Albion" was trying to play Germany and Russia off against one another, and sow discord between them. It confirmed him in his temperamental suspiciousness of British good faith. So the Chamberlain proposal of March, 1898, was not grasped by Germany, and came to nothing.

The utmost that could be secured was the Anglo-German Convention of August 30, 1898, for the contingent partition of the Portuguese colonies. As Portugal was supposed to be in financial straits and likely to wish to borrow money, Germany and England agreed to consult as to the terms of any loans made, and to divide the Portuguese colonial areas whose tolls were to be pledged as security for the loans. In case Portugal should default on payment, Germany and England would enter upon the administration of the tolls in the areas pledged to each. They agreed jointly to oppose any loans to Portugal by a third Power which

[50] G.P., XIV, 250 f.; Semenoff, p. 42, note, confirming the truth of the Tsar's statement says a British note to Russia of Feb. 12, 1898, formulated the conceptions of the British Cabinet concerning the delimitation of Russian and English spheres of influence both in Turkey and China. Russia was to enjoy freedom of action in Northern, and England in Southern, China; for O'Conor's note of Feb. 12 to Muraviev, see *British Documents,* I, p. 12.

involved pledging the revenue of the Portuguese colonies.[51]

This Convention is important because it aimed to remove one source of rivalry and friction between England and Germany, and became the basis of later negotiations in 1912-1914 for a fair and reasonable agreement for a further contingent rearrangement of colonial possessions. But it also became a source of irritation and suspicion on Germany's part. The Kaiser and Bülow overestimated Portugal's financial embarrassment. They waited in vain for the loan which would bring the expected results from the treaty. Lord Salisbury refused to hinder Portugal from making other loans which did not involve pledging the tolls as agreed in the treaty. In this he was justified by the wording of the treaty, but the Kaiser and his advisers thought it contrary to its spirit. They had expected England would use her influence to prevent Portugal finding any other sources of credit, thus hastening the moment for the contingent partition.

But, instead of this, the Germans soon observed closer relations between Lisbon and London after the visit of King Carlos to Windsor in the spring of 1899. And in fact, upon the outbreak of the Boer War, by the secret Anglo-Portuguese Declaration of October 14, 1899 (often inaccurately called the "Windsor Treaty"), Lord Salisbury renewed with Portugal the old treaty of 1661 by which England promised to defend and protect all the Portuguese colonies. In return, Portugal undertook not to permit the transporting of munitions of war for the Boers into the Transvaal, and not to issue any formal declaration of neutrality, inasmuch as that would hinder the supplying of coal to British warships at Delagoa Bay. Observing this close Anglo-Portuguese friendship and the failure of the Anglo-German treaty to produce the hoped-for results, the

51 G.P., XIV, 347-355; for the negotiations, see pp. 259-367; Eckardstein, II, 205 ff.; and *British Documents,* I, pp. 44-73.

German Foreign Office naturally suspected the sincerity of England's proffered friendship.[52]

Similarly unfortunate in its effects on the relations of England and Germany was the Yang-tsze Convention of October 16, 1900. It aimed to promote the common interests of the two countries in the Far East by preserving the territorial integrity of China and by keeping her ports open to trade for all countries without distinction; but a misunderstanding as to whether it applied or not to Manchuria, where Germany did not wish to antagonize Russia, ultimately led to friction and distrust on both sides.[53] Disillusionment and disappointment in regard to the Portuguese, Yang-tsze, and Samoa arrangements, as well as the British detention and search of a couple of German steamers bound for South Africa and other sources of friction growing out of the Boer War, were further motives for German coolness toward suggestions for an alliance which Chamberlain continued to make.

Though the German rejection of the Chamberlain proposals was one of the most momentous factors in shaping the fatal course of events in the following years, only a word can be said about them here.[54]

52 *British Documents,* I, pp. 74-99; G.P., XV, 429; XVII, 17 ff., 34 ff., 85. Brandenburg, p. 133, is incorrect in stating that the so-called Windsor Treaty was signed during the visit of King Carlos in the spring of 1899.

53 *British Documents,* II, pp. 1-31; G.P., XVI, 197-491; XVII, 85, 103; Eckardstein, II, 201-203, 210-223; O. Franke, *Die Grossmächte in Ostasien* (Hamburg, 1923), pp. 149-177.

54 The details can easily be found in G.P., XV, 410-426; XVII, 1-118; Eckardstein, *Lebenserinnerungen, passim;* Brandenburg, pp. 114-155; G. P. Gooch, *History of Modern Europe, 1898-1919,* pp. 310-332; and E. Fischer, *Holsteins grosses Nein,* Berlin, 1925. Fischer however fails to note adequately Germany's reasons for distrusting England, and, wise by later events, condemns unduly the German failure to come to an understanding with England. The same criticism may also be made of E. N. Johnson and J. D. Bickford, "The Contemplated Anglo-German Alliance: 1890-1901", in *Political Science Quarterly,* XLII, 1-57 (Mar. 1927). The fact that the new *British Documents* contain practically nothing on the Chamberlain proposals of 1899 indicates that again, as in 1898, he was making a private venture and not representing the official policy of the Cabinet;

In November, 1899, a few weeks after the outbreak of the Boer War and the consequent anti-English outburst all over the Continent, the Kaiser and Bülow visited England. Chamberlain seized upon the occasion for long talks with both. He suggested closer relations between England, Germany, and the United States. The detailed notes which Bülow made of the conversations [55] do not indicate that he gave Chamberlain much encouragement to think that Germany would abandon the relatively favorable position which she then enjoyed in exchange for the risk of an alliance with England. Nevertheless a few days later, in a famous speech at Leicester, the English Colonial Secretary spoke glowingly of the community of German and British interests, and publicly proposed an alliance: "At bottom, the character of the Teutonic race differs very slightly indeed from the character of the Anglo-Saxon race. If the union between England and America is a powerful factor in the cause of peace, a new Triple Alliance between the Teutonic race and the two great branches of the Anglo-Saxon race will be a still more potent influence in the future of the world." [56]

But the poisonous effects of the Boer War were already at work. German, as well as French and Russian, newspapers were attacking England violently. Germans, as Bülow himself noted, were more stirred up about the Boer War than the English themselves; the anti-English feeling in Germany was stronger than the anti-German feeling in England. In view of this Anglophobia, Bülow did not have the courage, speaking in the Reichstag on December 11 in favor of the German Navy Law, to take up sympathetically Chamberlain's Leicester proposal. On the contrary, he

this tends to justify the German scepticism as to the real possibility of an Anglo-German Alliance. See also Friedrich Meinecke, *Geschichte des Deutsch-Englischen Bündnisproblems, 1890-1901,* Berlin, 1927.

[55] G.P., XV, 413-420.

[56] Quoted by Gooch, p. 311.

poured cold water on it, as being quite unnecessary for Germany. It was a rude rebuff to England. Moreover, if it be true, as Chamberlain told Eckardstein,[57] that he had made his Leicester speech at Bülow's own suggestion, and with the expectation that it would find a friendly echo across the North Sea, Bülow's Reichstag speech was a treacherous act greatly resented by Chamberlain. At any rate, the British Foreign Office became more suspicious of the Wilhelmstrasse,—a suspicion which was now beginning to be further fostered by Tirpitz's plans for building up the German navy.

Nevertheless, in 1901, after the Kaiser's much appreciated visit to Osborne at the news that Queen Victoria was dying, Chamberlain again opened negotiations for a defensive alliance between England and Germany, or even between England, Germany and Japan. England still had her hands tied in South Africa where the Boers were resisting with dogged determination. In the Far East, following the suppression of the Boxer Revolt, English friction with Russia had reached an acute stage, because the Tsar's forces would not evacuate Chinese territory. Under these circumstances, a German alliance would have afforded a valuable support to Great Britain. But for this very reason Germany was not at all anxious to commit herself. The negotiations, which were taken over by Lord Lansdowne, dragged on through the year. They were finally dropped in December, 1901, because the British Cabinet felt unable to meet Germany's conditions that the treaty should include the Triple Alliance and that it should be approved by the British Parliament. Whether such approval could have been secured was, in fact, very doubtful. A bitter antagonism had been aroused in both countries by the Boer War and the

[57] *Lebenserinnerungen*, II, 107, 111, 124. A current, but inaccurate and misleading English version of this unfortunate Chamberlain-Bülow episode is given by H. H. Asquith, *The Genesis of the War* (N.Y., 1923), pp. 43-49.

Press attacks on both sides which accompanied it. Moreover, the British Cabinet was by no means solid in support of the alliance with Germany. Lord Salisbury had always been sceptical, and finally left on record a strong memorandum against it. Lansdowne and Balfour were not enthusiastic. Chamberlain, except for support from the Duke of Devonshire, had rather been compelled to play a lone hand; and even he, after Bülow's rebuff of his Leicester proposal, did not want to burn his fingers again.[58]

Looking back at the whole series of negotiations, it is possible that some kind of an Anglo-German defensive alliance could have been arranged, if Germany had been more receptive to Chamberlain's offers at the beginning. This would have laid the basis for a better mutual understanding and rendered less painful the popular antagonism caused by the Boer War, in which the German Government's attitude, as distinct from that of the German people and the German Press, was tolerably correct.[59] It would have helped to prevent the mutual suspicions which were nourished by the increase of naval armaments on both sides of the North Sea. It would probably have averted the German fright of 1904 that England was planning "to Copenhagen" the German fleet,[60] as well as the English

58 G.P., XVII, 16-19, 53, 67, 115, 221-224, 297, 316 f. Eckardstein, II, 337 f., 397 ff. According to the Germans, the initiative in reopening these negotiations in March, 1901, came from the British; according to the *British Documents,* II, pp. 60-88, it came from the Germans. For Lord Salisbury's memorandum condemning the inclusion of England in the Triple Alliance, *ibid.,* II, 68 f.

59 The German Government realized from the outset that the cause of the Boers was hopeless, and that Germany was impotent to help them owing to the lack of any adequate German fleet. The German Government had therefore tried to dissuade Kruger from defying England to the point of war. Later, the Kaiser refused to receive Kruger on his mission to Europe, and refused to join in Russian and French mediation projects. (G.P., XV, 367-437, and note 35 above).

60 G.P., XIX, 353-380: "Das erste Deutsch-Englische 'War Scare', Nov.-Dec., 1904," with the quotation (p. 354) from *Vanity Fair* of Nov. 17, 1904 about "the precedent of Copenhagen in 1807." This was just after Sir John Fisher had "purged the navy of obsolete vessels" and carried

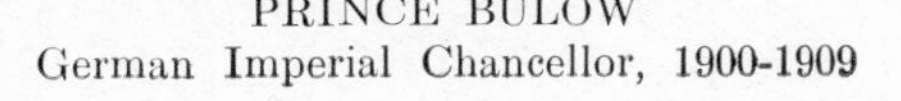

PRINCE BULOW
German Imperial Chancellor, 1900-1909

ADMIRAL TIRPITZ
German Secretary of Navy, 1897-1916

panic in 1908-09 at the specter of a German invasion of England.[61] It might even have established a basis of mutual goodwill which would have brought success to the numerous efforts made later for some kind of an agreement to limit the mad competition in Anglo-German naval armaments. And it would have doubtless prevented the formation of the Triple Entente.

But Holstein, Bülow and the Kaiser miscalculated the situation and let the golden opportunity slip by. They were irritated at what seemed England's unwillingness to afford Germany colonial acquisitions in Samoa and the Portuguese colonies. They were unable, or unwilling, to defy German public opinion by allying with a country which was crushing the Boers. They doubted whether the British Parliament would really sanction such an alliance. Their fundamental miscalculation was their persistent conviction that England would never draw close to her traditional French enemy, and certainly not to her bitter Russian rival. Anglo-Russian antagonism was so axiomatic in the Wilhelmstrasse that Holstein and Bülow were convinced that, even if England did establish a *rapprochement* with France, this would not be dangerous to Germany, since it would undoubtedly lead to the rupture of the Franco-Russian Alliance; an Anglo-Franco-Russian combination seemed impossible. As things stood during the Boer War and the Far Eastern troubles, at the turn of the century, Germany, dominating the Triple Alliance, seemed to stand with hands free between England on one side and the Franco-Russian

out other revolutionary reforms to make the British navy more effective; see his *Memories and Records,* II, 128-153; he himself admits (*ibid.,* I, 22) that in 1908 he urged King Edward to "Copenhagen" the German Navy, while England had seven dreadnoughts and Germany had none. *Cf.* B. E. Schmitt, *England and Germany, 1740-1914,* pp. 178-182, 205-207. For an excellent summary of the broad aspects of Anglo-German relations during the decades after Bismarck, see Friedrich Meinecke *Geschichte des Deutsch-Englischen Bündnisproblems, 1890-1901,* Berlin, 1927.

91 *Cf.* the play, "An Englishman's Home."

Alliance on the other. Germany enjoyed, they believed, the advantage of holding the Balance of Power between them. It made her, as Bülow once proudly said, *arbiter mundi.* He saw no reason to abandon lightly her advantage, and to assume instead the risk of defending British possessions all over the world. England needed Germany, he believed, needed her badly, and would probably need her more, rather than less, in the future; therefore Germany could afford to defer assuming the risk of an Anglo-German alliance until English Ministers showed more consideration to Germany's wishes in colonial and other matters.[62] Why should Germany pull the British chestnuts out of the fire? Why allow herself to be shoved forward by the British against the Russians? What could the British Navy do to protect the East Prussian frontier from a Cossack attack? [63]

These are the ideas which occur again and again in the reasoning of Bülow and Holstein, and which were readily accepted by the Kaiser. Though at times he seems to have inclined sincerely to an alliance with England, he was

[62] *Cf.* Bülow to the Kaiser, who was visiting at Osborne, Jan. 21, 1901: "Your Majesty is quite right in feeling that the English must come to us. They have just lost a good deal of hair in Africa; America is uncertain; Japan is not to be depended upon; France is filled with hate; Russia is perfidious; public opinion in all countries is hostile. . . . At present it is beginning gradually to dawn on the mind of the English that they will not be able merely by their own power to hold their World Empire against so many opponents.

"Now the important thing is neither to discourage the English, nor yet allow ourselves to be bound by them prematurely. The English difficulties will increase still further in the coming months, and with them will increase the price which we can demand. We ought not to show England too great eagerness, which would only increase the English demands and diminish our chances of gain; but at the same time we ought to maintain the English in their conviction that we desire the continuance of a powerful England; that we believe in the solidarity of Anglo-German political, cultural, and also commercial, interests; and therefore that we shall in time be ready for this or that agreement with England if we receive proper treatment from the English side. . . . The English threat of an understanding with the Dual Alliance is a spectre invented to frighten us. which the English have used for years"; G.P., XVII, 20 f.

[63] G.P., XVII, 1-129. *passim;* XVIII, 510; XX. 15.

nevertheless, to judge by his letters and marginal notes, obsessed by a strong dislike of most British political leaders, including "Uncle Bertie," which almost amounted to a kind of Anglophobia. Psychoanalysts, perhaps, would say that he suffered from an "anti-English complex" caused partly by a reaction against early maternal influence, and partly by an "inferiority complex"—by an acute realization of Germany's inferiority in naval and colonial power. "Our future upon the Seas," "the trident in our hands," the building of the German navy, and the eager desire for colonies may have been a form of "compensation for the repressed envy with which he regarded England's proud position in the world." [64]

Thus, from a variety of reasons, Holstein, Bülow, and the Kaiser failed to take advantage of the English offers. They held off in the hope of getting better terms—and got nothing. They let slip the golden moments which were never to return. The English, failing finally to arrange an alliance with Germany, turned elsewhere. In 1902 they signed with Japan the well-known alliance which protected their mutual interests in the Far East. In 1904 they signed with France the treaties which were the first step in the formation of the Triple Entente.

ITALY'S DUBIOUS LOYALTY TO HER ALLIES

Italy, like Germany, had been occupied so long establishing her own national unity that she came late into the race for colonial possessions. But if she were to play the part of a Great Power in Europe, and find an outlet for her rapidly increasing population, she felt that she too must

[64] On the curious psychology of "the most brilliant failure in history", as Edward VII called his nephew, see the by no means friendly or sympathetic accounts of Emil Ludwig, *Wilhelm der Zweite* (Berlin, 1925); especially pp. 174-196, 218-265, for the Kaiser's baneful influence on Anglo-German relations; and [F. C. Endres], *Die Tragödie Deutschlands* (Leipzig, 1922; 3rd ed., Stuttgart, 1924), pp. 121-146, with extensive bibliography.

acquire colonies. She had naturally cast her eyes on Tunis. But the French had stepped in ahead of her. She had then sought alliance with Germany and Austria in the hope of getting their support. Bismarck, however, was not at first inclined to allow the Triple Alliance to be exploited for Italy's colonial ambitions. But in 1887, when the Boulanger crisis in France and the Bulgarian situation in the Balkans cast heavy clouds over Europe, Italy was able to extort, as the price of her renewal of the Triple Alliance, new clauses looking toward future acquisitions in North Africa, the Balkans, and the Eastern Mediterranean. As Germany's interests were not identical with those of Austria in the Balkans, and as Austria was unwilling to commit herself in regard to Italy's North African ambitions, it was decided that these matters should be dealt with in separate treaties to be signed by Austria and Italy, and by Germany and Italy, on February 20, 1887, the same day that the Triple Alliance Treaty of 1882 was renewed.

Accordingly, Austria and Italy,

> "having in mind only the maintenance, so far as possible, of the *status quo* in the Orient, engage to use their influence to forestall any territorial modification which might be injurious to one or the other. . . . However, if, in the course of events, the maintenance of the *status quo* in the regions of the Balkans or of the Ottoman coasts and islands in the Adriatic and in the Aegean Sea should become impossible, and if, whether in consequence of the action of a third Power or otherwise, Austria-Hungary or Italy should find themselves under the necessity of modifying it by a temporary or permanent occupation on their part, this occupation shall take place only after a previous agreement between the two Powers aforesaid, based on the principle of a reciprocal compensation. . . ."[65]

[65] Art. I of the Austro-Italian Treaty of 1887, which was embodied as "Art. VII" in the Triple Alliance Treaty of 1891 and its subsequent renewals; Pribram, pp. 44, 66, 94, 99 f., 103, and 175-304, *passim;* G.P.,

Germany, on her part, undertook "to use her influence to forestall, on the Ottoman coasts and islands in the Adriatic and Aegean Seas any territorial modification which might be injurious" to Italy. As to North Africa: "If it were to happen that France should make a move to extend her occupation, or even her protectorate or her sovereignty, under any form whatsoever, in the North African territories, whether of the Vilayet of Tripoli or of the Moroccan Empire, and that in consequence thereof Italy, in order to safeguard her position in the Mediterranean, should feel that she must herself take action," Germany promised her armed support, if war should ensue.[66]

In 1891, at the third renewal of the Triple Alliance, Italy made a number of new requests, but the only one which was finally conceded to her was an extension of Germany's obligation to support her in North Africa. Germany and Italy engaged to exert themselves for the maintenance of the *status quo* in Cyrenaica, Tripoli and Tunis. But, "if unfortunately, as a result of a mature examination of the situation, Germany and Italy should both recognize that the maintenance of the *status quo* has become impossible, Germany engages, after a formal and previous agreement, to support Italy in any action in the form of occupation or other taking of guaranty which the latter should undertake in these same regions with a view to an interest of equilibrium and of legitimate compensation." In such an eventuality both Powers would seek to place themselves likewise in agreement with England.[67]

This opened the door, as the Italians hoped, to a possi-

IV, 179-260; VII, 51-123; XI, 267-300; XVIII, 499-647, 681-759; XXI, 351-419; XXX, 493-579; and Crispi, *Memoirs,* III, 301-349.

66 Arts. I and III of the Italo-German Treaty of 1887, embodied as Arts. VI and X in the Triple Alliance Treaty of 1891 and subsequent renewals.

67 Art. IX of the Triple Alliance Treaty of 1891 and subsequent renewals.

ble annexation of North African territory. But Germany still hoped to be able to restrain Italy from African adventures which might antagonize England, France or Turkey. She had therefore insisted on the insertion of the phrases "as a result of mature examination" and "after a formal and previous agreement." She also struck out the reference to Morocco, which was in the 1887 treaty and in the first Italian draft of the new clause, in order not to encourage Italy to collide with possible French, English, or Spanish ambitions in that region.

The Italians, however, were bitterly disillusioned in their hopes that these treaty arrangements would speedily enable them to acquire Tripoli. The following years were filled with demands and reproaches toward her allies, which became louder as the Abyssinian adventure went from bad to worse. Crispi complained that he was being browbeaten by France, threatened by Russian intrigues in the Near East and in Abyssinia, and neglected by England—and that for all this Germany and the Triple Alliance were to blame. The French, he said, were dominated by the thought of getting back Alsace-Lorraine, and had warned him to expect no concessions from them as long as Italy remained in the Triple Alliance; on the contrary they would "aim to make life as sour as possible for him." [68]

However, after Crispi had been overthrown as a result of the Abyssinian disaster, his successor, Rudini, began a *rapprochement* with France. By the Franco-Italian Tunis Convention of 1896, Italy at last virtually recognized the French protectorate in Tunis and received in return certain political and commercial privileges. The next year, the Italian Crown Prince, Victor Emmanuel and his Montenegrin bride, visited Paris, and the fêtes in their honor tended to draw the two Latin nations together. Two years later

68 Crispi's report of a French official statement, Feb., 9, 1896; G.P., XI, 288.

a Franco-Italian commercial treaty put an end to the long tariff war which had had a ruinous effect on the trade between the two countries and had caused great bitterness.

The *rapprochement* between Paris and Rome was helped by the new turn which Delcassé gave to Anglo-French relations. After the bitter humiliation of Fashoda, Delcassé had determined to put an end to the traditional hostility between France and England. By a convention of March 21, 1899, Delcassé came to an agreement with England in regard to the delimitation of spheres of influence in the regions between the Congo and the Upper Nile, and at the same time quieted Italian apprehensions by indicating that the French had no aspirations to the east of Tunis, in the Tripoli region coveted by Italy. This opened the way for the secret Franco-Italian accord of December, 1900. By an exchange of notes between Visconti-Venosta and Barrère, the active French Ambassador at Rome, Italy recognized French aspirations in Morocco, and France recognized Italian aspirations in Tripoli.[69]

The growing intimacy between France and Italy was now emphasized outwardly in every possible manner. President Loubet bestowed upon Victor Emmanuel the Grand Cross of the French Legion of Honor. The Italian fleet visited Toulon and was received with demonstrations of friendship which recalled the visit of the Russian fleet at the formation of the Franco-Russian alliance. On December 14, 1901, Prinetti, who was decidedly Francophil, revealed in the Italian Chamber of Deputies the existence of the secret Franco-Italian accord made twelve months before by Visconti-Venosta and Barrère. At the same time he protested profusely to the German and Austrian ambassadors that Italy was thoroughly loyal to the Triple Alli-

69 *Livre Jaune: Les Accords franco-italiens de 1900-1902* (Paris, 1920), pp. 1-4; Pribram, *The Secret Treaties of Austria-Hungary, 1879-1914*, ed. Coolidge, II, 227, 240-245.

ance, though he admitted it had been an act of disloyalty on his predecessor's part not to inform Italy's allies at once of the exchange of notes with France. He tried to excuse it by alleging that he had supposed Visconti-Venosta had already notified Germany and Austria of it.[70]

Bülow was worried at Italy's defection. He feared that Italy might proceed to the annexation of Tripoli, thus antagonizing Turkey and jeopardizing German interests in the Near East. But publicly he attempted to appear unconcerned, declaring in his famous Reichstag speech of January 8, 1902, that "the Triple Alliance still enjoys the best of health, and will, as I believe and hope, continue to do so, like persons who are mistakenly announced as dead but continue still to live for a good long time." And he added jauntily, "In a happy marriage the husband must not get angry right off if his wife innocently takes an extra dance with another partner. The main thing is that she does not elope with him; but she will not elope, if she realizes that she is better off with her husband." This warning to Italy he emphasized by remarking further that the Triple Alliance was "not a business concern for making gains, but an insurance company."

Italy, however, did not heed the warning. While carrying on negotiations for the renewal of the Triple Alliance, she at the same time listened to the wooing of Barrère, who was determined to secure a promise from Italy that she would not attack France and would give up any military conventions or other treaty obligations which might compel her to join in a German aggression against France.[71] And in fact on June 4, 1902, several weeks before the renewal of the Triple Alliance, Prinetti secretly assured Delcassé that it contained nothing either directly or indirectly aggressive toward France. Though he stipulated that "this

70 G.P., XVIII, 730 ff.

71 Barrère to Delcassé, May 8, 1902; *Les Accords franco-italiens,* p. 5.

communication is destined to remain secret," Delcassé soon announced its substance in the French Chamber of Deputies.

Delcassé was not yet satisfied. He wanted to get from Prinetti a signed document which would bind Italy to observe strict neutrality in case France should take the initiative in declaring a war to which she had been provoked.[72] Accordingly, by an exchange of notes between Prinetti and Barrère on November 1, 1902, it was mutually agreed:

> "In case France [Italy] should be the object of a direct or indirect aggression on the part of one or more Powers, Italy [France] will maintain a strict neutrality.
>
> "The same shall hold good in case France [Italy], as the result of a direct provocation, should find herself compelled, in defense of her honor or her security, to take the initiative of a declaration of war. In that eventuality, the Government of the Republic [the Royal Government] shall previously communicate its intention to the Royal Government [the Government of the Republic], which will thus be enabled to determine whether there is really a case of direct provocation."[73]

Practically this meant that Italy was now no longer a loyal member of the Triple Alliance. To be sure, Prinetti might soothe his conscience by maintaining that his promise to France merely "defined the character" of Italy's Triple Alliance obligations, and was not directly contrary to them.[74] It is true his promise was not contrary to the *letter* of Italy's obligations to Germany; since, according to Art. II of the Triple Alliance Treaty, Italy was bound to assist Germany only in case Germany was attacked by France "without direct provocation." Italy reserved the

[72] Delcassé to Barrère, June 18, 1902; *Les Accords franco-italiens,* p. 6

[73] Barrère to Delcassé, Nov. 1, 1902; *Les Accords franco-italiens,* 7-9.

[74] This is the aspect of the affair which Barrère gave to Poincaré in 1912, *Les Accords franco-italiens,* 11-14; it was, he said, not "a counter-treaty but a *counterpart* of the Triple Alliance."

right to decide what would constitute "direct provocation." But the interpretation of this phrase might be made as elastic as rubber. When asked by Barrère to define what it meant, Prinetti had cited as examples of "direct provocation" the Schnaebele incident, the Ems telegram, and King William's refusal to receive Benedetti in 1870.[75] This meant that at any time in the future, if some similar incident arose, which France considered a provocation, and which compelled her, "in defense of her honor or her security," to declare war on Germany, Italy would remain neutral. Thus, owing to the inclusion of the phrase "direct provocation," the Franco-Italian accord of 1902 was not exactly contrary to the *letter* of Italy's Triple Alliance obligation; but it was certainly contrary to its spirit and purpose.[76] Italy would no longer help Germany in case of a French attack, which had been one of the original essential purposes of the Triple Alliance. It all depended on how Italy would choose to interpret the essentially indefinite and elastic conception of "direct provocation." Being incapable of precise or judicial definition, this interpretation was likely to depend, as events proved, on what Italy considered her interests at the moment. M. Poincaré shrewdly summed up the real situation when he told Izvolski in December, 1912, that "neither the Triple-Entente nor the Triple Alliance can count on the loyalty of Italy; the Italian Government will employ all its efforts to preserve the peace; and in case of war, it will begin by adopting a waiting attitude and will finally join the camp toward which victory will incline." [77] Henceforth Italy had a foot in both camps and could jump in either direction, though she was

[75] *Les Accords franco-italiens,* 7.

[76] Even such a stout champion of France and severe critic of Germany as Pagès admits that Italy's new promise to France was "difficilement conciliable" with her prior obligation to Germany; Bourgeois et Pagès, p. 301, note 1.

[77] *Livre Noir,* I, 365.

not wholly trusted by either her old ally or her new friend.

In the fall of 1903, shortly before Germany was surprised by the conclusion of the Anglo-French Entente which threatened to draw Italy further to the side of these two Mediterranean Powers, she began to fear more seriously that Italy's "extra dance" might develop into an elopement after all. Victor Emmanuel explained to Emperor William that French friendship was important for Italy's commercial relations and for enabling Italy to borrow needed money. Though he was reported to have said of Barrère, "I don't like him, he is a liar and a nasty man," [78] nevertheless he paid a visit a few months later to Paris, which was made the occasion for further demonstrations of Franco-Italian friendship. At about the same time there was a violent renewed outburst of Italian irredentist feeling against Austria, which the Italian Government made little effort to check.[79] In April, 1904, President Loubet returned Victor Emmanuel's visit, going to Naples with the French fleet, and then even going on to Rome, though no French President hitherto had thus snubbed the Pope to honor the King. In the toasts given to Loubet at Naples, the Italians emphasized Franco-Italian friendship, but made no mention of Italy's position in the Triple Alliance. Germany protested against this omission, demanding that if further toasts were exchanged some reference should be made to the Triple Alliance and its peaceful character, in order that the world might not think that Italy had shifted to the side of France. The Italian Minister promised to heed the German protest. But he did not keep his promise. Two more Franco-Italian toasts were exchanged in which the Triple Alliance was passed over in dead silence.[80]

Monts, the German Ambassador at Rome, urged that

[78] G. P., XVIII, 615.
[79] G. P., XVIII, 616-636.
[80] G.P., XX, 37-64.

the way to make Italy return to a more loyal attitude was to take a severe tone toward her. "If we now are polite, friendly, and helpful, the Italians will become altogether intractable. The only motives which appear to be effective here are fear and a feeling of respect." [81] This advice was in accord with Bülow's past warnings to Italy not to let the flirtation with France develop into a permanent *liaison.* But Bülow now decided cordiality was wiser than scolding. He tried to win Italy back by assuring her that Germany had no objections to her taking Tripoli. He also believed it far better that Italy's colonial ambitions should be afforded an outlet in North Africa rather than in Albania and the Adriatic, where she was sure to antagonize Austria. Some months later, as Tittoni expressed contrition and promised "not to do it again," [82] and as the Moroccan cloud was gathering on the horizon, Bülow felt particularly anxious not to offend the Italians, or take a stiff attitude which might drive them further into the arms of France and England. "The façade of the Triple Alliance must be kept as intact as possible," he wrote to the Kaiser, "especially so, because as long as the Italians are still in the Triple Alliance, they will be regarded with distrust on the enemy's side. But in case of complications, we need certainly give ourselves no illusions as to active Italian coöperation. However, it will be a gain, not to be lightly valued, if Italy remains neutral instead of going with France." [83]

In his public utterances, and in the volume defending his policies which he published just before the War, Bülow naturally sought to maintain as far as possible the fiction of Italian loyalty—that is, to give the façade as good an appearance as possible. "Neither at Algeciras, nor during her Tripolitan expedition, nor shortly before this, at the interview of Racconigi, did Italy ever contemplate severing

81 Monts to Bülow, May 6, 1904; G.P., XX, 69.

82 G.P., XX, 81-95. 83 Bülow to the Kaiser, Mar. 5, 1905; G.P., XX, 95.

her connection with us." [84] This has often misled persons into thinking he placed more confidence in Italy after the Franco-Italian agreement of 1900-02 than was really the case. Even such a well-informed scholar as Professor Pribram says: "By the end of 1905, Bülow believed that no danger existed of Italy's alienation from the Triple Alliance." He quotes Bülow as declaring in 1905: "Italy has cast in her lot with the Triple Alliance, not for reasons of mawkish sentimentality, but because she finds it to her advantage to do so. The reasons which originally brought the three great states together are still in existence; nothing has happened to work a change in them." [85] But pre-war declarations of this kind are merely examples of the optimistic Chancellor's usual policy of *"faire bonne mine au mauvais jeu"*—of putting a good face on a bad matter. Privately and in reality he was much worried by Italy's double-dealing.

At the Algeciras Conference, by voting with France and England against Germany, Italy gave another rude shock to the façade of the Triple Alliance, and showed that Bülow had reason to be worried. Speaking in the Chamber of Deputies on March 8, 1906, Sonnino attempted to explain Italy's double policy, saying: "Loyal from our heart to the Triple Alliance, we shall maintain the traditions of intimacy with England and our honest friendship with France." On this the German Emperor commented significantly:

> " 'No one can serve two masters,' it says in the Bible; certainly therefore not three masters! France, England and the Triple Alliance, that is wholly out of the question! It will turn out that Italy stands in the British-French group! We shall do well to reckon with this, and write this 'ally' off as smoke!" [86]

[84] Bülow, *Deutsche Politik,* Berlin, 1913; Eng. trans. *Imperial Germany,* N. Y., 1914, p. 59.

[85] Pribram, pp. 263-4; Pribram-Coolidge, II, 135-6.

[86] G.P., XXI, 353.

THE ANGLO-FRENCH ENTENTE OF 1904

M. Delcassé, who became French Minister of Foreign Affairs in June, 1898, is said to have declared that the first object of his policy would be to secure a *rapprochement* with England. If France were to expand her colonial empire and some day recover Alsace-Lorraine, the age-long hostility with England must be ended. Delcassé therefore took steps toward a reconciliation with "perfidious Albion." He approved a treaty settling a long-standing dispute as to Anglo-French boundaries in the Niger Valley. A few months later, in the face of Kitchener's troops and in defiance of traditional French feelings, he had yielded to the British at Fashoda. On March 21, 1899, he reached an agreement with England delimiting French and English spheres of influence in the region between the Upper Nile and the Congo. He had done what he could to open the way for better Anglo-French relations.

But public opinion in the two countries was still hostile. It was further aggravated by the Boer War. To overcome this was part of the work of Sir Thomas Barclay. Looking at the two countries from a commercial rather than a diplomatic point of view, he secured the approval of Salisbury and Delcassé for a visit to Paris of British Chambers of Commerce in 1900. The banquet of 800 at which he presided proved an encouraging success. This was the year of the great Paris Exposition, and thousands of other British visitors flocked to the French capital. These visits were followed by delegations of French Chambers of Commerce to England, and by a similar exchange of visits by members of Parliament and their wives. With the ground thus prepared, Sir Thomas Barclay began to agitate for the conclusion of an Anglo-French Treaty of Arbitration, which should remove possible causes of friction and place the future of the two countries beyond the dangerous reach of popular

M. THÉOPHILE DELCASSÉ

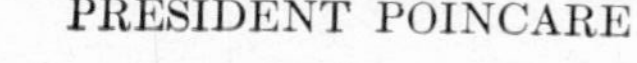

PRESIDENT POINCARÉ

emotions. Such a treaty, referring to the Hague Arbitration Tribunal all disputes between the two countries (except those touching vital interests, honor, or independence), was finally signed on October 14, 1903.[87]

Meanwhile, the death of Queen Victoria in 1901, and the retirement of Lord Salisbury in 1902, opened the way for two men who were more enthusiastic than their predecessors for closer relations with France—Edward VII and Lord Lansdowne.

The new King, Edward VII, had spent much of his time as Prince of Wales in Paris or on the Riviera. He spoke French with perfect ease, had formed many warm attachments in France, and had a strong liking for the people as a nation. In the spring of 1903, on his own initiative, he paid to Paris his first formal visit as King, and was delighted by his reception. Though it was not at first enthusiastic, it was respectful, and soon decidedly sympathetic. In one of those tactful speeches, in which he knew how to combine flattering appreciation and hearty personal good-will, thereby winning so many personal friends, he declared to the French:

> "It is scarcely necessary to tell you with what sincere pleasure I find myself once more in Paris, to which, as you know, I have paid very frequent visits with ever-increasing pleasure, and for which I feel an attachment fortified by so many happy and ineffaceable memories. The days of hostility between the two countries are, I am certain, happily at an end. I know of no two countries whose prosperity is more interdependent. There may have been misunderstandings and causes of dissension in the past, but that is all happily over and forgotten. The friendship of the two countries is my constant preoccupation, and I count on you all

[87] *Cf.* Sir Thomas Barclay, *Thirty Years of Anglo-French Reminiscences, 1876-1906,* Londo 1914, pp. 175-229, 340-354. *British Documents,* II, 261, 289 ff., 318 f.

who enjoy French hospitality in their magnificent city to aid me to reach this goal."[88]

The warmth of this royal utterance, and his hearty enjoyment of the state banquet at the Élysée, the military review at Vincennes, and the races at Longchamps, all went a long way toward wiping from the French mind the bitter memories of Fashoda and the Boer War. Two months later (July 6-9, 1903) President Loubet paid King Edward a return visit. This was marked on both sides by the greatest cordiality. "France," the French President said to his royal host, "preserves a precious memory of the visit which you paid to Paris. I am sure that it will have the most happy results, and that it will greatly serve to maintain and bind still more closely the relations which exist between our two countries, for their common good and as a guarantee of the peace of the world." In return Edward VII expressed the hope "that the welcome you have received today has convinced you of the true friendship, indeed I will say the affection, which my country feels for France." And upon President Loubet's departure, the King sent a farewell message which found a warm response on both sides of the English Channel: "It is my most ardent wish that the *rapprochement* between the two countries may be lasting."

Delcassé had accompanied President Loubet on this visit and began those conversations with Lord Lansdowne which were to bear fruit eight months later in the famous Anglo-French *Entente Cordiale.* This was signalized by the signing on April 8, 1904, of a series of conventions which settled amicably long-standing disputes concerning the Newfoundland fisheries, Senegambia, Siam, Madagascar, the New Hebrides, and other subjects. The most important convention was that by which France at last gave the English a free hand in Egypt in return for a free hand in Morocco.

[88] Quoted by Gooch, *History of Modern Europe, 1878-1919,* pp. 338-339. *Cf.* also Sidney Lee, *King Edward VII,* II, 221 ff.

Egypt for more than a quarter of a century had been one of the most acute sources of friction between Downing Street and the Quai d'Orsay. It had been the Achilles heel of British foreign policy. All the Great Powers had certain political and financial rights in Egypt which continually hampered England's freedom of action and threatened the efficiency of Egyptian administration. Egyptian finance was now in a flourishing condition. But owing to the international fetters originally imposed under conditions which no longer existed, the Khedive, that is to say, his English advisers, were unable to derive any real profit from the surplus funds. The situation, says Lord Cromer, had become intolerable.[89] It was therefore a great relief to England to obtain a waiver of the financial restrictions and to receive the assurance that "the Government of the French Republic will not obstruct the action of Great Britain in Egypt by asking that a date should be fixed for the British occupation or in any other matter." [90] England's new freedom of action was embodied in a Khedivial Decree which England speedily notified formally to the Powers and to which she secured their assent.[91] Egypt was no longer a vulnerable point in English diplomacy. Within six months, as Kühlmann wrote from Tangiers, "The Egyptian question is dead, but the Moroccan question is very much alive." [92]

Morocco, on the other hand, was pregnant with trouble

[89] Cromer, *Modern Egypt,* ch. 48. For Lord Cromer's active influence on the Anglo-French negotiations, see *British Documents,* II, 298 ff., 323, 332 f., 339 f., 354 ff., 364, 400.

[90] Art. I of the convention concerning Egypt and Morocco. For the text of the Anglo-French Conventions see the *British Blue Book* of 1904 (Cd. 1952) and the *French Livre Jaune* of 1904, *Accords conclus le 8 avril, 1904 . . . au sujet du Maroc, de l'Egypte, de Terre Neuve,* etc.; for the secret articles, first revealed in the Paris *Temps,* in 1911, see the *English Blue Book, Treaty Series,* 1911 (Cd. 5969); E. D. Morel, *Morocco in Diplomacy,* London, 1912, p. 234 ff.; *Amer. Jour. of International Law,* VI (1912), supplement, pp. 26 ff; and *British Documents,* II, 374-407.

[91] For the negotiations to secure Germany's assent, see G.P., XX, 121-165.

[92] G.P., XX, 33.

for France and was soon to become a diplomatic nightmare for all Europe. At the close of the nineteenth century it was virtually an independent country of some four or five million inhabitants—Arabs, Berbers, Jews, negroes and others—under the nominal rule of a Sultan at Fez. But this rule was a shaky one. There were continual uprisings from hostile tribes, or from rival claimants to the Umbrella, which was the symbol of sovereignty in that sunny land. Arab marauders continually jeopardized the life and property of European traders and travelers. Little satisfaction could be obtained from the Sultan's government. As a result of these turbulent conditions, the thirteen Powers, including the United States, who had once coöperated to suppress the Barbary Pirates, signed with the Sultan of Morocco in 1880 the Convention of Madrid. This provided for the proper protection of foreigners in Morocco and promised the most-favored-nation treatment to all the Signatory Powers.[93] The two European countries which were most directly interested in Morocco, because of geographical propinquity and historic associations, were Spain and France.

Spain had inherited or conquered during the sixteenth century a number of settlements on the North coast, between the Straits of Gibraltar on the West, and the French territory of Algeria on the East. These, however, were separated from the Moroccan interior by the line of Riff Mountains, so that Spain did not aspire to acquire any of the Moroccan *hinterland*. If a partition of Morocco was to take place, Spain merely wished to be assured of the Mediterranean coastal strip and of some seaports on the Atlantic coast opposite the Canary Islands for their protection.

France, though further removed from Morocco geographically, had in reality a closer and more vital interest

[93] *Amer. Jour. of International Law,* VI (1912), supplement, pp. 18-24.

in the country. Beginning in 1830, she had gradually built up a great colony in Algeria, or, to speak more correctly, had extended France into Algeria, for Algeria was not a colony in the ordinary sense of the word. It was divided into departments like France, was represented in the French Chamber of Deputies, and persons born in Algeria enjoyed all the full rights of French citizens. As the French extended their control southward toward the Sahara, there was no effective natural boundary separating their territories from those of the Sultan of Morocco. Algeria in consequence was subjected to continual raids from the plundering Moroccan tribesmen.[94] France could have no peace on the western border of Algeria so long as turbulent conditions continued to prevail in Morocco. The French, therefore, came to feel that the safety and destiny of Algeria, as well as their aspirations for a great North African Colonial Empire, made it imperative for them to extend their control over Morocco, either by police supervision, or by a protectorate, or by direct annexation.

But Italy, England, and Germany also had political, as well as commercial, interests in Morocco.[95]

94 The mournful tale of them is to be found in the despatches in the French *Livre Jaune: Affaires du Maroc* (Paris, 1905), *passim*.

95 Sir Thomas Barclay, well informed, as to the relative commercial interests of the various nations, says: "As it is still currently supposed in both England and France that Germany's brusque entry upon the scene was more or less gratuitous and that she intervened in view of possible interests to come, I may mention as explanatory facts that Germany had considerable interests in Morocco, in some respects greater interests than France. In 1901 the tonnage of ships calling at Moroccan ports was 434,000 for Great Britain, 260,000 for Germany, 239,000 for France, and 198,000 for Spain. At all ports, except Safi, England is an 'easy first', but as between France and Germany the latter is ahead at Casablanca, much ahead at Mazagan, and overwhelmingly ahead at Safi. At Mogador Germany shows a tonnage of 44,000 against France with 24,000. As regards imports into Morocco, Great Britain in 1901 stood first with 24,000,000 f., against France with 10,000,000 f., and Germany and Belgium with 3,000,000 f., each. Spain could only show 600,000 f. Of exports from Morocco, Great Britain received 12,000,000 f., France 6,000,000 f., Spain 5,000,000 f., and Germany 4,000,000 f. Germany's interest,

Italy, being without colonies, cast her eyes covetously toward Morocco, especially after the French had stepped into Tunis ahead of her. But in 1900 France bought off Italy's claims by the secret promise not to oppose Italian aspirations to Tripoli.

England, possessing one of the Pillars of Hercules at Gibraltar, was determined that the other Pillar at Ceuta must never come into the hands of a strong European Power like France; otherwise the English navy and English commerce would lose that vital control of the entrance to the Mediterranean, which Gibraltar had assured to her for two centuries. Ceuta belonged to Spain, but Spain was so weak, especially after the Spanish-American War, that England was content to have her retain it; she had no fear that Spain would ever dispute British control of the Straits. England also coveted Tangier, partly because of her large trade there. If she could not acquire Tangier for herself, she was at least determined not to let it fall into the hands of any other Great Power. England likewise wished to prevent any European Power from establishing a coaling station or naval base on the Atlantic coast of Morocco.

Germany was chiefly interested in preserving and extending her rapidly growing commercial interests in Morocco. Some Germans, including some Foreign Office personages, wanted a German colony in West Morocco which would open new markets for German goods, afford a much needed source for iron ore, and offer a convenient coaling station and naval base for the German fleet in the Atlantic. But the Kaiser was opposed to pressing this, for fear of antagonizing England and France.

By the opening of the twentieth century, it became increasingly evident that the Sultan, in spite of the Madrid

it is seen, was substantial, and among Morocco ports Mazagan and Mogador were places at which Germany was developing a considerable Morocco trade"; Barclay, *Thirty Years Anglo-French Reminiscences*, p. 276.

Convention, was unable to maintain order and protect foreigners properly. As the scramble for colonial possessions became more intense among the Powers, there was danger that one or another of them, probably France, would find reasons for intervening and depriving the Sultan of his independence, or his territories, or both. The future of Morocco therefore became one of the most lively subjects of secret discussion among the diplomats of Europe.

Mr. Joseph Chamberlain broached the question very privately to the German Ambassador on November 3, 1899, suggesting a secret convention: Germany was to renounce all claims to the Mediterranean coasts of Morocco, including Tangier; in return, "England could make Germany the most extensive concessions on the Atlantic coast." [96] Chamberlain, however, wanted the matter kept secret for the present from his Prime Minister, Lord Salisbury. Bülow was interested in the suggestion, and it was discussed behind Lord Salisbury's back by the Kaiser on his visit to England a few weeks later. But the Kaiser, foreshadowing the consistent attitude he adopted in the following years, had no great desire for German territorial acquisitions on the West coast or anywhere else in Morocco. "He himself had never had great interest in this question," he told Eckardstein, "and he had never understood why Germans placed such interest in it." [97] In spite of fresh misgivings aroused everywhere by the French occupation of Moroccan territory at Touat, in the spring of 1900, Chamberlain's suggestion came to nothing, owing in part to Salisbury's reserved and negative attitude.[98]

Bülow did not care to interfere in the Touat affair, "because today this would be equivalent to the possibility of a war with France.[99] He adopted his usual prudent but sphinx-like policy of "wait and see." In spite of recurring

[96] G.P., XVII, 297.
[97] Eckardstein, II, 93.
[98] G.P., XVII, 299-323
[99] G.P., XVII, 331.

rumors of possible Anglo-French and Franco-Spanish agreements contemplating a possible partition of Morocco, he maintained this attitude for nearly three years.[100] Then, on March 16, 1904, he received a telegram from the Kaiser, recounting a visit to King Alfonso at Vigo. William II had congratulated the Spanish King upon the rumored Franco-Spanish arrangements for a partition of Morocco, and had declared that Germany wished no territorial acquisitions; Germany wanted only the safeguarding of her commercial interests—"open ports, railway concessions, and the importation of manufactures;" and perhaps by way of compensation the Spanish Island of Fernando Po in the Gulf of Guinea off the German Kamerun coast, for which Germany would pay generously.[101] This declaration of German disinterestedness in Moroccan territory caused some dismay to Bülow and his Foreign Office colleagues, who had been inclined to think Germany might well secure some share of the disintegrating Sherifian Empire. But the Kaiser's declaration tied their hands. In spite of the clamorings of Pan-Germans on the one hand, and of Anglo-French suspicions on the other, the Kaiser's declaration laid down one of the guiding principles of German Moroccan policy in the following years.

Within a few days of the Vigo declaration, one of the Sultan's officials cast into prison a Moroccan in German employ, without giving reasons to the German consul in accordance with custom. The consul protested, but could get no satisfaction and no release for the imprisoned man. German officials suspected that the Sultan was being encouraged in his defiant attitude by the English or the French. They were the more indignant because some months earlier a German citizen (Genthe) had been robbed and murdered in Morocco, and the Sultan had replied

100 May, 1901, to March, 1904; G.P., XVII, 332-362.
101 G.P., XVII, 363-5; XX, 268.

evasively to demands for an indemnity to the murdered man's family. Bülow and his German Foreign Office colleagues feared that unless energetic steps were taken, German prestige, and consequently German trade and influence in Morocco, would suffer seriously. Bülow begged the Kaiser to consent to sending a German warship to Tangier to impress upon the Sultan the advisability of giving speedy satisfaction to German demands in these two matters. But the Kaiser was unwilling to sanction such a demonstration.[102] He knew that Anglo-French negotiations concerning Morocco were on the point of being signed, and wisely decided that sending a ship to Tangier just at this moment would arouse suspicion as to the genuineness of his Vigo declaration of Germany's territorial disinterestedness. He believed that,

> "forceful pressure by Germany against Morocco ought to be considered only after our grievances against Morocco have been brought fully with the facts to the knowledge of the three Powers most interested in Morocco [England France and Spain]. It could then be pointed out that remedial measures against the attitude of the Moroccan Government lay in the interests, not of Germany alone, but of all Europeans, and that Germany would gladly have the support and cooperation of the three aforesaid Powers in restoring by proper measures the injured prestige of Europeans in Morocco."[103]

Accordingly, in spite of arguments by Bülow, Lichnowsky, and German officials in Morocco, the Kaiser's decision prevailed and no German naval demonstration took place. But the Kaiser's hope that disorders in Morocco could be dealt with through the friendly coöperation of all the Powers most directly concerned was vain.

At this very moment, Lord Lansdowne and M. Paul

[102] Bülow to the Kaiser, Mar. 30, 1904; G.P., XX, 197-199.
[103] April 3, 1904; G.P., XX, 200.

Cambon, the French Ambassador in London, were signing the famous Anglo-French Convention of April 8, 1904, concerning Egypt and Morocco which has been indicated above. Its "Public Articles" disclaimed, of course, any intention of altering the political status of Morocco, but at the same time "recognized that it appertained particularly to France to preserve order there":

> Art. I. [France gives England a free hand in Egypt as indicated above at note 90].
>
> Art. II. The Government of the French Republic declare that they have no intention of altering the political status of Morocco. His Britannic Majesty's Government recognise that it appertains to France, more particularly as a Power whose dominions are coterminous for a great distance with those of Morocco, to preserve order in that country, and to provide assistance for the purpose of all administrative, economic, financial and military reforms which it may require. They declare that they will not obstruct the action taken by France for this purpose, provided that such action shall leave intact the rights which Great Britain enjoys in Morocco in virtue of treaties, conventions and usage. . . .
>
> Art. VIII. The two Governments, inspired by their sincere feeling of friendship for Spain, take into special consideration the interests which that country derives from her geographical position and her territorial possessions on the Moorish coast. . . .
>
> Art. IX. The two Governments agree to afford one another their diplomatic support, in order to obtain the execution of the clauses of the present declaration regarding Egypt and Morocco.

Important "Secret Articles," however, contemplated an eventual partition of Morocco between France and Spain:

> Art. II. [England has no present intention of proposing changes in Egypt, but, in case she should consider it desirable to introduce reforms, France] will not refuse to enter-

tain any such proposals, on the understanding that His Britannic Majesty's Government will agree to entertain the suggestions that the Government of the French Republic may have to make to them with a view of introducing similar reforms in Morocco.

Art. III. The two governments agree that a certain extent of Moorish territory adjacent to Melilla, Ceuta, and other *présides* should, whenever the Sultan ceases to exercise authority over it, come within the sphere of influence of Spain and the administration of the coast from Melilla as far as, but not including, the heights on the right bank of the Sebou shall be entrusted to Spain.

Nevertheless, Spain would . . . have to undertake not to alienate the whole, or a part, of the territories placed under her authority or in her sphere of influence.[104]

It is curious to note how casually Viscount Grey and M. Poincaré speak of these secret articles contemplating the partition of Morocco and seek to minimize their importance. Grey says the agreement with France "was all made public except a clause or two of no importance."[105] It is characteristic of his psychology that when he has to deal with something disagreeable or repugnant, which does not fit in with his conception of things, he rationalizes it into thinking it "of no importance."[106] M. Poincaré likewise speaks of the secret Moroccan arrangement as destined to remain "temporarily" secret.[107]

Upon the announcement of the public articles, the Spanish professed to be furious: they had not been consulted; they had been treated as *quantité négligeable;* this humilia-

[104] See note 90 above.

[105] *Twenty-Five Years,* I, 49.

[106] So, for instance, in explaining the omission from the report of his speech in Parliament on Aug. 3, 1914, of the last sentence in his 1912 note to Paul Cambon, Grey says, "Perhaps I thought the last sentence unimportant"; *ibid.,* II, 17. Similarly he continually seeks to minimize the political importance of the vital naval and military "conversations" carried on with France in the following years.

[107] *Au Service de la France,* I, 107.

tion endangered their dynasty; with clenched fists (prudently kept in his pocket), the Spanish Ambassador declared to Delcassé that "this Anglo-French Convention will have serious consequences and involve unforeseeable complications."[108] But Delcassé speedily bought off Spanish objections by providing that Spain should have her proper share when Morocco was partitioned. By the Franco-Spanish Moroccan Convention of October 3, 1904, in secret articles, Spain gave her approval to the Anglo-French agreement of April 8, 1904, and both France and Spain piously declared that they would remain firmly committed to the integrity of the Moroccan Empire under the sovereignty of the Sultan. But secret articles, which of course were communicated to Lord Lansdowne, frankly contemplated quite the opposite.

In delimiting the spheres of influence, the Spanish were to be given the northern coastal strip on the Mediterranean and the Atlantic, and the French were to have the vast *hinterland*. The boundaries were virtually identical with those which were actually adopted for the French and Spanish protectorates which were arranged by M. Poincaré in 1912.[109]

It has been asserted by a German historian,[110] though without proof, that the German Government in some unofficial way speedily became informed of the secret articles, and saw in them an evidence of the hostile feeling which France had nurtured against her ever since 1870. The assertion has been endorsed by Mr. Gooch [111] and others, but appears to be without foundation. There is no tangible

108 Report of Prince Radolin, German Ambassador at Paris, April 29, 1904; G.P., XX, 169; *cf.* pp. 170-194 for the cautious German attitude during the ensuing Franco-Spanish negotiations.

109 *Cf.* Poincaré, I, 106-118.

110 Veit Valentin, *Deutschlands Aussenpolitik* (Berlin, 1921), p. 54.

111 *Cambridge History of British Foreign Policy*, III, 340; *cf.* also G. Lowes Dickinson, *The International Anarchy*, p. 124.

evidence in *Die Grosse Politik* that Germany was definitely acquainted at this time with the double-faced bargain which Lansdowne and Delcassé had made and in which Spain participated. Had it been definitely known to Germany, it would surely be indicated in the recent German documents, as an evidence of Albion's perfidy and Delcassé's deviltry. It was not necessary, however, for Germany to have been definitely told what had been done. Given the knowledge of French ambitions and interests in Morocco, she could easily surmise the truth. She correctly suspected that there was more to the Anglo-French agreements than met the eye in the published articles. But though not without suspicions as to the fate awaiting Morocco, Bülow and Holstein seem chiefly to have suspected that France and England had made some secret deal in regard to the partition of China,[112] or had entered into some sort of an alliance aimed against Germany.[113]

Who were the originators of the Entente Cordiale and what were their motives? M. Tardieu, who stood close to Delcassé and had good information, says, "The English King was the initiator of the *rapprochement*. He it was who both conceived and facilitated it while many still believed that the moment was premature."[114] Lord Cromer spoke of it as the "work of that very eminent diplomatist, His Majesty the King, and Lord Lansdowne."[115] That the main impulse to it came from the side of England and not France grew to be a very general opinion both in England and on the Continent, and it was certainly greeted with more general enthusiasm in England than in France.[116] Tardieu,

[112] G.P., XIX, 548.

[113] G.P., XX, 16, 27-30, 599-698.

[114] Tardieu, *France and the Alliances,* p. 60.

[115] Speech on receiving the freedom of the City of London, Oct. 28, 1907; *Annual Register,* 1907, p. 242.

[116] *Cf.* J. A. Farrer, *England Under Edward VII,* pp. 89-94. See, however, Lee, *King Edward VII,* II, 216-257, and the recent *British Documents,* II, 253-407, which show that King Edward's influence has com-

however, throughout his volume seems to over-emphasize England's rôle and England's advantages from the Moroccan agreement. There is no doubt that Delcassé, from the moment he took charge of the French Foreign Office in 1898, had worked eagerly for the extension of French influence in Morocco. He had made a treaty with Spain with this in view in 1900, but the treaty was bound to be abortive so long as the greatest Naval Power with large Moroccan interests did not give her consent. Hence, one of his reasons for a *rapprochement* with England. His Minister of Colonies, M. Etienne, and his London Ambassador, Paul Cambon, energetically supported him and were warmly seconded by Lord Lansdowne and Lord Cromer.

As to the motives, those on the English side were primarily somewhat as follows. Having decided to abandon splendid isolation and having failed to receive a satisfactory response from Germany to Chamberlain's alliance feelers, England naturally turned to France. In view of the growing friction between Russia and Japan, ending in the outbreak of war between the two in February, 1904, and the fact that England was allied to Japan, and France to Russia, it was important to establish cordial relations with France to prevent the Russo-Japanese War from involving England and France against one another. England desired to avoid the danger of having the war in the Far East spread to Europe. She perhaps also wanted to forestall the possible renewal of the Triple combination of 1895 (Russia, Germany, France) for concerted pressure against Japan in the Far East.[117] England sincerely desired to wipe off the slate the numerous causes of friction which had so fre-

monly been exaggerated, and that the chief initiative came from Delcassé and the French.

117 According to the belief of Bernstorff, German Chargé d'Affaires in London, which was at first shared by Bülow and the Kaiser, this was a strong English motive in the *rapprochement* with France; G.P., XX, 14-21; and also 23, 31, 173.

quently brought her to the verge of war with France in the past.[118] Finally, and perhaps the most important, as Lord Cromer believes, was the desire for freedom of action in Egypt. There is little conclusive evidence that at the outset England planned to isolate Germany or to encourage France to count on England for more than *diplomatic* support, and even this was to be limited to the case of Morocco. On the other hand, there is much evidence that, within a few months, the Anglo-French Entente came to have a far wider significance inimical to the peace of Europe—partly owing to Germany's clumsy and alarming diplomatic gestures.

On the French side the motives were in part somewhat the same. The French were determined to avoid being involved in war on account of the ambitions of her Russian ally in the Far East. They wished to end the long-standing friction with England. They desired freedom of action in Morocco. And they hoped to secure England as a friend, or possibly as an ally, in order to build up a combination of Powers, equal to, or stronger than, the Triple Alliance. France had come painfully to realize that her alliance with Russia was of less value than she had anticipated, at the time of its formation, that it would be. Russia had given her little or no support at Fashoda and on other critical occasions, and now she appeared to be so involved in the Far East as to be of little support to France in case of a Franco-German war. Delcassé had no thought of abandoning the alliance with Russia, but he believed that close relations with England would help to compensate France for the lessened value of the Franco-Russian alliance.

By 1904 Delcassé had thus bought off the Moroccan claims of Italy and England, by promising these countries a free hand in Tripoli and Egypt respectively, and he had

118 Grey, I, 48 ff., emphasizes this motive.

satisfied Spain with a sphere of influence in northern Morocco. He assumed that he could now proceed leisurely to the "pacific penetration" of the rest of the Sherifian Empire without paying any attention to the natural claims of Germany. He believed that France at last had risen to such a strong diplomatic position, with Russia as an ally and England as a friend, that she could risk ignoring the country which had seized Alsace-Lorraine and long dominated Europe.[119] In this he was mistaken. He was grievously mistaken. As a French critic has well said, "With incredible blindness the Government took precautions with everybody, except the only one of its neighbors whom it had serious cause to fear." [120] And as Mr. Gooch has justly pointed out, "It is regrettable that the British Cabinet did not perceive—or at any rate did not help France to perceive—the wisdom of securing German consent by a *solatium.* Though the Secret Treaties of 1904 reserved no share for Great Britain in the contingent partition of Morocco, and though it has been argued that it was reasonable for the contracting parties to make alternative arrangements in the event of Morocco collapsing from internal weakness, our share in the transaction which suggested double-dealing involves the British Government in partial responsibility for the crises of 1905 and 1911." [121]

THE MOROCCO CRISIS OF 1905

It is commonly believed in France and England that the Kaiser's spectacular visit to Tangier on March 31, 1905, followed by Delcassé's fall on June 6, were the results of a German effort, by a threat of force, at a moment when France's ally lay prostrate in the Far East, to test or break up the newly formed Entente Cordiale and separate Eng-

119 Tardieu, *France and the Alliances,* pp. 178-182.

120 R. Millet, *Notre Politique extérieure,* p. 224.

121 Gooch, *Cambridge History of British Foreign Policy,* III, 340

land from France.[122] But this belief, as the recently published German documents show, is not altogether correct. The misconception has arisen in part from prejudice and ignorance, and in part from the fact that writers have supposed that the Kaiser's Björkö maneuver and Bülow's Morocco moves formed parts of one and the same consistent German policy.

Confronted suddenly with the accomplished fact of an Anglo-French Agreement, in which Germany had not been consulted though German interests were involved, and in which there were good reasons for suspecting that secret clauses lurked behind the public declarations, Bülow and the Kaiser both felt that something must be done. But they differed as to what this should be.

Bülow preferred to adopt a sphinx-like silence, waiting until Delcassé should formally notify Germany of the Moroccan agreement, and offer guarantees for her commercial interests and some equivalent compensations. When Delcassé had continued to ignore Germany for nearly a year, Bülow tried to serve notice on him by forcing the Kaiser to make the spectacular diplomatic gesture at Tangier in March, 1905. This was altogether repugnant to the Kaiser. Nothing shows this more strikingly than a phrase in one of his letters to Bülow:

> Do not forget that you persuaded me *personally, against my will,* to go to Tangier for the sake of the success of your

122 *Cf.* Tardieu, pp. 170 ff; Bourgeois et Pagès, pp. 307 ff.; Viscount Grey reiterates this belief in at least four passages, *Twenty-Five Years,* I, 51, 69, 75, 99; *cf.* also 108 f. So for instance p. 51: "In British minds, certainly in my own, the Anglo-French Agreement was not regarded as more than I have described it. It was the subsequent attempts of Germany to shake or break it that turned it into an Entente. These attempts were not long in coming. The German Emperor made a visit that was like a demonstration at Tangier, and in 1905 the German Government forced the French, by what was practically a challenge, to dismiss M. Delcassé (their Minister for Foreign Affairs who had made the Franco-British Agreement) and to agree to an international conference about Morocco".

> Morocco policy. Read through my telegrams prior to the Tangier visit. . . . It was to please you, for the sake of the Fatherland, that I landed, mounted a strange horse in spite of my equestrian disability due to my shrivelled left arm, and might have come within a hair of losing my life—*which was your venture* [*was Ihr Einsatz war*]. I rode among Spanish anarchists *because you wanted it and your policy* was to benefit by it! [123]

Their divergence in views is further indicated by the fact that Bülow did not keep his imperial master fully informed on all phases of the Moroccan affair, which he and Holstein were conducting. The greater part of the documents in *Die Grosse Politik* on the Morocco Crisis bear no marginal notes by the Kaiser, and were apparently not so regularly submitted nor so fully summarized for him as was usually the case. It is also likely that one reason for Bülow's later threat of resignation was his hope that the Kaiser would beseech him to remain, and he would then retain office with a stronger and freer hand.

The Kaiser, on the other hand, wished to avoid antagonizing French susceptibilities. With his "anti-English complex" and his inherited traditional friendship between Hohenzollern and Romanov, he wished to avert the possible danger lurking in the Anglo-French Agreement by realizing his dream of a "Continental League." This flitted frequently before his imagination throughout his reign.[124] It was a method of reviving the Alliance of the Three Emperors so far as was possible after the Tsar had entered into alliance with France. He hoped to use his personal influ-

[123] Kaiser to Bülow, beseeching him not to resign, Aug. 11, 1905; G.P., XIX, 497 f.

[124] *Cf.* G.P., XI, 67-92; XIV, 559 f. marginal note 2, XIX, 303-350; 435-528; and XX, *passim*. According to Kuropatkin's *Diary*, Nov. 17, 1902 (*Krasnyi Arkhiv*, II, 10), the Kaiser at maneuvers in 1896 or 1897 had discussed with General Obruchev how desirable would be a Franco-Russian-German Coalition as a means of dictating to England. Obruchev had mentioned it to President Faure who thought it "worth being studied".

ence over the weak-willed Tsar to draw Russia into a defensive alliance with Germany. Russia would then get her ally France to join it. By thus associating the Triple and Dual Alliances, he would form a league of the five great Continental Powers. This would put an end to the danger to Europe which existed from the antagonism of the two groups. It would help to assure the peace of the world. It would also be able to hold in check England's overweening naval and colonial power. Incidentally, it would increase his own prestige and influence, because Germany would be the dominating member of the league. This dream perhaps was fantastic and impossible of realization, but it formed the burden of the interesting letters from "Willy" to "Nicky" during the Russo-Japanese War.[125] At last, for a brief moment of ecstatic joy in July, 1905, it did seem about to come true.

(a) THE KAISER'S BJÖRKÖ POLICY

The Kaiser had been cruising in northern waters and suddenly suggested to the Tsar that they meet on their yachts at Björkö. The fact that France had just dropped Delcassé, as we shall see later, and was inclined to accept Germany's proposal for a Moroccan Conference, seemed to indicate that France had abandoned hopes of *revanche* and might at last be brought into more satisfactory relations with Germany through the Tsar's influence. So the Kaiser decided to take advantage of the Björkö interview and of

125 *Cf.* my article, "The Kaiser's Secret Negotiations with the Tsar, 1904-05", in the *Amer. Hist. Rev.*, XXIV, 48-72 (Oct., 1918). This may now be supplemented by G.P., XIX, *passim* (especially 435-528); A. Izvolski, *Memoirs,* ch. ii; E. J. Dillon, *The Eclipse of Russia,* chs. xvi-xviii; H. von Moltke, *Erinnerungen,* p. 325 ff.; Witte, *Memoirs,* pp. 415-430; A. Savinsky, "Guillaume II et la Russie", in *Rev. des Deux Mondes,* Dec., 1922, 765-802; the Russian documents in "Russko-germanskii dogovor 1905 goda, zakliuchennyi v Bërke" [Russo-German treaty of 1905, concluded at Björkö], in *Krasnyi Arkhiv,* V, 5-49 (1924), also in German translation in KSF, II, 453-500 (Nov., 1924); and A. Savinsky, *Recollections of a Russian Diplomat,* London, 1927. *Cf.* also Taube, pp. 45-84.

the Tsar's difficulties arising from the war with Japan to reopen the negotiations of the preceding autumn with the Tsar and secure his signature to a treaty of alliance. Some months earlier such a treaty had been discussed between them and a draft had been drawn up only to be rejected by Russia for fear of offending France. Now, perhaps, was the time for getting it signed after all.

The *Hohenzollern* steamed into the harbor of Björkö and dramatically dropped anchor along side of the *Polar Star*. "Willy" and "Nicky" exchanged visits. It was a scene which appealed vividly to the Kaiser's histrionic temperament. His exaltation of mind may be judged by a few selections from his autograph letter to Bülow, which covers six printed pages, giving the story of what happened in the cabin of the *Polar Star:*

Wisby, July 25, 1905

My dear Bülow:

By my telegrams you have already learned that the work of *rapprochement* has been crowned and the game won. . . .

And now that it is done, one is surprised and says: How is such a thing possible? For me the answer is very clear! God has ordained and willed it thus; in spite of all man's wit, in scorn of all man's intrigues, He has brought together what belonged together! What Russia rejected in pride last winter, and what she tried in her love of intrigue to turn against us, that now she has most joyfully accepted as a gracious gift after the fearful, stern, and humiliating hand of the Lord has brought her low. I have done so much thinking in the last days that my head has throbbed to be sure that I am acting aright, always to keep in mind the interests of my country no less than those of the Monarchical Idea in general.

Finally, I raised my hands to the Lord above us all and committed myself to Him and prayed Him to lead and guide me as He wished; I was only the tool in His hands and I would do whatsoever He would inspire me to do, though the task be ever so hard. And finally I also uttered the wish of the Old Dessauer at Kesselsdorf, that if He did not wish to help me He should at least not help the other side. Then I felt myself wonderfully strengthened, and the will and purpose became ever firmer and clearer within me: "You will put it through no matter what the cost!" So I looked forward to the interview full of confidence.

And what did I find? A warm, amiable, enthusiastic reception, such as one receives only from a friend who loves one heartily and sincerely. The Tsar threw his arms around me and pressed me to him as though I were his own brother, and he looked at me again and again with eyes that revealed his gratitude and joy. [The Kaiser noted the absence of Lamsdorf, to whom he applied an unprintable epithet.]

The Tsar said he was burning to have a thoroughgoing discussion. We lighted our cigarettes and were soon *in medias res*. He was uncommonly pleased with our Morocco agreement [for a conference at Algeciras] which would open the way for permanent good relations with France. He heartily approved my hope that from it a lasting understanding, perhaps even an "agreement," with France might blossom forth.

When I pointed out that in spite of egging on by England, France had down-right refused to take up our challenge [in consenting to drop Delcassé] and therefore no longer wanted to fight for Alsace-Lorraine, he said quickly: "Yes, that I saw; it is quite clear that the Alsace-Lorraine question is closed once for all, thank God!" Our talk then turned on England, and it very soon appeared that the Tsar feels a deep personal anger at England and the King. He called Edward VII the greatest "mischief-maker" and the most dangerous and deceptive intriguer in the world. I could only agree with him, adding that I especially had had to suffer from his intrigues in recent years. . . . He has a passion for plotting against every power, of making "a little agreement," whereupon the Tsar interrupted me, striking the table with his fist; "Well, I can only say he shall not get one from me and never in my life against Germany or you, my word of honor upon it!"

[After dinner on the *Hohenzollern* the Kaiser next day, with a draft of the hoped-for treaty in his pocket, visited the *Polar Star.* The conversation again turned on the subject of England's intrigues against Russia in connection with the war with Japan.]

I soon observed how deeply injured the Tsar felt by the attitude of France in the Dogger Bank Affair, and how, at England's behest, Rodjestvenski had been chased out of Cochin-China, virtually into the hands of the Japs: "The French behaved like scoundrels to me; by order of England, my Ally left me in the lurch; and now look at Brest! How they fraternize with the English. . . . What shall I do in this disagreeable situation?"

Now I felt the moment was come! . . . "How would it be, if we, too, should make a 'little agreement?' Last winter we talked about it . . ." "O yes, to be sure, I remember well, but I forget the contents of it. What a pity I haven't got it here." "I have a copy, which I happen to have quite by chance in my pocket."

The Tsar took me by the arm and he drew me out of the dining room into his father's cabin and immediately shut all the doors himself. "Show it to me, please." His dreamy eyes sparkled.

I drew the envelope out of my pocket and unfolded the paper on Alexander III's writing desk in front of the portrait of the Tsar's mother. He read once, twice and a third time, the text which has already been sent you. I prayed God that He would be with us now and incline the young ruler. It was still as death. There was no sound but that of the sea. The sun seemed gay and cheerful in the cozy cabin. Right before me, glistening white lay the *Hohenzollern,* and aloft in the morning breeze, fluttered the imperial flag; on its black cross I was reading the letters, *Gott mit Uns,* when the Tsar's voice near me said: "That is quite excellent. I quite agree!"

My heart beats so loudly that I can hear it; I pull

> myself together and say, casually, "Should you like to sign it? It would be a very nice souvenir of our interview." He scanned the paper again, and then he said: "Yes, I will." I opened the ink-well and gave him the pen, and he wrote with a firm hand "Nicolas," then he handed the pen to me and I signed. When I arose he clasped me into his arms deeply moved and said: "I thank God and I thank you; it will be of the most beneficial consequences for my country and yours; you are Russia's only real friend in the whole world. I have felt that through the whole war and I know it." Tears of joy stood in my eyes—to be sure drops of water were trickling down my forehead and back—and I thought of Frederick William III, Queen Louise, Grandpa and Nicholas I. Were they not close by at that moment? Undoubtedly they were looking down from above and were all surely full of joy!
>
> Thus has the morning of July 24, 1905 at Björkö become a turning point in the history of Europe, thanks to the grace of God; and a great relief in the situation for my dear Fatherland which at last will be freed from the frightful Franco-Russian pincers.[126]

The Kaiser's prayerful optimism and emotional fervor were soon given a dash of cold water by Bülow. His Chancellor threatened to resign. His pretext was that the Kaiser had ventured on his own responsibility to modify slightly the draft sent him from the Foreign Office. The Kaiser had added the two words, "in Europe," so that Article II read: "In case one of the two Empires shall be attacked by a European Power, its Ally will aid it in Europe with all its military and naval forces." The Kaiser's added words had the positive advantage for Germany that she assumed no obligations to help the Tsar on the frontier of India or in the Far East, where Russia was most likely to

[126] G.P., XIX, 458-465. The quoted passages are in English in the original, as the Kaiser was evidently giving as nearly as possible the Tsar's exact words. English was the language which "Willy" and "Nicky" regularly used to one another.

come into conflict with England. Bülow's threatened resignation was an unexpected and stunning blow. The Kaiser could not part with him. He offered to get the Tsar to change the treaty back to its original form and made an appeal which Bülow could not refuse:

> You are worth 100,000 times more to me and the Fatherland than all the treaties in the world. . . . No, my friend, stay in office and with me, and we will work further in common together *ad majorem Germaniae gloriam*. . . . After the receipt of this letter, telegraph me, "All right," so that I shall know you will stay. Because the morning after the arrival of your letter of resignation would no longer find your Emperor alive. Think of my poor wife and children![127]

The Kaiser was soon to suffer a still more stunning blow, which knocked his whole dream into a cocked hat. When the Tsar revealed the treaty to his Minister of Foreign Affairs, Count Lamsdorf "could not believe his eyes or ears." After studying over the problem for most of the night, he explained to the Tsar the serious significance of the document signed in the cabin of the *Polar Star*. He made it clear to his master how contrary the Björkö Treaty was to the spirit of the Franco-Russian Alliance, and how unlikely it was that France could be forced, *volens nolens,* into such a combination with Germany and Russia. Nicky therefore had to write as tactfully as he could to Willy:

> This document, of immense valour, ought to be strengthened, or made clearer, so as to enable all parties concerned to fulfill their duties honestly and frankly. . . .
>
> During your stay at Björkoe I did not have with me the documents signed by my Father, which clearly define the principles of the Franco-Russian Alliance. . . .
>
> The first steps taken with the object of trying to find out whether the French Government could be induced to

[127] G.P., XIX. 497 f.

join our new treaty showed us that it is a difficult task, and that it will take a long time to prepare to bring it over of its free will. . . .

Therefore I think that the coming into force of the Björkoe Treaty ought to be put off until we know how the French will look upon it.[128]

Great was the Kaiser's vexation upon the receipt of this letter postponing indefinitely the Björkö Treaty. He urgently appealed to Nicky to stand by his written agreement, arguing that the treaty did not conflict with the Franco-Russian Alliance, and that anyway,

> Your Ally has notoriously left you in the lurch during the whole [Russo-Japanese] war, whereas Germany helped you in every way as far as it could, without infringing the laws of neutrality. This puts Russia morally also under obligations to us; *do ut des.* Meanwhile the indiscretions of Delcassé have shown the world that, though France is your Ally, she nevertheless made an agreement with England and was on the verge of surprising Germany, with British help, in the middle of peace, while I was doing my best to help you and your country, her Ally! . . . Our Moroccan business is regulated to entire satisfaction, so that the air is free for better understanding between us. Our treaty is a very good base to build upon. We joined hands and signed before God, who heard our vows! I therefore think that the treaty can well come into existence. . . . What is signed is signed! and God is our testator! [129]

His appeals were unavailing. The Kaiser's hopes for a Continental League were permanently dashed to the ground.[130]

(b) BÜLOW'S MOROCCO POLICY

To return from the Kaiser's attempt to secure a defensive alliance with Russia to his Chancellor's Moroccan

128 Nicky to Willy, Oct. 7, 1905; G.P., XIX, 512.
129 Willy to Nicky, Oct. 12, 1905; G.P., XIX, 513-514.
130 For the details of the fate of the treaty, see G.P., XIX, 515-528.

moves. The latter are the more important, because they gave rise to the Morocco Crisis of 1905, and led to the intimate naval and military "conversations" between France and England, which are of the highest significance in the development of the system of secret alliances.

At a dinner given in his honor at the German Embassy, and again a few days later, on March 23, 1904, M. Delcassé mentioned informally to Prince Radolin the negotiations for the Anglo-French Agreement which was about to be signed on April 8. Delcassé indicated the regions it would deal with—Newfoundland, Egypt, Morocco, Sokoto, and Siam. As to Morocco, he repeated that "he wished above all else to maintain the *status quo* as long as possible." But he said that the weakness of the Sultan's government endangered commerce in Morocco, and that France felt it desirable to strengthen the Sultan's position and end the anarchy. "France does not wish to have any special interests in Morocco," he said, "but it is her task, in the interest of all nations carrying on trade, to put an end as far as possible to the anarchy in this neighboring state."[131] This was the first definite knowledge which Bülow received of the impending Anglo-French Agreement. Aside from this informal notification and the fact that the Public Articles were soon printed in the newspapers, Germany was not officially notified of the text, nor formally consulted by France about this agreement, which threatened seriously to interfere with German commercial rights and political interests in Morocco. Bülow felt that Germany had been slighted, and that her prestige as well as her material interests had been injured. To be sure, he at once instructed the German newspapers to accept the news, without irrita-

[131] Radolin to Bülow, March 23, 1904; G.P., XX, 5-7; *cf.* also 266 ff., 329 f., 396. Delcassé to Bihourd, the French Ambassador in Berlin, March 27, 1904, *Livre Jaune: Affaires du Maroc,* I, 122; *cf.* 167 f., 196 f., 202 ff.

tion and jealousy, as a new indication of the peaceful situation in the world.[132] And in his much-quoted speech in the Reichstag on April 12, he attempted, as usual, to put a good face on a bad matter by appearing to welcome any agreements between France and England which removed causes of friction. In answer to an interpellation on the subject he cautiously stated that he could hardly say much, because the English and French Ministers had not yet explained it publicly. In a delicate matter of foreign affairs, he added,

> I can only say that we have no reason to suppose that this agreement is directed against any Power whatever. It seems to be an attempt to eliminate the points of difference between France and Great Britain by means of an amicable understanding. From the point of view of German interests we have nothing to complain of, for we do not wish to see strained relations between Great Britain and France, if only because such a state of affairs would imperil the peace of the world, the maintenance of which we sincerely desire. Concerning Morocco, which constitutes the essential point of the agreement, we are interested in this country, as in fact in the rest of the Mediterranean, principally from the economic point of view. . . . We must protect our commercial interests in Morocco, and we shall protect them.[133]

Though Bülow certainly underestimated at first the political significance of the new Anglo-French Entente, he was far from taking it as lightly as one might be led to infer from his Reichstag speech, which was intended to quiet the fears of the German public. In fact, it caused him and his Foreign Office assistants to do a good deal of serious thinking during the following weeks. He and Holstein gradually reached a determination to hold to Germany's rights under the international Morocco Treaty of 1880, and to ignore the Anglo-French Moroccan Convention

[132] G.P., XX, 12 (April 9).

[133] *Affaires du Maroc,* I, 127.

until Delcassé should invite a discussion of it and give Germany an opportunity to be heard and perhaps get some equivalent compensations. England and France, they felt, could not by separate agreement deprive third parties of their rights in Morocco. France, now given a free hand in Morocco by England, would try to establish a French economic monopoly there, as she had done in all her other colonies. She would "Tunisify" Morocco by "peaceful penetration." So Germany's commercial rights and interests would be threatened, as the French would get exclusive trading and financial privileges, and a monopoly of railway and mining concessions. Furthermore, German prestige would suffer, if she allowed Morocco to be disposed of by France and England as if Germany did not exist. Holstein summed the matter up: "If we let our toes be trodden upon in Morocco without saying a word, we encourage others to do the same thing elsewhere."[134]

There were two ways by which Germany might give expression to her wishes. The first was to tell Delcassé in a frank and friendly manner that the published Anglo-French Convention aroused concern in Germany in regard to her commercial interests, and to ask more fully what guarantees France would offer for the protection of these interests. This was the more neighborly way. But it was not adopted. The second way was to maintain an impassive and sphinx-like silence, neither recognizing nor protesting against the Anglo-French Agreement, but acting as if it did not exist for Germany, since Germany had not been officially informed of the text of it. This second plan would consist in Germany's going step by step with France in Morocco in the matter of police measures to curb the anarchy. If France sent warships to Tangier, Germany could do likewise. In this way, without infringing any

134 Holstein's Memoir of June 3, 1904; G.P., XX, 207-9; *cf.* also Bülow to Radolin July 21; G.P., XX, 210-214.

rights, Germany might compel Delcassé to be the first to speak and inquire as to German intentions. The less Germany explained her steps in the newspapers, the more uncertain and uncomfortable the French would become. Then when once Delcassé saw that Germany was in earnest, Germany ought to make concessions and abandon any thought of establishing a foothold in Morocco. This policy was more adventurous and dangerous to the peace of Europe. But it was the one which Bülow and Holstein adopted.[135]

But this sphinx-like waiting policy did not bear fruit as rapidly as had been hoped. Delcassé was evidently becoming increasingly nervous, but he avoided broaching the question. To bring him out of his silence Germany began to encourage the Sultan to resist the police measures which the French at last, in the winter of 1904-05, planned to put into effect. Kühlmann, the German Chargé d'Affaires in Tangier, had already reported that there seemed to be friction between France and England, and that it was not likely that Delcassé could count on more than Platonic support from the British. The Dogger Bank Affair had just occurred and given rise in England to violent indignation against Russia. Kühlmann felt sure that France was in no position to settle the fate of Morocco without Germany's sanction. In fact he believed M. Delcassé to be in the unenviable position of resting one leg on Russia and another on England, and thus to be in danger of falling between two stools as the tension between these two hostile countries tightened. He had also heard that the American Vice-Consul had said to a leading Moor, "Germany has not spoken, and until then we cannot believe that anything definite has been decided." [136]

During the summer of 1904 the Sultan continued to

[135] G.P., XX, 7-33, 195-234, especially 215 ff.

[136] Kühlmann to Bülow, Nov. 9, 1904; G.P., XX, 232.

answer evasively Bülow's demands in regard to Genthe, a German citizen murdered in Morocco. The German Minister at Tangier, therefore, wanted Germany to assert her prestige by an ultimatum to the Sultan, to be followed, if necessary, by the sending of a warship to Moroccan waters as a diplomatic demonstration. Bülow favored it, but the Kaiser forbade it, and it did not take place.[137] Soon afterwards Germany put aside her grievance over the Genthe murder and began to assume an attitude of friendliness to the Sultan. This was to encourage him to resist the "Tunisification" program which Delcassé was now believed to be preparing to force upon him. This would consist, as was gathered in Tangier from St. René Taillandier, the head of the French Mission, mainly of three points: the reorganization of the Sultan's army by French instructors; the signing by the Sultan of a treaty with the French excluding the political influence of other nations; and the control by France of the Sultan's finances. To Kühlmann this looked very much like the establishment of a virtual protectorate.[138] Germany therefore secretly encouraged the Sultan to resist the imposition of the French program. When he called together a patriotic Assembly of Notables from all Morocco to examine the French demands, Kühlmann approved the measure as "a skilful anti-French move."[139] Then, when the French Press began to demand that the Assembly of Notables be dismissed, Bülow secretly advised the contrary, believing that the proud Moroccan chieftains would declare against the French program. He did not think it likely that the French would go to the point of trying to bluff the Sultan with a threat of war, because the new Rouvier Cabinet did not wish to risk the expenditure

137 G.P., XX, 222-230.

138 Kühlmann to Bülow, Nov. 28, 1904; G.P., XX, 237 ff. For the detailed aims of the Taillandier Mission, see *Affaires du Maroc,* I, 178-184.

139 G.P., XX, 246 ff.

of men and money in a Moroccan campaign, or weaken France's position toward Germany by transferring troops to Africa. Bülow, however, had been careful to warn Kühlmann not to encourage the Sultan to expect that Germany would support him to the point of making war on France on his behalf.[140]

(c) THE KAISER'S TANGIER VISIT

It was during these rival efforts in Morocco on the part of Kühlmann and Taillandier to win the ear of the Sultan, that Bülow suddenly decided to have the Kaiser stop on his trip from Hamburg to Corfu at Tangier and greet the Sultan. The original schedule of the Kaiser's trip did not provide for this, but Bülow had the *Kölnische Zeitung* print a despatch from Tangier announcing that the Kaiser would land there on March 31. He then sent the clipping to the Kaiser, adding, "Your Majesty's visit will embarrass M. Delcassé, block his plan, and benefit our economic interests in Morocco."[141] The Kaiser at first agreed, but when he learned from the newspapers that the Tangier population, including the English, were planning to exploit his visit against the French, he wrote Bülow: "Telegraph at once to Tangier that it is *most* doubtful whether I land, and that I am only travelling *incognito* as a tourist; therefore, no audiences, no receptions." Bülow, however, shrewdly pointed out to him that a public announcement of the visit had been made, and if it was given up, Delcassé would spread abroad the idea that it was owing to French representations in Berlin that the visit had been abandoned. Delcassé would make a diplomatic triumph out of it. So the Kaiser again agreed, though at Lisbon, and even at the last moment in the harbor at Tangier, he had further hesitations. But he finally yielded to the advice of those with

140 G.P., XX, 243.

141 Bülow to Kaiser, Mar. 20, 1905; G.P., XX, 262.

him, and carried out the program which had been arranged for him.[142]

In spite of the difficulties of landing in a very rough sea and the fright caused to the Kaiser's horse by the din of Arab yelling, music, and the promiscuous discharge of firearms, the Kaiser's visit passed off smoothly enough with brilliant Oriental color. At the German Legation he received the members of the German colony and the Diplomatic Corps. To the French representative he said that his visit meant that Germany wanted freedom of trade and equality with others; that he wished to deal directly with the Sultan as a free and equal sovereign of an independent country, and he expected that France would respect his wishes. To the Sultan's Great Uncle and Plenipotentiary, he emphasized the same points, adding that such reforms as were made ought to be in accordance with the Koran and Mohammedan tradition; that European customs ought not to be blindly adopted; and that the Sultan would do well in this matter to heed the advice of his Notables.[143]

Bülow then proposed the calling of an international conference of all the Powers who had signed the Madrid Treaty of 1880.

He thought this the best way of settling the Moroccan question and securing the commercial interests of Germany, as well as of other nations, against the danger of Delcassé's "Tunisification" of the country. Here, he rightly believed, he was on solid ground. He renewed Germany's declaration of territorial disinterestedness, and made it clear that Germany was not seeking any special advantages for herself,

142 G.P., XX, 263 ff. Baron Schoen, who accompanied the Kaiser, gives a good account in his *Memoirs of an Ambassador,* pp. 19-26.

143 As the speeches were informal, and in the midst of a large and somewhat noisy assemblage, the reports of what he said vary considerably in the accounts of Schoen (G.P., XX, 286), Kühlmann (Schulthess, *Europäischer Geschichtskalender,* 1905, p. 304), and Chérisey, the French representative (*Affaires du Maroc,* I, 205).

but was only acting in the interest of all countries having commercial interests in Morocco.

He felt sure that he would have the support of a majority of the Powers in such a conference. President Roosevelt was sounded and was thought to favor it, as he had always favored an "open door" policy throughout the world.[144] Bülow hoped that Roosevelt's attitude would have a favorable effect on England and strengthen the influence of the London *Times* correspondent at Tangier,[145] who had supported the German point of view. Austria and Italy, he believed, could be counted on as allies. Russia was too much absorbed by the defeats in Manchuria to interpose objections. The Sultan of Morocco himself grasped eagerly at the conference idea, when it was suggested to him, as an easy way of avoiding a virtual French protectorate. France, therefore, would be left in a minority and would have to consent to see her secret agreements with England and Spain replaced by an international settlement. As the whole French Morocco policy had been peculiarly the work of Delcassé, the thwarting of it by the holding of an international conference would probably render his position in France insecure, especially if Germany firmly insisted on a conference. Meanwhile, Bülow continued to maintain toward France his very disconcerting attitude of sphinx-like and impassive silence, still ignoring the Anglo-French Moroccan Agreement of 1904.[146]

As Bülow had calculated, the French in general, and Delcassé in particular, now became very uneasy. They felt that they were being menaced by Germany, but did not understand exactly what she wanted. Some suspected she was looking for a pretext for war, which was certainly not the case, as the recently published German documents

144 G.P., XX, 256 ff. J. B. Bishop, *Roosevelt,* I, 467 ff.
145 Mr. W. B. Harris, G.P., XX, 261 ff. See also Harris' own memoirs.
146 G.P., XX, 293 ff.

clearly prove. Within France there was a strong and growing party which felt that Delcassé had been pursuing an adventurous and dangerous imperialist policy; he was involving the risk of war with the Sultan of Morocco, and even with Germany, at a time when France was unprepared from a military point of view and weakened by the defeats of her Russian ally. This party, which included the French Ambassador in Berlin,[147] wanted to yield to Germany's proposal for a conference, even though it meant the humiliation and the probable resignation of Delcassé as Minister of Foreign Affairs. This also was the feeling of M. Rouvier, the Prime Minister, and eventually of a majority of the Cabinet.

On April 26, M. Rouvier dined with Prince Radolin at the German Embassy, and told him with evident emotion that under no circumstances would he wish to see trouble between Germany and France; that the French people inclined much more to the German than to the English side, though there were foolish irresponsible patriots who preached *revanche.* France and Germany must stand together and preserve the peace of the world. So long as he was at the head of affairs, this would be his purpose. As far as Morocco was concerned, he guaranteed that there would be no change in the *status quo* and no limitation on the commerce of foreign nations. "It is impossible and it would be criminal," he concluded, with great emotion, "that the two countries which are called to come to an understanding and draw closer to one another should quarrel—and that simply on account of Morocco!" M. Rouvier's remark had all the more significance from the fact that a few minutes before the dinner, Prince Radolin had been informed by a person in M. Rouvier's confidence that "the Prime Minister by no means identified himself with Delcassé, since he knew that the English navy did not run on

147 *Cf.* Bihourd's reports, *Affaires du Maroc,* I, 202 ff., 215 f., 240.

wheels" and, therefore, could not protect Paris. From all this Prince Radolin gained the impression that M. Rouvier would not be unwilling to sacrifice his Minister of Foreign Affairs.[148]

(d) DELCASSÉ'S FALL AND ITS CONSEQUENCES

This hint from Rouvier was sufficient to determine Bülow to work henceforth to overthrow the man whom he regarded as dangerous to Germany and to the peace of Europe. Not only did he regard Delcassé as the incarnation of French aggressive imperialism and of the *revanche* spirit, but he believed that so long as he continued at the head of the French Foreign Office, with his intrigues and misrepresentations, there could be no satisfactory relations between the countries on the two sides of the Rhine.[149]

Another party in France, however, made up of a considerable group of newspapers and chauvinists, protested loudly against the German menace. Delcassé counted on them for support, and made a strong fight for his political life. The exciting story of this internal French conflict, as witnessed by the German representative in Paris, may now be followed in detail in the new German documents.[150]

148 Radolin to Bülow, April 27, 1905; G.P., XX, 344. This telegram, according to a letter of Paléologue's in the Paris *Temps* of March 15, 1922, was deciphered by the French during the war. Its publication by Paléologue gave rise to a lively discussion in 1922, as to whether the German Government had demanded the head of Delcassé, or whether it had been offered to them. Mr. O. S. Hale, of the University of Pennsylvania, in an unpublished study, indicates that there is no truth in the commonly repeated legend, based on an article in *Le Gaulois,* June 17, 1905, that Prince Henckel von Donnersmarck was sent on a special mission by the German Government to demand the resignation of Delcassé. On internal and other evidence Mr. Hale thinks the report in *Le Gaulois* is apocryphal. This confirms the present writer's conclusion that the "Donnersmarck Mission" was a product of French journalistic imagination.

149 *Cf.* G.P., XX, 393 ff. for a list of half a dozen cases in which Bülow believed Delcassé guilty of misrepresentations and broken promises.

150 G.P., XX, 344-409. *Cf.* R. Pinon, *France et Allemagne* (Paris, 1913), which is, on the whole, favorable to Germany and critical of Del-

Delcassé insisted on holding out against the German proposal for a conference. He alleged it would put the Sultan under international tutelage, but in reality he feared it would wreck his own program. Moreover, to yield in the face of German pressure would be an intolerable humiliation for France, as well as for himself personally. He declared to his colleagues that Germany was "bluffing," and he wanted to call their bluff even at the risk of war. He would rather resign than yield.

But meanwhile his position was being undermined both at Fez and at Paris. At the end of May the Sultan finally rejected the French demands and adopted the German proposal of inviting the Powers to an international conference. In Paris the German Ambassador maintained a firm and unyielding attitude, and gave the impression that Germany would back up the Sultan with force if necessary.

M. Rouvier was in a most distressing position. He feared that M. Delcassé was leading France to the brink of war. Through a confidential agent he sounded Germany further, and gathered that if he consented to drop Delcassé from the Cabinet, and accepted the idea of a conference, the critical situation would be happily relieved and Germany would not make too great difficulties when the conference met. He therefore finally went to President Loubet, taking M. Delcassé with him, and told the President that he was absolutely opposed to M. Delcassé's policy. He said that

cassé; A. Mevil, *De la paix de Francfort à la conférence d'Algésiras* (Paris, 1909), which takes the opposite point of view. Tardieu *La Conférence d'Algésiras*, as usual, is strongly nationalist. The French Yellow Book, *Affaires du Maroc,* is singularly barren on this important aspect of the Moroccan affair; it contains nothing at all on the critical week of Delcassé's final fall. The material in the recent German documents on Björkö, Delcassé, and the Morocco Crisis of 1905 is summarized by E. Laloy, in *Mercure de France,* CLXXXVI, 594 ff.; CLXXXVII, 564 ff.; CLXXXIX, 293 ff.; CXC, 568 ff.; CXCII, 72 ff. (March-November, 1926); and by R. J. Sontag, in *Amer. Hist. Rev.,* XXXIII, 278-301 (Jan., 1928).

next day he would hold a Cabinet meeting, and would resign, if a majority of his colleagues did not agree with him. Accordingly, on June 6, the Cabinet was forced to choose between M. Rouvier and M. Delcassé. All the Ministers sided with the Prime Minister, according to information conveyed to Radolin. M. Delcassé resigned, and M. Rouvier took over his portfolio.

M. Delcassé's fall did not relieve the tension so much as Rouvier had hoped. There followed many weeks of difficult negotiations before the two countries could find a formula establishing the basis on which the conference should meet. Meanwhile England supported every French argument so strongly, and the English Press launched such a campaign against Germany, that the Moroccan question became almost more of an Anglo-German than a Franco-German conflict. Thanks in part to President Roosevelt's enjoying the confidence of M. Jusserand and Baron Speck von Sternburg at Washington, he was able tactfully and skilfully to secure first a French acceptance of the conference idea, and then the basis on which it should proceed.

When the conference finally met at Algeciras in January, 1906, there still remained the fundamental clash between the Anglo-French and the German positions. France and England pulled every possible political wire to secure decisions which would carry out the intention of the Anglo-French Agreement of 1904 and give France control. Germany pulled with equal energy, but less success, to secure equal rights for all nations and the establishment of a control in Morocco which should be genuinely international and not purely French. In sketching the development of the system of secret alliances, it is unnecessary to go into these Algeciras intrigues. Suffice it to say that Germany won in principle, but France won in practical results. The main importance of the First Morocco Crisis lies in the fact that from the outset it strengthened the ties between

France and England, and led to new secret understandings between them.

Bülow's Morocco policy seemed to have resulted in a brilliant diplomatic victory. The Kaiser, who had had no great share personally in bringing it about nor even full knowledge of its progress, accepted it with pleasure. He signalized it, not very tactfully as the French felt, by raising Bülow to the rank of Prince the day after Delcassé's fall, and by bestowing a decoration upon Betzold, the secret go-between in the unofficial negotiations between Rouvier and Radolin. Bülow had asked that Betzold be given the Order of the Red Eagle, "Third Class"; the Kaiser ordered it raised to "Second Class," "because he saved us from war."[151]

Blissfully oblivious of the psychological effect such a diplomatic humiliation as Delcassé's fall was bound to have on a proud people like the French, to say nothing of the impropriety of meddling in the internal politics of a Great Power, the Kaiser seems sincerely to have regarded Delcassé's departure from the French Foreign Office as really opening the way, not only for better relations with France, but even for a new era in the system of alliances. The French, he believed, had given evidence that they were no longer minded to pursue the *revanche* policy which Delcassé had personified. "France," he wrote to Bülow from Björkö, "refused to take up our challenge." And the Tsar had agreed that it was "quite clear that the Alsace-Lorraine question is closed once for all, thank God."[152] It opened the way, he hoped, for the success of his Björkö effort for a defensive alliance with Russia, in which France would be included as soon as the Russo-Japanese War was ended.

151 G.P., XX, 409.

152 G.P., XIX, 460. A few weeks later the Kaiser appears to have made a similar remark to Izvolski at Copenhagen; *Memoirs of Alexander Izvolski,* p. 78; *cf.* also Izvolski's letter in the Paris *Temps,* Sept. 15, 1917, quoted in my *Amer. Hist. Rev.* article on the Björkö meeting, note 48.

He and President Roosevelt had already taken energetic steps to bring about the peace negotiations which soon took place at Portsmouth.[153] The Kaiser, therefore, was in a great hurry to tell Roosevelt of the Björkö meeting, and directed the following telegram to him:

> The Emperor and I have concluded an agreement to lend each other mutual help in case any European power should attack one of us, and France is to be cosignatory to it. In fact Germany enters the dual-alliance—originally concluded against it—as third party. It being the leading power of the triple-alliance, the latter and the dual-alliance —instead of glaring at each other for [no] purpose at all— join hands and the peace of Europe is guaranteed. This is the fruit of our understanding with France about Morocco, the fact, upon which you sent me so kind compliments. I am sure, that this grouping of powers is leading to a general "détente," will be of great use in enabling you to fulfil the great mission of peace, which Providence has entrusted tc your hands for the good of the world.[154]

In reality, however, Bülow's Morocco policy of 1905 was one of those victories which are worse than a defeat. In seeking to preserve the independence of the Sultan and the open door in Morocco by his sphinx-like policy of studied silence, which gave the impression of a menace, all the more alarming because of its mysteriousness, Bülow had been striving for the right thing in the wrong way. In trying to frighten

[153] For the Kaiser's initiation and Roosevelt's carrying out of mediation between Russia and Japan, see G.P., XIX, 529-630; J. B. Bishop, *Theodore Roosevelt and His Time* (N. Y., 1920), I, 374-424; H. C. Lodge, *Correspondence of Theodore Roosevelt and Henry Cabot Lodge* (N. Y., 1925), II, 130-192; and A. Hasenclever, "Theodore Roosevelt und die Marokkokrisis von 1904-1906," in *Archiv f. Politik und Geschichte,* VI, Heft 3, 184-245 (1928).

[154] G.P., XIX, 466. The telegram was not sent, because Bülow objected that the arrangement with the Tsar was strictly secret, and might leak out prematurely in Washington; but it is highly interesting, as indicating the Kaiser's interpretation of the Björkö Treaty, and his close relations with Roosevelt at this time.

Rouvier into ousting his Minister of Foreign Affairs, he had been egregiously guilty of aiming at the wrong thing in the wrong way. The incident made a painful impression on the French. It contributed not a little to the ultimate revival of a new determination on the part of some of her leading men that they would rather risk war than accept another such humiliation. M. Poincaré, for instance, in his public speeches and his writings never tires of referring to the "brutality" and "odious violence" of Germany's bellicose diplomatic methods. More fatal still for Germany, it helped rouse the British Government to enter into those naval and military "conversations" which brought England into the World War and thus made certain Germany's ultimate catastrophic defeat.

ANGLO-FRENCH MILITARY AND NAVAL "CONVERSATIONS," 1905-1912

As the Franco-Russian Entente of 1891 was followed by a secret Military Convention, so the Anglo-French Entente of 1904 was soon supplemented by momentous but very secret naval and military arrangements, or, as Sir Edward Grey euphemistically calls them, "conversations." These lacked, at first, the rigid and binding character of the Franco-Russian Alliance, but they gradually came to be, in fact if not in form, a most vital link in the system of secret alliances. In spite of the meticulous nicety with which Sir Edward Grey was careful to state that "England's hands were free," and that "it would be left for Parliament to decide," he allowed the French to hope confidently that, in case Germany caused a European war, England would take the field on the side of the French. He permitted the English and French Naval and Military Staffs to elaborate technical arrangements for joint war action, which became the basis of the strategic plans of both countries. These came to involve mutual obligations which were virtually as entangling as a formal alliance. It is always dangerous to allow the military authorities of two countries to develop inter-dependent strategic plans. They come to make arrangements which, by their very nature, necessarily involve obligations which are virtually binding upon the political authorities. Here is where Sir Edward Grey's great responsibility and mistake began. It is therefore important to note in some detail the origin, character, and consequences of these naval and military "conversations." They reach back in part to the time of his predecessor at the Foreign Office, Lord Lansdowne.[155]

In Art. IX of the Anglo-French Convention of 1904, England had promised merely *diplomatic* support to France in connection with Morocco. But after the Kaiser's visit

[155] The secrecy and subleties of diplomatic language in which these conversations were carried on has given rise to a wide literature of apology and accusation. From the English side the most authoritative *apologias* are: Grey, *Twenty-Five Years,* I, 48 ff., 59-118; II, 1 ff., 39 ff., 310 ff.; H. H. Asquith, *The Genesis of the War,* pp. 92-110, 142-216; Lord Haldane, *Before the War, passim;* J. A. Spender, *Life of Sir Henry Campbell-Bannerman,* II, 245-268; C. A. Repington, *The First World War,* ch. i; and W. S. Churchill, *The World Crisis,* I, 1-191. The most noteworthy criticisms of Grey's policy are: Lord Loreburn, *How the War Came, passim;* E. D. Morel, *Ten Years of Secret Diplomacy;* G. P. Gooch, *Camb. Hist. of Brit. Foreign Policy,* III, 338 ff., 438 ff; J. A. Farrer, *England under Edward VII, passim;* G. L. Dickinson, *The International Anarchy, 1904-1914,* pp. 127 ff., 375 ff.; and the indictment, drawn with a lawyer's skill, by J. S. Ewart, *The Roots and Causes of the Wars,* chs. v, xxii.

From the French side, besides the volumes of Pinon, Mévil, and Tardieu mentioned above in note 150, see R. Poincaré, *Les Origines de la Guerre,* p. 72 ff., *Au Service de la France,* I, 146-235, and the criticisms of his policy in the volumes of Fabre-Luce, Judet, Pevet, Victor Margueritte, Morhardt, and Demartial.

From the German side there is abundant material in G.P., XX-XXV, XXVIII-XXXI, *passim; cf.* also H. Herzfeld, "Der deutsche Flottenbau und die englische Politik", in *Archiv. für Politik und Geschichte,* IV, 117 ff. (1926); H. Lutz, *Lord Grey und der Weltkrieg* (Berlin, 1927, English trans., N. Y., 1928); and A. von Tirpitz, *Politische Dokumente: I, Der Aufbau der deutschen Weltmacht* (Stuttgart and Berlin, 1924), *passim.*

American accounts, severely critical of Grey and Poincaré, may be found in H. E. Barnes, *The Genesis of the World War,* ch. viii; and E. F. Henderson, *The Verdict of History: The Case of Sir Edward Grey* (privately printed, 1924).

to Tangier, the English Press and the English Government became obsessed with the idea that Germany was endeavoring to break up the Entente by bullying France. It jarred the sporting spirit of the British to see France menaced because of her new friendship with England, at a moment when France's ally was being so disastrously defeated in the Far East.[156] The English were also irritated by the rapidly growing German navy, as well as by the undercurrent of political and commercial rivalry which had existed for some years in Africa, Turkey, and elsewhere in the world. Level-headed observers in the German Embassy at London, like Count Metternich and Freiherr von Eckardstein, who were not at all blinded by Anglophobia, reported the anti-German feeling in the newspapers and in society as dangerously strong.[157] They found the British Press, in the Morocco question, "more French than the French." They warned the German Government that if war arose over Morocco, "there can be no doubt that England will stand unconditionally and actively on the French side, and go against Germany, even with enthusiasm." [158]

In accord with this public feeling, Lord Lansdowne and M. Paul Cambon entered into discussions for an exchange of notes, by which England should "take a step further," and offer the French something more substantial than mere diplomatic support. Mr. Gooch, on the basis of information supplied to him by the British Foreign Office, implies that the initiative came from France,[159] while M. Poincaré, on

[156] Looking back six months later, the German Ambassador in London summed up the situation: "The impression here is that 'Germany has been acting as a bully', and that because we felt ourselves to be the stronger, we wanted to force measures upon the French"; Metternich to Bülow, Dec. 20, 1905; G.P. XX, 689; *cf.* also, XXI, 46 f.

[157] G.P., XX, 601 ff., 618 ff., 627 ff., 647 ff., 669 ff., 685 ff.

[158] Metternich to Bülow, May 1, 1905; G.P., XX, 607, 618.

[159] "In the middle of May, the French Ambassador complained to Lord Lansdowne of the general attitude of the German Government, which was seeking in all parts of the world to sow discord between France and Great Britain. . . . Lord Lansdowne replied that the moral seemed

COUNT BENCKENDORFF
Russian Ambassador in London, 1903-1917

M. PAUL CAMBON
French Ambassador in London, 1898-1921

the basis of Paul Cambon's reports, implies that it came from Lord Lansdowne.[160] From these discussions the French gathered that Lord Lansdowne was ready to offer an agreement, veiled from Parliament and the public under the form of an exchange of notes, to exchange views in common—an agreement which might lead to a real alliance.[161] As M. Cambon wrote, later on, in April and September, 1912:

> I know that the British Government does not have the right to bind itself without the authorization of Parliament; but there is no need of a duplicate agreement, of a treaty drawn up and signed [pas besoin d'un accord en partie double, de traité signé et paraphré]; we could content ourselves with an exchange of declarations. This is what we would have done in 1905 with Lord Lansdowne, if the resignation of M. Delcassé had not cut short our conversations.[162]

to be that each Government should continue to treat the other with the most absolute mutual confidence, should keep it fully informed of everything which came to their knowledge, and should, so far as possible, discuss in advance any contingencies by which they might in the course of events find themselves confronted"; Gooch, *Camb. Hist. of Brit. For. Policy,* III, 342.

[160] "In the month of April, 1905, Lord Lansdowne had appeared disposed to take one step further, and had proposed to M. Cambon a general formula for an Entente. . . ."; Poincaré, *Les Origines de la Guerre* (Paris, 1921), p. 79. That M. Poincaré is correct seems to be indicated by Mr. Spender, who says that on April 25, 1905, Sir Francis Bertie informed M. Delcassé, on Lord Lansdowne's instructions, that the British Government would join the French in opposing Germany's acquisition of a port on the coast of Morocco, and hoped to be given a full opportunity to concert with the French Government the measures which might be taken to prevent it. The French were pleased. A month later, after further conversations, on May 25, Lord Lansdowne suggested "that the two Governments should treat one another with the utmost confidence and discuss all likely contingencies"; J. A. Spender, *Life of Sir Henry Campbell-Bannerman* II, 248.

[161] M. Poincaré says in his recent memoirs (*Au Service de la France,* I, 187, 221); "The Conservative Government had been able to contemplate an alliance in 1905." "M. Paul Cambon had written me that at the time [1905] an agreement of this kind [for an exchange of views in common] would have been only a beginning on the part of Lord Lansdowne. . . . The forced resignation of M. Delcassé had perhaps made us lose in 1905 an opportunity for a veritable alliance with England".

[162] Paul Cambon to Poincaré, April 18, 1912, *Au Service de la France,* I, 174.

> Would it not be possible [said Cambon to Grey] to return, at least partially, to the proposals of Lord Lansdowne, to bind ourselves, for example, to exchange views in common [de se concerter] in case of menacing complications, and to settle that, in such a hypothesis, we should seek together the means most suited to protect us mutually from the peril of war? In a word, if, faced with this peril, we judge the best method to be an alliance and a military convention, we will employ it.[163]

Now it is interesting to observe how, on the one hand, Lord Lansdowne's proposal encouraged M. Delcassé's hopes and were given an extravagant interpretation by him; and how, on the other, its existence was reported to, or suspected by, the Germans, and then flatly denied by the British.

The Lansdowne-Cambon negotiations seem to have advanced to the point where the notes to be exchanged had already been drawn up and transmitted in written form to M. Delcassé for his final approval.[164] This was just at the moment when the Morocco Crisis was at its height, and he was fighting to persuade his colleagues to reject the German proposal for an international conference. He interpreted the Lansdowne proposal as an assurance of a British alliance and armed support. He used it as an argument to try to persuade President Loubet and the Cabinet to stand by him in refusing the German demands. But, as we have seen, the Rouvier Cabinet and President Loubet declined

163 Paul Cambon to Poincaré, Sept. 21, 1912; *Au Service de la France*, I, 218 f.

164 Both M. Delcassé and M. Chaumié, Minister of Justice at the time, appear to leave no doubt on this point. M. Delcassé, in a letter published in the *Figaro* of March 24, 1922, says: "Le 6 juin je n'avais que depuis quarante-huit heures l'offre anglais de concours". M. Chaumié, in notes on the decisive Cabinet meeting of June 6 made at the time and later published by his colleague in the Ministry of Justice, M. Bienvenu-Martin, in the *Temps* of March 19, 1922, says explicitly: "Ces ouvertures ne sont pas bornées à de simples pourparlers; des notes écrites ont déjà été échangées"

to take the risk of war with Germany, and M. Delcassé resigned.[165]

In October, 1905, the *Matin* published a series of revelations concerning the events of M. Delcassé's overthrow. They included the startling assertion, as coming from Delcassé, that he had been promised by the British Government that, in case of a German attack on France, the English fleet would be mobilized to seize the Kiel Canal and would land 100,000 men in Schleswig-Holstein. The revelations made a sensation at the time, and have remained ever since something of a puzzle to historians, inasmuch as the British have always denied that they made any offer of alliance or armed assistance to France. Mr. Gooch suggests that Delcassé's mistakenly wide interpretation of Britain's attitude may be explained by the probability that King Edward VII, during a visit to Paris, intimated to the French Minister that, in case of need, England would intervene on the French side.[166] One of the editors of *Die Grosse Politik* suggests that the offer came, not from Lord Lansdowne, but from Sir Francis Bertie.[167] This British Ambassador in Paris was certainly strongly pro-French, but it is hardly likely that he would have taken so serious a step without authorization, and there is no convincing evidence that he

[165] On June 7, Flotow, the German Chargé d'Affaires in Paris reported (G.P., XX, 623-5) information coming from the owner of the *Matin* that "a regular offer of an offensive and defensive alliance with an anti-German aim has been made here", but not yet accepted, partly on account of the effect on Russia, and partly because a majority of the Cabinet hoped still for a satisfactory settlement with Germany. On the same day, Flotow was able to sound M. Rouvier through their mutual confidential agent, and the French Premier had declared positively that an Anglo-French alliance was out of the question. It is quite possible that Delcassé, after his fall, may have given Paris newspaper editors a hint of the English proposals—both to justify his own policy, and with the idea that the news would be passed on to Germany and further irritate Anglo-German relations; *cf.* G.P., XX, 623 note, and 631 note.

[166] Gooch, *l.c.*, p. 343. Eckardstein, III, 105.

[167] A. Mendelssohn Bartholdy, in *Wissen und Leben,* Feb. 1, 1925, cited by Dickinson, *The International Anarchy,* p. 129, note 1.

did so. Possibly the idea of landing 100,000 men in Holstein came from Sir John Fisher. It was the kind of strategy which he often urged and commended, and accords with his advice to King Edward in 1908: "We should 'Copenhagen' the German Fleet at Kiel à la Nelson." [168] Admiral Fisher's idea may have been handed on to the French by King Edward, or it may have come to them as a result of the direct naval "conversations" which the French and English Staffs were already carrying on in 1905.[169] Sir John Fisher was a very lovable old sea dog, with all the freshness of the salt spray which he loved so well, but he had an indiscreet habit of expressing himself promiscuously.[170] At a dinner in December, 1905, he told Colonel Repington that "he was prepared, on his own responsibility, to order our fleets to go wherever they might be required. He told me that he had seen on paper Lord Lansdowne's assurances to M. Cambon, and that they were quite distinct in their tenor. He had shown them to Sir Edward Grey, and declared that they were part of the engagements taken over from the last Government, and would hold good until denounced." [171] It is not at all unlikely that he conveyed to the French the

[168] *Cf.* Fisher, *Memories and Records,* I, 22, 47 ff., 188, 207, 211, 233; II, 176, 208 ff., 218 f., 225 ff.

[169] Grey, I, 74; II, 2. Sir Alfred Beit and the Kaiser, in an interesting conversation soon after the *Matin* revelations, assumed that the idea came from Fisher; G.P., XX, 694. Fisher, *Memories,* p. 49, in connection with this conversation, says: "The German Emperor did say to Beit that I was dangerous, and that he knew of my ideas as regards the Baltic being Germany's vulnerable spot, and he had heard of my idea for 'Copenhagening' the German Fleet. But this last I much doubt. He only said it because he knew it was what we ought to have done."

[170] For example, upon the news of Tirpitz's dismissal, he addressed him a letter which got into a London newspaper: "Dear old Tirps: Cheer up, old chap! . . . Yours, till Hell freezes, Fisher"; *Memories,* p. 45. To a Russian Grand Duchess, who had written him of a picnic, pleasant except for the gnats biting her ankles, he telegraphed: "I wish to God I had been one of the gnats"; *ibid.,* p. 231. Winston Churchill (*The World Crisis,* pp. 72-79) paints a brilliant picture of Fisher and of his indiscretion in the "Bacon letters affair."

[171] Repington, *First World War,* p. 4.

prospect of British naval support and a British diversion upon the German rear in Holstein or Pomerania.

At any rate, it seems clear that M. Delcassé greatly exaggerated the nature of Lord Lansdowne's offer, whatever assurances he may have received from other high English sources. Perhaps, the wish being father to the thought, he really believed that Lord Lansdowne was holding out the offer of a British alliance. Perhaps he was deliberately overstating its character, in order to persuade his hesitating colleagues to stand firm against Germany. In either case, here was a dangerous example of the way Frenchmen of his character would misinterpret, either unconsciously or deliberately, proposals contemplating something more than mere diplomatic support. It should have been a warning to Sir Edward Grey of the danger of permitting the naval and military "conversations," and of the later exchange of notes with M. Cambon in 1912—the danger of arousing expectations and involving obligations at Paris that England would come in on the side of France in case of a European war.

It is equally interesting to note the German suspicions of an Anglo-French alliance,[172] and the flat denials on the part of the British. On June 16, 1905, Lord Lansdowne told the German Ambassador that "the news that England had offered France an offensive and defensive alliance was completely fictitious [*vollkommen erfunden*]. Since Lord Lansdowne rejected the alliance rumor with the greatest decisiveness and without equivocation, as made out of air," the Ambassador said he would regard the subject as settled. He did not think that Lord Lansdowne, after such a downright declaration, was capable of trying to deceive.[173]

But a few days later, Count Metternich received further

[172] G.P., XX, 494, 615 f., 623 ff., 634 f., 638 ff., 662 ff., and Flotow's report of June 7 (see above, note 165).

[173] Metternich to Bülow, June 16. 1905; G.P., XX, 630. *Cf.* also Gooch, *l.c.*, p. 342 f.

information, apparently coming through confidential sources from M. Rouvier himself, that England had promised naval aid to France. He therefore asked Lord Lansdowne about it, tactfully saying that he did so unofficially, without instructions from Berlin:

> Lord Lansdowne replied that I knew that diplomatic support was assured to the French Government within the corners of the Anglo-French Agreement. This has the natural result that the questions which the Agreement touched would be discussed by the two Governments in friendly fashion, and the most suitable ways and means would be considered to maintain unimpaired the various points of the Agreement. The question of an alliance with France, however, had never been discussed in the English Cabinet, nor had an English alliance ever been offered to the French Government either in recent times or earlier. However, he would not conceal from me that in the eventuality, which he however regarded as wholly out of the question, that Germany should light-heartedly let loose a war against France, one could not foresee how far public opinion in England would drive the Government to the support of France.[174]

Similarly, in October, 1905, Lord Lansdowne's Under Secretary, Sir Thomas Sanderson, felt obliged by the *Matin* revelations to reiterate the denial:

> The English Government has never held out to the French Government the prospect of military aid. A possible rupture between France and Germany has never been even discussed by the Government, and the promise of landing 100,000 men in Schleswig-Holstein belongs to the realm of myth. . . . [Sanderson said] Perhaps French imagination played some part in this. One could well imagine Delcassé had said to his colleagues that he was convinced that England would stand beside France in case of a Franco-German war. This subjective conception, supposing Delcassé had it, was however very different from an English promise or

174 Metternich to Bülow, June 28, 1905; G.P., XX, 636.

> an English offer of assistance. These had never been made, and, as he had said, the eventuality of a war between Germany and France had never even been discussed on the English side.[175]

In view of the seriousness with which the British Government viewed the Morocco Crisis in the early summer of 1905, it is difficult to believe this last statement of Sanderson that "the eventuality of a war between Germany and France had never even been discussed on the English side." Probably these sweeping denials were as correct in letter, and as misleading in spirit, as the similar denials made in Parliament later by Mr. Asquith and Sir Edward Grey after the Grey-Cambon exchange of notes in 1912.

On December 11, 1905, Sir Henry Campbell-Bannerman formed a Cabinet, in which Sir Edward Grey replaced Lord Lansdowne at the Foreign Office.[176] Viscount Grey tells us in his engaging and charmingly written retrospect,[177] no doubt with perfect sincerity, that he accepted the post with reluctance. It brought no joy to him or to his wife, for it meant exile from his home in the country, from his fishing, from his walks in the woods. Perhaps his reluctance may unconsciously have been in part owing to his lack of experience, his inability to speak any foreign language, and also to a sense of inadequacy for the exacting work of the Foreign Office. Perhaps also, in composing his memoirs, his realization of the failure of his long and sincere efforts to preserve the peace of Europe may have led him unconsciously in later years to exaggerate the reluctance with which he took office in 1905. But, as he tells us, he could not justify to his constituents or to his friends a refusal to take up the work. He seemed as well qualified as any one in the Liberal Party.

175 Metternich to Bülow, Oct. 9, 1905; G.P., XX, 663.
176 Spender, *Life of Sir Henry Campbell-Bannerman*, II, 188 ff. 245 ff.
177 *Twenty-Five Years*, I. 59-66.

One of the first tasks which claimed his attention was to quiet the fears of the French. The Algeciras Conference was about to meet. Germany was thought to be pursuing a threatening policy, and the French were nervous to know whether the new Liberal Government would sustain the assurances of Lord Lansdowne, or go even further. On January 10 and 15, 1906, Cambon asked Grey the pressing question whether the British Government "would be prepared to render France armed assistance," in case of German aggression, and whether it would sanction the continuation of the naval and military conversations. Grey replied that he could not at the moment make any promises, as the Ministers were all dispersed, taking part in the elections. He could only state as his personal opinion, adopting the attitude of Lord Lansdowne, that if France were to be attacked by Germany in consequence of a question arising out of the Morocco Agreement, public opinion in England would be strongly moved in favor of France. As to the naval and military conversations which had been going on, the former had been direct between the French and English Naval Staffs. They were already on a satisfactory basis, having been conducted on the English side by Sir John Fisher. But the plans for military coöperation were less satisfactory, being at the moment in the hands of an unofficial intermediary. Between January 10 and 15, however, Sir Edward Grey had managed to see the Secretary for War, Mr. Haldane, at an election meeting in Northumberland. Mr. Haldane had authorized Grey to say that these military communications might now proceed directly and officially between General Grierson and the French Military Attaché, but it must be understood that these communications did not commit either Government.[178]

The story of the new turn now given to the military

178 Grey to Bertie, British Ambassador in Paris, Jan. 10, 15, 1906; Grey, I, 70-74.

conversations has been interestingly told by the intermediary in question, Colonel Repington, the military correspondent of the London *Times*.[179] Although Anglo-German tension was relaxed at the moment and there seemed to be a prospect of better relations between the two countries,[180] Colonel Repington wrote an alarm article in the *Times* of December 27, which gave a warning of what he supposed to be Germany's threatening intentions. Next day, in response to it, he received a visit from Major Huguet, the French Military Attaché, dined with him, and was told that the French Embassy people were greatly worried about the general situation. Sir Edward Grey, who had just taken over the Foreign Office, had not renewed the assurances given by Lord Lansdowne, and M. Cambon was at the moment absent in France. Major Huguet said he knew the British navy was ready, and he trusted it, but he did not know what it would do to coöperate in case of trouble. The French Army also was ready, but he feared the Germans might attack suddenly, probably through Belgium. He therefore wanted the British to stiffen the Belgians, if war came. Colonel Repington at once reported this by letter to Sir Edward Grey. A couple of days later he discussed the whole situation at dinner with Sir John Fisher, who said he had perfect confidence in the navy and was prepared to order it to go wherever it might be required. On New Year's Day Repington received the reply from Grey: "I am interested to hear of your conversation with the French Military Attaché. I can only say that I have not receded from anything Lord Lansdowne said to the French, and have no hesitation in affirming it." [181] Colonel Repington then dined with General Grierson, Head of the Operations Bureau, who told him that, on the assumption

179 Repington, *The First World War,* ch. i.
180 Metternich to Bülow, Dec., 4, 20, 1905; G.P., XX, 681, 685.
181 Repington, p. 4.

that Germany violated Belgium, England could put two divisions into Namur by the thirteenth day of mobilization, and the Field Army, such as it then was, into Antwerp by the thirty-second day. After getting the approval of various officials, including Sir George Clark, Secretary of the Imperial Defense Committee, Colonel Repington saw Major Huguet again, and gave him a short list of questions to be submitted to the French General Staff. Major Huguet hurried to France and soon brought back a set of interesting and satisfactory answers which he was able to show to Colonel Repington on January 12.[182] With the authorization of Haldane and Grey these then became the basis for official discussions direct between the French and British military authorities through Major Huguet and General Grierson.

Sir Edward Grey returned to London on January 26 and found M. Cambon anxiously waiting for a more definite statement as to whether France could count upon British assistance. After talking further with Haldane and the Prime Minister, but without accepting the latter's suggestion that the statement to be made to Cambon should be approved in a meeting of the whole Cabinet, Grey gave Cambon his momentous answer on January 31. The long summary of it which he sent to Bertie in Paris shows clearly enough its double character. With one hand he held out what he withdrew with the other. He encouraged the French to expect aid, if needed; but he made no promises of armed support and reserved liberty of action. He told M. Cambon encouragingly that since their last interviews on January 10 and 15,

> A good deal of progress has been made. Our military and naval authorities had been in communication with the French, and I assumed that all preparations were ready, so

182 Repington's questions and the French replies, printed *ibid.*, pp. 6-10.

> that, if a crisis arose, no time would have been lost for want of a formal engagement. . . . I had taken an opportunity of expressing to Count Metternich my personal opinion, which I understood Lord Lansdowne had also expressed to him [Cambon] as a personal opinion, that, in the event of an attack upon France by Germany arising out of our Morocco Agreement, public feeling in England would be so strong that no British Government could remain neutral.[183]

Sir Edward Grey also pointed out to M. Cambon the possible disadvantages to France of making a more formal statement of Anglo-French relations: at present, under the Agreement of 1904, France had an absolutely free hand in Morocco, with the promise of English diplomatic support; but, if England extended her promise beyond this, and made a formal alliance which might involve her in war, he was sure the British Cabinet would say that England must from time to time be consulted with regard to French policy in Morocco, and, if need be, be free to ask for alterations in French policy to avoid war. Was not the present situation so satisfactory that it was better not to alter it by a more formal engagement?

M. Cambon was not convinced by this. He pointed out that if the Conference broke up, and Germany placed herself behind the Sultan, "war might arise so suddenly that the need for action would be a question not of days, but of minutes, and that, if it was necessary for the British Government to consult, and to wait for manifestations of English public opinion, it might be too late to be of use." [184]

To M. Cambon's request for "some form of assurance which might be given in conversation," Grey replied that he could give no such formal assurance,

[183] Grey to Bertie, Jan. 31, 1906; Grey, I, 76. For Grey's conversation with Metternich, here referred to, see Grey, I, 80, and G.P., XXI, 45-51; and for Lansdowne's statement to Metternich, which Grey now adopted as his own, see above at note 174.

[184] Grey to Bertie, Jan. 31, 1906; Grey, I, 77.

without submitting it to the Cabinet and getting their authority, and that were I to submit the question to the Cabinet I was not sure that they would say that this was too serious a matter to be dealt with by a verbal engagement but must be put in writing. As far as their good disposition towards France was concerned, I should have no hesitation in submitting such a question to the present Cabinet. Some of those in the Cabinet who were most attached to peace were those also who were the best friends of France; but, though I had no doubt about the good disposition of the Cabinet, I did think there would be difficulties in putting such an undertaking in writing. It could not be given unconditionally, and it would be difficult to describe the conditions. It amounted, in fact, to this; that, if any change was made, it must be to change the "Entente" into a defensive alliance. That was a great and formal change, and I again submitted to M. Cambon as to whether the force of circumstances bringing England and France together was not stronger than any assurance in words which could be given at this moment. I said that it might be that the pressure of circumstances—the activity of Germany, for instance—might eventually transform the "Entente" into a defensive alliance between ourselves and France, but I did not think that the pressure of circumstances was so great as to demonstrate the necessity of such a change yet. I also told him that, should such a defensive alliance be formed, it was too serious a matter to be kept secret from Parliament. The Government could conclude it without the assent of Parliament, but it would have to be published afterwards. No British Government could commit the country to such a serious thing and keep the engagement secret.[185]

When M. Cambon, in summing up, dwelt upon Grey's expression of personal opinion that "in the event of an attack by Germany upon France, no British Government could remain neutral," Grey was careful to point out that "a personal opinion was not a thing upon which, in so seri-

185 Grey to Bertie, Jan. 31, 1906; Grey, I, 77-78.

ous a matter, a policy could be founded," and added: "Much would depend as to the manner in which the war broke out between Germany and France. I did not think people in England would be prepared to fight to put France in possession of Morocco. They would say that France should wait for opportunities and be content to take time, and that it was unreasonable to hurry matters to the point of war. But if, on the other hand, it appeared that the war was forced upon France by Germany to break up the Anglo-French 'Entente,' public opinion would undoubtedly be very strong on the side of France. . . . If the French Government desired it, it would be possible at any time to reopen the conversation. Events might change, but, as things were at present, I did not think it necessary to press the question of a defensive alliance." [186]

This long and critical interview, which we have tried to summarize without bias or essential omissions, is significant for several reasons. In the first place, it reveals Sir Edward Grey's very strong sympathy with France, his evident desire to go as far as possible in giving her diplomatic support, but at the same time his unwillingness to make any formal engagement, written or verbal, which might bind England to go to war. Such an engagement must be sanctioned by Parliament, but it was very unlikely that Parliament would assent. Moreover, it would greatly increase the irritation between England and Germany. He gave France as much encouragement as he could, without going to the point where he thought he ought to inform the Cabinet and Parliament. He was satisfied in his own mind that he had avoided changing the Entente into a formal alliance. As he wrote to his wife next day, in a letter which she was never to read on account of the carriage accident which caused her sudden and tragic death: "I had tremendously difficult talk and work yesterday, and

[186] Grey to Bertie, Jan. 31, 1906; Grey, I, 78-79.

very important. I do not know that I did well, but I did honestly."[187]

In the second place, Sir Edward approved and confirmed the official military and naval conversations between the British and French Staffs. He assumed, as he told M. Cambon, "that all preparations are ready." As will be indicated further on, Haldane at once set very actively to work to reorganize the British Army and prepare for its coöperation with the French. These preparations continued right down to the outbreak of war in 1914, and inevitably came to involve England in increasingly binding obligations of honor to support France in case of a European war arising out of any question whatsoever—not merely one arising out of the Morocco question—provided that France did not appear to be the active aggressor. Probably Sir Edward Grey did not at the time see the full implications and danger of these "conversations." But his Prime Minister saw them. For we know that Sir Henry Campbell-Bannerman wrote to Lord Ripon on February 2, a couple of days after Grey's talk with Cambon: "Cambon appears satisfied. But I do not like the stress laid upon joint preparations. It comes very close to an honorable undertaking, and it will be known on both sides of the Rhine. But let us hope for the best."[188] He showed a true prophetic instinct, but it was submerged and lost to sight under the secret activities of the military authorities and the Foreign Secretary's strange silence or ignorance in regard to them for the next five years. It was not until 1912 that circumstances caused the military and naval "conversations" to be revealed to the whole Cabinet, and not until Grey's speech

187 Grey, I, 79.

188 Spender, *Life of Sir Henry Campbell-Bannerman,* II, 257. In spite of his just misgivings, the Prime Minister appears, however, to have acquiesced in the military conversations, provided they "were not talked about" and "should not commit either Government", if we are to believe the statements of Haldane (*Before the War,* p. 162), and Repington. (p. 13).

on August 3, 1914, that Parliament and the British public had any inkling of them.

In the third place, neither Sir Edward Grey's statement to M. Cambon, nor his approval of the naval and military conversations, was made with the knowledge and sanction of the Cabinet. The Prime Minister had written him on January 21: "Would you like the answer to the French to be confirmed by a Cabinet before it is given?" He suggested the 30th, the 31st, or the 1st of February. Viscount Grey in his memoirs says he has no recollection or record of any answer to this question.[189] His only explanations of why no Cabinet sanction was given are rather feeble: the Ministers were dispersed seeing to the elections, and the earliest date suggested by the Prime Minister was January 30, and "the French had been kept long enough waiting for a reply."[190] But, as his interview with Cambon did not take place until the 31st, this is hardly a satisfactory explanation. Moreover, a Cabinet meeting was actually held on this very day.[191] It would have therefore been perfectly easy for him to have pursued the proper course of consulting the Cabinet before talking with Cambon, or at least of informing his colleagues immediately afterwards of what he had said to the French and of the naval and military conversations which were already going on. But he did not do so. Why? One can only conjecture as to this strange aspect of his psychology. Possibly he felt that his talks with Campbell-Bannerman and Haldane after reaching London gave sufficient sanction. Possibly he considered that he was merely continuing Lord Lansdowne's policy, and that a continuation of policy in a matter like foreign affairs, which is not ordinarily supposed to be radically altered by change in parties, did not need to be brought before a new Cabinet. Perhaps he feared that the more

[189] Grey, I, 84.

[190] Grey, I, 84.

[191] Loreburn, *How the War Came,* p. 80 f.

cautious and pacifically inclined members of the Cabinet, like Mr. Morley and Lord Loreburn, and even the Prime Minister himself, would not be willing to go as far as he himself did in encouraging the French and in making joint military preparations. Throughout his memoirs and in his dealings with the Germans, as revealed in the new German documents, one finds that Sir Edward Grey had a very strong undercurrent of sympathy with the French and a correspondingly strong suspicion of Germany's intentions. Probably therefore he preferred to be free to give Cambon his personal friendly views, in a way that he might not have been able to do, if a Cabinet had discussed the subject and adopted a formal statement of policy which would have tied his hands.

At any rate he concealed the matter from the majority of his colleagues in a way which seems hardly to accord with the seeming honesty and frankness of his memoirs. He entered upon that slippery path of thinking that he could encourage the French with joint military preparations, and yet keep his "hands free"—a fatal double policy which he pursued for eight years. After the War, with more experience and with a realization of the seriousness of the criticisms of men like Lord Loreburn, he admits in his memoirs, rather sadly and regretfully, "I think there should have been a Cabinet." [192] In this he is right.

Lord Haldane has left an account of these secret preparations for military coöperation with France. He has told how, in the midst of the General Election of January, 1906, he "at once went to London, summoned the heads of the British General Staff, and saw the French Military Attaché, Colonel Huguet, a man of sense and ability. I became aware at once that there was a new army problem. It was,

[192] Grey, I, 84, and again, p. 96: "I have always regretted that the military conversations were not brought before the Cabinet at once: this would have avoided unnecessary suspicion."

how to mobilize and concentrate at a place of assembly to be opposite the Belgian frontier, a force calculated as adequate (with the assistance of Russian pressure in the East) to make up for the inadequacy of the French armies for their great task of defending the entire French frontier from Dunkirk down to Belfort, or even farther south, if Italy should join the Triple Alliance in an attack."[193] He began therefore at once to organize a British expeditionary force which should coöperate with the French to solve this problem. Impressed with the importance of high morale and quality in modern warfare, he believed that even a small force, if sufficiently long and closely trained, added to French and Russian troops, would be able to defeat any German attempt to invade and dismember France. A close investigation showed that it was not possible under the existing conditions to put in the field more than about 80,000 men, and these only after an interval of over two months.[194] The French naturally pointed out that so slow-moving a machine would be of little use to them; they might be destroyed before it arrived. In their interests, therefore, Haldane had to make "a complete revolution in the organization of the British Army." He accomplished this by the end of 1910. He made it possible "rapidly to mobilize, not only 100,000, but 160,000 men; to transport them, with the aid of the navy, to a place of concentration which had been settled between the Staffs of France and Britain; and to have them at their appointed place within twelve days."[195]

In view of Lord Haldane's own statements of how he saw Colonel Huguet, personally authorized the direct negotiations between the French and British Staffs represented by Huguet and Grierson, and at once reorganized the British

[193] Haldane, *Before the War,* p. 30; see also pp. 28-35 and 156-182.

[194] Haldane, p. 32. If Haldane is correct, General Grierson's assurances to Repington, referred to above at note 182, appear to have been unduly optimistic.

[195] Haldane, p. 33.

Army for coöperation with the French, a sinister light is thrown on the obliquity of the British secret preparations and the denials of their existence, by a statement which Lord Haldane himself made to the German Ambassador in London. It was occasioned by a French deputy who had inconsiderately interpellated M. Clemenceau as to the existence of an Anglo-French military convention. M. Clemenceau had replied evasively, seeming to admit a naval, but not a military, convention. This had naturally roused German fears and suspicions, especially in view of Sir John Fisher's sweeping reorganization of the British Navy, his beginning of the building of dreadnoughts,[196] and the threatening speech of one of the civil Lords of the Admiralty, Mr. Arthur Lee, that the British Fleet would know how to strike the first blow before the other party had read the news in the papers. When questioned by Count Metternich in regard to Clemenceau's declaration, Lord Haldane made a sweeping denial which it is difficult to reconcile with the facts. Taken in conjunction with the secret Anglo-French "conversations" and preparations which had been going on for more than a year, it made an impression in Berlin which may be seen from the Kaiser's marginal notes. According to Count Metternich's report:

> Mr. Haldane replied most definitely that a military convention between France and England did not exist, and had not existed; and also that no preparations had been made for the conclusion of one. Whether non-committal conversations between English and French military persons had taken place or not, he did not know [Kaiser: "Impudence! He, the Minister of a Parliamentary country, not supposed to know that! He lies!"]. At any rate, no English officer has been authorized by the English Government [Kaiser: "Indeed! He did it himself!"] to prepare military arrangements with a French military person for the eventuality of

196 Fisher, *Memories and Records,* II, 65 ff., 128-153.

war. It was possible that a General Staff Officer of one country might have expressed himself to the General Staff Officer of another country as to war-like eventualities. He, the Minister of War, however, knew nothing of this [Kaiser: "Magnificent lies!"].[197]

In the course of these Anglo-French joint military preparations, British and French Staff Officers thoroughly reconnoitered the ground upon which their armies were to fight in Belgium and in France. Sir Henry Wilson, Director of Military Operations, spent his holidays going all over it on his bicycle. The whole wall of his London office was covered by a gigantic map of Belgium, indicating the practicable roads which armies might follow. "He was deeply in the secrets of the French General Staff. For years he had been laboring with one object, that, if war came, we should act immediately on the side of France. He was sure that war would come sooner or later."[198]

Not only the French, but the Russians also, soon came to count upon Haldane's Expeditionary Force as a certain and essential part of their strategic plans in case of a war against Germany. This is significantly indicated, at least as early as 1911, in the secret report, since published by the Bolshevists, of the annual conference between the heads of the French and Russian Staffs. In August, 1911, at Krasnoe Selo, General Dubail was able to assure his Russian colleagues, as a matter of course, "that the French army would concentrate as quickly as the German army, and that from the twelfth day it would be in a position to take the offensive against Germany, *with the aid of the English army on its left wing,*" that is, on the Belgian frontier.[199]

[197] Metternich to Bülow, Jan. 31. 1907; G.P., XXI, 469. On German fears and suspicions of British naval and military intentions, 1904 to 1907, see G.P., XIX, 351-380, "The First German-English War Scare"; XX, 599-698; XXI, 421-521; and Tirpitz, *Politische Dokumente: Der Aufbau der deutschen Weltmacht,* 14 ff.

[198] Churchill, *The World Crisis,* p. 53.

[199] Protocol of the seventh annual Franco-Russian Military Conference, Aug., 31, 1911; L.N., II, 421; M.F.R., p. 698. As early as the annual

THE ANGLO-RUSSIAN ENTENTE OF 1907

An Anglo-Russian Entente, settling the long-standing sources of friction between the two countries in the Middle East, was an obvious complement to the Anglo-French Entente. It appears to have been discussed between King Edward VII and M. Izvolski during the Russo-Japanese War, and to have been warmly received by him and some of the Russian Liberals, though not by the Tsar and the Russian reactionaries and militarists.[200]

Izvolski, though occupying at the time the comparatively unimportant diplomatic post at Copenhagen, was already ambitiously counting upon promotion to a more important position, either as ambassador at one of the great capitals of Europe, or as Russian Minister of Foreign Affairs. He was naturally flattered to be made the recipient by King Edward of a proposal of such far-reaching possibilities. Henceforth he made it one of the cardinal aims of his policy. He saw that Russia was greatly weakened by her war with Japan (which he declares he had tried to avert), and that the Franco-Russian Alliance had conse-

conference of 1908, the Anglo-French connection had become so close that the French officers persuaded the Russians to agree to mobilize all their forces even in case of a German mobilization *against England.* A. Zaiontchkovski, *Les Alliés contre la Russie* (Paris, 1926), pp. 20-21.

200 *The Memoirs of Alexander Iswolsky* (London, 1920), pp. 20, 35, 81 ff.; Ph. Crozier, "L'Autriche et l'Avant-guerre", in *Revue de France,* April 1, 1921, pp. 275-277. According to Witte (Georges Louis, *Carnets,* Paris, 1926, II, 63 f.; Dillon, *Eclipse of Russia,* pp. 350-353; Witte, *Memoirs,* pp. 432-434), Edward VII sent to him, Witte, on his way back from Portsmouth, N. H., in Sept., 1905, the draft of an Anglo-Russian accord. This may be the basis for "Nicky's" letter to "Willy" of Nov. 10/23, 1905 (G.P., XIX, 523): "England is trying hard to get us round for an understanding about Asiatic frontier questions and this directly after the renewed Anglo-Japanese alliance! I have not the slightest wish to open negotiations with her, and so it will drop of itself". Sidney Lee, *King Edward VII,* II, 308 f., mentions only an invitation from Edward VII to Witte to visit England, but says nothing of the draft of an Anglo-Russian accord. For King Edward's urging upon Izvolski an Anglo-Russian Entente in a conversation at Copenhagen in April, 1904, see *ibid.,* II, 284 ff.

quently lost weight in the balance as compared with the Triple Alliance. Both Russia and the Franco-Russian combination needed the strengthening which would come from closer relations with the greatest sea-power in the world.

Izvolski believed that Russia was subject to two serious dangers. One was a possible renewal of trouble with Japan, who had made humiliating demands at Portsmouth and was suspected of preparing for a new struggle in the Far East.[201] Russia needed long years of peace to recover from the effects of the war, and the only method to assure it was to make certain that the Japanese would remain quiet. The best way to accomplish this was to come to an understanding with them by a virtual partition of interests in Manchuria by a secret treaty, though publicly both were pledged to an observance of the "open door." The natural bridge between Russia and Japan was England, Japan's ally since 1902. A *rapprochement* with England would facilitate a sincere reconciliation with Japan, fortify Russia's position as an ally of France, and give a new and more solid basis to the somewhat weakened Franco-Russian Alliance.

The other danger for Russia was that trouble might develop with England as a result of the long-standing conflict of interests in the Near and Middle East. Men still remembered the Crimean War, the strained situation when the British Fleet threatened the Dardanelles in 1878, and the Pendjeh incident which nearly led to war between the two countries in 1885. More recently the Dogger Bank Affair and other incidents of the Russo-Japanese War had inflamed popular feeling in both countries. But a conflict with England would throw Russia into the arms of Germany, and this would endanger the Franco-Russian Alliance which was the foundation rock of Russian policy, in spite of the disappointments which both allies had suffered in connection with it. On the other hand, if Russia could

201 G.P., XXV, 25, 28, 53 ff., 233 f.

wipe the slate clean of her rivalries and quarrels with Great Britain, this would greatly strengthen her own international position. It would allow her to return to an active forward policy in the Balkans after being checkmated in the Far East. It would also be welcomed by France, who would be glad to see her ally and her new friend on better terms with one another. An Anglo-Russian Entente and a reconciliation with Japan might tend toward the formation of a quadruple combination which would quite outmatch the Triple Alliance and could hold in check Austrian ambitions in the Balkans and German ambitions in Turkey. This therefore was the program which Izvolski determined to carry out upon taking up his new position of Russian Minister of Foreign Affairs in May, 1906.

King Edward and Sir Edward Grey were also favorable to an understanding with Russia. The first Morocco crisis and the growing German navy had filled them with suspicions of Germany's intentions and with the desire to remove the danger of Russian enmity in case of possible trouble with Germany. Sir Charles Hardinge was another ardent advocate of a *rapprochement* with Russia. He had been British Ambassador at St. Petersburg since 1904, but was recalled in the fall of 1905 to become Permanent Under Secretary in place of Sir Thomas Sanderson. He took pains to explain in St. Petersburg and London that his recall would afford him an opportunity to work with further success for close Anglo-Russian relations.[202] Henceforth he was to exert a strong pro-Russian influence on Sir Edward Grey in the direction of creating the group of Powers which came to be known as the Triple Entente. In this he was actively seconded by Sir Arthur Nicolson who went to St. Petersburg in his place.[203]

Within a few months after Izvolski took over the Foreign Office from Count Lamsdorf, the Anglo-Russian nego-

[202] G.P., XXV, 3, 10. [203] Grey, I, 155 ff.

tiations were well under way. In passing through Berlin on October 29, 1906, Izvolski admitted that, owing to fears of Japan's aggressive intentions, he was compelled to seek an understanding with England concerning Tibet, Afghanistan, and Persia.[204] Grey and Nicolson worked out draft proposals.[205] These provided for the partition of Persia into spheres of influence. This idea at first met with no approval in St. Petersburg. Russian imperialists demanded that Persia come entirely under Russian influence, and that Russia must build a trans-Persian railway and press on to the Persian Gulf. But Izvolski believed such an aggressive policy was impossible of realization and likely to lead to a conflict with England. So the English proposal for a partition of Persia into English and Russian spheres of influence was adopted.[206] In March, 1907, the visit of a Russian fleet to Portsmouth foreshadowed the coming Anglo-Russian agreement. Upon King Edward's invitation, a deputation of Russian officers and sailors visited London, were entertained as guests at the Admiralty, and given a special show in their honor at the Hippodrome. After a banquet in the evening, there was a gala performance for them at the Alhambra, attended by the First Lord of the Admiralty, Sir John Fisher, and Sir Edward Grey. "It has certainly never happened before," commented the German Ambassador, "that an English Minister of Foreign Affairs has gone to a variety theatre to greet foreign guests." [207]

But, as in the case of the Franco-Russian negotiations two decades earlier, the divergence in political ideals on the Seine and the Neva had delayed an understanding, so now the divergence between English liberalism and Russian autocracy hampered the conclusion of a settlement. The

204 G.P., XX, 39 ff.; XXV, 233 f.

205 Grey to Nicolson, Nov. 6, 1906; Grey, I, 156.

206 Russian Ministerial Council of Feb. 1/14, 1907; Siebert-Schreiner, p. 474 ff.

207 Metternich to Tschirschky, Mar. 28, 1907; G.P., XXV, 32 note.

Russian reactionaries and militarists, and also the Tsar, were at first opposed to a *rapprochement* with England. Izvolski later told Sir Edward Grey that he eventually had great difficulty in getting it accepted.[208] In England likewise the criticism in the Liberal Press of Russian pogroms, the oppressive character of Tsarist absolutism, the suspension of the Duma, and the misunderstanding and friction caused by Sir Henry Campbell-Bannerman's phrase, "La Duma est morte; vive la Duma!", did not facilitate the work of Grey, Hardinge and Nicolson.[209] Nevertheless, the gulf was eventually bridged, owing apparently more to the eagerness and pressure of the British, rather than the Russian, Foreign Office.[210]

Another cause of delay was the English desire that Russia should come to a satisfactory reconciliation with Japan. Grey held it important that the Russo-Japanese and Anglo-Russian negotiations should proceed simultaneously and be concluded practically *pari passu*.[211] As it happened, the Russian agreement with Japan was finally signed on July 30, 1907, a month before that with England. It included a mutual declaration to respect the *status quo* and the rights of one another in the Far East, and a recognition of the independence and territorial integrity of China and the principle of the "open door."[212] These laudable clauses were made known to Germany, but there were evidently secret supplementary clauses, because the secret Russo-Japanese Treaty of 1910 speaks of the demarcation of

208 Grey, I, 177. *Cf.* also Grey to Nicolson, Nov. 6, 1906 (Grey, I, 156): "Of course, I understand M. Izvolski's difficulty with the military party"; and G.P., XXV, 40 ff.

209 Grey, I, 149 ff.; G.P., XXV, 21 ff.

210 This, at any rate was the impression of German observers; *cf* G.P., XXV, 5, 21, 27, 54, 67.

211 Grey to Nicolson, April 1, 1907; Grey, I, 158.

212 See the text in A. M. Pooley, *The Secret Memoirs of Count Tadasu Hayashi* (London, 1915), pp. 224-238, 327-328. *Cf.* also G.P., XXII. 67; and XXV, 53-64.

spheres of interest in Manchuria "as defined in the supplementary article to the Secret Treaty of 1907."[213] And in reality an astonished and disillusioned world, which had counted upon Russo-Japanese rivalry to see to it that the "open door" was preserved in Manchuria, soon discovered that the two empires which had so recently engaged in deadly struggle, had found it convenient to pool their interests in exploiting Manchuria to the practical exclusion of third parties. In various underhand ways, and in virtual defiance of their public declarations in favor of the principle of equal commercial opportunities for all, they practically partitioned Manchuria between themselves.[214] The Russo-Japanese Treaty of July 30, 1907 had been preceded by an agreement[215] settling commercial and fishery questions arising out of the Treaty of Portsmouth between the two countries, and also by a treaty between Japan and France, providing for their mutual interests in the Far East.[216] These treaties of Japan with Russia and France, together with her alliance with England, renewed in 1905, established a basis for friendly coöperation in the Far East on the part of the three Western Powers who were soon to form the so-called Triple Entente. Germany felt diplomatically isolated. She put out some feelers to President Roosevelt for an Entente with the United States for the preservation of China and of their mutual interests in the Far East. But these feelers were not successful.[217]

Finally, on August 31, 1907, there was signed the Anglo-Russian Agreement dealing with the Middle East—Tibet,

[213] Siebert-Schreiner, p. 17.

[214] *Ibid.*, pp. 8-43. G.P., XXXII, *passim*. T. F. Millard, *America and the Far Eastern Question* (New York, 1909), chs. xv-xx. S. K. Hornbeck, *Contemporary Politics in the Far East* (New York, 1916), ch. xv. O. Franke, *Die Grossmächte in Ostasien* (Hamburg, 1923), pp. 308-343; Tyler Dennett, *Americans in Eastern Asia* (New York, 1922).

[215] July 28, 1907; *cf.* Pooley, *l.c.*, pp. 229 ff.

[216] June 10, 1907; *ibid.*, pp. 212-223, 325-6; and G.P., XXV, 53 ff., 67 ff.

[217] G.P., XXV, 67-99.

Afghanistan, and Persia.[218] Both contracting Powers recognized the territorial integrity of Tibet under the suzerainty of China, and agreed not to interfere with the country's internal concerns or attempt to secure special concessions there. The land of the Lamas was to remain a barrier between the Russian bear and the British lion in India.

As to Afghanistan, in return for an English promise not to occupy or annex it so long as the Ameer fulfilled his obligations, Russia declared the country to be outside her sphere of influence; she withdrew her diplomatic agents from Herat and agreed to deal with the Ameer only through the British authorities. Afghanistan therefore was no longer to be a field for Russian intrigue against India, and the English were freed from a great bugbear that had worried them for a century.

Persia was by far the most important subject of the Agreement. Though the preamble piously declared that the two Great Powers mutually agreed to respect the "integrity" and "independence" of Persia, the Agreement went on to divide Persia into three regions: the northern and largest region, bordering on Russia and comprising the richest and most populous parts of Persia, was to be a Russian sphere of influence, in which Great Britain would not seek for herself, or any third Power, any concessions of a political or commercial nature. The southern region, largely barren desert but containing roads leading to India, was in like manner to be a British sphere, in which Russia would seek no concessions. Between these two lay a central neutral region, including the head of the Persian Gulf, in which neither Great Power was to seek concessions except in agreement with the other. In all this the Shah was not consulted in the least. A cartoon in *Punch* hit off the

218 For the text see *British Foreign and State Papers,* vol. 100, pp. 555 ff.

arrangement aptly enough: the British lion and the Russian bear are seen mauling between them an unhappy Persian cat; the lion is saying to the bear, "Look here! *You* can play with his head, and *I* can play with his tail, and we can *both* stroke the small of his back"; while the poor cat moans, "I don't remember having been consulted about this." [219]

In his memoirs Viscount Grey argues, but unconvincingly, that England had the better of the bargain: "What we gained by it was real—what Russia gained was apparent." [220] In fact, the reverse was true. Though England gained peace of mind in regard to the Indian frontier, she also lost much. She lost her independence of action in Persia. Hitherto she had been free to protest and object to the encroachments of the Russian imperialist steam-roller crushing southward upon defenseless Persia. Henceforth she found herself involved as an accomplice in the destruction of the financial and political independence of the Shah's empire. Sir Edward Grey soon found himself drawn along in the wake of Russian aggression and intrigue, in a way most embarrassing to him when questioned on the subject in the House of Commons. He protested frequently against the activities of Russian agents in Persia. He even hinted he would resign. "Persia," he says, "tried my patience more than any other subject." [221] Russian unscrupulousness and double-dealing in the Middle East continued to be a recurrent source of annoyance to him almost up to the outbreak of the World War. One of President Poincaré's objects in visiting St. Petersburg in July, 1914, was to smooth this discord in the harmony of the Triple

219 "The Harmless Necessary Cat," *Punch,* CXXXIII, 245, Oct. 2, 1907.

220 Grey, I, 155.

221 Grey, I, 164. *Cf.* Siebert-Schreiner, p. 550 (where Grey's irritation and talk of resignation were due to Russia's "Potsdam agreements" in 1910-11), and p. 615 (where they were due to Russian action in Persia).

Entente.[222] But Grey was helpless to make his protests effective, because his distrust of Germany made him unwilling to take a really stiff attitude to Russia, or to recede from the Agreement of 1907, lest he should thereby endanger the solidarity of the Triple Entente. The Russians were quite aware of this, and took advantage of it. Sazonov put the situation in a nutshell in a significant letter to the Russian Minister in Teheran:

> The London Cabinet looks upon the Anglo-Russian Convention of 1907 as being important for the Asiatic interests of England; but this Convention possesses a still greater importance for England from the viewpoint of the policy which is being pursued by England in Europe. . . . The English, engaged in the pursuit of political aims of vital importance in Europe, may, in case of necessity, be prepared to sacrifice certain interests in Asia in order to keep a Convention alive which is of such importance to them. This is a circumstance which we can, of course, exploit for ourselves, as, for instance, in Persian affairs.[223]

Though the Anglo-Russian Convention was all made public, included no obligations of military or diplomatic support, and did not at once lead to a closely knit diplomatic partnership, it did nevertheless complete the circle for a closer political coöperation between Rusisa, France and England. The Press of these countries began to talk of the new "Triple Entente."

222 Poincaré, *Les Origines de la Guerre,* p. 201 f. *Cf.* K.D., 52.

223 Oct. 8, 1910; Siebert-Schreiner, p. 99. The dismal and disgraceful story of how Russia did this may be read in Siebert-Schreiner, pp. 49-141, and in the engaging personal narrative of the blunt financial American adviser who tried—in vain—to rescue the Persian cat from the deadly grasp of the Russian bear: W. Morgan Shuster, *The Strangling of Persia* (New York, 1913).

CHAPTER IV

THE SYSTEM OF SECRET ALLIANCES, 1907-1914: TRIPLE ALLIANCE AND TRIPLE ENTENTE IN OPPOSITION

BETWEEN the years 1907 and 1914 there was an increasing crystallization of opposition between the two groups into which the six Great Powers of Europe had now become divided. During the first four years it developed slowly; then, with the French occupation of Fez, the German threat at Agadir, the Italian seizure of Tripoli, Anglo-German naval rivalry, the failure of the Haldane Mission, and the Balkan Wars, it proceeded more rapidly. It was reflected in Morocco, Mesopotamia, the Balkans, and in many other matters, ranging all the way from European armaments to Chinese loans. In the case of the Balkans, it was so fundamental and so closely bound up with the immediate causes of the World War, that a separate chapter on "Balkan Problems," following the present one, will be devoted to some aspects of it in that troubled region. But to give a full account of this crystallizing opposition in all its complicated and disputed phases would go far beyond the limits of this volume. Fortunately, it has been excellently summed up by others.[1] No attempt therefore is here made

[1] Bernadotte E. Schmitt, "Triple Alliance and Triple Entente, 1902-1914" in *Amer. Hist. Rev.*, XXIX, 449-473 (April, 1924); G. P. Gooch, *History of Modern Europe, 1878-1918* (New York, 1923), chs. xi-xvi; E. Brandenburg, *Von Bismarck zum Weltkriege* (Berlin, 1924), chs. xi-xvii, of which the second edition (1926) is now available in an English translation; G. L. Dickinson, *The International Anarchy, 1904-1914* (London, 1926); and many others. Professor C. R. Beazley also is said to be preparing a considerable work on the diplomatic situation preceding the War.

to give any detailed account of this period. The aim has been rather to indicate, in the light of the new German documents, M. Poincaré's *Memoirs,* and other recently published material, the more important factors which increased this crystallizing opposition and gave it the fatal turn which it took in 1914.

This opposition of Triple Alliance and Triple Entente was accompanied and accentuated by four sets of tendencies.

(1) Both systems of alliance tended to be deformed from their originally defensive character. They tended to become widened in scope to cover policies involving offensive military action. For example, Germany felt compelled to back up Austria, if her ally became involved in war with Russia by her efforts at self-preservation from the "Greater Serbia" danger—in a way which Bismarck would hardly have tolerated. In precisely the same way, France under M. Poincaré felt compelled to back up Russia, if her ally became involved in war with Austria and Germany by her efforts to safeguard her Balkan ambitions—in a way which M. Poincaré's predecessors would hardly have permitted.

(2) Germany tried to strengthen the Triple Alliance, and, similarly, M. Poincaré tried to tighten up and strengthen the Triple Entente. But the latter was more successful than the former. The Triple Alliance, in spite of its renewal in 1907 and in 1912, tended to become relatively weaker. It was weakened by Austria's internal troubles and Balkan complications, by the deep-seated distrust between Austria and Italy, and by Italy's *sacro egoismo,* which often made her oppose her allies, especially Austria, in diplomatic questions and caused her allies to doubt her loyalty in case of war. The Triple Entente, on the other hand, became relatively stronger, because its members were not divided from one another by any such sharp conflicts of interest as between Austria and Italy, and because England, France, and Russia were able to make in-

creasingly close arrangements for military and naval coöperation.

(3) Although the Triple Alliance and Triple Entente—and especially the latter—were tightened up and strengthened, there still remained more occasions of friction, distrust, and suspicion within each diplomatic group than is commonly supposed. This will be seen also in the next chapter on "Balkan Problems." There was in fact by no means so much harmony and mutual confidence within the Triple Alliance as was usually assumed by writers a few years ago—nor was there so much within the Triple Entente as has been assumed by "revisionist" writers more recently. Italy's "extra dance" with France after 1902, and with Russia after Racconigi in 1909, were the most notable examples of this kind of domestic unfaithfulness within a diplomatic group, and continued to be a source of uncertainty and worry on all sides. But Italy's case was merely an example of what the Triple Entente feared might happen within its own circle. France, for instance, was much worried whenever England entered into confidential negotiations with Germany, as in the Haldane Mission or in the Bagdad Railway question; or when Russia made with Germany the Potsdam Agreements of 1910-1911, or seemed inclined to undertake diplomatic maneuvers in the Balkans without first fully informing her French ally, as happened on several occasions. Sir Edward Grey was worried lest the Entente with Russia concerning the Middle East would break down, if he did not give her the diplomatic support which M. Sazonov desired at critical moments, as in the Liman von Sanders affair—and in July, 1914. When he made friendly arrangements with Germany in regard to the Bagdad Railway and the Portuguese colonies, he thought it prudent to counter-balance them, as it were, by consenting to the desire of his two Entente friends that he should enter into negotiations for an Anglo-Russian naval con-

vention. Germany also found herself frequently embarrassed by the "stupidities" in which Austria indulged in the Balkans, against Germany's better judgment or without her approval. Within each group therefore special efforts were continually being made to lessen the friction and suspicion, and to increase the harmony, solidarity, and security of the group. This was done by making concessions to the selfish aims or special interests of the fellow members, or by giving "blank cheques" to one's ally in the shape of assurances of "complete fulfilment of the obligations of the alliance," even in matters which might easily develop into a European war. The acquiescence or encouragement which M. Poincaré gave to Russia, and which Germany gave to Austria, is to be explained in large part by this desire to preserve the solidarity of the group, rather than by any desire for a war to recover Alsace-Lorraine in the one case, or to gain the hegemony of Europe in the other. But it had the effect of encouraging Russia and Austria along the slippery Balkan path which eventually led to the yawning chasm of 1914.

(4) In both groups of Powers there was a rapid increase of military and naval armaments. This caused increasing suspicions, fears, and newspaper recriminations in the opposite camp. This in turn led to more armaments; and so to the vicious circle of ever growing war preparations and mutual fears and suspicions. In 1907, before the opposition had crystallized clearly, the Triple Alliance and Triple Entente, in Professor Schmitt's happy phrase, "had stood side by side; in 1914 they stood face to face."

GERMAN FEAR OF "ENCIRCLEMENT" AFTER 1907

Germany at first gave an outward appearance of accepting the Anglo-Russian Convention of 1907 with equanimity. Even before its conclusion, Count Bülow, in his Reichstag speech of April 30, 1907, had referred to the negotiations with quiet optimism. Afterwards, when the Anglo-Russian Convention was published, he instructed the German Press to be moderate and practical in its comments, and to accept the Convention for what it professed to be—a settlement of Anglo-Russian differences and not a combination inimical to German interests.

But in reality Germany felt very uneasy. She feared that the clauses in regard to Tibet, Afghanistan, and Persia were not merely an end in themselves, but rather a means to an end—the formation of a diplomatic combination on the part of England, France, and Russia. This Triple Entente would outmatch the Triple Alliance in diplomatic strength because Italy, owing to her hatred and jealousy of Austria in the Balkans and her desire to stand well with France and England, would vote with them, rather than with her own allies, as she had done at Algeciras. The Triple Entente Powers would also outmatch the Triple Alliance in economic resources and in military and naval strength. They would therefore feel able to block Germany's construction of the Bagdad Railway, obstruct her industry and commerce, and thwart her colonial ambitions, wherever these came into competition with their own. Moreover, in the most inflammable subjects, like Alsace-Lorraine, Morocco, the Middle East, and naval competition, one or other of the Entente Powers stood in direct opposition to Germany. The Balkans also might easily prove another highly inflammable subject. If Russia's reconciliation with England should prove (as it turned out to be the case) the preliminary to a Russian effort to revive her old aggressive Balkan policy, and to recover in the Near East the prestige which she had lost in the Far East, the ally of France would almost inevitably come into conflict with the ally of Germany. If a crisis should arise over any of these questions, Germany, supported by Austria and perhaps by Italy, would be likely to find herself faced by the Triple Entente and its superior strength. Germany would either have to back down or fight. Neither prospect, under the circumstances, was attractive.

These were the considerations which preyed upon the minds of the Germans and created a nervous *malaise* which finally took form in the conviction that they were being "encircled." Though Russia and England had protested abundantly that the Anglo-Russian Convention was in no way directed against Germany and had no ulterior purposes, their words did not carry conviction at Berlin, and their attitude in regard to the Bagdad Railway seemed to indicate a collective determination to obstruct one of Germany's dearest projects.

In 1902 Germany secured from Turkey the concession for the Bagdad Railway. This was to extend the rail connection from the eastern terminus of the Anatolian Railway at Konia, already in German hands, all the way via Bagdad to the Persian Gulf. The next year the Deutsche Bank made arrangements with the Ottoman Bank for financing the construction of the line. Germany desired and invited the participation of foreign capital in the costly enterprise. But she soon met with opposition, instead of coöperation, on the part of Russia, France, and England.[2]

Russia, on various political, economic, and strategic grounds, had been opposed from the outset to the whole German railway project. Moreover, since she had no surplus capital for investment, there was never any serious question of her financial participation in it. Her policy was to obstruct a scheme to which she had many objections and in which she was unable to take a part.

In France, the bankers, for the most part, favored par-

[2] *Cf.* G.P., XVII, 371-517; XXV, 177-280; and the excellent account in E. M. Earle, *Turkey, the Great Powers, and the Bagdad Railway* (New York, 1923), chs. iv-viii, with bibliographical notes. These are now supplemented to some extent by the *British Documents,* II, 174-196.

ticipation, both because they already had large investments in Turkey, and because this looked like another good business proposition. The French Government, however, favorable at first, then hesitating, finally declared its opposition to the investment of French capital in the German undertaking. M. Delcassé even went to the point of preventing Bagdad Railway bonds from being quoted on the Paris Bourse.[3] This hostile attitude of the French Government was partly owing to the vigorous representations made by French commercial interests, clericals, and politicians, and partly also, if we are to believe M. Izvolski, to French desire to support the policy of their Russian ally.[4]

In England Mr. Balfour and Lord Lansdowne had stated at first, on April 7, 1903, that the British Government approved the bankers' negotiations for the participation of British capital in the construction of the Bagdad Railway. But at once an outcry was raised in the British Press and in Parliament against the Government's favorable attitude: the railway would injure British vested interests in Mesopotamia and the Persian Gulf; it would increase the influence of the Germans in Turkey at British expense and bring them too close to India; it would rouse suspicions in Russia as to British intentions; and, in any case, the English ought not to participate, unless they did so on equal terms and to the same extent as the Germans. So Mr. Balfour was forced to announce in the House of Commons on April 23 his repudiation of the approval which he had given on April 7.[5] Henceforth the British also were inclined to obstruct the railway in various indirect ways. They long refused to consent to the raising of the Turkish tariff from eight to

3 G.P., XXV, 195; Earle, p. 147 ff.

4 G.P., XXV, 231. Russian influence was also suspected of causing England's change of attitude from one of favor to one of opposition; G.P., XVII, 443.

5 *Parliamentary Debates, House of Commons* (1903), CXX, 1247-8, 1358, 1361, 1354-7, 1371-4; CXXI, 271 f.; G.P., XVII, 431 ff.; Earle, p. 176 ff.

eleven per cent. Their ostensible reason was that the burden of the increase would largely fall on themselves, because they had the largest share of the trade with Turkey. But the practical result was that it made it more difficult for the Turkish Government to finance the kilometric and income guarantees which the Bagdad Railway agreement called for, and which seemed necessary for its construction.

In spite of this policy of opposition and non-participation on the part of the three Entente Powers, the Germans managed to push rapidly the building of the first 200-kilometer section from Konia to Eregli. Within something over a year, on the Sultan's birthday, October 25, 1904, they were able to open this first section to traffic with pompous ceremonies and justifiable self-congratulation. But here construction came to a sudden stop, and the rail ends were left sticking out into space. The next 200-kilometer section, reaching toward the Taurus Mountains, involved innumerable engineering difficulties and a far greater expenditure per kilometer of construction. The Turkish Government could not arrange the financing of additional bonds to meet the guarantees for this section without an increase in her customs revenues. Yet it was impossible for Turkey to raise her tariff, as she desired to do, because by existing treaties she could not do so without the consent of the Great Powers; and Russia, France, and England for a long time refused to give their consent.[6] By their refusal they practically blocked the further construction for the next few years.

In the course of 1905 and the following year Germany attempted some negotiations in a renewed effort to secure

6 G.P., XXII, 329-400; Earle, p. 95 f. They finally gave their consent in September, 1906, to become effective in July, 1907, but attached numerous conditions which made it difficult to divert any of the increased revenue to the payment of railway guarantees. One condition was that three-fourths of the increased revenue must go to Macedonian reform.

the financial participation and political coöperation of the French and the British in the building of the Bagdad Railway. After Delcassé's fall there was talk of a deal with M. Rouvier, by which Germany's Moroccan claims should be abandoned in exchange for French support to the Bagdad Railway. But the talk came to nothing.[7] In the summer of 1906 some members of the new Liberal Government in England, including Grey and Haldane, were believed to desire a Bagdad settlement with Germany. But Sir Edward Grey, in the spirit of the Entente with France, insisted that if England participated, France also must participate.[8] The English Press also demanded that, either the whole Bagdad Railway ought to be internationalized, or, if Germany controlled the railway as far as Bagdad, then England ought to control the section from Bagdad down to the Persian Gulf.[9] But no practical arrangement could be found for satisfying these English demands. Similarly, long German negotiations with Izvolski, contemplating German abstention from activity in Persia if Russia would withdraw her opposition to the Bagdad Railway, reached no definite conclusion.[10]

Three months after the signature of the Anglo-Russian Convention of 1907 the Kaiser visited Windsor and was cordially received. He took advantage of the occasion to reopen the Bagdad Railway discussion with Lord Haldane and Sir Edward Grey. He found that the former, as Minister of War, was anxious that the British should control the section from Bagdad to the Persian Gulf, as a "gate," to protect India from the possibility of troops coming down the new railway. The Kaiser at once declared, "I will give you the gate," and telegraphed to Bülow to this effect.[11] A lively exchange of views followed for a few hours in

[7] G.P., XX, 356, 395 f., 431; XXV, 180 f., 194 ff.; Earle, p. 169 ff.
[8] G.P., XXV, 226. [9] G.P., XXV, 240 ff. [10] G.P., XXV, 103-175.
[11] G.P., XXV, 261 ff.; Haldane, *Before the War*, p. 48 ff.

Windsor, London and Berlin. The British "recognized that the object of the commercial development of Mesopotamia was one that should not be opposed." But they desired "that the quickest route between West and East should not be under the exclusive control of a virtually foreign company, which would be in a position to affect seriously commercial relations between England and India, or to sanction its use for strategic purposes in hostility to British interests"; they "could not, however, discuss this question *à deux,* but only *à quatre,* for the various interests, strategical, political and commercial, affect France and Russia as well."[12] Sir Edward Grey's insistence that France and Russia must be associated with England in the discussions proved a fatal obstacle to reaching any satisfactory agreement on the Kaiser's proposal. Lord Haldane laid the blame for this on the German Foreign Office, which he thinks did not approve of the Kaiser's move. And there is some truth in this view.[13] But it is also true that Sir Edward Grey's insistence on conversations *à quatre* was a main cause of the Kaiser's offer of the "gate" remaining abortive. Germany objected that, since France had no special interests in Mesopotamia and the Persian Gulf, and since Russia's interests related largely to Persia, she could satisfy these two countries in separate negotiations. But if the whole Bagdad Railway question was to be dealt with in conversations *à quatre,* Germany would inevitably be in a minority of one to three. Germany therefore could not be expected to negotiate at such a disadvantage and subject her interests to the united opposition of the other three.[14] Sir Edward Grey's insistence on the solidarity of England, France and Russia, in this matter of the Bagdad Railway

12 Note of a private conversation between Sir Edward Grey and Mr. Haldane on Nov. 14, 1907, given by the latter to the Kaiser; G.P., XXV, 263.

13 *Cf.* Bülow to Schoen, Nov. 14, 1907; *ibid.,* 261.

14 G.P., XXIV, 77, 83; XXV, 264 ff.

in the fall of 1907, foreshadowed the solidarity of the Triple Entente in wider fields later. It also put an end to any important further discussions of the Bagdad question until Russia deserted her friends in making with Germany the "Potsdam Agreements" of 1910-1911.

ANGLO-GERMAN NAVAL RIVALRY, 1904-1908

The German suspicion that England was aiming to limit Germany's freedom of action also arose in connection with the Second Hague Peace Conference and the naval discussions at the beginning of the period of *Dreadnought* construction and rivalry. The British navy had just been reorganized and strengthened by Sir John Fisher, while the German navy was just beginning to grow in power. The proposal to discuss the limitation of armaments, urged by England, looked like a scheme to arrest naval development. It seemed to prevent Germany from catching up in strength at a moment when England still enjoyed a marked naval superiority. Nor could Germany, with Austria weakened by internal difficulties and Italy an ally of doubtful loyalty, consent to limit her army. There was the danger of a war on two fronts, when Russia should have recovered from her war with Japan and revived her active Balkan policy. So Germany insisted that the limitation of armaments should not be one of the subjects included in the call for the Conference. When the subject was nevertheless raised in the course of the Conference by England and the United States, Germany's opposition to it was, to be sure, largely but tacitly shared by France and Russia. But these two countries left it to the German delegates to voice the opposition and thereby incur the odium of wrecking the proposals.

No doubt Germany made a great mistake. Though limitation of armaments is a most difficult problem, as the long and sterile efforts of the League of Nations and the failure of President Coolidge's Conference have abundantly shown, it is possible that, had Germany taken a different attitude in 1907, the other European Powers might have followed her, and a beginning might have been made to check the fatal increase in rival armies and navies. At any rate Germany could not have been branded as the country which was most responsible for thwarting an effort to lessen a progressive danger which was one of the main causes of the World War.[15]

By the irony of history it was during the Hague Peace Conference that Anglo-German naval rivalry reached a new and hitherto unequalled stage of mutual suspicion and bitterness. By the Navy Laws of 1898 and 1900 Admiral von Tirpitz and the Kaiser laid the foundations for a strong German navy. Their motives were many and mixed. They wished to give expression to the greatness of the New Germany by creating a fleet which should be comparable to her growing commerce and colonial interests and afford them protection. They desired preservation from the danger of being blockaded from food and raw materials in case of war. But above all, they wanted to have a naval force which could be used to back up German diplomatic arguments in the struggle for colonial and commercial advantages. The Kaiser's marginal notes are filled with the idea that other countries, and particularly England, paid little or no heed to Germany's legitimate desires, simply because Germany had no force to back up her demands. If Germany had a navy, even a much smaller one than that of England, the British would be willing to make diplomatic concessions rather than take the risk of a naval conflict. This was Tirpitz's fundamental notion when he speaks of the new German navy as a "risk navy." He had no thought

15 On the Second Hague Conference, see G.P., XXIII, 99-397, and the writings of A. P. Higgins, F. W. Holls, J. B. Scott, A. H. Fried, O. Nippold, P. Zorn, L. Renault, and E. Lémonon. The Reichstag Investigating Committee is soon to publish an important work on Germany's influence at the Second Hague Peace Conference.

of attacking England in any near future. That would be folly for many years to come. But a respectable German sea force would compel England to make concessions in the colonial world rather than take the "risk" of a naval struggle. For this it was not necessary for Germany to build a fleet fully equal to that of England; some proportion like 2:3 or 10:16 would suffice.[16]

But in fact Admiral Tirpitz completely misconceived the psychological effect which his creation of even a "risk navy" would have on the British mind and policy. Though it may have contributed to induce the British to make various proposals for limiting naval competition and to enter into various diplomatic negotiations, it did not intimidate them or cause them to make important concessions. On the contrary, it rather created an atmosphere of suspicion and antagonism which was altogether unfavorable for friendly diplomatic agreements concerning the Bagdad Railway and other matters. Every increase in the German navy, instead of frightening the British into making concessions, tended to stiffen their opposition and their determination to maintain the wide margin of British naval superiority deemed vital to the safety and very existence of the British Empire.

So, for instance, in 1904, as the English observed the new-born German navy, still in its infancy but already showing signs of robust growth, they began a wide-sweeping rearrangement and reorganization of the British Fleet. They proceeded to create a strong force in the North Sea and make it ready for instant action against Germany. Sir John Fisher, with his characteristically energetic policy of "Ruthless, Relentless, and Remorseless!"[17] "brought home some 160 ships from abroad which could neither fight nor run away,"[18] and effected other revolutionary changes,

[16] *Cf.* Tirpitz, *Der Aufbau der deutschen Weltmacht* (Berlin, 1926), *passim.*

[17] Fisher, *Memories and Records*, II. 135.

[18] Fisher, II, 65 f., 139 ff.

so that, as he himself said, "We shall be thirty per cent. more fit to fight and we shall be ready for instant war!" [19]

The next year he laid the keels for the first *Dreadnoughts.* These were to be far superior to anything afloat and give the British navy a strength which no country could menace. But their introduction more than doubled the cost of capital ship construction. Furthermore, they rendered relatively less important the older and smaller types of vessel which had hitherto constituted England's naval superiority. It enabled Tirpitz to follow England's example, and be only a little behind her in the race in the construction of this new type of vessel, which neither country had possessed hitherto; whereas in the older types of vessel Germany was hopelessly behind. To express the same thing in figures: England had authorized the laying down by 1908 of 12, and Germany of 9 Dreadnoughts; whereas the ratio between England and Germany in vessels of the older pre-Dreadnought type was 63:26. Tirpitz also believed that Germany, where sailors were conscripted instead being paid wages for voluntary enlistment, and where cost of ship construction was relatively low, could stand longer and more easily than England the heavy strain of naval expenditure. With this double advantage on Germany's part, as it seemed to him, he was always skeptical about the sincerity and motives of British proposals for restriction of naval construction. He was steadily opposed to any serious limitation on his own program, by which he believed the German navy could gradually approach nearer in strength to the British navy, though it might never actually equal it. It would have to pass through the "danger zone" of inferiority, during which England might possibly attack and destroy it in a "preventive" war. But he did not think this danger great, especially if German diplomacy avoided irritating England in other fields. Once safely

[19] Fisher, *Memories and Records,* II, 134.

through the "danger zone," after a dozen years, Germany would have a very respectable "risk navy." Germany could stand the financial strain; in the long run England could not. So all Germany had to do was to push construction.

Thus, by a third Navy Law in 1906, Tirpitz secured the authorization of six new capital ships; and by the law of 1908, reducing the replacement period from 25 to 20 years, he provided for the early replacement of old obsolete vessels by new ships, not of the same size as the discarded ones, but of the new Dreadnought type. This law of 1908 fixed the construction of new and replacement ships of the Dreadnought type at the rate of four a year from 1908 to 1911, and two a year from 1912 to 1917. Meanwhile the German Navy League was clamoring for a big German navy. The Press on both sides of the North Sea was whipping up national passion, and the rumors of the Kaiser's ill-considered letter to Lord Tweedmouth added fuel to the flame. All this led to the British "war-scare" of 1908, and to further futile negotiations for some kind of a naval understanding.[20]

Sir Henry Campbell-Bannerman, in a speech on December 21, 1905, setting forth the platform of the new Liberal Government, had lamented the great expenditures on armaments: "A policy of huge armaments keeps alive and stimulates and feeds the belief that force is the best, if not the only, solution of international differences. It is a policy that tends to inflame old sores and to create new sores. . . . We want relief from the pressure of excessive taxation, and

[20] On Anglo-German naval relations 1904-1908, see Fisher, I, ch. xii; II, chs. ix, x; Churchill, pp. 19-41; Hurd and Castle, *German Sea-Power* (New York, 1913); Schmitt, *England and Germany, 1740-1914* (Princeton, 1916), 173-187; and, in more detail, from the German side, G.P., XIX, 351-380; XXIII, 27-53; XXIV, 3-210; Tirpitz, *Der Aufbau der deutschen Weltmacht,* 1-162; Bülow, *Imperial Germany* (Berlin, 1913); Haller, *Die Aera Bülow* (Berlin, 1922); Brandenburg, ch. xi; Herzfeld, "Der deutsche Flottenbau und die englische Politik," in *Archiv f. Politik u. Geschichte,* IV, 1926, 115-146, and Admiral Karl Galster *England, Deutsche Flotte, und Weltkrieg* (Kiel, 1925).

at the same time we want money for our own domestic needs at home, which have been too long starved and neglected owing to the demands on the taxpayer for military purposes abroad. How are these desirable things to be secured if in time of peace our armaments are maintained on a war footing?"[21] In the course of the next three years, the English made many proposals for reducing naval expenditure and thereby lessening the growing friction with Germany. It was proposed that the subject should be discussed at the Hague Peace Conference;[22] that Sir John Fisher should have a talk with Admiral Tirpitz; or that there should be a mutual inspection of shipyards and communication of naval programs.[23] It was informally intimated that, if Germany was uneasy at England's "insurance policy" of closer relations with France and Russia, the best way to dissipate this uneasiness and revive the former cordial Anglo-German relations would be for Germany to retard her naval program, or come to some understanding for an agreed-upon ratio between the English and German navies.[24]

But England could never get a satisfactory answer from Germany to any of these proposals. Being made after Sir John Fisher had so greatly strengthened the Home Fleet in the North Sea and begun to build Dreadnoughts, these proposals looked to the German mind like an intimation from the Supreme Naval Power that it desired naval competition to cease at the moment of its own greatest preponderance. Coinciding also with Lord Haldane's organization of the

[21] The London *Times,* Dec. 22, 1905; *cf.* also Spender, *Life of Sir Henry Campbell-Bannerman,* II, 208, 327-332.

[22] G.P., XXIII, 25-253 *passim; cf.* also Campbell-Bannerman's cordial and conciliatory article, "The Hague Conference and the Limitation of Armaments", in the first number of the London *Nation,* Mar. 2, 1907; Campbell-Bannerman's views, however, were severely criticized in the Paris *Temps* of March 4; the French, at bottom, had no more sympathy with disarmament proposals than the Germans.

[23] G.P., XXIII, 39 ff., 52.

[24] G.P., XXIV, 99 ff.

British Expeditionary Force and with England's closer diplomatic relations with France and Russia, they looked like a concerted plan on the part of these three Powers to put pressure on Germany. Any yielding to such pressure was sharply resented as inconsistent with Germany's dignity as a Great Power. As Bülow wrote privately to Bavaria and some of the other German Governments on June 25, 1908, after President Fallières's visit to London and King Edward's famous meeting with the Tsar at Reval: "Agreements which aim at a limitation of our defensive power are not acceptable for discussion by us under any circumstances. A Power which should demand such an agreement from us should be clear in its mind that such a demand would mean war." [25] By the Kaiser especially, the British proposals were indignantly repudiated as unjustifiable attempts to interfere with his sovereign right and duty to take all measures necessary for the dignity and defense of the German Empire. Commenting upon Count Metternich's report of July 16, 1908, of an informal luncheon discussion with Sir Edward Grey and Lloyd George, in which it had been intimated that a naval discussion would improve diplomatic relations, the Kaiser wrote:

> Count Metternich must be informed that good relations with England at the price of the building of the German navy are *not* desired by me. If England intends graciously to extend us her hand only with the intimation that we must limit our fleet, this is a groundless impertinence, which involves a heavy insult to the German people and their Kaiser, which must be rejected *a limine* by the Ambassador. . . . France and Russia might with equal reason then demand a limitation of our land armaments. The German Fleet is not built *against* anyone, and also not *against* England! But

[25] G.P., XXV, 478. For other German intimations that any attempt to put pressure on Germany to limit her navy would be answered by declaration of war, see G.P., XXIV, 53, 103, 127.

> according to *our* need! That is stated quite clearly in the Navy Law, and for 11 years has remained unchanged! This law will be carried out to the last iota; whether it suits the British or not, is no matter! If they want war, they can begin it; we do not fear it! [26]

The Kaiser's fears that England was trying to put a check upon Germany's navy, and "encircle" her in other ways, were increased by the numerous visits and interviews which Edward VII had with French and Russian rulers and ministers in the summer of 1908. In May President Fallières was very cordially received in London and given a dinner at the Foreign Office to which the only person invited, outside a French and English group, was the Russian Ambassador—a distinction which seemed to embarrass good Count Benckendorff.[27] The French Press made the most of the visit, and Tardieu in the *Temps* expressed the hope that Anglo-French relations were taking a firmer form, provided England made fundamental changes in her military system —a hint at the universal military service which Lord Roberts and others were now beginning urgently to advocate in public speeches. In June, King Edward's visit to the Tsar at Reval seemed more than a mere act of family courtesy, since he was accompanied by Admiral Fisher, Sir John French, and Sir Charles Hardinge, who had long talks with Izvolski and the Russian Premier, Stolypin. Hardinge told Izvolski that England had no hostile feelings toward Germany and was anxious to maintain the most friendly relations with her, but that "owing to the unnecessarily large increase in the German naval program, a deep distrust in England of Germany's future intentions had been created." This distrust was likely to increase with the progress

26 G.P., XXIV, 104

27 G.P., XXIV, 63. On President Fallières's visit, the French Press, and Delcassé's talks with Asquith, Grey, and Sir Charles Hardinge on his "private visit" to London a month later, see G.P., XXIV, pp. 57-78; and Sidney Lee, *King Edward VII*, II, 584 ff.

of time, the realization of the German program, and the heavier taxation entailed by England's necessary naval counter-measures. "In seven or eight years' time a critical situation might arise, in which Russia, if strong in Europe, might be the arbiter of peace, and have much more influence in securing the peace of the world than at any Hague Conference. For this reason it was absolutely necessary that England and Russia should maintain towards each other the same cordial and friendly relations as now exist between England and France." [28] Izvolski got the impression that the English wanted Russia to build up her army and navy as much as possible as a future check to Germany.

Sir John Fisher relates that he sat several times next Stolypin and Izvolski, and urged them to build up the Russian army on the Western frontier against Germany: "Stolypin said to me, 'What do you think we need most?' He fancied I should answer, 'So many battleships, so many cruisers, etc., etc.,' but instead I said, 'Your Western Frontier is denuded of troops and your magazines are depleted. Fill them up and then talk of Fleets!' Please see enclosure from Kuropatkin's secret report: 'The foundation of Russia's safety is her Western boundary!' " [29]

[28] Grey, I, 203. Viscount Grey prints Hardinge's report on the Reval conversations (I, 202-209), and calls it (p. 196) "the real, full, authentic confidential record of what took place"; but he indicates on p. 209 that sundry details concerning Macedonian reforms, Persia, and Crete are omitted. For Hardinge's complete report, see B.D., V, 232-246. *Cf.* Izvolski's account of the Reval meeting in his despatch to Benckendorff in London, June 18, 1908 (Siebert-Schreiner, p. 478), according to which Hardinge said: "If Germany should continue to increase her naval armaments at the same accelerated pace, in six or seven years a most alarming and strained situation might arise in Europe. For this reason we in the interest of peace and the preservation of the Balance of Power, desire that Russia shall be as strong as possible on land and on sea." Izvolski added, "Sir Charles reiterated this idea more than once, whereby he apparently wished to have it understood that he is expressing not his own personal opinion, but the decided political conviction of the London Cabinet." For German uneasiness as to the Reval meeting, see G.P., XXV, 441-494.

[29] Fisher to Lord Esher, Sept. 8, 1908; Fisher, *Memories,* p. 186f.

Aside from this renewal of Anglo-Russian cordial relations and English encouragement to Russia to build up her armaments again—which she soon proceeded to do—the Reval interview actually dealt mainly with the question of Macedonian reforms, Persia, Crete, the Sanjak railway project, and the attitude of the Russian Press. There was no attempt to build up a closer Anglo-Russian combination against Germany, and Izvolski was profuse in his assurances that it was in no way unfriendly to Germany. But the Kaiser was not convinced, and Reval marks a cooling off in Anglo-German relations. It also made him more positive in his refusal to discuss with England any limitation of his naval program, when Hardinge broached the subject directly to him at the time of King Edward's brief visit to Kronberg on August 11, 1908. There was a heated discussion. Hardinge, according to the Kaiser's lively account in dialogue form, complained that Germany was building Dreadnoughts so rapidly that in a few years she would be as strong as England in these capital ships. The Kaiser said this was "absolute nonsense," sent for a copy of *Nauticus,* an almanac of detailed naval statistics of all nations which Hardinge appeared never to have heard of, and showed him his errors. When Hardinge persisted that the competitive naval construction must cease, the Kaiser used his regular argument that Germany was not building in competition with England, but only for her own needs as laid down in Tirpitz's Navy Laws. When Hardinge still insisted, "You must stop or build slower," the Kaiser looked him sharp in the eye and replied, "Then we shall fight, for it is a question of national honor and dignity." Hardinge turned red, and, seeing he was on dangerous ground, begged the Kaiser's pardon, asked him to forget words said in private conversation, and changed the subject. In conversation later in the day with the Kaiser, Hardinge was as affable and friendly as could be, and was not a little surprised to be decorated with the Order of the Red Eagle, First Class.[30] The English Cabinet, whose views Hardinge had been representing, were determined to preserve England's supremacy of the seas and keep ahead of Germany in Dreadnought construction. But they foresaw the bitterness which would be engendered between the two countries by further naval competition, as well as the terrible financial burden it would impose on England. They therefore sincerely desired and tried to come to some sort of understanding with Germany on the subject. It was a tragic mistake of Tirpitz and the Kaiser that they should have so flatly refused discussion and thereby pushed England further into the arms of France and Russia, thus strengthening the Triple Entente and helping to crystallize its opposition.

The effect on Germany of England's opposition to the Bagdad Railway, of her efforts to limit the German navy, of the Reval meeting and the apparent consolidation of France, Russia, and England into a Triple Entente, was to produce a conviction that Germany was being "encircled." Germans believed that this encirclement was Edward VII's personal work, and that it aimed at strangling German commercial and colonial expansion, and even at crushing Germany's political and military position. There is no substantial evidence that there was any deliberate encirclement with such aims on the part of King Edward or the British Government. Such notions were the product of German imagination, fear, and suspicion. But there was nevertheless something of a diplomatic encirclement. Germany was now surrounded by three Great Powers, whose combined strength was supposed to be equal or superior to that of the Triple Alliance, and who were growing increasingly ready to coöperate in defense of their own interests whether

30 Kaiser to Bülow, Aug. 11-13, 1908; G.P., XXIV, 124-129; *cf.* also Hardinge's report to Grey of Aug. 16, 1908, printed with other material on the Kronberg visit, in B.D., VI, 173-200.

in Morocco, Mesopotamia, or the Balkans. Though Izvolski hoped that the Triple Entente would give him greater freedom of action in the Near East and Middle East, and though the French counted on it in the same way in Morocco, so far as England was concerned it aimed at the preservation of peace through the establishment of a balance of power. It was insurance against the supposed danger of possible German aggression, and not for any aggression against Germany's existing position in Europe and in the commercial world. But to German eyes it had a more ominous and irritating appearance. This finds expression in extreme form in the Kaiser's marginal notes on reports of the Reval meeting and of English efforts for slowing down German Dreadnought construction. It is also reflected in his indiscreet speech to German officers at Döberitz. His feeling was: "A strong navy; a strong army; and powder dry!" [31]

Bülow on the other hand, with his characteristic policy of putting the best face on an unpleasant situation, believed Germany should scrupulously avoid showing any signs of nervousness and uneasiness. To do so would simply be playing into the hands of Russia and France. While agreeing that Germany must keep herself in the highest possible state of defense, she must do so quietly. He chided the Kaiser as much as he dared for the Döberitz indiscretion,[32] and was inclined to agree with Metternich, the German Ambassador in London, that Germany ought not to close the door to all English suggestions for some arrangement to prevent the evils of Anglo-German naval competition.[33]

He also believed that the consolidation of the Triple Entente made it all the more important that Germany must stand firmly behind her Austrian ally. In a long very confidential circular to the Prussian Ministers in Bavaria

[31] G.P., XXV, 454.

[32] G.P., XXV, p. 466.

[33] G.P., XXVIII, 1-199, *passim*.

and the other leading states in the German Empire, he summed up the situation as optimistically as he honestly could. The Reval meeting, preceded by President Fallières's visit to London, has caused uneasiness in Germany. Grey and Izvolski have given assurances that nothing is being planned against her. Nevertheless it would be a fatal mistake, if, trusting in these assurances, we do not recognize that our freedom of movement may be limited by what has happened. It is Germany's economic and political power, and the fear that she may misuse them, which is driving other states into the Entente against us. "These Ententes and Alliances are therefore in their origin rather of a defensive character. But perhaps they will not hesitate to proceed aggressively against us and hold us down where possible, when they think they have the power to do so." Our ally, Austria-Hungary, is threatened just as we are by this new combination, and especially so, because the passions and intrigues directed against the very existence of the Dual Monarchy arouse in other nations expectations for a successful destructive blow from the outside. The supposedly imminent break-up of Austria-Hungary is a favorite standing theme in the French and other foreign Press. Because of her greater interests in the Balkans, Austria-Hungary is also more exposed than are we to the danger of a conflict with the Entente Powers. Germany and Austria, standing together as a solid block, may be able to withstand all storms. "A loyal coöperation with Austria-Hungary will and must remain in the future also the fundamental basis of German foreign policy." Germany cannot enter into a discussion with other Powers to limit her armaments, but she should avoid as far as possible giving any irritation to others and restrain all jingoistic expressions in the German Press.[34]

There was much shrewd wisdom in this statement.

[34] Bülow's circular, June 25, 1908; G.P., XXV, 474-479.

GERMANY'S RELATIONS WITH FRANCE, 1908-1911

While the naval friction with England continued, and the Young Turk Revolution and Bosnian Crisis led to a new tension with Russia, Germany managed to improve her relations with France in the years from 1908 to 1911.

The Algeciras Conference had not produced very satisfactory conditions in Morocco. The Sultan's brother, Mulai Hafid, had gained a strong following among the chieftains who resented the Franco-Spanish efforts to maintain order. Mulai Hafid finally revolted against his brother's authority. In the disorders which took place a French doctor was murdered, which gave the French occasion to occupy Moroccan territory at Oudjda near the Algerian frontier in the spring of 1907. Further outrages on Europeans led the French to land troops in Casablanca in August, and to place French police in other seaports on the West Coast. The Sultan, losing his authority more and more, was driven from his capital to the coast at Rabat, and finally declared deposed by Mulai Hafid's followers. Bülow and the Kaiser, recognizing that Germany's Morocco policy in the past had consolidated the Anglo-French Entente, refrained from any serious interference with these French measures, though German influence had contributed to the trouble between the rival sultans.[35]

While negotiations were going on concerning the terms under which Abdul Aziz should agree to abdicate in favor of Mulai Hafid, there occurred the Casablanca incident, which for a moment threatened to cause a new flare-up between France and Germany. On September 25, 1908, the German Consul at Casablanca attempted to assist six deserters from the French Foreign Legion to escape on board a German ship. But the deserters were forcibly seized, and

[35] For the details, see the French Yellow Book, *Affaires du Maroc*, III-IV, 1906-1908; and G.P., XXI, 601-689; XXIV, 215-326.

the consular secretary and soldier escorting them were somewhat mishandled by French soldiers. The German Consul was blamed by France for having exceeded his powers, contrary to international law, in affording protection to persons within French military jurisdiction. The local French military authorities were accused by Germany of having infringed the inviolability of consular rights. In spite of some excitement in the French and German Press, good sense fortunately prevailed in the Foreign Offices at Paris and Berlin. Both soon agreed to submit the matter to arbitration, which ultimately resulted in a compromise decision that both sides had been partly in the wrong. Both Powers were glad to see the incident disposed of in a conciliatory fashion so that it should not add a new danger to the peace of Europe which at the moment was threatened by the uncertain state of affairs growing out of the Turkish Revolution and the Bosnian Crisis. The Kaiser especially displayed as much wisdom and energetic influence in favor of friendly conciliation as he had lacked in dealing with the English suggestions for a restriction of naval competition. Never in sympathy with the Bülow-Holstein Morocco policy of the past, he now condemned it sharply, having come to the conclusion that it was impossible to check the extension of French political control in Morocco without resorting to force. On October 4 he informed his Foreign Office that, so far as still practicable, Germany should withdraw with dignity, and come to an understanding with France as quickly as possible, in spite of the incident at Casablanca. A couple of days later, after being painfully surprised by the Austrian annexation of Bosnia, he wrote more energetically to Bülow: "In view of these circumstances this wretched Moroccan affair must now be brought to a conclusion, quickly and definitely. There is nothing to be made of it; it will be French anyway. So let us get out of the affair with dignity, so that we may finally have done with this friction with France, now that great questions are at issue." To which Bülow replied characteristically that he agreed, but must not let the French see this too clearly, or they would never give any compensations for Germany's withdrawal; and he added, "The most desirable thing would be that we should come to an understanding with France and England about Morocco, as well as about other African and Asia Minor questions." [36]

Soon afterwards Germany gave her approval to the terms which the French had drawn up, highly favorable to themselves, as the conditions on which Mulai Hafid was to be Sultan. At the same time Schoen, the German Secretary of State, told Jules Cambon, the French Ambassador in Berlin, that it was time for Germany and France to shake hands on Morocco, and that the Kaiser wished it.[37] This led to negotiations which resulted in the Franco-German Agreement of February 9, 1909. "To facilitate the execution of the Act of Algeciras," France, still professing to respect the independence and integrity of Morocco, promised equality of economic opportunity to the Germans; and Germany, professing to pursue only economic aims, recognized France's special political interests in preserving peace and order, and promised not to interfere with them.[38]

The final negotiations took place very rapidly. This was owing to several reasons. The Bosnian Crisis was becoming dangerously acute as Austria and Serbia armed against one another, so that it was desirable to get the Moroccan question out of the way. In the second place, Bülow had taken up the idea of the German Ambassador in England, in spite of the Kaiser's absolute negative of the preceding summer, of conceding to England a modification of Germany's naval program in return for some politi-

36 G.P., XXIV, 440 f. On the Casablanca incident itself, *cf. ibid.*, pp. 329-374.

37 Oct. 28, 1908; G.P., XXIV, 454.

38 G.P., XXIV, 489.

cal equivalent, such as an exchange of colonial territory, or, better still, an English promise of neutrality in case of a European war.[39] For success in any such negotiation it was most important to remove all Franco-German friction in Morocco, which had been one of England's original and most persistent reasons for standing by the side of France. It was reported to Bülow that the English Minister in Tangier had had instructions to stir up trouble between the French and Germans, and he felt sure that anti-German propaganda by the English in Paris was likely to continue so long as England had cause to be alarmed over Germany's rapid construction of Dreadnoughts.[40] To cut the ground from under this propaganda and to remove England's anxiety as to German intentions in Morocco it was highly desirable "to shake hands with France" once and for all in regard to Morocco. A final reason for the speed with which the Franco-German Agreement was concluded lay in the fact that King Edward was to visit Berlin on February 9; Bülow wished to be able to publish the Agreement before his arrival in order to avoid any impression among the public that Edward VII had helped to bring it about.[41]

The Agreement was warmly welcomed in the French Press as putting an end to a long-standing source of irritation between France and Germany, and as assuring to the one the political, and to the other the economic, advantages necessary to each. Grey and Hardinge congratulated Bülow on it, expressing pleasure that a question which had been a constant source of anxiety to England and in which England was bound by the Entente of 1904 to give France diplomatic support was now so happily settled.[42] The Kaiser hastened to decorate the French Ambassador in Berlin with the Order of the Red Eagle and present him

39 G.P., XXVIII, 1-87, especially pp. 66, 74.
40 Bülow to the Kaiser, Dec. 29, 1908; G.P., XXIV, 465.
41 Bülow to the Kaiser, Feb. 9, 1908; G.P., XXIV, 488
42 G.P., XXIV, 491-4.

with an autographed portrait, "because the path I ordered in our Morocco policy has had such a brilliant success in the whole world, and because we owe much to the unselfish and devoted work of Cambon as well as to his loyalty." [43] Schoen instructed the German Minister in Morocco that he was to coöperate fully with the French, prevent all friction, and observe loyally in every way the spirit and purpose of the new convention. Though this Moroccan Agreement of 1909 did not have all the happy results expected from it, it did bring about much more cordial relations between the two countries, until new disorders arose in Morocco in the spring of 1911, which led to the French march to Fez and the German threat at Agadir.

GERMANY'S RELATIONS WITH RUSSIA, 1908-1911

Though the Anglo-Russian Convention of 1907 seemed to Germany an indication that Russia was turning away from the old friendly relations which had united the Hohenzollerns and the Romanovs, it did not at first seriously cloud the relations between the two countries. Izvolski had been profuse in his assurances that the Convention merely aimed to do away with Anglo-Russian friction in the Middle East, and was in no way directed at Germany or inimical to her interests. As Russia's interests seemed deeply centered in Persia, Germany carefully sought to avoid antagonizing her in that quarter. When Persia in 1906 had asked for the establishment of a German Bank at Teheran, with the hope of support against Russian encroachments, Germany had hesitated to heed the request, and informed Izvolski that Germany had no political aims or interests in Persia.[44] In return, early in 1907, Izvolski proposed an agreement by which Russia would withdraw her opposition to the construction of the Bagdad Railway,

[43] Kaiser's note, Feb. 11, 1909; G.P., XXVIII, 87.
[44] G.P., XXV, 103-121.

in return for Germany's recognition of Russia's monopoly in political, strategic, and economic matters in Northern Persia.[45] Izvolski carried on negotiations for such a Russo-German agreement during the spring and early summer of 1907, at the same time with his negotiations on the same subject with England, evidently playing off the two countries against one another.[46] But when he had the Anglo-Russian Convention safely in his pocket, he dropped the conversations with Berlin.[47] Russia's objections to the Bagdad Railway would be safeguarded by Sir Edward Grey's policy of insisting that all conversations on the subject must be *à quatre*, in which the Entente Powers would outnumber Germany three to one. Germany for her part felt sure that Russia's aggressive designs in Persia would inevitably lead to serious friction with England without any German stimulation. Therefore in Bülow's inelegant phrase: *"Il faut les laisser cuire dans leur jus."* [48]

In 1908, however, Germany's relations with Russia began to be less satisfactory. Izvolski wished to recover in the Near East some of the prestige which Russia had lost in her disastrous war in the Far East. He believed that the alliance with France and the Entente with England assured him their benevolent attitude, and that he could proceed to open the Straits for Russian warships. Germany had often declared that she had no objections to this, and Austria could be satisfied by being invited to annex Bosnia and Herzegovina. This was the substance of his "Buchlau Bargain" with the Austrian Foreign Minister, Aehrenthal, which will be described in more detail in the next chapter on Balkan Problems. Aehrenthal, however, acted quickly and made sure at once of his half of the bargain. But

[45] Feb. 20, 1907; G.P., XXV, 122 ff. [46] G.P., XXV, 124-145.

[47] There were, to be sure, some unimportant discussions arising from the conflicts between Hartwig and Richthofen, the overzealous representatives of Russia and Germany at Teheran; G.P., XXV, 147-173.

[48] G.P., XXVII, 735.

Izvolski found that his plan for opening the Straits did not meet with French and English approval, and his consent at Buchlau to having Orthodox Greek Bosnians placed under the Roman Catholic sovereignty of the Hapsburgs was violently denounced by the Pan-Slavs in Russia, as well as by the Serbians, who had coveted Bosnia as part of a future "Greater Serbia." Thereupon Izvolski tried to nullify the Buchlau bargain by insisting that the modification of the Berlin Treaty of 1878, which was involved by the Austrian annexation of Bosnia, should be subjected to revision by a Conference of the Powers. Austria refused. Serbia and Austria began to mobilize against each other.

Though the Kaiser was indignant at the sudden way in which Aehrenthal had annexed Bosnia, Bülow persuaded his master that Germany could not afford to refuse support to her ally's *fait accompli.* Germany was now surrounded by the Entente Powers, and Austria was her only reliable ally. So Germany supported Austria's refusal to accept a Conference, and hastened to propitiate France and England by the Moroccan Agreement of 1909. Meanwhile, by March, 1909, Serbia and Austria seemed on the verge of war. Serbia counted on Russian, and Austria on German, support. Unluckily for Izvolski, Russia's exhaustion and military disorganization after the war with Japan made it out of the question for her to back up by force his demand for a Conference; France was not yet ready to extend the scope of the Franco-Russian alliance to cover Russian ambitions in the Balkans; and England gave Russia little support.

To avert an actual clash of arms between Austria and Serbia, Germany then proposed a solution to extricate Izvolski from the *cul-de-sac* into which he had strayed, and demanded a yes or no answer in regard to it; if Russia rejected it, Germany would let the Austro-Serbian quarrel take its course, and the outcome under the circumstances would certainly not have been in Serbia's favor. Izvolski thereupon accepted the German solution, and the Bosnian Crisis was ended.[49]

The outcome of the Bosnian Crisis was a diplomatic victory for Austria and Germany, and a corresponding humiliation for Russia and Serbia, with all the feeling of soreness which such humiliations leave behind. Izvolski never forgave Aehrenthal for his quick action in annexing Bosnia without further consultation and in refusing a Conference. He claimed that in both these matters Aehrenthal had broken his word and was no gentleman. Aehrenthal denied the truth of the allegations and threatened to publish the documents, whereupon Izvolski begged Germany to prevent the publication; upon Germany's advice, Aehrenthal refrained from carrying out his threat.

This personal feud between Izvolski and Aehrenthal had been transferred to the pages of the English *Fortnightly Review*, where the recriminations further embittered the two men. Count Berchtold, then Austrian Ambassador in St. Petersburg, became involved, because Dr. Dillon had found material for one of the *Fortnightly* articles at Berchtold's castle at Buchlau. So for nearly a year it was virtually impossible for Izvolski and Berchtold to carry on diplomatic intercourse with one another. In the meantime Izvolski succeeded in making a secret agreement with Italy at Racconigi,[50] by which, among other things, Italy promised to regard with benevolence Russia's interest in the Straits in return for Russia's similar promise in regard to Italy's interests in Tripoli. Izvolski was thus getting Italy's consent to what he had failed to secure by the Buchlau bargain, and Italy was taking another "extra dance" outside the circle of her own Triple Alliance partners.

It was not until early in 1910 that Izvolski and Aehrenthal again took up "normal diplomatic" relations. Rumors

49 For the details, see below, ch. v.

50 Oct. 24, 1909; see below, ch. v.

of their *rapprochement,* and even of a secret agreement between them, caused terror: at Belgrade it was feared that Russia was about to abandon Serbia to Austria's tender mercies; and at Constantinople it was feared that the partition of Turkey was being contemplated.[51] Even at Berlin there were fears that Izvolski, aided and abetted by France and England, was trying to make a secret agreement with Austria in order to drive another wedge into the Triple Alliance and sow discord between Berlin and Vienna.[52] For weeks Izvolski tried to pin Aehrenthal down to signing an agreement which would put Austria on record in favor of the *status quo* in the Balkans and which could be confirmed by being communicated to all the Great Powers. Izvolski wished publicly to tie Austria's hands in the Balkans, until Russia should have reorganized her army and navy and tightened up the Triple Entente to a more active support than France and England had given Russia during the Bosnian crisis. Aehrenthal, however, though ready to sign a private agreement with Russia, saw no need to communicate it to the Powers. After misunderstandings and recriminations, Izvolski finally published some of the correspondence without asking Aehrenthal's consent, an unfriendly act which still further accentuated the personal feud between them.[53] Meanwhile Izvolski went ahead with other maneuvers for securing Russia's ambitions in regard to the Straits and for forming a Balkan league under Russian patronage.[54]

The Bosnian Crisis had less disastrous effects upon the relations between Russia and Germany than upon those between Russia and Austria just described. Germany's

51 Despatches from Russia's representatives at Constantinople and Belgrade, Feb. 2 and 4, 1910; Siebert-Schreiner, p. 285.

52 G.P., XXVII, 438 ff.

53 On this whole episode of an Austro-Russian "rapprochement", see Siebert-Schreiner, pp. 282-300· G.P., XXVII, 435-555.

54 See below, ch. v.

intervention to end the crisis was, to be sure, soon exaggerated by Izvolski and Sir Arthur Nicolson, into a "brutal ultimatum" and denounced by the Pan-Slavs.[55] But though the Pan-Slav Press reserved its bitterest shafts for Germany and not Austria, the Russian Foreign Office, knowing the truth about Germany's intervention, manifested less resentment against Berlin than against Vienna. This was indicated in many ways. While Izvolski and Berchtold were not on speaking terms for months, the genial Pourtalès remained on the most cordial personal relations with the Russian Foreign Minister, partly because Izvolski found he could pour out into the German Ambassador's ear all his complaints about Aehrenthal's conduct.[56] Similarly, when the Tsar went to Racconigi in October, 1909, he ostentatiously avoided Austrian soil, although his obvious path lay across it;[57] but with the German Emperor, the Tsar had cordial meetings near Finland[58] and at Kiel.[59]

In September Izvolski passed through Berlin. Though travelling *incognito,* he made a point of dining with Bethmann-Hollweg and becoming acquainted with the new German Chancellor. They had a frank and friendly discussion of the general political situation, past, present, and future, in which Izvolski poured out his usual complaints about Aehrenthal "in a passionate and excited fashion, as if he had come directly from a duel with Aehrenthal";[60] Izvolski hoped that Germany would restrain Aehrenthal from further reckless aggression in the Balkans, and assured Bethmann that Russia was far from pursuing any policy hostile to Germany. Both men agreed that the Press, especially the Russian Press, had done great harm.[61] This friendly relation was aided by Germany's continued policy of care-

55 G.P., XXVI, 738 ff., 783 ff.

56 G.P., XXVI, 810 ff.

57 G.P., XXVII, 403 ff., 425; Siebert-Schreiner, pp. 148, 152.

58 G.P., XXVI, 817-836.

59 G.P., XXVI, 849 f.

60 G.P., XXVI, 854.

61 Bethmann's memorandum, Sept. 15, 1909; G.P., XXVI, 852-855.

fully refraining from all political interference in Persia,[62] where revolution and disorders were causing a sharp conflict of interests between Russia and England [63]—a situation which Germany regarded with perfect complacency. Germany's non-interference with Russia's "strangling" of Persia was ultimately rewarded by Russian concessions in regard to the Bagdad Railway embodied in the Potsdam Agreements. But before these are described a word may be said about Bülow's resignation and the new men who entered the German and Russian Foreign Offices in 1909 and 1910—the men who in July, 1914, were to have in their hands the fate of the world.

When Herr von Bethmann-Hollweg replaced Count Bülow at the Wilhelmstrasse in July, 1909, and Kiderlen-Wächter became Secretary of State a little later, Germany's international position seemed considerably improved. Count Bülow in his volume on *Imperial Germany* has pictured with characteristic optimism and excessive self-complacency the favorable position in which he left the country at his resignation. But the new Chancellor, reviewing the situation of 1909 in his *Reflections on the World War,* shows that the tasks which he inherited from Bülow were by no means light and easy.

The Moroccan Treaty of February 9, 1909, with France and the diplomatic triumph of Austria in the Bosnian Crisis had brought a feeling of relief at Berlin. The Triple Entente seemed definitely weakened and the danger of "encirclement" less alarming. On June 3, 1909, at a secret meeting attended by Tirpitz, Bethmann, Moltke, and Metternich, who had come over from London for it, Bülow declared that not for twenty years had Germany been so respected and feared in the world. The one dark cloud on

62 G.P., XXVII, 721-824.

63 *Cf.* Siebert-Schreiner, 49 ff.; Grey, I, 147-165; W. M. Shuster, *The Strangling of Persia* (New York, 1912).

the horizon was the Anglo-German situation; this looked like a thunder-storm; therefore he had called this meeting to consider it.[64] In April the Kaiser had severely scolded Metternich, among other things, for telling England that Germany intended no new naval program in the future; now it appeared that Tirpitz and the Kaiser were contemplating a supplementary navy law in 1912. Metternich replied that he had been expressly authorized by the Kaiser to speak as he had done, and that it was a pity he had not been told sooner, if Tirpitz now had it in mind to ask in 1912 for a further increase of the navy. He closed the letter with words which are as noble a tribute to his own character, as they are a condemnation of the Kaiser and his Admiral: "I am well aware that my attitude in the naval question, in which I have followed my duty in reporting repeatedly that this is the question which chiefly poisons our relations with England, does not meet the approval of His Majesty, and also that the Secretary of the Navy attacks my attitude in his talks with His Majesty. Naturally it is not pleasant for the head of the Navy that our building program and our relations to England depend on one another. But I should be falsifying history, if I reported otherwise than I do, and I cannot sell my convictions, even for the favor of my Sovereign. Also I am doubtful whether smooth and pleasant despatches, up to the point when we suddenly find ourselves face to face with war with England, would be a service to His Majesty."[65]

In the meeting of June 3, Bülow defended his Ambassador against the unmerited criticisms of Tirpitz and the Kaiser: "The first duty of His Majesty's representative abroad is to report the truth and picture conditions as they really are. He, Bülow, would always stand behind an Ambassador who did that, heedless of whether the unvar-

64 Protocol of the meeting of June 3, 1909; G.P., XXVIII, 168-176.
65 Metternich to Bülow, June 2, 1909: G.P., XXVIII, 167.

nished truth was pleasant or not to hear. It does no good to scold the barometer because it points to bad weather." [66]

In the course of the discussion Bethmann, Minister of the Interior, suggested that an agreement with England might be reached on the basis of Germany "slowing down" naval construction from four to three ships annually, if England would make concrete political offers in return. But Tirpitz blocked the path at every turn, refusing even the 4:3 ratio for British and German capital ships to which he had previously assented, and revealing a sly *reservatio mentalis:* if Germany slowed down from four to three new ships a year from 1909 to 1912, she might counterbalance this loss by speeding up from two to three in the following years, so that Germany's total number of Dreadnoughts would be the same around 1915 in either case. Though accepting in principle Bethmann's suggestion for slowing down, Tirpitz declined to fix or work out any formula to accomplish it, until the English had made concrete proposals. And in general he was in favor of "quietly waiting." This was very discouraging to Metternich and Bülow, and probably had much to do with Bülow's resignation on June 26, which was accepted by the Kaiser on July 14.

The ostensible reason for Bülow's resignation was the refusal of the Blue-Black-Bloc (the Conservative-Clerical coalition) on June 24 to vote the new finance bill, including a heavy inheritance tax, made necessary by the insatiable demands of new armaments. This gave Bülow a good excuse to retire from office. It was a motive which looked perfectly obvious to the public and has generally been accepted as the reason for his abandoning the Chancellorship after ten years of weary work. But as one reads his long struggle to defend Metternich's view in favor of naval limitation against Tirpitz's stubborn and slippery evasion

[66] G.P., XXVIII, 168 f.

of all worth-while concessions, and especially as one reads the protocol of the secret meeting of June 3, 1909, and the documents connected with it, one gets the impression that one of Bülow's main reasons for resigning was the opposition of Tirpitz and the Kaiser to the efforts for a reasonable naval agreement with England. Like Metternich, Bülow would no longer sell his convictions even for his Sovereign's favor. This reason, however, involving internal friction within the Government, the Kaiser's political influence, and relations with England, was one of which no hint must be given to the public. So the world has been left to believe that he parted from the Kaiser mainly for two reasons: first, because his finance bill was voted down in the Reichstag; and second, because the Kaiser was displeased with his inadequate defense of His Majesty in the *Daily Telegraph* affair some months earlier. But if Bülow's resignation was motivated, as suggested, by the naval question, then nothing in the exercise of his Chancellorship became him like the manner of his leaving it.

Bülow's "resignation with brilliants" was accepted on July 14. He received the Order of the Black Eagle, the highest distinction of the kind in the gift of the Kaiser. He had earned it, for no German Chancellor had so difficult a personal position, and yet acquitted himself so brilliantly. Easy-going, *débonnaire,* good-natured, and with an ever-ready wit, he had known how to handle Reichstag majorities no less cleverly than he had handled the All Highest. With something of Tirpitz's shrewd patience in evading commitments, but lacking the Admiral's powerful determination, clearness of purpose, and absolute self-reliance, Bülow had preferred to gain his ends by gentler methods, by his clever dialectical skill, and by his occasional withholding of the full truth or more often by obscuring it with his witty subtlety. He knew also how to humor, flatter, and disarm his opponents (enemies he had few or none), and the literary turn of his speeches and despatches makes them delightful reading. But his flippant habit of darkening counsel by amusing metaphors and his assumed optimism silenced healthy criticism and resulted in his piloting the ship of state into dangerous currents at the moment when he handed over the helm to Bethmann. He (and Holstein) were mainly responsible for the failure to grasp Chamberlain's proffered hand at the turn of the century, and for the other policies which led to the formation of the Triple Entente. The real hollowness of his achievement, which he painted *couleur de rose* in *Imperial Germany*, was revealed in the catastrophe of 1914. His reputation has exceeded his deserts. He will go down in history as a Chancellor of lost opportunities.

Some months before his resignation, Bülow had called to Berlin from the obscurity of Bucharest a man whom many regard as the best horse in the German stable since Bismarck's day. Herr von Kiderlen-Wächter certainly had something of the Iron Chancellor's forceful dominating energy and direct methods, but he lacked the readiness to see an opponent's point of view, and as far as possible meet it, which had been one of the secrets of Bismarck's diplomatic success. With his light-hearted Swabian warmth of temperament and levity of conversation, Kiderlen lacked also the moral force which gave Bismarck such a hold on the old Emperor and the German people. In his highly diverting daily letters to the beautiful blond whom he first met when he was forty and she thirty-eight, who never became his wife, but who often lived in his house, Kiderlen has left a fascinating record of personal devotion and of public affairs. Indiscreet, but not uninteresting, are the nicknames which he used to designate even the great ones of this world: "Eel" (Bülow, who was slippery); "Earthworm" (Bethmann, whom the Kaiser could tread upon); "Poor Beauty Boy" (a pun upon Schoen, whom Kiderlen replaced as Secretary of State in 1910); "Hippopotamus" (Marschall von Bieberstein); "The Sudden One" ("Der Plötzliche," *i.e.*, the Kaiser); and "Uncle *motu proprio*" (the Pope).[67] Kiderlen was a career diplomat with excellent training and opportunities for observation. Entering the Foreign Office in 1879 as a specialist in commercial matters, he had served as Embassy Secretary at St. Petersburg, Paris, and Constantinople (1881-1888), and then for ten years accompanied the Kaiser on his journeys as reporter for the Foreign Office. But some of his indiscreet witticisms were brought to the ears of the Kaiser, probably by a jealous Admiral, and the imperial displeasure was visited upon him by his being "exiled" to Bucharest.[68] As German Minister there from 1900 to 1910, he did much to cement the relations between Rumania and the Triple Alliance. In spite of the Kaiser's displeasure, Kiderlen's ability was recognized as so indispensable that his advice was often sought by Bülow. In the winter of 1908-1909, during Schoen's sickness, Kiderlen was at Berlin as Acting-Secretary of State. It was he, rather than Bülow, who brought about the Morocco Agreement of 1909 and the final settlement of the Bosnian Crisis. A year after Bülow's resignation, when Bethmann needed a strong and skilful diplomat at his elbow, Kiderlen was at last brought back from Bucharest for good, and given the office of Secretary of State, made vacant by Schoen's appointment as Ambassador to Paris (June, 1910). For two years and a half, until his sudden death at the very end of 1912, Kiderlen was Bethmann's *spiritus rector* at the Foreign Office, casting his influence in favor of keeping Austria in check, of good relations with Russia, of a naval understanding with England, and of the abandonment of all

[67] E. Jäckh, *Kiderlen-Wächter, der Staatsmann und Mensch* (2 vols., Berlin, 1925), *passim*. This delightful biography is largely made up of selections from Kiderlen's letters to Hedwig Kypke.

[68] E. Jäckh, I, 100 f.

claims in Morocco in return for compensations in the French Congo.[69]

Herr von Bethmann-Hollweg, who took over Bülow's difficult inheritance, lacked his predecessor's brilliance, but inspired more general confidence by his diligence, sincerity, and upright nobility of character, for which he was esteemed by all who knew him at home and abroad. "Somewhat idealistic and weak, but a suitable person," was Kiderlen's comment on hearing that out of the various candidates the Kaiser had picked an old friend of his youth.[70] Trained as a jurist, Bethmann had risen by ability and hard work in the civil administration to the position of Imperial Secretary of State for the Interior, with which he was far better acquainted than with Foreign Affairs. But he at once applied himself very diligently to getting personally well acquainted with all Germany's ambassadors and foreign ministers, and studied the Foreign Office despatches so assiduously that his subordinates feared he would lose himself in the details. With the Kaiser Bethmann kept on intimate and friendly terms.

When both were in Berlin, they rode or walked almost daily together, discussing all political questions, in which the Kaiser had much wisdom as well as many prejudices. Bethmann was something of an idealist. He ardently desired peace in Europe. Therefore at heart he was opposed to greatly increased armaments. He hoped for an understanding with England on the naval question, and believed it could be reached—Germany slowing down her rate of naval construction, and England in return making political concessions in connection with the Bagdad Railway and perhaps even some kind of agreement to be neutral. The English were convinced of his sincerity in this purpose. Sir Edward Grey declared in 1912, after the Haldane Mission, that any possible differences between Germany and

69 Jäckh, II, 79-232.

70 Jäckh, II, 32.

DR. THEOBALD VON BETHMANN-HOLLWEG
German Imperial Chancellor, 1909-1917

England would never assume dangerous proportions, "so long as German policy was directed by the Chancellor"; upon which the Kaiser commented indignantly, "This shows that Grey has no idea who is really Master here and that I rule. He prescribes to me who my Minister shall be if I am to make an agreement with England." [71]

Bethmann's disinclination for increased armaments and his wish to make naval concessions brought him into conflict with the Kaiser, and he twice offered his resignation. But the Kaiser would not accept it because he had such confidence in Bethmann's character, and because he knew how highly he was esteemed abroad as an influence for peace. One may argue that Bethmann, for his own honor and conscience, ought to have insisted on his resignation being accepted, when he could not persuade the Kaiser to follow his advice rather than that of Tirpitz; that he ought to have put loyalty to his own conscience above personal loyalty to the Kaiser. But as he wrote rather pathetically to Kiderlen at New Year's, 1912: "Really this whole policy [of increased taxation for larger armaments] is such that I cannot join in it. That you know. But I ask myself ever and again whether I should not make the situation still more dangerous, if I should leave now, and then probably be not the only one." [72] Thus, it was really loyalty to his country, rather than mere personal loyalty to the Kaiser, that made him compromise with his own conscience and remain in office as the spokesman of part at least of the measures demanded by the army and navy and approved by the Kaiser. It was the misfortune of Bethmann and of Germany that he never had a wholly free hand to carry out the policies which he favored. He continually had to contend against the influence of the army and navy officials who had direct access to the Emperor at any time, whereas

71 Metternich to Bethmann, Mar. 17, 1912; G.P., XXXI, 182 f.
72 Jäckh, II, 174.

Germany's ambassadors and Foreign Office secretaries could usually present their views only through the medium of the "civilian Chancellor."

In the Russian Foreign Office also a change took place. In September, 1910, Izvolski finally secured for himself the Russian Embassy in Paris and the generous salary attached to it. Ever since the fiasco of his effort to open the Straits by the Buchlau bargain and the humiliating outcome of the Bosnian Crisis, he had been the target of Pan-Slav attacks at home. He was also criticized by level-headed men like Kokovtsev and Krivoshein, the Ministers of Finance and Agriculture, who felt that he had brought Russia into a perilous situation in antagonizing Austria and Germany while the Russian army and navy were still a negligible quantity. Izvolski would have been glad to escape this fire of criticism at once by exchanging the Russian Foreign Office for the Paris Embassy. But he did not like to resign immediately after the Bosnian Crisis; this would be too patent an evidence of his own failure or the Tsar's displeasure. Nor had the Tsar any suitable person to put in his place. So Izvolski remained Minister of Foreign Affairs for a year and a half after the Bosnian Crisis, but spent many months abroad. During his absence in April and May, 1909, Charykov was in charge at the Singer's Bridge. When Charykov went as Ambassador to Constantinople in June, Sazonov took his place as Izvolski's chief assistant at the Foreign Office.[73]

M. Sergei Dimitrijevitch Sazonov, who became Russian Minister of Foreign Affairs upon Izvolski's transfer to Paris in September, 1910, was by nature of a mercurial and emotional temperament. In his youth it is said that he intended becoming a monk, but gave it up on account of his bad

[73] On Izvolski and his critics in Russia from March, 1909, to Sept., 1910, see the despatches of Hintze and Pourtalès, in G.P., XXVI, 737 ff., 777 ff., 801 ff., 855 ff.; XXVII, 521 ff; and Sazonov, *Fateful Years,* ch. i

health and entered the diplomatic service. Slim and rather small of stature, with a nervous and abrupt manner, he always gave an impression of being frail in body and changeable in mind. In June, 1904, he became Counsellor to the Embassy in London, where he remained three years and acquired a friendly attitude toward England. In 1907, he was transferred to the Vatican, a pleasant but unimportant post which he filled for two years. In June, 1909, he returned to St. Petersburg as Assistant Minister of Foreign Affairs under Izvolski. His selection to succeed Izvolski in 1910 was, therefore, not unnatural. His appointment was recommended by Izvolski, who thought there was no one else better fitted for the office.

In Russian domestic politics, Sazonov was conservative, solidly in favor of the retention of old Russian institutions and little in sympathy with the constitutional movement brought about by the Russo-Japanese War. In foreign politics, he was an ardent patriot. His lips trembled with emotion as he once remarked that he could not survive a second defeat such as Russia had suffered in her unfortunate war with Japan.[74] The German Ambassador at St. Petersburg described him as "filled with glowing patriotism bordering on chauvinism. When he talks of past events in which he thinks Russia has suffered injustice, his face assumes an almost fanatical expression. Nevertheless, discussion with him is much easier and pleasanter than with Izvolski, because he always observes form, remains master of himself, and does not emphasize personal matters." [75]

Toward Germany Sazonov was favorably inclined personally. His grandmother was German and he had many personal relations with Germany. When he talked with Bethmann, he preferred to use German rather than French.

[74] Mühlberg, German Ambassador in Rome, to Bülow June 11, 1909; G.P., XXVI, 809.

[75] Pourtalès to Bethmann, Aug. 23, 1910; *ibid.*, 867.

He had much sympathy with the large group at the Tsar's court who wished to see restored the old cordial relations between Germany and Russia, who looked to Berlin rather than to Paris and London, and whose shibboleth was monarchical solidarity rather than constitutional democracy. To this group belonged Baron Fredericks, the venerable, influential, and universally respected Master of the Tsar's Household; Kokovtsev, Minister of Finance; Krivoshein, Minister of Agriculture; to a certain extent Stolypin, the Premier; Witte, who was out of office, but still influential; and a large number of "Baltic Germans" who by their ability had acquired a great number of civil and military offices in the Tsar's empire. But Sazonov also believed, like so many Pan-Slavs, that Bismarck had done Russia a great injustice at the Congress of Berlin, as had Bülow in the Bosnian Crisis. Nevertheless, he wanted to coöperate with Germany and reëstablish mutual confidence. He therefore welcomed the visit which the Tsar was to pay the Kaiser at Potsdam in November, 1910.

Sazonov, like Bethmann, was sincerely desirous of peace. But, as will appear in more detail in the next chapter, he was very nervous at any advance of Austrian or German influence in the Balkans which might endanger Russia's historic mission of acquiring control of the Bosphorus and the Dardanelles and even of Constantinople. He was also very sensitive to the criticism of the Pan-Slav Press. It is true that hardly ten per cent of the Russian people could read at all, and a still smaller proportion paid any attention to newspapers, so that there was in Russia no general "public opinion" in the Western sense of the word. Nevertheless Russian newspapers did exercise a much stronger influence on Russian foreign policy than is usually supposed, both through their criticisms of ministers at home and through their attacks on statesmen abroad. With the Russian Revolution of 1905, the establishment of the Duma, and the formation of the Entente with the two great democracies of the West, a majority of the Russian Press had become "liberal" in domestic matters, and strongly Anglophil and Francophil in foreign politics. It attacked Germany as the stronghold of absolutism and reaction, and as the instigator and protector of Austrian aggressions in the Balkans. It demanded that Russian Foreign Ministers should extend protection and help to the Slavs of the Balkans in their struggle to emancipate themselves from the Turkish and Hapsburg yoke. It had therefore been very bitter in condemning Izvolski's Buchlau bargain, which had placed Orthodox Greek Serbs under Austrian rule. It attacked Germany no less than Austria as the enemy of the Slav cause. It was this Pan-Slav Press of which Sazonov, timid by nature and none too secure in his official position, was in constant fear during the next four years. It drove him at times into a stronger support of Serbia and a sharper antagonism to Austria and Germany than he personally favored himself. It partly accounts for the changeableness and instability of his policies, which worried France and England as well as Germany. Pourtalès, the shrewd German Ambassador at St. Petersburg frequently noted how Sazonov's attitude seemed to shift, now one way and now another, in accordance with the rise and fall of the wave of Pan-Slav Press criticism and the militarist influence of the Grand Duke Nicholas and his bellicose circle. In fact, between 1908 and 1914, there was no single topic which was so frequently a subject of complaint and discussion between representatives of Germany and Russia as the malign influence of the Pan-Slav and Pan-German Press in stirring up bad blood between the two countries. After the Bosnian Crisis, for instance, "Willy" wrote to "Nicky":

> A few weeks ago, when affairs threatened to become dangerous, your wise and courageous decision secured peace among the nations. I was most gratified that by my co-

operation you were able to fulfil your task. I very naturally expected that you and I would win universal applause, for I ventured to think that we have earned the gratitude of all well-meaning people. But to my regret and astonishment I observe that a great many blame us both instead. Especially the press has behaved in the basest way against me. By some papers I am credited with being the author of annexation and am accused amongst other rot and nonsense of having humiliated Russia by my proposal. Of course you know better. Yet the fact must be taken note of that the papers mostly create public opinion. Some of the papers err through their ignorance and lack of correct information; they can scarcely see farther than their nose's length. But more dangerous and at the same time loathesome is that part of the press which writes what it is paid for. The scoundrels who do such dirty work, are in no fear of starving. They will always incite the hostility of one nation against the other and when at last, by their hellish devices, they have brought about the much desired collision, they sit down and watch the fight which they organized, resting well assured that the profit will be theirs, no matter what the issue may be. In this way in 99 cases out of a hundred, what is vulgarly called "public opinion" is a mere forgery.[76]

To this the Tsar replied: "Everything you write about the Press, as you know from our previous conversations, I agree with completely. It is one of the curses of modern times." [77]

In his discussions with the German Ambassador at St. Petersburg concerning the Press, Sazonov sometimes argued that what the Russian Press said was of little or no importance; that the German Government and the German Press made a mistake in paying so much attention to it; that it represented the views only of a small group of uninfluential Russian fanatics. But at other times the Russian Foreign

[76] May 8, 1909; G.P., XXVI, 786 f. [77] G.P., XXVI, 788 note.

Minister contradicted himself by using an exactly opposite line of argument: he must do this or he could not do that, because he had to have regard for public opinion and what the newspapers would say. His opponents might force him from office if in the interests of the peace of Europe he made too great concessions to Germany or failed adequately to safeguard Russia's national ambitions and to protect the Balkan Slavs. When he took this line he was much nearer the real facts of the situation. Pourtalès recognized this, and frequently urged the German Government not to make Sazonov's position unnecessarily difficult and embarrassing.

But it would be a mistake to think that Sazonov was wholly innocent of all connection with the Press which he genuinely feared. On the contrary, the Russian Foreign Office stood in close touch with *Novoe Vremia* and other papers which were most chauvinist and critical in tone. Sazonov (or his subordinates) often furnished the information and arguments which these papers were to use against Germany. He thus stirred them up to a nationalist campaign, behind which he would take refuge as a justification of the policy which he was "compelled by public opinion" to adopt. In critical negotiations with Germany, as in the Potsdam Agreements and the Liman von Sanders affair, important secrets often "leaked" from the Russian Foreign Office to the representatives of the Russian (and also of the French and English) Press in St. Petersburg; when matters thus got into the newspapers, they raised questions of prestige which made it more difficult for both Governments to make concessions toward a reasonable compromise settlement.[78]

There were also journalists outside Russia who wrote in the Pan-Slav cause, and who exercised an influence on

[78] For a few of Pourtalès's more important accounts of the Russian Press and Sazonov's relations with it, see G.P., XXVII, 844 f., 851 ff., 885, 890 ff., 924 ff.; XXXVIII, 226, 253 ff., 269, 293 ff., 300 f.; XXXIX, 540-589, *passim*. *Cf.* also *Journal Intime de Alexis Souvorine*, Paris, 1927.

Sazonov while at the same time receiving funds from the Russian Foreign Office. Of these the most important was Wesselitzki, the London correspondent of the *Novoe Vremia.* He had been given subsidies and the use of a summer villa at St. Petersburg when Izvolski was Minister of Foreign Affairs. "These expenditures were not in vain," wrote Izvolski in 1911, when urging that his successors at the Russian Foreign Office should continue to subsidize Wesselitzki.[79] As president of the Foreign Press Association in London, and in his frequent visits to foreign capitals, as well as in the materials which he contributed to the *Novoe Vremia,* Wesselitzki took every opportunity to sow discord between Russia and Germany and to tighten up the bonds between the members of the Triple Entente. Complaints of his mischievous activities and of the articles which he wrote under the pseudonym "Argus," appear frequently in the recently published German documents.[80]

After this brief digression on Bethmann and Sazonov, and the forces which influenced their policies, we may now return to an account of their negotiations in 1910-1911.

Izvolski's departure to Paris in September, 1910, left Sazonov and the Tsar free to carry out their desire of establishing more cordial relations with Germany. Though the Kaiser was still suspicious and much irritated at what he regarded as Russia's unfriendly Anglophil attitude since 1907, Bethmann and Kiderlen were ready to meet the Russians more than half way on their visit to Potsdam in November, 1910. Kiderlen hoped to clear up misunderstandings and so to lessen the opposition which had grown

79 Izvolski to Neratov, Nov. 23, 1911; M.F.R., p. 138; Stieve, I. 181. For a detailed statement of the "reptile funds" distributed to Russian newspapers in 1914, with names and amounts, totalling nearly a million rubles, see I. I. Tobolin, "Reptilnyi Fond, 1914-1916", in *Krasnyi Arkhiv,* X, 332-338 (1925).

80 *Cf.* especially G.P., XXV, 442 ff., and the index references, *ibid.*, p. 701; also XXVII, 440, 447 ff., 501 ff.

up between the Triple Entente and Triple Alliance. Neither Germany nor Russia were to be expected to modify in any way their respective alliances. But he was ready to assure Russia that Germany was neither bound nor inclined to support any new Austrian ambitions in the Balkans. Nor was Germany pursuing any political aims of her own in the Near East; she regarded the Badgad Railway primarily as an economic enterprise; and she merely wanted to see Turkey maintained intact, in the interests of peace and the *status quo*. There were many subjects in which Russian and German interests ran parallel, and it would be desirable to discuss them confidentially but frankly, and thus put an end to mutual recriminations and restore the friendly contact which had been lost under Izvolski's management of Russian foreign policy.[81]

These views met with a warm response from the new Russian Minister. Sazonov declared that the Bosnian Crisis belonged to the past and would not influence Russian policy in the future. Russia no longer had any expansionist policy. Her single task was her own internal consolidation. Russia's agreement of 1907 aimed purely to put an end to friction in the Middle East. If England pursued an anti-German policy, she would not find Russia on her side. Russia and Germany were neighbors and ought to live on good terms.[82]

As to Persia, the Germans again declared that they had no political aims in that troubled country, but wanted the "open door" for their commerce, which was handicapped by the Russian tariff charged upon goods in transit and by

[81] Kiderlen's memorandum, Oct. 30, 1910. G.P., XXVII, 832-834. Also Bethmann's private letter to Aehrenthal of Nov. 14, in which the German Chancellor frankly informed Aehrenthal of the Potsdam conversations, and especially of the fact that he had felt able to assure Sazonov "that Austria-Hungary is not contemplating any kind of expansion policy in the Balkans", and that Germany had never bound herself to support any such Austrian plans (*ibid.*, 850).

[82] Bethmann to Kaiser Nov. 1, 1910; G.P., XXVII, 835-837.

lack of good communications. Sazonov replied that the anarchical conditions in Northern Persia made it impossible for Russia to withdraw her troops. But if Germany would withdraw from all railway and telegraph projects in the Russian sphere in Persia, Russia would withdraw all discriminating tariffs and other obstacles to the importation of German goods into Persia. To open up the country Russia proposed to extend her railway system from the Caucasus via Tabriz and Teheran to the western frontier of Persia at Khanikin; and the Germans could then build a line to connect Khanikin and the Bagdad Railway. Bethmann understood that "Russia would no longer lay any obstacles in the way of the construction of the Bagdad Railway as far as Bagdad." In his report to the Tsar on the Potsdam meeting, Sazonov said "the question of the Bagdad Railway was not raised"; though he admitted that he told Bethmann that "if other interested Powers were to participate in this line, Russia could not remain empty-handed and would then want to have the Khanikin-Bagdad section." [83]

In his audience with the Kaiser Sazonov had been impressed with the Kaiser's irritation against England's naval policy, his fears of a "preventive attack," and his hope that the German fleet would soon have assumed proportions which would make England afraid to incur this risk. He had also tried to draw the Kaiser's attention to the danger to Russia, with her twenty million Mohammedan subjects, arising from the Pan-Islam propaganda.

The Potsdam conversations were cordial and frank on both sides. Bethmann and Sazonov each got a very favorable impression of the other. An excellent start was made in removing suspicions and in bringing the two countries

83 Bethmann to Pourtalès, Nov. 8, 1910; G.P., XXVII, 840 ff.; Sazonov's report to the Tsar, Nov. 4/17, 1910; *Krasnyi Arkhiv*, III, 5-8; L.N., II, 331-334.

back into the old paths from which they had strayed as a result of Izvolski's active Entente policy and unsuccessful Balkan ambitions. As the substance of the conversations had not been confirmed in writing, Bethmann drew up for Sazonov's approval a statement in general terms as the basis of a reference which he wished to make on the subject in his coming Reichstag speech. He also drafted nine paragraphs which he hoped Sazonov would sign, with such modifications as he saw fit, as a more precise written formulation of the Potsdam conversations.[84]

But Sazonov caused difficulties. On returning home, he seems to have feared criticism from the Pan-Slav Press. He had therefore, without consulting Germany, given an interview to the *Novoe Vremia*. This paper then published an account exaggerating the points conceded by Germany and minimizing those conceded by Russia. Sazonov explained apologetically to Pourtalès that he wished to turn aside the possible wrath of this section of the Russian Press.[85] To Pourtalès he gave also his full approval of the statement which was to be the basis of Bethmann's Reichstag speech. One sentence of this hinted at a point to which Kiderlen attached the greatest importance: "The result of the last interview I might sum up as a renewed assurance that both Governments will not enter into any sort of combination which could have an aggressive tendency against the other." [86] But neither to the Tsar, nor to the Press, nor apparently to the Ambassadors of France

[84] G.P., XXVII, 846 ff. [85] G.P., XXVII, 844 f., 851 ff.

[86] G.P., XXVII, 849, 855. One may note an interesting difference between Bethmann, the sincere seeker for a business-like agreement on economic questions like commerce in Persia and the Bagdad Railway, and Kiderlen, the more subtle politician concerned in the play of the system of alliances. To Bethmann, "the only essential things in the Potsdam conversations are the Persian and the Bagdad Railway questions" (*ibid.*, 842), But for Kiderlen, "the assurance of Russia concerning her relation to England is for me the alpha and omega of the whole agreement" (*ibid.*, 862).

and England, did Sazonov say a word of this general political understanding by which Russia promised not to support any policy hostile to Germany which England or France might undertake. He doubtless feared it might cause irritation in London and Paris. Therefore he gave evasive or dilatory replies to Pourtalès's efforts to get him to sign a written statement, such as the nine paragraphs which Bethmann had drafted, in which were precisely formulated the points relating to general policy as well as the specific agreements concerning Persia and the Bagdad Railway. He suggested that the two sets of points be dealt with in separate documents, and finally preferred not to sign any statement at all on general policy, asserting that the verbal promises of ministers, and especially of the Kaiser and the Tsar, were much more valuable than any exchange of written notes.[87]

Meanwhile Bethmann's Reichstag speech of December 10, 1910, summing up the Potsdam interview as a renewed assurance that Germany and Russia would not enter into any hostile combinations one against the other, had fallen like a bomb in Paris and London,[88] where Sazonov had allowed the impression to prevail that Persia and the Bagdad Railway were the only important questions discussed. The newly appointed English Ambassador in St. Petersburg, Sir George Buchanan, now hastened to present his credentials to the Tsar. He emphasized England's earnest wish to see the Anglo-Russian understanding maintained and consolidated, and expressed his anxiety concerning Sazonov's negotiations with Germany. Whereupon the Tsar, always inclined to agree with whoever had his ear at the moment, assured Buchanan that Russia "would conclude no arrangement with Germany without first submitting it to His Majesty's Government." [89]

87 G.P., XXVII, 879 ff. 88 G.P., XXVII, 888 ff.; XXIX, 61 f.

89 Buchanan, *My Mission to Russia,* I, 93; *cf.* Sazonov, *Fateful Years* ch. ii.

Pourtalès, shrewdly suspecting that English pressure explained Sazonov's evasive attitude, decided it was useless to press further for a signed statement on general policy. He therefore accepted with apparent grace and trust Sazonov's suggestion that merely verbal promises sufficed concerning general policy, and that the details of the Persian question could be left to a written agreement. Sazonov was much relieved in his mind at this.[90]

Accordingly, in the course of the next six months, a Russo-German agreement on the Middle East was gradually worked out. The negotiations were delayed by England's constant efforts to limit the entrance of German influence into Persia, and to secure control or participation in the section of the railway from Bagdad down to the Persian Gulf. There was also some recrimination over the publication in the London *Evening Times* of the secret draft treaty under discussion, the Russians and Germans each suspecting the other of being responsible for the "leak." But the Agadir Crisis caused Germany to make concessions and the agreement was finally signed on August 19, 1911. Germany disclaimed economic concessions (railways, roads, navigation, and telegraphs) in the Russian sphere in Persia; there were provisions for an eventual Russian railway in Persia from Teheran to the western border at Khanikin, and for linking this by a German branch line to the Bagdad Railway; and most important for Germany—Russia would no longer place obstacles in the way of the construction of the Bagdad Railway or in the participation of foreign capital.[91]

The Potsdam conversations in no way troubled the solidarity of the Triple Alliance, because Germany had kept

[90] G.P., XXVII, 875-883.

[91] *Krasnyi Arkhiv,* III (1923), 10-13; G.P., XXVII, 957 f.; for the negotiations, *ibid.,* 905-963; Siebert-Schreiner, pp. 501-576; the Izvolski-Sazonov correspondence, *passim,* in M.F.R., L.N., and Stieve; and Earle, ch. x.

Austria promptly informed of all her steps, and because Austria had no special interests in the Middle East. But the serenity of the Triple Entente was considerably ruffled by Sazonov's separate negotiations with Germany in a field where England and France had very active interests. M. Pichon, the French Minister of Foreign Affairs, was severely criticized in the Chamber of Deputies and in the Press for not safeguarding French interests and the solidarity of the Entente. Prominent men like M. Hanotaux in France, and Mr. Lloyd George in England, asked whether Sazonov's conduct was not leading to a dissolution of the Triple Entente. No little irritation was felt in Paris and London at Sazonov's independent course of action and departure from the Anglo-French standpoint that all Bagdad Railway negotiations ought to be *à quatre*.[92]

In the end, however, Russia's withdrawal of opposition to Germany's cherished desire of pushing the Bagdad Railway to completion opened the way for Germany's successful negotiations with Turkey and with England for further mutually advantageous arrangements. Germany acquired docks at Alexandretta and a branch line from there northward by which railway materials could be more easily imported for extending construction east of the Taurus Mountains. The Powers consented to an increase of the Turkish tariff from 11% to 15%, which would provide funds for paying the railway guarantees. England was given two of the seats on the Board of Directors of the Bagdad Railway Company, assured a dominant position in the navigation rights and oil resources of southern Mesopotamia, and largely relieved of her fears that the Bagdad Railway would be a German menace to the safety of India. The negotiations for all these arrangements were protracted

92 *Cf.* G.P., XXVII, 855, 887 ff.; XXIX, 61 ff.; Siebert-Schreiner, pp. 527 ff.; Earle, p. 241 ff.; Sazonov, p. 34 f.; and Stieve and Montgelas, *Russland und der Weltkonflikt,* p. 39 f.

over three years, but had been successfully concluded on June 15, 1914, two weeks before the Sarajevo assassination; the agreements lacked only the final signatures at the moment they were tossed to the winds by the outbreak of the World War.[93]

The Potsdam conversations and agreements of 1910-1911 are another indication of the fact that questions of economic imperialism are far easier for Governments to handle successfully than questions affecting prestige, alliances, or armaments; in fact the former may sometimes serve as a convenient bridge to the latter.

While Germany was thus on the way toward better relations with Russia in the summer of 1911, her relations with the two other members of the Triple Entente were suddenly made much worse by a new Morocco crisis.

THE AGADIR CRISIS, 1911

The Franco-German Morocco Agreement of 1909 was at first lived up to loyally by both parties. Pichon and Bethmann both made cordial public statements to that effect in the fall of 1909. But gradually friction developed again. The Mannesmann Brothers had acquired from Mulai Hafid certain mining rights not recognized by the French, which conflicted with the claims of the international "Union des Mines Marocaines." The Franco-German consortium for the development of the Cameroon-Congo trade had finally to be given up, on account of the protests of the French nationalists that the Germans were getting the greater advantage, and the Germans were then left seriously embarrassed. The disorders in the country gave the French a pretext for a steady extension of their police and military control, and Mulai Hafid was forced by an ultimatum to accept a loan which brought him more

93 On the Bagdad Railway negotiations between 1911 and 1914, see G.P., XXXI, 71-377; XXXVII, 141-470; Earle, pp. 244-274.

completely under French domination. It gradually became clearer and clearer that with this extension of French influence the equality of economic opportunity contemplated in the 1909 Agreement, and the idea of an independent Sultan at the head of a well-regulated government, were both fictions in contradiction with the actual trend of events. Nevertheless the fictions served as a basis for friendly relations between France and Germany for two years.[94]

The military and financial methods of the French had not endeared them to the Moroccan chieftains. The latter resented Mulai Hafid's subservience to the French and the continual encroachments upon their own national independence. The native discontent came to a head in March, 1911, after Colonel Mangin's public execution of a couple of Moroccan soldiers caught in the act of deserting. A revolt broke out in Fez. Alarming reports were sent out by the French that the lives of Europeans in Fez were in danger. On April 5, Jules Cambon, the French Ambassador in Berlin, informed Germany that the murder of Captain Marchand and the other disorders in Morocco would probably make it necessary for the French to occupy Rabat and send a punitive expedition into the Shawia district as well as a military force to rescue the Europeans in Fez. He added that this action was only due to extreme necessity, to preserve the sovereignty of the Sultan, and would be exercised in accordance with the spirit of the Algeciras Act. Kiderlen, who mainly directed Germany's policy in the Agadir affair, replied that he understood perfectly the anxiety of the French Government as to the fate of the

[94] On Moroccan affairs after 1909 see French Yellow Book, *Affaires du Maroc,* V, VI; the German White Book of 1910, *Denkschrift und Aktenstücke über deutsche Bergwerksinteressen in Marokko;* G.P., XXIX, 1-70; P. Albin, *Le Coup d'Agadir* (Paris, 1912); A. Tardieu, *Le Mystère d'Agadir* (Paris, 1912); J. Caillaux, *Agadir, Ma Politique Extérieure* (Paris, 1919).

Europeans in Fez, but that the French occupation of a second port like Rabat, in addition to Casablanca, would be likely to excite rather than allay the passions of the natives; it might also arouse public feeling in Germany and look like a further step toward the elimination of the Algeciras Agreement. He hoped that the French would delay military occupation as long as possible, and that Moroccan affairs could be satisfactorily arranged between Germany and France—a hint at compensations for Germany which Cambon clearly understood.[95] A little later Cambon reaffirmed that France would respect the Act of Algeciras and withdraw the troops as soon as order had been restored at Fez.

Kiderlen did not give an approval nor lodge a formal protest, but pointed out warningly that in cases like Fez it was easier to occupy a city than to withdraw again; and if French troops remained in Fez, so that the Sultan reigned only under cover of French bayonets, Germany could no longer regard him as the independent sovereign contemplated by the Algeciras Act; this and the Agreement of 1909 would fall to the ground, and Germany would reassume complete liberty of action.[96] The Kaiser, on the other hand, when he heard the news of massacres in Fez and the flight of Mulai Hafid into the French Consulate, said the French ought to send a large force; Germany had no reason to hinder it, as it would divert French troops and military expenditure from Germany's western frontier; if the French infringed the Algeciras Agreement, let other Powers, like

[95] *Affaires du Maroc,* VI, 179 f., 185, 189 ff; Caillaux, *Agadir,* 257 ff.; G.P., XXIX, 78 ff.

[96] Kiderlen's note of April 28; G.P., XXIX, 97 f.; *Affaires du Maroc,* VI, 247 f. The English at first had somewhat the same feeling; Sir Arthur Nicolson, said the Russian Ambassador in London, "did not conceal from me the fact that the Morocco question is disquieting the London Cabinet. . . . The experience of all European States, beginning with England, shows that it is easier to occupy a city than to withdraw again" (Benckendorff to Neratov. May 9. 1911; Siebert-Schreiner, p. 581).

Spain, protest; the Foreign Office ought to check the clamor that warships should be sent to Morocco.[97]

How far the French reports of disorders represented a genuine fear that their authority and European lives were endangered, and how far they were exaggerated as a pretext for securing a stronger grasp on the country, it is difficult to say. That they had been steadily extending their political grip on Morocco, and intended eventually to reduce it to a French protectorate, there is no doubt. Kiderlen likened it to the spread of oil upon water.[98] When the Russian Ambassador in Paris asked M. Cruppi, the French Minister of Foreign Affairs, how long the French would remain in Fez, the Minister answered evasively.[99] And Caillaux, who became Prime Minister in June 1911, has declared: "Our problem was nothing less than to regain all the ground lost since 1905, and to repair the consequences of the serious diplomatic check which we had suffered."[100]

In 1905, it will be remembered, Delcassé had been forced from office; but Delcassé was now back in the Cabinet again, just as the French were preparing to occupy Rabat and march to Fez. To be sure, he had only the naval portfolio, and the Prime Minister, Monis, had assured the German Ambassador that, "he had taken Delcassé into his cabinet on account of his notable work in the navy, and because his great technical knowledge was indispensable. Delcassé has firmly promised not to mix in foreign policy; anyway, his views today differ from those of some years ago."[101] But it was natural that, with his restless energy and memory of the past, Delcassé was suspected by the German Press of having a hand in the Moroccan policy, and later events

97 Kaiser to Bethmann, April 22; XXIX, 89.

98 G.P., XXIX, p. 169 f.

99 Izvolski to Neratov, May 24, 1911; L.N., I, 107.

100 Caillaux, *Agadir*, p. 29.

101 Schoen to Bethmann, March 4, 1911; G.P., XXIX, 74 note.

proved he had remained as determined an opponent of Germany as ever.[102] He told Izvolski that "his entrance into the Cabinet indicated the special care which would be devoted to France's military forces. His first task was the creation of a strong navy, and the efforts for the army would be redoubled. Although he had no intention of overstepping his office and arousing distrust in Germany," he was anxious to tighten up the relations with Russia. "According to general opinion, he will inevitably influence the activity of M. Cruppi, as the latter is very little versed in foreign affairs." [103]

Germany's intentions were a puzzle to the French at the time, and have remained something of a mystery, but they are now clear from a long memorandum which Kiderlen drew up on May 3 (greatly condensed):

> Three years have shown that the independence of Morocco, as contemplated in Algeciras Act, cannot be maintained in the face of native rebellion and imperialistic pressure from France and Spain. Sooner or later Morocco will inevitably be absorbed by these two neighbors. It is unlikely that a walled city like Fez can be captured by the natives and the revolt seems to be on the ebb. But the French fear for its safety and are preparing to send an expedition. This they have a right to do, and one must await the development of events. But if they march to Fez, it is hardly likely that they will withdraw; even if French public opinion approved withdrawal, it would be regarded by the natives as a sign of weakness. This would lead to new uprisings and new French military expeditions. The course of events shows that the provisions of the Act of Algeciras cannot be carried out. A Sultan who can only assert his authority with the aid of French bayonets can-

102 "In some of the German papers, Delcassé is regarded as the true originator of French Moroccan policy" (Russian Chargé d'Affaires at Berlin to Sazonov, April 28, 1911; Siebert-Schreiner, p. 580).

103 Izvolski to Sazonov, March 3 and 14, 1911; M.F.R., pp. 41, 43; L.N., I, 45, 48; Stieve I, 38, 41.

not maintain the independence which was the purpose of the Algeciras Act. Germany must recognize these facts and readjust her policy in accordance with them. After the French have been in Fez a while, we shall ask in a friendly way when they expect to withdraw. When they say that they cannot withdraw, we shall say that we understand this perfectly, but we cannot longer regard the Sultan as a sovereign independent ruler as provided by the Act of Algeciras; and since this is a dead letter, the Signatory Powers regain their freedom of action. It will do no good to protest against the French absorption of Morocco. We must therefore secure an object which will make the French ready to give us compensations. Just as the French protect their subjects in Fez, we can do the same for ours at Mogador and Agadir by peacefully stationing ships there. We can then await developments and see if the French will offer us suitable compensations. If we get these, it will make up for past failures and have a good effect on the coming elections to the Reichstag.[104]

The Kaiser was persuaded to approve this policy, though he ought to have foreseen that the *modus operandi* was dangerously analogous to that of Bülow and Holstein in 1905. He then departed for England to attend the unveiling of a memorial to Queen Victoria. Here he was cordially received, and got the impression that the English regarded the French Morocco action with regret. Sir Ernest Cassel and Prince Louis of Battenberg hinted that they hoped that German policy would not differentiate itself from that of England. But the Kaiser and Bethmann saw no reason for taking the hint, because Germany had not been consulted by England about Morocco in 1904, nor by Russia at Reval.[105]

104 G.P. XXIX, 101-108.

105 Bethmann's memorandum, May 23; *ibid.*, p. 120 f. Sir Edward Grey, however, reminded the German Ambassador on May 22, that in Moroccan questions England was bound by her agreement of 1904 to support France (*ibid.*, p. 119; Siebert-Schreiner, p. 583).

At the outset Kiderlen's program bade fair to work excellently. As the Pan-German Press began to demand compensations or the partition of Morocco, and the German Government maintained an ominous silence as to how it would use its freedom of action, the French began to be worried. Izvolski reported that so far as he was able to judge, "the Berlin Cabinet has chosen a very advantageous and skilful position: without protesting as yet against the French manner of action, it reserves the power of announcing at any moment that the Algeciras Act has been infringed—in this way German diplomacy dominates the situation and can, not only according to the development of events on the spot, but also according to the general trend of her domestic or foreign policy, suddenly render the Moroccan question more acute. . . . Sir Francis Bertie is personally convinced that Germany is only awaiting a suitable moment to declare the Act of Algeciras non-existent and then occupy one or two ports (including Mogador) on the Atlantic coast of Morocco." [106] A fortnight after the French military expedition occupied Fez, the Spanish troops landed at Larache. The French in turn denounced this action as a blow to the Algeciras Act and as endangering the international situation.[107]

By the middle of June the French intimated that they were ready to talk of a compensation for Germany; Cambon hinted at it very guardedly on June 11, when speaking of Morocco as a ripe fruit which must inevitably fall to France; [108] and Cruppi in Paris mentioned it in connection with a Congo-Cameroon railway project, but Kiderlen regarded this as a mere bagatelle. He wanted the whole French Congo! [109] But he did not want to ask for it until

[106] Izvolski to Sazonov, May 11, 1911; M.F.R., p. 88; L.N., I, 104; Stieve, I, 98 f.

[107] G.P., XXIX, 140 ff.; *Affaires du Maroc,* VI, 332 ff.

[108] G.P., XXIX, 124, 177 note; *Affaires du Maroc,* VI, 349 f.

[109] G.P., XXIX, 149 ff.

the appearance of a German ship at Agadir had frightened the French into coming forward with a very generous offer in return for Germany's abandoning Morocco to them completely.[110]

When therefore Cambon came to Kissingen to broach the subject with him on June 20, Kiderlen took an attitude of reserve. When Cambon intimated that France would be willing to make concessions in the Congo, but that there was no use talking further if Germany wanted part of Morocco, Kiderlen agreed completely. When Cambon left Kissingen for Paris to see how much his Government would offer, Kiderlen's last words were, "Bring us back something from Paris." [111] As several days passed without any French offer being made, and as the Kaiser was about to start on his northern cruise, Kiderlen went to Kiel to report on the situation and get a renewal of his consent to send warships to Morocco. On June 26 Kiderlen's laconic telegram, "Ships granted," indicated that he had secured the Kaiser's approval. Accordingly, the gunboat *Panther,* returning from southern Africa, was ordered to drop anchor at Agadir on July 1.[112]

On Saturday afternoon, July 1, as the *Panther* steamed into Agadir, Germany notified France and the other Powers that German business houses, alarmed at the fermentation among the natives caused by recent events, had asked for protection for their life and property in southern Morocco; the German Government had therefore sent a warship to Agadir, which would withdraw as soon as affairs in Morocco had calmed down.[113] It was true that German firms had petitioned the Foreign Office to protect their interests in southern Morocco,[114] but it is clear Kiderlen was using this

110 Zimmermann's memorandum, June 12, and Kiderlen's comments; *ibid.,* 142 ff., 177 ff., 184 ff.; also Jäckh, II, 123 ff.

111 *Affaires du Maroc,* VI, 372 ff.; G.P., XXIX, 142 note.

112 G.P., XXIX, 152 f.

113 G.P., XXIX, 153 ff.

114 G.P., XXIX, 153 note.

merely as a pretext. His real motive was to bring the French to the point of making a generous offer of Congo territory, and to emphasize to the Powers that the Algeciras Act had broken down.

On July 9, Cambon came again to see Kiderlen. He was deeply depressed and disturbed at the Agadir action, of which Germany had given no preliminary notice, whereas France had given ample notification of her march to Fez. The interview was long and difficult, and punctuated by silences. Each wanted the other to make proposals. Finally the words "Congo" and "Togo" were mentioned. But neither speaker would commit himself further, each declaring that he must get further information and instructions.[115] This delay and diplomatic fencing drew from the Kaiser the impatient comment:

> After four weeks! This is a cursed comedy! Nothing accomplished! What the devil is to be done now? This is a sheer farce, negotiating and negotiating and never getting any further! While we are losing precious time, the British and the Russians are stiffening up the frightened French and dictating to them what they at the most can condescend to allow us.[116]

Kiderlen was now in a very difficult position. When Cambon came to see him again on July 15, and spoke only of insignificant compensations, he decided to beat about the bush no longer. He took a map, pointed to the French Congo, and said Germany ought to have the whole of it. Cambon nearly fell over backward in astonishment. He declared that no French Government could ever give up a whole colony, but that part of it might be surrendered, if Germany gave up Togo and some of the Cameroons. From this interview Kiderlen received the impression that "to

[115] *Affaires du Maroc,* VI, 403 f.; Caillaux, 278 ff; G.P., XXIX, 173 ff.; Jäckh, II, 123 ff.

[116] G.P., XXIX, 177 f.

get a satisfactory result it would be necessary to take a very strong stand." [117] The whole matter was telegraphed to the Kaiser, who was still on his northern cruise. He was more dissatisfied than ever, and also alarmed at Kiderlen's attitude. He ordered positively that no steps involving threats to France should be taken in his absence. Realizing that it would be easier for the French Government to cede Congo territory to Germany, if Germany gave in exchange some small African territories of her own, he authorized Kiderlen to proceed with Cambon on this basis.[118] At the same time Treutler, the Foreign Office Minister who accompanied the Kaiser, telegraphed to Kiderlen: "As you know, it would be very difficult to get His Majesty's consent to steps which he assumes might lead to war." [119] Kiderlen was now ready to resign, because of the Kaiser's attitude, and because he himself believed the way to make the French yield was to make them feel that their refusal might mean war. But Bethmann persuaded him to stay in office and continue to negotiate on the basis indicated by the Kaiser.[120]

It was at this moment, when the Kiderlen-Cambon negotiations seemed to be making little progress, that England intervened. Many weeks before the *Panther* went to Agadir, Sir Edward Grey had feared that Germany meant to seek her compensation in West Morocco and establish the naval base on the Atlantic coast. To this England had been resolutely opposed for years; it had been one of her main motives for supporting France in Morocco. The *Panther* seemed to confirm Grey's fears. Therefore on July 4 he warned Germany that "a new situation has been created by the despatch of a German ship to Agadir; future developments might affect British interests more directly than they had hitherto been affected; and, therefore, we

117 G.P., XXIX, 184 ff.

118 Treutler to Bethmann, July 17; G.P., XXIX, 187 f.

119 G.P., XXIX, 188.

120 G.P., XXIX, 189 ff.; Jäckh, II, 128-134.

could not recognize any new arrangement which was come to without us."[121] Grey would have been less disturbed in his mind if he had known that Germany's real objective was the Congo and not a naval base on the Atlantic coast of Morocco. Kiderlen made a mistake in not reassuring him on this point. But Kiderlen, Bethmann and the Kaiser had all been bent on carrying the discussion of compensations directly with France alone, and had intimated politely that intervention by others was not desired.[122] They hoped to get more from France if others were not admitted to the discussion. Grey waited for more than two weeks for Germany to make some reply to his statement of July 4 that England wanted to be consulted in regard to any Moroccan settlement; but Germany remained silent. Grey was ready to accept a Franco-German settlement based on an exchange of French Congo territory for German African possessions, provided the terms of the settlement were acceptable to the French, and provided the Germans abandoned all intentions of having a foothold on the Moroccan coast. He had welcomed the suggestion of finding a solution in the French Congo.[123] But when Kiderlen demanded the whole Congo, the French told Grey that the German demands were unacceptable, reminded him of England's obligations under the Moroccan Agreement of 1904, and suggested that he take the initiative in calling another conference of the Powers to deal with the question.[124]

This hint that the Franco-German direct negotiations were likely to break down revived Grey's fears that the Germans would stay at Agadir. He therefore asked the German Ambassador to come to him, and told him informally that he understood that "there was danger that the negotiations

[121] G.P., XXIX, 167; Grey, I, 214. On the same day Grey told Paul Cambon that the Moroccan question ought to be discussed *à quatre*—by France, Spain, Germany, and England (*Affaires du Maroc,* VI, 392 ff.)

[122] G.P., XXIX, 155 ff.

[123] Grey, I, 223 f.

[124] De Selves to Paul Cambon, July 20; *Affaires du Maroc,* VI, 418 f.

would end without success, and then the question would come up: What is Germany doing in Agadir and its hinterland?" This was a question, he said, which involved English interests. So long as there had been a prospect that France and Germany might reach a settlement by exchanging colonial territory in Central Africa, he had kept aside; but as this now seemed unlikely, and as serious British interests were involved, he wished to suggest privately that it was time for England also to be heard—time for a discussion *à trois*—between France, Germany, and England. Grey was wise in wishing to find out Germany's real purpose and deal with it by the usual secret diplomatic methods without the noisy and embarrassing interference of the Press everywhere. But Metternich had no instructions to tell him that Germany wanted compensations in the Congo and not a naval port at Agadir. Grey therefore evidently came to the conclusion it was time to give Germany an unmistakable public warning, even though involving all the dangers of newspaper excitement and questions of "prestige." That very same evening without giving Metternich time to get new instructions from Berlin, Grey allowed Lloyd George to announce to the world that England demanded that she be consulted. In this famous Mansion House speech of July 21, Lloyd George said:

> But I am also bound to say this—that I believe it is essential in the highest interests, not merely of this country, but of the world, that Britain should at all hazards maintain her prestige amongst the Great Powers of the world. Her potent influence has many a time been in the past, and may yet be in the future, invaluable to the cause of human liberty. It has more than once in the past redeemed continental nations, who are sometimes too apt to forget that service, from overwhelming disaster, and even from national extinction. I would make great sacrifices to preserve peace. I conceive that nothing would justify a disturbance of in-

ternational good-will except questions of the gravest national moment. But if a situation were to be forced upon us in which peace could only be preserved by the surrender of the great and beneficent position Britain has won by centuries of heroism and achievement, by allowing Britain to be treated, where her interests were vitally affected, as if she were of no account in the Cabinet of nations, then I say emphatically that peace at that price would be a humiliation intolerable for a great country like ours to endure.[125]

This speech caused an explosion of wrath in Germany, where it was interpreted as a threat, and where it was felt that England was interfering in Franco-German negotiations which were none of her business. It made all the more effect that it was delivered, not by Grey himself, who was regarded as being unduly anti-German, but by the Chancellor of the Exchequer who had the reputation of being a man of peace and generally favorable to Germany. When he spoke out in this way he was regarded as having been selected by the Government in order to make the warning all the more emphatic. Both the Prime Minister and Sir Edward Grey had been consulted, and approved Lloyd George's action. Winston Churchill, the Home Secretary, was enthusiastic for it.[126] But he makes plain that he knew it was playing dangerously with fire. It greatly increased the already existing tension between England and Germany growing out of the naval competition. It might indeed have easily led to war, had not the Kaiser and Bethmann been determined not to allow the Moroccan affair to cause a European conflict. It did, however, produce two results which ultimately contributed to a peaceful solution of the Moroccan question. It led Germany to inform England at once that she had no intention of estab-

125 Grey, I, 216.

126 Asquith, *Genesis of the War,* p. 148; Churchill, I, 46 ff. Grey (I, 217) says he did not instigate it, but welcomed it.

lishing herself on the Atlantic coast of Morocco, which had been Grey's great cause of alarm. And it also caused Germany to moderate somewhat her demand on France. After four months of protracted and difficult negotiations, Kiderlen and Cambon were able to sign the agreement of November 4, 1911. By this Germany virtually acknowledged that the French might establish their desired protectorate over Morocco; in return France ceded more than 100,000 square miles of the French Congo, giving the Germans two much-needed river outlets to the Congo for the export of their Cameroon products; to give the appearance of an exchange of territories and make it easier for the French Government to justify the agreement to French public opinion, Germany ceded to France the "duck's bill," a small tract of valueless Cameroon territory east of Lake Chad. That the agreement represented a tolerably equitable compromise is evidenced by the fact that it met bitter criticism and opposition from the nationalists and colonial enthusiasts in both countries.[127]

As between England and Germany, the Agadir Crisis not only increased the friction between the two governments at the time, but it seems to have deepened Grey's suspicions of Germany's warlike inclinations. This is evident from his observations on the subject in his memoirs,[128] where he implies (quite contrary to facts) that "the Agadir Crisis was intended to end either in the diplomatic humiliation of France or in war;" and adds: "The militarists in Germany were bitterly disappointed over Agadir, and when the next crisis came we found them with the reins in their hands."[129] His feeling at the time was significantly expressed in his statement to the Russian Ambassador in London: "In the event of a war between Germany and

127 On these later negotiations and the Moroccan Convention of November 4, 1911, see G.P., XXIX, 293-454; *Affaires du Maroc,* VI, 423-635; and D.D.F., 3me Série, I, *passim,* especially No. 160.

128 Grey, I, 210-239.

129 Grey, I, 231, 233.

France, England would have to participate. If this war should involve Russia [the Ambassador had just assured him that it would], Austria would be dragged in too, for, although she has not the slightest desire to interfere in this matter, she will be compelled by force of circumstances to do so. There is no doubt that in such an event the situation in Albania will become aggravated. Consequently, it would no longer be a duel between France and Germany—it would be a general war." [130] Grey added, however, that he did not believe Emperor William wanted war. Two weeks earlier the Russian Ambassador had reported: "There is no use concealing the fact—one step further, and a war between England and Germany would have broken out as a result of the Franco-German dispute, although independent of it."

Between England and France the Agadir Crisis, like the Morocco Crisis of 1905, led to a tightening of the bonds between the two. France was grateful for Lloyd George's speech, and for the indications that England would not only give her the diplomatic support promised in the agreement of 1904, but also the military support contemplated in the military and naval "conversations" which had been going on between the two countries since 1906. On July 20, after Kiderlen's demand for the whole Congo and the day before Lloyd George's Mansion House speech, there took place at the French Ministry of War a Conference between General Wilson, the Head of the Department for Military Operations of the English General Staff, and General Dubail, the French Chief of Staff. It was "to determine the new conditions for the participation of an English army in the operations of the French armies in the North-East in case of a war with Germany." [131] The protocol of the Conference

130 Benckendorff to Neratov, August 16, 1911; Siebert-Schreiner, p. 598

131 French General Staff History, *Les Armées Françaises dans la Grande Guerre* (Paris, 1925), I, 49.

took care, as usual, to state that these "conversations, devoid of all official character, cannot bind either Government in any way," and aimed merely "to foresee the indispensable preparatory measures." But six weeks later, General Dubail stated to the Russians, as if there were no doubt in the matter, that the French army was ready to take the offensive against Germany "with the aid of the English army on its left wing." [132]

Russia, having just established more friendly relations with Germany as a result of the Potsdam agreements, did not wish to endanger these by too active a support of France in the Agadir affair. At the beginning, when requested by her ally to make representations at Berlin, Russia had done so in a perfunctory way, but without exerting any real pressure.[133] Later during the long Franco-German negotiations for a Congo-Cameroon exchange of territories, Izvolski himself says he worked "with all his strength" to moderate the French and urged them to yield to many of the German demands.[134] This is confirmed by Caillaux,[135] and by the French Ambassador in Russia, M. Georges Louis, who reported that Russia would honor her signature on the alliance, but that Russian public opinion would hardly understand a Franco-Russian war occasioned by a colonial question like Morocco. And when M. Louis pointed out to the Tsar that Morocco was as much of a vital interest to France, as the Caucasus and the control of the Black Sea to Russia, Nicholas II replied: "Keep in view the avoidance of a conflict. You know our preparations are not complete." [136] Russia did not at this time want to be

132 Protocol of the Franco-Russian Military Conference of August 31, 1911; M.F.R., p. 698; L.N., II, 421.

133 G.P., XXIX, 112, 117, 158 f., 168 ff.

134 Izvolski to Neratov, Sept. 14, 1911; M.F.R., p. 114; L.N., I, 132 f.; Stieve, I, 146.

135 Caillaux, *Agadir,* p. 142 ff.

136 Louis to De Selves, Sept. 7, 1911; Judet, *Georges Louis,* 156 f.; *cf.,* however, Poincaré, I, 294 ff.

drawn into a war over Morocco any more than France had wished hitherto to be drawn in over Balkan questions. Russia needed to build up her army and navy much further before risking a European War. But the very fact of this lukewarm support by Russia of French colonial interests, and by France of Russia's Balkan ambitions, became an added spur to Izvolski to tighten up the Franco-Russian Alliance after 1911. And in this he was soon aided by M. Poincaré, who became Minister of Foreign Affairs in France early in 1912.

Another effect of the Agadir Crisis and the consequent strengthening of the French grip on Morocco and the Western Mediterranean was Italy's decision that the time had come for her to seize Tripoli. This so weakened Turkey that Serbia and Bulgaria hastened to take steps toward the formation of a Balkan League, with Russia's assistance, which led to the Balkan Wars. These in turn further embittered the relations between Serbia and Austria, and so contributed to one of the main causes of the World War.

THE HALDANE MISSION, 1912

In 1908, as has been indicated above, Tirpitz had secured the adoption by the Reichstag of a naval program providing for the construction of four capital ships annually from 1908 to 1911, and for two annually from 1912 to 1917. The English had become greatly alarmed, both for their actual safety and for the disastrous effect upon Anglo-German relations. They had therefore made efforts to call a halt, or come to some understanding, but these had failed owing to the Kaiser's decisive opposition, culminating in his interview with Sir Charles Hardinge at Cronberg in August, 1908.

During the following months English alarm steadily increased, and frightened imaginations pictured a German invasion of England. Further antagonism between the two countries was caused by the unfortunate *Daily Telegraph* affair. The Kaiser had allowed an English friend to summarize a confidential talk in which the Kaiser refuted the idea that he was hostile to England. The English were "mad, mad as March hares," he had said, to suspect the German navy, which was simply to protect German commerce and not to attack England. The Kaiser was the friend of England. He wished to restrain the German people, whose prevailing sentiment was not friendly to England. But the English suspicions and Press attacks made his task of preserving peace difficult. As proof of his friendly attitude in the past, he recalled that during the Boer War he had refused to join France and Russia in putting pressure on England in favor of the Boers; on the contrary, he had even sent Queen Victoria a plan of campaign for use against the Boers. The Kaiser sent the manuscript of this summary to Bülow at his summer home at Nordeney on the shore of the North Sea, and Bülow, without studying it, sent it to the Foreign Office for examination and comment. But here an official, supposing that it had received Bülow's approval, allowed it to go out, and it was published in the London *Daily Telegraph* on October 28, 1908.[137]

The Kaiser had hoped the article would disarm England's suspicions and improve the relations between the two countries. It had precisely the opposite effect. It caused a storm of newspaper attacks on both sides of the North Sea, many of which were directed against himself personally. The English doubted his sincerity; they ridiculed and resented the idea that any advice of his had helped them win the Boer War; but they noted as ominous his admission that the prevailing sentiment in Germany was unfriendly

137 Reprinted in G.P., XXIV, 170-174; for the details of this incredible mistake and the storm which the article raised in both Germany and England, see *ibid.*, pp. 167-210.

to England. In Germany, the Liberals and Socialists protested bitterly against his ill-considered act and the dangers of his personal rule. Bülow tendered his resignation, but withdrew it after the Kaiser promised in the future not to talk politics without his Chancellor's advice. But in the great Reichstag debate growing out of this affair, the Kaiser felt that Bülow did not adequately defend his sovereign's position. He no longer regarded his Chancellor with the same favor and confidence.

Count Metternich, the German Ambassador in England, was greatly distressed at seeing the two countries drifting into mutual misunderstandings and recriminations which one day might lead to war. English public opinion was demanding that the Cabinet should assure the "Two Power Standard" (that the English navy should be as strong as the combined navies of any other two Powers), and that if Germany built four Dreadnoughts annually, England should build eight. Lord Roberts began to tour the country trying to arouse England to the creation of a huge army and the adoption of the continental system of universal military service, naming Germany as the enemy of the future. A year ago, reported Metternich, these speeches would have been regarded as so exaggerated that they would have made no impression; today they are taken more seriously. The fundamental cause of all this alarm and agitation, Metternich believed, was the rapid increase of the German navy. He therefore suggested the desirability of slowing down Germany's program of construction from four to three ships annually, and of trying to come to some understanding with England.[138]

Bülow personally was in favor of the suggestion. To facilitate an understanding with England he hastened to make the Morocco settlement of 1909, which he hoped

[138] Metternich to Bülow, Nov. 22, 27; Dec. 11, 20, 29, 1908; Jan. 1, 14, 20; G.P., XXVIII, 23-75.

would remove one of the political causes of England's distrust. He sent Metternich's despatches to Tirpitz for comment.

But the Admiral disagreed fundamentally with the wise Ambassador's diagnosis of the English situation. Tirpitz received part of his information about England from the German naval attachés, whose reports often sound like an echo of their master's voice and wishes. Tirpitz insisted that the fundamental cause of British alarm and agitation was not the German navy, but German industrial and commercial competition. The British were now getting accustomed to the idea of a respectable German navy, but what troubled them was the fact that Germany, like Holland in the seventeenth century, was everywhere taking their trade and capturing their markets. It would do little good to slow down the naval program; and, anyway, it was fixed by law and could not be altered. To alter it as a result of the English clamor would be an intolerable humiliation for Germany and encourage the navy propaganda in England. Therefore Germany ought to go ahead with the creation of the "risk navy," and trust to passing safely through the "danger zone" without a British attack. He also rejected Bülow's suggestion that it would be wiser to spend more money on naval defense—coast fortifications, torpedo-boats, and submarines—to which England would have no objection, rather than on so many Dreadnoughts, which Metternich believed were the main sources of irritation and alarm in London. He finally threatened to resign, if Bülow insisted.[139]

So Bülow, weakened in favor with the Kaiser after the *Daily Telegraph* affair, gave way before Tirpitz, and virtually abandoned Metternich's suggestion for the time being. He let slip the opportunity of taking the initiative afforded by King Edward VII's visit to Berlin in February, 1909,

139 Tirpitz to Bülow, Jan. 4, 1909; G.P., XXVIII, 51-55.

when Lord Crewe touched upon the question of naval competition.

As Metternich had forecast, the British agitation continued, and under its influence Mr. McKenna, First Lord of the Admiralty, proposed that for three years England should lay down six Dreadnoughts a year against Germany's four. A considerable number in the Cabinet and in Parliament thought that four British ships would still be enough to maintain a safe margin of British superiority. To overcome their objections and carry his bill, Mr. McKenna exaggerated the rate of speed at which the German ships were being completed. He alleged that Germany was exceeding the "normal rate" by secretly assembling materials beforehand, so that she might have 13 completed as early as 1911, instead of in 1912, as contemplated in the German navy law and as Metternich had expressly assured Grey beforehand was the actual intention.[140] Thus, Germany might have 13 Dreadnoughts to England's 16 in 1911, and an even more dangerous proportion in the following years. These statements of the First Lord of the Admiralty crystallized the general feeling of uneasiness into a first-class "navy scare." The public believed that Germany was trying to steal a march on England, and now clamored for eight ships, instead of the six which Mr. McKenna had asked for. "We want eight and we won't wait," was the popular cry. In the end, eight were voted, four at once, and four contingent upon Germany's continuing to build according to her program.

The effect on Anglo-German relations was deplorable. The Kaiser boiled with indignation at McKenna's "lies," and blamed Metternich for letting the wool be pulled over his eyes and for not taking a stiffer tone to Grey.[141] He was particularly displeased that Metternich had given the Eng-

140 Metternich to Bülow, Mar. 3, 10, 17, 1909; G.P., XXVIII, 93-112.

141 *Cf.* Kaiser's comments, G.P., XXVIII, 99, 102, 105, 113, 126.

lish to understand that Germany did not intend further to increase her program in the future—"a colossal personal concession, given right out of hand without getting the slightest thing from England in return, except untold lies, slanders, suspicions, and incivilities." [142]

Although Mr. McKenna later admitted his statements to have been incorrect,[143] they had done their damage in further increasing Anglo-German antagonism. In view of the offer implied in the English plan for four contingent ships, Bülow called a special meeting which was attended by Tirpitz, Bethmann, Moltke, and Metternich who came over from London. But the conditions demanded by Tirpitz and the Kaiser were such that there was no prospect of success in opening a negotiation.[144] Three weeks later Bülow was defeated in the Reichstag on his finance bill and resigned. Shortly afterwards the British voted to lay down the keels of the four contingent ships.

In this domestic conflict between Metternich and Bülow on one side, and Tirpitz and the Kaiser on the other, there is no doubt that wisdom lay with the former. Though it is true, as Tirpitz maintained, that commercial and industrial competition caused Anglo-German antagonism, it is much more true, as Metternich believed, that the naval question was the fundamental cause, and that the British were determined, cost what it might, to maintain the naval superiority which was vital for their commerce and for the very existence of the Empire. Metternich was quite right when he observed: "The services of Tirpitz in the development of our navy are unquestioned and great. But it is again evident that military, technical, and organizing ability are not necessarily united with correct political judgment. His judgment in regard to England is in such contradiction

142 Kaiser to Bülow, April 3, 1909; G.P., XXVIII, 145.

143 G.P., XXVIII, 391-395.

144 Proctocol of meeting, June 3, 1909; G.P., XXVIII, 168 ff.; *cf.* above 256 ff.

COUNT METTERNICH
German Ambassador in London, 1901-1912

PRINCE LICHNOWSKY
German Ambassador in London, 1912-1914

to the actual facts, that it almost seems as if he closed his eyes to them." [145]

Bethmann-Hollweg, who succeeded Bülow as Chancellor, agreed with Metternich as to the need for coming to a naval agreement with England. He believed that Germany could not be expected to have her 1908 program modified by a formal Reichstag amendment, but she might "retard the rate" of construction, by laying down less than the authorized four Dreadnoughts annually; he hoped that in return England might make concessions in regard to colonial questions and the Bagdad Railway and perhaps give some kind of neutrality promise. With this in view he opened negotiations with the British Ambassador, Sir Edward Goschen, in August, 1909, but they came to nothing.[146] In the course of the next two years he took up this idea several times, as well as various minor proposals to mitigate naval rivalry and suspicions, such as a mutual visiting of navy yards and exchange of information by naval attachés. But he had no success.[147] Finally, in the fall of 1911, after the heat of the Agadir Crisis had somewhat cooled down, the idea was taken in hand more definitely by two business men.

Albert Ballin, the head of the Hamburg-American Line, believed that the rapid building of the German navy was the main cause of Anglo-German antagonism and might some day lead to war. He considered this naval rivalry a far more serious threat to the peace of Europe than the Franco-Russian alliance. He was also on intimate and very friendly terms with Tirpitz and the Kaiser, as well as with Bethmann. He was aware that the German Government intended to lay a new navy law before the Reichstag in the spring of 1912, and he wished to bring about some

[145] Metternich to Bülow, Nov. 27, 1908; G.P., XXVIII, 19.

[146] G.P., XXVIII, 201-278.

[147] G.P., XXVIII, 281-423; *cf.* Grey to Goschen, May 5 and Oct. 26, 1910 (Grey, I, 244-247).

understanding with England before this made matters worse. His friend, Sir Ernest Cassel, was a rich and influential London banker. Born in Germany, Cassel had emigrated to England as a boy, and had at heart the interests of the land of his birth no less than of his adopted country. Like Ballin in Germany, he enjoyed in England a social and political position of great influence without holding any office in the Government. He had become an intimate friend of Edward VII, both as his banker and political adviser. He carried great weight among English business men in the "City," as well as in English political circles. Ever since July, 1909, Ballin and Cassel had been consulting together how to bring about an understanding between Germany and England.[148] In the winter of 1911-12, while the Berlin and London Foreign Offices were discussing possible colonial agreements,[149] and the English were becoming worried over rumors of an imminent new German Navy Law,[150] Ballin saw Cassel, who thereupon got into touch with Sir Edward Grey. This paved the way for the Haldane Mission. On January 29, 1912, Cassel came to Berlin with a memorandum[151] which had been approved by Sir Edward Grey, Winston Churchill, and Lloyd

[148] G.P., XXVIII, 205 ff.; Huldermann, *Albert Ballin,* 216 ff.

[149] G.P., XXXI, 71-94.

[150] G.P., XXVIII, 3-67.

[151] The full details of the Haldane Mission can now be followed in G.P., XXXI, 95-251; Tirpitz, *Erinnerungen,* p. 185 ff.; *Der Aufbau der deutschen Weltmacht,* pp. 197-338 (including many documents most of which were later published in G.P.); "Warum kam eine Flottenverständigung mit England nicht zur Stande?", in *Suddeutsche Monatshefte,* 23. Jahrgang (Nov., 1925), pp. 95-155, including polemical articles by Fritz Kern, Hans Hollmann and others, for and against the Tirpitz publication of documents; Bethmann-Hollweg, *Betrachtungen,* I, 48 ff.; Huldermann, *Albert Ballin,* pp. 235-270; E. Jäckh, *Kiderlen-Wächter,* II, 155 ff.; Siebert-Schreiner, pp. 613-639; Haldane, *Before the War,* pp. 55-72; Churchill, *The World Crisis, 1911-1914,* pp. 94-115; Asquith, *Genesis of the War,* 153-160; Grey, I, 240-248; Poincaré, I, 163-188. The subject is excellently summarized by B. E. Schmitt, in an article in *The Crusades and Other Historical Essays presented to Dana C. Munro* (N. Y., 1928), pp. 245-288.

George. This memorandum was to serve as a basis for opening official negotiations, and ran as follows:

> 1. Fundamental. Naval superiority recognized as essential to Great Britain. Present German naval program and expenditure not to be increased, but if possible retarded and reduced.
>
> 2. England sincerely desires not to interfere with German Colonial expansion. To give effect to this she is prepared forthwith to discuss whatever the German aspirations in that direction may be. England will be glad to know that there is a field or special points where she can help Germany.
>
> 3. Proposals for reciprocal assurances debarring either power from joining in aggressive designs or combinations against the other would be welcome.[152]

Sir Ernest Cassel showed this memorandum to the German Chancellor, who replied in writing that he welcomed this step taken by the British Government, and was in full accord with the memorandum, except that the new 1912 German naval estimates had already been arranged. He added that he and the Kaiser would be greatly pleased if Sir Edward Grey would visit Berlin, as the most effectual way of bringing the negotiations rapidly forward. He also gave Cassel a sketch of the proposed new Supplementary Navy Law, which indicated the creation of a third and new Naval Squadron to be formed from five existing reserve ships and three new ships; these three new ships, to be constructed during the next six years represented an augmentation of the 1908 program by three capital ships; that is, whereas by the 1908 program two capital ships were to be laid down annually between 1912 and 1917, by the new proposal three ships would be laid down in 1912, 1914, and 1916.[153] Cassel returned with this, and replied on Grey's behalf that if the German naval expenditure could be so

[152] G.P., XXXI, 98.

[153] G.P., XXXI, 99 note.

arranged, by a modification of the German rate of construction or otherwise, as to render unnecessary any serious increase of British naval expenditure, "British Government will be prepared at once to pursue negotiations, on the understanding that the point of naval expenditure is open to discussion and that there is a fair prospect of settling it favorably."[154] If this understanding was acceptable, a British Minister would come to Berlin. Bethmann replied that it was acceptable, provided England gave adequate guarantees of a friendly orientation of her general policy. "The agreement would have to give expression to a statement that both Powers agreed to participate in no plans, combinations or warlike engagements directed against either Power."[155]

Sir Edward Grey himself was unwilling to accept the cordial invitation to Berlin. His reasons, according to his memoirs of a dozen years later, were his fears that "the visit might arouse suspicion and distrust at Paris"; that the whole plan might be "one of those petty unofficial manoeuvres that could be avowed or disavowed at Berlin as best might suit German convenience"; and that he "had no great hope that anything would come of it."[156] Probably at the time his strongest motives were his deep distrust of Germany, and his fear of alarming France and so weakening the Entente. He decided not to go to Berlin himself, but arranged that Lord Haldane, the Minister of War, should go in his place. He desired that Haldane's visit "should be private and informal, so that, if nothing came of it, there should be no sensation and little disappointment to the public."[157] In 1910, when Bethmann was trying to secure an understanding with England, Grey had written to the British Ambassador in Berlin: "The mutual arrest

[154] Cassel to Ballin, Feb. 3, 1912; Churchill, p. 98; G.P., XXXI 102.
[155] G.P., XXXI, 103 f.
[156] Grey, I, 241 ff.
[157] Grey, I, 242 f.

or decrease of naval expenditure is *the* test of whether an understanding is worth anything," and that in Bethmann's overtures "the naval question was not sufficiently prominent." [158] He apparently did not think that there was any better chance of German naval reduction in 1912. He seems to have been convinced that the Kaiser had taken the initiative,[159] and then, if he had gone to Berlin and the negotiations had come to nothing, the German Government would have tried to put the blame upon him, Grey. But above all, Grey was determined not to endanger in the slightest degree the Entente with France. He had been told by Winston Churchill that the Admiralty was contemplating bringing home the Mediterranean ships, in order to meet the new Third Squadron which Tirpitz wanted; and that this meant relying on France in the Mediterranean (as was later actually arranged), so that certainly no change in the Entente would be possible, even if Grey desired it.[160] To allay French fears Grey at once informed the French Ambassador of the projected negotiations and assured him that he would do nothing with Germany that would tie his hands.[161] His statement to Paul Cambon shows what a restricted conception he had of the Haldane Mission: Haldane was "to find out whether Germany's recent overture was serious or not. He was also to attempt to gather information about the Bagdad Railway. But there is no question of entering upon negotiations. We desire only to

158 Grey to Goschen, May 5, 1910; Grey, I, 245.

159 Grey gave Paul Cambon the impression that the initiative had not come from England but from the Kaiser (Poincaré, I, 165, 168), and Churchill said the same to the German naval attaché, (G.P., XXXI, 104). But the Kaiser denied this at once in a marginal note, saying that he knew nothing of the proposal until Sir Ernest Cassel came to him with Grey's offer (*ibid.*, p. 122). The fact seems to be that the initiative came from Ballin and Cassel, and that only after the latter had talked with Grey, did the Kaiser suggest that the best way to facilitate the negotiations would be for Grey to come to Berlin.

160 Jan. 31, 1912; Churchill, p. 97.

161 Grey, I, 242.

learn the intentions of the German Government and to inquire about its plans for a naval program."[162] This attitude on Sir Edward Grey's part in itself foredoomed the Haldane Mission to failure.

Two other circumstances were hardly calculated to facilitate it. On February 7, the day of Lord Haldane's arrival in Berlin, the Kaiser in his speech at the opening of the Reichstag had announced in general terms that projects for the increase of the army and navy would be introduced later in the session. To this Winston Churchill immediately replied in a defiant speech at Glasgow, characterizing the German Navy as a "luxury": "The British Navy is to us a necessity and, from some points of view, the German Navy is to them more in the nature of a luxury. . . . We shall make it clear that other naval Powers, instead of overtaking us by additional efforts, will only be more outdistanced in consequence of the measures which we ourselves shall take." The speech offended Mr. John Morley and some of the other more pacific members of the British Cabinet, who sincerely hoped for an understanding with Bethmann, and it created no little indignation in Germany.[163]

In spite of these inauspicious circumstances Lord Haldane's reception at Berlin was most cordial and aroused considerable optimism, both in his own mind and especially in that of the Kaiser. His first interview on February 8 was with Bethmann at the British Embassy. He got the impression, which he always retained, that the Chancellor was as sincerely desirous of avoiding war as he was himself. Next day he lunched with Tirpitz and the Kaiser, and had a long and friendly discussion. He emphasized England's

162 Poincaré, I, 166. Haldane himself while in Berlin, also made a point of visiting the French Embassy and informing Jules Cambon that, even if a naval accord were reached, it would respect the existing ratio and not disturb the Entente (Poincaré, I, 167; G.P., XXXI, 126).

163 *Cf.* Churchill, 99-101; and G.P., XXXI, 55, 62, 126.

necessity of having a fleet large enough to protect her commerce and vital supply of food and raw materials. He admitted that Germany was free to build as she pleased, but so was England, and England would probably lay down two keels to every one which Germany added to her program. After a long discussion between him and Tirpitz about the Two Power Standard and naval ratios, in regard to which they could find no mutually satisfactory basis, the Kaiser proposed that it would be better to avoid for the moment discussing shipbuilding programs; instead of attempting to define ratios between the two navies, it would be better to have the agreement deal with the political question of general policy and colonial matters; after this was concluded and published, the Kaiser would have Tirpitz tell the Reichstag that the new political agreement with England had entirely altered the situation, and the three extra ships which the new navy law proposed to lay down in 1912, 1914, and 1916, would not be asked for until 1913, 1916, and 1919. Haldane tactfully assented to his suggestion and it was agreed that next day he should try to work out with Bethmann some formula of political agreement.[164]

In a long final interview on February 10, 1912, Bethmann proposed the following formula for a political agreement:

> I. The High Contracting Powers assure each other mutually of their desire for peace and friendship.
>
> II. They will not, either of them, make any combination, or join in any combination, which is directed against the other. They expressly declare that they are not bound by any such combination.
>
> III. If either of the High Contracting Parties becomes entangled in a war with one or more other Powers, the other of the High Contracting Parties will at least observe toward

164 Kaiser to Bethmann, Feb. 9; and Tirpitz's memorandum; G.P., XXXI, 112 ff.; 225 ff.; Haldane, *Before the War*, p. 57 ff.; Bethmann. *Betrachtungen*, I, 50 ff.; Tirpitz, *Memoirs*, I, 218 ff.

the Power so entangled a benevolent neutrality, and use its utmost endeavor for the localisation of the conflict.

IV. The duty of neutrality which arises from the preceding Article has no application in so far as it may not be reconcilable with existing agreements which the High Contracting Powers have already made. The making of new agreements which make it impossible for either of the Contracting Parties to observe neutrality toward the other beyond what is provided by the preceding limitation is excluded in conformity with the provision contained in Article II.[165]

Haldane objected to Article III as being too wide-reaching. It would preclude England from coming to the assistance of France should Germany attack her and aim at getting possession of such ports as Dunkirk, Calais and Boulogne. This England could never tolerate, because it was essential to her island security that these ports should remain in the friendly hand of France. Suppose, he said, that England were to attack Denmark, to seize a naval station, or for some other object disagreeable to Germany, Germany must have a free hand. Similarly, if Germany fell upon France "with her tremendous army corps," England could not bind herself to remain neutral. Furthermore, such a formula might also hamper England in discharging her existing treaty obligations to Belgium, Portugal and Japan. Lord Haldane therefore proposed to modify Articles II and III so that they would read:

II. They will not either of them make or prepare to make *any unprovoked attack* upon the other, or join in any combination or design against the other *for purposes of aggression,* or become party to any plan or naval or military enterprise alone or in combination with any other power directed to such an end.

165 Haldane, p. 64; G.P., XXXI, 116 ff. Kiderlen was not present at any of the conversations with Haldane, but he assisted Bethmann in drawing up this formula.

III. If either of the High Contracting Parties becomes entangled in a war with one or more other powers, *in which it cannot be said to be the aggressor,* the other of the High Contracting Parties will at least observe towards the power so entangled a benevolent neutrality and use its utmost endeavor for the localisation of the conflict.[166]

In his eagerness to secure an agreement Bethmann bit at this bait, without committing himself to accept it. Later, however, Germany argued, and with good reason, that the words "unprovoked" and "aggressor" were too uncertain in interpretation. In the complex situations which lead to war, it is always difficult to tell which side is really the aggressor. To make neutrality dependent on this uncertainty of interpretation would be robbing the agreement of all its value. Suppose Germany were drawn into a war with Russia and France, England's neutrality would then depend on whether or not she judged that Germany had "provoked" the war.

On colonial questions it was much easier for Haldane and Bethmann to come to a tentative agreement, which, however, was not to be regarded as binding upon either. In disposing of the Portuguese colonies Germany was to get Angola, and England Timor. Germany might buy the Belgian Congo, in return for giving a right of way to a Cape-to-Cairo Railway. England would cede Zanzibar and Pemba, in return for a satisfactory arrangement concerning the Bagdad Railway, such as 51% control of the section from Bagdad to Basra near the Persian Gulf.[167]

In regard to naval rivalry, Haldane agreed that the new Navy Law, having been publicly announced by the Kaiser, would have to be brought before the Reichstag, but he doubted very much whether the British Cabinet would regard as satisfactory the slight postponement in construc-

[166] G.P., XXXI, 118 f. Italics are by the present author.
[167] G.P., XXXI, 119 f.

tion which the Kaiser had mentioned the day before. England would be compelled to take counter-measures, and English public opinion would not be likely to sanction any "political agreement" between the countries at a moment when both were increasing naval expenditures.

After all these points had been noted down for further discussion by the London and Berlin Governments, Lord Haldane returned to England, carrying in his pocket the draft of the proposed German Navy Law. This had been confidentially given to him by the Kaiser, with permission to show it privately to his colleagues, although its contents was still unknown to the Reichstag and the German public. As it was a bulky document requiring technical knowledge, Haldane had not attempted to study it in Berlin. When he handed it over to Winston Churchill and the Admiralty for examination, they believed that it would entail very serious naval expenditures on the part of both England and Germany. The British therefore drew up and forwarded to Berlin a memorandum calling attention not merely to the three new capital ships contemplated, but to the great increase in personnel and expenditure by which Germany was proposing to provide for her new Third Squadron. To meet it England would have to lay down two keels to one for every capital ship added to the German Navy above the existing law; and she would make a further concentration of the Fleet in Home Waters, all involving £18,500,000 spread over the next six years. Public opinion would hardly regard these serious measures and counter-measures as appropriate to the coincident reëstablishment of cordial relations.[168] In other words, as Metternich bluntly reported, the "political agreement" was in danger of being shipwrecked on the Navy Law. To save the former, Germany must abandon or greatly modify the latter. In fact Grey told him flatly a few days later that it would be

168 G.P., XXXI. 134 f.

impossible to sign any political agreement at the moment when both countries were making increased naval expenditures, because public opinion would regard this as inconsistent.[169]

At Berlin this memorandum made a bad impression. Grey seemed to have damped all hopes of an understanding. He had abandoned the basis of discussion agreed to by Haldane at Berlin, shifting it away from the neutrality agreement, and giving priority to a criticism of the Navy Law and naval details, some of which (like the question of increase of personnel) had not been mentioned at all by Haldane. Even in colonial matters Grey seemed to be withdrawing what he had held out at first, and to be making difficulties: he had discovered that the Dutch had a prior right to purchase Timor; that England could hardly give up Zanzibar and Pemba without receiving some German territory in return; and that the suggested Bagdad Railway concession was insignificant and unsatisfactory.[170]

The Kaiser was especially indignant at the change in England's attitude. He was willing to proceed with negotiations on the basis of Haldane's conversations at Berlin, but not on the new basis which Grey was taking in London. A memorandum to this effect was drawn up for Metternich, but was held back by Bethmann for several days. In spite of everything, he and Kiderlen were still making a valiant struggle to satisfy Grey. They were trying to persuade Tirpitz and the Kaiser to abandon the three extra capital ships and postpone still further the publication of the Navy Law.[171] But the Kaiser was impatient to have the Navy Law laid before the Reichstag, inasmuch as it had already been announced in his speech, and been in English

[169] Metternich to Bethmann, Feb. 22, 24, 29; G.P., XXXI, 128-145.
[170] G.P., XXXI, 137-154.
[171] G.P., XXXI, 148-153; Tirpitz, *Der Aufbau der deutschen Weltmacht,* 290 ff., 306 ff.

hands for more than a fortnight. At Bethmann's insistence it had been withheld from publication hitherto, in order not to jeopardize the negotiations with England. Finally, on March 5, the Kaiser telegraphed to Bethmann that the memorandum for Metternich must be delivered to Grey on the morning of March 6, so that the Navy Law could then be laid before the Reichstag in the evening. He also took the unusual step of telegraphing himself directly to Metternich: it appeared that England had abandoned the basis agreed upon by Haldane; the Kaiser would stick to it and to the Navy Law except for a partial postponement of capital ships; but navy personnel was not to be a subject of discussion with England; if England withdrew her ships from the Mediterranean to the North Sea, this would be regarded as a threat of war and would be replied to by an increased Navy Law and by possible mobilization.[172]

Bethmann now sent in his resignation: he could no longer assume responsibility for such a policy or for such a direct dictation by the Kaiser to Germany's Ambassadors, without previous consultation with the Chancellor. The Kaiser hastened back to Berlin, persuaded Bethmann to remain in office, and agreed to a further postponement of the Navy Law and the continuance of the negotiations with England. Thereupon Tirpitz in turn threatened to resign, if the Navy Law were dropped altogether.[173] After a sharp domestic conflict between the two Ministers, the Admiral virtually triumphed over the civilian Chancellor. It was decided that no reduction in the Navy Law should be made beyond the minor matter of retarding the date for the capital ships, which Tirpitz had already grudgingly conceded.

Meanwhile Bethmann had been continuing his negotiations with England,[174] but they never had any chance of

172 G.P., XXXI, 156.
173 *Ibid.,* 157 note; Tirpitz, pp. 317-325.
174 G.P., XXXI, 159-210.

success as far as a neutrality agreement or naval limitation was concerned. They were virtually abandoned as hopeless on March 29, when Grey informed Metternich that the English Cabinet had finally decided definitely against Bethmann's original neutrality formula. Grey offered instead another much more restricted formula, which Germany rejected as not giving any satisfactory security against war with England.[175] Already, on March 18, Winston Churchill had laid before Parliament the British Navy Estimates, providing for two keels to every additional German one, and for the other greatly increased naval expenditures which he had threatened as England's reply to the expected German Navy Law. The Atlantic fleet would be moved from Gibraltar to Home Waters and replaced at Gibraltar by the Mediterranean ships which had hitherto had their base at Malta. He indicated, however, that if Germany made no increase, neither would England; the two navies would then stand in the same ratio to each other as before, and both countries would be spared enormous expenditures.[176] He did not make this proposal officially to Germany, however. On April 14 the German Navy Law was finally laid before the Reichstag, and accepted by it, unmodified, on May 14.[177]

The Haldane Mission failed primarily from two causes: England's unwillingness to make any political agreement concerning neutrality which would in any way limit her freedom to aid France; and Germany's unwillingness to make any worth-while reductions in the Supplementary Navy Law which would satisfy England. Each country was seeking a concession which dominant ministers in the other were determined not to make. Only in the third group of subjects under consideration—colonial matters and the

[175] G.P., XXXI, 210 ff.
[176] G.P., XXXI, 193-201; Churchill, 107 ff.
[177] Tirpitz, 334 ff.

Bagdad Railway—was it possible to continue successful negotiations; in this less difficult field of economic imperialism mutually satisfactory agreements were gradually worked out, and were complete for signature on the eve of the World War.[178] Thus, the Haldane Mission, like the Potsdam negotiations with Russia in 1910, resulted in removing some causes of friction, but they both failed in one of their main objects—the securing of some written agreement which would lessen Germany's political isolation and loosen the bonds of the Triple Entente.

THE TIGHTENING OF THE TRIPLE ENTENTE, 1912

Germany's overthrow of M. Delcassé in 1905, and her sudden sending of the *Panther* to Agadir, were regarded by the French as "brutal acts"—as exhibitions of the German habit of thumping the green table with the mailed fist to secure diplomatic victories. On both occasions they had been frightened by what they feared were German threats of war if they did not yield. In both cases therefore they had been forced to make what they felt to be humiliating concessions, because they were not prepared to take up the German challenge. Or as M. Poincaré puts it: "Germany's policy continued to be dominated by the arrogant spirit which since the war of 1870 had led to the Franco-German incidents of 1875 and 1887, and which between 1905 and 1911 had constantly poisoned affairs in Morocco. After the insult of Tangiers came the threat of Agadir. Instead of being stung into action by these repeated provocations, France, in her desire for peace,"[179] agreed to the Algeciras Conference, and to territorial concessions in the Congo in exchange for liberty of action in Morocco. These acts of Germany, as well as her ultimatum to Russia in the Bosnian Crisis and the Kaiser's bellicose gestures, had

178 G.P., XXXI, 255-305; XXXVII, 1-470.
179 *Foreign Affairs* (N.Y.), Oct., 1925, 7.

gradually aroused in a group of French politicians a new national spirit. They had revived the desire for *revanche* and the recovery of Alsace-Lorraine. They had created the feeling that France had suffered long enough from the German menace from across the Rhine. There had grown up the determination that in the future, if Germany made a new threat of force, it would be better to risk war than accept a new humiliation. This new national spirit, determination, and self-confidence was greatly increased by the friendship of England and the growing conviction that in case of a conflict with Germany, England would not only stand behind France with her fleet, but would send English troops to strengthen the left wing of the French army in northern France. This would give a good prospect of victory, and the fruits of victory would be the recovery of the lost provices and the end of the nightmare of the German menace. Most of these French leaders, like the mass of the French people, did not want war; but if Germany's desire for the "hegemony of Europe" and her attempt again to use the mailed fist to force a diplomatic triumph brought on another international crisis, it would be better to fight than to back down. As they had little doubt that Germany would attempt some new aggression, this would make war "inevitable." France must therefore prepare for it by increasing her own army and navy at home, and by tightening her relations with her ally on the other side of Germany and with her friend across the Channel.

This new national feeling was personified in M. Raymond Poincaré and the little group of men with whom he was closely associated. Not only was he the embodiment of the *réveil national*. By his determination, firmness, and ability, he did more than any other man to strengthen and to stimulate it. It found expression in the overthrow of the Caillaux Ministry, which was accused of having been too yielding to Germany in the Agadir Crisis, and in the formation, on January 13, 1912, of the "Great Ministry" or "National Ministry," in which M. Poincaré was Prime Minister and Minister of Foreign Affairs, M. Millerand Minister of War, and M. Delcassé Naval Minister. In announcing its program, M. Poincaré declared that its first task would be to unite all groups of Republicans by a single national feeling, to organize the new protectorate in Morocco, and to maintain courteous and frank relations with Germany; and, he added,

> As always, we intend to remain loyal to our alliances and our friendships—we shall make it our duty to unite, like twin convergent forces, the financial strength which is such a help for France, with her military and naval strength. However profoundly pacific our country may be, it is not master of all eventualities and it intends to live up to its duties. The army and the navy will be the object of our attentive solicitude.[180]

Born at Bar-le-Duc in Lorraine, M. Raymond Poincaré was ten years old when the German armies overran France in 1870, and took his home from his country. Son of a distinguished meteorologist, brother of a distinguished physicist, and related to a distinguished mathematician, M. Poincaré himself soon showed an ability at the bar which brought him into the Chamber of Deputies at the early age of twenty-seven, and into the Cabinet as Minister of Education six years later in 1893. Later he was Vice-President of the Chamber and twice Minister of Finance, before taking the Premiership and Foreign Affairs portfolio in 1912. No one since Bismarck's day has equalled him in sheer ability. His length of public service, his extraordinary vitality and endurance, his capacity for mastering and remembering detail, his clearness of purpose and determination to achieve it, have all combined to make him one of

180 Poincaré, I, 24; G.P., XXXI, 379.

the most remarkable of modern statesmen. All these native qualities, united with his dialectical skill and legal training, enabled him easily to vanquish his opponents in the Chamber of Deputies and to dominate his colleagues or subordinates in the Cabinet. One may not always approve of his aims, but one must admire the skill and ability with which he has achieved them. He knew precisely what he wanted, and he set about to secure it with singular directness and determination. The simplicity and brevity of his despatches are a refreshing contrast to the usual diplomatic circumlocutions and verbiage. His natural timidity was more than compensated by his bold energy. Such was the man who mainly directed and controlled French foreign policy from 1912 to 1914. In his memoirs he frequently denies that he pursued a personal policy as Minister of Foreign Affairs, or exceeded his constitutional position after he became President of the Republic in February, 1913, by imposing his wishes on the Ministers of Foreign Affairs who succeeded him. But with his ability, energy, and strong personality, it was inevitable that he should be the guiding spirit. In spite of his denials, we believe that he exercised a strong influence in the direction of an aggressive and dangerous policy, which was not a reflection of the wishes of the great majority of the truly peace-loving French people from 1912 to 1914, and which they would not have approved, had they been fully aware of it and the catastrophe to which it was leading.[181]

The man who coöperated most closely with M. Poincaré in his task of tightening the Triple Entente was the Russian Ambassador at Paris. It now is clear that Izvolski was vain, self-important, inclined to intrigue, and not always trustworthy. Consequently his reports must be

[181] Next to the revelation of his character and aims in his own Memoirs (see above, ch. i, at notes 45-47), the best-informed and most fair-minded account of M. Poincaré in English is the biography by Sisley Huddleston, *Poincaré*.

taken *cum grano salis.*[182] Nevertheless, his characterizations of M. Poincaré in the following quotations seem to be substantially accurate. He describes the new Minister of Foreign Affairs as "a very strong personality"; a man whose sensitive *amour propre* must be "taken into account"; one who "while often displaying useless rudeness and breaking windows without reason, has never given me cause to doubt his veracity"; "a passionate character and one who goes in a straight-line," whose "energy and decision" it is important to have wholly on Russia's side and turn to advantage.[183] After his election to the Presidency, M. Poincaré told Izvolski that he would still "have full opportunity to influence directly the foreign policy of France, and that he would not fail to take advantage of it to insure intact the policy founded on a close alliance with Russia. In his opinion it is of the highest importance for the French Government to prepare French opinion in advance to take part in a war which might break out over the Balkan question. For this reason the French Government requests us not to undertake any personal action of a nature to provoke such a war without an exchange of views beforehand with France."[184] Thenceforth, to the World War, the Russians found him "an ardent and convinced partisan of a close union between France and Russia and of a constant exchange of views between the two allies on all the most important questions of international policy";[185] and in

182 M. Poincaré has much to say on this score (e.g., I, 294 ff., 317 ff.; II, 335 ff.; III, 90 ff.). He has even said that he had so little confidence in Izvolski that in August, 1912, he "made energetic representations about him to M. Kokovtsev, President of the Russian Council, asking for his recall" (*Foreign Affairs* (N.Y.), Oct. 1925, p. 10). If this is true, and if he had so little confidence in Izvolski before the War as he indicates in his post-war memoirs, it is a pity he did not make his energetic representations to the Tsar and to Izvolski's official superior, M. Sazonov, and really secure his recall. Probably he feared that to do so might antagonize Sazonov and weaken the Alliance.

183 L.N., I, 203, 216, 266, 281 f.

184 L.N., II, 14 f.

185 L.N., II, 360. Kokovtsev had the same impression (*ibid.*, II, 393).

general, in a view of the Balkan situation, a man who would never fail Russia in case of a war with Germany.[186]

One of the first tasks which occupied M. Poincaré's attention, after forming his "National Ministry," was the cementing of closer relations with England. The Haldane Mission and the possibility of an Anglo-German *rapprochement* caused him some uneasiness, in spite of Sir Edward Grey's assurances. He therefore welcomed a curious step taken by Sir Francis Bertie, the English Ambassador at Paris. Although Grey was making no concessions which would satisfy Germany, Bertie feared that in the future he might change his mind under the influence of men like Lord Loreburn, Harcourt, and the other members of the Cabinet who were more eager for an understanding with Germany, and who might make trouble if they learned of the Anglo-French military and naval "conversations" which had been going on for six years but of which they had not been informed. Bertie therefore quite privately and unofficially suggested to Poincaré that he would do well to point out firmly to Grey the dangers involved in any neutrality agreement with Germany. Taking the hint, but not revealing where it came from, Poincaré sent an energetic despatch to Paul Cambon to this effect. Cambon presented the substance of it to Grey on March 29.[187] This was the very day on which the British Cabinet finally decided to give its negative answer to Bethmann's neutrality formula, and buried the hopes which had centered in the Haldane Mission.[188] It is not clear whether Cambon's interview came before or after the Cabinet meeting, nor whether it had any decisive effect on England's action. That Poincaré may have boasted later to Izvolski of having wrecked the

186 L.N., I, 326, 346 ff.; II, 10, 15, 345, 570.

187 Poincaré, I, 170-178.

188 G.P., XXXI, 210 ff. Germany suspected that Grey's negative attitude was partly caused by French pressure (*ibid.*, 144, 476 ff., 489 ff.).

Haldane Mission is quite possible.[189] But in view of Sir Edward Grey's evident determination from the outset not to concede any neutrality agreement which would limit his freedom in taking sides with France in case of a Franco-German war, and in view of the fact that even before March 29 the Haldane negotiations had virtually broken down, it seems very doubtful whether Poincaré's intervention had the decisive effect which Izvolski implies. Of course, it may be that Poincaré made earlier representations to Grey on the subject than those which he gives in his memoirs. Grey in his memoirs says nothing of this intervention on Poincaré's part. On this point, as on so many others, we must await a full publication from the English archives to learn the precise truth.

The Haldane Mission, however, impelled Poincaré to try to secure from England a binding statement in writing. Winston Churchill's plan to withdraw British ships from the Mediterranean for a stronger concentration against Germany in the North Sea, foreshadowed in his speech of March 18, 1912,[190] aroused a lively discussion in the British and French Press. It was urged that the time had come for naval coöperation between the two countries. If England withdrew her naval forces from the Mediterranean and protected the north coast of France against the possibility of a German attack, France could withdraw her fleet from

189 Izvolski to Sazonov, Dec. 5, 1912 (M.F.R., p. 609; L.N., I, 365 f.; Stieve, II, 377): "In my conversation with Poincaré and Paléologue I have been able to learn *in a very confidential way* that, *à propos* of the famous trip of Lord Haldane to Berlin, . . . Poincaré told the British Government that so long as France and England had no written agreement of a general political character, the signing of such an agreement between Germany and England would at once put an end to the existing Anglo-French relations. His protest had the expected effect and the London Cabinet rejected the German proposition." Poincaré made these confidences to Izvolski in December, 1912, if correctly reported, just at the time he was trying to convince Russia of the strength and solidarity of the Triple Entente and to persuade Sazonov in consequence to take a stiffer attitude in support of Serbia.

190 Churchill, pp. 97, 111 ff.; G.P., XXXI, 147 f., 156, 198, 218.

Brest and look after British interests, as well as her own, in the Mediterranean. In connection with this discussion, many British newspapers urged that the Anglo-French Entente should be definitely extended to a regular defensive alliance. "The only alternative to the constant menace of war is a new system of precise alliances."[191] This also was the feeling of M. Poincaré. Upon instructions from him, Paul Cambon spoke to Sir Arthur Nicolson about the need of strengthening the Entente Cordiale through a written agreement:

> "You see there is a cause of weakness in M. Poincaré's situation. More than anyone else, he is a partisan of the Entente with England, but to the important politicians, to his colleagues in the Cabinet, to the leaders of French public opinion who question him, he cannot give them to understand that there exist between us other bonds than those of sympathy. This is enough between two Governments sure of their reciprocal intentions. It is not enough for public opinion. The enemies of England in France (they are few but they exist) proclaim that our relations with you offer no security. I have, therefore, asked myself if we could not find together a formula which would permit us to reassure uneasy and doubting spirits. I know that the British Government does not have the right to bind itself without the authorization of Parliament, but there is no need of an agreement in duplicate, of a treaty drawn up and signed; we could content ourselves with an exchange of declarations. This is what we would have done in 1905 with Lord Lansdowne, if the resignation of M. Delcassé had not cut our conversation short."[192]

Sir Arthur Nicolson was personally favorable to making such an agreement, which, according to M. Poincaré, would

[191] *London Daily Express* of May 27, 1912; see also summaries of the British and French Press concerning the desirability of changing the Entente Cordiale into a regular alliance in G.P., XXXI, 475-556; Siebert-Schreiner, pp. 640-646.

[192] Cambon to Poincaré, April 18, 1912; Poincaré, I, 173 f.

have been a step further in the transformation of the Entente into an alliance.[193] But Sir Edward Grey, who had already been severely criticized in Parliament for subserviency in following in the wake of the French and Russian imperialism in Morocco and Persia, did not feel like taking such a momentous step without the knowledge of the whole Cabinet. The majority of them were still uninformed even of the military "conversations" which had been going on since 1906. Cambon's suggestion, therefore, remained for the moment without results. Meanwhile M. Poincaré strengthened the Triple Entente and the naval position of France in the Mediterranean by a Naval Convention with Russia.[194]

In May, 1912, Winston Churchill, accompanied by Mr. Asquith, visited Malta to confer with General Kitchener as to the situation in Egypt and the British position in the Mediterranean. Upon his return he announced more definitely in Parliament, on July 22, the Admiralty plan for withdrawing ships from the Mediterranean for concentration in the North Sea. At the same time he proposed to the French Military Attaché a draft plan for the coöperation of the British and French fleets. But the French hesitated to accept it, because its cautious preamble stated that it was not to affect the liberty of action of either party; this robbed it of its value in the eyes of the French.[195]

But Grey and Churchill did not want to tie their own hands by any binding written obligation. Even a naval arrangement, by which England withdrew her Mediterranean fleet to the North Sea, while the French shifted their Brest fleet to Toulon, was in danger of creating an obligation on England's part to protect the northern

193 Poincaré, I, 174. France and England kept Russia in the dark about this; denials were made by Nicolson to Benckendorff in London, and by Poincaré to Izvolski in Paris; Siebert-Schreiner, pp. 641-644.

194 See below, at notes 205-207.

195 Poincaré, I, 215-219.

coasts of France, as Grey had gathered in conversations with Cambon in July.[196]

Churchill also was well aware of this danger. Like Mr. Campbell-Bannerman in 1906,[197] and like Mr. Asquith in 1911,[198] he perceived that the French would be encouraged to count upon British assistance; this would virtually create an obligation and thus limit England's freedom of action. As he pointed out to Grey: "Freedom will be sensibly impaired if the French can say that they had denuded their Atlantic seaboard and concentrated in the Mediterranean on the faith of naval engagements made with us. [He did not think that such a statement by the French would be true, because such a distribution of the fleets was the best policy for both Governments anyway.] Consider how tremendous would be the weapon which France would possess to compel our intervention if she could say, 'On the advice of and by arrangement with your naval authorities, we left our northern coasts defenseless.' Everyone must feel, who knows the facts, that we have the obligation of an alliance without its advantages, and above all without its precise definitions."[199]

While these Anglo-French negotiations were going on but before a decision had been reached, it was announced prematurely, through an inadvertence on the part of one of M. Delcassé's subordinates, that the Brest fleet was to be transferred to the Mediterranean. This news, says M. Poincaré, caused great excitement, and was interpreted by the Press as a sign that an Anglo-French naval agreement had been definitely concluded.[200] This incident gave a new

196 Poincaré, I, 218.

197 See above, ch. iii, at note 188.

198 *Cf.* Asquith to Grey, Sept. 5, 1911 (Grey, I, 92): "Conversations such as that between Gen. Joffre and Col. Fairholme seem to me rather dangerous; especially the part which refers to possible British assistance. The French ought not to be encouraged, in present circumstances, to make their plans on any assumptions of this kind."

199 Churchill to Grey, Aug. 23, 1912, Churchill, p. 112.

200 Poincaré, I, 217.

impulse to the negotiations. Poincaré again instructed Cambon to ask Grey for a written agreement. Grey finally consented to give one. But before taking such an important step he rightly believed that it should be known to and approved by the whole Cabinet, and all its members were at last informed of the Anglo-French "conversations" which had been going on since 1906. He also insisted that it should not take the shape of a formal diplomatic document, but merely of a personal correspondence between himself and M. Cambon.[201] Accordingly, on November 22, he handed M. Cambon a letter which had been approved by the Cabinet, and received one in similar terms from him in exchange next day. Grey's cautiously expressed letter was as follows:

FOREIGN OFFICE,
My dear Ambassador, November 22, 1912.

From time to time in recent years the French and British naval and military experts have consulted together. It has always been understood that such consultation does not restrict the freedom of either Government to decide at any future time whether or not to assist the other by armed force. We have agreed that consultation between experts is not, and ought not to be regarded as, an engagement that commits either Government to action in a contingency that has not arisen and may never arise. The disposition, for instance, of the French and British fleets respectively at the present moment is not based upon an engagement to cooperate in war.

You have, however, pointed out that, if either Government had grave reason to expect an unprovoked attack by a third Power, it might become essential to know whether it could in that event depend upon the armed assistance of the other.

I agree that, if either Government had grave reason to expect an unprovoked attack by a third Power, or something that threatened the general peace, it should immediately discuss with the other whether both Governments should act

201 Poincaré, I, 219 ff.; Grey, I, 93 ff.

together to prevent aggression and to preserve peace, and, if so, what measures they would be prepared to take in common. If these measures involved action, the plans of the General Staffs would at once be taken into consideration, and the Governments would then decide what effect should be given to them.

Yours, &c.
E. GREY.[202]

These Grey-Cambon letters fixed the relations between the French and British Cabinets, so far as any written statements were concerned, down to the outbreak of the War. Sir Edward Grey continued to cherish the illusion that he still had his "hands free"; and this was true as far as the wording of the letters went. But as Mr. Campbell-Bannerman and Mr. Asquith had pointed out, the military conversations were dangerous in the encouragement they gave to the French; and as Winston Churchill warned, the new arrangement of the British and French navies, which took place in the fall of 1912, tied England to France more closely still. It created for England an inescapable moral obligation to protect the coast of France in case of a war between France and Germany—that is, to participate on the French side no matter how the war arose. To be sure, Poincaré was aware that Grey had carefully stated that if there was reason to expect "an unprovoked attack," the two Governments would "discuss" whether they would act together. He knew that Grey would have to reckon with a strong pacific group within the British Cabinet and among the British people; with them it would make a great difference how the war arose. Hence he was very careful, as will appear in connection with the crisis of July, 1914, to make it appear that Austria and Germany were the aggressors. The French military authorities also, in drawing up "Plan XVII" (which in a modified form was the plan of

[202] Grey, I, 94 f.

campaign used by the French in 1914), were aware that they could not count with certainty upon the coöperation of the British army; but they had no doubt that they could depend upon the British navy:

> On the sea, however, we can count without risk upon the effective support of the British fleet. On land, an understanding established between the General Staffs of the two countries has provided for the employment on our extreme left of an English army comprising . . . 120,000 men. [But this support remains doubtful.] We should therefore act prudently in not taking into consideration these English forces in our plan of operations."[203]

This, however, did not mean that General Joffre did not expect English military aid, but merely that the French mobilization plan should not be made absolutely dependent upon British military coöperation. The further details of "Plan XVII" show that not only was the British Expeditionary Force expected, but elaborate provisions were made for its transportation and concentration on the Belgian frontier.[204]

Significant from the political point of view is this French conviction that they could count on the British navy, for this would involve British participation in the war, with all advantages to France and Russia which would accrue from England's great naval superiority in the way of blockading Germany and shutting her off from food and war materials, to say nothing of the great moral effect of having the British Empire actively engaged on the side of the Franco-Russian Alliance.

Closely connected with these Anglo-French naval arrangements was the Franco-Russian Naval Convention of July 16, 1912. Russia wished to have absolutely undis-

203 Basis of "Plan XVII"; French General Staff History, *Les Armées françaises dans la Grande Guerre,* I, 19.

204 *Les Armées françaises dans la Grande Guerre,* I, 47 ff.

puted naval domination of the Black Sea. She had also long wished to control the Straits and Constantinople. A first step in this direction would be to secure a free passage for her warships through the Bosphorus and the Dardanelles. Izvolski had several times attempted to gain this but without success.[205] Italy's naval activity and closing of the Dardanelles during the Tripolitan War again made Russia acutely sensitive to the importance of the Straits Question. She believed that her French ally could and ought to aid the Russian fleet to retain its supremacy in the Black Sea, by hindering the Austrian or Italian naval forces from passing the Straits. In case of a European War this would safeguard the left flank of the Russian army; this in turn would be of advantage to the Triple Entente in the other theatres of war. Russia also wished to be able to transfer some of her Baltic fleet to augment her Black Sea fleet, and to have a possible naval base in the Mediterranean. This could be provided if the French would develop the port of Bizerta in Northern Africa and allow the Russians to use it. Such were some of the considerations which made the Russians desire a closer naval agreement with France. The French, on their part, were glad to meet all Russian wishes as far as possible, in order to strengthen the solidarity of action between the two countries.[206]

The Franco-Russian Military Convention of 1894 contained nothing concerning the coöperation of the navies of the two countries. This was owing to the relatively late establishment of Naval Staffs as distinct from the Army Staffs, the French Naval Staff not being formed until 1902,

[205] See below, ch. v, *passim.*

[206] *Cf.* *L'Alliance Franco-Russe,* pp. 133-139; Poincaré, II, 112-114; V. Egoriev and E. Schvede, "La Convention Navale de 1912," in *Les Alliés contre la Russie* (Paris, 1926), pp. 54-64 (containing new material from the Russian archives); Izvolski correspondence, July 18, Aug. 2, 5, 6, 10, 14, 17, 18; and Sazonov's report to the Tsar of Aug. 17, 1912 (M.F.R., pp. 229-256; L.N., I, 296-309; II, 338 f., 527-534; Stieve, II, 194-228); G.P., XXXI, 520-546.

and the Russian not until 1908. But by 1911 both countries recognized the desirability of extending their alliance by a Naval Convention analogous to the Military Convention. In the spring of 1912, upon the initiation of the Russians, negotiations to secure this took place in Paris between army and navy officers of both countries. They resulted in the secret Naval Convention signed on July 16 by Admirals Aubert and Lieven and by the Naval Ministers, Delcassé and Grigorovitch, and confirmed by an exchange of notes between Sazonov and Poincaré a month later, upon the latter's visit to Russia. It declared: "The naval forces of France and Russia will coöperate in all the eventualities in which the alliance contemplates and stipulates the combined action of the land armies." It also provided in time of peace for the preparation of this coöperation by means of conferences at regular intervals between the Naval Staffs of the two countries. The protocols of these subsequent conferences are not given in the *French Yellow Book,* but their substance has recently been revealed from the Russian archives. They dealt with the development of Bizerta as a naval base for the French and Russian fleets, for its connection with Sebastopol by wireless telegraph and for secret naval codes. In general it was agreed that naval domination was to be secured by France in the Mediterranean, by England in the North Sea, and by Russia in the Baltic and Black Seas.

When Poincaré visited Russia in August, 1912, one of his main topics of conversation with Sazonov was the closer coöperation of the naval forces of the Triple Entente. He confided to Sazonov, according to the latter's report to the Tsar, that "although there does not exist between France and England any written treaty, the Army and Navy Staffs of the two countries have nevertheless been in close contact. This constant exchange of views has resulted in the conclusion between the French and English Governments of a verbal agreement, by virtue of which England has declared herself ready to aid France with her military and naval forces in case of an attack by Germany."[207] He begged Sazonov to "preserve the most absolute secrecy in regard to the information," and not give the English themselves any reason to suspect that he had been told of it. He also urged Sazonov to take advantage of his coming visit to England to discuss the question of a possible Anglo-Russian naval agreement, which would thus complete the naval coöperation of the three Triple Entente Powers in case of a conflict with Germany.[208]

Sazonov followed Poincaré's suggestion. On his visit to Balmoral in September, he informed Grey of the substance of the new Franco-Russian Naval Convention, saying that the French would endeavor to safeguard Russian interests in the southern theater of war by preventing the Austrian fleet from penetrating into the Black Sea; he then asked whether England would perform the same service for Russia in the North by keeping the German fleet out of the Baltic. According to Sazonov's report to the Tsar, Grey declared that, if the contemplated conditions arose, England would make every effort to strike the most crippling blow at German naval power:

> On the question of military operations he said that negotiations had already taken place between the competent authorities concerned, but in these discussions the conclusion had been reached that while the British fleet could easily penetrate into the Baltic, its stay there would be very risky. Assuming Germany to succeed in laying hands on Denmark and closing the exit from the Baltic, the British fleet would be caught in a mouse-trap. Accordingly, Great Britain would have to confine her operations to the North Sea.

[207] Sazonov's report to the Tsar of Aug. 17, 1912; M.F.R., p. 256; L.N., II, 339.

[208] *Ibid.*

> On his own initiative Grey then gave me a confirmation of what I already knew through Poincaré—an agreement exists between France and Great Britain, under which in the event of war with Germany Great Britain has accepted the obligation of bringing assistance to France not only on the sea but on land, by landing troops on the Continent.
>
> The King touched on the same question in one of his conversations with me, and expressed himself even more strongly than his Minister. When I mentioned, letting him see my agitation, that Germany is trying to place her naval forces on a par with Britain's, His Majesty cried out that any conflict would have disastrous results not only for the German navy but for Germany's overseas trade, for he said, "We shall sink every single German merchant ship we shall get hold of."
>
> These words appeared to me to give expression not only to His Majesty's personal feelings but also to the public feeling predominant in Great Britain in regard to Germany.[209]

Whether Sazonov correctly reported what Poincaré and Grey had said to him is very doubtful.[210] But the fact that he made such statements to the Tsar shows how much the French and the Russians—and especially the Russians—were encouraged by the existence of the Anglo-French military and naval "conversations" and inclined to interpret them as a promise of British support in case of a general European War. This Naval Convention also gave rise to evasive statements on the part of the Entente Powers which naturally increased Germany's suspicions of their aggressive intentions. By some "leak" in the French or Russian Foreign Office, the French Press soon indicated the existence of the Franco-Russian Naval Convention. This led to inquiries by Germany. At St. Petersburg Kokovtsev denied that any such convention had been signed, but natu-

209 *Krasnyi Arkhiv,* III, 18; L.N., II, 347 f.; Stieve, II, 290 f.

210 *Cf.* Grey, I, 286-289.

rally refused to confirm his denial by a public statement, "because every word of it would be twisted around and the outcry would be all the greater."[211] Other Russian and French officials gave evasive answers to the effect that no agreement had been signed, but that since France and Russia were allies, their military and naval staffs must from time to time consult together.[212] Similarly, after the Grey-Cambon exchange of letters, Mr. Asquith and Sir Edward Grey continued to deny solemnly in Parliament that England had any secret agreements which bound her to participate in a continental war, although, as we have seen, this is what the French and Russians confidently counted upon. Inasmuch as the German Government by the spring of 1914 had in some secret way become informed[213] of the Grey-Cambon letters all these denials caused uneasiness in Germany. This was especially the case in connection with the negotiations for an Anglo-Russian naval convention just before the War.

The Grey-Cambon letters, following the consistent diplomatic support which England had given France throughout the Morocco crises, established a very satisfactory basis of mutual confidence between the French and British Governments. This confidence and harmony was strengthened by many factors: by the common distrust of Germany; by the cordial personal relations between Sir Edward Grey and Paul Cambon; by the fact that England had no aggressive aims which conflicted with French interests; and by the care with which M. Poincaré sought to consult Sir Edward Grey's wishes and as far as possible conform French policy to them. There was in fact more harmony and mutual confidence between France and England, though

211 G.P., XXXI, 523 f., 528.

212 G.P., XXXI, 523 ff.; *L'Alliance Franco-Russe,* 138; Poincaré, II, 114.

213 G.P., XXXI, 544 note; Grey, I, 286. Presumably the information came through Siebert, a secretary in the Russian Embassy in London, see ch. i, note 68.

they were only "friends," than between France and Russia who were allies. It was a striking example of the fact that a well established friendship is better than an alliance. Many writers, however, especially the "revisionists" and critics of Poincaré, have argued that there was a complete unity also between Paris and St. Petersburg; that Poincaré and Izvolski worked harmoniously hand in hand, though they are not agreed as to whether the Frenchman was the tool of the Russian, or *vice versa.* Their arguments rest largely on the Izvolski correspondence and their conviction that Izvolski and Poincaré were both working for war, the one to get Constantinople and the Straits, the other to recover Alsace-Lorraine. But we believe that a closer examination of the Izvolski correspondence, of M. Sazonov's character and methods, and of M. Poincaré's memoirs would show that there was by no means that perfect unity between the two allies which has often been assumed.

As has been pointed out in the second chapter, the Franco-Russian Alliance in its origin was essentially defensive in its wording and purpose. For nearly twenty years it remained so. It was not interpreted to cover Russian ambitions in the Balkans and the Far East, nor French ambitions in North Africa and the lost provinces on the Rhine. Russia had given France only lukewarm support in 1905, at Algeciras, and in the Agadir Crisis. France's negative attitude had been one of the reasons for Izvolski's failure to open the Straits after the Buchlau bargain; and again in 1911 France refused to be "nailed down" to support another of Izvolski's efforts to open the Straits in the Charikov affair.[214] But in 1912, under the Premiership of M. Poincaré, the character of the alliance began to be changed. France began to support more actively Russia's aggressive policies in the Balkans, and assured her that France would give her armed support if they involved

214 For the details, see below, ch. v.

Russia in war with Austria and Germany. One of the first signs and causes of this change is to be found in connection with the intrigues against M. Georges Louis.[215]

M. Georges Louis, a trained diplomat, served as Political Director in the French Foreign Office from 1904 to 1909, and then as Ambassador to Russia until his recall in February, 1913. He had used his influence to restrict the application of the Franco-Russian Alliance to its originally defensive character. He favored the Anglo-French policy of maintaining the integrity of the Ottoman Empire in contrast to Russia's designs upon it. He feared Russia's Balkan ambitions might involve France in war, and he was suspicious of the aims and intrigues of Izvolski. In the fall of 1911, when temporarily filling again the vacant office of Political Director at Paris, he had thwarted Izvolski's efforts to "nail France down" to a written agreement to support a plan for opening the Straits to Russian warships.[216] He had thereby incurred the displeasure of Izvolski and Sazonov. They also complained that as Ambassador he did not transmit accurately to Paris the views of the Russian Minister of Foreign Affairs. If this was true, it was certainly not wholly the Ambassador's fault, but was in part owing to M. Sazonov's lack of frankness in stating his views, and also to the fact that he often shifted them suddenly. He had, for instance, drawn up and shown to Georges Louis a *questionnaire* on February 14, 1912. This raised a whole

215 This unsavory affair has been dealt with at great length by M. Ernest Judet, *Georges Louis* (Paris, 1925) and by M. Poincaré, I, 294 ff., 333 ff.; II, 32 ff.; Judet, championing the cause and memory of his friend, bases his account in considerable part on official despatches contained among Georges Louis's papers and on his *Carnets* (2 vols., Paris, 1926), which is made up of Georges Louis's notes of conversations with prominent persons. M. Poincaré's reply to Judet's stinging attack is largely based on official despatches which he has been able to select from his own papers or from the French archives. In the following paragraphs only a bare summary of the facts can be given.

216 See below, for the details, ch. v. at notes 114-126; also Judet, pp. 131-167; Poincaré, I. 333-347.

series of fundamental questions about the Balkans growing out of Italy's Tripolitan War, and seemed to indicate that Sazonov was contemplating some important action to which he wished to secure French assent. "These are the most serious questions which Russia can raise for her ally," Louis wrote to Poincaré next day.[217] But Sazonov then apparently changed his mind suddenly; to Louis's repeated efforts to induce him to discuss the *questionnaire* and the intentions which lay back of it, Sazonov only answered evasively. On many other occasions, as in the case of the Potsdam negotiations, Sazonov took important steps or consulted with Germany without first informing Georges Louis; this lack of regard for Franco-Russian solidarity was very irritating to Poincaré. It was his great aim to have the Triple Entente present a solid diplomatic front to the Triple Alliance.

M. Sazonov also nourished a personal grievance against Georges Louis. This arose from the curious fact, which one would hardly have expected between two allies, that Sazonov's agents had discovered how to decipher the French secret diplomatic code, and were spying upon the telegrams between Georges Louis and the French Government. M. Louis suspected this and repeatedly warned Poincaré that the cipher ought to be changed more frequently. In April, 1912, in one of Georges Louis's deciphered telegrams, Sazonov thought he discovered that Louis had accused him of being dilatory in regard to a Chinese loan.[218] Thereupon he instructed Izvolski to try to get Georges Louis recalled and have someone else sent as French Ambassador to St. Petersburg. Izvolski readily undertook the task, though it was a very delicate and embarrassing one. Poincaré at

217 Judet, p. 174; *cf.* Poincaré, II, 24 ff.

218 Judet, p. 85. In reality Louis had referred to the dilatoriness of the "ministry" before Sazonov became Minister of Foreign Affairs, but Sazonov's agent had made the mistake of deciphering "minister" instead of "ministry" and Sazonov had taken this to be a personal reference to himself.

once complied with the request. On May 8, 1912, he had M. Paléologue, the new Political Director, telegraph to Georges Louis:

> With as much surprise as regret, the President of the Council has been officially notified that the Russian Government wishes to see France represented by an Ambassador who displays more activity in his political functions and social relations. . . .
>
> The diplomatic problems which are at present being discussed between Paris and St. Petersburg are too serious for our efforts to be paralyzed soon by the fact that M. Sazonov declares that he does not feel in touch with you. . . .
>
> M. Poincaré therefore invokes your patriotism to resign your Embassy, with the intention of finding another place for you as soon as possible. I am forced to recognize, as well as he, the imperative necessity of providing for your replacement.[219]

On receipt of this Georges Louis was at first dumfounded. Then, suspecting that Sazonov and Izvolski were intriguing against him, and being assured by Kokovtsev, the President of the Russian Council, that the Russian Government knew nothing of any request for his recall, he telegraphed to Poincaré begging him to delay his decision, and hurried to Paris to lay his suspicions before Poincaré in person. One of the most influential members of the Cabinet, M. Léon Bourgeois, opposed yielding to Izvolski's request for the Ambassador's dismissal, and other friends rallied to his support. Meanwhile, something of the affair had leaked out, and several newspapers raised an uproar against Izvolski's unwarranted interference in French affairs. The incident threatened to become a scandal, seriously troubling Franco-Russian relations. So Poincaré found it more prudent to issue a sweeping denial that any

219 Judet, p. 28 f.

request had been made to him for Georges Louis's recall, and the Ambassador was allowed to return to his post until the outcry had died down and a more suitable occasion should occur for his removal.[220]

This Georges Louis incident is important because it increased Poincaré's distrust of Izvolski, and made him all the more anxious to get into closer relations with Sazonov and so keep a more solid hold on the policies of France's ally. To secure Sazonov's confidence and loyal coöperation in maintaining solidarity of action on the part of the two Allied Powers was M. Poincaré's great aim henceforth. He sought to accomplish this in many ways: by visiting Russia in August, 1912, and in July, 1914; by reiterating that France was ready to support Russia in case of war; by backing up Russia's Balkan policies much more actively; by arranging French loans for Russian military preparations against Germany; by strengthening France's own armaments; and by the ultimate removal of Georges Louis.

By his visit to Russia in August, 1912, M. Poincaré did much to strengthen the bonds between the two allied countries. He sought to counteract the effect of the Tsar's recent meeting with the Kaiser at Port Baltic, and make sure that Russia made no further separate arrangements with Germany after the fashion of the Potsdam Agreements.[221] He also wished to clear up and smooth out the Georges Louis incident. He discussed with Sazonov, Kokovtsev, and the Tsar all the chief matters in which France and Russia had common interests—Asia Minor, the Chinese loan, the Turco-Italian War, the recent Naval Convention, the prospect of English coöperation, and the preparations made by the French and Russian Staffs for

220 Judet, pp. 83-130; Poincaré, I, 333 ff.

221 On the meeting of the Tsar and the Kaiser at Port Baltic, see Poincaré, I, 310 ff.; 379 ff.; Sazonov, *Fateful Years* (N. Y., 1928), p. 43 ff.; and G.P., XXXI, 427-454.

military action in case of war with Germany. He particularly urged Russia to develop her strategic railways to the West to facilitate the rapid concentration of the Russian forces against Germany. On all these points there was substantial harmony. But on one question, the most important one of all, Poincaré discovered another alarming evidence of Sazonov's lack of frankness: he had not revealed the terms of the secret Balkan League which had been drawn up with Russian assistance during the preceding winter. This had been signed on March 13, 1912, but Sazonov had given no hint of its contents and the fact that it was likely to lead to war in the Balkans. When he now read it to his French guest, Poincaré shrewdly perceived its dangerous character and exclaimed: *"C'est un instrument de guerre."* [222] He justly protested to Sazonov at having been kept so long in the dark about a matter which might involve Russia, and consequently France in war. He urged that each should keep the other fully informed as to his intentions. He defined the alliance in its originally defensive form, but immediately added words which encouraged Sazonov to believe that in a crisis Russia could count upon France. As Sazonov reported, among other things, to the Tsar:

> After having confirmed our reciprocal intention of observing with vigilance events in the Balkans, and of exchanging continuously our news and views on the subject, we agreed anew with M. Poincaré to set up a common action to prevent by diplomatic means an aggravation of the situation so soon as any complication should arise and according to circumstances.
>
> M. Poincaré considered it his duty to emphasize the point that public opinion in France would not permit the Government of the Republic to decide on a military action for the

[222] So he told Izvolski; M.F.R., p. 273; L.N., I, 324; Stieve, II, 250. See also below, ch. v.

sake of purely Balkan questions if Germany did not take part and if she did not provoke on her own initiative the application of the *casus foederis*. In this latter case we could certainly count on France for the exact and complete fulfilment of her obligations toward us.

On my part I declared to the French Minister that, while always being ready to range ourselves on the side of France in the cases contemplated by our alliance, we also could not justify to Russian public opinion taking an active part in the military operations provoked by colonial questions outside Europe, so long as the vital interests of France in Europe were not touched. . . . I am very glad to have had the occasion for making the acquaintance of M. Poincaré and of entering into personal relations with him, all the more so, because the exchange of views which I have had with him has left me with the impression that in his person Russia possesses a sure and faithful friend endowed with exceptional political ability, and with an inflexible determination. In case of a crisis in international relations, it would be very desirable that our ally should have as her head, if not M. Poincaré himself, at least a personality possessing the same decision and as free from the fear of responsibility as the present French Prime Minister.[223]

Faced with the *fait accompli* of the Balkan League and the potential dangers involved in it, Poincaré took steps with the other Powers to try to prevent the Balkan States from actually going to war. But they came too late. The Balkan Wars of 1912-1913 increased the delicacy and the importance of Franco-Russian relations, and also of relations between the Triple Entente and Triple Alliance. During the first weeks of the Balkan Wars his policy remained the same as on his visit to Russia; restraint of Sazonov from rash steps through insistence on a preliminary exchange of views, coupled, however, with assurances of

[223] Sazonov's report to the Tsar, Aug. 17, 1912; M.F.R., p. 255 ff.; L.N., II, 338 ff.; Stieve, II, 219 ff.; and (in part) Siebert-Schreiner, pp. 652-655. *Cf.* also Poincaré, II, 99-169, especially 114 ff.; and below, ch v.

complete loyalty to the obligations of the alliance; subordination of Russia's Balkan interests to the greater question of the preservation of peace between the Great Powers; the establishment of complete solidarity of purpose and action on the part of the Triple Entente Powers, coupled, however, with a willingness to coöperate with the Triple Alliance so long as the latter did not make excessive claims. But as the War proceeded and the Balkan allies won their great victories, there was some change, or rather shift of emphasis, in his guidance of French policy. This change, however, was not nearly as great as many of his critics have asserted, nor as considerable as Izvolski was inclined to represent in his despatches to St. Petersburg.

Poincaré found that Sazonov's purposes were not always clear and easy to reckon with. Sazonov did not always exchange views and come to a prior understanding with France. He had been dilatory or non-committal in replying to French proposals. At the beginning of the War he had rejoiced with the Pan-Slavs at the astonishing military successes of the Balkan States over Turkey. But the overwhelming victories of Kirk Kilissé and Lulé Burgas, and the rapid advance of Ferdinand's troops toward Constantinople, was an unpleasant damper on his enthusiasm. A Bulgarian occupation of the Turkish capital threatened to thwart indefinitely Russia's own historic hopes in that quarter. Even if the Powers who had political and financial interests there should refuse to permit the Bulgarians to have the city, they might take advantage of the opportunity to carry out Sir Edward Grey's idea of an internationalization of the Straits. Accordingly, even while the battle of Lulé Burgas was still in progress, Sazonov had urged the Bulgarians to recognize "the necessity for prudence and to halt in time," endeavoring to bribe them to listen to reason by promises of future diplomatic support. At the same time he informed France and England that he would greatly welcome intervention at Sofia and Belgrade in favor of mediation to restrain the victorious Slavs—in the war which Russia had helped to cause by her part in the formation of the Balkan League.[224] Three days later, in spite of the fact that Poincaré had already taken the initiative in the direction desired by Russia, and without any warning or prior consultation, Sazonov presented all the Powers with a complete program for immediate intervention: the maintenance of the Sultan in Constantinople with a defense zone including Thrace and Adrianople; an autonomous Albania; compensations to Rumania for remaining neutral; Serbian access to the Adriatic; and free transit for Austrian goods through the new Serbian territory.[225]

Except for Serbian access to the Adriatic, this whole program was in the nature of concessions to the Triple Alliance. As compared with Constantinople, Sazonov cared very slightly for "the little Slav sisters" or for the solidarity of the Triple Entente. Without giving Poincaré time to recover from his astonishment at the proposed concessions, Sazonov sent him the further startling news that if the Bulgarians occupied Constantinople the whole Russian Black Sea Fleet would "appear before the Turkish capital."[226] The Russian Admiralty plans went further: "For the protection of our Embassy and our interests in general, it will naturally be necessary to land, and in order not to weaken the navy crews, the despatch of some troop divisions with machine guns is desired. . . . The occupation of the Bosphorus one would not extend very far, but it would then be easier to remain there forever. If we have the Bosphorus tight in hand, the troublesome Straits Question is already half settled. If a favorable opportunity for such an advance

224 Sazonov to Benckendorff and Izvolski, Oct. 31, 1912; *Krasnyi Arkhiv,* XVI, 19; Siebert-Schreiner, p. 381 f.; Stieve, II, 326.

225 Sazonov's circular, Nov. 2; M.F.R., p. 293; L.N., II, 565; Stieve, II, 328.

226 Sazonov to Izvolski, Nov. 4; L.N., I, 339; Stieve, II, 331.

cannot be found, then it must be artificially created; because, if it is impossible to get possession of the whole Straits, we should at least have an eye to the enormous political advantage which the Bosphorus has." [227]

French public opinion, however, had been reassured by the Balkan victories and began to take a new interest in Russia's Balkan policies. A public declaration by Poincaré of French loyalty to Russia had aroused great enthusiasm. "Nothing succeeds like success," Izvolski reported; "under the influence of recent events one notices here a marked change in feeling in favor of the Balkan States and the Russian point of view"; and he added that he would do all he could to strengthen this new attitude, especially by influencing the Press, but for this he needed more money at his disposal.[228] Poincaré was not enthusiastic for Sazonov's program of intervention which would antagonize Bulgaria and Serbia. He was impressed by the new weight and influence which the Balkan victories had given to the Slav cause and to the Triple Entente in the Balance of Power in Europe. He also suspected that Austria, backed by Germany, might take advantage of the situation to attempt territorial aggrandizements, and this he was determined to prevent, not only in the interests of Russia and Serbia, but of France and the prestige of the Triple Entente. He was more concerned over what Austria might do, than at Sazonov's anxiety about Constantinople. As Izvolski reported on November 7: "Whereas France up to the present has declared that local, so to speak, purely Balkan events could not induce her to take any active measures, the French Government now appears to admit that an acquisition of territory on the part of Austria in the Balkans would affect the general European equilibrium and consequently also the

227 Admiralty Staff Report, Nov. 2, 1912; *Krasnyi Arkhiv,* VI, 52.

228 Izvolski to Sazonov, Oct. 28, M.F.R., p. 292; L.N., II, 564; Stieve, II, 320. On Izvolski's activities in bribing the French Press, see below, ch. V, note 117.

special interests of France. . . . Poincaré is perfectly conscious of the fact that France may thus become involved in a warlike action. For the present, of course, he submits this question merely for our consideration, but in a conversation with me Paléologue plainly admitted that the proposed agreement might lead to some kind of active step." [229]

Serbia's occupation of Northern Albania and desire for a port on the Adriatic soon became a dangerously acute question. Austria threatened to use force if necessary to prevent this, and had the support of both her allies. Sazonov naturally favored the Serbian demand, but not to the point of making war. He was secretly inclined to find some compromise proposal, such as giving Serbia a railway outlet on the Adriatic, but not part of Northern Albania to which Austria and Italy particularly objected. When he inquired what would be the attitude of France if an active intervention by Austria could not be avoided, Poincaré replied, according to Izvolski:

> It is for Russia to take the initiative in a question in which she is the most interested party. France's task is to lend her the most effective support. If the French Government should take the initiative it would risk falling short of, or overstepping, the intentions of its ally. . . . In short, added M. Poincaré, if Russia goes to war, France will do the same, for we all know that Germany will stand behind Austria in this question.[230]

This statement, which has been much quoted by Poincaré's critics as showing the triumphant influence exerted on him by the intriguing Izvolski, is severely criticized by Poincaré in his memoirs as being inaccurate. As a matter of fact, he was again insisting that he did not wish to make promises until Sazonov had taken the initiative in saying

229 M.F.R., p. 296; L.N., I, 342; Stieve, II, 336.

230 Izvolski to Sazonov, Nov. 17, M.F.R., p. 300; L.N., I, 346; Stieve, II, 346. *Cf.* however, Poincaré, II, 336 ff.

clearly what he wanted. Then France would be able to make her views known. As to war, he again defined the obligations of the alliance in the same terms he had used to Sazonov in August: France would go to war if the particular case of the *casus foederis* provided in the Alliance were fulfilled, namely, "if Russia is attacked by Germany or by Austria supported by Germany." Until then he would keep his hands free. A couple of days later he took care to warn Georges Louis of Izvolski's misrepresentations and asked him to correct any false impressions which they may have caused. Izvolski's report is therefore undoubtedly inaccurate as a representation of Poincaré's words; but it is accurate as a representation of what Sazonov was being told by his Russian Ambassador in Paris were Poincaré's views. And it indicates that Poincaré was now ready to consider seriously the question of war arising out of Balkan problems in which Russia was interested. In 1912, however, Russia was not prepared for war; none of the Great Powers wanted it, and the Serbian question was referred for settlement to the London Conference of Ambassadors.

With a person of Izvolski's intriguing, ambitious, and not wholly trustworthy character as Russian Ambassador at Paris, it was all the more important that France should have at St. Petersburg a man of Georges Louis's views, who was on his guard against the danger of Russia's ambitions in regard to the Straits. But on February 17, 1913, Georges Louis was suddenly notified of his definite dismissal and replacement by M. Delcassé. M. Poincaré had just become President of the Republic and the responsibility for the change in the French Embassy at St. Petersburg could be technically placed upon the shoulders of the Briand Cabinet in which M. Jonnart succeeded Poincaré as Minister of Foreign Affairs.[231] After being thus "politically assassi-

[231] Judet, pp. 205-234; Poincaré, II, 70; *Foreign Affairs* (N. Y.), IV, 11, Oct., 1925.

nated," as his friends called his dismissal, Georges Louis's diplomatic career was ruined. No new place was found for him. He died in 1917 in the midst of the War which it had been his aim to avert. Doubtless there is some truth in Poincaré's explanation that Louis's frail health and his lack of intimate relations with Sazonov and influential circles at St. Petersburg made it desirable in the interests of allied solidarity that he should be replaced by someone who would coöperate more cordially with Sazonov and his Balkan policies. The fact that he was succeeded by Delcassé, and then by Paléologue, who were both strongly in favor of strengthening the bonds of the alliance by giving Russia strong support, did make for harmony between the Cabinets of Paris and St. Petersburg. It did tend thereby to tighten the Triple Entente, but it also encouraged Sazonov in his support of Serbia and his stiff attitude to Austria and Germany which was one of the main causes of war in 1914.

THE RENEWAL AND WEAKNESS OF THE TRIPLE ALLIANCE, 1912

Bismarck, who regarded the Austro-German Alliance of 1879 as strictly defensive, had refused to permit military agreements between the German and Austrian Staffs, for fear that they might hamper the political freedom of action of the civilian authorities. This Alliance, therefore, as well as the Triple Alliance, had long remained without being supplemented by any such definite military convention, stating the number of troops which each ally was bound to furnish in case of war, as in the case of the Franco-Russian Military Convention in 1894.[232] Nor for many years were

[232] Two minor exceptions to this general statement were the convention of 1888 providing for the service of Italian troops on the Rhine frontier in case of a Franco-German war (*cf.*, G.P., VI, 247), and a convention of 1900 providing for naval coöperation by the Triple Alliance in case of war with France and Russia (Pribram, I, 241). See also W. Foerster, "Die deutsch-italienische Militärkonvention," in KSF, V, 395-416, May, 1927.

there any regular periodical conferences between the Staffs of the Triple Alliance Powers, with written protocols fixing in detail the coöperation of their armies, as in the case of the annual conferences between the French and Russian Staffs from 1900 onwards.[233] But in January, 1909, when the Bosnian Crisis began to look alarming, Moltke and Conrad, the Chiefs of Staff of the German and Austrian armies did enter into a correspondence concerning possible military coöperation.[234] It was carried on with the knowledge and approval of the civilian authorities of the two countries, and was continued intermittently during the following years. It was also supplemented by personal meetings between the two generals at visits during military maneuvers and other occasions. One Austrian writer sees in this correspondence a "military convention" which transformed the Austro-German Alliance from its originally defensive character into an offensive agreement. He even makes it the "key" to the whole question of responsibility for the war.[235] But nowhere did Moltke and Conrad, or any other persons in authority, ever refer to this exchange of views as a "military convention." On the contrary, it was more in the nature of a general discussion of the political situation, and an exchange of information as to the plan of campaign which each intended to put into operation if war should be declared by the civilian authorities. Conrad was trying to persuade Moltke to make Germany's mobilization plan provide for as many troops as possible against Russia, so as to lessen the number which the Tsar would have available against Austria. Moltke, in turn, wanted to have Conrad plan to use few troops in Serbia, and send as many as possible into Galicia against Russia, in order to

233 For summaries of the earlier Franco-Russian military conferences, see *Les Alliés contre la Russie,* pp. 8-39; and for the protocols of those in 1911, 1912, and 1913, see M.F.R., pp. 697-718; and L.N., II, 419-437.

234 Conrad, I, 379-406; II, 54-62.

235 H. Kanner, *Der Schlüssel zur Kriegsschuldfrage,* Munich, 1926

relieve the pressure on Germany's eastern frontier, while the bulk of the German forces were being thrown against France. Their arrangements with one another were hardly as definite or as binding as those which were being made by the French and Russian Staffs. Though some of the Moltke-Conrad letters were shown to the civilian authorities, they did not legally modify the terms of the Alliance. This remained fixed in writing, and its interpretation and application rested with the civilian, and not the military, authorities.

On the other hand, it is undoubtedly true that this Moltke-Conrad correspondence tended to foster the conviction at Vienna, that if Austria attacked Serbia, she could count on a threat of German mobilization to bluff Russia into remaining inactive; or upon German support, if Russia made war. In this sense it did tend to give the Alliance a potentially offensive, rather than defensive, character. Another result of their correspondence was the fact that Moltke and Conrad made mobilization plans which were dependent for success on one another, and, as in all such cases, this enabled the military authorities in a time of crisis to exert pressure on the civilian authorities in favor of war. To what extent this was actually the case in July, 1914, will be discussed later in the second volume. In the years before the final crisis, the personal friendship and mutual confidence between Moltke and Conrad had been one of the factors in strengthening the bonds between these two allies.

Italy was the element of weakness in the Triple Alliance. Ever since the Algeciras Conference Germany had regarded her loyalty with doubt. Conrad was so convinced not only of her probable disloyalty to her treaty obligations, but of her positive hostility, that he speaks of her as Austria's "principal opponent." He made plans for mobilization against her, and even wanted a "preventive war" against her.[236] Italy's war with Turkey for the possession of Tripoli had further displeased her allies, not only because they had not been fully consulted beforehand, but because it embarrassed them to have their nominal ally attack the Turks, whose friendship and good-will they were trying to cultivate. To be sure, the events of the war and Italy's establishment as a sea-power in the Mediterranean had led to a decided coolness in her relations with France. But these had improved again by the summer of 1912 so that Poincaré and Sazonov both agreed that it was best to keep Italy as a "dead weight" in the Triple Alliance, where she would be useful to both France and Russia.[237]

Though the Triple Alliance was to run until 1914, the question of its renewal had already begun to be discussed in the summer of 1911. Italy favored its early renewal as a means of placating her allies on the eve of her Tripolitan adventure. Germany favored it, being always glad of anything which might make for better relations between her two allies, and thus help to counter-balance the growing strength and solidarity of the Triple Entente. Aehrenthal at first was not opposed to it.[238] But Conrad and the military officers were so incensed at Italy's insults and treacheries that they saw no use in trying to keep her even as a nominal ally. General Auffenberg related with childish indignation to the German Ambassador in Vienna evidences of Italian animosity which he had just seen in the Southern Tyrol: every day or two a patrol had to be detailed to clean up the insulting epithets scribbled on a war memorial; he had seen cigarette boxes in which all the Austrian territory from Fiume to the Brenner Pass was marked as belonging to Italy; irredentist propaganda even took the form of calling the horses and mules by the names of Austrian

236 For the period 1907-1912, *cf.* Conrad, I, 110, 128, 141, 173, 224, 272.

237 Sazonov's report to the Tsar, Aug. 17, 1912; L.N., II, 340.

238 G.P., XXX, 495-510.

cities like Trent and Trieste! "In case of a war Italy would explode against us like a keg of powder," he added, declaring that the best thing for Austria to do would be to crush the irredentist hopes by war, and then Austria would be freer to deal with Serbia or meet a Russian attack.[239] Aehrenthal, however, had Francis Joseph on his side, and secured the dismissal of Conrad because the latter was urging war with Italy and friendship with Russia. The Tripolitan War delayed the negotiations for the renewal of the Triple Alliance. It was finally renewed, however, on December 5, 1912, without modification, being extended for six years from July 8, 1914.[240] A couple of weeks later, Italy notified Germany that, in view of the existing political conditions, frankness compelled her to say that she would be unable to carry out her agreement of 1888 for sending troops to coöperate with a German army on the Rhine.[241]

THE EFFECTS OF THE BALKAN WARS

The outbreak of the Balkan Wars and the consequent intensification of the conflict of interests between all the Powers, great and small, affected the system of alliances in several ways.

It increased the internal friction within the Triple Alliance and Triple Entente. A study of the daily and even hourly interchange of telegrams which went on between the members of each group during the succession of crises and kaleidoscopic changes which took place in the Balkans during 1912 and 1913 shows, for instance, that Germany was constantly irritated by the selfish policies and rash acts of her Austrian ally. She was irritated because Austrian policies sometimes ran counter to her own views on Balkan affairs, and sometimes because they might endanger the

239 Tschirschky to Bethmann, Nov. 18, 1911; *ibid.*, 514 ff.

240 Tschirschky to Bethmann, 568; Pribram, I, 268-298.

241 G.P., XXX, 574-579; Pribram, I, 299.

peace of Europe. For example, Germany had no great desire for the creation of an autonomous Albania. The Kaiser did not think that the country was capable of governing itself, and he thought it very doubtful whether any European prince could be found who could succeed in the difficult task.[242] In spite of this, however, Germany consented to support Austria's wishes (and also Italy's) for the creation of an autonomous Albania which should exclude Serbia from access to the Adriatic. Similar clashes of interest existed between France and her ally. France desired the maintenance of the integrity of the Ottoman Empire, in which she had large financial interests, and wanted the right to construct railways in northern Asia Minor, which would strengthen and develop Turkey. Russia opposed these railways because they might aid Turkey to move troops more easily to prevent the Russian advance south of the Caucasus. An interesting example of this internal conflict within each group is seen in the intrigues in regard to the disposal of Kavala at the close of the Balkan Wars. Austria and Russia, for various reasons to be explained in the next chapter, wanted to give Kavala to the Bulgarians; their allies, Germany and France, instead of agreeing with them respectively, were in favor of letting the Greeks keep it. The Greeks kept it.

This internal friction, however, was more than counterbalanced by the feeling in each group that it must do everything possible to preserve unity and solidarity among its members. Allies must stand together and support one another's policies, consenting to policies which were unpalatable, or even consenting to acts which might involve dangers to the peace of Europe. In this way Austria was often a liability, rather than an asset, to Germany, as was also Russia to France. Sometimes the dominant member exerted successfully a restraining influence on her ally in favor

[242] G.P., XXXVI, 127-745, *passim.*

of moderation and the preservation of the peace, as in the case of Germany's veto on Austria's contemplated intervention against Serbia in July, 1913, or France's unwillingness to approve Sazonov's proposed measures for exerting pressure on Turkey in connection with Liman von Sanders affair.[243]

In the recently published German documents and in Conrad's memoirs one finds many cases indicating that Germany encouraged Austria to take steps against Serbia for putting an end to the "Greater Serbia" danger in the belief that it threatened the existence of the Dual Monarchy and consequently of Germany's only remaining reliable ally.[244] They occur in official despatches from the German Foreign Office to the German Ambassador in Vienna, in the correspondence and interviews between Moltke and Conrad, and occasionally in the meetings between the German Kaiser and Franz Ferdinand. On the other hand, however, one finds as many, if not more, cases of an exactly opposite kind, in which German officials, especially the Kaiser, urged Austria to come to some arrangement with Serbia and warned her against using force.[245] On the whole, we believe we are justified in saying that Germany's influence was in favor of moderation and peace rather than the contrary—until the provocation of the Sarajevo assassination.

243 See below, ch. v.

244 G.P., XXVI, *passim* (Bosnian Crisis); XXX, 253; XXXIII, 274 ff., 330, 373 f.; XXXIV, 34 ff.; XXXVI, 386 ff.; XXXIX, 325 ff. (Konopischt Meeting). Conrad, I, 95 f., 106 ff., 129 ff., 202 f., 369 ff.; II, 54 ff.; III, 38 f., 143 ff., 294, 328, 368 f., 424 ff., 469 f., 474, 609 ff., 667 ff. *Cf.* also W. Schüssler, *Oesterreich und das deutsche Schicksal* (Leipzig, 1925), pp. 8 ff., 177 ff.; and H. Kanner, *Der Schlüssel zur Kriegsschuldfrage* (Munich, 1926), *passim.*

245 G.P., XXXIII, 42, 80, 92 ff., 116, 150, 295 ff., 355 ff., 371 ff., 426 ff., 478 f.; XXXIV, 444 ff., 455 ff., 538 ff., 619 ff., 674 ff., 820 ff.; XXXV, 52 ff., 66 ff., 122 ff., 319 ff. (Kavala affair and non-revision of the Treaty of Bucharest); XXXVI, 27 ff.; XXXVIII, 335, 342 ff. Conrad, I, 156, 165; III, 78 ff., 143 ff., 164 ff., 318, 404, 410, 417, 429 ff., 448, 597 f., 627 f., 632, 644 f., 729. *Cf.* also H. Friedjung, *Das Zeitalter des Imperialismus* (Berlin 1919-1922), III, *passim.*

To what extent France in the same way gave dangerous encouragement or exercised wise moderation on Russia, it is difficult to say. The evidence furnished by Sazonov's correspondence with Izvolski and Benckendorff, his reports to the Tsar, and other Russian material on the one hand, is often contradicted, on the other, by Poincaré's memoirs and by the *French Yellow Book* on Balkan Affairs. But it must be remembered that this *Yellow Book* is very far from complete, the documents in it evidently being selected to support the view that M. Poincaré's policy was always in the interests of the peace of Europe. On this question, no wholly satisfactory answer can be given until the French make a full publication of their pre-War documents, similar to that already made by Germany and to that in course of publication by England.

One effect of the Balkan Wars, which was most serious to the peace of Europe and to the crystallization of opposition between the Triple Alliance and the Triple Entente, was the intensification of the general movement for an increase of armaments on the part of all the Continental Powers. We have already noted above the antagonism between England and Germany caused by the rapid construction of Dreadnoughts and the failure of the Haldane Mission. At the same time that Germany passed the Naval Bill of 1912 she made a considerable increase in her army. In 1913 a new Army Law provided for a much larger increase to take place in the following years. Before France was aware of this German Army Law of 1913, Poincaré and the little group associated with him had already decided to bring in a bill greatly increasing the strength of the French army. Convinced that sooner or later a war was "inevitable," they persuaded the French Chamber of Deputies to vote the law extending the French term of active military training from two to three years, and the liability for service in the reserve from the age of forty-five to forty-eight. According to the opinion of Colonel Buat, who was one of the ablest French experts and officially in charge of one section of the French General Staff, France would have in 1914 a slightly larger army than Germany in the first weeks of a war.[246] The idea that Germany was overwhelmingly superior in numbers in her invasion of Belgium and France in 1914 is a myth. In Russia also strenuous efforts were being made to organize and train a greater number of her vast population. The increases in Austria and Italy were relatively slight. We refrain at this point from giving any figures as to the relative size of armies and military expenditures because such figures are apt to be extremely misleading. Figures comparing English and German naval expenditures have no significance unless allowance is made for the cheaper costs of construction in Germany and the system of obligatory service instead of voluntary enlistment. Similarly the size and strength of armies is not indicated merely by the numbers of troops, but depends in large part upon efficiency of equipment, rapidity of mobilization, and other technical matters which would require long comment if trustworthy and really just bases of comparison are to be made. By the spring of 1914 all these armaments in progress of preparation had raised in both Triple Alliance and Triple Entente a growing uneasiness and suspicion. Everywhere thoughtful observers were alarmed at the situation, but little was accomplished to alleviate it. Colonel House went to Europe with the hope of doing something about it, and wrote to President Wilson, a month before the assassination of the Austrian Archduke:

> The situation is extraordinary. It is militarism run stark mad. Unless someone acting for you can bring about a different understanding, there is some day to be an awful cataclysm. No one in Europe can do it. There is too much

[246] E. Buat, *L'armée allemande pendant la guerre de 1914-1918,* Paris, 1920; Montgelas, *Leitfaden,* 81-87.

> hatred, too many jealousies. Whenever England consents, France and Russia will close in on Germany and Austria. England does not want Germany wholly crushed, for she would then have to reckon alone with her ancient enemy, Russia; but if Germany insists upon an ever-increasing navy, then England will have no choice. The best chance for peace is an understanding between England and Germany in regard to naval armaments and yet there is some disadvantage to us by these two getting too close.[247]

One beneficial consequence of the Balkan crisis was the increased effort sincerely made to establish a "Concert of Europe," which should counteract the opposition between the Triple Alliance and Triple Entente. This was the aim of the London Conference of Ambassadors, and it succeeded in its task of finding peaceful solutions of most difficult problems. Possibly if such another conference could have been arranged in July, 1914, it also might have averted the catastrophe. In this matter of the Concert of Europe each statesman was continually torn between two conflicting purposes. On the one hand, he wished to preserve and strengthen the solidarity of the group which he represented —Triple Alliance or Triple Entente as the case might happen to be. He therefore aimed to reach a prior agreement within his own group which would safeguard the prestige and interests of the other two members and thus of the group as a whole; and then to try to impose the acceptance of this prearranged agreement upon the members of the opposing group. This of course tended to accentuate the crystallization of opposition between Triple Alliance and Triple Entente, and if carried too far, as in 1914, would precipitate war. At the same time, on the other hand, most of the statesmen of Europe were aiming at an altogether different purpose. In the interests of peace, they were

247 Charles Seymour, *The Intimate Papers of Colonel House* (Boston and New York, 1926), I, 249; *cf.* also G.P., XXXIX, 107-117.

genuinely trying to maintain the Concert of Europe, that is, to have all six Great Powers arrive at collective action and common views in a conciliatory spirit and by means of compromises. This often involved sacrificing to some extent the interests of his own country, or at least those of his ally. In Balkan questions Austria and Russia had the greatest interests and were therefore the countries most frequently expected to make sacrifices. England, whose interests were least, and who was not bound by any formal alliance, could most easily afford to serve as a medium in smoothing out opposition between the others. It is not here possible to review in detail the extent to which each of the leading statesmen of Europe pursued each of these two opposite purposes. As one reads the complicated diplomatic negotiations of the years immediately preceding the War one gets the impression, beyond all doubt, that Sir Edward Grey was the man who most sincerely and tirelessly placed the Concert of Europe above the interests of any single Power or group. Next to him in support of the Concert of Europe would come Bethmann-Hollweg and the German Secretary of State, Kiderlen-Wächter; but Kiderlen died in December, 1912, and after that the German Chancellor was less able to make his influence prevail over that of Tirpitz and the Kaiser. In France, M. Poincaré was more interested in the solidarity of the Triple Entente, than in the Concert of Europe; but in order to preserve the confidence and friendship of England, which was one of his primary aims, he also frequently took the lead in steps for initiating or upholding collective action by the Powers. Sazonov and Izvolski cared less for the Concert of Europe, and Count Berchtold least of all.

It was while Europe was thus divided into two opposed groups that a new danger arose from the assassination of the Austrian Archduke and a new intensification of Balkan problems.

CHAPTER V

BALKAN PROBLEMS, 1907-1914

The Balkan situation was one of the most important factors in causing the World War. It sharpened the antagonism between the Triple Alliance and the Triple Entente, stimulated a general increase in armaments, and led to the assassination of the Austrian Archduke with its catastrophic consequences. It was an old and complicated question which had troubled the peace of Europe for a century and a half. No attempt can be made here to trace its development, which has been ably dealt with by many writers.[1] It arose from many elements. The progressive disintegration of the Ottoman Empire, caused by external as well as internal causes, produced a continual unrest in the Near East. This was increased by Russia's persistent desire to acquire increased influence in the Balkan Peninsula and to realize her age-long dream for control of the waterways to the Mediterranean. The Hapsburgs, sitting astride the Danube for centuries, were trying to preserve authority over subject peoples, many of whom had become fired with nationalism and a desire to break away and unite with their brothers living in the independent States bordering on Austria-Hungary. The ambitions of Serbia, Bulgaria, Rumania and Greece to extend their territories to include all peoples of their own nationality brought them into constant conflict with Turkey, Austria-Hungary or

[1] For a very useful list of works on the Balkans see R. J. Kerner, *Slavic Europe: A Selected Bibliography in the Western European Languages* (Cambridge, Mass., 1918), especially Nos. 737-842, 3121-3144, 3592-4186, 4357-4411, 4490-4518.

one another. The antagonism between Austria-Hungary and Serbia was increased by the Austrian annexation of Bosnia and Herzegovina, the creation of Albania, and the Serb agitation for national unity at Austria's expense. To understand how the World War had its beginnings in this corner of Europe, it will be convenient to review some of the Balkan problems between 1908 and 1914.

THE BEGINNINGS OF AUSTRO-SERBIAN ANTAGONISM [2]

Serbian national poets and historians love to recall to their people the heroic days of Stephen Dushan in the fourteenth century, when the great Greek Orthodox Serbian Empire stretched from the Danube nearly to the Gulf of Corinth, and from the Aegean to the Adriatic. From those far-off days to the decades immediately preceding the World War, when Serbian nationalists began to dream of again extending their boundaries to include "Old Serbia" and even more territory, the Serbian people suffered long

[2] In addition to the works cited by Kerner, as indicated in the preceding footnote, the more important recent books from the Austrian point of view are: H. Friedjung, *Das Zeitalter des Imperialismus, 1884-1914* (3 vols. Berlin, 1919-22); F. F. G. Kleinwächter, *Der Untergang der österreichisch-ungarischen Monarchie* (Leipzig, 1920); L. Mandl, *Die Habsburger und die serbische Frage* (Vienna, 1918); Theodor von Sosnosky, *Die Balkanpolitik Oesterreich-Ungarns seit 1866* (2 vols. Stuttgart, 1913-1919); J. Redlich, *Oesterreichische Regierung und Verwaltung im Weltkrieg* (New Haven), 1925; H. Delbrück, "Serbien, Oesterreich und Russland," in *Deutschland und die Schuldfrage* (ed. W. Ziegler, Berlin, 1923; pp. 95-112); and the works of Burian, Conrad, Hoyos, Musulin, Pribram, and Szilassy. Above all, Oe.—U.A., I-VIII, *passim.*

From the Serb and Croat point of view: H. Wendel, *Der Kampf der Südslawen um Freiheit und Einheit* (Frankfort, 1925), written in a somewhat lyrical vein, but containing a valuable bibliography (pp. 757-773) including numerous Slavic works; R. W. Seton-Watson, *Sarajevo: A Study in the Origins of the Great War* (London, 1926), giving the best account in English of the Jugoslav Movement; L. von Südland [Pilar], *Die Südslawische Frage und der Weltkrieg* (Vienna, 1918); Goricar and Stowe, *The Inside Story of Austro-German Intrigue* (New York, 1920); and the works of Cvijitch, Jevtitch, Markovitch, and Stanojevitch.

From a more general point of view: *Die Grosse Politik, passim;* H. Wickham Steed, *Through Thirty Years, 1892-1922* (2 vols. London, 1924); and the works of Bogitchevitch, Brandenburg, Kanner, and Valentin.

years of oppression and hardship. First came the Turks. On Vidov-Dan, 1389, an army of Serbs, Albanians and Croats was terribly crushed at Kossovo, and submerged under the Turkish flood. But from the field of battle there rose up a Serb hero who penetrated to the victorious Sultan's tent and there slew him, as the hateful oppressor of the Slav peoples. So the anniversary of Kossovo became a great day in the Serb calendar: Vidov-Dan was a day of sorrow for the national defeat of 1389, but a day of rejoicing for the assassination of the cruel foreign oppressor.[3] For more than four centuries after Kossovo the greater part of the Serb people lived and suffered under Turkish rule. Some Serbs, for obvious reasons of convenience, abandoned Greek Orthodoxy for Mohammedanism, especially in Bosnia, and remained Moslems ever afterwards.

Austria was the European Power which first brought to the Serbs some relief, and caused the Turkish flood to recede. It was Prince Eugene, with his Hapsburg army, who recaptured Belgrade in 1717 and helped arouse in the Serbs a longing for independence from Turkish misrule. When Hapsburg troops had to retreat twenty years later, many Serb peasants followed on the soldiers' heels to escape servitude under the Sultan. They settled north of the Danube in the southern fringe of the Hapsburg lands. There they lived and multiplied and were joined by other fugitives from south of the Danube. At first these Serb settlers were well treated by their new rulers, and were appreciated as good soldiers to defend the country against the Turks. But in the later eighteenth century Roman Catholic propaganda and economic oppression by feudal Magyar landlords made existence so bitter for the Serb settlers that many preferred to escape back to their brothers

[3] Vidov-Dan, St. Vitus's Day, June 15/28, 1914, the day of the Archduke's assassination, was the 525th anniversary of the Battle of Kossovo.

of the South. As between Magyar exploitation and Turkish misrule, the latter was the lesser of two evils. So began an antagonism, which persisted ever afterwards, and was aggravated in 1867 when Emperor Francis Joseph withdrew the special privileges which had long been enjoyed by the Serbs of the "Military Frontiers."[4] Nevertheless, common enmity to the Turks generally tended to preserve a political friendship between the ruling authorities at Vienna and Belgrade.

In the year 1878, to be sure, Austria "occupied" the provinces of Bosnia and Herzegovina, which were largely inhabited by peasants of Serb blood and were coveted by the new Kingdom of Serbia; but the pill was coated by the fact that, at the Congress of Berlin, Austria secured for Serbia the valuable Pirot and Nish districts, which Russia would have assigned to her own protégé, Bulgaria. Political friendship between the Austrian and Serbian Governments, though not between the peoples of the two countries, was again secured by the secret Austro-Serbian Treaty of 1881, signed for ten years, in which both States promised to pursue a mutually friendly policy, and not to tolerate within the territory of one any intrigues against the other.[5] In the year following, a tariff agreement admitted Austrian manufactured articles into Serbia at half the tariff rates asked of other countries, and in return special advantages were given to Serbian pigs and prunes imported into Austria-Hungary. In 1885 it was the support of Austria which saved the Serbian army from destruction after its fatal defeat by the Bulgarians at Slivnitza. King Milan, both off and on the throne, squandered much of his money and spent much of his bizarre existence in Vienna. And so,

[4] *Cf.* Michael Pupin, *From Immigrant to Inventor* (New York, 1923), ch. i.

[5] Pribram, I, 18; also his article, "Milan IV von Serbien und die Geheimverträge Oesterreich-Ungarns mit Serbien, 1887-1889," in *Historische Blätter*, I, 1922.

in spite of Russian intrigues from within, Serbian policy, generally speaking, continued to be Austrophile until the great assassinations of 1903.

It was the misfortune of the Serbian people that, at the beginning of the movement for national independence in the days of Napoleon, there arose not one, but two, national leaders. Instead of one great man dominating the movement, and establishing a single strong dynasty, there were two rivals: Kara George and Milosh Obrenovitch. Ever since the assassination of the former in the interests of the latter, in 1817, the unhappy country was torn by the feuds of these rival families, and by a series of palace revolutions and violent changes of dynasty. These culminated in 1903. On the night of June 11, a band of conspirators, consisting mainly of Serbian army officers, entered the royal palace at Belgrade, dragged King Alexander Obrenovitch and his unpopular wife from their hiding place, and brutally murdered them.[6] Belgrade rejoiced; the church bells were rung; the city was decorated with flags; and the Legislature unanimously thanked the assassins for their work. Though he may not have been directly privy to the plot, Peter Karageorgevitch, grandson of the man murdered nearly a century before, profited by it, and he ascended the throne as Peter I. This hideous crime, "brutal but not unprovoked," and the favors shown to those who were responsible for it, outraged the sense of decency in the crowned heads of Europe, most of whom soon withdrew their representatives from Belgrade as a sign of their disapproval. Great Britain did not renew diplomatic relations for three years.

[6] For a recent vivid account of this deed, see the article of Dragisha Vasitch, in *Knjizhevna Republika,* summarized in *The Living Age,* Jan. 3, 1925; and the detailed contemporary narrative of Pomiankowski, the Austrian Military Attaché, in the Berlin *8-Uhr-Abendblatt,* Nos. 46-50, Feb. 23-28, 1928; for its importance in internal Serbian politics, see below, Vol. II, ch. ii.

Though frowned on at first by Europe, the new reign marked a notable revival in Serbian life. A freer, more democratic, spirit prevailed. A patriotic national movement developed, which expressed itself in new economic activity, in newspapers and literature, and in the spread of the "Greater Serbia" idea. Peter I was personally popular, devoted to the interests of his country, and noted for his soldierly qualities of loyalty and simplicity. The fact that he had fought for the Serbian cause in the revolt of Herzegovina gave him an added popularity far beyond the bounds of his own kingdom; it made him "our King" to the Serbs beyond the Danube and the Drin. Many a Bosnian peasant is said to have made a pilgrimage to Belgrade, merely to hang about the streets till he could catch a near view of the new sovereign and future "liberator." He was to lead Serbian "Piedmont" in the movements for reuniting all races of Serb blood—Serbs, Bosniaks, Slovenes, Croats, and Dalmatians—into a "Greater Serbia," as the House of Savoy had led in the unification of Italy half a century earlier. His marriage with Princess Zorka, daughter of Nicholas of Montenegro, seemed to forecast close relations between these two Slav states. Many of his years of exile had been passed in Russia. His brother, Prince Arsene, had served as an officer in a crack regiment of Russian Guards. His two Montenegrin sisters-in-law married Russian Grand Dukes. These facts all seemed to suggest a Russophile orientation in Serbian policy with the accession of Peter I in 1903. And such proved to be the case. It was actively hastened also both by encouragement from the Pan-Slav elements in Russia, and by the irritating attitude adopted by Austria-Hungary.

Austrian ministers soon observed with dismay this growth of Serbian nationalism and pro-Russian feeling. If unchecked, it threatened the integrity of the Hapsburg lands. It meant that the Kingdom of Serbia would act as a dangerous magnet, tending to draw away Austria's Serb subjects to form the "Greater Serbia." If the decaying Turkish Empire should ever fall to pieces, if nationalist revolts should break out in Austria-Hungary in some crisis, such as the death of Emperor Francis Joseph, or if war should be declared in the Balkans or in Europe, Serbia would be likely to try to annex territories inhabited largely by Serbs. Probably Pan-Slav interests would lead Russia to support the Serbians. If Serbia secured Bosnia, her next step would be to attempt to unite the Croats, the Dalmatians, the Slovenes, and the Serbs in the Banat in southern Hungary. This would encourage the other subject nationalities under Hapsburg rule—the Rumanians, Czechs and Slovaks—to break away. This would spell *Finis Austriae.*[7]

In view of the danger to the Dual Monarchy from its subject nationalities, Austrian officials began to adopt measures to stifle this growing movement in Serbia for political and economic independence from Hapsburg influence. Serbia, having no direct outlet to the sea, had been virtually dependent upon Austria-Hungary for a market for her agricultural products. To strengthen herself, Serbia began in 1905 to negotiate with Bulgaria for a customs-union; but Austria interfered. In 1906, when the Austro-Serbian tariff treaty expired, feeling in both countries ran so high that it was not renewed, especially as the Magyar landlords found that Serbian products came into competition with their own. As a consequence, a bitter tariff war—the so-called "Pig War"—ensued. But instead of crushing Serbia economically, Austria only caused the Serbians to seek other markets, especially in Germany; and at home the Serbians began to erect slaughter houses and factories of their own. Germany easily managed to supply the Serbian peasants with goods which had formerly come from Austria. This displacement of Austrian by German goods

[7] *Cf.* Conrad, I, 13-28.

caused not a little hard feeling between Vienna and Berlin which persisted for years.[8] Austria's attempt at economic intimidation, far from compelling Serbia to return to an Austrophile policy, had just the opposite effect; it embittered Peter I's Ministers, and drove them more than ever into the open arms of Russia. It made them realize more clearly Serbia's need for a direct economic outlet to the sea, such as a railway connection with a port on the Adriatic in Albania or Montenegro, or on the Aegean at Salonica.[9] They welcomed negotiations for a railway crossing Serbia from the Danube to the Adriatic which was urged on their behalf by Russia in the spring of 1908, as a counter-measure to Austria's project for a railway from Bosnia through the Sanjak of Novi Bazar to Salonica.[10] The outbreak of the Young Turk Revolution in the summer hastened the negotiations, but led them to a fiasco in the most unexpected manner. It brought to a crisis the question, often discussed since 1876, and several times conditionally assented to by Russia, of Austria's "annexation" of the "occupied" provinces of Bosnia and Herzegovina. This in turn was closely connected with Russia's much-desired aim of opening the Bosphorus and the Dardanelles to the passage of Russian ships of war.

[8] Stanojevitch, *Die Ermordung der Erzherzogs Franz Ferdinand* (Frankfort, 1923), p. 38; Conrad (III, 407), in 1913, spoke of, "Deutschland, welches in gierigem Egoismus die Monarchie aus Serbien und überhaupt vom Balkan kommerziell zu verdrängen trachtet." The figures for Germany's displacement of Austria in Serbia in the years 1905, 1906, 1907, are significant: imports from Germany, in millions of dinars, 6.2, 9.7, 20.3; exports to Germany, 2.1, 19, 32; imports from Austria-Hungary 33.3, 22.2, 25.5; exports to Austria-Hungary 64.7, 30, 12; *Statesman's Year Book.*

[9] *Cf.* Dr. Baernreither, "Unsere Handelsbeziehungen zu Serbien," in *Oest. Rundschau,* XXIX, 1 ff., 1911; and "Aehrenthal und Milovanovitch" in *Deutsche Revue,* Jan., 1922. Dr. Baernreither was an enlightened Austrian enjoying the confidence of the Archduke Franz Ferdinand, who disapproved of Aehrenthal's policy and wished to make reasonable economic concessions to Serbia; see the selections from his diaries published by Josef Redlich, in *Foreign Affairs* (N. Y.), VI, 645-657, July, 1928

[10] G P., XXV. 281-382.

RUSSIA AND THE STRAITS

In the course of the nineteenth century, especially after the events of 1878, Russia had come to regard the closure of the Dardanelles against foreign warships by the Sultan as a valuable protection and asset for Russia. As Count Kapnist remarked in May, 1897: "Russia needs this gate-keeper [portier] in Turkish clothes for the Dardanelles, which under no circumstances ought to be opened. The Black Sea is a Russian *mare clausum.*"[11] This remained one of the corner-stones of Russian policy down to the World War. Russia did not desire any modification of the treaties which excluded warships of the other Great Powers from ingress into the Black Sea.

But the treaties which excluded Russian war vessels from passing inward or outward through the Straits of the Bosphorus and Dardanelles were quite a different matter. These were humiliating restrictions. They were inconsistent with Russia's prestige as a Great Power. They were contrary to her ambitions since Peter the Great's day for the control of a free outlet to the Mediterranean. They were a serious and positive handicap when she was engaged in war,

[11] G.P., XII, 285. On the earlier history of the closure of the Straits, see above, ch. ii, note 27; on the later history, E. A. Adamov, *Konstantinopol i Prolivy* [Russia and the Straits], 2 vols., Moskva, 1925-26; E. A. Adamov, *Razdel Aziatskoe Turtsii* [Partition of Asiatic Turkey], Moskva, 1924; I. M. Zakher, "Konstantinopol i Prolivy" in *Krasnyi Arkhiv,* VI, 48-76; VII, 32-54 (1924); A. Popov, "Pervaia Balkanskaia Voina" [First Balkan War], *ibid.,* XV, 1-29; XVI, 3-24 (1926); M. N. Pokrovski, *Drei Konferenzen,* Berlin, 1920; B. Shatzky: "La question de Constantinople et des Détroits," in *Rev. d'Hist. de la Guerre Mondiale,* IV, 289-309; V, 19-43 (Oct., 1926; Jan., 1927); G.P., X, 1-41, 70 f., 109-114; XI, 99-106; XII, 47-87; XIV, 531-563; XVII, 34, 84, 102; XVIII, 409-446; XIX, 229-244; and XXII, XXVI, XXVII, XXX-XXXIX, *passim; Livre Jaune: L'Alliance Franco-Russe,* p. 19 ff.; *Affaires Balkaniques,* M.F.R., L.N., Stieve, and Conrad, *passim;* a good brief account by G. Frantz, "Die Meerengenfrage in der Vorkriegspolitik Russland," in *Deutsche Rundschau,* LIII, 142-160 (Feb., 1927); P. Mohr, "Konstantinopel und die Meerengenfrage," in *Meereskunde,* Heft 178 (1927); and the references below in the present chapter.

as in the case of the Russo-Japanese War, because they prevented her from freely using her Black Sea Fleet where it might be most needed. Furthermore, they prevented the augmentation of this Black Sea Fleet for war against Turkey by any other means except naval construction on Russia's southern shores; it could not be increased by construction on the Baltic, or by the purchase of warships in England, as the Tsar sorrowfully observed in January, 1914.[12]

So the opening of the Straits to Russian warships became one of the first aims of Russian ministers in the decades immediately preceding the World War. This was quite distinct from two other aims which are often confused with it, but which were really different and would have involved even more serious European complications; one was the forcible seizure of Turkish territory along the heights of the Bosphorus; the other was the acquisition of control over Constantinople itself. To be sure, Russian warships once in the Straits would be in an easy position to accomplish either of the two other aims. But, generally speaking, the temerity of Russian ministers, though considerable, did not usually go to the point of planning to seize Constantinople itself. This city, they were inclined to admit, must remain in the hands of the Sultan so long as the Ottoman Empire survived; to try to seize it would meet with too great opposition from the Great Powers, not to mention Bulgaria and Greece. Constantinople, however, must in no case be allowed to fall under the control of any other Power —neither under Bulgaria during the Balkan Wars, nor under Germany through the appointment of General Liman von

12 M. W. Rodzjanko, *Erinnerungen,* p. 90 (Berlin, 1927). For England's persistent opposition to Russia's sending a couple of torpedo boats even though under a commercial flag, into the Black Sea in 1902, and also to Russia's sending any of her Black Sea Fleet out of the *mare clausum* during the Russo-Japanese War, see G.P., XVIII, 407-446; XIX, 229-244; and B.D., IV, 44-60.

Sanders to the command of a Turkish army corps in the Sultan's capital, as will be seen later.

Occasionally, however, ambitious Russian ministers seriously considered in secret the project for a sudden descent with a landing force to seize in time of peace the heights of the Bosphorus in the neighborhood of Constantinople. One of these occasions was in the winter of 1896-97. A word may be said of it, because it is the forerunner of several similar projects later, and because it typifies the confusion of authority and purposes which existed in the higher spheres at St. Petersburg.

To M. Nelidov, the Russian Ambassador at Constantinople, the frightful Armenian massacres caused a revulsion of feeling in Europe against the Sultan and anarchic conditions in his capital which seemed likely to afford Russia a good opportunity to make a bold *coup de main* to seize the heights of the Bosphorus above Constantinople. In the latter part of 1896 Nelidov came up to St. Petersburg to set forth his plan. Nicholas II at once approved it, even though it threatened, as Witte pointed out, a general European War. Nevertheless it was seriously considered in a special secret ministerial council and was favored by Vannovskii and Tyrtov, Ministers of War and Marine, and by Durnovo, President of the Council. Nelidov's plan was to despatch suddenly 30,000 troops on warships and transports from Odessa to the Upper Bosphorus and land them to seize control of the Straits, before England or any of the other Great Powers could prevent the filibustering expedition. Europe would be faced with a *fait accompli.* Nelidov was to return to his post at Constantinople; when he judged that the situation in the Sultan's capital had reached the proper critical point, the signal for the sudden descent of the Russian landing force was to be given by a harmless sounding telegram, "Long without news." But when the plan was further studied by the military and naval authorities, it appeared that, even with the most secret precautions, it would be almost impossible to concentrate and despatch a sufficiently large number of troops and transports without attracting the attention and opposition of England. Moreover, Count Witte and Pobiedonostev were opposed to it on economic, political and moral grounds, and cast the weight of their personal influence against the rash project, so that it was ultimately abandoned by the Tsar. But that Nelidov's plan was seriously considered, and was even thought by Witte to have been on the point of being carried out, is significant of the aims of Russian diplomats and of the readiness with which the weak-willed Nicholas II at first assented to it.[13]

THE BALKAN QUESTION "PUT ON ICE," 1897-1907

Soon after the abandonment of Nelidov's project, Emperor Francis Joseph visited Nicholas II at St. Petersburg. Friendly conversations took place which resulted in an important Austro-Russian Balkan agreement. It was at this time that Russia was embarking more actively on her

13 Nelidov's project of 1896-97, first hinted at anonymously by E. J. Dillon, and then by several memoir writers, has recently been confirmed by documents published by the Bolshevists. See E. J. Dillon, *The Eclipse of Russia* (N. Y., 1918), pp. 231-244; S. I. Witte, *Memoirs* (Garden City, 1921), pp. 186-189; Baron Rosen, *Forty Years of Diplomacy* (N. Y., 1922), I, ch. xiv; M. Pokrovski, "Russko-germanskie otnosheniia" [Russo-German relations], in *Krasnyi Arkhiv,* I, ch. i (1922), part of which is publishd in German translation, "Lange ohne Nachricht," in KSF, IV, 175-181 (Mar., 1926); G. N. Trubetzkoi, *Russland als Grossmacht* (Stuttgart, 1913), pp. 161-162. Sazonov refers to it in his report to the Tsar of Nov. 23/Dec. 6, 1913, in L.N., II, 367. That Germany got wind of Nelidov's plan is evident from G.P., XII, 67-69. Probably one reason that Russia did not dare to carry out Nelidov's plan was the fear of offending her French ally; for nine hundred years France had had large interests in the Eastern Mediterranean which she did not care to see jeopardized by a too active advance even of her own ally. Hanotaux, who had served as secretary at the French embassy in Constantinople, had often said to the German Ambassador at Paris: "La question des détroits nous touche de trop près et j'espére toujours que la Russie n'y touchera pas, car cela pourrait devenir trop gros pour nous!" (Münster to Holstein. April 25, 1896; G.P., XII, 51).

policy of economic and political penetration in the Far East, and wished to be freed from possible complications in the Balkans. In case her aggressive attitude in Manchuria should lead to trouble with China or Japan, it was important that her Balkan rear should not be endangered from the side of Austria, or otherwise. In the spring of 1897, therefore, consequent upon Francis Joseph's visit, the Austrian and Russian foreign ministers exchanged friendly notes declaring in favor of the *status quo* in the Balkans, and asserting their intentions to pursue "a policy of perfect harmony." Austria reserved her claims to Bosnia and Herzegovina, and expressed herself in favor of an independent Albania. The status of Constantinople and the Straits, "having an eminently European character," was not to be modified by any separate Austro-Russian arrangements.[14] By this agreement the Balkan question was said to be "put on ice," and for a decade the tension between the rival aims of Russia and Austria was in fact somewhat relieved.

But it would be a mistake to assume, as most writers do, that Russia had abandoned, even temporarily, the consideration of her ambitions in the Near East while pressing her imperialist policy in the Far East. This misconception arose largely from the inspired Russian Press and from misinformed persons who believed that the Russian Bear had shifted his appetite completely to the plains of Manchuria. In reality, though the Tsar and his ministers talked of "Port Arthur," they were at the same time thinking of "Constantinople." Of this there are several indications.

14 Notes of Goluchowski and Muraviev of May 8 and 17, 1897; Pribram, pp. 78-82; G.P., XII, 273-305. For further efforts to extend Austro-Russian Harmony in the Balkans by the Mürzsteg Program, the Neutrality Declaration of 1904, and the Macedonian reform plans of 1904-1907, see Pribram, p. 98; G.P., XVIII, 85-405; XXII, 3-8, 19-522; and *British Documents,* I, 281 f., 295-305.

In 1899, Muraviev, the Russian Minister of Foreign Affairs, uneasy at the rapid growth of German activity in Turkey and the beneficial effect which it might have upon the Sick Man's health, spoke bluntly to the German Ambassador about Russia's "exclusive claim to Constantinople"; and added, "Already the Tsar's Government must now have a watchful eye that no other Power assumes a dominating position on the Bosphorus." [15] He then tried to bluff Germany into signing a written agreement guaranteeing the Bosphorus to Russia; he threatened that he would come to an understanding with England, if Germany refused. But Bülow preferred to adhere to Germany's traditional policy of declaring that Germany did not oppose Russia's aspirations at the Straits (because he felt sure that England would still do so); but he was unwilling to put anything into writing, for fear that Russia might reveal it to England, and thus endanger Anglo-German good relations.[16]

In 1900 Muraviev drew up a long secret memorandum, for discussion by the army and navy authorities, in which he urged the preparation of measures by which Russia might at any given moment take possession of the shores of the Bosphorus; and the Sultan must be prevented from doing anything which would strengthen his position on the Straits.[17]

On March 1, 1903, General Kuropatkin, the Minister of War, noted in his diary:

> I told Witte that our Tsar has grandiose plans in his head: to capture Manchuria for Russia, and to annex Korea. He is dreaming also of bringing Tibet under his dominion.

15 G.P., XIV, 550.

16 G.P., XIV, 531-563; especially No. 4022.

17 M. Pokrovski, "Tsarskaia diplomatiia o zadachakh Rossii na Vostoke v 1900 g." [Imperial diplomacy concerning Russia's aims in the East in 1900], in *Krasnyi Arkhiv,* XVIII (1926), pp. 3-29, especially pp. 9-11 and 17.

He desires to take Persia, and to seize not only the Bosphorus but also the Dardanelles.[18]

In the spring of 1904, Izvolski, who had just been transferred from Tokio to Copenhagen, was already contemplating a revolution in Russian diplomacy: the abandonment of the long-standing Asiatic conflict with England in favor of an entente which he hoped would enable Russia to open the Straits for her own war vessels. In one of his first conversations with King Edward VII at Copenhagen (which in view of Sir Edward Goschen's presence was something more than a purely private and personal talk), Izvolski set forth his views about Russia's necessities for a free passage of the Straits. King Edward replied that the closure of the Straits was not "absolute and eternal," but that for the moment British public opinion was so absolutely opposed to any opening of the Straits that he could not and would not at present do anything in defiance of it.[19]

Similarly, in the later negotiations for the Anglo-Russian Agreement of 1907, at least so far as they were carried on by Benckendorff, the Russian Ambassador in London, Izvolski again tried to carry out his fond hope of opening the Straits. He did this by offering the concession, unusual for Russian diplomacy, that England and the other Powers might send their vessels of war through the Dardanelles, but not into the Black Sea.[20] Russia would thus

18 *Krasnyi Arkhiv,* II, 31 (1923). Six weeks earlier he had written in his diary (Jan. 5/18; *ibid.,* p. 20): "I emphasized [to the Tsar] the necessity of shifting our main attention from the Far East to the West. The Tsar formulated it something like this: not to take our eyes off the East, but to pay the greatest attention to the West."

19 Ph. Crozier, "L'Autriche et l'Avant-guerre," in *Revue de France,* April 1, 1921, p. 276; *cf.* also Izvolski, *Memoirs* (London, 1920), pp. 20 81 ff.; Lee, *King Edward VII,* II, 283 ff.; and G.P., XIX, 177 ff., 188.

20 The proposal "which Count Benckendorff had discussed with me at the time of the Anglo-Russian Convention . . . had been that, while Russia should have egress from the Black Sea through the Straits, other

retain her *mare clausum,* while Russia and England would share equally in the favorable position which their fleets would have for exercising control over Constantinople and the Dardanelles. But Sir Edward Grey, in view of British public opinion and the fact that other Powers had a right to be consulted in any modification of the Straits treaties, did not want any mention to be made of the Bosphorus and the Dardanelles in the Anglo-Russian Convention which dealt primarily with the Middle East. So Izvolski failed to induce England to abandon her traditional attitude. Thereupon Izvolski decided to turn to Baron Aehrenthal and seek a solution of the Straits Question through coöperation with Austria.

THE BUCHLAU BARGAIN OF SEPTEMBER, 1908

In 1906 the direction of Foreign Affairs in Russia and in Austria passed into the hands respectively of two men who represented more aggressive and ambitious policies than their predecessors. At St. Petersburg, Alexander Izvolski, shrewd, subtle, proud, belonging to the Russian rural nobility but supposed to be a great admirer of British Liberalism, wished to win back for Russia in the Balkans the prestige which she had recently lost in her disastrous ad-

Powers should have liberty to send their vessels of war into the Straits without going into the Black Sea;" Grey to Nicolson, Oct. 14, 1908; Grey, I, 179. Izvolski also says there had been negotiations with England twice concerning the Straits, "une fois par l'intermédiaire de Benckendorff, et la seconde fois par mon intermédiaire, lors de mon séjour à Londres, en automne 1908;" L.N., I, 148; Stieve, I, 163; M.F.R., p. 122. And Hintze, Emperor William's personal representative in Russia, gathered from Sir Arthur Nicolson that the Straits question had been discussed in connection with the Anglo-Russian Convention negotiations (G.P., XXII, 80-81, note; XXVI, 127, 218-219, note). We may therefore reject as untrue both Viscount Grey's later statement that "the question of the Straits was not mixed up with those Anglo-Russian negotiations about Persia" (Grey, I, 159), and Izvolski's "particular assurance" to Aehrenthal in September, 1907, "that he had not spoken of the question to the English" (G.P., XXII, 80-81); for Benckendorff's equally untrue denial, see G.P., XXV, 306.

venture in the Far East. At Vienna, Baron Aehrenthal, energetic, ambitious, the courtier-aristocrat, wished to free Austria from the excessive dependence on Germany which had characterized his predecessor's policy. He wished to strengthen the Dual Monarchy in the Balkans, by putting an end to the Serbian danger which he believed threatened to disrupt the Hapsburg Empire.

Here were two political adventurers, equally ready to fish in troubled waters to satisfy their ambitions, even to the extent of upsetting international treaties and endangering the peace of Europe. On Aehrenthal has usually fallen the odium for the Bosnian "Annexation Crisis" of 1908-09, but recently published Russian and German documents indicate that Izvolski had quite as much to do with the initiation of this plan for modifying the Treaty of Berlin as did Aehrenthal.

A few days after signing the Convention of 1907 with England and thus relieving Russia from the danger of complications in the Middle East, Izvolski visited Vienna. He was decorated with the Grand Cross of the Order of St. Stephen, received in audience by Francis Joseph, and had a long conversation with Aehrenthal. He hinted very confidentially that he intended to solve the Straits Question in the manner desired by Russia, which was true; and he particularly assured Austria that he had not spoken of the question to the English; which was untrue.[21] He went on to tell Aehrenthal:

> Russia has lost Manchuria with Port Arthur and thereby the access to the sea in the East. The main point for Russia's military and naval expansion of power lies henceforth in the Black Sea. From there Russia must gain an access to the Mediterranean.[22]

[21] G.P., XXII, 76, 79 ff., and preceding note.
[22] G.P., XXII, 83 f.

Aehrenthal thanked him for his confidence, but, following Bismarck's earlier advice to take a reserved attitude until Russia should show her hand and declare more definitely her intentions, gave a dilatory and non-committal reply. He merely remarked that it was a difficult problem, and that if the Straits Question were really opened up, Austria would want to define her attitude, adding:

> I beg you to inform me in good time before the moment comes for putting the Russian plans into action, precisely as I should feel myself under obligations to inform the Russian Government in case Austria-Hungary should ever intend to annex Bosnia and Herzegovina.[23]

Shortly afterwards Aehrenthal told Conrad, the Austrian Chief of Staff, that Russia, having limited her policy in Asia, "will now take up again her Western Balkan policy and demand freedom of the Straits for Russian vessels, but not for others"; and the two discussed the annexation of Bosnia and Herzegovina as possible compensation for conceding the freedom of the Straits to Russia.[24] Here then at Vienna, in September, 1907, in the confidential conversation of Izvolski and Aehrenthal, was foreshadowed the bargain which was struck between them at Buchlau just a year later.

Izvolski apparently did not proceed immediately with his plans, possibly because of Aehrenthal's reserved attitude and because of England's known opposition to them. But a few months later, after Aehrenthal had "thrown a bomb between his legs" [25] by his statement in the Delegations of

[23] G.P., XXII, 81, 84. [24] Conrad, I, 513 f., 528, 530.

[25] "C'est une bombe qu'il m'a jetée entre les jambes," said Izvolski to the German Ambassador in St. Petersburg, referring to Aehrenthal's announcement of the Sanjak railway project; G.P., XXV, 313. Izvolski at once countered with a Danube-Adriatic railway project which would cut Austria's projected line at right angles, and greatly benefit Serbia by giving her direct access to the sea. On these rival railway projects see G.P., XXV, 281-382; Schwertfeger, *Zur Europäischen Politik,* III,

Austria's desire for a railway from Sarajevo to Mitrovitza, to connect up with the Macedonian and Greek railways, Izvolski took up again Nelidov's idea of accomplishing Russia's historic mission by force rather than by diplomacy. In a secret Ministerial Conference of February 3, 1908, he pointed out that if Russia continued the passive defensive policy of 1897 of leaving the Balkan Question on ice, Russia "runs the risk of losing all at once the fruits of her century-long efforts, ceasing to play the rôle of a Great Power, and falling into the position of a second-rate State to which no one pays attention." After calling attention to the situation in the Caucasus, Persia, and the Balkans, and also to Russia's recent *rapprochement* with England, he suggested that joint Anglo-Russian military action in Turkey "offered an extremely attractive prospect, which might lead to dazzling results and to the realization of Russia's historic mission in the Near East." But this would involve the whole Turkish and Near Eastern Question. He, therefore, sought the advice of the other Ministers as to how far they could back up an active aggressive policy.

In reply General Palitsyn, Chief of the General Staff, said he had urged three months earlier the use of force in the Caucasus, but that now the situation no longer demanded it; he called attention to Russia's military unpreparedness. General Polivanov, of the War Ministry, agreed with him that "Russia lacks artillery, machine guns, uniforms. The restoration of order, of complete order in the army and fortresses, will take stupendous sums and much time." The Minister of Marine confessed that the Black Sea Fleet was not ready for war, needing sailors, coal, ammunition, guns, and mines. M. Kokovtsev, the Finance Minister, complained that neither he nor the whole Council had been kept informed of Izvolski's warlike and expensive

64-72; Conrad, I, 555; G. Giolitti, *Memoirs of My Life* (London, 1923), pp. 207-211.

plans; he was energetically opposed to military action in Persia and to pulling chestnuts out of the fire for Foreign Powers; such a policy would not be understood in Russia, "and it is also not clear whom we should be defending in Persia." As to the Balkans, the question was still more serious; he would limit Russia's action to the possible protection of Bulgaria in case of a Turco-Bulgarian war. Meanwhile money must be raised by every means for reorganizing the army and navy and making adequate military preparations.

Izvolski therefore again emphasized the unfavorable consequences of a strictly defensive policy. But Premier Stolypin summed up the discussion by declaring that Izvolski must not count on support for an aggressive and adventurous policy at present. Otherwise a new revolution might break out in Russia and endanger the dynasty. "But after some years, when we have secured complete quiet, Russia can speak again as in the past."

At present she must limit herself to what could be accomplished by the diplomatic skill of the Minister of Foreign Affairs. In approving this policy of avoiding war for the present, and preparing for the future, Nicholas II noted in pencil: "God helps those who help themselves." [26]

Unable to get unanimous Russian backing for active military measures, Izvolski then turned again to Aehrenthal and Austria, to secure by diplomacy a more modest part of Russia's Historic Mission—the opening of the Straits for the Russian warships of the future. A year before he had tried to win England's consent to this as part of the Anglo-Russian Entente, but without success.

Count Aehrenthal on his side had been secretly consider-

[26] Protocol of the Ministerial Council of Jan. 21/Feb. 3, 1908; printed by M. Pokrovski, *Drei Konferenzen* (Berlin, 1920), pp. 17-31; and in part by Adamov, *Konstantinopol i Prolivy,* I, 8 ff.; *cf.* also Polivanov's diary [in Russian], quoted by G. Frantz, *Russland auf dem Wege zur Katastrophe* (Berlin, 1926), pp. 7-10.

ing for some months the desirability of converting the occupation of Bosnia and Herzegovina into full ownership, both on account of administrative difficulties and of the growing danger of the "Greater Serbia" propaganda.

The administration of Bosnia was in the hands of a military governor (*Landeschef*), but his authority was restricted at every point by a civilian assistant (*Ziviladlatus*) on the spot, who represented the supreme authority of the Austro-Hungarian Joint Minister of Finance in Vienna. By the Dual Compact in 1867 the Hapsburg Monarchy could acquire no territory except by the common consent of both halves of the Monarchy. This was one of the reasons why, in 1878, Bosnia and Herzegovina had been merely "occupied" jointly by Austria-Hungary, instead of being directly annexed to Austria. It was also the reason the administration of the provinces had been placed under the Austro-Hungarian Joint Minister of Finance. This Minister, however, occupied with other matters and far away in Vienna, was often out of touch with the exact situation in Bosnia and Herzegovina. In consequence he often sent orders to his representatives there, which conflicted with the views of the military governor on the spot. The result was frequent friction between the *Landeschef* and the *Ziviladlatus*.

Though the Hapsburgs had done much, during the period of occupation, for the material improvement of Bosnia and Herzegovina, by building roads, establishing schools, and enforcing order, there was also much in their administration which could be justly criticized, and they had failed to win the loyalty of all the inhabitants. The Mohammedans, and most of the Roman Catholic elements in the population, were fairly well disposed, but the great majority of the Greek Orthodox Serbs were persistently hostile.

With the outbreak of the Turkish Revolution, the administrative and revolutionary dangers threatened to become more serious. The Young Turks, who had announced the calling of a democratic parliament for the whole Turkish Empire, might demand that representatives from Bosnia should sit in it. They might even seek to nullify the Austrian occupation which had existed since 1878. Moreover, if war should break out between Austria and Turkey, would it be the duty of the Bosnians to fight on the side of their "sovereign," the Sultan, or on the side of the actual Austrian rulers of the district? The situation offered an excellent opportunity for anti-Austrian agitation, and the "Greater Serbia" propaganda made the most of it. By annexing Bosnia and Herzegovina, Aehrenthal hoped to put an end once and for all to any doubts that the provinces were to belong to Austria-Hungary.[27]

The sudden Young Turk Revolution of 1908, and the vista of uncertain possibilities which it opened, seemed to both Izvolski and Aehrenthal to offer a favorable opportunity for a mutually advantageous bargain at Turkey's expense. Russia might settle the "Straits Question," by securing the right to send Russian warships through the Bosphorus and the Dardanelles; and Austria might strengthen her position in Bosnia and Herzegovina, by converting the occupation which she had enjoyed for thirty years into a direct annexation. This was the substance of an *aide-memoire* which Izvolski sent to Aehrenthal on July 2, 1908,[28] in connection with the negotiations concerning the Sanjak and the Danube-Adriatic railway projects. Aehrenthal was delighted with Izvolski's proposal, which fell in so nicely with his own plans. In order to arrange the details

[27] Conrad, I, 13-28, 87-109; 170-4; 518-524, 527-9, 540-3, 557; G.P., XXVI, 1-22; Freiherr von Musulin, *Das Haus am Ballplatz* (Munich, 1924), p. 163 ff.; Brandenburg, pp. 261-269 (Eng. trans., pp. 305-314); Stephan, Count Burián, *Austria in Dissolution* (N. Y., 1925), pp. 265-310.

[28] Conrad, I, 107 f.; printed, with Aehrenthal's reply of Aug. 27, in G.P., XXVI, 190-195.

of the bargain, he invited the Russian Minister of Foreign Affairs to a meeting at Count Berchtold's castle at Buchlau in Moravia.

As the conversations between Izvolski and Aehrenthal at Buchlau on September 15, 1908, took place without witnesses or definite agreements in writing drawn up on the spot, conflicting versions arose a few weeks later, when the bargain did not turn out as had been anticipated. Izvolski declared that he had been tricked and misrepresented. But the facts can be stated with considerably certainty, on the basis of what each Minister stated privately to third parties within a few days.[29] Izvolski assented to the Austrian annexation of Bosnia and Herzegovina, and Aehrenthal to the opening of the Straits to Russian ships of war. Aehrenthal also promised to abandon his Sanjak railway project and all intentions of extending Austrian influence toward Salonica, and to withdraw the Austrian military garrisons from the Sanjak of Novi Bazar. As these changes modified important terms of the Treaty of Berlin, Izvolski thought that they would have to be confirmed by a Conference of the Powers which had signed the Treaty. To this Aehrenthal apparently did not object at the time. Less important points discussed and agreed upon were the abolition of Austria's rights over the Montenegrin coast, the annexation of Crete to Greece, and acquiescence in the independence of Bulgaria, if Prince Ferdinand should finally decide to proclaim himself full sovereign. The one important matter which was not made definite, and gave rise to endless and bitter controversy, was the date at which these changes were to be made and published. Aehrenthal claims to have told Izvolski explicitly that the annexation of Bosnia would have to be made prior to the meeting of the Austro-Hungarian Delegations, which was fixed for October 8, when he would have to make a public state-

[29] G.P., XXVI, 25-64.

ment.[30] Izvolski, however, got the impression that the Austrian Minister would merely lay the annexation plan before the Delegations for consideration, not that he would inform them of it as a *fait accompli.* He seems to have anticipated that this bargain would meet with some serious difficulties, and he evidently did not expect that Aehrenthal would take any definite steps until the substance of the Buchlau conversations had been confirmed in writing. Later, after the annexation, he complained bitterly that Aehrenthal was "no gentleman," and had "broken faith" in proceeding so speedily with the annexation.[31]

Possibly at Buchlau Aehrenthal had not made up his mind exactly as to his procedure. But by September 26 he had evidently decided to act quickly, for he sent Bülow a long private letter informing him of the Buchlau agreement and justifying his own part in it, but not indicating any date for the annexation.[32] On September 29 personal letters

30 Tschirschky, German Ambassador at Vienna to Bülow, Nov. 2, 1908; G.P., XXVI, 31 note, 234. See also G.P., XXVI, 35 ff., 186 ff., 228 ff., 307 ff., 837; and note 61 below. H. Friedjung, *Zeitalter des Imperialismus,* II, 226 ff.; Th. von Sosnosky, *Die Balkanpolitik Oesterreich-Ungarns seit 1866,* II, 167 ff.; L. Molden, *Alois Graf Aehrenthal,* p. 59 ff.; and Eduard Ritter von Steinitz, "Iswolski und die Besprechungen in Buchlau," in KSF, V, 1151-1179, Dec., 1927; also Count Berchtold, "Russia, Austria and the World War," in *Contemporary Review,* CXXXIII, 422 ff., April, 1928.

31 For his first expectations see G.P., XXVI, 35 ff., 55 ff.; for his later complaints, G.P., XXVI, 118 ff., 135 f., 147 ff., 180 ff., 206 ff., 235 ff., 396 ff.; and below, note 75. See also Ph. Crozier, "L'Autriche et l'Avant-guerre," in *Revue de France,* April 15, 1921, pp. 566-574; and the anonymous articles in the *Fortnightly Review* for Sept. and Nov., 1909, "Baron Aehrenthal and M. Iswolski: Diplomatic Enigmas" and "M. Iswolski and Count von Aehrenthal: A Rectification," the first inspired by Izvolski, and the second inspired by Aehrenthal and written by Mr. E. J. Dillon after a visit with Count Berchtold at Buchlau—a fact which soon gave rise to an unpleasant scene between Berchtold and Izvolski (*cf.* G.P., XXVII, 442-446; J. von Szilassy, *Der Untergang der Donau-Monarchie,* 194 ff.); Georges Louis, *Carnets,* I, 66-69, 115.

32 G.P., XXVI, 35-39. Two days later Aehrenthal told the German Ambassador in Vienna that "circumstances might compel him to begin even in the very immediate future with the accomplishment" of his annexation plans; the circumstances to which he referred were the propagandist agitation of the Serbians and the probability that Prince Ferdi-

from Emperor Francis Joseph, to be presented on October 5 to the rulers of the leading states, were sent to the Austrian ambassadors abroad. The letters announced that he would proclaim the annexation of Bosnia and Herzegovina on October 7.[33]

Meanwhile Izvolski, not expecting that Aehrenthal would act so precipitately with a *fait accompli,* started on a leisurely tour to sound the Powers on the Buchlau bargain and to secure their consent thereto. On September 26, at Berchtesgaden, he saw Schoen, the German Secretary of State for Foreign Affairs, and emphasized the difficulties which Serbia was likely to make, adding that he thought a European Congress would be necessary to sanction the new arrangements. Schoen listened, and indicated that perhaps Germany would expect some services in return for consenting to the opening of the Straits. On September 29 and 30, at Desio, Izvolski took Tittoni into the secret. This was the first definite information that the Italian Minister had had of the impending changes, and his feelings were hurt. He straightway begged urgently at Vienna for a postponement of the annexation, but his prayer fell on deaf ears, and was overtaken by the course of events. Though indignant at Aehrenthal's Balkan plans and silence in regard to them, Tittoni was willing enough to satisfy Izvolski's ambitions in regard to the Straits in return for a favorable attitude on Russia's part toward Italy's eventual seizure of Tripolis. In the communiqué issued to the press on the Desio interview and in Tittoni's speech in Parliament on December 4, 1908, emphasis was laid on the complete har-

nand of Bulgaria was about to proclaim his independence of Turkey; *ibid.,* 43 f.

33 G.P., XXVI, 97-101; for Francis Joseph's letter to Nicholas II, see *Krasnyi Arkhiv,* X, 42-43 (1925) and KSF, IV, 238-240 (April, 1926). Since Ferdinand of Bulgaria proclaimed his independence on Oct. 5, Aehrenthal hurriedly notified Turkey of the Bosnian annexation on Oct. 6, one day earlier than the date announced in the Emperor's letters (G.P., XXVI, 112).

mony of Russo-Italian views—which was set down in a formal written agreement at Racconigi thirteen months later, in October, 1909.[34]

From Desio Izvolski started for France. At Meaux, just before his train reached Paris, he bought a newspaper and was startled at the indications that Aehrenthal and Prince Ferdinand of Bulgaria appeared about to put into immediate effect part of the plans which had been discussed at Buchlau.[35] The news was confirmed by a letter from Aehrenthal which was handed to him upon his arrival at Paris.

THE BOSNIAN CRISIS OF 1908-1909

In Serbia the news caused great indignation and excitement. Newspaper "extras" bitterly denounced the infringement of the Treaty of Berlin and demanded preparations for a life and death struggle against Austria. Only thus could the Powers be aroused to support Serbia.[36] Serbian Ministers assumed that war was inevitable. The Skupshtina was hurriedly called together; credits were voted for war; preparations for mobilization were made; armed irregular bands, the famous "Comitadjis," were formed; and the "National Defense" (*Narodna Odbrana*) society was estab-

[34] G.P., XXVI, 43, 55-64; XXVII, 319 ff., 399 ff. Writing on Nov. 4, 1909, Izvolski speaks of this identity of Russo-Italian views on Balkan questions between himself and Tittoni as having been formulated "nearly two years ago"; *ibid.*, p. 424; Siebert-Schreiner, p. 151. This Desio interview and earlier negotiations concerning the Sanjak railway project may explain Giolitti's curious mistake (*Memoirs of My Life*, London, 1923, pp. 202-204) in giving 1907, instead of 1909, as the date of the Racconigi bargain.

[35] Crozier, *op. cit.*, p. 571. The Austrian Ambassador at Paris, hearing that President Fallières would be out of town on Oct. 5, decided to present Francis Joseph's letter to him on Oct. 3 under strict secrecy, but Pichon at once telegraphed the news to the French ambassadors abroad and something of it leaked out to the French papers (Crozier p. 567 f.; G.P., XXVI, 101 f.).

[36] Report of Austrian Chargé d'Affaires in Belgrade, 9 P.M., October 5, 1908; Conrad, I, 113; G.P., XXVI, 247 ff.

lished by leading citizens to prevent the annexation.[37] Prince George Karageorgevitch hastened to Russia to beg help from the Tsar, and was soon followed by Pashitch, the powerful leader of the pro-Russian Radicals. Milovanovitch, the Serbian Premier and Minister of Foreign Affairs, started on a tour of the European capitals to secure assistance in preventing Aehrenthal from taking sovereign possession of the two provinces, which were regarded as the very heart of the hoped-for future South Slav Kingdom.

But while Serbian Ministers protested loudly in one breath against the wicked infraction of the Treaty, in the next they suggested "autonomy" for Bosnia and Herzegovina, and "territorial compensations" for their own Kingdom.[38] They urged the partition of the Sanjak between Serbia and Montenegro. This would connect these two Slav countries by a common boundary and form a barrier against further penetration by Austria to the South; it was part of the region through which the projected Danube-Adriatic railway would run, giving Serbia direct access to the sea, and cutting off Aehrenthal's projected railway to Salonica at right angles. What would the Powers do for Serbia? And in particular what would Russia, the Protectress of the Slavs, do?

Izvolski was now in great embarrassment. He feared that Aehrenthal was about to secure the advantages of Austria's half of the Buchlau bargain, before he had gotten French and English consent to Russia's half. Therefore he did not want the Serbians to stir up trouble until he had the Straits safely in his pocket. So he told the Serbians to keep quiet for the moment, and wait for a conference of the Powers:

37 Stanojevitch, 47; for further details, see below, Vol. II, ch. ii, "The Assassination Plot."

38 Reports of Vesnitch from Paris, Oct. 5; of Milovanovitch from London, Oct. 29; and of Pashitch from St. Petersburg Nov. 25, 1908; Bogitchevitch, 147 ff. (French edition, 1925, p. 171 ff.); G.P., XXVI, 252 ff

> You Serbians surely cannot be thinking of driving Austria-Hungary out of Bosnia and Herzegovina by force of arms. And we Russians, on the other hand, cannot wage war on Austria on account of these provinces. . . . I have foreseen this step of Austria-Hungary's, and it did not surprise me. For that reason I made our acceptance of it dependent upon her renunciation of her rights to the Sanjak of Novi Bazar; and then will follow the revision or alteration of the Treaty of Berlin, which we shall demand; upon this occasion Serbia, too, will be able to present her wishes as regards the rectification of her frontiers. . . . I do not understand your state of agitation. In reality you lose nothing, but gain something—our support. I trust that the Serb people in Bosnia and Herzegovina will continue as hitherto their cultural activity for their own renaissance, and, awake as they are, it will never be possible to denationalize them.[39]

But Izvolski soon found that in Paris he could get no effective backing for his projected opening of the Straits. M. Pichon was "sympathetic" but non-committal, wishing first to know what England's attitude would be.[40] On crossing the Channel, Izvolski discovered, to his great chagrin, that England was still opposed to it, in spite of the more intimate relations which he expected from the Entente of 1907. Sir Edward Grey tactfully told him that a request for opening the Straits was "fair and reasonable," and not objectionable "in principle," provided they were opened "on terms of perfect equality to all," *i.e.*, including the English. But Grey was absolutely opposed to Izvolski's project, which consisted in opening the Straits to Russian warships, while leaving them still closed against war vessels of the other Great Powers. Any such purely one-sided modification of existing treaties, exclusively for the benefit of the Russians, would give them in time of war "the advantage of having the whole of the Black Sea as an inviolable harbor,

[39] Report of Vesnitch, Serbian Minister in Paris, of conversation with Izvolski, Oct. 5, 1908; Bogitchevitch, 151-154; and in the same strain Prince Urusov to Simitch at Vienna, Oct. 10; *ibid.*, 154-156.

[40] L.N., I, 145 f.; G.P., XXVI, 133-136.

from which cruisers and commerce destroyers could issue, and retire at will from pursuit by a belligerent." Any modification of the existing treaties closing the Straits to warships "must be one which would contain such an element of reciprocity as would, in the event of war, place belligerents on an equal footing." [41] This, of course, was not at all what Izvolski intended. Like Saburov thirty years earlier he wanted to have the door to Constantinople and the Black Sea bolted from the inside, so that Russia, and no one else, could open and lock it at pleasure. In vain he tried to frighten Grey into accepting his proposal by hinting that a refusal might break up the Anglo-Russian Entente. "M. Izvolski went on to say that the present was a most critical moment. It might either consolidate and strengthen the good relations between England and Russia, or it might upset them altogether. His own position was at stake, for he was entirely bound up with the policy of a good understanding with England, which he had advocated against all opposition." [42]

Izvolski now began to lose all hope of securing the opening of the Straits to Russian warships after all. If he could not secure his half of the Buchlau bargain, perhaps it would still be possible to thwart Aehrenthal, by insisting that the annexation question be laid before a Conference of the Signatory Powers. Unless he succeeded in this, he would have to confess to a humiliating diplomatic defeat and a severe loss of personal prestige. Already the Pan-Slavs in Russia had begun to criticize him angrily and bitterly for being outwitted by Aehrenthal, for allowing Prince Ferdinand to assert his independence unaided instead of receiving it from the hands of the Tsar, and especially for having sacrificed the Orthodox Slavs of Bosnia to the Romanist

[41] Grey's memorandum to Izvolski, Oct. 14, 1908; M.F.R., p. 530; L.N., II, 458.

[42] Grey to Nicolson, Oct. 14, 1908; Grey, I, 178. *Cf.* also G.P., XXVI, 140, 144, 149 ff., 157 ff., 173 ff., 195 f.

sovereignty of the Hapsburgs. Even one of his own ambassadors did not hesitate to denounce the folly of his superior for raising the Straits Question and for his leisurely tour of Europe after Buchlau instead of returning to Russia; the whole affair might cause Izvolski's fall from office:

> M. Izvolski is undoubtedly very intelligent and highly cultivated, but unfortunately he is weighed down by excessive irritability and pride. An unfavorable newspaper article costs him his night's rest. In his combinations he is too subtle and tricky, so that he often does not see the forest for the trees and what is simplest. All his arrangements aim only at the enhancement of his personal prestige. His eventual successor will be M. Charykov.[43]

Izvolski, therefore, in view of his weakened position at home and his failure at Paris and London, began to pretend to the Serbians, in spite of what he had just said to M. Vesnitch in Paris, that he had never approved Austria's annexation of Bosnia. While still in London he "did not conceal his vexation at Austria, and protested most energetically against the affirmation that he had given his approval to the annexation." He declared that he would do everything to protect Serbian interests and secure compensation for them.[44] Stopping at Berlin on his way home from Paris and London, he denounced Austria in still stronger terms to Milovanovitch: "He condemned Austria-Hungary, which has entirely lost the confidence of Russia and of the Western Powers; he expressed the conviction and the hope that her action in this affair would be avenged upon her in a sanguinary manner." But in Berlin he found that Germany was firm in supporting her Austrian ally's refusal to submit the annexation to a Conference unless its

[43] Remarks of Muraviev at Rome, as reported by Monts to Bülow, Oct. 25, 1908; G.P., XXVI, 220. On the feeling in St. Petersburg, *ibid.*, pp. 124-129, 169-173, 199, 235-239, 265 ff.

[44] Report of Gruitch from London, October 13, 1908; Bogitchevitch, 157-161.

decisions, including recognition of the annexation, were agreed upon beforehand. In the face of this opposition, he now feared that he might not be able to thwart Austria, by insisting on a Conference, without endangering the peace of Europe. For such a conflict he knew that Russia was wholly unprepared. Therefore, he told the Serbians to avoid war for the present, but intimated to them, that, even if the annexation was allowed to stand, it need not be regarded as a final settlement:

> His [Izvolski's] policy was directed toward a goal, which, after liquidation of all Russian questions outside of Europe, would lead Russia on to her European objectives; Serbia was an important factor in this policy as a center of the Southern Slavs. Bosnia was, in the opinion of Russia and Western Europe, now more certainly assured to Serbia than ever, even if the Annexation should be recognized; Serbia must take the first steps toward the realization of her national tasks in the direction of the Sanjak and Bosnia. For the present a conflict must be avoided, as the ground had not yet been prepared either militarily or diplomatically. If Serbia brought on a war, Russia would have to abandon her, and she would be vanquished, although this would be a very severe blow, not only for the Russian national sentiment, but also for Russian interests and future plans.[45]

In the course of the next four months Izvolski's embarrassment increased. But he continued to encourage the Serbians with the hope that the Annexation Question would be submitted to a Conference of the Powers for revision, and he tried by every means to accomplish this. But it became evident that he would not be successful.[46]

Meanwhile, excitement in Serbia, as well as among the

[45] Report of Milovanovitch from Berlin, Oct. 25, 1908; *ibid.*, 161-163. On Izvolski's interviews with Bülow in Berlin, see G.P., XXVI, 201-212.

[46] G.P., XXVI, 247-363; Siebert-Schreiner, pp. 229-272.

Slavs in Bosnia and Croatia, continued to increase. Demonstrations of defiance against the Hapsburgs became more frequent. Austria, on her side, redoubled her repressive measures and made wholesale arrests of agitators and suspected traitors. In a notorious treason trial some of her officials even resorted to the use of documents said to have been forged in the Austrian Embassy at Belgrade, which the Austrian historian, Friedjung, unfortunately for his reputation, made the mistake of accepting as genuine.[47]

The situation in Bosnia and Serbia became so threatening for Austria, that in December, 1908, Conrad, the Chief of Staff, was permitted to carry out "brown mobilization," a supposedly inconspicuous measure, by which Austrian troops were pushed up toward the Serbian frontier without disturbing the normal peace traffic on the railways.[48] This threatened a local conflict between Austria and Serbia, which might easily develop into a general European war. Russia, however, wished to avoid any armed conflict at this time, since she was as yet wholly unprepared for a general European war, and would be unable to give Serbia armed support. Neither could she count on her ally, for France was not at all inclined to be dragged into a war with Germany over a Balkan dispute. So Russia was forced to continue to beg the Serbians to submit for the present, and to trust in the future. Guchkov, a leading member of the Russian Duma, told the Serbian Minister in St. Petersburg:

> When our armament shall have been completely carried out, then we shall have our reckoning with Austria-Hungary. Do not begin any war now, for this would be your

[47] J. Goricar and L. B. Stowe, *The Inside Story of Austro-German Intrigue* (New York, 1920), pp. 28-48; H. Wickham Steed, *Through Thirty Years* (London, 1924), I, 308-316; T. G. Masaryk, *Der Agramer Hochverratsprozess und die Annexion von Bosnia und Herzegovina*, Vienna, 1909; R. W. Seton-Watson, *The Southern Slav Question and the Hapsburg Monarchy* (London, 1911).

[48] Conrad, I, 120.

suicide; conceal your purposes, and make ready; the days of your joy will come.[49]

Izvolski himself was reported as saying:

> Serbia will be condemned to a pitiful existence until the moment for the downfall of Austria arrives. The Annexation has brought this moment nearer, and when it comes, Russia will unroll and solve the Serbian question. Izvolski sees that the conflict with Germandom is inevitable, but Russia's policy must be purely Slavophile.[50]

A few days later Kosutitch noted that these were also the views of Nicholas II:

> The Tsar said the Serbian sky is overcast with black clouds by this blow. The situation is frightful, because Russia is unprepared for war, and a Russian defeat would be the ruin of Slavdom. The Tsar has the feeling that a conflict with Germandom is inevitable in the future, and that one must prepare for this.[51]

As the situation on the Serbian frontier became increasingly threatening, and as the Powers, in spite of a lively interchange of despatches,[52] could come to no solution, Germany finally made a proposal for preserving the peace of Europe, by helping Izvolski to extricate himself from his embarrassment, while at the same time satisfying Austria.

GERMANY'S SOLUTION OF THE CRISIS

It is often said that Germany instigated Aehrenthal's annexation program in the interests of the Bagdad Railway and German imperialism. There is no truth in any such statement. As a matter of fact, Germany had not even been given a timely and definite warning by her ally of the

49 Report of Kosutitch, Mar. 3, 1909; *Deutschland Schuldig?*, p. 112.
50 March 10, 1909; *ibid.,* 114.
51 Mar. 19., 1909; *ibid.,* 114; Bogitchevitch, 150-151.
52 G.P. XXVI, 385-770. Siebert-Schreiner, pp. 229-272.

step she was contemplating, and consequently had no opportunity to interpose a restraint until it was too late.[53]

When Aehrenthal wrote Bülow on September 26 of the Buchlau bargain, the German authorities were scattered at various summer resorts. Bülow was at his villa at Norderney on the North Sea coast; Schoen, the Secretary of State for Foreign Affairs, was at Berchtesgaden in the Bavarian Tyrol; and the Kaiser was at Rominten in East Prussia. Aehrenthal's letter of September 26 wandered first to Norderney, and then, after a delay, to Rominten, so that the Kaiser did not learn of Austria's intentions until the very day of annexation. He was highly indignant, not only that he had been kept so long in ignorance, but also at Austria's action itself. He regarded it as an unjustifiable attack on Turkey, which would be disastrous to German influence in Constantinople, threaten the Bagdad Railway, and sow suspicion in England against the Central Powers. "Vienna will be charged with duplicity and not unjustly. She has duped us in a most unheard-of fashion." "My personal feelings as an ally have been most seriously wounded." Such were some of the Kaiser's marginal comments. He feared that this was the beginning of the partition of Turkey, and might lead to a European war. "If the Sultan in his necessity declares war, and hoists in Constantinople the green flag of the Holy War, I should not blame him." "With a policy of this kind Austria will drive us into a dangerous opposition to Russia." He was afraid that if

[53] Aehrenthal had preferred to face even his ally with a *fait accompli*. At the end of August, he had twice assured Germany he had no intention of annexing Bosnia and Herzegovina (G.P., XXVI, 20-22). On Sept. 5, he hinted to Schoen of the bargain he was planning with Izvolski (*ibid.*, p. 26 f.); but the first definite information was his letter to Bülow of Sept. 26 (*ibid.*, p. 35), which did not reach the Kaiser at Rominten until Oct. 6 (*ibid.*, 53, note). The Austrian Ambassador in Paris presented Emperor Francis Joseph's letter concerning the annexation on Oct. 3; thus the President of France was officially informed three days before the German Emperor,—a fact which greatly incensed the Kaiser (*ibid.*, 53, 102).

Germany did not take a stand against the Annexation, everyone would believe that it had taken place with his approval.[54] His Ambassador at Constantinople, Baron Marschall, favored disavowing it, even at the risk of forfeiting the alliance with Austria.[55]

Bülow, however, differed from his master. Convinced that Germany must support Austria in the Balkans, lest otherwise the Triple Alliance would be weakened, he believed that Germany must uphold Austria in the step which she had taken. If Germany assumed a negative or hesitating attitude in this question, Austria would never forgive her. Though Germany had a right to be indignant with Austria for not consulting her earlier, it would do no good to protest now. Anyway, Russia appeared to have given her consent. The Kaiser finally accepted Bülow's point of view; but he regretted that "Aehrenthal's frightful stupidity has brought us into this dilemma, so that we are not able to support and protect our friends, the Turks, when our ally has outraged them." Bülow thereupon informed Vienna, that, "In case difficulties or complications arise, our ally can count upon us," and that Austria was to judge of what must be done in the Serbian question.[56] But the Kaiser's feeling of irritation remained; he may have had the shrewd political instinct to realize that in thus giving a blank cheque to Austria, he was assuming a risky liability, and creating a dangerous precedent.

After proclaiming the Annexation of Bosnia and Herzegovina, Aehrenthal entered into negotiations with the Young Turks to satisfy their claims. They, like the Serbians, had at first made a loud outcry against the nullification of the clauses of the Treaty of Berlin. They assembled troops and attempted to boycott Austrian goods. But they gradually became convinced that none of the

54 G.P., XXVI, 39, 43, 45, 53, 102, 112.

55 G.P., XXVI, 99-103.

56 G.P., XXVI, 106, 160 ff.

European Powers would actually go to the length of giving them armed support. In view of Germany's strong stand behind Austria, the Young Turks finally decided, on February 26, 1909, to accept the Austrian offer of £T2,500,000 "for the loss of crown property," as a solace for abandoning their nominal sovereignty over the annexed provinces.[57]

Turkey's acceptance of Aehrenthal's *fait accompli* did not settle the question, however. It only increased the embitterment of the Serbians. Hitherto they had comforted themselves with the hope that Turkish claims, supported by the Entente Powers, could be used as a basis for forcing Austria to submit the Annexation to a Conference of the Powers, at which Serbia could at least secure "autonomy" for the provinces and "compensation" for herself. These hopes, too, were shattered, as Austria firmly refused to make concessions.

In the weeks following Austria's settlement with Turkey, the Great Powers telegraphed urgently back and forth in an attempt to reconcile Izvolski's promise to the Serbians that a Conference should be held, and Aehrenthal's steady refusal to submit the Annexation to revision. No solution was reached, until Germany finally made a proposal which eventually relieved the situation. To avert the possibility of an outbreak of hostilities on the Austro-Serbian frontier, which seemed imminent, and to bridge the gulf between Izvolski and Aehrenthal, Germany, on March 14, confidentially proffered mediation to Russia: Germany would request Austria to invite the Powers to give their formal sanction by an exchange of notes to the Austro-Turkish agreement, involving the nullification of Article 25 of the Treaty of Berlin, provided Russia promised beforehand to give her sanction, when invited by Austria to do so.[58]

This proposal had a threefold advantage: it secured to Austria a recognition by the Powers of the change in the

[57] G.P., XXVI, 415-488. [58] G.P., XXVI, 669 ff.

status of Bosnia and Herzegovina and deprived Serbia of legal grounds and hopes that the *fait accompli* would be overturned; it satisfied the Entente demand that no change in a treaty is valid unless formally recognized by all who signed it; and, finally, by omitting any reference to a Conference, which might still meet to consider other Balkan questions which had been raised, it avoided humiliating Russia by a direct rejection of the Conference idea which Izvolski had been steadily demanding for months. It let Izvolski easily out of the embarrassing blind alley into which he had strayed. Izvolski appreciated the proposal and was inclined to accept it.[59] He "recognized the conciliatory spirit . . . of this effort of Germany to bring about a relaxation of the tension."[60] But he still hesitated to give a definite answer, as he continued to cling to the hope of a Conference and the avoidance of another diplomatic defeat. His inclination to accept the German proposal, however, was stimulated by the fact that a Russian Ministerial Council on March 17 decided that Russia was totally unprepared to support Serbia by force of arms, and also by a hint from Aehrenthal that Austria might publish the documents relating to the Buchlau bargain and thus prove the untruthfulness of the assertions which Izvolski had been spreading everywhere about the origin of the Bosnian affair. Izvolski instantly begged Bülow to dissuade Aehrenthal from any such publication, and Germany accordingly did so, suggesting to Austria that it was better to keep this trump in one's hand as long as possible.[61]

59 Pourtalès to Bülow, Mar. 16, 18, 20; G.P., XXVI, 673-692.

60 Izvolski to the Russian Ambassadors in London and Paris, March 17, 1909; Siebert-Schreiner, p. 254.

61 G.P., XXVI, 668; *cf.* also pp. 230, 234-246, 308, 668-671, 825. In order to hide his own mistakes and misrepresentations, Izvolski apparently did not tell the Tsar the frank truth about the Buchlau bargain; this is indicated by the contents of the Tsar's letters to William II and Francis Joseph (Semenoff, *Correspondance entre Guillaume II et Nicolas II*, pp. 230-251; Zaionchkovski, "Vokrug anneksii Bosnii i Gertsegoviny" in

Aehrenthal was willing to accept the German mediation proposal, provided Serbia made a formal declaration admitting that the annexation of Bosnia had not infringed her rights and promising in the future to give up her attitude of opposition and protest.

Meanwhile an internal struggle was going on in Austria itself as to peace or war with Serbia. Conrad, the Austrian Chief of Staff, was again urging that the Hapsburg Monarchy should seize this favorable moment for the "inevitable" war with Serbia. By a "preventive war" now, "the dangerous little viper" could be crushed and rendered harmless for the future. Russia and Italy, he urged, were not sufficiently prepared to fight. Rumania was still loyal, and Turkey was satisfied. France and England might disapprove, but would not intervene. No such favorable moment for the reckoning with Serbia and averting the "Greater Serbia" danger was likely ever to recur, because, in the future, Russia and Italy would have reorganized and increased their armies. Austria might then have to reckon with a war on three fronts. Aehrenthal and Franz Ferdinand, on the other hand, had been inclined to peace, but Bülow feared they might at any time yield to Conrad's arguments. On March 15 Aehrenthal did, in fact, advise Francis Joseph to approve the calling up of more troops and their secret transportation toward the Serbian frontier.[62] The situation was therefore critical. To prevent an Austro-Serbian outbreak, Bülow believed it was necessary to press his mediation proposal and secure a definite answer from Izvolski. On March 21, he sent instructions to this effect to the German Ambassador at St. Petersburg:

Krasnyi Arkhiv, X, 41-53, partly translated in *Die Kriegsschuldfrage,* IV, 238-250, April, 1926), and also by the fact that Izvolski removed the Buchlau papers from the Russian archives (statement of Zinoviev, a Foreign Office secretary, to the French Ambassador, Aug. 26, 1912; Georges Louis, *Carnets,* II, 30). See also below, note 66.

62 Conrad, I. 138-157.

> Say to M. Izvolski that we learn with satisfaction that he recognizes the friendly spirit of our proposal and seems inclined to accept it . . . and that we expect an answer—yes or no; we must regard any evasive, conditional or unclear answer as a refusal. We should then draw back and let things take their course. The responsibility for further events would then fall exclusively on M. Izvolski, after we had made a last sincere effort to help him clear up the situation in a way which he could accept.[63]

By this Izvolski understood that he was "placed before the following alternatives: either an immediate regulation of the annexation question by an exchange of notes, or the invasion of Serbia."[64] He consulted the Tsar and next day gave the formal affirmative answer desired. The Tsar had already telegraphed the Kaiser that he was heartily pleased that Germany's proposal had made a peaceful compromise possible.[65]

Such were the events which soon became distorted into the legend that Germany had threatened Russia with force and humiliated her with an ultimatum. The legend was exploited in the Russian Press, spread in England by Sir Arthur Nicolson, and used by Izvolski as a means of saving his face before his critics in Russia.[66] But it was not an ultimatum. It was an attempt on Germany's part to bridge

[63] Bülow to Pourtalès, Mar. 21, 1909; G.P., XXVI, 693 ff. Though Bülow signed this note, it was Kiderlen-Wächter, who composed it and gave it its friendly but decisive tone; see E. Jäckh, *Kiderlen-Wächter, der Staatsmann und Mensch* (Berlin, 1925), II, 26-29.

[64] Izvolski to the Russian Ambassadors in London and Paris, March 23, 1909; Siebert-Schreiner, 259 ff.

[65] Tsar to Kaiser, Mar. 22, 1909; G.P., XXVI, 700.

[66] For the long controversy which arose over the nature of Germany's action, see G.P., XXVI, 693 note, and 777-855 *passim*. Bülow proposed to publish the documents to set the matter in its true light and counteract the legend of a German threat of force. The proposal was favored by Charykov, the Acting Minister during Izvolski's absence; but it was abandoned upon Izvolski's return, on account of his opposition to making documents public which would have shown how he and the Pan-Slav Press misrepresented things (*ibid.*, pp. 788-793, 796-801, 811, 814).

the gulf between Russia and Austria and prevent outbreak of war between Serbia and Austria. Sir Edward Grey had meanwhile come forward with a similar mediation formula and told Austria in language almost identical with that of Bülow to Russia, that, "if this fails, he would draw back and let things take their course." [67]

After Russia had accepted Germany's proposal, England, France and Italy soon followed suit. Upon Austria's invitation the Powers accordingly exchanged notes, giving a belated sanction to the unilateral action by which Aehrenthal had presumed to nullify the solemn clause of a European treaty.

Before the news of Russia's yielding had reached Vienna, or in spite of it, the war party had gotten the upper hand. A Ministerial Council of March 29 finally decided to order "Yellow Mobilization" or "Mobilization B" (Balkans). This involved the full mobilization of five of the total fifteen army corps which at that time composed the Austro-Hungarian army. It was thus a "partial mobilization" for the case of a war against Serbia and Montenegro only, but was complete for the five corps involved. Conrad left the Council with the conviction that now, at last, the reckoning with Serbia, which he had so often urged, was about to begin.[68]

Serbia, however, finally heeded the warnings she had been receiving from Russia, to avoid war for the present and to trust to the future. She decided at the eleventh hour to yield to the advice of the Powers. On March 31, 1909, she made at Vienna the formal declaration which had been agreed upon by Aehrenthal and Sir Fairfax Cartwright, the English Ambassador at Vienna, in the following terms:

67 Metternich to Bülow, Mar. 22, 1909; G.P., XXVI, 701.

68 Conrad, I, 162; for the technical mobilization measures, I, 116 ff. 160, 640 ff.

> Serbia recognizes that she has not been affected in her rights by the *fait accompli* created in Bosnia, and that consequently she will conform to the decisions that the Powers may take in regard to Article 25 of the Treaty of Berlin. In deference to the advice of the Great Powers, Serbia undertakes to renounce the attitude of protest and opposition which she has adopted since last autumn with regard to the Annexation. She undertakes, moreover, to modify the direction of her present policy toward Austria-Hungary, and to live in future on good neighborly terms with the latter.
>
> In conformity with these declarations and with confidence in the peaceful intentions of Austria-Hungary, Serbia will replace her army, as far as concerns its organization and the location and number of the troops, to the state in which it was in the spring of 1908. She will disarm and disband the volunteers and irregular forces and prevent the formation of new irregular corps on her territory.[69]

Within the next few weeks the Serbian and Austrian armies were demobilized and the Annexation Crisis was relieved. But, as will be seen later, the Serbians, encouraged by Russia, did not live up to the promises which they had been forced to give, and Conrad repeatedly complained later that Germany had prevented Austria in 1909 from settling the Serbian danger in the only permanently satisfactory way, viz., by the use of force.

THE CONSEQUENCES OF THE BOSNIAN CRISIS

We have dealt in some detail with these events, because the effects of the Annexation Crisis continued to be felt long afterwards,[70] and are to be counted among the causes of the War of 1914. In 1909, to be sure, Aehrenthal seemed

69 G.P., XXVI, 731; *cf. Austrian Red Book* of 1914, no. 7.

70 For interesting contemporary comment on the immediate effects of the Bosnian Crisis, see G.P., XXVI, 773-871.

to have achieved a diplomatic victory as brilliant for Austria, as it was humiliating for Russia and Serbia. He was congratulated on his success from all sides, and was rewarded with the title of Count. It was, however, one of those pyrrhic victories, which seem brilliant at the moment, but which bring more misfortune than success, if looked at from a longer perspective. Aehrenthal had, indeed, secured a clearer legal title to Bosnia. He had shown that the Hapsburg Monarchy was still able to pursue a vigorous and independent policy of its own, and gain the prestige which comes with a successful diplomatic move. But, on the other hand, he had caused Europe to distrust the methods of Austrian diplomacy, and incurred the odium of an unjustifiable breach of a solemn treaty. This fact was hardly obscured by the exchange of notes with which the Powers ultimately sanctioned his illegal nullification of treaty stipulations. He had also forced from Serbia a humiliating declaration, which he hoped would put an end to the "Greater Serbia" propaganda. But such a humiliation of one nation by another is hardly ever statesmanlike or really successful in achieving its aim. On the contrary, it usually leaves a bitter sting, which is likely to give trouble later. Serbia did not, in fact, live up to her promise to live on good neighborly terms with Austria. She allowed her soil to be the hearth from which a subversive agitation was spread, encouraging disloyalty and treason among the Bosnians and other Slav subjects of the Hapsburg Monarchy. Aehrenthal was soon to find that he had failed in the main purpose for which he had undertaken Annexation—the strengthening of the Austrian hold on Bosnia and Herzegovina. He had achieved a momentary success at the cost of future difficulties. "I hope our action will succeed," he had said to the German Ambassador at the beginning of the crisis; "if not, I am naturally done for, but in that case, at least, we shall have met defeat with honor;

otherwise we should have continued to sink miserably step by step." [71]

Germany, likewise, incurred some of the suspicion and odium which fell upon her ally. This distrust and antagonism was to be found, however, much more among the Entente Powers, particularly in Russia and England, than, as one might have expected, in Serbia.[72] Though Germany had not actually had definite foreknowledge of Aehrenthal's Annexation step, nor encouraged him to take it, the Powers —and many historians—were hardly convinced by Germany's assertions, at the time and later, as to the real facts. They naturally suspected, from the way in which Berlin firmly supported Vienna during the whole crisis, that Germany was Austria's accomplice from the outset and thoroughly approved of her action.[73] Germany's effort to find a solution, which would sanction Austria's *fait accompli,* and at the same time offer Izvolski a line of retreat from a position which Russians more sensible than he realized was untenable, was twisted into a "threat of force" or "ultimatum." It was represented as a brutal German attempt

[71] Brandenburg, p. 287.

[72] Stanojevitch, pp. 36-42, shows that the Serbians felt no particular animus against Germany during the following years. This was owing in part to the greatly increased trade relations between the two countries during and after the "Pig War." It may have been also owing partly to Serbia's realization that Germany often used her influence to restrain Austria from an aggressive Balkan policy. Though Izvolski's bitter hatred was mainly directed against Aehrenthal, that of the Russian people, led by the Pan-Slav Press, was henceforth directed more against Germany; see Pourtalès' reports, Mar.-Sept. 1909; G.P., XXVI, 777-858. The English Government's attitude was colored by the strongly Russophil attitude of Sir Arthur Nicolson, British Ambassador to Russia, who was soon to become permanent Under-Secretary in the British Foreign Office and to exert a strong pro-Russian influence on Sir Edward Grey; *cf.* Grey, I, 182, 304 ff.; and G. P., XXVI, 732, note; 738 ff., 866.

[73] "We have to deal with an action which permits of no contradiction, which has been agreed upon between Vienna and Berlin," telegraphed Izvolski to the Russian ambassadors in London and Paris on Mar. 23, 1909, in reporting the last stage of the crisis; Siebert-Schreiner, p. 260.

to humiliate Russia and drive a wedge into the Triple Entente by forcing Russia to abandon the Entente with England in favor of some new agreement between the three Eastern Emperors. It was set down as a new evidence of the brutality of Germany's diplomatic methods. Unfortunately for Germany, confirmation seemed to be given to this feeling by Emperor William's vainglorious and tactless speech, when on a visit to Vienna in 1910, he proclaimed to the world that he had stood by his ally "in shining armor."

The effect of the whole episode on the third partner in the Triple Alliance was thoroughly unfortunate for the Central Powers. Italy had not been fully consulted beforehand by her ally, nor had she been able to take any important part in the solution of the crisis. Italian pride had been offended, and Italian ambitions seemed threatened by Austria's further grip upon the Balkan Peninsula. The latent emotional hatred of Austria in Italian hearts was rekindled by a feeling of military and naval inferiority at the sight of Austrian troops dominating the frontiers, the fortifications of Pola, and the contemplated construction of Austrian Dreadnoughts. The tradition of Venetian domination in the Adriatic seemed threatened by Aehrenthal's more aggressive policies. Hitherto Italian hopes had been protected by the *status quo* principle of *quieta non movere,* but Austria's action looked like an alarming departure from it. To these fears were added the perennial irredentist friction, the fact that Austria was the only Power which had not answered the invitation for the International Exposition planned for 1911, and the bitter memories revived by the semi-centennial celebrations of the Wars of 1859. This bitter feeling found vent in a passionate and loudly applauded oration by ex-Premier Fortis: "There is only one Power with whom Italy sees a possibility of conflict, and that, I regret to say, is our ally. The Government must invite the nation to new sacrifices to adjust our military forces to the needs of the situation." Italy's doubts of the value of the Triple Alliance to herself were increased. She was quite ready a few months later to sign with Russia the secret agreement of Racconigi. This aimed at Russo-Italian diplomatic coöperation against Austria in the Near East, and marked another mile-stone in Italy's shift from the Triple Alliance to the Triple Entente.[74]

It was in Russia, however, that the Bosnian Crisis had the most serious effects. The Pan-Slav Press was excited to a long and violent campaign against Germany, the burden whereof was that a war between Slavdom and Teutondom was "inevitable," and that Russia must consequently hasten to make preparations for it. And, in fact, it was shortly after this that Russia undertook the sweeping reorganization and increase of her army and navy which was still in progress in 1914. To Izvolski, personally, this diplomatic defeat, which he had to some extent brought upon himself, was the most bitter experience of his life. It affected his behavior all the rest of his days, filling him with a desire for revenge and for the recovery of lost personal prestige. The bitterness which he felt is hardly conveyed in the formal despatch in which he announced to his Ambassadors in Paris and London that he had been forced to accept the German solution of the crisis. The storm of criticism to which he was subjected by the Pan-Slav elements in Russia was one of the reasons which forced him to give up his position of Minister of Foreign Affairs in September, 1910, and take in exchange the Russian Ambassadorship in Paris.[75] There he was henceforth in a position to devote his untiring energy and wily intrigues to knitting together more closely Russia's bonds with France and England. He now realized that only by their support and by increased arma-

[74] G.P., XXVI, 793 ff., 819 ff.; XXVII, 397-431.

[75] G.P., XXVI, 777-793, 796-817, 823-828, 834-840, 853-858, 971; see also *supra*, notes 31, 61, 66.

ments could he avert another such diplomatic defeat, or, if need be, risk a decision by war. His efforts to accomplish these aims can be traced in detail in recently published documents,[76] as has been briefly indicated in the preceding chapter.

The prevailing feeling among Russian diplomats, after the Annexation Crisis, was characteristically expressed by the Russian Ambassador in Paris:

> Foreseeing the further development of the European situation, many newspapers come to the conclusion that precisely as Germany and Austria have now achieved a brilliant victory, so must the two Western Powers, together with Russia, now pay their attention to the systematic development of their forces in order to be able, once they are in a position not to fear a challenge of the Triple Alliance—and in this case Italy would separate herself from the Triple Alliance—to set up on their part demands which would restore the political balance which has now been displaced in favor of Germany and Austria. . . . All these circumstances show how necessary it is for us to bind ourselves still more closely to France and England in order to oppose in common the further penetration of Germany and Austria in the Balkans.
>
> Such an opposition need not, under all circumstances, lead to an armed conflict with the Triple Alliance. Just as Austria, supported by Germany, concentrated her fighting forces and threatened Serbia without listening to the just demands of Europe, so might we, too, in agreement with France and England, after our military strength will have been re-established, force Austria-Hungary in a favorable moment to give up her Balkan plans and to restore to the now subjugated Serbians their freedom of action. The experience of the last crisis has proved that if military meas-

[76] G.P., XXVII-XXXVII; Siebert-Schreiner; M.F.R.; L.N.; Stieve; and in the works of Barnes, Bogitchevitch, Brandenburg, Churchill, Ewart, Fabre-Luce, Gooch, Grey, Judet, Montgelas, Poincaré, Schmitt, Stieve, and Valentin.

> ures are already prepared in times of peace, diplomatic questions may all the easier be solved by threats and the exercise of strong pressure. The art of diplomacy consists in selecting the favorable moment, and in utilizing a favorable general situation, so that, conscious of one's own strength, one may hold out to the end. Thus we shall undoubtedly be able to weaken the unfavorable impression which the failure of our policy has now produced and in this way we will gradually succeed in liberating the kindred Balkan States from the Austro-German influence.[77]

To the Serbians Izvolski continued to give secret encouragement, urging them to prepare for a happier future in which they could count upon Russian support to achieve their Jugo-Slav ambitions. He never really accepted the annexation of Bosnia and Herzegovina as a final settlement, but regarded it, and encouraged the Serbians to regard it, as a Serbian Alsace-Lorraine. For the liberation of these provinces all Serbs, both in Serbia and Austria-Hungary, should continue to make secret preparations. This was the policy which inspired his secret negotiations with Italy and Bulgaria in October and December, 1909, and which ultimately led to the formation of the Balkan League of 1912. All of these contemplated the possibility of changes in the Balkans which might ultimately lead to that triumph of Slavdom over Germandom which the Tsar and his Ministers had assured the Serbians was "inevitable." [78] These encouraging assurances from Russia for the future realization of the "Greater Serbia" ambitions partly explain Serbia's failure to keep the promises made to Austria at the close of the Bosnian Crisis. That Serbia from the very outset had no serious intention of living up to her new promises, but intended merely to shift the basis and

[77] Nelidov to Izvolski, Mar. 19/Apr. 1, 1909; Siebert-Schreiner, 266-268. Nelidov, of course, depended on his dispatches from Izvolski for his version of the Bosnian Crisis.

[78] See above, at notes 49-51.

method of her secret underground campaign against Austria, is seen from the following illuminating document, drawn up only a few days after the promises of March 31 were solemnly made:

Instructions of the Royal Serbian Government of April 17, 1909, to the Serbian Minister in Vienna concerning the continuation of the Great Serbia propaganda in Austria-Hungary.

The Royal Serbian Government, whose foreign policy embraces the interests of all Serbdom, trusting in the support of England, France and Russia, is firmly determined to await the moment when Serbia can with the best prospects of success proceed to the realization of her legitimate interests in the Balkans and in the whole Slavic South. Till then the Royal Government wishes to maintain with Vienna merely purely routine and scrupulously correct relations, without any political agreement of any kind. For this reason the Government will undertake no step to promote a renewal of the commercial treaty with the Monarchy; for this reason also, it must establish its national activity in the territory of the Hapsburg Crown Lands on new bases.

[The Instructions then warn the officials of the Serbian Legation and consulates in Austria-Hungary that, henceforth, in contrast to the past, they must refrain from all active and personal participation in national Serbian propaganda, and must wipe out all traces of such activities of the Serbian Ministry of Foreign Affairs, so that all correspondence which had been carried on hitherto with political agents in Austria-Hungary should definitely cease. After April 28th, the Serbian Legation and consulates in Austria-Hungary were no longer to be furnished with funds for these purposes, except 250,000 dinars in connection with the Agram treason trial, and 4,000 dinars for "influencing" the Austro-Hungarian Press. Funds for obtaining military information will no longer be needed by the Serbian Legation in Vienna, because henceforth the necessary sums for this will be placed at the disposal of the Serbian Ministry of War and its agents. The Instructions then go on to explain the secret new basis on which the "Greater Serbia" propaganda is henceforth to be carried on.]

In order that the foreign policy of the Royal Government, which embraces the whole of Serbdom, may remain intact, in spite of the above mentioned renunciation of all direct activity in Austria-Hungary, the Royal Government has placed its national propaganda in the Slavic South under the Pan-Slav national propaganda; its organization will receive its definite form in fraternal Russia July 1 of this year. Through a backing of this kind, the support of the all-powerful Government of the Russian Empire will be assured for our aspirations in decisive questions. This organization will be provided with considerable means. A new focus [of agitation] is being projected in the fraternal Czech Kingdom, around which can rally all those who wish to seek, or must seek, the salvation of their national individuality in the triumph of the Pan-Slav idea.

So far as a revolutionary propaganda appears necessary it is to be cared for henceforth from St. Petersburg and from golden Prague. We shall also promote this activity through connections which in the future it will also be the business of the General Staff to maintain.[79]

That Serbia counted confidently on Russian assistance in seizing Bosnia and Herzegovina by force in the future is further indicated by a secret circular emanating from the executive committee of a Pan-Slav Conference in St. Petersburg a few weeks later. It is addressed to the Slav organizations in the Balkans and in summary is as follows: Russia is on the point of reorganizing her army and reforming her internal administration. Until this double work of consolidation is completed, the Slav peoples must have patience and continue to trust in Russia. The Serb delegates at the Slav Conference in St. Petersburg and Moscow have been able

[79] Quoted by Conrad, I, 181 For a summary of this or a similar document, see G.P., XXVI, 776 f.

to convince themselves on the spot that all classes of Russian society are inspired with the desire to have Russia able to take up energetically her mission as the Protectress of the Slav world. Serbia and Montenegro must hold themselves ready to complete their union by the occupation of Novi Bazar and to invade Bosnia and Herzegovina. Bulgaria must be ready to seize the territories promised to her in the Treaty of St. Stefano and extend herself to the gates of Constantinople. The Young Turk régime cannot last much longer and the liquidation of Turkey is much nearer than one might suppose. This will be the moment for Russia, in union with the other Slav peoples, to realize Slav ideals and prevent Austria and Germany from exploiting Turkey to their own advantage. Meanwhile all Slav peoples must unite in solidarity and work especially to increase their economic strength. They must shut out German commerce and industry from their territories by a radical boycott. As for the money needed by the Slavs of the Balkans for their military preparations, Russia will furnish this directly or procure it with the help of France and England. Certainly within two or three years at the most, the time will come when the Slav World under Russian leadership must strike the great blow.[80]

80 Brockdorff-Rantzau, German Chargé d'Affaires in Vienna to Bethmann, July 25, 1909; G.P., XXVI, 844 f. For Russian efforts to provide financial aid, both directly and by means of loans from France, to provide the Balkan states with munitions of war, see L.N., I, 283 ff.; II, 155 ff., 233 f., 242 f., 262 f.; Stieve, Nos. 280, 283, 317, 346, 1070, 1082, 1101, 1169, 1201, 1205, 1217-8, 1223-4, 1233-5, 1245-1250, 1322, 1328, 1330, 1335, 1346, 1348, 1356, 1363, 1365, 1374; Siebert-Schreiner pp. 312, 339 ff., 451 ff.; Poincaré, II, 35, 49 ff.

French investments, including both Government loans and private banking investments, in the Balkan states (not including Turkey) rose from 920 million francs in 1902 to 3,130 million in 1914, an increase of 242%; her investments in Russia rose from 6,900 million in 1902 to 11,300 in 1914, an increase of 63%; while French total foreign investments, even including her own colonies, rose from 20,860 million in 1902 to 38,230 in 1914, an increase of only 83%; figures for 1902 from *Bulletin de Statistique et de Législation Comparée,* Oct. 1902; figures for 1914 from H. G. Moulton *The French Debt Problem* (N. Y., 1925), p. 20. As French

It was this encouragement to Serbia, secretly on the part of the Russian Government and more or less openly by the Pan-Slav Press, which helped to stimulate the violent nationalist agitation among the Serbs both in Serbia and Bosnia and also among the Croats. It helped further to unsettle the unbalanced minds of pro-Serb youths who carried out a series of attempts to assassinate Austrian officials which finally culminated in the tragic assassination of the Austrian Archduke at Sarajevo and thus led directly to the World War. Austrian Ministers were more or less aware of this encouragement and suspected that Russia rather than Serbia was the root of the Austro-Serbian antagonism.

From the formal and external point of view, however, Austro-Serbian relations appeared to be improved after Serbia's declaration of March 31, 1909, that she would henceforth live on proper friendly terms with the Dual Monarchy. Austrian and Serbian troops were demobilized on both sides of the frontier. Serbian propagandist agitation against the Dual Monarchy ceased to be open and public, but it did not become less dangerous because it was secretly taken over by Serbian military officers and driven underground. The Austro-Serbian antagonism remained almost as keen as before on both sides of the frontier. While the "Narodna Odbrana," and later the "Black Hand," carried on the secret subversive work of Serbian agitation, the Austrian authorities on their part did their full share in keeping the wound open, and in stirring Serb hatred by wholesale arrests of suspected agitators in Austria-Hungary. The further story of this antagonism and of the Archduke's assassination will be taken up later.

foreign loans were very closely connected with French foreign policy, these figures give some indication of the rapid increase of French political interest in the Balkans; they help explain the fact that M. Poincaré was often more pro-Serbian than M. Sazonov himself, and very determined in 1914 to see that Serbia received Entente support against Austria.

The three years from 1909 to 1912—from the end of the Annexation Crisis to the completion of the Balkan League—were free from acute conflicts over Balkan problems (except for the effects of Italy's Tripolitan War against Turkey). During these years Austria was busy consolidating her position in the newly annexed provinces. She had renounced her project for an extension of her railway system from Bosnia down the Vardar Valley to Salonica, and had withdrawn her military garrisons from the Sanjak of Novi Bazar, as a concession to Serbian and Montenegrin (and Russo-Italian) desires.

In Germany, Bülow resigned as Chancellor in July, 1909, for reasons which have already been indicated above, and was succeeded by Bethmann-Hollweg, an old personal friend of William II's university days at Bonn.

The new Chancellor lacked diplomatic experience and was devoid of the highest qualities of statesmanship. He possessed none of the happy literary facility and cleverness of speech, by which Bülow had been able to gloss over the mistakes of his neglected opportunities and to represent Germany's situation in a more rosy light than was warranted by the facts.[81] But Bethmann possessed much native shrewdness, a high sense of honor and honesty, and a sincere desire to preserve the peace of Europe. During the Tsar's visit to Potsdam in November, 1910, he assured Sazonov, the new Russian Minister of Foreign Affairs, that if Austria should pursue expansionist plans, which he believed would not be the case, Germany was neither "bound

81 This literary facility and optimism, which characterized Bülow's Reichstag speeches, is also reflected in his *Deutsche Politik* (1913, revised ed., 1916), intended as a defense of his administration. The best and severest indictment of it is by J. Haller, *Die Aera Bülow* (Berlin, 1922). Bethmann's more simple honesty and lack of *finesse* is seen in his *Betrachtungen zum Weltkriege* (2 vols., Berlin, 1919-1921). Severe criticisms of his policy are to be found in the writings of Tirpitz and in H. von Liebig. *Die Politik von Bethmann Hollwegs* (3rd ed.. Munich, 1919).

nor inclined to support her." Sazonov on his side declared that he desired the maintenance of Turkey, and sought to give the impression that Russia's interests were again being directed toward Asia and the Far East. On this understanding, mutually advantageous arrangements were then agreed upon in regard to Persia and the Bagdad Railway. Bethmann's reserved attitude toward Austria, which was in accord with the originally defensive character of the Austro-German treaty of 1879 and Bismarckian traditions, coincided with the views of the German Ambassador at Vienna, who, a year after the Annexation Crisis, wrote:

> Germany is not a Balkan Power. During the past year, for reasons of higher policy, we threw the weight of our political influence into the scales in favor of Austria. In my opinion we should do well to prevent, as far as possible, a repetition of this procedure. For the future, we ought to preserve a free hand for ourselves, and allow ourselves to be drawn as little as possible into Balkan questions, so that we shall be able at the psychological moment to choose our policy freely or to use it as profitably as possible.[82]

Henceforth, until July, 1914, Germany, while still assuring Austria of her readiness to fulfil her obligations as an ally, repeatedly exercised a restraining influence on Austria, especially during the Balkan Wars, in the interests of the peace of Europe. This was so much the case that Vienna officials, notably the Austrian Chief of Staff, often felt exasperated at the lack of support from Berlin in Balkan affairs. In spite of the generally good understanding between the heads of the German and Austrian army staffs, Moltke and Conrad, there was more friction between the two allies than has generally been supposed. Occasionally, Bethmann felt it necessary to renew promises to support policies which Austria deemed essential for her vital

[82] Tschirschky to Zimmermann, May 1, 1910; G.P., XXVII, 537.

interests in the Balkans, because he would otherwise have caused such dissatisfaction at the Ballplatz as to have seriously weakened the alliance which still remained the corner-stone of German foreign policy. But much more often his instructions to the German Ambassador in Vienna were in the direction of holding back Austria from taking action against Serbia, from antagonizing Russia, and from other reckless measures. Sometimes Austria heeded the advice, and sometimes she did not. But to represent Germany as exercising a complete control over her ally, as so many writers have done, is altogether incorrect. It was not until after the World War began and Austria exhibited such military weakness and failure that Germany gradually assumed that complete control over her ally's destiny which popular opinion ordinarily attributes to her.[83]

THE RACCONIGI BARGAIN OF OCTOBER, 1909

While Germany was thus working, on the whole, to restrain Austria and lessen the tension in the Balkans, Russia was actively preparing for the "inevitable" conflict between Slavdom and Germandom, which would bring about the final realization of Russia's historic mission in regard to Constantinople and the Straits, and incidentally the realization of Serbia's ambition for a "Greater Serbia" at Austria's expense. With this in view, Izvolski arranged that the Tsar should visit Victor Emmanuel at the castle of Racconigi, south of Turin, in October, 1909. He indi-

[83] On Austro-German relations, 1909-1914, see G.P., XXVII-XXXVII, *passim;* Pribram, pp. 268-298; Brandenburg, pp. 315 ff., 337 ff., 362 ff. For some examples of Germany's restraint upon Austria or non-support of her policies, see for instance, Conrad's comments in regard to Serbia (III, 77, 78, 164-9, 258, 404, 595-8), Albania (III, 63-64, 77, 108, 136, 268-9, 323, 586), Rumania (429-432, 671), Montenegro (III, 166-7, 318-9), Turkey (III, 27, 644-5), the preservation of peace (78-81, 102, 239), and in general (III, 407, 410, 417, 421, 429, 627-8, 632, 729). For the interesting but opposing views of Jagow and Lichnowsky in July, 1914, in regard to the Austro-German alliance, see K.D., 62, 72.

cated his resentment over the Annexation by ostentatiously making a wide detour to avoid stepping on Austrian soil, and the fact was widely commented upon in the Press everywhere.[84] The important secret Russo-Italian agreement signed here by Izvolski and Tittoni begins with the usual pious wish for the preservation of the *status quo* in the Balkans, but goes on to state that, if this should prove impossible, as both Powers expected, they would agree to support the principle of nationality in the development of the Balkan states. The important clauses were the 4th and 5th:

> 4. If Russia and Italy wish to make agreements concerning the European East with a Third Power, beyond those which exist at present, each will do it only with the participation of the other.
>
> 5. Italy and Russia engage themselves to regard with benevolence, the one Russia's interests in the question of the Straits, the other Italian interests in Tripoli and Cyrenaica.[85]

These clauses ran so counter to Izvolski's and Tittoni's solemn public and private assurances that they were kept even more closely secret than was the case with most secret treaties. Izvolski does not appear to have informed the Russian Ambassadors in Paris and London of their exact nature at once.[86] He did not even tell M. Poincaré until after the outbreak of the Balkan War three years later, and even then he merely read the text aloud on the promise that the French Premier would not reveal it to the Cabinet

[84] *Cf.* G.P., XXVII, 403 ff., 425; Siebert-Schreiner, pp. 148, 152. For the earlier negotiations between Izvolski and Tittoni, see above at note 34.

[85] M.F.R., p. 298; L.N., I, 358; Stieve, II, 363; KSF., IV, 415-417 (June, 1926).

[86] Siebert-Schreiner, pp. 146-177, contains many telegrams concerning the Racconigi meeting, but they do not reveal the essential character of the agreement until Italy seized Tripoli in 1911; then the London Ambassador was told of the 5th clause (p. 158), and Izvolski reminded Tittoni "not to forget Italy's obligations in regard to our claims to the Turkish Straits" (p. 161).

or even his closest collaborators. M. Poincaré nevertheless at once informed his colleagues of its contents, though he "did not read them the text of the agreement, because it had not been handed to him." [87]

M. Tittoni similarly was careful that no inkling of it should reach Germany or Austria though they were Italy's allies. With characteristic duplicity, at the same time he was promising to make no agreements concerning the Balkans without Russia's participation, Tittoni was actually negotiating an agreement with Austria on the very subject. He had begun the negotiations in the preceding June, by proposing to Austria "an agreement that neither of the two states without the knowledge of the other should make an agreement concerning the Balkans with a third state." [88] A week before the Racconigi meeting Tittoni wished to add more definitely that Italy and Austria should "agree not to conclude agreements with Russia without the participation of one another." [89] Then he signed the Racconigi agreements. A few days later, nevertheless, Italy signed an agreement with Austria, behind Russia's back and in total disregard of the Racconigi promise, embodying essentially the proposals which Tittoni had been negotiating since June.[90] To such deceit toward both Russia and Austria did Italian ambitions for Balkan and African territory lead M. Tittoni and the Italian Government! Racconigi betrays the same morality on Italy's part as in the agreements with France in 1902.

Notwithstanding the extreme secrecy in which Izvolski and Tittoni wrapped their arrangement, rumors and suspicions of what they had done were widespread. By Italy and the Entente Powers, the meeting of Nicholas II and Victor Emmanuel was hailed with enthusiasm. The British

[87] Poincaré, II, 365. [88] G.P., XXVII, 319. [89] G.P., XXVII, 334.

[90] Austro-Italian Agreement of Nov. 30, 1909, defining "Art. VII" of the Triple Alliance Treaty; Pribram, 99 f., G.P., XXVII, 336.

Under-Secretary, Sir Charles Hardinge, expressed to the Russian Chargé d'Affaires his "intense satisfaction," saying it "was most opportune and of great importance not only to Russia, England and France, but even more so to Italy. . . . He [Hardinge] shares the opinion of a part of the European Press regarding the strange position which Italy has assumed in respect to the grouping of the Powers. Chiefly in the event of complications in the Near East, Italy would either have to be untrue to her ally or act counter to her own national interests. These words confirm the deep impression made on Government circles here [in London] by the meeting at Racconigi; they seem to incline to the belief that Italy in the future will stand closer to the Entente than to the Triple Alliance." [91] Germany, Austria and Turkey were correspondingly alarmed, but they were given the solemn but lying assurance that nothing had been agreed except the laudable desire of Italy and Russia to preserve the *status quo* in the Balkans and to allow the Balkan states their normal and peaceful development.[92]

The Racconigi Agreement, which contemplated the possible partition of Turkey and the satisfying of Russia's ambitions in regard to the Straits, also served admirably another of Izvolski's purposes—that of tending to draw Italy away from the side of the Triple Alliance to that of the Triple Entente, or at least of neutralizing Italy as a "deadweight" in the Triple Alliance.[93] It played henceforth an important part in Izvolski's Balkan policy no less than in Tittoni's African ambitions. It was further consolidated by the very intimate relations between the two when they were later Ambassadors in Paris together in close touch with M. Poincaré.[94]

[91] Siebert-Schreiner, p. 148 f.

[92] Siebert-Schreiner, pp. 149-152. G.P., XXVII, 409-431, *passim*.

[93] G.P., XXVII, 411, 421.

[94] *Cf.* M.F.R., L.N., and Stieve, *passim*; Judet, *Georges Louis*, p. 150 ff., 173; Poincaré, I, 32 ff., 336 ff.; II, 363 ff.

Along with his Racconigi policy, Izvolski undertook to consolidate the Balkan States into a solid block under Russian guidance and protection. Hitherto the greatest obstacle to harmonious action by the mutually jealous Balkan Powers had been the fact that Serbia, Bulgaria, and Greece all made claims to the greater part of Macedonia, which was still in constant ferment under Turkish misrule. This obstacle could be overcome if Serbia abandoned some of her claim to Macedonia in favor of Bulgaria, and was promised compensation out of territories belonging to the Hapsburg Monarchy, when this should finally be disrupted, either by the death of the aged Emperor Francis Joseph,[95] or by the disintegrating influence of the restless nationalities under Hapsburg rule. Accordingly, in the summer and fall of 1909 Izvolski endeavored to bring about a *rapprochement* between Serbia and Bulgaria in the common interests of Slavdom, but Balkan jealousies and suspicions were too strong to permit success to these first efforts, and the negotiations came to a standstill.[96]

At Constantinople an active newly-arrived Russian Ambassador, Charykov, appeared to be working for an entente or league between Turkey and the Balkan States, which might greatly increase Russia's influence in the Balkans and form a barrier to "the advance of Germanism."[97] But Charykov had little chance of success with the Turks, who were suspicious of Bulgaria, Serbia, and Greece, all of whom coveted Turkish territory. With Bulgaria, however, Russia opened negotiations for a secret military convention, extending the scope of the secret treaty of 1902 by which Russia undertook to protect Bulgaria against attack by

95 As contemplated by Delcassé in his letter of 1899, urging the indefinite prolongation of the Franco-Russian Alliance; *Livre Jaune, L'Alliance Franco-Russe,* p. 131.

96 *Cf.* Siebert-Schreiner, pp. 273-281; G.P., XXVII, 157-174; and the telegrams of the Serbian Minister, Milovanovitch, in *Deutschland Schuldig?* (Berlin, 1919), pp. 115-119.

97 G.P., XXVII, 159 ff., 170 ff.

Rumania. Izvolski's new proposal to King Ferdinand provided for mutual aid in certain contingencies in case of wars against Turkey and Austria, and promised the utmost possible Russian support to secure for Bulgaria the great gains in territory once contemplated in the Treaty of San Stefano of 1878. Article V of the proposed military convention declared,

> The realization of the high ideals of the Slav peoples upon the Balkan Peninsula, so near to Russia's heart, is possible only after a favorable outcome of Russia's struggle with Germany and Austria-Hungary.[98]

The negotiations did not ultimately result in the signing of the proposed military convention,[99] but they are indicative of Russian efforts, successful later, for forming a Balkan bloc which it was hoped would help the Triple Entente to triumph over the Triple Alliance.

Russia's Racconigi Agreement with Italy and negotiations with Bulgaria and Serbia did not mean, however, that she intended any immediate warlike solution of the Balkan problem. They were merely part of that "preparation for the future," which was Russia's policy until she had finished reorganizing her army and navy, and had succeeded in winning more definite assurances from France and England for support of her Balkan ambitions. During 1910, partly through the influence of Germany, a certain ostensible *rapprochement* had been brought about between Russia and Austria which for the moment relieved the tension be-

98 Proposed Russo-Bulgarian Military Convention of Dec., 1909; Bogitchevitch, 115-121; Laloy, *Les Documents Secrets Publiés par les Bolcheviks* (Paris, 1919), pp. 52-58.

99 V. Radoslavov, "Der russisch-bulgarische Vertragsentwurf von 1909," in KSF, IV, 272 f., May, 1926. The negotiations were continued in 1910 during the visit of Ferdinand of Bulgaria to St. Petersburg (*cf.* G.P., XXVII, 176, 183, notes). They are apparently referred to by Neratov in a telegram to Sofia of Nov. 23/Dec. 6, 1911 (*Krasnyi Arkhiv,* IX, p. 11, 1925), when he speaks of "our confidential proposal to Bulgaria in 1910."

tween these two Great Powers over the Balkan Problem.[100] But this understanding was merely temporary, and intended, at any rate by Russia, merely as a stop-gap until Sukhomlinov's army reorganization had produced results and a new Black Sea Fleet been created. As the Russian Ambassador in Paris wrote to Izvolski in February, 1910:

> An agreement of this sort, concluded for a certain number of years, would leave the Balkan States at perfect liberty, both in regard to their internal development as well as to their mutual relations, which they might develop in every possible way. At the same time Russia would be placed in a position which would enable her to develop her military forces in all security and to prepare herself for those events which cannot be avoided. In the meantime the further evolution of the Ottoman Empire would be clearer—the problems would mature, and we should be able to meet the events that are to be foreseen much better equipped than otherwise.[101]

Similarly M. Nekliudov relates that in 1911, when he was received by the Tsar before taking up his post at Sofia, Nicholas II said to him, "after an intentional pause, stepping backwards and fixing me with a penetrating stare: 'Listen to me, Nekliudov; do not for one instant lose sight of the fact that we cannot go to war. I do not wish for war; as a rule I shall do all in my power to preserve for my people the benefits of peace. But at this moment, of all moments, everything which might lead to war must be avoided. It would be out of the question for us to face a war for five or six years—in fact till 1917. . . . Though if the most vital interests and the honour of Russia were at stake, we might, if it were absolutely necessary, accept a challenge in 1915; but not a moment sooner—in any circumstances or under any pretext whatsoever.' "[102]

100 *Cf.* Siebert-Schreiner, pp. 282-303; G.P., XXVII, 433-517.

101 Nelidov to Izvolski, Feb. 3, 1910; Siebert-Schreiner, p. 283.

102 Nekliudov, *Diplomatic Reminiscences*, p. 5.

As Mr. Lowes Dickinson justly observes: "Had this remark been the Kaiser's instead of the Tsar's, all our war-historians would have been citing it as a definite proof of the guilt, and the sole guilt of Germany. I do not cite it as a proof of the guilt, still less the sole guilt, of Russia. I cite it as one more illustration of the state of mind of all ministers and all princes—'The war will come. We don't want it; but we must be ready. And when it comes . . . !' "[103]

IZVOLSKI'S EFFORT TO OPEN THE STRAITS IN 1911

Izvolski had made two futile and unfortunate efforts to realize his ambition of opening the Straits to Russian warships. The first was made during the negotiations for the Anglo-Russian Convention of 1907, and the second in the Buchlau Bargain of 1908. Both had failed on account of opposition from Sir Edward Grey and lack of support from the French. But in the fall of 1911, Izvolski believed that the European situation invited a more successful effort. The French march to Fez, and the resulting Agadir Crisis, had drawn closer the ties between the Entente Powers, particularly the bonds between France and England. Germany, having roused England to the verge of war in defense of France and the Morocco Agreement, had been compelled to accept a settlement, which was on the point of being signed, by which she abandoned all claims in Morocco in exchange for portions of the French Congo. Russia had not given France any such active and effective diplomatic support as had Sir Edward Grey and Mr. Lloyd George. On the contrary, Izvolski had worked "with all his strength" to moderate France and urged her to give in to many of the German demands.[104] M. Neratov, who had charge of the

103 Dickinson, p. 303 f.

104 Izvolski to Neratov, Sept. 1/14, 1911; M.F.R., p. 114; L.N. I, 133; Stieve, I, 146. Neratov's telegram to Izvolski of 18/31 Oct. (Stieve, I,

Russian Foreign Office during Sazonov's long illness, gave repeated warnings that "Russian public opinion would hardly understand a [Franco-German] war occasioned by colonial questions." The Tsar took the same attitude. Even when M. Georges Louis, the French Ambassador in St. Petersburg, pointed out to him that North Africa was as much of a "vital interest" to France as the Caucasus to Russia, Nicholas II had replied, "Keep in view the avoidance of a conflict. You know that our preparations are not complete." [105] Yet in spite of this indifference to the very vital interests of the French, Izvolski flattered himself that he could coax from them a promise of support in the question of the Straits, as a *quid pro quo* for accepting without objections the Franco-German Morocco settlement. When he learned from Tittoni in September, 1911, that Italy, stirred by the establishment of the French protectorate in Morocco, and taking advantage of the various secret promises made to her by the different Powers, was about to seize Tripoli, he believed that the favorable moment had come to cash in his part of the Racconigi Bargain.

Russia's raising of the Straits Question in 1911 has usually been explained as the unauthorized act of M. Charykov, the Russian Ambassador at Constantinople—"The Charykov kite," Mr. Gooch calls it [106]—intended to be merely a feeler to see how the wind was blowing in regard to the question. The fact that Charykov's action was soon disavowed by the Russian Foreign Office has given color to

170) shows that he also, though more guardedly, advised France to yield to German demands.

105 Georges Louis to M. de Selves, Sept. 7, 1911; Judet, *Georges Louis*, p. 156 f.

106 *History of Modern Europe, 1878-1919*, p. 488. Mr. Gooch attributes the initiation of the affair to Sazonov, but Sazonov was absent from the Foreign Office from early July to mid-December, 1911, because of ill health, leaving the direction of affairs to Izvolski in Paris and Neratov in St. Petersburg. In September he was at Davos recovering from an operation; *cf.* M.F.R., pp. 66, 113 f.; Stieve, I, 72, 136, 147.

this view; but the truth is the whole affair originated with Izvolski, while Charykov was made the scapegoat, and recalled when it failed. This seems to be the conclusion to be drawn from the more recent material available on this interesting incident.[107]

On learning of Italy's intended action, Izvolski immediately wrote to Neratov on September 26, recalling the Racconigi secret agreement, rejoicing in the embarrassment which Italy would cause for Germany and the Triple Alliance, and urging that the moment had come "to draw the greatest possible advantages for our own interests from the approaching events." Now was the time, while Turkey was weakened by war with Italy, to force the Young Turks to settle such questions as the railways in Asia Minor, the Turco-Persian boundary, and above all the question of the Straits.

Izvolski at once saw Tittoni at Paris, "to remind him of the conditions on which we promised on our side to recognize Italy's freedom to action in Tripoli," and to beg him that "Italy, at the moment when she was proceeding to carry out her program in Tripoli, should give us assurances in return that she would not forget in the future to fulfill the parallel obligations undertaken by her in regard to our rights to the Turkish Straits." Tittoni answered affirmatively and promised Izvolski precise written assurances.[108] Having written to Neratov initiating a revival of

[107] M.F.R., pp. 114-145, 530-538; L.N., I, 134-179; II, 458-470; Stieve, I, 150-200; II, 20-27. Siebert-Schreiner, pp. 161, 319-330. G.P., XXX, 201-255. E. A. Adamov, *Konstantinopol i Prolivy,* p. 14 ff. Bogitchevitch, p. 167. E. Judet, *Georges Louis* (Paris, 1925), pp. 142-167, 245, exaggerates the divergence of views between Izvolski and Georges Louis, while Poincaré, *Au Service de la France,* I, 328-354, makes a skilful brief to beguile the unwary reader into thinking that Izvolski was perfectly satisfied with Georges Louis, and that Poincaré's own policy did not diverge from that of former French Cabinets in the matter of the Straits and the Franco-Russian Alliance.

[108] Izvolski to Neratov, Sept. 13/26, 14/27, 1911; M.F.R., p. 115; L.N., I, 134-138; Stieve, I, 150-152; Siebert-Schreiner, p. 161.

the Straits Question, Izvolski went on a vacation to his family at Tegernsee in Bavaria.

M. Neratov at once fell in with Izvolski's idea. He despatched instructions to Charykov at Constantinople to take advantage of the circumstances of the Turco-Italian War, the Franco-German Moroccan negotiations, and the very feeble character of the new Grand Vizier, to open conversations on the subject of Asia Minor railways, and, if Charykov deemed it wise, on the question of the Straits (and certain other subjects) on the following basis:

> The Imperial Government engages to give the Ottoman Government its effective support for the maintenance of the present régime of the Straits of the Bosphorus and the Dardanelles, extending it also to the territories adjacent. To facilitate the execution of the above clause the Imperial Ottoman Government engages on its side not to oppose the passage of Russian warships through the Straits, on condition that these ships do not stop in the waters of the Straits unless by agreement.[109]

Charykov was also informed that the plan was, first to secure the assent of Turkey, and to reserve the right to make explanations to the Powers concerning this modification of international treaties. Charykov therefore saw the Grand Vizier, Said Pasha, discussed with him all the subjects suggested by Neratov, and handed him a letter containing the proposal for opening the Straits and for settling other questions. He asked for a reply within a week.

Said Pasha did not at all fancy the proposal. He naturally saw that it would place Constantinople at the mercy of a Russian Fleet. The clause referring to Russian support in the Straits and "also the territories adjacent" had an ominous sound. It threatened to reduce Turkey to the posi-

[109] Neratov to Charykov, Sept. 19/Oct. 2, 1911; M.F.R., p. 530 f.; L.N., II, 458 f.

tion of a dependent vassal of the Tsar at a moment when Turkey was helplessly involved in war with Italy. The Grand Vizier therefore resorted to the usual Turkish dilatory tactics in dealing with disagreeable demands. For several weeks he evaded a definite reply, telling Charykov that he was delayed by having to consult other Ministers.[110]

M. Charykov also confided his proposal to the French Ambassador in Constantinople. M. Bompard thought it opportune, but shrewdly suggested the need of getting England's assent, and telegraphed to Paris. The French Government was much alarmed, and at once inquired in St. Petersburg about the meaning of Charykov's confidences to Bompard.[111]

Neratov and Izvolski were now faced with the very delicate task of securing the assent of the Powers to this modification of international treaties concerning the Straits. With Italy and Germany this was easy enough. Italy needed Russia's diplomatic support in putting pressure upon Turkey to cede Tripoli. Tittoni quickly gave to Izvolski a definite promise, written down at Izvolski's own dictation, and guaranteed the Italian Government's approval.[112] Germany also gave her full assent; Bethmann-Hollweg and his Secretary for Foreign Affairs, Kiderlen, shrewdly calculated that England would object anyway, and that there was, therefore, no occasion for Germany to offend Russia needlessly. For Germany to object would simply be pulling the chestnuts out of the fire for the British.[113]

Austria also, influenced by Germany, was ready to give her consent, qualifying it only with a reservation which would protect Austria from an attack by the Russian

110 M.F.R., pp. 531-535; L.N., II, 460-464; *cf.* also G.P., XXX, 203-213.

111 M.F.R., p. 118 f., 535 f.; L.N., I, 143 f., 464 f.; Stieve, I, 158 f.

112 M.F.R., pp. 118-537; L.N., I, 142; II, 468; Stieve, I, 157.

113 G.P., XXX, 206-214, 219 f., 233-240, 251-255; M.F.R., p. 537 f.; L.N., II, 468 f.

Fleet.[114] With France and England, however, the task was much more delicate.

When Izvolski returned from Tegernsee to his post, he found a "very secret" letter from Neratov, telling of Charykov's communications to Said Pasha and Bompard and of the French inquiry, and suggesting to Izvolski that now was the time to nail down the French Government to giving its written promise of assent. He even suggested the very words in which it should be given:

> France engages to consider with benevolence the Russian interests in the question of the Straits of the Bosphorus and the Dardanelles, and not to oppose the realization of the projects which Russia might have in view relative to the Straits and the territories adjacent.[115]

Accordingly, on October 11, M. Izvolski made a long and persuasive plea to M. de Selves, the French Minister of Foreign Affairs,

> not to refuse to formulate in some fashion the French Government's attitude toward the means which we shall sooner or later consider it necessary to take in regard to the Straits and the territories adjacent. . . . In view of M. de Selves' very feeble knowledge in questions of foreign policy, I limited myself to the above mentioned general discussion. I intend to return to the theme a little later and then state our concrete desires.[116]

114 G.P., XXX, 207-211, 232 ff.; M.F.R., p. 538; L.N., II, 469 f.

115 Neratov to Izvolski, 22 Sept./5 Oct. 1911; M.F.R., pp. 114, 535; L.N., I, 140; II, 464 f.; Stieve, I, 155. A little later, impatient at French and English hesitation, he became more urgent: "It is desirable to make use of the present political situation in order to induce the French and British Governments to express their views on the question of the Straits, in so far as Russia is concerned, in a concrete form and in writing, independently of any agreements which we shall eventually conclude with Turkey;" Neratov to Benckendorff in London, Oct. 20/Nov. 2, 1911; Siebert-Schreiner, p. 326. On 14/27 Oct. he wrote in the same strain to Izvolski in Paris; M.F.R., p. 125; L.N., I, 153; Stieve, I, 169 f.

116 Izvolski to Neratov, Sept. 28/Oct. 11, 1911; M.F.R., p. 119 ff.; L.N., I, 144 ff.; Stieve, I, 160 ff.

Next day M. Izvolski again complained of M. de Selves' ignorance. "The misfortune is that M. de Selves is very little informed on all these questions, and at the same time is wholly absorbed with the Morocco and Congo question." He also added a word on the desirability of bribing French newspapers:

> It is very important to take care that we have here "a good Press." In this matter, however, I lack unfortunately the chief weapon, because my requests to be provided with special funds for the Press have resulted in nothing. I shall naturally do all I can; but this [Straits question] is precisely one of those questions in which public opinion, as a result of old traditions, is rather predisposed against us. An example of how advantageous it can be to hand out money for the Press here is shown in the Tripoli Affair. I know that Tittoni has worked the principal French papers in a very thorough fashion and with a very generous hand. The results are evident.[117]

Though M. Justin de Selves was in fact probably not well informed on the Balkan Problem, his "encyclopaedic ignorance" has been exaggerated. He was cautious, sincere, and honest, and did not want to be precipitated into a rash promise which might encourage France's ally to risky Balkan adventures or which might displease the friend of France across the English Channel. He therefore quickly got into touch with Downing Street. He learned from Paul Cambon that news had reached London, by way of Italy, that Charykov had made an official request at Constantinople, and that England took the same stand as in 1908: England was ready to see the Straits opened, provided they were opened to the warships of all nations alike, but not if

[117] Izvolski to Neratov, Sept. 29/Oct. 12, 1911; M.F.R., p. 121; L.N., I, 148 f.; Stieve, I, 163. For interesting but exaggerated accounts of the bribery of the French Press see *Hinter den Kulissen des französischen Journalismus; Von einem Pariser Chefredakteur* (Berlin, 1925), and Poincaré, III. 97-114

they were opened only to Russia, thus converting the Black Sea into a potential Russian naval fortress.[118] Sir Arthur Nicolson "doubted whether the moment was well chosen." Sir Edward Grey would go no further than to confirm his declarations of 1908. The Russian Ambassador in London, though he "had convinced himself how highly Sir Edward values the Entente and how firmly determined he is to preserve it and avoid anything which might endanger its existence," soon had to confess sadly that "it is always difficult to induce the British Government to assume engagements on principle for future eventualities."[119] Further interviews merely made it clearer that it was impossible to persuade Sir Edward Grey to alter his attitude.

On November 4, Izvolski finally sought "to nail France down" to a written promise, while de Selves was in a pleasant mood of relief at the conclusion of long negotiations with Germany, and before the inexperienced Minister should have time to get advice from England or elsewhere about the problem of the Straits:

> In view of the signing of the Franco-German Agreement, it seemed to me indispensable, immediately and without waiting for our official acceptance of it, to nail down[120] the results of my conversations with de Selves concerning the Straits and North China. I therefore wrote M. de Selves a letter on November 4, in which I expressed, approximately in the form you proposed to me in your last letters to me,[121] our confidence in the assent of France to our wishes in these questions. . . . I hope to receive from de Selves an unconditional confirmation of the contents of this letter, the text of which I shall send you by Thursday's courier.

118 P. Cambon to de Selves [early in Oct.]; L.N., I, 149 f.; Stieve, I, 164 f.

119 Benckendorff to Neratov, Oct. 10/23, and Oct. 26/Nov. 8 1911; Siebert-Schreiner, pp. 321, 327.

120 Russian *zakriepit* "to nail down," "clinch," or "rivet."

121 See above, note 115.

> I have preferred quick procedure rather than more formal negotiations chiefly in order not to give de Selves a chance to discuss our demands with England or perhaps with the other Powers.[122]

In his letter to M. de Selves, Izvolski complimented him on the Morocco settlement "to which Russia would give her full and complete agreement," and coaxingly "expressed his firm hope that at the moment at which France, the friend and ally of Russia, is proceeding to establish her position in North Africa on a new and firm foundation, the French Government, to which the Imperial Cabinet has unceasingly given its most sincere diplomatic support, is ready on its side to assure us that it recognizes our liberty of action in the Straits as well as in North China, and will not deny its assent to the measures which we might be put in a position to take for the safe-guarding of our interests and strengthening of our position there." Even to M. de Selves these honeyed words must have seemed hypocritical, since Russia's diplomatic support in the Agadir Affair had been *nil* and whatever success France had secured in the negotiations with Germany had been chiefly due to British support and to M. Caillaux's efforts. M. Izvolski was arriving after the event and claiming a reward which he had done nothing to earn,—a reward which threatened to suck France into the wake of Russia's risky Balkan course and to displease England.

M. de Selves, however, was not to be taken in so easily. His suspicions of the Russian Ambassador are indicated by the fact that he inquired at St. Petersburg whether Izvolski had written the letter on his own initiative or upon instructions from Neratov.[123] He was shrewd enough to

122 Izvolski to Neratov, Oct. 24/Nov. 6, 1911; M.F.R., p. 123; L.N., I, 154; Stieve, I, 171 f. On Nov. 9, he again pointed out the advantage of "eliminating conferences between Paris and London."

123 Neratov to Izvolski, Oct. 29/Nov. 11, 1911; M.F.R. p. 125; L.N., I, 162; Stieve, I, 177 f.

consult Sir Edward Grey again, and learned that England had no intention of approving a Russian guarantee of "the *status quo* of the Straits and the territories adjacent," which went far beyond Izvolski's proposal of 1908. Grey gave Russia "a dilatory reply." He approved the non-committal reply which de Selves proposed to make verbally to M. Izvolski as "very wise and conceived in the same spirit of courtesy and prudence as that which he [Grey] has made to the Russian Ambassador."[124] De Selves therefore avoided committing himself to Izvolski. In explaining to Neratov his failure to "nail France down," Izvolski several times laid it to M. de Selves' "unfortunate ignorance" and his preoccupation in defending the Moroccan Agreement against attacks in the Chamber of Deputies.[125] Perhaps M. de Selves was wiser than M. Izvolski supposed.

Fortunately for France, M. de Selves was able to hand over to M. Georges Louis the delicate task of framing an answer to Izvolski's letter of November 4. M. Louis had been French Ambassador to St. Petersburg, but at this moment was temporarily filling a vacancy in the French Foreign Office.

Thoroughly acquainted by experience with the question and with M. Izvolski's shifty methods, M. Louis cautiously raised objections to the looseness of the phrase concerning Russia's "liberty of action in the Straits." M. Izvolski made elaborate explanations, and was willing to change it. After long discussions M. Louis drew up a polite but non-committal formula, which formed the basis of the answer which M. de Selves finally handed to M. Izvolski on January 4, 1912:

124 Daeschner, Chargé d'Affaires in London, to de Selves, Nov. 14, 1911; Judet, p. 163. For Grey's own courteous but non-committal replies to Benckendorff, see Siebert-Schreiner, pp. 321-329.

125 Izvolski to Neratov, Nov. 8, 23, and Dec. 7.

> In a general way I am happy to confirm to Your Excellency the declarations of the French Government on the occasion of the events of 1908, relative to the satisfactions which the Russian Government may be led to seek in the question of the Straits of the Bosphorus and the Dardanelles. The French Government remains disposed to exchange views with the Russian Government, if new circumstances render necessary an examination of the question of the Straits.[126]

While Sir Edward Grey and M. de Selves, by polite but dilatory answers, were saving themselves from being nailed down in advance to definite support of an indefinite program, events had been taking place at Constantinople which also contributed to Izvolski's chagrin. After Charykov had tried in vain for weeks to secure an answer from the Grand Vizier, Said Pasha, he turned to the Turkish Minister of Foreign Affairs. On November 27, he officially presented to Hassim Bey a note embodying Russia's request for opening the Straits and settling other points. Hassim Bey was furious. He feared that Russian warships in the Bosphorus would mean Russian domination at Constantinople, the establishment of a Russian protectorate over the Turkish Empire, or even the beginning of its final dismemberment. Russia had destroyed the independence of Persia and was preparing the same fate for Turkey.

In his peril and perplexity, Hassim Bey hurried to inform his good friend the German Ambassador. "The great blow has just been struck us," were his first words to Baron Marschall. He then proceeded to tell of Charykov's demands, and to pour out all his fears and indignation against Russia, and against the Triple Entente which he suspected (quite wrongly) was standing behind Russia. Beside the danger from Russian warships before the walls of Constantinople, Charykov's proposal in regard to railways in North-

[126] M.F.R., p. 536; L.N., II, 466; Stieve, II, 22. *Cf.* also Judet, pp. 164-9, and Poincaré, I, 341-7.

ern Asia Minor meant that railways which were for the strategic defense of Turkey against Russia would be put into the hands of Russia and her ally France! Baron Marschall sympathized with him completely. He, too, saw shattered at a blow all his own efforts of twenty years in strengthening German influence in Turkey, in trying to save the Ottoman Empire from disintegration, and in building the Bagdad Railway. He foresaw that an acceptance of Russia's demands would be interpreted by the Balkan States as indubitable evidence of the great superiority of the Triple Entente over the Triple Aliance. The Balkan States would be quick to line up on the side of the former, because superior strength was the unfailing argument which determined their political allegiance. He pleaded at great length with the German Foreign Office to aid Turkey in resisting Russia. When he was told that Germany would not oppose the opening of the Straits because there was little doubt that England would oppose it, and that Germany would only be playing England's game and offending Russia needlessly, Baron Marschall sent in his resignation. Later, however, he was persuaded to withdraw it, when it soon appeared that the German Foreign Office had quite correctly surmised England's attitude.[127]

Rumors of Charykov's negotiations had meanwhile leaked out and caused no less indignation among the Young Turks and in the Turkish Press than Hassim Bey had expressed to Baron Marschall. On December 6, the *Jeni Gazette,* though it usually inclined to favor England, published a leading article to the effect that, "The Russians want to degrade the great and glorious Turkish Empire into a province standing under a Russian protectorate, but the Ottomans will never tolerate this." Hassim Bey was further encouraged to resist Charykov's demands on learning that Sir Edward Grey had told the Turkish Ambassador in

127 Marschall to Bethmann, Dec. 1 to 15, 1911; G.P., XXX, 212-245.

London that "Russia's step seems to me out of place at this moment," and that the assent of all the Signatory Powers would be necessary.[128]

As a result of the attitude of England, France and Turkey, it began to be clear that Izvolski's idea could not be realized at the moment. Accordingly, M. Sazonov, who had just come to Paris after his long rest at Davos, gave an interview to Stéphane Lauzanne:

> There is no "Dardanelles Question" such as is printed every day a little everywhere. A "question" in the diplomatic sense of the word presupposes in effect a demand formulated by a Government, as well as diplomatic steps [*démarches*] or negotiations. But Russia demands nothing, has undertaken no negotiations, nor attempted any diplomatic step.[129]

How little truth there was in Sazonov's disavowal, the reader of the preceding pages may judge for himself. On December 15, Charykov was now instructed to tell Hassim Bey that since Russia's proposals had been prematurely divulged, and not by Russia's fault, it was impossible to continue the negotiations. Sazonov sent a telegram to Russian Ambassadors abroad trying to give the impression that Charykov had exceeded his instructions in extending private conversations into official negotiations. In March, 1912, Charykov was recalled and replaced at Constantinople by M. Giers. So ended Izvolski's third effort to open the Straits.

Izvolski still entertained some forlorn hopes that he might use de Selves' answer of January 4, 1912, as a basis for securing future French assent to his favorite project. M. Poincaré [130] would have us believe that the Russian

128 Marschall to Bethmann, Dec. 6, 1911; G.P., XXX, 218.

129 Paris, *Matin*, Dec. 9, 1911; G.P., XXX, 233 ff., 245 ff. In passing through Berlin two days later Sazonov told Bethmann that the interview was authentic; G.P., XXX, 234, 239.

130 Poincaré, I, 344 ff.

Ambassador was "entirely satisfied" with the attitude of France. But he gives this impression by quoting merely three sentences out of a letter of Izvolski to Neratov; the whole tenor of the rest of the letter, however, indicates that Izvolski was really sadly disappointed, was trying to put the best face on his failure, and was merely advising Neratov to accept the French answer because there was no present prospect of getting a more satisfactory one. As a matter of fact, Izvolski was almost as bitterly disappointed over this fiasco as over that of 1908, only he could not voice aloud his dissatisfaction at France and England, who were chiefly to blame, as he had done after 1908 against Austria; France and England were fellow members of the Triple Entente, whereas Austria belonged to the rival group. He seems to have come to the conclusion after this that there were only two ways to open the Straits; either by pouncing upon them in time of peace, or as the result of a general European war. On several occasions between 1912 and 1914 Russian Ministerial Councils seriously considered the first alternative only to abandon it as impractical. So there was left only the second alternative, a general European war. To prepare for this Izvolski worked persistently and consistently during the two following years, and, when at last it suddenly burst forth, was said to have claimed exultingly: *"C'est ma guerre!"*

RUSSIA AND THE BALKAN LEAGUE

Five centuries of Turkish oppression, combined with the rising tide of nationalism in the nineteenth century, had inspired the Christian peoples of the Balkans with a passion for national unity and independence. By the year 1911, owing to the progressive decay of the Ottoman Empire, long steps had already been made toward the realization of their ardent hopes. Greece, Serbia, Bulgaria and Rumania had been constituted into independent kingdoms

But there were thousands of Greeks, Serbs, Bulgarians and Rumanians, not to mention Macedonians and Albanians, still living under the foreign rule of Turkey or Austria. They, too, longed to be liberated and united with their brothers in the independent kingdoms. The supposedly democratic revolution in Turkey, and Austria's annexation of Bosnia and Herzegovina in 1908, for a moment seemed to indicate that these two States were showing signs of rejuvenation and that the day of Slav liberation was likely to be delayed. But the impractical ideals of the Young Turks and their foolish disregard of traditional rights and prejudices only resulted in antagonizing more completely the non-Turkish elements, and in weakening still further the decaying Empire which Abdul Hamid's skill and ruthless methods had managed to preserve. The Tripolitan War gave it another staggering blow, and led directly to the formation of the Balkan League, which finally drove the Turks almost completely from Europe. This natural ambition of the Balkan States, to liberate and annex their brothers under alien rule, was the main cause of the Balkan League, but it is doubtful whether it could have been formed except for the very active part taken by MM. Hartwig and Nekliudov, the Russian Ministers at Belgrade and Sofia.

During the early months of the Tripolitan War various Russian representatives were pursuing three quite different Balkan policies—a striking example of lack of unity and discipline in the Russian diplomatic service. They all wanted to take advantage of Turkey's difficulties with Italy to strengthen Russia's position in the Balkans and in Europe, but they had altogether different ideas of how this must be done. Izvolski, with the coöperation of Neratov and Charykov, had tried to open the Straits to Russian warships, and had failed. Meanwhile Charykov, on his own initiative, had at the same time been renewing his efforts for the formation of a Balkan League of which Turkey (!) should be a member. He had offered his "good offices" to Said Pasha and Hassim Bey to bring about close relations between Constantinople, Sofia and Belgrade. Such a league might be used to preserve the *status quo* in the Balkans, and to support Russia in a war against Austria. It would reduce Turkey to a kind of vassalage to Russia, because Turkey would be dependent on Russia for protection from the Balkan States.[131] But Charykov's fantastic idea had not the slightest chance of being realized. It was at the antipodes of Russia's traditional policy, which was to push the Balkan States *against* Turkey. It was regarded with suspicion by the Turks. And it was anathema to the Slavs of the Balkans.[132] It ended with Charykov's dis-

131 M.F.R., pp. 531-535; L.N., II, 460-465; G.P., XXVII, 159 ff., 171 ff.; XXX, 205, 218.

132 Hartwig to Neratov, Oct. 23/Nov. 5, 1911, *Krasnyi Arkhiv,* 1925, VIII, 45 ff.: "The affair of the famous Balkan Federation under the supremacy of the Ottoman Empire is up again. Every time Turkey finds herself in some external troubles, this political combination comes up for consideration . . . among those few remaining European diplomatists, politicians, and publicists who are still wont to believe in Turkey's regeneration. But it is interesting to raise the question: What is the attitude of the Balkan States themselves? . . .

"The passionate sermons about the importance to the Slavs of an alliance with Turkey seem to carry very little conviction with them; under certain conditions, particularly under pressure from Russia, they might not refuse to start on this road, not, however, because they would expect any great benefits from Turkey's friendship, but exclusively for the sake of gaining a respite from the troubles chronically rising in the Balkans, to gain time, and gradually gaining strength, when the favorable moment should arise, to square up accounts with their ancient enemy. The Slavs can have no other point of view on the Federation. . . .

"In my opinion Russia should pursue two clear, quite definite, final aims: (1) to make easier for the Slav nations, called by her into an independent existence, the attainment of their sacred ideals, which means an amicable division amongst them of all Turkish possessions on the Balkan Peninsula; and (2) to accomplish her own century-old problem—the planting of a firm foot on the shores of the Bosphorus at the gates to the 'Russian Lake.' . . .

"The Serbian Government would consider it extremely dangerous to approach the Turks now with any offers of alliance such as Hofmeister Charykov urged upon the Serbian Minister to Turkey. Every favor

missal in March, 1912, just at the moment a very different kind of Balkan League was actually being signed.

While the policies of Izvolski and Charykov were doomed to failure, a third policy, ardently pursued by Hartwig and Nekliudov in Belgrade and Sofia, ripened into success. They aimed at the formation of a Balkan Slav League under Russian patronage, nominally for the preservation of the *status quo,* but capable of being directed against Turkey or Austria. Active Russian efforts to create such a league had been made from time to time ever since the Young Turk Revolution and the Austrian annexation of Bosnia in 1908.[133] But they had all failed, owing in large part to the inherent hatred and jealousy of Serbia and Bulgaria toward one another, and to the distrust with which the wily King of Bulgaria was regarded by everybody, including even his own ministers. The idea of a Slav Balkan League was galvanized into life again by the news of Italy's war on Turkey in September, 1911.

M. Geshov, the Bulgarian Premier and Minister of Foreign Affairs at the time, has given a dramatic and authentic narrative of his part [134]—how he heard the news of the Tripolitan War at Vichy, hurried home to Sofia via Paris and Vienna, having interviews with de Selves and Aehrenthal, returned to Vienna for secret conferences with King Ferdinand and with Milovanovitch of Serbia, and finally, in a three-hours' talk between stations in a railway compartment outlined a Balkan Agreement to him. It was in the course of this interview, after they had touched upon

seeking step of the Serbians in Constantinople would inevitably arouse distrust in Sofia and injure the prospects of the Serbo-Bulgarian Agreement, which by its political importance will open a new era in the history of the Slavs."

133 Siebert-Schreiner, pp. 273-281; 304-316; G.P., XXVII, 155-194; Bogitchevitch, 28 ff., 113 ff.

134 I. E. Guéchoff, *L'Alliance Balkanique,* Paris, 1915, pp. 14-63. This book contains much the same material as I. E. Guéchoff, *La Genèse de la Guerre Mondiale: la Débâcle de l'Alliance Balkanique,* Berne, 1919.

the thorny question of the future division of Macedonia that the Serbian Premier exclaimed:

> Ah! Yes! If, at the same time with the liquidation of Turkey, the disintegration of Austria could take place, the solution would be enormously simplified: Serbia would get Bosnia and Herzegovina, as Rumania would get Transylvania, and we should not have to fear the intervention of Rumania in our war with Turkey.[135]

But M. Geshov's narrative tells relatively little of the part played by Russia in the long and difficult negotiations which followed. This can now be traced in detail in the correspondence of Hartwig and Nekliudov with Neratov at St. Petersburg.[136] These two Russian Ministers at Belgrade and Sofia worked indefatigably to smooth out the mutual jealousies and suspicions of the Serbian and Bulgarian Ministers toward one another, and to help them in the almost superhuman task of reaching an agreement as to the division of spoils to be conquered from Turkey. At the same time they kept Neratov fully informed of each step forward in the negotiations. Finally, on March 13, 1912, Serbia and Bulgaria agreed on a Treaty and signed it.

By this Treaty of March 13, 1912, Serbia and Bulgaria mutually guaranteed each other's territory and independence, and agreed to support one another in case any of the Great Powers should attempt to acquire by force, even temporarily, any territory in the Balkans. This protected Serbia against any attempts of Austria to reoccupy the Sanjak of Novi Bazar or to seize the parts of Macedonia and Albania coveted by Serbia. Serbia had hoped in the early negotiations that the alliance would be primarily directed against Austria. But Bulgaria had little interest

135 Guéchoff, *L'Alliance Balkanique,* p. 27.

136 *Krasnyi Arkhiv,* VIII, 1-48; IX, 1-22 (1925). A. Nekludoff, *Diplomatic Reminiscences* (London, 1920), pp. 39 ff., 51 ff., gives only a very brief account.

in seeing Serbia acquire Bosnia and Herzegovina or other Hapsburg territory. King Ferdinand's eye was directed primarily toward Macedonia, Thrace, and even perhaps Constantinople; he therefore wished the new alliance directed against Turkey. Accordingly, a secret annex provided that if disorders broke out in Turkey and the *status quo* in the Balkans was threatened, Serbia and Bulgaria would enter into an exchange of views for joint military action. If Russia had no objections to their plan of action, the two Balkan Allies would then carry on military operations as agreed; any dispute which might arise was to be referred to the Tsar for arbitration, and his decision was to be binding. A detailed statement set forth the division of the spoils to be acquired in Macedonia from Turkey, and provided among other things that Serbia should lay no claim to territory in the direction of Salonica south of a line from Mt. Golem to Lake Ochrida.[137]

On taking charge of the Foreign Office again at the beginning of 1912, M. Sazonov found the Serbo-Bulgarian Treaty well on the way to completion. Negotiated during his absence, and containing a clause for rigid secrecy, he did not know whether he ought to inform the other members of the Triple Entente of it. Though professing to preserve the *status quo,* and giving Russia a kind of veto on making war (at least so he said), he appears to have realized that it might easily encourage the Balkan States to a war which in turn might involve Russia and her French Ally. For a moment in February, 1912, he apparently thought of engaging France in a full discussion of the new

[137] The texts of the Balkan Treaties and Military Conventions are printed by Guéchoff, *L'Alliance Balkanique,* pp. 191-234; by [George Young], *Nationalism and War in the Near East* (London, 1915), pp. 387-428; and by [S. Radev] *La Question Bulgare et les États Balkaniques* (Sofia, 1919), pp. 171 ff., including maps and documents on the later dispute over Macedonia. For a recent keen appreciation of the treaties, see Dickinson, p. 308 ff.

aspect of the Balkan problem. He drew up a *questionnaire* as a basis of discussion: what should France and Russia do in case of an internal Turkish revolution, an Austrian attack on Albania or the Sanjak, or an outbreak of war between Turkey and one of the Balkan states? He showed it to M. Georges Louis. But the French Ambassador was again exceedingly cautious and saw great dangers ahead. "These are the greatest questions," he wrote M. Poincaré, "with which Russia can face her ally." "It would be better for us to consent to discuss them in academic conversations, than to risk being drawn along in Russia's wake by the rapidity of events, without being able to discuss either her action or to set forth our conditions. . . . For M. Sazonov as for M. Izvolski, it is neither in China nor in Persia, but in the Balkans that Russia will direct at present her principal political effort." [138]

Observing M. Georges Louis' extreme reserve, and aware of Izvolski's failure to nail France down to support an opening of the Straits, Sazonov drew back, and contented himself with merely informing France and England of the existence of a Serbo-Bulgarian Treaty, but not of its details and potentially aggressive character.[139] He did not bring up again for discussion his *questionnaire,* and evaded all French efforts to draw him out as to what he had had in mind.[140]

It was not until Poincaré visited St. Petersburg in August, 1912, that he learned for the first time the full text of the Serbo-Bulgarian Treaty, and exclaimed in alarm: "*Mais c'est lá une convention de guerre!,*" exactly the expression which Nekliudov had used when forwarding the document to St. Petersburg. M. Poincaré was indignant

138 Louis to Poincaré, Feb. 15 and 21, 1912; Judet, *Georges Louis,* p. 174 f.

139 Sazonov to the Russian Ambassadors in Paris and London, Mar. 30, 1912; Siebert-Schreiner, p. 339.

140 Poincaré, II, 24-60.

that the details of a treaty, likely to lead to war in the Balkans and arranged under Russia's patronage, had been so long withheld from France by her Ally. As he noted at the time:

> I did not conceal from him [Sazonov] that I could not well explain to myself why these documents had not been communicated to France by Russia. . . . The Treaty contains the germ not only of a war against Turkey, but a war against Austria. It establishes further the hegemony of Russia over the Slav Kingdoms, because Russia is made the arbiter in all questions. I observed to M. Sazonov that this convention did not correspond in any way to the definition of it which had been given to me; that it is, strictly speaking a convention for war, and that it not only reveals mental reservations on the part of the Serbs and Bulgarians, but that it is also to be feared lest their hopes appear to be encouraged by Russia, and that the eventual partition will prove a bait to their covetousness.[141]

Nothing better characterizes the Serbo-Bulgarian Treaty than these words of the French Premier, unless it be what he himself said a week after the outbreak of the Balkan War:

> It is certain that she [Russia] knew all about [the Serbo-Bulgarian Treaty], and, far from protesting against it she saw in this diplomatic document a means of assuring her hegemony in the Balkans. She perceives today that it is too late to wipe out the movement which she has called forth, and, as I said to MM. Sazonov and Izvolski, she is trying to put on the brakes, but it is she who started the motor.[142]

[141] Note by Poincaré of his conversation with Sazonov in August, 1912; *Affaires Balkaniques,* I, 38, 111 ff. Poincaré, II, 114 ff. For Sazonov's report to the Tsar of this same conversation see M.F.R., p. 255 ff.; L.N., II, 338 ff.; see also Judet, 178-203, and Sazonov's recent account in his memoirs, *Fateful Years,* p. 52 ff.

[142] Poincaré to P. Cambon, Oct. 15, 1912; *Affaires Balkaniques,* I, 112.

THE BALKAN DANGER AND THE POWERS IN 1912

Though M. Poincaré, with his characteristic quickness and accuracy of judgment, was quite correct in his view of the dangers latent in the Serbo-Bulgarian Treaty, he and M. Sazonov took no immediate steps to consult with the Powers to avert an outbreak of war in the Balkans. He merely told M. Sazonov that public opinion in France would not allow the French Government to take up arms for Russia over a purely Balkan question—so long as Germany did not intervene. In this latter case, Russia "could certainly count on France for the accomplishment of her exact and entire obligations" as an ally. He confidentially informed Sazonov of the secret Anglo-French "verbal agreement in virtue of which England has declared herself ready to aid France with all her naval and military forces in case of a German attack." He discussed the new Franco-Russian Naval Convention, and urged Sazonov to try to make a similar convention with Sir Edward Grey for the coöperative action of the Russian and English navies. In fact, aside from his brief comment of warning on hearing the terms of the Serbo-Bulgarian Treaty and some discussion of an Austrian peace proposal, virtually all of his conversations during his stay in Russia from August 9th to 16th were devoted to strengthening the bonds of the Triple Entente and securing solidarity of action between France, Russia and England.[143]

After returning to France, though now fully aware of the impending danger of war in the Balkans, M. Poincaré made no proposals to avert it until September 22. Even then he consulted only with the two other members of the Triple Entente, being ever anxious to preserve Entente solidarity and to get concerted agreement to proposals

143 Sazonov's report to the Tsar, Aug. 17, 1912; M.F.R., 255-262; L.N., II, 338-345; *Affaires Balkaniques,* I, 34-39; Poincaré, II. 99-169.

which could then be notified to the Triple Alliance Powers for their acceptance or rejection.[144]

This tended to sharpen the division of the Great Powers into two hostile groups, whereas Germany, and also Sir Edward Grey and Sazonov, for the most part, took the broader and wiser stand of desiring to have the Powers act collectively and in concert, in order to prevent a possible conflict between the Triple Entente and Triple Alliance.

At times, to be sure, M. Poincaré asserted his solicitude for collective European action. Thus, on August 28, he told the German Chargé d'Affaires that "his policy aimed that the Triple Alliance and Triple Entente should not seek to range themselves on opposite sides, but should work for the establishment of the European Concert." [145] This sounded well. But did his acts correspond to his words? On this same August 28 he telegraphed to London, "It seems to me desirable that an Entente should take place between

[144] M. Poincaré's great insistence on what may be called "Entente Solidarity" is seen on page after page of his own memoirs, in his innumerable public speeches, and in the documents. We give a few examples taken merely from his memoirs within the eight weeks between his visit to Russia and the First Balkan War. On leaving Russia, "the last words spoken to M. Sazonov were to beg him to act with England and with us" (II, 164). The communiqué issued to the Press announced that he and Sazonov "have recognized once more the Entente of the two friendly and allied countries" (II, 164). His reply of August 22 to Berchtold's proposal for preserving peace makes the reservation, "It goes without saying that we shall arrive at an agreement in concert with Russia and England." . . . (II, 176). On Sept. 1, concerning further communications from Berchtold, "I shall examine them with England and Russia;" and he instructed the French Ambassador at Vienna: "Henceforth you can express as your personal opinion that the French Government, firmly attached to the Triple Entente, does not aim at any exclusive interests in the East, and that *the cooperation of all the Powers seems to it necessary for the solution of the Balkan Problem*" (II, 184). It is seldom that M. Poincaré ventures to put into one sentence two such essentially contradictory phrases as "firmly attached to the Triple Entente" and the words which he now italicizes in his *apologia,* but which he did not italicize in 1912. M. Poincaré then asks a rhetorical question which the reader may answer for himself: "Was it possible to take at the beginning of the crisis a more clear and a more pacific position?" (II, 184).

[145] G.P., XXXIII, 79; *cf.* Poincaré, II, 181.

France, England and Russia so that completely harmonious advice can be given at the Sublime Porte." [146] Two days later he emphasized both at London and St. Petersburg: "It remains understood that the concert of the three [Entente] Powers is necessary for every collective action." [147]

In contrast to Poincaré's policy of "Entente Solidarity," Count Berchtold proposed on August 13 that all the Great Powers enter collectively into a discussion, with a view to securing reforms from Turkey and restraining the Balkan States from disturbing the *status quo*.[148] Count Berchtold was thus the first of the European diplomatists to propose collective European action in view of the increasing tension between Turkey and the Balkan States, although he had no such definite knowledge of the explosive material hidden in the secret Balkan Treaties as had Sazonov and Poincaré. He acted without first consulting his own Ally, and, at first sight, one is inclined to praise him for taking a statesmanlike stand, in favor of preserving peace by the Concert of Europe.[149] But it appears his proposal was dictated mainly by a desire to "be important," to offset newspaper criticisms of his indolent do-nothing methods, and to seem to take the initiative in the Balkan Problem before Sazonov and Poincaré should announce something from St. Petersburg.[150] Moreover, Berchtold's proposal was so vague, both in its wording and in his own mind, that it did not commend itself

[146] *Affaires Balkaniques,* I, 45.

[147] *Affaires Balkaniques,* I, 50 f. In this case, though not always, Sir Edward Grey and M. Sazonov agreed with him in placing "Entente Solidarity" ahead of the "Concert of Europe."

[148] *Affaires Balkaniques,* I, 34 ff.; G.P., XXXIII, 47 ff.

[149] Fabre-Luce, *La Victoire,* Paris, 1924, p. 165, takes M. Poincaré severely to task for declining "the first part of these proposals" of Berchtold. Poincaré's reply (II, 160 ff.) to Fabre-Luce is not just; he talks about a different stage in the Berchtold proposals.

[150] G.P., XXXIII, 50 f., 61 f., 89 ff., 99. Kiderlen contemptuously speaks of Berchtold's *Wichtigtuerei* as "stirring up much dust," but as impractical.

to any of the Powers, and was later pushed aside when M. Poincaré took the initiative out of Count Berchtold's hands.

During mid-summer Sazonov had been very optimistic, trusting perhaps too confidently to the power of veto which he says the Balkan Treaty gave him; he thought he could restrain his protégés from a war which he probably wished at this time to avoid. But by September 17, the news of Turkish atrocities and Bulgarian war excitement became so alarming, that he suddenly became frightened. He therefore made a suggestion to all the Powers, "not as a rival but as a supplementary action" to that of Berchtold, that the Powers should advise Turkey to make immediate reforms in Macedonia.[151] As quick action seemed urgent to prevent the Bulgarians taking things into their own hands in Macedonia, Sazonov gave his advice to Turkey immediately, without waiting to hear from his Entente friends. But his proposal had no effective results for several reasons: Sir Edward Grey did not want to put pressure on the Turks; Poincaré did not wish to act except in coöperation with England; and Germany, after past experiences, had little confidence in the success of any reforms by the Turks in Macedonia.[152]

Finally, on September 22, M. Poincaré took the initiative by proposing to England and Russia a formula for restraining the Balkan Powers, which the Triple Entente should agree upon and then present to Germany and Austria for acceptance. Izvolski told him that he feared that this procedure would not receive the assent of Sazonov nor of England, "because it emphasized the division of Europe into two groups." M. Poincaré replied that it could be kept

151 M.F.R., p. 276; L.N., II, 547; Stieve, II, 253; G.P., XXXIII, 106 ff.; *Affaires Balkaniques,* I, 58.

152 Poincaré, II, 208 ff.; *Affaires Balkaniques,* I, 58 f.; G.P., XXXIII, 106 ff.

secret,[153] and, after some modifications to please England and Russia, secured an accord with them: the Entente Powers were to invite Germany and Austria to agree to join in advising the Balkan States not to disturb the peace, and warning them that, even if they broke it, they would not be allowed to make territorial gains. On September 28, M. Jules Cambon broached the subject to M. Kiderlen-Wächter at Berlin and found a cordial reception. The only remaining question seemed to be who should assume the ungrateful office of making the announcement to the Balkan States. M. Kiderlen suggested that Russia and Austria should act in the name of the Great Powers, and his suggestion was adopted. But there were further delays due to objections raised by Russia and England. On October 7, the assent of all the Great Powers was finally secured, and the next day Russia and Austria issued the agreed warning to the now highly excited Balkan States.[154] It was too late. On this very day, October 8, Montenegro declared war on Turkey and was speedily joined by the other Balkan Allies.

THE BALKAN WARS OF 1912-1913

In an outline of Balkan Problems from 1907 to 1914 it is obviously impossible to enter into all the complicated kaleidoscopic questions which now arose between the Great Powers and between the Balkan States themselves. Any adequate treatment of them would fill a book in itself. The Balkan Wars therefore must be dealt with very briefly here.

When Bulgaria, Serbia, and Greece joined Montenegro in war upon Turkey in October, 1912, they quickly astonished themselves and the world by the rapidity and com-

153 Poincaré to P. Cambon, Sept. 22, 1912; *Affaires Balkaniques,* I, 61. In his memoirs (II, 214 ff.) M. Poincaré omits to mention his own advocacy of concealment, but notes that Sazonov urged that the three Entente Powers should concert measures in secret.

154 *Affaires Balkaniques,* I, 63-104; G.P., XXXIII, 133-181; Poincaré II, 219-249.

pleteness of their victories. The Greeks occupied Salonica; the Bulgarians marched victoriously to the defensive forts outside Constantinople; and the Serbians swept over the whole upper valley of the Vardar, the Sanjak of Novi Bazar, and the northern part of Albania. This gave them at last an outlet on the Adriatic. Only the Turkish fortresses of Adrianople, Janina, and Scutari held out against the victorious allies.

The Serbians were greatly elated by these conquests which doubled their territory and seemed to foreshadow the possibility of the early realization of their "Greater Serbia" ambitions at Austria's expense. They were actively encouraged by Hartwig, the Russian Minister at Belgrade. He was said to have declared to his Rumanian colleague that Serbia could not possibly renounce her outlet on the Adriatic; Serbia must be the Slavic advance-post in the Balkans, and must annex Bosnia, Herzegovina, and the South Slav districts of Hungary; Rumania, he hinted, had better look out for her interests in the same way and annex Transylvania. When this was called to Sazonov's attention, he denied emphatically that Hartwig could have made such remarks, but a little later admitted that "Hartwig has great sympathy for the Slav cause, is of a passionate character, and perhaps lets himself be carried away occasionally by his Slavophil sympathies." [155] But there was little doubt

[155] G.P., XXXIII, 319, 388, 439. Hartwig, in his zeal for the Pan-Slav cause, very probably made the remarks attributed to him. There are indications that he often went beyond his instructions and was dangerously indiscreet. *Cf.* Nekliudov, *Diplomatic Reminiscences,* pp. 47 ff. Even Izvolski now complained of "the conviction which is enrooted here [in Paris], as in London, that Hartwig is acting at Belgrade contrary to the instructions which he receives. . . . I cannot conceal from you that Poincaré is firmly convinced that Hartwig, who has known how to acquire a great influence at Belgrade, is not making any use of it at all to make the Serbians wise and calm;" Izvolski to Sazonov, Nov. 21, 1912; L.N., I, 351-352. M. Georges Louis had no doubt that Hartwig was encouraging Serbia against Austria; on Nov. 18 he reported another remark of Hartwig's on the Balkan victories: "The affair of Turkey is settled. Now it is the turn of Austria;" Judet, 200-201.

that Russia was energetically supporting the Serbian claim to Northern Albania and ports on the Adriatic. Reports came from St. Petersburg that the Pan-Slav and militarist party of the Grand Dukes was using pressure upon the peace-loving Tsar to resort to war, if necessary, on Serbia's behalf.[156]

To Austria and Italy, as well as to the Albanians themselves, the extraordinary and unexpected victories of the Serbians were most unwelcome. Though the Albanians, numbering less than two million, were still in a relatively primitive state of civilization, and divided into hostile quarreling groups of varying religious affiliations—Roman Catholic, Greek Orthodox, and Mohammedan—they scouted the idea of coming under the rule of the Serbians. They had no mind to exchange the Turkish for a Serbian yoke.[157] Though Albania could not look back to a great historic past, like Greece under Pericles, or like Serbia and Bulgaria in the later Middle Ages, the more intelligent Albanian chieftains now desired an independent, or at least an autonomous, Albanian State. When the Serbian and Greek armies overran their territory and threatened their independence, Ismael Kemal saved the situation by hastily calling an assembly of representative chieftains from all parts of Albania. On November 28, 1912, the national flag, the black double-headed eagle of Scanderbeg on a blood-red ground, was hoisted over Valona, and Albania's independence and neutrality was proclaimed. This was done with the approval of Austria and Italy.

Both Austria and Italy urged the establishment of an Albanian State, though under different forms and for different reasons. Allies, yet rivals, both were in favor of creating Albania as a means of excluding Serbia from the Adri-

156 G.P., XXXIII, 335 f., 383 ff.

157 Conrad, II, 157 ff., III, 56 ff., 101 ff.; and M. Edith Durham, *High Albania* (1909), *The Struggle for Scutari* (1914), and *Twenty Years of Balkan Tangle* (1920).

atic, which both aspired to dominate. But both were extremely jealous and suspicious of each other. Both had sought secret support from Russia for the exclusion of the other from all influence in Albania—Austria by Goluchowski's exchange of notes with Muraview in 1897, and Italy by the secret Racconigi Agreement of October, 1909, as has been indicated above. These two jealous Powers differed, however, as to the details of the desired Albanian principality. Austria wanted a completely independent Albania, either under a native chieftain, or under some other ruler whom Austria could more or less control and influence. She hoped to find in a newly created Albania an ally against Serbia on the east and a check upon Italy on the west. Austria therefore desired that the new state be as strong as possible, and that it should include Ipek, Djakovo, Dibra, and Prizren, as well as Scutari and Janina. "An Albania without Scutari, Janina, and Prizren, would be a body without a heart and stomach." [158] An Albania of such size and strength as Austria desired would deprive Serbia of part of the fruits of her unexpected victories, and also tend to check the dangerous "Greater Serbia" movement in the future.

Italy, on the other hand, did not want too strong an Albania, where Italy had political, commercial, and military ambitions. Italy wanted to control the harbor of Valona, build a railway across the mountains to Salonica, and check the northern advance of Greek influence. In possession of Brindisi on one shore of the Adriatic, and in control of the Albanian coast on the other, Italy aspired virtually to close up the Adriatic into an Italian lake. Italy was satisfied merely to have the Serbians shut out from the coast. Rather than give Albania wide frontiers and a prince who might be under Austrian influence, Italy preferred leaving

[158] Report of an Austrian expert on Albania in January, 1913; Conrad, III, 59.

the region under nominal Turkish suzerainty, with a governor appointed by the Great Powers and assisted by a *gendarmerie* under Swedish, Spanish, Swiss, or Belgian officers. Italy foresaw, as proved to be the case, that a weak Albania under the joint direction of the Great Powers would be far more favorable to Italian interests, than a strong independent Albania under Austrian influence; because in Balkan questions, the grouping of the Great Powers tended to be 4-2 or even 5-1 against Austria—after the Racconigi Agreement Italy inclined more and more to the Entente, and Germany often sided with the Entente when she considered Austria's Balkan policy to be dangerously aggressive.

By the end of November, this Albanian question, together with all the other rivalries and suspicions which had been accentuated by the Balkan War, began seriously to threaten the peace of Europe. Russia, in spite of some wavering on Sazonov's part, inclined to back the Serbians in their actual possession of Northern Albania, and Austria and Italy were determined to support the Albanian chieftains in their opposition to Serbia. Russia began mobilizing part of her forces against Austria. Austria had already made preparations for war against Serbia, and was believed to have mobilized three army corps in Galicia against Russia. On December 7, Conrad, the head of the Austrian militarist group, was reappointed to his old position as Chief of Staff. Russia, however, drew back when the risk of war became imminent. Poincaré, who had warned Russia from a too risky support of Serbia on his visit to Russia, before the Balkan Allies had won their great victories, now encouraged Russia to take a stiff stand. He saw that the new Balkan Alliance was virtually equivalent in strength to a Great Power. With this on the side of Russia, the prospects were highly favorable for French *revanche,* if Austria should attack Russia, and thus involve France and Germany in a general war. He counted on Italy's doubtful loyalty to the Triple Alliance, and he hoped for England's armed support to the Triple Entente, in view of the exchange of notes which had just taken place between Paul Cambon and Sir Edward Grey in London.

Peace between the Great Powers, however, was preserved, thanks largely to efforts of the English and German Governments. Concessions were made on all sides. On December 16, the London Conference of Ambassadors accepted Sir Edward Grey's compromise proposal for an independent Albania whose boundaries were to be determined later.

Like most compromises, this satisfied neither of the two states most directly interested in the fate of the unhappy little country. Serbia felt very bitterly at being deprived of the fruits of her victories and her long hoped-for economic outlet on the Adriatic. Deprived by the Great Powers of territory which she had expected to get in this direction, Serbia quite naturally felt she had a right to ask Bulgaria to revise the terms of the Serbo-Bulgarian Treaty, and to give her some of Macedonia south of the line from Mt. Golem to Lake Ochrida. Bulgaria refused. This eventually led to the second Balkan War, when Bulgaria made her sudden treacherous attack upon Serbia at the end of June, 1913.

Austria also complained bitterly that nearly everything which occurred in connection with Albania in the months following the adoption of Sir Edward Grey's proposal was done in opposition to her wishes and was prejudicial to her interests. This was either because the majority of the Conference took sides against her in favor of Serbia, Russia, and Italy; or because the Serbians and Montenegrins acted in defiance of the decisions of the Powers, by placing *faits accomplis* before the Conference, which the latter was unwilling or unable to remedy. The most notorious and grotesque case of the kind was the way in which King Nicholas of Montenegro snapped his fingers in the face of the Powers and their international fleet and continued the siege of Scutari, which the Conference had assigned to Albania. On the other hand, Ipek, Djakova, Dibra, and Prizren were not included within the boundaries of the new state. This meant, according to Austria's contention, that something like half a million Albanians, forming a compact group within the watershed which constitutes the natural geographical boundary of Albania, were to be left to the mercy of Serbian and Montenegrin troops. In the south, Greece demanded that the boundary be drawn in such a way that the Greek Orthodox Albanians would be assigned to her. Conrad, the Austrian Chief of Staff, wanted to compel Greece to abandon these claims on Southern Albania, either by diplomatic action, or by a joint Austro-Italian show of force. But here Austria met with opposition from her own Ally.

Although the Albanian compromise averted the danger of an immediate war between the Great Powers, it remained a highly disturbing factor in Balkan politics until it disappeared into relative insignificance at the outbreak of the World War. It was indirectly the cause of the fratricidal Serbo-Bulgarian conflict of June, 1913, and it led to a new Austro-Serbian crisis in the following November.

When Bulgaria suddenly attacked Serbia in the quarrel over Macedonia, and started the Second Balkan War (June 30-August 10, 1913), she was speedily crushed. Rumania and Greece seized the favorable opportunity to settle their grievances against her by joining forces with Serbia. Even Turkey returned to the attack to recover the Thracian territory which she had just lost. Attacked on four sides, and already exhausted by her efforts during the First Balkan War, Bulgaria was quickly forced to beg for peace and sign the Treaty of Bucharest. This deprived her of a large part of her recent conquests from Turkey and some of her own former territory which was ceded to Rumania. It increased the power of her Balkan rivals, and left her isolated and embittered. Henceforth she was eager to gain the support of Austria or Russia—whichever offered her the best prospect of overthrowing the Bucharest Treaty. But she had forfeited the confidence of every one. Russia hesitated to ally with her for fear of antagonizing Serbia, and Austria hesitated similarly for fear of offending Rumania.

Serbia came out of the Balkan Wars greatly increased in power and prestige, and fired with a renewed self-confidence and determination to realize her ambition of a "Greater Serbia." She had nearly doubled her territory, and increased her population from three to nearly four and a half millions. To be sure, the newly acquired districts in Macedonia were predominantly Bulgarian in character, and would therefore present a difficult problem of assimilation and administration as Serbia's first task of the future. But her acquisition of part of Novi Bazar and the upper Vardar valley, and her running frontier with Montenegro, would enable her effectively to bar the progress of Austria toward Salonica. Together these two Slav states partially surrounded the Austrian provinces of Bosnia and Herzegovina. There were soon rumors that Serbia and Montenegro might merge together, as the first step in the formation of "Greater Serbia." The next step would be to take Bosnia, Herzegovina, Dalmatia, and the other South Slav districts belonging to Austria-Hungary.

These dangerous and reckless territorial ambitions, which were taking stronger and stronger hold of all Serbians, even of their greatest leader and Prime Minister, M. Pashitch, are reflected in the remark which he made to his Greek colleague, M. Politis, as they finished dividing up the spoils of the Second Balkan War at the Bucharest Peace Conference: "The first round is won; now we must prepare the second against Austria."[159] Even more indicative of his megalomania is the statement he made to the Serbian Chargé d'Affaires at Berlin, whom he met a few days later at Marienbad:

> Already in the first Balkan War I could have let it come to an European war, in order to acquire Bosnia and Herzegovina: but, as I feared that we should then be forced to make large concessions to Bulgaria in Macedonia, I wanted first of all to secure the possession of Macedonia for Serbia, and only then to proceed to the acquisition of Bosnia.[160]

It would be a mistake, however, to think that M. Pashitch intended "the second round" against Austria immediately. Cooler reflection told him that before proceeding to this, it was necessary to consolidate the gains in Macedonia and to make more certain of Russian support. Hence his visit to Russia in January, 1914, to ask for a marriage alliance between the Serbian Crown Prince and the Tsar's daughter, as well as for "120,000 guns and ammunition and some few cannon, especially howitzers."[161] Although M. Pashitch was willing to await the favorable moment, this was not the feeling of many nationalist Serb youths and especially of the Serbian military officers of the secret "Black Hand." Highly elated by their recent victories, they looked forward with increasing eagerness and impatience to the day, so often promised by Russia, when the great Slav Empire of the north would be ready to help them in the "inevitable" struggle between Slavdom and Germandom, and the final creation of a "Greater Serbia" at the expense of the Hapsburg Empire.[162]

[159] Bogitchevitch, 65. [160] Bogitchevitch, 65. [161] Bogitchevitch, 175.

[162] On May 6, 1913, Sazonov wrote to Hartwig in Belgrade (*Deutschland Schuldig?* p. 99): "Serbia's Promised Land lies in the territory of the present Austria-Hungary, and not there where she is now making efforts and where the Bulgarians stand in her way. Under these circumstances it is of vital interest to Serbia to maintain her alliance with Bulgaria on the one hand, and, on the other, to accomplish with steady

In proportion as Serbia was elated and strengthened, Austria felt discouraged and weakened in power and prestige by the results of the Balkan Wars. Though she had taken no part in them, and lost no territory, her position was seriously undermined. Her subject nationalities grew more restless and more accessible to subversive propaganda. Rumania was becoming a less reliable ally, and Serbia a more certain and active enemy. The ever-present friction and distrust between Italy and Austria had been increased, and the danger that Austria might one day have to fight a war upon four fronts—Italian, Serbian, Rumanian and Russian—had become more threatening. Realizing these increased dangers, the militarist party at Vienna again seriously considered whether Austria ought not to deal at once with the Greater Serbia danger.[163]

GERMANY'S WARNING TO AUSTRIA, JULY, 1913

When Bulgaria treacherously attacked Serbia at the end of June, 1913, and began the short but disastrous Second Balkan War,[164] Berchtold at first adopted a reserved "wait

and patient work the necessary degree of preparedness for the inevitable struggle of the future. Time works on the side of Serbia and for the ruin of her enemies, who already show evident signs of decay. Explain all this to the Serbians! I hear from all sides that if ever any voice can have a full effect at Belgrade, it is yours." For the Tsar's long encouraging interview with Pashitch on Jan. 20/Feb. 2, 1914, see *ibid.,* 130-136; and Bogitchevitch, 170-180. For Hartwig's attitude, see above, note 155.

[163] Conrad, III, 11 ff., 74 ff., 98 ff., 238 ff., and especially 303 ff. and 329 ff.

[164] For the oft-repeated assertion that Austria egged Bulgaria on to the attack on Serbia we find no clear and definite confirmation in all the voluminous documents which have now been published. As early as May 6, from reports from Bulgaria and talks with Bulgarian officers, Conrad was convinced that an early war between Serbia and Bulgaria was inevitable, and urged Berchtold to make up his mind to take advantage of it; but Berchtold hesitated (Conrad, III, 302-316). On May 26 Conrad says he heard from the Austrian Military Attaché in Sofia that Berchtold had offered to support Bulgaria, protect her from loss of territory, and loan her money, if Bulgaria would refrain from following in the wake of Russia (Conrad, III, 330); but Conrad's own correspondence and frequent interviews with Berchtold at this time and during the following

and see" attitude, which accorded with his own hesitating nature and the wishes of Germany and Italy.[165] But he did not intend to tolerate any further great increase of Serbian territory, in spite of the moderating counsels of the German Ambassador in Vienna. According to the latter's despatch of July 1, 1913:

> If Russia, in case of decisive Bulgarian victories, should intervene in favor of Serbia, they would oppose it here [Kaiser's marginal comment: "Unbelievable"]. To my question, how this would be done, Count Berchtold thought either by direct steps at St. Petersburg, or perhaps by the occupation of Belgrade [Kaiser: "Totally crazy; that is then war!"].

Interference by Austria-Hungary without Russian provo-

weeks contain nothing which confirms this doubtful report. Neither does *Die Grosse Politik,* unless it be Tschirschky's vague phrase on July 2 that Berchtold "seems to begin to fear the Bulgarian spirits which he called" (G.P., XXXV, 147 note). The editors of the latter declare (G.P., XXXV, 52 note): "The Russian assumption that the Bulgarian Government was egged on to its final intransigence by Austria-Hungary finds no confirmation either in the German documents nor in the Austrian sources." To be sure, the *argumentum ex silentio* is negative and not conclusive. There is no doubt that Berchtold rejoiced at the prospect of the collapse of the Balkan League formed under Russian patronage, though he still suffered from the illusory nightmare that Triple Entente intrigues and Rumanian demands on Bulgaria for territorial compensations might cause its reconstitution (G.P., XXXV, 7, 40, 68 f.). There is also no doubt that Berchtold refused to support the Russian proposal early in June, 1913, that the Great Powers invite the Balkan States to demobilize at once (G.P., XXXV, 26, 41, 240; *Affaires Balkaniques,* II, 209 ff.); that he recognized the "parallelism of Austrian and Bulgarian interests" in their common opposition to a Greater Serbia (G.P., XXXIV, 822; XXXV, 117 f., 320, 329 f., 346 ff.); and also that he was "Bulgarophil" to the extent of trying to bring about a peaceful arrangement between Rumania and Bulgaria without too great territorial concessions on the latter's part (G.P., XXXIV, 577 ff., 843, 873 ff.; XXXV, 17, 56, 61 f., 66 ff., 77, 115 ff.). But that he positively egged Bulgaria on in her suicidal attack on Serbia seems not proven. Had he done so, Germany would have been likely to have known of it, and some allusion would be found to it in the German documents, especially in the frequent uncomplimentary remarks which the Kaiser and his German officials indulged in concerning Berchtold's diplomacy (*cf.* G.P., XXXV, 40, 54, 116, 147 note, 148 note, 365, 378; XXXVI, 28-30, 32).

165 G.P., XXXV, 7 f., 16 ff., 52 ff., 115.

cation would only be necessary in case Serbia should win decisively and a "Great Serbia" threaten to arise. . . . I called the Minister's attention to the fact that, just as Russian intervention on behalf of Serbia might call forth counter action by Austria-Hungary, just so Austrian interference against Serbia would bring Russia to a counter action. Berchtold observed, "Perhaps." [166]

Two days later Berchtold again expressed his anxieties to the German Ambassador, who reported to Berlin:

Count Berchtold asked me to call on him today. The Minister said he considered it his duty not to leave the German Government in the dark as to the gravity of the position for the Monarchy. The South Slav question, that is to say, undisturbed possession of the provinces inhabited by South Slavs, is a vital question for the Monarchy as well as for the Triple Alliance. The Monarchy's South Slav provinces could not be held if Serbia became too powerful. As to that, all competent opinions here agree. The Monarchy might accordingly possibly be compelled to intervene, in the event of Serbia inflicting a crushing defeat on Bulgaria in conjunction with Rumania and Greece, and annexing tracts of country in excess of the territory of Old Serbia, or something approximating to that. Serbia cannot be left in possession of Monastir, in any case.

To my question, when and how he thought of intervening, the Minister replied that it would no doubt be possible to find the psychological moment. Naturally he could not say anything now as to the method of procedure; that would depend on circumstances. He thought they would have to begin with a diplomatic conversation in Belgrade, which must be supported by military pressure, if it led to no conclusion. Then, if Russia came into the arena, St. Petersburg would become the scene of action.

The Minister again expressed a hope that the Monarchy's difficult position would be understood in Berlin. Far from

166 Tschirschky to F.O., July 1, 1913; G.P., XXXV, 115f.

wishing to pursue an adventurous policy, or being bent on conquest, her only object was to safeguard her South Slav possessions, which of course included Trieste. Naturally the most acceptable solution of the question would be a small Serbia, defeated by the enemy, and he would very much prefer this to a possible occupation of Serbia by the Monarchy. But, failing the first alternative, the Monarchy would be compelled to take action, in order to safeguard her possessions. There must be no mistake as to the danger of a Great Serbian "Piedmont," weighing as a military factor, on the borders of the Monarchy.[167]

This telegram arrived at Berlin while Bethmann-Hollweg and Jagow, the German Secretary of State, were absent at Kiel at the Kaiser's annual yachting festival, at which the Italian King and Queen, accompanied by their Minister of Foreign Affairs, San Giuliano, were also present. Zimmermann, the Under-Secretary at Berlin, forwarded the telegram to Kiel, with the moderating German comment:

> For the moment there hardly seems to be any ground for special nervousness on Vienna's part, because one can scarcely talk as yet of the danger of a Great Serbia. Our business should be to exercise a quieting influence on Vienna, and see that she keeps us regularly informed of her intentions and takes no decisions before hearing what we have to say.[168]

Meanwhile Berchtold had become increasingly nervous. He feared that Rumania was about to fall upon Bulgaria and so weaken her that Serbia would have a complete victory, and then the Greater Serbia danger would be greater than ever. He therefore telegraphed to the Austrian Am-

[167] Tschirschky to Bethmann, July 3, 1913; G.P., XXXV, 122 ff.; previously published by Count Montgelas in the *Deutsche Allgemeine Zeitung* of March 7, 1920 No. 123, and in his *Leitfaden zur Kriegsschuldfrage* (Berlin, 1923), p. 61 f.

[168] G.P., XXXV, 124; Montgelas, *l. c.,* p. 62. The Kaiser approved Zimmermann's comment and Tschirschky was so informed (G.P., XXXV, 125).

bassadors in Berlin and Rome on July 4, expressing much the same views as in his conversations with the German Ambassador quoted above, and particularly urging that Austria's two allies should "make representations at Bucharest to hold off Rumania from further steps against Bulgaria." [169] Bethmann refused to do this, and made it clear, as he had often done before, that the way to prevent Rumania from falling upon Bulgaria was for Austria to exert energetic pressure at Sofia to induce King Ferdinand to satisfy King Carol's justifiable demands for territorial compensations. For Berchtold's edification Bethmann added the further sapient observations and effective warnings:

> Austria-Hungary from the outset declared that in the present Balkan crisis she is striving after no territorial conquests. She has defined her interest as to the outcome of the Balkan War to the effect that Serbia must not reach the Adriatic, and that a viable Albania must be delivered. The first point she has smoothly accomplished. As to the boundaries of Albania, she has triumphed in the Scutari question, and along with Italy also in the question of the southern boundary of Albania along the coast. The questions still open—the southern boundary on the mainland, the constitution, and the choice of a ruler, etc., will, it is to be hoped, be satisfactorily settled. At any rate the hostilities which have now broken out between Bulgaria and Serbia-Greece in no wise disturb as yet the rule of policy hitherto traced by Austria-Hungary. On the contrary, these hostilities are not undesirable for specifically Austro-Hungarian interests, aside from the further disturbance they cause to trade and travel. It can only benefit the Dual Monarchy, if Bulgaria and Serbia are weak and discordant at the end of the war. Austria gains time thereby to restore the *modus vivendi* with Serbia which under all circumstances is necessary.

169 G.P., XXXV, 128 f.; Pribram, p. 301, note 424.

How the present hostilities between Bulgaria and Serbia will end, no man knows. But this is certain, that whichever wins, both will be weakened and filled with hatred against one another! Austria-Hungary should not interfere with this result. Even if Serbia should win, it is still a long way to a Great Serbia. For even then, Serbia will not reach the Adriatic, and a few strips of land more or less will not put the fat in the fire. Should Austria-Hungary now try by diplomatic means to chase Serbia out of her newly won territories, she would have no luck, but would certainly rouse deadly hatred in Serbia. Should she try to do this by force of arms, it would mean a European war. Germany's vital interests would thereby be most seriously affected, and I must therefore assume that before Count Berchtold makes any such decisions he will inform us.

I can therefore only express the hope that the people in Vienna will not let themselves be upset by the nightmare of a Great Serbia, but will await further developments from the Serbo-Bulgarian theatre of war. Only insistently can I warn against the idea of wanting to gobble up Serbia, for that would simply weaken Austria.[170]

This speedy and decisive warning from Germany on July 6 effectually deterred Berchtold and Conrad from rashly entering upon any reckless adventure which would have endangered the peace of Europe. We have given the episode in some detail, partly to suggest that Germany might have done the same in July, 1914; partly to illustrate the divergence in views between Berlin and Vienna; and partly to correct false impressions which M. Giolitti has spread concerning this incident, and which have been generally accepted by Entente writers.

Speaking in the Italian Parliament on December 5, 1914, in an attempt to justify Italy's neutrality in the World War by an historical precedent in 1913, M. Giolitti said:

170 Bethmann to Szögyényi, and Zimmermann to Tschirschky, July 6. 1913; G.P., XXXV, 129 f.

During the Balkan War, on the 9th of August, about a year before the present war broke out, during my absence from Rome, I received from my hon. colleague, Signor di San Giuliano, the following telegram:

"Austria has communicated to us and to Germany her intention of taking action against Serbia, and defines such action as defensive, hoping to bring into operation the *casus foederis* of the Triple Alliance, which, on the contrary, I believe to be inapplicable. (*Sensation.*)

"I am endeavoring to arrange for a combined effort with Germany to prevent such action on the part of Austria, but it may become necessary to state clearly that we do not consider such action, if it should be taken, as defensive, and that, therefore, we do not consider that the *casus foederis* arises.

"Please telegraph to me at Rome if you approve."

I replied:

"If Austria intervenes against Serbia it is clear that a *casus foederis* cannot be established. It is a step which she is taking on her own account, since there is no question of defence, inasmuch as no one is thinking of attacking her. It is necessary that a declaration to this effect should be made to Austria in the most formal manner, and we must hope for action on the part of Germany to dissuade Austria from this most perilous adventure." (*Hear, hear.*)

This course was taken, and our interpretation was upheld and recognised as proper, since our action in no way disturbed our relations with the two Allied Powers. The declaration of neutrality made by the present Government conforms therefore in all respects to the precedents of Italian policy, and conforms also to an interpretation of the Treaty of Alliance which has been already accepted by the Allies.

I wish to recall this, because I think it right that in the eyes of all Europe it should appear that Italy has remained completely loyal to the observance of her pledges. (*Loud applause.*)[171]

171 *Collected Diplomatic Correspondence* (London, 1915), p. 401.

M. Giolitti repeats his statement in his memoirs, and it has been blindly copied by Entente writers generally—even by such a well informed and cautious writer as M. Poincaré.[172] But the statement is incorrect in many respects.

In the first place, Giolitti places the incident on August 9 instead of July 9—that is, at the end instead of at the beginning of the Second Balkan War; in placing it after Serbia had made her great gains from Bulgaria and after Austria was correspondingly dissatisfied with the situation, he gives his account a more plausible character. In reality what appears to have happened was this. Berchtold's telegram of July 4, asking for pressure on Rumania and saying that Austria could not allow Serbia to be greatly increased,[173] reached Rome when Giolitti and San Giuliano were both absent from the city, San Giuliano being at Kiel. In the absence of the Prime Minister and the Minister of Foreign Affairs, the subordinate Foreign Office officials, who received Berchtold's communication, "got a fright such as they had never had in their lives"; [174] but they were greatly relieved when they soon learned from the German Ambassador in Rome of the vigorous warning which Berlin had at once given Vienna. When San Giuliano returned from Kiel to Rome, he found the Austrian communication which had terrified his subordinates, consulted Giolitti by telegraph on July 9, and then replied to the Austrian Ambassador on July 12 (nearly a week after Bethmann had already given his warning to Berchtold), protesting against any Austrian military action against Serbia, and adding,

172 G. Giolitti, *Memoirs of My Life* (London, 1923), p. 372; Poincaré, III, 231. See, however, G.P., XXXV, 122 note; Pribram, p. 301; Jagow, *Ursachen*, p. 71, and article in *Deutsche Allgemeine Zeitung*, Feb. 21, 1923; Montgelas, *Leitfaden*, p. 60 ff.; and A. von Wegerer, *Kritische Bemerkungen zu Kapitel XIII aus Vivianis "Réponse au Kaiser"* (Berlin, 1923), p. 28 ff.

173 G.P., XXXV, 128 ff., 164; Pribram, p. 301, note 424. *Cf.* above, p. 451.

174 Flotow, German Ambassador in Rome, to Bethmann, July 15, 1913; G.P., XXXV, 165.

"We shall hold you back by the coat-tails, if necessary."[175]

Giolitti is also incorrect in implying that it was Italy, rather than Germany, who deterred Berchtold from taking rash action;[176] it was not San Giuliano's reply of July 12, but Bethmann's prompt warning of July 6, which was of decisive influence at Vienna. Nor is there anything in the documents hitherto published by Germany and Austria which confirms M. Giolitti's assertion that the Triple Alliance *casus foederis* was discussed on this occasion. Nor, finally, is the righteous attitude of the Italian statesmen of December, 1914, quite so admirable and convincing if it be true, as it probably is, that San Giuliano, after his return from Kiel in 1913, confided to the German Ambassador in Rome that he himself, in Berchtold's place, would have followed the path which he feared Berchtold was preparing to follow—action against Serbia, possibly involving a European war.[177]

INTRIGUES OVER KAVALA IN 1913

The Second Balkan War, resulting in the conquest from the Bulgarians of Kavala by the Greeks and of Adrianople by the Turks, led to some very interesting diplomatic intrigues which illumine the methods of pre-War diplomatists. They throw a curious light on the support—or rather lack of support—which allies give one another when their own selfish interests are involved. In fact, the Kavala question caused such an internal split within each diplomatic group,

175 Merey, Austrian Ambassador in Rome, to Berchtold, July 12, 1913; Pribram, p. 301 f., and note 425.

176 Giolitti's statement of Dec. 5, 1914, quoted above, that San Giuliano was "endeavoring to arrange for a combined effort with Germany to prevent such action on the part of Austria" etc. *Cf.* similarly Poincaré (III, 321): "A la demande de l'Italie, l'Allemagne retint, en effet, le bras de l'Autriche." It is greatly to be wished that Italy should publish her documents for the pre-War period, as Germany and England are doing, but there seems little prospect of this at present.

177 Flotow to Bethmann, July 19, 1913; G.P., XXXV, 192 f.

that in the resulting Franco-Russian newspaper recriminations the *Novoe Vremia* demanded a revision of the Franco-Russian Alliance;[178] and, similarly, the Vienna *Neue Freie Presse* regretted sorrowfully the hitherto incredible "rift and serious weaknesses" in the Austro-German Alliance, "which for more than thirty years had rooted itself in our consciousness like an oak tree in its soil."[179] While allies were thus at odds with one another, French and German ministers were felicitating each other on their successful coöperation and their hopes of defeating the desires of their own respective allies, and Sir Edward Grey joyfully observed in this curious inversion of the usual diplomatic rôles a happy augury for the peace of Europe.[180]

Kavala was a Macedonian walled town and seaport situated about half-way between Salonica and the Dardanelles. Its tolerably good harbor was the best port available for the Bulgarians on the Aegean. It was near the center of a rich agricultural region where millions of dollars worth of the best Turkish tobacco was produced annually. Aside from Turks and Spanish Jews, its population was predominantly Greek, though the hinterland was predominantly Bulgarian.[181] Greeks and Bulgarians both coveted it. In the first Balkan War the Bulgarian armies got there first and occupied it. But in the following war between the Balkan States, Bulgaria was attacked on all sides and had to yield it up to the Greeks. On both occasions the usual unspeakable atrocities were committed.

As to the final fate of Kavala, it soon appeared that the

178 M.F.R., p. 407; L.N., II, 132; Stieve, III, 241; *Affaires Balkaniques,* II, 294 f.; III, 3-7.

179 Aug. 11, 1913; on these Press feuds, see G.P., XXXV, 368-381.

180 *Affaires Balkaniques,* II, 294; G.P., XXXV, 368 f.

181 *Cf.* ethnographic map in *Petermann's Mitteilungen,* 1915, map 44; Bulgarian Ministry of Foreign Affairs, *La Question Bulgare et les Etats Balkaniques,* (Sofia, 1919), pp. 78-87, 200-205, 275; *Carnegie Endowment Report on the Balkan Wars* (Washington, 1914), pp. 78-106, 186-207, 285-290; G.P., XXXV, 319-383, *passim.*

Great Powers held very divergent views. Austria and Russia, usually diametrically opposed on Balkan matters, were both very anxious to give it to Bulgaria. Berchtold and Sazonov therefore began intrigues in which their methods were precisely analogous and parallel, but in which their objectives were altogether different. Germany and France, on the other hand, were equally insistent that Kavala should go to Greece. England and Italy, less directly interested, were at first inclined to give it to Bulgaria, but both soon acquiesced in letting the Greeks stay in the coveted seaport, because, as Sir Edward Grey observed, "it would be difficult to drive the Greeks out." [182]

Berchtold, by trying to secure Kavala for Bulgaria, hoped to set up a stronger counter-weight to Serbia, now so swollen in size and conceit by her conquests in two Balkan Wars. He hoped also to win King Ferdinand's Government over to the side of the Triple Alliance, thereby frustrate Franco-Russian intrigues at Sofia, and bring about a reconciliation between Bulgaria and Rumania. He was encouraged in these hopes by the fact that the Bulgarian Government, *in extremis* at the end of July, had made positive offers to join the Triple Alliance and Rumania.[183] If this could be brought about, and Bulgaria and Rumania became reconciled, Rumania would then enjoy greater liberty of action, in case of a European war, for directing her main forces against Russia, instead of being compelled to leave them on her own southern frontier for protection against Bulgaria. So Berchtold, at the beginning of the Bucharest negotiations, secretly promised Kavala to the Bulgarians, without informing Germany as a frank and loyal Ally should have done. For this concealment he was

182 Lichnowsky to Bethmann, Aug. 8, 1913; G.P., XXXV, 368 f.; on the English and Italian attitude see also *ibid.*, pp. 328-332, 339-345, 357, 366.

183 G.P., XXXV, 329 f., 348.

very properly and severely reproached by Germany when the truth came out a little later.[184]

Sazonov's conceptions and methods were precisely analogous to those of Berchtold. He calculated, by giving Kavala to Bulgaria, to win her definitely to the side of the Triple Entente, checkmate suspected Austrian intrigues at Sofia, and bring about a reconciliation between Bulgaria and Serbia; then, in case of a European war, Serbia need not worry about Macedonia and the Bulgarian frontier, but could turn her main attack against Austria—a possibility of which Berchtold and his Chief of Staff were very much afraid. Furthermore, Sazonov believed that Kavala in Bulgarian hands would be a protection against Greek naval interference with Russia's cherished ambitions in regard to the Dardanelles, especially as the King of Greece was the German Kaiser's brother-in-law. So Sazonov used all his efforts at the Bucharest Peace Conference to get Kavala restored to the Bulgarians. But he did not at once inform his French Ally of the importance which he attached to this policy. He did, however, secure from the Russian treasury, at the suggestion of Izvolski and the French Minister of the Interior, a second sum of 100,000 francs with which to bribe the French Press, stipulating that the money was to be used for propaganda in favor of Russia's Balkan interests as well as in favor of the new law increasing the French army. But the Turks were reported by the Russian financial agent in Paris to be spending much more generously for bribery in the opposite direction—five million francs, with 100,000 to *La Libre Parole* alone. France did not support Sazonov's Kavala policy, and the Franco-Russian newspaper feud, mentioned above, burst forth. Izvolski naturally complained: "This incident is for me personally extremely painful." He bluntly criticized Sazonov for not informing the French Government frankly at the beginning

184 G.P., XXXV, 320-331, 338 ff., 346 ff., 378.

that the Kavala question was "of first-class importance" for Russia, instead of leaving France to learn this from the Triple Alliance Powers rather than from her own Ally.[185]

Why did Germany and France fail to support their respective allies in this Kavala question?

The Kaiser's philhellenism was strengthened by his annual spring visit to Corfu and the building of the Achilleion. He might also naturally be expected to give political support to his brother-in-law. King Constantine did not hesitate to capitalize his imperial connection as far as possible. On July 31, at "Tino's" direction, "Sophy" telegraphed to "Willy," begging him to put in a good word with King Carol of Rumania on behalf of the Greek claims to Kavala. Whereupon the Kaiser telegraphed to King Carol in restrained and considerate terms: "Can you do anything about Kavala? I should regard the question sympathetically. Hearty congratulations and good wishes on your successes.—Wilhelm." [186]

Much more important than these personal considerations, however, was the German Government's hope that German support of Greek claims to Kavala would counteract Gallophil influences at Athens and draw Greece more definitely into the wake of the Triple Alliance, thus securing Greek strategic and diplomatic support in the Eastern Mediterranean and Asia Minor. This at the moment seemed quite possible. Threatened with a deadly struggle with Bulgaria in a Second Balkan War, M. Venizelos had sought German good-will by assuring her that, "Greece would never join the Triple Entente so long as Constantine was King and he was Minister. Greece wants to keep clear of every complication of the Great Powers, but hopes by

[185] Sazonov-Izvolski correspondence, July 12 to Aug. 14, 1913; M.F.R., pp. 392-411; L.N., II, 120-135; Stieve, III, 203-244. *Cf.* also *Affaires Balkaniques,* II, 279-295; III, 3-13. The phrases quoted in the last sentence are from Izvolski's letter of Aug. 14.

[186] Aug. 1, 1913; G.P., XXXV, 323.

closer coöperation with Rumania and Turkey to be useful to the Triple Alliance as a counterweight against the Slavs." [187] A few days later Theotokis, the Greek Minister at Berlin, definitely stated that, "Greece was ready to join the Triple Alliance at any time," in return for support of her claims to Kavala, certain districts on the South Albanian frontier, and the Aegean Islands.[188] But the German Foreign Office, correctly suspecting that Theotokis had exceeded his authority, gave him a dilatory answer. Meanwhile the Berlin officials at once loyally informed their allies at Vienna and Rome of Theotokis' offer and their doubts concerning it, and asked at Athens for confirmation of it.

Venizelos replied that Theotokis had in fact exceeded his instructions, being authorized only to propose an alliance with Rumania, but not one with the Triple Alliance. Venizelos added that King Constantine at his recent accession had expressed a desire to join the Triple Alliance, but he himself had opposed alliance with either group, and had so informed the Triple Entente. Therefore he could not now change his attitude all at once, without seeming to be guilty of bad faith. He had told Constantine, however, he said, that if the King wished to carry out his desire of joining the Triple Alliance, he (Venizelos) was quite ready to resign; he added generously that he would then do all he could in Parliament to support the King's new orientation of Greek policy in favor of the Triple Alliance. Bethmann and the Kaiser, instead of urging Constantine to take advantage of his Prime Minister's generous gesture, advised

187 Quadt, German Minister at Athens, to Bethmann, June 7, 1913; G.P., XXXV, 19; *cf.* also p. 105 f. The Greek Minister at Vienna, Zaimis, expressed the same idea to Berchtold: Greece was very ready to enter into good relations with the Triple Alliance Powers, but must avoid becoming mixed in their affairs; "Ce que nous voulons, c'est de ne pas être poussé ni par un groupe ni par l'autre" (June 24, *ibid.*, p. 97).

188 Jagow's memorandum, June 18; G.P., XXXV, 89.

him that Venizelos' resignation at this critical time might be disastrous for Greece, but that he might well negotiate with Rumania. Germany could not endanger her own policy of preserving peace in Europe, as she might do if she should guarantee Greek boundaries and become involved in Balkan complications. But she would welcome joyfully a Greek orientation toward the Triple Alliance, and the question might be advantageously taken up after the close of the present crisis.[189]

Meanwhile, to encourage Greece in her new attitude, Germany decided it was imperative to support the Greek claims to Kavala, even though Austria insisted on taking the opposite line of championing the Bulgarian claims. In the ensuing lively conflict between the Wilhelmstrasse and the Ballplatz, the Berlin authorities pointed out that they could not afford to abandon the Greek claims and run the risk of losing the prospect of Greece joining the Triple Alliance. They feared that otherwise Greece would fall back into the wake of the Triple Entente. Berchtold rejoined that he too, having promised Kavala to Bulgaria, could not stultify himself by reversing his attitude and run the risk of losing the prospect of Bulgarian adherence to the Triple Alliance. He feared that if he did so Franco-Russian intrigues would triumph at Sofia. Berlin also pointed out very properly that the Greek offers had come first, were more dependable and had at once been loyally communicated by Germany to her two allies, while the Bulgarian offers had come afterwards, were very uncertain in view of King Ferdinand's treacherous character, and moreover had been disloyally concealed from Germany by Berchtold.[190]

As to French policy, according to M. Poincaré, who cites the highly selective and relatively meager *French Yellow Book* on the Balkan Wars, "The preoccupation of

[189] G.P., XXXV, 89-97. [190] G.P., XXXV, 344-355.

France was always the same—to put an end to a war which might become general; she took the side of Greece against Bulgaria, that is in this case of Germany against Russia, solely in the hope of preventing a renewal of hostilities." [191] But in reality, French policy in the Kavala question was dictated also by the traditional policy of France of friendship for Greece, by the French instructors loaned to drill the Greek armies who were supplied with French guns, and by the large investments of French in Greek loans and in the tobacco monopoly in the Kavala region (which the Bulgarians had threatened to confiscate if it came into their possession), all of which tended to make French public opinion philhellenic. But above all, according to Izvolski, it was dictated by "the fear that Germany would gain the upper hand in Athens," that French interests in the Near East would suffer, and that France must get the strategic support of the Greek navy against the rival power of Italy in the Mediterranean.[192]

As to the Balkan States themselves, Greece, Serbia, and Rumania were firm in opposing the Bulgarian claims to Kavala. It looked as if the Bucharest Peace Conference might be broken up, if Bulgaria refused to accept the terms

191 Poincaré, III, 230. "But who opens the Yellow Books?" he asks (III, 233). The present writer has opened them, and finds that Pichon's despatch to Delcassé of Aug. 9 (*Affaires Balkaniques,* II, 294 f.), which M. Poincaré refers to but refrains from quoting, hints also at quite other motives than the laudable one he mentions. Pichon declares the French attitude "justifiée par notre politique traditionnelle, par le souci de l'équilibre méditerranéen, par les conditions de la guerre entre la Bulgarie et la Grèce, par les victoires et les sacrifices de cette dernière, par l'attitude de l'Allemagne, enfin et surtout par la certitude que j'avais d'une reprise d'hostilités dans l'hypothèse d'une tentative de règlement différent."

192 See quotation in preceding note. Izvolski to Sazonov, Aug. 2, 5, 12, and 14, 1913; M.F.R., pp. 399-409; L.N., II, 122-135; Stieve, III, 220-224. Jules Cambon to Pichon, Aug. 2 (*Affaires Balkaniques,* II, 281) "quelle que soit l'attitude de la Russie, nous ne saurions, sans péril pour notre influence à Athènes et sans y laisser le champ libre à l'Allemagne, nous départir de l'appui que nous avons donné jusqu'ici aux revendications helléniques."

demanded by the victors. When Austria and Russia realized this, and found that they were not supported by their respective allies, they each tried indirectly to save the situation for Bulgaria. They proposed, separately and in slightly different terms, that the Kavala clauses, or even the whole Bucharest Treaty, should be subject to revision later by the Great Powers. But these proposals, highly offensive to the three Balkan victors, naturally also met with the same negative from Germany and France as in the direct discussion of the Kavala question, the motives being much the same. The revision idea was given the deathblow by the publication of King Carol's telegram to the Kaiser announcing the certainty of peace, "which thanks to You remains a definite one." [193] The Kaiser telegraphed in reply his hearty congratulations. The cautious and considerate Bethmann doubted the advisability of making these telegrams public, for fear of offending Austrian susceptibilities. But the Kaiser insisted, and his Foreign Office Under-Secretary, Zimmermann, thought that their publication, though "hardly agreeable" to Vienna, would have the advantage of checking Berchtold's "zeal for revision." They were therefore published by the Wolff Telegraph Bureau from Bucharest on August 10, 1913, the day the Peace of Bucharest was finally signed, and caused no little irritation in Austria.[194]

THE AUSTRIAN ULTIMATUM TO SERBIA OF OCTOBER 18, 1913

In the summer of 1913, after the First Balkan War and the decision to establish an independent Albania, the Lon-

[193] Aug. 7, 1913; G.P., XXXV, 359.

[194] G.P., XXXV, 359-379. One of the Kaiser's secretaries later tried to smooth Conrad's ruffled feelings by assuring him that the telegrams had been published upon the initiative of King Carol and not of the Kaiser, but this was "not wholly in accord with the historical facts" (G.P., XXXIX, 442). The text of the Bucharest Treaty is printed in *Affaires Balkaniques,* II, 296 ff.

don Conference of Ambassadors agreed to create three commissions which, it was hoped, would help bring into existence an Albanian state capable of life and survival. One commission was to delimit the southern frontier between Albania and Greece, another the northern one toward Serbia and Montenegro, and the third, the Commission of International Control, was to attempt to administer Albania until the Great Powers could find and agree upon an acceptable Prince for the country.[195]

But there were long delays before the boundary commissions were ready to begin work on the spot. Even when they finally set forth into the rough mountainous country, with automobiles which continually broke down and had to be abandoned for horses or even procedure on foot, there were more delays and difficulties. In the South, local Greek officials resorted to all sorts of naïve and futile efforts to deceive the Commission into thinking that the majority of the inhabitants spoke Greek and were wildly enthusiastic for incorporation into Constantine's kingdom. With suspicious regularity processions of peasants came forth from the villages garbed after the Greek fashion and bellowing at the top of their lungs, ἕνωσις ἤ θάνατος, "Union or Death." But the Commission was so convinced that they had been imported for the occasion, and that strong-arm methods were being used to keep the Albanians and Mohammedans shut indoors and silent, that an official protest had to be made at Athens. In the North, the Serbians were less naïve and more circumspect, but the members of the Commission were often stopped or arrested by the Serbian troops. In both Boundary Commissions the representatives of the six Great Powers soon tended to divide into three groups corresponding to the political attitude of their superiors in London. The French and Russian delegates took every occasion to favor the Greeks, Serbians and Montenegrins, while the

[195] G.P., XXXV, 235-315; *Affaires Balkaniques,* II, 209-222.

Austrian and Italian were bent on giving Albania the widest extent possible. Between these two extreme groups, whose bickerings over picayune trifles several times threatened to break up the work of the Commissons altogether, the English and German Commissioners tried to find satisfactory compromises, and at the same time conscientiously reach decisions which accorded with the facts on the spot and the instructions they received from London.[196]

Owing to the delays of the Commissions in fixing the Albanian boundaries and to the mutual enmity of Serbians and Albanians, a frontier conflict broke out. Serbian troops reoccupied Albanian territory. The Albanians, upon this provocation, took revenge by attacking and routing a

[196] For an account, often highly diverting, of these delays and bickerings, see the reports of the German Commissioners in G.P., XXXVI, 129-260. In this boundary matter Germany wanted to preserve the solidarity of the Triple Alliance by supporting all the reasonable desires of her allies, but she did not want to oppose too strongly what Constantine had set his heart upon, for fear of driving him into the arms of the Entente. Germany therefore tried to persuade both sides to be moderate and reasonable. To King Constantine, upon his visit to Berlin on Sept. 6, 1913, the Kaiser pointed out persuasively how great were the gains he had already made: "Janina, Salonica, Kavala, and last not least Crete, all regular basic hellenic Pelita, which it would have taken centuries to acquire. . . . In comparison with all this, a trifling rectification of the Epirus frontier plays absolutely no rôle and is worthless." The Kaiser also pointed to Germany's self-restraint at Nikolsburg in 1866 as an example of the wisdom of moderation after victory, and hinted that, if Constantine refrained from antagonizing Italy in regard to the South Albanian frontier, Rome might eventually concede to him the Aegean Islands, which were of far greater importance (*ibid.*, pp. 144-6). Similarly, in regard to Austria and Italy, the Kaiser noted: "If Austria and Italy are unreasonable toward Greece, we are not to blame! We do not have to join in *every* folly which they perpetrate. We have already taken over abundantly much at our expense for love of our allies. If the latter just go on making their situation worse in relation to the Triple Entente, we can warn them, but we cannot prevent them. But we do not need to join with them" (G.P., XXXV, 251). Instructions to this effect, in more diplomatic but sufficiently clear language, were sent by Berlin to Vienna and Rome. For Jagow's personal advice to the German delegate on the South Albanian Frontier Commission, see G.P., XXXVI, 160 f. On the general merits of this whole Epirote question, with a full bibliography, see Edith P. Stickney, *South Albania in European Affairs, 1912-1923*, Stanford, 1926.

Serbian detachment. Serbia then mobilized part of her army. The Serbian Press demanded a punitive expedition and the occupation of a considerable part of Albania. It was pointed out that the Scutari and Adrianople incidents had demonstrated the impotency of the Great Powers, who were likely to bow before a *fait accompli* rather than attempt to expel those who were *beati possidentes.* Some of the Powers individually warned Serbia to respect the decisions of the London Conference, but the Conference as a whole could not bring itself to a collective warning, which alone would be effective. Sir Edward Grey's patience threatened to become exhausted. From the point of view of English interests he was indifferent as to whether this or that Balkan village was Turkish, Greek, Serbian, Bulgarian, or Albanian. He conceived of his rôle as that of an honest broker whose Balkan efforts should be directed toward serving the one British interest of preserving the peace of Europe. But he was becoming so wearied with the almost daily complaints and counter-complaints that finally, "he wanted to hear the name 'Albania' as seldom as possible, and one would not be surprised if, yielding to his feeling of irritation, he laid the Albanian flute down on the table and recalled Admiral Burney and the English contingent." [197]

Under these circumstances, and in view of the fact that Serbian troops persisted in remaining in occupation of Albanian territory, Berchtold and the Austrian Chief of Staff, Baron Conrad, again considered what more drastic measures they ought to take.

Conrad again urged that now at last Austria should

[197] Kühlmann, German Chargé d'Affaires in London to Bethmann, Sept. 24, 1913; G.P., XXXVI, 165; on Grey see also pp. 377, 394. On the first part of this paragraph, see *ibid.*, pp. 131-174, 361-382; *Affaires Balkaniques,* III, 46-54; and *Oesterreich-Ungarisches Rotbuch: Diplomatische Aktenstücke betreffend die Ereignisse am Balkan, 13 Aug. bis 6 Nov., 1913* (Vienna, 1914), *passim.*

GENERAL CONRAD VON HÖTZENDORF
Austro-Hungarian Chief of Staff, 1906-1917

COUNT BERCHTOLD
Austro-Hungarian Minister for Foreign Affairs, 1912-1915

have her final reckoning with Serbia. He learned from Prince Hohenlohe, who had recently returned from St. Petersburg, that Russia was not likely to interfere, if Austria acted quickly and energetically against Serbia; now was better than later, because Russia was trying to win over Rumania from the side of the Triple Alliance to that of the Triple Entente. This was also the view of Baron Nopsca, who had recently been going about in Rumania disguised as a shepherd. He reported to Conrad that public opinion there was entirely against Austria-Hungary, and that Rumania was falling wholly into Russian and French leading strings. But Berchtold, timid and hesitating, was inclined to be content with gestures and half-measures.[198]

In long Ministerial Councils on October 3 and 13, Austrian officials earnestly discussed what should be done. Three views were represented respectively by Baron Conrad, Count Tisza, and Count Berchtold. Conrad, as usual, insisted that Serbia must be dealt with once and for all, before it was too late, especially as Rumania was falling away from Austria and coming under Russian and French influence. Serbia must either be compelled to accept peaceful incorporation into Austria-Hungary, being given a position somewhat like that of Bavaria or Saxony in the German Empire, and involving "trialism"—a reorganization of the Dual Monarchy into a federal "triple state." Or, if this was not possible, then Conrad favored an ultimatum to Serbia; if no satisfactory reply was forthcoming, he would then urge immediate and energetic war. At its conclusion—he had no doubt but that Austria would be victorious—Austria could annex some parts of Serbia, and could gratify Rumania, Bulgaria and Greece by offering other parts of Serbia to them—the Timok district to Rumania, and Macedonia to Bulgaria and Greece. This would be an effective revision of the Bucharest Treaty very beneficial to Austria.

[198] Conrad, III, 442-447, 453-458.

But above all, no half-measures should be tried, such as a mere occupation of a few Serbian towns as a pledge. The Austrian army, once mobilized, must not be expected to lay down its arms until Serbian territory had been conquered; the morale of the army could not tolerate mobilization without war for a third time [i.e. in addition to 1909 and 1912]. In short, "either the complete incorporation of Serbia by peaceful means—or the use of force."[199]

Count Tisza, the all-powerful Magyar leader, who had become Hungarian Minister-President on June 6, 1913, though recognizing the Serbian danger, was inclined to trust to diplomatic action. He agreed that the London Conference had brought nothing but disillusionment, and therefore favored having Austria-Hungary strike out an independent policy of her own. One could not allow Serbians, Montenegrins, Greeks, and Italians to go on treating Albania as *res nullius*. He was unalterably opposed to the incorporation of more Serbs into the Dual Monarchy either by a peaceful arrangement or by the use of force; it would be impracticable, disadvantageous to the Monarchy itself, and certain to meet with the opposition of Europe. Serbia should be energetically requested to remove her troops from Albanian soil; if this did not suffice, one might send an ultimatum, and inflict a diplomatic, and even, if necessary, a military, defeat. But in no case should Serbian territory be annexed. Tisza hoped that the anti-Austrian Balkan group—Serbia, Montenegro, Rumania, and Greece—could be offset by winning over Turkey and Bulgaria, who were on the point of coming to terms with one another. Such a diplomatic regrouping would reëstablish a favorable Balkan Balance of Power, parallel with the European Balance of Power between the Triple Alliance and Triple Entente. It would also avoid the financial burden of a large increase in the Austro-Hungarian army, to which he himself,

[199] Conrad, III. 442 ff., 461, 465 ff., 724-746.

as Minister-President of Hungary, was opposed. In short, Tisza's program was: restoration of the waning Austrian prestige, by the diplomatic humiliation, but not the territorial partition, of Serbia, and the avoidance of war, if possible. In case Austria had to resort to mobilization, she must still avoid war, if Serbia yielded at the last minute and agreed to pay the costs of mobilization.[200]

In contrast to the clear-cut program of Conrad for military action, and that of Count Tisza for diplomatic action, Count Berchtold, the Minister of Foreign Affairs, had no definite idea of what ought to be done. He was as helpless and incompetent a person as was ever called to fill a responsible position in time of danger. He set forth the *pros* and *cons,* and oscillated timidly and uncertainly between conflicting influences. He hesitated to decide for military action against Serbia for fear that Germany and Italy would not support him. He feared also the danger of Russian interference. He felt the difficulty of persuading Francis Joseph to approve war, and he knew Franz Ferdinand's opposition to it. He was finally inclined to think that some concession to Serbia in regard to the Albanian boundary might be given for the moment, and that military preparations should be made for the future, with the hope that in the meantime the general diplomatic situation might improve.[201]

The result of the discussion was that no definite decision was taken, except the adoption of proposals in regard to finance and a small army increase to be laid before the Delegations the following November. In spite of the fact that the Serbians had burned several villages and massacred Albanians in the neighborhood of Dibra, so that the population was in flight toward the coast,[202] Berchtold contented

200 Conrad, III, 461, 464-6, 727-730, 735-741. This foreshadows interestingly Tisza's Memoir of 1914, urging a diplomatic shift in the Balkans, as well as his initial attitude in the crisis of July, 1914.

201 Conrad, III, 463, 466, 724-729, 735.

himself on October 14 with an "amicable request" to Serbia to withdraw her troops from Albania and respect the decisions of the London Conference, within a date which Serbia herself might fix. Sazonov and Pichon also advised Pashitch to withdraw his troops at once, as we learn from Sazonov's report to the Tsar a fortnight later:

> My stay in Paris coincided with the new sharpening of Austro-Serbian relations in consequence of the occupation of several strategic points on Albanian soil by the Serbian troops. In the fear that Austria might give way to the desire to win an easy diplomatic victory in this matter, Pichon and I advised the Serbian Minister [in Paris] to inform his Government that it was preferable to yield to the friendly advice of Russia and France, rather than await threats from Austria. Vesnitch agreed completely, and telegraphed at once in this sense to Belgrade. . . . Pichon promised me to use all his influence to have the Serbian loan admitted to the Paris Bourse.[203]

But the Serbian Prime Minister did not follow this good advice, possibly because he may not have received it in time, or more probably because he was being influenced by the ardent Pan-Slav Russian Minister, Hartwig, and by subterranean pressure from the secret society of Serbian

202 Report of the French Consul in Scutari, Oct. 9; *Affaires Balkaniques,* III, 65. A few weeks later the Boundary Commission observed between Dibra and Prizren that "Nearly all the villages have been wholly or partially burned down by the Serbians. . . . The Serbian outposts here have been pushed some ten kilometres beyond the provisional boundary" (G.P., XXXVI, 241).

203 Sazonov's report to the Tsar, Oct. 24/Nov. 6, 1913; L.N., II, 360; Stieve, III, 328 f. See also Izvolski to Neratov, Oct. 18 (M.F.R., p. 430; L.N., II, 161; Stieve, III, 313), where Izvolski says that the French Government's decision not to withhold the loan any longer was "to make it easier for the Serbian Government to take this step" of withdrawing her troops from Albania. One may doubt, however, whether the furnishing of French money would tend to make Serbia more yielding and pacific. According to Poincaré (III, 306 f.), who says nothing of the French loan, Vesnitch did not send his telegram to Belgrade until Oct. 16.

military officers known as the "Black Hand."[204] On the contrary, Pashitch replied to Austria that the withdrawal of Serbian troops would depend on future conditions in Albania, where the anarchical state of affairs endangered the safety of his own peace-loving subjects. He even asked the London Conference to revise its former decisions, and assign some new strategic positions to Serbia. At the same time, Montenegro, to whom a new loan had just been authorized by the French Government,[205] occupied Albanian territory, and was reported to be on the point of ordering a general mobilization against the people whom the Great Powers were supposed to protect and govern. It was again rumored that Montenegro was about to merge with Serbia toward the formation of a "Greater Serbia." It looked to Vienna as if Serbia, Montenegro, and Greece were seriously intending to reoccupy the unhappy distracted country and present the impotent Powers with a new *fait accompli*.[206]

Meanwhile Berchtold informed Germany of the situation, reiterated that Albania's existence was necessary as a barrier against the Slav advance to the Adriatic, and de-

204 " . . . Finally it is unmistakable that since M. Hartwig's return, opposition [to Austria's requests] has been increasing" (Griesinger, German Minister in Belgrade, to Bethmann, Oct. 17; G.P., XXXVI, 396).

From the German reports (*ibid.*, pp. 397, 399, 415, 417) it appears that Neratov, in charge of the Foreign Office at St. Petersburg during Sazonov's absence, was consulted by Hartwig and endorsed Pashitch's negative reply to Austria. This was in flat contradiction to Sazonov's alleged attitude at Paris. One wonders whether Sazonov quite stated the truth in his report to the Tsar, or whether this is another of the many instances in which Russian ministers pursued divergent policies.

"From conversation with the English Chargé d'Affaires here [in Belgrade], who is usually well informed and can also get his information from the Russian Legation, I gather that the Serbian Government . . . has been forced to attempt to carry through a revision of the frontier, through the influence of the Military Party—through the subterranean activities of the group of officers known here as the '*crna ruka*' ['Black Hand']" (Report of the Austrian Military Attaché in Belgrade, Oct. 18; Conrad III, 475).

205 Oct. 8; *Affaires Balkaniques,* III, 65.

206 *Affaires Balkaniques,* III, 66; Conrad, III, 462, 472 f.

clared that further acquiescence would be an abdication on Austria's part. He therefore expressed "the hope that Germany, who herself has a great interest in damming back the Slav flood, would stand morally solid behind Austria in this matter; because, as far as one could see, it would only be a question of moral support, since neither Russia nor France wanted war. One could also therefore hope that Serbia was only bluffing." [207]

The Berlin Foreign Office assured Berchtold of the moral support desired, and instructed Germany's diplomatic representatives to back up Austria's efforts in preserving the life of Albania. It urged that Sir Edward Grey use his influence, at Belgrade and in the London Conference, to see that the decisions of the Powers were respected, adding that, "if the warnings of the Vienna Cabinet at Belgrade remain unheeded, it is to be feared from the form and content of Count Berchtold's representations in Berlin that Austria will go ahead independently." [208] But Sir Edward Grey was

[207] Oct. 15; G.P., XXXVI, 384 ff.

[208] Zimmermann to Lichnowsky, Oct. 16; G.P., XXXVI, 389; *cf.* also pp. 384-396. The Kaiser, who was absent from Berlin, was informed of the steps taken by his Foreign Office, and approved them heartily. But his approval, and his remarks to Conrad (III, 470) at the Battle of Leipzig Centennial celebration, that patience has its limits and that Austria must soon take the sword, did not influence Berchtold in sending his ultimatum to Serbia, as they were still unknown to him when he sent it. For Dr. Heinrich Kanner's errors in this connection, see the present writer's comments in the *Amer. Hist. Rev.*, XXXII, 317 ff., 944 ff. (Jan. and July, 1927). Some weeks earlier the Kaiser had approved of Conrad's idea of the peaceful incorporation of Serbia into the Dual Monarchy, like Bavaria in the German Empire, rather than forcible Austrian action, because "it would be much more advantageous for Germany, if Austria-Hungary were united with Serbia in one structure, than if she has a South Slav state as a neighbor who will always fall upon her rear" (Conrad, III, 431). But after the latest events, upon a report from the German representative at Vienna that "the solid stand of Germany, of which Berchtold never doubted, strengthens him in the conviction that Serbia will heed the eight-day time limit and not go to extremes," the Kaiser noted impulsively: "That would be very much to be regretted! Now or never! One must finally have order and quiet down there!" (G.P., XXXVI, 399).

out of town over the week-end. His Under-Secretary, Sir Eyre Crowe, would take no step without first getting Sir Edward's instructions. Nor was the Under-Secretary's response encouraging: he thought it was merely a question of a few strategic positions in Albania which had been occupied simply *provisionally;* every inch of Albanian territory would of course have to be evacuated, and England would coöperate in this; but he did not think that Grey would favor an immediate demand on Serbia for evacuation, nor one to which a time-limit was attached.[209]

Suddenly, in the middle of the night of October 17-18, Berchtold, gratified at Germany's moral support but without saying anything further to her, and influenced by the latest reports concerning Albania, despatched an ultimatum to Belgrade. It insisted that Serbia respect Albanian territory and withdraw her troops within eight days; "otherwise Austria would be forced, with regret, to have recourse to the proper measures to secure the realization of her demands."[210]

Berchtold's unexpected exhibition of decisive energy took all Europe aback with surprise. To Sazonov it caused much chagrin, because, as he claims to have foreseen would be the case, Austria won an easy diplomatic victory. But he not unjustly complained of Berchtold's "policy of surprises," which her allies were unable to prevent: "As long as Austria asks us beforehand, before taking a momentous decision, he was wholly satisfied, he said. But there is unfortunately no assurance of this, as the last incident shows. Austria is always facing her allies with *faits accomplis;* and they are then compelled to honor their treaty signa-

209 Kühlmann to Bethmann, Oct. 18; G.P., XXXVI, 394.

210 Note to Serbian Government, 12:10 A.M., Oct. 18, 1913; Conrad, III, 473, 747; G.P., XXXVI, 394-402. By diplomatic euphemism it was called a "Note with a time-limit" [befristete Note], as in the case of its fatal successor of July 23, 1914 (as will be indicated below, vol. II, ch. v), but it was in fact essentially an ultimatum.

tures." [211] At Belgrade Pashitch and Hartwig learned of the ultimatum with rage and dismay, especially as it was soon followed by strong warnings from all the Great Powers, now suddenly awakened to the possible danger of serious complications, that Serbia should respect the decisions of the London Conference. Even Rumania added her warning. So Serbia decided at once to yield, and gave orders to her troops to evacuate the occupied Albanian territory. "I do it," said Pashitch, the Serbian Premier, "not under pressure of Austria, but out of regard for the friendly advice of Russia." [212]

These events of 1913 in connection with Albania help to explain Austria's course of action, under much greater provocation, in July, 1914. The decisions of the London Conference had brought her little or nothing, in her own opinion, except disappointments and illusions. Its delays and ineffectiveness in protecting Albanian interests, when defied by the Montenegrins at Scutari and the Serbians at Dibra, explain to some extent why Austria was absolutely unwilling, after the murder of Archduke Franz Ferdinand at Sarajevo, to submit her latest grounds of complaint against Serbia to another Conference of the Powers. "The course of the London Conference was so horrible to recall to memory, that all public opinion would reject the repetition of such a spectacle." [213] On the other hand, when Austria had acted quickly and energetically on her own account, by sending a peremptory ultimatum, Serbia had

[211] Lucius, German Chargé d'Affaires in St. Petersburg, to Bethmann, Oct. 28, 1913; G.P., XXXVI, 420. For Neratov's "complete surprise" and irritation, *ibid.*, 399, 409. *Cf.* also Sazonov's report to the Tsar, Nov. 6, 1913.

[212] Dumaine to Pichon, Oct. 21, 1913; *Affaires Balkaniques,* III, 70. *Cf.* also *ibid.*, III, 67-72; G.P., XXXVI, 401-422; Conrad, III, 474; and Sazonov's report to the Tsar, Oct. 24/Nov. 6, 1913 (L.N., II, 360 f., and Stieve, III, 328 f.).

[213] Bilinski's remark in the Ministerial Council of July 31, 1914; A.R.B., III, 79.

heeded her demands immediately, Russia had not interfered, and the Vienna Foreign Office had accomplished its immediate purpose.

Another factor in the Balkan situation, which was pregnant with danger for Austria-Hungary and became more evident after the Balkan Wars, was the change which took place in Rumania.

THE RUMANIAN RIDDLE

The very secret treaty of 1883, by which Rumania joined the Triple Alliance Powers, had been renewed at various times, the last occasion being on February 5, 1913.[214] During the early years of the treaty, Austria and Germany had no serious fear that Rumania would ever fail to fulfil her treaty obligations. King Carol, a Hohenzollern educated in Germany and sympathetic in his whole being with the German point of view, was universally regarded as an honest, upright man, whose personal loyalty was trusted up to his very death in October, 1914. Self-interest likewise seemed to assure Rumania's loyal adherence to the Triple Alliance: it guaranteed the little Balkan State against domination or transgression by Russia in any advance toward Constantinople, and against attack by Bulgaria or Turkey for possession of the Dobrudja.

But by 1914 the situation had greatly altered. King Carol remained as loyal as ever. Sentiment among the Rumanian people, however, had changed so greatly that

[214] See above, ch. ii, p. 88 ff.; Pribram, I, 29-34, 69-77, 85-90, 107, 209, 245 f.; G.P., III, 261-282; VII, 149-187; XI, 301-307; XXVIII, 649-680; XXVII, 195-235; XXX, 581-593. Though the renewal of the Austro-Rumanian Treaty (to which Germany acceded on Feb. 26 and Italy on March 5) was signed on Feb. 5, 1913, King Carol delayed for a week his ratification, giving as his excuse that he feared an impending ministerial crisis "and did not want it signed by various ministers." His more real reason was that, by delaying ratification and threatening "a new orientation of Rumanian policy," i.e., away from the Triple Alliance, he hoped to frighten Austria into a more energetic support of the Rumanian claims to Silistria against Bulgaria (G.P., XXXIV, 337, 357 ff., 364).

Austria, and to some extent Germany, began to be seriously worried as to whether King Carol's personal prestige would be strong enough to carry his country with him. He was after all a constitutional monarch. Anti-Austrian popular sentiment in a parliamentary democracy might override the monarch's personal preference.

Three factors had contributed toward the development among the Rumanians of a hatred toward Austria, which threatened to undo the alliance: (1) the Magyar policy toward Transylvania, (2) the Austrian policy toward Bulgaria, and (3) the Russo-Serb wooing to win Rumania away from the Triple Alliance to the side of the Triple Entente.

For the first of these factors the Magyar nobility were chiefly to blame. In order to retain the dominant position which they had exercised since the Middle Ages, they had steadily refused, even at the opening of the twentieth century, to grant any really democratic suffrage to the Rumanian and Slav subject peoples in Hungary. The Rumanians in Transylvania were refused a fair number of seats in the Hungarian Chamber of Deputies, and their nationalistic desires in regard to school and language questions had been blindly disregarded. This galling denial of political rights naturally contributed toward the bitterness and irredentist longings which were shared by Rumanians on both sides of the Carpathian Mountains.

The second factor which embittered the people of Rumania, and threatened to transfer Rumania from the side of the Triple Alliance to that of the Triple Entente, was Austria's attitude toward the Bulgaro-Rumanian conflict which arose out of the First Balkan War. By their astonishing victories over Turkey in the first weeks of the war, Bulgaria, Serbia and Greece had occupied wide stretches of territory, which vastly extended their frontiers and greatly increased their prestige, power, and population. Rumania, meanwhile, had maintained a dignified neutrality, remaining at peace with Turkey, while her rivals were growing strong. She alone had gained no new frontiers during the First Balkan War. She alone had liberated and annexed no suppressed nationalities crying to be free. Her people therefore were swept in the spring of 1913 by a new wave of irredentist nationalism and indignation. There was a strong popular demand on the Rumanian Cabinet that something must be done to redress the Balance of Power in the Balkans, which had existed since the Treaty of Berlin in 1878, but which had now been completely upset to Rumania's disadvantage.

Rumanian newspapers bitterly complained of the mistaken policy of folded hands: King Carol should have intervened while the Bulgarian armies were tied up in front of Adrianople and Constantinople and insisted that Bulgaria cede to him the Silistria-Balchik district south of the Dobrudja, as "compensation" for Rumania's benevolent neutrality. Instead of adopting an active selfish policy of this kind, Rumania had pursued a waiting attitude, trusting in the generosity of Bulgaria and in a favorable pressure by the Great Powers to secure her adequate "compensations." But she had been deceived in both hopes. Throughout the early months of the Balkan War, Bulgaria remained obdurate and deaf to Také Jonescu's pleas for "just compensations." And when the question was finally left to the decision of the Great Powers at the St. Petersburg Conference, in March, 1913, Rumania did not get as much as her nationalists thought she had a right to expect.[215]

It was in connection with these negotiations about "compensations" that Rumanian Ministers and public opinion turned more sharply against Austria-Hungary.

215 *Affaires Balkaniques,* II, 30-35, 40-42, 56, 60 f., 67, 70 f., 74-81, 83-90, 93-109, 130 f., 137, 154 f., 229 f., 236-248, 253, 256, 263, 280; Conrad, III, 26, 33 ff., 39-56, 74 f., 103 f., 113 f., 129-131, 140 ff., 204 ff., 305 ff., 335-339, 365 f., 381 ff.; G.P., XXXIV, 245 ff., 301 ff., 337 ff., 357 ff., 418 ff., 575 ff.; XXXV, 115 ff.; XXXIX, 433 ff.

Austria was suspected (and rightly) of giving slight support to the demands of her ally against Bulgaria for Silistria and a strip of territory south of the Dobrudja. King Carol's Ministers not only demanded this territory, but insisted that Rumania's prestige obligated Austria to show as much zeal and energy in securing Silistria for Rumania as in opposing Serbia's access to the Adriatic. With Germany's attitude they were satisfied. Although Germany gave them salutary advice—to leave prestige aside, be content with moderate compensations, and not to listen to the wooing of Russia, who would not lift a finger for them as soon as she had achieved her purpose of breaking up her alliances—Germany did strongly back up Rumania's claims.[216] But with Austria they suspected it was otherwise. "People are especially irritated against Austria-Hungary, because her support [to Rumania], in comparison with what Russia gives Bulgaria, is much too weak to lead to any favorable result. Feeling already runs so high that the King [Carol] will be compelled in a very short time to come to a grave decision. The decision will be either for war with Bulgaria, or for peace, but with the summoning of a Russophil ministry, which would mean that the course of Rumanian policy, hitherto friendly to the Triple Alliance, would give way to dependence on the Triple Entente." [217] Austria was suspected of being "more Bulgarian than the Bulgarians." When Rumania finally threatened to mobilize against Bulgaria, in order to secure the coveted territory, Austria tried to hold her back. Prince Fürstenberg, the Austrian Minister at Bucharest, warned King Carol that a Rumanian attack on Bulgaria would be totally opposed to Austrian policy; and that if Rumania persisted, Austria might eventually intervene; King Carol should keep on good terms

216 See below, notes 241-244.

217 Pomiankowski to Conrad, quoting the Rumanian Military Attaché in Constantinople, Jan. 28, 1913; Conrad, III, 39 f.

with Bulgaria; because, otherwise, he would be playing into the hands of the Russian Pan-Slavs.[218]

This restraint which Austria exercised, or rather tried to exercise, upon King Carol weakened and isolated the King still more among his own people. "King Carol is following Austria's advice for peace in Bulgaria's interests," it was said. The popular pressure became so strong that the King finally had to yield to public opinion. He joined Serbia and Greece in the Second Balkan War against Bulgaria, and secured her coveted "compensations"—a generous slice of Bulgarian territory south of the Dobrudja, stretching from Silistria on the Danube to Constanza on the Black Sea. Rumanian nationalistic aspirations and irredentist ambitions were strongly stirred by this short successful war. As the French proverb says, *"L'appetit vient en mangeant."* As a result, Austria-Hungary now found herself seriously menaced by a "Greater Rumania" movement, which aimed at the ultimate detachment of the Rumanians in Transylvania, just as the "Greater Serbia" propaganda aimed at detaching the Serbs in Bosnia and other parts of the Dual Monarchy. In November, 1913, a Rumanian Minister gave France to understand that the old friendship with Austria was "no longer anything but a shadow; the question of the Rumanians in Transylvania has become the only important one in public opinion, which frankly desires a *rapprochement* with Russia." [219] And in December King Carol himself finally admitted to the Austrian Minister at Bucharest, that public feeling was such that, "to his great regret, he was not in a position to be able to guarantee to fulfil the existing secret treaty between Rumania and the Dual Monarchy." [220]

218 Conrad, III, 335-338; Jonescu, *Origins of the War.* p. 25; G.P., XXXIV, 843, 873 ff.; XXXIX, 434 ff., 504 f., 512.

219 *Affaires Balkaniques,* III, 74.

220 Austrian Military Attaché in Bucharest to Conrad, Dec. 12, 1913; Conrad, III, 496; see also G.P., XXXIX, 464 ff., and Alexander Hoyos,

By his double-faced and futile policy of pretending to support the interests of two opposed states like Rumania and Bulgaria, Berchtold had fallen between two stools. He had lost the confidence and good-will of the one before he had secured that of the other. This "desertion" on Rumania's part was one of the most important facts in Austrian foreign policy in the spring of 1914. The Serbian question has received a great deal more attention from writers, because it ultimately became the occasion of the World War; but, next to it, nothing bothered the heads of the men at the Ballplatz more seriously than this Rumanian question in the months before the War. This brief survey of it will also help to clarify a number of other obscure points, such as the conflicting policies at Vienna, Berchtold's hesitations and mistakes, Austro-German friction, and the Konopischt interview of Emperor William and Franz Ferdinand, about which so many mysterious insinuations have been made.

Russia meanwhile was taking advantage of the situation to win Rumania over to a seat beside the Triple Entente and form a new Balkan group under Russian patronage to replace that which had been broken up by Bulgaria in the Second Balkan War. Though the Tsar ruled over Rumanian populations in Bessarabia, Russian ministers at Bucharest sought to divert Rumanian irredentist ambitions away from Bessarabia to Transylvania. Russia had shrewdly used her influence on the side of Rumania to secure for her the "compensations" in the Treaty of Bucharest.[221] Rumanians noted with gratitude that, in contrast

Der deutsch-englische Gegensatz und sein Einfluss auf die Balkanpolitik Oesterreich-Ungarns (Berlin, 1922), pp. 36 ff.

[221] G.P., XXXIX, 433 ff., 445 ff., 464 ff. *Cf.* also Izvolski to Sazonov, Aug. 1/14, 1913, congratulating him on his Russian policy at Bucharest: "Your diplomatic *chef d'oeuvre* has been the detachment of Rumania from Austria, which I had always dreamed of, but which I had not been able or known how to accomplish;" M.F.R., p. 408; L.N., II, 133; Stieve, III, 243.

to Austria's "perfidious" effort to bring about a revision of the Treaty, Russia had finally joined with Germany in preventing a revision.

Russia's purpose in winning Rumania as part of her preparation for a general European war is well indicated in Sazonov's secret report to the Tsar in December, 1913:

> While repeating my wish for the prolongation as far as possible of the *status quo,* it is also necessary to repeat that the Straits Question can hardly advance a step except by the favor of European complications. These complications, to judge by present circumstances, would find us in alliance with France, and in a possible but not at all assured, alliance with England, or at least with her as a benevolent neutral. In the Balkans, in case of European complications, we could count on Serbia, and perhaps on Rumania. From this there results clearly as the task of our diplomacy the creation of conditions for as intimate a *rapprochement* as possible with Rumania. This policy ought to be as persistent as it is circumspect and devoid of rashness. The position of Rumania in the Balkans recalls in many respects that of Italy in Europe. These two powers are subject to megalomania, and, not having strength enough to accomplish their projects openly, are obliged to content themselves with an opportunist policy, observing always on which side lies force, in order that they may range themselves on this side. . . .
>
> Two factors play a great rôle in the instability of the present situation in the Balkans. The first is Austria-Hungary, with the manifest increase of the nationality movement caused by the success of the Serbs and the Rumanians, and the effect of these successes upon their racial brothers within the frontiers of the Hapsburg Monarchy. The second factor is that it is impossible for Bulgaria to resign herself to the painful results of the Treaty of Bucharest.[222]

[222] Secret report of Sazonov to Nicholas II, Nov. 23/Dec. 6, 1913; Adamov, *Konstantinopol i Prolivy,* 74 f.; L.N., II, 371-2; Stieve, III, 382.

Partly as a result of Sazonov's policy, when a new Russian Minister arrived at Bucharest in January, 1914, he found an exceedingly warm welcome in Governmental circles:

> Again and again, sentiments of genuine friendship for Russia have been expressed to me. I found the same welcome in society here. I have spoken to former Ministers, Senators, Deputies, and various leaders of the Rumanian army. . . . To my mind, all this corroborates the fact already pointed out by my predecessor, and also emphasized by my French and English colleagues, that an important and perhaps decisive change in public opinion has been brought about here in favor of Russia. The events of last year which have inspired the Rumanians, and above all their military leaders, with confidence in their own strength, have at the same time also encouraged the efforts of the Irredentists. These are not so much directed against Russia, as toward Transylvania with its three million Rumanians. This latter circumstance also naturally tends to enhance Rumania's sympathy for Russia.[223]

Early in 1914 Russia took further steps to win Rumania. She promoted a Serb-Greek-Rumanian combination, which, while ostensibly aiming at peace and the preservation of the *status quo* in the Balkans, might be used by Russia to solve the Straits Question at a time of "European complications." It also fell in with Russia's policy of supporting Serbia against Austria. In order to bring about such a combination, Sazonov had long interviews with the Serbian and Greek Premiers, M. Pashitch and M. Venizelos, in February, 1914.[224] M. Pashitch also had an encouraging

[223] Poklevski-Koziel, Russian Minister at Bucharest, to Sazonov, Jan. 11/24, 1914; Siebert-Schreiner, p. 436.

[224] Doulcet, Chargé d'Affaires at St. Petersburg, to Doumergue, Feb. 5, 1914; "M. Venizelos has made an excellent impression . . . [Sazonov] has the impression that a very close accord exists between Greece and Serbia against every attack of the Turks; with Rumania the ties are less close, but the visit of M. Venizelos to Bucharest will tend to tighten them;" *Affaires Balkaniques,* III, 112.

and significant talk with the Tsar, of which he has left an interesting account:

> The audience lasted a full hour. The Tsar received me in his cabinet. When I entered, the Tsar was already there and at my entrance he came to meet me at the door, stretched out his hand without waiting for my greeting and invited me to be seated. . . . I set forth the Serbian policy which amounts to this, that she desires the maintenance of peace in the Balkans, and that new complications be avoided, since Serbia needs peace in order to recuperate, and in order that she may arm herself afresh for the defense of Serbian national interests. I also set forth the difficulties which Serbia will have to meet in the pursuit of her peaceful policy. Bulgaria, Turkey, and Austria are dissatisfied: Turkey because she lost in the war with the Balkan States; Bulgaria because she could not retain or acquire all that she wished; and Austria because she lost the prospect of an advance to Salonica. . . .
>
> Thereupon the Tsar answered: We have confidence in the new Rumanian [Bratianu] Government, that it will attach itself as closely as possible to Russia. He did not believe that matters would be allowed to go so far as to call in question the Peace of Bucharest. . . . I took occasion to remark that at the time of my stay in Bucharest I had a conference with Bratianu, and Bratianu was at that time very enthusiastic over the idea of an alliance with Greece and Serbia. I also remarked that I intended to return home by way of Bucharest in order to see whether Bratianu still retained the same willingness and views which he had revealed to me when I was in Bucharest. The Tsar said that would be very good, and that Rumania had three and a half million co-nationals in Austria-Hungary and that these desired union with Rumania. Thereupon, I said to him that the Transylvanian Rumanians were better nationalists than the Rumanians in Rumania. . . .
>
> I led the conversation around to a discussion of Austria's deliveries of arms to Bulgaria, namely that Austria had

furnished arms and munitions out of her magazines and that Bulgaria had received cannon also. And again the Tsar added that Germany too was supporting Bulgaria. I begged him that Russia should likewise aid us, and that out of her magazines she should deliver to us 120,000 rifles and munitions and some few cannon, particularly howitzers, if they could spare them, because the Turks had held up delivery of our heavy guns when they were in transport immediately before the war. The Tsar asked me if I had spoken about the matter to any of the Russian Ministers. I said, to the Minister of War, Sukhomlinov, and to Sazonov; and the Minister of War had said, it would be all right if Russian policy permitted it. And here I took occasion to tell the Tsar how pleased we were that Russia had armed herself so thoroughly; it gave us a feeling of security and hope for a better future. The Tsar said that they had done a great deal, and were still doing much. For that reason their munition establishments could not assume the task of manufacturing arms for us. This gave me occasion to say to the Tsar that immediately upon my return from Tsarskoe Selo, I would furnish Sazonov with an estimate of what we needed. He said that was all right, for he would receive Sazonov on the morrow, and would see what we needed. They would do all they could to lighten the situation for us. He asked me what we needed. I told him what I had noted down on the slip I had prepared for Sazonov. . . .

The Tsar inquired how many Serbo-Croats lived in Austria-Hungary, and what they were now believing and desiring. I replied about six millions, and told him where they lived. I also told him of the Slovenes, that they, too, were gravitating to the Serbo-Croats, and would adopt the Serbo-Croatian language, owing to the fact that their dialect is bad and that they have long lost their national independence. Then I told him that just at this time there was a Slovene stopping at St. Petersburg who was working for the establishment of a South-Slav Bank, and was trying to win over the Russian banks to the project. This was quite agreeable to the Tsar, and he said it was very necessary that the Russian banks should take a greater interest in the Slavic countries, and that it would be a good thing if Hribar should succeed with his mission.

I then told the Tsar how great a change in sentiment had taken place among the Slavs of Austria-Hungary—how many Starcevitch followers there were who formerly expected salvation from Austria, but now comprehended that this salvation could come to them only from Russia or Serbia, and that they could scarcely await the opportunity to see their desires fulfilled. Then I told him that for every rifle we received, we would have a soldier from these countries to carry it. . . . He asked how many soldiers Serbia could put into the field. Serbia, said the Tsar, had astonished the world when she marched out 400,000 men. I replied: We believe that we can put half a million well clothed and armed soldiers into the field. "That is enough; that is no trifle; one can go a great way with that" [said the Tsar].

Thereupon we discussed the need of fostering the alliance with Greece, for, aside from other considerations, we shall thus safeguard our incoming and outgoing commerce. Furthermore, we must labor to bring about an alliance upon a broader basis with Rumania, and not alone upon the basis of safeguarding the Treaty of Bucharest. . . .

[Pashitch then begged the Tsar to permit a marriage between the Serbian Crown Prince and a Russian Grand Duchess. The Tsar replied smilingly that he had no objections, but followed the principle of allowing his children to choose for themselves.]

Upon my taking leave, the Tsar accompanied me to the door and asked me especially and repeatedly to present greetings to the King, not only from himself, but also from the Tsarina and his family, and wished him good health: "For Serbia we shall do everything; greet the King for me and tell him [in Russian]: For Serbia we shall do everything." [225]

[225] Report of Pashitch of his audience with the Tsar, Feb. 2, 1914; Bogitchevitch, pp. 170-180; *Deutschland Schuldig?*, pp. 130-136.

While thus protesting to the Tsar his desire for peace, M. Pashitch, it is to be noted, asked for "120,000 rifles and munitions and some few cannon"; he spoke of the Slavs in Austria-Hungary "who now comprehend that their salvation can come only from Russia and Serbia, and who can scarcely wait"; and he urged an alliance with Rumania, "not alone upon the basis of safeguarding the Treaty of Bucharest" but with a view to the "three and a half million Transylvanian Rumanians who were better nationalists than the Rumanians in Rumania." Having indicated his real desires to the Tsar, he then set out with Venizelos for the Rumanian capital. Their visit was at once reported to Conrad at Vienna by the Austrian military attaché at Bucharest:

> Premiers Pashitch and Venizelos have spent two days together in Bucharest, highly pleased with their visit, as they both say, and today started together on their return journey to Belgrade and Athens. Their visit is said to concern measures to be taken in case any other State threatens to overthrow by force the terms of the Peace of Bucharest. Pashitch proceeds from the fixed assumption that Turkey and Bulgaria have signed a convention directed against Serbia and Greece, and that its unquestioned existence demands that these two States and Rumania shall join together. The result of the conference here, according to my informant, is a complete agreement of views as to the future attitude of the three States, though Rumania has not entered into any binding engagements. . . . Undoubtedly Russia wants a new Balkan League, and is working in this direction at high pressure.[226]

[226] Hranilovitch to Conrad, Feb. 11, 1914; Conrad, III, 555. That Hranilovitch was substantially correct is seen from the reports of the Russian and French Ministers at Belgrade: Hartwig to Sazonov, Feb. 11/24, 1914 (Siebert-Schreiner, p. 440); and Descos to Doumergue, Feb. H. (*Affaires Balkaniques,* III, p. 113): "M. Patchou [Acting Minister of Foreign Affairs in Serbia] tells me that, according to news from Bucharest, the Bratianu Cabinet will be much more decided and more hostile to

As a further link to bind Russia and Rumania together the Tsar invited the Crown Prince with his wife and son, Prince Carol, to visit Russia. They started on March 27, 1914, and stayed three weeks. One of the objects in view was believed to be the possibility of arranging a marriage between Prince Carol and one of the Tsar's daughters. Such a marriage would obviously strengthen the increasingly close relations between Bucharest and St. Petersburg, and help swing Rumania away from the Triple Alliance into the current of Sazonov's active Balkan policy. Prince Carol, who would ultimately be the ruler of Rumania, had none of King Carol's sympathies for Germany and the Hohenzollerns. He had been educated under the influence of M. Jorga, one of Rumania's strongest nationalist and anti-Austrian leaders.[227] The visit met with such success that in May, Sazonov told the French and English Ambassadors, that, though no marriage was definitely settled, the Tsar's second daughter had declared herself ready for the match.[228]

On June 14, 1914, the Tsar and Tsarina, accompanied by M. Sazonov, returned the visit of the Rumanian Princes. As they stepped ashore from the imperial yacht at Constanza, the sun broke through the clouds after days of heavy rain and added its warmth and brightness to the welcome of the cheering Rumanian populace. King Carol, wearing the uniform of a Russian field marshal, was photographed with his imperial guests, and an enterprising Rumanian Press saw to it that even the most remote villages of Transylvania had full news of the Tsar's visit, with all sorts of exaggerated hopes as to the coöperation of Russia with Rumania. M. Sazonov and M. Bratianu even went on a

Austria than the preceding Ministry, and that Serbia is absolutely sure of Rumania."

227 Conrad, III, 481 ff., 494 ff., 549 ff., 633 ff.; G.P., XXXIX, 456, 474 ff., 496 501, 566.

228 Adamov, *Konstantinopol i Prolivy,* I, 357, note 1. The World War put an end to the projected match.

walking tour together to Transylvania. "I did not hear of this tactless excursion until it was over" writes the Austrian Minister, Count Czernin, "but I shared Berchtold's surprise at such a proceeding."[229] In the private political conversations which M. Sazonov had with M. Bratianu, the Russian Minister gave the impression that important changes were coming in the European political situation, and that Rumania would not fare badly "if she understood the signs of the times and listened to counsels of wisdom."[230]

M. Bratianu in return assured Sazonov that "Rumania was not obligated in any way to take part in any war whatever, except where her own individual interests were directly concerned." Not finding this Delphic utterance sufficiently clear, and wishing to press him to a more definite statement, Sazonov bluntly asked Bratianu the significant leading question: "What would be Rumania's attitude in case of an armed conflict between Russia and Austria-Hungary, if the former were obliged by circumstances to resort to military action?" Bratianu replied that "the attitude of Rumania in this case would depend on the circumstances which led Russia to resort to military action against Austria-Hungary, as well as upon what Rumania's interests demanded at the given moment." From this conversation Sazonov carried away the comfortable conclusion that, "Rumania is not bound by any obligation which would force her to act with Austria and against us under all circumstances, but, in reality, in case of war between us and Austria-Hungary, Rumania will take the side which will be

229 Czernin, *In the World War,* p. 112.

230 P. Lindenberg, *König Karl von Rumänien,* II, 240 ff., 288 ff. Lindenberg writes with warm feeling for King Carol and with some resentment against Russia. He cites no documents but appears to have had access to King Carol's papers, as well as the King's own assistance, in writing the work which was nearly completed when the War broke out. For accounts of the Constanza meeting as reported to Berlin, see G.P., XXXIX, 520-529.

strongest and which will be in a position to promise her the greatest gains." [231]

Vienna had been viewing with increasing fears and suspicions the signs of growing intimacy between Bucharest and St. Petersburg, as well as the formation of a Serb-Greek-Rumanian combination, which originated primarily in common hatred of Bulgaria but which might easily be directed against the Dual Monarchy. How was Austria to deal with this danger that Rumania would gravitate to the side of the Triple Entente?

Baron Conrad, while willing to agree with any measures which aimed at winning back Rumania, or making her declare her position more definitely, either for or against Austria, had his staff work out plans for a campaign against Rumania. He advised the building of defensive fortifications on the Rumanian frontier, or better still, a preventive war against Serbia, which would rid Austria once and for all of the Greater Serbia danger and clarify the general political situation.[232] But his advice was not followed, because Emperor Francis Joseph, Archduke Franz Ferdinand, Count Tisza, and the German Emperor were all opposed to any steps which might further antagonize Rumania.[233]

Count Berchtold, like other weak and undecided persons, preferred to wait and see; he hoped Rumania could be won

231 Sazonov's report to the Tsar, June 11/24, 1914; Adamov, pp. 356-363; L.N., II, 377-384. Sazonov also pointed out to the Tsar how he had successfully flattered Rumania and increased her prestige among the other Balkan States by associating her with the Great Powers in the discussion for keeping the Straits open to commerce during the Tripolitan War. Similarly on July 24, 1914, upon the news of the Austrian ultimatum to Serbia, M. Diamandi, the Rumanian Minister in St. Petersburg, was invited to the important luncheon with M. Sazonov, M. Paléologue and Sir George Buchanan. Such flattery often counts for much in diplomacy, as elsewhere. M. Diamandi has related his version of the Constanza meeting in *Revue des Deux Mondes,* Jan. 1, 1928, pp. 129-143.

232 Conrad, III, 404 f., 554, 626, 640-648.

233 G.P., XXXIX, 333 ff., 358 ff., 511, 515 f.

back by concessions. With this in view, Tisza undertook negotiations to conciliate the Rumanians in Transylvania; but, owing to the selfish obstinacy of the Magyars on one side, and the excessive demands and bitterness of the Rumanians on the other, these negotiations proved futile, and were abandoned at the end of March, 1914.[234] In the hope of winning back Rumanian sentiment in favor of Austria, Berchtold also sent Count Czernin as Minister to Bucharest in October, 1913, in place of Prince Fürstenberg, who was personally obnoxious to some of the Rumanian Cabinet. Czernin was expected to be *persona gratissima* at Bucharest. He was a protégé of Franz Ferdinand, and had written a pamphlet some years before advocating the rights of the nationalities oppressed by the Magyars. He had taken pains to inquire into the wishes of the Transylvanian Rumanians. After reaching Bucharest he made it a point to express publicly his hopes that the Hungarian Government would make concessions in the negotiations which Tisza was then carrying on. He earnestly tried to carry out Berchtold's instructions to secure better relations between the two countries who were allies in form, but were becoming enemies in fact. But in a few months Czernin realized that his mission was hopeless. He found that King Carol stood almost alone in his sympathy with the Triple Alliance. The treaties which attached his country to Germany and Austria had been kept so secret that they were known only to the King himself, to the Premier, M. Bratianu, and to one or two others. No other Ministers knew of them or felt bound by them, so that it often happened that Rumanian diplomats abroad worked on the side of the Triple Entente. So seriously did King Carol feel his own weakness in the face of Rumanian popular sentiment, that he ad-

234 Conrad, III, 553, 556, 636. For the views of William II and Franz Ferdinand at Konopischt on this Rumanian problem, see below, Vol. II, ch. i; and G.P., XXXIX, 364-370.

mitted to Count Czernin in December, 1913, that "under existing circumstances he would be unable to side with Austria in a war." [235]

So Count Czernin became convinced that Berchtold's optimistic do-nothing policy was folly. Like Conrad, he too came around to thinking something more positive must be done. In March, 1914, he closed one of his pessimistic despatches with the prophetic warning:

> I am in duty bound to call your attention to the fact that we are slipping down an inclined plane here with frightful speed, and there is no time to be lost. It would be an ostrich policy to shut our eyes and let things go on as they are here. For I must most energetically and emphatically repeat, a hundred times if necessary, the Austro-Rumanian Treaty [of Alliance] is a worthless scrap of paper. In case of war, Rumania will not take a stand on the side of the Dual Monarchy. The present situation is the most unfavorable imaginable for us, since it binds us without benefiting us. A passive policy of hesitation, of floating with the current, of *laissez faire, laissez aller*, will not improve this situation. Nothing but a clear-cut positive action on Austria's part, nothing but an iron, unbending determination to compel Rumania to show her colors, can avert at the twelfth hour unfathomable disaster.[236]

Czernin suggested several alternative plans of action which the Dual Monarchy might adopt. One was the cession of Transylvania to Rumania, with the stipulation that the Rumanian Kingdom, thus enlarged, be incorporated into the Hapsburg Empire, similar to Bavaria's position in the German Empire. Czernin thought this plan desirable, but impracticable of realization. As to a preventive war against Serbia, urged by Conrad, Czernin was not one of

[235] Conrad, III, 634.

[236] Closing paragraph of a long and remarkable report to Berchtold on the Rumanian situation, March 11, 1914; Conrad, III, 781-789; *cf.* also Czernin's despatch of April 2; *ibid.*, 633-638.

those who, like Tisza, argued that a war with Serbia was useless and undesirable because Austria-Hungary was already oversaturated with Slavs; no one, to be sure, wanted any more Serbs in the Dual Monarchy, he said; but after a successful war against Serbia, it would be possible to use Serbian territory to win the good-will of the other Balkan states; Greece and Bulgaria could be given what they wanted in Macedonia; Albania could be rounded out to the east; and Rumania be given the Timok-Njotin district, a corner in northeast Serbia partly populated by Rumanians. The point, however, which Czernin particularly urged, was that the status of the Treaty of Alliance be cleared up. In the present situation it was not worth a scrap of paper to Austria, because King Carol no longer controlled the situation and would be forced by public opinion to repudiate it or to resign, in case a Russian attack on Austria should give rise to the *casus foederis.* Austria meanwhile had her hands tied by the treaty, and could not enter into other diplomatic negotiations which might offend Rumania. To make Rumania take a stand openly, either for or against Austria, Czernin therefore suggested a newspaper "indiscretion" by which the existence of the treaty should be allowed to leak out; one could then tell by the way the Rumanian Government denied the accuracy of the newspaper account, and the way public opinion in Rumania discussed it, what Austria could count upon. But Berchtold rejected all these suggestions. He merely gave a half-hearted authorization to Czernin to sound King Carol tactfully as to whether the King would not be willing that the treaty should be made public. But, as Czernin had foreseen, when he broached the subject, King Carol delicately evaded it. So Berchtold and his associates were left uncertain whether, in a crisis, the secret treaty with Rumania would hold or not.

Another suggestion by which Austria might offset the

probable loss of Rumania was that Austria should follow Russia's example, and build up a Balkan League under her own patronage to balance the feared Serb-Greek-Rumanian league under Russian patronage. Bulgaria and Turkey, smarting from recent defeats and eager for support, might be brought together by Austria and be eventually drawn into the Triple Alliance circle to make up for Rumania's "desertion." In other words, Austria might shift the pivot of her Balkan policy from Bucharest to Sofia. Such a Bulgarophil diplomatic program had already been attempted by Berchtold during the Balkan Wars; but it had met with no success and had caused serious differences of opinion between Vienna and Berlin. In the spring of 1914, it was taken up again at Vienna and a long memorandum for its accomplishment had been worked out at the moment that Franz Ferdinand was assassinated at Sarajevo. But there was still the serious difficulty: would Germany consent to this program of her Austrian Ally? Of late Emperor William had become strongly philhellene, supporting Greek claims to the Aegean Islands against Turkish interests.[237] Would he ever consent to abandon a Hohenzollern like King Carol, whom he greatly respected and trusted, and take in his place Ferdinand of Bulgaria, for whom he had a personal aversion and who was universally regarded with distrust? This question of shifting the pivot from Bucharest to Sofia had long been argued without agreement between Berlin and Vienna during and after the Balkan Wars. It also formed the larger part of the fateful memoir and royal missive from Francis Joseph which the Austrian Ambassador handed to William II after lunch at Potsdam on July 5, 1914, as will be related in the second volume, "After Sarajevo."

This Rumanian problem was one of the many points on

[237] Conrad, III, 644, 655 ff., 662. On the Kaiser's philhellenism see above, notes 186-190, in connection with intrigues over Kavala.

which there was a sharp divergence between German and Austrian policy. Though the relations between Bucharest and Vienna had become increasingly strained, Bucharest and Berlin had remained on terms of firm cordiality, and Germany had done much to keep King Carol and his people loyal to the Triple Alliance. These ties had been originally cemented through the kinship of the Hohenzollern rulers. They had been strengthened by the long residence at Bucharest of Kiderlen-Wächter, one of Germany's ablest diplomats since Bismarck's day. Even when Kiderlen was called to Berlin to pilot the Foreign Office in the last months of Bülow and the first years of Bethmann, he continued the close friendly relations which he had established with King Carol and influential Rumanian politicians.[238] Jon Bratianu the Younger, the leader of the so-called Liberal Party, at heart tended more and more to the side of the Triple Entente. He had been educated in France, visited Paris annually, and naturally had Gallic sympathies. These were strengthened by the political calculation as far back as 1909 that the Entente might prove a stronger combination than the Triple Alliance in a general European war, and might therefore be a safer group for Rumania to join.[239] In spite of this, however, he had confidentially assured Kiderlen that "he had inherited from his father the fundamental principle that Rumania's path to Vienna lies through Berlin, and that he had the firm conviction that everything which Berlin advised was for Rumania's genuine best interests."[240] He adhered to this principle and Germany did nothing to forfeit his well-placed confidence.

During the First Balkan War, when Rumania demanded territorial "compensations" from Bulgaria, Germany recognized her demands as justified. Berlin privately urged wise moderation and concessions both at Bucharest and Sofia, in

238 *Cf.* E. Jäckh, *Kiderlen-Wächter,* I, 179-219; II, 161-237, *passim.*

239 G.P., XXVII, 200.

240 G.P., XXVII, p. 223.

order to prevent a Bulgaro-Rumanian war, which would add another Balkan complication and still further threaten the peace of Europe. But at the same time, both before and during the St. Petersburg Conference, Germany exerted her influence strongly in favor of Rumania's claims. She refused all Berchtold's Bulgarophil projects for giving Bulgaria Salonica, Samothrace, or money, as a solace for ceding Silistria to Rumania; she feared that such gifts would be frowned upon by Rumania and increase her distrust of the Triple Alliance—not to mention other objections.[241]

When the Second Balkan War broke out, and Rumanian indignation ran high against Berchtold's suspected Bulgarophilism, Germany refused to join him in putting pressure on Rumania to keep quiet. Berlin regretted his ill-judged effort, believing it would not be successful, and would only deepen Rumanian indignation—as proved to be the case. On the contrary, Germany recognized that Bulgaria's attack on Serbia was the psychological moment for King Carol to make good the claims which Bulgaria had been refusing; Germany could not assume the responsibility of advising Rumania to neglect her vital interests for the sake of Austria's desire to see a strong Bulgaria in Serbia's rear. Resentment would be so great in Bucharest that Rumania would certainly swing over from the Triple Alliance to the Triple Entente. It was a poor policy for Austria to risk losing a faithful ally like King Carol for the hope of getting a treacherous friend like King Ferdinand of Bulgaria. Austria made a mistake in letting herself be so obsessed with the fear of a Greater Serbia and in forgetting that she ruled over Rumanians as well as Slavs. Germany accepted the Rumanian point of view: Austria says that she cannot tolerate a Greater Serbia, but no more can Rumania tolerate a Greater Bulgaria.[242] Berchtold was so

[241] G.P., XXXIV, 444 ff., 456, 459 ff., 520 f., 660 ff., 674 f., 687 ff., 820 ff., 873 ff.

[242] G.P., XXXV, 46 ff., 61 ff., 66 ff.

put out with Germany's solicitude for Rumania's feelings, that he thrice made formal representations in Berlin against it.[243] But the German Secretary of State, Jagow, while admitting some of his arguments, noted: "Yes, but we do not need by a long shot to join in all Vienna's stupidities."[244] Accordingly, after King Carol mobilized his army and seized the New Dobrudja by force from Bulgaria, Germany confirmed him in his new territories by helping to prevent the Austrian and Russian efforts to have the Treaty of Bucharest subjected to revision by the Great Powers.

This divergence of views between Berlin and Vienna continued during the months following the Balkan Wars. Bethmann and the Kaiser still placed their hopes on Rumanian loyalty, while Berchtold and his advisers inclined toward closer relations with Bulgaria, since Rumania seemed to be lost. In the spring of 1914 Rumania's "desertion" seemed more and more probable. This was partly owing to the active wooing by Russia, and to the propagandist articles by French journalists and professors, who visited and lectured at Bucharest. It was also partly owing to the Magyar oppression of the Rumanians living in Transylvania and to Austria's suspected Bulgarophilism. The anti-Austrian demonstrations of the chauvinistic Rumanian "League of Civilization" became louder, and the attacks of the Rumanian Press more virulent. An anti-Hapsburg play, "Mr. Notary," written by a Transylvanian, was being performed at the National Theatre in Bucharest. It roused the people to a frenzy. They marched past the royal palace singing war songs and crying, "Down with Austria" and "Long live Russia." King Carol genuinely regretted all this. But he feared to censor "Mr. Notary," lest it serve only to advertise it and make matters worse.[245] In the

243 G.P., XXXIV, 820 ff.; XXXV, 66 ff., 115 ff.

244 G.P., XXXIV, 824.

245 Despatches of Waldthausen, German Minister at Bucharest, January-April, 1914; G.P., XXXIX, 471-497. These despatches hardly bear

winter he had admitted that, if the anti-Austrian feeling kept up, Rumania would not march with Austria in case of a European war; a treaty of alliance was not enough by itself; it must have popular support. In the spring he confessed that his country was "in a complete paroxysm," and that he was helpless to stem the tide of popular hatred of Austria.[246]

This situation disturbed Berlin considerably. It led the Kaiser to make the Rumanian danger the main subject of his discussions with Franz Ferdinand and the Austrians on his visits to Vienna, Miramar, and Konopischt shortly before the Sarajevo assassination. He hoped that Count Tisza the Hungarian Premier, would make concessions to the Rumanians in Transylvania. Germany urged that nothing be done like Conrad's plan of fortifying the Carpathian frontier which would certainly be unfavorably interpreted in Bucharest, or like Czernin's schemes for getting the Rumanian treaty made public.[247] But on the whole Germany was inclined to take a less tragic view of the Rumanian situation than Austria, and tried to calm the latter's fears. She hoped that the paroxysm would pass, and that Rumania would swing back to her traditional loyalty, if the Triple Alliance Powers did not show too much uneasiness and nervousness. It might be that in case of a European war King Carol might have difficulty in fulfilling his

out Czernin's reports to Berchtold (April 2, 1914; Conrad, III, 634) that Waldthausen had no real insight into the situation, allowed the wool to be pulled over his eyes, and was nothing more than "a human phonograph," reporting credulously to Berlin whatever he was told by the Rumanian ministers, "who are a hundred times cleverer than he." Czernin, who was not lacking in a sufficiently good opinion of his own astuteness, says of himself: "Bratianu reports to me daily that I am his real friend, that he has never been able to speak with a diplomatic representative so frankly as with me, and all such words. He thinks I am more of a fool than I really am. . . . But I do not trust him around the corner" (*ibid.*, p. 786).

[246] Waldthausen to Bethmann, Dec. 6, 1913, and Mar. 30, 1914; G.P., XXXIX, 466, 481.

[247] G.P., XXXIX, 506, 511, 515 f.

treaty obligations. But even so, it was still a long step from this to his active participation on the enemy's side, "quite aside from the fact that complications between the Great Powers are hardly to be expected in the immediate future."[248] Rumania's future remained a puzzling riddle, adding still further to Balkan instability, uncertainties, and intrigues.

THE LIMAN VON SANDERS AFFAIR

Hitherto we have been considering the Balkan Problems chiefly from the point of view of the rival interests of Austria and Russia and the nationalist aspirations of the Balkan States themselves. In the latter part of 1913 the appointment of the German General Liman von Sanders at Constantinople caused friction between Russia and Germany, which for several reasons deserves more attention than it has usually been given. It was the last diplomatic crisis of importance before July, 1914, and, like the latter, involved the influence and prestige of these two Great Powers in the Near East. But it is a good example of how such a crisis can be settled, if there is sufficient good will on both sides. Its satisfactory settlement is a proof of the proposition that war is not "inevitable." We are at last in fairly full possession of the essential documents relating to the affair,[249] and are therefore able to follow the inner

248 Jagow to Waldthausen, April 24, 1914; G.P., XXXIX, 505 f. *Cf.* also the much more pessimistic views of Vienna as to Rumania, *ibid.*, pp. 434-515, *passim;* and Conrad, III, 549-563, 633-648, 781-789.

249 From the Russian side, M.F.R., pp. 629-693 contains a satisfactorily abundant correspondence between Sazonov and his diplomatic agents—Giers at Constantinople, Izvolski at Paris, and Benckendorff at London; only part of this is included in L.N., II, 173-279; Stieve, III, 352-439, IV, 1-28; and Siebert-Schreiner, pp. 678-708. The interesting report to the Tsar of the conversations of the Russian Premier, Kokovtsev, with Emperor William and Bethmann-Hollweg on the subject is printed in M.F.R., pp. 624 ff.; L.N., II, 414 ff.; Stieve, III, 415 ff. For the minutes of the Secret Ministerial Councils concerning counter-measures to compel Germany and Turkey to abandon the German Military Mission, see Adamov, *Konstantinopol i Prolivy*, I, 61-77 (with Sazonov's reports to the Tsar);

workings of Sazonov's mind, with its blunt rudeness of expression, its fickle alternations of pessimism and optimism, its fear of Russian "public opinion," and its dangerous inclination to resort to military measures as a "bluff" to force a diplomatic victory. We are also enabled to get an insight into the domestic cross currents at St. Petersburg, the secret workings of the Triple Entente, and the exceedingly moderate and conciliatory attitude of Germany.

M. Sazonov was highly indignant when he heard in November, 1913, that a German General, Liman von Sanders, was to command Turkish troops at Constantinople. In his mind it was a sly, unjustifiable, and not-to-be-permitted move on Germany's part to gain further power and prestige in the Ottoman Empire and so to thwart Russia in her "historic mission" of securing control of Constantinople and the Straits—regions which he curiously but significantly speaks of as "bordering on our frontier." He instantly telegraphed from Ialta in the Crimea to the Russian Ambassador in Berlin:

> Learning about the agreement of Germany with Turkey relating to the military instructors, I am extremely astonished that this serious question was not touched upon by the [German] Chancellor at the time of my frank and friendly explanations with him. Of itself, a German Military Mission in regions bordering on our frontier could not but

I. Zakher, "Konstantinopol i Prolivy" in *Krasnyi Arkhiv,* VI, 48-76; VII, 32-54, 1924 (with important and significant Russian Admiralty Reports); Pokrovski, *Drei Konferenzen,* pp. 32-45; Stieve, *Iswolski und der Weltkrieg* (Berlin, 1924), pp. 234-266 [English trans., appendix, 11]; Stieve, however, fails to observe the distinction between Old Style and New Style in discussing these councils. See also *Affaires Balkaniques,* III, 81-107, which evidently omits many important telegrams from the German side; *Deutschland Schuldig?* (Berlin, 1919), pp. 159-181; and, most important of all, G.P., XXXVIII, 193-318.

Good brief accounts of the Liman von Sanders affair may be found in Liman von Sanders, *Fünf Jahre Türkei* (Berlin, 1920), pp. 9-30; Montgelas, *The Case for the Central Powers,* 93-95; Brandenburg, pp. 393-395; Dickinson, pp. 348-9; and more fully, R. J. Kerner, in the *Slavonic Review,* VI, 12-27, 344-363, 543-560 (June, Dec., 1927; March, 1928).

> provoke violent irritation in Russian public opinion, and would certainly be interpreted as an act manifestly hostile to us. Especially also, the placing of Turkish troops in Constantinople under a German general must necessarily arouse suspicion and apprehension among us. Please speak in this sense to the German Government.[250]

Sazonov's indignation was shared and whetted by M. Delcassé—though for somewhat different reasons. The French Ambassador feared it foreshadowed a German "attempt to bring about a seizure of Turkey by the Triple Alliance Powers, to which the Triple Entente could not shut its eyes without prejudice to itself." [251] Germany already enjoyed tremendous economic and political power in Asia Minor because of the Bagdad Railway, Delcassé argued; now she would have a fleet in the Eastern Mediterranean and be getting a naval base and coaling station for it. Italy, too, would get concessions—the building of a harbor and railway at Adalia and the establishment of an Italian sphere of influence in southern Asia Minor. Austria would likewise want something for herself. As far as Italian and Austrian ambitions in Asia Minor were concerned, Delcassé was not so far astray; but Germany was opposed to satisfying them, even though they were her allies, fearing that the other Powers would demand similar "compensations," and that this would mean the final carving up of Turkey. To this surgical operation Germany was strongly opposed

250 Sazonov to Sverbeev, Oct. 28/Nov. 10, 1913; sent also to Giers at Constantinople; M.F.R., p. 633. *Cf.* G.P., XXXVIII, 206-209.

251 *Cf.* Delcassé's Tgs. 700, 701, omitted from the French Yellow Book, but quoted in part by Adamov, p. 59. The first reference to the Liman von Sanders affair in the French *Affaires Balkaniques* (III, 81) is the apparently mild and laconic telegram from Delcassé of Nov. 17, 1913: "The sending of the new German military mission, whose head is to have the command of the Constantinople Army Corps, is preoccupying M. Sazonov." For other indications that Delcassé and Pichon *at first* encouraged Sazonov in his attitude of protest, see *ibid.*, pp. 84, 88, 92 f., 96 f.; G. P., XXXVIII, 211, 224 ff.; and Siebert-Schreiner, p. 678 f.; see also below, note 294.

at this time, because she feared it might lead to a conflict between the Great Powers; and also because, being tolerably well situated in Asiatic Turkey and enjoying much influence at Constantinople, she wanted to preserve the *status quo* as long as possible, or at least until the Powers could agree upon an amicable and mutually satisfactory basis of division.[252] A few days later Delcassé sent the French Government the gloomy warning: "The falling to pieces of Turkey has already begun, or is about to begin, and Germany will occupy a position guaranteeing to her all the advantages of a partition." [253]

The Liman von Sanders Mission originated with the Young Turk desire to westernize and modernize the administration of the Ottoman Empire. Soon after seizing power they had invited a number of distinguished foreigners to help them: two Frenchmen, M. Laurent, as financial adviser, and M. Baumann, to train the Turkish gendarmerie; a French trained jurisconsult, M. Léon Ostrorog, to assist in judicial reforms; Sir Richard Crawford to reorganize the customs service; Sir William Willcocks to start irrigation works in Mesopotamia; two other Englishmen, Admiral Sir Douglas Gamble and Admiral Limpus were to reorganize and train the navy, while a German General, Von der Goltz, who had already been in Turkish service, was to spend part of his time in training the Turkish army.

Von der Goltz, however, had found his position difficult on account of the lack of unity among the Young Turk officers, their tendency to mix politics with military matters, and their unwise system of promotions. He also complained of the lack of authority in his own hands, and eventually

252 For evidences that Germany was strongly opposed to the partition of Asiatic Turkey, though of course if the Entente Powers forced it, she wanted to have her fair share, see G.P., XXXIV, 207, 219 ff., 229 f., 255 f.; XXXVII, 474 ff.; XXXVIII, 41-48, 54-66, 93 ff., 129, 196-202; Conrad, III, 569 ff.; and Brandenburg, 389 ff. [Eng. trans. p. 456 ff.].

253 Adamov, I, 59.

abandoned the work.[254] The old Turkish officers and soldiers, into whom he had tried to infuse Prussian discipline and methods, proved poor material, and made a lamentable exhibition of themselves when Turkey was attacked by the Balkan Allies in the fall of 1912.

On January 2, 1913, during the armistice in the First Balkan War and the pending negotiations in London, the Young Turk Noradunghian confidentially asked Wangenheim, the German Ambassador in Constantinople, to find out for him as quickly as possible the terms on which the French General Eydoux had been engaged to reorganize and train the Greek army.[255] He was evidently contemplating something of the same kind for Turkey after the overwhelming defeats she had suffered in the past three months. The assassination of Nazim Pasha and the Cabinet Revolution in Constantinople, following the concessions made by the Turkish delegates in London, delayed whatever plans Noradunghian may have had in mind, but they brought into power Mahmud Shevket Pasha. With him were a group of patriotic and determined Young Turks, who were bent on energetic reforms in Turkey, with the assistance of European advisers, as the only hope of saving their country from an early and complete dissolution. As Von der Goltz and his companions had already given the Turks a start in German military methods, it was obvious that Mahmud Shevket should turn to Germany rather than to any other Power for new military instructors. Accordingly he begged the Kaiser, through the German Military Attaché in Constantinople, for the services of some Prussian officers for the strengthening of Constantinople. The Kaiser favored the idea, and on April 2 asked his Foreign Office whether it saw any political objections to the plan, adding that the

[254] G.P., V, 182, 186; IX, 3 f., 36 ff., 41, 226; XII, 134, 562, 566 ff.; XXIV, 150; XXV, 490, 527, 541, 612-622; XXVII, 243, 275-284; XXXVIII 214 f.

[255] G.P., XXXVIII, 193.

matter was not urgent, as it was not desired that the officers should go to Turkey until peace had put an end to the Balkan War. The Foreign Office had no objections.[256]

Long negotiations then began between the Turkish and German military authorities, which finally resulted by November in the signing of a definite contract for a German Military Mission of some forty-two German officers, headed by General Liman von Sanders.

Though it is commonly stated by Entente writers that Germany instigated the Liman von Sanders Mission, there is no indication of this in the German documents; in fact, the weight of evidence is against it, and in favor of the view that it was initiated by the Turks themselves for their own salvation.[257]

More important, however, than the origin of the German

[256] G.P., XXXVIII, 195 f.

[257] On Jan. 28, 1913, the Austrian Military Attaché in Constantinople, after hearing Wangenheim set forth "in his usual lively manner" Turkey's need of a general reorganization, reported to Conrad (III, 40): "As I now learn from a sure Turkish source, this reorganization plan does not originate with Baron Wangenheim, but with the former Turkish Ambassador in Paris, Munir Pasha. The latter put his views down in a memoir which he recommended to his friends and to Mahmud Shevket Pasha." Hilmi Pasha, the Turkish Ambassador in Vienna, correcting Dumaine's assertion to the contrary, assured Tschirschky that "the initiative came exclusively from the Turkish side" (G.P., XXXVIII, 228). Djemal Pasha, who was Minister of Public Works in January, 1913, and then became Military Governor of Constantinople in charge of the Army Corps which he later handed over to General Liman, explains in detail (*Memories of a Turkish Statesman, 1913-1919,* London, pp. 65-70), quoting Mahmud Shevket, how the German Military Mission originated with the latter's determination to strengthen the Turkish army by reorganizing it along the lines which German instructors for thirty years had been trying to introduce. His statements on this point deserve all the more credibility as they coincide very closely with Mahmud Shevket's expression of views to Wangenheim at the time, as now revealed in the German documents (especially G.P., XXXVIII, 198 ff.). Against this unanimous Turkish evidence is only the casual remark of General Liman himself (*Fünf Jahre Türkei,* pp. 12, 25) that the Mission was due to Wangenheim's initiative; but General Liman knew nothing of the whole matter until several months after it had been first broached; he may have gotten this erroneous idea from Wangenheim's zeal in furthering the Mission, or from the German Ambassador's tendency to magnify his own importance.

Military Mission were its aims and potential effects as viewed by the Turks, the Germans, and the Russians.

Mahmud Shevket and the Young Turks, in fear of Russian intrigues south of the Caucasus and in response to pressure for reforms in Armenia, decided in the spring of 1913 to ask for seventeen English inspectors for the Anatolian gendarmerie and civil administration. Grey at first assented, but later cut the number down to five out of regard for Russian and German susceptibilities.[258] At the same time Mahmud Shevket desired that Germany should send new military instructors to Turkey. He believed that it was only through Anglo-German coöperation that Turkey could be regenerated. As he explained to the German Ambassador on April 26, 1913:

> Turkey can only bring about her resurrection if she can count on Germany and England. That these two countries have hitherto been in opposition has been the chief cause of our misfortunes. I must therefore take care that Turkey becomes the ground on which an Anglo-German understanding shall take place. [After discussing the internal reforms needed, he continued.] We have few trained and reliable officials. Here foreign countries must help. I shall therefore turn to the various Cabinets with a request for reformers. For the reorganization of the army I count definitely upon Germany. This is the most important point in my program. The army must be reformed from the bottom up; politics must be driven out of the [Turkish] officer group. For this the activity of the officers of instruction, in the way they have been shoved in here and there into our organization as mere advisers, is not sufficient. Also for the reform of education I count upon the support of the German Government. I shall ask Italy for gendarme officers for Syria, and France for reorganizers for finance and for the postal and telegraph service. Austria's help I would rather not have. On the other hand, I need the Eng-

[258] G.P., XXXVIII, 32-41, 49-54, 58 f., 98.

> lish for the different administrative branches in the provinces of North and East Anatolia. . . . The navy also will be further reformed by the English. On the basis of a proposal by Admiral Limpus the ships will receive as commanders English officers not in active service.[259]

The German Ambassador listened eagerly to these plans of the Grand Vizier. He urged Germany to accede to the request for military instructors. He warmly welcomed Mahmud Shevket's idea of Anglo-German coöperation for strengthening Turkey, and let his imagination wander in happy political vistas of the future: "It opens for us prospects for an understanding with England, or at least the possibility of coöperation for the maintenance of the Turkish Empire. On the other hand, if England should refuse such coöperation with us, she could not ignore the influence which we should acquire by our controlling position in military matters and in the instruction of the youth. We should always be in a position through a skilful use of the German military reformers to control or paralyze possible separate efforts by the British." [260] But Wangenheim was such an optimistic enthusiast about the future of Turkey that his friends said he was "turkified," and he was so much inclined to exceed his functions and meddle in Turkish politics that he had sometimes to be called to order by the Kaiser.[261] One must therefore take his despatches with a grain of salt and be on one's guard against accepting completely his opinions as representing those of his Government.

259 Wangenheim to Bethmann, April 26, 1913; G.P., XXXVIII, 198 ff. These views of Mahmud Shevket, set forth on April 26, are the key-note and first elaboration of the Military Mission plan, and are echoed a month later in Wangenheim's despatches of May 21 and 29 (see next paragraph) which Professor Kerner quotes at length (*l.c.*, pp. 15-18).

260 Wangenheim to Bethmann, May 29, 1913; *ibid.*, p. 59; *cf.* also his despatch of May 22 repeating and endorsing Mahmud Shevket's request for a German military mission; *ibid.*, 201 f.

261 *Cf.* G.P., XXXIII, 323, 340.

The Kaiser was much more skeptical, and did not altogether endorse Wangenheim's enthusiasm. Commenting on Mahmud Shevket's plans quoted above, he wrote: "Many good intentions, but much that is fantastic! In reality this employment of various European nations for Turkey's internal affairs is a grand bridge to intrigues and the partition of Turkey! It is not so simple to set bounds to the Powers and restrict them to their duties! Especially not the British;" and he feared that a reorganized Turkish army might "also be used against us or the Bagdad Railway." [262] However, in spite of these reflections of the moment, the Kaiser had already approved the idea of German military instructors, and later urged that the slow arrangements for it be hurried up. On the whole, as he told the Russians in the fall, he seems to have regarded the mission as primarily a military, rather than a political, affair.

The Porte early notified the British Government of the project,[263] and it was discussed in a general way with the Tsar and King George upon their visit to Berlin on May 24 to attend the wedding of the Kaiser's daughter to the Guelf Duke of Brunswick. The Kaiser informed them of the Turkish request for German officers: "The Tsar as well as King George were wholly agreed. The King said: 'It is quite natural that they should turn to you for officers to reorganize their Army. We are asked to send people

[262] G.P., XXXVIII, 201.

[263] Wangenheim to Berlin Foreign Office, May 26, 1913 (*ibid.*, p. 49): "In the undeveloped conditions here the administration and gendarmerie need unconditionally the support of the army. Therefore a basic Anglo-German understanding concerning the work of reform is imperative. The Porte has informed London that the reorganization of the army and instruction is to fall to Germany. The English Embassy counsellor said to me day before yesterday of his own accord: 'Whether Germany and England want to or not, they will be led by necessity to uphold Turkey.'" Grey told Lichnowsky on May 30 that he agreed with Germany in wishing to preserve and strengthen Turkey, but thought all the Powers ought to assist in the reform work (*ibid.*, p. 55 note).

to reorganize their Police and Gendarmerie, which we shall do.' The Tsar also said that it was necessary to fortify the Tchataldja Line very strongly, so that the Bulgarians should not be able to get in [Constantinople]." [264]

Later Sazonov repeatedly objected that the German Government had acted unfairly in concealing everything from Russia about the matter until the news came out in November. He even complained of it to the King of Rumania at the Constanza meeting in June, 1914. This caused the Kaiser to make the pertinent, if not parliamentary, comment: "The old liar! I told it in the spring *personally* to the Tsar; if he did not inform Sazonov, that is not my affair. . . . If the Tsar did not tell him anything of it, he regarded the matter as not important enough to mention and as wholly natural." [265]

However, aside from the undoubted discussion by royalty at the wedding festivities in May, secrecy shrouded the plans for German officers in Turkey while the Balkan Wars (including Turkey) were still going on, and while the details of General Liman's contract were being worked

[264] Kaiser's marginal note, Dec. 3, 1913; *ibid.*, p. 232; *cf.* also to the same effect the Kaiser's statements to Kokovtsev, the Russian Prime Minister, in November, 1913; *ibid.*, 216, 219 comment 2; M.F.R., p. 638; Siebert-Schreiner, p. 676 f. Professor Kerner also mentions this marginal note of Dec. 3 (*l.c.*, p. 18), but later seems to cast doubt upon its trustworthiness, for he speaks of "a vague reference in May, 1913," which the Kaiser "asserts" (p. 25) and "claims" (p. 26) he made to the Tsar and George V. One might doubt the trustworthiness of the Kaiser's memory or sincerity in his notes and statements six months after the event, were it not that this Willy-Nicky-Georgie May conversation is confirmed by Jagow's contemporary despatch to Lichnowsky (May 27; G.P., XXXVIII, 52), and by the fact that the Tsar himself subsequently "admitted that the plan to send a German Military mission to Turkey had been told to him by the Kaiser at the time of the marriage festivities in Berlin" (Pourtalès to Bethmann, Jan. 31, 1914; *ibid.*, 307). What King George replied, when he was asked by Grey about this May conversation, does not appear (*cf.* Siebert-Schreiner, p. 705).

[265] G.P., XXXVIII, 318. For the quite different light in which Sazonov represented this Constanza conversation in his report to the Tsar, *cf.* Adamov, I, 357 f.; L.N., II, 378.

out. Such secrecy was only natural, because their publication might bring upon the Germans "the reproach of taking sides and cause political difficulties." [266] This secrecy was nevertheless unfortunate, both for M. Sazonov's personal feelings and consequently for the friendly relations between Russia and Germany. It was particularly unfortunate that no mention of the contract was made to him confidentially, when he passed through Berlin in October and had a frank and cordial discussion with the German Chancellor on the general political situation in Europe. Sazonov not unnaturally felt injured in his feelings by what seemed to him to be a lack of reciprocal frankness and friendliness on Bethmann's part. Bethmann on his part was genuinely innocent of any deliberate *suppressio veri.* He apparently failed to mention it simply because it did not occur to him. This explanation accords with his character, with his statement to Kokovtsev later, and with the fact that he had really known little about the Liman von Sanders arrangements, which had mainly been made through the military and not the diplomatic channels.[267]

General Liman von Sanders himself knew nothing of the project until it was proposed to him on June 15.[268] He was rightly believed to be a much abler man than Von der Goltz. Never having been to Turkey, he at once began to read through his predecessor's correspondence to get an idea of the kind of difficulties he would have to meet. He had plenty of time for this, as it was still many months before a contract was signed with Turkey defining his powers and duties and those of the forty-one subordinate

266 Jagow to Wangenheim, Aug. 24, 1913; G.P., XXXVIII, 204.

267 G.P., XXXVIII, 212 ff. Bethmann and the Foreign Office did not learn the final terms of General Liman's contract until they received a copy of it on Jan. 8, 1914, from the Prussian Ministry of War (*ibid.*, p. 213 note).

268 Liman, p. 9 ff. Bethmann was not informed of Liman's selection until June 30; G.P., XXXVIII, 202 f.

officers who eventually accompanied him. These were details which had to be worked out by the German and Turkish military authorities. In this connection General Liman says, and with truth:

> The work of the members of the Mission was to be strictly military. The wording of the contract shows this clearly. The charge made on many sides, in writings and newspapers, that it was also to have political activity is wholly incorrect.[269]

At the end of November, when the contract was finally ready and signed, General Liman was commanded to an audience with Emperor William. The Kaiser said to him in substance:

> You must not care in the least whether the Young Turks or the Old Turks are in power. You have only to do with the army. Get politics out of the Turkish corps of officers. Dabbling in politics is its greatest mistake. In Constantinople you will meet Admiral Limpus who is at the head of the English Naval Mission. Be on good terms with him. He works for the navy and you for the army. Each of you has his own separate field of work.[270]

On December 14, 1913, he finally arrived at the Turkish capital and was received with martial music and an honorary escort from the Constantinople Fire Department. But already, a month before his arrival, he had become the object of a diplomatic conflict which threatened to involve Russian and German prestige, or even the Triple Entente and the Triple Alliance.

On November 2, 1913, M. Giers, the Russian Ambassador at Constantinople, telegraphed to St. Petersburg announcing the rumor of a coming German Military Mission. According to the friendly explanations of his German colleague, Baron Wangenheim, it was to be like the French

269 Liman, 11.

270 Liman, 11.

Military Mission to Greece. But three days later Giers learned that General Liman would also have command of the Turkish Army Corps stationed at Constantinople. This was a new feature to which Russia and France at once, and eventually England, objected. It gave General Liman quite a different position from that of Von der Goltz before him, or from that of the French military instructor in Greece.[271]

On the day the news of the German Military Mission reached St. Petersburg, Sazonov was absent in the Crimea making a report to the Tsar. M. Kokovtsev, the Russian Premier and Minister of Finance, was in France arranging for the five-hundred-million-franc loan for the construction of Russian strategic railways, but he was planning to stop in Berlin on his way home to thank the Kaiser for decorating him with the Order of the Black Eagle. It was therefore decided that Kokovtsev should take advantage of his visit in Berlin to set forth Russia's objections to the new German Military Mission. His report to the Tsar of his interviews with Bethmann-Hollweg and the Kaiser gives an excellent statement of the Liman von Sanders affair at the moment it became a serious diplomatic question. After mentioning Sazonov's injured feelings at not having been told of the projected Military Mission, Kokovtsev continues [his prolix circumlocutions being somewhat abbreviated]:

> Both the Chancellor and the Emperor left me with the impression that the project was born last Spring, and that

271 Giers to Sazonov, Tgs. 928, 936, Oct. 20/Nov. 2, and Oct. 23/Nov. 5, 1913; M.F.R., p. 631. Neratov to Sverbeev, Russian Ambassador in Berlin, Tg. 3032, 25 Oct./7 Nov. (M.F.R., p. 632): "Discuss in a friendly way . . . the very undesirable impression which would be made upon us by the placing of divisions and corps in Constantinople under German officers. Acts of this sort, causing unnecessary suspicion, hinder friendly relations with the Berlin Cabinet which are maintained on our side at such serious cost. We should not object to a command, not in the capital, but in other parts of Turkey not in our neighborhood."

the Chancellor, according to his affirmation during a completely sincere talk, was scarcely acquainted with it. He had merely learned that the Turkish Government had invited Germany to undertake the instruction of the Turkish army, that this question had been touched upon by the German Emperor in a private talk with Your Majesty in Berlin last May, and that Your Majesty had made no objection in principle, in view of the fact German officers have served as instructors in the Turkish army for more than twenty years; but that afterwards the ultimate arrangements for the organization of a Model Army Corps, under German command in the capital of Turkey, had remained wholly unknown to him and had followed the routine through military departments of the Empire.

In repeated and entirely sincere talks, the Chancellor did not hide from me how particularly painful to him was the possibility of the thought that he had participated in the preparation of a project disagreeable to Russia, and that he had not given a timely notification to our Minister of Foreign Affairs.

"During my four years of office," said Herr von Bethmann-Hollweg, "in the relations between the two Empires which are bound together by traditional ties of friendship and confidence, I have made every effort to avoid every occasion for the smallest misunderstanding, and my honesty guarantees that I shall never lend my hand to an act of disloyalty toward Russia." I have the impression that he was wholly sincere, and I do not think I am mistaken in judgment in saying that the very idea of an army corps at Constantinople under the command of German officers was really not known to him until the last few days just before my arrival, or even in part through my own explanations.

[After admitting the reasonableness of the Germans giving military instruction to the Turks and explaining mildly Russia's objections to Germans exercising command over troops in Constantinople, Kokovtsev summed up] with a demand having the character of an alternative: either give up completely the command over Turkish troops and merely exercise a right of inspection as formerly; or, if that seemed impossible on account of the promises Germany had made to Turkey, concentrate the Model Army Corps, not at Constantinople, but at some other point, e.g. Adrianople or in Asia Minor, but naturally not near our frontier nor in the sphere of interests belonging to France.[272]

The suggestion that General Liman exercise his command, not at Constantinople where his presence might seem to overawe the Ambassadors of the Powers, but at some Turkish provincial town, at first sight seemed a hopeful way out of the objections raised by Russia. Giers, Sverbeev, and Neratov, as well as Kokovtsev, favored this solution. Smyrna and Adrianople were suggested. But at once difficulties arose from the selfish interests of France and Russia themselves. France was strenuously opposed to having General Liman at Smyrna, "where a German command would be very dangerous to French interests."[273] Pichon, however, thought that "at the worst, it might be possible to agree to Adrianople."[274] But the choice of Adrianople, as the Russian Ambassador in Berlin shrewdly pointed out, "would probably cause great excitement in Bulgaria, and still further estrange this country from us [Russians]."[275] Bethmann, on the other hand, in accordance with his conciliatory attitude in the whole affair and his sincere desire to find a solution satisfactory to Russia, was quite ready

272 Kokovtsev's report to the Tsar, 19 Nov./2 Dec., 1913; M.F.R., 624 ff.; L.N., II, 411 ff. The accuracy of Kokovtsev's report is confirmed by G.P., XXXVIII, 212-217.

273 Izvolski to Sazonov, Tg. 550, Nov. 12/25; M.F.R., p. 641, but omitted from L.N., and Stieve. *Cf.* also Izvolski's Tg. 555 (M.F.R., p. 642; L.N., II, 189; Siebert-Schreiner, p. 678): "Pichon has again insisted on the fact that France cannot consent that Germans shall command at Smyrna or Beirut; he has suggested Adrianople to the Porte."

274 Izvolski's Tg. 550.

275 Sverbeev's confidential letter to Sazonov, Nov. 8/21; M.F.R., p. 639; Siebert-Schreiner, p. 677.

to consider this. General Liman, therefore, was to be asked whether it would be possible to change the arrangements which had been made.[276] But, as Sverbeev was informed at the same time, the military authorities in Berlin were of the opinion that unless the Model Corps was established at Constantinople, the activity of the German instructors would be reduced to nil, because the Military Academy and the General Staff were situated in Constantinople and with these the German officers would have to be in uninterrupted relations. This eventually proved to be General Liman's opinion after arriving at Constantinople. But on being informed of Russia's objections, he "came to the conclusion that there is no necessity for the General to command the Army Corps if there are only a sufficient number of troops to give the military schools an opportunity for practice exercises. A German general could command the Army Corps in Adrianople." [277] This solution was favored by the Russian Ambassador in Constantinople, but it was indignantly rejected by the Turks, who resented what they regarded as unwarranted Russian efforts to interfere in Turkey's internal affairs.[278]

Without waiting to hear General Liman's answer, Sazonov had hastened to suggest that France and England better join him in demanding "compensations." Such a demand for "some equivalent" was a common enough second-line form of attack in diplomacy when a direct effort at the main objective had failed. So now M. Sazonov, after protesting "how difficult it would be for us to permit our Embassy to remain in a city in which, so to speak, a German garrison was quartered," suggested to France and

276 Sverbeev to Sazonov, Tg. 277, Nov. 13/26; M.F.R., p. 643.

277 Giers to Sazonov, Tg. 1069, Dec. 7/20; Siebert-Schreiner, p. 694.

278 Giers to Sazonov, Tgs. 1072, 1073, 1078, 1086, Dec. 7/20 to Dec. 11/24, M.F.R., 670-672, and in part in Siebert-Schreiner, p. 695. Wangenheim's despatches of Dec. 16, 17, 18, 19; G.P., XXXVIII, 259-268; Liman, p. 14f.

England that "if it should appear inexpedient to raise further objections in Berlin, a joint step could be taken in Constantinople to point out that the concessions made to Germany raised the question of equivalent compensations for the other Powers." [279] France at first agreed instantly. Pichon "is entirely of your opinion. . . . If the Porte does not renounce the realization of this plan, France will demand extraordinary compensations of a moral and political nature." [280]

Sir Edward Grey, however, did not at first favor Sazonov's suggestion. He diplomatically "conceded in principle" the possibility of compensations, but feared "it might be difficult actually to find such compensations. Pichon's first proposal, that officers of other countries should also receive such posts of command, he deems inpracticable and not in keeping with our [Russian] interests, because our main object, the removal of the Germans from Constantinople, would not thereby be attained. Besides this would mean the first step in the partition of Turkey. . . . Grey thinks it best to continue friendly negotiations with Germany, in order to move her to change her original plan. . . . He believes that Emperor William, as well as the Imperial Chancellor, are seeking a pretext to extricate themselves from this situation." [281] Somewhat ignorant of Balkan problems, he also had a certain distrust of Russian diplomacy on account of Persian affairs and he feared that Sazonov's fickleness of mind might easily lead to some disaster.[282]

Unable to force Germany to yield, and abandoning the

279 Sazonov to Benckendorff and Izvolski, Tg. 3220, Nov. 12/25; M.F.R., p. 642; Siebert-Schreiner, p. 678. *Cf.* G.P., XXXVIII, 235 f., 241.

280 Izvolski to Sazonov, Nov. 13/26; M.F.R., p. 642; L.N., II, 189; Stieve, III, 354.

281 Benckendorff to Sazonov, Nov. 15/28; M.F.R., p. 644; Siebert-Schreiner, p. 679.

282 *Cf.* Sazonov to Benckendorff, Nov. 29/Dec. 12, 1913; Siebert-Schreiner, p. 687.

idea of accepting "compensations," M. Sazonov decided to try to coerce Turkey into annulling or revising the contract by presenting her with something like an ultimatum from the Triple Entente. In order to secure Sir Edward Grey's coöperation in this line of attack, Paul Cambon was instructed to persuade Grey to join "in making the Porte understand the inadmissible consequences which would result from placing the Constantinople Army Corps under a German general. It would, in short, place the Diplomatic Corps which resides in Constantinople under German guardianship. It would be virtually handing over to this Power the key to the Straits. It would make possible military interventions by the German general which might strike directly at the sovereignty of the Sultan. It would destroy the balance among the Powers which is the guarantee for the existence of Turkey. It might eventually bring these Powers into antagonism toward, or even into conflict with, the German Military Mission in case they had to exercise some action or demonstration at Constantinople." If Sir Edward agreed with these views he was to be flattered by being asked to formulate the note which the Entente Powers would present to the Porte.[283]

Cambon's potent argument, that General Liman's contract would put into German hands "the key to the Straits" —where Admiral Limpus was supposed to assure England's domination—did not fail to have the calculated effect upon Sir Edward Grey. It brought him out of the fogs of the Irish question and galvanized him into an energetic action (which a little later he regretted and reversed). He fell in with the French proposal, and speedily formulated a vigorous "declaration" embodying its arguments and amounting almost to an ultimatum. It warned the Turkish Government that if General Liman retained his command "the other Powers would demand analogous advantages for

283 Pichon to Cambon, Nov. 29; *Affaires Balkaniques,* III, 91 f.

themselves." It was approved by the Prime Minister, M. Asquith, and forwarded to the two other Entente Powers as a basis for identical warnings to be presented by their Ambassadors at Constantinople. In transmitting it to the French Ambassador in Turkey, M. Pichon added, "It is essential that the Ottoman Government can have no doubt as to the absolute agreement which has been established between England, France and Russia on this question." [284]

Sazonov was now assured, as he supposed, of "the absolute agreement" of both France and England. He now suddenly decided to try to use this as a lever at Berlin to bluff Germany into backing down, before the Entente Ambassadors should take action at Constantinople. Such a success at Berlin would be a more signal diplomatic victory and settlement of the affair than one secured in Constantinople. He accordingly telegraphed to Izvolski at Paris to have Bompard delay in presenting the note to Turkey.[285]

At the same time he instructed Sverbeev in Berlin to invite the German Government's attention to the proposed action of the Entente Powers at Constantinople if Germany did not give a satisfactory reply. Jagow, the German Secretary for Foreign Affairs, answered that he could not yet give a definite reply; he had written to General Liman to look into the local conditions in Constantinople; and if he came to an agreement with the Turkish authorities that no technical difficulties prevented the removal of the Model Corps to another center, then the German Government could easily revise General Liman's contract. Next day, December 5, Sazonov was told by the German Ambassador that "notwithstanding the embarrassment of its situation, the German Government was getting on with a possible

[284] Pichon to Bompard at Constantinople, Dec. 3, 1913; *ibid.*, III, 96.

[285] Tgs. 3281 and 3282, indicated in Izvolski's reply Tg. 565, Nov. 21/Dec. 4; M.F.R., p. 648; this telegram is not included in L.N., Stieve or Siebert-Schreiner.

settlement of the difficulty which has arisen, but some time would be necessary for this in order not to give the impression of yielding to pressure." Sazonov replied he "was ready to receive the proposal if the German Government did not postpone its decision to a too protracted date." But at the same time he instructed Sverbeev in Berlin to point out Pan-Slav Press criticisms of himself and "the necessity for us [Russians] to be able to remove the plausible reproaches printed as to the perfidy of German policy, and the desirability of winding up this whole incident as quickly as possible. If the German Minister talks about his Government's being unable to settle with the Porte, tell him that we should readily adopt the point of view that the question ought to be deliberated upon, not in Berlin, but in Constantinople, and that we shall take the agreed-upon steps immediately."[286]

Sazonov in fact was in no mood to wait. He concluded that it was impossible to pry Germany into giving an immediate decision, and that his lever had therefore failed. He also heard that the Sultan had issued on December 4 an iradé announcing General Liman's appointment as Member of the War Council and Commander of the Constantinople Corps. He therefore telegraphed to London and Paris on December 7: "We consider it desirable that the three Ambassadors should at once address themselves to the Turkish Government with the following identical note which has been drawn up according to the English proposal."[287]

But M. Sazonov was now chagrined to discover that Sir Edward Grey had meanwhile changed his mind, during the interval in which Sazonov himself had desired a delay in the Entente action at Constantinople. Sazonov now found that the agreement was not so "absolute" as he had

[286] Sazonov to Sverbeev, Nov. 22/Dec. 5, 1913; M.F.R., p. 648.
[287] Tg. 3309; M.F.R., 650; Siebert-Schreiner, p. 681.

supposed. His proposed "note" had a sharper tone than Grey's "declaration."

A misunderstanding also arose as to the form in which the Entente declaration should be presented to the Grand Vizier. Sazonov and Pichon wanted a very strong diplomatic procedure: the simultaneous presentation by the Entente Ambassadors of an identical written note. Sir Edward Grey, however, characteristically desired to treat the Grand Vizier more gently: "In the opinion of Grey the notes ought to be identical, but not presented simultaneously." [288]

Meanwhile also Grey had begun to hear from the German Chargé d'Affaires in London an account of the German Military Mission very different from that which had been pictured to him by Paul Cambon. He was informed by Kühlmann that the arrangement for a German command over the Constantinople Army Corps was simply intended to obviate the inherent weakness in the position of General Liman's predecessor. General Von der Goltz's efforts had been paralyzed by lack of authority and by Turkish inertia which blocked the reforms he tried to introduce. The new plan was to give General Liman a Model Corps over which he would have command, and in which he would therefore enjoy sufficient authority to compel real reforms. The Corps at Constantinople had been chosen as the Model Corps, because that was the seat of the Military School and the General Staff, with which the German instructors would have to be in constant touch. General Liman was simply to have a position in the army analogous to that of the English Admiral Limpus in the navy, against whom no Powers had

[288] Etter to Sazonov, Tg. 799, Nov. 19/Dec. 2; M.F.R., p. 646; Siebert-Schreiner, p. 681. *Cf.* Cambon to Pichon, Dec. 2 (*Affaires Balkaniques,* III, 93): "The Prime Minister [Asquith] has approved the proposal of Sir Edward Grey for an action at Constantinople. He thinks this ought not to be collective but identical, and that the Ambassadors could express themselves in about the same terms."

protested. The point about Admiral Limpus made a deep impression on Grey. He began to see that he might be getting into a very illogical position if he should demand that General Liman give up the command of a single Turkish Army Corps in Constantinople while Admiral Limpus kept the command over the whole Turkish fleet. He may well have imagined the poor figure he would cut in the House of Commons if he were questioned and forced to defend such an illogical attitude. As the Russian Ambassador ruefully reported a few days later: "Grey did not know until now the exact details of the contract of the British Admiral. . . . The position of the British Admiral really furnishes Germany with an argument which is causing difficulties here. Nicolson has spoken to me about it several times." [289]

In addition to Kühlmann's arguments, Grey was also put on his guard against Sazonov's maneuvers by the correct information which he began to get from Sir Louis Mallet in Constantinople: the importance of continuing the Anglo-German coöperation in the construction of naval docks for Turkey at Ismid; Admiral Limpus' declaration that his powers were really wider than General Liman's; the fact that he had leased the house in Constantinople picked out for the German General; and finally Sir Louis Mallet's warning that out of the Russian demands for Liman's withdrawal might easily arise a dangerous situation like the French demand for the withdrawal of the Hohenzollern Candidacy in 1870.[290]

[289] Benckendorff to Sazonov, Tg. Nov. 29/Dec. 12, 1913; M.F.R., p. 657; Siebert-Schreiner, p. 688. *Cf.* also Tg. 813, Dec. 1/14: "I asked Nicolson, for what reason Grey had changed his original standpoint. He replied, that meantime details concerning the position of the British Admiral in Constantinople had come to hand from the British Ambassador in Constantinople, which had deprived Grey of every possibility of agreeing to the draft proposed by you."

[290] G.P., XXXVIII, 232 ff., 240 f., 245 f., 249 ff., 270 ff., 282 f.; and preceding footnote.

On learning more about the facts of the case, and especially about Admiral Limpus, Grey in fact virtually reversed his attitude. He came to the opinion that Sazonov's projected "note" to Turkey (though based closely on his own and Cambon's proposals) was "premature"; there must not be "any kind of threats at its close"; instead of warning the Sultan of the dangerous consequences of General Liman's appointment, he now suggested a mere "verbal inquiry," politely asking the Turks for information as to the contract made by them with the German General, and the extent of the functions he was to exercise.

M. Sazonov was now much upset in his mind, as may be seen from his telegram to the Russian Ambassador in London on December 12:

> I hear from a very secret source [291] that Grey has explained to the French Ambassador, that he did not wish to go too far in Constantinople, as he is afraid of a change in my attitude, which might lead to a diplomatic failure. I should like to remark, that as to the instructors, it is not a question of a change in our attitude, but of a regrettable change in England's attitude. For Grey will have nothing more to do with a note, which had been based on a telegram of Grey's to the British Ambassador [in St. Petersburg].
>
> Should we be finally obliged to change our attitude in this question, as already in so many others, this is to be attributed only to the lack of confidence in the effectiveness of England's support, and, indeed, this confidence will only be shaken still more by such actions on the part of England. This lack of homogeneity and solidarity between the three Powers of the Entente arouses our serious apprehension, for it constitutes an organic fault of the Triple Entente,

291 This "very secret source" may have been another case of Sazonov's deciphering telegrams sent by the French Government to the French Ambassador in St. Petersburg, similar to the case which contributed to the famous attempted dismissal of M. Georges Louis in May, 1912; *cf.* Judet, *Georges Louis,* pp. 85-88, 99; Poincaré, I, 377 f.

which will always place us at a disadvantage in face of the firm block of the Triple Alliance.

Such a condition of affairs might under certain circumstances entail grave consequences, and most seriously endangers vital interests of every Power of the Triple Entente.[292]

In spite of his irritation and chagrin at Sir Edward Grey's disconcerting change of attitude, Sazonov perceived that there was nothing to be done but accept it. On December 13, therefore, the three Entente Ambassadors at Constantinople made, one after another, their mild "verbal inquiry" as to the nature of General Liman's contract and position, and whether it threatened Turkey's sovereign independence and authority over Constantinople and the Straits. They were given the desired information about the contract, but were told by the Grand Vizier that their other question was Turkey's own private affair. He compared General Liman's position to that of Admiral Limpus, and therefore saw no reason for cancelling or changing the German contract.[293] In view of Sir Edward Grey's attitude there was nothing more to be gained by M. Sazonov through negotiations at Constantinople. Though there was some

[292] Sazonov to Benckendorff, Nov. 29/Dec. 12, 1913; Siebert-Schreiner, p. 687. See M.F.R., p. 657 ff. for Benckendorff's replies. *Cf.* also Buchanan, *My Mission to Russia,* I, 149 f., and the approximately correct surmise of the situation by Kühlmann in London, with the Kaiser's comments (Dec. 12; G.P., XXXVIII, 250): "Apparently an extraordinarily strong pressure is being exercised from the Russian side [Kaiser: 'Rascals!']. The Russian Government is said to have gone so far as to say to Sir Edward Grey that it must regard his attitude in this question as a touchstone for his feelings toward Russia in general [Kaiser: 'Aha']. Because Sir Edward in his policy wants to avoid a break with Russia [Kaiser: 'Ass! He betrays his country's own interests'], he is said to have decided to participate formally in the inquiry in the matter but without showing a strong interest in it himself [Kaiser: 'Then the Grand Vizier can calmly be rude']."

[293] M.F.R., pp. 658-662; Siebert-Schreiner, pp. 688-692; G.P., XXXVIII, 250-268.

talk of altering the status of both General Liman and Admiral Limpus, it came to nothing.

M. Bompard, the French Ambassador at Constantinople did not believe that Russia would ever achieve her purpose by peaceful means; he suggested privately that Russia "should dispatch a warship to the Bosphorus and declare that it would not be withdrawn until the contract with General Liman and his officers had been altered." M. Paléologue, Political Director in the French Foreign Office, thought that "the Turkish batteries would scarcely dare to open fire." And M. Izvolski added that "in the event of our resolving upon an energetic action of this sort, public opinion in France would take our part, since it is susceptible to everything which touches national dignity, and feels most keenly the inadmissibility of German influence in Turkey.[294] M. Sazonov, as will be seen in a moment, was actually contemplating military measures to coerce Turkey. But France and England both intimated that it would be better to await the results of the efforts which the German Government was making to find a solution which would satisfy Russia without seeming to involve the prestige of Turkey or of any of the Great Powers. Though impatient of delay because of the criticisms being levelled against him in the Pan-Slav Press, Sazonov fortunately heeded the advice.

Meanwhile the German Ambassador at Constantinople had been active in trying to find a sensible and peaceful solution of the whole affair. He had urged Turkey to yield and modify Liman's contract. He tried to have the German and Russian military attachés in Constantinople work out an agreement. He finally hurried back to Berlin and there arranged the successful solution. General Liman was ad-

294 Izvolski to Sazonov, Dec. 19/Jan. 1; M.F.R., p. 602; L.N., II, 222; Stieve, IV, 10; Siebert-Schreiner, p. 701. For pacific assurances by the French to Germany and Germany's impressions thereof, see G.P., XXXVIII, 241, 247, 255, 272, 274 ff., 286 f., 307.

vanced a grade in the Prussian army; by the terms of his contract, this automatically resulted in his advance in the Turkish army to rank of Field Marshal which relieved him of the command of the First Army Corps in Constantinople. He remained Inspector of Turkish troops and Director of the Military School, but did not exercise command over troops in the Turkish capital—the point to which Sazonov had so strenuously objected. This solution, which was satisfactory to Russia, was publicly announced on January 15, 1914.[295] It brought the affair peacefully to an end, without involving the danger of a test of strength between the Triple Entente and the Triple Alliance. As the Russian Ambassador in Berlin wrote to M. Sazonov: "The Berlin Cabinet has actually done everything in its power in order to fulfil our justifiable wishes, and this has not been easy for it, in view of the newspaper campaign directed against the Government."[296]

The whole affair shows how even a serious Russo-German diplomatic crisis could be sensibly and peacefully settled, provided that Germany was willing to make some concessions, and that Russia was restrained by France and England from taking too extreme and hasty steps; and provided also that neither side paid too much attention to the hounding criticisms of its own jingo newspapers and military alarmists. Though Germany had had no intention of suddenly springing a surprise which would embarrass Sazonov, the unfortunate failure of the Tsar in May, and of Bethmann in October, to mention the Military Mission to the Russian Minister of Foreign Affairs gave the latter a natural feeling of grievance. This was accentuated by his fears that the Liman Mission might ultimately block Russia's ambitions in regard to the Straits—a fact which

295 G.P., XXXVIII, 265-302.

296 Sverbeev to Sazonov, Jan. 3/16, 1914; M.F.R., p. 689; Siebert-Schreiner, p. 707.

is significant of the great importance he attached to Russia's "historic mission"—as is further indicated by his measures of preparedness presently to be described. The effect of the Liman von Sanders affair in Berlin was to strengthen the feeling that though Sazonov was inclined to get excited and even to bluff, it was doubtful whether he would have England's support for his bluff. This was one reason why Germany at first believed it probably safe to support Austria in July, 1914.

M. SAZONOV'S PLANS FOR PREPAREDNESS

M. Sazonov is pictured by many "revisionist" writers as being "converted" in the fall of 1913 to the "Franco-Russian war plot" which MM. Poincaré and Izvolski had been weaving since 1912 by "Balkanizing of the Franco-Russian Alliance."[297] But this picture does too little justice to M. Sazonov's independence of attitude, and gives too much weight to the influence exerted by Izvolski and Poincaré on Russian foreign policy. M. Sazonov often pursued Balkan policies which by no means wholly harmonized with those of Izvolski and still less with those of Poincaré. In the winter and spring of 1914, Russian policy can be more accurately followed in his reports to the Tsar and in the minutes of Russian Councils than in the self-important despatches of the Russian Ambassador in Paris. Izvolski's influence on Russian policy has been exaggerated by Izvolski himself and by writers who take him at his own valuation. M. Poincaré, to be sure, in his recent self-righteous memoirs, goes much too far to the other extreme in attempting utterly to discredit Izvolski. But there seems to be little doubt that in the early months of 1914 Izvolski's influence was somewhat on the wane both in Paris and St. Petersburg. He

[297] *Cf.* Stieve, *Izvolski and the World War,* pp. 186 ff.; H. E. Barnes, *The Genesis of the World War,* pp. 110 ff., 138 ff.; and note 299 below.

was terribly alarmed by the rumor that he might be superseded by Kokovtsev.

M. Sazonov's real views are well revealed in a long report to the Tsar early in December, 1913.[298] In this he summed up the general situation after the Balkan Wars, and especially the danger to peace caused by the long failure of Turkey and Greece to come to terms. In view of Turkey's weakened position, Sazonov concluded that the final dissolution of the Ottoman Empire was not far distant, that all the Powers were calculating the parts which they would appropriate when the final partition took place, and that Russia must therefore decide what attitude she would take in the premises.

An impartial reading of his report, which is too long to quote in full, shows that he did not desire to bring about a European war. On the contrary, he repeatedly stated that he wished to preserve the *status quo* as long as possible. But the situation in the Balkans was very unstable. Russia could never permit the Straits to pass into the hands of any other Power, as they had been in danger of doing when the Bulgarians advanced to the outposts of Constantinople in 1912. Therefore he and the other Russian Ministers must concert plans of preparedness to seize the Straits, in case of European complications which he feared might occur at any moment. Hence he requested the Tsar to allow him to consult with the other Ministers on these measures of preparedness:

> It is not at all in our direct interest to strive for any increases of territory whatever. All the needs of our internal development make the task of maintaining peace of first importance. However, while not abandoning this principal and primary task, we cannot close our eyes to the

[298] Sazonov's report of Nov. 23/Dec. 6, 1913; L.N., II, 363-372; Stieve, III, 374-383 (with the date, Nov. 25/Dec. 8); summarized by Adamov, pp. 70-75; approved by the Tsar at Livadia, Nov. 27/Dec. 10.

dangers of the international situation, dangers the prevention of which does not depend on us alone. That is why we cannot neglect, any more than the other Powers, to raise the question of preserving in advance our rights and interests, if events should demand that we defend them by armed force.

Uncertainty as to the stability and longevity of Turkey raises for us the historic question of the Straits, and a weighing of their importance for us, both from a political and an economic point of view. . . . In case of a change in the *status quo*, Russia cannot permit a solution of the question counter to her interests; in other words, she cannot, under certain circumstances, remain a passive spectator of events. . . .

At present the question of safeguarding the Straits is settled at bottom in a fairly satisfactory manner as regards our direct interests. Turkey is a State neither too strong nor too weak—unable to be a danger to us, but at the same time obliged to give consideration to Russia, which is stronger than she. The very weakness of the Ottoman Empire, and its inability to regenerate itself on the basis of law and civilization, have hitherto been to our advantage, creating among the peoples subjected to the Crescent that aspiration toward Orthodox Russia, which is one of the fundamental bases of our international position in the East and in Europe. . . .

Can we permit the transfer of the Straits into the full possession of another State? To put the question, is to answer it in the negative. The Straits in the possession of a strong State would mean that the economic development of all South Russia would be subjected to it. . . . He who possesses the Straits will not only hold the keys of the Black Sea and the Mediterranean; he will have also the key to the penetration of Asia Minor and the hegemony of the Balkans; consequently, the State which replaces Turkey on the shores of the Straits will probably aspire to follow the paths followed formerly by the Turks. . . .

[Rejecting as unsatisfactory all proposals for neutralizing and demilitarizing the Straits, Sazonov reiterated the need of a detailed program of preparedness.] We must study the measures which can be taken to increase our military and naval strength in the Black Sea. What ought the War and Navy Departments to do to accelerate mobilization, by means of new railways and the development of our means of transport? . . . Is it possible, or not, to determine the task of our army and navy in forcing the Straits and seizing Constantinople, if circumstances should demand it?

Returning to the political aspect of preparedness, one must again repeat that an early dissolution of Turkey could not be desirable for us, and it is necessary to do everything possible, through diplomacy, to postpone such an outcome.

[M. Sazonov then indicated the principal questions to be discussed: (1) the accelerated mobilization of an adequate expeditionary force; (2) the preparation of the lines of communication necessary for this mobilization; (3) the increase of the Black Sea Fleet so that it will surpass the Turkish Fleet, and be able to force the Straits and occupy them temporarily or permanently, if necessary; (4) the increase of naval transports; and (5) the construction of strategic railways in the Caucasus.]

Renewing the wish expressed above for the prolongation as far as possible of the *status quo*,[299] it is also necessary

[299] Stieve, *Izvolski and the World War*, p. 189 ff., quoting this paragraph, suppresses the important clause "Renewing . . . *status quo*" as well as other similar phrases, in which Sazonov expresses his desire to preserve peace and the *status quo*. Having suppressed the words which do not fit in with his theories, he says: "this passage is an admission of enormous import," and proceeds with the misleading and unwarranted conclusions: "The kernel lies in the first [!] clause, with the declaration that 'the question of the Straits can hardly be advanced a step except *through European complications*' [italics are Stieve's]. . . . The passage establishes Sazonov's conversion to the idea of world war. Thus at the end of 1913 the Russian Foreign Minister had, as regards the attainment of the specifically Russian aims, completed that fateful change of course which Poincaré on behalf of France had resolutely made as long ago as the end of 1912, when he was ready to attack Austria and Germany. . . . It was this that sealed the doom of Europe," etc. Barnes, p. 139, follows

> to repeat that the question of the Straits can hardly be advanced a step except through European complications. These complications, to judge from present conditions, would find us in alliance with France, and in a possible, but not at all assured, alliance with England, or at least with her as a benevolent neutral. In the Balkans, in case of European complications, we could count on Serbia, and perhaps on Rumania. . . .[300]

The Tsar approved Sazonov's report, and the discussion by various Ministers, as proposed, took place cn January 13, 1914. Sazonov also sent a copy of it to M. Grigorovitch, the Naval Minister, who passed it on to the Admiralty Staff for examination. The latter naturally endorsed very heartily Sazonov's proposal for strengthening the Black Sea Fleet. They urged that only by this means could Russia make her voice heard in the concert of Europe and in dealings with Turkey, where Russia's influence was already sadly inadequate. The Admiralty Staff suggested several measures for the immediate strengthening of the Black Sea Fleet: speeding up the construction of vessels already being built; the purchase of Dreadnoughts abroad, and the prevention of their purchase by Turkey; and the preparation of plans for the combined action of the Baltic and the Black Sea Fleets against Turkey.[301]

On the basis of these suggestions the Naval Minister made a long report to the Tsar, endorsing Sazonov's ideas:

> The systematic and successful preparations of operations of our fleet for the dominating control on the sea at the Constantinople channel and in the waters of the Aegean and Mediterranean adjacent to it demand careful and persistent

Stieve in suppressing passages in which Sazonov expresses his desire to preserve peace and the *status quo*.

300 For the continuation of Sazonov's report, concerning Rumania, Serbia, and Austria, see above at note 222.

301 Report of the Admiralty Staff, Dec. 9/22, 1913; Zakher, "Konstantinopol i Prolivy," in *Krasnyi Arkhiv,* VII, 33 f.

work, not only by the Navy Department, but also by the War Ministry and some others, especially the Ministries of Foreign Affairs, Commerce, Industry, and Finance. This preparedness can be completed only in the course of some years. Therefore the Navy Department wholly agrees with the proposal of the Minister of Foreign Affairs (after the termination of certain preparatory studies) about the necessity of holding a Special Council for the working out of these guiding principles, which result from the idea approved by Your Majesty that Russia cannot allow any Power whatever to establish itself on the Straits of the Bosphorus and the Dardanelles; and that Russia must therefore be ready to take possession of the Straits, in case great European complications should bring up the Eastern Question for a final settlement.[302]

Meanwhile, on January 5, 1914, Sazonov drew up a memorandum for circulation among the other Ministers to serve as a basis for discussion at the Special Council. It summarized the Liman von Sanders negotiations, and went on to declare:

3. Decisions must now be taken to provide for the possible necessity of supporting our demands by measures of compulsion.

4. The measures of compulsion on our part might take the form of the occupation of some point in Asia Minor, e.g. Trebizond or Bayazid, with a declaration that we should stay there until our demands were satisfied.

5. After it had been clearly established what measures of compulsion we should be able to employ, a confidential exchange of views on the subject must be set on foot with the British and French Governments, since measures of compulsion can, necessarily, only be undertaken after we have ascertained whether we can count on corresponding steps on the part of these two Powers.

302 Grigorovitch's report, approved by the Tsar Dec. 30, 1913/Jan. 13, 1914; *Krasnyi Arkhiv,* VII, 35 ff.

6. In the negotiations with the said Governments, the necessity for extremely cautious and unanimous action on the part of the three Powers must be insisted on, in order, if possible, to prevent the conflict becoming more acute, as a European war might result. At the same time efforts must be made on our part to prepare France and Great Britain for the necessity of pursuing to the end an action once begun in the common interests.

7. Should this point of view be accepted by all three Powers and the negotiations in Berlin not lead to the desired result, an understanding must be arrived at as to an ascending scale in the measures of compulsion:

(a) A rigid financial boycott of Turkey;

(b) Should this method fail to produce the required effect, as in the case of the Adrianople question, the three Powers might withdraw their representatives from Constantinople;

(c) At the same time the Governments of Russia, France, and Great Britain would acquaint the Porte with the date fixed for the fulfilment of their demands, after which the measures of compulsion might begin to be put into force, with the warning that they would not be withdrawn until the demands had been complied with.

8. Should certain preparatory steps of a military nature, such as reinforcements of troops in the Caucasus, be necessary to enable us promptly to put measures of compulsion into effect, it would be desirable to keep these steps as secret as possible. From the political point of view, however, it is clearly necessary that it shall be possible, after issuing a threat, should that become necessary, to take prompt steps to translate the threat into action.[303]

This memorandum indicates clearly Sazonov's desire, "if possible, to prevent the conflict becoming more acute, as a European war might result," but at the same time his

[303] Pokrovski, *Drei Konferenzen,* 32 f.; Stieve, *Izvolski and the World War,* 219 f.

determination to resort to "measures of compulsion" and a threat of force as a bluff to secure a diplomatic victory, and his readiness, if necessary, "to take prompt steps to translate the threat into action"—provided he could feel sure of British and French support. He told the Tsar on January 9 that he believed a firm stand on Russia's part would probably have the desired effect on Germany and Turkey, "but the risk of serious European complications must undoubtedly be kept in view." He was determined that Russia must not accept the Liman von Sanders Mission as a *fait accompli,* because "a yielding would be equivalent to a political defeat and might have altogether ruinous consequences." It would make Germany and her allies more arrogant, and "in France and England there would be strengthened the dangerous conviction that Russia will accept any conditions whatever for the sake of preserving peace. Once such convictions were strengthened in our friend and our ally, the not very close solidarity of the Triple Entente Powers might be finally broken up, and each of them would endeavor to seek security for its interests by making agreements with the Powers of the opposing camp."

Sazonov feared particularly that England and Germany might come to some separate solution of the Liman von Sanders affair by changing the status of Admiral Limpus, and then Russia would be left alone to face Germany. "Russia would be finally left in complete political isolation, because it would hardly be possible to reckon separately even upon France, who also, even without this [possible Anglo-German agreement], is inclined to sacrifice great political interests for the sake of the financial advantages of a settlement. . . . If, however, the replies of France and England [in regard to the use of measures of compulsion] should be regarded as satisfactory, then, reserving all necessary strength and caution for the complications necessity may demand, it would remain for us to defend firmly our interests to the end." [304]

That Sazonov should suspect England's loyalty to Russian interests in the Balkans is not altogether surprising. But that he should also speak thus of France indicates what a strong element of suspiciousness there was in his character, especially in view of the fact that Izvolski had informed him only a few days before that "Poincaré, in the most decisive terms, confirmed Doumergue's declaration . . . that France is firmly determined to act with us in this connection. From Poincaré's words, I have been able to conclude that the expressions of the declaration mentioned have been most carefully weighed by him and his Ministers, and that, in spite of France's love of peace, these words express, with full and deliberate intent, a quiet resolution not to withdraw, under existing circumstances, from those obligations imposed upon her by her alliance with us." [305] It was this suspiciousness which led him to intercept and decipher from time to time the despatches between the French Government and the French Ambassador in St. Petersburg. It was perhaps a realization of this suspiciousness which caused M. Poincaré so frequently to assure Russia that France would support her; these assurances are probably to be interpreted as efforts to strengthen the Franco-Russian alliance and tighten up the Triple Entente, rather than as incitements to bring about a European war by which France might recover Alsace-Lorraine.

On January 13, 1914, just as the Liman von Sanders Affair was about to be given a satisfactory solution, the

[304] Sazonov's report to the Tsar, Dec. 27/Jan. 9; Adamov, pp. 62-64. It is possible that Sazonov used this argument—that Russia was in danger of being politically isolated—in order to persuade the peace-loving Tsar to approve the discussion of plans for preparedness.

[305] Izvolski to Sazonov, Dec. 23/Jan. 5; M.F.R., p. 686; Siebert-Schreiner, p. 704; Stieve, IV, 17. *Cf.* also Izvolski to Sazonov, Dec. 17/30, 1913, and Jan. 2/15, 1914; M.F.R., pp. 478-481, 674; L.N., II, 218, 229; Stieve, III, 437; IV, 25-28; Siebert-Schreiner, p. 697.

Special Conference, which M. Sazonov had proposed several weeks earlier, finally met under the chairmanship of the Premier and Minister of Finance, M. Kokovtsev. There were present only the most important officials: the Ministers of War (Sukhomlinov), Navy (Grigorovitch), Foreign Affairs (Sazonov), the Chief of Staff (Zhilinski), and a couple of recording secretaries from the Near East Division of the Ministry of Foreign Affairs.[306] M. Sazonov reported that, according to the latest news, General Liman was about to be promoted to the highest rank in the Turkish army and would therefore give up the command of the Army Corps in Constantinople; this seemed good news, but the promotion was not yet an accomplished fact, and one should not therefore be too optimistic.

General Sukhomlinov energetically expressed the opinion that Turkey ought to be persuaded to abandon the German Military Mission altogether, and that all discussion about modifying the terms of its activity was a subordinate matter. Sazonov replied that any advice given in Constantinople would be without result unless accompanied by measures of compulsion such as he had proposed.

M. Kokovtsev, however, wise, peace-loving, and conciliatory, wished to put the brakes on any hasty aggressive action. Before proceeding to discuss measures of compulsion, he begged to lay stress on two matters of primary importance:

> 1. The German Government is looking for a way out of the situation created by Russia's demands. In this connection the Berlin Cabinet points to the necessity, in the interest of a satisfactory solution of the question, of Russia's avoidance of any categorical declaration, of the character of an ultimatum to Germany, as this might compel Ger-

[306] The Minutes of this Conference of Dec. 31/Jan. 13 were published by M. N. Pokrovski in Russian in 1919; in German in 1920 (*Drei Konferenzen,* pp. 32-45); and in English by Stieve, *Izvolski and the World War,* pp. 219-229.

many to adhere still more firmly to her standpoint, since regard must be had to the difficult position of the German Government in the face of public opinion in its own country.

2. The negotiations with the Berlin Cabinet, which have now been going on for two months, should be continued until the Russian Government is convinced that it is impossible to attain in this manner the object indicated.

M. Kokovtsev also pointed out that even the measures of compulsion ought to be taken only "in closest association with the other Powers of the Triple Entente. Before any decision is come to, the Russian Government must know to what extent it will receive the support of France, and whether active participation by Great Britain in the pressure on the Porte can be relied on."

M. Sazonov replied that he contemplated this, and added: "It seems still to be uncertain how far Great Britain would be prepared for energetic action. As regards France, the Russian Government can count on effectual support to the uttermost limit. M. Delcassé has assured the Minister, in the name of the French Foreign Minister, that France would go as far as Russia may wish."

M. Kokovtsev was of the opinion that any measures of compulsion such as the occupation of Asia Minor territory "would inevitably be followed by war with Germany, and put the question: "Is war with Germany desirable, and can Russia wage it?" In reply, Sazonov agreed with Kokovtsev "that in principle a war with Germany would be undesirable;" as to whether Russia could wage it, Sazonov "did not consider himself called upon to decide this." But "the Minister of War and the Chief of Staff declared categorically the complete readiness of Russia for a duel with Germany, not to mention one with Austria. Such a duel is, however, hardly likely; those Powers would be much more likely to have to deal with the Triple Entente." This categorical statement of the Russian militarists disposes of

M. SAZONOV
Russian Minister for Foreign Affairs, 1910-1916

GENERAL SUKHOMLINOV
Russian Minister of War, 1909-1915

the argument that Russia did not want war in 1914 because they did not think her preparations were sufficiently complete.

M. Kokovtsev, in opposition to all the others, again insisted that an occupation of Trebizond or Bayazid would inevitably lead to intervention by Germany. But Sazonov thought this "would be a very effective measure, and might deter Germany from intervening." His views were shared by the Ministers of War and Navy and by the Chief of Staff. "M. Kokovtsev, who considered that a war at the present moment would be the greatest misfortune for Russia, expressed the opinion that it would be most undesirable to entangle Russia in a European conflict—a view which was shared by the other members of the Conference."

M. Kokovtsev finally summed up the sense of the meeting to the effect that negotiations were to be continued at Berlin to secure General Liman's removal from the command of troops in Constantinople; if it became quite clear that the negotiations would fail, measures of compulsion might be applied, if the Entente Powers were in agreement; but "Should Russia not be assured of the active participation of France and England in common steps with Russia, it does not seem possible to adopt measures of compulsion which might lead to a war with Germany." It was to secure the closer support of England, which was necessary to enable Russia to carry out her ambitions in the Near East, which made Sazonov redouble his efforts in the spring of 1914 to get more definite and binding obligations from Sir Edward Grey in the shape of an Anglo-Russian Naval Convention. Negotiations for this were soon begun, but had to be dropped when news of them leaked out.

From the minutes of this Special Conference one sees clearly that Sazonov sided fully with the militarists in being ready to adopt measures of compulsion to oust General Liman from the command of the Turkish Corps in Constantinople. While not desiring war with Germany and preferring a diplomatic victory, he was nevertheless quite ready to adopt measures which would probably lead to war with Germany, provided he was sure of the support of the Entente. He was ready to use a threat of force, and "to translate the threat into action," if the threat did not prove to be an effective bluff. This was his attitude in July, 1914, and it led to war. In January, 1914, it did not lead to war, because Germany made timely conciliatory concessions in the Liman von Sanders Affair, and because M. Kokovtsev used his influence to prevent any over-hasty provocative action on Russia's part, like the occupation of Trebizond or Bayazid. This Conference reveals sharply the contrast between Kokovtsev's moderate, conciliatory, and restraining influence on the one hand, and, on the other, the dangerous policy of military pressure urged by Sazonov and the military and naval officials. Kokovtsev, as Minister of Finance, looked at affairs more from a business man's point of view than from that of a politician. Like Count Witte, he had an eye for economic, as well as purely political, considerations. He was not blinded by the diplomatist's shibboleths about Pan-Slav interests, Russia's "prestige," and her "historic mission." He kept in view the probable catastrophic effects which a European War would have upon Russia's commerce, finance, and internal political structure. When he put bluntly the question, "Is a war with Germany desirable?" the other members of the Conference were forced to agree with him that it was not. It was therefore an incalculable misfortune for Russia and the world that, a few days after this Conference, M. Kokovtsev followed Count Witte into political retirement, and left the field free to M. Sazonov and the Russian Pan-Slavs and militarists.[307]

307 For the intense nationalism of influential men like the President of the Duma, see M. W. Rodzjanko, *Erinnerungen* (Berlin, 1926; Eng.

M. Kokovtsev's retirement from the Premiership gave rise to a rumor that he might be appointed Russian Ambassador at Paris, and that Izvolski would be transferred to Rome or some other post. This threw Izvolski into a panic. He abjectly besought Sazonov to prevent it:

> A transfer to Rome would involve me in the greatest financial difficulties, since every moving causes great expenditures, and the salary at Rome is 40,000 francs less than here. Dismissal through appointment to the Council of the Empire on the other hand would be for me a direct catastrophe. . . . You know my personal means are very limited, and that I have not yet put my son on his feet nor provided for my daughter. I am compelled to place especial value on my office. [If he lost it, he says, he would have to seek private employment with some bank.] After nearly forty years of diplomatic service, this would be very hard and bitter for me.

Izvolski's plea was effective. A few days later he thanked Sazonov effusively for having "prevented M. N. Kokovtsev's effort to sit himself in my seat." [308]

It is interesting to speculate on how the course of history might have been changed, if Kokovtsev had replaced Izvolski at Paris, or if he had still been able as Premier to exert a restraining influence at St. Petersburg in July,

trans., *The Reign of Rasputin,* London, 1927), *passim.* How strongly Russian diplomacy seems to have been influenced during the Liman von Sanders Affair and the spring of 1914 by the Grand Duke Nicholas, the militarists, and the Pan-Slav Press (which Sazonov apparently often encouraged yet always feared), is indicated in the shrewd and carefully balanced observations of Pourtalès, the German Ambassador in St. Petersburg (G.P., XXXVIII, 253 ff., 269 f., 293 ff.; XXXIX, 540-589, *passim*); Pourtalès, however, was not an alarmist; in fact, after July, 1914, he was criticized for not having been sufficiently so. On this subject in general, see also A. Fischel, *Der Panslawismus bis zum Weltkrieg* (Stuttgart, 1919); E. H. Wilcox, *Russia's Ruin* (New York, 1919); G. Frantz, *Russlands Eintritt in den Weltkrieg* (Berlin, 1924), and *Russland auf dem Wege zur Katastrophe* (Berlin, 1926).

[308] Izvolski to Sazonov, Jan. 30/Feb. 12, and Feb. 12/25, 1914; M.F.R., 488 f.; L.N., II, 238 f.; Stieve, IV, 52, 56.

1914. With his sweet reasonableness, his firm character, and his friendly personal relations with the Kaiser and the Berlin authorities, he might have been able to prevent the over-hasty steps which helped cause the World War. It was Russia's misfortune that she discarded real statesmen like Count Witte and M. Kokovtsev in favor of prestige diplomats like Izvolski and Sazonov.

Although the Liman von Sanders Affair had been happily settled in January, 1914, M. Sazonov, freed from M. Kokovtsev's pacific influence, continued his examination of preparedness plans, and even took up again the discussion of the aggressive project for a sudden seizure of the Straits by an armed landing force, which had been seriously contemplated in 1896 and 1912, but in both cases postponed because of lack of preparations.[309] At another Special Conference on February 21, 1914, presided over by himself, and including military and naval experts and also M. Giers, the active and aggressive Russian Ambassador at Constantinople, Sazonov called attention to his report of December 5, approved by the Tsar,

> that it was necessary to proceed without delay to the preparation of a program, elaborated in every direction, which should aim at the assurance in our favor of the historic question of the Straits. [Though admitting that at the moment political complications in the Balkans were not likely, Sazonov] expressed the firm conviction that should events result in the Straits slipping from Turkey's control, Russia could not permit any other Power to establish itself on their shores. Russia might thus be compelled to seize possession of them, in order then to secure in one shape or another a state of things along the Bosphorus and the Dardanelles corresponding to her interests. The success of this operation would depend in large degree on the rapidity with which it was carried out. . . . [He therefore asked for

309 On the 1896 project, see above, note 13; and on that of 1912, Zakher, in *Krasnyi Arkhiv,* VI, 50-61, with Admiralty Staff reports.

a technical discussion of measures for expediting the mobilization and transportation of a sufficiently strong landing force; the strengthening of the Black Sea Fleet, so as to be able, jointly with the landing force, to occupy the Straits; and the construction of strategic railways in the Caucasus.]

[With reference to the possibility that Russia's seizure of the Straits might be opposed by Greece and Bulgaria, Sazonov remarked that] in view of their historical enmity and their present conflicting interests, there was a good deal of reason to suppose that, if one of these States came out as our enemy, the other would range itself on our side, so that they would cripple one another. . . . Sazonov said that it could not be assumed that our operations against the Straits could take place without a general European war, and that it was to be assumed that under such circumstances Serbia would direct all her forces against Austria-Hungary. . . . The favorable turn in Rumanian policy and public opinion, now to be observed, justified a certain doubt whether, in the event of our being at war with Austria, Rumania would actually come out against us. . . . In the event of our coming into collision with the Triple Alliance, Germany and Austria would send no troops towards the Straits, and, at the worst, Italy might send landing parties, though it would be dangerous for Italy to expose her frontiers to attack from France.[310]

Thus, according to Sazonov, the diplomatic situation seemed not unfavorable for landing an armed force to seize the Straits, even though it might lead to a collision with the Triple Alliance. But General Zhilinski, the Chief of Staff, "expressed the conviction that the struggle for Constantinople would hardly be possible without a general European war," in which case the troops which it was proposed to send to seize the Straits would be needed on the Western Front against Germany; success there would also

[310] Minutes of the Special Conference of Feb. 8/21, 1914; Pokrovski, *Drei Konferenzen,* p. 46 ff.; Stieve, *Isvolsky and the World War,* p. 232 ff.

mean success in the question of the Straits. M. Giers suggested that the troops for the landing expedition might be taken from the Caucasus Front; but General Zhilinski and General Danilov declared that this would be impracticable, both because they would be needed in the Caucasus in case of war with Turkey, and because, for technical reasons, they could not be mobilized quickly. Both these military experts were agreed that, with a battle proceeding or expected on the Western Front, the diversion of considerable troops to the Straits must be regarded as indefensible and impossible: "The only good strategy is strong strategy. The war on our Western Front would demand the utmost application of all the forces of the State, and we could not dispense with a single army corps to be left behind for special tasks. We must direct our energies to ensuring success in the most important theatre of war. With victory in this theatre, we should secure favorable decisions in all secondary questions." [311]

In spite of more optimistic arguments by the naval experts in favor of a landing expedition in the Straits, the Chief of Staff seemed to express the general sense of the Conference that such an expedition could only take place during a crisis which would lead to a general European war and that the troops for it would be needed on the Western Front against Germany and Austria. Therefore no separate landing expedition should be attempted for the present. Nevertheless, everything should be done to prepare for one. Accordingly, after a long discussion of the technical details involved, the Conference decided to recommend to

311 Minutes of the Special Conference of Feb. 8/21, 1914; Pokrovski, *Drei Konferenzen,* p. 46 ff.; Stieve, *Isvolsky and the World War,* p. 232 ff. This strategic point of view, always urged on the Russians by the French (*cf.* A. Zaiontchkovski, *et al., Les Alliés contre la Russie,* Paris, 1926), and embodied in General Danilov's detailed plan of campaign drawn up for the Russian General Staff in March, 1914 (printed by Frantz, *Russlands Eintritt in den Weltkrieg,* pp. 112-162), was of course the one actually put into operation four months later.

the Tsar a series of preparatory measures. These included increasing the strength and rapidity of mobilization of the expeditionary landing army; the gathering and subsidizing of adequate naval transports provided with sufficient collapsible horse-boxes and small boats for speedy embarkation and disembarkation; the increasing of the Black Sea Fleet by a second squadron of most modern and powerful battle cruisers, if possible, by the purchase of ships abroad; and the building of more strategic railways in the Caucasus, in order to speed up mobilization there, as a necessary part of "the measures required in preparation for our offensive on the Bosphorus."[312] The minutes of this Special Conference were laid before the Tsar on April 5, and received his entire approval.

The Duma also voted 110 million rubles to carry out the naval program for strengthening the Black Sea Fleet during the years 1914-1917.[313] As only 25 millions of this were to be spent in 1914, it would appear that no immediate expedition against Constantinople was intended unless something should occur to threaten the *status quo* and cause a general European war.

From the minutes of this Special Conference it appears that Sazonov contemplated the forcible seizure of the Straits. But the military experts regarded it as impracticable; they wished to reserve the troops for use in the main theatre of war against Germany and Austria. All were agreed, however, that Russia could not allow the Straits to fall into the hands of any other Power. Therefore the fullest preparatory measures must be taken for a landing expedition at the Straits in case European complications should afford an opportunity. This was regarded as probable in the future, but not as immediately imminent.

[312] Pokrovski, pp. 65-67; Stieve, pp. 244-246.

[313] Duma vote of Mar. 17/30, 1914; Zakher, in *Krasnyi Arkhiv,* VII, 51.

SUMMARY

We may now sum up very briefly the main Balkan Problems.

The origin of the trouble lay in the progressive decay of the Ottoman Empire, which was no longer able to maintain control over the Christian subject nationalities. These had become filled with a natural desire for political freedom and national unity. But, owing to the events of past history, considerable sections of these peoples still lived under Turkish or Hapsburg rule, and could not fulfil their nationalistic aspirations except by the further disintegration of Turkey and the partial dismemberment of Austria. Hence the Balkan Wars of 1876-78 and 1912-13. Hence also the antagonism between Austria and Serbia, which grew steadily more acute, because each had a vital interest at stake—Austria to preserve her very existence as a State, Serbia to satisfy twentieth century ideals of political liberty and national unity.

As Turkey declined in power, Russia and Austria became increasingly jealous of each other's influence in the Balkans, Russia wishing to achieve her "historic mission," and Austria to prevent the danger threatening to her from too great Slav power on her southern frontier. Bismarck and the League of the Three Emperors, and later Russia's venture in the Far East, for many years prevented this rivalry from disturbing the peace of Europe. But with the ambitious aims of M. Izvolski and Count Aehrenthal the rivalry became acute through the outcome of the Buchlau Bargain. Aehrenthal succeeded in annexing Bosnia and Herzegovina, while Izvolski failed to open the Straits, because Austria had the support of Germany, but England was unwilling to accept Izvolski's one-sided proposal to open the Straits to Russian warships but not to those of the other Great Powers. Though the Annexation Crisis was settled without war, thanks to the solution proposed by Germany, it increased the antagonism between Austria and Serbia on the one hand, and between Austria and Russia on the other. Henceforth Russia encouraged Serbia to prepare for the future, when, aided by Russia, she could achieve a "Greater Serbia" at Austria's expense. Until Russia was ready, however, Serbia was to wait.

Having made the Racconigi Bargain with Italy, and believing that he could count on the support of the Triple Entente, Izvolski took advantage of the Tripolitan War to make a third diplomatic effort to open the Straits by means of the Charykov negotiations with Turkey. But again he failed largely on account of lack of support from France and direct opposition from England. Henceforth he came to the conclusion that his aim could be achieved only in connection with a general European war, and used all his efforts to strengthen and tighten the Triple Entente for this "inevitable" conflict.

Meanwhile MM. Neratov, Hartwig, and Nekliudov had used the unrest caused in the Balkans by the Tripolitan War to help bring about the Balkan League, its nominal purpose being the preservation of the *status quo,* but its practical effect being an encouragement to the Balkan States to open war on Turkey. Though the Great Powers, especially England and Germany, managed to prevent Europe from being involved in a general conflict, the Balkan Wars resulted in a universal increase of suspicion, hatred, intrigues, and uncertainty, not only among the Great Powers who increased their armaments, but among the Balkan States themselves, and especially in Austria and Serbia. Serbia, greatly embittered at her exclusion by the Powers from a political and economic outlet on the Adriatic, had found some compensation in Macedonia. But this involved Bulgaria's deadly hatred. Serbia therefore tightened her relations with Greece and Rumania under Russian patronage, partly as a protection against Bulgarian revenge and partly with a view to the future struggle as the "Piedmont" of the Balkans, against the hated Hapsburg rule. Though M. Pashitch and the Serbian civil authorities did not want or plan war in 1914, they tolerated an agitation which contributed to a series of assassinations which culminated in the tragedy of Sarajevo. Austria meanwhile became more and more alarmed at the dangers threatening her very existence: the "Greater Serbia" agitation within and without her frontiers, the "desertion" of Rumania, and the closer ties which Russia was establishing with these two countries whose nationalist aspirations could only be satisfied through the dismemberment of Austria-Hungary. Whether Austria *could* have averted the danger from the "Greater Serbia" and "Greater Rumania" irredentist agitation, by giving democratic and reasonably liberal rights to her Slav and Rumanian subjects, or by some form of "trialism," is a hypothetical question to be touched upon later; at any rate she *did* not do so. Instead she chose to see her salvation in a war in which Serbia would be reduced in power by having to cede territory to Bulgaria, Rumania, and Albania. Several times Austria was ready to wage such a war on Serbia, but was held back either by Germany, as in July, 1913, or by concessions on the part of Serbia, as in March, 1909, and October, 1913. But in July, 1914, as will be seen later, Austria welcomed the opportunity for a localized war on Serbia afforded by the assassination of the Austrian Heir to the Throne.

M. Sazonov, though caring little for the Serbs themselves, and leaving them in the lurch in crucial moments, nevertheless encouraged and supported them at other times as an outpost of Slavdom in the Balkans and as an asset in a future war with Austria. Desiring peace, but fearing the power and criticism of the Russian Pan-Slavs and militarists, M. Sazonov was anxious to fulfil Russia's "historic mission." Observing Izvolski's failures to open the Straits by peaceful diplomatic means and his own failure to coerce Germany into an instant modification of General Liman's command at Constantinople, owing in each case chiefly to Sir Edward Grey's attitude, the Russian Foreign Minister came to the conclusion that he could succeed in his Balkan aims only as a result of "European complications." While Izvolski had attempted the more modest task of merely opening the Straits to Russian warships, Sazonov wanted to achieve the wider Pan-Slav "historic mission" of obtaining possession of the Straits and controlling Constantinople. It was because the Liman von Sanders Mission seemed to lessen the likelihood of this that Sazonov was so alarmed by it. Hence his proposal of "measures of compulsion" to force Turkey to abandon it; these, however, were not put into effect, owing to Germany's timely concessions and M. Kokovtsev's restraining influence. Hence also Sazonov's contemplation of a landing force to seize the Straits, which the military experts declared was impracticable at the moment but should be prepared for in case of European complications in the future. During the spring of 1914, together with M. Izvolski and President Poincaré, he worked to tighten the bonds with England by negotiations for an Anglo-Russian Naval Convention, in order that, when the "inevitable" war broke out, the solidarity of the Triple Entente should be more perfect than on former occasions. Consequently, if a new crisis arose, Germany and Austria would have to yield—or fight a war in which the superior forces would be on the side of the Triple Entente. In July, 1914, with the restraining hand of Kokovtsev removed, Sazonov believed that this Entente solidarity was virtually assured, when the murder of the Archduke and the Austrian ultimatum caused the "European complications" by means of which he calculated that Russia could finally achieve her "historic mission."

Turkey and the Balkan States were in unstable equilibrium. An inherent opposition of interests necessarily caused persistent enmity between Greece and Turkey, between Turkey and Russia, and between Austria and Serbia. But Bulgaria and Rumania were pursuing opportunist policies, and were ready to side with whichever group of the Great Powers seemed likely to prove the stronger and offer the greatest gains. No Power ever wants to yield on a matter of prestige, but this Balkan situation made an additional reason why neither France, Russia, Germany nor Austria was at first willing to yield in the Austro-Serbian conflict of July, 1914—it might have a determining effect on the policy of Bulgaria and Rumania. For several years it had been recognized that a strong Balkan bloc would have an influence in a general European war almost equal to that of a Great Power. Hence, in the spring of 1914, Russia was seeking to win Rumania and build up such a bloc including Serbia and Greece, while Austria in turn was preparing to form a counter-bloc with Bulgaria and Turkey. Such was the situation when the shots at Sarajevo precipitated the Austro-Serbian conflict and caused a crisis involving the prestige and power of the Triple Alliance and Triple Entente.

The writer of these lines does not believe that the World War was "inevitable." But he is quite ready to admit that, of all the major conflicts of interest which have been alleged as making it "inevitable," the Balkan problems were those most nearly incapable of a peaceful solution.

APPENDIX

FIFTH TREATY OF THE TRIPLE ALLIANCE

BETWEEN AUSTRIA-HUNGARY, THE GERMAN EMPIRE, AND ITALY

VIENNA, DECEMBER 5, 1912 *

THEIR Majesties the Emperor of Austria, King of Bohemia, etc., and Apostolic King of Hungary, the Emperor of Germany, King of Prussia, and King of Italy, firmly resolved to assure to Their States the continuation of the benefits which the maintenance of the Triple Alliance guarantees to them, from the political point of view as well as from the monarchical and social point of view, and wishing with this object to prolong the duration of this Alliance, concluded on May 20, 1882, renewed a first time by the Treaties of February 20, 1887, a second time by the Treaty of May 6, 1891, and a third time by the Treaty of June 28, 1902, have agreed upon the following Articles:

ARTICLE I. The High Contracting Parties mutually promise peace and friendship, and will enter into no alliance or engagement directed against any one of their States.

They engage to proceed to an exchange of ideas on political and economic questions of a general nature which may arise, and they further promise one another mutual support within the limits of their own interests.

ARTICLE II. In case Italy, without direct provocation on her part, should be attacked by France for any reason whatsoever, the two other Contracting Parties shall be bound to lend help and assistance with all their forces to the Party attacked.

* Pribram, I, p. 101 (Amer. ed. I, p. 245).

This same obligation shall devolve upon Italy in case of any aggression without direct provocation by France against Germany.

Article III. If one, or two, of the High Contracting Parties, without direct provocation on their part, should chance to be attacked and to be engaged in a war with two or more Great Powers nonsignatory to the present Treaty, the *casus foederis* will arise simultaneously for all the High Contracting Parties.

Article IV. In case a Great Power nonsignatory to the present Treaty should threaten the security of the states of one of the High Contracting Parties, and the threatened Party should find itself forced on that account to make war against it, the two others bind themselves to observe towards their Ally a benevolent neutrality. Each of them reserves to itself, in this case, the right to take part in the war, if it should see fit, to make common cause with its Ally.

Article V. If the peace of one of the High Contracting Parties should chance to be threatened under the circumstances foreseen by the preceding Articles, the High Contracting Parties shall take counsel together in ample time as to the military measures to be taken with a view to eventual cooperation.

They engage, henceforth, in all cases of common participation in a war, to conclude neither armistice, nor peace, nor treaty, except by common agreement among themselves.

Article VI. Germany and Italy, having in mind only the maintenance, so far as possible, of the territorial status quo in the Orient, engage to use their influence to forestall on the Ottoman coasts and islands in the Adriatic and the Aegean Seas any territorial modification which might be injurious to one or the other of the Powers signatory to the present Treaty. To this end, they will communicate to one another all information of a nature to enlighten each other mutually concerning their own dispositions, as well as those of other Powers.

Article VII. Austria-Hungary and Italy, having in mind only the maintenance, so far as possible, of the territorial status quo in the Orient, engage to use their influence to forestall any territorial modification which might be injurious to one or the other of the Powers signatory to the present Treaty. To this end, they shall communicate to one another all information of a nature to enlighten each other mutually concerning their own dispositions, as well as those of other Powers. However, if, in the course of events, the maintenance of the status quo in the regions of the Balkans or of the Ottoman coasts and islands in the Adriatic and in the Aegean Sea should become impossible, and if, whether in consequence of the action of a third Power or otherwise, Austria-Hungary or Italy should find themselves under the necessity of modifying it by a temporary or permanent occupation on their part, this occupation shall take place only after a previous agreement between the two Powers, based upon the principle of a reciprocal compensation for every advantage, territorial or other, which each of them might obtain beyond the present status quo, and giving satisfaction to the interests and well founded claims of the two Parties.

Article VIII. The stipulations of Articles VI and VII shall apply in no way to the Egyptian question, with regard to which the High Contracting Parties preserve respectively their freedom of action, regard being always paid to the principles upon which the present Treaty rests.

Article IX. Germany and Italy engage to exert themselves for the maintenance of the territorial status quo in the North African regions on the Mediterranean, to wit, Cyrenaica, Tripolitania, and Tunisia. The Representatives of the two Powers in these regions shall be instructed to put themselves into the closest intimacy of mutual communication and assistance.

If unfortunately, as a result of a mature examination of the situation, Germany and Italy should both recognize that the maintenance of the status quo has become impossible, Germany engages, after a formal and previous agreement, to support Italy in any action in the form of occupation or other taking of guaranty which the latter should undertake in these same regions with a view to an interest of equilibrium and of legitimate compensation.

It is understood that in such an eventuality the two Powers

would seek to place themselves likewise in agreement with England.

ARTICLE X. If it were to happen that France should make a move to extend her occupation, or even her protectorate or her sovereignty, under any form whatsoever, in the North African territories, and that in consequence thereof, Italy, in order to safeguard her position in the Mediterranean, should feel that she must herself undertake action in the said North African territories, or even have recourse to extreme measures in French territory in Europe, the state of war which would thereby ensue between Italy and France would constitute *ipso facto,* on the demand of Italy, and at the common charge of Germany and Italy, the *casus foederis* foreseen by Articles II and V of the present Treaty, as if such an eventuality were expressly contemplated therein.

ARTICLE XI. If the fortunes of any war undertaken in common against France by the two Powers should lead Italy to seek for territorial guaranties with respect to France for the security of the frontiers of the Kingdom and of her maritime position, as well as with a view to stability and to peace, Germany will present no obstacle thereto, and, if need be, and in a measure compatible with circumstances, will apply herself to facilitating the means of attaining such a purpose.

ARTICLE XII. The High Contracting Parties mutually promise secrecy as to the contents of the present Treaty.

ARTICLE XIII. The Signatory Powers reserve the right of subsequently introducing, in the form of a Protocol and of a common agreement, the modifications of which the utility should be demonstrated by circumstances.

ARTICLE XIV. The present Treaty shall remain in force for the space of six years, dating from the expiration of the Treaty now in force; but if it has not been denounced one year in advance by one or another of the High Contracting Parties, it shall remain in force for the same duration of six more years.

ARTICLE XV. The ratifications of the present Treaty shall be exchanged at Vienna within a period of a fortnight, or sooner if may be.

In witness whereof the respective Plenipotentiaries have

signed the present Treaty and have affixed thereto the seal of their arms.

Done at Vienna, in triplicate, the fifth day of the month of December, one thousand nine hundred and twelve.

L. S. Berchtold
L. S. von Tschirschky
L. S. Avarna

SUPPLEMENTARY NOTES

I, 3, note 3. Mr. Gooch's *Recent Revelations of European Diplomacy,* (London, 1927), are brought nearly up to date by supplementary volumes (London, 1928, 1929).

I, 23. Ex-President Poincaré's extraordinary capacity for historical work in addition to all his political activities, and his readiness to reply to his critics, is illustrated in a little book: *Les Responsabilités de la Guerre: Quatorze Questions par René Gerin; Quatorze Réponses par Raymond Poincaré* (Paris, 1930). M. Gerin propounded fourteen shrewd questions to M. Poincaré, begging him to answer them, and promising that, if he did so, he, Gerin, would refrain from making any counter-replies. M. Poincaré accepted the challenge, and set forth his fourteen answers in some one hundred and fifty pages. Though he contributes a little new information, his material is for the most part drawn from his already published memoirs. The weak points in his answers have been thoroughly dissected by G. von Jagow, G. Frantz, A. von Wegerer, and M. Montgelas, in KSF, VIII, 601-665, 705-730, July, August 1930. *Cf.* also the criticism of Poincaré by A. Bach, *Poincaré und der Kriegsausbruch, 1914* (Berlin, 1929); and the volume of Demartial quoted above, p. 6.

I, 47-49. During the past two years many writers have become increasingly aware of the importance of the influence of the Press as one of the causes of the World War, and have devoted monographs to various aspects of the subject. Among the most important of these may be noted: G. Arbouin, *Les Nations d'après leurs Journaux: Petit Essai de Psychologie de la Presse* (Paris, 1917); I. Grüning, *Die russische öffentliche Meinung und ihre Stellung zu den Grossmächten 1878-1914* (Berlin, 1919); R. Ibbeken, *Das aussenpolitische Problem Staat und Wirtschaft in der deutschen Reichspolitik 1880-1914* (Schleswig, 1928); "Irenäus" (pseud. August Stein), *Es War Alles Ganz Anders* (2nd ed., Frankfurt, 1922); A. Jux, *Der Kriegsschrecken des Frühjahrs 1914 in der europäischen Presse* (Berlin, 1929); S. M. von Propper, *Was nicht in die Zeitung kam: Erinnerungen des Chefredakteurs der "Birschewyja Wedomosti"* (Frankfurt, 1929); C. Schoen, *Der "Vorwärts" und die Kriegserklärung* (Berlin, 1929); W. Zimmermann, *Die Englische Presse zum Ausbruch des Weltkrieges* (Charlottenburg, 1928); and in general, O. Groth, *Die Zeitung* (3 vols., Manheim, 1927-30), especially, II, 192-236. See also the present writer's brief account of the pre-war British and German Press in his review of the sixth volume of the *British Documents* in *Current History,* Oct. 1930.

I, 80, note 37. See also Italicus, *Italiens Dreibundpolitik, 1870-1896* (Munich, 1928); the early pages of W. L. Langer's excellent analysis of the general European situation after 1878, *The Franco-Russian Alliance*

(Cambridge, 1929), with an extensive bibliography; the thoughtful survey of B. Molden, "Das deutsch-österreichische Bündnis und der grossdeutsche Gedanke," in KSF, VIII, 312-323, April 1930; and L. D. Steefel's review of recent Bismarck literature in the *Journal of Modern History,* II, 74-95, March 1930.

I, 123, note 36. Later on, to be sure, after England had become the friend of France, the English Foreign Office was inclined to accept the French assertion that the initiative in the discussions for intervention in the Boer War had come from Germany and not from Russia; B.D., III, 411-12, 425-6, 432-3, 436-7; and especially VI, 204-6.

I, 129-141. On the negotiations for an Anglo-German alliance at the turn of the century, see: Lord Newton, *Lord Lansdowne, A Biography* (N. Y. and London, 1929), ch. vi, who concludes that "The failure of the negotiations in 1901 may be described as a turning-point in the history of the world, and will doubtless, provide a subject of endless speculation as to what would have occurred had they ended favorably; but one thing is certain, and that is that William II. would have been almost intolerable as an ally" (p. 208); Willy Becker, *Fürst Bülow und England* (Greifswald, 1929), who lays the blame for failure on Bülow and Holstein (cf. the review by W. Frauendienst in KSF, VIII, 532-9, June 1930); G. Ritter, *Die Legende von der verschmähten englischen Freundschaft* (Freiburg, 1929); the review of both Meinecke and Ritter by O. Becker, in the *Deutsche Literaturzeitung*, 1929, Heft 19, p. 903 ff.; and the article of G. Roloff, "Die Bündnisverhandlungen zwischen Deutschland und England, 1898-1901," in KSF, VII, 1167-1222, Dec., 1929.

I, 152-192. On the Anglo-French Entente of 1904 and the First Morocco Crisis of 1905-06, the full documents from the British side are given in B.D., II and III, "The Anglo-Japanese Alliance and the Franco-British Entente" and "The Testing of the Entente, 1904-06 (London, 1927-28). Excellent accounts are to be found in Lord Newton's *Lord Lansdowne* (N. Y. and London, 1929), chs. x, xiv, and p. 488; in Mr. Harold Nicolson's life of his father, *Lord Carnock* (London, 1930), chs. vi, vii; and especially in the detailed and scholarly volume of Mr. Eugene N. Anderson, *The First Moroccan Crisis,* 1904-1906 (Chicago, 1930).

I, 181. For an interesting account of the Dogger Bank Affair, by one who was behind the scenes and perceived Delcassé's effort to turn the affair into a stepping-stone for an Anglo-French-Russian Triple Entente, see Baron Taube, *La Politique Russe d'avant-Guerre* (Paris, 1928), pp. 1-43; and for the documents on the British side of the affair, B.D., IV, 5-41.

I, 209 f. What is said at this point of Sir Edward Grey's reasons for failing to consult and inform the Cabinet concerning the Anglo-French military "conversations" and for his preferring them to any other more definite or written agreement seems to be confirmed by an interesting Memorandum of a Permanent Under-Secretary, Sir T. H. Sanderson. In a Memorandum of Feb. 2, 1906, giving a summary of a conversation which he had just had with M. Paul Cambon concerning the Grey-Cambon "conversations," Sanderson said unofficially and privately to Cambon:

In the first place, in the course of my experience, which was a pretty long one, I knew of no instance of any secret Agreement by the British Government which pledged them further than that if a certain policy agreed upon with another Power were in any way menaced, the two Powers should consult as to the course to be taken. That I thought was the limit to which the Government could properly bind itself without in some way making Parliament aware of the obligations that it was incurring.

Secondly, it was a maxim which had been impressed upon me by several statesmen of great eminence that it was not wise to bring before a Cabinet the question of a course to be pursued in hypothetical cases which had not arisen. A discussion on the subject invariably gave rise to divergences of opinion on questions of principle, whereas in a concrete case unanimity would very likely be secured. [And Grey here noted on the margin: "I am glad this point was so well pointed out to M. Cambon."] M. Cambon observed that this view was a perfectly just one.

Thirdly, I told him that I thought that if the Cabinet were to give a pledge which would morally bind the country to go to war in certain circumstances, and were not to mention this pledge to Parliament, and if at the expiration of some months the country suddenly found itself pledged to war in consequence of this assurance, the case would be one which would justify impeachment, and which might even result in that course unless at the time the feeling of the country were very strongly in favor of the course to which the Government was pledged (B.D., III, 184 f.).

I, 213. The Anglo-Belgian military conversations began on Jan. 18, 1906, upon instructions from General Grierson, between the English Military Attaché, Col. Barnardiston, and the Belgian Chief of Staff, General Ducarne. They had the express sanction of the Foreign Ministers of both countries, as well as of the military authorities. They quickly led to an agreement for the landing of 100,000 British troops on the continent for the defense of Belgium (*cf.* B.D., III, 186-203; and Carl Hosse, *Die englisch-belgischen Aufmarschpläne gegen Deutschland vor dem Weltkrieg,* Vienna, 1930; Hosse prints for the first time interesting details of the technical railway schedules worked out for the British; he uses photographs of Belgian documents which were taken by the Germans during the war, but restored after the Treaty of Versailles). General Wilson, who succeeded General Grierson as Chief of Military Operations in August, 1910, arranged with Belgium and France for the rapid transport of 160,000 British, who were to take a position on the French left wing. In 1912 there were some doubts for a while about Belgium's readiness to cooperate with the French and British (*cf.* D.D.F., 3e Série, I, No. 522), and the British Foreign Office, in spite of its obligation to observe Belgian neutrality, appears to have considered the question of marching British troops into the little country, without invitation and even against Belgium's consent, "in order to meet the approach of German troops on the other side" (Harold Nicolson, *Lord Carnock,* London, 1930, p. 399). In 1913 Belgium increased her army and was again ready to enter into close military relations with the French and British at the outbreak of the war. For a good summary of the Anglo-Belgian military conversations, see A. Bach, "Die 'conventions anglo-belges' im Lichte neuer Dokumente," in KSF, VIII, 547-560, June, 1930.

I, 214-222. The negotiations for the Anglo-Russian Entente of 1907 can now be followed in great detail in the fourth volume of the *British Documents,* "The Anglo-Russian Rapprochment, 1903-7" (London, 1929). From them it appears that as early as November, 1903, King Edward had "spoken very earnestly" to Count Benckendorff, the Russian Ambassador, during the latter's visit to Windsor, "His Majesty expressing his desire that an attempt should be made to establish a better understanding between the two Governments" (B.D., IV, 186). For King Edward's conversation with Izvolski on the same subject at Copenhagen in April, 1904, see *ibid.,* p. 188 ff. The impression mentioned by the present writer (I, 218, note 210), that the bridging of the gulf between Russia and England was owing apparently more to the eagerness and pressure of the British, rather than the Russian, Foreign Office, is amply confirmed in the recent British documents (cf. B.D., IV, 183, 188, 195 ff., 232, 237, 400, 410 ff.). A delightful and authoritative account of the long negotiations which led to what came to be known as the "Triple Entente" is to be found in Mr. Harold Nicolson's *Lord Carnock* (London, 1930), chs. viii, ix; he notes (p. 308) that his father, Sir Arthur Nicolson, who conducted the negotiations in St. Petersburg, was requested by Sir Edward Grey to discontinue his habit of using "in official telegrams and despatches the expression 'triple entente' when referring to the joint action of England, France and Russia. The expression is one which is no doubt convenient, but if it appeared in a Parliamentary Bluebook it would be assumed to have some special official meaning and might provoke inconvenient comment or inquiry."

I, 229. The British Government's sudden change of attitude in April, 1903, in refusing to participate in the construction of the Bagdad Railway, is ascribed by Willy Becker, *Fürst Bülow und England* (Greifswald, 1929), to Lansdowne's new policy of an entente with France. But the material in the British documents, private information in my possession, and Lord Newton's *Lord Lansdowne* (N. Y. and London, 1929), p. 253 f., seem to confirm my statement that it was the outcry in the British Press and Parliament which caused the British Government, against Landowne's own better judgment, to make the *volte-face* and to refuse British participation. Possibly also underground Russian influences were at work against British participation, for Russia worked persistently to block or delay the construction of the Bagdad Railway.

I, 230-232. For the details of later British obstruction to the building of the Bagdad Railway during the years 1905-10, so long as Germany did not consent to Grey's conditions that the negotiations must be *à quatre* (that is, include also England's friends, Russia and France) and that Turkey ought not to be burdened with further kilometric guarantees, see the documents in B.D., VI, 91-105, 325-433. The British insistence on negotiations *à quatre* was partly owing to the expectation of being able to get a better bargain from Germany, and partly out of political deference to Russia; but Russia showed small gratitude for this deference when she made a separate bargain without England in the Potsdam Agreements. Besides preventing the Germans from getting Turkish money for the construction of the Bagdad Railway by refusing British consent to an increase of the Turkish customs, (cf. B.D., V, 168 ff., 199, 208 f., 502; and

VI, 325-433 *passim*), other British suggestions for thwarting the Germans were rival railways: an Anglo-Russian line from the Persian Gulf through Persia toward Russia, which "would completely crowd out the Bagdad Railway" and "reduce it to a purely local railway" (B.D., VI, 359); and a British line from Bagdad and the Persian Gulf by way of the Euphrates Valley to Damascus and the Mediterranean; a concession for this was demanded from Turkey (*ibid.*, 371 ff.).

I, 237, note 20. For British fears and suspicions in regard to the German navy in 1907 and 1908, with summaries of the German Press, and with long reports from the British Naval Attaché in Berlin concerning the German navy, see the full details now available in B.D., VI, 1-226. A brief review of these documents, so far as concerns the mischievous influence of the German and British Press, may be found in the present writer's article in *Current History* for Oct., 1930.

Many English officials even believed that Germany was secretly making plans for the invasion of England. One of the most suspicious of these officials was Sir Eyre Crowe. As Senior Clerk in the Foreign Office it fell to him to write the first long comments on the despatches as they came in from Germany's diplomatic representatives abroad. Inevitably his hostile dissection of the reports from Germany greatly influenced Sir Edward Grey and the other officials who next read them, and who generally endorsed with brief comments Crowe's long criticisms. Crowe, whose mother and wife were both German, appears to have been accepted as an infallible authority on Germany. But unfortunately he was prone to accept baseless gossip as gospel truth. For instance, he cites in 1908 three alleged circumstances as evidence that Germany was making plans for the invasion of England. (1) "So great an authority as Moltke regarded the invasion of England as practicable. It is certain that the Great General Staff at Berlin is of the same opinion." (2) "It is only 2 or 3 years ago [in reality *seven* years earlier, in 1901] that Baron von Edelsheim then a captain of that Staff published, with the authorization of his chief, a pamphlet dealing in detail with the measures to be taken for that purpose." (3) "Some 2 or 3 years ago, I think, the Emperor with his own hand made a number of blue pencil corrections or alterations in the designs of 2 new liners [of the Hamburg-American Line], then about to be built, because His Majesty maintained that the designs as submitted to him would not permit of these ships taking their allotted part in the transport of 2 divisions to England" (B.D., VI, 117). The statements in regard to Moltke, the General Staff, and the Emperor are untrue; and Edelsheim was dismissed from the General Staff because he had published his pamphlet *without the approval of his chief,* General von Schlieffen, and because the views expressed in it were *in contradiction* with those of the General Staff. Something has been said above of the malign influence of Herr von Holstein in the Wilhelmstrasse; that of Sir Eyre Crowe in Downing Street deserves further attention.

I, 256-264. For the impressions of Sir Edward Goschen, the British Ambassador in Berlin, in regard to Bülow's resignation, and in regard to his successor, Bethmann-Hollweg, and Kiderlen-Wächter, see B.D., VI, 276 ff.

I, 291. The close relations between the English and French military authorities during the Agadir Crisis are reflected in the confidential report of Aug. 24, 1911, of the British Military Attaché in Paris, Colonel Fairholme, of his conversation with General Joffre:

General Joffre said that he and his Staff have been, and still are, hard at work settling the details of their plans of campaign, which, he stated, will be ready in every particular in a few days' time.

The General went on to discuss the strategical problem.

The one unknown factor is whether the Germans mean to come through Belgium or not. "I wish I knew that," he observed, "and I wish I knew that they intend doing so; it would be better for us." . . .

The new Chief attaches the very greatest importance to the co-operation of a British expeditionary force, which concentrating somewhere between Douai and Cambrai, and falling on the right flank of the German advance, might produce great, and even decisive, results. But it would have to be sent early in the day; its intervention, for instance, on the 18th day of the French mobilization, might not prove a bit too soon. . . .

"In any case," he said, "Germany must pour a large force into Alsace-Lorraine, as, if they allowed us to gain a footing there, the populations of both provinces would rise. *This we know for certain.* And then every possible difficulty would be created for their transport, etc." . . .

I gathered that, if the Germans should advance in force *via* Belgium, the French plan would be to hold them in check on that flank, and to attack vigorously on Alsace and Lorraine. . . .

On my mentioning Italy, the General said very positively, "Italy will make no move. Her interests lie on our side, not on that of Germany and Austria." (B.D., VI, 643 f.)

Harold Nicolson, in the life of his father (*Lord Carnock,* p. 346 ff.) indicates that British preparations for war in the late summer of 1911 were far more advanced than was realized by British public opinion, and that the state of "war preparedness" was not relaxed until September 22, on receipt of news from Berlin that Kiderlen-Wächter was weakening.

I, 293-299. For English comments on the *Daily Telegraph* affair, see B.D., VI, 201-226; and for the English side of the long but futile negotiations for some kind of an agreement to lessen the growing tension over Anglo-German naval rivalry during the years 1909-12, *ibid.,* 227-324, 434-665. The official attitude of the members of the British Foreign Office on them may be well summed up in their "Minutes" on a telegram from Sir Edward Goschen, the British Ambassador in Berlin, to Sir Edward Grey on May 9, 1911 (*ibid.,* 622 f.):

MINUTES.

The German government now at last confess what we suspected from the outset to be the case: they have definitely withdrawn from their promise to submit proposals for a reduction of armaments, on the ground that they consider any such scheme impossible. In view of the repeated public utterances of high German officials, including successive Chancellors, and of the Emperor himself, it is clear that they never did believe that they could put forward such proposals. Their statement to the contrary was used, as was pointed out here at the time, for the purpose of leading H[is] M[ajesty's] G[overnment] on to the conclusion of a general Anglo-German agreement, such as they knew Great Britain was unwilling even to discuss.

They have gone some considerable way in gaining their point. They have induced H[is] M[ajesty's] G[overnment] in the first instance to abandon their original attitude which was that no discussion of a reduction of armaments was of any use if the existing German naval programme was to be carried out in its integrity. The Chancellor on the contrary explained that any negotiation would have to start from the basis of the actual completion of that programme. We abandoned our position, and continued the discussion.

Germany insisted that before a naval understanding could be thought of, there must be a general Anglo-German agreement of a political nature, which would preclude the possibility of war between the two countries in any circumstances. The essential feature of such an agreement was that not only would the two countries refrain from ever attacking the other, but they would undertake each to remain neutral in any war in which the other was engaged. The object of this clearly is to allow Germany to deal with other Powers, such as France and Russia, without any fear of British intervention. . . .

With the view of assuring the success of this negotiation, the German government, being always farsighted in these matters, have for a considerable time carefully laid their plans for leading H[is] M[ajesty's] G[overnment] further on in the same road. The means employed have been those placed at their disposal by the organization of their press bureau, the direct and indirect influence they exercise over the British press, and personal connection, through the Berlin Foreign Office, and through the German ambassador in London, with the leaders of the so-called "pacifist" propaganda in this country. By these means the German gov[ernmen]t have encouraged, if not created, over here an agitation—to which nothing in practice corresponds in Germany—in favour of an Anglo-German understanding as such, of the exact purport of which its promoters and supporters have not the shadowiest notion.

Finally, in order to put still further pressure on H[is] M[ajesty's] G[overnment], they have so played their cards that, if the negotiations come to nothing, they will be able to say,—and they will say it loudly and have it re-echoed throughout Europe—that it is all the fault of H[is] M[ajesty's] G[overnment]. . . .

We are fast drifting back into the position which was summarized in the memorandum of Jan[uary] 1st, 1907. [Cf. B.D., III, 397-420, *App.* A.] Now again, as on former occasions, the German gov[ernmen]t after a period of much unfriendliness on their part, come to woo us with assurances that if we will only do what they wish, it will lead to peace, the end of all friction, and the definite establishment of Anglo-German friendship. This time, if we fall into the same trap, the consequences will be still more serious than before. We shall have to reckon not only with renewed German unfriendliness, and further German demands, passed by the added weight of a strengthened Germany, but we run the imminent risk of practically breaking up the *entente* with France and Russia. . . .

E. A. C[rowe, Senior Clerk, Foreign Office].

The "tempo of construction" proposal has turned out as shadowy as was expected.

Whatever unfavourable comment our failure to conclude an Agreement may expose us to, an agreement which leaves the naval question unsettled would, I believe, command still less support.

W. L[angley, Assistant Under-Secretary of State].

Sir Eyre Crowe's minute is an admirable summary of what has passed and merits the most careful consideration. I entirely agree with his views and am also of his opinion that the object of the German Gov[ernmen]t is to lay on one side the naval agreement and lead us into "a general understanding." We have hitherto resisted, and rightly resisted, going further with Germany as regards an understanding than we have done with France and Russia. I trust that we shall firmly maintain this attitude. . . . A. N[icolson, Permanent under-Secretary of State].

It would be well to have the papers put together, which give the history of the question and will bring out the points of Sir E. Crowe's minute. I remember one occasion on which Count Metternich reproached us because the Prime Minister had stated in Parliament that there could be no question of Germany altering her naval law and had thereby ignored the offer to reduce the "tempo." I am sure I recorded this conversation and it should be included in the collection of papers. [Cf. B.D., VI, 496-7].

The last decision of the Gov[ernmen]t was that an agreement under which Germany undertook not to increase her naval programme might be worth consideration. From the point of view of naval expenditure the German reply is most unsatisfactory. On the other hand the last paragraph apparently makes it easier for us to avoid being entangled in separate political negotiations with Germany to which other Powers are not parties.

We must wait for the full text, which I will circulate to the Cabinet when received.

E. G[rey, Secretary of State].

I, 299-312. On the Haldane Mission itself, see B.D., VI, 666-761. The "Minutes" quoted above help to explain why it was foredoomed to failure.

I, 317-8. Volume VII of *British Documents,* which will deal with Anglo-French relations during the Agadir Crisis and the Haldane Mission, has not yet (June, 1930) been published. But Volume VI, covering Anglo-German naval and political negotiations from 1907 to 1912, confirms my view of the dubiousness of Izvolski's allegation that Poincaré's intervention prevented the success of the Haldane Mission. Long before Poincaré became Prime Minister, it is perfectly clear from numerous letters and "Minutes" that Grey, Nicolson, and Crowe were determined to make no "political understanding" or neutrality agreement with Germany which would in any way limit England's freedom to aid France. As Sir Arthur Nicolson wrote to Lord Hardinge on April 19, 1911:

I sincerely hope that we shall keep clear of any understanding which would tie our hands in any way, or which would in the slightest degree affect our understanding with France and Russia. I hope that our Government now fully realize that the aim of Germany in these negotiations is to smash up, as far as she is able to do, the Triple *Entente* and that her chief object is to isolate France as much as possible (B.D., VI, 621).

After the failure of the Haldane Mission, Nicolson wrote to Goschen: "I need hardly tell you that I feel great relief at the idea that the Formula question is in process of interment; it has always been my dream to be on cordial relations with Germany *without* any definite political understanding, and if, as I hope, the recent conversations have that result no one will be more pleased than I" (B.D., VI, 750). And Grey summed up the Foreign Office view tersely to Nicolson: "Although we cannot bind ourselves under all circumstances to go to war with France against Germany, we shall also certainly not bind ourselves to Germany not to assist France" (BD., VI, 751).

Although Grey was meticulous in keeping the French fully informed of all the negotiations, the French were nevertheless a little nervous (*cf.* B.D., VI, 664, 669 f., 675, 687 f., 690 f., 726 ff.). This nervousness of the French naturally confirmed Grey in his determination not to make any agreement with Germany which might increase French nervousness.

I, 319-20. Mr. Harold Nicolson, in the recent life of his father, draws a very interesting contrast between the attitude of Sir Arthur Nicolson and that of Sir Edward Grey in regard to the Entente with France (*Lord Carnock,* p. 330 ff.; *cf.* also B.D., VI, 739, 747-751). He says:

He [Sir Arthur Nicolson] desired, above all, that the solidarity of the Triple Entente should be patent and proclaimed. He regarded the existing arrangements with France and Russia as possessing all the disadvantages, and none of the benefits, of an alliance. He feared that the Ententes were sufficiently binding to encourage people in St. Petersburg and Paris, but not sufficiently binding to discourage people in Berlin. He considered that in this vital matter the indolent British indulgence in half-measures was not only dangerous but unfair. Unfair to Germany: unfair to France and Russia: unfair, above all, to British public opinion. He urged Sir Edward Grey, in season and out of season, to make it clear to the world exactly where we stood.

The Secretary of State, somewhat naturally, was annoyed by this persistence. It is always irritating for a gentleman in a false position to be assured by other gentlemen that his position is false. And from 1906 onwards Sir Edward Grey's position had been very illogical indeed. His ignorance of Continental psychology had tempted him in the early days of his office to under-estimate the importance which would be attached abroad to "conversations" between General Staffs. His expert knowledge of Ministerial and Parliamentary psychology convinced him, on the other hand, that, once these conversations had been taken seriously by the foreigners, the Cabinet would be extremely annoyed at not having been informed at the time. . . . In wishing to come into the open, to show the solidarity and reliability of the Entente, Nicolson desired solely to avert a European war. Whereas Grey's apprehensions were disturbed by his simultaneous desire to avert a Parliamentary crisis.

I, 342, note 232. See also Graf Waldersee, "Von Deutschlands militärpolitischen Beziehungen zu Italian," in KSF, VII, 636-664, July, 1929.

I, 350. The reference to the myth of Germany's overwhelming superiority in numbers refers of course to the total forces available in Germany, and in France and Belgium at the beginning of the war, and not to the forces actually present in northeast France and Belgium at the moment of the German invasion. Germany had a great military advantage during the first weeks of the war owing to the fact that the French deployed their main forces eastward between Mezières and Belfort instead of northeast to stop a German sweep through Belgium, either because they did not feel sure that the Germans would come through Belgium rapidly, or because of diplomatic policy—the fear that a French deployment toward Belgium might look like a threat to Belgian neutrality—or because of the political and strategic hope of occupying quickly Alsace and Lorraine and so being *beati possidentes* in the peace negotiations at the close of a short war.

I, 357, note 6. On the assassination of King Alexander in 1903, see also D. A. Loncharevich, *Jugoslaviens Entstehung* (Vienna, 1929), pp. 318-323; and, for the hesitation of the Great Powers as to whether they should show their abhorrence of the crime by withdrawing their ministers from Belgrade, B.D., V, 124-148.

I, 360, note 9. For the details on Austria's economic intimidation of Serbia, see B.D., V, 148-167; and Joseph N. Baernreither, *Fragments of a Political Diary,* (edited and introduced by Joseph Redlich, London, 1930), chs. i-v, *passim.*

I, 367, note 20; 369, note 21. In connection with the negotiations for the Anglo-Russian Agreement of 1907 the question of the Straits was several times mentioned (B.D., IV, 254-5, 272, 279-284, 286-7, 289-291, 293-6, 414). The apparent contradiction between the statements of Sir Edward Grey and Izvolski on the one hand, and the contemporary evidence cited in note 20 on the other, is explained by the fact that, though the Straits were considerably discussed, they were not made the subject of formal negotiations for inclusion in the Agreement of 1907. On March 15, 1907, Grey said to Benckendorff, the Russian Ambassador in London:

"I had felt all through these negotiations that good relations with Russia meant that our old policy of closing the Straits against her, and throwing our weight against her at any conference of the Powers, must be abandoned. It was this old policy which, in my opinion, had been the root of the difficulties between the two countries for two generations. And, for us and Russia to settle our difficulties in Asia, and then to find ourselves afterwards in opposition on some other important matter, would be to undo the good which would be done by the present negotiations as to Asiatic frontiers.

I felt, however, that it would be difficult for us to put anything concerning the Straits in the form of an engagement, and it would be necessary for me to speak to the Prime Minister before I could say anything very definite" (B.D., IV, 280).

Four days later, in writing to Sir Arthur Nicolson at St. Petersburg, Grey pointed out some of the difficulties in acceding to Russian desires about the Straits. But Izvolski appears to have overlooked the difficulties and to have jumped eagerly at Grey's statement that the old policy of closing the Straits against Russia would have to be abandoned. Nicolson reported a few days later:

"M. Izvolski said that the conversation [reported from London] constituted to his mind a great evolution in the relations of the two countries, and that though the matter was one which would have to be most carefully considered from all points of view, especially as to the method and moment of advancing further in the question, still he was highly gratified with the tone and tenor of your remarks. . . . I have rarely seen M. Izvolski so contented and satisfied" (B.D., IV, 281-2).

And two days later, in a private letter to Grey, Nicolson repeated: "M. Izvolski is beaming with pleasure over the report which Poklewsky brought to him of your communication to Count Benckendorff in regard to the Bosphorus and the Dardanelles. He quite grasped the sense of your observations and will study the question thoroughly before making an overture; but the fact that the British Government are willing to discuss the question is, he considers, and as he expressed it, a great evolution in our relations and a historical event" (B.D., IV, 283-4). The importance of these conversations lies in the optimism with which Izvolski felt encouraged to proceed to the Buchlau negotiations (without informing England beforehand), and in the pessimistic despair with which he learned on visting England after Buchlau that Grey refused after all to concede opening the Straits to Russian warships alone, according to Izvolski's plan, as I have indicated on pp. 380-1.

I, 368-378. The Buchlau Meeting, and the preliminaries leading up to it, can now be followed in great detail from the Austrian side in Oe.-U.A., I, 1-92. Baron Taube, p. 173 ff., adds some light from the Russian side. But precisely what was said cannot be exactly determined and probably never can be. It had been agreed at Buchlau by Izvolski and Aehrenthal that Izvolski should make a memorandum of their conversations at Buchlau and submit it to Aehrenthal. Unfortunately Izvolski neglected to do this at once. He had not even done it at the time of his return to St. Petersburg six weeks later at the end of October (Oe.-U.A., I, 90, 144, 252). By this time, however, he had learned to his great sorrow that he would be unable, on account of Sir Edward Grey's attitude and on account of domestic criticism in Russia, to pocket his expected share of the Buchlau bargain; his chagrin seems to have warped his recollection of what was said at Buchlau. Aehrenthal also drew up a memorandum of the Buchlau conversations (Oe.-U.A., I, 86-92), but it is not clear that it was strictly contemporary.

I, 378-406. On the long Bosnian Crisis of 1908-09 and its immediate consequences, see Oe.-U.A., I, 92-895; II, 1-285; B.D., V, 366-815; and Harold Nicolson, *Lord Carnock,* chs. x, xi; he points out (p. 311 f.) that it is not true to say that Sir Arthur Nicolson was at the bottom of Izvolski's resistance. And in fact we know that at the end of the crisis Izvolski suddenly capitulated without waiting to hear his advice—much to Nicolson's regret (*cf.* B.D., V, 736-7). Nicolson was also properly and shrewdly skeptical as to Izvolski's account the Buchlau affair; on Jan. 2, 1909, for instance, he wrote confidentially to Grey:

"At the time the preliminary explanations which M. Izvolski gave me did not seem to me to be quite convincing. . . . and it may be that M. Izvolski committed himself a little further than he is willing to admit. His position on the question is a little tangled and hampered by various secret arrangements which seem to be emerging piecemeal into publicity, concluded between Russia and Austria-Hungary; but it would create a painful impression here if it were believed that during M. Izvolski's tenure of office, and after the Sanjak railway incident, *pourparlers* had taken place in respect to the incorporation of Bosnia and Herzegovina" (B.D., V, 547-8).

I, 413-426. On Izvolski's efforts to open the Straits in 1911, see the documents between Nov. 4 and Dec. 30, 1911, listed in D.D.F., 3me Série, I, pp. xxif.

I, 439, note 155. For English complaints of Hartwig's earlier unreliability and aggressive attitude in Persia, see B.D., IV, 199 ff., 403 ff., 420, 425 f., 588 f., 598; and for numerous references to Austria's suspicions of his later Russian intrigues in Belgrade, see the index volume, Oe.-U.A., IX, 53, under "Hartwig."

The Balkan Wars and the other remaining topics in my chapter on "Balkan Problems" are now illustrated in great detail from the Austrian side in Oe.-U.A., IV-VII, *passim;* and from the Serbian side in *Die Auswärtige Politik Serbiens* (edited by M. Bogitchevitch, Berlin, 1929), II, *passim.*

II, 3, note 4. Several interesting studies have recently been added to the biographical material on the Archduke Franz Ferdinand: Theodor von Sosnosky, *Franz Ferdinand* (Munich and Berlin, 1929); Leopold von Chlumecky, *Erzherzog Franz Ferdinands Wirken und Wollen* (Berlin, 1929); and Victor Eisenmenger, *Erzherzog Franz Ferdinand* (Vienna, 1929).

II, 46, note 59. For further details on the Bosnian maneuvers, with a good sketch map, see L. Schnagl, "Die Manöver in Bosnien im Jahre 1914," in KSF, VI, 873-881, Sept., 1928.

II, 55, note 3. Recently M. Albert Mousset has published a French translation, said to be complete, of the stenographic report of the trial, entitled, *L'Attentat de Sarajevo* (Paris, 1930); it contains some of the less important passages omitted by "Pharos."

The information which Potiorek, Governor of Bosnia, collected during the days immediately following the assassination, and which he forwarded in daily cipher telegrams to Vienna, is now available in the recently published Austrian documents. This information is doubly interesting, partly because it contains the first confessions extracted from the assassins when they were trying to conceal their accomplices, and partly because it indicates just how much information the Vienna authorities possessed at the time they had to make up hurriedly the ultimatum to Serbia and the *dossier* to be presented to the Powers. This information is contained in Oe.-U.A., VIII, Nos. 9939, 9940, 9947-9, 9975, 9991-2, 10023, 10066-7, 10109, 10137, 10184-6, 10207, 10224-5, 10249-50, 10272, 10313-4, 10346, 10372, 10374, 10390-1, 10426-9, 10467-9, 10505-9, 10558-62.

II, 58. In connection with the origin of the "Black Hand," it is perhaps not quite correct to speak of Dimitrijevitch as "its organizer." The first steps toward its organization appear to have been taken by Bogdan Radenkovitch and Voja Tankositch (whose names appear as nos. 1 and 7 in the facsimile at p. 89) and one or two others. But Dimitrijevitch very quickly became its leading spirit; for further light on him see numerous references to him in Oe.—U.A., *passim;* M. Bogitchevitch, *Le Colonel Dragoutine Dimitriévitch Apis* (Paris, 1928); A. Szanto, *Apis der Führer der "Schwarzen Hand"* (Berlin, 1928); and the references in the following Supplementary Notes.

II, 74. My conclusions about M. Pashitch's guilty knowledge of the murder plot seems to be confirmed by the statement of a Serbian officer in 1915 to L. Magrini, who gives it in his book, *Il Dramma di Saraievo* (Milan, 1929), p. 106 f.

II, 76-92. On the dark question of the *Narodna Odbrana* and the "Black Hand" much additional light has been thrown from several sides: numerous passages in Oe.—U.A., *passim;* several articles by C.A. Popovitch and "Marco" [?pseudonym for Popovitch] for 1927-28 in the Zagreb magazine *Nova Evropa* (a publication which for several months was suppressed because "inconvenient" to the present Jugoslav régime); Oskar Tartaglia, *Veleizdajnik* [Traitor] (Agram-Spalato, 1928); L. Magrini, *Il Dramma di Seraievo* (Milan, 1929); J. A. Zhibert, *Der Mord von Sarajewo und Tiszas Schuld an dem Weltkriege* (Laibach, 1919); A. von Wegerer, *Die Widerlegung der Versailler Kriegsschuldthese* (Berlin, 1928); Friedrich, Ritter von Wiesner, "Die Schuld der serbischen Regierung am Mord von Sarajewo," in KSF, VI, 307-395, April, 1928; most of these are utilized by Professor Bernadotte E. Schmitt in his admirable account of the *Narodna Odbrana* and the "Black Hand" in his forthcoming book, *The Coming of the War, 1914* (New York, 1930), I, 179-228.

II, 80. The story of the telegram, "Both horses well disposed of," published in the newspapers and reprinted by Conrad, now appears to be wholly without foundation; investigation by the Austrian authorities a few weeks after the Archduke's assassination revealed that no such telegram had been handed in at Sarajevo or delivered to Pribichevitch; Oe.-U.A., VIII, Nos. 10425, 10468.

II, 90, note 54. The main facts about Ciganovitch are given in Oe.-U.A., VIII, No. 10505; for numerous other references to him, see Oe.-U.A., IX, 24, under "Ciganovitch."

II, 94, note 61. See also Stefan, Freiherr von Sarkotić, "Der Hochverrats-Prozess von Banjaluka," in KSF, VII, 30-47, Jan., 1929; Josef Brauner, "Bosnien und Herzegowina, Politik, Verwaltung und leitende Personen vor Kriegsausbruch," *ibid.*, 313-344, April, 1929.

II, 103, note 84. Various dubious rumors concerning Chabrinovitch are examined by Schmitt, I, 212-218. For the main facts concerning him, so far as they appear in the *Austrian Documents,* see Oe.-U.A., VIII, Nos. 9940, 9943, 9947, 9991-2, 10056, 10073, 10109, 10117, 10123-4, 10139, 10152.

II, 111, note 103. Oskar Tartaglia, who claims to have been himself a member of the "Black Hand," declares in a series of articles in the Sarajevo *Vecernja Posta,* Sept. 29—Oct. 6, 1928 (Summarized in KSF, VII, 91-94, Jan. 1929) that Princip acted primarily as the agent of the "Black Hand," and that Freemasons as such had nothing to do with the plot.

II, 116, note. If Mr. Jovan M. Jovanovitch's story is true that five more youths, other than Princip, Chabrinovitch and Grabezh, set out from Belgrade for Bosnia intent on murder, and if he has seen the *dossier* concerning them (Cf. B. E. Schmitt, *The Coming of the War, 1914,* New York, 1930, I, 224, note), Mr. Jovanovitch could make an interesting contribution to history by giving the facts of the *dossier* in detail; but he would hardly weaken the general Austrian complaint against Serbia that Belgrade was a dangerous center of conspiracy against the Dual Monarchy.

II, 131, note 9. At the trial Chabrinovitch denied the truth of this testimony by Mitro; A. Mousset, *L'Attentat de Sarajevo* (Paris, 1930), p. 484-5.

II, 142-146. The story of the domestic conflict between the Serbian civilian and military authorities, and of the "priority question," can now be pieced together in much more detail from the despatches in Oe.-U.A., VII-VIII, Nos. 9216, 9260, 9485, 9649, 9673, 9702, 9734, 9809, 9819, 9844, 9864, 9908, 9919, 9922.

The view that I have expressed (II, 61 ff., 145 f., 550), that Pashitch and the members of his cabinet were aware of the plot before the assassins set out from Belgrade, seems to be further confirmed by the statement which Ljuba Jovanovitch is said to have made to M. Mousset in 1925 (quoted by Schmitt, I, 235): "The preparations for the *attentat* were revealed to Pashitch, Jovan Jovanovitch, Serbian Minister at Vienna, and myself—no doubt in rather vague form *'en termes assez imprécis'*—at the end of May or the beginning of June by Milan Pribichevitch." This also confirms my conclusions (II, 152-166) that Pashitch conveyed some hint about it to Jovan Jovanovitch in Vienna, who thereupon gave the vague warning in general terms to Bilinski.

II, 167-182. Much new and interesting information concerning the growth of the legend of the "Potsdam Council" has been collected and printed by Dr. Kurt Jagow, "Der Potsdamer Kronrat," in *Süddeutsche Monatshefte,* XXV, Heft 11, Aug., 1928, pp. 775-825; a considerable part of this information has been made conveniently available in English by Professor Schmitt, I, ch. v, especially pp. 329-341.

II, 198-223. Berchtold had at first hoped he might win Germany's support for action against Serbia by talking personally with Emperor William, who had originally intended to come to Vienna for the Archduke's funeral. But after he learned that Emperor William had changed his mind about coming to the funeral, he decided to send the Memorandum on Balkan policy, with the letter from Francis Joseph, to Berlin by an ordinary courier. Finally, however, he decided that they should be taken by Count Hoyos. Hoyos arrived in Berlin about 9:30 A.M. Sunday morning, and went at once to Szögyény to deliver the Memorandum and letter. What he may have said to Szögyény can only be surmised. Toward noon, after Szögyény's departure for Potsdam, Hoyos went to the German Foreign Office, and had a conversation with Zimmermann; but what they said to one another cannot be determined with certainty, as neither preserved a record of their talk. Next day, on Monday afternoon, Hoyos was present at the conversations between Bethmann, Zimmermann, and Szögyény, of which somewhat divergent accounts were immediately given by Bethmann and Szögyény in their respective telegrams to Tschirschky and Berchtold. (For the facts concerning these various Hoyos conversations, see Kurt Jagow, *Der Potsdamer Kronrat,* 780 ff.). How far Hoyos "may well have received instructions" from Berchtold to explain verbally his intentions and to interpret the Memorandum and the letter of Francis Joseph, and how far he merely "spoke of his own initiative and without authorization" (Schmitt, I, 279; 343, note) it is also impossible to determine with certainty. In spite of Professor Schmitt's arguments, I still believe it is impossible to say with precision just what impression as to Berchtold's intentions was left on the minds of Emperor William, Bethmann, and Zimmermann by whatever

Hoyos may have said. I am inclined to think that the impression which the three Germans received directly or indirectly from Hoyos as to Austrian intentions was somewhat more definite than I have indicated in my account, and somewhat less definite than Professor Schmitt indicates in his.

II, 208. How sharp a shock was given to Emperor William's impressionable feelings by the news from Sarajevo is indicated by the telegram of condolence which he instantly despatched to Francis Joseph, and by telegrams which he sent to Bethmann and the Grandduchess Louise a few hours later. To the Chancellor he wired: "The cowardly detestable crime, to which my dear friend, His Imperial Highness the Heir Presumptive, and his wife, have fallen victim, has shaken me to the depths of my soul." And to the Grandduchess: "The unutterable misfortune has also shaken me to the very depths. Only 14 days ago I was with him and saw him in his happy family circle. God comfort the unfortunate children and the poor old Emperor" (Kurt Jagow, *Der Potsdamer Kronrat,* 779).

II, 210. The Kaiser took the auto merely from his palace to the Wildpark Station at Potsdam; the rest of the trip to Kiel was by special train (*cf.* Kurt Jagow, *l.c.,* 785 f.).

II, 216-218. Professor Schmitt, I, 306, note, speaks of my view (216 ff., note 43; 413 ff., note 40) that Szögyény, being already old did not always report quite accurately and promptly, as an "artificial hypothesis," and says that "the somewhat elaborate reasoning of Fay, II, 217, to prove that Bethmann could not have consented to keeping Italy in the dark is refuted by the simple fact that the German Ambassador in Rome, when informed of the decision to support Austria-Hungary, was instructed not to mention the matter to the Italian Foreign Office. Jagow to Flotow, 11 July." But Jagow's telegram of July 11 is not certain evidence as to what was said five or six days earlier; nor does it say that Bethmann agreed to keep Italy in the dark; it is probably merely a reflection of remarks which Hoyos may have made to Zimmermann (to which I allude on p. 218, and to which Zimmermann may have unofficially assented)—but not necessarily to Bethmann. A distinction should be made, as I have pointed out, p. 220 ff., between Bethmann, Zimmermann, and the Kaiser. Jagow, who was not present at the Berlin conversations on July 5 and 6, may have at first approved of Zimmermann's assent in regard to Italy (supposing that Zimmermann gave it); but Jagow's better knowledge of the situation in Rome, where he had formerly been ambassador, soon convinced him that it was folly to keep Italy in the dark, and consequently he sent on July 15 the telegram I quote on p. 217, and later those to which I refer in note 41. Szögyény telegraphed on July 12 (A.R.B., I, 16): "The German Government [by which he probably meant Zimmermann, possibly Jagow, but certainly not Bethmann who was away at Hohenfinow], with whom matters are proceeding in the most complete agreement, is of the opinion shared by me that the Italian Government should not be initiated into the secret." This is in flat contradiction with Jagow's telegrams of July 15 and the following days.

II, 222, note 50. The clause in the second sentence should be corrected to read: "which probably took place at Berlin with Zimmermann about noon on Sunday after Szögyény had gone to Potsdam, or possibly on Monday afternoon after the Kaiser had left for Kiel." *Cf.* Kurt Jagow, *l.c.*, p. 787, who makes it clear that Hoyos' second conversation was on Monday about 3 P.M.

II, 246-249. Some Vienna newspapers also tended to defeat Berchtold's efforts to deceive Europe. The *Neue Freie Presse* of July 11 published such a shrewd surmise of his intentions, as indicated in the discussion at the Ministerial Council of July 7, that Berchtold suspected that Bilinski had "leaked" to a reporter. But one of Bilinski's subordinates pointed out that practically the same information had appeared two days before in the *Frankfurter Zeitung,* which had probably been informed by its Vienna correspondent, Hugo Ganz. Tisza was inclined to scout the idea of a "leak," and believed that some reporter had simply made a very shrewd guess at the truth; Oe.-U.A., VIII, Nos. 10209, 10211, 10251.

The Austrian Ambassador in Italy believed that Italy's apparent foreknowledge of Austria's intentions was due to a "leak" from German sources, and Berchtold was greatly disturbed by it, for fear of the effect it would have on Italy, which would try to block his plans. (Oe.-U.A., VIII, Nos. 10364, 10398.)

II, 262. My statement near the bottom of the page, to the effect that the British Foreign Office were convinced of the sincerity of Bethmann's proposals for a rapprochement with England, needs some modification in view of the new evidence of the great suspiciousness of Grey, Hardinge, Nicolson, and especially of Sir Eyre Crowe, in regard to Germany's intentions and methods. See, for instance, their "Minutes" in B.D., VI, 298 ff., 316 f., 557, 566, 574 f., 614 f., 620, 622 f., 702 f., 738. My statement was based on Metternich's reports but Metternich did not fully realize how suspicious the English ministers were in regard to those in high authority in Berlin.

II, 277-286. On M. Poincaré's visit to Russia in 1914, see also the article of the Rumanian Minister at St. Petersburg, Mr. C. Diamandy, "Ma Mission en Russe," in *Revue des Deux Mondes,* Feb. 15, 1929; and the critical study of August Bach, *Poincaré und der Kriegsausbruch, 1914* (Berlin and Leipzig, 1929), 23-78.

II, 333, note 8. For a detailed analysis of British newspapers of different shades of opinion during the July crisis, 1914, see Walter Zimmermann, *Die Englische Presse zum Ausbruch des Weltkrieges,* Charlottenburg, 1928.

II, 343, note 41. An interesting facsimile of a page of the Serbian reply, in which erasures indicate the haste in which the final copy was made, is also printed with Oe.-U.A., VIII, No. 10648.

II, 474. The *Lokal-Anzeiger* episode has been treated in a very detailed and interesting fashion by A. von Wegerer, "Das Extrablatt des 'Lokal-Anzeigers', in KSF, VII, 1035-1076, Nov., 1929; and "Der bekannte und der unbekannte Markow," in KSF, VIII, 157-161, Feb., 1930.

II, 492-6. For the sharp division in the British Cabinet between those who wished to stay out of war and those who wished to join with France, and for very interesting details on the last days of the July Crisis in England, see Lord Morley, *Memorandum on Resignation* (London, 1928), and Harold Nicolson, *Lord Carnock* (London, 1930).

II, 526, note 110. See also J. V. Bredt, *Die belgische Neutralität und der Schlieffensche Feldzugsplan* (Charlottenburg, 1929).

II, 550-552. The 10,000 documents recently published by the Austrian Government incline me in some respects to a less severe judgment on Austrian policy as compared with that of Russia. They make more clear how much Austria had to bear with from Serbia (more or less backed by Russia), in the years before the Archduke's assassination, and how convinced Austrian officials were that their country's very existence was at stake unless something decisive was done to put an end to the Greater Serbia agitation and danger. As Sir Fairfax Cartwright, the British Ambassador at Vienna, wrote to Arthur Nicolson, January 31, 1913:

> Serbia will some day set Europe by the ears, and bring about a universal war on the Continent. I cannot tell you how exasperated people are getting here at the continual worry which that little country causes to Austria under encouragement from Russia. It will be lucky if Europe succeeds in avoiding war as a result of the present crisis. The next time a Serbian crisis arises, I feel sure that Austria-Hungary will refuse to admit of any Russian interference in the dispute and that she will proceed to settle her difference with her little neighbor coûte que coûte.
>
> [And a little later, on May 23, he wrote again:] This country cannot allow any dismemberment of her provinces without incurring the danger of the whole edifice crumbling down; we have all the elements in the near future of another violent crisis in this part of the world. . . . (Nicolson, *Lord Carnock*, p. 390.)

Austria, in acting against Serbia, was taking the only step by which she believed she could preserve her very existence as a state. Russia, however, in claiming to protect Serbia and to exercise a kind of protection over the Balkan Slavs, did not have any such vital interest at stake; her existence as a state was not in jeopardy; her interest was more to preserve and increase her prestige. Austria's action aimed at a localized war. Russia's action made inevitable a European War.

II

AFTER SARAJEVO

IMMEDIATE CAUSES OF THE WAR

CHAPTER I

THE ARCHDUKE FRANZ FERDINAND

Archduke Franz Ferdinand, who became Heir-Presumptive to the Austrian throne after the death of his father, Karl Ludwig, in 1896, has remained, both living and dead, one of the most enigmatic of political personages. Even Austrians themselves held the most contradictory views as to the supposed purposes and influence of this sphinx. By many he was regarded as the chief of the Austrian militarists, eager for a "preventive war" against Italy or Serbia. Others, however, believed that he had little active influence on Austrian policy. Still others even thought the Heir to the Throne was almost a pacifist. There was the same wide divergence of opinion as to his views on domestic politics. He was commonly believed to hate the Magyars and to favor the Serbs. He was credited with having in mind a regeneration of the Monarchy by giving to the Slavic nationalities an equal political recognition with that enjoyed by the Germans in Austria and by the Magyars in Hungary—that is, he was thought to favor a federalistic "triple" organization of the Monarchy known as "Trialism" in place of the existing "Dualism." By fanatical Serbs, however, he was blindly hated as being a powerful and determined enemy and oppressor, as a man who might well be assassinated in the interests of a Greater Serbia. In fact at the trial of the Sarajevo assassins in October, 1914, Chabrinovitch, who threw the bomb, frankly declared, "The Heir-Presumptive was a man of action—I knew that at the Ballplatz there existed a clique, the so-called war-party, which wanted to conquer Serbia. At its head stood the Heir-Presumptive. I believed that I should take vengeance on them all in taking vengeance on him." And Princip, who fired the fatal shots, defiantly asserted, "I am not at all sorry that I cleared an obstacle out of our path. He was a German and an enemy of the South Slavs."[1] By Russians likewise he was regarded as an enemy, of whom the Tsar was fortunately rid by the crime of Sarajevo. "Not only in the press, but also in society, one meets almost nothing but unfriendly judgments concerning the murdered Archduke, with the suggestion that Russia has lost in him an embittered enemy," reported the German Ambassador at St. Petersburg. The German Kaiser, on the other hand, in one of those marginal notes which unrestrainedly expressed his inmost thoughts and first impressions, wrote in comment on this report, "The Archduke was Russia's best friend. He wanted to revive the League of the Three Emperors."[2]

The misconceptions and conflicting views current about the Archduke alive, were as nothing to those which circulated upon his death. It was said that he had plotted to displace his uncle; and was planning to break up the Dual Monarchy in alliance with Emperor William by seizing Poland and Venice and by creating two new states over which his sons might ultimately rule, while German Austria was to be added to the German Empire as Emperor William's reward. It was darkly hinted that his tragic death was due to the connivance of Austrian officials, who wanted to prevent these suspected designs, or at least wanted to throw the blame on Serbia and so have a pretext for the annihilation of this neighboring kingdom. Other rumors alleged that his assassination was due to the fact that, as a

[1] Pharos, *Der Prozess gegen die Attentäter von Sarajevo* (Berlin, 1918), pp. 11, 13, 30. The idea that Franz Ferdinand headed the militarist clique and was an enemy of the Serbs was, as will be seen below, wholly incorrect.

[2] Pourtalès to Bethmann, July 13, 1914; K.D., 53.

ARCHDUKE FRANZ FERDINAND

Roman Catholic, he was planning to attack Italy and restore the Temporal Power of the Pope. One widely-read German author devotes half a chapter to showing that the Scottish-Rite Masons had decreed his death and worked for that purpose through the Masonic Lodge at Belgrade.[3] Amid this mass of conflicting gossip and rumor, where lies the truth about this mysterious man whose death served as the spark which lit the conflagration in Europe?[4]

Franz Ferdinand of Austria-Este, born on December 18, 1863, was the eldest son of Karl Ludwig, brother of Emperor Francis Joseph. His consumptive mother, a daughter of the late Bourbon King of the Two Sicilies, Ferdinand II, died while he was a child, but he was affectionately cared

[3] Reventlow, *Politische Vorgeschichte des grossen Krieges,* Berlin, 1919, pp. 28-38. See below, p. 111, note 103.

[4] There is no satisfactory complete biography of Franz Ferdinand. Of the older biographies written during his lifetime, Paul von Falkenegg, *Erzherzog Franz Ferdinand von Oesterreich-Este* (Vienna, 1908), and H. Heller, *Franz Ferdinand* (Vienna, 1911), deserve mention. In celebration of his fiftieth birthday on December 18, 1913, the *Oesterreichische Rundschau* published a special illustrated edition containing interesting, though superficial, articles by Chlumecky, Sosnosky, Admiral Mirtl, Professor Mycielski and others on Franz Ferdinand as soldier, sailor, traveler, hunter and collector, etc. *Franz Ferdinands Lebensroman* (Stuttgart, 1919), purports to be based on the diary of one of the Archduke's instructors and intimate friends; the anonymous author has a romantic touch, but appears to give much reliable and solid fact. Conrad von Hötzendorf, *Aus Meiner Dienstzeit,* (5 vols., Vienna, 1921-1925), throws much light on the Archduke from the pen of one of those who knew him best. Freiherr von Margutti, personal adjutant to Francis Joseph, was in a position to know intimately the relations between the old Emperor and his imperial nephew; in his interesting reminiscences, *Vom Alten Kaiser* (Vienna, 1921), the chapter on the Archduke reflects unfriendly Vienna gossip. It needs to be corrected by the loyal devotion and intimate personal account of the Archduke's private secretary for a dozen years, Paul Nikitsch-Boulles, *Vor dem Sturm: Erinnerungen an Erzherzog Thronfolger Franz Ferdinand* (Berlin, 1925); and by the affectionate appreciation of his military adjutant, Karl Freiherr von Bardolff, "Franz Ferdinand," in KSF, V, 599-608, July, 1927. See also the fair-minded and friendly accounts by Count Czernin, *In the World War* (New York, 1919), ch. ii; and the more complete life by Horstenau, in the *Neue Oesterreichische Biographie;* the references in G.P., XL, 45; and the less favorable accounts by R. W. Seton-Watson, *Sarajevo* (London, 1926), ch. iv; and by Eugene Bagger, *Francis Joseph* (New York, 1927), p. 524 ff.

for by a Portuguese stepmother. In his youth he had not been seriously thought of as a possible successor to the throne, until the tragic death of Crown Prince Rudolph at Meyerling in 1889 left Francis Joseph without a direct male heir. Franz Ferdinand had not therefore at first been given any special training in politics, but, like Austrian Archdukes generally, had been placed in the army for a military career. His health had never been robust, owing perhaps to tubercular tendencies inherited from his mother. This tendency at times became so threatening that he often had to spend months at Brioni or Miramar on the warm shores of the Adriatic, where he came to have an intense interest in the creation of an Austrian navy; at other times he sought better health in the dry air of Switzerland at Davos, or in a ten months' trip around the world in 1892-1893. In the fatal spring of 1914 there were those who prophesied that the old Emperor at eighty-four would actually outlive his nephew who had just passed fifty.

Franz Ferdinand's lung trouble appears to have influenced somewhat his life and character. It had not sweetened his temper; it had made him feel that fate had been unfair to him, and had developed in him a tendency to shun society life. The undisguised haste with which many people, especially those connected with the Court, deserted him when he was seriously ill and seemed unlikely ever to come to the throne, hardened the Archduke's character, which was not naturally gentle, increased his distrust of the men who surrounded him, and heightened his contempt for mankind in general. His ill health may also have contributed somewhat to his intense zeal for the Catholic Church, especially after his marriage to a strict Catholic; and it strengthened his iron determination to overcome obstacles and fit himself for the task of ruling the Hapsburg dominions. He learned the languages of the nations over which he seemed likely some day to rule. He also took instruction from men of science in special branches of knowledge; his later collections in natural science and in art formed a notable museum. To the organization and improvement of the army, and later to the creation of a navy, he began to devote himself with persistent energy and more than average ability.

Since the Archduke had a family to provide for, he spent a considerable part of each year on his estate at Konopischt, where he established a model farm, which, like Wallenstein, he managed very profitably. This determination to live may actually have contributed toward the more vigorous health which he enjoyed in his last years. But he never outgrew his tendency toward aloofness from society and from the public. He had, in fact, very few intimate friends. He did not try to make them. Quite characteristic of his aloofness is a remark which he once made to Conrad von Hotzendorf; they had been discussing the proper basis for the promotion of officers in the army, and the Chief-of-Staff had said that it was his own tendency to think well of a man until he knew something against him, and that he had therefore been sometimes too quick in advancing new officers. The Archduke replied, "We hold opposite views. You think every man is an angel at the outset, and have unfortunate experiences afterwards. I regard every one whom I meet for the first time as a cheap fellow (*gemeiner Kerl*) and wait until he does something to justify a better opinion in my eyes."[5] This was hardly an attitude of mind to make friends, and partly accounts for the hostile and malicious tittle-tattle which circulated so freely about him and his wife at Vienna, and which has found its way into many accounts of him in the Entente countries. But the few friends whom he did admit to his intimacy, who saw him sitting on the floor playing with his children, like his secretaries or like Emperor William, were affectionately devoted to him.

[5] Conrad, I, 338.

FRANZ FERDINAND AND THE ARMY

Franz Ferdinand's chief interests in life, aside from his hobbies as a hunter and collector and gentleman farmer, were the army, the navy and his wife and children.

In 1906, with the appointment of Major Brosch as his personal adjutant, the Archduke began to exercise a more direct influence on the army. Brosch was an extremely intelligent and able officer, anxious to increase his own influence and also that of the Archduke in military matters. After long opposition he was able to bring it about that the Archduke was given a military chancery (*Militärkanzlei*) of his own, similar to that of the Emperor. Henceforth all the important military documents, as well as the reports of the military attachés, were made out in duplicate so that Franz Ferdinand received a copy at the same moment that the Emperor received his, and the nephew was kept as fully informed as his uncle. In fact he soon came to take a more active part in military reforms and reorganization than the Emperor himself. His activity is indicated by the fact that his military chancery quickly grew from a personnel of two to one of fourteen persons—only two less than the Emperor's own chancery.[6]

Franz Ferdinand regarded the Austro-Hungarian army as a potentially important unifying political instrument for counteracting the disintegrating elements in the Dual Monarchy, as well as for defending it in case of foreign war. He wanted one language of command—German—to be the tongue of at least all the officers, though those who commanded non-German regiments should also be masters of the tongue spoken by the rank and file under their command. It was one of his main aims in life to strengthen and increase the army. It was this aim that lay at the bottom of his hatred of the Magyar politicians who refused

6 Nikitsch-Boulles, p. 60 f.

to vote the military credits asked for, and who insisted that Magyar should be the language of command in the Hungarian half of the army.[7] How strongly Franz Ferdinand felt this need for an increase in the army is seen in the characteristic letter to Conrad, complaining of the Magyar refusal to vote taxes for an increase in the number of Hungarian recruits: "You can imagine, dear Conrad, what I have had to go through in the way of rage and desperation, especially on account of the attitude of the Minister of War [Schönaich] and the two [Austrian and Hungarian] Governments! On the one hand they proclaim to all the world that there is a surplus of 200 million kroner, give the civilian officials 20 million here and the railroad employees the same there, and yet do not even grant the paltry nine million for the poor army officers. And all this because of a few traitorous Hungarian political wind-bags. This means that this is only a pretext; the fundamental reason is that the Monarchy has fallen into the hands of Jews, Free Masons, Socialists and Hungarians, and is ruled by them; and all these elements make the army and its officers discontented and injure it so that at the moment when I need the army, I can no longer count upon it. . . . Do you know what I would do if I were Emperor? I would summon Weckerle, Beck, Sieghart and Schönaich and say to them: 'I'll send you all to the devil if I don't get the increased number of the recruits and the officers' pay for my army within a week,' and I wager that I should have it all within 24 hours!"[8]

The most important step in Franz Ferdinand's energetic efforts for improvement of the army was his insistence in 1906 upon the appointment of a new Chief-of-Staff. Beck, the officer who held this position at the time, was generally

[7] *Cf.* his Memorial to the Emperor, Jan. 5, 1909, summarized by Conrad, I, 134; and Conrad's own similar views, pp. 135-138, and 327-334.
[8] Conrad, I, 565.

recognized by experts as totally unfit for the place. He was a shrivelled-up old man belonging to the same generation as the aged Emperor. His days of usefulness were long outlived, and yet the kindly heart of Francis Joseph had hated to dismiss him. "One might see him any day going for a walk in Vienna, looking like a good-natured little monkey, a living picture of military inefficiency."[9] Beck was, however, an honest and upright officer and a thoroughly likable, easy-going personality, and enjoyed a certain popularity. He and the corps of officers whom he had carefully selected represented the chivalry, the dignity, and the *esprit de corps* of the best old Vienna society. They were regarded by Francis Joseph as one of the main supports of his ancestral throne. "Efficiency" had not been born to disturb their quiet routine; their ideal was "the development of Austria's defensive force gradually along the line of natural evolution." Owing to the terms of mutual confidence and intimacy on which he stood with the Emperor, Beck had been allowed to continue at the head of the Austrian Staff for twenty-four years. In spite of his excessive age—one might even say senility—Beck was still a painstaking official. At his home in Baden he had been trained in German "thoroughness." With his cautious, conservative, do-nothing policy, he had to a certain extent been an influence in favor of European peace. So no one had had the courage to insist on the retirement of the genial old chief, until Franz Ferdinand urged a new appointment. The Emperor finally gave way, and in November, 1906, a new Chief-of-Staff took up his quarters at the war office in Vienna—Conrad von Hötzendorf.

Conrad's appointment to the highest position in the Austrian army coincided with a change at the Foreign

[9] Kanner, *Kaiserliche Katastrophen-Politik,* p. 153. For a kindly but just estimate of Beck's qualities and deficiencies see Margutti, *Vom Alten Kaiser,* pp. 282-291.

Office. The timid Pole, Count Goluchowski, was replaced by the ambitious aristocrat, Baron Aehrenthal. A new era in Austrian policy was soon manifested. It was the beginning of a more aggressive and reckless activity in foreign affairs. Men came into control who felt that Austria was gradually disintegrating, and that desperate eleventh-hour efforts must be made to infuse fresh life and vigor into the body politic, and to check the tendencies to dissolution arising from the hot ambitions of the subject nationalities. Austria, it was said, was decaying like Turkey. Not the Ottoman, but the Hapsburg, ruler was now the "sick man of Europe." Conrad and Aehrenthal were the doctors who should try strong remedies to keep their patient from collapse. Unfortunately for the sick man, the doctors differed radically in their views and remedies, and they loved each other about as little as bedside specialists often do.

Conrad's appointment as Chief-of-Staff, urged by the Heir to the Throne and acquiesced in by the Emperor, never, however, really commended itself to Francis Joseph. The aged Monarch, who had taken the greatest pride in the old army at whose head he had fought so many years, now found himself importuned by Conrad to make sweeping changes and reforms. With impulsive self-confidence Conrad urged that the army maneuvers be speeded up to approximate war conditions as closely as possible, and that an early opportunity be seized for "preventive wars" against Italy and Serbia. At Christmas, 1906, scarcely a month after Conrad's appointment, the old Emperor remarked ruefully: "Conrad is a restless organizer! He is lacking in experience; one sees this from everything he puts his hand to! And moreover his hand does not look to me like a lucky one!"[10]

The Emperor's distrust of the new régime tended, as years went on, to estrange him from the army with which

[10] Margutti, p. 293.

he had grown up. It was one of the things which added loneliness and sadness to the last years of the loneliest and saddest of the Hapsburgs. Conrad's policy of conducting the great annual maneuvers, "under conditions like actual war" without carefully prepared plans, with the aim of developing initiative and self-reliance among his officers, often had the most distressing results. All emphasis was placed on a hasty offensive; the soldiers were totally exhausted by the forced marches; they often arrived at the objective completely worn out and in greatest confusion, too tired and hungry to have ears and eyes for anything, even for their King and Emperor. As he rode about the field, Francis Joseph would see hundreds of soldiers lying dead-tired in the ditches along the road, and cavalry and guns were strewn over fields where the horses had fallen from exhaustion. This was the Conrad régime, very different from the decorous and dignified ways of old Beck, when the Emperor had been greeted by the well-formed lines of troops standing at a respectful salute as he rode down the front. The old Emperor was terribly distressed by what he saw. Though very slow to find fault and criticize, he did give expression to his feelings on a visit to the German Emperor in 1909. A German regiment had just passed in review in perfect order and discipline. Francis Joseph turned to one of his own officers and said sharply: "Why is this kind of thing totally impossible with us?" The officer shrugged his shoulders, whereupon the Emperor continued more bitterly, "Well, owing to the misguided practices which have now become the fashion with us, any such parade is beyond even my dreams." [11]

Conrad had in fact alienated the Emperor and his army from one another. After 1909 Francis Joseph ceased to take pleasure in the maneuvers which had been one of the delights of his life. He allowed himself to be represented

[11] Margutti, p. 298.

at them instead by his nephew. It was as his representative that Franz Ferdinand went to Sarajevo in 1914 to attend the maneuvers of a couple of army corps.[12]

The fact that it was Franz Ferdinand who selected Conrad, secured his appointment, and remained intimately associated with him, was one of the reasons for the lack of cordiality between the Emperor and the Heir to the Throne. It was also one of the reasons that it was commonly believed, especially among Austria's enemies, that Franz Ferdinand held the same militaristic views which Conrad so freely proclaimed in memorials, interviews and coffee-houses. It is true that the Heir remained Conrad's staunchest supporter, except for occasional bursts of irritation, in spite of all the criticism and jealous opposition directed against the new Chief-of-Staff. When Conrad was forced to resign in November, 1911, because of his conflicts with Aehrenthal and Schönaich on foreign and military matters, it was Franz Ferdinand who secured his re-appointment the following year.[13]

[12] For many evidences and anecdotes of the Emperor's distrust of Conrad's system and his consequent distress of mind and gloomy forebodings, both before and during the war, see Margutti, *Vom Alten Kaiser,* pp. 291-306, 391-452. Alfred Krauss, *Die Ursachen unserer Niederlage* (Munich, 1912), *passim,* is a severe but not unjust estimate of Conrad by a high military expert in the Austrian General Staff. Kanner's sharp portrait of Conrad, (*Kaiserliche Katastrophen-Politik,* pp. 151-173) loses nothing in vigor because of the fact that Conrad's agents tried to suppress Kanner's Vienna newspaper, *Die Zeit.* Conrad's best defense, though not convincing, are his own five bulky volumes *Aus meiner Dienstzeit,* which contain invaluable documents of every sort. Nowak, who is one of his admirers and claims to have had access to his papers, writes panegyrics of him: *Der Weg zur Kastastrophe* (Vienna, 1920) and *Hôtzendorf's Lager* (Vienna, 1921). See also friendly biographies by Ludwig Pastor, *Conrad* (Vienna, 1916); François, *Conrad, Baron de Hötzendorf* (Berne, 1916); and *Unser Conrad, Von einem Oesterreicher* (Vienna, 1915). *Cf.* also General Auffenberg-Komarów, *Aus Oesterreichs Höhe und Niedergang,* Munich, 1921, *passim.*

[13] G.P., XXX, 525 ff.; Margutti, p. 302; Kanner, 157 ff.; Conrad, II, 218 ff., 373 ff.; Pribram, "Der Konflikt Conrad-Aehrenthal," in *Oest. Rundschau,* August, 1920.

Lacking authentic information, the public naturally tended to identify protector and protégé. But it is incorrect to regard Franz Ferdinand as one of the Austrian militarists, holding the same views as to strenuous maneuvers, preventive wars, and aggressive foreign policy as the Chief-of-Staff. The Archduke certainly disapproved the extreme strenuousness of Conrad's exhausting army maneuvers. He used his influence to moderate them after the distressing experiences at the Meseritz maneuvers in 1909, where he had exclaimed: "It is not necessary to teach death to the troops; least of all is that what the maneuvers are for!"[14] When the Annexation Crisis reached its height, and Austria and Serbia were preparing for war, the more cautious Heir to the Throne opposed the Austrian militarists who favored immediate war with Serbia, which involved the possibility of war with Russia. He approved the peaceful settlement of the crisis.[15] Later on, during the First Balkan War, when the Pan-Slav and militarist elements in Russia appeared very threatening to Austria, Conrad, as always, urged a final reckoning with Serbia, even at the risk of war with Russia; but Franz Ferdinand was absolutely opposed to it and insisted on the reduction of the Austrian forces in the interest of peace. "Under no circumstances did he want war with Russia, nor would he consent to it. He will not take from Serbia a single plum-tree, not a sheep. He will not hear of it."[16] He told the German Military Attaché that a war against Russia would be "absolutely nonsense," because there was no reason for it and no gain worth the price; that he was also opposed to a conflict with Serbia; and that in his opinion the internal

[14] Margutti, p. 303; *cf.* also Conrad, II, 323-328.

[15] Conrad, I, 146, 153, 155; Nikitsch-Boulles, p. 118 ff.

[16] Statement of Col. Bardolff, the Archduke's confidential secretary, to Conrad, Feb. 22, 1913; Conrad, III, 127; and Berchtold to Conrad, Feb. 22, 1913; "I cannot lend my name to a war with Russia; the Archduke Franz Ferdinand is absolutely opposed to a war;" *ibid.,* p. 129.

problems of Austria-Hungary were more pressing than the external ones.[17]

In conversation with Conrad, "the Archduke emphasized that their guiding star must be coöperation between Germany, Russia and Austria-Hungary, primarily out of regard for monarchical interests, and added, 'Possibly it may come to some action against Serbia, merely to chastise her, but under no conditions must a square kilometer be annexed! . . . War with Russia must be avoided, because France is stirring it up, especially the French Freemasons and anti-monarchists, who want to bring about a revolution by which monarchs will be cast down from their thrones.' He called attention to a letter of the German Emperor which represented the same views; hence his determination: 'No war!' "[18] One sees that both the Archduke and the German Emperor were altogether opposed to war with Russia and inclined toward the old policy of the League of the Three Emperors for protection against France and the safeguarding of monarchical interests.

A month later Franz Ferdinand sent Col. Bardolff to warn Conrad to stop trying to influence Berchtold in favor of war. Conrad's reply shows how incorrect is the common notion that the German Kaiser was always backing Austrian aggression in the Balkans: "I wish the Archduke would not let himself be so much influenced by the German Emperor; he held us back in 1909, and now he is staying our hand again. This is the result of our wholly unsuccessful Turkish policy. I have the conviction that the Germans are indifferent to our interests, but we have to think of them. Germany calmly uses us, while she sees that she is better secured against France, which is her chief fear, but

[17] Reports of Count Kageneck, Dec. 17, 1912, and Feb. 26, 1913; Brandenburg, p. 372; *cf.*, G.P., XXXIII, 473 ff., XXXIV, 229, 250 f., 309 ff., 318 ff., 323, 415 ff., 426 f.

[18] Conversation of Feb. 27, 1913; Conrad, III, 155 f. *Cf.* also pp. 236, 324, 329.

will eventually sacrifice us."[19] In consequence, Conrad even thought of resigning his position as Chief-of-Staff, rather than be responsible for letting slip another opportunity to settle with Serbia.

In the fall of 1913, when Serbia and Montenegro were defying the Powers by refusing to respect the Albanian frontier established by the London Conference, Conrad again urged military action on the part of Austria for the defense of Albania. Berchtold hesitated. Conrad then talked with Forgach. "Count Forgach agreed that a strong intervention would be the best thing, but he had lost hope that it could be brought about. The Emperor and the Heir to the Throne were opposed to it, and Berchtold would not force them to it."[20]

Toward Italy Franz Ferdinand always had a strong antipathy and deep distrust, based partly on political hatred for the country which had seized his family lands in Modena and Este, partly from bigoted religious dislike for the state which had dispossessed the Pope and seemed to be ruled by Freemasons and anti-clericals, and partly on a shrewd suspicion of the duplicity of Italian diplomacy. Nevertheless, he refused to support Conrad in his repeated efforts to let loose a preventive war against Italy in 1907 and again in 1911, when Italy was involved in war with Turkey.

The idea that Franz Ferdinand is to be wholly identified with the reckless fire-eating militarists of Austria is unsound. It is a legend which grew up later after the War began. He was one of those who thoroughly believed in the maxim, *Si vis pacem, para bellum.* But he was not the kind of a man to be swept away, as so many worshipers of this maxim are, by the desire to engage in war and put into

19 *Ibid.*, 169.

20 October 6, 1913; *ibid.*, p. 462. A few days later Czernin also told Conrad: "Here in Austria we have to reckon with the Emperor and the Heir to the Throne, who are not in favor of war, least of all the Heir; he clings blindly to peace;" *ibid.*, 464. See also p. 597.

actual use the military machine which has been created to preserve the peace. Baron Szilassy, a liberal-minded Hungarian magnate, who went as Austrian Minister to Athens in December, 1913, writes: "Two days before my departure, Archduke Franz Ferdinand invited me to visit him and discussed with me the whole international situation. He appeared to be even as pacifistic as his imperial uncle, and desired an entente with Russia. He regarded the realization of South Slav aspirations within the framework of the Monarchy as altogether possible later, and criticized severely Tisza's policy, which was making better relations with Serbia and Rumania impossible."[21] If he had been alive in July, 1914, it is quite possible that Franz Ferdinand would have used his influence and authority to check Conrad and Berchtold in the mad policy which led to the World War.

FRANZ FERDINAND AND THE NAVY

There was another subject on which Franz Ferdinand and Conrad did not see eye to eye. This was the Austrian navy. At the close of the nineteenth century the Austrian navy was almost negligible. It was Franz Ferdinand who, by his great energy and interest, virtually created the new navy, hoping it would be a counterweight to that of Italy in the Adriatic and Mediterranean. Before his day the view had prevailed that Austrian interests were purely continental; that any conflict with a foreign power would ultimately be decided by land armies; that the army therefore was the branch on which money should be spent, not the navy; a navy was merely a luxury. The Dual Monarchy, it had been thought, did not possess sufficient resources to maintain a proper army and at the same time to create a navy which could ever face that of Italy, to say nothing of opposing the great naval forces of France and England in

[21] Baron J. von Szilassy, *Der Untergang der Donau-Monarchie* (Berlin, 1921), p. 259. *Cf.* Czernin, *In the World War*, p. 43.

the Mediterranean. Conrad adhered to this older way of thinking. With his endemic suspicion of Italy, he naturally would have been glad to see the Austrian navy developed, but only if this could be done without detriment to the interests of the army. When, therefore, the legislatures drew the purse strings tight, and one was faced with the alternative of choosing between the absolutely necessary demands of the army, as he saw them, and the laudable desire of creating a navy, he used all his influence in favor of the former. With equal jealousy he opposed recruiting for the navy at the expense of the army.[22]

Emperor Francis Joseph had still less understanding for, or interest in, the navy. In his last years he did, to be sure, visit the ship-yards and witness naval evolutions, but he did it in a perfunctory way, merely to do his duty as a sovereign. He would stand on the bridge by the hour, almost never taking the marine glasses from his eyes. He gave an appearance of following the evolutions with intelligent interest. But it was remarked by those close to him that he never asked an intelligent question on naval matters, never showed any enthusiasm for the fleet, and never wore the naval uniform; in fact, he never even possessed one, though he had a large and very expensive wardrobe of military uniforms. The mighty battleship of the twentieth century, with its complicated mechanism of steel, steam and electricity, was a thing strange and new to him. He and Bismarck belonged to the older generation who felt at home in a general's uniform and knew what armies were good for. Emperor William and Franz Ferdinand were of the new age, who believed that "the future lies on the water." Interest in naval matters was in fact one of the common bonds which tended to draw the German Emperor and the Austrian Heir together.[23] In spite of this opposition, or lack of enthusiasm, from Conrad and the Em-

22 Conrad, I, 357-360.

23 Margutti, 125 f.; 306-311.

peror, Franz Ferdinand had succeeded by 1914 in raising the Austrian navy to a respectable size; though scarcely half as strong as that of Italy, it gave a good account of itself during the War and showed that the spirit of Admiral Tegetthoff was not dead.

FRANZ FERDINAND'S POLITICAL VIEWS

In his views on foreign affairs Franz Ferdinand was at one with his uncle in regarding the Dual Alliance with Germany as the corner stone of Austrian policy. This conviction was strengthened by his strong personal regard for William II, whose great tact in the matter of the Archduke's wife had won his heart. With Rumania Franz Ferdinand sought to strengthen the ties of loyalty and alliance. He and his wife were charmed with the visit they paid to King Carol and Carmen Sylva in July, 1909. They adored the simplicity of life of the Rumanian royal family at their summer castle at Sinaia, which was so different from the stiff ceremonial and stifling court atmosphere at Vienna. His heart was touched at the genuineness and friendliness with which the Queen of Rumania entertained his Countess, took her to ride, and served her tea at a rustic farm house. He long remembered it as one of the happiest visits of his life.[24]

Italy, however, the Archduke regarded with deep distrust, but not to the point of thinking it wise to unmask her suspected disloyalty to the Triple Alliance by a preventive war. On the contrary, he wanted to remain at peace with Italy and maintain as firm relations as possible with her. As heir of Francis V, Duke of Modena, he had inherited in 1875 the fortune of the Este family, but he had no notion of attempting to restore the ducal power which had been overthrown in 1859. In fact, in order to avoid giving offense to the ruling house of Savoy in Italy, he never

24 *Cf.* Nikitsch-Boulles, p. 129 ff.

wore the insignia of the Este Black Eagle Order, the grandmastership of which he had inherited as Francis V's heir.

With Russia Franz Ferdinand wanted to be on terms of friendly understanding. Autocratic himself by nature, he had admired the autocratic government of Russia before the Russo-Japanese War and the Russian Revolution of 1905 had begun to shake the Tsar's throne. But later he was disillusioned as to Nicholas II's stability. This may have been one of the reasons he sought more close personal relations with Emperor William and King Carol. The French he frankly disliked. He never forgot the humiliation imposed upon Austria by Napoleon I, and he regarded Napoleon III as responsible for Austria's downfall in the nineteenth century. Great Britain, on the other hand, he held in respect, and there had even been rumors at one time that he might marry Princess Mary.

Such are the views on foreign affairs ascribed to Franz Ferdinand by men who knew him well. There is no reason to doubt their substantial accuracy.[25]

Of Franz Ferdinand's views on the internal nationality problems of the Hapsburg Empire it is less possible to speak with certainty. It was the conviction of those who stood close to him, like Major Brosch,[26] and his private-secretary, Nikitsch-Boulles,[27] that if the Archduke had come to the Throne, he would have come to the rescue of the oppressed nationalities and attempted a federal organization of the Monarchy, substituting "Trialism" for the existing "Dualism." This was also the commonly expressed opinion in the Austrian and German obituary notices of the Archduke.[28] There are also several signs which point in this direction:

25 Margutti, pp. 126-138; Conrad, I-IV, *passim;* Czernin, *In the World War,* ch. ii.

26 Cf. Seton-Watson, *Sarajevo,* p. 83 ff.

27 *Vor dem Sturm,* p. 58, 62 ff.

28 The *Vossische Zeitung* was an exception; *cf. Belgian Documents,* **IV**, 97 ff.

the Archduke's energetic reforming temperament, his relations with Emperor Francis Joseph, the study he gave to the subject, and various draft projects which have come to light.

Though in many respects conservative, as one might expect from his Roman Catholic traditions, there is no doubt that Franz Ferdinand possessed qualities of character which indicate that he was quite the kind of man to undertake a reorganization of the Monarchy. He had no sympathy with preserving an institution simply because it had long existed. On the contrary, he looked to the future rather than to the past, and was inclined to reform in accordance with modern conditions rather than to conserve that which was old. Possessed of restless energy and an iron will, he had no patience with the traditional ceremonial of the Vienna Court or the antiquated methods of the old Austrian administrative machine which was managed in large part by old men who belonged to Francis Joseph's generation rather than to the twentieth century. His influence in substituting Conrad for the aged Beck as Austria's Chief-of-Staff, and in building up the army and navy, was typical of his reforming tendencies. Wherever he had authority, he showed his executive ability in modernizing and improving the arrangements which he found in existence. This is seen notably in his transformation of the Konopischt estate, which he built up into a flourishing landed property with rose gardens famous throughout Europe. He believed in dispatching business rapidly, making large use of the telephone and the telegraph. He was impatient with his secretaries if any business was left unfinished on his desk for more than twenty-four hours. In all this he was the exact opposite of his aged uncle.

Francis Joseph was a Monarch by the Grace of God in the old sense. He still ruled or wanted to rule in patriarchal fashion. One of his greatest faults was his insistence on dealing himself with all matters of minutest detail. His mind was so occupied with these minor matters that he had no breadth of view for the wider interests of the Monarchy. As was natural in his old age, he was inclined to live in the past rather than to look to the future. He was extremely conservative and hesitated to make any changes in the red tape of the old Hapsburg machine, even when it was pointed out to him what advantages could be secured by modern methods.

The contrast in attitude between the uncle and nephew is seen in an incident of 1911 concerning the administration of some Hapsburg family property left by the Empress Maria Theresa. This was still being administered under provisions a century and a half old, which were no longer adapted to modern conditions. The Archduke looked into the question carefully and ventured to hand the Emperor a long memorandum in which he pointed out how the administration of this family property needed reorganization. There were too many officials handling the property and they were often incapable and sometimes dishonest. He showed in detail how the Göding beet-root sugar factory was losing 200,000 crowns a year as a result of a foolish contract. Another estate was being rented for 47 crowns an acre when it might easily bring 70 to 80 crowns an acre, thus causing another loss of about 100,000 crowns a year. "A great part of the domains of the family are mostly leased for a long term of years for a rent which may have been suitable 40 or 50 years ago, but which today is simply ludicrous," he wrote. He therefore begged the Monarch to examine the question with a view to economic reforms corresponding to the twentieth century. The Emperor left the letter unanswered for weeks. After his attention had been called to it several times, he finally replied in characteristic fashion: "I have fully considered the question in its various aspects and come to the conclusion that as the responsible guardian of this family property, I cannot bring myself to permit an experiment which would so destroy a long tried administrative system which has worked without criticism for so many years for the advantage of our property."[29] This is a good example of Emperor Francis Joseph's opposition to innovation, and of his nephew's readiness for energetic administrative and political reforms.

Franz Ferdinand was very keenly aware, much more so than the Emperor, of the violent discontent among the subject nationalities of the Empire. He had one characteristic which is of great value in a ruler—he was ready and anxious to know the facts, even if they were unpalatable. Though he had a very violent temper, it was far more likely to be vented upon any one whom he suspected of trying to deceive him, than on one who told him disagreeable truths. He took pains to read opposition newspapers, with the result that he was well informed of the public feeling on the part of the Czechs, Transylvanians, Croats, and Serbs within the Dual Monarchy, and realized the danger which they constituted for the future unless something was done to satisfy them. His strong disapproval of the oppressive policy of the ruling Magyar magnates in Hungary was notorious, and will be indicated a few pages further on in connection with the Konopischt interview. He was criticized by the Magyar and German dominant factions for wishing to favor the small nationalities. It was a reproach which did honor to his wisdom and sense of justice. Here again he differed from the aged Emperor. Francis Joseph was inclined to half-measures and compromise. He regarded himself as the author of the Austro-Hungarian Compromise of 1867 and had no thought of modifying it. Franz Ferdinand, however, seems to have regarded this dual organization of the Empire as an unfortunate mistake, because it gave in practice so much power into the hands of

29 Letters of Franz Ferdinand and Francis Joseph, quoted in Nikitsch-Boulles, pp. 49-57.

the Magyar magnates. He therefore seems to have been quite ready to see the "Dualism" of 1867 replaced by some kind of "Trialism" when he himself should come to the throne. He had given much study to the question of a possible constitutional reorganization along federal lines. He had pondered the proposals of noted Austrian writers like Lammasch, Tezner and Steinacker. He had heard with great interest expositions of the American federal system by Professor J. W. Burgess of Columbia University; Professor Burgess had been invited to return to Vienna to give further information on the subject and was on the point of again sailing for Europe to do so at the moment the Archduke was assassinated.

A further indication of Franz Ferdinand's intention of making constitutional reforms in the direction of curbing the power of the Hungarian magnates and extending political rights to the minor nationalities is seen in various draft proposals which have been published from his papers.[30] One of the most recent of these is the draft Manifesto which he had prepared for publication in case the old Emperor's periodical bronchial trouble should sometime suddenly cause his death and open the way for a new régime. Though expressed in somewhat vague and general terms, it indicates that the Heir to the Throne was a true friend to the Croats and Bosnian Serbs and that he intended important constitutional reforms in the interests of all the minor nationalities before taking the oath to the Hungarian Constitution. The Manifesto runs in part as follows:

> Since it has pleased Almighty God to call out of this life after a long and richly blessed reign, My exalted Uncle, . . .
>
> We hereby solemnly announce to all people of the Monarchy Our accession to the Crown. . . .
>
> To all peoples of the Monarchy, to all ranks, and to

30 *Cf.* Seton Watson, *Sarajevo,* p. 84, note 1.

everybody that does his duty in the work of the nation, no matter what his race or creed, We return equal love. In high station, or low, poor or rich, all shall be equal before Our Throne.

The established constitutional arrangements and the judicial system of the state, in which every citizen has equal rights according to the laws, We will honor and protect with a strong hand. For the well-being and prosperity of all peoples in all parts of the Monarchy, We deem it Our first duty to bring about a concentration into a great unit and a harmonious coöperation according to just principles. . . . In the Constitution of the Empire all contradictions must be removed which exist in the laws of Austria and those of Hungary in regard to the common affairs of the Monarchy, and which make the giving of the prescribed oath on the Constitution impossible through the incompatibility of these laws. As pledge of Our most sacred duties as ruler, We shall thereupon confirm by solemn oath of coronation the unambiguous provisions of the Constitution together with the fundamental rights and privileges of all those who belong to the Monarchy. In order to create the possibility for this, Our Governments will inaugurate without delay the necessary measures. . . .

Since all peoples under Our scepter shall have equal rights in regard to participation in the common affairs of the Monarchy, this equality of rights demands that to every race be guaranteed its national development within the frame of the common interests of the Monarchy, and that to all races, ranks, and classes the preservation of their just interests be made possible through just laws of suffrage —wherever this has not yet been carried through.[31]

It is doubtful, however, whether Franz Ferdinand had come to any definite decision in his own mind as to the exact form which the reorganization should take. Count

[31] Published by J. A. Freiherr von Eichhoff in the *Berliner Tageblatt* No. 152 of Mar. 31, 1926, and reprinted in translation in the New York *Nation,* May 26, 1926.

Czernin, who was more intimately acquainted with Franz Ferdinand's ideas than most men, says: "The Archduke was a firm partisan of the Great-Austria program. His idea was to convert the Monarchy into numerous more or less independent National States, having in Vienna a common central organization for all important and absolutely necessary affairs—in other words, to substitute Federalism for Dualism. . . . However, it had many opponents who strongly advised against dissecting the State in order to erect in its place something new and 'presumably better,' and the Emperor Francis Joseph was far too conservative and far too old to agree to his nephew's plans. This direct refusal of the idea cherished by the Archduke offended him greatly, and he complained often in bitter terms that the Emperor turned a deaf ear to him as though he were the 'lowest serving man at Schönbrunn.' . . . There was a widely spread but entirely erroneous idea in the Monarchy that the Archduke had drawn up a program of his future activities. This was not the case. He had very definite and pronounced ideas for the reorganization of the Monarchy, but the ideas were never developed into a concrete plan—they were more like the outline of a program that was never completed in detail." [32]

Two projects closely connected with the federalization idea had been much discussed. One of them is suggested in Conrad's letter to the Archduke of December 14, 1912: "The unification of the South Slav race is one of those nation-moving phenomena which cannot be denied nor artificially prevented. The only point is whether this unification shall take place *within* the control of the [Dual] Monarchy—that is at the expense of Serbia's independence—or whether it shall be accomplished under the aegis of Serbia *at the cost of the Monarchy.* This cost for us would consist in the loss of our South Slav lands and thereby of nearly

[32] *In the World War,* pp. 41 f., 49.

all our coast. This loss in territory and prestige would depress the Monarchy into a Small State."[33]

This peaceful incorporation of all South Slavs into the Hapsburg Empire was often dwelt upon by Conrad. In June, 1913, on the eve of the Second Balkan War the Austrian Military Attaché in Belgrade reported that there was a party in Serbia in favor of it. The idea was that Austria-Hungary should cede to Serbia the South Slavs, and to Rumania her kindred populations in Transylvania, and that the Serbian and Rumanian Kingdoms, thus enlarged, should be incorporated into a federal Hapsburg Empire and have somewhat the same constitutional position as the Kingdoms of Saxony and Bavaria in the German Empire. But it was generally agreed that this peaceful incorporation of Serbia and Rumania was impracticable, because the two kindoms would never consent to give up their complete independence. The analogy with Saxony and Bavaria was hardly apt, since their population was solidly of the same nationality as the rest of the German Empire, while Rumania and Serbia were not only of absolutely different nationality from the Germans in Austria and the Magyars in Hungary, but had come to regard them with deep hostility. Moreover, Vienna and Budapest looked down in aristocratic contempt upon Belgrade and Bucharest as representing totally different and inferior civilizations. Doubtless also the Triple Entente would have raised strenuous objections to any such apparent strengthening of Austria and consequently of Germany.

A second scheme, which was regarded as more practical and hopeful by many, was altogether different and was in flat contradiction to Conrad's view of the inevitability of Jugoslav unification. It had long been favored by Count

[33] Conrad, II, 380. Baron Conrad reiterated frequently this view (III, 343 f., 362 ff., 419 ff., 456, 461, 729 ff.).

Aehrenthal.[34] It consisted in a policy of playing off the Croats against the Serbs and thus splitting the Jugoslavs apart according to the old maxim of *divide et impera.* It contemplated the creation of a "Greater Croatia" as a third unit with Austria and Hungary in a *regnum tripartitum.* Franz Ferdinand was very favorably inclined toward the Croats. They were Roman Catholics and had helped preserve Hapsburg authority in the revolutions of 1848. A "Greater Croatia," composed of the Slav elements in Croatia, Slavonia, Dalmatia, and Bosnia-Herzegovina, and given equal political federal rights with the remaining parts of Austria and Hungary, would form a valuable bulwark against the "Greater Serbia" propaganda. The plan had had many staunch adherents among the Croats themselves, and in view of the unhappy conflicts between the Serbs and Croats since the War can hardly be regarded as altogether Utopian if it had been adopted seasonably. But during the years just before the War this antagonism between Serb and Croat had been rapidly disappearing owing to the oppressive rule of the German and Magyar authorities on the one hand, and the active propaganda of Jugoslav intellectuals on the other. Baron Musulin, an observant Austrian diplomat and Foreign Office Secretary, who was born in Croatia, visited his old home in 1913 and noted with alarm the change which was rapidly taking place from Croat loyalty to Jugoslav agitation. He believed the Croatian peasantry were still true to the Hapsburgs and that a strengthening of the Croatian sentiment could still be used to offset the Jugoslav movement for uniting Croats and Serbs into a "Greater Serbia."[35] An incident in the trial of the Sarajevo assassins which moved the court to mirth

34 Musulin, *Das Haus am Ballplatz,* Munich, 1924, p. 205 ff. *Cf.* also G.P., XXVI, 28, 47.

35 Musulin, pp. 195-210. *Cf.* also Stephan Count Burián, *Austria in Dissolution,* New York, 1924, pp. 358-371 on the conflict between the Croatian and the Jugoslav tendencies.

seems to confirm Baron Musulin's view, and shows how the superficial Jugoslav agitation had not overcome the older inherent Croat dislike of Serbs. A certain Sadilo was being questioned:

Question: What are you according to your political convictions?
Sadilo: I belong to the Croatian Right Party.
Question: Do you like the Serbs?
Sadilo: Yes, when I don't see them. (Laughter.) [36]

This creation of a "Greater Croatia," perhaps under the historic name of "Illyria," offered possibly the nearest approach to a peaceful solution of the Austro-Serbian conflict. Austria-Hungary would then have been transformed into a federation of at least three component parts, instead of a kind of Siamese-twin state, in which one of the twins insisted on oppressing all the non-Magyar elements. But it would have amounted to a constitutional revolution and would have certainly provoked bitter opposition from Germans and Magyars. Whether Franz Ferdinand would have actually attempted to replace "Dualism" by "Trialism" had he come to the throne, and whether he would have been successful, must remain among the great unanswered questions of history.

Certain it is, however, that he was commonly credited with wide-reaching plans for reorganizing and strengthening the Dual Monarchy, as was stated by Count Czernin and in most of the obituary notices. The dread of what he might do was one of the factors which led fanatical Serbs to plot his assassination. It also unquestionably caused many Viennese and Budapest officials to heave a sigh of relief when they heard the news of Sarajevo.

[36] Pharos, p. 154. The preceding paragraphs were written prior to the Serbian assassination of Croatians in the Serbian Parliament on June 20, 1928. On Croatian desires, see [Dr. Pilar], *Die Südslawische Frage und der Weltkrieg,* Vienna, 1918.

FRANZ FERDINAND'S MARRIAGE

One of the most fateful influences on the Archduke's life was his marriage. In the early 'nineties it was rumored at Vienna that he was paying attention to the Archduchess Marie Christine, eldest daughter of the Archduke Frederick and the Archduchess Isabella. He paid such frequent visits to them in Pressburg, sometimes twice a week, that the parents began to flatter themselves that their daughter would one day be Empress. But in reality Franz Ferdinand had fallen deeply in love with one of the ladies-in-waiting in their household—Countess Sophie Chotek. She was a handsome, proud, tall woman with flashing eyes and an eager step. She belonged to an ancient but impoverished Czech family. For nearly a year their love ran on in secret and unsuspected. When absent from one another they exchanged letters weekly through one of the Archduke's trusted officers. But then came a catastrophe. After a tennis party at Pressburg Franz Ferdinand changed his clothes, but forgot his watch. A servant brought it to the Archduchess Isabella. She opened the locket, expecting perhaps to find a photograph of her daughter—and found instead that of her lady-in-waiting. One can imagine the feelings of a disappointed mother! Countess Sophie was instantly dismissed in disgrace and had to leave the house that very night.[37]

The tongues of the gossips at the Austrian capital began to wag vigorously. But Franz Ferdinand, with his usual determination and obstinacy, declared that he would marry her. All his Hapsburg relatives objected. She was not a princess and did not belong to a ruling family. She was only a countess and therefore debarred from an "eligible" (*ebenbürtige*) marriage with an Archduke. To the old Emperor, Francis Joseph, the announcement of his neph-

37 Nikitsch-Boulles, p. 26 ff.

ew's determination came as a terrible blow. It was a disgrace unworthy of the family. It seemed like the last drop in his cup of bitterness and family sorrows. His brother, Maximilian, had been shot against a wall in Mexico, and Maximilian's wife had gone insane with grief. His own and only son, Rudolph, had died by violence under the most suspicious circumstances—very probably by suicide. His wife, the Empress Elizabeth, was assassinated by an Italian anarchist in 1898. His wife's insane nephew, Louis of Bavaria, escaping from his guardian, strangled his pursuer and together the two were drowned in the Starnbergersee. His younger nephew, Otto, Franz Ferdinand's brother, living a riotous life and weakened by the disease which he had contracted, caused frequent shocks to the old Emperor's sense of dignity and decency. And now his own heir insisted on defying European traditions and Spanish etiquette by marrying a mere impoverished countess with a possible taint of insanity in her blood. "Was I not to be spared even this?" the Emperor was heard to murmur.[38]

For months Francis Joseph remained absolutely opposed to the marriage. But when he saw that this only increased the obstinate determination of his nephew, and that Franz Ferdinand would sooner give up the right to the throne than the hand of the woman he loved, the old formalist sadly gave his final consent to a compromise. The marriage might take place, but it was to be only a morganatic alliance. On June 28, 1900, the marriage declaration was solemnly registered in the small council room of the Vienna Hofburg in the presence of the Emperor, the Archdukes, and the leading government officials. At the same time the Archduke made a solemn Oath of Renunciation, signed and sealed in German and Magyar copies, declaring:

> "Our marriage with the Countess Chotek is not an eligible but a morganatic marriage, and is to be considered

[38] Margutti, p. 139.

> as such for now and all time; in consequence whereof neither Our wife nor the issue to be hoped for with God's blessing from this Our marriage, nor their descendants, will possess or be entitled to claim those rights, titles, armorial bearings, privileges, etc., that belong to the eligible wives and to the issue of Archdukes from eligible marriages. And in particular we again recognize and declare that inasmuch as the issue from Our aforesaid marriage and their descendants are not members of the Most High Arch-House, they possess no right to succeed to the Throne."

The Act of Renunciation was to be the source of untold unhappiness and bitterness in the days to come, since those whom he held dearest were deprived of rights and honors which would have been theirs except for the restrictions of feudal law and Spanish etiquette. June 28, fatal day! Precisely fourteen years later on another June 28 the assassin's revolver, which made no distinctions of birth, united in death the two human beings whose life in matrimony had been clouded by the morganatic bond. June 28! Nineteen years later, on another anniversary of the Archduke's renunciation, was signed the Treaty of Versailles which registered the tragic results from the War of which the Archduke's death was made the immediate occasion!

After the marriage Countess Chotek was raised in rank with the title of Duchess of Hohenberg through the graciousness of Francis Joseph. Yet notwithstanding this elevation in rank, she was still regarded as inferior in position to the youngest Archduchess. Her lot was far from happy. "Greatness is dearly bought," she is said to have confessed to an intimate friend a year before her death. The members of the Imperial family often inflicted cruel humiliations upon her, and there were stories of violent scenes between Franz Ferdinand and his relatives because of the slights which were put upon his wife. Ultimately things came to such a pass that the Heir Presumptive and the Duchess of Hohenberg preferred to absent themselves from Court functions altogether.[39]

As Franz Ferdinand found that his wife was slighted and rebuffed at Vienna, he was all the more grateful for the more generous attitude which Emperor William displayed towards her. This explains in part the increasingly close relations which developed in the years before the War between the German Kaiser and the Archduke. On his first visit to Berlin Franz Ferdinand had been captivated, as had been so many others, by the Kaiser's vivacity, intellectual interests, and efforts to please. In November, 1908, the German Emperor stayed for two days with Franz Ferdinand for hunting at Eckartsau on the Danube, and their relations grew more intimate. A year later the Archduke was invited to Potsdam and the Duchess of Hohenberg was included in the invitation. There she was received with all the honors due to an Archduchess. The Kaiser's tact was in striking contrast to the galling etiquette at Vienna. At dinners at the Austrian Court, the Duchess of Hohenberg had been compelled to sit far removed from her husband at the foot of the table, below all the Austrian Archduchesses. At Potsdam the embarrassment of having her sit at a long table above others who were of higher

[39] *Cf.* the clerical *Reichpost,* a journal regarded as the personal organ of Franz Ferdinand, Jan. 17, 1911: "We are not acquainted with the reasons for the absence of the exalted couple, but we should find it comprehensible if the position assigned to the Consort of the Heir to the throne by the present Court ceremonial should have been thought unnecessarily painful. According to this ceremonial, the wife of the Heir Presumptive is preceded not only by the married ladies of the Imperial House, but even by the youngest Princesses. We remember the disagreeable scene at the Court Ball two years ago, when the members of the Imperial House appeared in the Ballroom, each Imperial Prince with a lady on his arm according to rank, whereas the wife of the Heir to the Throne was obliged to enter the room last, alone and without escort. As several young Archduchesses appear this year at the Court Ball for the first time, the rigors of the ceremonial hitherto observed would, perhaps, have been even more conspicuous. It would be very intelligible if the Duchess Sophie of Hohenberg should have wished to avoid a painful situation, if only out of regard for her exalted husband."

rank was ingeniously obviated by having many small tables. The German Emperor and Empress and the Archduke and his wife dined at one table, while the other guests dined at similar small tables. In this way no precedent could be created, and it could not be said that the German Court had given the Duchess precedence over any princess of the blood royal. On subsequent visits to Vienna the German Emperor was careful to pay personal visits to the Duchess of Hohenberg and show her every mark of esteem. Such conduct touched the heart of the Archduke and was one of the reasons for the more intimate relations and frequent visits of the two men to one another. When the Kaiser went to Corfu the Archduke would take pains to meet him and have the Austrian navy draw up to salute him, or would invite him to visit at Brioni or Miramar.[40] In the course of this interchange of visits, it so happened that the Kaiser was invited to Franz Ferdinand's beautiful villa at Konopischt in Bohemia on June 12, 1914.

THE KONOPISCHT MEETING: LEGEND AND FACT

The meeting at Konopischt, according to the official announcement in the Austrian Press, was a purely personal affair, "in order that the Kaiser might see the Archduke's wonderful roses in full bloom." Horticulture and landscape gardening were in fact one of the Archduke's most passionate hobbies. Having bought the Konopischt estate in 1886, he had spent years of thought, and sums of money which shocked his stewards, in laying out one of the finest parks in Europe. A sugar-factory, a brewery and peasants' houses had been removed, an artificial lake had been created, and rare and beautiful plants had been set out, so that from every window in the castle only the most pleasing prospect met the eye. Here at Konopischt Franz Ferdinand knew every tree and every bush. Every bed of flowers was

40 Nikitsch-Boulles, pp. 114 ff., 143 ff.

designed according to his exact orders, and his roses were his especial delight and care.[41] But the fact that William was accompanied by Admiral von Tirpitz, and that the Austrian Foreign Minister, Berchtold, came to Konopischt the day after the Emperor left, quickly caused some newspapers at the time to suspect that this meeting had some more serious occasion than merely the viewing of roses. A few weeks later, after the Archduke's assassination and the mysterious events connected with his death and interment, the wildest rumors began to circulate about the "pact" which had been plotted at Konopischt and which had caused the World War. It is therefore worth while to examine a little more closely into this meeting and the rumors to which it gave rise.

According to the London *Times* correspondent, Mr. H. Wickham Steed, who based his account upon an anonymous informant "whose position and antecedents entitle his statements to careful examination," the German Emperor had been deliberately courting the good-will of Franz Ferdinand by attentions to his wife for political purposes, which found their expression in the "Pact of Konopischt." Mr. Steed would have us believe that "the Kaiser opened to the Archduke Franz Ferdinand a magnificent horizon, and spread out before him a grandiose plan which promised presently to place his sons, Maximilian and Ernest, at the head of two vast realms in Eastern and Central Europe." Russia was to be provoked to a war for which Germany and Austria were ready; France was to be reduced to impotence by a few vigorous strokes; and the abstention of England was considered certain. The result of the war was to be the transformation of Europe. The ancient kingdom of Poland, with Lithuania and the Ukraine, was to be reconstituted, stretching from the Baltic to the Black Sea. This was to be the inheritance of Franz Ferdinand; after

41 Nikitsch-Boulles, pp. 188-197.

his death it was to pass to his eldest son. For his younger son was reserved, under his father's direction, a new realm comprising Bohemia, Hungary, and the Jugoslav lands, including Serbia, Dalmatia, and Salonica. Franz Ferdinand, according to this story, saw great thrones prepared for his sons, and Sophie Chotek saw herself the mother of Kings. Emperor William, on his part, was to give up to the new Polish state a part of Posen, and to indemnify himself by bringing into the German Empire a new state comprised of German Austria and Trieste and ruled by Franz Ferdinand's nephew, the Archduke Charles Francis Joseph. Germany would thus acquire a coveted outlet upon the Adriatic, and would be enlarged by the addition of another state equal in importance to Bavaria. Between the enlarged German Empire, the reconstituted kingdom of Poland, and the new Bohemian-Hungarian-Jugoslav realm, a close and perpetual military and economic alliance was to be formed. This alliance would become the arbiter of Europe, and would command the Balkans and the route to the East.

Such, according to Mr. Wickham Steed, were the terms of the agreement. Knowledge of it, he thinks, came to the ears of the Austrian Imperial family, and herein lies the explanation of the shabby way in which Franz Ferdinand and his wife were unceremoniously hurried to their graves after being murdered at Sarajevo. He darkly hints that the Austrian Court itself was guilty of complicity in the murder. He then goes on to exaggerate or distort in sensational newspaper fashion a number of other circumstances calculated to leave the reader with the impression that the assassination of the Archduke was brought about through the complicity of Austrian officials and that Serbia was in no way responsible. "General Potiorek, who was sitting in the archducal car, escaped injury. Neither he nor any other military or civil dignitaries were punished for their failure to protect the visitors. General Potiorek remained Governor and presently commanded the Bosnian army through the first campaign against Serbia. After the defeat of his troops he was deprived of his command, was reported to have lost his reason, and was placed in a lunatic asylum. . . . When the Emperor Francis Joseph visited Sarajevo in June, 1910, the number of police available exceeded a thousand; probably double that number of secret agents were employed; yet when the Heir to the Throne visited the city the police were warned off! No evidence proving the complicity of the Serbian Government in the plot to assassinate the Archduke has ever been adduced. . . . It would certainly not be beyond the power of the Austro-Hungarian secret service agents to work up a plot at Belgrade or at Sarajevo . . . to 'remove' obnoxious personages or to provide a pretext for war." [42]

After describing at length the indignity of the funeral arrangements made for the murdered couple which "were hardly less astonishing than had been the circumstances of the assassination," Mr. Steed adds as a further incriminating circumstance the fact that it was at first announced that the German Emperor would attend the funeral, but "on the 2nd of July it was announced in Berlin that owing to a slight indisposition, the German Emperor had abandoned his journey to Vienna. He nevertheless gave audiences as usual on that day." He implies that the German Emperor and the other sovereigns were instructed from Vienna not to attend the funeral and that this is a further indication that the Archduke's death was contrived by Austrian officials because of his having plotted at Konopischt a partition of the Hapsburg lands to provide crowns for his sons. But as a matter of fact the failure of the Kaiser to attend the funeral was not due to any hint from the authorities in Vienna who wanted to deprive the Archduke and his wife

[42] Steed, "The Pact of Konopischt," pp. 265 ff.; see below, note 45

of due honors even after death. He abandoned his intention of going to Vienna because a warning had come from the German consul at Sarajevo that the Serbs might make an attack on his life also, and because his Chancellor declined to assume the responsibility of allowing the Emperor to risk his life by going to Vienna. As we learn from Bethmann-Hollweg's telegram to the German Ambassador at Vienna on July 2:

> As a result of warnings which have been received from Sarajevo, of which the first, in fact, dates back to April of this year, I have been obliged to request His Majesty the Emperor to give up the visit to Vienna. What confirmed me in the determination was the fact that the journey was not an act of national or political necessity, but one concerned with the voluntary announcement of friendly feelings beyond a point required by etiquette; that there is apparently a wide-spread conspiracy at the bottom of the Sarajevo crime; and that assassinations are well known to exercise a suggestive influence on the criminal elements. On the strength of these considerations, I was unable to undertake the responsibility of exposing His Majesty unnecessarily in a foreign land.
>
> For public purposes, the giving up of the visit will be laid to the physical indisposition of His Majesty. His Majesty wishes, however, that the true reason be communicated to His Majesty the Emperor Franz Joseph personally.[43]

Similarly all the other circumstances with which Mr. Steed and his followers have built up the theory of Austrian complicity are really to be explained quite simply and naturally on altogether different and less sensational grounds, as will be indicated below. There is not a shred of evidence that the Archduke was plotting at Konopischt, or that Austrian officials conspired for his assassination.

[43] K.D., 6 B; and the warning telegram from Sarajevo, K.D., 6 A.

Nevertheless Mr. Steed's astounding theory received wide acceptance among Austria's late enemies. Serbians naturally are glad to adopt it because it would remove all responsibility for the crime from their country.[44] It has been widely circulated with some reservations or amplifications by many over-suspicious French writers: by M. Raymond Recouly, a popular newspaper correspondent and magazine writer; by M. Alfred Dumaine, who was French Ambassador to Vienna, but who at the time appears to have known nothing of all this; by M. Chopin in his monograph on the Sarajevo murder; and even by such a sober historian as Professor Debidour.[45]

Fortunately for the cause of truth, documents have re-

[44] Mr. A. V. Seferovitch, Jugoslav Consul-General at Montreal, quotes Mr. Steed at length to prove "that the plot to murder the Archduke originated in Austria and served a twofold purpose, namely, the elimination of the Archduke as heir presumptive and a pretext for the long-desired attack on Serbia by Austria;" see his article, "The blame for the Sarajevo murder plot" in New York Times *Current History,* Dec., 1925, p. 385.

[45] H. Wickham Steed, "The Pact of Konopischt," in *Nineteenth Century and After,* Vol. 79, pp. 253-273 (Feb., 1916). Many months later Mr. Steed is said to have admitted in private conversation that he no longer believed in this fantastic story. Nevertheless he repeats it in abbreviated form in his interesting but unveracious work, *Through Thirty Years,* London, 1924, I, 396-403, where it will doubtless continue to deceive thousands of unsophiscated readers like Mr. Seferovitch. Among the French writers who have swallowed and broadcasted with variations his theory are Jean Pozzi, "Les Roses de Konopischt," in *Le Correspondant,* June 10, 1921; Recouly, *Les Heures Tragiques d'Avant-Guerre* (Paris, 1922), pp. 173-194; and also in *La Revue de France,* April 1, 1922, pp. 598-610; Dumaine, *La Dernière Ambassade de France en Autriche* (Paris, 1921), p. 126 ff.; Debidour, *Histoire Diplomatique de l'Europe* (Paris, 1918), II, 229; Jules Chopin (pseudonym of J. E. Pichon, a lecturer at the University of Prague who shares the characteristic Czech attitude of hostility towards the Hapsburgs) "La preméditation austro-hungroise," in *Mercure de France,* Vol. 115 (1916), pp. 577-599. In his much-quoted little book, *Le Complot De Sarajevo* (Paris, 1918), p. 82, Chopin sums up: "Il est certain que l'entrevue de Konopischt avait un tout autre but que celui d'échanger des politesses et de mettre à mal le gibier des parcs archiducaux. Nous croyons donc que son seul objet était justement de trouver le prétexte d'une guerre qui manquait en 1914, et de minutieusement régler la marche diplomatique et militaire de toute cette entreprise belliqueuse

cently been published which give precise and trustworthy accounts of what really took place at Konopischt and which will lead all serious students to consign Mr. Steed's amazing theory to the limbo of propagandist war myths.[46] One of these documents is the official report sent to the German Foreign Office the day after the interview by Baron von Treutler, the Minister in attendance upon William II.[47]

This gives a good account of the conversations between William II and Franz Ferdinand. They first touched upon the Balkan situation, in view of an alarming telegram from Athens that the Greeks had called up their marine reserves and were rumored to be planning an attack on Turkey. Franz Ferdinand and his guest agreed to sound King Carol of Rumania, to see whether he would use his influence in favor of peace and the preservation of the *status quo* as fixed by the Treaty of Bucharest. Both expressed their dislike of Ferdinand of Bulgaria. Franz Ferdinand gave vent to his suspicions of Italy's *mala fides* in Albania and in general. The German Emperor tried to allay his suspicions, and hoped that when Franz Ferdinand should meet the King of Italy at the German routine maneuvers later in the year, there would be an opportunity for establishing more cordial personal relations between Victor Emmanuel and the Heir to the Hapsburg throne.

The main topic of conversation at Konopischt, however, like that between William II and Francis Joseph at

46 Even Mr. Seton-Watson, whom no one will accuse of being over lenient toward Austria, has at last acknowledged (*Sarajevo,* p. 111): "Nothing which even remotely deserves the name of evidence has ever been adduced in proof [of the theory of official complicity on the part of Vienna and Budapest] and each of the many suspicious details is susceptible of a simpler and less sensational explanation;" similarly also pp. 114, 287.

47 In *Deutsche Politik,* May 14, 1920; G.P., XXXIX, 365 ff.; and reprinted by Montgelas, *The Case for the Central Powers,* pp. 232-235. Treutler's accuracy as to the first point discussed in the interview is confirmed by the telegram sent by the Austrian Minister in Athens on June 12, printed in Conrad, III, 660 f.

Vienna three months previously,[48] dealt with internal Austrian politics—Tisza's treatment of the Rumanians in Transylvania and its dangerous effect on public feeling in the Kingdom of Rumania. Franz Ferdinand assailed the medieval and anachronistic Magyar oligarchy, with Tisza at its head, which dominated Hungary and was trying to dominate Austria as well. "Already Vienna begins to tremble when Tisza starts for the city; everyone lies flat on his stomach when Tisza steps out at Vienna." Emperor William, on the other hand, urged that Tisza was such a powerful and unusual man that he "ought not to be thrown overboard, but be kept under a firm hand, and then used for his valuable qualities." The Archduke complained that "it was precisely Tisza who was to blame, if the interests of the Triple Alliance were badly looked after, since it was Tisza who, in contradiction with his own promises at Schönbrunn, had been maltreating the Rumanians in Hungary. The Archduke finally begged His Majesty whether he would not instruct Tschirschky [the German Ambassador at Vienna] to remind Tisza at every opportunity that he should not lose sight of the necessity of winning over the Rumanians through moderation in the treatment of their brothers who were living in Hungary. His Majesty promised that he would instruct Tschirschky continually to repeat to Tisza, 'Sir! Remember the Rumanians!' The Archduke greatly approved of this." Treutler gathered the impression from the Archduke's secretary that Franz Ferdinand felt that the Kaiser and the Berlin Foreign Office were too inclined to look at conditions in Austria-Hungary through Hungarian spectacles, owing to the fact that for decades the Dual Monarchy had been represented at Berlin by a Hungarian Ambassador. Franz Ferdinand in fact told William II confidentially that it was planned to replace Szögyény, a Hungarian, by Prince Hohenlohe, an Austrian.

[48] G.P., XXXIX, 333 ff., 358 ff.; Montgelas, pp. 229-231.

At the close of the conversation Franz Ferdinand expressed the opinion that Russia was not to be feared; her internal difficulties were too great to allow her to follow an aggressive foreign policy.

Treutler's report, showing that the main topic of conversation at Konopischt was Tisza's Rumanian policy, is further corroborated from the Austrian side. The day after the German Emperor left Konopischt, Berchtold was summoned thither, and upon his return to Vienna gave the German Ambassador a résumé of the conversations which Tschirschky reported as follows:

> After His Majesty the Kaiser left, Count Berchtold was invited to Konopischt by Archduke Franz Ferdinand. This Minister told me today that the Archduke expressed himself as greatly gratified at the Kaiser's visit. He had talked over in detail all possible questions with the Kaiser and was able to find that they were in complete agreement in their views.
>
> The Archduke also told Count Berchtold what he had said to the Kaiser in regard to Count Tisza's policy, especially the policy toward the non-Magyar nationalities. "Toward the Rumanians," the Archduke had remarked, "Count Tisza used fine words, but his deeds did not correspond to his words." It was one of the Hungarian Premier's cardinal mistakes that he had not given more parliamentary seats to the Rumanians in Transylvania.
>
> Count Berchtold told me that he had attempted often and emphatically to influence Count Tisza to make greater concessions to the Rumanians. But his efforts had been in vain. Count Tisza maintained that he had already conceded as much as possible to the Rumanians.
>
> For my part I will also use every opportunity, as I have been doing hitherto, in accordance with the Kaiser's directions, to point out to the Hungarian Premier the necessity of winning over the Rumanians.[49]

[49] Tschirschky to Bethmann, June 17, 1914; K.D., 4. On this report the Kaiser made the marginal note, "He [Tisza] must not by *his internal*

In view of these precise contemporary documents, one may therefore confidently relegate to the realm of legend all the fantastic tales of Mr. Wickham Steed and the French writers, that William II and Franz Ferdinand were planning a rearrangement of the map of Europe, or plotting a European war which was to be provoked by the Archduke's maneuvers near the Serbian frontier at Sarajevo. The Magyar oppression of the Transylvanian Rumanians, and the consequent indignation that was being stirred up among King Carol's subjects, involving as it did the danger that Rumania might cease to be loyal to her secret treaties with the Triple Alliance Powers, was a sufficiently serious question, aside from the roses and personal friendship, to account for the meeting at Konopischt. In this connection it is significant that the Rumanian question, and its relation to Germany and Austrian policy, fills a large place in the documents recently published by Conrad von Hötzendorf and by the German Government.[50]

policy, which through the Rumanian question has an influence on *the external policy of the Triple Alliance,* jeopardize the latter."

For further references to the Konopischt meeting and the possible subjects discussed there see the report of the Russian Ambassador in Vienna to Sazonov (printed in *Die Kriegsschuldfrage,* III, 169, June, 1925), alleging that Franz Ferdinand had discussed the Austrian naval program with Admiral Tirpitz in view of the danger that Russia would open the Straits Question. Tirpitz's brief memorandum on the visit, written immediately upon his return to Berlin (*ibid.,* III, 561 f., Sept. 1925), is mainly a description of the society and landscape gardening at Konopischt with which he was greatly impressed; "aside from the Kaiser's talk with the Archduke, politics were hardly touched upon at all;" the Kaiser had mentioned to Franz Ferdinand the possibility of sending the German fleet into the Mediterranean in case of war, "because it had been deduced from the naval manoeuvres that in view of the submarines, etc., we could not do much in the North Sea." For the Triple Alliance Naval Convention of June 23, 1913, fixing the conditions of naval coöperation in the Mediterranean, see Pribram, I, 282 ff. Conrad, III, 36 f., reports a conversation with Francis Joseph on July 5, 1914 in which the Emperor said, "I instructed Franz Ferdinand to request from the German Emperor at Konopischt information as to whether in the future also we could reckon unconditionally upon Germany. The German Emperor had evaded the question and given no answer."

50 Conrad, III, *passim;* G.P., XXXIII-XXXIX, *passim.*

The uncertainty as to Rumania's loyalty and the consequent advisability of a definite shift in the Balkan policy of the Triple Alliance is also, as we shall see, the main theme of a long memoir for preserving peace in the Balkans, which Tisza drew up in the spring of 1914, and which was being worked over in the Austrian Foreign Office at the moment Franz Ferdinand was assassinated.

The fact that the German Emperor was accompanied at Konopischt by Admiral von Tirpitz has caused some remark, and helped to spread the legend that great things were being plotted there. But Tirpitz's presence at Konopischt is probably sufficiently explained, as Jagow later asserted,[51] by the Archduke's interest in the upbuilding and reorganization of the Austrian navy, which he had so much at heart. Possibly it is also to be explained by the fact that the Kaiser was unquestionably greatly worried, as was the German Foreign Office, at the rumors of a naval agreement between Russia and England which was actually under discussion just at this time. France and Russia had supplemented the Military Convention of the Dual Alliance by an analogous Naval Convention in the spring of 1912. In November of the same year, France had secured from Sir Edward Grey a written promise that the French and British naval and military experts should continue to consult together in anticipation of a possible war. The British and French navies had been rearranged in such a way that the French increased their forces in the Mediterranean to protect British as well as French interests in that area, and the British on their part concentrated their fleet in the North Sea to protect the north coast of France from attack by Germany. Finally, in the spring of 1914, Poincaré, Izvolski and Sazonov were eagerly trying to arrange

51 Jagow, *Ursachen,* p. 181, n. 2: "That Secretary of State Tirpitz accompanied the Kaiser at Konopischt was due to the express wish of the Archduke who wished to hear the Grand Admiral's views concerning the construction of types of ships."

for a naval agreement between England and Russia which would consolidate the naval forces of the Entente against Germany. Naturally the Kaiser would be anxious to consult with Franz Ferdinand and his own Grand Admiral as to the significance of these negotiations, and as to the means of averting, if possible, what looked like naval "encirclement."

Perhaps after all, however, the most important result of the meeting at Konopischt was the effect that it had on the Kaiser's psychology. On his impetuous and emotional nature the murder made all the more vivid impression inasmuch as it had struck down a friend at whose home he had been visiting so intimately only a few days previously. The pistol shots at Sarajevo followed so closely upon the roses at Konopischt that they intensified all the more the horror with which he regarded all tyrannicide. Whereas heretofore he had been restraining Austria from rash action against Serbia, now he instantly envisaged Serbia as a den of murderers, and unwisely allowed Count Berchtold complete freedom to take any steps against Serbia which should be deemed advisable at Vienna.

THE TRIP TO SARAJEVO

The Archduke's fatal trip to Bosnia and Sarajevo in June, 1914, was decided upon many months beforehand. On September 16, 1913, during the Austrian army maneuvers in Bohemia he spoke to Conrad of it. On September 29 Conrad discussed it in Vienna with General Potiorek, Governor of Bosnia, who said it was the Archduke's intention to visit Bosnia as Heir to the Throne, to attend the maneuvers of the XVth and XVIth Army Corps, and to take advantage of the occasion to bring his wife with him.[52]

[52] Conrad, III, 445. Whether the original suggestion for the trip came from the Archduke himself, as is usually assumed, or whether it was due to the request of General Potiorek, Governor of Bosnia, as I think more probable, is not clear. Conrad says (III, 702): "On whose initiative the

This conversation indicates the three-fold purpose of the visit and explains the somewhat unusual details in connection with it.

From the political point of view it was highly desirable that a member of the imperial family should show himself in the recently annexed provinces. Among the impressionable simple peasant populations of Europe, who before the War had a deep-rooted respect for royalty and a traditional feeling of loyalty to a personal ruler, nothing was better calculated to stimulate and strengthen this feeling of personal loyalty than such official visits of princes. They flattered local pride. The simple peasant liked the pageantry of princes. He liked to see his ruler and find in him a flesh and blood human being like himself, who walks and rides about and eats three good meals a day. Merely to see him or hear him speak was to renew the human bond of common understanding and interests. So throughout history, from Henri Quatre and Frederick the Great in the past to the Prince of Wales in the present, it has been a common practice for popular princes and rulers to make royal progresses, which tend to strengthen the bonds between ruler and ruled.[53] With this in view Emperor Francis Joseph had visited Bosnia in 1910. It was with this same idea that Baron Musulin in 1913 had urged that Franz Ferdinand should make himself better known in Croatia, and that members of the Hapsburg family should make

decision for the Heir's trip originated, and who fixed the measures for it, I do not know. But that an imperial prince should finally again visit Bosnia, like Crown Prince Rudolf in earlier days, seemed to me only natural and in the interests of the dynasty; especially so if it was the Heir to the Throne himself who should undertake this trip." Nikitsch-Boulles (pp. 209-216), who accompanied the Archduke's wife, indicates that the Archduke made the trip rather against his will because of his dislike of the heat, and implies that it was undertaken to please General Potiorek and the military officers.

53 On the political importance of having princes present their traits familiarly to peasants, see the shrewd observations of Mr. H. A. L. Fisher, *The Republican Tradition in Europe,* Boston, 1911, pp 322-324.

longer visits there, in order to counteract among the loyal peasantry the propaganda of Jugoslav agitators.[54] Possibly his suggestion may have had something to do with the Archduke's decision to visit Bosnia and Herzegovina. Such a visit would strengthen the Roman Catholic and other loyal elements and tend to offset Jugoslav revolutionary propaganda and the Serb agitation for "Greater Serbia." This was the political aspect of his trip, and it partly explains why he did not wish to be protected by heavy guards of soldiers and secret police, but preferred to ride about freely in an open automobile. In 1909, when he had travelled through Hungary to visit King Carol, he had been highly indignant at the way the civilian authorities had shut off the railway stations with cordons of police and kept at a distance the crowds of peasantry who had come to wave their hats and handkerchiefs to the Archducal couple.[55]

The main object of the trip, however, was that the Archduke might attend the maneuvers of the XVth and XVIth Army Corps, which were regularly stationed in Bosnia. As Inspector-in-Chief of the Army he had in recent years regularly represented the Emperor at such maneuvers. The Bosnian maneuvers of 1914 are commonly represented by Austrophobe writers as "planned as a kind of rehearsal for military operations against Serbia." [56] Mr. Jovanovitch, the Serbian Minister in Vienna, says: "The plan was to hold the maneuvers in the **district between** Sarajevo and the Romanija and Han Pisesak [to the *east* of Sarajevo]—thus just against the Serbian frontier. **With maneuvers** so planned the 'enemy' was naturally Serbia. . . . The **maneuvers** were to be held in Bosnia on the Drin just opposite to Serbia." [57] There is no truth in these assertions. All the provisions for a campaign against Serbia were taken

[54] Musulin, pp. 206-210. [55] Nikitsch-Boulles, p. 130.

[56] Seton-Watson, *Sarajevo*, p. 115.

[57] Letter of Jovan Jovanovitch in *Neues Wiener Tageblatt*, No. 177, June 28, 1924.

care of in an altogether different way, namely by Baron Conrad's "Mobilization B"[alkan] plan. This included not merely the two Corps regularly stationed in Bosnia, but the use of five more Corps from the rest of Austria-Hungary comprising altogether about half the total army;[58] it contemplated of course a direct offensive against the Drin, which forms the boundary between Bosnia and Serbia. This plan had been worked out in all its details by Conrad and his General Staff, and, like the General Staff mobilization plans of all countries, was always in readiness. But the Bosnian maneuvers which the Archduke was to inspect comprised merely two Army Corps and were merely part of the routine training to which parts of the army were regularly subjected. They had no connection with any concrete war preparations, but simply had as their main object the practicing of considerable forces moving in a relatively difficult and varied terrain. Nor were they to be held in the Romanija *east* of Sarajevo "on the Drin just opposite to Serbia," as M. Jovanovitch states. On the contrary they were held some 30 kilometers to the *southwest* of Sarajevo in the Tarcin district. They did not in the slightest contemplate a theoretical attack on Serbia to the eastward, but looked in exactly the opposite direction—the theoretical protection of Sarajevo against an attack coming from the *west* from the direction of the Adriatic. The "Blue" defending army had a position southwest of Sarajevo and was to prevent the "Red" attacking force, advancing from the side of Mostar and the west, from capturing the Ivan Pass which guards the road which runs up from the Adriatic to Sarajevo.[59] It was in order to become acquainted with this region at the opposite side of Bosnia, as far away from Serbia as possible, that the Archduke travelled to

[58] Conrad, I, 361-423; IV, 112-124. For the disposition of the Austrian forces, see below, at the end of ch. vii.

[59] For the details of the maneuvers see the *Neue Freie Presse,* Nos. 17901-2, June 27, 28, 1914.

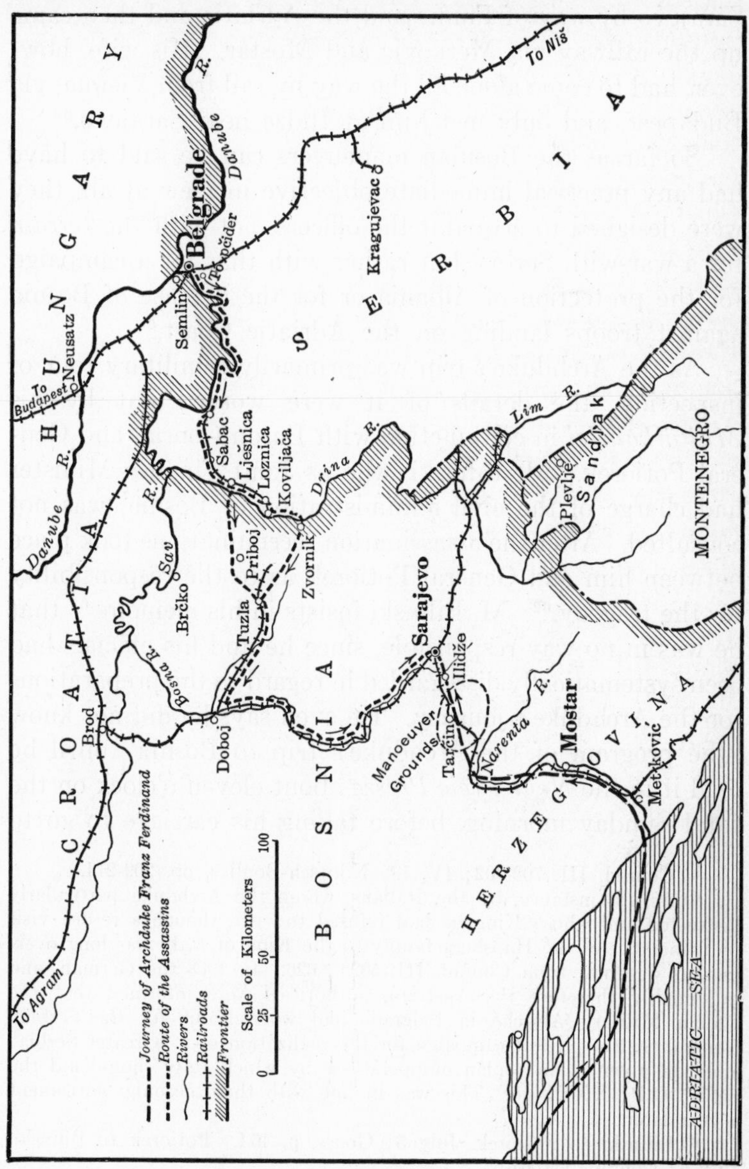
H U N G A R Y
C R O A T I A
B O S N I A
S E R B I A
H E R Z E G O V I N A
MONTENEGRO
Sandjak
ADRIATIC SEA
Journey of Archduke Franz Ferdinand
Route of the Assassins
Rivers
Railroads
Frontier
Scale of Kilometers
0 25 50 100
To Agram
To Budapest
Neusatz
Semlin
Belgrade
Topčider
Kragujevac
To Niš
Danube R.
Sav R.
Bosna R.
Drina R.
Lim R.
Narenta R.
Brod
Doboj
Brčko
Tuzla
Priboj
Sabac
Lješnica
Loznica
Koviljača
Zvornik
Sarajevo
Ilidže
Tarčin
Manoeuver Grounds
Mostar
Metković
Plevlje

Sarajevo by way of Fiume and the Adriatic and then came up the railway via Metkovic and Mostar. His wife, however, had to come alone all the way by rail from Vienna, via Budapest, and only met him at Ilidze near Sarajevo.[60]

So far as the Bosnian maneuvers can be said to have had any practical immediate objective in view at all, they were designed to acquaint the officers, not with the *terrain* for a war with Serbia, but rather with that for a campaign for the protection of Albania or for the defense of Bosnia against troops landing on the Adriatic Coast.[61]

As the Archduke's trip was primarily a military tour of inspection, the details of it were worked out by his *Militärkanzlei* in conjunction with Baron Conrad and General Potiorek. M. Bilinski, who as Joint Finance Minister had charge of the civil administration of Bosnia, was not consulted. After the assassination recriminations took place between him and General Potiorek as to the responsibility for the tragedy.[62] M. Bilinski insists in his memoirs [63] that he was in no way responsible, since he and his officials had been systematically disregarded in regard to the preparations for the Archduke's journey. He even says he did not know "the program of the Archduke's trip to Bosnia" until he read it in the *Neue Freie Presse* about eleven o'clock on the fatal Sunday morning, before taking his carriage to go to

60 Conrad, III, 700-702; IV, 13; Nikitsch-Boulles, pp. 209-214.

61 As, for instance, by the Italians, whom the Archduke particularly distrusted and whose King he had refused to visit, though a return visit by a member of the Hapsburg family to the King of Italy was long overdue, as we know from Conrad, III, 502 f., 626. In 1908 the German, and presumably therefore the Austrian, authorities were informed that the Italian Military Attaché in Belgrade had worked out for the Serbian General Staff a plan of campaign for the realization of a "Greater Serbia" and had given them a plan of operations by which Italy should aid the Serbs; G.P., XXVI, 18. This was in line with the Racconigi agreement a year later.

62 Bilinski to Potiorek, July 3; Gooss, p. 46 f. Potiorek to Bilinski, July 6; Conrad, IV, 64-67.

63 Léon Bilinski, *Wspomnienia i Dokumenty* [Reminiscences and Documents], 2 vols., Warsaw, 1924-25, I, 273-277.

church. He had a painful shock, he says, when he then learned for the first time that the program of the Archduke's trip contained, contrary to the Emperor's original permission for a military tour, a solemn entry into Sarajevo.[64] Bilinski's denial of any prior knowledge of the Archduke's intended entry into Sarajevo can hardly be true, because the *Neue Freie Presse* does not contain on June 28 any "program of the Archduke's trip to Bosnia"; it merely gives an account of the day's maneuvers there. Moreover, three weeks earlier, on June 4, it had already printed an outline of the Archduke's trip, including the proposed visit to Sarajevo, which he can hardly have failed to see. Furthermore, on June 24 there was printed a detailed private program of the trip for the information of officials.[65] Bilinski admits that a copy of this had been brought to him by one of his assistants.[66]

The point that Bilinski was not consulted has been made much of by writers who try to explain the responsibility for the crime by emphasizing the "bevy of assassins" lying in wait for the Archduke, the "criminal negligence" of the Austrian police, the arrogance of Potiorek, and headstrong obstinacy of Franz Ferdinand in ignoring the Joint Finance Minister.[67] In thus trying to put the blame on the Austrian authorities they obscure the true conspiracy which was developed at Belgrade. One of the main reasons which they cite for putting the preparations into the hands of Potiorek instead of Bilinski was said to be the Archduke's desire to eliminate Court officials who might have placed obstacles in the way of having the Duchess Sophie go to

64 Bilinski, I, 276.

65 Margutti, p. 146; *cf.* Seton-Watson, p. 107, note 2.

66 Bilinski, I, 274 f.

67 Seton-Watson, *Sarajevo,* pp. 106-117; Wickham Steed, in *The Nineteenth Century and After,* LXXIX, 253-273; Recouly, *Les Heures Tragiques,* pp. 180-182; Chopin, *Le Complot de Sarajevo,* pp. 89-100; Margutti, pp. 145 ff., 396 f.

Sarajevo. However this may be, the Emperor appears to have made no objection to her participation in the trip when the matter was laid before him by the Archduke on June 4.[68]

The Archduke appears finally to have undertaken the trip more from a sense of duty than from the desire, as usually stated, to have an opportunity to have his wife received with royal honors by his side. As already noted they travelled to Sarajevo by different routes. In the last weeks he had some doubts about going at all, because of his health and the heat. He discussed the point with the Emperor, who said, "Do as you wish." [68a] His private secretary has noted several remarks which indicate that Franz Ferdinand was the reverse of enthusiastic about the trip. On June 23 the special railway carriage regularly reserved for him had a hot-box, so that he and his wife had to travel in an ordinary first class compartment after leaving their three children at Chlumetz. Franz Ferdinand remarked sarcastically, "Well, the journey is beginning in a right promising fashion!" [69] A little later, when told that the train by which he and his wife intended to leave Sarajevo on June 29 would have to start at 5 A. M. instead of 6 A. M. as originally planned, he exclaimed, "Tell Colonel Bardolff that if he continues daily to make the Bosnian trip still more disgusting with new difficulties and unpleasantnesses he can hold the maneuvers alone, and I will not go down there at all." The secretary adds that the idea "that

[68] Conrad, III, 700. Bilinski had an audience with the Emperor on this same day (*Neue Freie Presse,* No. 17878, June 4, p. 2) and had plenty of opportunity to raise objections to the Archduke's proposed trip, but there is no indication that he did so. It was *after* the tragedy that he and his officials emphasize how worried they had been and how much they had disapproved of the plans. Mr. Seton-Watson, to be sure (*Sarajevo,* p. 106) quotes a second-hand statement by A. Mousset to the effect that Bilinski did instruct Sarajevo to sound the local authorities, who declined to take responsibility; but Mousset, though he passes for an authority on Serbian history, is strongly Austrophobe and not an altogether reliable writer.

[68a] Conrad, III, 700.

[69] Nikitsch-Boulles, p. 210.

the Archduke himself wanted the trip to Bosnia in order to provide a triumphal journey is a pure invention." [70]

However, in spite of these annoyances, and the fact that the electricity gave out in the train in which he rode from Vienna to Trieste, the rest of the journey passed off excellently and the Archduke was in the best of humor. He was greeted with enthusiasm at the railway stations on the way from the Adriatic to Sarajevo, and joined his wife on the afternoon of June 25 at the pleasant little resort of Ilidze, a dozen miles from Sarajevo, where they were to stay. The maneuvers passed off very satisfactorily in spite of heavy rain, and the Archduke complimented General Potiorek on the spirit and training of the troops.[71]

On Friday afternoon, June 26, after returning from the first day's maneuvers, Franz Ferdinand and his wife motored in to Sarajevo to do some shopping in the bazaars. The Mayor of the town had already issued a proclamation expressing the loyalty of the population to Francis Joseph and their pleasure that he had sent his Heir to visit Bosnia; he urged the people to decorate the stores and houses with flags and flowers, and this was done; everywhere his picture was in the windows.

On this afternoon Franz Ferdinand was in uniform and was continually recognized and acclaimed with loyal shouts of "*Zivio.*" The crowd was so dense that the officers accompanying him had some difficulty in making way for him from one shop to another.[72] Had there been really a "bevy of assassins" waiting to do away with him, here was ample opportunity. But the visit passed off without any incident, and the Archducal pair returned to Ilidze, much pleased with the town and the way they had been received.

On Sunday morning the Archduke telegraphed to his

[70] Nikitsch-Boulles, p. 211. [71] Conrad, IV, 13-15.

[72] Nikitsch-Boulles, p. 213; Conrad, IV, 14 f.; Jevtitch, *Sarajevski Atentat.*

children at Chlumetz that everything was going well with "Papi" and "Mami," and that they were looking forward to seeing them again on Tuesday. These were the last words he ever wrote.[73]

[73] Nikitsch-Boulles, p. 215

CHAPTER II

THE ASSASSINATION PLOT

THE immediate occasion of the World War was the murder of the Austrian Archduke at Sarajevo. Had it not occurred, there would have been neither an Austro-Serbian War, nor a World War, in the summer of 1914. In spite of the increasing tension between the Triple Alliance and the Triple Entente, it is probable that European diplomacy would have succeeded for months, perhaps for years, in averting a conflict which all statesmen foresaw as unspeakably terrible, and for which the Franco-Russian forces planned to be better prepared in 1917 than in 1914. The murder of the Archduke ignited material which would not otherwise have taken fire as it did, or perhaps not at all. It is, therefore, of importance to trace the origins of the plot to which he fell a victim and to determine the responsibility for the deed which was to have such awful and world-racking consequences.

What are the true details of the Sarajevo plot? What were the motives of the assassins? Who were their instigators or accomplices? These are dark and difficult questions which have remained more mysterious and baffling than most of the problems relating to the immediate causes of the War. Serious historians have devoted relatively little attention to them. Fantastic rumors and persistent misstatements, born of hatred and war propaganda, have passed current for a longer time on this subject than on any other aspect of those tragic days which set Europe aflame. There are many reasons for this. Historians have been mainly occupied with the question of the relative responsibility of the Great Powers. Information from Serbian sources was not only very meager, but such as there was consisted of contradictory assertions. Another reason was the fact that the official Austrian version of the plot, which laid the blame largely on the Serbian agitation for a "Greater Serbia," and especially on the subversive activities of the Serbian patriotic association known as the "Narodna Odbrana," was set forth in Austria's ultimatum to Serbia, and in the *dossier* offered to the Powers, containing the results of Austria's Sarajevo investigation and justifying the ultimatum.[1] But this Austrian version never inspired much confidence —to put it mildly—among most people in the Entente or neutral countries. The investigation at Sarajevo had necessarily been very hurried and had been carried on in strict secrecy. The *dossier* seemed to read like a hasty patchwork; appended to it are a couple of "supplements after the close of the printing." As the *dossier* did not reach the Powers until after they had begun seriously to suspect that Austria was bent on war against Serbia in any event, the statesmen of Europe were already so entirely absorbed with apprehension of a general European war that they had no time, in their hot, sleepless days and nights, to give any serious attention to what they suspected might be fabricated accusations.[2] There was fresh in everyone's mind

1 *Austrian Red Book* of 1914, Nos. 7-9, 19.

2 The *dossier,* in German, was dispatched by mail or messenger to twenty-two Austrian diplomatic representatives abroad on July 25, (A.R.B., II, 48). As there had been no time to translate it into French, as was usually done with Austro-Hungarian communications to the Powers, it was sent in the original German. It was delivered to Bienvenu-Martin in Paris on July 27 (F.Y.B., 75), but only the first part of it was printed in the French Yellow Book. It was not offered to Sir Edward Grey in London until July 29, and not printed at all in the English Blue Book. It is doubtful whether Sir Edward even read it at the time; *cf.* Grey to Bunsen, July 29 (B.D., 282): "The Austrian Ambassador told me today he had ready a long memorandum, which he proposed to leave and which he said gave an account of the conduct of Serbia toward Austria, and

the memory of the disgraceful Agram and Friedjung trials, in which Austrian officials had been detected in using forged documents in their efforts to incriminate Serb sympathizers. Was it not very probable that the *dossier* of 1914 was equally dishonest? People prejudiced against the Central Powers, therefore, were inclined to consign Berchtold's *dossier* to oblivion or incredulous ridicule, and to accept instead the Serbian Government's explicit denial of the Austrian charges and its sweeping assertion that it was in no way guilty of any complicity.

Later on, in November, 1914, the assassins and other suspects were brought to a formal trial at Sarajevo. A stenographic report of the essential part of it, translated into German from the Croatian original, was published in Berlin in 1918.[3] It is a fascinating human document, full

an explanation of how necessary the Austrian action was. I said I did not wish to discuss the merits of the question between Austria and Serbia." To Sazonov in St. Petersburg the *dossier* was apparently never shown at all, and is not printed in the Russian Orange Book. On July 24, when informed of the ultimatum, Sazonov told the Austrian Ambassador that he "was really not curious at all to see the *dossier;* the fact is, you want war and have burned your bridges." But on July 29, "Sazonov begged again urgently for the transmission of the *dossier,* which had been promised to the Powers, but had not yet been produced. One would like to see it before the war with Serbia should have begun. If war once broke out, it would be too late to examine the *dossier;*" Szápáry to Berchtold, July 24, 29; A.R.B., II, 19; III, 16.

The author of the *dossier,* Dr. Wiesner, has recently given an interesting account of the way it was compiled and the reasons for the delay in presenting it to the Powers; "Die unwiderlegt gebliebene Begründung für das Ultimatum Oesterreichs an Serbien vom Juli, 1914," in *Die Kriegsschuldfrage,* V, 492-503, June, 1927. He has recently summed up the responsibility of Serbia in an article, "Die Schuld der serbischen Regierung am Mord von Sarajevo", *ibid.,* VI, 307-395, April, 1928.

3 Professor Pharos, *Der Prozess gegen die Attentäter von Sarajevo: nach dem amtlichen Stenogram der Gerichtsverhandlung aktenmässig dargestellt; Einleitung von Josef Kohler.* Berlin, 1918, pp. 165. "Pharos" is said to be a pseudonym. The fact that he was evidently personally present at the trial, giving a personal description of each defendant and showing a strong bias against Free-Masonry, suggests that the pseudonym covers the identity of Father Puntigam, the Archduke's Jesuit Confessor. Pharos does not attempt in his German translation to reproduce all the evidence from the lesser defendants and the witnesses; he gives

of pathos and humor. It seems to indicate that the trial was full and fair. In contrast to the preliminary judicial investigation in July preceding, it was less strictly secret; in addition to the twenty-two defendants, more than a hundred witnesses, several soldiers and the judicial officials themselves, a small select "public" was admitted into the crowded, stuffy little court room. Several times the Judge had to suspend the session for five minutes to open the windows for fresh air. Twice he had to instruct feeble-voiced persons, "Speak louder! Because this is a public proceeding, and the rest, as well as I, want to hear what you say."[4] The report of the trial also throws much valuable light on the dark preparations within Serbia which culminated in the assassination. Yet few persons outside Germany appear ever to have given it any serious attention. This is partly because, at the time of its publication in 1918, Germany was cut off from communication with much of the world; and it is partly because war hatred and moral blindness condemned it in advance as another German

only the part of the record concerning the leading prisoners. A condensed summary of the whole trial, including some portions omitted by Pharos, was published anonymously at Berne in 1917: *Serajevo; La Conspiration Serbe contre la Monarchie Austro-Hongroise*, pp. 62-150. Mr. Seton-Watson gives no proof of his assertion (*Sarajevo*, p. 295) that these versions are "very incomplete and unreliable," and that they "were published by the Austro-Hungarian Government." A carbon copy of the original stenographic report is said (according to the Vienna paper, *Der Tag*, No. 84, April 7, 1925) to have come into the hands of the editor of the Sarajevo newspaper, *Vetchernje Posta* (Evening Post), and to have been placed by him at the disposal of the Jugoslav Government. It is significant that the Jugoslav authorities have been unable to extract from it anything for their own exculpation, or to publish a single word of evidence beyond what is contained in the two volumes just mentioned. Brief extracts, to be sure, were published by Mr. P. Slijepchevitch (*Nova Evropa*, June, 1925) and reprinted in translation by Mr. Seton-Watson in *The Slavonic Review*, IV, 645-656, March, 1926. There are significant (but unindicated) omissions in these extracts. Their aim is to conceal references to Serbia and to emphasize the idea that the murderers did not receive external prompting from Serbia, but were crude Bosnian fanatics, attempting to bring about Jugoslav unity.

[4] Pharos, pp. 120, 144, and photographs of court, defendants, exhibits, etc.

"falsification" or "piece of propaganda." Even so distinguished a historian as Sir Charles Oman thought "the whole evidence is falsified. . . . The record of the trial has been so much tampered with that no confidence can be placed in any word of it." [5] Yet the fact is, as we shall see below, that Austria's charges against Serbia in 1914, confirmed by the evidence at the trial, are really an understatement, rather than an overstatement, of Serbia's responsibility. So, for nearly a decade, the truth about the Sarajevo plot remained mysterious and unknown. The Austrian evidence was neglected, discredited, or ridiculed. Serbian writers, on the other hand, were careful to publish nothing in conflict with the attitude of injured innocence which their Government had assumed in 1914.

RECENT REVELATIONS

Within the last five years, however, there have come numerous Serb revelations, whose authors appear to be moved by various motives: simply to tell the truth and see that justice shall replace injustice; to play party politics; or, strangely enough, to claim the doubtful honor of being among those who planned the murder of the Archduke, which ultimately resulted in the establishment of the glorious Jugoslav Kingdom.

The first of these revelations to attract attention beyond the frontiers of Serbia [6] came from the pen of a well-known professor of history at Belgrade, Stanoje Stanojevitch.[7] He

[5] C. Oman, *The Outbreak of the War of 1914-1918,* London, 1919, p. 9.

[6] Among well-informed Serbians themselves it has long been an open secret that higher Serbian officials than those charged in the Austrian ultimatum shared in the preparation of the plot to murder Franz Ferdinand; see below the discussion of the "Black Hand" and the Salonica Trial of 1917.

[7] S. Stanojevitch, *Ubistvo Austriskog Prestolonaslednika Ferdinanda* [The Murder of the Austrian Heir to the Throne Ferdinand], Belgrade, 1923; German trans. by H. Wendel, *Die Ermordung des Erzherzogs Franz Ferdinand,* Frankfurt, 1923; summarized in English by M. Edith Durham, *The Serajevo Crime,* pp. 96-117. Stanojevitch's statements, though not

gives no references to his authorities, but, according to his preface, gathered much of his information at first hand from surviving Serbian conspirators with whom he was personally acquainted. In seeking to minimize the responsibility of the *Narodna Odbrana* (National Defense), and thus to discredit the Austrian version of the plot, he throws the blame on the leader of a less well-known secret Serbian revolutionary society, *Ujedinjenje ili Smrt* (Union or Death), commonly known as the "Black Hand." This was composed of a powerful clique of military officers who had plotted and carried out the murder of King Alexander and Queen Draga in 1903, and had since then played a sinister rôle in Serbian domestic politics and foreign relations. Its organizer, and its leader and moving spirit in 1914, was no less a person than the Chief of the Intelligence Department [including spy service] of the Serbian General Staff, Col. Dragutin Dimitrijevitch. Of this remarkable arch-plotter, who was put to death by the Pashitch Party in 1917, but who has become a hero in the eyes of a large part of the Serbian people, Professor Stanojevitch gives the following edifying picture:

> Gifted, cultured, personally brave, honest; full of ambition, energy, and willingness to work; and a convincing talker, Dragutin Dimitrijevitch had an extraordinary influence on those about him, especially on his companions and the younger officers, who were altogether inferior to him in feeling and character. He had the qualities which fascinate men [in Serbia]. His reasoning was always thorough and convincing; he understood how to make the worst deeds appear trifles, and the most dangerous schemes innocent and harmless. At the same time, he was in every respect a splendid organizer; he always kept everything in his own hands, and even his most intimate friends knew

free from inaccuracies, are in large part supported by the pro-Serb German writer, H. Wendel, *Die Habsburger und die Südslawenfrage*, Belgrade-Leipzig, 1924.

only what was on foot at the moment. But Dragutin Dimitrijevitch was also extraordinarily conceited and quite affected. Being very ambitious, he loved secret activity. He loved also that men should know that he was engaged in this secret activity, and kept everything in his own hands. Doubts about what was possible or impossible, or about the reciprocal relation of power and responsibility, never troubled him. He had no clear conception of political life and its limitations. He saw only the goal immediately before his eyes, and went straight at it, without hesitation and regardless of consequences. He loved danger, adventure, secret trystings, and mysterious doings. . . .

Restless and adventuresome, he was always planning conspiracies and assassinations. In 1903 he had been one of the chief organizers of the plot against King Alexander. In 1911 he sent someone to murder the Austrian Emperor or Heir to the Throne. In February, 1914, in concert with a secret Bulgarian revolutionary committee, he agreed upon the murder of King Ferdinand of Bulgaria. In 1914 he took over and organized the [Sarajevo] plot against the Austrian Heir to the Throne [Franz Ferdinand]. In 1916 he sent someone from Corfu to murder King Constantine of Greece. And in the same year he was apparently seeking to have dealings with the enemy, and organized a plot against the then heir to the Serbian throne, Prince Alexander. For this reason he was condemned to death and shot at Salonica in June, 1917.[8]

Stanojevitch goes on to describe in detail how this Serbian General Staff officer helped organize the plot in

[8] Stanojevitch (German ed.), pp. 50-51. This is the orthodox Pashitch version of the Salonica affair. There is some reason to believe, however, that this alleged plot against Prince Alexander was in part a mere pretext, trumped up as a convenient means of getting rid of a powerful political opponent. Another reason for closing his mouth forever may very probably have been the fear on the part of the Pashitch Party that he might reveal to the world the truth about his own part in the murder-plot which gave rise to the World War, and thus reveal the Serbian Government's own guilty knowledge of that plot. On the Salonica Trial, see below, notes 32, 33.

Belgrade and provide the Bosnian youths with the bombs and Browning revolvers actually used at Sarajevo. He gives a naïve motive for Dimitrijevitch's crime: when Dimitrijevitch heard, in addition to other rumors, that the Austrian Archduke was coming to hold manoeuvres in Bosnia, "he was thoroughly convinced that Austria-Hungary intended to carry out an attack upon Serbia," and, "after long consideration, came to the conclusion that the attack on Serbia and war itself could only be prevented by killing Franz Ferdinand." [9]

Some months after Stanojevitch made these admissions, which went far beyond the Austrian charges of 1914, a Jugoslav journalist, Borivoje Jevtitch, came forward with an interesting pamphlet.[10] It explains the rise of the new terrorist movement, with its fanatical "cult of assassination," which developed among the Bosnian youth in the decade before the War. It minimizes the influence of Serbia, and throws light mainly on the execution of the plot in Sarajevo, rather than on its preparation in Belgrade. Jevtitch had been one of the witnesses at the trial of the murderers in 1914. At that time he admitted frankly that he was a contributor to such Sarajevo newspapers as *Srpska Rijetch* (The Serbian Word) and *Narod* (Nation), and also that he was a member of the *Srpska Omladina* (Serbian Youth), an association devoted to fostering Serb nationalism in Bosnia. He even admitted having corresponded intermittently with the principal assassins, but stoutly denied that he knew anything of the plot to murder the Archduke, and managed to appear innocent. Such was

9 Stanojevitch, 55.

10 Jevtitch, *Sarajevski Atentat,* Sarajevo, 1924; some of his conclusions are summarized by Albert Mousset, "L'Attentat de Sarajevo," in *Revue d'Histoire Diplomatique,* XXXI, 44-68, 1925; in the Paris *Figaro,* May 23, 1924; and in the New York *Times,* June 22, 1924, E, p. 5. The first seven chapters are published in German translation in KSF, III, 657-686, Oct., 1925.

his testimony in 1914.[11] But in 1924, when his life was no longer in jeopardy at the hands of the Austrian police, and when his hopes for Jugoslav unity had been realized as a result of the assassination and the World War, he declared that he knew all about the plot. He even gives a vivid description of how he spent Saturday night, the eve of the crime, in company with Princip, who fired the fatal shots next morning. He claims that there were no fewer than ten ambuscades for the Archduke; that, if Franz Ferdinand had escaped Princip's bullet as he did Chabrinovitch's bomb, so many others were prepared to slay him that he could scarcely have left Sarajevo alive.

The most sensational revelation, important because made by a distinguished Serbian official who was Minister of Education in the Pashitch Cabinet in July, 1914, is that of M. Ljuba Jovanovitch. To celebrate the tenth anniversary of the outbreak of the World War, there was published in the summer of 1924, under the editorship of a Russian, a book of short articles by leading Serbians under the title, "The Blood of Slavdom." [12] The opening article, "After Vidov Dan, 1914," is by M. Jovanovitch. In it he suddenly lets the cat out of the bag in the most extraordinary fashion. The very thing that M. Pashitch and the Serbian Government had been concealing for years, he admits in the most matter-of-fact way:

[11] *La Conspiration Serbe,* p. 133; Mousset, p. 59 f.

[12] *Krv Slovenstva,* Belgrade, 1924. Mr. Jovanovitch's article is of such importance that it has several times been reprinted in English translation; in the *Journal of the Institute of International Affairs* for March, 1925; in the *National Review* for April, 1925; and in *The Living Age,* May 9, 1925. English attention was first called to it by the Balkan traveller and specialist, M. Edith Durham, in an address before the British Institute of International Affairs in Dec., 1924, and in an article, "Fresh Light on the Crime of Serajevo," in the *Contemporary Review,* 1-11, Jan., 1925, which is reprinted in *The Living Age,* March 7, 1925, pp. 532-539. She discusses it at length in her recent volume, *The Serajevo Crime,* pp. 127-147. "Vidov Dan" (St. Vitus' Day), June 28, was the anniversary of the Battle of Kossovo in 1389 A.D. and a national Serb festival: it was also the day of the Archduke's assassination.

At the outbreak of the World War I was Minister of Education in M. Nikola Pashitch's Cabinet. I have recently written down some of my recollections and some notes on the events of those days. For the present occasion I have chosen from them a few extracts, because the time is not yet come for everything to be disclosed.

I do not remember whether it was at the end of May or the beginning of June, when one day M. Pashitch said to us (he conferred on these matters more particularly with Stojan Protitch, who was then Minister of the Interior; but this much he said to the rest of us) that certain persons [*neki*] were making ready to go to Sarajevo to murder Franz Ferdinand who was to go there to be solemnly received on St. Vitus' Day. As they told me afterwards, this plot was hatched by a group of secretly organized persons and by patriotic Bosno-Herzegovinian students in Belgrade. M. Pashitch and the rest of us said, and Stojan agreed, that he should issue instructions to the frontier authorities on the Drina to prevent the crossing over of the youths who had already set out from Belgrade for that purpose. But the frontier "authorities" themselves belonged to the organization, and did not carry out Stojan's instructions, but reported to him (as he afterwards told us) that the instructions had reached them too late, because the youths had already crossed over.[13]

From this it appears that members of the Serbian Cabinet knew of the plot a month or so before the murder took place, but took no effective measures to prevent it. The Serbian Government was thus criminally negligent, to say the least. Not having nipped in the bud the plot prepared

[13] *Krv Slovenstva,* p. 9 f. In an explanatory letter in the *Novi Zivot* (New Life) and the Belgrade *Politika* of March 28, 1925, Jovanovitch makes it clear that by this phrase he meant the "Black Hand": [upon the news of the Austrian annexation proclamation in 1908] "private initiative founded the association *Narodna Odbrana,* and other elements, which were irreconcilably dissatisfied with the activity of official Serbia, later founded, under the name *Ujedinjenje ili Smrt* ['Union or Death,' commonly known as the 'Black Hand'] that 'group of secretly organized persons' which I mentioned in my article."

in their capital by one of their own General Staff officers, and not having prevented the youths from crossing over into Bosnia, either because Protitch did not give his instructions in time, or more probably, because "the frontier 'authorities' themselves belonged to the organization" of the "Black Hand," the Serbian Government should at once have notified the Austrian authorities, giving the names of the criminals and all other details which might have led to their arrest before their execution of the plot. But M. Pashitch and his Cabinet did nothing of the kind. Furthermore, after the crime had been committed, they should have made a searching inquiry into the incriminated secret organizations in Serbia, and arrested all the accomplices who had helped hatch or carry out the plot. Instead, as we shall see, they sought to conceal every trace of it, and denied all knowledge of it, in the hope that Austria would be unable to discover their complicity. No wonder that M. Jovanovitch, with his guilty conscience, was "overwhelmed with grave anxiety," when he heard the fatal news at his country house on Sunday afternoon, June 28. It was not regret for the crime, but fear of its consequences, which filled him with "terrible thoughts":

> About 5 P.M. an official from the Press Bureau rang me up on the telephone and told me what had happened that morning at Sarajevo. Although I knew what was being prepared there, yet, as I held the receiver, I felt as though someone had dealt me an unexpected blow; and a little later, when the first news was confirmed from other quarters, I began to be overwhelmed with grave anxiety.
>
> I did not doubt for a moment that Austria-Hungary would make this the occasion for a war on Serbia. I saw that the position of our Government and our country in regard to the other Powers would now become very difficult, in every way worse than after May 29, 1903 [N. S. June 11, the date of King Alexander's assassination], or than at the time of our later conflicts with Vienna and Budapest. I

was afraid that all the European Courts would feel themselves the targets of Princip's bullets, and would turn away from us, with the approval of the monarchist and conservative elements in their countries. And even if it did not come to that, who would dare to defend us? I knew that neither France, nor, still less, Russia, was in a position to match herself with Germany and her ally on the Danube, because their preparations were not to be complete until 1917. This especially filled me with anxiety and fear.

The most terrible thoughts crowded in upon me. This began at 5 P.M. on the Sunday of *Vidov Dan,* and continued day and night, except during a few fitful moments of sleep, until Tuesday forenoon. Then there came to see me a young friend, Major N—— (in the Ministry of Education). He was uneasy, but not in despair as I was. I poured out to him my apprehensions without restraint or reflection. He at once said to me, in the tone usual to him on such occasions, that is to say, pleasantly and quietly, but with real inspiration: "My dear Minister, I think it is quite unnecessary to despair. Let Austria-Hungary attack us! It must come to that sooner or later. The present is a very inconvenient moment for us for settling the account. But it is not now in our power to choose the moment. And if Austria chooses it,—well, so let it be! It may possibly end badly for us, but who knows? It may also be otherwise!"[14]

These words of Major N——, which suggest that the Serbian military circles did not take so gloomy a view, but felt sure, or speedily received assurances, of Russian protection, "quite pulled me together," M. Jovanovitch continues; "Happily, from the St. Petersburg Press—and so far as it was concerned we could assume in advance that it represented the Government view—we received the first favorable reports; it began to take up our defense against the Austro-Hungarian accusations. Russia would not deny us nor withdraw her hand from us. After Russia would

14 *Krv Slovenstva,* p. 11.

come her friends. And so it was." M. Jovanovitch therefore braced himself to the idea of an attack on Serbia and a European War. He noted as favorable circumstances the anti-Serb "pogroms" in Bosnia and the violence of the Austrian Press, which would turn European opinion against Austria. His colleagues, however, believed that war could be avoided. In the expectation "that Vienna would be unsuccessful in establishing any connection between official Serbia and the deed on the Miljacka" [the river flowing through Sarajevo near which the Archduke was murdered], it was decided to conceal everything, to pose as unconcerned and innocent, to make a demonstration of sorrow, and to try to get off as cheaply as possible in giving satisfaction to the country whose royal couple had been murdered:

> M. Pashitch therefore hoped that we should somehow pull ourselves through this crisis, and he made efforts, in which all the rest of us supported him, to preserve as far as possible the relations which we had so far established, in order that Serbia might get off as cheaply as possible with the unhappy task of giving satisfaction to Austria-Hungary, and that she might recover as quickly as possible from the blows which in such an affair were bound in any case to fall upon her.
>
> As is well known, the Government did not fail to do all it could to show their friends and the rest of the world how far removed we were from the Sarajevo conspirators. Thus, on the very same evening upon which it was known what Princip had done, Stojan gave orders that the Belgrade police should forbid all music, singing, and merry-making in public places; everything was suspended, and something like official mourning began. M. Pashitch expressed to the Vienna Government our regret at the loss which a great neighboring Power had suffered and his execration at the deed itself. At the Requiem in the Catholic Church of the Legation on June 20 [July 3], on the day when the funeral of the murdered Heir to the Throne and his wife took place

> in Vienna, the Government was represented by several Ministers. I, too, was among them. I wished to show that even I, who more than any of the others might have been thought to have approved of Princip's deed,[15] was on the contrary entirely in agreement with what our Cabinet were doing. Nevertheless, this occasion and the short stay in the church were unpleasant to me. I felt myself among enemies, who did not desire peace with us.[16]

What a study in the psychology of the guilty conscience! Knowing of the plot a month beforehand, doing nothing effective to forestall it, terrified at first that Serbia will be isolated and attacked, then hopeful that the truth could be concealed, the Minister of Education goes to church in pretended mourning for the murdered victim for the sake of the good impression it will make. No wonder he felt "unpleasant"!

Many more interesting details of these tragic days M. Ljuba Jovanovitch gives in his recent revelations, but they are too long to reprint here. So far as the present writer is able to judge them in the light of other evidence, the Minister's account is substantially accurate and trustworthy —in fact remarkably so, when compared with the memoirs of other politicians written ten years after the events. To persons not blinded by prejudice or propaganda, it will not come as such a total surprise that the serious historian can no longer maintain the theory that the war-guilt was all on the side of Austria, and that Serbia was an innocent victim. But among many Serbians and champions of Serbia, M. Jovanovitch's revelations have roused mixed feelings of surprise and sorrow, indignation and incredulity. M. Mousset, who passes for a leading French authority on Serbia, still writes in 1925: "Without doubt certain diplo-

15 M. Jovanovitch was one of the founders and active members of the *Narodna Odbrana,* and, in a paragraph which we have omitted, tells of his personal acquaintance with Princip at Belgrade.

16 *Krv Slovenstva*, p. 15.

matic archives [he does not name them] have been opened. They have made it possible to wash the Belgrade Government of the charge of complicity which Austria, without herself giving it much credence, brought against it." [17]

A more thorough English scholar and prolific writer on the Balkans, and long a stout champion of the Jugoslavs, Mr. R. W. Seton-Watson, has been much disturbed at M. Jovanovitch's revelations, but cannot bring himself to accept them as trustworthy and literally true. In 1925 he declared: "The whole article [of Jovanovitch] is written in a careless, naïve and reminiscent vein, and its author seems to be blissfully unaware how damning are his admissions if they are to be taken literally. . . . There thus rests upon Belgrade the onus of proving, either that the information at its disposal was much more vague than Ljuba Jovanovitch would have us believe, or that it conveyed an adequate warning of the danger in some way of which no record has yet reached us. The matter can hardly rest here. Public opinion in Europe and America is more interested than ever in the problem of responsibility for the Great War, and is entitled to demand a full and detailed explanation from Ljuba Jovanovitch and from his chief, M. Pashitch." [18] A little later Mr. Seton-Watson went in person to Serbia to demand this explanation—to make M. Jovanovitch eat his words on the spot or explain them away

[17] "L'Attentat de Sarajevo," in *Revue d'Histoire Diplomatique,* XXXI, p. 44. M. Alfred Mousset is the author of *Le Royaume des Serbs, Croates, et Slovenes,* Paris, 1921 (Bossard).

[18] *Foreign Affairs* (N.Y.), III, 507-9, April, 1925; *cf.* also Mr. Seton-Watson's recent volume, *Sarajevo* (London, 1926), pp. 153-159. In articles in the London *Times* of Feb. 16, 1925, the *Post* of April 7, the Zagreb *Obzor* of April 12 and May 13, and the Belgrade *Politika* of April 13, Mr. Seton-Watson admitted the seriousness of Ljuba Jovanovitch's statements for Serbia's good name, but still refused to believe they were to be taken literally at their face value; see the quotations and comments by A. von Wegerer, "Der ungläubige Seton-Watson," in KSF, III, 287-292, May, 1925; and "Der Anlass zum Weltkrieg," *ibid.,* 394-395, June, 1925.

in some fashion if possible, or failing in that to force the Serbian Government to clear its reputation by making a clean breast of all it knew about the plot in 1914. But he appears to have succeeded in neither the one effort nor the other, judging by a justly impatient open letter which was published in the Zagreb *Obzor* (Observer) of May 13, 1925:

> It is now more than two months since I requested the Belgrade Government to clear up those statements which Mr. Ljuba Jovanovitch made some time ago in the pamphlet, *Krv Slovenstva,* concerning the Sarajevo murder. But I have never yet received any answer. . . .
>
> A few weeks ago, to be sure, Ljuba Jovanovitch published some articles on responsibility for the war, but in them he evades the main issue and accuses me of an incorrect reproduction of his former statements. [Mr. Seton-Watson therefore put the two concrete questions, "Does Ljuba Jovanovitch stand by his statement, that *at the end of May or the beginning of June . . . one day M. Pashitch said . . . that certain persons were making ready to go to Sarajevo to murder Franz Ferdinand?*" And, second, "Does he actually mean it, when he says, in describing how he received the telephone news of the murder at Sarajevo, *although I knew what was being prepared there?*"]
>
> I can understand very well Mr. Ljuba Jovanovitch's hesitation in giving a downright answer. If he denies it, one must wonder how a responsible statesman could write in so frivolous a fashion. And if he admits it, then his colleague and Minister-President at the time, Mr. Pashitch, is placed under the unpleasant duty of speaking out clearly and frankly, and setting forth the facts in their true light.[19]

To this strong and clear letter of Mr. Seton-Watson's, M. Pashitch and the Serbian Government made no answer. The Belgrade Press, however, announced that the Jugoslav Government had decided to publish a new *Blue Book* on

19 Zagreb *Obzor,* No. 126, May 13, 1925; *cf.* KSF, III, 394 f., June, 1925.

the origins of the War. Mr. Seton-Watson then wrote a second letter to the London *Times*, begging its readers to suspend judgment until these documents could appear. But, as he has to admit in his recent volume,

> Eight months have passed, and nothing more has been heard of the *Blue Book;* and it seems probable that the announcement was merely tactical, intended to appease the critics until the whole agitation should die down. Unfortunately the Jugoslav Government, instead of demonstrating its innocence by a detailed statement of the facts, shrouded itself in mystery.[20]

M. Ljuba Jovanovitch's revelations attracted at first little attention in Serbia, where well-informed persons apparently saw in them nothing really new. Neither M. Pashitch nor anyone else thought of taking him to task for them. He was elected President of the Serbian Skupshtina, President of the Election Committee, and President of the Legislative Committee. But when it was learned how great attention was being given to them in England and America, where people began to wake up to the extent of Serbia's responsibility for the War, some Serbian newspapers began to attack M. Jovanovitch as a liar and a traitor. In self-defense, he wrote a series of long articles in the magazine *Novi Zivot* (New Life) setting forth and justifying his part in Serbian history for more than thirty years, from the time he first came to Belgrade in 1881 as an emigré from Herzegovina.[21] "I have made no revelations," he said, "the way people are now trying to make out. I only wrote what was essentially already known to everyone in 1914." [22] This may have been true enough as regards Serbia, which was well acquainted with the do-

[20] Seton-Watson, *Sarajevo,* p. 156.

[21] *Cf.* the Belgrade *Politika,* March 22, 29; April 6, 12, 17, 1925; and KSF, III, 211-220, 270-287, April, May, 1925.

[22] Interview in the *Politika,* April 17, 1925; KSF, III, 395, June, 1925.

ings of the "Black Hand" and its powerful leader, Dimitrijevitch, but it was not true of the Entente countries which had been taught to believe in Serbia's innocence.

But Mr. Seton-Watson, in spite of the stony silence of M. Pashitch and the Government, the non-appearance of any new *Blue Book,* and M. Jovanovitch's explanatory articles, still cannot bring himself to believe in the truth of M. Jovanovitch's revelations which we have quoted above. He devotes an appendix of several pages to them, concluding that "Mr. Jovanovitch, for reasons of his own, has misrepresented the true facts, and his former colleagues, for reasons of their own, have refrained from giving him the lie publicly." His line of argument is that Jovanovitch "is one of those politicians who like to exaggerate their own importance"; that in the struggle for increased political influence "he was making a bid for the support of the Bosnian youth by showing that the Belgrade Government had sympathized with the revolutionary movement," and "probably hoped to strengthen his own position in the Radical Party, as against those whose outlook is more narrowly identified with the old Serbian Kingdom"; that he feels on the defensive on account of the part he took in the Salonica Trial; and that M. Pashitch has made no public denial, because "he has always shown an astonishing indifference to public opinion, especially to foreign public opinion." [23]

The question of M. Jovanovitch's veracity, however, roused a storm of passionate discussion in the Serbian Press, where it is mixed up with questions of party politics and leadership. Some Serbian leaders demanded that M. Pashitch speak out and deny the truth of M. Jovanovitch's revelations. On February 26, 1926, M. Jovan Jovanovitch,

[23] *Sarajevo,* pp. 156-159. These hypotheses have been subjected to severe criticism by A. von Wegerer in KSF, IV, 767-785, Oct., 1926. See also above, note 18.

of the Peasant Party and former Serbian Minister in Vienna, at a meeting of the Budget Commission of the Skupshtina, called attention to the injury done to Serbia's reputation in Entente countries by the fact that Ljuba Jovanovitch's revelations were being widely circulated and received no official contradiction. He therefore earnestly begged M. Pashitch, in the interests of Serbia's good name, to speak out, lest otherwise Serbia should suffer eventually in the matter of foreign credits and Reparation Payments.[24]

Others, like Professor Jelenitch, formerly private secretary of Crown Prince Alexander, bitterly denounced Ljuba Jovanovitch as a traitor to Serbia and his revelations as "a lie, a most perfidious, Levantine lie." He went on with a fantastic development of Mr. Wickham Steed's legend that the assassination was the work of Austro-Hungarian authorities. His assertion that the deed was prepared in Berlin, developed at Konopischt, and "carried out through the coöperation of the Vienna and Budapest Camarilla with the 'Black Hand' in Belgrade" is so naïve and preposterous that it hardly needs comment. The notion that it was developed at Konopischt is tantamount to saying that Franz Ferdinand plotted his own assassination. M. Jelenitch appealed to Pashitch and the other surviving members of his Cabinet of 1914 to denounce Ljuba Jovanovitch.[25]

It is interesting to observe that Professor Jelenitch has not the slightest doubt that the "Black Hand" had an important part in the assassination plot, though he denies that M. Pashitch knew of it. But his insinuation that the "Black Hand" had coöperated with the hated Vienna authorities in the assassination instantly brought forth an

[24] *Cf.* KSF, IV, 260 ff., 343 ff.

[25] *Cf.* the Belgrade *Politika,* March 26, 1926; and KSF, IV, 345, 400-403. On Mr. Wickham Steed's legend, see above, pp. 32-43, "The Konopischt Meeting: Legend and Fact." It is naturally a favorite theme with Serbian writers and was again set forth in 1926 by Dr. Leo Pfeffer, of Sarajevo, and by others (*cf.* KSF, IV, 661, 722).

indignant denial from two surviving "Black Hand" members, Milan G. Milanovitch and C. A. Popovitch. They declared that they would be glad to see Jelenitch's alleged proofs of his assertions; "then we also shall produce all that we know about the Sarajevo murder, on the basis of facts at our disposal. The attack upon our dead companions whose patriotism has hitherto never been challenged in circles of earnest and impartial men releases us, in our opinion, for the future, from all considerations by which we have hitherto been bound." [26]

This press campaign rose to such a pitch that finally, at a committee meeting of the Radical Club on April 25, 1926, M. Pashitch spoke out against Ljuba Jovanovitch and tried to drive his former friend and colleague out of the party. According to the report of this speech in his party newspaper, he said,

> Foreign correspondents had asked him whether he had known that the Austrian Heir to the Throne would be murdered. He repudiated the idea. He had begged M. Jovanovitch to contradict it, because it was not true that he [M. Pashitch] had said this in a Cabinet Meeting. . . . M. Pashitch had waited for M. Jovanovitch's denial. M. Jovanovitch had delayed to make one, and had not made one. M. Pashitch repeated and maintained that he had not said what M. Jovanovitch ascribed to him [in the pamphlet *Krv Slovenstva*]. He also asked his ministerial colleagues: "Friends, have I perhaps not forgotten that I said that?" They all confirmed the fact that he had really not.
>
> It has not been contradicted, and now this question is alive. I must contradict it. Why M. Ljuba Jovanovitch said it, I do not know. But he said what was not true. . . . I have given evidence that I can keep still, but if Ljuba Jovanovitch wants to act independently, let him separate

[26] *Politika,* March 31, 1926; KSF, IV, 406. For a summary of many other articles, see *ibid.,* 403-408.

himself from us and work independently. That is a mistake of M. Jovanovitch's which cannot be pardoned.[27]

In reply to this attack, M. Ljuba Jovanovitch declared that he had never said in his pamphlet that M. Pashitch had given certain information in regard to the preparation of the assassination *at a Cabinet Meeting.* It was *in a private conversation.* To substantiate the truth of what he had written, he offered to bring forward documents and proofs, but demanded that the Prime Minister and Minister of Foreign Affairs assume the responsibility for his doing so. Thereupon these two responsible Ministers, MM. Uzunovitch and Nintitch, refused his offer, apparently in fear lest he might reveal more unpalatable secrets concerning the Serbian Government of 1914 and the origin of the World War.[28]

Many Serb newspapers at once proclaimed that at last M. Pashitch had spoken out and denied the truth of the charges, but on examining his carefully phrased statement it appeared that he denied a charge which had not been made. He denied that he had given the information about the assassins *in a Cabinet Meeting,* which M. Jovanovitch had never asserted.[29] As will be pointed out below, and as M. Jovanovitch had indicated in one of his articles in 1925, the truth of his assertion that M. Pashitch knew of the plot beforehand is indicated, among other things, by the fact that an order was actually given to stop the assassins from crossing over from Belgrade into Bosnia, but the order was not carried out because the Serbian frontier guards belonged to the "Black Hand" organization and did not obey the order. This is confirmed by the diary and papers of the

27 Belgrade *Politika,* April 26, 1926, KSF, IV, 408-9.

28 Belgrade *Politika,* April 26, 1926; *Obzor,* April 27, 1926; *cf.* KSF, IV, 408-413, 780-783; and the New York *Times,* April 30, 1926.

29 See Jovanovitch's own words, quoted above at note 12.

frontier guard, Todorovitch, which the Austrians captured during the War.

One may conclude, therefore, that there is no good reason to doubt the accuracy of M. Ljuba Jovanovitch's revelations of 1924. Mr. Seton-Watson's argument, that they were written in a "careless, naïve, reminiscent vein," is really an argument in favor of their genuineness. M. Jovanovitch evidently made no effort to elaborate them carefully as a political pamphlet to gain adherents or to show his own personal importance. As he explained in 1925, he had promised in the spring of 1924 to M. Ksjunjin, a Russian journalist and emigré, that he would write an article for a pamphlet on the tenth anniversary of the outbreak of the World War. Occupied with other matters, he did not write the article at once. Some months later, being asked for it and not wishing to disappoint M. Ksjunjin, he took some material from a manuscript of recollections and notes which he had already written down.[30] The fact that the MM. Uzunovitch and Nintitch intervened to prevent M. Jovanovitch from bringing forward his proofs, and that the "Black Hand" survivors also threatened to make revelations, seems to indicate that there are things which the Serbian Government still prefers to conceal. Until M. Jovanovitch's revelations are definitely proved to be untrue, impartial historians will conclude that M. Pashitch and members of the Serbian Government had a guilty knowledge of a murder plot, but concealed it, in oblivion of the fact that "murder will out."

Another series of revelations, said to be contained in some 2,000 documents which were seized by the Austrians in Belgrade during the War, relates to the propagandist and revolutionary activities of the Serbian nationalist organizations known as the *Narodna Odbrana* and the "Black Hand." Many of these documents were found in the houses

[30] *Politika*, March 25, 1925; KSF, III, 213; IV, 768.

of M. Pashitch and Milo Pavlovitch, a leading member of the *Narodna Odbrana.* They contain lists of "serviceable people," Bosnian editors, students and spies, and the amounts of money with which they were subsidized from Belgrade.[31]

Much new information concerning the "Black Hand" has also recently been brought to light by a careful examination of the official record of the famous Salonica Trial of 1917.[32] This thick volume, published officially in Salonica in 1918, was later withdrawn from circulation and suppressed so far as possible, apparently because it contained so much material damaging to the reputation of the Serbian Government of 1914. It is now almost impossible to get a copy. But it has been studied by students of Serbian affairs and the causes of the War, and is found to contain a great deal of information about the activities of the "Black Hand" before 1914, and about those of its members who participated in the plot to assassinate the Archduke Franz Ferdinand.[33]

[31] *Cf.* M. Edith Durham, in *Current History,* XXV, 661 f., Feb., 1927.

[32] *Tajna Prevratna Organisacija: Izvestaj sa pretresa u vojnom sudu zu offizire u Solunu, po beleskama vodjenim na samom pretresu.* Solun Stamparija "Velika Srbija," 1918 (A Secret Revolutionary Organization: Report of the Trial at the Court Martial of Officers at Salonica, from Notes Taken at the Trial Itself. Salonica Press "Great Serbia," 1918, pp. 638). Mr. Seton-Watson (*Sarajevo,* p. 295) incorrectly translates the title of this "strange book" as a secret "pre-war," instead of a secret "revolutionary," organization.

[33] *Cf.* M. Bogitchevitch's numerous articles: "Bemerkungen zum Saloniki Prozess, 1917," in KSF, II, 112-113; "Weitere Einzelheiten über das Attentat von Sarajevo," in KSF, III, 15-21, 437-444, Jan. and July, 1925; "Nouvelles dépositions concernant l'attentat de Sarajevo," in KSF, IV, 21-28, 87-95, Jan.-Feb., 1926; "La Société 'Union ou Mort' dite la 'Main Noire,'" in the French periodical *Evolution,* No. 7, 16-30, July 15, 1926, and in German and English trans. in KSF, IV, 664-689, Sept., 1926; M. Bogitchevitch has now collected much of this material and other new information on the "Black Hand" and Salonica Trial in his recent volume, *Le Procès de Salonique, juin, 1917* (Paris, 1927). See also M. Edith Durham, *The Serajevo Crime,* London, 1925, pp. 44-74, 158-201; "The Serajevo Murder Plot," in *Current History,* XXV, 656-662, Feb., 1927; S. B. Fay, "The Black Hand Plot that led to the World War," in

On the basis of this material, we may now outline briefly the main threads of the assassination plot, and the three factors which largely contributed to it: the *Narodna Odbrana,* the "Black Hand," and the revolutionary movement in Bosnia.

THE *NARODNA ODBRANA*

In the 'sixties and 'seventies of the nineteenth century many Serbian revolutionaries gathered in Switzerland and came under the influence of Russians like Bakunin, Kropotkin, and Herzen. They adopted a revolutionary program which was to be brought about by anarchist deeds of violence and terrorism. They were responsible for the Zajecar revolt against King Milan in Serbia in 1883. Their tendency toward revolution by violence and assassination has continued to exert an influence over a certain group of Serbs ever since. But not all the young Serbians studying in Switzerland adopted these views completely. Among the latter was M. Nikola Pashitch. He believed in the gradual building up of the moral and material forces of Serbia as a means for the eventual liberation and union of all Serbs

Current History, XXIII, 196-207, Nov., 1925; and Dr. Wiesner in KSF, VI, 362-395, April, 1928.

Some information on the "Black Hand" may also be found in the following: *Carnegie Report of the International Commission to Inquire into the Causes and Conduct of the Balkan Wars.* Washington, 1914, pp. 169 ff.; D. R. Lazarevitch, *Die Schwarze Hand.* Lausanne, 1917; Seton-Watson, "Serbia's Choice," in *The New Europe,* Aug. 22, 1918; *Sarajevo,* pp. 143, 158, 295; Pharos, pp. 14 f., 81 f.; Stanojevitch, pp. 49-56; Wendel, pp. 48-62; A. von Wegerer, "Der Anlass zum Weltkrieg," in KSF, III, 353-405, June, 1925; "Neue Ausschnitte zum Attentat von Sarajewo," in KSF, IV, 400-414, June, 1926; L. Mandl, "Ein düstere Gedenktag," in the Vienna *Neues 8 Uhr-Blatt,* Nos. 2906-2909, June 27-July 1, 1924; N. Nenadovitch, "Les secrets de la camarilla de Belgrade," in *La Fédération Balkanique,* Dec. 1, 1924; the articles by M. Vladimirov, N. Mermet, and V. Nikolitch, *ibid.,* May 31, 1925, and by N. Obarov, *ibid.,* July 15, 1925; and the statements of Colonel Bojin Simitch printed by Victor Serge in the Paris Periodical, *Clarté,* No. 74, May, 1925. The statements made at the Salonica Trial and by "Black Hand" members later, however, are often contradictory and inspired with animus against M. Pashitch, and must therefore be used with great caution.

in a powerful state, after the manner in which Italy had accomplished her unification in the generation immediately preceding. Serbia should be "the Piedmont of the Balkans." With this aim in view, M. Pashitch founded in Serbia in 1881 the Radical Party, which under his venerable leadership long preserved its original name, though in character it is today the very opposite of radical.

The program of the Radical Party, as stated in the first issue of its organ, *Samouprava,* on January 8, 1881, was: "The people's welfare and freedom at home, and the country's independence and unification with the other parts of Serbdom abroad." A special section was devoted to the importance of organizing and training the Serbian army; but until the time should come for the army to fulfil these tasks, the program provided, under the heading "Foreign Policy," that "there must be organized, in the field of intellectual development, a way of helping the divided and unliberated parts of Serbdom, as well as of keeping alive the sense of our national unity in the Serb provinces which, being far away, are exposed to the influence of foreign elements." In other words, discontent must be kept alive in the Serb districts of the Turkish and Hapsburg Empires until the future war of liberation should join them to a Greater Serbia.

These two political ideals—individual acts of assassination practiced by immature half-baked students and by military cliques on the one hand, and national unification by a well-prepared movement and eventual war with Turkey and Austria as advocated by the Radical Party—dominated Serb political leaders until the triumph of the latter in the World War. Sometimes the leaders of the two tendencies have been in harmony, as in the palace assassinations of 1903; at other times they have been in bitter opposition, as in the so-called "priority question" in the spring of 1914. This dualism of ideals is the key to the obscure and much disputed problem of the origin and relations of the *Narodna Odbrana* and the "Black Hand" with one another, as well as to the notorious "Salonica Affair" of 1917 which stirred political fury in Serbia much as did the Dreyfus Affair in France.

M. Pashitch and the Radicals soon became the implacable enemies of King Milan, on account of the brutal and bloody severity with which he had taken vengeance on the Zajecar rebels, his disgraceful neglect of Serbia's national interests, and his scandalous private life, much of which was spent in questionable society in Vienna. Later the same hostile attitude was assumed toward his successor, King Alexander, especially after the latter's marriage to the notorious woman who became Queen Draga. Being childless, Queen Draga was suspected by many of intending to secure the succession to the throne for one of her brothers. Fear and disgust gradually united many Radicals and revolutionary army officers against the existing régime. In the words of a Serbian historian:

> What went on at Court and outside of it was justly regarded as a shame to the State and the Nation. Every moment grave scandals became public, and by these scandals Serbia and the Serbian people were becoming notorious and in bad repute. . . . The finances were in a pitiful state, and for months officials and officers received no salary. After the King's marriage every thing was still worse in every respect. Fickle changes were the order of the day, and likewise scandals. The fabricated story of the Queen's pregnancy, and the overbearing, provocative behavior of her brothers, roused the public and especially the military officers still further. All this brought it about that some eighty officers and several civilians formed a conspiracy with the purpose of murdering the King, the Queen, and her brothers. The greater part of the conspirators consisted of young officers inspired by upright patriotism. They saw their country given over to decay and shame under

the rule of a bad and unscrupulous monarch. They came to the conviction that Serbia was neglecting or abandoning her ideals and tasks because of the bad administration. The deep conviction that they must save the State and the Nation brought these people to a wicked deed which they believed justified by their patriotic duty.[34]

On the night of June 11, 1903, these patriotic assassins suddenly forced their way into the palace, murdered the King and Queen cowering in hiding, shot down the Queen's brothers in cold blood, and killed several Ministers. One of the chief leaders in organizing this brutal palace revolution was a young army captain, Dragutin Dimitrijevitch, who received incidentally three bullets which he carried in his body the rest of his days. Another—the man who ordered the murder of the Queen's brothers—was a young lieutenant, Voja Tankositch. These two were the later leaders of the "Black Hand," and, as another "patriotic duty," helped to prepare the Sarajevo plot against the Austrian Archduke.[35]

After the tragic night in 1903, which placed Peter I. Karageorgevitch upon the blood-stained throne of Alexander Obrenovitch, the conspirators who had carried out the palace revolution remained bound together as a protection against a possible counter-revolution, and also for the sake of personal interests and political advantages. They met together often and intervened in party politics whenever they believed their own interests were concerned. But when the country regained its balance and the new régime they had inaugurated seemed to be fairly established, their organization was no longer needed for safety, and their interference in politics was resented by the Radicals and the public. So the military conspirators as an organized group gradually retired until a new crisis arose.

[34] S. Stanojevitch, *Die Ermordung des Erzherzogs Franz Ferdinand*, pp. 45-46.

[35] *Ibid.*, 54-56.

In 1908, on the day Austria proclaimed her annexation of Bosnia and Herzegovina, Dr. Milovan Milovanovitch, then Serbian Minister of Foreign Affairs, called together in the evening several ministers and notables, including Pashitch, Ljuba Stojanovitch, Professor Ljuba Jovanovitch, the Burgomaster of Belgrade, and others, to consider what action to take in the face of the Austrian "provocation." It was decided that the Burgomaster should summon next morning at the Town Hall a larger group of representative Serbians which included the historian, Stanojevitch.[36] In the course of this meeting next day, there was founded the *Narodna Odbrana* (National Defense). This association was to enrol and train volunteers and strengthen Serbia in other ways for an armed struggle to prevent Austria from carrying out her annexation program.

The universal indignation in Serbia at Austria's breach of the Berlin Treaty and incorporation of coveted Serb lands had again brought together in harmonious coöperation leading representatives of both the dualistic tendencies noted above. Thus, at its foundation, the *Narodna Odbrana* included political leaders of the Radical Party, as well as military officers like Dimitrijevitch, Tankositch, and General Bozo Jankovitch. It also included Zivojin Dashitch, Director of the Government Printing Office, in which Chabrinovitch was employed just before setting out to murder Franz Ferdinand; and Milan Pribichevitch, whose brother, Svetozar, was one of Austria's most bitter opponents in the Croatian Landtag, and who is said to have received from Sarajevo on the day of the assassination of the Archduke and his wife, a telegram, with apparent reference to the crime, "Both horses well disposed of." [37]

[36] S. Stanojevitch, p. 47.

[37] Conrad, IV, 73. Milan Pribichevitch remained active in the *Narodna Odbrana;* it was to him that Princip first thought of applying for the means to carry out the Sarajevo plot, which he later received from the "Black Hand" leaders. Pribichevitch fought as a colonel in the Serbian

The organization and the activity of the *Narodna Odbrana* began immediately. Its Central Committee, sitting at Belgrade, directed the work of the District Committees which were established in the chief towns and divided into sections for cultural work, physical training, collection of money, and in some cases relations with neighboring lands. Below the District Committees were "divisional committees," "local committees," and, at the bottom, "confidential men," "located in those places in the interior of the country where the establishment of a Committee is not necessary." In Serbia these committees and "confidential men" were rapidly organized everywhere. The *Narodna Odbrana* affiliated with itself and aided financially the existing patriotic associations like the Sokols, Riflemen's Clubs, and Horsemen's Clubs. It began its task of enrolling *comitadjis* and training them in bomb-throwing, the blowing up of railways and bridges, and similar activities to be carried on in a guerilla war against Austria. It collected funds and stirred the people to hatred against Austria by an active propaganda of fervid nationalism.[38] This activity was not limited to Serbian subjects. Bosnian émigrés in Serbia were similarly enrolled, trained for treasonable activity upon their return to Bosnia, and provided with funds.[39]

Army at the beginning of the World War, but the story that he was murdered by his own soldiers in the woods on Jastrebac Mountain (*cf.* Pharos, 8, 161-2), is incorrect; he disappeared to America to enlist Serbian recruits. *Cf.* also Wiesner's telegram of July 13, 1914 (*Austrian Red Book,* I, 17), and Krstanovitch's deposition in the Austrian *dossier,* appendix 5.

38 *Cf. Narodna Odbrana Izdanje Stredisnog Odbora Narodne Odbrane,* Belgrade, 1911, ch. i, "Origin and activity of the first Narodna Odbrana." This pamphlet and annual report, "issued by the Central Committee of the Narodna Odbrana," was read at the trial of the murderers in 1914, and a summary of it is printed in the Austrian *dossier,* appendix 2. The complete pamphlet, giving a vivid and full picture of the propagandist agitation of the *Narodna Obdrana,* is printed in German translation in KSF, V, 192-225, March, 1927.

39 *Cf.* the deposition of Trifko Krstanovitch in the Austrian *dossier,* appendix 5; he tells how he went from Bosnia to Belgrade in 1908, was given food and lodging by Voja Tankositch, trained in bomb-throwing,

Gatchinovitch, the chief leader of the terrorist wing of the revolutionary movement in Bosnia, was at first closely associated with the *Narodna Odbrana* in Belgrade and worked in its interests in Bosnia,[40] though he later joined the "Black Hand," and, in accordance with its ideals, instigated assassination plots in Bosnia. Princip, the Archduke's murderer, was, according to his own admissions at the trial, enrolled in the *Narodna Odbrana* in 1912, given money, and trained as a *comitadji*.[41]

Within Bosnia itself similar committees and "confidential men" were recruited to form a net-work of spies and serve as a "tunnel," or "underground railway," for conveying propagandist literature, weapons, and conspirators across the frontier from Serbia into Bosnia.[42] This is also evident from the subsequent report of a Serbian frontier officer, Kosta Todorovitch, to the commander of the Drin Division. His report, along with his diary and accounts, was captured by the Austrians in the first weeks of the War, and gives detailed evidence of the way the "tunnel" was originally established in the Annexation Crisis by the *Narodna Odbrana,* and later continued by the "Black Hand" military authorities. Todorovitch's report was, of course, unknown to the authors of the Austrian *dossier,* but it was read at the trial in October, 1914, and its trust-

and then became a paid spy and secret carrier of letters between the leaders of the *Narodna Odbrana* in Serbia and its agents in Bosnia. Some doubt, to be sure, has been cast upon the trustworthiness of this man (*cf.* Wendel, p. 46; Chopin, pp. 12-17; Conrad, IV, 83, where the Governor of Bosnia, Potiorek, speaks of him as "keine integre Persönlichkeit").

40 Jevtitch, p. 6.

41 Pharos, pp. 22-25. For other evidences of the activity of the *Narodna Odbrana,* see Pharos, pp. 5, 8, 14 f., 19, 21 ff., 34, 43, 55, 81-101, 108, 132, 162.

42 This "tunnel" still existed in 1914, and is several times referred to by the Archduke's murderers in their conversations with their accomplices in Belgrade; *cf.* Pharos, pp. 9, 16, 34, 91.

worthiness is incidentally vouched for by Ljuba Jovanovitch.[43] After referring to an enclosed letter from a "confidential man" in Bosnia, Todorovitch's report continues:

> The plan which I have begun to carry out and to which I have devoted the greatest care is the winning of "confidential men" [in Bosnia]. They had all belonged to the time of the Annexation Crisis, but have all been dropped, with the exception of the one mentioned [in the letter] and two or three others. Some have moved away to other districts. The *Narodna Odbrana* in Shabats has also found some "confidential men," as for example in Tuzla and Sokolac. The connection has hitherto been weak and insufficient, since it has been in the hands of people who devoted themselves to it but little and did not give it enough attention. In accordance with the wish of the Minister of War, I have tried to carry out as conscientiously as possible the tasks and directions sent to me, especially the organizing work on the ground. . . . In the Drin region the connection has been sufficiently restored; it goes *via* Zvornik and Dabovje. In the other places the connection formerly existing has broken down, because it is now superfluous since the garrisons have been removed from the points in question. The connection by way of the Bosnian Islands and Draljatcha Vrata is favorable. There are people here who are admirably fitted for smuggling across. The tunnels do not yet have their full numbers; but I hope soon to be able to send you information and news.[44]

[43] Jovanovitch wrote in the *Politika,* April 17, 1925: "It is known exactly how it was . . . about the measures which M. Pashitch took to prevent the crossing over of those who took part in the murder, about whom it was heard that they had obtained the weapons in Belgrade and gone over the Drin to Bosnia. Of these measures the Austrians found positive traces when they crossed the Drin for the first time in 1914, took Lozhnica, and found the diary of our frontier officer, the late Kosta Todorovitch, who recorded from day to day the orders received, and among them a strong order given by the then War Minister, Dushan Stepanovitch, that the youths from Bosnia who were mentioned were to be prevented from crossing the frontier."

[44] Pharos, pp. 91-92.

The report further states that the activity of these "confidential men" consists ostensibly in spreading education and the *Pobratimstvo* (an anti-alcohol brotherhood), "because thus they are splendidly masked" in their real work of spying, smuggling, and conspiring.[45]

After the settlement of the Annexation Crisis in March, 1909, when Serbia, deserted by Russia, had to promise to cease her subversive agitation and to maintain in the future friendly relations with the Hapsburg Monarchy, the *Narodna Odbrana* made a show of transforming itself from an aggressive and subversive organization into a society which emphasized more laudable "cultural" aims, such as education, physical training, and the fostering of national ideals. Though its official report still proclaimed that "Austria is our greatest enemy," it added by way of recapitulation: "While the *Narodna Odbrana* works in conformity with the times according to altered conditions, it also maintains all connections made at the Annexation Period; today therefore it is the same as at the Annexation Period. . . . Then the cry was for war; now the cry is for work. Then meetings, demonstrations, volunteers, weapons, and bombs were asked for; today steady, fanatical tireless work and again work is required to fulfil the tasks and duties to which we have drawn attention by way of present preparation for the fight with gun and cannon which will come." [46] Though there was undoubtedly some change in the character of the *Narodna Odbrana* after 1909 in the direction here indicated, it never became so completely innocent and "cultural" as

[45] Pharos, p. 94. *Cf.* map, at p. 47 above. Some of the "favorable" places here mentioned are precisely the ones actually used by the Sarajevo assassins; Chabrinovitch was smuggled over at Zvornik, and Princip and Grabezh with the bombs and revolvers, at the Bosnian Islands, the three meeting again at Tuzla; *ibid.,* 16, 19, 25-27, 36-40, 48-52, 56-58, 86-108, 126-151.

[46] Extract from the pamphlet report issued by the *Narodna Odbrana* Central Committee in 1911, printed in the Austrian *dossier,* appendix 2; and complete reprint in KSF, V, 223-225, March, 1927.

is often asserted.[47] Nor did it cease its propagandist work in the Hapsburg territories.

On the other hand, it is true that the direct connection of the *Narodna Odbrana* with the Sarajevo plot was exaggerated in the Austrian ultimatum and *dossier,* because the Austrians centered their attention more on its earlier and more aggressive, rather than its later and more "cultural" activity, and particularly because, in their ignorance of the secret work of the Serbian military authorities, they failed to distinguish sufficiently between the *Narodna Odbrana* and the "Black Hand." It is nevertheless clear that the *Narodna Odbrana* secretly continued its work of maintaining "tunnels" and smuggling revolutionary literature from Belgrade into Bosnia. It kept in touch with the "confidential men" who were later used by the "Black Hand" and who actually assisted the Archduke's murderers on their journey. And it inspired and assisted Bosnian emigrants who came to Belgrade. It thus helped to develop the revolutionary movement in Bosnia and to prepare the ground for the Sarajevo crime. The original membership of the *Narodna Odbrana* and the measures which the Radical Government took to give it the appearance of a "cultural" organization show that M. Pashitch and his colleagues were perfectly acquainted with its work of propaganda, espionage, and the recruiting of "confidential men" on Austrian soil. Even after 1909, M. Pashitch evidently did not regard the association as purely "cultural," because he himself has said, "as soon as he came back from Bucharest [in August, 1913] he advised the *Narodna Odbrana* not to undertake anything against Austria, because it would be dangerous." [48]

[47] E. g., Stanojevitch, pp. 49-54; Ljuba Jovanovitch, *Politika* articles, March 22-April 17, 1925; Wendel, pp. 46-49, 59-61; Seton-Watson, in *Foreign Affairs,* III, 499-500.

[48] M. Pashitch's speech against Ljuba Jovanovitch at the Radical Club as reported in *Politika*, April 26, 1926; KSF, IV, 409, June, 1926.

THE "BLACK HAND"

By 1911 the old divergence of views between the Radical political leaders and the more restless and reckless military officers began to show itself again. The Radicals, in view of Russia's attitude and the existing diplomatic situation in Europe, believed that Serbians must preserve correct and peaceful relations with Austria-Hungary and confine their work for the present to strengthening the State for the future struggle which would realize their ultimate aim—the creation of a Greater Serbia. This, as we have seen, was now the ostensible policy of the *Narodna Odbrana.* But some [49] of the more hot-headed and zealous military clique which had carried out the palace revolution of 1903 were impatient of the more moderate Radical policy. They wanted "deeds." They therefore revived their old organization of 1903 in a new secret association known in its statutes as *Ujedinjenje ili Smrt* (Union or Death), but commonly referred to as the "Black Hand."

The most authoritative information about the "Black Hand" is contained in its Rules and By-Laws. These were published in a mutilated form in *Tajna Prevratna Organisacija,* the report of the Salonica Trial printed in 1918, which has already been mentioned.[50] At this later time the Serbian Government, wishing to make it appear that the "Black Hand" was a revolutionary organization exclusively within Serbia aiming to overthrow the power of the Radical Party and even the reigning dynasty, deleted certain passages which referred to the subversive and terrorist activity

49 Some, not all; several of the former conspirators of 1903 refused to enter the new "Black Hand" organization on the ground that, though the murder of King Alexander was necessary, there was no need to plunge into new adventures which could only harm the State; these officers followed the Radical Party and were eventually rewarded after the crushing of the "Black Hand" in 1917 by being given the places of their rivals; they were commonly known as the "White Hand."

50 *Cf.* above, note 32.

of the Society outside Serbia. But M. Bogitchevitch, from information supplied by two surviving members of the "Black Hand," has been able to establish the complete text of its Rules and By-Laws.[51] He has also been able to establish the identity of a large number of its members and the secret numbers by which they were known, showing that they included many Serbian civilian officials, as well as military officers. It is from his text of the Rules that the following quotations are made.

The aim of the "Black Hand" was (Art. 1): "The realization of the national ideal: the union of all Serbs." "Art. 2. This organization prefers terrorist action to intellectual propaganda, and for this reason must be kept absolutely secret from non-members." To accomplish its aim, it brings influence to bear on Government circles and on the various social classes of the Kingdom of Serbia, which is regarded as "Piedmont." Then follow the clauses which were deleted in 1918, but which show clearly its terrorist activity in the Hapsburg lands:

> Art. 4. (b) It organizes revolutionary activity in all the lands inhabited by Serbs.
>
> (c) Beyond the frontiers of Serbia, it fights with all means those who oppose this idea.
>
> (d) It maintains friendly relations with all States, peoples, organizations, and private individuals who are friendly toward Serbia and the Serb element.
>
> (e) It lends help and support in every way to all peoples and all organizations struggling for national liberation and unity. . . .
>
> Art. 7. The Central Committee in Belgrade includes, besides the members of the Kingdom of Serbia, one delegate for each of the Serb lands abroad [Pokraine]: (1) Bosnia

[51] Bogitchevitch, "La Société 'Union ou Mort' dite la 'Main Noire,'" in the French periodical *Evolution,* No. 7, 16-30, July 16, 1926; in German and English trans. in KSF, IV, 664-689, Sept., 1926; and in his recent interesting volume, *Le Procès de Salonique* (Paris, 1927), pp. 41-53.

and Herzegovina, (2) Montenegro, (3) Old Serbia and Macedonia, (4) Croatia, Slavonia and Syrmia, (5) the Voivodina, (6) the Coast Lands [Primorje, i.e. Dalmatia]. . . .

Art. 18. The Central Committee in Belgrade is in touch with the committees of Serb territory abroad by authorized delegates, who are usually members of the Central Committee, or, in exceptional cases, are special delegates.

Art. 19. Liberty of action is left to the Committees in the Serb lands abroad; but the execution of more extensive revolutionary movements shall depend upon the approval of the Central Committee in Belgrade.

To enlarge the society and yet secure absolute secrecy, obedience, and devotion among its members, it was provided (Arts. 23-33) that it was the duty of each new member to enrol new members and pledge his own life for those whom he introduced. Members were not generally known to each other personally, but were designated by secret numbers. Only the Central Committee at Belgrade was to know their names. "The interests of the organization are to be put above all others. Every member on entering the organization must realize that by this act he forfeits his own personality and that he can expect within it neither glory nor personal profit." "When the Central Committee at Belgrade has pronounced penalty of death, the only matter of importance is that the execution shall take place without fail. The method of execution employed is a matter of indifference." The initiation of a new member took place in a darkened room, lighted only by a wax candle, before a small table covered with a black cloth on which lay a crucifix, a dagger and a revolver. The candidate took an oath "by the Sun that warms me, by the Earth that nourishes me, before God, by the blood of my ancestors, on my honor and on my life, that I will from this moment till my death be faithful to the laws of this organization, and that I will always be ready to make any sacrifice for it." The seal of the "Black Hand," with ominous significance, bore an unfurled flag, skull and cross-bones, dagger, bomb, and

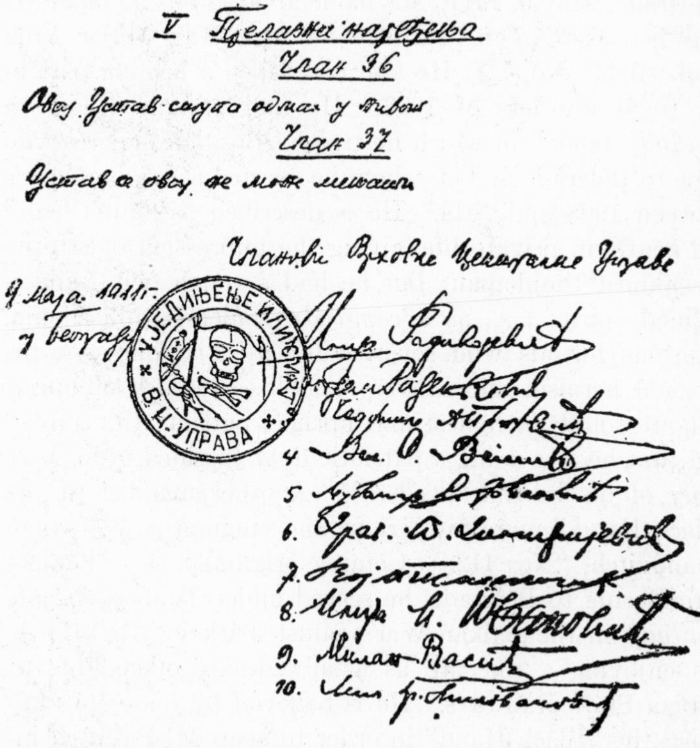
V Прелазна наређења
Члан 36
Овај Устав ступа одмах у живот
Члан 37
Устав се овај не може мењати
Чланови Врховне Централне Управе
9 маја 1911 г.
у Београду

Facsimile of the last page of the Rules of the Serbian Secret Society, "*Ujedinjenje ili Smrt*" ("Union or Death"), commonly known as the "Black Hand." Signature No. 6 is that of Dragutin Dmitrijevitch, the most influential leader in the Society. The Society's seal shows symbolically a skull and cross-bones, hand-bomb, dagger, and bottle of poison.

bottle of poison, with the inscription *Ujedinjenje ili Smrt*.

The inspirer and leader of this singular association, which seems to belong to the spirit of the sixteenth rather than of the twentieth century, was that reckless, generous, idolized, childish Renaissance figure, whose portrait by

Stanojevitch was given above,[52] Colonel Dragutin Dimitrijevitch—head of the espionage department of the Serbian General Staff. On the last page of the statutes, dated "Belgrade, May 9, 1911," his name appears on the membership list as "No. 6." His chief aide was Major Voja Tankositch, "No. 7." He also had taken a leading part in the royal murders of 1903. He had organized later a *comitadji* school, in which he trained Bosnian émigrés who came to Belgrade and on whom he exerted a large influence between 1908 and 1914. He is described as "quiet, calm and gentle in private life, giving the impression of a retiring, almost timid man; but he had a rough, wild, undisciplined spirit; . . . as a *comitadji* leader in Macedonia, notorious for his wild severity toward his followers, his personal heroism and bravery and his presence of mind; without doubt an honest and upright patriot; the conviction that he was doing a patriotic duty justified in his eyes many of his horrible deeds."[53] Another member of the "Black Hand," more mysterious and enigmatic, was Milan Ciganovitch, "No. 412." Coming originally as an émigré from Bosnia to Belgrade, he served under Tankositch as a *comitadji* in the Balkan War against Turkey. In 1914 he was enjoying a sinecure as a subordinate official in the Serbian State Railways. He is believed by many to have joined the "Black Hand" in order to keep M. Pashitch informed of its doings.[54] Tankositch and Ciganovitch were the two men who directly helped prepare the assassination plot in Belgrade, giving the three youths who were to murder Franz Ferdinand bombs, Browning pistols, and

[52] See quotation at note 8. For further characterizations of Dimitrijevitch, see Bogitchevitch, *Le Procès de Salonique,* pp. 61-69.

[53] Stanojevitch, p. 52. Jevtitch, p. 23, speaks of Tankositch as "an officer greatly beloved among the émigrés" from Bosnia in Belgrade.

[54] *Cf.* N. Mermet, "L'Agent Provocateur Milan Ciganovitch," in *La Fédération Balkanique,* pp. 270-272, May 31, 1925; Durham, *The Serajevo Crime,* pp. 80 ff., 174 ff., 182; and the obituary notice by Dr. Wiesner, in KSF, V, 1041-1048, Nov., 1927.

poison to be swallowed as soon as their deed was accomplished.

Another early member of the "Black Hand" was Vladimir Gatchinovitch, who appears as "No. 217" in the list of members published in *Tajna Prevratna Organisacija.* This interesting man, as we shall see a little later, carried on an active terrorist propaganda in Bosnia, both by his writings and by his organization of secret terrorist groups.

Among the other members of the "Black Hand" identified by M. Bogitchevitch were Dushan Obtrkitch, "No. 166," an intimate friend of M. Ljuba Jovanovitch; Michel Givkovitch, "No. 442," Secretary of the Serbian Court of Cassation; Demetrius Novakovitch, "No. 471," Secretary of the University of Belgrade; Dr. Milan Gavrilovitch, "No. 406," Secretary at the Ministry of Foreign Affairs and afterwards editor of the *Politika*; M. A. Jovanovitch, "No. 401," Secretary of the Railway Department; Bogoljub Vutchitchevitch, "No. 407," Commissioner of Police; and Stanoje Simitch, "No. 467," an employee at the Ministry of Foreign Affairs.[55] These names indicate that the "Black Hand" was not so exclusively a military organization as it has often been represented. Nor was it so divorced from, and opposed by, the *Narodna Odbrana,* as is often stated. While it is true, as pointed out above, that the *Narodna Odbrana* professed to work for Greater Serbia by "cultural" preparation, and the "Black Hand," more impatient, preferred terrorist action by assassination, the two Societies had the same ultimate goal and even had many members in common. Milan Vasitch, who was one of the ten members of the Supreme Central Committee of the "Black Hand" at Belgrade, was at the same time mentioned by the Archduke's murderers as "Secretary of the *Narodna Odbrana,*" and as having provided them with funds and revolutionary literature.[56] The two organiza-

[55] Bogitchevitch, in KSF, IV, 675, 688.

[56] Pharos, pp. 5, 22.

tions also made use of the same "confidential men" in Bosnia and the same "tunnels" of communication. Radé Malobabitch, for instance, who was one of the Austrian Serbs condemned for treason at Agram, and became a "confidential man" for the *Narodna Odbrana* in 1911, was introduced to Col. Dimitrijevitch in 1913 by Todorovitch, the frontier guard at Lozhnica, and thereupon became one of the chief spies for the "Black Hand" and the Intelligence Department of the Serbian General Staff.[57] So close was the connection between the two Societies that the members of the Carnegie Commission of Inquiry on the Balkan Wars failed to distinguish between them.[58] The three youths who planned to murder the Archduke sought to give the impression at their trial that their relations in Belgrade had been rather with the *Narodna Odbrana* than the "Black Hand." They declared that they knew of the latter only by hearsay or what they had read in the newspapers; but they admitted that they were aware that Tankositch and Ciganovitch were on bad terms with the *Narodna Odbrana,* and were perhaps providing the bombs and Browning pistols "because they were members of another society." [59]

THE REVOLUTIONARY MOVEMENT IN BOSNIA

For more than half a century before the World War, there had been an increasing antagonism between the Austro-Hungarian ruling authorities and the subject nationalities within the Dual Empire. This arose partly from the new feeling of nationality, which was an ever stronger force in the course of the nineteenth century, and partly from the oppressive rule of the Hapsburg Government and its disregard of the aspirations of its Slav and Rumanian subjects. This antagonism was particularly

57 *Tajna Prevratna Organisacija,* p. 201, quoted by Durham, *The Serajevo Crime,* p. 162.

58 Carnegie Report, p. 169.

59 Pharos, p. 82; *cf.* also pp. 14, 43, 47, 55, 80 f.

sharp in Bosnia and Herzegovina after the Austrian occupation of these provinces in 1878, and especially after their annexation in 1908. The unrest was heightened by the suspension of the Bosnian Landtag and by the repressive "Exceptional Laws" introduced during the popular ferment caused by the Serbian victories and the great extension of Serbian territory in 1912. But in 1913-14, under the administration of Count Bilinski, the Landtag was reopened, the Exceptional Laws withdrawn, wide freedom given to the Press, and great efforts were made to improve the political and economic conditions in Bosnia. Bilinski, being a Slav himself (a Galician Pole), had more sympathy with Serb aspirations than his German and Magyar colleagues. By a policy of conciliation in Bosnia, he hoped to win from the Serb population something of the same loyalty to Hapsburg rule which was found in the Croatian and Mohammedan elements of the recently annexed provinces.

In Bosnia and Herzegovina, according to the census of 1910, the population consisted, according to religion, which was the most vital factor, of Greek Orthodox, Mohammedans, and Roman Catholics, approximately in the proportion of 4, 3, and 2: 825,000 Greek Orthodox, mainly Serbs; 612,000 Mohammedans, mainly Serbs and Turks; and 442,000 Roman Catholics, mainly Croats; altogether, with Jews and a sprinkling of Protestants and gypsies, nearly 1,900,000. Generally speaking, the Greek Orthodox sympathized with the Serbians in the neighboring kingdom; the Roman Catholics were divided between loyalty to Austria and their higher cultural connections with the West on the one hand, and, on the other, their nationalistic desires for a national Serb-Croat union, either as a self-governing unit in a federalized "trialistic" Hapsburg state, or as part of a "Greater Serbia, or of an independent Jugoslav Federation; the Mohammedans were generally loyal to the Hapsburg Monarchy. These four political tendencies were represented respectively by the four main political parties: (1) *Srbska Rijec* (Serbian Party led by G. Jevtanovitch and Sola) and the *Narodna Stranka* (Nationalist Party), both in bitter opposition to Austrian rule; (2) the loyalist Serb minority led by Dr. Dimovich; and the loyalist Croats, formerly a part of the Starcevitch Party, but in 1914 having an anti-Serb tendency and known as the *Frankovacka Stranka* after their leader, a Hungarian Jew, Dr. Frank; (3) the *Starcevicanjka Stranka,* founded half a century earlier by the Croatian patriot Starcevitch; (4) the loyal Mohammedan Party.[60] But Bilinski's conciliatory efforts met with little or no response. On the contrary, they were interpreted as signs of Austrian weakness and decay. They were taken advantage of for further open newspaper attacks and secret subversive movements against Austrian authority.[61]

In 1914, however, the Bosnian parties and movements just mentioned represented what M. Jevtitch calls the "older generation." [62] They represented the politicians and

60 *Cf.* Conrad, *Aus meiner Dienstzeit,* I, 13-28; and the interesting memorials presented to the Russians in December, 1914, by the Jugoslav agents, MM. Supilo and Salviati and printed by Stieve, *Iswolsky im Weltkriege* (Berlin, 1925), pp. 136-161.

61 Leon Bilinski, *Wspomnienia i Dokumenty* (Reminiscences and Documents), 2 vols., Warsaw, 1924-25, I, 227-332; Bilinski, as Austro-Hungarian Joint Finance Minister from Jan., 1912, to the War, had supreme charge of the administration of Bosnia. See also the interesting views of his predecessor, Count Burián, *Austria in Dissolution,* N. Y., 1925, pp. 244-310, 358-371. Bilinski's conciliatory policy was not favored by Conrad nor by Gen. Potiorek, the military Governor of Bosnia (*cf.* Conrad, III, 95 ff., 157 ff., 370 ff., 442 ff.; IV, 13-124), nor by the Bosnian police officials (*cf.* Baron Carl Collas, "Auf den bosnischen Wegspuren der Kriegsschuldigen," in KSF, V, 11-27, Jan., 1927.

62 Jevtitch, *Sarajevski Atentat,* p. 3 ff.; *cf.* also Pharos, *passim;* and Seton-Watson, *Sarajevo,* ch. iii, "The Jugoslav Revolutionary Movement," in many respects an excellent and informing account, except that he minimizes the influence exerted from Belgrade upon the movement in Bosnia, as has been pointed out by M. Bogitchevitch, "Nouvelles dépositions concernant l'attentat de Sarajevo," in KSF, IV, 21-28, 87-95. Mr. Seton-Watson fails to note such significant points as the fact that the

the bourgeoisie who had been educated in the universities. Though they formed an opposition party in the Bosnian Landtag, they were content for the most part to follow legal means of action and counted on exacting larger political concessions from the Austrian authorities. They were the elements which Austria hoped to divide against one another. Hapsburg authority was to be maintained by the policy of *divide et impera.*

In contrast to this older generation was an altogether different "new generation." This arose in Bosnia in the early years of the twentieth century. It was known as *Mlada Bosna* (Young Bosnia). It was impatient with the politicians, the bourgeoisie, and all legal forms of opposition. It repudiated all notions of "trialism" as a solution of Serbo-Croat national aspirations. It was recruited from the youth of the "small and insignificant classes"—peasants, journeymen, school teachers, and sons of priests and young students.[63] Its members were impatient and "desperate." They had begun to feed upon Russian revolutionary and anarchistic literature, especially the writings of Herzen and Kropotkin. They were fired with the success of violence in the Russian revolution of 1905. They developed the "cult of the individual deed," that is, they believed that terrorist acts of assassination were the best means of putting a speedy end to the temporizing methods of Bosnian politicians and of throwing off all Austrian control to prepare the way for a new "Jugoslav" nationalism. Deeds of revo-

chief leader of the new movement, Gatchinovitch, was a member of the *Narodna Odbrana* and later of the "Black Hand," and that nearly all of the attempted assassinations of Austrian officials between 1910 and 1914 were made by youths who had just come from spending some months in Belgrade.

[63] *Cf.* the Bosnians directly connected with the preparation and execution of the plot to murder the Archduke: Chabrinovitch was a typesetter; Mehmedbashitch, a cabinet-maker; Mishko Jovanovitch, a merchant and cinema director; Ilitch, an ex-school teacher; Pushara, a town-clerk; the Kerovichi, peasants; Jakov Milovitch, a fisherman on the Drin; and Princip and Grabezh were students; *cf.* Jevtitch, p. 23.

lutionary terrorism served two great purposes: they created panic among the ruling authorities; and they uplifted the national spirit of the masses.[64]

The first most notable expression of this new cult was the "deed" of Bogdan Zherajitch, a Herzegovinian Serb. After being trained in revolver practice at Vranja by a Serbian officer, Bojin Simitch, who soon became a "Black Hand" member, "No. 111," [65] Zherajitch returned to Bosnia in 1910 and at Sarajevo fired five shots at the Governor, General Vareshanin. Zherajitch then committed suicide on the spot. The story of the General's contemptuous spurning of the corpse with his foot, as Zherajitch still lay sprinkled with mud and blood upon the bridge at Sarajevo, and his burial in the part of a cemetery where only suicides and criminals were interred, spread throughout the land, and did much to inflame Bosnian youths to imitate and avenge him.[66] He was speedily hailed as a hero and "first martyr" by the Serbs of Bosnia and Serbia. Two months later, on the occasion of Emperor Francis Joseph's birthday, August 18, 1910, the Belgrade *Politika* published a large portrait of Zherajitch, with an incendiary poem and laudatory article saying, "Today, we too light a candle at his grave and cry, 'Honor to Zherajitch.' " [67] His grave was kept fresh with flowers and became a place of pilgrimage for Bosnian youths filled with nationalistic fanaticism and a desire for the notoriety which would come to anyone who should follow his example. Thus, Princip, on the evening before he shot the Archduke, is said to have placed flowers on Zherajitch's grave and to have sworn by it that his hand should not waver next day.[68] Among Bosnian youths,

[64] *Cf.* Jevtitch's chapter (pp. 17-21) on "The Cult of Individual Action."

[65] Bogitchevitch, in KSF, IV, 24, 675, 688.

[66] *Cf.* Jevtitch, pp. 5, 20; Pharos, pp. 21, 30, 40.

[67] Austrian *dossier,* appendix 1.

[68] Jevtitch, p. 20; Pharos, p. 40.

whose mental balance had been unsteadied by a mixture of anarchism, socialism, and nationalism, it was not unnatural that the force of mental suggestion, in an act of political assassination like that of Zherajitch, should exercise a strong psychological influence.

The man most influential in developing the revolutionary movement in Bosnia and in inspiring the Bosnian students who carried out the plot against the Archduke was Vladimir Gatchinovitch.[69] He was the son of an orthodox priest in Herzegovina. His father wished him to follow the priesthood and sent him to school for the purpose, but he threw up his studies and began reading revolutionary Russian literature. In the spring of 1909, during the Annexation Crisis, he went to Belgrade, where he came in contact with the leaders of the newly organized *Narodna Odbrana* and also with the more violent spirits who favored "direct action" and later organized the "Black Hand." He remained in Serbia for a couple of years and came under the influence of Skerlitch, an active propagandist of anti-Austrian revolutionary ideas. Later he returned to Bosnia on behalf of the *Narodna Odbrana* and, in the words of one of his followers, "speaks, wakes people up, and again disappears like a shadow, as if he were swallowed up by the earth, feeling himself followed by the foot-falls of Austrian agents among whom were to be found some Serbians also."[70]

Gatchinovitch attended the University of Vienna; but

69 The best source of information of this arch-conspirator is to be found in *Spomenica Vladimira Gatchinovitch,* Sarajevo, 1921. This contains his famous pamphlet, *Smrt Jednog Heroja* (The Death of a Hero), glorifying Bogdan Zherajitch's attempt on General Vareshanin's life in 1910; it was published at Belgrade in 1912 by the "Piedmont" Press, the organ of the "Black Hand." It also includes some of his other writings and some interesting biographical notes by his friends and fellow conspirators. On Gatchinovitch, see also Jevtitch, pp. 5, 13, 15, 19-21; Seton-Watson, *Sarajevo,* pp. 69-79; and M. Edith Durham in *Current History;* XXV, 657-661, Feb., 1927.

70 Jevtitch, p. 6.

he spent more time in organizing a revolutionary movement among the Slav students than in study. Here also he wrote his famous eulogy on the murderer Zherajitch, which, as Mr. Seton-Watson well says, "by its strange, perverted idealism and high-falutin style gives a clear insight into the revolutionary movement which is now commencing." Gatchinovitch complained that Serbian public opinion did not pay due attention to "those who are coming," whose aim is "to kindle revolution in the minds and thoughts of young Serbs, so that they may be saved from the disastrous influence of anti-national ideas and prepare for the breaking of bonds and for the laying of healthy foundations for the shining national life that is to come." After quoting the example of Orsini, who tried to murder Napoleon III, and after lauding the Russian terrorists, he sang the praises of Zherajitch, as "a man of action, of strength, of life and virtue, a type such as opens an epoch, proclaims ideas and enlivens suffering and spell-bound hearts." He urged young Serbs to avenge Zherajitch's martyrdom by imitating his example.[71] This pamphlet was published anonymously at Belgrade at the office of *Piedmont,* the newspaper organ of the Greater Serbia movement and the "Black Hand" group. It was smuggled from Belgrade into Bosnia and circulated widely among young students upon whom it had a profound and decisive effect.

In 1912 Gatchinovitch was again in Belgrade, probably in connection with the printing of his pamphlet. Finding the *Narodna Odbrana* too mild, he joined the newly organized "Black Hand." His name appears as "No. 217" in the list of members published by the Serbian Government at the Salonica Trial. He is said to have received funds from both societies, and also a "scholarship" from the propagandist department of the Serbian Ministry of For-

[71] *Spomenica,* pp. 41, 47-8; see below, ch. iii, at notes 5-7.

eign Affairs. This enabled him to go to Lausanne for further study.[72] Here he came into direct touch with various Russian revolutionists, including Trotsky, who wrote an introduction, signed "L. T.," to a selection of Gatchinovitch's French articles.

Meanwhile Gatchinovitch had also found time to travel in Bosnia and organize the radical youth of *Mlada Bosna* into secret revolutionary "circles" known as *Kruzhoci*, "small groups of trustworthy persons, who do not know each other, but are in touch with one another through intermediaries."[73] This method of organization was also characteristic of the "Black Hand," from which Gatchinovitch got the idea. It gave the "Black Hand" a network of affiliated groups spread throughout Bosnia and the other Serb districts of Austria-Hungary. The students, peasants, and workmen who largely composed these "*Kruzhoci*" outside of Serbia were probably not regular members of the "Black Hand," but they could be used by the "Black Hand" for revolutionary agitation and terrorist action in Bosnia.[74] It is impossible to estimate the number of these *Kruzhoci*, but it is certain that they existed in all the towns with

[72] Bogitchevitch, in KSF, IV, 25 ff, 92 ff.; *Le Procès de Salonique*, p. 157 f. His statement is based on the deposition of two revolutionists, Mustapha Golubitch and Paul Bastaitch, who shared with Gatchinovitch in the plot against the Austrian authorities prepared at Toulouse. That Gatchinovitch was one of the many Bosnian students subsidized by the Belgrade authorities seems also to be indicated by the documents seized by the Austrian authorities during the War in the houses of MM. Pavlovitch and Pashitch; Durham, in *Current History*, XXV, 661, Feb., 1927.

[73] Jevtitch, pp. 6-7.

[74] One of the chief Serbian authorities on the "Black Hand," however, M. Boghitchevitch, *Le Procès de Salonique*, pp. 2-4, seems to regard the men in these *Kruzhoci* as regular "Black Hand" members. But I do not find proof of this. The evidence at the trial of the Sarajevo assassins appears to show a pretty general and probably genuine ignorance of the real and more restricted "Black Hand" in Serbia on the part of the suspects arrested in Bosnia after the assassination. He is undoubtedly correct, however, in contrasting the relatively humble social composition of the *Kruzhoci* in Bosnia with the "Black Hand" members in Serbia who were drawn mainly from the professional and especially the military class.

secondary schools—Banja Luka, Tuzla, Mostar, Trebinje, and especially in Sarajevo. One of the most active and alert groups, which gave directions to the others, was the one organized by Gatchinovitch at the house of Danilo Ilitch in Sarajevo. "Through it passed all that was most revolutionary. It was, in a way, the leading organ of all the nationalistic currents in the country. Its relations, direct and indirect, with the émigrés in Belgrade were very close." [75]

The revolutionary ferment among the Bosnian youth, which arose from exasperation at Austrian oppression, from a desire for Serbo-Croat national unity, and from the influence of Russian anarchistic writings and Serbian propaganda, manifested itself also in the widespread practice of young Bosnians migrating back and forth between Serbia and their own country. These "émigrés" liked to escape from the stifling atmosphere of Hapsburg control and roam about in the freer and more congenial air of Belgrade. Here they were well received, and it was easy for them quickly to secure a certificate of education. Princip, for instance, with the personal approval of M. Ljuba Jovanovitch, the Serbian Minister of Education, passed off three years' work in less than two years, in spite of the fact that meanwhile he was spending much of his time in political discussions and in travelling back and forth.[76] This practice of "emigration" is well illustrated by the case of the three youths who carried out the plot to assassinate Franz Ferdinand.

Gavrilo Princip was born at Grahovo, in Western Bosnia in the wild mountains near the Dalmatian border. Though at first diligent in school, his periods of application to study were frequently interrupted by excursions into po-

75 Jevtitch, p. 23; *cf.* also Seton-Watson, *Sarajevo,* pp. 74-77.

76 Pharos, pp. 22-24; Jevtitch, p. 71. Ljuba Jovanovitch describes his personal acquaintance with Princip in *Krv Slovenstva,* p. 10. Princip's fellow conspirator, Grabezh, also passed off examinations rapidly in Belgrade; Pharos, p. 44.

itical propaganda, so that he was often suspended, and finally came to Sarajevo, where he stayed for a month. In May, 1912, he went to Belgrade, ostensibly to study; but when asked at the trial why he went there, he replied, "That is my affair." [77] As this was just about the time that Gatchinovitch was organizing the *Kruzhoc* at Sarajevo and impressing upon the youth there the need of revolutionary agitation, it is probable that Princip's journey to Belgrade was inspired by him.[78] At any rate, Princip quickly came into touch with the "Black Hand" *comitadjis* in the Belgrade coffee-houses, and, according to his own declaration, was taken into the *Narodna Odbrana* by its secretary, Major Vasitch, who was also a leading member of the "Black Hand." When the Balkan War broke out, he went to the Turkish frontier to receive military training with *comitadjis* under Major Tankositch, another leading "Black Hand" terrorist and agitator. But being only sixteen years old, with a small weak body, he was sent home by Tankositch.[79] He had, however, become filled with the "Black Hand" ideas of terrorist action by political assassination, and spent the next fifteen months in plotting with Gatchinovitch and Ilitch, and in journeys between Belgrade and Hadzhici, a village half a dozen miles west of Sarajevo. At this village he passed the winter of 1913-14, and then returned to Belgrade in February, 1914.[80]

Nedjelko Chabrinovitch, who later threw the bomb at

[77] Pharos, p. 22. For the details of Princip's early life, see Jevtitich, p. 35 ff.; and Princip's own interesting confessions, made in prison to the Austrian psychiatrist, Dr. Pappenheim, and published in English translation by Mr. H. F. Armstrong in *Current History*, August, 1925, pp. 701-707; and in an anonymous pamphlet, *Gavrilo Princips Bekenntnisse*, Vienna, 1927.

[78] For Gatchinovitch's strong influence on Princip, see Jevtitch's biography of the former in *Spomenica*, p. 104 ff., and Miss Durham's summary of it in *Current History*, XXV, 657 f., Feb., 1927.

[79] Pharos, pp. 22-23; Jevtitch, p. 13.

[80] Pharos, p. 23; Princip's "Confessions," in *Current History*, Aug., 1927, p. 705.

the Austrian Archduke, left school because he made no progress and quarreled with his father.[81] He turned from one trade to another, and finally took up type-setting. After quarrelling with various employers, he went to Belgrade, where he found work in a shop which printed anarchist literature, and where he himself drank in anarchist views. But he fell sick and returned to Sarajevo, bringing anarchist books with him—some of which his mother burned. Here he worked for a couple of months in 1912, until his activity in a type-setters' strike and other complaints against him caused the Sarajevo authorities to order his banishment from the town, when he again sought refuge in Belgrade. Here he was in touch with Princip, though at this time they held somewhat different political views. Here also he came into contact with the *Narodna Odbrana.* Desiring travelling money to enable him to return to Sarajevo, he was advised by a friend to apply to this Serbian society which often secretly helped Bosnian émigrés. He did so, and the same Major Vasitch, who was also an active "Black Hand" member and who had befriended Princip, gave him fifteen dinars, a quantity of *Narodna Odbrana* literature, and the advice, "Be always a good Serb." [82] He then returned to Sarajevo in December, 1912. But after quarrelling with his friends there, he left the city and worked for a while on a newspaper in Trieste. From there he went to Abbazia in October, 1913, where, according to a recent statement,[83] he told a friend of his intention to assassinate the Archduke Franz Ferdinand. The friend aided him to go again to Belgrade, where he was given employment in the Serbian Government Printing Office, by its Director, Zhivojin Dachitch, one of the founders of

81 His father, who is said to have been an Austrian spy, committed suicide in 1924, near the tenth anniversary of his son's attempt on the Archduke.

82 Pharos, pp. 4-5.

83 By Dr. Orlitch, in the Zagreb *Rijetch* of July 10, 1927; quoted by Dr. Wiesner in KSF, V, 884, Sept., 1927.

the *Narodna Odbrana.* It was while there that he received from one of the members of the Sarajevo *Kruzhoc* at Easter, 1914, a newspaper clipping announcing the Archduke's coming visit to Bosnia. He at once determined to take advantage of this favorable opportunity to carry out his intention of assassinating Franz Ferdinand, and quickly found that "Black Hand" officers were ready to supply him and two fellow émigrés with the necessary bombs and revolvers.[84]

The third member of the student trio who conspired at Belgrade to go to Sarajevo to murder Franz Ferdinand was Trifko Grabezh. He was expelled from the Tuzla high school for slapping a teacher in the face during the fall of 1912, and went home for six months to his father's house at Pale, a dozen miles to the east of Sarajevo. Then he went to Belgrade to finish his studies, and managed to pass the fifth, sixth and seventh classes at Easter, 1914. Here he met Princip and other émigrés, and became fired with Serbian nationalism and an eagerness to participate in political assassination.[85]

Meanwhile, at Lausanne and Toulouse, Gatchinovitch was plotting the assassination of Austrian officials, though there is disagreement as to the details in the accounts left by his fellow conspirators. The version given by Mr. Seton-Watson, on the basis of what he learned from persons now living in Sarajevo is as follows. In January, 1913, Gatchinovitch invited certain young Bosnians—among them two Moslems, Mehmedbashitch and Mustapha Golubitch—to meet him at Toulouse. Here he provided them with weapons and poison, for the purpose of attempting the life of General Potiorek, the Governor of Bosnia, and

[84] Pharos, pp. 7 ff. For the false allegation of the Serbian authorities after the assassination that they had wished to expel Chabrinovitch but that he had been protected and vouched for by the Austrian Consulate in Belgrade, see the article by A. von Wegerer, in KSF, IV, 330-332, May, 1926.

[85] Pharos, pp. 24, 44 ff.

forestalling their own capture by suicide. But the youthful conspirators' nerve failed them; fearing a customs examination on their return across the Austrian frontier, they threw their weapons out of the railway carriage window, and nothing further came of this design.[86] A year later, "early in 1914, Danilo Ilitch set himself to collect youths ready for some desperate outrage," but without any clear idea against whom they were to act, until the announcement of the Archduke's intended visit to Bosnia. This was clipped from a newspaper by Ilitch's friend, Pushara, at Sarajevo, pasted on a piece of paper without comment, and mailed to Chabrinovitch at Belgrade. This news suggested to him and to Princip, whose "heads were already full of terrorist ideas," the idea of assassinating Franz Ferdinand. While they were winning over a third youth, Grabezh, and obtaining weapons from Tankositch and Ciganovitch, "Ilitch continued his preparations in Sarajevo quite independently of them, and armed three other youths, Cvetko Popovitch, Vaso Chubrilovitch, and Muhamed Mehmedbashitch, none of whom had any connection with Belgrade. . . . The initiative lay, not with those who so recklessly provided arms to the three in Belgrade, but with Ilitch and Pushara in Sarajevo, and above all with Gatchinovitch in Lausanne." [87]

Thus, according to Mr. Seton-Watson's version, the initiative for the assassination plot "came from Bosnia, not from Serbia," [88] and Danilo Ilitch took a very prominent part in it.

86 Seton-Watson, *Sarajevo,* p. 74. 87 Seton-Watson, p. 77 f.

88 Seton-Watson, p. 78. Lest his readers may not be convinced by his evidence, he again twice repeats (pp. 144, 145) his view that "the real initiative for the crime came from within Bosnia itself." It is natural that the Jugo-Slavs now living in Sarajevo or Jugoslavia, from whose statements he has largely drawn his information, should seek to magnify the Jugoslav Movement before 1914 and the oppression of the Austrian authorities in Bosnia, and to minimize the activity of Serbian officers in Belgrade, as the responsible causes of the crime.

According to another version, told to M. Bogitchevitch by two Serbs, Paul Bastaitch and Mustapha Golubitch, the latter of whom was himself present, the Toulouse meeting took place in January, 1914 (not January, 1913), in the Restaurant St. Jerome, Rue St. Jerome. Only Golubitch, Mehmedbashitch, and Gatchinovitch were present. The idea of the meeting came from Voja Tankositch in Belgrade. Its purpose was to prepare the assassination of the Archduke Franz Ferdinand and other important Austrian officials, with a view to rousing the Slav elements in the Hapsburg lands. After the meeting at Toulouse, Gatchinovitch wrote to Princip asking him to come to Lausanne with Danilo Ilitch to arrange the details of these assassinations. At the end of January, 1914, Mehmedbashitch returned from Toulouse to Herzegovina and soon afterwards went to see Ilitch at Sarajevo to put himself at his disposition for the murder of General Potiorek. But Ilitch at once said it was unnecessary to assassinate Potiorek because it had been decided to murder the Archduke, which was much more important. In fact, as soon as Ilitch and Princip had received Gatchinovitch's letter asking them to come to Lausanne, Princip had departed for Belgrade to ask authorization to make this journey. But Tankositch, who executed Dimitrijevitch's orders, said the journey was not necessary, as it had also been decided at Belgrade that the Archduke should be murdered. For this reason Princip was kept at Belgrade till the end of May, and trained by Ciganovitch in pistol practice.[89]

Several facts appear to confirm this second version, according to which there was already on foot an intention to murder the Archduke prior to the announcement of his intended visit to Bosnia; and the initiative for it came not from Bosnia but from Belgrade from Major Tankositch, a

[89] Bogitchevitch, in KSF, IV, 26-28, 93-95; reprinted in *Le Procès de Salonique*, pp. 151-163.

Serbian officer and one of the most active "Black Hand" leaders.

In the first place, there is every indication that the Toulouse meeting took place in January, 1914, and not in 1913. In view of the fact that Gatchinovitch fought in the First Balkan War at Scutari in the winter of 1912-13 and sent interesting reports of the fighting to the Sarajevo nationalist newspaper *Narod,*[90] it is hardly likely that he would have been at Toulouse in January, 1913. But a year later, when Serb nationalism and ambitions had been enormously swollen by the victories over Turkey and Bulgaria, would be the natural time for him to be plotting to assassinate Austrian officials as a means of hastening the further realization of Serb or Jugoslav nationalist aspirations. Furthermore, it is true that Princip went from Sarajevo to Belgrade in February, 1914; [91] this accords with the statement of M. Bogitchevitch's two informants that he departed from Sarajevo for Belgrade upon the receipt of a letter from Gatchinovitch shortly after the Toulouse meeting in January, 1914.

In the second place, the testimony concerning Danilo Ilitch at the trial of the assassins in many respects corroborates M. Bogitchevitch's version and contradicts that of Mr. Seton-Watson. Ilitch was one of the more active members of the Sarajevo *Kruzhoc*. He was some five years older than the other conspirators, who were mostly youths not out of their teens. He had been a schoolmaster, then worked in a bank, and in July, 1913, went to Belgrade.

Ilitch stayed there two months, frequented the coffeehouses used by Bosnian émigrés and "Black Hand" members like Ciganovitch and Tankositch, and "saw how indi-

90 Jevtitch, p. 13.

91 Princip's own testimony at his trial; Pharos, p. 23; and "Confessions," p. 705.

vidual *comitadjis* knew how to get hold of bombs." [92] Like other Bosnians who went to the Serbian capital, he drank in there the ideas current among the *comitadjis* of political agitation by terrorist acts like the assassination of high officials. Returning to Sarajevo, he devoted his time to writing articles for nationalist Serb newspapers, to spreading revolutionary propaganda among the Bosnian youth, and to plotting with Gatchinovitch at Lausanne and Toulouse. Having no regular livelihood, he lived at his mother's house, depending on the money she received from lodgers.[93] Though his statements after his arrest and at the trial in October, 1914, are often confused and contradictory, evidently with the aim to escape conviction, he admitted that he had talked with Mehmedbashitch early in 1914 about the need for a political assassination as the best means for realizing the Jugoslav ideal. This was evidently just after Mehmedbashitch had returned from Toulouse and before the news of the Archduke's intended visit to Bosnia. Ilitch relates that as a result of his talk with Mehmedbashitch: "We were completely agreed on the idea that an assassination must be executed. This was before they came upon the idea of carrying out an attempt against the Heir to the Throne. . . . Since we had no weapons, we decided to go to Serbia for them because here [in Bosnia] one cannot get them, and in Serbia they are cheaper. We did not decide which of us should go to Serbia, but whoever should first decide to make the journey should tell the other he was going to get the weapons." [94] But a little later he received a letter from Princip which made it unnecessary for either him or Mehmedbashitch to go to Serbia after weapons: "It was by chance about our Easter time, that one day—I no longer remember the date—I received a letter from Princip from Belgrade, in which he said he had the

[92] Ilitch's own testimony at the trial; Pharos, p. 62; *cf.* also Jevtitch, pp. 22-24.

[93] Pharos, 59 f.

[94] Pharos, p. 60.

intention of carrying out an assassination, and that he would have the weapons for it, and that I was to collect some fellow assassins. Later I did collect some. . . . When I received the letter from Princip, I wrote to Mehmedbashitch [at Mostar] and told him that the weapons would come." [95] Princip likewise stated at the trial: "I wrote to him [Ilitch] from Belgrade in very indefinite terms that I would carry out the assassination. . . . [After arriving in Sarajevo about three weeks before the crime] I said to him [Ilitch] that he should collect some other serviceable participants in the assassination, people who could be relied on." [96]

The independent testimony of these two conspirators against the Archduke's life makes it clear that Ilitch had no weapons except those which Princip and his two companions were to bring from Serbia; and furthermore, that the idea of recruiting more participants came from Princip and not from Ilitch; whether this suggestion was contained in Princip's letter, however, or whether it was made by him in person after his arrival at Sarajevo, is not clear. The leading spirit was not Ilitch but Princip, and the active impulse came from Serbia and not from Bosnia. The testimony of these two men clearly contradicts Mr. Seton-Watson's version, quoted above, that "early in 1914 Danilo Ilitch set himself to collect youths"; and that while Princip, Chabrinovitch and Grabezh were obtaining arms in Belgrade, "Ilitch continued his preparations in Sarajevo quite independently of them, and armed three other youths, Cvetko Popovitch, Vaso Chubrilovitch and Muhamed Mehmedbashitch, none of whom had any connection with

95 Ilitch's testimony; *ibid.*, pp. 60-62.

96 Ilitch's testimony, *ibid.*, p. 28 f. Similarly, in his "Confessions" in prison, Princip says he wrote in cipher to Ilitch, who "was under his [Princip's] influence though he was five years older and formerly a teacher," saying that "he himself would also take part," and "would procure five or six weapons" (*Current History*, Aug., 1927, p. 706).

Serbia." In reality Ilitch did not set himself to collect youths until after Easter, after receiving Princip's letter, and very probably not until Princip's arrival at Sarajevo about three weeks before the crime.[97] Nor can it be true that Ilitch, while Princip and his two companions were still in Belgrade, "continued his preparations in Sarajevo quite independently of them" and "armed three other youths," because he had no arms until Princip brought them. Incidentally it may be noted that neither Ilitch nor his Sarajevo recruits appear to have had the nerve or determination to do the deed. None of them raised a finger on the fatal day. Had it not been for the fixed purpose with which Princip and Chabrinovitch had come from Belgrade it is probable that the Archduke would have come and gone unharmed. More will be said on this point later in connection with the responsibility for the crime.

Furthermore, though there is no doubt that Mr. Seton-Watson's version is correct in so far as it relates to the newspaper clipping sent at Easter from Sarajevo to Chabrinovitch in Belgrade,[98] it is to be noted that Princip declared energetically that even before this clipping was received, he had formed the determination to carry out the deed: "I know positively that before Chabrinovitch received the clipping I said to him that I would carry out the assassination." [99]

As between these two accounts of Mr. Seton-Watson and M. Bogitchevitch, one may say that the latter is in many

[97] The testimony at the trial concerning Popovitch and Vaso Chubrilovitch seems to indicate that they were recruited by Ilitch for the deed only a few days before it was to be committed, and that they really lacked the nerve and determination for the actual deed (*cf.* Pharos, pp. 52 f., 64 f., 69 ff., 76 ff.). The idea of having a number of assassins armed was to make the demonstration of protest against Austria's rule appear to be as wide as possible; as Grabezh testified, "we wished to be as many as possible in order in this way more to show the discontent" (*ibid.*, p. 55).

[98] *Cf.* Pharos, pp. 7, 23; Jevtitch, p. 25 f.

[99] *Cf.* Pharos, p. 40, Chabrinovitch, however, claimed the doubtful honor of first suggesting it to Princip.

respects nearer the truth. Both contain certain statements which it is difficult to accept. But there seems to be no doubt that the effective impulse to the plot came from Princip at Belgrade and not from Ilitch at Sarajevo. Evidently the idea of carrying out a political assassination had been plotted in the winter of 1913-14 by Princip, Gatchinovitch and Ilitch, and this was the purpose of the Toulouse meeting, but probably these plotters had not yet definitely decided whether the victim should be the Austrian Archduke or General Potiorek, who was hated as being immediately responsible for the severity of the Austrian régime in Bosnia; the preference appears at first to have been to take vengeance on the Governor of Bosnia rather than on the Heir to the Throne.[100] At the same time, it is likely that Princip had, as he says, "formed the determination" to kill the Archduke. It is probable that he had been strengthened in this determination, if indeed it was not suggested to him, by Ciganovitch in Belgrade, who was an intimate associate of Major Tankositch, and who later secured from Tankositch the Browning revolvers to be used against the Archduke. Both Princip and Chabrinovitch declared at the trial that Ciganovitch had told them that the Freemasons had already decreed in 1913 that the Archduke must be killed, but the decree had not been executed because no assassins had yet been found to do the deed.[101] All three youths asserted that both Ciganovitch and Tankositch were members of a Masonic Lodge in Belgrade, and Chabrinovitch mentioned their dealings with a mysterious "man," who came and went and finally gave the word that it was time for them to cross over from Serbia to Bosnia to carry out the plot against Franz Ferdinand.[102] Whether the Freemasons had actually passed any such decree, or whether this idea arose from the fact that Franz Ferdinand was

100 Pharos, p. 8; Jevtitch, pp. 15 ff., 22; Princip's "Confession," p. 705.

101 Pharos, pp. 14, 33, 162.

102 Pharos, pp. 11 f., 14, 33 f., 58, 162.

known to be a zealous Roman Catholic and hence obnoxious to Freemasons, or whether Ciganovitch and his friends used "Freemasons" as a convenient screen for hiding the activities of the "Black Hand," cannot be determined with certainty.[103] But the statements of the youths in Belgrade concerning Ciganovitch, Tankositch, and the Freemasons indicates that there had been discussion by them of the question of the Archduke's assassination.

On the whole, one may conclude that at a Toulouse meeting in January, 1914, Gatchinovitch, in collaboration with Princip and Ilitch, plotted to terrorize the Austrian authorities by assassinating either Franz Ferdinand or Potiorek, probably the latter; but the plot came to nothing either because the assassins lost their nerve, or because it had meanwhile been decided at Belgrade to make the Archduke the victim. Princip then went to Belgrade in February, 1914, having formed the decision to assassinate the Archduke, and got into touch with Ciganovitch, and through him with Major Tankositch. When the newspaper clipping arrived with the announcement of the Archduke's intended visit to Bosnia, this visit was at once seized upon

103 "Pharos," judging by his preface, footnotes, and care in reproducing passages relating to Freemasonry at the trial of the assassins, evidently suspected the Freemasons of having contributed to the crime. *La Conspiration Serbe,* p. 33, quotes a prophecy alleged to have been made by a high Masonic official and published in the *Revue internationale des sociétés secrètes,* II, 788 (1912) to the effect that the Archduke made a good appearance and it was too bad that he had been condemned and that he would die upon the steps to the throne. The responsibility of the Freemasons has been a favorite theme of many writers: Karl Heise, *Die Entente-Freimaurerei und der Weltkrieg: ein Beitrag zur Historie des Weltkrieges und zum Verständnis der wahren Freimaurerei* (Basel, 1919); Ernst Reventlow, *Politische Vorgeschichte des Grossen Krieges* (Berlin, 1919), pp. 29-38; H. Gruber, *Der deutsche Katholizismus im Weltkriege.* But much of their evidence concerning the Freemasons seems to be fantastic. The present writer believes it very doubtful whether they had any responsibility for the plot, but thinks it very probable that their name may have been used as a means of throwing dust in the eyes of the Austrian authorities and of covering up the real activities of the "Black Hand."

by the three youths as offering an excellent occasion for carrying out an assassination which had already been discussed. Princip wrote to Ilitch at Sarajevo that he had determined to do the deed, and would come bringing weapons. In any case, the inspiration for the plot sprang from the group of Bosnian revolutionaries—Gatchinovitch, Princip, Ilitch, and others—all of whom had been in Belgrade and in close touch with "Black Hand" members. The idea of murdering the Archduke had certainly been discussed before his trip to Bosnia was announced. It would have been quite in keeping with the character of Major Tankositch and with the fact that he later procured the revolvers, as well as in keeping with the purposes and methods of the "Black Hand," that the idea should have originated with him or with his associate, Ciganovitch; but whether it really did originate with Tankositch, as asserted by M. Bogitchevitch's two informants, may be regarded as uncertain until further evidence confirms their assertion.

PREPARATION OF THE PLOT IN BELGRADE

In March, 1914, the Zagreb newspaper *Srbobran* published the announcement that the Austrian army would hold summer manoeuvres in Bosnia and that the Archduke Franz Ferdinand would be in command. This news at first greatly alarmed the little revolutionary group in the Sarajevo *Kruzhoc,* because it was well known that the Archduke was friendly to the Roman Catholic Croats and was believed to favor some form of "trialism." They feared that his visit would strengthen the Croatian bourgeoisie and political leaders who were ready to accept political concessions from the Hapsburgs, and that it would deal a blow at Jugoslav aspirations for national unity and independence. The Archduke's presence and the army manoeuvres would seem to be a demonstration of Hapsburg strength which might weaken the Orthodox Serb elements and the irredentist movement for a Greater Serbia. But the alarm of *Kruzhoc* members was only momentary. They at once saw that here was the opportunity for the best possible political assassination of the kind which Gatchinovitch had long been preaching. But in the temporary absence of Ilitch they did not have the courage to think of planning to commit the murder themselves. Instead, they bethought them of the more reckless and fanatical Bosnian émigrés at Belgrade with their *comitadji* friends in Serbia, and decided to inform them of the Archduke's intended visit. One of their number, Pushara, clipped the announcement from the newspaper, pasted it on a card without any commentary except "Greetings," and typewrote the address to Chabrinovitch at his coffee-house in Belgrade. In order not to draw any suspicion to themselves in case the letter was opened, Pushara took the letter to Zenica and mailed it there.[104]

When Chabrinovitch received the news clipping from Sarajevo, he showed it to Princip at the coffee-house where they were in the habit of meeting. In the evening they went to walk in the park to discuss it, and Princip invited Chabrinovitch to join him in murdering the Archduke. Chabrinovitch, according to his statement at the trial, had not hitherto thought of an attempt on Franz Ferdinand. He would have preferred to assassinate General Potiorek, as the personification of the Austrian system of oppression. But he now fell in with Princip's proposal.[105] Princip, however, claimed that he had had the idea of assassinating Franz Ferdinand even before Chabrinovitch received the clipping. "By myself alone I had already previously formed the decision to do the deed. When I was in Sarajevo earlier I had already determined upon it."[106] When confronted with one another at the trial, both claimed priority

[104] Jevtitch, pp. 25-26. [105] Pharos, pp. 7 ff., 23 f.; Jevtitch, p. 27.
[106] Pharos, p. 40.

for the idea, and a curious wrangle took place between them. Grabezh also claimed that he had already formed the idea independently during a brief visit to his home in Pale at Easter, 1914, when he read in *Istina* that Franz Ferdinand was coming to Bosnia. When he returned to Belgrade he showed the clipping to Princip, and the latter told him that he and Chabrinovitch were ready for the deed. "So am I," replied Grabezh, and from that moment the three youths discussed the ways and means for realizing their project.[107]

Among the Serbian *comitadjis* who frequented the coffee-houses with the Bosnian émigrés was Milan Ciganovitch, a Bosnian by birth, who had come to Belgrade some years before. He had been trained as a *comitadji* by Major Tankositch and fought under him during the Balkan Wars. He had joined the "Black Hand" as "No. 412," and in 1914 enjoyed a subordinate position on the Serbian State Railways. He had often talked with Princip about the oppressive conditions in Bosnia before this time,[108] fully approved the idea of murdering Franz Ferdinand, and offered to provide the weapons and other means. A little later he took Grabezh to his room, and showed him a chest full of bombs which he had either secured from the Serbian arsenal or saved from the Balkan Wars. But since bombs were somewhat uncertain, only exploding after a few seconds, it was agreed that the murderers ought also to be provided with revolvers.[109] To secure these, Ciganovitch turned to his fellow members in the "Black Hand"—to Major Tankositch, who got from Dimitrijevitch the money with which to buy them.[110] Ciganovitch also told the youths of the

107 Pharos, pp. 45 ff.; Princip's "Confessions," p. 706.

108 Pharos, p. 24.

109 Pharos, pp. 9, 24, 47.

110 Chabrinovitch testified at the trial, on being asked where Ciganovitch got the money and the Browning revolvers: "I do not know. He [Ciganovitch] got the money from Tankositch. This man endorsed a check with one of his colleagues [presumably Dimitrijevitch], cashed it, and bought the weapons. In our name Grabezh went to Tankositch

"tunnel," or underground railway, by which Serbian officials would help them over the frontier and put them in touch with "confidential men" on the Bosnian side. At the suggestion of Tankositch, who wanted to make sure that there would be no failure, Ciganovitch also gave the students revolver practice in a shooting park near Belgrade.[111]

So far during the preparations it was Ciganovitch with whom the students dealt chiefly. But Ciganovitch evidently was acting with the approval of Major Tankositch and Col. Dimitrijevitch, who were leading members of the Supreme Central Committee of the "Black Hand." Ciganovitch, in talking with the students, several times spoke of Tankositch. Shortly before the students left Belgrade, Ciganovitch took one of them—Grabezh—to the lodgings of Tankositch, who wanted to convince himself that the youths were determined in their purpose and knew how to use the weapons.[112] Tankositch, however, judging at least by the statements made at the trial, kept himself for the most part carefully in the background. Grabezh declared: "Ciganovitch had an understanding with Major Tankositch. But he was a side-figure. The man mainly guilty, if one wants to speak of guilt at all, is Ciganovitch."[113] The students denied knowing whether Tankositch was a member of the "Black Hand," but asserted that "he had a conflict" with the *Narodna Odbrana,* and was on bad terms with the Serbian civilian officials.[114]

Tankositch asked him: 'Are you ready?' When Grabezh answered 'Yes,' he asked him about us, whether we were reliable fellows. Grabezh assured him that he could guarantee us. What further dealings he had with Tankositch I do not know at all;" Pharos, p. 10. On Grabezh's visit to Tankositch's lodgings and talk with him, see *ibid.,* pp. 24, 47 f. Chabrinovitch's testimony about the money and revolvers coming from Tankositch and Dimitrijevitch is confirmed by Bogitchevitch who says (KSF, III, 440, note 1) that Dimitrijevitch actually showed him and others the receipted bill for the purchased revolvers.

111 Pharos, pp. 9 ff., 24 f., 47 f. 112 Pharos, p. 24. 113 Pharos, p. 47.

114 Pharos, pp. 14, 43, 55, 82. In the latter part of the preparations for the secret journey, with the aid of the frontier military officers, they

Dimitrijevitch kept himself even more completely in the background. The students declared that Ciganovitch had merely referred mysteriously to "a man" whom he had to consult about procuring the weapons, and that he seemed to get his instructions as to the time for their departure and other matters only after consulting some other important person.[115] Whether the students at their trial were really as ignorant of Tankositch and Dimitrijevitch and the "Black Hand" as they appeared to be, or whether they were carefully concealing from the Austrian authorities the real connection of these high Serbian military officers with the plot, one cannot say. In the first case, one must admire the secrecy with which the "Black Hand" leaders worked, or, in the second, the skill with which the students managed to throw the Austrian officials off the right track.

In order to avoid suspicion more easily and escape ar-

admitted that Tankositch took a direct and active part (*ibid.,* 47, 82).

In this connection may be noted the improbable story of Jovan M. Jovanovitch, in the *Politika,* December 4, 1926. When the plotters had first applied to Tankositch, he had disapproved of the idea of murdering the Archduke. Thereupon the youths had applied directly to Col. Dimitrijevitch, and he had sanctioned the plot, but without telling anyone else. There were at first five conspirators who got as far as Shabats, but before crossing over the frontier one of them turned traitor. The civil authorities got wind of it, and upon the order of Protitch, the Minister of Interior, the conspirators were brought back to Belgrade; so the first effort failed. But it contributed to the antagonism between the Radical Party and the "Black Hand" just at this time. Tankositch was not informed of this first effort, but after it he was importuned by Princip and Chabrinovitch to help them cross over into Bosnia; he then changed his attitude and did so. Such is the story told by the former Serbian minister at Vienna.

The three youths nowhere make any mention of this first arrest, which, if true, would be certain evidence that the Serbian Government had knowledge beforehand of the plot. And it would confirm the statement of Ljuba Jovanovitch, quoted above, at note 13, that, at the end of May or beginning of June, Pashitch learned of a plot. Jevtitch, p. 30, says: "Three weeks before Vidov-Dan [June 28th] these young people came through 'tunnels' to Bosnia. Probably due to someone's indiscretion, something was known about the movements of the émigrés. The Belgrade police immediately made several raids, but without any apparent success."

[115] Pharos, pp. 33 f., 162.

rest, the three assassins finally left Belgrade for Sarajevo some three weeks before the Archduke's arrival in Bosnia. Before their departure, Ciganovitch provided them with six bombs from his room, four Browning pistols and ammunition, 150 dinars in cash, and some cyanide of potassium with which they were to commit suicide immediately after killing the Archduke, in order to lessen the possibility of any confessions or statements which might incriminate the Serbian officers in Belgrade who had helped to prepare the plot.[116] They were also provided with a map of Bosnia showing the roads which they were to follow and the Austrian gendarmerie stations which they were carefully to avoid.

Meanwhile at Sarajevo, Danilo Ilitch, who had been in correspondence with Princip, soon recruited a number of local men who would be armed with the extra weapons which the three assassins from Belgrade would bring with them.

JOURNEY OF THE ASSASSINS FROM BELGRADE TO SARAJEVO

From Belgrade to Shabats, the three assassins went up the Save by boat. They carried a note from Ciganovitch to the frontier commander at Shabats, Major Popovitch, and were to say to him that they were being sent by Major Tankositch. But they were carefully warned not to make themselves known to the civilian authorities, lest they should be arrested and sent back.[117] Arriving at Shabats,

[116] This precaution, as it turned out, was not successful: Princip swallowed the poison, but threw it up immediately in great pain before it had taken effect. Chabrinovitch took his dose, but it did not work. Grabezh did not have any because Ilitch mislaid the dose which he was to take; Pharos, pp. 17, 18, 35, 55; Princip's "Confessions," in *Current History,* Aug., 1927, p. 702; Jevtitch, p. 29, is incorrect in saying that Chabrinovitch alone took the poison.

[117] Chabrinovitch testified: "Ciganovitch had expressly told us that we were to take care that none of the civilian authorities should learn anything of our journey and purpose. If it became rumored about the Ministry of Interior would have us at once arrested;" Pharos, p. 80 f.

they easily found Major Popovitch at a coffee-house, and told him that they were journeying secretly to Bosnia. He seemed to be already well acquainted with their mission, having probably learned of it directly from Tankositch during a visit to Belgrade a couple of days previously.[118] He conducted the three students to the guard-house and secured an order for them for buying half-fare tickets on the railway for the next stage of their journey from Shabats to Lozhnica, where they were to cross the frontier. He also gave them a card to the frontier authorities: "The officials concerned are requested to assist these people." [119] Finally, he filled out for them a false pass, making it appear that one of them was a Serbian exciseman and the other two his colleagues. With the half-fare railway tickets, they went by train to Lozhnica and delivered to the frontier captain the card from Major Popovitch. He immediately telephoned to the excisemen's watch-house directly on the border, but could get no connection. He therefore told the youths to return in the morning. Next day it was arranged that Chabrinovitch should take the false pass and go on to Zvornik, where he was helped over the frontier by a Serbian exciseman and later driven across Bosnia to Tuzla. Meanwhile Princip and Grabezh, with the bombs and revolvers, were driven back a few miles to a watch-house near Ljeshnica, where they were met by prearrangement by another Serbian exciseman who smuggled them over the Drin by way of the Bosnian Islands. There he handed them over to a peasant in whose hut they spent the night. Next day they were passed on to another peasant, who conducted them safely along by-paths in Bosnia toward Priboj until they were met by Veljko Chubrilovitch.[120]

Veljko Chubrilovitch was an Orthodox Serb school-

118 Pharos, pp. 15 f., 48, 82. 119 Pharos, p. 36 f.

120 Pharos, pp. 15 ff., 34 ff., 48 ff., 80 ff.; *cf.* Dr. Wiesner, in KSF, VI, 332 ff., April, 1928. For this region, see the sketch-map, above, p. 47.

master at Priboj and the "confidential man" of the *Narodna Odbrana* for this region. He had made trips to Serbia, had become a member of the *Narodna Odbrana,* and then chairman of the Priboj *Sokol,* one of the apparently harmless and "cultural" Serb organizations which were a medium, however, for active Serbian propaganda. He was in touch with *Narodna Odbrana* officials in Serbia and other "confidential men" in Bosnia and with local peasants who appeared to be in the habit of smuggling letters and information across the frontier.[121] He now took Princip and Grabezh to the house of another peasant, Jacob Kerovitch, and arranged that the latter's son should drive the two conspirators and their weapons on to Tuzla, where they would find another "confidential man," the cinema director, Mishko Jovanovitch. Princip and Grabezh accordingly set out that night in the peasant's cart. On approaching Lopare, where Austrian gendarmes were stationed, they let the peasant drive on alone with the weapons well hidden, while they made a detour on foot and mounted the cart again on the other side of the village. Arriving at Tuzla early in the morning, they went to the cinema director, Mishko Jovanovitch, as the Priboj school-master had directed, and found a ready reception.[122]

As Princip and Grabezh had just come from Serbia and had no travelling passes for Bosnia, they feared that they might be stopped and searched on entering Sarajevo at a time when the police might be expected to be keeping an especially sharp eye out for suspicious characters in view

121 Pharos, pp. 83 ff.

122 Mishko Jovanovitch was a middle-aged, well-to-do business man in Tuzla, being chairman of the Serbian parish school board, director of a local Serbian bank, and manager of a cinema. In 1912, at the urging of his relative, Chubrilovitch, he had gone to Shabats, become a member of the *Narodna Odbrana,* and then distributed its literature in Bosnia, for which his position in the Serb school gave him an excellent opportunity. Letters found in his house spoke of "working for beloved Serbia" and "risking one's life for Serbia;" Pharos, p. 83 ff.

of the Archduke's coming visit. They did not think it was safe that they should carry the bombs and revolvers any further. They therefore begged Jovanovitch to hide the weapons in his house until some safer person should come from Sarajevo to fetch them. He agreed, and hid them in his attic. It was arranged that the person who came for them should identify himself by offering a half-open package of Stephanie cigarettes. The three youths then went on safely by train from Tuzla to Sarajevo. Princip at once sought out Ilitch, took lodgings with him, and told him of the weapons at Tuzla. Grabezh went to his home in Pale. All three lived as quietly and inconspicuously as possible until the time for the deed. Thus, the "tunnel," often mentioned by Ciganovitch, which Serbian officials had long prepared, had worked to perfection.[123]

A few days later Ilitch went to Tuzla and identified himself to Mishko Jovanovitch in the agreed-upon way with the package of cigarettes. Fearful, however, that he might be arrested if seen carrying a large package in Tuzla where he was not known, he begged Jovanovitch to bring the weapons to Doboj on the way to Sarajevo, and hand them over to him there. This was finally agreed upon. Jovanovitch concealed the bombs and revolvers in an innocent-looking paste-board sugar box, and took them to Doboj. Not finding Ilitch at once as he had expected, he left the explosives under his raincoat in the railway waiting-room and later in a friend's shop in care of a child; in either place they might easily have been discovered. Finally Ilitch turned up, took charge of the precious package, carried it safely to Sarajevo by train, and hid it under a couch in his room. A few days before the crime he gave some of the weapons to two of his own Sarajevo recruits, and took them to a suburb to show them how to shoot.[124]

123 Pharos, pp. 28 ff., 51 ff., 103 ff.; Jevtitch, p. 30 ff.

124 Pharos, pp. 63 ff., 70 ff., 76 f., 105 ff.

Early on the morning of the day Franz Ferdinand and his wife were to make their formal visit to Sarajevo, Princip and Chabrinovitch met Ilitch at the back of the Vlajinitch pastry shop and received again from him some of the weapons they had brought from Belgrade—Princip took one of the Browning revolvers, Chabrinovitch a bomb, and Grabezh both a revolver and a bomb. Then they dispersed to take their stand at various places, as agreed upon, along the route which the Archduke was to pass.

THE ASSASSINATION, JUNE 28, 1914

Sarajevo, for some five hundred years, had been the capital of Bosnia and is still its principal city. It is crowded into a narrow valley at the foot of high hills. Through its center runs a little river, the Miljachka, half dry in summer. In the older parts of the city toward the cathedral the streets are crooked and narrow. But the Appel Quay, now known as the Stepanovitch Quay, is a fairly wide straight avenue lined with houses on one side, and with a low wall on the other, where the Quay follows the Miljachka. It leads towards the Town Hall, and is connected by several bridges with the other side of the town, where one of the principal mosques and the Governor's residence or Konak are situated. Along the Appel Quay, which was the route the Archduke and his wife were to follow, Ilitch had placed the various murderers to whom he had distributed the bombs and revolvers a few hours before the assassination. Mehmedbashitch, Vaso Chubrilovitch and Chabrinovitch were on the river side near the Cumurja Bridge. Ilitch and Popovitch were across the street, near the Austro-Hungarian Bank. Further along the Quay Princip at first stood near the Latin Bridge; after Chabrinovitch's attempt, while the Archduke was at the Town Hall, he crossed over the Quay to the corner of the narrow winding Franz Josef Street, now King Peter Street, where the actual assassination finally took place. Further on toward the Town Hall Grabezh was walking up and down, looking for a good place where he would not be interfered with by the police or bystanders.[125]

On Vidov-Dan, Sunday, June 28, 1914, the day opened with glorious summer weather. The streets, at the request of the Mayor, had been beflagged in the Archduke's honor. His portrait stood in many windows. Considerable crowds were abroad in the streets to see him pass. No effort was made to keep them back, by forming a line of soldiers, as had been done in 1910 when Francis Joseph visited the city. Several of the loyal newspapers welcomed the Archduke's presence, but the leading Serb newspaper, *Narod,* contented itself with the bare announcement of his visit, and devoted the rest of its issue to a patriotic account of the significance of Vidov-Dan, an account of the Battle of Kossovo, and a picture of King Peter of Serbia framed in the national Serbian colors.

Franz Ferdinand and his party reached Sarajevo from Ilidze about 10 A. M. After reviewing local troops, they started in autos toward the Town Hall for the formal reception in accordance with the announced program. The Heir to the Throne was in full uniform, wearing all his decorations. His wife, in a white gown and large hat, sat beside him. On the seat facing them was General Potiorek, the

[125] For various details of the assassination, see the testimony of the accused and the witnesses at the trial in Pharos, and *La Conspiration Serbe, passim,* and especially the accounts of General Potiorek and Count Harrach. One of the most trustworthy contemporary accounts is the report of the Archduke's military secretary, Col. Bardolff, to Conrad on July 3 (Conrad, IV, 19-22). Of the newspaper accounts that by René Gourdiat, the local correspondent of the Paris *Matin,* is the best; *Sarajevo, 28 juin, 1914* (Thionville, 1920); it appears to have attracted little notice, until largely drawn upon by R. Recouly, *Les Heures Tragiques d' avant Guerre* (Paris, 1923), ch. vii. Jevtitch, *Sarajevski Atentat,* exaggerates the part played by the local Sarajevo conspirators and the certainty of success of their arrangements. His account is largely followed by Seton-Watson, *Sarajevo,* ch. x, and by Clair Price, *N. Y. Times Magazine,* June 22, 1924, p. 2. Jules Chopin [J. E. Pichon], *Le Complot de Sarajevo* (Paris, 1918) is full of fantastic errors.

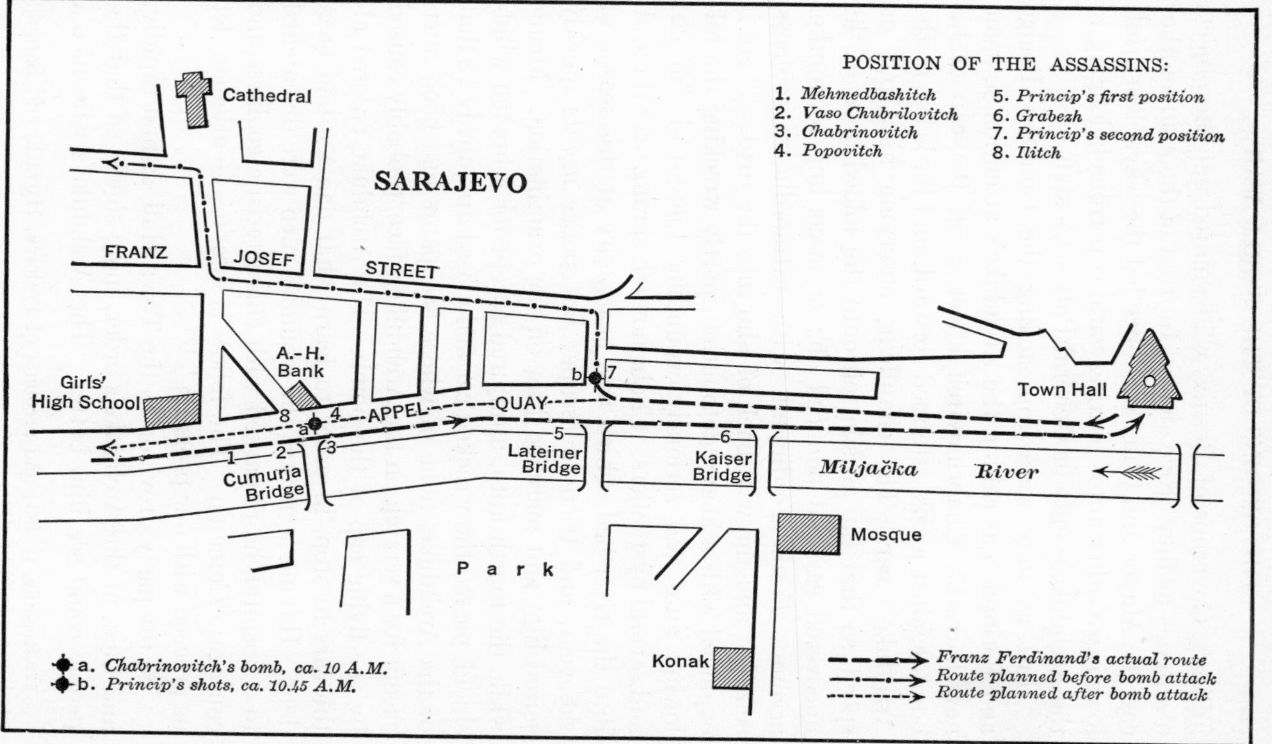

POSITION OF THE ASSASSINS:
1. Mehmedbashitch
2. Vaso Chubrilovitch
3. Chabrinovitch
4. Popovitch
5. Princip's first position
6. Grabezh
7. Princip's second position
8. Ilitch
Cathedral
SARAJEVO
FRANZ
JOSEF
STREET
Girls' High School
A.-H. Bank
APPEL
QUAY
Town Hall
Cumurja Bridge
Lateiner Bridge
Kaiser Bridge
Miljačka River
Mosque
Park
Konak
a. Chabrinovitch's bomb, ca. 10 A.M.
b. Princip's shots, ca. 10.45 A.M.
Franz Ferdinand's actual route
Route planned before bomb attack
Route planned after bomb attack

military Governor of Bosnia, who pointed out the objects of interest as they drove along. In front of them, in another car, the Mayor and Chief of Police led the way. Then followed two other autos bearing various persons belonging to the Archduke's suite or General Potiorek's staff.

Just as they were approaching the Cumurja Bridge and Potiorek was calling the Archduke's attention to some new barracks, Chabrinovitch knocked off the cap of his bomb against a post, stepped forward, and hurled it at the Archduke's car. The chauffeur, observing him, put on speed, so that the missile fell onto the folded hood of the uncovered car and bounced off; or, according to another account, Franz Ferdinand, with extraordinary coolness, seized it and threw it back of him into the road. There it exploded with a heavy detonation, partly wrecking the following auto and seriously wounding Lieut.-Col. Merizzi and several bystanders. Chabrinovitch sprang over the wall into the river-bed, which was nearly dry at this season of the year, and tried to escape; but police agents quickly seized him and marched him off for examination. Meanwhile the fourth auto, uninjured except for a broken windshield, passed the wrecked car and closed up quickly to that of the Archduke, none of whose occupants had been hurt, except for a scratch on the Archduke's face, probably caused by the flying cap of the bomb. The Archduke ordered all the cars to stop, in order to learn what damage had been done. Having seen that the wounded men were dispatched to a hospital, he remarked with characteristic coolness and courage: "Come on. The fellow is insane. Gentlemen, let us proceed with our program." [126]

So the party drove on to the Town Hall, at first rapidly, and then, at the Archduke's order, more slowly so that the people could see him better. The Archduke's wife met a

[126] Recouly, p. 183; and accounts of Potiorek, Harrach, and Bardolff cited in preceding note.

deputation of Mohammedan women, while the Archduke was to receive the city officials. The Mayor, who had written out his speech of welcome, started to read it, as if nothing had happened. But it hardly suited the occasion. It dilated upon the loyalty of the Bosnian people and the overwhelming joy with which they welcomed the Heir to the Throne. Franz Ferdinand, by nature quick-tempered and outspoken, roughly interrupted the Mayor, saying: "Enough of that. What! I make you a visit, and you receive me with bombs."[127] Nevertheless, he allowed the Mayor to finish his address. This terminated the formalities at the Town Hall.

The question then arose whether the party should still follow the prearranged program which provided for a drive through the narrow Franz Josef Street in the crowded part of the city and a visit to the Museum; or whether, in view of another possible attack, they should drive straight to the Governor's residence on the other side of the river for luncheon. The Archduke insisted that he wanted to visit the hospital to inquire after the officer who had been wounded by Chabrinovitch's bomb. General Potiorek and the Chief of Police thought it very unlikely that any second attempt at murder would be made on the same day. But as a punishment for the first, and for the sake of safety, it was decided that the autos should not follow the prearranged route through the narrow Franz Josef Street, but should reach the hospital and Museum by driving rapidly straight along the Appel Quay. Therefore the Archduke and his wife and the others entered the cars in the same order as before, except that Count Harrach stood on the left running-board of the Archduke's car, as a protection from any attack from the Miljachka side of the Quay. On reaching the Franz Josef Street the Mayor's car in the lead turned to the right into it, according to the original

127 Recouly, p. 184; *cf.* Jevtitch, p. 38.

program. The Archduke's chauffeur started to follow it, but Potiorek called out. "That's the wrong way! Drive straight down the Appel Quay!" The chauffeur put on the brakes in order to back up. It happened that it was precisely at this corner, where the car paused for a fatal moment, that Princip was now standing, having crossed over from his original position on the river side of the Quay. These chance occurrences gave him the best possible opportunity. He stepped forward and fired two shots point blank. One pierced the Archduke's neck so that blood spurted from his mouth. The other shot, aimed perhaps at Potiorek,[128] entered the abdomen of Sophie Chotek.

The car turned and sped over the Latin Bridge to the Konak. The Archduke's last words to his wife were: "Sophie, Sophie, do not die. Live for our children." But death overtook them both within a few minutes. It was about 11:30 A. M., St. Vitus's Day, Sunday, June 28, 1914.[129]

128 At his trial and in prison Princip maintained that his second shot was intended for Potiorek and that he had not meant to kill the Archduke's wife; Pharos, p. 30; Nikitsch-Boulles, p. 227.

129 Accounts of Potiorek, Harrach and Bardolff in Pharos, pp. 155-159, and Conrad, IV, 19-22.

CHAPTER III

THE RESPONSIBILITY FOR THE SARAJEVO ASSASSINATION

THE preceding chapters on Balkan Problems, Franz Ferdinand, and the Assassination Plot have given a brief narrative of the events and an account of the conditions which contributed to the fatal tragedy at Sarajevo. They will also have indicated to some extent the responsibility for it. But they left aside several much-disputed questions which can now be best dealt with separately, before one attempts to draw any final conclusions concerning the relative responsibility for the crime which was the immediate occasion of the World War. Chief among these disputed points are the motives of the assassins, the lack of Austrian police protection, the part played by Dimitrijevitch and the "Black Hand," M. Pashitch's cognizance of the plot and failure to prevent it, and the alleged Serbian warning to Austria.

MOTIVES OF THE ASSASSINS

A man's motives are ordinarily mixed, and often not even fully understood by himself. This is particularly true in the case of a political murderer, who has every reason to expect that one of the consequences of his act will be his own death. One would naturally expect to find each assassin assigning various reasons for his deed, and to find that the different conspirators differed somewhat from one another in the emphasis which they placed on their various motives. This is in fact the case with the half dozen youths who conspired against Franz Ferdinand. Princip and Chabrinovitch, however, may conveniently be considered together, not only because they may be regarded as the ringleaders, and because they had the courage of their convictions to make the actual attempts on the Archduke's life, but also because their motives were much the same.

The best materials for judging their motives are their statements after their arrest and at their trial, if due allowance is made for the fact that they were speaking as prisoners under indictment for murder and treason, and were trying to shield each other and their accomplices in Serbia. Of this attempt to shield each other and their accomplices among the Serbian officers in Belgrade there is abundant evidence. When first arrested, Princip declared that he alone was guilty, that he had acted as an anarchist, "convinced that there is nothing so fine as to commit a political assassination," and that his attempt had no connection with that of Chabrinovitch. "I have nothing in common, I repeat, with the author of the first attempt. When the bomb exploded, I said to myself, that there is someone else who thinks as I do." [1] This, of course, was totally false, as soon appeared when Chabrinovitch and Grabezh were arrested and their confessions made it clear how the three had conspired together at Belgrade and came to Sarajevo with the common purpose of murdering Franz Ferdinand. Even at their trial in October, 1914, when much of the truth was known about their activities and that of the *Narodna Odbrana,* all three students sought to shield the Belgrade authorities by asserting that the *Narodna Odbrana* was "purely cultural," that it did not extend to Bosnia, and that it had nothing to do with their preparations.[2] But these assertions were shown to be untrue, both by their own admissions, and by the evidence of the "confidential men" of the *Narodna Odbrana* in Bosnia, as to the way the three

[1] Princip's first confession, as published in the Budapest *Az Est* of July 1, 1914.

[2] Pharos, pp. 15, 34, 43, 55, 82, 162.

youths had been helped forward by the "tunnel" on their journey from Belgrade to Sarajevo.[3] Similarly Princip and Chabrinovitch denied knowing much of anything about the "Black Hand" except what they had read in newspapers, and denied having met Major Tankositch; they admitted, however, that he had procured the weapons and money, and that he had asked Grabezh to come to his room so that he could convince himself that the three youths were to be relied on.[4] How far these denials of knowledge of the "Black Hand" and its leaders were true, in which case the youths would be acting as the more or less ignorant tools of this secret Serbian terrorist organization, and how far the denials were purposely concocted to shield it and deceive the Austrians, one cannot at present say with certainty. Probably the latter hypothesis is closer to the truth than the former.

Making allowance for this tendency in their statements, one may say that the motives of Princip and Chabrinovitch were mainly of three kinds.

In the first place, there was a personal motive—a feeling of discontent with their own lives, of the desire to be martyrs and heroes after the fashion of Bogdan Zherajitch, who fired five shots at the Governor of Bosnia and then committed suicide at Sarajevo. Both Princip and Chabrinovitch had been unhappy at home, and received little or no financial support from their parents. Chabrinovitch had quarrelled often with his father and with his fellow Socialists at Sarajevo. Both youths had early left school but had not become established in any occupation. They drifted to Belgrade where they came under the influence of anarchist and terrorist propaganda, and heard the coffee-house talk about Austria's oppression and Serbia's future rôle as the "Piedmont" which would bring liberation to the Bos-

[3] See preceding chapter, at notes 40-48.

[4] Pharos, pp. 10, 24, 47 ff.; see also preceding chapter, note 110.

nian Serbs. Both, but especially Chabrinovitch, suffered from ill health and lack of proper food, and were probably already tubercular. Both died in prison not long afterwards, Chabrinovitch in January, 1916, and Princip in the spring of 1918. Life seemed to hold out little for either of them, but they could at least secure the glory of a martyr's crown by imitating the example of Zherajitch.

Princip declared, after being at Belgrade but before hearing of the Archduke's coming visit to Bosnia: "I often used to go out to the grave of Zherajitch. I often passed whole nights there, pondering over our conditions and our miserable situation and over him [Zherajitch], and then I determined upon the assassination. On his grave I made an oath to myself to carry out an assassination at some time or other." [5] Later, in prison, he told Dr. Pappenheim that, "in Sarajevo he used to dream every night that he was a political murderer, struggling with gendarmes and policemen; that he had read much about the Russian revolution, about the fightings; and that this idea had taken hold of him." [6]

Chabrinovitch also stated: "I too went to the grave of the late Zherajitch, when I came to Sarajevo. There I fixed upon the firm determination to die as he had done. I knew moreover that I had not long to live. I was continually occupied with the idea of suicide, because I was indifferent to everything." [7] His psychopathic thirst for notoriety is suggested by the fact that he had his photograph taken an hour or so before he threw the bomb and attempted suicide,[8] and also by his boast a moment after his

5 Pharos, p. 40. Jevtitch, p. 21 f., adds that on the eve of the assassination, Princip again went to the grave as to a holy shrine "to bid good-bye to Zherajitch with a big wreath."

6 *Current History,* August, 1927, p. 706.

7 Pharos, p. 40 f. He also said Gatchinovitch's eulogy of Zherajitch, "The Death of a Hero," had made a great impression upon him (*ibid.,* p. 21).

8 The photograph is reproduced in Pharos, p. 165.

attempt on the Archduke, "Yes, I am a Serb, a hero."[9] Both youths were clearly psychopathic, maladjusted by personal suffering, discontent and failure, and easily open to suggestive influences toward murder by the example of "heroes" and the talk of Belgrade *comitadjis*.

A second motive was to take vengeance on Austria for the oppressive régime in Bosnia, arouse opposition to it, and prepare the way for a revolution which should put an end to it. "What moved me primarily," declared Chabrinovitch, "was revenge for the oppression which the Serbs in Bosnia and Herzegovina had had to suffer, especially the 'Exceptional Laws' which last year continued for two full months. . . . I regarded revenge as the holy duty of a moral civilized man, and therefore I planned to take vengeance. . . . I knew that there existed at the Ballplatz [the Austro-Hungarian Foreign Office] a clique, the so-called war-party, which wanted to conquer Serbia. At its head stood the Heir to the Throne. I believed that I should take vengeance on them all in taking vengeance on him. . . . I hated him because he was an enemy of Serbia. . . . All the injustices of which I read in the newspapers—all this had collected in me until it burst forth on St. Vitus's Day."[10]

[9] Testimony of Josef Mitro, who helped arrest him; *La Conspiration Serbe*, p. 121.

[10] Pharos, p. 13 f. This declaration shows incidentally how the Serb Nationalist Press stirred up hatred and opposition against Austria by misrepresenting the facts. The "Exceptional Laws" were indeed very repressive and objectionable, but they had been cancelled in 1913 in accordance with Bilinski's policy of conciliation (see above, ch. ii, note 61). Franz Ferdinand, though a friend of Baron Conrad who headed the war-party in Vienna, was not a member of any Vienna war clique himself; on the contrary, he had often used his influence against it in favor of peace; he represented a friendly, rather than hostile, policy toward the Serbs; his policy of "trialism" would have favored them at the expense of the Germans and Magyars in the Dual Monarchy (see above, ch. i, *passim*).

At the close of the trial, giving his final defense, Chabrinovitch said the idea of killing Franz Ferdinand had not been a spontaneous idea with

Princip likewise, on being asked if he was sorry that he had killed the Archduke replied: "No, I am not sorry. I have cleared an evil out of the way. He [Franz Ferdinand] is a German and an enemy of the South Slavs. He treated them badly. . . . Every day a high treason trial. Every day it went worse with our people. They are impoverished. I have seen how our people fall more and more into decay. I am a peasant's son, and so I can convince myself of the misery of our people. I killed him and I am not sorry. I knew that he was an enemy of the Slavs. . . . I regarded him as an energetic man who as ruler would have carried through definite ideas and reforms which stood in our way." [11] "For union [of the South Slavs] one must sacrifice many lives, and it was for this reason that Franz Ferdinand fell. Nevertheless, the main motive which guided me in my deed was: the avenging of the Serbian people." [12]

A third motive was to kindle further opposition and hatred toward the Hapsburg rule, cause a revolution among the Serbs in Bosnia and Herzegovina, and so prepare the way for tearing these two provinces away from the Dual Monarchy and uniting them with Serbia in some kind of a national South Slav state. Princip had hinted at this in the passage just quoted, where he expressed the fear that Franz Ferdinand on coming to the throne might make some energetic reforms—such as the carrying out of his "trialistic" plan to unite the South Slavs, not by union with Serbia

himself and his two associates, but had been suggested to them by the milieu in which they lived in Belgrade, where the assassination was represented as a noble enterprise. The men with whom they associated had kept repeating that the Archduke ought to be done away with, because he was an obstacle to the realization of the Jugoslav idea. Although Princip remained defiant and unrepentant, the other defendants regretted what they had done. They had not known that the Archduke had children, and begged the forgiveness of these orphans; *La Conspiration Serbe*, p. 147.

11 Pharos, p. 30 f. Similarly Chabrinovitch: "People said that he [Franz Ferdinand] wanted to establish a federal monarchy including Serbia;" *ibid.*, p. 10.

12 Pharos, p. 36.

but by giving them an organic position under the Hapsburgs comparable to that enjoyed by the Germans in Austria and by the Magyars in Hungary. Asked if that was the kind of union he wanted, Princep exclaimed, "God forbid!", thereby causing laughter in the court room.[13] On the contrary, he believed unification would come through the action of Serbia: "I am a nationalist. I aimed to free the Jugoslavs. For I am a Jugoslav. This is to come from intimidation—from above. . . . As far as Serbia is concerned, it is her duty to free us, as Italy freed her Italians." [14]

This accords also with his later "Confessions" in prison: "The ideal of the young people was the unity of the South Slav peoples, Serbs, Croats, and Slovenes, but not under Austria. In a kind of state, republic or something of that sort. Thought that if Austria were thrown into difficulties then a revolution would come. But for such a revolution one must prepare the ground, work up feeling. Nothing happened. By assassination this spirit might be prepared." [15] "He considered that if he prepared the atmosphere, the idea of revolution and liberation would spread first among men of intelligence and then later in the masses. Thought that thereby attention of the *intelligentsia* would be directed upon it. As, for instance, Mazzini did in Italy at the time of the Italian liberation." [16] "Could not believe that a World War would break out as a result of an act like his. Did indeed think that a World War might break out, but not at that moment." [17] This was precisely the trend of opinion which was set forth at Belgrade in much

13 Pharos, p. 29.

14 Pharos, p. 23. Similarly Chabrinovitch: "We said we must organize the Serbs [in Bosnia], provide them with means, dynamite and bombs, so that they could make a revolution before the war, and so that Serbia could just come over and establish order;" *ibid.*, p. 11.

15 *Current History*, August, 1927, p. 703.

16 *Current History*, p. 706.

17 *Current History*, p. 704.

of the *Narodna Odbrana* propagandist literature and in the "Black Hand" newspaper *Piedmont* which inspired Princip and his companions.

Chabrinovitch agreed with Princip in working like Mazzini to prepare a revolution in Bosnia which should open the way for a reunion of all the Serb lands which had once formed the Empire of Stephen Dushan. But his political evolution had been somewhat different. He had at first held anarchist and social revolutionary opinions, but after living in Belgrade and mixing with *comitadjis* he had become more nationalist—"anarchistic with a mixture of nationalism," as he defined his position in 1914.[18]

His ideal was a Jugoslav republic, not a monarchy with a Serbian dynasty. The unification of the Serb peoples was to be accomplished, "after Mazzini's fashion. The ideal was to tear Bosnia away from the Dual Monarchy. We were all agreed in that. Some were for the [Karageorgevitch] dynasty; I was a republican. We could therefore have made a compromise, that King Peter should be king during his lifetime, and that after his death a republic should be proclaimed." [19]

Such were the three chief motives of the two principal plotters. But which was the strongest of the three—their personal psychopathic condition, or their desire for vengeance on Austria, or their Serb nationalism—it would be difficult to say. Jugoslav writers and sympathizers of today, like M. Jevtitch and Mr. Seton-Watson, emphasize Jugoslav nationalism as the main motive. But in 1914 the accused themselves hardly knew. Princip, being asked whether he had acted primarily from revenge or from the idea of national unity—i.e., whether the personal or the political motive predominated, replied, "The personal. But the other was also strong. They were evenly balanced." [20]

18 Pharos, p. 6. 19 Pharos, p. 7. 20 Pharos, p. 41.

It is often urged in mitigation or explanation of the crime that it was a wanton provocation on the Archduke's part to hold maneuvers in Bosnia, that the Serbs feared he meant to attack Serbia, and that they resented his visiting Sarajevo precisely on a Serb national anniversary like Vidov Dan. This has been stressed since the event by writers hostile to Austria and friendly to Serbia.[21] But Princip's and Chabrinovitch's own statements do not indicate that such considerations had any considerable influence upon them. They had in fact begun to organize their plot when they heard of the Archduke's coming trip to Bosnia but *before they were aware that he would visit Sarajevo on Vidov Dan.* They had decided to assassinate him in Bosnia, not because they resented the visit or feared an attack on Serbia, but because his presence in Bosnia afforded an excellent opportunity for giving effect to the three motives which have been sketched above.

THE "BEVY OF ASSASSINS" AND THE AUSTRIAN "NEGLIGENCE"

Most Jugoslav sympathizers, and most critics of Austria who follow the fantastic insinuations of Mr. H. Wickham Steed, like to represent the assassination of the Archduke as virtually inevitable, both because of the Austrian oppression, the wide-spread nationalist movement in Bosnia, and the "bevy of assassins" lying in wait for him, and also because of the "criminal negligence" of the Austrian authorities in not taking adequate precautions to protect him.[22]

21 E.g., Seton-Watson, *Sarajevo,* p. 110; Jevtitch, pp. 32-34; and Jovan Jovanovitch in his letter of 1924, concerning his "warning," quoted below at note 68. Fear of an Austrian attack under the Archduke's leadership is also often given as the motive for Dimitrijevitch's share in the plot (*cf.* Stanojevitch, p. 55 f.; Wendel, *Die Habsburger und die Südslawenfrage,* p. 50 ff.); but it is very unlikely that any such fear was really one of his motives (*cf.* Wegerer, in KSF, III, 385 f., June, 1925).

22 H. Wickham Steed, "The Pact of Konopischt," in *The Nineteenth Century and After,* LXXIX, p. 265 ff.; *Through Thirty Years,* I, 401; Recouly, *Les Heures Tragiques,* p. 108 ff.; Chopin, *Le Complot de Sarajevo,* pp. 89-100; Dumaine, *La Dernière Ambassade de France en Autriche,* p.

After the crime, in the recriminations of Austrian officials as to the responsibility for not averting it, and in the boasts of Jugoslav survivors at having participated (or intended to participate) in a glorious deed which has ultimately resulted in the creation of a Jugoslav state, it is easy to collect many expressions of opinion which seem to bear out these views. Thus, Mr. Wickham Steed quotes the Archbishop of Sarajevo as saying that "the Archduke could not have escaped, because he would have had to pass through 'a regular avenue of bomb-throwers.' "[23] Mr. Seton-Watson also quotes this, and unhesitatingly accepts all the stories which have been told to him of heroes who would have assassinated the Archduke had not Princip done so.[24] He even speaks of "a whole bevy of assassins on the streets of the capital."[25]

At the same time, both these writers blame the Austrian authorities for their lack of police protection. Says Mr. Steed: "When the Emperor Francis Joseph visited Sarajevo in June, 1910, more than one thousand uniformed police and probably double the number of 'plain clothes men' were employed to protect him. In June, 1914, when the Heir Presumptive went there the police were warned off."[26] Similarly Mr. Seton-Watson: "Every street [at the Emperor's visit in 1910] along which he passed was

147; Seton-Watson, pp. 77-79, 106-114, 144-152; Jevtitch, *passim;* Clair Price, in *N. Y. Times Magazine,* June 22, 1924, p. 2.

On Wickham Steed's fantasies concerning the Konopischt Meeting, see above, ch. i, pp. 32-43. Recouly and Dumaine intimate that at Sarajevo the Austrian authorities, instead of detailing proper police, assisted in placing the assassins at favorable points; and Chopin attempts to show that Chabrinovitch was an Austrian *agent provocateur* who had been sent to Belgrade before the crime in order to give the impression of Serbian complicity! Such intimations are pure fiction. Nor has there been any confirmation of the story of the Croatian, Rudolph Bartulitch, that the assassination was the result of Magyar connivance (*cf.* G. Beck, *Ungarns Rolle im Weltkriege,* Lausanne, 1917, pp. 215-218).

23 Steed, *Through Thirty Years,* I, 401.

24 Seton-Watson, *Sarajevo,* pp. 77-79, 147 f.

25 Seton-Watson, p. 110.

26 Steed, *Through Thirty Years,* I, 401.

lined with a double cordon of troops, and the town swarmed with special police and detectives from headquarters in Vienna and Budapest"; but in 1914 the police "showed itself strangely remiss or inefficient." "The contrast between 1910 and 1914 amply justifies us in speaking of criminal negligence on the part of those Austro-Hungarian authorities with whom the care of the Archduke lay."[27] But to assert that the assassins were so numerous that the Archduke could not have escaped, and at the same time to blame the police for negligence in not saving him, is illogical. As a matter of fact, neither was the danger to him from residents in Bosnia so great, nor the conduct of the Austrian authorities so strangely negligent, as these writers would have us believe.

On the Archduke's journey up through Bosnia from the Adriatic to Ilidze, and at the maneuvers, he was received with demonstrations of loyalty and there were no signs of danger. Soon after his arrival at Ilidze he and his wife motored in to Sarajevo, visited some of the shops, and were everywhere recognized and acclaimed. So great was the crowd about them that a passage had to be cleared for them. Here would have been an excellent opportunity for assassins.[28] On the fatal Sunday morning it is noteworthy that only those conspirators who had just come from Belgrade had the courage of their convictions. Chabrinovitch and Princip acted, and perhaps Grabezh would have done so also, if he had not had an uneasy feeling that he was being shadowed by police.[29] There was something about the atmosphere in Belgrade and the talk of the *comitadjis*

[27] Seton-Watson, *Sarajevo,* p. 109 f.; for his repeated assertions of "criminal negligence," see also pp. 129, 287.

[28] Conrad, IV, 14 f., 65 f.; Nikitsch-Boulles, p. 213; Jevtitch, p. 33, adds the piquant detail that, as the Archduke stopped in front of one of the bazaars, he came almost face to face with Princip; "Princip saw him, but did not move; behind him a stranger, undoubtedly a police agent, had carefully spread his hands. The same evening in the *kružnok* Princip told us about the meeting."

[29] Pharos, p. 53.

there which bred a firm determination to assassinate Austrian officials. It is significant that it was directly after being trained in Serbia by one of the officers of the later "Black Hand" group that Bogdan Zherajitch came to Sarajevo to assassinate the Governor of Bosnia in 1910. It was directly after a visit to Belgrade where he received a bomb from a Serbian major and a Browning revolver from a comrade, that Lukas Jukitch used this revolver to shoot the Commissioner of Croatia in 1912. Similarly Princip, Chabrinovitch and Grabezh had come straight from Belgrade with the firm determination to execute the plot prepared there.

But the resident youths who were recruited by Ilitch in Sarajevo and who had not been in Belgrade were a less robust sort of conspirators. Mr. Seton-Watson ascribes much importance to this Sarajevo group, in his effort to emphasize the Bosnian, and to minimize the Serbian, aspects of the plot. But he is in error, as has been pointed out above, in saying that the Sarajevo recruits were already being armed by Ilitch while Princip and his two companions were still in Belgrade. They had no arms until the Belgrade conspirators brought them.[30]

Ilitch himself appears to have lost his nerve, and to have advised abandoning the attempt. He asserted at the trial that he had tried to dissuade the Belgrade conspirators from carrying out their purpose. If his assertion stood alone and unsupported, one might well discount it as a fiction intended to exculpate himself. But it is confirmed

[30] See above, p. 107 ff. Nor can one accept his view that "the entire initiative came from Bosnia" and that the murder would have been committed anyway even without the bombs brought from Belgrade, because, "after all, it was a 'Browning' that did the mischief, and there were plenty of Brownings available without importing them from Serbia" (*Sarajevo*, p. 147). All the evidence at the trial shows that the youths had no money with which to buy revolvers, that Brownings were very difficult to get in Bosnia, and that Ilitch had planned to go to Serbia as the only place where he could secure them (*cf.* Pharos, pp. 9 f., 19, 23 f., 47 f., 61).

separately by Princip, Chabrinovitch, and Grabezh.[31] Asked why he had not destroyed the weapons, if he was really opposed to the assassination, Ilitch replied: "I did not dare. Princip had told me that he had received the bombs from *comitadjis,* and therefore I did not dare to throw them away, in view of my going to Serbia." [32] Shortly before the crime Princip told Chabrinovitch that he did not regard Ilitch as "reliable." [33] Certain it is that Ilitch himself did not raise a finger against the Archduke on Vidov Dan, nor did any of his three recruits. Mehmedbashitch let the procession of autos pass without taking any action, but, after hearing Chabrinovitch's bomb, fled precipitately to Montenegro—the only one of the seven armed men who was not speedily apprehended by the police. Similarly Popovitch and Vaso Chubrilovitch watched the Archduke's party go by—and did nothing; after the crime the latter, "all pale and trembling in his whole body," came to one of his friends and got him to take and hide his weapons.[34] Such was the "bevy of assassins"—three determined conspirators who had come from Belgrade, and

[31] Pharos, pp. 20, 29, 41 f., 52 f., 60, 62, 64, 66 f. 83.

[32] Pharos, p. 83. This fear of vengeance from Serbians, which arose from the "Black Hand" secret vows and terrorist methods, is also vividly given by several of the "confidential men" who formed the "tunnel' as their excuse for assisting the three conspirators on their journey from Belgrade to Sarajevo (*ibid.,* pp. 87 f., 95 f., 98, 104, 138). Thus, the Priboj schoolmaster, Chubrilovitch, declared: "I feared the annihilation of my family. Our house is only five miles from the frontier, and so we could be ruined in a night—all destroyed and murdered. . . . I had heard what horrors the secret organizations in Serbia had committed in Macedonia. Now I feared that Princip might be a member of one of those organizations, and so I was apprehensive about my head. I thought there must be some one standing behind Princip; because otherwise how would he have gotten the bombs? I had heard of a landowner in Old Serbia whose whole family had been annihilated" (p. 95). For actual examples of *comitadji* terrorist intimidation, see *ibid.,* p. 81, quoted below at note 46; and Miss Durham, *The Serajevo Crime,* pp. 55-74.

[33] Statements of both men; Pharos, pp. 20, 42. Grabezh also, on hearing the bomb explosion, at once concluded that it was Chabrinovitch's bomb, because he regarded Ilitch and his recruits as "of poorer quality as assassins" (*ibid.,* p. 53).

[34] Kranjchevitch's testimony, *ibid.,* p. 115.

a hesitating and "unreliable" Sarajevo ex-schoolmaster with three weak-kneed local recruits. If it had not been for the first three, and for the excellent chance opportunity afforded by the mistake of the Archduke's chauffeur in turning into the Francis Josef Street and stopping just at the point where Princip happened to be standing, it is altogether probable that there would have been no assassination.

MR. PASHITCH, THE *NARODNA ODBRANA* AND THE "BLACK HAND"

Some indication has already been given in the preceding chapter of the activity of the *Narodna Odbrana* and the "Black Hand," and of the probable cognizance of a plot on the part of Mr. Pashitch and some members of his Cabinet. But to understand more adequately the responsibility of Serbia something further must be said concerning the relation of these two Serbian organizations to one another and to the Serbian Government.

The Serbian Government may be regarded as responsible for the activities of the *Narodna Odbrana*. This society was publicly organized by prominent Serbians, including some members of the Serbian Cabinet of 1908. Its central committee sat in the Serbian capital and its president was General Jankovitch. Its statutes were published, and its activities, alleged to be "cultural," were publicly approved by members of the Serbian Government, with which it remained on intimate and friendly terms. It was organized originally to prepare forcible means for preventing Austria from carrying through her policy of annexing Bosnia and Herzegovina. But after the crisis of March, 1909, when Russia failed to back up Serbian hopes, and Serbia was forced to make to Austria her promise to live on good and neighborly terms, the *Narodna Odbrana* ostensibly changed its aims from the use of force against Austria to the "cultural work" of stimulating national feeling within the Kingdom of Serbia.

As a matter of fact, it continued a secret subversive work of propaganda in Bosnia: smuggling in nationalist Serb literature and recruiting "confidential men" who should organize ostensibly harmless local societies for education, physical training, and the anti-alcohol movement, but who in reality were to rouse Serbian nationalism and prepare the ground for the eventual unification with Serbia of the Serb populations in the Dual Monarchy. It had also given assistance and encouragement to Bosnian youths who came to Belgrade to study or to plot assassinations and revolution against the Hapsburg authorities. Though the *Narodna Odbrana* probably had no knowledge officially of the plot to assassinate Franz Ferdinand, its network of "confidential men" and its "tunnel" for secret communications between Serbia and Bosnia were certainly used by "Black Hand" officials and by the three youths who went from Belgrade to Sarajevo to commit the crime.[35] This interlocking activity between the two Serbian societies, which otherwise had somewhat different ostensible aims and were not altogether friendly, was facilitated by the fact that the Secretary of the *Narodna Odbrana,* Milan Vasitch, and other members of it were also members of the "Black Hand." Thus the Serbian Government may be regarded as responsible for an organization whose secret agents in Bosnia were preparing the way for the disruption of Austria-Hungary and were actually made use of to assist the Archduke's assassins on their journey to Sarajevo. Austria was therefore justified in her demand in the ultimatum to Serbia that the *Narodna Odbrana* be dissolved.

The relations of the Serbian Government to the "Black Hand" were quite different. This secret society had "budded itself off" from the *Narodna Odbrana,* in the words of one

[35] See above, ch. ii. at notes 56-59 and 117-123.

of the witnesses at the trial of the Sarajevo assassins,[36] being formed in 1911. The clique of military officers, who had murdered King Alexander and Queen Draga in 1903, had become impatient at the ostensibly "cultural" activities of the *Narodna Odbrana* and at the policy of the Pashitch Radical Party of postponing the final struggle with Austria until Serbia had liberated Serbians under Turkish rule, greatly consolidated her internal resources and strength, and made more certain of the support of Russia and France. The "Black Hand" was a very secret terrorist organization; its members were designated by numbers instead of by their names; and its curiously medieval statutes were never published until the famous Salonica Trial of 1917. The Serbian Government was well aware of the existence of this organization, which was a matter of common knowledge in Belgrade and was discussed in the newspapers,[37] but probably did not know at first in any detail its membership and all its subterranean activities.

At first the relations between the Serbian Government and the "Black Hand" leaders were tolerably harmonious. This Society included Dimitrijevitch, who was advanced in June, 1913, to the position of Chief of the Intelligence

36 Stanarinchitch; in *La Conspiration Serbe,* p. 109; see also above, ch. ii. p. 85 ff.

37 Chabrinovitch, being asked at the trial if he knew of a secret fraternity at Belgrade known as the "Black Hand," replied, "Yes, I know from my reading that the "Black Hand" exists in military circles"; Pharos, p. 14. *Cf.* also Potiorek to Bilinski, July 14, 1914 (Conrad, IV, 83): "There exists in Serbia by the side of the official Government a military secondary government [eine militärische Nebenregierung]. It is proven that active Serbian officers coöperated in the plot and in the whole propaganda in a preëminent way, and therefore are to be counted among the originators of the treasonable agitation stirred up in our country. To be sure the army is not part of the Government. But to try to maintain that the official Serbian Government does not know what the army is doing, is not at all allowable." For further evidence that the "Black Hand" was a matter of common knowledge in Belgrade and well known to the Serbian Government, see Bogitchevitch, *Le Procès de Salonique,* p. 31 ff.

Department of the Serbian General Staff, Major Tankositch, who was one of the most famous *comitadji* leaders, and a large number of other officers. It was regarded primarily as a group of military men, but it also included a considerable number of civilian officials, among whom were at least three employees in the Serbian Ministry of Foreign Affairs.[38] Prince Alexander at the outset favored it. He is said to have contributed 26,000 dinars toward the support of its newspaper organ, *Piedmont,* to have made various presents to the officers, and to have paid the expenses of Dimitrijevitch's illness in the fall of 1912. But when he intimated that he would like to be made head of it, the officers for various reasons did not take the hint; this rebuff wounded the Prince's pride and was the beginning of an estrangement which widened when he sided with the Pashitch Radical Party against the "Black Hand" in the so-called "priority-question." [39]

This "priority-question" arose after the Balkan Wars out of a dispute between the military and civilian officials

[38] Milan Gavrilovitch, No. 406; Y. Simitch, No. 420; and S. Simitch, No. 467, according to the partial list of members identified by Dr. Bogitchevitch, *Le Procès de Salonique,* pp. 53-58. He includes also in the list, though without giving his number, the name of Mr. Pashitch's nephew, Milutin Jovanovitch, formerly Secretary in the Ministry of Foreign Affairs, then Serbian Chargé d'Affaires at Berlin in 1914, and later Serbian Minister to Switzerland. For other details on the rules and membership of the "Black Hand," see above ch. ii., p. 86 ff.

[39] Bogitchevitch, *Le Procès de Salonique,* pp. 7 ff.; 34; Protocol of the Salonica Trial, p. 195. Shortly before the assasins left Belgrade, Prince Alexander visited the Government Printing Office, with the Director, Zhivojin Dachitch, an ardent Serbian nationalist. Here he was made acquainted with Chabrinovitch whom Dachitch had employed as a typesetter. Questioned after his arrest concerning this meeting, Chabrinovitch admitted it, but then suddenly refused to answer any further questions, as if fearing to incriminate Prince Alexander. These circumstances, together with evidence collected by the Austrians in Belgrade during the War, have suggested to some writers the possibility that Dachitch and Prince Alexander may have known something of the assassination plot; *cp.* Pharos, pp. 6, 11; and the articles by A. von Wegerer and Friedrich von Wiesner in KSF, IV, 485-489, 639-661, July, Sept. 1926. But this cannot be regarded as definitely established.

concerning the government of the territories which Serbia had conquered from Turkey. The Radical Party, headed by Mr. Pashitch, instead of extending the Serbian constitution to the new districts as demanded by the army officers, had introduced a Draconian régime which angered the inhabitants and quite surpassed in violence and oppressiveness anything which had occurred under Hapsburg rule in Bosnia.[40] The blame for this, according to the military officials and articles in *Piedmont,* lay with the selfish and incompetent civilian officials whom the Radicals placed in charge of the newly conquered districts. According to the Radicals, military officers were improperly refusing to admit the priority of authority decreed by the civilians. In this conflict the officers were supported by the Opposition political groups who demanded the resignation of the Pashitch Cabinet. The Minister of Interior tried to deal a blow to the "Black Hand" by seizing its club quarters. The conflict reached such a point at the beginning of June, 1914, that Pashitch asked King Peter to dissolve the Skupshtina and give the people an opportunity to express themselves on the matter in a new general election. The King at first refused. Pashitch thereupon actually did resign. He doubtless counted on strengthening his own hand, believing that no one else would be able to form a Cabinet in his place. At this point in the ministerial crisis Mr. Hartwig, the Russian Minister in Belgrade, is said to have intervened and helped smooth the way for the restoration of the Pashitch Cabinet as being indispensable for the policy of collaboration with Russia and France. On June 11, King Peter had to restore Pashitch to power, and a few days later, on grounds of ill health, retired from Belgrade, leaving his

40 For the text of this Serbian decree of Oct. 6, 1913, concerning government of the "liberated" territories, see *La Conspiration Serbe,* pp. 171-180. See also Stanojevitch, *Die Ermordung des Erzherzogs Franz Ferdinand,* p. 53 ff.; and Wendel. *Die Hapsburger und die Südslawenfrage,* 54 f.

COLONEL DIMITRIJEVITCH
Serbian "Black Hand" Leader

M. PASHITCH
Serbian Prime Minister, 1912-1918

son, Alexander, as Prince-Regent.[41]

This internal party conflict between the Pashitch Radicals and the "Black Hand" military officers is often cited as proof that Dimitrijevitch and the Sarajevo assassins were in no way in league with the Serbian Government and would have tried to conceal all knowledge of the assassination plot from it. This is probably true. There are several indications at the trial of the assassins that they were warned by their Serbian military friends to avoid letting the Serbian civilian authorities get wind of what was on foot.[42]

So it may be regarded as perfectly certain that Mr. Pashitch and his Cabinet had nothing to do with the originating of the assassination. It was hatched behind their backs. They probably had no knowledge of it until the preparations were nearly complete and the youths were about ready to go from Belgrade to Sarajevo. On the other hand, the fact that the Government and the "Black Hand" group were in political conflict over the "priority-question" is no proof that no knowledge of the plot came to the ears of the Government. We have, on the contrary, the clear and explicit statements of the Minister of Education, Mr. Ljuba Jovanovitch, that at the end of May or beginning of June, Mr. Pashitch knew that certain persons were preparing to go to Sarajevo to murder the Archduke; that he told some of his Cabinet of it; and that orders were given to the frontier authorities to stop the assassins, but the orders were not carried out because the frontier authorities were members of the "Black Hand" organization, and reported afterwards that the orders had arrived too late and the youths had already crossed over. We have already

[41] Bogitchevitch, *Le Procès de Salonique,* p. 8 ff.; Stanojevitch, p. 54; Seton-Watson, *Sarajevo,* p. 139 f.; and London *Times* and Vienna *Neue Freie Presse,* for May and June, 1914, *passim.*

[42] Pharos, p. 80 ff.

given our reasons for believing these statements of the Minister of Education to be true.[43]

THE SERBIAN NEGLECT TO ARREST THE ACCOMPLICES

The significance of the "priority-question" does not lie merely in the presumption that the Serbian Government was at first ignorant of the assassination plot. Even more important is the fact that it affords one explanation of two of the most serious charges which have been brought against Mr. Pashitch: his failure to give any definite warning to the Austrian authorities after he was aware that the assassins had gone to Sarajevo, and his remissness after the murder in failing to search for and arrest the accomplices in Belgrade.

In fact Serbian police officials appear to have actually aided one of them, Ciganovitch, conveniently to disappear from sight. To have attempted to arrest Ciganovitch, who was a member of the "Black Hand," and to have exposed the part taken by such prominent members of it as Dimitrijevitch and Tankositch, would have still further accentuated the political conflict and have strengthened the antagonism which had already caused the temporary downfall of the Cabinet. Mr. Pashitch apparently did not dare to take action against the leaders of such a powerful organization, and therefore adopted a purely passive attitude hoping that Austria and Europe would not learn the truth.

Precisely when and how Mr. Pashitch learned of the plot has not been revealed from Serbian sources. One commonly accepted theory is that he was secretly informed of it by Milan Ciganovitch, who is believed to have played a double rôle as a kind of *agent provocateur,* both conspiring with the "Black Hand" leaders, and at the same time being employed by Mr. Pashitch to spy upon them and keep him informed in the interests of the Serbian Government and

43 See above, ch. ii. p. 61 ff.

the Radical Party.[44] Ciganovitch was freely declared by all three of the Sarajevo plotters, both at their arrest and at their trial, to have taken a most active part in their preparations in Belgrade. He was a Bosnian Serb, who came as an émigré to Belgrade in 1908, was trained as a *comitadji* by Tankositch, and then given employment as a small official on the Serbian State Railways. In 1911 he was enrolled in the "Black Hand" as "No. 412," and fought as a *comitadji* under Tankositch in the Balkan Wars. In the preparation of the plot he served as the agent of Tankositch. He secured for Princip and his companions in Belgrade the bombs and revolvers which were to be used against the Archduke. He gave them the cyanide of potassium with which to poison themselves after the crime, and thus prevent revelations concerning Ciganovitch himself and his Serbian accomplices. Upon orders from Tankositch, Ciganovitch took the youths to a shooting park near Belgrade and gave them practice in the use of the revolvers. At the end of May, when they were ready to start, he supplied them with cards of introduction to "Black Hand" agents and "confidential men" who would help them forward on their journey to Sarajevo.[45] The reasons for believing that Ciganovitch informed Pashitch do not lie in any direct evidence prior to the assassination, but in the apparent collusion between them afterwards—in the action

[44] Bogitchevitch, *Le Procès de Salonique,* pp. 32, 131-133, 142 f.; and in KSF, III, 18 f., Jan., 1925; M. E. Durham, *The Serajevo Crime,* pp. 53, 80-85, 174-182; A. von Wegerer in KSF, III, 380-384, June, 1925; articles by Dimitrijevitch's personal friend and fellow "Black Hand" member, Col. Bozhin Simitch, in the French review *Clarté* for May, 1925, and in the Vienna publication *La Fédération Balkanique,* May 31, 1925; N. Nenadovitch, "Die Geheimnisse der Belgrade Kamarilla," *ibid.,* Dec. 1, 1924; and F. von Wiesner's obituary notice on Ciganovitch, who died Sept. 28, 1927, in KSF, V, 1041-1048, Nov., 1927. Most of these writers draw part of their conclusions from the records of the Salonica Trial, in which Ciganovitch was a prominent witness against Dimitrijevitch.

[45] Pharos, pp. 9-12, 14-17, 19, 24 f., 33 f., 37-39, 47 f., 55, 82; and Austrian *Dossier* of 1914, Appendix VIII.

of the Serbian authorities in attempting to conceal Ciganovitch and have him conveniently disappear from sight, and in the evidence which Ciganovitch gave in 1917 to aid the Radical Party in convicting Dimitrijevitch and in breaking the power of the "Black Hand."

Within a couple of days after the assassination, when rumors began to reach Belgrade of the confessions made by Chabrinovitch and Princip, both Tankositch and Pashitch appear to have tried to suppress all information about the Belgrade accomplices. On the evening of June 29 three *comitadjis* "came to Mr. Svetolik Savitch, owner of the newspaper *Balkan,* and told him in the name of Major Tankositch that under no circumstances was he to publish anything in his newspaper about any of the connections and relations of the assassin Chabrinovitch with their acquaintances here [in Belgrade]. Above everything he was not to write anything which might in any way compromise Serbians; *otherwise it would fare badly with him."* [46] This kind of intimidation—fear of violence and vengeance from *comitadjis* like Tankositch—was frequently mentioned by "confidential men" in Bosnia as one of their motives for assisting the assassins.[47] It suggests an additional reason why Mr. Pashitch did not care or dare to make any move to arrest this popular and powerful "Black Hand" leader, until finally forced by the Austrian ultimatum to detain him for a few days.

On June 30 the Austrian Chargé d'Affaires inquired of the Serbian Government what police measures it had taken, or proposed to take, "to follow up the clues to the crime which notoriously are partly to be found in Serbia," but was informed that "the matter had not yet engaged the

[46] Confidential report of the Belgrade Police to Protitch, Serbian Minister of Interior, June 30, 1914; discovered by the Austrians after the capture of Belgrade; published in the *Hrvatski Dnevnik* (Croatian Daily), No. 132, May 12, 1916; and reprinted in Pharos, p. 81, note 45. Italics by the present writer.

[47] See above, note 32.

attention of the Serbian police" [48]—"that up to the present nothing had been done, and that the matter did not concern the Serbian Government." [49] High words then passed between the two, as the Austrian expressed "his extreme astonishment that any Government which was continually asserting its desire to live on good terms with its neighbors should exhibit such indifference." [50]

On June 30, Zimmermann, the German Foreign Under-Secretary, gave the Serbian Chargé d'Affaires in Berlin some timely advice with a view to averting serious complications, as we know from the report of the Bavarian Minister at Berlin:

> At the Foreign Office they hope that Serbia will now neglect nothing in order to call to account those persons guilty of the conspiracy. Mr. Zimmermann immediately and seriously called the attention of the local Serbian Chargé d'Affaires to the consequences to which a Serbian refusal in this direction might lead, and, furthermore, suggested to the Russian Ambassador that he get his Government to give the same advice at Belgrade. Mr. Zimmermann offered this counsel on the ground that no one could tell what would happen should the Serbian Government fail to fulfil its obligations, considering the wrath which the Sarajevo deed had aroused in Austria-Hungary.[51]

Zimmermann also spoke to the diplomatic representatives of England and Russia in Berlin in the same sense, with the evident hope that they would give Serbia similar good advice,[52] but they do not appear to have done so. If the Serbian Government had at once taken energetic

48 Ritter von Storck to Berchtold, June 30; *Austrian Red Book* of 1914, No. 2.

49 Von Griesinger, German Minister in Belgrade, to Bethmann, July 2; K.D., 12; *cf.* also B.D. 27.

50 Von Griesinger, *ibid.*

51 Lerchenfeld to Hertling in Munich, July 2; Dirr, p. 118; K.D., IV, Anhang IV, No. 1.

52 *Cf.* Rumbold to Grey, June 30 and July 11; B.D., 22, 44.

action to arrest the Belgrade accomplices, and given genuine evidence of its often asserted desire to live on good neighborly terms with Austria, this would have mitigated Germany's indignation at the assassination, made her less ready to follow Austria's fatal path, and increased the chances of friendly mediation. In failing to do this, and in assuming the passive and negative attitude of waiting to see what definite incriminating evidence and charges Austria might be able to bring forward, Mr. Pashitch incurred a further serious responsibility for what befell.[53]

The Serbian Government was informed on July 6 by its Minister in Vienna that the Austrian evidence from Sarajevo indicated the Belgrade origin of the plot and implicated Ciganovitch.[54] In spite of this, and of Zimmermann's warning, it not only made no move to apprehend the accomplices in Belgrade, but it apparently actually facilitated the disappearance of Ciganovitch, the chief accomplice, in order that it might not have to hand him over to the Austrian authorities. As Ciganovitch was a Bosnian by birth, Austria might have demanded that he be extradited for trial, and Austria might have then learned the whole truth. So it was better that he should disappear. On July 8 the Austrian Government learned by a cipher despatch from its Legation in Belgrade that Ciganovitch had been in Belgrade the day of the assassination, but had left the city three days later, having been granted supposedly a month's

[53] Musulin, p. 221. *Cf.* Seton-Watson, *Sarajevo,* pp. 133-137, for some excellent remarks on this subject. We cannot agree, however, with his explanation that this passive attitude on Pashitch's part was owing to his "truly Oriental indifference to public opinion both about himself and about his country" (p. 136). We suspect it was his fear that Austria and Europe might learn more of the truth about the complicity of Serbian officers, and also his fear of further antagonizing the "Black Hand;" Mr. Seton-Watson concedes that "a further reason for the Serbian Government's inaction at this critical time was the rôle played by the 'Black Hand'" (p. 137 ff.). On Serbian efforts to conceal the truth and deceive Europe, see also Wegerer, "Wie Serbien England täuschte," in KSF, V, 238-29, March, 1927.

[54] S.B.B., 16.

vacation by the railway administration in which he was employed. The Belgrade prefect of police declared that he did not know anyone of the name of Milan Ciganovitch, but it soon appeared that it was the prefect of police himself who had brought about Ciganovitch's disappearance from Belgrade.[55] It later appeared also that his name was erased from the railway books and was reëntered under the name of Milan Danilov, and as such he continued to draw pay. When Serbian mobilization took place he quickly joined Tankositch's band. Dr. Bogitchevitch says that on August 3 or 4, 1914, he was told by Commandant Srb, who was in charge of an important Serbian railway station, that he had just assisted Ciganovitch to escape to the south.[56]

The Austrian authorities, having learned from the confessions of the assassins some of the facts about the Belgrade accomplices, demanded in the ultimatum of July 23 (Point 7) that Serbia "proceed without delay to the arrest of Major Voja Tankositch and of the individual named Milan Ciganovitch, a Serbian State employee." The Serbian Government replied a couple of days later that it had arrested Tankositch as requested, but "as regards Milan Ciganovitch, who is a subject of the Austro-Hungarian Monarchy and who up to June 15 [N. S. 28, that is, the day of the assassination] was employed (on probation) by the railway administration, he has not yet been able to be found (and therefore a writ of arrest has been issued against him)."[57] It is certainly a curious fact that the Serbian Government pretended to cease to have any knowledge of

[55] Wiesner, in KSF, V, 1046, Nov. 1927; and Austrian comment on Serbian reply to the ultimatum, Point 7; A.R.B., II, 96.

[56] Bogitchevitch, *Le Procès de Salonique,* p. 143.

[57] In its embarrassment to explain why Ciganovitch had not been arrested, the Serbian Government appears to have given its reply in various forms: as given in A.R.B., II, 47, the last clause reads: "il n'a pu encore être découvert et un mandat d'amener a été lancé contre lui;" but in S.B.B., 39, and F.Y.B., 49, "joint"—and in B.B.B., 39, "arrêté"—is substituted for "découvert," and no mention is made of "un mandat d'amener."

Ciganovitch precisely from the moment of the assassination. In view of the other facts given above, one may doubt the sincerity of their asserted ignorance of his whereabouts and their inability to find him. This doubt is increased by the fact that the Minister of Education, speaking of the period just after the assassination and before the Austrian ultimatum, when the Serbian authorities might have arrested Ciganovitch but did not do so, indicates clearly that his colleagues were informed about this accomplice:

> When the Austrian stories arrived from Vienna to the effect that the assassins had been sent to Sarajevo by an official of the Serbian Ministry of Public Works, a certain Milan Ciganovitch, Mr. Pashitch asked Mr. Jotsa Jovanovitch, then in charge of that department, who this official of his was; but Mr. Jotsa knew nothing about him, nor did anybody in his department. Under pressure from Mr. Pashitch, they at last unearthed Ciganovitch in some small clerical post in the railway administration. I remember that somebody (either Stojan or Pashitch) said, when Jotsa told us this: "There, you see! It is true enough what people say: if any mother has lost her son, let her go and look for him in the railway administration." After that we heard from Mr. Jotsa that Ciganovitch had gone off somewhere out of Belgrade.[58]

DID SERBIA "WARN" AUSTRIA?

This question is exceedingly important, because of the variety of conclusions which have been drawn from the affirmative and negative answers which have been given to it. On the one hand, if the Serbian Government gave a warning at Vienna, this can be interpreted either, (1) in favor of Serbia, as showing that the Pashitch Cabinet, on discovering the plot, did its utmost to avert a crime and thus went far in clearing itself of all blame in the matter; or, (2) in favor of Austria, as proving that the Serbian

58 Ljuba Jovanovitch, *Krv Slovenstva,* p. 14.

Government was aware of a plot, and as justifying the Austrian demand that Austrian officials be allowed to coöperate with Serbian officials in discovering the Belgrade accomplices, since the Serbian officials themselves had taken no steps in this direction. On the other hand, if no warning was given, then either, (1) the Serbian Government could claim—as in fact it did claim—that it knew nothing of any plot beforehand and was therefore wholly innocent; or, (2) in justification of Austria, it could be claimed that Serbia was guilty of concealing the plot and thus of conniving at the crime. With the possibility of these various interpretations in either direction, it is not surprising to find Serbian sympathizers arguing violently against each other, and Austrian sympathizers doing the same. Nor is it surprising that a great deal of conflicting evidence has been brought forward. In sifting it, it is helpful to fix the attention especially upon three points: To whom was the warning given, if given at all? Was it given on his own initiative and unofficially by Mr. Jovanovitch, the Serbian Minister in Vienna, or officially upon instructions from Belgrade? Did it contain any hint of a definite plot, or was it merely a vague general statement about the undesirability of the Archduke's visit to a troubled province?

The first important assertion that Serbia warned Austria came from the Serbian Minister to Russia, Mr. Spalaikovitch. In an interview in the St. Petersburg *Vechernee Vremia,* within a couple of days after the assassination, he declared the Serbian Government had given a warning in Vienna in regard to the Archduke's trip to Bosnia; it had learned that a plot was being planned by Bosnians who were embittered by the Austrian oppression and believed the Archduke was responsible for it; but in Vienna the warning was left unheeded.[59] But the truth of

[59] Summarized in the Vienna *Neue Freie Presse,* July 2, No. 17906, p. 4.

this assertion and others like it was officially denied at the Vienna Foreign Office on July 3.[60]

Here the matter rested for some months, being overshadowed by the Austrian ultimatum and the excitement of the War. It was revived again by the eminent French professor of Slavic history, E. Denis, who wrote: "Mr. Pashitch attempted in a discreet way to indicate to the Ballplatz the dangers which the Archduke was incurring; on June 21 the Serbian Minister [Jovan Jovanovitch] informed the Minister of Foreign Affairs that his Government had reason to believe that a plot was being prepared in Bosnia. The Chancellor [Berchtold] paid no attention to this communication." [61] Professor Denis's statement was generally accepted during the War by persons outside Germany and Austria, though it was emphatically contradicted by Berchtold when eventually brought to his notice.[62] It was later repeated, for instance, by Stano-

60 The London *Times*, July 1, p. 7, had already reported from its Vienna correspondent that he "understood on the best authority that there is no foundation for the reports that information of the existence of a plot against the Archduke was given to the Austro-Hungarian Government by the Serbian Minister in Vienna." Mr. Pashitch also, according to an interview published in the Budapest *Az Est* of July 7, and copied the same day in the *Neue Freie Presse*, No. 17811, p. 5, is reported as saying: "The statement is false that Serbia had knowledge beforehand of the preparation of the murder and that it therefore gave a warning." The Paris *Temps*, July 8, p. 8, printed a summary of the Pashitch interview of July 7 in the *Az Est;* but in the leading editorial of July 10 made the extraordinary statement: "M. Pashitch in an interview of day before yesterday showed in an irrefutable manner that the Serbian Government had given warning of the danger [*avait signalé le peril*], and that no notice had been taken of its warning [*avertissement*] by the Austro-Hungarian authorities."

61 E. Denis, *La Grande Serbie* (Paris, 1915), p. 277. As Denis wrote largely from Serbian sources he may have had his information from Pashitch or one of the Serbian ministers, or he may have merely copied the irresponsible *Temps* editorial quoted in the preceding footnote.

62 In a letter of May 9, 1917, to the Austrian historian, Leopold Mandl: "The fantastic statements of Professor E. Denis . . . are a pure invention from A to Z, both as to Jovanovitch's communication to me, as well as to my ignoring it. Whether an order of this kind was sent by Pashitch to Jovanovitch, but was ignored by the latter, I am of course

jevitch,[63] who even claimed that its truth could be proved by a certain bundle of documents in the Austrian Foreign Office marked "Reg. B. 28 VI, 1914"; but the archivists of the present Austrian Republic have searched the records, and state that no papers with any such marking are to be found; and Professor Stanojevitch has been unable or unwilling to tell what source of information led him to think there was such a record. These Austrian denials that Jovanovitch ever gave any warning of any kind to Berchtold or the Ministry of Foreign Affairs are unquestionably correct. If he gave a "warning," all the reliable evidence indicates that he communicated his fears, not in accordance with regular procedure to Berchtold or the Ministry of Foreign Affairs, but to Dr. von Bilinski, the Joint Finance Minister; to explain the curious reason for this irregular procedure we must digress for a moment.

Mr. Jovan Jovanovitch came to Vienna as Serbian Minister at the end of December, 1912, to take the place of Dr. Simitch. The latter was an elderly, experienced

unable to say;" Mandl, *Die Habsburger und die serbische Frage* (Vienna, 1918), p. 151 ff.; *cf.* also KSF, II, 29, 108 ff., Jan., Apr., 1924.

[63] Stanojevitch, *Die Ermordung des Erzherzogs,* p. 61: "Some days before the murder, the Serbian Minister in Vienna officially informed the Austro-Hungarian Government that the Serbian Government possessed indications that something was being prepared at Sarajevo against the Heir to the Throne."

On this whole controversy see KSF, II, 28-30, 108-111, 208-9, 231-8, 282-3, Jan.-July, 1924; III, 282-287, 293-299, 393-405, 437-444, May-July, 1925; and L. Mandl, in *La Fédération Balkanique,* pp. 272-3, May 31, 1925. By the Treaty of St. Germain (Art. 93) Serbia had the right to take all documents relating to the territories which she received from the former Austro-Hungarian Monarchy and she did actually take records going back as far as 1895. *Cf.* Ludwig Bittner, "Die zwischenstaatlichen Verhandlungen ueber das Schicksal der oesterreichischen Archive nach dem Zusammenbruch Oesterreich-Ungarns," in *Archiv f. Pol. u. Gesch.,* III, 58-96, Jan., 1925). If the Serbians found any such document as Stanojevitch claims, they would doubtless have taken a copy of it and could make it public. Moreover, they have their own Legation records and the correspondence of Pashitch and Jovanovitch; if these contain anything to their advantage in this question of an alleged warning, one would expect that they would have published it. But they have not done so.

diplomat of tact and dignity, who had had fair success in what was at best a very difficult office. Even in normal times the position of the Serbian representative in Vienna was no easy one after 1903, in view of the national antagonism between the peoples of the two countries and the constantly irritating questions of alleged spying, propaganda, oppression, and incitement to treason on both sides. At the moment when Jovanovitch arrived in 1912 the situation was particularly delicate and difficult on account of the exciting consequences of the First Balkan War and the Austrian efforts in the London Conference to deprive the Serbians of the fruits of their victories. Mr. Jovan Jovanovitch, in contrast to his predecessor, was a young man of hardly forty; even according to one of his best friends and colleagues, "with his unruly, bushy hair, dark eyes, and black moustachio across his face, the new arrival presented a less reassuring appearance than his venerable predecessor. In Vienna people made no bones of affirming that he had fomented trouble in 1908 against the annexation of Bosnia and Herzegovina, and even that he had commanded bands of *comitadjis.*" [64]

Upon his arrival in Vienna, therefore, Jovanovitch was not regarded altogether as a *persona grata.* In fact Austria is said to have delayed her assent when his name was first proposed, and afterwards have given hints that she would be glad to have him recalled—hints which Belgrade refused to take. His reception was far from cordial. When he was presented to Francis Joseph, the Emperor is said merely to have bowed to him, instead of extending him the handshake usual on such occasions. The Archdukes would not see him at all. Berchtold was chilly, and limited his relations to official business. Under these painful circumstances Jovanovitch appreciated all the more his cordial relations with Dr. von Bilinski. Bilinski, being recently appointed

64 Dumaine, *La Dernière Ambassade de France en Autriche,* p. 79 f.

Joint Finance Minister, had charge of the civil administration in Bosnia and Herzegovina, and as such had much in common to discuss with the Serbian Minister. Being a Slav himself (a Galician Pole), it was easier for him, than for an Austrian-German or a Magyar, to get on amicably with a Serb like Jovanovitch. In fact, in the interest of better relations between the two countries, it was soon agreed between the two, and approved by Francis Joseph and Berchtold, that Bilinski should handle diplomatic relations with the Serbian Minister, and then report upon them to Berchtold.[65] This was, of course, wholly anomalous and irregular. But further reasons for it, in addition to those just given, are doubtless to be found in Berchtold's natural indolence, and in Bilinski's ambition to gather as much power as possible into his own hands, and increase his own importance. It explains, however, why in June, 1914, Jovanovitch might prefer to choose Bilinski, rather than Berchtold or anyone in the Austrian Ministry of Foreign Affairs, as the person to whom to make his delicate suggestion that it might be dangerous for Archduke Franz Ferdinand to go to Bosnia.

In 1924, at the tenth anniversary of the Archduke's assassination, the controversy concerning Serbia's alleged "warning" to Austria was revived. A letter to a Vienna newspaper signed "X.Y.," but attributed to Mr. Josimovitch, secretary to the Serbian Legation in Vienna in 1914, declared: "On June 18, 1914, Mr. Jovanovitch received a cipher despatch from Pashitch directing him to dissuade the Archduke from his trip to Sarajevo, or at least to warn him of the dangers threatening him;" Jovanovitch then

65 Bilinski, I, 258 f.; Paul Flandrak, "Bilinski's Eingreifen in die Auswärtige Politik," in *Neues Wiener Journal,* No. 11289, April 26, 1925; Mandl, "Zur Warning Serbiens an Oesterreich" in KSF, II, 108-111, April, 1925; Ljuba Jovanovitch, "Sketches from the history of the relations between Vienna and Belgrade" in the Belgrade daily *Politika,* No. 6095 April 12, 1925, quoted *ibid.,* III, 281-287, May, 1925.

informed Bilinski of this "at noon on June 21." [66] At first sight this seems to confirm the allegations of Denis and Stanojevitch as to an official warning from the Belgrade Government. But this letter is of such doubtful authenticity that no reliance can be placed upon it.[67] It is also contradicted in several particulars by Mr. Jovanovitch himself, who a week later made to another Vienna newspaper the following interesting communication (slightly condensed):

> I am glad to give you an authentic account of the warning given to the Archduke which came from me and arose from my own initiative. I was at that time Minister Plenipotentiary and Envoy to Vienna. And I learned that the Heir to the Throne intended to be present at manœuvres in Bosnia. [After mentioning—incorrectly—some of the details of Franz Ferdinand's proposed visit to Bosnia, and asserting that it would be regarded as a "provocation" by Serbs, he continues:] After I had duly weighed all these circumstances, I resolved to visit Dr. von Bilinski, who was then Finance Minister and Minister for Bosnia. So far as I remember, my visit took place about June 5—thus 23 days before the assassination. I explained quite openly to the Minister what I had learned, namely, that the manœuvres were to be held in Bosnia on the Drin just opposite to Serbia, and that the Archduke himself would take command.[68] I said to Minister von Bilinski: "If this is true,

[66] *Wiener Sonn- and Montagszeitung,* No. 25, June 23, 1924; *cf.* KSF, II, 234, 282, June, 1924.

[67] Mr. Josimovitch is said to have denied that he wrote it (Seton-Watson, *Sarajevo,* p. 154). The statement that Jovanovitch informed Bilinski "at noon on June 21" is contradicted by the fact that Bilinski did not return to Vienna from a holiday at Lemberg until the *afternoon* of June 21 (*Neue Freie Presse,* No. 17896, June 22, p. 8). And a further assertion contained in the letter, that Bilinski then informed the Archduke's *Hofmeister,* Baron Rummerskirch, has been emphatically denied by the latter, KSF, II, 233, note 6).

[68] His information in 1914, or his remembrance of it in 1924, was not accurate: The maneuvers were not to be held "on the Drin just opposite Serbia," but the southwest of Sarajevo, in the Tarcin district toward

I can assure your Excellency that it will arouse the greatest discontent among the Serbs who must regard this as an act of provocation. Manœuvres under such circumstances are dangerous. Among the Serb youths there may be one who will put a ball-cartridge in his rifle or revolver in place of a blank-cartridge, and he may fire it, and the bullet might strike the man giving provocation. Therefore, it would be good and reasonable that the Archduke should not go to Sarajevo; that the manœuvres should not be held on Vidov Dan [St. Vitus's Day, June 28, a Serb holiday]; and they should not be held in Bosnia."

To these clear words Dr. von Bilinski replied that he took note of them, and would inform me what result they had with the Archduke, although he himself could not believe in any such result of the manœuvres as I foresaw: and that moreover, he was in possession of information that Bosnia was completely quiet. A few days later I again called on Minister von Bilinski about this matter. But nevertheless had shortly to learn that the original program would be followed and nothing changed in spite of my warning. The Archduke was certainly informed, but would heed none but himself.[69]

the Adriatic (about as far away as possible from the Drin and the Serbian frontier), as was clearly stated in the announcement in the *Neue Freie Presse,* No. 17878, June 4, 1914, p. 9. Nor was it true that "the Archduke himself would take command;" General Potiorek was in command, and the Archduke was merely an official onlooker.

69 *Neues Wiener Tageblatt,* No. 177, June 28, 1924.

In a private letter to Dr. Bogitchevitch, the Serbian Chargé d' Affaires at Berlin in 1914 but later a severe critic of Mr. Pashitch and Entente diplomacy, Mr. Jovan Jovanovitch had given a shorter account which says nothing about his having acted on his own initiative, and is less definite as to the date: "In the month of May, the end of May, 1914, I said to the Joint Finance Minister, von Bilinski, when I heard that the Archduke Franz Ferdinand was going to go to the Sarajevo manoeuvres in Bosnia on the very day of Vidov Dan, 14/15 [27/28] June, 1914, that it would be undesirable [nezgodno] that the Archduke should conduct manoeuvres there on Vidov Dan. This would mean a provocation to the Serbs, and something untoward [rgjavo] might happen, because at manoeuvres some real shots might often occur in shooting with blank cartridges;" Bogitchevitch, "Die Warnung vor dem Attentate in Sarajevo," in KSF, II, 235, July, 1924.

This account of Mr. Jovan Jovanovitch appears to be the closest approximation to the truth hitherto made from the Serbian side. It is in some respects confirmed, and in others contradicted, in a valuable statement by Mr. Paul Flandrak, who was Chief of the Press Section in Bilinski's Finance Ministry in 1914, and since the war the director of the Vienna *Depositenbank*. This evidently responsible and trustworthy man wrote recently:

"In May, 1914, when the first announcements about the Archduke Franz Ferdinand's trip to Dalmatia and Bosnia began to spread among the public, Jovanovitch appeared for the last time at the office of the Joint Finance Minister. Upon his arrival he began to speak at once about the proposed manœuvres and expressed the fear that the Serbian Government might regard them as a provocation. Furthermore he would like to bring to the serious consideration of the Joint Finance Minister whether the patriotic demonstrations inevitable at the appearance of the future ruler of the Monarchy would be likely to arouse bad feeling on both sides of the [Austro-Serbian] frontier. He begged Bilinski not to regard his remarks as an official communication. He was moved only by the desire to prevent everything which might possibly, even though only temporarily, disturb the negotiations which had begun for the improvement of the mutual relations [of Austria and Serbia].

Bilinski did not pay these declarations any sort of special attention, and I believe that he did not inform Count Berchtold of them at all, though otherwise he used to report on all his conversations with the Serbian Minister. . . . Though at the time of this conversation he did not yet know that out of the Archduke's military tour of inspection was to grow a political tour, yet he was convinced that the moment was at least premature for Franz Ferdinand's trip to the southern provinces; and he also frankly expressed to the Emperor his misgivings.

From this conversation of the Serbian Minister Jovanovitch, which Bilinski told me directly afterwards quite

> incidentally and to a certain extent as confirming his standpoint of the untimeliness of the Archduke's trip, there has developed in the course of years a cycle of legends; some have even gone so far as to construct out of Jovanovitch's remarks a warning of the murder or a hint at the possibility of it. Bilinski himself, who during his service as Finance Minister kept no notes, does not mention at all this last interview with the Serbian Minister in his memoirs written from memory—an evidence that he saw in it neither an open nor a hidden warning."[70]

It would be interesting to hear what the person who received the "Warning" has to say about it. But curiously enough, the late Dr. von Bilinski's two volumes of memoirs, though they deal fully with his public life otherwise, say nothing of this. From this fact some writers have drawn the conclusion that he never received any warning, as otherwise he would have surely mentioned it because of its crucial interest. But more probably he avoided recalling the painful fact that he did not dissuade the Archduke from his fatal trip, or that at least, as the Minister officially responsible for the administration of Bosnia, did not make sure that adequate arrangements were made for his protection and that Sarajevo was carefully combed for potential murderers. In view of the terrible consequences to Austria and the world, this neglect must have haunted him as the most dreadful nightmare of his life.[71] While the War was still raging, an Austrian historian applied to him for any light he could throw upon the alleged Serbian Warning

[70] P. Flandrak, "Bilinski's Eingreifen in die Auswärtige Politik," in *Neues Wiener Journal*, No. 11289, April 26, 1925.

[71] In the days following the assassination he tried to shove the blame upon General Potiorek, Governor of Bosnia, upon the military authorities, and even upon the Archduke himself for the irregular and headstrong way in which the trip had been planned. Margutti, *Vom Alten Kaiser*, pp. 45 ff., 397; Conrad, IV, 37, 41, 64-70, 82-85; Musulin, *Das Haus am Ballplatz*, p. 215; Seton-Watson, *Sarajevo*, pp. 106 ff., 154; and also the sentence from Bilinski's own memoirs to be quoted below.

concerning the Sarajevo plot. Bilinski's brief letter of reply is significant: he would gladly talk about every other aspect of this sad affair, except precisely this point, over which he "wished to draw the veil of oblivion." [72] In his memoirs he merely complains that he was not consulted about the arrangements because the Archduke had expressed the wish "that on this occasion the matter should be handled exclusively by the *Landeschef* [Gen. Potiorek, Governor of Bosnia and Herzegovina] as commanding general, without involving the Joint Finance Ministry in any arrangements. Against this I could raise no objections, because I did not interfere in regard to the organization of the province in affairs of military administration—with the exception of summoning recruits and paying the costs of this." [73] "The rumor that I warned the Emperor before the trip is not true, for I had no right to interfere in a purely military tour, and the extension of the trip into a political affair was permitted without my being asked or informed." He explained these facts, he says, in an audience with the Emperor two days after the assassination, and the Emperor exonerated him from all responsibility; except for this audience he "never talked about the Archduke's trip, never, either before, or after." [74]

From all this evidence, we may venture to draw the following conclusions:

1. On or about June 5 the Serbian Minister in Vienna, Mr. Jovan Jovanovitch, made a communication to Bilinski, the Austro-Hungarian Joint Finance Minister, but not to Berchtold or the Austrian Foreign Office as he should properly have done according to regular diplomatic procedure. His irregular diplomatic procedure on this occasion may

[72] L. Mandl, "Zur Warnung Serbiens an Oesterreich," in KSF, II, 108 ff., April, 1924; and "Ein düsterer Gedenktag," in the Vienna *Neues 8 Uhr Blatt,* No. 2907, June 28, 1924.

[73] Bilinski, I, 273.

[74] Bilinski, I, 277; *cf.,* however, Flandrak's statement to the contrary

have been unwise as matters turned out, but it was not unnatural, because it had been a practice for many months. Jovanovitch also doubtless realized that what he had to say was of a very delicate and difficult character, and that it would be far easier to say it to the cordial Bilinski than the chilly and suspicious Berchtold. He also did not want to give his communication a formal or official character; a communication to his friend Bilinski would seem less official than one to the Minister of Foreign Affairs. Bilinski, who was not especially alarmed about conditions in Bosnia, and was intending soon to make a trip there himself with his wife,[75] did not take Jovanovitch's communication very seriously and probably did not mention it either to the Emperor, to Franz Ferdinand, or to Berchtold.[76] The repeated denials of the Austrian Foreign Office officials of receiving any official warning from Serbia are therefore wholly correct.

2. It is possible that Jovanovitch, as he himself alleges, made his communication "on his own initiative." But it is to be observed that in his earlier letter to Dr. Bogitchevitch he says nothing of this. Moreover, it seems strange that he should take such an important step without authorization or instructions from the Serbian Minister of Foreign Affairs. If he really acted on his own initiative in suggesting that there was danger of the Archduke's being shot at the maneuvers through the disloyalty of his own troops—by the substitution of a ball-cartridge for a blank-cartridge—why did he wait until the beginning of June? As the trip had been announced in the papers in March—Jovanovitch himself says, "This was already fixed in March"—he would have known of it for some two months. He would have known as much concerning the general loyalty or

[75] Bilinski, I, 273.

[76] Possibly he may have communicated it to the local authorities in Sarajevo; *cf.* Mandl, in KSF, II, 109, April, 1924; and Seton-Watson, *Sarajevo,* p. 106.

disloyalty of the Bosnian troops earlier as later. One would have expected him to have pointed out this danger at a much earlier date, if he had been acting only on his own initiative.

Is it a mere coincidence that his "warning" was given very soon after Mr. Pashitch, "at the end of May or the beginning of June," told Ljuba Jovanovitch and others of his Cabinet that "there were people who were preparing to go to Sarajevo to kill Franz Ferdinand"? [77] May there not after all be some truth in Mr. Denis's statement that "Mr. Pashitch attempted in a discreet way" to indicate the danger the Archduke was incurring and therefore instructed his Minister at Vienna to take steps to avert the tragedy if possible. The venerable Serbian Prime Minister was a shrewd enough man to realize perfectly well the odium which would fall upon Serbia if any of the facts concerning the Dimitrijevitch and "Black Hand" complicity should leak out. Ljuba Jovanovitch's revelations are eloquent enough as to this "terrible" possibility. Serbia's record was already too spotted with blood to be able to stand the disgrace of another political murder of a prince of such rank. Serbia would be ostracized by Europe. Worse than that. Mr. Pashitch was well enough acquainted with Austro-Serbian tension in the past to realize that Austria would make very stiff demands on Serbia if the assassins should be successful, and perhaps even seize upon the crime as a pretext for war with her troublesome neighbor. But Mr. Pashitch did not want war at this time, and least of all a war occasioned by such an event. He knew that Serbia needed peace for many more months at least before the final life and death struggle with Austria, in order that his country might recover from the Balkan Wars and consolidate the new territories which she had just acquired. And he was doubtful whether Russia or France would sup-

[77] Ljuba Jovanovitch, *Krv Slovenstva,* p. 9.

port him in a conflict with Austria, if the truth should leak out that the murder had been hatched in the capital of Serbia with the aid of a high officer in the Serbian General Staff and other members of a secret Serbian society notorious for their political assassinations in the past. He was certainly in a very difficult and embarrassing position. He wanted to avert the murder because of its potential terrible consequences. But to have warned Austria of the facts, in the only way which would have been effective, would have been to reveal his own cognizance of a plot and to confess one more to the long list of assassinations plotted in Serbia against the Dual Monarchy. Under these circumstances may he not have sent the Serbian Minister in Vienna some hint which led the latter to express to Bilinski his doubts about the loyalty of Bosnian troops and the general undesirability of the Archduke's proposed trip? In such a case Jovanovitch would of course have sought to give the impression that he was speaking unofficially and merely on his own initiative. This is a very common practice in diplomacy. Innumerable examples of it may be seen in the recent publications from the German, Russian, and English archives. When one government desires to sound another, or to give a hint, on an especially delicate subject, it is a well-recognized ruse to instruct its ambassador to bring up the subject for discussion, but to preface it with the assurance that he is merely "expressing his own private personal opinion," or simply "acting on his own initiative."

The fact that Spalaikovitch in St. Petersburg could also issue so quickly after the assassination the statement that Belgrade had "warned" Vienna, suggests that Pashitch had hinted to him, as well as to Jovanovitch, something of the danger impending and the indirect step which had been taken to try to avert it. Furthermore, it was scarcely within the bounds of diplomatic etiquette and propriety for the Serbian Minister in Vienna to assume to interfere in such purely domestic affairs of another country as manoeuvres and journeyings of princes; it is therefore difficult to believe that Jovanovitch would have taken such an important step, infringing on diplomatic propriety, unless he had received some instructions from Belgrade. Until the Serbian authorities see fit to publish in full the correspondence exchanged between Pashitch and Jovanovitch in the weeks before the assassination, or at least the document in which Jovanovitch must have reported to Pashitch his interview with Bilinski, one may doubt whether he really acted "on his own initiative."

3. The "warning" was given in the most general terms; it contained no hint of the possibility of assassination by civilian conspirators or of any plot such as was actually on foot; of this there is complete agreement in all the accounts, otherwise so divergent. It referred only to the possible danger of disloyalty among the troops. It is therefore small wonder that Bilinski paid so little attention to it. Nor does it in any way relieve the Serbian Government of the guilt of withholding information concerning a plot to commit murder, connived at by its own officers—a crime known in private life as "compounding a felony."

CHAPTER IV

THE LEGEND OF THE "POTSDAM COUNCIL"

AFTER the publication of the *Kautsky Documents* and the report of the Reichstag Investigating Committee on the preliminaries of the War, it may seem superfluous again to refute the legend that, "This greatest of human tragedies was hatched by the Kaiser and his imperial crew at this Potsdam conference of July 5, 1914." [1] It may seem like "flogging a dead horse." But as it was cited by the Commission of the Peace Conference, presided over by Mr. Lansing as justification for Art. 231 of the Treaty; as it has been accepted by MM. Bourgeois and Pagès and appears to be endorsed by President Poincaré,[2] in spite of the full documents available to them when they wrote; and as the legend is still largely believed by those who have not kept abreast with recent investigations into the causes of the War, it is perhaps worth while to examine again this wide-spread legend, as a typical example of the way myths grow up and flourish during war-time hatred and propaganda.

The most interesting and picturesque account of the alleged "Crown Council" at Potsdam on July 5, as well as the one which had received widest currency, is that given by Mr. Morgenthau, in the volume just quoted, in a chapter entitled, "Wangenheim Tells the American Ambassador How the Kaiser Started the War:"

[1] Henry Morgenthau, *Ambassador Morgenthau's Story,* N. Y., 1918, p. 86. This book, which first appeared serially in *The World's Work,* beginning May, 1918, was also published in England under the title *Secrets of the Bosphorus,* and widely circulated in French and other translations.

[2] *Les Origines et Les Responsabilités de La Grande Guerre,* Paris, 1921, p. 76; Poincaré, IV, 196-199.

I shall always keep in my mind the figure of this German diplomat, in those exciting days before the Marne. . . . The good fortune of the German armies so excited him that he was sometimes led into indiscretions, and his exuberance one day caused him to tell me certain facts which, I think, will always have great historical value. . . .

The Kaiser, he told me, had summoned him to Berlin for an imperial conference. This meeting took place at Potsdam on July 5th. The Kaiser presided and nearly all the important ambassadors attended. Wangenheim himself was summoned to give assurance about Turkey and enlighten his associates generally on the situation in Constantinople, which was then regarded as almost the pivotal point in the impending war. In telling me who attended this conference Wangenheim used no names, though he specifically said that among them were—the facts are so important that I quote his exact words in the German which he used—*"die Häupter des Generalstabs und der Marine"*—(the heads of the general staff and of the navy) by which I have assumed that he meant Von Moltke and Von Tirpitz. The great bankers, railroad directors, and the captains of German industry, all of whom were as necessary to German war preparations as the army itself, also attended.

Wangenheim now told me that the Kaiser solemnly put the question to each man in turn: "Are you ready for war?" All replied "yes" except the financiers. They said that they must have two weeks to sell their foreign securities and to make loans. At that time few people had looked upon the Sarajevo tragedy as something that would inevitably lead to war. This conference, Wangenheim told me, took all precautions that no such suspicion should be aroused. It decided to give the bankers time to readjust their finances for the coming war, and then the several members went quietly back to their work or started on vacations. The Kaiser went to Norway on his yacht, Von Bethmann-Hollweg left for a rest, and Wangenheim returned to Constantinople.

In telling me about this conference Wangenheim, of

course, admitted that Germany had precipitated the war. I think that he was rather proud of the whole performance, proud that Germany had gone about the matter in so methodical and far-seeing a way, and especially proud that he himself had been invited to participate in so epoch making a gathering. I have often wondered why he revealed to me so momentous a secret, and I think that perhaps the real reason was his excessive vanity—his desire to show me how close he stood to the inner counsels of his emperor and the part that he had played in bringing on this conflict. Whatever the motive, this indiscretion certainly had the effect of showing me who were really the guilty parties in this monstrous crime. The several blue, red, and yellow books which flooded Europe during the few months following the outbreak, and the hundreds of documents which were issued by German propagandists attempting to establish Germany's innocence, have never made the slightest impression on me. For my conclusions as to the responsibility are not based on suspicions or belief or the study of circumstantial data. I do not have to reason or argue about the matter. I know. The conspiracy that has caused this greatest of human tragedies was hatched by the Kaiser and his imperial crew at this Potsdam conference of July 5, 1914. One of the chief participants, flushed with his triumph at the apparent success of the plot, told me the details with his own mouth. Whenever I hear people arguing about the responsibility for this war or read the clumsy and lying excuses put forth by Germany, I simply recall the burly figure of Wangenheim as he appeared that August afternoon, puffing away at a huge black cigar, and giving me his account of this historic meeting. Why waste any time discussing the matter after that?

Why discuss the matter any further? Because the contemporary documents now available prove conclusively that there is hardly a word of truth in this whole narrative, either as to (1) the persons present, (2) the Kaiser's attitude toward delay, (3) the real reason for delay, or, finally. (4) the alleged selling of securities in anticipation of war.

THE PERSONS ALLEGED TO BE PRESENT

Let us examine the narrative, taking the statements one by one.

"Nearly all the important ambassadors attended." The most important ambassadors would be those stationed at London (Lichnowsky), Vienna (Tschirschky), Paris (Schoen), and St. Petersburg (Pourtalès).

Lichnowsky at London was not at this Potsdam Council, because he himself says in his pamphlet that he learned of it "subsequently."[3]

It is also equally certain that Tschirschky at Vienna was not present, for otherwise Bethmann would not have telegraphed him as he did on July 6, giving an account of an important interview at Potsdam on July 5 between Emperor William and the Austrian Ambassador, Szögyény.[4] This interview and its significance will be described in detail later. Nor is there the slightest indication that Schoen and Pourtalès came from Paris or St. Petersburg.

Perhaps, however, the "important ambassador" whom Wangenheim referred to was no other than Wangenheim himself. Now it is true that Baron Wangenheim left Constantinople on July 2, arrived in Berlin on July 4 at 4:25 P. M., and was back again at Constantinople on July 15. But it is not true that "the Kaiser summoned him for an imperial conference." On the contrary, he did not see the Kaiser at all, but only reported to the Foreign Office. In fact, he was much irritated that in these uneasy days the Kaiser had not thought it worth while to arrange for an

3 *My London Mission,* p. 323.

4 K.D., 15.

interview with such an important person as his Ambassador to Turkey during the latter's visit to Berlin.[5]

"The heads of the General Staff and of the Navy." General von Moltke, the Chief of Staff, certainly was not at Potsdam on July 5. On April 15, 1914, Moltke went to Karlsbad for the "cure" which he had been in the habit for some years of taking there with members of his family.[6] Here he was visited on May 12 by the Austrian Chief of Staff, Baron Conrad, who came in civilian clothes, and talked with Moltke two or three hours on the general political situation. Conrad pointed out the unreliability of Rumania, the possible ways of employing Italian troops north of the Alps, and the desirability of Moltke's adopting a strategic plan which would send more German troops against Russia in case of war, and so relieve Russian pressure on the Austrians in Galicia. Neither General had any expectation of an immediate war. The whole conversation was merely a general one as to political conditions and military coöperation between the Central Powers, such as was natural between the Chiefs of Staff of two allied Powers,—such as the two men had carried on before, and such as the French and Russian Staff Officers had been carrying on for years. When Conrad left Moltke, to take the midnight train back to Vienna, it was understood that Conrad should attend the ordinary German manoeuvres later in the year.[7] Neither of the Generals had

[5] Private letter from Baroness von Wangenheim in the author's possession.

[6] Photographs of the police registration records at Karlsbad, which the writer has secured, show that Moltke was at Karlsbad in 1911, April 8-May 12; in 1912, April 15-May 8; in 1913, April 13-May 9; and in 1914, April 15-May 14; and again June 28-July 25; the latter record reads: "Angemeldet Stadtrath Karlsbad. 28 Juni 1914. No. 23673. Name: *Excellenz Helmuth v. Moltke*. Beruf: *Offizier*. Wohnsitz: Berlin. Angekommen in Karlsbad am 28, 6, 1914, und wohnt *Haus Bremen*, Abgereist 25. 7 nach *Berlin*."

[7] For a detailed summary of this interview see Conrad, *Aus Meiner Dienstzeit*, III, 667-674, 701.

the slightest idea that they were never to see each other again.[8]

On May 14 Moltke left Karlsbad to accompany one of the routine General Staff observation trips in the Vosges Mountains. At the close of this he had a talk with Eckardstein in Baden-Baden on June 1.[9] He was not a well man at this time—he died a few months later after his failure at the Battle of the Marne—and upon the advice of his physician, returned again to Karlsbad on Sunday, June 28, before he heard the news of Franz Ferdinand's assassination which occurred on the same day. He stayed in Karlsbad, as he had planned to do, until July 25, arriving in Berlin again July 26.[10] The evidence from the Karlsbad police register indicates that Moltke, even after the Sarajevo murder, was pursuing his normal routine life, and was living quietly at Karlsbad on July 5, instead of plotting war in a Council at Potsdam. A further proof that Moltke was not at Potsdam on July 5 is the interesting letter which Falkenhayn, the Prussian Minister of War, sent to him on July 5 at Karlsbad, giving him an account of the interview between the Austrian Ambassador and Emperor William on that day at Potsdam.[11]

Perhaps the author of the legend had in mind not Moltke, but the Acting Chief of Staff, Count Waldersee. But neither was he at Potsdam on July 5. Because of a death in his family he had gone to Hanover on July 4, leaving word to call him on the telephone if anything of importance arose. If there had really been an important Conference, such as the Potsdam Council myth describes, Waldersee would certainly have returned to Potsdam for it; but he did not come back from the funeral until July 7.

8 Private letter of Conrad's in author's possession.

9 Eckardstein, *Lebenserinnerungen,* III, 184-187.

10 Confirmed by K.D., 74, 197; by Moltke's letters to his wife in his *Erinnerungen,* p. 381; and by Tirpitz, *Erinnerungen,* p. 227.

11 Published by Montgelas, *Leitfaden zur Kriegsschuldfrage,* p. 196.

He learned from a subordinate, General Bertrab, of the interview between the Austrian Ambassador and Emperor William which had taken place on July 5 in his absence; but he considered it of so little importance that he again left Berlin on a short furlough which had been previously arranged. If any military plans were to have been made, or if war had been "plotted" and was thought to be impending, he certainly would not have left his post.[12]

The head of the Navy, Admiral von Tirpitz, was likewise absent from Berlin. He was enjoying a vacation at Tarasp in Switzerland from July 2 to July 27, and could not, therefore, have been at the famous council as the legend represents.[13]

What of the other notables, vaguely referred to by Wangenheim, "who were as necessary to German war preparation as the army itself"? Krupp v. Bohlen-Halbach, the head of the great Krupp munition works, was not at Potsdam on July 5, but saw the Kaiser at Kiel on the latter's way to his Northern cruise. There at Kiel he learned of the Kaiser's interview with the Austrian Ambassador on July 5, but did not believe that, because of it, his firm need make any special preparations.[14] One of Krupp's directors, who has been much quoted, Dr. Mühlon, himself admits that he heard nothing of the Austrian communication until the "middle of July" in a conversation with Dr. Helfferich, the Director of the Deutsche Bank. And in 1919 when invited to tell what he knew of the alleged meeting at Potsdam and of the consequent military preparations, Mühlon stated that he had nothing to say which would throw any more light on the matter.[15] Dr. Helfferich has vigorously denied that any war council took place at Potsdam, or that he received any official hint before the Aus-

[12] *Investigating Commission,* I, 63-64.

[13] Tirpitz, *Erinnerungen,* pp. 204 ff., 208 ff.; *Investigating Commission,* I, 60, 67, 72.

[14] *Investigating Commission,* I, 87. [15] *Ibid.*

trian ultimatum was delivered to Serbia that he ought to take any financial or economic measures preparatory to war. He suggests that the whole rumor may have started with a waiter in a Berlin hotel who overheard some mention of the interview between the Kaiser and the Austrian Ambassador.[16]

Herr Ballin, the head of the Hamburg-American Line, who had been absent from Berlin the early part of July at a health resort, was asked on July 15 if he would go to England and try to find out from Haldane what truth there was in the rumor as to an Anglo-Russian naval agreement. Neither he nor the director of the North German Lloyd could have been present at the "Potsdam Council," because they do not appear to have had any information until July 20 that there was a possible danger of warlike complications.[17] Von Jagow, the Secretary of State, did not return from his honeymoon in Switzerland until July 6.[18]

As a result of this evidence it appears that the very persons who would have been most likely to have been present at any such council, had it really taken place, can be proved to have been elsewhere on July 5, and to have taken no measures toward "plotting war." Finally, it is worth noting that neither Sir Horace Rumbold, who was in charge of the British Embassy in Berlin during the early days of July, nor any of his diplomatic colleagues, had at the time any inkling of such a conference as the Wangenheim story represents. If it had really taken place it is almost certain that they would have heard some rumor of

16 *Ibid.*, p. 88. Helfferich, *Vorgeschichte,* I, 175-186.

17 K.D., 56, 80, 90.

18 Jagow, *Ursachen und Ausbruch des Weltkrieges,* p. 97. The first document from his hand is of July 8; K.D., 18, note 2. Lichnowsky says (*My London Mission,* p. 323 f.) that soon after "the decisive conference at Potsdam on July 5 . . . von Jagow was in Vienna to talk over everything with Count Berchtold." There is not a shadow of evidence for this statement. In the hundreds of telegrams from the Berlin and Vienna archives now published, there is not the slightest hint of such a visit.

it within a few days or weeks. Later, in 1917, when the legend spread, Sir Horace was rightly inclined to believe that the newspapers had found a mare's nest.[19]

THE KAISER'S ATTITUDE TOWARD DELAY

Baron Wangenheim, according to the story above, represents the Kaiser and the Council as deciding to delay action for two weeks in order to give the bankers time to sell their foreign securities. This is the opposite of the truth. There is much contemporary evidence in the *Kautsky Documents* that the Kaiser wished that, whatever action Austria took against Serbia, *she should not delay.* She should take it as quickly as possible, while the sentiment of Europe, shocked by the horrible crime at Sarajevo, was still in sympathy with the Hapsburgs and indignant at regicide Serbs. When he read that the German Ambassador at Vienna, two days after Sarajevo, had "used every opportunity to warn [Austria] calmly but very energetically and earnestly against overhasty steps," the Kaiser made the marginal note: "Now or never! Who authorized him to do this? It is very stupid! It's none of his business, for it is purely Austria's affair to consider what to do in this matter, for it will be said afterwards, if things go wrong, that Germany was not willing!! Tschirschky will please drop this nonsense! Matters must be cleared up with the Serbs, *and that soon.* That's all self-evident and the plain truth." [20] The Austrian Ambassador at Berlin similarly reported that the Kaiser said to him that "he would be sorry if we left unused the present moment which was so favorable to us." [21] When Tschirschky reported on July 14 that Berchtold himself was at last convinced that the "speediest action was desirable," the Kaiser underlined the words twice; and when he heard that the ultimatum was

[19] Oman, *The Outbreak of the War of 1914-1918,* p. 16 ff.

[20] K.D., 7.

[21] Szögyény to Berchtold, July 5; A.R.B., I, 6.

to be delayed for more than two weeks, until after President Poincaré had left St. Petersburg, he noted, "A pity."[22] No, instead of urging delay, according to the Wangenheim story, the Kaiser, with his natural impetuosity, wanted Austria's action, whatever it might be, to be taken as quickly as possible.

THE REAL REASONS FOR DELAY

Equally without foundation is Wangenheim's alleged reason for the two weeks' delay in sending the ultimatum: "The financiers said they must have two weeks to sell their foreign securities and to make loans." The real reasons for the delay came wholly from Vienna and not at all from Berlin. They were mainly two, and are repeatedly referred to in the German and Austrian documents which were published in 1919. The first was that Berchtold, the Austro-Hungarian Minister of Foreign Affairs, could not act against Serbia until he had secured the consent of Tisza, the Premier of Hungary. It took two weeks to win Tisza over from his original opposition to violent action against Serbia. The second, and by far the more important, reason for the final delay, was the fact that Berchtold did not want to present the ultimatum to Serbia until it was certain that President Poincaré and the French Premier, Viviani, had left St. Petersburg and were inaccessible upon the high seas returning to France. For otherwise Russia, under the influence of the "champagne mood" of the Franco-Russian toasts and the chauvinism of Poincaré, Izvolski, the Grand Duke Nicholas and the others gathered at St. Petersburg, would be much more likely to give Serbia military support, and thereby thwart Austria's plans for "localizing" the conflict with Serbia.[23]

[22] K.D., 40, 50.

[23] For delay on account of Tisza, *cf.* A.R.B., I, 2, 8, 9, 10, 19, 26; K.D., 18, 19, 29, 40, 49, 50; and on account of Poincaré's presence in

THE ALLEGED SELLING OF SECURITIES IN ANTICIPATION OF WAR

Following upon the narrative as quoted from the lips of Baron Wangenheim, there appears in Mr. Morgenthau's volume a paragraph, which does not increase one's confidence in his account of "how the Kaiser started the War." As if to confirm the truth of Wangenheim's story this paragraph asserts:

> This imperial conference took place on July 5th, and the Serbian Ultimatum was sent on July 22nd [*sic*]. This is just about the two weeks' interval which the financiers had demanded to complete their plans. All the great stock exchanges show that the German bankers profitably used this interval. Their records disclose that stocks were being sold in large quantities and that prices declined rapidly. At that time the markets were somewhat puzzled at this movement, but Wangenheim's explanation clears up any doubts which may still remain. Germany was changing her securities into cash for war purposes. If anyone wishes to verify Wangenheim, I should suggest that he examine the quotations of the New York Stock Market for these historic weeks. He will find that there were astonishing slumps in prices, especially in the stocks that had an international market. Between July 5th and July 22nd Union Pacific dropped from 155½ to 127½, Baltimore and Ohio from 91½ to 81, United States Steel from 61 to 50½, Canadian Pacific from 194 to 185½, and Northern Pacific from 111⅜ to 108. . . . How little the Wall Street brokers and financial experts realized that an imperial conference which had been held in Potsdam and presided over by the

Russia A.R.B., I, 19, 21, 26, 39, 57, 62; K.D., 50, 65, 93, 96, 108, 112, 127. Two further but minor reasons for the two weeks' delay were Berchtold's desire to wait till the harvest had been gathered and to await the results of the judicial investigation at Sarajevo which was expected to afford grounds of accusation against Serbia; *cf.* Conrad IV, 72; and Dirr, p. 129.

Kaiser, was the real force which was then depressing the market.[24]

Now if one follows Mr. Morgenthau's suggestion and examines the quotations of the New York Stock Market for these weeks, and reads the accompanying articles in the New York *Times,* one does not find very much evidence, either in the price of stocks or the volume of sales, that large blocks of German holdings were being secretly unloaded and thereby depressing the New York market during these two weeks. The stocks that he mentions declined only slightly or not at all; such declines as did take place were only such as were to be naturally expected from the general trend downward which had been taking place since January, or are quite satisfactorily explained by local American "bearish" influences, like the publication of a very depressing report by the Interstate Commerce Commission. Here are the facts. The "astonishing slump" in Union Pacific from 155½ to 127½, alleged by Mr. Morgenthau, represented in fact *an actual rise* of a couple of points in the value of this stock. Union Pacific sold "ex-dividend" and "ex-rights" on July 20; the dividend and accompanying "rights" were worth 30⅝, which meant that shares ought to have sold on July 22 around 125. In reality they sold at 127½; that is, at the end of the two weeks' period, during which it is asserted that there was depressing "inside selling" from Berlin, Union Pacific, instead of being depressed, was actually selling two points higher.[25]

Baltimore and Ohio, Canadian Pacific, and Northern

[24] *Ambassador Morgenthau's Story,* p. 86 f.

[25] *Cf.* article "Taking off U. P. Dividend" in New York *Times* July 18: 8:3: "It will be some time before experienced traders become accustomed to Union Pacific stock as an 8% issue. Disregarding other factors over Sunday which may affect all stocks, Union Pacific should open Monday morning [July 20] ex-dividend around 125¾. The shares closed yesterday at 156⅜, and the value of the warrants, 30⅝, will be deducted after today's trading."

acific did in fact slump on July 14, and there was evidence of selling orders from Europe. But this is to be explained partly by the fact that Baltimore and Ohio had been already falling steadily since January, and partly to the very depressing influence exercised on all railroad shares by the sharply adverse report on the New York, New Haven, and Hartford Railroad which was made by the Interstate Commerce Commission. The comment of the New York *Times* of July 15 is significant: "Stocks which had lately displayed a stable character in the face of great weakness of particular issues, could not stand up under such selling as occurred in New Haven and some others today. There were times when it looked as though the entire market was in a fair way to slump heavily, and only brisk short covering toward the close prevented many sharp net declines. . . . For its own account, or on orders from this side, Europe was an unusually large seller of stocks in this market. The cable told that a very unfavorable impression had been created abroad by the Commerce Commission's New Haven report. The European attitude toward American securities is naturally affected by such official denunciations of the way in which an important railway property had been handled." [26]

Most extraordinary is the striking assertion concerning United States Steel Common. It states that between July 5 and 22 it fell from 61 to 50½. The real fact, as any one may verify from the Stock Market reports for himself, is that Steel during these two weeks never fell below 59⅝, and on July 22 was almost exactly the same as two weeks earlier.[27]

When the facts are examined, therefore, it does not appear that the New York Stock Market affords any confirmation of the widespread story of German bankers

[26] New York *Times,* July 15: p. 12, cols. 2, 3.

[27] July 5th, the date given by Mr. Morgenthau, was Sunday; the true quotation for Steel Common on Monday, July 6, was 61⅞; on July 22, 61⅜.

demanding a two weeks' respite in which to turn American securities into gold in preparation for a war already decided upon. A real and violent decline on the New York Market did begin, of course, *after July 23,* when universal alarm was caused by the publication and character of the Austrian ultimatum to Serbia.[28] Within a week it approached panic conditions and the Governors of the Stock Exchange, following the example already taken by all the European stock exchanges, decided to close the doors to all further trading until conditions again became more normal.

In this connection there is another bit of interesting evidence. Sir William Plender, Comptroller of "Enemy Banks, London Agencies" during the War, made a report to the Chancellor of the Exchequer on December 16, 1916, which was presented to the House of Commons. Among other things, he had been directed by the British Government to ascertain whether the London branches of German banks had executed any unusual sales of securities for foreign account during the weeks immediately preceding the outbreak of War; and also whether there had been any unusual shipments of gold or silver. He reported that, after a very thorough examination of the books of these German banks, he "did not find any unusual transactions nor anything to suggest that the banks shipped securities or bullion from London" during the weeks just before the War. On the contrary, the Deutsche Bank alone held assets of nearly $50,000,000 in London when War broke out, which it might have easily transferred by cable to Holland or Germany, if it had any anticipation of the war which the Kaiser is supposed to have plotted at the "Potsdam Council."

28 It is also true that the Vienna and Budapest markets, if not that at New York, had begun to show a disquieting decline before July 23, due, no doubt, to an inkling of the action which Berchtold was about to take.

CONCLUSIONS

It is clear that the "Potsdam Council" was a myth. It is an interesting example of the way a legend will grow up, flourish, and receive the widest currency in an atmosphere of war propaganda and readiness to believe anything about an enemy. There remain, however, several interesting questions. How did the legend first start? How did it reach the complete form in which it was cited by Mr. Lansing and his associates at the Paris Peace Conference as proof of Germany's guilt?

As will be indicated in the next chapter, the Kaiser had interviews separately with the Austrian Ambassador and various German officials on July 5 at Potsdam. It is quite possible, as Dr. Helfferich suggests, that the legend started with a waiter in a Berlin hotel who overheard mention of these conversations, and exaggerated them as he passed them on. In September, 1914, there appeared in a Dutch newspaper, the *Nieuwe Rotterdamsche Courant,* the tale of a meeting at Potsdam on July 5, attended by the leading German and Austrian officials, including even Berchtold, Tisza, Conrad and the Archduke Frederick, at which the outline of the fatal ultimatum was drawn up. The tale passed almost unnoticed at the time, owing to the fact that the Battle of the Marne was then engrossing the attention of the world. It was forgotten until revived again in 1917 and given great publicity by Socialists in Germany, by the allusion to it made by Prince Lichnowsky, and by the general discussion it attracted in the European Press. It was shortly after this that Mr. Morgenthau's books was written, and then cited in 1919 at the Peace Conference in assigning responsibility for the War.

Is it not extraordinary that Baron Wangenheim should have given to Mr. Morgenthau so many picturesque details which are in flat contradiction with the facts? How could he have dared to make such an important revelation so prejudicial to the interests of his Government? Germany at this time, in the early weeks of the War, was trying hard to win the good-will of the United States and make the world believe that she was fighting for self-defense in a war forced upon her. A statement such as Wangenheim's would have done Germany infinite damage.

And is it not difficult to understand why the American Ambassador did not report to Washington what was perhaps the most important thing he ever heard at Constantinople? Yet a careful search through the files of the State Department at Washington shows that there is no despatch or telegram recounting this interesting conversation with Baron Wangenheim; nor does Mr. Morgenthau in his book say anything about having made a report on the subject to Washington.

CHAPTER V

THE PREPARATION OF THE AUSTRIAN ULTIMATUM

The assassination of Franz Ferdinand and his wife shook Berchtold out of his undecided hesitating attitude of the past. It determined him to use the crime as a good excuse for clearing up the unsatisfactory situation with Serbia and for putting an end once and for all to danger to the Dual Monarchy from the Greater Serbia propaganda and the Russian intrigues against Austrian influence in the Balkans. For months and years past there had been a growing conviction among certain groups at Vienna that the political situation was becoming dangerous and intolerable for Austria in the Balkans. Serbia, as a result of the Balkan Wars, had grown greatly in territory, population, and pretensions. The Greater Serbia movement was gathering strength and received support from the growing nationalist movement among all the South Slavs living under Hapsburg rule. In the spring of 1914 there were rumors that Serbia and Montenegro were to be fused together. This would give Serbia an outlet on the Adriatic and threaten the existence of the struggling infant Albanian State, and so endanger the arrangements by which Austria had sought to protect herself against the Slav danger on her southern borders. Rumania could no longer be counted upon as a reliable ally, and the Rumanian irredentist agitation in Hungary was as violent as ever. It was suspected that a Serbo-Rumanian-Greek Balkan League was being secretly encouraged by Russia, and was only waiting for the favorable opportunity afforded by the death of the aged Francis Joseph or by a European War to disrupt Austria by liberating her oppressed nationalities, while Russia possessed herself of the long-sought control of the Straits and a free outlet to the Mediterranean. Russian armaments, military railway construction, and trial mobilizations were proceeding apace. France was loaning Russia millions of francs for these purposes, while at the same time increasing her own military establishment. Albania, Austria's pet creation to check Serbia, was in the throes of disorder and revolt against the weak prince who had finally been selected as its ruler. Prince William of Wied's flight had led to the sarcastic pun, "Les caisses sont vides; le trône est Wied; tout est vide."[1] The ever-latent irritation between Italy and Austria, arising from Italian irredentist aspirations for Trieste and the Trentino and from Austro-Italian jealousy and rivalry in the Balkans, had again become recently acute because of an Austrian decree excluding persons of Italian birth from holding municipal office at Trieste. Even Germany was felt to betray an irritating disregard for her Austrian ally's Balkan interests and dangers; the best way to make Germany respect Austria as a worthy ally— as *bündnisfähig*—would be to adopt a more vigorous policy, show that she was capable of decisive action, and prove that she was really an asset and not a liability in the Triple Alliance.

Thus, even before Sarajevo, there was a general feeling on the part of many officials at Vienna that something must be done to prevent the decaying Hapsburg structure from crumbling to pieces, either from its own internal weaknesses and hesitating indecisions, or from being violently thrown down before long by its enemies. The news of the Archduke's assassination enormously strengthened this feeling. If Austria accepted this blow to her dynasty without actively resenting it and taking vigorous measures to put

[1] Dirr, p. 13; K.D., IV, p. 130.

an end to the Greater Serbian danger once and for all, her prestige in the Balkans and in Europe would be gone forever. The currently expressed Serb opinions that she was "worm-eaten," would soon be dismembered like Turkey, and find a place only in a "historical museum," would gain strength. Her enemies would be all the more ready to disregard her interests or even fall upon her. She must therefore show that she had vitality to restore her prestige and build new buttresses. It was better to do this instantly, for the situation would only grow worse with the future, as Russian armaments reached completion and nationalist ambitions grew stronger. Austria's existence as a Great Power was at stake. As Conrad, the Chief of Staff and head of the militarist party at Vienna, has put it:

> Two alternatives stood sharply out against one another: either the preservation of Austria-Hungary as a conglomerate of various nationalities which should stand together as a whole toward the outside and find their common well-being under a single ruler; or the rise of separate independent national states which would seize upon the Austro-Hungarian territories inhabited by their co-nationals and so bring about the destruction of the Monarchy.
>
> The conflict between these two alternatives, long foreseen, had reached an acute stage through Serbia's procedure; its decision could not longer be postponed.
>
> For this reason, and not as vengeance for the assassination, Austria-Hungary must draw the sword against Serbia. . . .
>
> Austria-Hungary could no longer remain coolly indifferent, suffer this provocation quietly, and observe the Christian humility which demands that, after a blow, one shall turn the other cheek also. It was not a question of a knightly duel with "poor little" Serbia, as she liked to call herself, nor of punishment for the assassination. It was much more *the highly practical importance of the prestige of a Great Power,* and indeed of a Great Power

> which, by its continual yielding and patience (herein lay its fault), had given an impression of impotence and made its internal and external enemies continually more aggressive, so that these enemies were working with increasingly aggressive means for the destruction of the old Empire.
>
> A new yielding, especially now after Serbia's act of violence, would have unloosed all those tendencies within the Empire which were already gnawing at the old structure anyway, in the shape of South Slav, Czech, Russophil, and Rumanian propaganda, and Italian irredentism. . . .
>
> The Sarajevo assassination had torn down the house of cards erected by diplomacy in which Austria-Hungary had thought herself safe. The Monarchy had been seized by the throat, and had to choose between allowing itself to be strangled, and making a last effort to prevent its destruction.[2]

So Conrad, convinced that Austria must make war on Serbia as an act of self-preservation, urged Berchtold to approve immediate mobilization against Serbia. But Berchtold replied that there were difficulties: public opinion must be prepared; the grounds for war must first be established as a result of the investigation at Sarajevo; Francis Joseph was opposed to any immediate action; and Count Stephan Tisza, Minister-President of Hungary, was opposed to any war at all against Serbia, fearing that Russia would attack Austria and that Germany and Rumania would leave her in the lurch. Conrad was forced to admit that it was unsafe to make war on Serbia until they had made sure that Germany would protect Austria's rear from a Russian attack.[3] Berchtold had, however, like Conrad, become convinced of the necessity of a local war against Serbia. During the following days he proceeded to scheme to secure Germany's support, to build up a case against Serbia, and to overcome the two chief domestic obstacles to an imme-

2 Conrad, IV, 31 f.; *cf.* Berchtold, in *Current History,* July, 1928, p. 626 f.

3 Conrad, IV, 33 f.; interviews of June 29 and July 1.

diate local war against Serbia—the hesitation of Francis Joseph and the opposition of Count Tisza.

EMPEROR FRANCIS JOSEPH

Emperor Francis Joseph at the time of the Sarajevo assassination had hardly recovered from the illness of the preceding winter, which many observers had thought might prove fatal to the aged monarch. All the wars which he had waged in the past had resulted in defeat, or loss of territory, or generally both. He was not enthusiastic for Conrad as Chief of Staff, nor optimistic about the changes which had been made in the Austrian army. There is little doubt that he wanted to end his days in peace. But now, with the news of Hartwig's Pan-Slav intrigues at Belgrade, the Greater Serbia propaganda, and this final tragedy to his family, he had begun to fear that the Serbian situation might at last become intolerable. "I see a very dark future," he said to the German Ambassador on July 2; "what is particularly disquieting to me is the Russian practice mobilization which is planned for the fall, just at the time when we are shifting our recruit contingents. Hartwig is master at Belgrade, and Pashitch does nothing without consulting him." "Every one is dying around me," he added mournfully, referring to the sudden death of the Italian Chief of Staff, General Pollio, who was one of the few loyal adherents of the Triple Alliance in Italy. But though very sad and pessimistic, Francis Joseph evidently had no immediate expectation of even a local war with Serbia, for he spoke of his plans for the summer and the prospects for the stag-hunts.[4]

Three days later, on July 5, when Conrad urged mobilization measures, Francis Joseph refused to approve them. "No, that is impossible," he said, pointing out the danger of an attack from Russia and the doubtfulness of German

[4] Tschirschky to Bethmann, July 2; K.D., 9, 11.

support; before the Konopischt meeting he had asked Franz Ferdinand to get from Emperor William an unconditional declaration that Austria could count on Germany, but William II had avoided committing himself.[5] On July 7 the sad old man returned to his summer rest and repose at Ischl, having been unwilling to make any decision which might involve war. Some of the most important documents which Berchtold laid before him during the following days are pencilled in trembling hand with his signature as having been read, but they no longer bear the searching annotations of his earlier and more vigorous years. It is quite possible that the aged sovereign did not fully grasp the consequences of the policies which Berchtold was now pursuing.[6] We have no satisfactory accounts of the interviews which took place between him and his Minister of Foreign Affairs, but Berchtold seems not to have met with great difficulty in persuading his sovereign to approve the measures placed before him. Tisza, however, was a more difficult person.

TISZA'S PEACE PROGRAM

Count Stephan Tisza,[7] the famous son of a famous father, was perhaps the ablest and most striking political figure at this time in the whole Dual Monarchy. With close-cropped hair, square dark face, and flowing Hungarian cloak, he was like a little giant among the Magyar nobles, when he led the majority party as his father had done before him. He saw clearly the dangers ahead on all sides, and had the ability to reason coolly concerning them. He knew

[5] Conrad, IV, 36 f.

[6] Wilhelm Fraknói, *Die ungarische Regierung und die Entstehung des Weltkrieges* (Vienna, 1919), p. 34; Gooss, p. 40; Margutti, p. 391 ff.

[7] Tisza's own lips were sealed with blood when he was murdered on the threshold of his own hall at the very end of the War. It was the general impression that he was one of those primarily responsible for its origin. For the meager references in his papers to the July Crisis of 1914 and for articles in defense of his memory, see below at notes 77, 78.

exactly what he wanted, and having become Hungarian Minister-President in June, 1913, he was in an official position to compel attention to his views. He had already worked out, in the spring of 1914, as will be explained in detail, a diplomatic *"politique de longue main,"* which was to win Bulgaria to the side of Germany and Austria and secure peace in the Balkans for a few years at least. This peace program had been adopted with some changes by Berchtold, and made the basis for a long memorandum to Berlin—just before the news from Sarajevo made him suddenly change to Conrad's war program. Tisza, however, was not the kind of man to allow his matured judgments to be overturned in a moment, even by such a crime. On June 29, the day after the assassination, he hastened to Vienna to express his country's sympathy to Francis Joseph, but with no idea that the Monarchy's policy was to be altered because of what had occurred. After condoling with the Emperor, Tisza visited the Ballplatz, little suspecting the sudden change in the attitude of the Minister of Foreign Affairs. But here at the Foreign Office he learned with painful surprise of Berchtold's "intention of making the horrible crime of Sarajevo the occasion for the final reckoning with Serbia."[8]

Tisza thereupon told Berchtold frankly that the provoking of such a war with Serbia would be "a fatal mistake"; it would pillory Austrians "before the whole world as disturbers of the peace, besides beginning a great war under the most unfavorable circumstances." But he apparently made little impression on Berchtold. At any rate, upon his return to Budapest, Tisza considered it his duty to inform Francis Joseph of Berchtold's reckless plans and warn him against them. Since it was expected that Emperor William was about to come to Vienna to express his personal sympathy for his brother monarch, Tisza begged Francis Joseph

8 Tisza to Francis Joseph, July 1; A.R.B., I, 2.

to take advantage of the opportunity "to induce him to support us in our Balkan policy as intended," [9] i.e., winning Bulgaria and preserving peace in the Balkans. In his conflict with Berchtold, Tisza wanted to play German influence in favor of his own diplomatic peace program against Berchtold's new and reckless war program. But Berchtold proceeded to take this very arrow out of Tisza's quiver, and use it, as we shall see, against Tisza himself.

In view of the unreliability of Rumania as an ally, and the increasing dangers to the Dual Monarchy after the Balkan Wars, Tisza had drawn up a memoir in March, 1914. In this he set forth a program of peace, recuperation, and diplomatic readjustment in the Balkans, which he laid before Francis Joseph and Berchtold, and which he hoped would be adopted as the basis of a well-considered Austrian and German policy in the Balkans. It may be summarized as follows.[10]

The Balkan Wars and the Peace of Bucharest have created for Austria-Hungary an intolerable situation. Until this is improved there can be no real lasting peace. On the other hand, the general exhaustion and dismay have been too great to allow any advantageous military action in the immediate future. Hatreds and passions lie in the way of a sound, correct judgment of one's own interests, as well as of those of one's neighbors. The over-confidence of the victor impairs correct judgments, just as much as the bitterness of the vanquished. Austria cannot come to a correct appreciation of her own worth nor command a corresponding respect for her interests and advice among the Balkan States until the smoke has cleared away and

[9] Tisza to Francis Joseph, July 1; A.R.B., I, 2. *Cf.* also the post-War statements of Berchtold, Hoyos, Wiesner, Jagow, and Zimmerman, in *Current History,* July, 1928, pp. 626-636.

[10] Fraknói, pp. 7-13, gives the German text, which Tisza sent to Vienna. A German and English translation of the Tisza's original Magyar text is given by Marczali in *Am. Hist. Rev.*, XXIX, 303-310, Jan., 1924

cool reason holds sway. It would be a great mistake to precipitate matters, or to try to force a premature development which can only come as a result of time, patience, and a well-considered policy. Nevertheless one must not sink into apathetic resignation or passive inactivity. On the contrary, one must adopt a carefully thought out *"politique de longue main"* which shall gradually smooth away the internal difficulties and bring about a more favorable situation in the Balkans. "With this aim we must consider not only our own interests, but also come to a clear understanding with Germany. Our task is a difficult one. There can be no talk of success unless we have complete assurance of being understood, respected, and supported by Germany. Germany must see that the Balkans are of decisive importance not only for us but for the German Empire."

As to Russia, Tisza did not believe that she intended to make war immediately. Her aggressive attitude and saber-rattling was meant to impress the Balkan States and was encouraging the nationalist movement in Rumania and Serbia. It might even win Ferdinand of Bulgaria to the Tsar's side. Bulgaria, Tisza believed, could and ought to be deflected to the side of the Central Powers. Undoubtedly, Ferdinand had fallen into his desperate position after the Second Balkan War because of his own crazy policy and his failure to follow Austrian advice. Nevertheless, clamped in between Rumania, Serbia, and Greece, and still threatened by Turkey, Bulgaria would certainly throw herself into the arms of Russia, unless Austria came strongly to her support. Such a combination, in which Bulgaria should be reconciled with the other Christian States under Russian patronage, would lead to a successful war against Austria, Bulgaria being rewarded with Macedonia. Austria would be surrounded by the iron ring which Russia was so persistently forging, and the military superiority of the Triple Entente on the Continent would be complete. The long-sought moment would then have arrived in which Russia and France could attack Germany with overwhelming forces and begin the World War with a prospect of success.

The Triple Entente would not attack Germany, however, Tisza believed, until Russia had won over Bulgaria and so threatened Austria with a war on three fronts. The crux of the European situation lay, therefore, in the Balkans and particularly in attaching Bulgaria to the Central Powers. This was of just as much vital interest to Germany as to Austria. Therefore the Dual Monarchy should strive to oppose Russia's Balkan policy by a well-considered harmonious German-Austrian policy. The best way to win Bulgaria, Tisza believed, was to hold out to Ferdinand the prospect of acquiring Macedonia. This could not be accomplished at once. Bulgaria would need several years to recover strength and heal the wounds of war. Meanwhile the Central Powers must assure Bulgaria protection against attack from Turkey or Greece. Rumanian public feeling was very strong against Hungary, but an effort must be made to keep King Carol firm in his alliance and assure him that Rumania was in no danger of an attack from Bulgaria. Germany and Austria must henceforth coöperate together to effect a favorable grouping of the Balkan States; Rumania and Greece must be wooed away from Serbia, and reconciled with Bulgaria on the basis of an enlargement of Bulgaria at Serbia's expense.

Such, in outline, was the policy which Tisza thought ought to be urged upon Germany, so that the two Central Powers would support one another at Sofia, Bucharest, and Constantinople. At the end of his Memoir he again repeats that this is a policy of peace for the present, and that "it is only in a relatively distant future that Bulgaria can compensate herself with Macedonia." And in closing, he again says with emphasis: "In the Balkans we must first preserve the peace and prepare a favorable development. There is no time to be lost."

Tisza's program apparently met with the approval of Francis Joseph and Berchtold, who had Baron Flotow, the Foreign Office specialist on Balkan affairs, draw up a much longer memoir developing Tisza's ideas in more detail. Flotow emphasized the critically dangerous position in which Austria found herself. Rumania, in spite of King Carol's undoubted personal loyalty, could not be depended upon in view of the strong tide of anti-Austrian feeling among the Rumanian people. Austria must therefore compel Rumania to declare herself openly either for or against Austria. The best way to put pressure on Rumania for this purpose was for Austria to enter into an alliance with Bulgaria, and to make Sofia, instead of Bucharest, the pivot of Austria's Balkan policy. Bulgaria would guarantee to Rumania the existing boundary between Bulgaria and Rumania, so that King Carol would not be antagonized or alarmed. In fact he would then see the wisdom of holding to the Triple Alliance; he might even be induced to use his great influence with Serbia "to draw Serbia closer to the Dual Monarchy; in which case the Dual Monarchy, within the bounds of such a political situation, would meet Serbia most loyally half-way." [11] But if King Carol should not consent to make a satisfactory public declaration of his loyalty to the Triple Alliance, then Austria must revise her military arrangements, and seek to bring Turkey into alliance with Bulgaria, so that both would support the Triple Alliance.

Flotow's memorandum, somewhat amplified by Matscheko and Pogascher, was put before Berchtold about the middle of June. Whether it was shown to Franz Fer-

[11] Gooss, p. 5. Berchtold later went over Flotow's draft and deleted this clause contemplating mediation by Rumania for a possible friendly settlement between Austria and Serbia.

dinand during the visit which Berchtold paid to Konopischt the day after Emperor William's interview with the Heir to the Throne is not clear. At any rate it was decided that it should be worked out in greater detail and laid before the Berlin authorities as a memorandum for guidance of the two allies in Balkan affairs. Accordingly, an elaborate draft to this effect was completed by June 24. Berchtold then went over the draft, and gave it the final gentle form, which he hoped would prove unobjectionable and persuasive to the Berlin Foreign Office.[12]

Beginning with an analysis of the results of the Balkan Wars, Berchtold pointed out the dangers to Germany and Austria of the existing situation. "Turkey, which has a natural community of interests with the Triple Alliance and has formed a strong counter-weight against Russia and the Balkan States, has been almost entirely driven out of Europe and largely lost its position as a Great Power. Serbia, whose policy for years has been hostile to Austria-Hungary, and is now wholly under Russian influence, has gained unexpectedly in population and territory. Her proximity to Montenegro and the general spread of the Greater Serbia idea makes imminent the possibility of her further aggrandizement by a union with Montenegro. Finally, the relations of Rumania with the Triple Alliance have essentially altered during the crisis." Omitting for obvious reasons all Austria's own responsibilities for the bad situation, Berchtold emphasized the dangerously aggressive intrigues of Russia and France. "The idea of liberating the Christian peoples of the Balkans from the Turkish yoke in order to use them as a weapon against the Triple Alliance has long been the political main-spring of Russia's traditional interest in these peoples. Recently [i.e., in 1912] this idea, which has been sympathetically taken up in France, developed into a plan for uniting all

12 Printed in A.R.B., I, 1; K.D., 14; *cf.* Gooss, pp. 6-26.

the Balkan States into a Balkan League in order in this way to put an end to the superiority of the Triple Alliance. . . . But [the Second Balkan] War caused the Balkan States to split into two almost equally strong opposing groups: Turkey and Bulgaria on the one hand, and Serbia, Montenegro, Greece and Rumania on the other. To heal this split, in order to use all the Balkan States, or at least a decisive majority of them, to shift the balance of power in Europe, is the present task which Russia, aided by France, is attempting to accomplish. Since Serbia and Greece are already in alliance, and Rumania has declared herself in harmony with them, at least as far as the Treaty of Bucharest is concerned, France and Russia are anxious to remove the rancor which exists between Bulgaria and Greece and especially between Bulgaria and Serbia on account of Macedonia. They are anxious to find a basis on which Rumania would be willing to come over completely to the side of the Entente, and even to coöperate in a political combination with Bulgaria, whom she regards with suspicion; and they are anxious finally, if possible, to bring about a peaceful solution of the Aegean Islands question that would lead Turkey to approach or even to join the Balkan States. The basis on which Russian and French diplomacy intends to accomplish an adjustment of all this hostility and rivalry and build up a new Balkan League is undoubtedly founded upon a program directed against Austria-Hungary, at whose expense all the members of the League could be promised a successive extension of boundaries westwards."

After detailing all the intrigues by which Russia and France were seeking to build up this new Balkan League, aimed at the territorial dismemberment of the Dual Monarchy, Berchtold dealt as tactfully as possible with the Rumanian problem, pointing out Austria's embarrassments and hinting that Germany might use pressure to make

Rumania see the error of her ways. As the best method of thwarting Russia's projected Balkan League and compelling Rumania to return to the fold of the Triple Alliance, Berchtold then urged Tisza's program for an alliance with Bulgaria, adding that Turkey also might be included in it eventually. "Austria must accept the offer of a definite alliance made by Bulgaria a year ago and repeated several times since then. At the same time she must aim to bring about an alliance between Bulgaria and Turkey; both these states were recently so favorably disposed to this, that a draft treaty was worked out, though not signed afterwards. This is another instance in which the Dual Monarchy, if it continued delaying action out of consideration for Rumania, which is moved by no such reciprocal feelings, might cause itself serious and irreparable injury. Further delay and failure to begin a countervailing activity at Sofia would give Russia and France free scope for their intensive and wide-reaching plans. Rumania's attitude simply forces Austria to give Bulgaria that support which she has long been seeking, and which will frustrate Russia's otherwise unavoidable encirclement policy. And this must be done at once, while the road to Sofia and also to Constantinople is still open."

"The treaty with Bulgaria, the details of which will have to be examined more fully, must naturally be so framed as not to be in conflict with Austria's treaty obligations to Rumania. It also ought not to be kept secret from Rumania, since there is no hostility against Rumania in this step, but simply a serious warning to the authorities in Bucharest of the consequences of a persistent partisan dependence on Russia on their part."

Berchtold closed with an appeal to Germany for support for Tisza's program for a diplomatic shift in the Balkans, pointing out that Germany, no less than Austria, was threatened by Russia's aggressive policy. "Before Austria takes the step in question, she is most anxious to establish a full understanding with the German Empire, not only in consideration of old traditions and of what is due to a close ally, but more especially because grave interests of Germany and the Triple Alliance are at stake, and because its common interests can be successfully safeguarded only if the joint action of Russia and France is opposed by an equally joint counter-action of the Triple Alliance, and especially of Austria-Hungary and the German Empire. . . . While France aims to weaken the Dual Monarchy with the hope of promoting her plans for *revanche,* the intentions of Russia are much more comprehensive. If one considers the development of Russia during the last two centuries, the steady extension of her territory, the enormous increase of her population, exceeding so much that of all the other European Great Powers, and the vast progress of her economic resources and military strength, as well as the fact that this great Empire is as good as cut off from the sea by its geographical position and treaty obligations, one sees why Russia's policy has necessarily always had an inherently aggressive character. . . . For these reasons the Austrian Foreign Office is convinced that it is for the common interests of Austria no less than of Germany to oppose a timely and energetic counter-action to the development which is being pushed by Russian intrigues, and which perhaps at a later time could never be undone."

In this form the memorandum was complete and ready for transmission to Berlin. It was to "open Germany's eyes" to the need of supporting Austria more energetically in this diplomatic wooing of Bulgaria.[13]

Then on Sunday afternoon, June 28, came the terrible

[13] Hoyos at Vienna to Pallavicini at Constantinople, June 26: "Unterdessen wird ein langes Memorandum für Berlin ausgearbeitet, das demnächst abgehen soll, und der Minister [Graf Berchtold] tut sein Mögliches, Tschirschky die Augen zu öffnen." Gooss, p. 6. *Cf.* Berchtold's article in *Contemporary Review,* April, 1928, pp. 422-432.

telephone message that Franz Ferdinand and his wife had been murdered at Sarajevo. The news appears to have had a stimulating effect upon the ordinarily rather indolent and undecided mind of Count Berchtold. Many historians, and several Viennese with whom the present writer has talked, speak of Berchtold as a minister who allowed himself to be managed by others, especially by a number of Serb-haters in the Austrian Foreign Office, like Hoyos, Forgach, Macchio, and by Baron Conrad, the Austrian Chief of Staff. The Foreign Minister has been regarded as a mere "rubber stamp," approving what others urged upon him. While this view may be more or less true for the period before Sarajevo, it does not appear equally so for the crisis of July, 1914. The contemporary evidence seems to show that however much Berchtold may have been guided by his subordinates at the Ballplatz, and by the militarists, he took a very active and sinister part in the events which led directly to the World War. Hitherto he had vacillated between the two opposing groups of opinion represented respectively by Conrad and by Tisza. But now, after Sarajevo, he decided to use this crime as the final justification for clearing up, once and for all, Austrian relations with Serbia.

BERCHTOLD'S APPEAL FOR GERMAN SUPPORT

Berchtold was now finally converted to Conrad's desire for immediate war against Serbia. But owing to Francis Joseph's hesitation and Tisza's opposition he could not adopt it at once. Moreover, he realized that it would be madness to embark on any such hare-brained action without first getting from Berlin an assurance of German support. Germany during the last few years had been constantly restraining Austria from aggressive action in the Balkans which might involve the Triple Alliance in conflict with the Triple Entente. Two days after Sarajevo, when even serious people in Vienna "were expressing frequently the hope that Austria had now the excuse for coming to a final reckoning with the Serbians," the German Ambassador, Tschirschky, used every opportunity to warn calmly but very energetically and earnestly against any overhasty steps. He pointed out above all else that Austria must be clear as to exactly what she wanted, and remember that she did not stand alone in the world; she must consider her allies and the entire European situation, and especially the attitude which Italy and Rumania would take in regard to Serbia.[14] On July 2, Berchtold set forth to him all the dangers from the Greater Serbia propaganda. News had just come that twelve assassins were on the way to assassinate Emperor William. It was as much to Germany's, as to Austria's, interest to put an end to the Belgrade plottings. Tschirschky admitted this, but observed confidentially to the Austrian Minister that the reason Berlin had not given more definite promises of support in the past was that Austria "had talked much theoretically but had never formulated a fixed and definite plan of action"; only when such a plan was formulated, could Berlin promise full and complete support; and he again warned Berchtold of the danger of alienating Rumania and Italy.[15] Similarly from Berlin came expressions of sympathy, but they were accompanied with advice to be cautious. The Austrian Ambassador in Berlin telegraphed:

> Zimmermann [German Under-Secretary of State for Foreign Affairs] assured me that he would consider decisive action on the part of Austria, with whom the whole civilized world today was in sympathy, quite comprehensible, but still he would recommend the greatest caution, and advise that no humiliating demands be made upon Serbia.[16]

14 Tschirschky to Bethmann, June 30, K.D., 7.
15 Berchtold's summary, July 3, A.R.B., I, 3; Gooss, 37 ff.
16 Szögyény to Berchtold, July 4; A.R.B., I, 5.

In view of this attitude of caution and moderation on the part of Francis Joseph, Tisza, and Germany, Berchtold feared that an immediate mobilization against Serbia might result in Austria being left without German backing and the consequences might be disastrous. He saw that he must first gain an assurance of support from Berlin for whatever policy he should ultimately adopt. To secure this he decided to send Count Hoyos on a special mission to Berlin. Berchtold intended to have two strings to his bow. He would not openly abandon Tisza's peace program for winning over Bulgaria to the side of Austria and Germany, to which Berlin would probably assent; but at the same time he would do all he could to bring Germany as far as he could in the direction of approving energetic and immediate military action against Serbia. For this purpose he would exploit to the utmost the horror of Sarajevo; he would emphasize the fact that the threads of conspiracy certainly led to Belgrade, that the crime was merely the culmination of the series of intolerable Serbian outrages which must now at last be forcibly dealt with. Accordingly, with this double program in view, he decided to send at once to Berlin the long memorandum on policy mentioned above; but to it he added the postscript:

> "The above memorandum had only just been completed, when the terrible events of Sarajevo happened. The full significance of the villainous murder can hardly be estimated today. Most certainly, if a proof was needed that the gulf between the Monarchy and Serbia is beyond bridging over, or that the ambition of Greater Serbia in its intensity and recklessness does not stop at anything, that proof has been given. Austria-Hungary has not been lacking in good-will and readiness to bring about tolerable relations with Serbia. But it has recently been shown that all these efforts are in vain, and that the Monarchy must in future look to the persistent, implacable and aggressive enmity of Serbia. It is all the more necessary for the Monarchy to tear asunder

with a determined hand the threads which its enemies are weaving into a net over its head." [17]

Berchtold also drew up an ambiguous double-faced letter for Francis Joseph to sign and send to Emperor William. The greater part of it, like the memorandum on policy, was devoted to Tisza's pacific program for a diplomatic shift in the Balkans to strengthen the hold on Rumania, win Bulgaria, and isolate Serbia. But the beginning and the end of the letter, like the postscript above, were calculated to convince the two imperial Monarchs of Serbia's responsibility for the Sarajevo crime, and so to lay the foundation on which Berchtold might base military action. Military action, however, was not actually mentioned, for he did not want to alarm the Monarchs unduly and brusquely at first. But if he found that they accepted his view of Serbian responsibility, they might be willing to take the next step of approving armed invasion of Serbia; and if they did not, he could at any rate fall back on Tisza's diplomatic program. The royal missive ran as follows:

> . . . I am sending you a memorandum, drawn up by my Minister of Foreign Affairs prior to the frightful catastrophe at Sarajevo, which after that tragic event now appears especially noteworthy. The attack on my poor nephew is a direct result of the agitation of the Russian and Serbian Pan-Slavs, whose single aim is the weakening of the Triple Alliance and the disruption of my Empire. According to all indications, the crime of Sarajevo is not the deed of a single individual, but the result of a well-arranged plot whose threads reach to Belgrade; and though presumably it will be impossible to prove the complicity of the Serbian Government, there can be no doubt that its policy of uniting all the South Slavs under the Serbian flag promotes such crimes, and that a continuation of this situa-

[17] A.R.B., I, 1; K.D., 14; Gooss, p. 4.

tion spells lasting danger for my dynasty and for my territories.

This danger is heightened by the fact that Rumania, in spite of its existing alliance with us, is in close friendship with Serbia and permits in its own territory just as hateful an agitation against us as does Serbia. [In spite of Carol's loyalty and because of **popular feeling**] **I fear** that Rumania can only be rescued for the Triple Alliance in case we do two things: prevent the establishment of a new Balkan League under Russian protection by joining Bulgaria to the Triple Alliance; and give it clearly to be understood in Bucharest that Serbia's friends cannot be our friends, and that Rumania can no longer count upon us as allies, unless she cuts loose from Serbia and suppresses with all her power her own agitation in Rumania which is directed against the existence of my Empire.

The aim of my Government must henceforth be to isolate and diminish Serbia. The first step in this direction must be to strengthen the present Government of Bulgaria whose real interests tally with ours, and prevent her return to a Russophil policy. When Rumania realizes that the Triple Alliance does not hesitate to ally with Bulgaria and yet is ready to compel Bulgaria to guarantee Rumania's territorial integrity, Rumania will then perhaps retreat from the dangerous path into which she is led by her friendship with Serbia and her *rapprochement* with Russia. If this should succeed, a further attempt could be made to reconcile Greece with Bulgaria and Turkey, and so form a new Balkan League under the protection of the Triple Alliance; its purpose would be to set a dam to the Pan-Slav flood and assure peace to our lands.

This will only be possible when Serbia, which at present forms the pivot of the Pan-Slav policy, is eliminated as a political factor in the Balkans. After the last frightful events in Bosnia, you too will be convinced that a friendly settlement of the antagonism which divides Austria from Serbia is no longer to be thought of, and that the peace policy of all European monarchs is threatened so long as the source of criminal agitation in Belgrade lives on unpunished.[18]

THE POTSDAM CONVERSATIONS, JULY 5 AND 6

This royal letter, together with Berchtold's completed memorandum and postscript, were dispatched to Berlin by Berchtold's confidential Foreign Office Secretary, Alexander Hoyos, and then presented to the Kaiser by the Austrian Ambassador, Count Szögyény, at Potsdam on Sunday, July 5. According to Szögyény's report of what took place:

After I had brought it to the knowledge of Emperor William that I had an autograph letter to deliver, I received Their Majesties' invitation to lunch today at noon in the New Palace. I gave His Majesty the letter and the accompanying memorandum. He read both documents in my presence with the greatest attention. At first he assured me that he had expected an earnest action on our part against Serbia, but at the same time he must confess that the statements of Our Majesty raised the prospect of a serious European complication, and he therefore, wished to give no definite answer until he had consulted with the Chancellor.

After luncheon, when I again emphasized the seriousness of the situation, His Majesty authorized me to report that in this case also we could reckon on Germany's full support. He must, as he said before, first hear what the Imperial Chancellor had to say, but he did not doubt at all that Bethmann-Hollweg would agree with him completely. As regards any action on our part against Serbia, he thought such action ought not to be delayed. Russia's attitude would doubtless be hostile, but he had been prepared for that for years, and even if it should come to a war between Austria and Russia, we could be convinced that Germany would stand by our side with her accustomed

18 Francis Joseph to William II, drafted by Berchtold July 2, and presented by Szögyény July 5, K.D., 13; A.R.B., I, 1; Gooss, pp. 26-29.

faithfulness as an ally. Russia, furthermore, he thought, as things stand today, was in no way ready for war and would certainly ponder very seriously before appealing to arms. But she would stir up the other Powers of the Triple Entente against us and blow upon fire in the Balkans.

His Majesty said he understood how hard Francis Joseph, with his well-known love of peace, would find it to invade Serbia; but if we had really decided that military action against Serbia was necessary, he would be sorry if we left unused the present moment which was so favorable for us.

As to Rumania he would take care that King Carol and his counsellors should observe a correct attitude. He could not sympathize with the idea of concluding an alliance with Bulgaria; he had never trusted King Ferdinand, nor his former or present counsellors, and he did not trust him now. Still he would make no objections to a treaty between Austria and Bulgaria, but care must be taken that the treaty contained nothing to offend Rumania and it must, as the memorandum proposes, be communicated to Rumania.

Early tomorrow morning Emperor William intends to go to Kiel to start from there on his northern cruise. But first he will talk with the Chancellor, and for this purpose he has summoned him from Hohenfinow for this evening to the New Palace. In any case, I shall find an opportunity to speak with the Chancellor sometime tomorrow morning.[19]

What were Emperor William's feelings at the time of this interview? His emotional nature had been deeply shocked at the horrible news of the assassination of Franz Ferdinand and his wife, whom he had just been visiting at Konopischt. While yachting on the preceding Sunday afternoon at Kiel he espied a little launch steaming at full speed as if to board his boat. He made a peremptory gesture to her to keep off. But, instead, Admiral Müller, who was at the helm, made a sign that he had something to commu-

19 Szögyény to Berchtold July 5, 7:35 P. M.; A.R.B., I, 6; Gooss, pp. 30-32.

nicate. Holding up to view a piece of paper, he folded it into his cigarette case, and tossed it carefully on board. A sailor picked it up and handed it to the Emperor. William II opened the case, took out the paper, and turned pale as he read the fatal news from Sarajevo. He at once gave orders to tack about and give up the regatta.[20] He intended to go to Vienna to attend the Archduke's funeral and show his respect to the aged Francis Joseph in his latest bereavement. But when it was reported to him that a dozen Serb assassins were on their way from Belgrade to Vienna to bring about his own assassination, he allowed himself to be persuaded by his Chancellor to abandon his visit.[21] It was officially announced that the reason for his change of purpose was an attack of lumbago and not at all considerations for his personal safety,[22] but his sudden decision not to go to Vienna to pay the last honors to his late friend gave rise to all sorts of contradictory statements and fantastic rumors.[23]

[20] J. Cambon's account of what he heard a few days later direct from "a personage who was beside the Kaiser at this moment;" Recouly, pp. 19 f. Recouly adds that the Kaiser remarked, as he turned pale, "Tout est à recommencer!" He deduces from this, wholly without proof, that the Kaiser had persuaded Franz Ferdinand to some great project at Konopischt—he is careful not to be very definite as to just what this project was—and that now the whole plan was spoiled by the Archduke's death.

[21] K.D., 6a, 6b, 9, 13; *cf.* also Berchtold's statement to Tschirschky, July 2, that "today's news from Semlin, according to which twelve assassins are on their way with the intention of murdering Emperor William, will perhaps at last open people's eyes in Berlin to the danger which is threatening from Belgrade;" A.R.B., I, 3.

[22] Dirr, p. 120; B.D., 24.

[23] B.D., 11, 12, 18, 24, 26, 29; Wickham Steed, *Through Thirty Years,* I, 401; Seton-Watson, *Sarajevo,* p. 105. According to the British Ambassador in Vienna (B.D., 18; *cf.* also B.D., 26; and Dirr, p. 117) Berchtold had expressed the hope on June 29 that no missions of foreign princes would be sent to the Archduke's funeral, in order to spare Francis Joseph fatigue and to shorten the ceremonies as much as possible. Possibly he feared that a meeting of sovereigns at Vienna would exercise a moderating influence and tend to thwart him in his plan of making war on Serbia. That such a gathering of sovereigns might have perhaps have led to advice which would have found some other solution than war is the post-

It would be rash for any writer to attempt to give an adequate analysis of the Kaiser's psychology on July 5, 1914, or at any other time. Karl Kautsky, the German Socialist leader, thinks he was already something of a madman. Herman Lutz has made an elaborate study to show that the Emperor had long suffered from periods of maniacal depression, each of which coincided with one of the insensate bellicose gestures with which he had continually alarmed Europe.[24] Other writers, having read the Kaiser's emotional speeches during the War, alternating between exaltation and tearfulness, or his futile "Comparative Tables" and Memoirs composed after the War, think of him variously as a dangerous paranoiac, an incurable megalomaniac, or an egotistical simpleton; but they forget that to judge leaders, even in the Entente countries, by what they said under the stress of War or for political propaganda, is no fair indication of their pre-War views or mental condition. They forget, in reading the historically inaccurate effusions from Doorn, the disintegrating effect upon an emotional and excitable mind of the strain of years of war. To estimate the Kaiser's attitudes in July, 1914, there is no better material than the marginal notes which he jotted down on the despatches which were laid before him. This was a practice which he had long since adopted in imitation of Bismarck, who found it a great saving of time to indicate his wishes by marginal notes, rather than by writing out or dictating long instructions. Bismarck and William II supposed that these *verba privatissima* would always remain

War opinion of two high Austrian officials: General Auffenberg, *Aus Oesterreichs Höhe und Niedergang* (Munich, 1921), p. 255 f.; and A. Hoyos, *Der deutsch-englische Gegensatz und sein Einfluss auf die Balkanpolitik Oesterreich-Ungarns* (Berlin, 1922), p. 77, note.

24 Kautsky, *Wie der Weltkrieg Entstand* (Berlin, 1919); Herman Lutz, *Wilhelm II periodisch geisteskrank* (Leipzig, 1919). For a hostile but excellent brief study of the Kaiser's mentality, with a full bibliography, see [F. C. Endres], *Die Tragödie Deutschlands,* (Leipzig, 1922, 3rd ed. 1924).

secret in the archives; both would have been exceedingly astonished if they could have foreseen that they were so soon to be published to the world.[25] But while Bismarck's notes were carefully pondered and usually intended as instructions, the Kaiser's marginalia are more often merely the hasty emotional reaction to the document before him. In using them it must be remembered that they are often merely the first impressions of the moment, rather than the conclusions of mature reflections; that they are often contradictory and exaggerated; and that they frequently had no influence upon the actual course of events, because they were commonly made several days late on documents upon which the Foreign Office had already taken decisions. Nevertheless they do give some indication of the trend of his mind and the decisive impression made by the assassination of his friend.

Before Sarajevo Emperor William had been inclined to think that Austria was unnecessarily nervous about Serbia, and ought to try to come to some friendly understanding with her. In the spring of 1914, when Austria was greatly alarmed at rumors that Serbia, instigated by Russia, might attempt some union with Montenegro,[26] the Kaiser appeared to be pro-Serbian rather than pro-Austrian. Austria's efforts during the Balkan Wars to exclude Serbia from access to the Adriatic he regarded as "nonsense"; her new effort to prevent Serbia from reaching the Adriatic by union with Montenegro he pronounced "Unbelievable! This union is absolutely not to be prevented. And if Vienna attempts it, she will commit a great stupidity, and stir up the danger of a war with the Slavs, which would leave us quite cold."[27] He agreed with Tisza, who calmly accepted the union as imminent, rather than with Berch-

[25] In *Die Grosse Politik* and *Kautsky Documents, passim.*

[26] *Cf.* G.P., XXXVIII, 325-358; Conrad, III, 661-665.

[27] Marginalia on Griesinger's despatch from Belgrade, Mar. 11, 1914; G.P., XXXVIII, 335. Similarly on a despatch of May 12: "One must

told and Franz Joseph who were declaring it unacceptable. He telegraphed from Corfu to Bethmann on April 5:

> It is absolutely necessary that the people in Vienna should face the possibility [of union of Serbia and Montenegro] seriously, and be clear in their minds whether under all circumstances they would stand by the position taken by the Emperor and Count Berchtold, or whether they adopt Tisza's view. The first would only be possible in case they were absolutely firmly determined to prevent the planned union by force of arms. In any case Austria must not put her prestige at stake, and publicly declare unacceptable things which she will ultimately be willing to permit. If they will agree to the sensible views of Tisza, Austrian policy will without further ado be able to adapt itself to the changed conditions in the direction which we have been preaching for years. There must be found a *modus vivendi* with the Dual Monarchy which will be attractive to Serbia.[28]

While the German Kaiser had hitherto generally inclined to protect Serbia from dangerously excessive demands by Austria and hoped for a peaceful settlement of their difficulties,[29] now, after the murder of one of his best friends, whom he had just been visiting, by assassins who had admittedly come from Belgrade, his indignation against the Serbians was thoroughly roused. His marginal notes excoriate them as "murderers," "regicides," and "bandits." He sincerely felt that the monarchical principle was in danger; that the spirit which led them to murder their own king and queen in 1903 still dominated the country; that

realize that in the long run Serbia and Montenegro will come together anyway, just as Tisza said;" G.P., XXXVIII, 352.

28 G.P., XXXVIII, 337 f.

29 Tisza in his letter of July 1 to Francis Joseph had spoken of "the Kaiser's preference for Serbia" (A.R.B., I, 2). Bethmann wrote to the German Chargé d'Affaires at Bucharest, July 6: "The Kaiser, as King Carol is aware, has always intervened at Vienna in favor of an understanding with Serbia" (K.D., 16).

all monarchs, Nicholas II most of all, ought to support, instead of opposing, any action on Austria's part which aimed at the suppression of the unscrupulous agitation which had been going on for years among Serbians and which, as he was now informed by Berchtold, threatened the very existence of his Austrian ally, and had made his own personal friend its victim. When therefore he read that Tschirschky, his Ambassador at Vienna, was "using every opportunity to warn [Berchtold] calmly but energetically and earnestly against any overhasty steps," he noted in the margin, as already pointed out in the preceding chapter: "Now or never! Who authorized him to this? That is very stupid! It's none of his business, for it is purely Austria's affair to consider what to do in this matter, for it will be said afterwards, if things go wrong, that Germany was not willing!! Tschirschky will please drop this nonsense! Matters must be cleared up with the Serbians, *and that soon.* That's all self-evident and the plain truth." [30] With his natural impetuosity he wanted Austria to take action in regard to the Serbians as quickly as possible, while the whole civilized world, still under the vivid impression of the terrible assassination, sympathized with her.

What this action of Austria's was to be, the Kaiser did not know definitely on July 5, and did not care to advise. But neither he nor Bethmann thought it at all probable on that day that the Austro-Serbian dispute would lead to a European war. He could therefore quite safely depart on his northern cruise early next morning, as he had long planned, and as Bethmann advised. This he would hardly have done, if he had thought that the action, which he wished Austria to take at once instead of delaying more than two weeks, would probably involve a European conflagration. It is significant that the moment he heard the kind of ultimatum Berchtold had presented to Serbia, he

[30] K.D., 7; *cf.* also 29, 120, 288, 290, 335, 337.

started in a hurry to return to Berlin. The "Potsdam Council" legend represents him as leaving the scene of action with the Machiavellian intent of lulling Europe into unsuspecting security before his sudden attack on France and Russia; but such a notion he characterized at the time as "childish," in a marginal note on a despatch from Vienna reporting that this was exactly what the Austrian Chief of Staff and Minister of War were doing.[31] Furthermore, the Kaiser was not the kind of man to leave Berlin if he seriously expected European complications. And to have suddenly given up the northern cruise, which he had been accustomed for years to take at this season, and which had been long announced in the papers, would have been the very thing which would have excited uneasy comment abroad and played into the hands of the militarists everywhere. Therefore the Kaiser decided to carry out previously made arrangements, in spite of the Sarajevo assassination—precisely as Poincaré decided to carry out his previously arranged visit to Russia.

Nevertheless, the Kaiser realized that, while it was not probable that Austria's action would kindle a European war, it was possible. It was likely at any rate to give rise to rumors of war during his absence, and therefore he deemed it prudent quietly to inform representatives of the army and navy who happened to be in Berlin, as well as Bethmann, of his interview with Szögyény.

Accordingly, on Sunday afternoon or early Monday, before taking the auto from Potsdam for Kiel on July 6 at 9:15 A.M., the Kaiser had brief interviews with representatives of the army and navy. He informed each of his con-

31 Tschirschky to Bethmann, July 10: "Der Kriegsminister wird morgen auf *Urlaub gehen,* auch Freiherr Conrad von **Hötzendorf** Wien zeitweilig verlassen. Es geschieht dies, wie Graf Berchtold mir sagte, absichtlich, um *jeder Beunruhigung vorzubeugen,*" on which the Kaiser noted "kindisch!" and underlined the words italicized; K.D., 29. See below, pp. 243 f., 249.

versation with the Austrian Ambassador. He told them privately to inform their chiefs who were absent on vacation, but added that they need not cut short their vacations to return to Berlin, and that no orders for military preparations need be given, as he did not expect any serious warlike complications.[32]

On Sunday afternoon the Kaiser also telephoned to Falkenhayn, the Prussian Minister of War, to come to Potsdam. Upon his arrival he received him at once, read him the communications from Szögyény, and suggested the

32 The officers whom he saw were General Falkenhayn, Prussian Minister of War, and Captain Zenker of the Navy Staff on Sunday afternoon; and Lieut. Gen. Bertrab of the Army Staff and Admiral Capelle, Acting Secretary of the Navy, on Monday morning. In answer to a questionnaire sent out by the Foreign Office of the German Republic in October, 1919, they replied in letters, which were apparently written without consultation together but which are in substantial agreement, that they talked separately with the Kaiser, that he did not expect any warlike complications; that he did not order any military preparations; and that no such orders were given in the period July 5-23 covered by the questionnaire. Their letters are printed in the K.D., I, pp. xiv-xvi. The accuracy of their statements is confirmed by the results of an investigation into the responsibilities for the War undertaken by a subcommittee of the Reichstag in December, 1919; *cf. Investigating Comm.,* especially pp. 58-67, 70-72. Bertrab's letter may be cited as typical: "In reply to the Foreign Office, I respectfully state that on July 6, 1914, His Majesty personally informed me, without witnesses being present, of his view of the situation created by Austria's measures, in order that I, as the senior representative officer of the General Staff present in Berlin, might inform the Chief of the General Staff who was staying at Karlsbad. Present in the background were Her Majesty, the Empress, an adjutant, and a servant. Just before this His Majesty had been speaking apparently with the same purpose and likewise with no one in hearing with a naval officer who withdrew directly after the interview. After the Kaiser had dismissed me he entered his auto for the northern journey. No orders were given then nor as a result of the interview. In fact His Majesty emphasized the point that he did not consider it necessary to give any special orders, as he did believe there would be no serious complications as a result of the Sarajevo crime." Capelle likewise declared: "The Kaiser said he did not believe there would be any great warlike complications. The Tsar would in his opinion in this case not place himself on the side of regicides. Moreover, Russia and France were not ready for war. England was not mentioned by the Kaiser. Upon the advice of his Chancellor, in order not to create any unrest, he would go on his northern cruise. Still he wished to inform me of the strained situation so that I could weigh the future."

possibility of serious complications. When Falkenhayn asked if any military preparations ought to be made, the Kaiser said "No,"—and the short interview was at an end. No one was present except Plessen and Lyncker, two military secretaries regularly in attendance upon the Kaiser. Falkenhayn gave in consequence no orders for military preparations at this time nor until after the ultimatum had been presented to Serbia.[33] On the contrary, he left Berlin on July 8 for an official visit, then joined his family on vacation at the sea-side, and did not return to Berlin until Saturday, July 25, the day after the ultimatum had been published in the newspapers.[34]

One might object that these statements of 1919, as to events in 1914, are open to question. But they are confirmed by a noteworthy letter which Falkenhayn wrote to Moltke immediately after the interview with the Kaiser. This letter, being a private communication from one high army officer to another, deserves quoting in full as giving a fairly exact account of what the Kaiser said and thought on July 5:

> This afternoon His Majesty commanded me to the New Palace to inform me that Austria-Hungary appeared determined to tolerate no longer the intrigues stirred up against Austria in the Balkans, and with this in view to invade Serbia soon in case it should be necessary; should Russia not be willing to consent to this, even then Austria would not be willing to give in.
>
> His Majesty believed this was the view to be gathered from what the Austrian Ambassador said when he delivered today at noon a memorandum from the Government at Vienna and a letter from Emperor Francis Joseph.
>
> I did not hear their conversation, and cannot therefore permit myself any judgment in regard to it. On the other

[33] Statement of Falkenhayn in December, 1919; *Investigating Comm.*, p. 62 f.

[34] Letter of Wurtzbacher to the Foreign Office, Oct. 19, 1919; K.D., I, p. xvi.

hand, His Majesty read me the letter as well as the memorandum; and from them so far as it was possible to arrive at an opinion from hearing them read rapidly, I did not get a convincing impression that the Vienna Government had come to a firm determination. Both documents gave a very gloomy picture of the general position of the Dual Monarchy as a result of the Pan-Slav intrigues. Both also regarded it as necessary that something should be done as quickly as possible to check them. But neither of them spoke of any warlike issue; it was rather some "energetic" political steps which seemed indicated; for example, the making of a treaty with Bulgaria, for which they wished to be assured of the support of the German Empire.

This support is to be promised to them, with the statement that it is primarily and solely Austria's affair to take steps necessary for her own interests.

The Imperial Chancellor, who also came to Potsdam, does not believe any more than I do that the Austrian Government with its talk, though more decided than formerly, is in earnest. At least, not only has he raised no objections to the departure for the northern cruise, but he has even advised it. A long time will pass before the treaty with Bulgaria is signed. Your Excellency's stay at the baths will therefore hardly need to suffer any curtailment. Nevertheless, though I have no instructions to do so, I thought it proper to inform you of the strain in the situation, so that sudden events, which in the end may always occur, should not take you wholly by surprise.

With best wishes for the success of your cure, I remain with sincere devotion and high esteem, as always,

Your devoted,

v. Falkenhayn.[35]

[35] Falkenhayn to Moltke, July 5; Alfred von Wegerer, *Kritische Bemerkungen zu Kapitel XIII aus Vivianis "Réponse au Kaiser"* (Berlin, 1923), appendix ii; Montgelas, *Leitfaden,* p. 196. Moltke also evidently did not expect any immediate complications, for he wrote to his wife from Karlsbad on July 18; "I am looking forward a great deal to our meeting in August when you come back from Bayreuth;" Moltke, *Erinnerungen,* p. 380.

Falkenhayn's letter, it will be seen, has quite a different tone from Szögyény's report of the luncheon interview quoted above. Falkenhayn did not at all expect any immediate danger to the peace of Europe, nor "that the Austrian Government with its talk, though more decided than formerly, is in earnest." He got the impression that the main point of Berchtold's ambiguous missives was the diplomatic action to secure Bulgaria, and that even this would take "a long time."

As the Kaiser had very properly told Szögyény that he could give no definite answer until he had consulted his Chancellor, Bethmann-Hollweg also was summoned to Potsdam the same afternoon. With him went Zimmermann, Acting-Secretary of State of Foreign Affairs during Jagow's absence on a honeymoon in Switzerland.[36] The results of their conference, embodying Germany's official decision, were stated next day by Bethmann to Szögyény at Berlin, and notified to the German Ambassador in Vienna in the following telegram:

> The Austro-Hungarian Ambassador delivered yesterday to His Majesty a private letter from Emperor Francis Joseph, which describes the present situation from the Austro-Hungarian point of view and the measures contemplated by Vienna, copies of which are now being sent to you.
>
> I replied today to Count Szögyény, thanking him for Francis Joseph's letter, to which the Emperor will soon send a personal answer. In the meantime His Majesty wishes to emphasize that he is not blind to the danger threatening Austria, and consequently the Triple Alliance, from the agitation carried on by Russia and Serbian Pan-Slavs. Although His Majesty, as is known, has no great confidence in Bulgaria and its ruler, and is naturally more inclined toward his old ally Rumania and its Hohenzollern prince,

36 *Cf.* Bethmann, *Betrachtungen zum Weltkrieg,* I, 135 ff.; *Investig. Comm.,* I, pp. 9-10, 28, 31-33.

nevertheless he can understand that Emperor Francis Joseph should want to join Bulgaria to the Triple Alliance in view of Rumania's attitude and of the danger from the formation of a new Balkan League pointed directly against the Danubian Monarchy. His Majesty will therefore direct his minister in Sofia to support steps in this direction taken by Austria's representative, if requested to do so. His Majesty will also use his efforts at Bucharest, as suggested by Francis Joseph, to bring King Carol to fulfil his duties as an ally, to drop Serbia, and to suppress the agitation in Rumania against Austria-Hungary.

Finally, concerning Serbia, His Majesty naturally can not take any stand in the questions between Austria and Serbia, for they are beyond his competence, but Francis Joseph may be sure that His Majesty, in accordance with his treaty obligations and old friendship, will stand true by Austria's side.[37]

Bethmann also telegraphed immediately to the German Chargé d'Affaires in Bucharest, for King Carol's information, concerning Francis Joseph's letter to the Kaiser, the Sarajevo assassination, and Germany's resulting consent to accept Tisza's Balkan policy of winning Bulgaria:

The Kaiser, as is known to King Carol, has constantly intervened at Vienna in favor of an understanding with Serbia. In spite of this, the Austro-Serbian relations have grown steadily worse. In view of the assassination at Sarajevo, which evidently appears to be the result of a well organized plot and of the policy promoted by the Government at Belgrade for uniting all South Slavs under the Serbian flag, His Majesty understands that Emperor Francis Joseph regards an understanding with Serbia as impossible,

[37] Bethmann to Tschirschky, July 6; K.D., 15. The original draft made by Zimmermann had said Germany would stand true by Austria's side "under all circumstances;" but these last three words were stricken out by the more cautious Bethmann and not sent to Tschirschky. The Kaiser's personal reply to Francis Joseph, drawn up by the Foreign Office on July 9 and sent on July 14, after expressing condolences, is of similar tenor; K.D., 26.

and, by approaching Bulgaria, is seeking to counteract the dangers threatening his dynasty and his empire from the side of Serbia. His Majesty has therefore agreed that Francis Joseph should receive favorably Bulgaria's expressed desires for adhesion to the Triple Alliance.[38]

Szögyény also, after an interview with Bethmann on the morning of July 6, at which Hoyos and Zimmermann were present, sent a second telegram to Berchtold. The first part of this substantially reproduced what Bethmann had telegraphed to Tschirschky as Germany's decision in regard to the new diplomatic action at Sofia and Bucharest; and as to Serbia: "Austria must judge what is to be done to clear up her relation with Serbia; but whatever Austria's decision may turn out to be, Austria can count with certainty upon it, that Germany will stand behind her as an ally and friend."

Szögyény then went on to make other assertions of which there is no trace in Falkenhayn's letter or in Bethmann's telegrams as to Germany's position on July 5 and 6:

> In the course of further conversation, I made certain that the Chancellor, as well as the Emperor, regards an immediate action by Austria against Serbia as the most radical and best solution of our Balkan difficulties. From an international point of view he regards the present moment as more favorable than a later one. He is in complete agreement that we should not inform either Italy or Rumania beforehand of an eventual action against Serbia. On the other hand, Italy ought to be informed now by Germany and by us of the intention of bringing about Bulgaria's adhesion to the Triple Alliance. At the close of the interview the Chancellor asked about the state of affairs in Albania, and warned us most energetically against any plans

[38] Bethmann to Waldburg, July 6; K.D., 16. The German Minister at Sofia was also instructed to support Austrian steps to win Bulgaria; K.D., 17.

which might endanger our relations with Italy and the existence of the Triple Alliance.[39]

It is easy to see why Szögyény alleged that Bethmann was "in complete agreement" with him that Austria should not inform Italy beforehand of action against Serbia. Like most Austrian officials, he now wanted war with Serbia, and by this statement encouraged Berchtold not to inform Italy beforehand, for fear that Rome would let the cat out of the bag at Belgrade, or at least that Italy would make demands for territorial compensation which Austria had no intention of giving. But this policy of deceiving Italy, or of delaying to inform her, was so completely contrary to the German attitude just before and after July 5, that one is forced to doubt the accuracy of the Austrian Ambassador's assertion. Germany's whole effort in recent years had been to keep Italy loyal and to restrain Austria from doing things in the Balkans which would unduly offend her, and make her likely to abandon completely her treaty obligations in the Triple Alliance. On July 3 Tschirschky had expressed to Berchtold Germany's unvarying attitude, by reminding him of "Italy, which, in view of her relations as an ally, ought to be consulted before the adoption of any military action." Berchtold had replied: "If we should put this question before the Cabinet at Rome, they would probably demand Valona as compensation, but we cannot concede this." [40]

Similarly, a little later, on July 15, Jagow reiterated Tschirschky's statement that Austria should inform Italy beforehand: "It is, according to my opinion, of the *greatest* importance that Austria should come to an understanding with the Cabinet at Rome as to her aims in case of a conflict with Serbia, and that she should hold her on her side,

[39] Szögyény to Berchtold, July 6, 5:10 P. M.; A.R.B., I, 7; Gooss, p. 32. *Cf.* Berchtold to Merey in Rome, July 12; A.R.B., I, 16.
[40] A.R.B., I, 3.

or (since a conflict with Serbia alone does not give rise to the *casus foederis*) keep her strictly neutral. Italy has the right, according to her agreements with Austria, in case of any change in the Balkans in favor of the Dual Monarchy, to claim compensations." [41] Thus Szögyény's assertion that Bethmann agreed that Italy should not be informed beforehand of an eventual action against Serbia is directly contrary to the whole tenor of German policy. It even seems to be contradicted by Szögyény's own words at the end of his despatch, that Bethmann "warned us most energetically against any plans which might endanger our relations with Italy." Nothing would be more calculated to do this, as the event proved, than the presenting Italy with a *fait accompli* of which she had been told nothing by her ally. Hoyos, however, in the course of reckless conversation with Zimmermann, seems to have indicated Berchtold's intention of keeping Italy in the dark, and secured Zimmermann's assent, and so stated later in Vienna.[42] But it is doubtful whether the Kaiser or Bethmann gave any such assent. If such is the case, and if Szögyény attributed to Bethmann a concession made only by Zimmermann, this would be one of the instances in which Szögyény did not report quite accurately, and exerted an influence in the direction of encouraging Austria in her reckless policy.[43]

41 Jagow to Tschirschky, July 15; K.D., 46. For Germany's repeated attempts to persuade Austria to come to a seasonable and reasonable understanding with Italy, see K.D., 57, 68, 87, 89, 94, 104, 119, 150, 202, 212, 244, 267, 269, 287, 326, 396, 573, 577.

42 Stolberg to Jagow, July 18, K.D., 87; and Berchtold's statement to Tschirschky, July 20 (Journal No. 3425; A.R.B., I, 35): "I cannot make up my mind to enter at present into an exchange of views with the Italian Government concerning our action, a point moreover which was discussed between Hoyos and Zimmermann at Berlin."

43 For other instances, *cf.* Gooss, pp. 31, note 1, 173 ff., 235 ff., 248, note 3, and 253, note 2; and below ch. ix, at notes 33-36.

CONCLUSIONS AS TO GERMANY'S ATTITUDE ON JULY 5 AND 6

If one compares the two accounts of Germany's attitude as stated by Bethmann and by Szögyény, he will find that they are somewhat different in substance and spirit. Bethmann devotes four-fifths of his attention to the innovation in German policy involved in the Austrian diplomatic project of winning Bulgaria to the Triple Alliance. He only touches briefly, at the end of his telegram, on the question of Austro-Serbian relations, and then only to repeat a principle which he and Kiderlen had stated at one of the crises in the Balkan Wars—Germany will continue to act as a loyal ally, but must leave with Austria the decision as to what her vital interests require.[44] Szögyény, on the other hand, is mainly interested in Berchtold's projected military action against Serbia, of which he had been made acquainted by Count Hoyos. His telegrams represent both the Kaiser and Bethmann as believing "an immediate action by Austria against Serbia as the most radical and best solution" and "the present moment as more favorable than a later one"; and he says Bethmann is "in complete agreement" that neither Italy nor Rumania should be informed beforehand.

What is the explanation of this divergence in the two accounts? Probably it is partly to be found, as Gooss suggests, in the fact that Szögyény was already suffering from old age, and did not always grasp and report conversations accurately. His inaptitude had been responsible for some of the diplomatic friction between Berlin and Vienna during the Balkan Wars. He was a personal favorite with Em-

[44] *Cf.* Kaiser's conversation with Bethmann Nov. 9, 1912 (G.P., XXXIII, 302-305), and Kiderlen to Tschirschky, Nov. 19, 1912 (*ibid.*, p. 361); "We are not the arbiter of what Austria regards as her vital interests or as possible concessions in regard to Albania; but we have expressly supported in diplomacy what Austria has indicated to us as her necessary demands, and we shall continue to do so."

peror William, but also moved in Berlin militarist circles, whose ideas did not always accord with the more moderate and cautious policies of Bethmann. Owing to Szögyény's superannuation, and perhaps to his bellicose tendencies and Magyar sympathies, Franz Ferdinand several weeks before the Sarajevo tragedy had raised the question of replacing him by a more capable representative. His successor, Prince Gottfried Hohenlohe, had already been selected and approved in Berlin on June 12. But unfortunately, in view of the sudden development of the July crisis, the change was not made until August 19, 1914.[45] In the case of these Potsdam conversations Szögyény seems to have over-emphasized Berlin's approval of the indefinitely stated second part of Berchtold's appeal.

Probably also the divergence is partly to be explained as reflecting a slight divergence of attitude on the part of Bethmann, the Kaiser, and Zimmermann. Bethmann, more optimistic and idealistic in character, desiring better relations with England and the Triple Entente, and encouraged by the Bagdad and Portuguese colonial treaties now ready for final signature, hoped that the Austro-Serbian crisis might be sufficiently dealt with by the peaceful diplomatic plan of winning over Bulgaria. He was less affected emotionally by the Archduke's death. He had recently been alarmed at the reckless way Berchtold had antagonized Italy in connection with Montenegro and thereby endangered the increasingly tottering Triple Alliance structure. "Vienna is beginning to emancipate herself from us somewhat rudely [*etwas stark*]) and in my opinion needs to be reined in before it is too late," [46] he had written a few weeks earlier, and had accordingly sent a strong warning to Berchtold. So now, after Sarajevo, he did not want to encourage Berchtold to other reckless adventures; and,

45 G.P., XXXIX, 362 f., 546; Dirr, p. 114.
46 Bethmann to Jagow, May 8, 1914; G.P., XXXVIII, 349 ff.

while forced to agree with the Kaiser that Germany must promise to support Austria, he had stricken out the words "in all circumstances" from the telegram as drafted by Zimmermann.[47]

The Kaiser, with shrewder insight than Bethmann, with longer acquaintance with the Balkan question, and bound by close personal ties to Franz Ferdinand and Francis Joseph, but with less self-control and less regard for the political consequences of his acts, expressed his feelings in the marginal note, "Now or never, etc.," which has already been quoted.[48] He was willing to assent to the Austrian plan of winning Bulgaria, though this did not accord with his past policy and his personal distrust of King Ferdinand. He was more impressed with the last part of Berchtold's memorandum and Francis Joseph's letter urging the necessity for some energetic action to put an end to the Greater Serbian danger. In view of Austria's hesitations and vacillations in the past, he advised her to act quickly while she had the sympathy of Europe; but, as Falkenhayn's letter to Moltke indicates, it was doubted whether Berchtold really would make any immediate and decisive moves.

Zimmermann, Acting-Secretary of State until Jagow's return to Berlin after these conversations of July 5 and 6, had at first reflected Bethmann's cautious views. Immediately after Sarajevo he "recommended the greatest caution" to Szögyény, advised Serbia "to call to account the persons guilty," and urged the Entente Ambassadors to back up this timely advice in order to avert dangerous consequences.[49] But on July 4 the Kaiser's marginal note, "Now or never, etc.," was received at the Foreign Office, and Zimmermann thereafter took his cue from it. He apparently made no objections when Hoyos confided to him

[47] K.D., 15; see above, note 37.

[48] K.D., 7; see above, at note 30.

[49] A.R.B., I, 5; Dirr, p. 118; B.D., 22, 44; see above at note 16, and ch. iii, at notes 51, 52.

that "Austria had in mind a complete partition of Serbia." Berchtold had carefully avoided saying anything of this in the missives which Szögyény was to present to the Kaiser. When Hoyos returned to Vienna and reported what he had said to Zimmermann about partitioning Serbia, his remarks were promptly disavowed: "Berchtold, and especially Tisza, want it expressly emphasized that Hoyos was uttering merely a purely personal opinion." [50]

Such were the views of the three leading Berlin officials at the moment Germany had to make her decision on July 5 and 6. It would be a mistake to exaggerate the divergence of attitudes, but it helps to explain the way in which the "blank check" was given at Berlin, and the way it was interpreted and used at Vienna. During the following days the Kaiser was absent on his northern cruise and Bethmann was on his estate at Hohenfinow, so that they exerted little influence on the course of affairs. This left the German Foreign Office in charge of Zimmermann, and then of Jagow who returned to Berlin and took up again his duties as Secretary of State soon after the departure of Hoyos on July 6. Jagow, though in general agreement with Zimmermann, soon began to adopt a more cautious attitude. He forwarded some good advice to Vienna—which Berchtold disregarded. In order to find out where the Austrian path was leading, he began to offer advice and ask questions—which Berchtold did not answer fully and frankly.[51]

Thus the Kaiser and his advisers, influenced by the

50 Tschirschky to German Foreign Office, July 7, 3:25 P. M.; K.D., 18; *cf.* also 61 and 361. Evidently the Kaiser was unaware on Sunday afternoon of this reckless talk of Hoyos, which probably took place on Monday morning after he had left for Kiel. This explains why this passage relating to the Hoyos incident was cut out from Tschirschky's despatch when it was forwarded by Jagow for the Kaiser's perusal; K.D., note 2.

51 *Cf.* Jagow's despatches, July 9-18; K.D., 23, 31, 33, 36, 39, 46, 61, 67-70, 72; and the information gathered from Zimmermann and Jagow by the Bavarian Legation in Berlin, in Dirr, pp. 4-13, 123-129.

Sarajevo assassination and confronted with Berchtold's appeal for support, made their decision. Toward Bulgaria they agreed to adopt a new policy; and in regard to Serbia, they stated, according to Szögyény: "Austria must judge what is to be done to clear up her relation to Serbia; whatever Austria's decision may turn out to be, Austria can count with certainty upon it, that Germany will stand behind her as an ally and friend." [52] They gave Austria a free hand and made the grave mistake of putting the situation outside of their control into the hands of a man as reckless and unscrupulous as Berchtold. They committed themselves to a leap in the dark. They soon found themselves involved, as we shall see, in actions which they did not approve, and by decisions which were taken against their advice; but they could not seriously object and protest—at least until the eleventh hour when it proved too late—because they had pledged their support to Austria in advance, and any hesitation on their part would only weaken the Triple Alliance at a critical moment when it most needed to be strong. The Kaiser and his advisers on July 5 and 6 were not criminals plotting the World War; they were simpletons putting "a noose about their necks" [53] and handing the other end of the rope to a stupid and clumsy adventurer who now felt free to go as far as he liked. In so doing they were incurring a grave responsibility for what happened later.

[52] Szögyény to Berchtold, July 6; A.R.B., I, 7; see above, at notes 19, 37, 39.

[53] As the Kaiser himself noted frantically on July 30, after hearing of Grey's warning, Russian mobilization measures, and Berchtold's persistent disregard of all proposed peaceful solutions: in addition to encirclement by the Entente, "the stupidity and clumsiness of our ally has been made a hangman's noose for us" [wird uns die Dummheit und Ungeschicklichkeit unseres Verbündeten zum Fallstrick gemacht]; K.D., 401.

BERCHTOLD'S EFFORTS TO CONVERT TISZA

Having been informed by Szögyény that Germany assented to the second part of his double-faced appeal, i.e., that Germany would stand firm as an ally in whatever Austria should decide to undertake against Serbia, Berchtold no longer pretended to advocate the first part, i.e., the peace program of Tisza.[54] For he had now overcome half his difficulties. He now needed only to persuade his aged monarch and Tisza to agree to the extirpation of the Serbian danger, which Conrad had long urged,[55] and which he himself had finally decided upon. How was this to be done?

Tisza's *"politique de longue main"* to win Bulgaria and secure peace in the Balkans for a few years at least had been adopted by Berchtold and made the basis for his memorandum to Berlin—until the news of Sarajevo made him suddenly change to Conrad's war program. Tisza, however, was not the kind of man to allow his matured judgments to be overturned in a moment even by such a crime. He had told Berchtold frankly that the provoking of such a war with Serbia would be "a fatal mistake"; it would pillory Austrians "before the whole world as disturbers of the peace, besides beginning a great war under the most unfavorable circumstances." But he apparently made little impression on Berchtold. Tisza had also informed Francis

54 In fact he not only abandoned it, but on July 8 suggested to Berlin to drop taking further steps at Bucharest and Sofia for the winning of Bulgaria; and Berlin acquiesced; A.R.B., I, 11; K.D., 19, 21, 22. This only increased Berlin's belief in the "vacillation" of the "ever timid and undecided authorities in Vienna;" Schoen's report of July 18; Dirr, p. 7; K.D., IV, Anhang iv, No. 2.

55 Not counting the period 1906-1912, covered by the two first volumes of his memoirs, it may be noted that in the seventeen months from January 1, 1913 to June 1, 1914, the Chief of Staff had, according to his own statements, urged war against Serbia no less than twenty-five times; *cf.* Conrad, III, 12 ff., 74, 78, 82, 84, 114, 165, 178 ff., 183 f., 249, 257 f., 261, 267, 302 f., 333, 342, 354 f., 375 f., 405 f., 453 f., 457, 461, 463, 467, 477, 661, 694 ff.

Joseph of Berchtold's reckless plans and warned him against them.[56]

After Tisza had returned to Budapest, Berchtold added the postscript to the memorandum for Berlin, denouncing Serbia, and drew up the royal missive from Francis Joseph to Emperor William which, like the memorandum, set forth Tisza's peace program, but which also at its close hinted at more vigorous action against Serbia: peace "will only be possible when Serbia . . . *is eliminated as a political factor in the Balkans.* After the last frightful events in Bosnia, you too will be convinced that *a friendly settlement of the antagonism which divides Austria from Serbia is no longer to be thought of,* and that the peace policy of all European monarchs is threatened so long as this source of criminal agitation in Belgrade lives on *unpunished.*"[57]

Berchtold could not properly or constitutionally send such an important message on foreign policy, suggesting, as it did, a modification of what had already been agreed upon, without informing the Hungarian Premier. He therefore sent a copy to Tisza; but Tisza, on reading it, was not at all pleased with it. He feared it would make Berlin "shy off" from approving the peaceful diplomatic program. He suspected the truth, that Berchtold was scheming to get the backing of Germany for military action against Serbia rather than for the agreed-upon "*politique de longue main.*" He therefore telegraphed at once to Berchtold urging the omission of the words printed in italics above.[58] But at the very moment he was sending this telegram, Szögyény was already putting the unmodified text of the letter into Emperor William's hands at Potsdam. Berchtold had sent

[56] Tisza to Francis Joseph, July 1; A.R.B., I, 2.

[57] Francis Joseph to William II, drafted by Berchtold July 2, and presented by Szögyény July 5; K.D., 13; A.R.B., I, 1, Gooss, pp. 26-29; see above, at note 18. Words italicized were objected to by Tisza.

[58] Tisza to Berchtold, July 5, 11:50 A.M.; Gooss, p. 28 f.; Fraknói, p. 16.

it off without waiting to hear from Tisza. He had resorted to the sharp practice, which he was to employ later in similar fashion but in far more serious matters, of making use of a *fait accompli.* Disliking argument because of his natural indolence, his ignorance of detail, and his consequent dependence on his secretaries for information,[59] he always found it easier to take a step first, and avoid argument about it until after the moment had passed when the step could not very well be undone, and argument about it would therefore be futile.

The best lever with which to pry Tisza from his firm stand, as Berchtold, Hoyos and Forgach believed, was to represent to Tisza that Berlin wanted immediate and energetic action against Serbia; to make it appear that if Austria did not take advantage of the present favorable opportunity, Germany would more than ever regard Austria as *bündnisunfähig,* i.e., as a weak, hesitating, decrepit state of little value to Germany as an ally; and that consequently Berlin would disregard Austria's interests and treat her even more cavalierly in the future than in the past. In this purpose they were assisted by, or perhaps it would be more correct to say, they made use of, Tschirschky, the German Ambassador in Vienna.[60]

On July 4, at Forgach's suggestion, Berchtold sent to Francis Joseph and Tisza a rumor, gathered by one of the press agents in the Foreign Office, that "Tschirschky is re-

59 For indications of Berchtold's incompetence and aversion to the hard study necessary to master the intricate subject of foreign affairs, see H. Kanner's portrait of "Graf Berchtold, der aristrokratische Dilettant" in *Kaiserliche Katastrophen-Politik* (Vienna, 1922), pp. 87-93; and Dumaine, *La Dernière Ambassade de France en Autriche* (Paris, 1921), pp. 22, 34 ff., 99 f.

60 *Cf.* Berchtold to Tisza, July 8: "Aus den weiteren Aeusserungen des Botschafters [Tschirschky] konnte ich ersehen, dass man in Deutschland ein Transigieren unsererseits mit Serbien als Schwächebekenntniss auslegen würde, was nicht ohne Rückwirkung auf unsere Stellung im Dreibunde und die künftige Politik Deutschlands bleiben könnte;" A.R.B., I, 10.

ported to have declared, with the evident intention that it should be reported in the Ministry of Foreign Affairs, that Germany would support the Dual Monarchy through thick and thin, whatever should be decided against Serbia. . . . The sooner Austria attacked the better. Yesterday would have been better than today; today would be better than tomorrow. Even if the German press, which is wholly anti-Serbian today, should preach again in favor of peace, Vienna should not allow herself to be in doubt that the [German] Emperor and Empire would stick unconditionally to Austria-Hungary. One Great Power cannot speak more clearly to another than this." [61]

Again on July 6, the moment he received from Berlin Szögyény's version of the interviews with the Kaiser and Bethmann, Berchtold had Forgach forward the news to Tisza,[62] and for Tuesday, July 7, he summoned a Ministerial Council to approve the repressive measures in Bosnia and the warlike action against Serbia which he desired. Before the Council met, he arranged for a preliminary meeting, including himself, Tisza and Stürgkh, the Premiers respectively of Hungary and Austria, Tschirschky, and also Hoyos, who had just come back from Berlin and was one of the most active instigators for war with Serbia. Hoyos read aloud the two despatches from Szögyény and a memorandum of his own talk with Zimmermann. Berchtold

[61] Austrian Foreign Office *Journal* No. 3117; Gooss, p. 40, n. 1. How far Tschirschky was correctly reported here, and how far his words were twisted by Berchtold and his agents for their own purposes does not appear. Even if correctly reported, Tschirschky was evidently giving expression merely to his own personal views, for there is no indication in any of the documents that he had at this time received from Berlin any instructions to this effect; and if he had received instructions he would certainly have stated them officially to Berchtold, who would have been only too glad to emphasize the fact to Francis Joseph and Tisza. For Tschirschky's genuine views, given on June 30, July 2 and 3,—expressions of Austro-German solidarity, coupled with warnings against any hasty and reckless steps which would disturb the general European situation, see K.D., 7, 11; A.R.B., I, 3; and above, at notes 14 and 15.

[62] Forgach to Tisza, July 6, 1:30 P.M.; Gooss, p. 65.

expressed to Tschirschky his gratitude to the Kaiser and Bethmann "for their clear attitude which was in accordance with treaty obligations and friendship," but promptly disavowed what Hoyos had said to Zimmermann about Austria's intention to partition Serbia.[63]

At the Ministerial Council of July 7, Berchtold raised the question:

> whether the time had not come to make Serbia harmless once for all through the use of force. Such a decisive blow could not be struck without diplomatic preparations. So he had got into touch with the German Government. The discussions in Berlin had led to a very satisfactory result, inasmuch as Emperor William, as well as Bethmann-Hollweg, had given emphatic assurance of unconditional German support in case of a warlike complication with Serbia.[64] Italy and Rumania must still be reckoned with; and here he was in accord with the Berlin Cabinet that it was better to act first without consulting them, and then await any possible demands for compensation.[65]
>
> He [Berchtold] was aware that a passage of arms with Serbia might result in a war with Russia. But Russia was following a policy, that, looking to the future, was aiming at a combination of the Balkan states, including Rumania, for the purpose of using them against the Monarchy when the time seemed opportune. He was of the opinion that Austria must take into account the fact that

[63] K.D., 18; see above, at note 50.

[64] The words, "inasmuch as . . . with Serbia," were added by Berchtold afterwards to the minutes which were noted down by Hoyos; Gooss, p. 51, n. 3. Berchtold's alteration of the record would make it easier for him to persuade Francis Joseph to consent to war with Serbia when the minutes of the Council were presented to him for approval.

[65] Berchtold here implies that it was the Berlin Cabinet which made the suggestion that Italy and Rumania be not informed. In reality, (even admitting the fact of Bethmann's assent on this point which is doubtful; see above, at notes 39-42), it is clear from Szögyény's own phrase, "Bethmann as well as the Emperor is in complete agreement with us," that it was from the Austrian, and not from the German, side that this shortsighted suggestion was first made.

her situation in the face of such a policy was bound to become increasingly worse, especially as passive toleration would be interpreted by her South Slavs and Rumanians as a sign of weakness, and would lend strength to the magnetic power of the two border states.

The logical conclusion of what he had said was that Austria should get ahead of her enemies, and, by a timely final reckoning with Serbia, put an end to the movement which was already in full swing, a thing which might be impossible later.[66]

Tisza thereupon replied, at least according to the minutes which were made by Hoyos but which were somewhat touched up afterwards by Berchtold:

He [Tisza] agreed with Berchtold that the situation had changed somewhat in the last few days as a result of the investigation [at Sarajevo] and the attitude of the Serbian press, and emphasized that he also regarded the possibility of warlike action against Serbia as nearer than he had believed just after the crime at Sarajevo. But he would never agree to a surprise attack on Serbia without preliminary diplomatic action, which seemed to be intended [by Berchtold], and which had been unfortunately mentioned by Hoyos in Berlin, because in this case we should stand, in his opinion, in a very bad position before the eyes of Europe, and in all probability would have to reckon with the hostility of all the Balkan States except Bulgaria; and Bulgaria, which is at present very weak. would be unable to give us any corresponding support.

Unquestionably demands must be made on Serbia, but

[66] This and the following quotations are from the minutes of the Ministerial Council of July 7 in A.R.B., I, 8; English translation in the N. Y. Times *Current History,* Dec., 1919, pp. 445-460; Gooss, pp. 50-62, indicates the alterations which Berchtold made in the minutes See also Conrad, IV, 43-56, who was present with an Admiral at the afternoon session from 3-5 P. M., and gave secret military information, which he records in his memoirs but which was omitted for reasons of prudence from the official minutes of the Council; Fraknói, pp. 18-27; the reports of Tschirschky (K.D., 19) and of Tucher, the Bavarian Minister in Vienna, Dirr, p. 125 f.; and *Investigating Comm.* I, p. 90.

no ultimatum must be sent until Serbia had failed to comply with these demands. These demands, to be sure, must be severe, but not such as could not be complied with. If Serbia accepted them, we should be able to point to a notable diplomatic success, and have increased our prestige in the Balkans. If the demands were not complied with, he too would favor military action, but must still emphasize that we aim at the diminution, but not the complete annihilation, of Serbia, both because this would never be permitted by Russia without a life-and-death struggle, and because he, as Hungarian Premier, could never consent to have the Dual Monarchy annex any part of Serbia.

Refusing to be shaken by Berchtold's assertion that Germany was in favor of immediate military action, Tisza declared further:

It is not Germany's affair to decide whether we should attack Serbia now or not. He personally was of the opinion that it was not unconditionally necessary to make war at the present moment, and that in view of the excited state of public opinion in Rumania we should have to reckon with a Rumanian attack, and in any case should have to maintain considerable forces in Transylvania to intimidate the Rumanians. At present, when Germany had happily prepared the way for the adhesion of Bulgaria, there was opened a promising prospect for successful diplomatic action in the Balkans; by joining with Bulgaria and Turkey, and by securing their adhesion to the Triple Alliance, we could out-balance Rumania and Serbia, and so compel Rumania to return to the Triple Alliance. As to Europe, one must bear in mind that the strength of France, in comparison with that of Germany, was steadily decreasing on account of her lower birth-rate, and that Germany therefore in the future would have more troops available for use against Russia. . . . [He concluded therefore that the Bosnian situation could be improved by internal administrative reforms, and that] he could not decide unconditionally for war, but would consider a corresponding diplomatic success

> with the severe humiliation of Serbia as the proper means for improving Austria's position and making possible a successful Balkan policy.

Berchtold answered in reply that the last few years had shown that, though diplomatic victories had raised the prestige of the Monarchy temporarily, they had only increased the existing tension in Austro-Serbian relations. Neither the success in the Annexation Crisis, nor that in connection with the creation of Albania, nor the later backing-down on Serbia's part in October, 1913, had actually changed the situation materially. "A radical settlement of the problem raised by the Greater Serbia propaganda, systematically carried on from Belgrade, whose disruptive force could be detected as far as Agram and Zara, was only possible through an energetic intervention." The Rumanian danger he did not think serious. And as for the relative strength of the Great Powers, Russia's increasing population more than offset France's declining birth-rate.

After a long discussion through the morning and afternoon, in which all the ministers except Tisza expressed views in virtual agreement with Berchtold, and in which Conrad set forth secret military plans which he asked not to be recorded in the minutes, no complete agreement was reached. Tisza was willing that specific demands should be made upon Serbia, but insisted that they should not deliberately be made so hard that Serbia could not comply with them, and that they should not be in the form of an ultimatum. He also insisted that he should see them before they were sent, so that he should not be faced with another *fait accompli*. All the other ministers, however, agreed with Berchtold against Tisza, "that a purely diplomatic victory, even if it ended with a striking humiliation of Serbia, would be worthless, and that consequently the demands presented to Serbia must be so far-reaching that their rejection would be a foregone conclusion, and so the way would be prepared for a radical solution through a military attack." As to military preparations, Tisza made his view prevail to the extent that the others consented that there should be no mobilization until after specific demands and an ultimatum had been successively presented and rejected.

At the close of the meeting Berchtold stated that he would present its results to Francis Joseph at Ischl next day. Tisza, however, who had to return to Budapest, feared that his own views against deliberately forcing war upon Serbia might not be effectively presented by Berchtold to the aged sovereign. He therefore requested Berchtold to delay his audience until he, Tisza, could draw up a memoir to be laid before the Emperor along with Berchtold's report on the Ministerial Council. This Berchtold consented to do, and postponed his audience with the Emperor until Thursday morning, July 9.

In his memoir of July 8 Tisza still urged the advisability of his original diplomatic program to win Bulgaria; but in view of the unanimity of the opinion against him in the Council the day before, he devoted most of his long memoir to what had now become the main secret question at Vienna: should the demands on Serbia, as Tisza insisted, take the form of a polite note, humiliating but not impossible for Serbia, stating specific grievances, and asking remedies which Austria was ready, *bona fide,* to accept as satisfactory; or, should the demands, as Berchtold and the majority wished, be a general indictment of Serbia in the form of an ultimatum, deliberately worded to provoke immediate war with Serbia? In favor of the former, Tisza argued to the Emperor, as he had done in the Council:

> I [Tisza] am not pleading at all that we should swallow all these provocations [of Serbia], and I am ready to assume the consequences of a war caused by a rejection

of our just demands. But, in my opinion, it must be made possible for Serbia to avoid war by accepting a severe diplomatic defeat, and if it comes to war it will be clear to the world that we stand on the basis of justifiable self-defense. A note in moderate, but not threatening, language should be addressed to Serbia, which should set forth our specific grievances and our precise demands in connection with them. [He suggests, for example, the remarks of the Serbian Minister, Spalajkovitch in St. Petersburg, and Jovanovitch in Berlin, the fact that the bombs in Bosnia came from the Serbian arsenal at Kragujevac, that the assassins crossed the border with false passes issued by Serbian authorities; and the general attitude of the Serbian press, societies, and schools.]

Should Serbia give an unsatisfactory answer, or try dilatory tactics, an ultimatum should follow, and after its expiration, the opening of hostilities. . . . After a successful war Serbia could be diminished in area by the cession of some of the conquered districts to Bulgaria, Greece, and Rumania, but we ourselves should ask at most merely certain important boundary modifications. To be sure, we could claim a war indemnity, which would give us the chance to keep a firm hand on Serbia for a long time. . . .

Should Serbia yield, we must accept this solution *bona fide,* and not make her retreat impossible.[67]

This possible peaceful solution urged by Tisza was not at all what Berchtold wanted. Shortly after Tisza had left Vienna, he again tried to apply the German lever, by alleging in a letter to Tisza on July 8:

Tschirschky has just left me, after informing me that he has received a telegram from Berlin in which his Imperial Master directed him to declare here *most emphatically* that Berlin expects Austria to act against Serbia, and that it would not be understood in Germany if we should let this opportunity go by without striking a blow. . . . From

67 Tisza to Francis Joseph, July 8; A.R.B., I, 12.

further things the Ambassador said, I could see that in Germany any yielding on our part toward Serbia would be interpreted as a confession of weakness, which would not fail to react on our position in the Triple Alliance and on Germany's future policy.

These statements of Tschirschky's seem to me of such importance as possibly influencing your conclusions that I wanted to inform you of them at once, and beg you, if you see fit, to send me a cipher telegram to this effect at Ischl, where I shall be tomorrow morning and could interpret your view to His Majesty.[68]

Tisza was apparently unmoved by this, and did not telegraph as requested. Accordingly, although Berchtold had gone to Ischl to get Francis Joseph's approval for such demands upon Serbia "that their acceptance would be out of the question," [69] he did not succeed, as we learn from Tschirschky's report of July 10:

. . . The Minister informed the Emperor of the two possible methods of procedure against Serbia which are in question here. His Majesty thought perhaps the difference between them could be bridged over. But in general His Majesty inclines to the view that specific demands should be addressed to Serbia. Count Berchtold likewise would

[68] Berchtold to Tisza, July 8, *ca.* 8 P. M.; A.R.B., I, 10; Gooss, p. 68 ff. There are serious grounds for thinking that Berchtold himself fabricated these statements which he attributed to Tschirschky, his purpose being, as stated in the second paragraph, to "influence" Tisza: (1) The *Kautsky Documents* do not contain any such telegram to Tschirschky, nor does Tschirschky make any acknowledgment of its receipt or the carrying out of its instructions, as he usually does in such cases; (2) Tschirschky, in reporting his interview with Berchtold on July 8, (K.D., 19) does not make the slightest mention of any such statements as Berchtold alleged to Tisza; (3) Berchtold speaks of "a telegram from Berlin in which his Imperial Master etc.," whereas the Kaiser had already left Berlin two days earlier to go on his northern cruise. It may be noted that Berchtold did receive a telegram from Szögyény on July 8, alleging that Berlin was waiting with impatience for a decision (Gooss, p. 39 f.); perhaps it was the contents of Szögyény's telegram which Berchtold fathered upon Tschirschky to serve his purpose of "influencing" Tisza.

[69] Tschirschky to Berlin F.O., July 8; 8:10 P. M.; K.D., 19.

not deny the advantages of such a procedure. . . . He thinks one might demand among other things the establishment of an Austro-Hungarian agency in Belgrade to watch from there the Greater Serbia machinations, and also the dissolution of societies and the dismissal of compromised officers. The time-limit for this answer ought to be made as short as possible, perhaps 48 hours. To be sure, even this short time-limit would suffice for Belgrade to get directions from St. Petersburg. Should the Serbians accept all the demands made, this would be a solution which would be "very unwelcome" to him, and therefore he was thinking how he could frame demands which would make Serbia's acceptance wholly impossible.

Finally the Minister complained again of Count Tisza's attitude, which made difficult for him an energetic action against Serbia. Count Tisza maintained that one must proceed "gentleman-like," but this was hardly appropriate, when such important interests of state were at issue, and especially toward such an opponent as Serbia.[70]

Thus, by July 9, Berchtold had secured the approval of Francis Joseph and Tisza to the idea that some demands should be presented to Serbia, but not in the form of an ultimatum, the terms of which were to be deliberately framed to make acceptance impossible. Nevertheless, he secretly proceeded with this second purpose. On July 11 he told Tschirschky that he had summoned Tisza to Vienna for a conference on July 14, when he hoped the document would be finally drafted:

So far as he [Berchtold] could say today, the chief demands on Serbia would be to request that the King should officially and publicly make a declaration, and publish it as an army order, that Serbia abandons the policy of a Greater Serbia; secondly, the institution of an Austro-Hungarian Government agency which should watch over the strict observance of this declaration. The time-limit

70 Tschirschky to Berlin, F.O., July 10; K.D., 29.

for the answer to the note would be as short as possible, perhaps 48 hours. If the answer was not regarded in Vienna as satisfactory, mobilization would take place at once.[71]

WIESNER'S REPORT OF JULY 13

During the first two weeks after the murder of Franz Ferdinand, all action proposed against Serbia, both in Vienna and Berlin, had been based on the conviction that "the crime was the result of a well-organized plot, the threads of which reach to Belgrade." To gather proof of this Berchtold sent Dr. Wiesner, a legal counsellor of the Foreign Office, to Sarajevo on July 11 to investigate on the spot. Wiesner was a cautious and conservative lawyer who did not want to make any charges against Serbia except what were clearly established by documentary evidence and could satisfactorily stand examination in a court of law. Having to examine the material hurriedly during a couple of days and nights at Sarajevo, he learned only a small part of what we now know concerning the way the plot was organized in Belgrade.

Wiesner telegraphed from Sarajevo on July 13 that it was the prevailing conviction of all persons of influence in Bosnia that the Greater Serbia propaganda there was carried on with the knowledge and approval of the Serbian Government, but that the evidence laid before him gave "no support for the charge that this propaganda is promoted by the Serbian Government. The evidence that this

[71] Private letter of Tschirschky to Jagow, July 11; *Investig. Comm.*, I, p. 120 f. This private letter and the telegram of July 10 quoted above, were to prove important, as they evidently formed the basis of the famous despatch of Schoen, the counsellor of the Bavarian Legation at Berlin, on July 18, which was published in mutilated form by Kurt Eisner and cited at the Peace Conference as one of the proofs of Germany's war responsibility; its publication also gave rise to a famous libel suit at Munich (*cf.* Dirr *passim*). These two reports of Tschirschky were evidently the basis also of Tirpitz's statement in his polemic against Bethmann that "on July 13 the Chancellor was acquainted with the essential points of the ultimatum;" Tirpitz, *Erinnerungen,* p. 212 f.

agitation is stirred up by societies in Serbia and is tolerated by the Serbian Government is sufficient, although scanty." As to the crime itself, "there is nothing to prove, or even to cause suspicion of the Serbian Government's cognizance of the steps leading to the crime, or of its preparing it, or of its supplying the weapons. On the contrary, there are indications that this is to be regarded as out of the question." [72] On the other hand, there was "hardly a doubt that the crime was resolved upon in Belgrade, and prepared with the coöperation of Serbian officials, Ciganovitch and Major Tankositch, who provided bombs, Brownings, ammunition, and cyanide of potassium"; that the bombs came from the Serbian Kragujevac arsenal; and that the three assassins, with bombs and weapons upon them, were secretly smuggled across the frontier to Bosnia by Serbian agencies through the assistance of Ciganovitch and the frontier-captains at Shabats and Loznica. He also reported that there was valuable material in regard to the *Narodna Odbrana* which had not yet been sifted, but which he was bringing back to Vienna next day for further study. This was incorporated in the Austrian *dossier* later. Meanwhile he suggested the following demands as justified by the evidence already found:

[72] These two sentences, and these only, were cited from the Wiesner report by Mr. Secretary Lansing and Mr. J. B. Scott, the American members of the Commission on the Responsibility of the Authors of the War, at the Paris Peace Conference, April 4, 1919 (*German White Book concerning the Authors of the War,* Eng. trans., N. Y., 1924, p. 28). But in stating that these two sentences were the "essential portion" of the Wiesner report, they gave a totally misleading impression of its true character. Whether they did this deliberately, or whether they were supplied with the report only in this mutilated form (possibly by Mr. Vesnitch, the Serbian Minister in Paris, who, as they admit, supplied them with other documents), they have never stated, so far as the writer knows. For other cases in which the "evidence" for Germany's responsibility for the World War was later proven to be of an unsound or misleading character, thereby constituting a moral justification for a "revision" of the Versailles Treaty, see A. von Wegerer, "Die Unterlagen des Versailler Urteils über die Schuld am Ausbruch des Weltkrieges," in KSF, V, 1087-1106, Nov., 1927; and in *Current History,* Aug., 1928, p. 810 ff.

A. Suppression of the coöperation of Serbian official agencies smuggling persons and goods across the frontier.
B. Dismissal of Serbian frontier-captains at Shabats and Loznica as well as the implicated customs officials.
C. Prosecution of Ciganovitch and Tankositch.[73]

Dr. Wiesner also showed General Potiorek a copy of this telegram to Berchtold absolving the Serbian Government from direct complicity in the Sarajevo crime, though not from the responsibility for the subversive agitation against Austria. Potiorek thought the report much too conservative. He at once wrote to Conrad, expressing his own convictions, which, as we now know from the activities of the "Black Hand," were very much closer to the truth. "It is downright impossible that some person or other in a democratic government in such a small country as Serbia should not have had knowledge of the preparation of the crime and the traitorous working methods of the whole propaganda. According to the investigations so far, several persons in Bosnia-Herzegovina certainly knew what was going to happen on June 28. According to one of the assassins the preparations were talked over in a tavern in Belgrade. . . . Furthermore, in Serbia, by the side of the official Government, there is a rival military government, which takes its existence from the army. That Serbian officers in active service participated in the preparation of the assassination, and also participated prominently in the whole propaganda, and are therefore among the instigators of the traitorous agitation stirred up in our country, is proven. The army, to be sure, is not part of the Government. But to try to main-

[73] Wiesner to Berchtold, July 13; 1:10 and 2 P. M.; A.R.B., I, no. 17; Gooss, p. 91 ff. For the difficulties under which Dr. Wiesner labored in drawing up this preliminary report, owing to the shortness of the time at his disposal and his desire to make no charges not fully proven, and also for Entente misrepresentations concerning it, see his two valuable articles: "Der Serajevoer Mord und die Kriegsschuldfrage," in Das Neue Reich, No. 44, August 2, 1924; and "Der verfälschte und der echte Text des 'Dokument Wiesner,'" in KSF, III, 641-657, Oct., 1925.

tain that the official Serbian Government does not know what the army is doing, is by no means tenable." Potiorek added new information which he had just received concerning the treasonable activities of the Sokol Societies in which Serbian military officers and high officials had an active part. He declared that he could not assume the responsibility of remaining in office unless vigorous measures were taken at once. Mere demands such as those suggested by Wiesner were not enough. It was necessary to crush the machine behind all this agitation, i.e., the Serbian army. "All this sort of thing would have been wholly impossible, unless it had been known and tolerated, if not furthered, by the Serbian Government." [74]

Potiorek's views, strengthened by long residence in Bosnia and close contact with Serbia, corresponded more nearly to what Berchtold and the Ballplatz officials suspected was the truth than Wiesner's more judicial and conservative preliminary conclusions. The three demands which Wiesner had suggested were incorporated in the ultimatum to Serbia, but otherwise Berchtold appears to have made little or no immediate use of his report. Wiesner was left at work sifting the material and drawing up the *dossier* of evidence to be presented to the Powers. Meanwhile Berchtold continued with the plan, desired by Conrad and Potiorek, of bringing about a localized preventive war against Serbia.

THE CONVERSION OF TISZA

On July 14 Berchtold finally succeeded in persuading Tisza to give up his opposition to an ultimatum with a short time-limit. But he had to yield to Tisza's unalterable demand that before the ultimatum was presented, a full Ministerial Council should adopt the formal resolution that "Austria, aside from slight regulations of boundary,

[74] Potiorek to Conrad, July 14; Conrad, IV, 82-85.

seeks no acquisition of territory as a result of the war with Serbia"—a resolution calculated both to safeguard what Tisza regarded as the special interests of Hungary, and to prevent Italian claims to compensation and intervention on the part of the Powers. It was also decided that the ultimatum should not be presented until it was certain that Poincaré had left Russia. For otherwise Berchtold feared that "to take such a step at the moment when the President of the French Republic was being fêted as the guest of the Tsar might conceivably be interpreted as a political affront, which we wish to avoid." Moreover, he feared it would be unwise to threaten Belgrade while "the peace-loving, hesitating Tsar and the cautious Sazonov were subject to the immediate influence of the two instigators, Poincaré and Izvolski"; then Russia, under the influence of the "champagne-mood" of the warm Franco-Russian toasts and the chauvinism of the French President, Izvolski, and the Grand Duke Nicholas, would be more likely to intervene with military action.[75] After the date had been changed several times, it was ultimately decided that if the ultimatum were not presented in Belgrade until after 5 P.M. on Thursday, July 23, the news could not reach St. Petersburg until after Poincaré and Viviani had embarked on the waters of the Baltic, and were safely out of touch with the Russian authorities.[76]

Why did Tisza change his mind and consent to an ultimatum and the idea of immediate local war with Serbia?

[75] Berchtold's report to Francis Joseph, July 14; and Berchtold to Szögyény, July 15; A.R.B., I, 19, 21; K.D., 49, 50.

[76] For the high importance of waiting until Russia had recovered from the "champagne-mood" and Poincaré's influence, see telegrams between Berchtold and the Austrian Ambassador in Paris, July 12-16, deciphered by the French and published by Poincaré, IV, 283 f.; A.R.B., I, 19, 21, 26, 36, 39, 57, 62; K.D., 50, 65, 69, 80, 93, 108, 112, 127. That Berchtold's fears were not without foundation may be seen from the accounts which Paléologue, Buchanan, and Szápáry, the French, British, and Austrian Ambassadors in St. Petersburg, have given of the Poincaré visit; see below, ch. vi.

We do not know with certainty. Probably Berchtold's use of the German lever had something to do with it. Several months later, when some recriminations were passing privately between Austrian and German officials concerning responsibility for the war, Tisza wrote to Tschirschky: "Before beginning our action against Serbia we went to Germany for advice; and upon the direct encouragement and declaration of the German Government that it regarded the present situation as favorable for the ever more threatening settlement [with Serbia], we presented our Note in Belgrade."[77] This, as we have seen, was what Berchtold had been continually urging upon Tisza as Germany's attitude and as an argument for seizing the present moment for the final reckoning with Serbia.

But a stronger influence which made Tisza change his mind, with a heavy heart, was the growing conviction that unless Austria acted now she would be throttled by her enemies later. As he wrote to his niece a month afterwards: "My conscience is clear. Already the noose had been thrown around our necks with which they would have strangled us at a favorable moment, unless we cut it now. We could not do otherwise, but it agonized me that we had to do as we did."[78] This conviction arose from the evidence collected at Sarajevo and especially from what Tisza regarded as the "downright intolerable" utterances of cer-

[77] Tisza to Tschirschky, November 5, 1914; *Gróf Tisza István összes munkái,* 4 Sorozat, II, Kötet, Kiadia a Magyar Tudományos Akademia [Count Stephan Tisza's Collected Works, 4th Series, Vol. 11, edited by the Hungarian Academy of Sciences], Budapest, 1924, p. 267.

[78] Tisza to Margaret Zeyk, Aug. 26, 1914; *Ibid.,* p. 90. These are almost the only references in his letters to his change of attitude during the July crisis. See also A. Weber, "Graf Tisza und die Kriegserklärung an Serbien," in KSF, III, 818-826. Dec., 1925; H. Marczali, "Papers of Count Tisza, 1914-1918," in *Am. Hist. Rev.,* XXIX, 301-315, Jan., 1924; Ernest Ludwig, "The Martyrdom of Count Stephan Tisza," in *Current History,* Jan., 1925, pp. 542-549; and by the French brothers, Jérome and Jean Tharaud in their articles in the *Revue des Deux Mondes,* Dec. 15, 1920, and April 15, 1921, and more at length in their recent volume, *Die Herrschaft Israels*, Zürich and Leipsig, 1927.

tain Serbian diplomatists and of the Serbian press. In his letter of July 8 to Francis Joseph he had already protested against the statements of Spalajkovitch and Jovanovitch, representing Serbia in St. Petersburg and Berlin, and of "the well-known abuses in connection with the Serbian press, societies, and schools, of which we have complained." [79] On July 14, after his conference with Berchtold, Tisza went to see Tschirschky, and told him of his change of mind:

> Count Tisza said that hitherto he had always been the person who had urged caution, but every day had strengthened him in the feeling that the Monarchy must come to an energetic action, prove its ability to exist, and put an end to the downright intolerable conditions in the south-east. The language of the Serbian press and of Serbian diplomatists was so presumptuous as simply not to be borne. "I have found it hard to decide to advise in favor of war," said Tisza, "but I am now firmly convinced of its necessity, and shall apply all my strength for the greatness of the Monarchy." [80]

Another decisive factor with Tisza was Berchtold's reiteration of Conrad's militarist argument that "everything must be avoided in the way of diplomacy which by delays or by any kind of successive application of diplomatic steps might give the enemy time to take military measures, and so put us at a military disadvantage." [81] And so, as Berchtold reported to Francis Joseph after the conference of July 14, "Count Tisza gave up the objection which he had brought forward in regard to an ultimatum with a short time-limit, because I pointed out the military difficulties which would be involved in a delayed procedure. I also used the argument that even after mobilization had taken

79 Tisza to Francis Joseph, July 8; A.R.B., I, 12.
80 Tschirschky to Bethmann, July 14; K.D., 49.
81 Conrad to Berchtold, *ca.* July 10; A.R.B., I, 14.

place, a peaceful settlement would still be possible, in case Serbia yielded sufficiently quickly."[82]

Thus, for various reasons—Germany's supposed attitude, the provocative tone of Serbian Ministers and newspapers, military considerations, and the general conviction that the very existence of the Dual Monarchy depended upon putting an end to Serbian propaganda—Tisza decided to abandon his attitude of opposition.

Berchtold had now overcome his main obstacles to an ultimatum with which Serbia could hardly be expected to comply. The precise form of these demands had not been fixed in the conference of July 14, but Berchtold promised Tschirschky that same evening that as soon as the precise wording had been fixed at a second Ministerial Council to be held on July 19, he would immediately show him a copy in great confidence, even before it had been submitted to Francis Joseph for approval.[83] Berchtold, however, did not keep this promise, as will appear later.

Meanwhile Berchtold and one of the Foreign Office secretaries, Baron Musulin, set to work at once on the ultimatum.

AUSTRIAN EFFORTS TO DECEIVE EUROPE

During these days while the ultimatum was being drafted and Berchtold was waiting for the Poincaré visit to Russia to run its course, he made every effort to preserve the greatest secrecy as to its contents. He alleged that he was waiting for the final results of the Sarajevo investigation before making demands on Serbia.

In order to allay all suspicions everywhere as to his real purpose, Berchtold arranged that the Austrian Chief of Staff and Minister of War should leave Vienna as if on

[82] Berchtold to Francis Joseph, July 14; A.R.B., I., 19; Gooss, p. 85 f.
[83] Tschirschky to Bethmann, July 14; K.D., 50.

vacation,[84] and all Austro-Hungarian officials adopted a more pacific and conciliatory tone in their utterances.

Tisza, on returning to Budapest and being interpellated in the Hungarian Diet next day, gave the non-committal declaration:

> "Our relations with Serbia, to be sure, need to be cleared up, but in what manner. . . . I cannot in the nature of the case state, as the question is still under discussion. I can only emphasize again that the Government is fully conscious of all the weighty interests in favor of the maintenance of peace. The Government is not of the opinion that the clearing up will necessarily involve warlike complications. In this connection, therefore, I shall not indulge in any prophecies, but merely observe that war is a sad *ultima ratio,* which one should not adopt until every possibility of a settlement has been exhausted. But every state, every nation, must be in a position to carry on war as an *ultima ratio,* if it is to continue as a state and as a nation." [85]

This Delphic utterance produced on the whole a reassuring impression. In Vienna "some people saw in it signs of an intention quietly to await the development of events and of calmness in the attitude of the Austro-Hungarian Government, while others saw in it hidden intentions for an action as yet undecided." [86] At Paris even the *Temps* had a good word to say for his moderation and for the Austrian Government, though the other French newspapers sought to contrast the tone of the Hungarian Premier's speech with the hitherto intransigent attitude of the Hungarian press

[84] Conrad, IV, 77 f., 87, 94 f., K.D., 29; and above note 31, Conrad left Vienna on July 14, returned for a few hours to take part in the Ministerial Council of July 19, left again immediately after it, and did not return until July 22, the day before the Austrian Note was delivered to Serbia.

[85] Fraknói, p. 38.

[86] J. M. Jovanovitch, Serbian Minister at Vienna, to Pashitch, July 15, S.B.B., 23; *cf.* however, Dumaine, French Ambassador at Vienna, to Viviani, July 15, F.Y.B., 12; and the reports of Bunsen in Vienna and Max Müller in Budapest to Grey; B.D., 70, 81-83, 85.

and the fiery speech of the opposition leader, S sanyi.[87]

Fortunately for Berchtold, the Hungarian D was the only legislative body before which explanations as the given. Neither the Delegations nor the Austrian o be were in session at the moment. rat

In order further to avoid possible embarrassin tions, Berchtold also gave up his usual weekly tions, and ceased to discuss the Sarajevo outrage wit representatives of foreign countries; or, if discussions arise at the Ballplatz, they were such as to dispel all ap hensions and suspicions that Austria was preparing a seri step against Serbia. The Foreign Office officials acknow edged that some step would be undertaken at Belgrade a soon as the results of the investigation in Bosnia should have established the connection between Belgrade and the Sarajevo outrage. But, at the same time, it was said that this step would not be such as to give rise to any uneasiness. Dumaine, the French Ambassador in Vienna, reported that the expected "requirements of the Austro-Hungarian Government with regard to the punishment of the outrage, and to guarantees of control and police supervision, seem to be acceptable to the dignity of the Serbians; M. Jovanovitch believes they will be accepted. Pashitch wishes for a peaceful solution, but says he is ready for a full resistance."[88]

Shebeko, Russian Ambassador at Vienna, spoke several times on the situation with Forgach, in the absence of Berchtold, but was unable to discover the true nature of Austria's intentions. He was told by Szápáry, the Austro-Hungarian Ambassador at St. Petersburg, who, for family reasons happened at the time to be in Vienna, that the step to be taken at Belgrade would be of a conciliatory character and not such as to cause Russia any dissatisfaction. In con-

[87] Fraknói, p. 39; Kanner, p. 246 f.

[88] Dumaine to Viviani, July 22, F.Y.B., 18. A couple of days earlier, however, Dumaine had been less optimistic (see F.Y.B., 13 and 14, quoted below at note 96).

sequence ese reassuring explanations Shebeko left for a trip to a, and was not at Vienna during the first days of the which soon followed.[89]

At de Baron Giesl assured a Hungarian journalist on Ju hat at the conclusion of the Sarajevo inquiry "we sha ventual steps in the most conciliatory fashion an the bounds of international diplomatic propriety nd a week later he told his English colleague that ly he was not in favor of pressing Serbia too hard, was convinced that the Serbian Government was take whatever measures can reasonably be de- of them, and that he did not view the situation in mistic light."[91] Yet Giesl was the Serbophobe gen hose appointment to Belgrade a few months before een likened to the throwing of a lighted match into a er magazine.[92] And Giesl himself, at the end of a long t jeremiad against Serbia, reported his conviction to htold on July 21, that the best thing was "to crush the my which has been threatening us, and so give Austria iet after years of crisis. Half-measures, a presentation demands, long negotiations, and finally a rotten com- romise would be the worst blow which could happen to Austria-Hungary's prestige in Serbia and position in Europe."[93] Such was the Machiavellian deceit with which Berchtold and his officials sought to lull Europe into a false security before the explosion of his diplomatic bomb.

Berchtold, however, was not so successful in these efforts

89 Dumaine to Bienvenu-Martin, July 22, 26; F.Y.B., 18, 55; Jovanovitch to Pashitch, Aug. 16; S.B.B., 52; Szápáry also told Sazonov on July 18 that "they are convinced in Vienna that Serbia will meet our possible demands;" Szápáry to Berchtold, July 18, A.R.B., I, 25.

90 Kanner, p. 248.

91 Crackanthorpe to Grey, July 18; B.D., 57.

92 Giesl, formerly Austrian Minister to Montenegro, had been an ardent champion of Austrian interests against Serbia during the Balkan Wars.

93 Giesl to Berchtold, July 21; A.R.B., I, 37.

to deceive Europe concerning his real intentions, as has usually been assumed on the basis of the "colored books" published in 1914. At the opening of the War, Serbia and the Entente countries tried as much as possible to make it appear that they were taken totally by surprise by Austria's note to Serbia.[94] But as we know now from more recently published documents, the Great Powers suspected and knew more of Berchtold's intentions than has usually been supposed.

On July 16 the English Ambassador in Vienna telegraphed to Sir Edward Grey:

> A kind of indictment is being prepared against the Serbian Government for alleged complicity in the conspiracy which led to assassination of the Archduke. Accusation will be founded on the proceedings in the Sarajevo Court. My informant states that the Serbian Government will be required to adopt certain definite measures in restraint of nationalist and anarchist propaganda, and that Austro-Hungarian Government are in no mood to parley with Serbia, but will insist on immediate unconditional compliance, failing which force will be used. Germany is said to be in complete agreement with this procedure, and it is thought that the rest of Europe will sympathise with Austria-Hungary in demanding that Serbia shall adopt in future more submissive attitude. . . .
>
> I asked if Russia would be expected to stand by quietly in the event of force being used against Serbia.
>
> My informant said that he presumed that Russia would not wish to protect racial assassins, but in any case Austria-Hungary would go ahead regardless of results. She would lose her position as a Great Power if she stood any further nonsense from Serbia.[95]

94 *Cf.* Seton-Watson, *Sarajevo,* ch. viii, "The Duping of Europe."

95 Bunsen to Grey, July 16; B.D., 50 (suppressed from B.B.B.). Sir Eyre Crowe noted on this: "Count Trauttmansdorff spoke to me (quite informally) at great length to-day, giving expression to very much the same views." In a letter to Sir Arthur Nicolson at the British Foreign

Similarly, on July 21, President Poincaré at St. Petersburg, as we shall see, believing that "Austria is preparing to strike a blow," [96] undertook to give the Austrian Ambassador a rude and severe warning, saying significantly, "The Russian people are very warm friends of the Serbians, and France is Russia's ally." [97] He was trying to bluff Austria out of doing precisely what Berchtold was intending to do, and at the same time encouraging Sazonov to stand firm in support of Serbia.[98]

Italy also appears to have gotten some inkling of what was preparing at Vienna—possibly from Count Lützow or from Bunsen. On July 16 the Italian Ambassador in St. Petersburg, "having the impression that Austria was capable of taking an irrevocable step with regard to Serbia,"

Office next day Bunsen explained that he had this information from "Count Lützow, ex-Ambassador at Rome. He has a place near us in the country and we motored over to luncheon. He had seen both Berchtold and Forgach at the Ballplatz the day before, and had long conversations. He put on a serious face and said he wondered if I realized how grave the situation was. This Government was not going to stand Serbian insolence any longer. No great Power could submit to such audacity as Serbia had displayed, and keep her position in the world. . . . If Serbia did not at once cave in, force would be used to compel her. Count Lützow added that Count Berchtold was sure of German support and did not believe any country could hesitate to approve—not even Russia. . . . I expressed my doubts whether, if it really came to fighting, which I could not believe, Russia would allow Austria and Serbia to have it out in a cockpit. Count Lützow said Austria was determined to have her way this time and would refuse to be headed off by anybody" (B. D., 56).

96 Paléologue, *La Russie des Tsars,* I, 7. The French Ambassador in Vienna had already forwarded as "accurate information" a memorandum stating: "The French Government would be mistaken to have confidence in disseminators of optimism; much will be demanded of Serbia; she will be required to dissolve several propagandist societies, repress nationalism, to guard the frontier in cooperation with Austrian officials, and to keep a strict control over anti-Austrian tendencies in the schools; and it is a very difficult matter for a Government to consent to become in this way a policeman for a foreign Government. . . . The tenor of the Note and its imperious tone almost certainly ensure that Belgrade will refuse. Then military operations will begin" (Dumaine to Viviani, July 19 and 20; F.Y.B., 13, 14).

97 A.R.B., I, 45, 60; K.D., 134; and Poincaré, IV, 253 f.

98 See below, ch. vi.

advised Russia to warn Vienna that "Russia would not endure any infringement by Austria of the integrity and independence of Serbia."[99] On the evening of July 23 a Counsellor of the Italian Embassy definitely informed Prince Trubetzkoi that "Austria-Hungary would today present to Serbia a quite unacceptable ultimatum."[100]

THE FINAL DRAFTING OF THE ULTIMATUM

The precise terms of the ultimatum, or "Note with a time-limit" (*befristete Démarche*) as it was euphemistically called,[101] were laid before a second secret Ministerial Council on Sunday, July 19. To make secrecy doubly sure, the meeting was held at 10 A.M. at Berchtold's private residence, instead of at the Foreign Office, and those who attended it came in ordinary autos instead of in their own official "unnumbered" cars. Tisza's renewed trip to Vienna was "explained" as being due to his need of getting further information—an explanation which was plausible enough since the Hungarian Diet was still in session and thirsting for news. Conrad made a brief flying trip back to the capital, which was given out as being caused by the illness of his son.[102]

> Before the Joint Ministerial Council was called to order for business by the presiding officer [Berchtold], an informal discussion took place as to wording of the Note to be sent to Serbia, and its definitive text was fixed. The presiding officer then opened the Council, and requested approval for the presentation of the Note to the Serbian Government about 5 P.M. on Thursday, July 23, so that after the expiration of the 48-hour time-limit at 5 P.M. on Saturday, July 25, the mobilization orders could be sent out in the night between Saturday and Sunday. According to the

99 Schilling's *Diary,* p. 25.

100 Schilling's *Diary,* p. 28. As early as July 18 Berchtold suspected that Italy had learned something of his intentions; A.R.B., I, 24; Gooss, pp. 79, 117 ff.

101 *Cf.* Berchtold to Giesl, July 23, A.R.B., I, 65, 66; and B.D., 105.

102 Kanner, p. 250; Conrad, IV, 78, 87, 94 f.

opinion of Count Berchtold, it was not probable that our step would become known in St. Petersburg before the departure of the President of the French Republic, but even if this should happen, he would see no great disadvantage in it, as we had observed sufficient regard for courtesy in waiting for the end of his visit. On the other hand, for diplomatic reasons, he would be decidedly opposed to any further postponement, since they were already beginning to get nervous in Berlin and news of our intentions had already leaked out at Rome, so that he could not be responsible for undesirable incidents if they should postpone the matter longer.[103]

After Conrad, the Chief of Staff, had made a statement about military operations, and had reassured Tisza as to the safety of Transylvania from possible Rumanian uprisings or invasion, Tisza renewed the request which he had made on July 14, that the Council unanimously declare that "no plans of conquest by Austria were connected with the action against Serbia, and that, with the exception of rectifications of frontier necessary for strategic reasons, Austria did not wish to annex a single bit of Serbian territory." Berchtold remarked that he would accept this "only with a certain reserve":

Austria, in case of victory over Serbia, ought not to annex any of her territory, but should seek to reduce her size so that she would no longer be dangerous, by ceding as large parts of Serbian territory as possible to Bulgaria, Greece, Albania, and possibly to Rumania also. The situation in the Balkans might change; it was not at all impossible that Russia might succeed in overturning the existing cabinet at Sofia, and in bringing into power again there a government hostile to Austria; Albania also was no de-

103 Minutes of the Ministerial Council, July 19; A.R.B., I, 26; Gooss, p. 101 ff. The date of presentation at Belgrade was later changed from 5 P.M. to 6 P.M., in order to make more certain that Poincaré should have left Russia before the news reached St. Petersburg; Berchtold to Giesl, July 23, A.R.B., I, 62; see also note 76 above.

> pendable factor; as the person responsible for foreign affairs, he must reckon with the possibility that at the end of the war, on account of conditions then existing, it would no longer be possible not to annex anything, if we wanted to establish better conditions along our frontier than exist at present.[104]

Count Stürgkh, the Austrian Premier, pointed out that a public disclaimer of any intention to annex Serbian territory would not prevent "necessary strategic rectifications of the frontier" or "the bringing of Serbia into a position of dependence on Austria by overthrowing the dynasty, by a military convention, or by other appropriate measures." The Minister of War was willing to vote for such a disclaimer only on condition that it did not exclude a permanent occupation of a bridge-head over the Save into Serbia, as well as "rectifications of the frontier."

Tisza, however, made his consent and that of the Hungarian Government which he represented, inflexibly dependent upon a unanimous acceptance of his request. Whereupon it was unanimously voted:

> Immediately at the beginning of war a declaration shall be made to the Foreign Powers that the Monarchy is not waging a war of conquest, and does not intend to incorporate the Kingdom [of Serbia]. This vote naturally does not preclude rectifications of the frontier strategically necessary, nor the diminution of Serbia for the benefit of other states, nor the temporary occupation of parts of Serbia which may eventually be necessary.[105]

This solemn obligation to declare to the Powers at the beginning of war Austria's "territorial disinterestedness" was another of the promises, as we shall see, which Berchtold did not honestly live up to. Even when the declaration was finally made, its insincerity is indicated by these mental reservations of several of the Ministers, and by

104 A.R.B., I, 26; Gooss, p. 101 ff.
105 A.R.B., I, 26; Gooss, p. 101 ff.

Conrad's remark to the Minister of War as they were leaving the Council: "Well, we shall see; before the Balkan War the Powers talked about the *status quo*—but after the war no one bothered himself about it." [106]

The next day, July 20, the Note was dispatched by courier to Giesl at Belgrade, with instructions to present it to the Serbian Government on Thursday the 23rd.[107] It was also sent on July 20 under the seal of strictest secrecy to the Austro-Hungarian Ambassadors at Berlin,[108] Rome, Paris, London, St. Petersburg, Constantinople, and the Ministers at the lesser courts. Each was given appropriate instructions that on Friday morning, July 24, he was to inform the Government to which he was accredited of the "Note" presented to Serbia the night before, make a statement of the justice of Austria's cause, and in some cases say that a *dossier* giving fuller details of the Austrian case against Serbia was at the disposal of the Powers for examination.[109]

[106] Conrad, IV, 92.

[107] Berchtold to Giesl, July 20; A.R.B., I, 27, 28. It was post-dated "July 22"; Gooss, p. 101, note 1. Berchtold perhaps thought it would look better if it did not appear that it had been dispatched before it had been shown to Francis Joseph and received his approval; or if the Emperor demurred, there was the *fait accompli* that it had already been sent out. It is dated "July 22" in the original *Austrian Red Book* of 1915, and "July 24" in the copies presented to the Powers on the morning of July 24; B.B.B., 4; F.Y.B., 24.

[108] Szögyény at Berlin had received it by July 21, for on that day at 7:30 P.M. he urgently requested to be allowed to show it to the German Government ahead of the time stated in his instructions; A.R.B., I, 39, 41; Gooss, p. 110 f. The Austrian representatives in Rome, Paris and Cettinje had received their copies of the ultimatum by July 22; *ibid*, 50, 51, 55. Szápáry in St. Petersburg cannot have received the note on July 20, as incorrectly stated by Mr. Seton-Watson (*Sarajevo,* p. 207; and pp. 221, 227 for similar misstatements as to its reception in Paris and London). There was deceit enough in Austria's actions without accepting Mr. Seton-Watson's further allegation that Szápáry had "this secret explosive in his breast" when he made "the grossly dishonest statement" to Poincaré at the reception to the diplomatic corps in St. Petersburg.

[109] Berchtold's instructions, 3401-3406, 3426-3436, July 20; A.R.B., I, 29-31. As to the *dossier* see above, ch. ii, note 2.

Berchtold had despatched the ultimatum without the knowledge or approval of Francis Joseph. The aged Emperor, who was away at Ischl and had been told that the "Note" was to be settled at the Ministerial Council of July 19, had heard nothing further of it, and therefore telegraphed on the 20th to know about it.[110] Berchtold hastened to reply that it had not been possible to complete it on July 19[!], but that it was now finished and would be sent to Ischl by a courier, and that he himself would arrive next morning, July 21, for an audience. There is no record of the explanations which he may have given to Francis Joseph in this audience on Tuesday morning, except that at its close he telegraphed to his subordinate, Baron Macchio, in Vienna: "His Majesty has approved without change the text of the Note to Serbia and that to the Powers. I beg you to inform the German Ambassador, Tschirschky, that he cannot be given the Note until early tomorrow morning since some corrections are still to be made in it."[111] Why this falsehood? Why did Berchtold here break the promise which he had made a few days before to Tschirschky that "as soon as the text [of the Note] had been fixed on Sunday [July 19, at the Ministerial Council], he would immediately communicate it to the Imperial [German] Government in great confidence, even before it had been submitted to Francis Joseph for approval"?[112] If the "definitive text was fixed"[113] on July 19, secretly forwarded to all the Austrian Ambassadors on July 20,[114] and "approved without change" by the Emperor on July 21, why did Berchtold still want to withhold it from Tschirschky and allege that "some corrections are still to be made in it"? Probably

110 Telegram from Ischl from Baron Schiessl, head of the Emperor's cabinet chancery, to Berchtold, July 20, 11 A.M.; Berchtold's reply, July 20, 1:30 P.M.; Gooss, p. 101.

111 Berchtold to Macchio, July 21, 12:30 P.M.; A.R.B.,I, 46.

112 Tschirschky to Bethmann, July 14; K.D., 50; *cf.* K.D., 88.

113 Minutes of the Ministerial Council, July 19; A.R.B., I, 26.

114 A.R.B., I, 29-31.

because Berchtold feared that even the Berlin Foreign Office would disapprove the extreme and intransigent tone of the Note, and might, at the last moment, stretch out a restraining hand. Berlin, as he had already alleged to the Council on July 19, was becoming "nervous," and he could "not be responsible for undesirable incidents if they should postpone the matter longer." Therefore Berlin must not know the text of the Note until it was too late to do anything. Berlin must accept the *fait accompli* that a very severe ultimatum had been dispatched, and that it was practically too late to recall or modify it.[115]

AUSTRIA'S DISREGARD OF GERMAN ADVICE

In this connection, and in view of Germany's repeated statements later that she did not have foreknowledge of the Austrian ultimatum, it is important to observe the change in Berchtold's treatment of Germany before and after July 14, the day on which he finally secured Tisza's consent to a severe ultimatum. Before this date Berchtold had kept Germany quite fully informed of the plans which were developing to deliver a stiff ultimatum to Serbia, and some of the probable terms to be included in it had been indicated to Berlin. He had intimated that they would be so exacting that Serbia could hardly accept them, and that

115 *Cf.* Merey to Berchtold, July 27 (Gooss, p. 114): "I have the feeling that the German Cabinet . . . is aiming and hoping in various ways, for example at Rome and Bucharest, to work against our military conflict with Serbia. In this way sufficient diplomatic and political barriers will be erected on all sides, by friend and foe, to prevent our fighting, in the period between the delivery of the Note and the outbreak of hostilities on all sides. Should Germany succeed in this, Serbia would finally be compelled to yield in the main, but as a matter of form would be spared to a certain extent in its dignity as a state. This in the end would be the outcome which Your Excellency has regarded as such a horrible contingency, and which in fact would be a situation far worse for us than that which preceded it. But Germany would again reap in Vienna a cheap and undeserved jubilation for having again stood by us 'in shining armor.'"

an acceptance would be "very disagreeable" to him.[116] He had asked advice, and appeared ready to receive it and act upon it. Germany, having given a *carte blanche* on July 5, acquiesced in these plans. Knowing Berchtold's hesitations and indecisions in the past, and desiring that Austria should act quickly before the horror and sympathy aroused in Europe by the Sarajevo crime had died away, Germany had not only acquiesced, but encouraged Berchtold to speedy action. Not knowing the precise text of the intended note, and being still optimistic that any possible Austro-Serbian conflict could be "localized," Germany began to take steps and to offer advice which would help assure such localization. But now Berchtold, after July 14, having been promised German support and having converted Tisza, no longer showed the same consideration for Germany, and gave little heed to her advice and requests.

Jagow, for instance, advised Vienna to "assemble sufficient evidence to prove that there exists a Greater Serbia agitation in Serbia which endangers the Dual Monarchy, in order that the public opinion of Europe may be convinced as far as possible of the justice of Austria's cause. This material would best be published, not separately but as a whole, shortly before submitting to Serbia the demands, or the ultimatum, as the case may be." [117] But Berchtold did not heed this excellent advice. The *dossier*, which set forth in detail Austria's grievances against Serbia and the results of the Sarajevo investigation, was not laid before the Powers until several days after the presentation of the ultimatum. It came so late, after a serious diplomatic crisis had begun to develop, that the Powers paid little or no

116 See Tschirschky's nine despatches, July 7 to 14; K.D., 18, 19, 27, 29, 35, 40, 41a, 49, 50; three of these have been quoted in part above at notes 69-71; see also Schoen, the Bavarian Chargé d'Affaires in Berlin, to Hertling in Munich, July 18 (Dirr, p. 4ff.; K.D., IV, Anhang, iv, No. 2) for the fullest statement of the extent of Germany's knowledge up to that date of Austria's intentions.

117 Jagow to Tschirschky, July 11; K.D., 31.

attention to it,[118] and Austria lost completely the advantage which she might have had of influencing public opinion in her favor and against Serbia.

Germany also urged Berchtold to come to a timely understanding with Italy. The Italian Government, owing to the threatening outpourings of the Austrian Press against Serbia and to the suspiciously silent attitude of the Vienna authorities, was becoming very uneasy. Baron Flotow, the German Ambassador at Rome, reported on July 14 that San Giuliano was very pessimistic as to plans which Berchtold might be hatching. The Italian Minister had said that he could not admit in international law that a Government could be made responsible for a criminal act of an individual, nor for political propaganda, if the propaganda did not amount to an overt act. He feared therefore that the Italian Government could not support the demands which he suspected Austria might make upon Serbia, especially as they would be contrary to the deep-seated feelings of the Italian people, contrary to liberal principles, and contrary to the principle of nationality, which Italy, with her traditions, could never oppose. Flotow concluded that San Giuliano "apparently wanted to warn us that Italy would not remain on Austria's side in case of further complications."[119] During the following days he sent a series of increasingly emphatic and alarming telegrams that Italy would not support Austria against Serbia, because of the prevailing popular hatred of Austria and sympathy for the Serbian nationalistic "Piedmont" movement, so similar to Italy's own struggle for national unity in the face of Hapsburg oppression half a century before. He also said that it was virtually impossible to influence the Italian Press.[120]

Jagow, realizing the importance of keeping Italy from

118 See above, ch. ii, note 2.

119 Flotow to Bethmann, July 14; K.D., 42.

120 Flotow to Bethmann, July 15, 16, 17, 19; K.D., 51, 54, 59, 60, 64, 73, 75. 78.

siding with Serbia, and the difficulty of bribing or bargaining with the Italians, sent Flotow's telegram on to Tschirschky at Vienna, and told him to discuss the Italian situation confidentially with Berchtold. He declared that any territorial extension of Austria, or even an extension of her influence in the Balkans, would absolutely horrify Italy; every time there was a question of Austria threatening Serbia, Italy became extraordinarily nervous; and Italian support to Serbia would materially increase Russia's lust for action. It was therefore of the greatest importance, he believed, that Austria should come to an understanding with the Cabinet at Rome, and hold out as a bait the prospect of some compensations, such as Valona, which formed part of Albania and would cost Austria nothing but might not satisfy Italy, or even such a fat morsel as the Trentino, which would certainly stop the mouths of Austrophobe public opinion in Italy.[121]

In accordance with these instructions, and in the absence of Tschirschky, Stolberg, a Counsellor of the German Embassy at Vienna, "asked Berchtold whether he intended to get into touch with Italy prior to a possible action against Serbia. Berchtold replied that up to now he had not breathed a word of it, and indeed intended to face the Italian Government with a *fait accompli,* because he was not quite sure whether it could keep a secret, and with its Serbophil attitude might easily let some hint leak out at Belgrade." [122] Stolberg did not press the point with Berchtold, preferring to leave the delicate question of compensations for Tschirschky to deal with. Stolberg, however, had a long talk with Berchtold's confidential agent, Hoyos, and urged conciliation toward Italy, but got little satisfaction. Hoyos suggested compensating Italy with another territory—which did not belong to Austria—namely, the Dodecanese..

121 Jagow to Tschirschky, July, 15; K.D., 46.
122 Stolberg to Jagow, July 18; K.D., 87.

Two days later, on July 20, Tschirschky had a long interview with Berchtold and set forth emphatically Jagow's arguments in regard to the importance of winning and compensating Italy before it was too late. But he too had little success. Berchtold blindly insisted that Italy had no claim to compensation; that he did not need Italian coöperation or support, but only Italy's abstention from interference; that the best way to keep Italy out was to keep intended action secret from her until after the *fait accompli*; and that he had strictly forbidden Merey, the Austrian Ambassador in Rome, to speak of the Serbian question, because he was sure that the slightest hint would be at once communicated by Italy to St. Petersburg, and be seized upon at Rome as an excuse for some counter-action or for claims to compensations. Berchtold gave such a down-right refusal to have Italy get even Valona that Tschirschky apparently refrained from the more delicate proposal that Austria give up the Trentino.[123]

Instead of acting on Germany's wise and prudent suggestion of bargaining reasonably with Italy, Berchtold sent Merey a long argument, in which he tried to contradict the interpretation held by Germany, as well as by Italy, in regard to Art. VII of the Triple Alliance, relating to compensations for Italy in case of a change in the Balkans in Austria's favor.[124] And on the same day, after sending Merey the text of the ultimatum, he instructed him to say to San Giuliano, if questioned, that "he had no precise information as yet in regard to the conclusion of the investigation at Sarajevo and the step which Austria would take at Belgrade as a result of it." [125] Merey was also to avoid, if possible, any discussion of Art. VII because "neither side would be able to bring the other to its own interpretation,

123 Tschirschky to Bethmann, July 20; K.D., 94; and report of the interview in the Austrian F.O. Journal, No. 3425, A.R.B., I, 35.

124 Berchtold to Merey, July 29; A.R.B., I, 32, 33.

125 A.R.B., I. 34.

and there was danger that the discussion of it might give rise to heated feelings and in the end endanger the whole Triple Alliance Treaty." [126]

Berchtold had promised Tschirschky that, as an act of courtesy to Italy as an ally, he would inform the Cabinet at Rome of the ultimatum before it was delivered to Serbia, so that San Giuliano and his colleagues should not have to learn of it from the newspapers, and that at the same time he would declare that Austria in her action against Serbia did not aim at any extension of territory for herself.[127] But he kept neither of these promises fully. As to giving Italy preliminary notification, he sent a series of contradictory orders to Merey, who was sorely perplexed what to do. In the end he had to take to his bed and send his secretary by automobile to San Giuliano in the country on the afternoon of July 23 at about the time the ultimatum was being handed in at Belgrade; and even then no copy of it was given to the Italian Minister, merely the meager information that the Note, with a 48-hour time-limit, contained a number of demands based on the Sarajevo inquiry and aimed to protect Austria against Greater Serbia propaganda.[128]

Berchtold likewise did not make any clear and timely declaration to Italy or to any of the Powers that Austria would not seek any extension of territory for herself at Serbia's expense, a declaration such as was desired by Tisza and by Germany.[129] Thus, after having converted Tisza on July 14, Berchtold paid no more attention to Germany's advice in regard to Italy than in regard to publishing the

126 Berchtold to Merey, July 21; A.R.B., I, 42.

127 Tschirschky to Bethmann, July 20; K.D., 94.

128 A.R.B., I, 22, 30, 34, 50, 56; II, 8; Gooss, pp. 114-127.

129 Merey did tell San Giuliano on July 21 that Austria did not intend to incorporate any territory, but refused to allow San Giuliano to publish this in the papers "because it was not to be understood as a promise;" A.R.B., I, 43. For the hesitating and unconvincing statements to Russia and the other Powers on the same subject, see below.

Sarajevo evidence simultaneously with the demands on Serbia.

WHAT FOREKNOWLEDGE DID GERMANY HAVE OF THE ULTIMATUM?

Similarly Berchtold paid little heed to Germany's requests after July 14 to be informed as to Austria's final intentions and the precise terms of her contemplated demands on Serbia. This fact, together with Jagow's repeated assertions a few days later that "he had no previous knowledge of the contents of the Austro-Hungarian Note,"[130] and the new facts revealed in subsequently published German documents, have given rise to much controversy as to the extent of Germany's foreknowledge of the Austrian ultimatum.[131]

During the first week after the Potsdam Conversations, as has already been pointed out, Berchtold had kept the German Ambassador in Vienna quite fully informed of the progress of his plans, and of several of the probable demands which he intended to include in the ultimatum.[132] This information was passed on to the Bavarian Chargé d'Affaires in Berlin, who summed it up in a long despatch on July 18:

> As Zimmermann told me, the Note, so far as yet determined, will contain the following demands:
>
> 1. The issuing of a proclamation by the King of Serbia which shall state that the Serbian Government com-

[130] Rumbold to Grey, July 25; B.D., 122; *cf.* also his statement to the French Ambassador on July 24 that "the Berlin Cabinet had been entirely ignorant of Austria's requirements before they were communicated to Belgrade" (F.Y.B., 30); and on the same day Sazonov was informed by the German Ambassador in St. Petersburg that "the German Government had no knowledge of the Austrian note before it was presented" (R.O.B., 18).

[131] For a discussion of opposing views on this question, see the articles of G. von Jagow and B. E. Schmitt in *Current History,* Dec., 1927, pp. 393-398.

[132] See above, at notes 69-71 and 116.

pletely dissociates itself from the Greater Serbia movement, and disapproves of it.

2. The opening of an investigation against persons guilty of complicity in the Sarajevo assassination, and the participation of an Austrian official in this investigation.
3. Proceedings against all persons who have participated in the Greater Serbia movement.

For the acceptance of these demands a 48-hour time-limit will be granted. It is evident that Serbia cannot accept such demands, which are incompatible with her dignity as an independent state. Thus the result would be war.

Here [in Berlin] they are thoroughly willing that Austria use this favorable moment, even at the risk of further complications. But whether they will actually rise to the occasion in Vienna, still seems doubtful to Jagow as well as Zimmermann. The latter expressed the opinion that Austria-Hungary, thanks to her indecision and breaking-up, has now become really the Sick Man of Europe, like Turkey formerly, for whose partition Russians, Italians, Rumanians, Serbians and Montenegrins are now waiting. A vigorous and successful move against Serbia would have the result that Austrians and Hungarians could feel themselves once more to be a national power, would again revive the decayed economic life, and would suppress the foreign aspirations for years to come. . . .

What attitude the other Powers will take toward an armed conflict between Austria and Serbia will chiefly depend, according to the view here, on whether Austria is content to chastise Serbia, or will also demand territorial compensations for herself. In the first case, it would be possible to localize the war; in the other case, on the other hand, more serious complications would probably not be lacking.

The German Government will immediately after the presentation of the Austrian Note at Belgrade, initiate diplomatic action with the Powers, in the interest of the localization of the war. It will claim to have been just

> as much surprised as the other Powers by Austria's action, pointing out that the Kaiser is on his northern cruise and that the Chief of the General Staff as well as the Prussian Minister of War are absent on vacation. . . . It will emphasize that it is a matter of common interest for all monarchical Governments that "the Belgrade nest of anarchists" be rooted out once and for all; and it will try to get all the Powers to accept the view that the settlement between Austria and Serbia is a matter concerning these two states alone. The mobilization of the German Army is to be refrained from, and they are also going to work through the military authorities to prevent Austria from mobilizing her entire Army, and especially not the troops in Galicia, in order to avoid bringing about automatically a counter-mobilization on Russia's part, which in turn would cause us, and then France, to take similar measures, and thereby conjure up a European War.[133]

The first part of this famous report indicates that Germany had received only a brief outline of a part of the actual later ultimatum, namely, the issuing of a proclamation by the Serbian Government dissociating itself from the Greater Serbia agitation, the 48-hour time-limit, and two demands which roughly correspond to four of the total ten points elaborated in the ultimatum (viz. points 2, 4, 5 and 6, concerning Austrian coöperation in an investigation of persons guilty of complicity, and concerning proceedings against persons who have participated in propaganda). Beside the ten points, the eventual ultimatum contained a long introductory statement of Serbia's breach of the promises of friendly behavior made in 1909. Incidentally it may also be noted that Schoen reported that it "still seemed doubtful" to Zimmermann and Jagow whether "the always

133 Schoen to Hertling, in Munich, July 18; K.D., IV, Anhang iv, No. 2; Dirr, p. 4 ff., gives in parallel columns Schoen's report in its authentic form and in its abbreviated or "forged" version as published by Kurt Eisner in 1918.

timid and undecided authorities at Vienna" [134] would actually "rise to the occasion," and take the action which had been intimated.

On the other hand, while it is true that the German Government did not know half the demands nor the actual wording of the ultimatum (which in fact had not yet been definitely drawn up even in Vienna), it knew the substance of some of the probable demands which were most important; and it knew that the ultimatum was to be so framed that Serbia would not be likely to yield to it. Jagow was therefore virtually lying when he repeatedly asserted a few days later that "he had no previous knowledge of the Austro-Hungarian Note." This is a matter to which we shall return in a moment. Though it is no justification of his lie, it may be pointed out that Sir Edward Grey, who is often extolled as an example of honesty and sincerity, lied just as deliberately in regard to his foreknowledge of the probable terms of the ultimatum. He had learned on July 16, from a friend of Berchtold's who told the English Ambassador in Vienna, that "a kind of indictment is being prepared against the Serbian Government for alleged complicity in the conspiracy which led to the assassination of the Archduke. . . . The Serbian Government will be required to adopt certain definite measures in restraint of nationalist and anarchist propaganda; the Austro-Hungarian Government are in no mood to parley with Serbia, but will insist on immediate unconditional compliance, failing which force will be used." [135] Nevertheless on July 20, Sir Edward Grey, having "asked the German Ambassador today if he had any news of what was going on in Vienna with regard to Serbia," and having received a negative reply, remarked that he also "had not heard anything

134 Dirr, p. 4 ff.

135 Bunsen to Grey, received July 16, 3:15 P.M.; B.D., 50; quoted above at note 95.

recently," except that Count Berchtold had spoken reassuringly to the Italian Ambassador.[136] Either Sir Edward Grey was ignorant of Bunsen's important despatch received at the British Foreign Office four days before this (such ignorance seems hardly likely), or he too was making an untrue assertion of ignorance concerning what was going on at Vienna. This kind of diplomatic lying, unfortunately, was not the monopoly of any one country, but was indulged in all too freely by Foreign Secretaries and Ambassadors almost everywhere in July, 1914.

Though Germany possessed, within the first week or ten days after the Potsdam Conversations, such knowledge concerning the ultimatum as has just been indicated, this was still regarded at Berlin as too indefinite. After July 14, therefore, she repeatedly requested further information as to Austria's ultimate aims and the precise terms of the ultimatum, in order to prepare public opinion in favor of "localization." Thus, on July 17, Jagow recognized that Berchtold's "plans may be influenced or modified by the course of events," but assumed that "he has in mind a general picture of the aims to be sought, including the matter of territory;" Jagow therefore instructed the German Ambassador in Vienna to "get some information on this point," and "about where the road is likely to lead us."[137] And again on July 20: "For dealing with public opinion, it is of the greatest importance for us to be precisely informed beforehand, not only of the contents of the Note, but also as to the day and hour of its publication. Reply by telegraph."[138] But now Berchtold paid little

[136] Grey to Rumbold, July 20; B.D., 68; *cf.* also the account of this interview by the German Ambassador, who was given the impression that Grey "was still viewing the Austro-Serbian quarrel optimistically, and believed that a peaceful solution would be reached. He [Grey] said that he had received no information that would indicate anything to the contrary;" Lichnowsky to Bethmann, July 20; K.D., 92.

[137] Jagow to Tschirschky, July 17; K.D., 61.

[138] K.D., 83.

heed to these requests, and Germany was virtually unable to learn anything further, except as to the date when the ultimatum would be presented and Berchtold's obstinacy in rejecting German advice as to Italy.[139]

The German Foreign Office also applied for information to the Austrian Ambassador in Berlin. Szögyény's instructions were that he was not to show the ultimatum to Germany until July 24, the morning after it had been delivered in Belgrade. But Szögyény now felt himself compelled to telegraph to Berchtold, that he "considered it unconditionally necessary to inform the German Government at once, that is, before the other Powers, in a strictly confidential manner." And in a letter of the same day he wrote: "Jagow gave me clearly to understand that Germany would naturally stand behind us unconditionally and with all her strength, but for this very reason it was of vital interest to Germany to be informed betimes as to 'where our path is leading to.' "[140] Accordingly, on the following afternoon, July 22, Berchtold finally gave his consent, and Szögyény then showed the text of the ultimatum to Jagow.

After reading it on Wednesday evening, July 22, Jagow told Szögyény it was, in his opinion, "too sharp," and went too far in its demands. He reproached the Austrian Ambassador for thus communicating it only at the eleventh hour. Szögyény replied that nothing could be done about it, as it had already been dispatched to Belgrade, and would be presented there next morning, and officially published by the Vienna telegraph agency at the same time.[141]

[139] See the despatches from Tschirschky and Stolberg in Vienna, July 17-21; K.D., 65, 87, 88, 94, 95, 103, 104, 106.

[140] Szögyény to Berchtold, July 21; A.R.B., I, 39, 41.

[141] Jagow, *Ursachen,* p. 110, and Bethmann, *Betrachtungen,* I, 139, both state that Szögyény said it would be presented "next morning;" if they are correct, this would be another instance of Szögyény's inaccuracies tending in the direction of aggravating the situation; it would make the *fait accompli* seem even more irrevocable. Szögyény himself made no report to Berchtold on this conversation, or if he did, it has not been

While Jagow was considering the ultimatum, another copy of it was brought to him which had just arrived from Tschirschky. Curiously enough, on the preceding day at Vienna, Forgach, in ignorance of Berchtold's order to Macchio not to show Tschirschky the text of the ultimatum "since some corrections are still to be made in it,"[142] actually handed it to him for transmission to Berlin. Forgach "expressly emphasized that it was for Your Excellency's strictly personal information, as the Emperor's approval is still lacking, though there is no doubt that he will give it."[143] Tschirschky sent it by mail instead of by telegraph, probably because he feared that its subsequent publication might endanger the secrecy of the German cipher. It thus did not reach Berlin until the evening of July 22, as Jagow was knitting his brows over the copy which Szögyény had just given him. Bethmann, who was at Hohenfinow at this time, apparently did not know of the text of the note until late on the night of the 22nd or the morning of the 23rd,[144] but when he saw it, he too, like Jagow, was of the opinion that it was too sharp. Emperor William, away at sea on the *Hohenzollern*, first heard the contents of the ultimatum later still, through a newspaper agency and not officially from the German Foreign Office, as we know from an irritated telegram which he sent to his "civilian Chancellor."[145]

published. The time decided upon for presenting the note at Belgrade was not "next morning," but next afternoon, July 23, at 5 P.M.; at the last moment the hour was changed, at Jagow's suggestion, from 5 to 6 P.M., to make certain that the news should not reach St. Petersburg until after Poincaré had departed; K.D., 112, 127; A.R.B., I, 62; and above at note 76.

142 See above, at note 111.

143 Tschirschky to Bethmann, July 21; K.D., 106.

144 Bethmann's telegram of July 22 at 11:40 P.M. (*ibid.*, no. 116), speaks of "the wording of the Austrian note which is not yet known to me."

145 Kaiser to Bethmann, July 26, 7:30 P.M.; K.D., 231. This telegram, together with what has been said above, shows the incorrectness of the much-quoted despatch from the English Ambassador at Vienna:

Thus it is essentially true that Germany knew the general tenor of some of the terms of the ultimatum, and was aware that they were likely to lead to a localized war with Serbia, but she did not know the text of it beforehand in time to modify or recall it. Berchtold's *fait accompli* methods had prevented that. At the time Jagow finally saw the text, on the evening of July 22, there remained less than twenty-four hours before the Austrian Minister was to present it at Belgrade. The text of it was already in his hands. Even in these modern days of the telephone and telegraph it would have been virtually impossible for the German and Austrian officials in Berlin, Vienna and Belgrade to communicate with each other within the brief time and agree upon a modification of the ultimatum. And even if Bethmann and Jagow had been informed of the text much earlier, it is not to be assumed that they would have modified or stopped it. They would have probably still adhered to the policy adopted on July 5, that the Austro-Serbian question was "beyond the competence of Germany," but that Germany must support her ally in the action she had decided upon to protect herself against the Greater Serbia danger. They felt they had to accept Berchtold's *fait accompli*. It was a consequence of their folly in giving him a free hand on July 5. To have disavowed Austria's action at the last moment, would of course, as events turned out, have been wiser. But it would have meant that the Triple Alliance would have been greatly weakened further in the face of the Triple Entente which was growing closer and stronger. The internal dissolution of Austria would have been accelerated through the encouragement to restless Slav subjects. Austria's evaporating prestige in the Balkans would have completely

"Although I am not able to verify it, I have private information that the German Ambassador [Tschirschky] knew the text of the ultimatum to Serbia before it was despatched, and telegraphed it to the German Emperor;" Bunsen to Grey, July 30; B.B.B., 95; *cf.* B.D., 307.

dried up, and Russia, with her growing population and ambitions, would have dominated the Balkans and hastened the day for controlling Constantinople and the Straits.

Bethmann and Jagow concluded that the more energetically they appeared to support Austria, the more likely they would be to succeed in "localizing" the conflict and in preventing Russia and the other Powers from interfering. Therefore on the morning of July 24, when Austria notified the Powers of Europe of the Note delivered to Serbia the night before, Germany immediately followed with declarations endorsing Austria's charges against Serbia and emphasizing the importance of localizing the conflict. Jagow made the assertions which we have quoted above as to Germany's having no foreknowledge of the contents of the ultimatum. But in pretending to be wholly ignorant of Austria's step and at the same time approving it when taken, the German Foreign Office stupidly put itself in a false and self-contradictory position which not unnaturally made the Entente Powers suspect that it was acting in bad faith; it made them suspect that the German authorities were more responsible for Austria, and were harboring more reprehensible plans of their own, than was really the case —that Germany had not only approved but had instigated Austria's action; that this action was not aimed merely at Serbia, but was the pretext for a general war which would realize the ambitions voiced by irresponsible Pan-German orators and newspapers. These suspicions were not unnatural under the circumstances, and though they were far from accurate, they were assiduously spread, especially by the representatives of France, and contributed much to the later fatal course of events. Later, when Germany perceived that it might not be possible after all to "localize" an Austro-Serbian war, and therefore made genuine efforts to restrain Austria and avoid a general European War, less credence was given to her statements because of the suspicions which had been aroused by Jagow's untrue assertions that Germany had been ignorant of the ultimatum. Reputation for good faith once weakened is difficult to restore. This is what made so serious her adding to the first blunder of giving Berchtold a blank check on July 5 the second blunder of saying what was not true in regard to foreknowledge of the ultimatum.

THE ULTIMATUM

The Note which Austria addressed to Serbia on July 23 at 6 P. M., and notified to the Powers next morning, was as follows:

> On the 31st March, 1909, the Serbian Minister in Vienna, on the instructions of the Serbian Government, made the following declaration to the Imperial and Royal Government:—
>
> "Serbia recognises that the *fait accompli* regarding Bosnia has not affected her rights, and consequently she will conform to the decisions that the Powers may take in conformity with article 25 of the Treaty of Berlin. In deference to the advice of the Great Powers, Serbia undertakes to renounce from now onwards the attitude of protest and opposition which she has adopted with regard to the annexation since last autumn. She undertakes, moreover, to modify the direction of her policy with regard to Austria-Hungary and to live in future on good neighborly terms with the latter."
>
> The history of recent years, and in particular the painful events of the 28th June last, have shown the existence of a subversive movement with the object of detaching a part of the territories of Austria-Hungary from the Monarchy. The movement, which had its birth under the eye of the Serbian Government, has gone so far as to make itself manifest on both sides of the Serbian frontier in the shape of acts of terrorism and a series of outrages and murders.
>
> Far from carrying out the formal undertakings contained

in the declaration of the 31st March, 1909, the Royal Serbian Government has done nothing to repress these movements. It has permitted the criminal machinations of various societies and associations directed against the Monarchy, and has tolerated unrestrained language on the part of the press, the glorification of the perpetrators of outrages, and the participation of officers and functionaries in subversive agitation. It has permitted an unwholesome propaganda in public instruction, in short, it has permitted all manifestations of a nature to incite the Serbian population to hatred of the Monarchy and contempt of its institutions.

This culpable tolerance of the Royal Serbian Government had not ceased at the moment when the events of the 28th June last proved its fatal consequences to the whole world.

It results from the depositions and confessions of the criminal perpetrators of the outrage of the 28th June that the Sarajevo assassinations were planned in Belgrade; that the arms and explosives with which the murderers were provided had been given to them by Serbian officers and functionaries belonging to the Narodna Odbrana; and finally, that the passage into Bosnia of the criminals and their arms was organised and effected by the chiefs of the Serbian frontier service.

The above-mentioned results of the magisterial investigation do not permit the Austro-Hungarian Government to pursue any longer the attitude of expectant forbearance which they have maintained for years in face of the machinations hatched in Belgrade, and thence propagated in the territories of the Monarchy. The results, on the contrary, impose on them the duty of putting an end to the intrigues which form a perpetual menace to the tranquillity of the Monarchy.

To achieve this end the Imperial and Royal Government see themselves compelled to demand from the Royal Serbian Government a formal assurance that they condemn this dangerous propaganda against the Monarchy; in other words, the whole series of tendencies, the ultimate aim of which is to detach from the Monarchy territories belonging to it, and that they undertake to suppress by every means this criminal and terrorist propaganda.

In order to give a formal character to this undertaking the Royal Serbian Government shall publish on the front page of their "Official Journal" of the 13/26 July the following declaration:—

"The Royal Government of Serbia condemn the propaganda directed against Austria-Hungary—*i.e.,* the general tendency of which the final aim is to detach from the Austro-Hungarian Monarchy territories belonging to it, and they sincerely deplore the fatal consequences of these criminal proceedings.

"The Royal Government regret that Serbian officers and functionaries participated in the above-mentioned propaganda and thus compromised the good neighborly relations to which the Royal Government were solemnly pledged by their declaration of the 31st March, 1909.

"The Royal Government, who disapprove and repudiate all idea of interfering or attempting to interfere with the destinies of the inhabitants of any part whatsoever of Austria-Hungary, consider it their duty formally to warn officers and functionaries, and the whole population of the kingdom, that henceforward they will proceed with the utmost rigor against persons who may be guilty of such machinations, which they will use all their efforts to anticipate and suppress."

This declaration shall simultaneously be communicated to the Royal army as an order of the day by His Majesty the King and shall be published in the "Official Bulletin" of the Army.

The Royal Serbian Government further undertake:

1. To suppress any publication which incites to hatred and contempt of the Austro-Hungarian Monarchy and the general tendency of which is directed against its territorial integrity;

2. To dissolve immediately the society styled "Narodna Odbrana," to confiscate all its means of propaganda, and

to proceed in the same manner against other societies and their branches in Serbia which engage in propaganda against the Austro-Hungarian Monarchy. The Royal Government shall take the necessary measures to prevent the societies dissolved from continuing their activity under another name and form;

3. To eliminate without delay from public instruction in Serbia, both as regards the teaching body and also as regards the methods of instruction, everything that serves, or might serve, to foment the propaganda against Austria-Hungary;

4. To remove from the military service, and from the administration in general, all officers and functionaries guilty of propaganda against the Austro-Hungarian Monarchy whose names and deeds the Austro-Hungarian Government reserve to themselves the right of communicating to the Royal Government;

5. To accept the collaboration in Serbia of representatives of the Austro-Hungarian Government for the suppression of the subversive movement directed against the territorial integrity of the Monarchy;

6. To take judicial proceedings against accessories to the plot of the 28th June who are on Serbian territory; delegates of the Austro-Hungarian Government will take part in the investigation relating thereto;

7. To proceed without delay to the arrest of Major Voja Tankositch and of the individual named Milan Ciganovitch, a Serbian State employee, who have been compromised by the results of the magisterial enquiry at Sarajevo;

8. To prevent by effective measures the co-operation of the Serbian authorities in the illicit traffic in arms and explosives across the frontier, to dismiss and punish severely the officials of the frontier service at Shabats and Loznica guilty of having assisted the perpetrators of the Sarajevo crime by facilitating their passage across the frontier;

9. To furnish the Imperial and Royal Government with explanations regarding the unjustifiable utterances of high

Serbian officials, both in Serbia and abroad, who, notwithstanding their official position, have not hesitated since the crime of the 28th June to express themselves in interviews in terms of hostility to the Austro-Hungarian Government; and, finally,

10. To notify the Imperial and Royal Government without delay of the execution of the measures comprised under the preceding heads.

The Austro-Hungarian Government expect the reply of the Royal Government at the latest by 6 o'clock on Saturday evening, the 25th July.

In the light of what has been said in the preceding chapters concerning the Sarajevo assassination, the circumstances leading up to it, Serbia's failure to take prompt steps to discover and arrest the accomplices, and Austria's conviction that her very existence was at stake, one cannot say that the demands, though very severe, were excessive from the Austrian point of view. If they had been honestly calculated merely to exact punishment for those connected with the Sarajevo assassination and to obtain guarantees of security for the future, they might be regarded as justified. But having been deliberately framed with the expectation that they would be rejected, and that their rejection would lead to a localized war with Serbia, they must be condemned on both moral and practical grounds as one of the main causes of the World War. And Germany, in so far as she assented to them and endorsed them, must share in this condemnation.

CHAPTER VI

THE RUSSIAN DANGER

The first news of the assassination of the Archduke Franz Ferdinand made a painful impression in Russia, as everywhere else in the civilized world. But the feeling of hatred toward Austria-Hungary which prevailed in Russia, and which had been steadily increasing since the Balkan crises, soon overshadowed all expressions of sympathy for the aged Austrian monarch in the latest of his many tragic bereavements. At the memorial services arranged in St. Petersburg by the Austrian Ambassador there was, to be sure, a full attendance of Russian officials, including Grand Dukes Boris and Nicholas, who had been requested by the Tsar to represent the Imperial family. But aside from this perfunctory expression of feeling, the German Ambassador, Pourtalès, did not notice any genuine sympathy with Austria's loss. Not only in the newspapers, but also in society, he heard virtually nothing but unfriendly comments on the murdered Austrian Archduke: that Russia, by his death, was now rid of a bitter enemy.[1]

At the close of the memorial service, Pourtalès took the opportunity to talk with Sazonov, the Russian Minister of Foreign Affairs. It was the first time he had seen him since the assassination. Sazonov began by sharply criticizing the Sarajevo officials for their conduct after the crime: they had not only permitted attacks on the Serbs, but had

[1] Pourtalès to Bethmann, July 13; K.D., 53. The Kaiser's marginal note at this point was much nearer the truth: "He [Franz Ferdinand] in fact always wanted to renew the old League of the Three Emperors! He was the best friend of Russia!"

deliberately given a free rein to the popular fury. He did not believe that there was any population worth mentioning in Bosnia and Herzegovina which was really loyal to the Hapsburgs—at most merely some Mohammedans and Roman Catholics. He denied Austria's assertion that the assassination was the result of a Greater Serbian plot; at least, he said, there was not the slightest proof of this so far, and it was exceedingly unjust to hold the Serbian Government responsible, as the Austro-Hungarian newspapers were doing. This was no more justifiable than it would have been for Russia to call the French Government to account for the crimes which were plotted on French soil and committed in Russia. Championing the official Serbian attitude, he declared that the Sarajevo crime was only the isolated act of immature young persons, and there was no proof of their connection with any deep-laid political plot. When Pourtalès urged "monarchical solidarity" against such dangerous anarchists and murderers, he found that Sazonov responded to this ancient theme with less warmth than usual, and concluded that Sazonov, like nearly everyone else in Russia, was blinded by his hatred of Austria-Hungary. He noticed also everywhere in Russia a boundless contempt for the condition of affairs in the Dual Monarchy.[2]

During the middle of July, Sazonov spent several days at his country estate near Grodno. He wanted a rest before the exacting demands on his strength, which would be made by the approaching visit of the French President and Prime Minister. Such an absence from St. Petersburg seemed, at that time, quite safe. But when he returned to the Russian Foreign Office on July 18, he began to grow nervous at the ominously silent attitude of the Vienna authorities, and the heated recriminations between the Austrian and

[2] K.D., 53. Beside the last remark the Kaiser penciled, "Pride goeth before destruction!"

Serbian Press. The Italian Ambassador had told the Secretary, Baron Schilling, of his impression that Austria was about to take an irreparable step against Serbia, and that it would be well to serve a warning at Vienna.[3] To the Austrian and German Ambassadors Sazonov therefore reiterated his views, that it was unjust to make the whole Serbian people responsible for the crime of a single individual, as the Austrian newspapers were doing. "Russia," he said to the Austrian Ambassador, "would not be indifferent to any effort to humiliate Serbia. Russia could not permit Austria to use menacing language or military measures against Serbia. In short, *'La politique de la Russie est pacifique, mais pas passive!'* "[4] Szápáry, who had unexpectedly returned from his vacation the day before, said that Austria could not continue to tolerate the Serbian terrorist activities, but that his Government were convinced that Serbia would yield to any such demands as might result from the investigation going on at Sarajevo. He gave the impression in peace-loving phrases that Austria had not the slightest intention of rendering more acute her relations with Serbia. Sazonov was fully quieted, and told Schilling that there was no need to resort to threats, as the Ambassador had assured him emphatically of his Government's love of peace. *"Il a été doux comme un agneau."*[5]

Sazonov had feared that some sudden stroke might be attempted by Austria, which would humiliate Serbia

[3] Schilling's *Diary,* p. 25; on the high value of this Diary, see above, vol. I, ch. i, at notes 14 and 15. Baron Schilling was Director of the Chancellery of the Russian Foreign Office. His position corresponded to that of the Permanent Under-Secretary for Foreign Affairs in England. He was reported to be "an extraordinarily clever, skilful, and influential man", who really directed foreign policy more than Sazonov (*cf.* G. P., XXXIX, 526).

[4] Szápáry to Berchtold, July 18; A.R.B., I, 25; Pourtalès to Bethmann, July 21, K.D., 120.

[5] Schilling's *Diary,* p. 27. *Cf.,* however, Buchanan to Grey, July 18, 8:50 P.M. (B.D., 60) for evidences of Sazonov's great nervousness and anxiety.

directly, and thereby Russia indirectly. He was always very much afraid that Germany or Austria would do something to diminish Russia's prestige in the Balkans and in Europe. It was a point on which he was very sensitive, particularly in view of the strong Pan-Slav sentiment of the Russian Press and the militarists, who were not wholly friendly to him, and who might drive him from office if he suffered a diplomatic defeat. He did not want a repetition of anything like the Liman von Sanders episode. However, the main matter immediately at hand, until Austria should finally break her sphinx-like silence, was the reception of President Poincaré and M. Viviani, and the ceremonial renewal of the Franco-Russian solidarity.

POINCARÉ'S VISIT TO RUSSIA

In January, 1914, at the height of the Liman von Sanders crisis, the French had asked Sazonov when it would be convenient for President Poincaré to repeat the summer visit to Russia, which he had made in August, 1912, shortly before the outbreak of the Balkan War. It was finally arranged that he should arrive at Kronstadt at 2 P. M. on July 20, and leave at 11 P. M. on July 23.[6] When the Sarajevo assassination occurred the French Cabinet raised the question whether it was desirable for him to leave France, but decided, as did the Kaiser in going on his northern cruise, that it would seriously alarm public opinion as to the European situation, if important arrangements long announced should be abandoned.[7] Jean Jaurès, however, the veteran French Socialist and historian, distrusting the policies of Izvolski and Poincaré, refused to vote credits for the trip, declaring that it was dangerous for France to become increasingly entangled in adventurous Near East questions, and in treaty arrangements of which the French

[6] Poincaré, IV, 3-6, 221-285; K.D., 96, 108; Paléologue, I, 1-19.
[7] Poincaré, IV, 211; *Les Origines de la Guerre,* 197 ff.

public knew neither the text nor the consequences.[8] But the French President and his Prime Minister embarked from Dunkirk on the cruiser, *France,* on July 15, and were welcomed five days later off Peterhof by Sazonov, Paléologue, and Izvolski, and then by the Tsar. Poincaré and Paléologue in their memoirs have left elaborate and picturesque accounts of all the ceremonial occasions with which the three following days were filled, but they say very little of private conversations which were exchanged.

One of Poincaré's aims was to reduce Anglo-Russian friction over Persia, in order to secure closer coöperation between the ally and the friend of France,[9] and so perhaps pave the way for a renewal of the negotiations for an Anglo-Russian Naval Convention; these had been interrupted owing to the rumors of it which had leaked out, and to Sir Edward Grey's unwillingness to continue negotiations in secret which he had publicly denied in Parliament.[10] But among the main subjects of their discussion were certainly the strengthening of the bonds of the Franco-Russian Alliance, as well as of the Triple Entente,[11] and especially

8 *Cf.* G. Demartial, *L'Evangile du Quai d'Orsay* (Paris, 1927), p. 11 f. Demartial has given a most penetrating analysis of the French Yellow Book, showing how French official telegrams were suppressed and altered by its editor (M. Berthelot?), to conceal the truth concerning Poincaré's visit and the Russian mobilization measures. His revelations and those of August Bach and others (*cf.* KSF, II, 129-152; IV, 879-884; V, 262-5; 1228 f.) make all the more welcome the eventual prospect of a complete and honest publication of the French diplomatic correspondence during the July crisis. Such a publication will perhaps clear M. Poincaré's reputation of the suspicions which have been leveled against him at home and abroad. *Cf.* R. Gerin et R. Poincaré, *Les Responsabilités de la Guerre* (Paris, 1930).

9 Poincaré, *Les Origines de la Guerre,* p. 201 f; *cf.* also B.D., pp. x-xi, and Nos. 49, 75, 164.

10 *Cf.* Benckendorff, Russian Ambassador in London, to Sazonov, July 2, 1914; Siebert-Schreiner, p. 733; see also G.P., XXXIX, 612-628.

11 Just before Poincaré's arrival, the Tsar said to the French Ambassador: "There is one question which preoccupies me above everything else; our Entente with England. We must get her to enter our alliance. . . . It is all the more important that we should be able to count upon the English in case of a crisis;" Paléologue, I, 2 f.

the measures to be taken in view of the increasing indications that Austria was preparing to deliver a stiff ultimatum to Serbia.[12]

In all the conversations which took place in the course of the next three days it was Poincaré, as one might expect from his dominating and energetic personality, who took the lead, and sounded the key-notes. At the very outset, as the guests were leaving the *France* in a launch, Paléologue observed: "The Emperor and the President, sitting in the stern, enter at once into conversation. . . . It is Poincaré who guides the discussion. Soon it is he alone who is talking. The Emperor only acquiesces." [13] At the gala banquet at Peterhof in the evening the Tsar, in his toast of welcome, hoped the two countries "will continue to enjoy the benefits of the peace, which the fullness of their strength ensures, by constantly tying more tightly the bands which unite them." [14] Poincaré in a longer reply, which Paléologue thought had a remarkably significant force and note of authority,[15] recalled that the Franco-Russian Alliance had existed nearly twenty-five years, and added:

> Founded upon community of interests, consecrated by the peaceful desires of the two Governments, supported by armed forces on land and sea which know and value each other and have become accustomed to act as brothers, strengthened by long experience and augmented by valu-

12 For the fact that the Entente Powers knew more of Austria's intended action than they admitted in their documentary publications of 1914, see above, ch. v, at notes 95-100. As early as July 5 the British Ambassador in Vienna had reported that, "Dumaine, my French colleague, is full of serious apprehension. His country is known to be in sympathy with the Serbian aspirations and he is in a position to know what is being said and done by Serbians in Vienna. He has repeatedly spoken to me during the past week of the dangers of the situation, which he fears may develop rapidly into complications from which war might easily arise;" Bunsen to Grey, July 5; B.D., 40, but omitted from B.B.B.

13 Paléologue, I, 4.

14 Schilling's *Diary,* Appendix, p. 113 f.

15 Paléologue, I, 6.

able friendships, the Alliance to which the sublime Tsar Alexander III and the lamented President Carnot gave the initiative has ever since constantly afforded proof of its beneficial activity and its unshakable strength. Your Majesty can be assured that France in the future, as always in the past, will, in sincere and daily co-operation with her ally, pursue the work of peace and civilization for which both the Governments and both the peoples have never ceased to labour.[16]

Next morning, July 21, Poincaré and the Tsar talked over the general European situation, and especially the Persian Question. The Tsar assured him that "he would not allow Persia to cause division between England and Russia."[17] In the afternoon the French guests went to St. Petersburg to receive the French colony and the Diplomatic Corps, but were surprised that the Tsar did not accompany them. This was probably because of the severe strikes which had broken out there, the workingmen being more interested in their own grievances than in the representatives of French capitalism.[18] In the reception at the Winter Palace, Paléologue presented his diplomatic colleagues to the French President, who spoke affably to all except the Austrian Ambassador: to Pourtalès, about his French ancestors, but not a word about politics; to Motono, virtual assent to Japan's acting with the Triple Entente; to Buchanan, he repeated the Tsar's assurances about Persia; it was probably also on this occasion that he rejected emphatically Sir Edward Grey's first proposal for settling peacefully European complications which might grow out of the Austro-Serbian question by means of "direct-conversations" between Austria and Russia,[19] though

16 Schilling's *Diary,* Appendix, p. 114.

17 Buchanan to Grey, July 22, 23; B.D., 75, 164.

18 *Cf.* Pourtalès to Bethmann, July 23; K.D., 130, 291; and B.D., 164.

19 Poincaré "expressed opinion that a conversation *à deux* between Austria and Russia would be very dangerous at the present moment;"

neither Paléologue nor Poincaré mention this in their accounts. When Szápáry, the Austrian Ambassador, came forward in his turn, Poincaré seized the occasion to try to draw him out as to Berchtold's intentions, and to warn him almost threateningly against Austria's holding Serbia responsible for Sarajevo:

> After some words of condolence over the assassination of the Archduke Franz Ferdinand, the President asked Szápáry:
>
> "Have you any news from Serbia?"
>
> "The judicial investigation is advancing," replied Szápáry coldly. Poincaré went on:
>
> "The results of this investigation do not fail to disturb me, Mr. Ambassador; for I remember two former investigations which did not improve your relations with Serbia. You remember the Friedjung Affair and the Prochaska Affair?"
>
> Szápáry replied drily: "We cannot tolerate, Mr. President, that a foreign Government shall allow murderous attacks to be prepared on its soil against our sovereignty."
>
> Poincaré tried in a most conciliatory tone to show him that, in the present state of feeling in Europe, all Governments ought to be doubly prudent. "With a little good-will, this Serbian affair is easy to settle. But it is easy also for it to become envenomed. Serbia has very warm friends in the Russian people. And Russia has an Ally, France. What complications are to be feared here!" [20]

This description by Paléologue of Poincaré's conversation with the Austrian Ambassador is confirmed in its essentials by Szápáry himself, who concluded his long report of it with the shrewd observation:

> This action of the President, tactless, considering that it came from the head of a foreign state, who was here on a visit, sounding like a threat and so strikingly different from

Buchanan to Grey, July 22; B.D., 76. On the significance of this, see below ch. viii, at notes 27-37.

20 Paléologue, I, 9 f.

> Sazonov's reserved and cautious attitude, confirms the expectation that M. Poincaré will have anything but a calming effect here. Significant is the close resemblance between the President's juristic deductions and the arguments by Pashitch in the *Leipziger Neueste Nachrichten.* Spalajkovitch [Serbian Minister at St. Petersburg], whom Sazonov characterized to me only recently as "unbalanced" [déséquilibré], may have had a hand in this game.[21]

When Szápáry had bowed and departed, Poincaré remarked to Paléologue that the interview had made an unfavorable impression on him: Austria seemed to be preparing some sudden stroke which Szápáry was concealing; "Sazonov must be firm, and we must support him." These words sum up better than anything else the significance of Poincaré's trip to Russia. Aware of Sazonov's changeable and mercurial temperament, of his ardent Russian nationalism, alternating, however, with a genuine desire for peace and a certain timidity which made him shrink at critical moments from supporting the Serbians to the point of war,[22] Poincaré wanted to strengthen Sazonov's attitude toward Austria. He wanted him to warn Austria against making inacceptable demands on Serbia, and to prevent him, in case of need, from accepting any compromise settlement which might be regarded as a diplomatic defeat for the Triple Entente at the hands of Germany and Austria.

Poincaré's visit also greatly strengthened the militarist group in Russia, headed by the Grand Duke, who wanted Sazonov to take a more aggressive attitude and who were continually trying to exert pressure on the peace-loving

[21] Szápáry to Berchtold, July 21, A.R.B., I, 45.

[22] E.g. in the Albanian crisis in November, 1913; see also below, ch. viii, at note 85, Sazonov's remark to Szápáry on July 26, that he "had no sympathy at all for the Balkan Slavs," and his apparently momentary inclination to abandon them, if he could reach a compromise settlement with Austria which would save Russia's prestige.

Tsar. The war spirit and "champagne mood" which was stirred by the presence of the French guests is well described by Paléologue in his account of the banquet which Grand Duke Nicholas gave in Poincaré's honor on the evening of July 22, after a military review at Krasnoe Selo. Paléologue arrived a few minutes early and found the Montenegrin Princesses, Anastasia and Melitza, wives of Grand Duke Nicholas and Grand Duke Peter respectively, decorating the tables; they both began to talk to him excitedly:

> "Do you know that we are passing through historic days, blessed days! Tomorrow, at the review, the bands will play nothing but the *Marche Lorraine* and *Sambre et Meuse*. Today, I had a telegram from my father in the proper style; he tells me we shall have war before the month is out. What a hero, my father! He is worthy of the Iliad. Here, look at this little box—it never leaves me; it has Lorraine soil in it, yes, Lorraine soil, which I collected beyond the frontier when I was in France two years ago with my husband. And now look at that table of honor! It is decorated entirely with thistles; I would not have any other flowers put on it. Now then! They are thistles from Lorraine! I picked a few stalks on the territory annexed [by Germany]; I brought them here and had the seeds sown in my garden. Melitza, talk to the Ambassador some more; tell him all this day means to us, while I go and receive the Tsar."
>
> During the meal I sat next the Grand Duchess Anastasia and the dithyrambics continued, mixed with prophecies: "War is going to break out. Nothing will be left of Austria. You will get Alsace-Lorraine back. Our armies will meet in Berlin. Germany will be annihilated."
>
> Then suddenly—"I must control myself, the Tsar is looking at me." [23]

Late that same night, at 4 A. M., Sazonov sent off to the Russian Chargé d'Affaires at Vienna the warning telegram

[23] Paléologue, I, 14 f.

which before Poincaré's visit he had told Schilling was unnecessary:

> Please point out in a friendly but firm manner the dangerous consequences of any Austrian action of a character inacceptable to the dignity of Serbia. The French and English Ambassadors are trusted to give councils of moderation.[24]

Poincaré completely approved of this, and the French Ambassador at Vienna was instructed accordingly.[25] But the British Foreign Office realized the danger of a veiled threat of this kind. Sir Eyre Crowe noted: "Any such communication at Vienna would be likely to produce intense irritation, without any benefical other effect." Sir Arthur Nicolson was "afraid that it is not a judicious move." And Sir Edward Grey decided to postpone any action until next day.[26]

This Franco-Russian move to head off Austria from making demands on Serbia, however, came to nothing, because the Russian Chargé d'Affaires in Vienna did not receive his instructions until 3 P. M. on July 23. He went at once to the Ballplatz, but was told that Berchtold was very busy and could not see him until next morning. In

24 Sazonov to Kudashev, Tg. 1475 (much condensed); July 22 [23], 4 A. M.; Schilling's *Diary,* pp. 27; and p. 85 for unabridged text; also L.N., II, 275. Renouvin says (p. 77) Sazonov sent this telegram "during the night on July 21-22 about 4 A.M.," but he is in error; it was really sent on July 23 at 4. A. M., as is clear from the serial number (1475 is close to 1487 sent on July 24; *cf. Krasnyi Arkhiv,* IV, p. 45), and from the fact that it was received in Vienna at 3 P. M. on July 23 (Schilling's *Diary,* p. 38), that is, within the 10-12 hours which was the normal interval for telegrams between St. Petersburg and Vienna. To be sure, the telegram is dated "July 22, 4 A. M.," but this is evidently one of the many cases in which telegrams written late in the evening and not put on the wire until after midnight, were stamped at the telegraph office with an early morning *hour* which had the misleading effect of antedating by 24 hours the *day-of-the-month* date which the writer of the telegram had correctly put upon it before he went to bed.

25 F.Y.B., 22, 23.

26 Minutes on Buchanan's tg. to Grey, which was received July 23, 3 P.M.; B.D., 84.

the meantime the ultimatum was presented at Belgrade at 6 P. M. on July 23.[27] Even had the instructions arrived earlier, they would almost certainly have failed to deter Berchtold, especially in view of England's do-nothing attitude and of the Vienna Cabinet's firm determination.

Meanwhile in Russia the final festivities of the Poincaré visit took place in blissful ignorance of the fact that Austria had already presented her demands at Belgrade, and that the Franco-Russian move to prevent it would prove abortive. In the farewell toast on board the *France,* the President thanked the Tsar for the warmth of his reception, which afforded "an emphatic affirmation of the indissoluble alliance which unites Russia and my native France"—two countries which would continue to coöperate in the future as in the past, because "both have many times experienced the advantages accruing to each from the regular coöperation, and because they are both animated by the same ideal of peace combined with strength, honor and dignity." The words were acclaimed with tumultuous enthusiasm, and made on all present a vivid and lasting impression of Poincaré's complete determination to stand firmly behind Russia. A few days later Paléologue cited them to the Under-Secretary, as an evidence of such perfect Franco-Russian accord that they would bluff Germany out of making war in support of Austria.[28]

The result of Poincaré's visit, as the English Ambassador was confidentially informed by Sazonov and Paléologue next morning, had been to establish the following points:

[27] Kudashev to Sazonov, July 26; Schilling's *Diary,* p. 38 f. The French Ambassador did not receive his instructions until July 24, so that the "observations intended to prevent presentation of the Note or to cause its terms to be modified would now be out of place;" Bunsen to Grey, July 24, 7:50 P.M., B.D., 97. Renouvin is in error (p. 79) in speaking of the Franco-Russian move as "made at Vienna on July 22."

[28] Schilling's *Diary,* p. 32; Paléologue, I, 16 ff.

1. Perfect community of views on the various problems with which the Powers are confronted as regards the maintenance of general peace and balance of power in Europe, more especially in the East.
2. Decision to take action at Vienna with a view to the prevention of a demand for explanations or any summons equivalent to an intervention in the internal affairs of Serbia which the latter would be justified in regarding as an attack on her sovereignty and independence.
3. Solemn affirmation of obligations imposed by the alliance of the two countries.[29]

The second of these points, as we have just seen, had already been frustrated by Austria's prompt action at Belgrade before the Russian and French Ambassadors were able to carry out their instructions. The first and third points find their interpretation in the events which followed. By the French Ambassador in St. Petersburg they were treated as a blank check by which France promised full support to Russia in whatever measures she should take to prevent Austria from carrying out the plans which Berchtold had decided to carry out, but which were not yet fully known to the rest of Europe. This is seen in the assurances which Paléologue repeatedly gave to Sazonov as the latter took progressive steps toward secret Russian military measures preparatory to mobilization and to a general European War.

SAZONOV'S PLAN FOR "PARTIAL MOBILIZATION," JULY 24

On the morning of Friday, July 24, the Austrian Ambassadors everywhere notified the Governments to which they were accredited of the ultimatum which had been presented at Belgrade the preceding evening. Everywhere, except

[29] Buchanan to Grey, July 24: B.D., 101; this important part of Buchanan's telegram was suppressed from B.B.B., 6. For Poincaré's summary of the results of his visit, see Viviani's despatch from Reval to Bienvenu-Martin, July 24, 1 A.M., F.Y.B., 22.

PRESIDENT POINCARÉ'S VISIT TO RUSSIA IN JULY, 1914

at Berlin, its severe demands and intransigent tone made a painful impression and caused the most serious misgivings.

Sir Edward Grey called it "the most formidable document he had ever seen addressed by one State to another that was independent." But he did not care to discuss the merits of the dispute between Austria and Serbia; that was not England's concern. It was solely from the point of view of the peace of Europe that he would concern himself with the matter, and he would wait to hear the views of the other Powers.[30] After talking with the French and German Ambassadors, he began to make a series of proposals for preserving the peace of Europe which will be discussed later.

In Paris, M. Bienvenu-Martin, Minister of Justice, who was Acting-Minister of Foreign Affairs during the absence of Poincaré and Viviani, was completely nonplussed. He did not know what to do, beyond informing the absent President and Minister of the new developments and giving Serbia some cautious advice.[31] But he soon received instructions sent by wireless from the *France,* where Poincaré and Viviani had learned by a radiogram from Russia the substance of the ultimatum. Viviani had at once sent wireless messages to St. Petersburg, London, and Paris, "that, in his opinion, (1) Serbia should immediately offer all the satisfaction compatible with her honor and independence; (2) that she should request an extension of the twenty-four hour [*sic*] time-limit within which Austria demanded a reply; (3) that England, Russia and France should agree to support this request; and (4) that the Triple Entente should see whether it would be possible to substitute an international investigation in place of an

30 Grey to Bunsen and the other British Ambassadors, July 24, 1 P. M.; B.D., 91; *cf.* also B.D., 98, 99, 100; A.R.B., II, 14, 15; K.D., 157; and F.Y.B., 32.

31 *Cf.* F.Y.B., 24-34.

Austro-Serbian investigation." [32] Bienvenu-Martin proceeded to take some steps accordingly, but they came too late to produce any positive results.

It was in St. Petersburg, however, that the ultimatum caused the greatest excitement and alarm. The Russian Ministers and Entente Ambassadors did not get to bed until long past midnight, after the *France* had steamed away under the stars carrying Poincaré down the Gulf of Finland. They had not yet recovered from the fatiguing festivities and bountiful banquets, when they were rudely awakened toward 7 A. M.,[33] after very few hours of sleep, by the news of a telegram from Belgrade telling of the ultimatum. During the succeeding fortnight of almost sleepless days and nights, the fatigue and mental demands were far greater than during Poincaré's visit. Not only in St. Petersburg, but everywhere in the Foreign Offices of Europe, responsible officials now began to fall under a terrible physical and mental strain of overwork, worry, and lack of sleep, whose inevitable psychological consequences are too often overlooked in assessing the blame for the events which followed. But if one is to understand how it was that experienced and trained men occasionally failed to grasp fully the sheaves of telegrams put into their hands at frequent intervals, how their proposals were sometimes confused and misunderstood, how they quickly came to be obsessed with pessimistic fears and suspicions, and how in some cases they finally broke down and wept, one must remember the nerve-racking psychological effects of continued work and loss of sleep, combined with the conscious-

32 Poincaré, *Les Origines de la Guerre*, p. 213; this and the other important wireless messages to and from Poincaré and Viviani on board the *France* are suppressed from the *French Yellow Book*.

33 Paléologue, I, 22 f.; Sazonov, *Fateful Years*, p. 152, says that, having learned during the night of July 23-24 of the presentation of the ultimatum, he left Tsarskoe Selo next morning to return to St. Petersburg.

ness of the responsibility for the safety of their country and the fate of millions of lives.

"C'est la guerre Européenne," were the words with which Sazonov greeted Baron Schilling, on arriving from Tsarskoe Selo at the Russian Foreign Office about 10 A. M. on Friday morning. He at once telephoned the news to the Tsar, who exclaimed, "This is disturbing," and gave orders that he be kept informed as to further developments.[34]

A few minutes later Szápáry arrived to read the full text of the ultimatum and to explain and justify Austria's action. Sazonov, who had not yet had time to consult with the other Russian Ministers or to learn how far England would back him up, received Szápáry by saying that he knew what brought him, but could not state what Russia's attitude would be. Szápáry then read aloud the ultimatum, but was frequently interrupted by Sazonov's questions and objections to its statements. At the mention of the *dossier*, which was to place the full Austrian evidence against Serbia before the Powers, Sazonov asked why Austria bothered with it, when she had already sent an ultimatum, showing she wanted war and not an impartial investigation; as things were, after the ultimatum, he said, he was not at all curious to see the *dossier*. "The fact is, you want war, and have burned your bridges." When Szápáry protested that Austria was peace-loving, and merely wanted security for her territory against foreign revolutionary agitation and for her dynasty against bombs, Sazonov remarked sarcastically, "One sees how pacific you are, now that you are setting Europe on fire." There followed a long discussion for an hour and a half. Sazonov sought to defend Serbia against the Austrian charges, and criticized the form and severity of the demands, especially the shortness of the time-limit. He kept saying from time to time:

34 Schilling's *Diary,* p. 28 f.

"I know what it is. You want to make war on Serbia! I see what is happening, the German newspapers are egging you on. You are setting fire to Europe. It is a great responsibility you are assuming; you will see the impression this will make here and in London and Paris and perhaps elsewhere. They will consider this an unjustifiable aggression." He recalled the scandals of the Friedjung trial, but, contrary to Szápáry's expectation, Sazonov did not argue about the pressure from Russian public opinion, Slavdom, or Greek Orthodoxy. He spoke rather of England, France and Europe, and the effect which the ultimatum would have outside Russia. Szápáry got the impression that the Russian Minister was more dejected than excited, and was being careful not to say anything which would prejudice Russia's future action. On the whole he thought Sazonov "relatively calm."[35]

Sazonov, however, was more excited and disturbed than Szápáry appeared to think. Of a naturally mercurial temperament, he was now particularly indignant at Berchtold's methods. The short time-limit, the withholding of the *dossier*, and the humiliating demands on Serbia, all seemed to him to indicate that Austria was determined on war at once with Serbia. It was particularly deceitful on Austria's part to have pretended for three weeks that the demands would be mild, such as Serbia could surely accept, and then to face the little kingdom with an ultimatum which seemed to indicate that Austria wanted war and would soon cross

[35] Szápáry to Berchtold, July 24, 3:35, 8:00 and 8:25 P.M.; A.R.B., II, 16, 17, 18. The *Austrian Red Book* of 1915 condenses these three telegrams into one and suppresses seven passages. On this interview between Sazonov and Szápáry, see also Pourtalès to Bethmann, July 24; K.D., 148. For Berchtold's simultaneous interview with Kudashev, the Russian Chargé d'Affaires in Vienna, in which Berchtold sought to be as conciliatory as possible, saying that he had no desire to humiliate Serbia but only to require necessary guarantees of security for Austria, and that he had no intention of annexing Serbian territory but only of maintaining the *status quo*, see A.R.B., II, 23; and Schilling's *Diary*, p. 39 f.

the frontier into Serbian territory. Moreover, Poincaré and the French Prime Minister had left Russia only a few hours previously. They were now out on the Baltic, where it was difficult for him to get into touch with them. Furthermore, he suspected that much that Szápáry said was not true. Therefore Russia must be prepared for war, or at least a strong diplomatic bluff, and he must make sure of British and Rumanian support. Accordingly, while he had been talking with Szápáry, he had Baron Schilling notify the Ministers of War,[36] Navy, and Finance of the course of events and summon them to a Council of Ministers at 3 P. M. Schilling warned Izvolski and Shebeko to return to their posts at Paris and Vienna, and recalled Neratov, Prince Trubetzkoi and other Foreign Office advisers from their leaves of absence. He also pointed out to the Finance Minister the necessity of withdrawing without delay as far as possible all State deposits in Germany.[37]

Sazonov himself consulted with General Ianushkevich, the Chief of the General Staff, and proposed preparations for a partial mobilization of the Russian army, directed exclusively against Austria, the announcement of which might serve as a warning to Germany and an effectual bluff to stop Austria from attacking Serbia. This at any rate seems to be the conclusion to be drawn from the following narrative of General Dobrorolski.[38] Dobrorolski was Chief

36 Sukhomlinov later denied that he took part in the Council of Ministers on July 24 (*cf.* Wegerer, in *Pol. Sci. Quart.*, XLIII, 204 f., June, 1928), but we seriously doubt whether his post-War denial is trustworthy.

37 Schilling's *Diary*, p. 29.

38 Sergei Dobrorolski, "Mobilizatsia russksoi Armii v 1914 G.," in the Belgrade *Voennii Sbornik*, I, pp. 91-116; Aug.-Sept., 1921; German translation, *Die Mobilmachung der russischen Armee, 1914*, Berlin, 1922; and French translation, "La Mobilisation de l'Armée Russe en 1914," in *Revue d' Histoire de la Guerre Mondiale*, I, April-July, 1923.

Other valuable material on Russian military preparations and mobilization in 1914 may be conveniently noted at this point. Among the memoirs of Russian Generals: V. A. Sukhomlinov, *Erinnerungen*, Berlin, 1924, more valuable on his army reforms before 1914, than on July, 1914, in which he minimizes his part. I. Danilov, *Russland im Weltkriege*,

of the Mobilization Section of the General Staff in 1914, and therefore in a position to know authoritatively all the technical details and preparations of Russia's mobilization measures. Driven into exile by the Bolshevist revolution, and writing his narrative in Belgrade in 1921 without access to his notes and papers, he made a few minor slips of memory. But his remarkable frankness, authoritative information, and general accuracy is confirmed by all the

Jena, 1925 (Russian ed. Berlin, 1925; and French trans., Paris, 1927), chs. i-vi; Danilov was Quartermaster General from 1909-1914, and supplements Dobrorolski's account at certain points in an article in *Rev. d'Hist. de la Guerre Mondiale,* I, 259-266, Oct., 1923. V. I. Gurko, *Russia, 1914-1917,* N. Y., 1919, pp. 1-24; A. S. Lukomski, *Vospominaniia* [Memoirs], 2 vols., Berlin, 1922. A. A. Polivanov, [Memoirs containing extracts from his diaries, in Russian] ed. A. M. Saiontschovski, Moscow, 1924.

Very illuminating are the numerous Russian mobilization telegrams and other military documents captured by the Germans during the war, published and analyzed by R. Hoeniger, *Russlands Vorbereitung zum Weltkrieg,* Berlin, 1919; and more completely by G. Frantz, *Russlands Eintritt in den Weltkrieg,* Berlin, 1924 (quoted hereafter as "Frantz"). B. von Eggeling, *Die russische Mobilmachung und der Kriegsausbruch,* Berlin, 1919, is the first-hand account of the German Military Attaché in St. Petersburg in 1914.

Sazonov's memoirs, *Fateful Years* (N. Y., 1928) cannot be relied on.

The contradictory testimony and confused newspaper reports of the famous Sukhomlinov Trial of 1917 were summarized by the present writer in his third article in the *Amer. Hist. Rev.,* XXVI, 225-254, Jan., 1921, together with the other literature then available; extracts from the Russian newspaper reports of the trial are also given by R. Hoeniger, in the *Deutsche Rundschau,* April, 1918, pp. 15-80; in an anonymous pamphlet, *Suchomlinow, Die russische Mobilmachung im Lichte amtlicher Urkunden und der Enthüllungen des Prozesses,* Bern, 1917; and by P. Renouvin, in *Rev. d'Hist. de la Guerre* Mondiale, II, 49-69, April, 1924; but this testimony from the Sukhomlinov Trial is now of relatively small value.

For more recent accounts, see the military histories in Russian by I. K. Zichovich (Moscow, 1922), and N. N. Golovine (Prague, 1925); H. von Kuhl, *Der deutsche Generalstab in Vorbereitung und Durchführung des Weltkrieges,* Berlin, 1919, 2nd ed. 1920; G. Frantz, *Russland auf dem Wege zur Katastrophe,* Berlin, 1926; Michael T. Florinsky, "The Russian Mobilization of 1914," in *Pol. Sci. Quart.,* XLII, 203-227, June, 1927; the reply to this by A. von Wegerer, *ibid.,* XLIII, 201-228, June, 1928; the articles by Danilov, Demartial, Dobrorolski, Frantz, Montgelas, Sukhomlinov, and von Wegerer, in KSF, I, 97-104; II, 18-21, 78-98, 205-207, 225-231; III, 27-38, 753-762; IV, 207-219, 430-435; by Montgelas, in the *Deutsche Rundschau,* May, 1922, pp. 113-124, and July, 1922, pp. 1-6; and by G. Frantz, in *Current History,* March, 1927, pp. 852-858.

documents which have since come to light, as well as by talks which the present writer was privileged to have with him in 1923. Dobrorolski writes:

> On July 11 [N. S., 24], St. Olga's Day, between 11 o'clock and noon, the Chief of the General Staff, General Ianushkevich, called me on the service telephone and told me to come immediately to his office.
>
> "The situation is very serious," he said as I entered. "Austria has delivered a wholly unacceptable ultimatum to the Serbian Government and we cannot remain indifferent. It has been decided to announce this publicly and decisively. Tomorrow there will appear in the *Russkii Invalid* a short official warning, saying that all Russia is following with close attention the course of the negotiations between the Austro-Hungarian and the Serbian Governments, and will not remain inactive if the dignity and the integrity of the Serbian people, our blood brothers, are threatened with danger.[39] Have you everything ready for the proclamation of the mobilization of our army?"
>
> Upon my replying in the affirmative, the Chief of the General Staff said to me, "In an hour bring to me all the documents relative to preparing of our troops for war, which provide, in case of necessity, for proclaiming partial mobilization against Austria-Hungary only. This mobilization must give no occasion to Germany to find any grounds of hostility to herself."
>
> I pointed out that a partial mobilization was out of the question. But General Ianushkevich ordered me anew to make a detailed report to him after an hour in accordance with his decision already made. . . . The absolute impossibility of a partial mobilization of the army was evident. By what motives was our strategy to be guided? By political considerations. [Dobrorolski then explains that on account of the system of alliances Russia was convinced that a war between Austria and Russia would inevitably

[39] For the text of the announcement as actually made on July 25, see R.O.B., 10.

> involve Germany, and therefore no mobilization plan had been worked out for war against Austria alone.]
>
> What then could be the purpose of any partial mobilization against Austria-Hungary alone? A threat which was not supported by a convincing evidence of one's own power would give rise to an attempt to despise this threat. A partial mobilization of our forces would have had exactly the opposite consequences of those which we reckoned upon.
>
> From a strategic point of view the partial mobilization was simply folly. It was the intention to mobilize four Military Districts: Kiev, Odessa, Moscow and Kazan. In the territory covered by these military districts thirteen army corps had their standing peace quarters.[40]

Dobrorolski goes on to explain all the technical dangers and difficulties of any such partial mobilization as was proposed. After mobilization the troops of these four districts would necessarily advance to the frontier, but to strike at Austria effectively from the East and North, it was necessary for some of them to advance through the Warsaw District. Yet in order not to alarm Germany the Warsaw District was to remain untouched! And if no preparations were made in the Warsaw District, the part of it which bordered on Austria would remain uncovered and unprotected. Moreover, if a general mobilization should follow the partial mobilization, the utmost confusion would take place, because the reservists for the Warsaw District were drawn partly from the Moscow and Kazan Districts, where partial mobilization would already have taken place. These dangers and difficulties were not apparently, however, at first fully grasped by Sazonov, or even by Ianushkevich, who had been in office only a few months, and, as we shall see, this plan of partial mobilization was proceeded with, to the utter dismay of the military technicians like Dobrorolski and General Danilov.

[40] Dobrorolski, pp. 99-101 (German trans., pp. 17-19).

After his interview with Szápáry and his arrangement with Ianushkevich, Sazonov hurried to the French Embassy, where he lunched with Paléologue and Buchanan. Diamandi, the Rumanian Minister, was also invited to join them, because "it was of the greatest advantage for us that Rumania should be drawn in on our side, while for Rumania it was manifestly flattering to participate as an equal in the diplomatic steps taken by the Great Powers." [41] Sazonov said that "the step taken by Austria meant war," and he hoped that England would proclaim her solidarity with France and Russia. He said that Austria's conduct was "immoral and provocative," that some of her demands were absolutely inacceptable, and that she never would have acted as she had done without first having consulted Germany. He told Buchanan of the perfect agreement of views which had been established between France and Russia during Poincaré's visit,[42] and Paléologue added, "France would not only give Russia strong diplomatic support, but would, if necessary, fulfil all the obligations imposed on her by the alliance." Buchanan replied that he could not speak for England, but would telegraph Grey all that they had said; he personally could hold out no hope that England would make any declaration of solidarity that would entail armed support of France and Russia; England had no direct interest in Serbia, and public opinion in England would never sanction a war on her behalf. Sazonov replied that the Serbian question was but part of the general European question and that England could not efface herself; that he personally thought Russia would have to mobilize, but no decision would be taken until a Council of Ministers had been held. Buchanan then suggested bringing influence to bear on Austria to extend the time-limit, but Paléologue "replied that time did not permit of this; either Austria was bluffing, or had made up her mind to act

41 Schilling's *Diary,* p. 30.

42 See above, at note 29.

at once. In either case a firm and united attitude was our only chance of averting war." As Sazonov and Paléologue both continued to press Buchanan for a declaration of complete solidarity, he said he would telegraph a full report to Sir Edward Grey. He even went so far as to express his personal opinion that Grey, "might be prepared to represent strongly at Vienna and Berlin the danger to European peace of an Austrian attack on Serbia, . . . and that if war became general it would be difficult for England to remain neutral." Sazonov remarked that if war did break out, England would be sooner or later dragged into it, and if she did not make common cause with France and Russia she would have rendered war more likely, and would not have played a "beau rôle." Buchanan concluded from Paléologue's language that "it almost looked as if France and Russia were determined to make a strong stand even if we declined to join them." [43]

Sazonov, disappointed at being unable to secure England's immediate declaration of Entente solidarity which he had hoped might give pause to Austria, still avoided seeing the German Ambassador. He was not yet ready to indicate to him what Russia's policy would be. Moreover, he wished first to consult his ministerial colleagues. Accordingly, on leaving the luncheon conference at the French

[43] Buchanan to Grey, July 24, 5:40 P.M.; B.D., 101; *cf.* also Sir George Buchanan *My Mission to Russia* (2 vols., London, 1923), I, 189 ff.; and Paléologue, I, 23 f., where it is clear that the French Ambassador was exerting all his influence to make Sazonov stand firm, even if it led to war, and where a very different impression is given from that in his telegram of July 24 as published in F.Y.B., 31; one suspects that here also the editor of the *French Yellow Book* has used the blue pencil very generously. In the original serial form in which Paléologue published this part of his memoirs (*Rev. des Deux Mondes,* Jan. 15, 1921, p. 248), he represents Buchanan as saying regretfully at this luncheon meeting, "Ah! if only the Conservative Party [in England] were in power now, I am sure that they would understand what the national interest now so clearly imposes on us;" but he discreetly omitted this and several other passages when he published his memoirs in book form. Buchanan (I, 210) takes exception to some of Paléologue's statements.

Embassy about 3 P. M., he proceeded to the meeting of the Ministerial Council. Here he set forth the diplomatic situation and probably argued at length to persuade the reluctant military authorities to accept his partial mobilization plan. We have no precise and satisfactory record of the discussion, but after several hours the Council adopted the following resolutions: (1) to get into touch with the other Powers to request Austria to extend the time-limit, and so give them time to become acquainted with and to investigate the *dossier* of Sarajevo documents which Austria had declared she would communicate; (2) to advise Serbia not to offer armed resistance, if Austria should invade her territory but to announce that she was yielding to force and entrusting her fate to the judgment of the Great Powers; (3) to authorize the Ministers of War and Marine to ask the Tsar's consent to announce, depending on the course of events, mobilization in the four Military Districts of Kiev, Odessa, Moscow and Kazan, and of the Baltic and Black Sea Fleets; (4) to fill up immediately the stocks of war-supplies, and (5) to recall instantly state funds in Germany and Austria.[44]

Thus, an effort was to be made to have the Great Powers examine the merits of the Austro-Serbian question—to "Europeanize" it, instead of "localizing" it, as Austria and Germany wished; and, if this was unsuccessful, to arrange that much of the Austrian army would be tied up in Serbia at the moment Russia should finally have to take up arms. Sazonov accordingly telegraphed to Belgrade that "if the helpless situation of Serbia is indeed such as to leave no doubt as to the outcome of an armed conflict with Austria," it would be better not to make resistance, but retreating, let Austria occupy territory without a fight and appeal to

[44] Journal of the Council of Ministers, July 24, approved by the Tsar, July 25; printed from the copy in the Hoover War Library by Robert C. Binkley, in *Current History,* Jan., 1926, p. 533; *cf.* also Schilling's *Diary,* p. 30.

the Powers to intervene.[45] He also sent a circular telegram to the Powers urging an extension of the time-limit, so that, if Austria enabled the Powers to acquaint themselves with the results of the Sarajevo investigation, they would be in a position to give Serbia corresponding advice.[46]

As these efforts might not be successful, the Council had also decided "in principle" in favor of Sazonov's "partial mobilization" plan, that is, the mobilization of 1,100,000 men—thirteen army corps in the four southern districts near Austria; this was only to be announced, however, when Sazonov should decide it was necessary, and this decision of the Council was not final until approved by the Tsar next day.[47]

All these arrangements were made by Sazonov before he received Pourtalès and heard Germany's views on the ultimatum and policy of "localization." Pourtalès had been told in the morning that Sazonov could not receive him after Szápáry, because he must go to a meeting of the Council of Ministers,[48] whereas in reality he had gone to the luncheon conference at the French Embassy. It was not until toward 7 P. M. that Pourtalès was finally admitted. When he attempted, in accordance with the instructions given to him and the other German Ambassadors,[49] to justify Austria's action and to urge that the Austro-Serbian conflict should remain "localized," Sazonov, "who was very much excited and gave vent to boundless

45 Sazonov to the Russian Chargé d'Affaires in Belgrade, July 24; Schilling's *Diary,* pp. 33, 86. Cf. Crackanthorpe to Grey, July 28 (B.D., 221): Serbian Government expected immediate attack on Belgrade on departure of Austrian Minister and so removed at once. Plan of campaign is now to draw into interior as large a portion as possible of Austrian army so as to weaken Austria elsewhere. Under-Secretary of State tells me that Russian support is assured."

46 Schilling's *Diary,* pp. 33, 40; R.O.B., 4, 5; B.D., 125.

47 *Cf.* Buchanan to Grey, July 25; B.D., 125; and statement of a former Russian Minister of War to the present writer.

48 Pourtalès to Bethmann, July 24, 6:10 P.M.; K.D., 148.

49 K.D., 100.

reproaches against Austria-Hungary, stated in the most determined manner that it would be impossible for Russia to admit that the Austro-Serbian quarrel could be settled between the two parties concerned." He argued shrewdly that the Serbian promises of 1909, to which Austria made reference in the ultimatum, were given, not to Austria alone, but to the Powers; consequently, the question whether Serbia had lived up to these promises was a European one; it was for Europe to examine the *dossier*, and see whether Austria's charges were well founded.[50] Moreover, Austria could not be both prosecutor and judge.

Pourtalès replied that it was not practical to submit the question for adjudication by the six Great Powers, because the general political attitude of the Powers and their allied grouping would be the decisive factor in their judgment of the case. What would be the practical use of such a "judicial procedure," if the political friends of Austria took one side, and her opponents the other? Who would decide in such a case? He promised, however, to report Sazonov's idea to Berlin, but "he doubted whether Germany would expect her ally to lay the results of her investigation before a European Areopagus. Austria would refuse, as any Great Power must, to subject to arbitration a question in which her vital interests were at stake." Pourtalès then urged "monarchical solidarity" and the danger of countenancing regicides, but Sazonov quickly shifted the conversation to the broader political ground that a whole Government and Nation could not be held responsible for the act of an individual, and that Austria's charges were by no means convincing. He launched into

[50] Sazonov's argument was shrewd and technically quite correct, because, as Szápáry regretted (A.R.B., II, 19), in the ultimatum itself, Serbia was accused, in failing to live up to the promises of 1909, of "acting in opposition to the will of Europe," and because a copy of the ultimatum had been sent "to all the other Signatory Powers" who were interested in any modifications of the Treaty of Berlin.

such unrestrained accusations against Austria that Pourtalès expressed the fear that he was blinded by his hatred of Austria. "Hate," replied Sazonov, "is foreign to my nature. I do not hate Austria; I despise her." Finally he exclaimed: "Austria is seeking a pretext to gobble up Serbia; but in that case Russia will make war on Austria." Pourtalès sought to calm him by expressing his conviction that, at most, Austria was only intending to inflict a deserved chastisement on Serbia, and was far from thinking of making territorial gains. But Sazonov shook his head doubtingly: "First Serbia would be gobbled up; then will come Bulgaria's turn; and then we shall have her on the Black Sea." [51]

The interview was a tense one, and served only to accentuate more sharply the conflict between two views which were now coming into dangerous conflict—should the Austro-Serbian question remain "localized," or be "Europeanized." As Pourtalès was leaving Sazonov's office, Paléologue was waiting to come in and learn the decisions taken by the Ministerial Council and the outcome of the interview with Pourtalès, but his reports as published do not give a satisfactory account of what passed between him and the Russian Foreign Minister.[52]

WARLIKE PORTENTS AT KRASNOE SELO, JULY 25

On Saturday, July 25, the wave of midsummer heat which had been hanging over St. Petersburg for a month seemed to reach its climax. The trains were crowded with peace-loving people pouring out for the summer holidays. Out on the sun-baked plain at Krasnoe Selo, the Tsar and all St. Petersburg's high society were gathered to witness

51 Pourtalès to Bethmann, July 25, 1:08 A. M., and detailed report later in the day; K.D., 160, 204. *Cf.* also Szápáry to Berchtold, July 25, 2:30 A.M.; A.R.B., II, 19; and Schilling's *Diary*, p. 31.

52 Paléologue to Bienvenu-Martin, July 25 [24?]; F.Y.B., 38; Paléologue, I, 24-26; and Schilling's *Diary*, p. 31 f.

the summer review of the Russian troops. Late in the forenoon an important Ministerial Council was held at which the Tsar presided. It lasted so long that the maneuvers had to be postponed an hour. Even when they finally took place, they were cut short, and an unusual military excitement pervaded all the officers. The foreign Military Attachés got the impression that the Ministerial Council had considered mobilizing the Russian army, and perhaps had even decided to order it, at least in the four Southern Military Districts facing Austria.[53] General Adlerberg, the Governor of St. Petersburg, by a slip of the tongue, in talking with the German General Chelius, actually spoke of measures "for mobilization." Baron Grünwald, the Tsar's chief equerry, sitting next to Chelius at the banquet that evening, said to him, "The situation is very serious. What was decided this noon, I am not permitted to tell you. You yourself will soon learn it. But take it from me, it looks very serious." He touched glasses with Chelius and drank his health with the words, "Let us hope we shall see each other again in better times!" [54]

[53] Major Eggeling, German Military Attaché, in the *Nordd. Allg. Zeitung,* No. 261, Oct. 21, 1917; Eggeling, *Die Russische Mobilmachung,* pp. 23-25.

[54] Chelius to the Kaiser, July 26; K.D., 291. Chelius was Emperor William's personal representative at the court of the Tsar. For many years "Willy" and "Nicky" had each kept at the court (*à la suite*) of the other such a personal representative, in addition to the regular ambassadors, consuls, and military and naval attachés. They were accorded special intimacy, and served to keep the two autocrats in closer personal touch with each other. Owing to their privileged position and their intimate contact with the Sovereign's entourage, they were often able to get a closer view of the currents of feeling and the personages of influence than the regular formal diplomatic representatives. Chelius, who gives the best account of these events on July 25, gives evidence here and elsewhere of this close touch. Tatishchev, the Tsar's representative at the Kaiser's court, happened during these critical days to be in Russia. On July 30, 1:20 A.M., the Tsar telegraphed to the Kaiser: "Am sending Tatishchev this evening with instructions," but apparently this emissary of peace was stopped by Sazonov at the railway station just as he was departing for Berlin; R. Rosen, *Forty Years of Diplomacy* (London, 1923),

After the military review had been held, in an unusually curtailed form, it was announced that the maneuvers at Krasnoe Selo and in the whole Empire were to be broken off, and that the troops were to return at once to their standing quarters, as they would have to do in case of war.

The idea that mobilization and war were imminent was increased by the immediate promotion that same evening of the St. Petersburg Military Academy cadets to the position of regular officers in the army, instead of later in the year as customary. At the banquet following the Tsar's address to these new appointees, says the German Military Attaché, "young officers openly expressed their joy to me that now at last they were starting something 'against Austria.' Others aired their rage against 'Austrian presumption.' Even Prince Peter of Montenegro, who was present just at this time, thought he had to tell me that in his country there reigned a distinct enthusiasm for war, and that mobilization was in full progress. Not a man seemed to recollect that we [Germans] were in alliance with Austria!" [55]

Following the banquet there was a theatrical performance, which, under the leadership of the Grand Duke Nicholas, was made the occasion of a great demonstration for war. On this same evening St. Petersburg was startled out of its stillness by the unexpected sound of the hoofbeats of the Imperial Guards hurrying back through the mist to the capital, although they were to have been quartered out at Krasnoe Selo for another month.[56] "At seven o'clock," writes Paléologue, "I go to the Warsaw Railway

II, 171; Schilling's *Diary*, p. 64 ff.; K.D., 390, 399; and details by A. Bach in KSF, II, 508 ff, Nov., 1924.

[55] Eggeling, in *Nordd. Allg. Zeitung*, No. 261, Oct. 17, 1917.

[56] On the events at Krasnoe Selo on this fateful Saturday, July 25, see K.D., 194, 291; Eggeling, *Die Russische Mobilmachung*, pp. 22-27; A.R.B., II, 37, 60, 61; Meriel Buchanan, *The City of Trouble* (New York, 1918), pp. 10-12.

Station to say good-bye to Izvolski, who is returning to his post in haste. On the platforms, there is lively animation: the trains are crowded with officers and soldiers. This already looks like mobilization. We exchange rapidly our impressions, and come to same conclusion, *'Cette fois, c'est la guerre.'* "[57] Next day Princess Paley, who was in close touch with the Grand Dukes, sent an urgent telegram to her mother and daughter who were at Bad Kissingen in Germany to leave immediately for Switzerland or Italy;[58] and General Danilov, who had been hurriedly recalled from a tour in the Caucasus, telegraphed to his family in Podolia near the Austrian frontier begging them to return at once to St. Petersburg.[59]

THE RUSSIAN "PERIOD PREPARATORY TO WAR"

What took place on July 25 at this important Ministerial Council (often incorrectly called a Crown Council) in the presence of the Tsar to cause all these impressions of impending war? Again we have no precise record of what was said by each person present, but we know the final decisions taken. We may surmise that a conflict took place between Sazonov, who adhered to his "partial mobilization" plan, and the military leaders, led by the Grand Duke Nicholas, who feared that the technical and political difficulties of a partial mobilization would be disastrous.[60]

General Sukhomlinov, Minister of War, later claimed to have taken a passive attitude during the July crisis,[61] but his *apologia* is not convincing. General Danilov, speaking of the Ministerial Council, says: "It is easy to understand the decision of those members of the Council who had little knowledge of purely military problems and were

57 Paléologue, I, 27 f.

58 Princess Paley, "En Russie à la veille de la guerre," in *La Revue de Paris,* Nov. 15, 1923, p. 592.

59 Danilov, p. 16.

60 *Cf.* Dobrorolski, as quoted above at note 40.

61 Sukhomlinov, *Erinnerungen,* pp. 357-379.

not acquainted with the technical side of mobilization. They were solely guided by the natural desire of safeguarding the honor of Russia and of avoiding at the same time anything that could suggest a hostile attitude towards Germany. But how can it be explained that General Sukhomlinov, who took part in the Council, deemed it possible to agree even without a word of protest to a decision which put Russia in a very dangerous position? Was it mere negligence or utter incompetence?"[62] Whether General Ianushkevich was now fully aware of the dangers of a partial mobilization, or whether he still had to be convinced that it was folly, is not certain. In any event the military leaders felt that a war between Austria and Serbia was necessarily a war between Austria and Russia, and therefore between Russia and Germany. They had no doubt that Austria was about to begin the invasion of Serbia as soon as the time-limit expired. In fact, later in the day, a Russian officer looking at his watch at six o'clock, remarked to General Chelius, "The cannon on the Danube will have begun to fire by now, for one doesn't send such an ultimatum except when the cannon are loaded."[63] They were probably convinced that war was "inevitable," and that here was Russia's heaven-sent opportunity to have her final reckoning with Germany, and to acquire that control of Constantinople and the Straits, which had been so seriously considered at the secret conference on February 8/21, 1914, and for which preparations had been ordered, in order that, when a crisis should break out, Russia should be able to secure her historic aims at the Bosphorus.[64] Therefore the sooner general mobilization was declared the better.[65]

62 Danilov, p. 15.

63 Chelius to the Kaiser, July 26; K.D., 291.

64 *Cf.* above, I, ch. v, "Balkan Problems," at notes 309-311

65 For indications of the conflict of opinions among the various Ministers on the question of military measures, see K.D., 130, 194, 203.

It is quite possible that one of the arguments at the Ministerial Councils on Friday and Saturday was the dangerous domestic situation. St. Petersburg and all the larger cities in Russia were in the throes of an extensive working-men's strike. By a strange irony of fate, at the same moment when the Russian military bands, in the camp at Krasnoe Selo, had been welcoming Poincaré with the *Marseillaise,* the Cossacks in the suburbs of St. Petersburg had been striking down working-men for singing this same martial anthem.[66] An apparently well-informed Russian sympathizer, writing at length in the *Gazette de Lausanne* of September 7 and 8, 1917, in comment upon the Sukhomlinov trial, asserts that in 1914 general mobilization was strongly urged as a salutary measure against this internal industrial and revolutionary danger, rather than as a necessary military precaution against German attack; it would also counteract, it was urged, the feared autonomous and separatist agitation among the non-Slavic elements in the Russian Empire. The idea of a foreign war to avert domestic troubles is, of course, a very familiar one in the history of many countries.[67] The militarists may quite probably have believed that the leading forth of the specter of threatening internal revolution and anarchy would serve as a good bogey with which to persuade the peace-loving Tsar to consent to a general mobilization, and they were ready to assure him that, in case of mobilization

204, 338; A.R.B., II, 60, 61, 73, III, 19, 71; Dobrorolski, Danilov, and Sukhomlinov, *passim;* Nekliudov, *Diplomatic Reminiscences,* pp. 284-285.

[66] Pourtalès to Bethmann, July 23; K.D., 130; *cf.* also V. A. Wroblewski, "Die russischen Arbeiterunruhen im Juli, 1914," in KSF, III, 325-331, May, 1925.

[67] *Cf.* Jules Cambon's similar suspicions about Germany in his report to Pichon, July 30, 1913 (F.Y.B., 5): "Some want war . . . for social reasons, i.e., to provide the external interests which alone can prevent or retard the rise to power of the democratic and socialist masses . . . This social class [the Junkers], which forms a hierarchy with the King of Prussia as its supreme head, realizes with dread the democratization of Germany and the increasing power of the Socialist Party."

and war, the strikes would offer no serious obstacle,[68] as in fact proved to be the case.

At any rate, whatever the arguments used at this Council, Sazonov prevailed in maintaining his plan for "partial mobilization." But a concession was made to the militarists in the adoption of a series of preparatory military measures which would facilitate a "general mobilization" when the Tsar should finally be persuaded to consent to it. In all, five decisions were taken by the Ministerial Council. The details of the fifth, and most important, of these were kept very secret. The others were soon evident, or were communicated to Paléologue and Buchanan at once, and to Pourtalès a little later.

What were these five decisions?

1. The Tsar's approval of the decision "in principle" for contingent "partial mobilization" against Austria—the decision which had been reached at the Ministerial Council of the preceding afternoon. This was reported to the French Government in Paris, which was able to inform Poincaré on July 26 on his voyage homeward:

> At the Ministerial Council on the 25th, which was held in the presence of the Tsar, the mobilization of thirteen army corps, intended in case of need [*eventuellement*] to operate against Austria was considered; this mobilization, however, would only be effective if Austria were to bring armed pressure to bear on Serbia, and not until notice had been given by the Minister of Foreign Affairs, upon whom falls the duty of fixing the day, liberty being left to him to go on with the negotiations, even if Belgrade should be occupied. Russian opinion makes it clear that it is both

68 Pourtalès to Bethmann, July 25 (K.D., 205): "From a trustworthy source I hear that in the Ministerial Council here yesterday [July 24] the question of first consideration discussed was whether the present internal condition of Russia is such that the country could face external complications without trouble. The majority of the Ministers present are said to have expressed themselves to the effect that Russia need not hesitate before such complications on account of the internal situation."

politically and morally impossible for Russia to allow Serbia to be crushed.[69]

This decision in favor of partial mobilization, in case of need, to bluff Austria, is confirmed by the testimony of Ianushkevich at the Sukhomlinov trial in 1917: "At first it had been decided to proclaim a partial mobilization—the four districts—to frighten off Austria-Hungary."[70] It was welcome to Sazonov because he hoped it would check Austria, and give a turn to the diplomatic negotiations which would result in a settlement acceptable to Serbia and Russia. It avoided the danger of the "general mobilization," which was desired by the military leaders, but which would probably lead Germany to retaliate with a counter-mobilization, and so bring on a general European war. It would also gain time for diplomatic negotiations, during which wide-reaching measures preparatory to war could be carried on under cover of a secret "Regulation concerning the Period Preparatory to War," to be mentioned a little later.

In 1912, at the height of the Balkan Wars, at a diplomatic crisis with Austria in many respects similar to that of 1914, a secret Russian Military Commission, in annulling for technical reasons the order that "the proclamation of mobilization is equivalent to the declaration of war," had stated significantly:

69 Bienvenu-Martin's summary to Viviani on board the *France*, July 26; F.Y.B., 50. Paléologue's telegram on which this summary is supposed to be based is suppressed from F.Y.B.; it may have been his telegram of July 26, at 1:55 P. M., which M. Bourgeois, though he had access to the French archives, has published in two variant and evidently garbled forms; Bourgeois et Pagès, pp. 39, 137. *Cf.* also Buchanan to Grey, July 25, 8 P. M.; Sazonov told us "this morning Emperor had sanctioned drafting of Imperial Ukase, which is only to be published when Minister of Foreign Affairs considers moment come for giving effect to it, ordering mobilization of 1,100,000 men. Necessary preliminary preparations for mobilization would, however, be begun at once;" B.D., 125 (but also suppressed from B.B.B.).

70 As reported in the *Novoe Vremia*, No. 14,852, Aug. 13 [26], 1917.

> It will be advantageous to complete concentration without beginning hostilities, in order not to deprive the enemy irrevocably of the hope that war can still be avoided. Our measures for this must be masked by clever diplomatic negotiations, in order to lull to sleep as much as possible the enemy's fears.[71]

Thus, if the announcement of partial mobilization should not after all succeed in checking Austria, it could at least be used conveniently to explain and screen the measures of the "Period Preparatory to War," which it was decided were to take place over the whole empire and which would therefore greatly facilitate the general mobilization against Germany as well as against Austria, if eventually necessary. Sazonov believed that he now had the trump cards in his hand. He could continue to negotiate, and he held in his hand the threat of force to strengthen his bluff; but at the same time military preparations would be going on preparatory to a general mobilization if his bluff of partial mobilization was called. Also the militarists in Russia could not get out of control, because a decision as to mobilization was dependent on the course of the diplomatic negotiations, which were also in his hands. Sazonov was highly delighted with this arrangement. He was also agreeably surprised to find that Austria did not attack Serbia at once after the expiration of the time-limit and the rupture of Austro-Serbian diplomatic relations on this same Saturday afternoon. During the next three days (July 26-28) of "direct conversations" with Vienna, he appeared to be much more conciliatory and optimistic, so much so, in fact, that it was specially remarked by a number of persons.[72] But this optimism was not shared by the Russian

71 Protocol of the Special Military Commission of Nov. 8 [21], 1912, quoted by Hoeniger, p. 34 f., and by Frantz, p. 236.

72 By Pourtalès, "I found Sazonov much quieter and more conciliatory today" (July 26, 3:15 P.M.; K.D., 217); by Buchanan, "I found Sazonov this afternoon very conciliatory and more optimistic" (July 27, 8:40

military authorities, and came to a sudden end with the news of the Austrian declaration of war on Serbia on July 28.[73]

2. The second of the decisions taken by the Ministerial Council of July 25 was the recall of the troops to their standing quarters.[74]

At the moment of the Sarajevo murder and during the following weeks, the Russian troops throughout the empire were dispersed in camps for maneuvers and summer training, often at a considerable distance from their regular standing quarters. It was in these standing quarters that was kept the full equipment, which was necessary for war, and which the soldiers must have before they could start for the front. It was necessary therefore that they should be recalled as quickly as possible to the point at which they would be given their full equipment and be ready for transportation to the designated area of concentration on the frontier. This is why the camp at Krasnoe Selo was broken up at the close of the maneuvers on Saturday afternoon, as has already been indicated. Ianushkevich lost no time in putting this decision into operation also for all the rest of the troops in the empire. At 4:10 P.M. he had the General Staff send out secret cipher telegram No. 1547:

P.M.; B.D., 198); by Paléologue, "Sazonov has used conciliatory language to all my colleagues" (July, 27; F.Y.B., 64); and especially by Szápáry, the Austrian Ambassador, as will be indicated later in connection with the "direct conversations" between St. Petersburg and Vienna.

[73] *Cf.* Dobrorolski, p. 104 (German trans., p. 22 f.); "The unlucky idea of a partial mobilization was not yet dropped. It had its adherents, but not in the military departments. . . . Among the optimists was Sazonov. By this optimism only can one explain the fact that he persistently advocated a partial mobilization, and supported at Peterhof [to the Tsar] confidence in its success. . . . On July 15 [28], the day of the Austro-Hungarian declaration of war on Serbia, Sazonov suddenly abandons his optimism. He becomes filled with the idea that a general war is inevitable, and calls the attention of Ianushkevich to the necessity of not delaying any longer the [general] mobilization of our army."

[74] Dobrorolski, p. 102 (German trans., p. 20); Sukhomlinov, p. 360; K.D., 194, 339; A.R.B., II, 60; Eggeling, p. 25.

St. Petersburg, July 12 [25], 1914, 4:10 P.M.

Prepare quickly transport plans and provisions for the return of all troops to their standing quarters. Time for the completion of the work: twenty-four hours. 1547.

[Signed] General Dobrorolski.[75]

This was followed later the same night by telegram No. 1557:

St. Petersburg, July 12 [25], 1914, 11:59 P.M.

His Majesty commands that upon the arrival of this telegram the troops are to return from their camps to their standing quarters. If their simultaneous return involves difficulties, the Staffs and Administrations of the Corps, Divisions, and independent formations are to have precedence. The troop divisions close to their standing quarters can remain there and do not need to return to their winter barracks. 1557.

[Signed] Bieliaiev.[76]

This breaking off of maneuvers and return of the troops to their standing quarters was not, however, in any way equivalent to mobilization. It was, to be sure, a necessary preliminary to mobilization, but was not in any way a menacing or hostile act.[77] Nevertheless, the execution of the unexpected order which began on Sunday, July 26, involved the movement of more than a million men throughout the empire, and gave rise to military excitement

[75] Telegram to the Chief of Staff of the Warsaw District, captured later by the Germans, and published by Hoeniger, p. 80, and by Frantz, p. 258.

[76] Hoeniger, p. 80; Frantz, p. 259.

[77] Similar orders for the return of troops to their standing quarters were given in France as early as July 27 (K.D., 341, note 3), but in Germany not until July 28 for the nine corps to be "hastily" mobilized, and not until July 29, between 1 and 1:30 P.M., for the greater number of remaining corps (*Investigating Commission,* II, p. 68. Anlage 17, and p. 69, Anlage 20); for the best detailed analysis of the French and German preliminary military measures, based on a study of the French official General Staff History of the War, which show in every case that the French preparations considerably antedated the German, see M. Montgelas, "Das französische Generalstabwerk," in KSF, V, 1206-1220, Dec., 1927.

among Russian officers everywhere similar to that which had prevailed at Krasnoe Selo on the preceding evening. It also naturally led to disturbing reports being sent to Berlin and Vienna from German and Austrian agents in Russia.

3. The promotion of cadets to be officers.[78]

The Russian army lacked in 1914, even on a peace footing, some 3000 younger officers. These were being trained in the St. Petersburg Military Academy and similar schools, but the cadets would normally not be graduated and made officer until later in the year. To fill this deficiency as far as possible at once, it was decided to make the promotion immediately. The cadets of the St. Petersburg Academy were advanced to the rank of officer at Krasnoe Selo just before the banquet on Saturday evening; the Tsar himself made them an address, saying, "Believe in God, as well as in the greatness and glory of our country. Seek to serve Him and Me with all your strength." The promotions in the other military schools followed almost immediately.[79] Also the organizations in which officers were receiving practical training were dissolved so that they should be free to take active command. These measures not only created a large number of much-needed subaltern officers, but also freed for active service in the field many mature officers who had hitherto been detailed on educational work. But in spite of these efforts, one of the most serious defects in the Russian army, as the War was soon to show, was the inadequacy of the officers, both as to quality and quantity.

4. The proclamation of the "state of war" in towns containing fortresses and in the frontier sectors facing Germany and Austria.

[78] Dobrorolski, pp. 102, 114; K.D., 194, 291; A.R.B., II, 60, 77; Paléologue to Bienvenu-Martin, July 26; Bourgeois et Pagès, p. 39.

[79] *Cf.* Paumgartner in Odessa to Berchtold, July 27; "Reserve officers who were to have been let go, have been retained; also school cadets have already been enrolled; in Odessa alone 390. Great excitement among officers;" A.R.B., II, 77.

The order for this was sent out by Gen. Ianushkevich still later this same night, i.e., at 1 A.M. on July 26.[80] That the order was speedily obeyed on the frontier toward Germany is indicated by the proclamation of the Commander of the fortress of Kovno: "In accordance with the command of the Tsar and of General Rennenkampf's order No. 13,482, July 26, I declare the fortress and district of Kovno placed in a 'state of war.'"[81] The purpose of this proclamation was to give the local military commanders full powers, as under martial law, to take all actions necessary to secure the success of mobilization, and to prevent trouble from spies or other hostile-minded persons. It also forbade the newspapers to publish any news in regard to military and naval preparations, such as the movements or provisioning of troops or naval vessels, the recall of officers on leave, military transportation, or the collection of merchant ships in harbors.[82]

One incident which grew out of the order shows the desire for peace and friendly relations between Russia and Germany which was sincerely held by the Tsar and by Pourtalès, the German Ambassador. The *Prinz Eitel Friedrich,* a German merchant ship lying in the harbor near the fortress of Kronstadt, aroused the suspicions of the commander of the fortress, because she had a wireless outfit and was observed to be sending radiograms. As a "state of war" had been proclaimed in the fortress sector and the wireless outfit might be used for espionage purposes, the

80 General Staff tg. no. 1566; printed by Hoeniger, p. 80; and by Frantz, p. 242; *cf.* also Paléologue to Bienvenu-Martin, July 26; Bourgeois et Pagès, pp. 39, 137.

81 E. Mueller-Meiningen, *Diplomatie und Weltkrieg* (Berlin, 1917), p. 930. Bülow, German consul at Kovno, was able to telegraph from Eydkuhnen in East Prussia on July 27, at 5:35 P. M., presumably having heard the news many hours earlier: "Kovno has been placed in a state of war;" K.D., 264. For similar orders of July 26 for other fortresses, see Frantz, pp. 243-250.

82 Dobrorolski, pp. 102, 104 (German ed., pp. 21, 23); Hoeniger, pp. 66-67.

commander of the fortress reported the case to the Grand Duke Nicholas who commanded the whole Petrograd Military District, including Kronstadt. The Grand Duke at once ordered the German captain to be arrested, the wireless apparatus to be seized, and the ship forbidden to leave the harbor. As Germany and Russia were still at peace, this arbitrary action led Pourtalès to make a vigorous protest to Neratov at the Foreign Office. As a result, the Tsar, the same day, sent an autograph letter to the Grand Duke ordering him to set the captain free and not detain the ship, and expressing condemnation of the measures taken against the ship of a friendly state. Sazonov also telephoned in a friendly way, and apologized for the Grand Duke's action. Pourtalès then said that he considered the incident closed, and would say nothing of it to the Government at Berlin.[83]

5. The secret orders for the "Period Preparatory to War."

Though the decision for contingent partial mobilization may have been regarded by Sazonov and the Tsar seriously, as a satisfactory military measure in case of need, it was by no means so regarded by the militarists and the General Staff. Besides the technical and political difficulties and the total lack of perfected plans, what would Russia's ally think of such a measure? In the negotiations for the Franco-Russian alliance in 1892, General Obruchev, the Russian Chief of Staff at the time, had energetically denied the possibility of a partial mobilization against Austria; Russia must and would order general mobilization, even in case of a war with Austria alone.[84] And General Vannovski, the Minister of War, had likewise declared to General

83 There is therefore nothing about it in the *Kautsky Documents*, but the details are given by Dobrorolski, and by Pourtalès, *Am Scheideweg*, p. 34.

84 "En ce qui concerne la Russie, il lui est absolument impossible, en cas de guerre avec l'Autriche, de faire une mobilisation partielle. Il leur faut faire et ils feront une mobilisation générale;" Aug. 10, 1892; *Livre Jaune: L'Alliance Franco-Russe*, p. 68.

Boisdeffre, the French Chief of Staff: "You tell me in this case [of an attack by Austria alone] to make a partial mobilization, but this is absolutely impossible for us, because the troops which we shall assemble in Poland come from all the points of the Empire and are mixed together. Beside this being impossible, in making a partial mobilization, we should expose ourselves to too great dangers with the menace of a rapid attack from Germany."[85] This point of view was as true in 1914 as in 1892.

For all these reasons the Russian General Staff regarded this partial mobilization project as the height of folly; nevertheless, since the Ministerial Council and the Tsar had decided in favor of it, they hurriedly began to work out plans for it, secretly hoping, however, that it would never be carried out.[86] But at the same time, as a measure of far greater importance and safety, they persuaded the Tsar to approve the putting into operation of the wide-reaching measures preparatory to general mobilization comprised in the very secret "Regulation Concerning the Period Preparatory to War."[87] The Regulation was to become effective

[85] *Livre Jaune: L'Alliance Franco-Russe,* p. 73.

[86] Dobrorolski, p. 102 f. (German trans. p. 21).

[87] For the facsimile of the Council's decision, approved by the Tsar on July 25, the writer is indebted to the courtesy of the Hoover War Library. This reads:

Copy
Confidential

On the original is written in His Imperial Majesty's own hand: "Agreed to," at Krasnoe Selo, July 12 [25], 1914.

Countersigned: President of the Council of Ministers,
Secretary of State Goremykin.

Special Journal of the Council of Ministers, July 12 [25], 1914.

Concerning the bringing into effect of the Regulations Concerning the Period Preparatory to War, sanctioned by His Majesty on February 17 [March 2], 1913. [The first paragraph mentions the Tsar's approval of the recommendation of the Council of July 24 for partial mobilization, already published by Mr. Robert C. Binkley from the same volume in the Hoover War Library, and summarized above at note 44].

Today, in accordance with the present trend of the diplomatic negotiations and with the aim of taking measures necessary in all departments for preparing and guaranteeing the success of the mobilization of the Army, Navy, and Fortresses, and the concentration of the armies at

48 *Копія.*
Довѣрительно.

На подлинномъ Собственною Его Императорскаго Величества рукою начертано: „Согласенъ", въ Красномъ Селѣ, 12 Іюля 1914 года.

Скрѣпилъ: Предсѣдатель Совѣта Министровъ,
Статсъ-Секретарь *Горемыкинъ.*

ОСОБЫЙ ЖУРНАЛЪ СОВѢТА МИНИСТРОВЪ

12 Іюля 1914 года.

О приведеніи въ дѣйствіе Высочайше утвержденнаго, 17 Февраля 1913 года, Положенія о подготовительномъ къ войнѣ періодѣ.

Вашему Императорскому Величеству благоугодно было, 12 сего Іюля, Высочайше утвердить особый журналъ Совѣта Министровъ 11 Іюля 1914 года, по заявленію Министра Иностранныхъ Дѣлъ о послѣднихъ выступленіяхъ Австро-Венгерскаго Правительства въ отношеніи Сербіи. Журналомъ этимъ, между прочимъ, предоставлено Военному и Морскому Министрамъ, по принадлежности, испросить Высочайшее Вашего Императорскаго Величества соизволеніе на объявленіе, въ зависимости отъ хода дѣлъ, мобилизаціи четырехъ военныхъ округовъ—Кіевскаго, Одесскаго, Московскаго и Казанскаго, Балтійскаго и Черноморскаго флотовъ, а также незамедлительно ускорить пополненіе запасовъ матеріальной части арміи.

Нынѣ, въ соотвѣтствіи съ современнымъ оборотомъ дипломатическихъ переговоровъ и въ цѣляхъ приня-

к. 11516. 1

8

FACSIMILE OF THE MINUTES OF THE RUSSIAN COUNCIL OF MINISTERS OF JULY 25, 1914

See note 87

on July 26, and Ianushkevich lost no time in putting it into force, as is seen from two secret cipher telegrams, numbers 1566 and 1575, which he sent out from the General Staff before dawn on Sunday morning, July 26, to the commanders of the troops in the Warsaw Military District:

St. Petersburg, July 13 [26], 1 A.M.

His Majesty commands all the fortresses of the District to be placed in a state of war. It is ordered to begin with the works which are indicated in Lists 1 and 2 attached to the Regulation Concerning the Period Preparatory to War, approved by His Majesty on February 17 [March 2], 1913. 1566.

[Signed] Lieut.-Gen. Ianushkevich.[88]

St. Petersburg, July 13 [26], 3:26 A.M.

His Majesty commands that July 13 [26] is to be reckoned as the beginning of the Period Preparatory to War in the whole territory of European Russia. You are to take, in accordance with Lists 1 and 2 of the Regulation Concerning the Period Preparatory to War, all the measures which are to be carried out under the direction of the District Staffs, Provisioning Boards, Corps Commanders, Fortress Commanders, Troop Divisions, and Administrative Bureaus. The Regulation was sent on March 22 [April 4], 1913 under No. 813. 1575.

[Signed] Lieut.-Gen. Ianushkevich.[89]

the frontiers of our possible enemies, the Council of Ministers declares that the time has come for bringing into effect, beginning with July 13 [26] in all lands of the Empire the Regulations Concerning the Period Preparatory to War, for both lists; and authorizes moreover the Minister of War to request the supreme consent of Your Imperial Majesty for the taking by the War Department of these and other measures not provided for in the aforesaid lists, which he shall duly consider necessary according to circumstances, and which shall be reported to the Council of Ministers. . . .

88 Captured Russian telegram, printed by Hoeniger, p. 80; and by Frantz, p. 243; for the execution of the order concerning the fortresses, see above, at notes 80-81.

89 Hoeniger, p. 81; Frantz, p. 243. It is to be noted that this telegram shows that the "preparatory measures" were to be carried out "in the whole territory of European Russia." This proves the incorrectness of

What is the significance of this cryptic "Period Preparatory to War" with its "Lists 1 and 2"?

One of Russia's greatest handicaps to the successful beginning of war had been the relative slowness of mobilization. Owing to her vast areas, inadequate railway systems, and somewhat inefficient local military authorities, the Russian mobilization machine had not been able in the past to work with anything like the speed of the German, or even the Austrian, military machine. To remedy this defect as far as possible had been the aim of one of Sukhomlinov's reforms. It had been discussed as early as the spring of 1912, and was finally solved at a secret conference in February, 1913, sitting under the presidency of General Lukomski, and containing representatives of the Navy and Interior Departments as well as of the War Department. This conference drafted, and the Tsar approved on March 2, 1913, a very secret "Regulation Concerning the Period Preparatory to War." [90]

According to this Regulation,

> "Period Preparatory to War" means the period of diplomatic complications preceding the opening of hostilities, in the course of which all Boards must take the necessary

the commonly made assertion (e.g. by Recouly, p. 157, and by Paléologue, I, 28) that measures preparatory to war were ordered only in the Military Districts of Kiev, Odessa, Kazan and Moscow.

[90] Dobrorolski, p. 102 f. (German trans. p. 21 f.); Sukhomlinov, p. 343 f., Hoeniger, 8-12, 17-20; Frantz, pp. 22-24. Dobrorolski speaks of this as the "Pre-mobilization Period" (*Predmobilizatsennoe Period*), but the official journal given in facsimile above and the captured Russian telegrams regularly speak of it as the "Period Preparatory to War." Ordered before dawn on July 26 for the whole Russian Empire, it may very roughly be compared with the Austrian "Alarmierungstag" (ordered on the night of July 25-26, for five of the eight corps which were to operate against Serbia and for two others—one on the Rumanian front and one for the protection of the Danube bridges; *Investig. Comm.*, II, pp. 19, 83; Conrad, IV, 122); with the French *"alerte"* (ordered July 30; Poincaré, *Les Origines de la Guerre,* p. 255; Recouly, p. 76; Montgelas, in KSF, V, p. 1214, Dec., 1927); and with the German *"Drohender Kriegsgefahrzustand"* (ordered *ca.* 1 P. M., July 31; K.D., 479, 499).

> measures of preparation for security and success at the mobilization of the Army, the Fleet, and the Fortresses, as well as for the march of the Army to the threatened frontier.[91]

These preparatory measures are grouped under two headings, known as "List 1" and "List 2." Under "List 1" are the measures which are to be taken at once, upon the order of the Minister of War, as soon as the Tsar has approved the recommendation of the Ministerial Council in favor of putting into effect the Regulation Concerning the Period Preparatory to War. The expenditures incurred are to be paid for out of the ordinary funds assigned to the local Boards. According to "List 1," in the districts on Russia's Western frontier, it is decreed:

> Upon the order of the Minister of War [not upon that of the Tsar] the reservists and the territorial reserve are to be called up for reserve exercises in such a way that the reservists may be assigned as far as possible according to the existing mobilization plan among the frontier troop divisions. Out of the territorial reserve will be formed troops for securing the frontiers, the lines of communication, the telegraph system, and other objects of military importance. The expenditures incurred are to be labelled in the accounts under the head of funds granted for reservist training and for "trial mobilization."[92]

91 Quoted by Hoeniger, p. 17; and by Frantz, p. 189.

92 Hoeniger, p. 19; Frantz, p. 195. The Belgian Minister in St. Petersburg reported on March 27, 1914, that the Duma committee on national defense had approved almost without exception the credits demanded, and that the extraordinary credits for military purposes would amount to the enormous sum of 450 million rubles (*Investig. Comm.*, II, pp. 98-99). On these "trial mobilizations," which often took place in time of peace for local areas, see Hoeniger, pp. 58-66; and Dobrorolski, p. 114: "Beside these 'control mobilizations' or *'povyerochnie mobilizatsii'*, there existed another form of mobilization practice—'trial mobilization' [*opitnia mobilizatsia*], including the calling up of reservists and the furnishing of horses by the population. Sufficient money was granted for these, and this practice had a double advantage: They were instructive both for the troops and the reservists, as well as for the local

Detailed regulations under "List 1" also explained that the frontier posts are to be made ready for mobilization, are to be completely armed for the campaign in the field, and are to guard the frontier. All orders for mobilization, for advance to the concentration area, and for protecting this advance are to be carefully examined. The troops are to be instructed as to the uniforms and probable dispositions of the enemy. Horses are to be reshod. No more furloughs are to be granted, and officers and men on furlough or detailed elsewhere are to return at once to their troop divisions. Espionage suspects are to be arrested. Measures to prevent the export of horses, cattle, and grain are to be worked out. Money and valuable securities are to be removed from banks near the frontier to the interior. Naval vessels are to return to their harbors and receive provisions and full war equipment.[93]

"List 2" represents a still further stage in preparatory measures. According to it, upon the order of the Minister of War, "the calling up of reservists and the territorial reserve takes place to an extent which exceeds the funds of the current year fixed for training and trial mobilization. It also includes in the frontier districts the buying of horses and wagons for the baggage trains, and the transport of baggage to its destination. Officers' families receive free transportation from the frontier to places of safety in the interior. Freight cars having the standard gauge of European railways (4 ft. 8½ in. instead of the Russian 5 ft. gauge) are no longer to be allowed to leave Russia. The harbors are to be closed by the setting of mines, and Rus-

authorities charged with the registration and the calling up of the reservists and horses. Just two months before the actual mobilization [in July, 1914], a trial mobilization of this kind took place in the Odessa Military District, for the 34th Artillery Brigade at Ekaterinoslav. Experience showed that one need not worry about the mobilization of our field troops."

93 Frantz, pp. 190-198.

sian merchant ships destined for military or naval uses are to be detained in port.[94]

One important elastic clause in the Regulation also provided: "The Ministerial Council will further decide the question whether still other measures in addition to those set forth in the 'Lists' are to be carried out during the Period Preparatory to War." [95]

Thus, under cover of "trial mobilizations" and the "Period Preparatory to War," military measures could be ordered by the Minister of War, which did not require the approval of the Tsar or a public announcement of mobilization, but which nevertheless were almost equivalent to mobilization in the frontier districts. Such a "trial mobilization" had been undertaken on a wide scale in the fall of 1912 close to the German frontier, and had called forth a strong protest from the German Chief of Staff, Moltke—a protest which Sazonov, at that time, appeared to admit was well founded.[96]

Highly significant is Dobrorolski's own admission that the militarists and the General Staff, at least, on July 25, already regarded war as a settled matter; and also that the local authorities on the frontier, in their zeal or nervousness, may have even gone further than the Regulation properly permitted. This is what he says:

> The following days [after Sazonov had been informed of the Austrian ultimatum] are well known to everybody through the "colored books" and documents published by the European Governments. The war was already a settled matter [*"Voina byla uzhe predrieshena"*], and the whole flood of telegrams between the Governments of Russia and

94 Frantz, pp. 190-192, 198-200. *Cf.* Pourtalès to Bethmann, July 27, 7:17 P.M. (K.D., 274): "Swedish consul at Riga reports mouth of the Düna closed by mines. In Riga all the freight cars have been unloaded and placed at the service of the military administration."

95 Frantz, p. 190.

96 G.P., XXXIII, 128-9 in footnote, 316 f.; 407 f.; Hoeniger, p. 25; *Deutschland Schuldig?*, pp. 141-142.

Germany represented merely the stage setting [*mise en scène*] of a historical drama.

The postponement of the final moment of decision was, to be sure, very useful for the preparatory measures, but it augmented the tension on both sides of the frontier.

The establishment of the Pre-Mobilization Period, as it had been defined, did not give authority to undertake measures having the character of mobilization; but it was evident that in the frontier zones, where the population and the officials were nervous, it was possible that they would allow themselves to be drawn into taking measures which went beyond instructions, in order to insure the safety of mobilization.

Especially was this naturally the case on the German frontier, where there was the danger that the requisitioning of horses and the calling up of the reservists would be exploited by an enterprising neighbor.

In the Suwalki Government [near East Prussia] there were actually cases where horses were prematurely brought together at the concentration points, which gave the German Ambassador at St. Petersburg, Count Pourtalès, occasion to address protests to our Government, and especially to the Minister of War, through the Military Attaché. Sukhomlinov denied in the most categorical manner that any mobilization measures had been taken on our side; but one cannot guarantee that not a single frontier military commander would not take such measures on his own initiative, when the Pre-mobilization Period was once decreed. Frontier incidents are indeed always possible, and all the more so at such a moment.[97]

There was thus the danger that the Russian military authorities would take such wide-reaching "preparatory measures" that Germany would become alarmed and resort to counter-measures, which in turn would lead to a general European war. The German Foreign Office in fact received, as the *Kautsky Documents* show, between the morning of

[97] Dobrorolski, p. 103 (German trans. p. 21 f.).

July 26 and the evening of July 30 twenty-eight reports of Russian military preparations, no less than sixteen of which related to the Russian frontier against Germany; and the German General Staff and Navy Department received many more such reports.[98] But in spite of this, Germany refrained from corresponding preparatory measures (*Drohender Kriegsgefahrzustand*) until she received on July 31 official news that Russia had taken the final military step of openly announcing by placards throughout the streets of St. Petersburg a general mobilization of the whole Russian army and navy. These secret "preparatory measures," which had been decided on at the Ministerial Council on the afternoon of the 25th, and ordered before dawn of the 26th, enabled Russia, when war came, to surprise the world by the rapidity with which she poured her troops into East Prussia and Galicia.

DIPLOMATIC NEGOTIATIONS AND MILITARY PREPARATIONS

Though the military authorities had objected very strenuously to "partial mobilization," to be undertaken only "in the four southern districts toward Austria," they found it a very convenient form of camouflage by which to attempt to mislead the Germans as to the secret "preparatory measures," which General Ianushkevich had ordered "in the whole territory of European Russia" on July 26 at

98 *Cf.* especially K.D., 216, 230, 242, 255, 264, 274-276, 291, 294, 296, 310a, 327, 330, 331, 333, 335a, 338, 339, 343, 344, 348, 349, 365, 365a, 370, 372, 375a, 390, 401, 410, 412, 422, 429, 431a, 445; *Investig. Comm.*, II, p. 28 f., and note 8; Eggeling, *Die Russische Mobilmachung,* pp. 25-28; and compare also Bogitchevitch, p. 83: "On July 28, in company with several Serbian officers, I arrived at Warsaw [from Berlin]. As far as the German frontier, not the slightest indications were seen of military measures. But immediately after crossing the German frontier [into Russian Poland], we noticed mobilization steps being taken on a grand scale (assembly of freight cars in the several stations, military occupation of the railway stations, massing of troops in the several cities, transport of troops at night, mobilization signalling). When we arrived at Brest-Litovsk, July 28, the state of siege had already been proclaimed."

3:26 A.M.,[99] and which were taking place while Sazonov was carrying on his diplomatic negotiations. This does not necessarily imply, as many Germans believe,[100] that "partial mobilization" was deliberately and primarily agreed upon as a ruse to deceive the Germans or that Sazonov's diplomatic negotiations for a peaceful solution were pure hypocrisy, "war being already a settled matter," as Dobrorolski says. There seems little doubt, as indicated above, that the partial mobilization plan was seriously regarded by Sazonov and the Tsar, if not by the General Staff, as a good means of checking Austria without provoking Germany. And if it provoked Germany, Russia would wait for Germany to declare war or attack first, and thus be branded before the world as the aggressor.[101] There seems equally little doubt that between July 26 and 28 Sazonov honestly carried on diplomatic negotiations with the optimistic hope, not shared by the Russian military authorities, of securing a peaceful solution satisfactory to Russia.[102] Pourtalès, however, like Buchanan,[103] had become very apprehensive as to the danger of even a partial mobilization against Austria. He was clear-minded enough to realize that it would be an exceedingly dangerous means of exerting diplomatic pressure. If Russia should attempt a bluff of this kind, he feared that the militarists everywhere would gain an increased influence, and soon take the question beyond

99 See above, at note 89.

100 Hoeniger, 44-54; Eggeling's comment on the German edition of Dobrorolski, pp. 39-48; and Frantz, in *Current History,* March, 1927, p. 855.

101 *Cf.* Sukhomlinov's statement to Paléologue: "The Minister of War has repeated his wish to leave to Germany the eventual initiative of the attack," Paléologue to Bienvenu-Martin, July 26; Bourgeois et Pagès, p. 39.

102 It is noteworthy that Pourtalès has always maintained this view of Sazonov's honesty of purpose; see his comment on the German edition of Dobrorolski, p. 38.

103 For Buchanan's apprehensions, see his despatches to Grey on July 24, 25 and 27 (B.D., 101, 125, 170); and *My Mission to Russia,* I, 192 ff.

the control of the diplomatists, by the purely technical and strategic arguments which they knew so well how to urge.[104] He had also received from Bethmann-Hollweg the following telegram:

> After Count Berchtold has declared to Russia that Austria does not aim at any territorial acquisitions in Serbia, but only wishes to secure repose, the maintenance of the peace of Europe depends on Russia alone. We trust in Russia's love of peace and in our traditional friendly relations with her, that she will take no step which would seriously endanger the peace of Europe.[105]

Accordingly, on Sunday evening, July 26, having heard many rumors of Russian preparatory mobilization measures, Pourtalès deemed it wise to give Sazonov a friendly but firm warning, "concerning the news current among the foreign Military Attachés, according to which it is supposed that mobilization orders have been issued to several Russian Army Corps on the Western Frontier." He "called his attention to the great danger of such measures, which might easily call forth counter-measures." Sazonov "replied that he could guarantee that no mobilization order of the sort had been issued; that, on the contrary, in the Ministerial Council it had been decided to delay with any such order until Austria-Hungary adopted a hostile attitude toward Russia. M. Sazonov admitted that there had already been taken 'certain military measures in order not to be taken by surprise.' "[106]

Sazonov evidently felt that he had been rather vague in his assurance that the mobilization order "would be de-

104 Pourtalès, *Am Scheideweg,* pp. 24-26.

105 Bethmann to Pourtalès, July 26, 1:35 P.M.; K.D., 198.

106 Pourtalès to Bethmann, July 26, 9:30 P.M., K.D., 230; *cf.* also A.R.B., II, 61. The German General Staff, though doubting the sincerity of these assurances, telegraphed to the German Military Attaché in St. Petersburg that no military measures were contemplated by Germany, but he was to observe and report the Russian measures; K.D., 267a.

layed until Austria-Hungary adopted a hostile attitude toward Russia." Did he mean partial or general mobilization? Did "hostile attitude toward Russia" mean an Austrian invasion of Serbia, or an Austrian mobilization in Galicia facing against Russia? He must have realized that his admission about "certain military measures in order not to be taken by surprise" was hardly calculated to have a very reassuring effect upon the German Ambassador. He may also well have had a somewhat uneasy conscience in view of what we know about the wide-reaching measures of the "Period Preparatory to War" which were already in full swing on the western frontier toward Germany as well as toward Austria. He therefore decided it would be well to have a more definite statement made, and telephoned to the Minister of War. He asked Sukhomlinov to make it plain to the German Military Attaché, as one military man speaking to another, that nothing was contemplated except measures preparatory to a contingent partial mobilization against Austria. Accordingly, late on Sunday evening, Eggeling was invited to an interview with Sukhomlinov, which Eggeling thus reports, with his own shrewd conclusions:

> Sazonov requested him to enlighten me on the military situation. The Minister of War gave me his word of honor that no sort of mobilization order had yet been issued. For the present merely preparatory measures were being taken. Not a horse had been recruited, not a reservist called in. If Austria crossed the Serbian frontier, such Military Districts as are directed against Austria, *viz.* Kiev, Odessa, Moscow, Kazan, would be mobilized. Under no circumstances those on the German front, Warsaw, Vilna, St. Petersburg. Peace with Germany, he said, was earnestly desired.
>
> Upon my inquiry as to the object of the mobilization against Austria, he shrugged his shoulders and indicated the

diplomats. . . . I got the impression of great nervousness and anxiety. I consider the wish for peace genuine; military statements in so far correct, that complete mobilization has probably not been ordered, but preparatory measures are very far-reaching. They are evidently striving to gain time for new negotiations and for continuing their armaments. Also the internal situation is unmistakably causing serious anxiety. The general feeling is: hope from Germany and for the mediation of His Majesty [the Kaiser].[107]

Pourtalès also communicated these dubious assurances of Sazonov and Sukhomlinov to his Austrian colleague. Szápáry reported them in turn to Vienna, with conclusions which well sum up the situation:

Although the direct informing of the German Military Attaché [by Sukhomlinov] indicates nervousness on Sazonov's part, and although mobilization against Austria only in case the Serbian frontier is crossed appears rather to reveal the purpose of exerting diplomatic pressure, it must not be left out of account that, in addition to the lack of veracity in the assurances here, there is a lack of harmony between the doings of the diplomats and the militarists, as well as the importance of gaining time for Russian mobilization.

The character of the military preparations now in progress seems specially suited to the mentality of the Tsar, Nicholas, since, though avoiding regular war measures, which to him particularly are repugnant, a certain preparedness is nevertheless arrived at.[108]

SUMMARY OF THE RUSSIAN DANGER

The Russian danger lay in the fact that Sazonov naturally felt bound to protect Serbia, whose hopes and aspirations Russia had encouraged in the past, and whom she

107 Eggeling's report, sent by Pourtalès to Bethmann, July 27, 1 A.M.; K.D., 242.

108 Szápáry to Berchtold, July 26 (telegraphed July 27, 4:30 A. M.); A.R.B., II, 61.

could not abandon now without loss of prestige to herself and the Triple Entente. Still more, he was determined to prevent Austria from gobbling up Serbian territory and upsetting the *status quo* in the Balkans. He had jumped to the conclusion that this was the meaning of the Austrian ultimatum, and that an Austrian invasion of Serbia was likely to begin immediately upon the expiration of the 48-hour time-limit. He was strongly encouraged by the French Ambassador to stand firm in protecting Serbia and in checking Austria. Therefore on July 24, even before hearing the German Ambassador's justification of Austria and plea for "localization," Sazonov had decided to take the side of Serbia, if necessary, even if it should involve war. He adopted the plan of "partial mobilization," which was a dangerous method of exerting diplomatic pressure. At the luncheon conference with Paléologue and Buchanan, "he personally thought that Russia would have to mobilize." To be sure, he desired to avert war, and he made several proposals which he hoped might avert it. He begged Buchanan for an English declaration of Entente solidarity, which Buchanan did not feel able to give. And he proposed to extend the time-limit and give the European Powers an opportunity to pass upon the Austro-Serbian question, a proposal which was met evasively at Berlin and negatively at Vienna.

Then, on July 25, even before Austria had broken off diplomatic relations with Serbia, Sazonov and the Tsar conceded to the Russian militarists the putting into effect of various military measures, including those of the "Period Preparatory to War," which roused anticipations of war among the Russian officers, and gave an impression, as Dobrorolski puts it, that "war was already a settled matter." Henceforth the army leaders, recognizing that partial mobilization was folly on account of the technical and political difficulties involved in it, exerted steadily increasing pressure for general mobilization; and the danger was that Sazonov would accept their views, and add the weight of his pressure to that of the General Staff in persuading the Tsar to consent to the final military step which would probably make a general war inevitable. Even on Saturday evening, July 25, Sazonov himself, in spite of his hopes to the contrary, seems to have thought war likely, and to have been ready to resort to it if his partial mobilization bluff did not work. Meeting again with Paléologue and Buchanan, he told them of his partial mobilization plan, and again received active encouragement from Paléologue, as we now know from the interesting parts of Buchanan's dispatch which were suppressed or altered when published in 1914:

> French Ambassador said he had received a number of telegrams from the Minister in charge of the Ministry of Foreign Affairs, that no one of them displayed the slightest sign of hesitation, and that he was in a position to give his Excellency [Sazonov] formal assurance that France placed herself unreservedly on Russia's side.
>
> [After thanking Paléologue, Sazonov turned to the British Ambassador with the question, "And your Government?" Buchanan replied that Sir Edward Grey did not yet despair of the situation, and that the great thing was to gain time. He repeated that] England could play the rôle of mediator at Berlin and Vienna to better purpose as a friend who, if her counsels of moderation were disregarded, might one day be converted into an ally, than if she were to declare herself Russia's ally at once. Sazonov said that unfortunately Germany was convinced that she could count upon our [British] neutrality. . . . He did not believe that Germany really wanted war, but her attitude was decided by ours. If we took our stand firmly with France and Russia there would be no war. If we failed them now, rivers of blood would flow and we would in the end be dragged into war

French Ambassador remarked that French Government would want to know at once whether our fleet was prepared to play part assigned to it by Anglo-French Naval Convention. He could not believe that England would not stand by her two friends, who were acting as one in this matter.

[Buchanan urged prudence on Sazonov and warned him, if Russia mobilized, Germany would not be content with mere mobilization, or give Russia time to carry out hers, but would probably declare war at once. Sazonov repeated that] he did not wish to precipitate a conflict, but unless Germany can restrain Austria, I can regard the situation as desperate. Russia cannot allow Austria to crush Serbia and become predominant Power in Balkans, and, secure of support of France, she will face all the risks of war.[109]

At the close of this meeting between the representatives of the Triple Entente, Sazonov threatened England with a point on which Sir Edward Grey and his advisers were very sensitive. "For ourselves," Buchanan reported, "the position is a most perilous one, and we shall have to choose between giving Russia our active support, or renouncing her friendship. If we fail her now, we cannot hope to maintain that friendly coöperation with her in Asia, that is of such vital importance to us." [110]

Sazonov's fears as to Austrian intentions were partly owing to Szápáry's failure to make at once the declaration

[109] Buchanan to Grey, July 25, 8:00 P.M.; B.D., 125; *cf.* B.B.B., 17, where much is suppressed, and where the paraphrase of the last sentence altered materially the meaning by adding the words, "if she feels," so that it read, "if she feels secure of the support of France, she [Russia] will face all the risks of war." Whether Paléologue actually received "a number of telegrams," as he asserted, does not appear from F.Y.B.; but his remarks here and elsewhere, and his inquiry about the British fleet, leave no doubt that Sazonov felt "secure of the support of France." Until the French documents are published in full, we shall not know how much this feeling was the result of Poincaré's assurances during his visit, how much it may be that Paléologue went beyond his instructions in encouraging Russia and failed to keep his own government sufficiently informed, and how much Sazonov exaggerated the nature of Paléologue's assurances.

[110] B.D., 125.

—which had been promised to Tisza should be made [111]—that Austria intended no territorial gains at Serbia's expense.[112] It was not until after he had been assured of Austria's territorial disinterestedness by Pourtalès and later by Szápáry,[113] and until after he had been agreeably surprised to find that the expiration of the time-limit was not immediately followed by an Austrian attack on Serbia, that Sazonov was visibly eased in his mind and became again somewhat optimistic. Thereupon, from July 26 to 28, he carried on conciliatory diplomatic negotiations, while at the same time the Russian military authorities were secretly making wide-reaching military preparations which would facilitate an eventual "general," as well as a "partial," mobilization. Rumors of these preparations began to cause alarm in Germany. This situation continued until the news of Austria's declaration of war on Serbia on July 28 put an abrupt end to Sazonov's optimism and gave a new and fatal turn to the Russian danger. But before discussing this, we must consider the Serbian reply to the Austrian ultimatum, and various proposals offered by the Powers for a peaceful solution of the question.

[111] See above, ch. v, at notes 104-106.

[112] *Cf.* A.R.B., II, 19, 40.

[113] By Pourtalès on the evening of July 24 (K.D., 204; A.R.B., II, 19), and again on July 26 (K.D., 198, 230); and by Szápáry on July 26 (K.D., 238; A.R.B., II, 73).

CHAPTER VII

THE SERBIAN REPLY

THE first reports of the Sarajevo assassination which reached Belgrade caused the gravest consternation among Government officials. Mr. Pashitch, the Prime Minister, went to bed to give undisturbed thought to the problem, and remarked to his first visitor, "It is very bad. It will mean war." [1] Mr. Ljuba Jovanovitch, the Minister of Education, "overwhelmed with grave anxiety," did not doubt for a moment that Austria-Hungary would make this the occasion for war on Serbia.[2] Hartwig, the Russian Minister in Belgrade, is said to have exclaimed, "In Heaven's name! Let us hope that it was not a Serbian." [3]

The Serbian Government at once realized that in view of all the anti-Austrian propaganda in the past and of the fact that the plot had been prepared in Belgrade, the Austrian Government would be likely to hold the Serbian agitation, if not the Serbian Government, responsible, and use

1 H. F. Armstrong, "Three Days in Belgrade," in (N. Y.) *Foreign Affairs,* V, 267-275, Jan., 1927, gives a very interesting account, largely based on conversation with Serbian officials, of the presentation of the Austrian ultimatum and the composition of the Serbian reply, July 23-25.

2 See above, ch. ii, at note 14.

3 Gooss, p. 72; K.D., 10. He did not, however, cancel a quiet bridge-party which he had arranged for that same evening, and later, during the requiem mass for the murdered couple, it was charged that he did not follow the example of the other Legations in placing his flag at half-mast. He claimed on the other hand that he had done so, and that the flag had unfortunately become twisted about so that it did not show plainly. It was after a discussion with the Austrian Minister, Giesl, on this point that he suddenly fell dead from a heart attack in the Austrian Legation on July 11—an incident that gave rise to a wild unfounded rumor that he had been poisoned. *Cf.* Baron Wladimir Giesl, *Zwei Jahrzehnte im nahen Orient,* Berlin, 1927; and B.D., 48, 62.

it as a pretext for war. The Serbian Government therefore sought to preserve as correct an attitude as possible. It cancelled the festivities which were celebrating Vidov Dan, published in the official paper a severe condemnation of the crime, expressed proper condolences, and declared its readiness to hand over to justice any subjects who might be shown to have been guilty of complicity. It did not, however, take any proper steps to make an inquiry of its own as to the origins of the plot in Belgrade; on the contrary Dr. Grouitch, the Secretary General of the Serbian Foreign Office, told the Austrian Chargé d'Affaires on July 1 "that up to the present nothing had been done, and that the matter did not concern the Serbian Government." [4] It waited to see how much Austria would be able to discover and what accusations she would bring forward.

Nor did the Serbian Government take any effective steps to curb the violent attacks on Austria in the Belgrade Press, whose comments on the Sarajevo assassination, according to the British Ambassador in Vienna, contained "expressions amounting almost to condonation and even approval of the dastardly outrage." [5] Pashitch took the attitude that he was unable to prevent these provocative polemics, seeing that the Serbian Constitution guaranteed complete freedom of the press and prohibited all censorship or seizure of newspapers.[6] The Serbian attacks, to be sure, were in part provoked by the equally bitter and insulting attacks of the Austro-Hungarian Press, which now took special pains to reprint selections from the more outrageous Serbian newspaper articles, with the aim of circulating them in Europe and turning public opinion against the Belgrade

[4] Griesinger to Bethmann, June 30, July 2; K.D., 10, 12; and Crackanthorpe to Grey, July 2; B.D., 27.

[5] Bunsen to Grey, July 4; B.D., 34. Even the Serbian Minister in Vienna found it necessary to warn his Government to moderate the tone of the Press (Jovan Jovanovitch to Pashitch, June 30, July 1; S.B.B., 2, 9).

[6] Pashitch to the Serbian Legations abroad, July 14, 19; S.B.B., 20, 30.

Government. There thus developed during the three weeks after the Archduke's murder an intensely bitter press campaign of vilification between Austria and Serbia, which whipped up the war spirit among the masses on both sides of the frontier. It was the psychological preparation for war.[7]

The propaganda of the Austrian newspapers, which enjoyed a wider circulation, was on the whole much more successful at first than that of Serbia in influencing public opinion in Europe, especially in England. On July 16 the London *Times* denounced "the reckless and provocative language which a good many Serbian newspapers are alleged to have used, both before and after the crime that has shocked Europe." It issued the warning that "Serbia ought herself, and of her own motion, to make the inquiry, which she has reason to suppose that Austria-Hungary will call upon her to make, and lay the full report of the proceedings before the Powers." Next day the influential *Westminster Gazette* justified Austria's desire to clarify her relations with Serbia, after a crime believed to have its origins in Belgrade and to be part of a deliberate attempt to tear away the Serb provinces of the Dual Monarchy; Austria "cannot be expected to remain inactive; and Serbia will be well advised if she realizes the reasonableness of her great neighbor's anxiety, and does whatever may be in her power to allay it, without waiting for a pressure which might involve what Count Tisza calls 'warlike complications.'" This attitude on the part of powerful English papers gave great encouragement to Austrian hopes that England would remain inactive toward a "localized" Austro-Serbian conflict. But they caused a correspondingly

[7] *Cf.* B.D., 29, 34, 35, 46, 55, 64, 70, 81; S.B.B., *passim;* Appendix ix of the Austrian *dossier* (A.R.B., II, 48), giving choice extracts culled from the Serbian Press; H. Kanner, *Kaiserliche Katastrophenpolitik* (Vienna, 1922), pp. 309-327; and J. F. Scott, *Five Weeks: the Surge of Public Opinion on the Eve of the Great War* (N. Y., 1927), pp. 20-98.

great uneasiness and nervousness on the part of Serbia; and were made the subject of some diplomatic protest and many comments.[8]

Pashitch finally became seriously alarmed at the attitude of the Austrian, German and British Press, at the ominous silence of Vienna, and perhaps also at the news of Berchtold's intentions which had leaked out through Count Lützow to the British authorities on July 16.[9] This news had been at once passed on to the British resident in Belgrade,[10] and may have been hinted to the Serbian Minister in London, who telegraphed to Pashitch on July 17: "The Austrian Embassy is making great efforts to win over the English Press against us, and to induce it to favor the idea that Austria must give a good lesson to Serbia. . . . No reliance should be placed in the ostensibly peaceable statements of Austro-Hungarian official circles, as the way is being prepared for diplomatic pressure upon Serbia, which may develop into an armed attack." [11]

The despatches from the Serbian Minister in Vienna were also alarming, as to the incitement of public opinion by the Austrian Press Bureau and the secret steps which were probably being taken. "Austria has to choose between two courses: either to make the Sarajevo outrage a domestic question, inviting us to assist her to discover and punish the culprits; or to make it a case against the Serbians and Serbia, and even against the Jugoslavs. After taking into consideration all that is being prepared and done, it appears

[8] *Cf.* B.D., 58, 61, 73, 80, 125, 153, 156; K.D., 55, 92. Shortly after the *Times* article of July 16, Mr. Wickham Steed used his great influence to swing the *Times* around to an anti-Austrian and anti-German attitude (*cf.* Steed, *Through Thirty Years,* I, 402-412), but the greater part of the English Liberal Press remained sympathetic to Austria and severe on Serbia, until after Austria declared war on Serbia (*cf.* J. F. Scott, pp. 206-246; and Irene Cooper Willis, *England's Holy War,* N. Y., 1928, Part I.

[9] See above, ch. v, at note 95.

[10] B.D., 50, "Repeated to Belgrade."

[11] Boshkovitch to Pashitch, July 17; S.B.B., 27.

to me that Austria will choose the latter course. Austria-Hungary will do this in the belief that she will have the approval of Europe . . . and that she will thus raise her prestige internally as well as externally." [12] All this appears to have made the Belgrade Cabinet nervous as to the wisdom of their passive waiting policy and their neglect to search for and arrest accomplices in Serbia.

On July 18, when the British Chargé d'Affaires at Belgrade alluded to the *Times* article that the wisest course for Serbia would be to undertake herself an enquiry into the conspiracy on Serbian soil, Dr. Grouitch of the Serbian Foreign Office replied that, when the Sarajevo investigation was completed, Serbia would be ready to comply with any requests, compatible with international usage, for a further investigation. But until then she could not act. He then tried to deceive the British as to the Serbian Government's knowledge of the assassins. "Of Princip the Serbian Government knew nothing," he said,[13] a statement manifestly untrue in view of the admission of the Serbian Minister of Education that he was personally acquainted with Princip and had twice examined him,[14] and also in view of what has been said above in the chapters on the assassination plot and the responsibility for it. Grouitch added that, "should it come to the worst and Austria declare war, Serbia would not stand alone. Russia would not remain

12 Jovanovitch to Pashitch, July 15; S.B.B., 25; *cf.* also 15-17 and 22-24.

13 Crackanthorpe to Grey, July 18; B.D., 80. A few days later the Serbian Minister in London similarly tried to deceive the British as to the other conspirator, Chabrinovitch, repeating the false statement current in Belgrade newspapers, that "the Serbian authorities, considering him [Chabrinovitch] suspect and dangerous, had desired to expel him, but on applying to the Austrian authorities, the latter had protected him and said that he was a harmless and innocent individual" (B.D., 87). For the details as to the extent to which this was false, see A. von Wegerer, "Die angebliche Bürgschaft der k. u. k. Regierung für Chabrinovitch," and "Wie Serbien England täuschte," in KSF, IV, 330-332 (May, 1926), and V, 238-249 (March, 1927).

14 Ljuba Jovanovitch, *Krv Slovenstva,* p. 10.

quiet, were Serbia wantonly attacked, and Bulgaria would be immobilized by Rumania."

Next day Pashitch sent a long telegram of a similar tenor to the Serbian Ministers abroad, denouncing the activities of the Austrian Press, which, he said, were to blame for such excesses as appeared in the Serbian newspapers. He instructed his diplomatic representatives to impress upon the Governments to which they were accredited Serbia's "desire to maintain friendly relations with Austria-Hungary," and her willingness, if requested, "to subject to trial in our independent courts any accomplices in the outrage who are in Serbia—should such, of course, exist. But," he added, "we can never comply with demands which may be directed against the dignity of Serbia, and which would be inacceptable to any country which respects and maintains its independence."[15] Shortly after this, Pashitch departed from Belgrade on an electioneering campaign caused by the dissolution of the Skupshtina which had been brought about by his conflict with the "Black Hand" over the "priority question." He was therefore absent from the capital at the moment that the Austrian Minister, Baron Giesl, presented the Austrian ultimatum on the afternoon of July 23.

FRAMING THE SERBIAN REPLY

Berchtold had taken care that Serbia should not evade giving a reply punctually within the 48 hours required. Neither the absence of Pashitch, nor the possible resignation of his Cabinet, was to be allowed as an excuse for delay, because a resigning Cabinet was to be regarded as responsible for the carrying on of business until a new one

[15] Pashitch to the Serbian Legations abroad, July 19; S.B.B., 30. In London, Boshkovitch, acting on these instructions, was advised that Serbia should "meet the Austrian requests in a conciliatory and moderate spirit" (B.D., 87); in Berlin, the Serbian Chargé d'Affaires begged the German Government to use its influence in reconciling Austria and Serbia, but was told that, in view of Serbia's attitude, it could well understand that Austria might take energetic measures (K.D., 86, 91, 95).

was formed. To make certain that there would be someone to receive the ultimatum when it was presented, and to enable Pashitch to be recalled quickly, Giesl notified the Belgrade Foreign Office on the morning of July 23 that he would have an important communication to make between 4 and 5 o'clock that afternoon. At the appointed hour Dr. Grouitch and the three Cabinet Ministers who happened to have remained in Belgrade met in anxiety at the Foreign Office. They had already dispatched a telephone message to Pashitch and arranged for a special train to hurry him back to the capital. But Giesl did not appear. Instead he sent a secretary, begging to say that he would come instead at 6 o'clock. His delay was caused by an eleventh hour instruction from Vienna. Berchtold, upon further information from Berlin as to Poincaré's movements, wanted to make doubly sure that the French President be well out on the Baltic before the news of the ultimatum could reach Russia, and therefore Giesl was to postpone delivery for an hour.[16]

Finally at 6 o'clock Giesl arrived, handed in the Note, and said, "Unless a satisfactory reply is given on all points by 6 o'clock on Saturday, the day after tomorrow, I shall leave Belgrade with all the personnel of my Legation." He was told that it would be difficult to answer so important a communication in so short a time, especially in the absence of several Cabinet Ministers. He replied that in this age of railways, telegraphs and telephones, in a country as small as Serbia, this need be only a matter of a few hours, and that he had already suggested in the morning the desirability of Pashitch's return. Without any further discussion Giesl then departed, leaving the dismayed Ministers to study the Note which still lay unread upon the table.[17]

16 Berchtold's instructions to Giesl, July 21 and 23; A.R.B., I, 36, 62, 63; see also K.D., 110, 112, 127; and ch. v, notes 75-76.

17 Giesl to Berchtold, July 23; A.R.B., I, 64, 65, 67; and H. F. Armstrong, *op. cit.*, pp. 268-272.

The Serbian Ministers then began to go through the fateful document. Their emotion grew as its tenor and object became clear. Nobody cared to be the first to speak. At last Ljuba Jovanovitch got up, and said, "Well, there is nothing to do but die fighting." [18] Obviously the first thing to do was to telegraph the news of Giesl's action to the Serbian Ministers in foreign countries, stating that "the demands are such that no Serbian Government could accept them in their entirety." [19] The representatives of the Powers at Belgrade were similarly notified at once. A special appeal for help was instantly dispatched to Russia,[20] reaching Sazonov and Paléologue, as we have seen, very early next morning before they had slept off the fatigue of the Franco-Russian festivities. This was followed by a moving plea from the Prince Regent of Serbia to the Tsar: "We are unable to defend ourselves and beg your Majesty to come to our aid as soon as possible. The much-appreciated goodwill which your Majesty has so often shown toward us inspires us with the firm belief that once again our appeal to your noble Slav heart will not pass unheeded." [21] The King of Italy also was invoked, to use his good offices to induce his Austrian ally to prolong the time-limit and moderate the demands.[22]

Meanwhile the Cabinet Ministers who were away, taking part in the electoral campaign, had been summoned back in all haste to the capital. Pashitch arrived within a few hours at 5 o'clock on Friday morning, July 24. At 10 o'clock the Cabinet began a long and gloomy session, but no decision as to an answer was reached. It met again in the evening, and still again on Saturday morning, knowing that an answer of some kind must be given before 6 P.M.

18 Armstrong, p. 272.

19 Pachu to the Serbian Ministers abroad, July 23; S.B.B., 33.

20 Russian Chargé d'Affaires at Belgrade to Sazonov, July 23; R.O.B., 1, 2.

21 S.B.B., 37; R.O.B., 6.

22 B.D., 96.

Pashitch saw the Montenegrin and Greek Ministers. The former assured him emphatically that Montenegro would march side by side with Serbia. But the Greek Minister was uncertain what attitude his Government would take; M. Venizelos, the Premier, was absent from Athens, but telephoned from Munich to Berlin next morning that if Bulgaria took advantage of an Austro-Serbian conflict to attack Serbia, Greece would oppose such Bulgarian interference.[23] Far more important, however, was the attitude which the Triple Entente Powers would take.

Unfortunately for Serbia, it happened that these three Great Powers were not represented at Belgrade at this moment by regular Ministers. Hartwig, the energetic Russian Minister and strong champion of Serbia, had dropped dead a few days previously when talking with Giesl, and his successor had not arrived. No British Minister was on the spot, though Mr. des Graz was on his way from London to Belgrade. The French Minister was suffering from a nervous breakdown and was invisible; his successor, M. Boppe, was only just arriving from Constantinople and was unacquainted with his new post. So the Chargés d'Affaires of the Entente Powers could do little for Serbia except report home the news of Austria's unacceptable demands, and await instructions. These were slow in coming, so slow, in fact, that they were probably too late to have had any decisive influence on Serbia's decision.

Sazonov talked with the Serbian Minister on Friday evening about 7 o'clock, and is said to have "advised extreme moderation in respect to the Serbian reply."[24] But no such advice appears in the Serbian Minister's account of this conversation. On the contrary, as he was leaving Sazonov, he met the German Ambassador, and told him "he

[23] Giesl to Berchtold, July 24; A.R.B., II, 3, 4; Russian Chargé d'Affaires in Berlin to Sazonov, July 25; *Krasnyi Arkhiv,* I, p. 166.

[24] Schilling's *Diary,* p. 31.

would see before long that this was not a question merely between Serbia and Austria, but a European question."[25] Later in the evening, Sazonov telegraphed to his Chargé d'Affaires in Belgrade that if the Serbians felt helpless in case of an Austrian invasion, they had better offer no resistance, but retire without fighting and appeal to the Powers for protection.[26] But whatever advice Sazonov gave is said not to have reached Belgrade until after the Serbian reply had been handed to Giesl at 6 o'clock on July 25.[27]

Sir Edward Grey telegraphed on Friday at 9:30 P.M. that "Serbia ought certainly to express concern and regret that any officials, however subordinate, should have been accomplices in murder of the Archduke, and promise, if this is proved, to give fullest satisfaction;" for the rest, "to reply as they consider the interests of Serbia require;" and, in order to avert military action by Austria, "to give a favorable reply on as many points as possible within the limit of time, and not to meet Austria with a blank negative." He added, with an eye to preserving Entente solidarity, "Consult with your Russian and French colleagues as to saying this to Serbian Government. Serbian Minister here implores us to give some indication of our views, but I cannot take responsibility of giving more advice than above, and I do not like to give that without knowing what Russian and French Governments are saying at Bel-

[25] Spalajkovitch to Pashitch, July 24; S.B.B., 36. If Spalajkovitch or Sazonov may have sent other messages to Belgrade while the Serbian reply was being framed, either advising moderation or promising Russian support, they have not been published. The Serbian Minister at Vienna, however, stated "that active exchange of telegrams is taking place between Belgrade and St. Petersburg, and that, in his opinion, reply of Serbian Government will depend on result of this correspondence" (Bunsen to Grey, July 24, 1:30 P.M.; B.D., 93).

[26] Tg. 1487, July 24; Schilling's *Diary,* pp. 33, 86. See also B.D., 125; and B.D., 221, quoted in preceding chapter, note 45.

[27] Seton-Watson, p. 257 note; *cf.* also Crackanthorpe to Grey, July 25, 12:30 P.M.: "My Russian colleague and new French Minister . . . are as yet without instructions" (B.D., 111).

grade." [28] This advice also came too late materially to influence the Belgrade Cabinet. Crackanthorpe replied at 12:30 P.M. next day that his colleagues were still without instructions; in view of this, and of the proposed conciliatory terms of the Serbian reply, of which Dr. Grouitch had already given him an advance summary, he had abstained from offering Grey's advice to the Serbian Government.[29]

M. Berthelot, the Political Director at the Quai d'Orsay, advised the Serbian Minister in Paris on July 24 that Serbia should "try to gain time," by offering satisfaction on all the points not inconsistent with her dignity and sovereignty, and by asking for further information on others; above all, Serbia should "attempt to escape from the direct grip of Austria by declaring herself ready to submit to the arbitration of Europe." [30] Whether this advice arrived at Belgrade in time to influence the Serbian reply is uncertain. The fact that Serbia's reply did substantially follow the line Berthelot suggested makes it seem likely.

In any case, however, Pashitch and his colleagues, rather than any of the Great Powers, must be given the main credit for the cleverness with which they met a difficult situation. They framed a reply which not only won the approval and sympathy of all the Powers except Austria, but which also commanded the admiration of the man who framed the Austrian ultimatum itself, "as the most brilliant example of diplomatic skill which I have ever known." [31] They had instantly decided that "no Serbian Government could accept the Austrian demands in their entirety." [32]

[28] B.D., 102.

[29] Crackanthorpe to Grey, July 25; 12:30 P.M.; B.D., 111, 114.

[30] Bienvenu-Martin's circular telegram, July 24; F.Y.B., 26; *cf.* also A.R.B., II, 11.

[31] Musulin, *Das Haus am Ballplatz,* p. 241. Berchtold, reporting to Francis Joseph on July 28, spoke of "the very cleverly composed reply of the Serbian Government, which however is wholly worthless in content, though yielding in form" (A.R.B., II, 78).

[32] Pachu to the Serbian Ministers abroad, July 23, S.B.B., 33.

Such being the case, they now concluded that Austria would treat any reply they could make as unsatisfactory, and make war. Therefore they "would appeal to the Governments of the friendly Powers to protect the independence of Serbia. If war was inevitable, Serbia would carry it on."[33] Since Austria would evidently reject any reply which did not yield on all points, they could afford to give their reply a very conciliatory form, apparently yielding on many points, and even suggesting submitting the question to the arbitration of the Hague Tribunal. This kind of a conciliatory reply would help gain the sympathy and protection of the Powers, and tend to place Austria in the wrong when she rejected it. It was, however, more yielding in form than in substance, and it is significant that two or three hours before they handed it to Giesl at the expiration of the time-limit, they had already ordered the general mobilization of the whole Serbian army.[34] In fact they had at once begun to make such frantic military preparations for defence and for the transport of the Government archives, treasure and officials from an exposed position in Belgrade to the interior,[35] that the German Minister was misled into telegraphing his Government at 11:50 P.M. on Friday night, "Mobilization is already in full swing."[36]

This ordering of Serbian mobilization before handing in the conciliatory reply, which was regarded more as a diplomatic gesture than a serious effort to satisfy Austria, had another advantage. Serbian hatred against Austria had been so stimulated by the newspaper campaign, and Serbian military officers of the "Black Hand" group were so eager for war and ready to overthrow Pashitch, that if he had

33 Pashitch to Spalajkovitch, July 24; S.B.B., 34.

34 At 3 P.M., July 25, according to Giesl, A.R.B., II, 23.

35 *Cf.* Giesl to Berchtold, July 25, 1 P.M.; A.R.B., 22; and Armstrong, p. 272 f.

36 K.D., 158. The Austrian Chief of Staff also received news late on Friday night from an officer near the frontier that mobilization had been proclaimed at Shabats in Serbia at 4 P.M. on July 24 (Conrad, IV, 109).

made his conciliatory reply involving some humiliating concessions, there might have been danger of a military revolt against the civil Government. Even before the presentation of the ultimatum, Serbian officials had pointed out the danger from the excited national feeling in their country,[37] and the German Minister reported that Pashitch's "position is a very difficult one, in view of the coming elections and of the agitation that has arisen throughout the country. Every concession to the neighboring Monarchy will be charged against him by the united Opposition as weakness. In addition to that, is the fact that military circles, blinded by their megalomania and chauvinism, are forcing him to roughness which is otherwise wholly opposed to his conciliatory nature." [38] This became even more true after the ultimatum became known. "The military categorically demand the rejection of the Note and war." "In case of the proclamation of the Order of the Day [which Austria demanded should be published in the official Bulletin of the Army], a military uprising is feared." [39] But the preparations for war and the proclamation of mobilization, before making known that the Government had yielded to some of the Austrian demands, satisfied the military officers and averted this danger.

The main points of the Serbian reply were substantially threshed out at the long Cabinet meeting on Saturday morning. The representatives of the friendly Powers were given an advance summary of it and informed that "it will be drawn up in most conciliatory terms and will meet Austrian demands in as large measure as possible." [40] The actual wording was drafted mainly by Stojan Protitch, the Minister of Interior, but every phrase was discussed and re-discussed by the other Ministers, and changes made up

37 F.Y.B., 19; B.D., 27, 40.

38 Griesinger to Bethmann, July 21; K.D., 137.

39 Griesinger to Bethmann, July 24; K.D., 158, 159.

40 Crackanthorpe to Grey, July 25, 12:30 P.M., B.D., 114.

to the last moment. The final Serbian text, as handed over to Grouitch for translation into French and typing, was so full of erasures and corrections that only one who had been working on it could decipher the sense. As he was dictating the translation to the typist and the minutes were flying by, the only remaining typewriter broke down, and in the end the text was copied out in a rather shaky hand by a secretary. It was then given to Pashitch, who started off a little before six o'clock to deliver it in person to the Austrian Minister.[41]

THE SUBSTANCE OF THE SERBIAN REPLY

The Serbian reply was more conciliatory in form than in substance. To make this clear the Austrian authorities delayed making it public until they had time to make comments upon it. These they published in parallel columns with the Serbian reply, showing that the concessions at many points were so guarded with limitations and conditions as to be virtually worthless as guarantees of security for the future, as well as failing to be the complete assent which they had demanded. But they were not able to publish this annotated edition of the Serbian reply until July 28, and it then came too late to have the effect in Europe for which they had hoped.[42] Meanwhile Serbia had circulated her reply and the advance summary of it, and created the good impression which she had hoped for.[43]

41 Armstrong, *op. cit.*, pp. 273-275; Mr. Armstrong gives a facsimile of a part of the Serbian reply and of other interesting Serbian documents connected with the July Crisis, in *Current History,* Oct., 1927.

42 Berchtold did not inform even Germany of the Serbian reply for more than two days. Berlin telegraphed for it in vain on July 26 (K.D., 226), and again on July 27 (K.D., 246): "Please telegraph text of the Serbian reply immediately." Finally on July 28 at 1:45 A.M. (K.D., 280) Tschirschky telegraphed that he had urgently requested the text of the reply, but had only just received it in printed form with the Austrian annotations; as it was being given to the Press and was a long document, he dispensed with sending it by telegraph.

43 *Cf.* B.D., 114, 115, 171; K.D., 271, 293.

A summary of the Serbian reply, and of the Austrian parallel comments which are here indicated by brackets, follows.

"Convinced that their reply will remove any misunderstanding which may threaten to impair the good neighborly relations" between the two countries, the Serbian Government protest that at no time since their promises of 1909 have they or their agents attempted to change the political and legal state of affairs created in Bosnia and Herzegovina. [This was trying to shift the argument, since the ultimatum did not maintain that the Serbian Government or their official agents had attempted to change the situation created in 1909, but that in failing to suppress the movement directed against Austria, they had not lived up to their promise to adopt a friendly and neighborly attitude].

The Serbian Government "cannot be held responsible for manifestations of a private character, such as articles in the press and the peaceable work of societies. . . . They are prepared to hand over for trial any Serbian subject, without regard to his situation or rank, of whose complicity in the Sarajevo crime proofs shall be forthcoming." They also agree to publish on the first page of the *Journal Officiel* the declaration condemning all propaganda "which may be" directed against Austria-Hungary, and regretting that, "according to the communication from the Imperial and Royal Government," certain Serbian officers and functionaries participated in the above-mentioned propaganda. [In altering the declaration from the form demanded by Austria, by the insertion of the quoted phrases, the Serbian Government were insincere in implying that no such propaganda existed, or that they were not aware of it].

Coming to the ten Austrian demands, the Serbian Government then undertook:

1. "To introduce at the first regular meeting of the

Skupshtina a provision into the Press law providing for the most severe punishment of incitement to hatred and contempt of the Austro-Hungarian Monarchy," and also proposing a modification of the Constitution which would permit the confiscation of newspapers. [This was unsatisfactory—it did not assure a definite result within a given time, and if the bills were rejected by the Skupshtina everything would be as it was before].

2. "To dissolve the *Narodna Odbrana* and every other society which may be directing its efforts against Austria-Hungary," although the Serbian Government possesses no proof, and Austria furnishes none, that the members of these societies have committed criminal acts. [Austria could not admit the reservation in the last clause; nor did Serbia comply with Austria's further demands that the means of propaganda possessed by these societies should be confiscated, and that their reëstablishment under other names be prevented].

3. "To eliminate without delay from public instruction in Serbia everything that serves, or might serve, to foment the propaganda against Austria-Hungary, whenever facts and proofs are furnished." [Serbia asks proofs when she must know that the school books contain objectionable matter, and that many of the teachers are enrolled in the *Narodna Odbrana*].

4. To remove from the military service all persons proved by a judicial inquiry to be guilty of acts directed against Austria-Hungary, after information had been furnished by the latter. [This confined removals to officers convicted by a judicial inquiry of crimes punishable by law, but Austria demanded removal of officers who fomented propaganda, a proceeding which was not generally punishable by law in Serbia].

5. As to the demand to accept the collaboration in Serbia of Austrian representatives for the suppression of

subversive propaganda, the Serbian Government "do not clearly grasp the meaning and scope of the demand . . . but will admit such collaboration as agrees with the principles of international law, criminal procedure, and good neighborly relations." [The reservation is vague and calculated to lead to insurmountable difficulties in reaching an arrangement].

6. The Serbian Government "consider it their duty to open an inquiry [*enquête*], against all such persons as are, or eventually may be, implicated in the plot"; but "as regards the participation in this inquiry of Austro-Hungarian agents, cannot accept such an arrangement, as it would be a violation of the Constitution and of the law of criminal procedure." [Serbia has misinterpreted Austria's clearly expressed demand which was for two distinct things: (1) the opening of a judicial inquiry [*enquête judiciaire*], in which, of course, no Austrian collaboration was expected: and (2) Austrian collaboration in the preliminary police investigations [*recherches*] for the collection and verification of evidence, for which numberless precedents exist].

7. The Serbian Government arrested Tankositch the very evening the ultimatum was delivered, but has not been able to arrest Ciganovitch. [The Prefect of Police at Belgrade contrived the departure of Ciganovitch, and then declared that no man of the name existed in Belgrade].[44]

8. The Serbian Government will take measures to prevent the smuggling of arms and explosives across the frontier, and will severely punish the frontier officials who allowed the Sarajevo assassins to cross over.

9. The Serbian Government will gladly give explanations as to the remarks in interviews made by their officials in Serbia or abroad, alleged to be hostile to Austria, as soon as Austria specifies the passages and it is shown they were

44 On Serbian complicity in Ciganovitch's sudden disappearance, see above, ch. iii, at notes 44-45 and 55-58.

actually made. [The interviews in question must be well known to the Serbian Government; their request for details and proof indicate unwillingness to comply seriously with this demand].

10. The Serbian Government will inform Austria of the execution of the above measures as soon as each has been carried out.

If Austria is not satisfied with this reply, the Serbian Government "are ready, as always, to accept a peaceful agreement, by referring this question either to the decision of the International Tribunal of the Hague, or to the Great Powers which took part in drawing up the declaration made by the Serbian Government on March 31, 1909." [45]

Though some of the Austrian comments are pettifogging in character, they show that it is by no means true, as often stated, that Serbia virtually yielded to all the Austrian demands except one. Nos. 1, 2, and 3 were accepted to a very reasonable extent, and Nos. 8 and 10 completely. But Nos. 4, 5, and 9 were answered evasively or with serious reservations. No. 7 contained an implication concerning Ciganovitch which was untrue. No. 6 concerned the collaboration in Serbia of Austrian officials in searching out (though not in trying and judging) Serbian accomplices in the assassination plot; this was refused, though most important, either because Pashitch and his colleagues misunderstood it, deliberately or unconsciously; or because it seemed to infringe upon Serbia's sovereignty; or because they feared it would lead to inconvenient discoveries concerning the complicity of the "Black Hand" and other Serbian officials, as well as concerning the Serbian Government's cognizance of a plot which they had failed to prevent.

The general impression, however, made upon contemporaries by the Serbian reply was favorable. At the British Foreign Office Sir Eyre Crowe noted: "The answer is

[45] S.B.B., 39; A.R.B., II, 96; B.D., Appendix B.

reasonable. If Austria demands absolute compliance with her ultimatum, it can only mean that she wants war."[46] The German Emperor, after reading it on the morning of July 28, jotted down at the end of it, "A brilliant performance for a time-limit of only 48 hours. This is more than one could have expected! A great moral success for Vienna; but with it every reason for war drops away, and Giesl ought to have remained quietly in Belgrade! After such a thing, *I* should never have ordered mobilization!—W."[47]

Giesl, however, was justified by his instructions in rejecting it as unsatisfactory. One cannot accept, on the other hand, the arguments sometimes made by Austrians, that the rejection of the Serbian reply was justifiable on the ground that it did not give Austria adequate guarantees of security; because it was not primarily guarantees which Austria aimed at in her ultimatum, but an excuse for weakening Serbia and putting an end to the Greater Serbia danger by making war on her.

THE DIPLOMATIC BREAK BETWEEN AUSTRIA AND SERBIA

The time-limit was to expire at 6 P. M. on Saturday afternoon, July 25. A few minutes before six, Pashitch arrived at the Austrian Legation and handed in the Serbian reply. Giesl said he would have to compare it with his instructions, and that he would then give an immediate answer. As he knew that Serbia had already ordered mobilization, he had little expectation that the reply would be wholly satisfactory, and had probably written his answer to it before he saw it. He now hurriedly glanced at it to make sure that Serbia had not completely yielded on every point, and that, as Berchtold desired, he could reject it as unsatisfactory and break off diplomatic relations. Pashitch

46 Minute on Serbian Reply, July 28; B.D., 171.

47 K.D., 271. See also his letters to Jagow and to Moltke (K.D., 293) quoted below, ch. ix, at note 56.

had hardly returned to his office in the Ministry of Foreign Affairs, when he received a note from Giesl, that as the time-limit "has now expired and as I have not received a reply which is satisfactory, I have the honor to inform your Excellency that I am leaving Belgrade tonight together with the Staff of the Imperial and Royal Legation; . . . that from the moment this letter reaches your Excellency the rupture in the diplomatic relations between Serbia and Austro-Hungary will have the character of a *fait accompli*."[48] So great was Giesl's speed that he and his whole staff were able to catch the 6:30 P. M. train from Belgrade. He certainly established the speed record for the rupture of diplomatic relations.

In order that the measures for Austrian partial mobilization against Serbia might follow the diplomatic break as quickly as possible, Berchtold had made elaborate preparations to get the news from Giesl with the utmost promptness. After leaving Belgrade at 6:30 P. M., Giesl was to arrive at Semlin across the frontier at 6:40 P. M., and there to use the railway telephone which would be held open for him to inform Tisza at Budapest, who in turn would forward the message at once to Vienna.[49] Berchtold himself had gone to Ischl to attend an early dinner which Emperor Francis Joseph was giving to the Duke and Duchess of Cumberland. Toward noon he received an urgent telegram from the Russian Chargé d'Affaires begging an extension of the time-limit, on the grounds that the Powers had been taken by surprise and had not yet had an opportunity to study the *dossier* of Sarajevo evidence which Austria had promised them. But Berchtold replied that he could not grant any such extension. He added, however, that even after diplomatic relations with Serbia should have been broken off, a peaceful settlement could be brought about

48 Giesl to Pashitch, July 25; S.B.B., 40.

49 Berchtold to Giesl, July 24, 1:30 P.M.; A.R.B., II, 1.

afterwards by Serbia's complete acceptance of the Austrian demands. But in such a case Austria would expect to be indemnified by Serbia for the expenses incurred in military preparations.[50] It was clear that he counted confidently on a diplomatic break with Serbia to be followed by military measures against her.

In the evening Berchtold sat impatiently in the Emperor's Cabinet at Ischl waiting for the expected message, and finally went out to take a turn in the air. At quarter to eight the telephone rang. Count Kinsky took the message at Vienna and repeated it to Ischl:

> Minister Giesl telephones from Semlin to Budapest: two minutes before six P.M. answering note delivered; since unsatisfactory on several points, Baron Giesl has broken off relations and left. At 3 P.M. general mobilization was ordered in Serbia. The Government and Diplomatic Corps left for Kragujevatch.[51]

Baron Margutti jotted down the message on a slip of paper and ran with it to Francis Joseph. The old man took the paper in trembling hands, and sank into his chair, muttering in a choked unaccustomed voice, "*Also doch!*" ["So it has come after all"], as if he had hoped and believed to the last that a rupture might be avoided. Then, after staring at the paper for a while, lost in thought, he remarked, half to himself, "Well, the rupture of diplomatic relations still does not mean war." [52]

Meanwhile Berchtold had been quickly called in, and was closeted with the Emperor. He had been urged by Tisza, by Conrad, and by the Austrian Ambassador in Berlin, that Austria ought to order mobilization against Serbia at once; any delay or hesitation would be regarded

[50] A.R.B., II, 27-30.

[51] A.R.B., II, 26. Pashitch (S.B.B., 41) gives 5:45 P.M., and not "two minutes before six," as the time at which he handed the Serbian reply to Giesl.

[52] Margutti, p. 404.

as a sign of weakness and increase the likelihood of Russian intervention.[53] Using these arguments, it did not take him long to persuade his aged Emperor of the necessity of ordering immediately the partial mobilization contemplated in case of war against Serbia and Montenegro alone. The Kaiser's assent reached the Chief of Staff at 9:53 P. M., and was at once put into execution: July 27 was ordered as the "alarm" day, and July 28 as the first day of actual mobilization.[54]

The task of the Austrian Staff was a very difficult one. If there was to be war merely with Serbia and Montenegro, the situation was simple. It was calculated that the mobilization of about half the Austrian army—8 Army Corps with 20 infantry divisions—would be sufficient to secure a satisfactorily quick victory over the 12 Serbian and 4 Montenegrin infantry divisions. But if Russia made war, either before Serbia, or simultaneously, or after Serbia, it was all important that Austria should throw as great a mass of troops as possible toward the northeast, into the main theater of war in Galicia, leaving only a minimum number in the Balkan theater. Serbia's fate would be decided by the outcome of the fighting against Russia; moreover, Germany wanted Austria to send as many troops as possible against Russia, to relieve the Russian pressure on eastern Germany, while the bulk of the German Army was attempting to crush the French in the west.

Conrad and Berchtold were uncertain whether Russia would intervene or not. They hoped of course that she would not, and that the war with Serbia would be "localized." There is much evidence that this was also their expectation, though they were ready to risk the danger that Russia might move.[55] To provide as far as possible for the uncertainty whether Austria could fight Serbia without

[53] A.R.B., II, 21, 22, 32; Conrad, IV, 109 ff.

[54] Conrad, IV, 122.

[55] *Cf.* Conrad, IV, 110-124; 266 ff

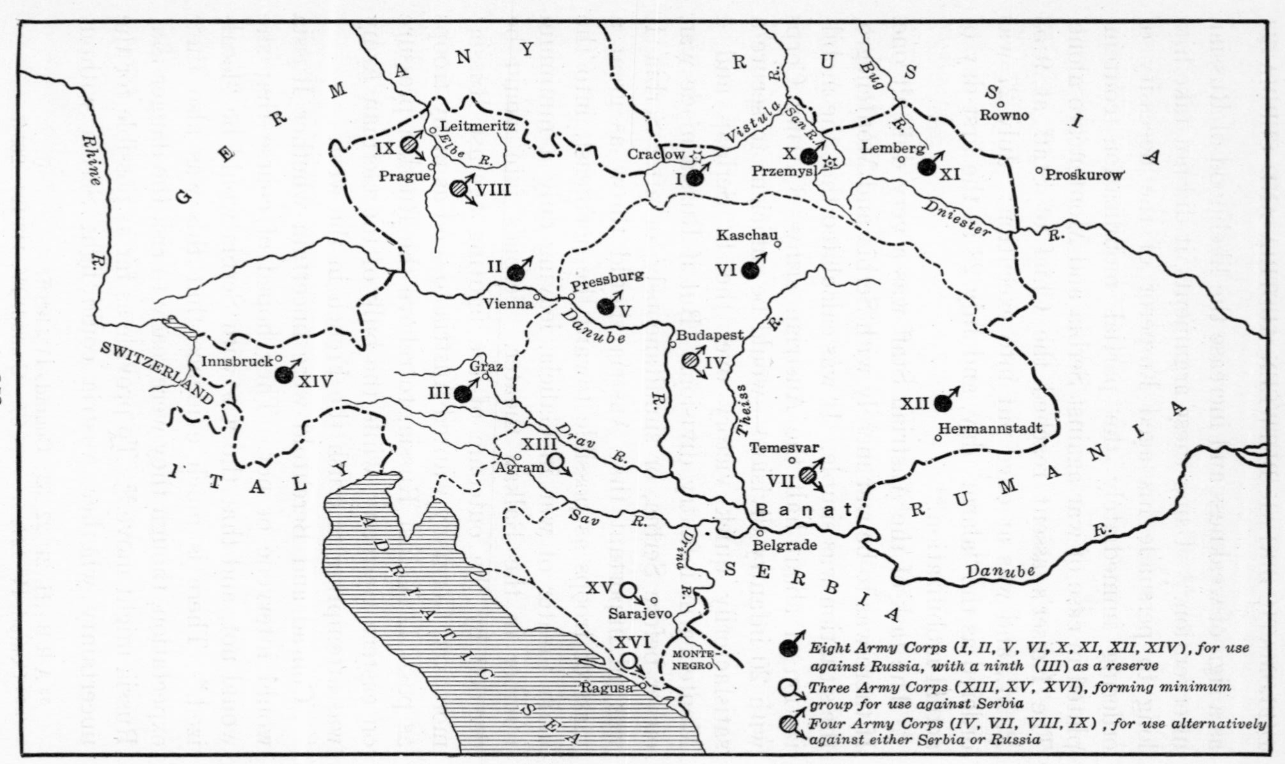

GERMANY
RUSSIA
ITALY
RUMANIA
SERBIA
ADRIATIC SEA
SWITZERLAND
MONTENEGRO
Banat
Rhine R.
Elbe R.
Vistula R.
San R.
Bug R.
Dniester R.
Danube
Drav R.
Sav R.
Drina R.
Theiss R.
Leitmeritz
Prague
Cracow
Przemysl
Lemberg
Rowno
Proskurow
Kaschau
Vienna
Pressburg
Budapest
Innsbruck
Graz
Agram
Temesvar
Hermannstadt
Belgrade
Sarajevo
Ragusa
I
II
III
IV
V
VI
VII
VIII
IX
X
XI
XII
XIII
XIV
XV
XVI
Eight Army Corps (I, II, V, VI, X, XI, XII, XIV), for use against Russia, with a ninth (III) as a reserve
Three Army Corps (XIII, XV, XVI), forming minimum group for use against Serbia
Four Army Corps (IV, VII, VIII, IX), for use alternatively against either Serbia or Russia

fighting Russia, or *vice versa,* Conrad had worked out mobilization plans which divided the Austrian forces into four groups: (1) a minimum Balkan group, consisting of three Army Corps—the XVth and XVIth in Bosnia and Herzegovina, and the XIIIth at Agram; (2) a group of eight Army Corps for use against Russia and if necessary against Rumania—I, Cracow; X, Przmysl; XI, Lemberg; XII, Hermannstadt, all near the Northeast Frontier; and II, Vienna; V, Pressburg; VI, Kaschau; and XIV, Innsbruck; (3) an alternative group of four Army Corps—IV, Budapest; VII, Temesvar; VIII, Prag; and IX, Leitmeritz—which could be used either against Serbia or Russia; in case of war with Serbia alone this group would roll toward the Danube to attack Belgrade and Serbia from the north while the first group were attacking from the west; but if Russia made war before it had become engaged on the Danube, it could be shifted north to the Galician front; and (4) the IIIrd Army Corps at Graz, to be held as a reserve, which could also be used either against Serbia or Russia. These strategic arrangements made it possible to mobilize half the Austrian army without mobilizing any troops near the Russian frontier, thus avoiding as far as possible giving Russia grounds for alarm. The eight Army Corps, accordingly, to which Conrad issued mobilization orders on the evening of July 25, were those comprised in groups (1), (3), and (4) above.[56]

As Austria and Serbia had now broken off diplomatic relations and were mobilizing against one another, the Great Powers began to put forward a variety of proposals for preserving peace.

[56] Conrad, IV, 122 ff., 266 ff.; R. Kiszling, "Die österreichisch-ungarischen Kriegsvorbereitungen und die Mobilisierungsmassnahmen gegen Russland 1914," in KSF, IV, 365-377, June, 1926; and the Diary Notes of General F. Demus-Morau, *ibid.,* IV, 549-552, Aug., 1926.

CHAPTER VIII

PROPOSALS FOR PRESERVING PEACE

EVERYWHERE it was anticipated that the Sarajevo assassination would tighten dangerously the long-standing tension between Austria and Serbia. Numerous proposals were therefore made by all the Great Powers to prevent this tension from developing into an armed conflict between the two exasperated countries, and, if this did break out, to prevent it from involving the other Powers in a general European conflagration. Some of these proposals—such as Sir Edward Grey's suggestion for "direct conversations" between Austria and Russia, Germany's plan of "localization," and the Poincaré-Sazonov move to head off an Austrian ultimatum—were made prior to the publication of Berchtold's demands on Serbia. After the stiff ultimatum became known, and especially after the diplomatic break and commencement of mobilizations in Serbia and Austria, the proposals for preserving peace came in a flood, sometimes running parallel and sometimes counter to one another. They were often confused, and not always kept perfectly clear and distinct even in the minds of their authors. Sir Edward Grey, for instance, both in writing his memoirs and in July, 1914, did not grasp clearly the importance of the distinction between mediation between Austria *and Russia* and between Austria *and Serbia*.

Sazonov also, in his nervousness, put forth in rapid succession so many suggestions that they became bewildering: a suggestion to head off an Austrian ultimatum,[1] to

[1] See above, ch. vi, at notes 24-27.

extend the time-limit,[2] to have Serbia appeal to the Great Powers,[3] to have England and Italy collaborate with Austria to end the tension,[4] to have Austria modify her ultimatum, even after it had been presented and answered,[5] to have the Great Powers institute a kind of informal international supervision over Serbia to prevent anti-Austrian plots in the future,[6] and above all to have England restrain Austria and Germany by proclaiming unmistakably her solidarity with France and Russia.[7] No wonder that at the British Foreign Office Sir Arthur Nicolson complained on July 27: "This is confusing. In three consecutive days M. Sazonov has made one suggestion and two proposals all differing from each other. . . . One really does not know where one is with M. Sazonov, and I told Count Benckendorff so this afternoon." [8]

Germany's main solution, until she read the conciliatory Serbian reply and began seriously to realize that Russia would not remain quiet, was the "localization" of the conflict which she had been urging for a week. But this was absolutely unacceptable to Russia and France, and therefore to England. As Sir Arthur Nicolson wrote to Buchanan: "The talk about localizing the war merely means that all the Powers are to hold the ring while Austria quietly strangles Serbia. This to my mind is quite preposterous, not to say iniquitous." [9]

Italy, embarrassed by her obligations to both groups of Allied Powers, and therefore especially desirous of preventing a European war, hoped to work with England to this end. On July 27 and 28 she made an excellent proposal.

2 R.O.B., 4, 5; Schilling's *Diary*, 33, 40; B.D., 117, 118; A.R.B., II, 27-30.

3 See above, ch. vi, at note 45; and B.D., 125, 221.

4 B.D., 170.

5 See below on "Direct Conversations" at notes 84-87.

6 B.D., 198, 203.

7 B.D., 101, 125.

8 Minute, B.D., 179.

9 July 28; B.D., 239; and Minute, B.D., 249. See also below, ch. ix, "Germany's Belated Peace Efforts."

If the Powers would give the advice, even after the diplomatic break of July 25, Serbia might be induced even still to accept the Austrian demands in their entirety; Austria would then be satisfied; Serbia would save her face by yielding to Europe and not to Austria alone; and the Powers could adjust the details by which Serbia would carry out the demands of Austria. The proposal seemed to be substantially acceptable to the Serbian Minister in Rome. But in the end it came to nothing, largely because it was not taken very seriously by the Entente Powers and was crowded aside by their other proposals, and because Austria quickly complicated the situation by declaring war on Serbia.[10]

To attempt to give an account of all these numerous proposals for preserving peace in July, 1914, would be tedious and futile. But it will be useful to review briefly at this point a few of those which were made before July 28, and which were of special significance, or seemed to have the greatest prospect of being successful, or have often been not clearly understood. They are the various proposals of Sir Edward Grey, and the so-called "Direct Conversations" between Vienna and St. Petersburg.

ENGLAND'S KEY POSITION

In most of the peace proposals, England was generally recognized as holding the key to the situation, for several reasons. Her direct interests in the Balkans were less than those of the other Great Powers, and, as Grey reiterated, the merits of the Austro-Serbian dispute were not his concern; it was only from the point of view of the peace of Europe that he would concern himself with the

[10] B.D., 202, 231, 276, 328; F.Y.B., 72; K.D., 249, 357, 432; Dirr, p. 152 f.; an anonymous article [by the French Ambassador in Rome, Barrère?], "L'Italie et les Responsabilités Austro-Allemandes de la Guerre," in *Rev. des Deux Mondes,* Oct. 1, 1927; M. Morhardt, *Les Preuves* (Paris, 1924), pp. 249-274.

matter, and about this he felt great apprehension. Now, just as during the Balkan Wars, he was looked to as the man most impartial and best able to take steps toward calling an international conference or providing some other means of preventing the two groups of Great Powers from coming into conflict. Moreover, England was not bound by any formal alliance with either group. And finally, it was realized that with her great sea-power she would probably be able to exercise a decisive pressure, by whatever attitude she might assume, both upon Franco-Russian and Austro-German, as well as upon Italian, policy. Therefore Russia and France besought Grey to preserve peace by indicating energetically to Germany that if war came, England would support them. And Germany besought him to preserve peace by putting pressure on Russia to remain quiet.

But Grey was unwilling, early in the crisis, to warn Germany energetically, because his Cabinet was divided on the question of England's eventual intervention; he could not make a threat which he might not be able to carry out; and he was fearful of saying anything which might encourage France and Russia to let themselves in for war, counting on support which the British Cabinet and Parliament might not be willing to render when the ordeal came. It was only very gradually that he acceded to the urgings of Russia and France, seconded by his own Secretaries, Crowe and Nicolson, and gave warning hints to Germany in the shape of announcements concerning the British Fleet, and later in plainer terms to the German Ambassador. Nor, on the other hand, was he willing to put restraint upon Russia, for fear it might break down the solidarity of the Triple Entente, cause "misunderstandings," and possibly wreck the Anglo-Russian Entente concerning the Middle East.

In the early summer of 1914, before the Sarajevo tragedy, and even during the days immediately following it, English minds were far more absorbed as to what might happen in Ireland than in the Balkans. The eternal Irish question threatened at last to reach a tragic culmination. Ulster was arming, and openly defying the Asquith Government to apply force through Sir John French's army. The Irish Nationalist Volunteers had also begun to arm. Ireland seemed on the verge of civil war. Hardly anyone in England appeared to realize how the European situation might be seriously menaced by a double murder in faraway Bosnia. Only a few men who had closely followed Continental politics, like Sir Arthur Nicolson and Sir Eyre Crowe, and perhaps Sir Edward Grey, at the Foreign Office, or who were responsible for the safety of the British Empire, like Lord Haldane at the War Office and Winston Churchill at the Admiralty, became somewhat apprehensive. Yet Lord Haldane had created a little standing army ready to be sent across the Channel at a moment's notice, and had been organizing a larger territorial force for the protection of England herself. And Winston Churchill had assembled for maneuvers at Portsmouth what he proudly but justly calls "incomparably the greatest assemblage of naval power ever witnessed in the history of the world. The King himself was present and inspected ships of every class. On the morning of the 19th [July] the whole Fleet put to sea for exercises of various kinds. It took more than six hours for this armada, every ship decked with flags and crowded with bluejackets and marines, to pass, with bands playing and at 15 knots, before the Royal Yacht, while overhead the naval seaplanes and aeroplanes circled continuously. Yet it is probable that the uppermost thought in the minds both of the Sovereign and those of his Ministers there present, was not the imposing spectacle of British majesty and might defiling before their eyes, not the oppressive and even sultry atmosphere of Continental politics, but the haggard, squalid, tragic Irish quarrel which threatened to divide the British nation into two hostile camps. One after another the ships melted out of sight beyond the Nab. They were going on a longer journey than any of us could know." [11]

Aside from the fact that Sir Edward Grey's time and attention were largely absorbed at this time in Parliamentary affairs and the acute Irish situation, there were many reasons why he at first felt no serious alarm for the peace of Europe. In spite of the persistent and fundamental undercurrent of friction caused by Germany's naval policy, his relations with Germany were on the whole better than they had been for many months. The treaties concerning the Bagdad Railway and the Portuguese colonies had been completed and initialed; they awaited only the final signature, which was delayed owing to the fact that Germany had to complete some arrangements with Turkey concerning the railway, and Sir Edward wanted to publish the secret Anglo-Portuguese Guarantee Declaration of 1899 along with the new German treaty, while Germany wished to delay publication.[12] Sir Edward Grey hoped that the signing of these two treaties, settling two long-standing sources of irritation, would do much to produce a better political atmosphere between Germany and England.

Another happy augury for more cordial relations was the visit of the British Fleet at Kiel. Though it was unfortunately interrupted by the tragic news of Sarajevo, this Kiel visit, according to the British Naval Attaché, was a great success, all the more so because of its non-political character. The Germans were honestly glad to see their guests and were looking forward eagerly to a return visit to an English port, being sick to death of the sight of

[11] Churchill, *The World Crisis* (London, 1923), p. 190 f.

[12] G.P., XXXVII, 96 ff., 452 ff.; Grey, I, 293, note; Gooch, *Camb. Hist. of Brit. Foreign Policy,* III, 477-481; B.D., p. x.

Heligoland, round which their monotonous naval work centered. One surprise for the British was the fact that they were beaten in football and the other sports, in which they had always supposed they had a monopoly of superiority.[13] Altogether the utmost good fellowship prevailed between officers and men on both sides, and the comments of the Press were less acrid and irritating than usual.

Also, the alarm and suspicion which had been aroused in Germany by the "leak" of the secret negotiations for an Anglo-Russian naval convention, intended to strengthen the solidarity of the Triple Entente and to satisfy Russia and France as an offset to England's Bagdad and Portuguese settlements with Germany, seemed to have been relieved, if not entirely dispelled, by Grey's denials in Parliament. Lichnowsky assured him that his statement in Parliament "had given great satisfaction in Berlin and had had a reassuring effect," and that Bethmann hoped that, if new developments or emergencies arose in the Balkans, they would be discussed as frankly between Germany and England as during the last Balkan crisis.[14] Grey agreed cordially, so that when Lichnowsky left for Kiel and a ten days' vacation in Germany, the two countries seemed to be on unusually good terms. Grey believed that he could successfully continue the main aims of his foreign policy: the cultivation of more intimate relations with France and Russia as a protection against Germany; the smoothing out of causes of friction with Germany; and at the same time the preservation of the peace of Europe by preventing any questions which arose from throwing the two systems of alliance into opposition.

13 Captain Henderson's report, July 3; B.D., 7.

14 Grey to Goschen, June 24; B.D., 4; Grey I, 293. *Cf.* also Jagow's statement a week earlier to Goschen, that he had so much confidence in Grey's "loyalty and straightforwardness that his mind was now completely at rest;" Grey, I, 283. For German alarm at the negotiations for an Anglo-Russian Naval Convention, see G.P., XXXIX, 591 ff.

It has often been said that war could have been avoided in 1914 if a Conference of the Powers could have met and discussed the Austro-Serbian quarrel. This is quite probable. As none of the responsible statesmen wanted a European war, it is possible, even probable, that a way out of even this most difficult Balkan conflict might have been found in a Conference, as it had been found during the crises of the Balkan Wars. The Conference which Sir Edward Grey proposed in 1914, however, it may be noted, was of four Powers—England, France, Germany and Italy—while the Conference which had succeeded in averting a general European conflagration during the Balkan Wars was of the six Great Powers, Russia and Austria being also included.

It is also commonly asserted by Entente writers that Sir Edward Grey did his utmost to bring about a Conference, but that Germany vetoed it, and that her veto places on her shoulders a further responsibility for the World War. This is the impression which Viscount Grey gives in his memoirs. He devotes most of a chapter to this question of "the Conference." Sazonov was ready, he says, "to let the Conference have its chance, if Austria would hold her hand. France and Italy were ready to coöperate. Germany did not raise the objection I had feared, but, while agreeing in principle, vetoed the Conference. . . . They [Bethmann and von Jagow] vetoed the only certain means of peaceful settlement without, as far as I knew, even referring it to Austria at all. . . . I remember well the impulse to say that, as Germany forbade a Conference, I could do no more, and that it was on Germany that the responsibility must rest if war came." [15] But this explanation is too simple, and is far from being wholly true. Viscount Grey does not adequately indicate all vicissitudes which his Conference idea met with, arising from various

[15] Grey, I, 308, 311.

other actions of his own, and from the objections and hesitations with which it was received by Russia and France, as well as by Germany and Austria. He did not in fact stick steadily to any one clearly defined Conference proposal, but, in his genuine desire to do anything and everything to avert a European war, made a variety of suggestions. Some of these, before being examined more in detail, may be summarized as follows:

(1) An early suggestion for "direct conversations" between Vienna and St. Petersburg, which was vetoed by President Poincaré. The "direct conversations" which did take place between Austria and Russia, July 26-28, which Grey and Nicolson regarded as "the best method," and which the Russian and German Governments both thought preferable to a Conference, were the consequence of a suggestion, not by Grey, but by the German Ambassador at St. Petersburg.

(2) A proposal for mediation between Austria *and Russia* by the four less directly interested Powers, "accepted in principle" by Germany, but disliked by Russia and France.

(3) A proposal for mediation between Austria *and Serbia* in a Conference of Ambassadors, made under the influence of Russia and M. Paul Cambon, at first rejected by Germany and Austria, but later accepted in modified form and *bona fide* by Germany, though not by Austria.

GREY'S PROPOSAL FOR "DIRECT CONVERSATIONS" BETWEEN VIENNA AND ST. PETERSBURG

In the intervals of the Irish trouble Sir Edward Grey had conversations with Prince Lichnowsky on July 9, 15, and 20.[16] The German Ambassador urged England to exercise restraint upon Russia. But Sir Edward Grey became more cautious and more regardful of Russia's point of

[16] B.D., 41, 68; K.D., 30, 52, 92.

view. It would all depend, he told Lichnowsky, on what kind of measures Austria might take. "Should a tremendously excited feeling arise in Russia as a result of Austrian military measures, he would not be in a position to hold Russian policy in check, and, in view of the vexation existing at the moment in Russia against England,[17] he would have to have some regard for Russia's sensitive feelings."[18] He gently hinted that "the more Austria could keep her demand within reasonable limits, and the stronger the justification she could produce for making any demand, the more chance there would be of smoothing things over." And, he added, he "hated the idea of a war between any of the Great Powers, and that any of them should be dragged into a war by Serbia would be detestable."[19] Lichnowsky, on his part, remained pessimistic as to his own Government's intentions, but optimistic as to Grey's efforts for peace and belief that "a peaceful solution would be found." To his hope that Russian and English influence would persuade Serbia to agree to justifiable demands, Grey replied that "everything would depend on the form of satisfaction demanded. . . . He [Grey] hoped that the quarrel might be settled and localized, for the idea of a war between the Great Powers of Europe must be repelled under all circumstances."[20]

Meanwhile, however, the vituperations of the Austro-

17 This vexation arose from British irritation at the aggressive conduct of Russian consuls in Persia, and from Russian irritation at the Anglo-Persian Oil Agreement of 1913, which secured to the British Admiralty oil monopolies at the head of the Persian Gulf in the "neutral sphere;" these were valued at $200,000,000, and would provide fuel for the newest and largest type of English naval vessels which Winston Churchill had just decided should be equipped as oil-burners (*cf.* Churchill, pp. 129-135; B.D., p. x.). To smooth away this vexation and to strengthen the solidarity of the Triple Entente was one of President Poincaré's objects in his visit to Russia at this time (*Cf.* Poincaré, *Les Origines de la Guerre,* pp. 201 f.; B.D., 49, 75, 164, 318).

18 Lichnowsky to Bethmann, July 15; K.D., 52.

19 Grey to Rumbold, July 20; B.D., 68.

20 Lichnowsky to Bethmann, July 20; K.D., 92.

Serbian Press campaign became more bitter and dangerous, and the reports from the Balkans more alarming.[21] Official reports reached Sir Edward Grey from Vienna, based on confidential information from Count Lützow, formerly Austrian Ambassador in Rome and now an intimate associate of Count Berchtold, which foreshadowed a very stiff ultimatum.[22] From Paris Grey received militaristic clippings from the *Matin* and the *Temps;* the latter was publishing a series of very chauvinistic articles from their Russian correspondent, setting forth Russia's great increase in military strength and preparedness for war with Germany.[23] And from St. Petersburg Buchanan reported in no uncertain terms Sazonov's statement that "anything in the shape of an Austrian ultimatum at Belgrade could not leave Russia indifferent, and she might be forced to take some precautionary military measures." [24]

Noting these more stormy indications on the sinking political barometer, Sir Edward Grey deemed it opportune to throw out a cautious peace proposal. Acceding neither to Lichnowsky's desire that he should put restraining pressure on Russia, which he knew would be resented by the two other members of the Triple Entente, nor to the desire of Russia for restraining pressure upon Austria,[25] which he feared would be equally resented at Vienna and at Berlin,[26] Sir Edward Grey chose a more cautious middle course. He made the confidential suggestion to Sir George Buchanan in Russia of what were later called "direct conversations" between Vienna and St. Petersburg:

> It is possible that the Serbian Government have been negligent, and that proceedings at the trial at Sarajevo will

[21] B.D., 43, 45, 53, 55, 61, 62.
[22] B.D., 50, 55, 56; quoted above, ch. v, at note 95.
[23] B.D., 52, 66.
[24] Buchanan to Grey, July 18; B.D., 60.
[25] B.D., 39, 60.
[26] *Cf.* Minutes on B.D., 76.

show that the murder of the Archduke was planned on Serbian territory. If Austrian demands in Serbia are kept within reasonable limits, and if Austria can produce justification for making them, I hope every attempt will be made to prevent any breach of the peace. It would be very desirable that Austria and Russia should discuss things together if they become difficult. You can speak in this sense if occasion seems to require it.[27]

A couple of days later Sir Edward Grey set forth his idea for "direct conversations" more fully to the Russian Ambassador in London, who evidently did not relish it, and to Buchanan:

I spoke to Count Benckendorff to-day of the apprehension felt about Austria and Serbia. . . . I said it was very desirable that the Russian Government should communicate directly with the Austrian Government. . . . Count Benckendorff spoke of the difficulty of making a friendly communication in Vienna; at present there was nothing to go on.

I said I had been thinking what might be done if I were in M. Sazonov's place. It might be possible for M. Sazonov to send for the Austrian Ambassador in St. Petersburg; to refer to the statements in the press that Austria was going to make some demand on Serbia; to emphasize the strength of pro-Serb feeling in Russia, and how strong and irresistible this feeling might become if there was a crisis; and then to ask the Austrian Government to take Russia into their confidence by telling them exactly the extent and nature of their grievance against Serbia, and what they felt it necessary to ask. It might be then possible for the Russian Government to get the Austrian demand kept within reasonable limits.

I also said that I had told Mr. des Graz, who was proceeding to Belgrade at the end of this week as our Minister there, that it was not our business to take violent sides in this matter, and that what he could say in Belgrade must depend on what case the Austrians presented. If they

[27] Grey to Buchanan, July 20; B.D., 67.

> proved that the plot to assassinate the Archduke Franz Ferdinand had been prepared and organized on Serbian territory, and that Austria had real grounds of complaint against Serbia, it would be possible for him to urge in Belgrade that the Serbian Government really ought to give to Austria the utmost assurances they could for the prevention of such plots against Austria being carried on in Serbia in future.[28]

This suggestion of Sir Edward Grey's was an excellent one, but it met with instant and emphatic condemnation from President Poincaré, when Buchanan proposed it to him during the visit to St. Petersburg:

> His Excellency [President Poincaré] expressed opinion that a conversation *à deux* between Austria and Russia would be very dangerous at the present moment, and seemed favorable to moderating counsels by France and England at Vienna.[29]

"Very dangerous" to have Austria and Russia converse with a view to coming to a friendly and peaceful solution of the Austro-Serbian conflict? One rubs one's eyes to see if one has read aright. Very dangerous to what? Certainly not to the peace of Europe. But perhaps to M. Poincaré's policy of having the Triple Entente stand as a solid block in opposition to Germany and Austria, refusing conciliatory arrangements with either of them, and preparing to force them to accept diplomatic defeat or fight against superior forces. For more than two years he had sought to tighten the Triple Entente in every way possible, and to prevent separate understandings by any one of its members with Germany or Austria. He had repudiated M. René's efforts

[28] B.D., 79. For Grey's proposals to the Austrian Ambassador for "direct conversation," see B.D., 86; and A.R.B., I, 59.

[29] Buchanan to Grey, July 22; B.D., 76 (omitted from B.B.B.). Poincaré (IV, 252) merely alludes to this in a couple of sentences, and gives an incorrect reference in his footnote ("73" for "75").

at conciliation by greater autonomy to Alsace-Lorraine.[30] When M. Crozier, the French Ambassador at Vienna, sought to establish better relations between Austria and Russia and France, and the listing of Austrian securities on the Paris Bourse, M. Poincaré thwarted his efforts; then he recalled him and replaced him by M. Dumaine, a less capable man, but a more docile instrument of his own policies. And in his memoirs he seeks to discredit M. Crozier by heaping ridicule upon his "Olympian thoughts," "vague suggestions which he mistook for ideas," and "cloudy vaporings." [31] According to Izvolski, M. Poincaré claimed also to have prevented the success of the Haldane Mission and the Anglo-German negotiations for a naval understanding.[32] During the Balkan Wars he never wanted Sazonov to enter upon any separate negotiations without first concerting a policy with the two other members of the Triple Entente.

M. Poincaré's contemporary telegrams and his later memoirs continually reiterate the desire to have the Triple Entente always concert together their line of action before any one of them approached Germany or Austria.[33] So now, in the more serious crisis of July, 1914, quite in keeping with his whole policy since he became Minister of Foreign Affairs in January, 1912, he thought "a conversation *à deux* between Austria and Russia would be very dangerous."

After Poincaré's decisive disapproval of "direct conversations" it is doubtful whether Buchanan even mentioned the idea to Sazonov, since his telegram to Grey, quoted above, does not speak of it, but continues:

30 *Cf.* Bourgeois et Pagès, p. 343 f.; Poincaré, I, 125 ff, 138 ff.; and the retraction which he was forced to make in the *Rev. des Deux Mondes*, Feb. 15, 1926, p. 885 ff.

31 *Cf.* Poincaré, I, 238-274; Ph. Crozier, "L'Autriche et l'avant-guerre," in *La Revue de France,* April 1 to June 1, 1921.

32 Izvolski to Sazonov, Dec. 5, 1912; M.F.R., p. 309; L.N., I, 365; Stieve, II, 377; *cf.* also Poincaré, I, 165 ff.

33 See above, Vol. I, chs. IV, V, *passim*.

> I also spoke to the Minister of Foreign Affairs, whom I met later in the day. His Excellency said that if Austria could prove plot had been hatched in Serbia there was no objection to her asking Serbian Government to institute judicial inquiry, and this, he believed, Serbia was ready to do. He thought, however, it would be advisable for three Governments [Russia, France and England] to counsel moderation at Vienna. This should be done in friendliest manner, and should not take the form of any collective action. He begged me to telegraph to you in this sense, and said he would speak to the President of the Republic to-day on the subject.[34]

These telegrams from Sir George Buchanan show that both Poincaré and Sazonov wanted to have Russia, France and England put pressure on Austria, which would force her to abandon her plans at the behest of the Triple Entente. And in fact, before President Poincaré's departure from Russia, Sazonov told Buchanan that the Russian Ambassador in Vienna was being instructed to concert with his French and British colleagues "with a view to giving friendly counsels of moderation," and hoped that Grey would give similar instructions. But the British Foreign Office Secretaries disapproved the suggestion and Grey decided not to act on it until next day.[35] Next morning he was informed of the text of the ultimatum which had already been presented at Belgrade the night before. Since England had delayed to fall in with the Poincaré-Sazonov plan and the ultimatum had already been presented, the French and Russian Ambassadors at Vienna made no use of their instructions to have the Triple Entente give Austria the intended warning.[36]

Thus Sir Edward Grey's first peace proposal for "direct

[34] Buchanan to Grey, July 22; B.D., 76.

[35] Buchanan to Grey, July 23, and Minutes; B.D., 84; for the details of this abortive move, see above, ch. vi, at notes 24-27.

[36] Bunsen to Grey, July 24; B.D., 97.

conversations" between Vienna and St. Petersburg fell to the ground, owing to Poincaré's decisive disapproval and desire to substitute in its place Triple Entente pressure at Vienna. The direct conversations which Sazonov consented to undertake later, July 26-28, after Poincaré had left Russia and no longer exercised such an immediate influence on the Russian Minister of Foreign Affairs, were owing to the initiative, not of Sir Edward Grey, but of the German Ambassador in St. Petersburg.[37]

GREY'S PROPOSAL FOR MEDIATION BETWEEN AUSTRIA AND RUSSIA

On the morning of Friday, July 24, Count Mensdorff called at Downing Street to communicate the Austrian Note to Serbia and the reasons for it. Sir Edward Grey's report of the interview shows his alarm for the peace of Europe:

> I said . . . that I thought it a great pity that a time-limit, and such a short time-limit, had been introduced at this stage, and the note seemed to me the most formidable document I had ever seen addressed by one State to another that was independent. . . .
>
> I was not, however, making these comments in order to discuss the merits of the dispute between Austria-Hungary and Serbia; that was not our concern. It was solely from the point of view of the peace of Europe that I should concern myself with the matter, and I felt great apprehension.
>
> I must wait to hear the views of other Powers, and no doubt we should consult with them to see what could be done to mitigate difficulties.[38]

This was a very busy and harassing day for Sir Edward. The Buckingham Palace Conference had just broken down and failed to bring about any solution of the Irish question.

37 See below, at notes 80-83.

38 Grey to British Ambassadors in Europe, July 24, 1:30 P.M.; B.D., 91. Confirmed by Mensdorff to Berchtold, July 24, 2:50 P.M.; A.R.B., II 14.

A Cabinet Meeting was to be held on it in the afternoon. On top of this problem now came Mensdorff's news of the ominous Austrian ultimatum. Grey had to talk with M. Cambon and Prince Lichnowsky, and he naturally took the French Ambassador first. Grey proposed to him mediation between Austria *and Russia* by the four less directly interested Powers—Germany and Italy representing the Triple Alliance, and England and France representing the Triple Entente. As this might mean that France would be expected to exert a moderating influence on her ally, Cambon did not like the idea. He preferred mediation between Austria *and Serbia,* which would probably mean that Austria would have to back down in some of her demands upon Serbia and accept a diplomatic defeat. How Cambon subtly tried to shift Sir Edward Grey over from mediation between Austria *and Russia* to mediation between Austria *and Serbia* may be seen in Grey's despatch to the British Ambassador in Paris:

> I told M. Cambon that this afternoon I was to see the German Ambassador, who some days ago had asked me privately to exercise moderating influence in St. Petersburg. I would say to the Ambassador that, of course, if the presentation of this ultimatum to Servia did not lead to trouble between Austria and Russia, we need not concern ourselves about it; but, if Russia took the view of the Austrian ultimatum, which it seemed to me that any Power interested in Serbia would take, I should be quite powerless, in face of the terms of the ultimatum, to exercise any moderating influence. I would say that I thought the only chance of any mediating or moderating influence being exercised was that Germany, France, Italy, and ourselves, who had not direct interests in Serbia, should act together for the sake of peace, simultaneously in Vienna and St. Petersburg.
>
> M. Cambon said that, if there was a chance of mediation by the four Powers, he had no doubt that his Government would be glad to join in it; but he pointed out that

we could not say anything in St. Petersburg till Russia had expressed some opinion or taken some action. But, when two days were over, Austria would march into Serbia, for the Serbians could not possibly accept the Austrian demand. Russia would be compelled by her public opinion to take action as soon as Austria attacked Serbia, and therefore, once the Austrians had attacked Serbia, it would be too late for any mediation.

I said that I had not contemplated anything being said in St. Petersburg until after it was clear that there must be trouble between Austria and Russia. I had thought that if Austria did move into Serbia, and Russia then mobilised, it would be possible for the four Powers to urge Austria to stop her advance, and Russia also to stop hers, pending mediation. But it would be essential for any chance of success for such a step that Germany should participate in it.

M. Cambon said that it would be too late after Austria had once moved against Serbia. The important thing was to gain time by mediation in Vienna. The best chance of this being accepted would be that Germany should propose it to the other Powers.

I said that by this he meant a mediation between Austria and Serbia.

He replied that it was so.

I said that I would talk to the German Ambassador this afternoon on the subject.[39]

In short, Grey said: mediation at Vienna *and St. Petersburg,* but only "after it was clear that there must be trouble between Austria *and Russia.*" Cambon said: intervene with mediation *at Vienna* between Austria *and Serbia at once,* and get Germany to propose it.

Cambon's account of this interview with Grey, however, supposing it is correctly given in the *French Yellow Book,* never mentioned Grey's mediation proposal in the form Grey really made it to him. Already, earlier that same

[39] Grey to Bertie, July 24; B.D., 98.

morning, Cambon had heard of the Austrian ultimatum from the Serbian Minister in London, and had hastened to get into touch with Benckendorff:

> In consultation with my Russian colleague, who thinks it extremely difficult for his Government not to support Serbia, we have been asking ourselves what intervention could avert the conflict. As Sir Edward Grey has summoned me for the afternoon, I propose to suggest that he ask for the semi-official intervention of the German Government at Vienna to prevent a sudden attack.[40]

Cambon did in fact urge upon Grey mediation at Vienna to prevent an Austrian attack on Serbia, as is seen from Grey's long despatch to Bertie quoted above. But Cambon either failed to get the point of Grey's own original suggestion as to mediation between Austria *and Russia*, or he purposely Cambonized it to fit in with what he had already agreed with the Russian Ambassador, as we see from his own account of his interview with Grey:

> Sir Edward Grey having discussed with me his desire to leave no stone unturned to avert the crisis, we agreed in thinking that the British Cabinet might ask the German Government to take the initiative in approaching Vienna with the object of offering mediation between Austria and Serbia, of the four Powers which are not directly interested. If Germany agrees, time will be gained, and this is the essential point.
>
> Sir Edward Grey told me he would discuss with Prince Lichnowsky the proposal I have just explained. . . . [After the interview with Grey, Cambon again talked with his Russian colleague]. Count Benckendorff thinks it right to attempt the *démarche* upon which I have agreed with Sir Edward Grey.[41]

[40] P. Cambon to Bienvenu-Martin, July 24; F.Y.B., 33.

[41] P. Cambon to Bienvenu-Martin, July 24; F.Y.B., 32; evidently this telegram, which the editors of the *Yellow Book* print under No. 32 should follow, not precede, that printed under No. 33, and quoted just above.

Cambon then departed from London to Paris this same Friday afternoon or evening, and did not return until late Monday night, July 27.[42] What his purpose was in going thither, or what he did there, is not revealed by any of the documents in the *French Yellow Book*. Perhaps it was merely to give aid and counsel to Bienvenu-Martin, who was inexperienced in foreign affairs and somewhat at sea as to his bearings, with a storm gathering and the pilot and captain of the French ship still absent somewhere in the Baltic. The temporary withdrawal of Cambon's strong personality and influence on Sir Edward Grey seriously worried the Russian Ambassador who wrote to Sazonov on Sunday: "Unfortunately Cambon is away, and will not return until Tuesday morning. I have asked that he be begged to speed his return. I fear that Grey is not sure of his public opinion, and he doubts if he will be supported, if he engages himself any further." [43]

On Friday afternoon, after his interview with Cambon, and after a long and wearisome Cabinet on the Irish question, Sir Edward Grey saw Prince Lichnowsky. After the latter had given him the German *communiqué* defending Austria's action and urging a "localization" of the conflict, Sir Edward Grey replied that if the ultimatum did not lead to trouble between Austria and Russia, he "had no concern with it." But he was apprehensive of the view Russia might take. Referring to Lichnowsky's previously

[42] The next despatch from the French Embassy in London, reporting Grey's Friday evening interview with Lichnowsky (F.Y.B., 37), is signed, not by Cambon, but by Fleuriau, the French Chargé d'Affaires. Fleuriau continued to sign despatches (F.Y.B., 40, 63, 66, 68, 69, 71) for the next three days, and on July 27 informed the British Foreign Office (B.D., 173): "M. Cambon returns at 11 this evening." His presence in Paris is indicated in F.Y.B., 53, and B.D., 183. In telling his story of the tragic days before the War to M. Recouly, Cambon says nothing of his Paris visit, and does not begin his narrative until the events of July 31; Recouly, *Les Heures Tragiques d'avant Guerre,* ch. ii, "A Londres—Récit de M. Paul Cambon."

[43] Benckendorff to Sazonov, July 26; L.N., II, 329.

expressed hope that he would exercise moderating influence at St. Petersburg, he said that now, in view of the extraordinarily stiff character of the Austrian Note, he "felt quite helpless as far as Russia was concerned." He then made his own mediation proposal, and added to it Cambon's plan for restraining Austria:

> The only chance I could see of mediating or moderating influence being effective, was that the four Powers, Germany, Italy, France and ourselves, should work together simultaneously at Vienna and St. Petersburg in favor of moderation in the event of the relations between Austria and Russia becoming threatening.
>
> The immediate danger was that in a few hours Austria might march into Serbia and Russian Slav opinion demand that Russia should march to help Serbia; it would be very desirable to get Austria not to precipitate military action and so to gain more time. But none of us could influence Austria in this direction unless Germany would propose and participate in such action at Vienna.[44]

Next day, having heard from Buchanan that M. Sazonov "thought that Russia would at any rate have to mobilize,"[45] Sir Edward Grey made to Russia his proposal for mediation between Austria and Russia by the four less directly interested Powers.[46]

In view of the sweeping statement often made that Germany blocked all Sir Edward Grey's peace proposals, it is interesting to note the attitude of Germany, and compare it with that of Russia and France.

Germany at once expressed approval. On Saturday

[44] Grey to Rumbold, July 24, 7:45 P.M.; B.D., 99. For Lichnowsky's account of this conversation see K.D., 157, and A.R.B., II, 15. Grey's telegram was also sent to British Ambassadors in Paris, St. Petersburg, Vienna, and Rome for their information.

[45] B.D., 101.

[46] He explained it directly to Count Benckendorff in London (B.D., 132), and telegraphed it to Buchanan in St. Petersburg (July 25, 2:15 P.M.; B.D., 112).

morning, July 25, when the British Chargé at Berlin presented it, the German Foreign Office was still optimistic that the conflict could be localized. It had been informed that Berchtold had told the Russian Ambassador in Vienna that "Austria-Hungary had no intention of seizing Serbian territory." It thought that this assurance might exercise a calming effect at St. Petersburg, but if not—if the relations between Austria and Russia became threatening—then Germany "was quite ready to fall in with your [Grey's] suggestion as to the four Powers working in favor of moderation at Vienna and St. Petersburg."[47] Meanwhile, in London, before the arrival of this, Sir Edward Grey and the German Ambassador again discussed the proposal for mediation between Austria and Russia. Prince Lichnowsky said "he thought Austria might with dignity accept it, and expressed himself personally favorable." Grey endorsed this, and said that "between Serbia and Austria I [Grey] felt no title to intervene, but as soon as it was a question between Austria and Russia, it was a question of the peace of Europe, in which we must all take a hand. . . . The participation of Germany would be essential to any diplomatic action for peace."[48] In response to Lichnowsky's report of this conversation and urgent advice to coöperate with England, the German Foreign Office immediately reaffirmed its approval of mediation between Austria and Russia, should "localization" become impossible:

> Sir E. Grey's distinction between Austro-Serbian and Austro-Russian conflict entirely to the point. In the former we do not want to interfere any more than England; as hitherto we hold that the question ought to remain localized through the non-interference of all the Powers. . . . Should

[47] Rumbold to Grey, July 25, 3:16 P.M.; B.D., 122.

[48] Grey to Rumbold, July 25, 3 P.M.; B.D., 116. *Cf.* Lichnowsky to Bethmann, July 25, 2:02 P.M. (K.D., 180), and his letter to Jagow (K.D., 179).

an Austro-Serbian strife arise, we are ready, reserving our known treaty obligations, to have mediation begin between Austria and Russia.[49]

After receiving this, Lichnowsky informed Grey, who was out of town, in a written note: "My Government accepts your suggested mediation *à quatre.*" [50]

What was the attitude of Russia and France toward the British mediation proposal? The Russian Ambassador objected to it, as we learn from a despatch of Grey to Buchanan which was suppressed from the *British Blue Book* of 1914:

> I told Count Benckendorff to-day of what I had said to the German Ambassador this morning as to the possibility of Germany, Italy, France and ourselves working together in Vienna and St. Petersburg to secure peace after Austria and Russia had mobilized.
>
> Count Benckendorff was very apprehensive that what I said would give Germany the impression that France and England were detached from Russia.[51]

[49] Jagow to Lichnowsky, July 25, 11:05 P.M.; K.D., 192.

[50] B.D., 145. Some writers, to prove that Germany blocked Grey's proposal, point to the fact that it was wirelessed to the Kaiser in Norway, who made the marginal note: "This is superfluous! Austria has already explained to Russia, and Grey cannot propose anything else. I will not join in—unless Austria expressly requests it, which is not likely. In questions of honor and vital interests one does not consult others" (K.D., 157). This marginal note, like so many of the Kaiser's annotations, is interesting for a study of his psychology. But it exercised no practical influence upon the actual course of events as far as this mediation proposal of Grey's was concerned; because the German Government had already expressed their approval through Lichnowsky, and, by the time the marginal note reached the German Foreign Office on July 27 (*ibid.,* note 13), the situation had already essentially changed, and Grey had made another proposal. On this same day, July 27, the Kaiser himself returned to Potsdam, and was very soon ready, as indicated later, to accept mediation on the basis of the Austrian occupation of Belgrade.

[51] Grey to Buchanan, July 25; B.D., 132, and note. The note, however, is misleading in saying that, while Benckendorff demurred to Grey's proposal, "M. Sazonov according to No. 125, was prepared to accept the idea;" Sazonov, in B.D., 125, was talking about mediation between Austria *and Serbia,* not between Austria *and Russia.* This letter of Grey's

France also, like Russia, took a negative attitude toward Sir Edward Grey's proposal for mediation between Austria *and Russia.* As has been indicated above, it was made to Cambon around mid-day on Friday, July 24; but it made little or no impression on him, owing perhaps to his eagerness to impress upon Grey the plan for mediation between Austria *and Serbia,* which he and Count Benckendorff had agreed upon together. Nor did Cambon report it to his Government. Sir Edward waited in vain for any reply from the French. He had to admit next day to Lichnowsky that "he did not yet know whether France would participate. He had talked with Cambon, but had so far received no reply. He counted firmly on the assent of France, although he did not know how far she was already committed to Russia." [52]

Thus, it was not so much Germany, as Russia and France, who failed to give approval to Sir Edward Grey's proposal for mediation by the four Powers if Austria and Russia should mobilize.

GREY'S PROPOSAL FOR A CONFERENCE OF AMBASSADORS, JULY 26

On Saturday evening, July 25, the European situation had taken a decided turn for the worse. Austria had broken off diplomatic relations at Belgrade, and Austria and Serbia had ordered mobilization against each other. In Russia war excitement and the military party were in the ascendant, the Tsar had sanctioned provisionally the mobilization of 1,100,000 men, and measures of the "Period Preparatory to War" were about to be put into effect. But the news of these ominous events had not yet reached London, where a more hopeful tone prevailed than the day before,

of which a part is here quoted, was at first included in the draft copy of the *Blue Book* of 1914 as No. 28, but then deleted by Sir Edward Grey's direction, and No. 28 was marked *"Nil."*

[52] Lichnowsky to Bethmann, July 25; K.D., 180; *cf.* also B.D., 116.

upon the first news of the Austrian ultimatum. There came a rumor—untrue as it turned out—that Serbia had accepted the Austrian demands. Germany had expressed approval of mediation by the four Powers at Vienna and St. Petersburg, if "localization" failed and the situation between Austria and Russia became threatening. As the situation seemed more hopeful, some of the British Cabinet left London for Sunday in the country. Winston Churchill, who had arranged to spend the day with his family at Cromer, decided not to alter his plan, and went peacefully to bed with a feeling that things might blow over. Sunday morning he went down to the beach and played with his children, damming up the little rivulets which trickled down to the sea as the tide went out. Sir Edward Grey, for his part, went down for Sunday rest to Itchen Abbas and his beloved birds and woods. Sir Arthur Nicolson was left in charge at the Foreign Office.

But on Sunday morning, those who had remained in London began to realize that the danger was greater than ever. At noon, Winston Churchill was called up from the Admiralty, and decided to return to London that evening. Without waiting for him, but with his approval, the Admiralty sent out at 4 P. M. the secret and significant order that the fleet was not to disperse for maneuvers as hitherto intended, but was to remain concentrated at Portland.[53] At the Foreign Office Sir Arthur Nicolson found much bad news which had come in overnight. Austria and Serbia had severed diplomatic relations. Serbia had ordered mobilization and removed the Government from Belgrade to Nish. From Vienna Bunsen reported that "war is thought to be imminent." It was reported that the German fleet had received orders to concentrate off the Norwegian coast and that the Kaiser had given up his northern cruise and was returning direct to Kiel, a step which the German

[53] Churchill, p. 199 ff.; Corbett, *Naval Operations*, I, 24.

Foreign Office regretted as likely to cause speculation and excitement.[54] From Buchanan in St. Petersburg came a long telegram:

> [Sazonov] thought that, in the event of an Austrian attack, Serbian Government would abandon Belgrade and withdraw their forces to the interior, while they would at the same time appeal to Powers to help them. His Excellency was in favor of such an appeal. . . . Were Serbia to appeal to Powers, Russia would be quite ready to stand aside and leave question in hands of England, France, Italy and Germany.
>
> [After telling of the Tsar's approval of the contingent mobilisation of 1,100,000 men, Paléologue's "formal assurance that France placed herself unreservedly on Russia's side," and his inquiry "whether the British fleet was prepared to play part assigned to it by Anglo-French Naval Convention," Buchanan continued:] His Excellency [Sazonov] assured me once more that he did not wish to precipitate a conflict, but unless Germany can restrain Austria I can regard situation as desperate. Russia cannot allow Austria to crush Serbia and become predominant Power in the Balkans, and, secure of support of France, she will face all the risks of war. For ourselves position is a most perilous one, and we shall have to choose between giving Russia our active support or renouncing her friendship. If we fail her now we cannot hope to maintain that friendly coöperation with her in Asia that is of such vital importance to us.[55]

This telegram, indicating that "Russia, secure of support of France, will face all the risks of war," might well have prompted Sir Edward Grey to the conclusion that it

[54] For all this bad news, see B.D., 130-138.

[55] Buchanan to Grey, July 25, 8 P.M., received 10:30 P.M.; B.D., 125. *Cf.* B.B.B., 17, in which the paraphrase of 1914 alters the meaning in the second sentence of the last paragraph by adding three words to read, "*if she feels* secure of support of France, she [Russia] will face all the risks of war." See also above, ch. vi, at note 109, for important passages omitted from the *British Blue Book* of 1914.

was high time to attempt to exercise a moderating influence at St. Petersburg—if he preferred to place the preservation of the peace of Europe above the maintenance of the Triple Entente. But he did not. Although Buchanan at St. Petersburg in the early part of the crisis attempted to exercise restraint upon Russia, no such effort was made from London. The British Foreign Office took the stand expressed in a minute by Sir E. Crowe on July 25:

> The moment has passed when it might have been possible to enlist French support in an effort to hold back Russia.
>
> It is clear that France and Russia are decided to accept the challenge thrown out to them. Whatever we may think of the merits of the Austrian charges against Serbia, France and Russia consider that these are the pretexts, and that the bigger cause of Triple Alliance versus Triple *Entente* is definitely engaged.
>
> I think it would be impolitic, not to say dangerous, for England to attempt to controvert this opinion, or to endeavor to obscure the plain issue, by any representation at St. Petersburg and Paris. . . .
>
> Our interests are tied up with those of France and Russia in this struggle, which is not for the possession of Serbia, but one between Germany aiming at a political dictatorship in Europe and the Powers who desire to retain individual freedom.[56]

England expected Germany to exercise restraint upon Austria not to move against Serbia, but unless Germany did so England was unwilling to exercise any restraint upon her Entente friends. Here was the evil of the system of alliances. On neither side was a Power willing to put out a restraining hand upon its ally or friend for fear of destroying the alliance or friendship. Instead, therefore, of dispatching a moderating telegram to St. Petersburg, England now merely decided to make a new peace proposal. Sir

[56] B.D., 101.

Arthur Nicolson, noting Sazonov's suggestion to Buchanan quoted above, wrote to Sir Edward Grey at Itchen Abbas:

> I think that the only hope of avoiding a general conflict would be . . . that you should telegraph to Berlin, Paris, Rome, asking that they shall authorise their Ambassadors here to join you in a Conference to endeavour to find an issue to prevent complications and that abstention on all sides from active military operations should be requested of Vienna, Serbia, and St. Petersburg pending results of conference.[57]

Grey at once approved, and on July 26, at 3 P. M., this proposal for a Conference of Ambassadors of the four Powers was dispatched to Paris, Berlin and Rome. It was also repeated to the British representatives at St. Petersburg, Nish and Vienna with instructions to endeavor to prevent active military operations pending the results of a Conference, as soon as they had received similar instructions from their Italian, French and German colleagues.[58]

This proposal for a Conference of Ambassadors at London at first sight seemed a good one and was certainly made with sincerity. A similar Conference of Ambassadors at London under Sir Edward Grey's leadership had functioned successfully during the Balkan Wars to prevent that cancerous trouble from spreading to the rest of Europe. Incidentally, however, its decisions had exasperated the authorities in Vienna and made the very word "Conference" anathema to them.[59] But the Ambassadorial Conference during the Balkan Wars was not quite the same thing as that which Grey was now proposing. The London

57 B.D., 139.

58 Grey to Bertie and others July 26, 3 P.M.; B.D., 140, 141.

59 A.R.B., III, 79. Sir Francis Bertie also gathered from the German Ambassador in Paris "that Austrians are particularly suspicious of words 'intervention,' 'mediation' and 'conference,' and suggested therefore that care should be taken to speak of conversations, moderating advice, etc.;" Bertie to Grey, July 27; B.D., 183.

Conference of 1912-13 had been composed of the Ambassadors of all the Great Powers of Europe, who represented the two opposing groups into which Europe was divided, instead of four only, as Grey had proposed. All the members of the London Conference, except perhaps Austria, had at that time, been genuinely anxious to preserve the peace of Europe. In 1912-13, Russia was not ready for war; France did not want a war over Balkan questions; and Germany did not want to be dragged into a war because of Austria's difficulties. But in 1914 these Powers were, for various reasons, less disinclined for war than in 1912-13. Moreover, the London Conference of 1912-13 had merely been called upon to settle differences between Turkey and the Balkan states, and among the Balkan states themselves. Though Austro-Russian rivalry had been strong, the London Conference had not been compelled to decide vital questions at issue between these two Great Powers.

But now in 1914, Grey was proposing the far more delicate task of attempting to decide a question which involved the prestige of the Triple Alliance and Triple Entente. He was virtually proposing a tribunal which was ostensibly fair and possible, being composed of two allies of Austria (Germany, Italy), and two friends of Russia (England and France). But, in view of Italy's nationalist hostility to Austria, of her ambitions in the Balkans which conflicted with those of Austria, and of her secret agreements with France (in 1900 and 1902) and with Russia (at Racconigi in 1909), it was likely that Italy would be more inclined to side with the Entente than with her ally.[60]

[60] At this moment, July 26, the British Ambassador in Rome was telegraphing to Grey: "I gather . . . that inasmuch as Austria did not consult Italy before delivering Note, and inasmuch as by her mode of attack on Serbia she would be constructively provoking Russia, the *casus foederis* contemplated by Alliance would not arise" (B.D., 148). See also Flotow to Bethmann, July 24 (K.D., 156) quoted below, ch. ix, at note 18; and Bethmann-Hollweg, *Betrachtungen zum Weltkrieg,* I, 133, 144.

In the proposed Conference, therefore, the "four less directly interested Powers" would be likely to stand three to one against Austria and Germany, instead of being evenly balanced two to two. This fact probably explains in large part Germany's ultimate rejection of this European "Areopagus." To Germany, the proposal had the additional objection that, though "active military operations" were to be suspended pending the result of the Conference, Russia could still continue her "preparatory measures," and so deprive Germany of her advantage of being able to mobilize much more quickly than Russia.

Whether purposely or not, in wording his draft, Nicolson had avoided indicating whether he intended that the Conference of the four Ambassadors should mediate between Austria *and Serbia,* which would be unpalatable at Berlin and Vienna, or between Austria *and Russia,* which would be equally unpalatable at Paris and St. Petersburg. Essentially, however, it was bound to mean intervention between Austria *and Serbia,* in order to prevent Austria from invading Serbian territory. This was clear from the way it was explained, to the German Ambassador in London:

> I have just spoken with Sir A. Nicolson and Sir W. Tyrrell. . . . Both men look at Sir Edward Grey's proposal to hold a Conference *à quatre* here as the only possibility of avoiding general war; and they hope it will secure full satisfaction to Austria, since Serbia would be more ready to yield to the Powers and give way to their joint wishes than to the threats of Austria, but the absolute condition for the success of the conference and the maintenance of peace would be that no military movements should take place. Should the Serbian boundary once be crossed, all would be lost, for the Russian Government could not tolerate this. . . . The localization of the conflict hoped for in Berlin, they said, was wholly impossible and must be discarded from practical politics.[61]

[61] Lichnowsky to Bethmann, July 26, 8:25 P.M.; K.D., 236.

In other words, Grey's new proposal was the kind of mediation which Paul Cambon had been desiring from the outset—mediation between Austria *and Serbia.* Though it was made with sincerity, Nicolson was not at all hopeful, as he wrote to Grey a little later on Sunday afternoon: "It seems to me the only chance of avoiding a conflict—it is I admit a very poor chance—but in any case we shall have done our utmost. Berlin is playing with us. . . . I am not hopeful. Still no chance should be neglected." [62]

What was the attitude of each of the Powers towards Sir Edward Grey's new proposal for a Conference of Ambassadors at London?

Italy immediately "welcomed the proposal," just as she had already welcomed the earlier proposal for mediation between Austria and Russia.[63]

Lichnowsky in London was in favor of accepting Grey's proposal, believing that the "localization" hoped for by Germany was no longer practicable and should be dropped. If, however, Germany should coöperate with Grey in preserving the peace of Europe, "German-English relations would be placed on a firm foundation for time everlasting." If not, everything would be doubtful, and it was necessary "to spare the German nation a struggle in which it has nothing to gain and everything to lose." [64] But when the proposal was made at Berlin, Bethmann telegraphed to Lichnowsky:

> We could not take part in such a conference, as we should not be able to summon Austria before a European court of justice in her case with Serbia. Sir Edward Grey

[62] B.D., 144.

[63] Rodd to Grey, July 26; B.D., 154. *Cf.* also B.D., 133, 189; F.Y.B., 72.

[64] Lichnowsky to Bethmann, July 26, 8:25 P.M.; K.D., 236; *cf.* also his despatches of July 27 (K.D., 258, 265, 266). The British proposal was formally made in Berlin on the morning of July 27 by an *Aide Mémoire* from Goschen to Bethmann; K.D., 304.

> makes a sharp distinction, as Your Excellency has expressly reported, between Austro-Serbian and Austro-Russian conflict, and is concerned about the former just as little as ourselves. Our mediation activities must be confined to a possible Austro-Russian clash. In regard to the Austro-Serbian conflict, the method of a direct understanding between St. Petersburg and Vienna . . . appears to me to be feasible. I therefore request you most urgently to advocate in London the necessity and the possibility of localization.[65]

Similarly Sir Edward Goschen, the British Ambassador to Germany, who had just returned to his post and talked with Jagow, reported:

> Conference you [Grey] suggest would practically amount to a court of arbitration and could not, in his opinion, be called together except at the request of Austria and Russia. He could not therefore, desirous though he was to cooperate for the maintenance of peace, fall in with your suggestion. . . . He added that the news he had just received from St. Petersburg showed that there was an intention on the part of M. Sazonov to exchange views with Count Berchtold. He thought that this method of procedure might lead to a satisfactory result, and that it would be best, before doing anything else, to await outcome of the exchange of views between the Austrian and Russian Governments.[66]

Germany rejected Grey's conference proposal for several reasons. She had not quite yet abandoned her hope, though she was to do so in a few hours, that the Austro-Serbian conflict could be treated as one to be "localized." She hoped, as Jagow told Goschen, that the "direct conversations" which were being opened between St. Petersburg and Vienna, might prove a more satisfactory method of averting trouble between these two countries. She knew also that a Conference would not be palatable to her ally,

[65] K.D., 248.

[66] Goschen to Grey, July 27, 6:17 P.M.; B.D., 185.

for Austria retained bitter memories of the decisions of the London Conference during the Balkan Wars, and of its impotency in enforcing its decisions against Serbia. Bethmann naturally feared that in such a Conference of four Powers as Grey proposed, Germany would inevitably be in a minority of one to three; Italy would side with the Triple Entente rather than with her own nominal allies, and so Germany at the Conference would stand alone in representing Austria's point of view against England, France and Italy.[67] Furthermore, from a military point of view, a conference of ambassadors might work to Germany's disadvantage; its decisions would be likely to drag out for days or weeks; but meanwhile Russia was making active military preparations; if the Conference should break down and war come eventually, Germany would be deprived of much of the military advantage which she enjoyed in being able to mobilize more rapidly than Russia, an advantage which she counted on partly to offset the superior numbers of the French and Russian armies. A final, and probably decisive, reason for the rejection of Grey's conference proposal was the fact that the German Foreign Office had received simultaneously a strongly worded annotation from Emperor William emphatically rejecting Grey's earlier proposal for mediation between Austria and Serbia.[68]

Though there are thus many reasons which made it natural for Germany to reject Grey's conference proposal, and though she herself a few hours later abandoned her "localization" plan, accepted the idea of mediation, and began to put pressure on Austria also to accept it, her

[67] Bethmann-Hollweg, *Betrachtungen zum Weltkriege,* I, 133, 144 f. Jagow, *Ursachen,* p. 118 f.

[68] For the Kaiser's annotation, which reached Berlin by wireless from on board the *Hohenzollern* at 12:07 A.M. on July 27, (K.D., 157, final note), see above, note 50. Lichnowsky's despatch containing Grey's proposal was also received July 27, 12:07 A.M. and when ultimately submitted to the Kaiser, "His Majesty disapproved of Lichnowsky's point of view" (K.D., 236, note 2).

rejection of the Conference was a grave political mistake. It was another stupid blunder, comparable to giving Austria a free hand at Potsdam on July 5, and to endorsing and justifying the Austrian ultimatum when urging "localization" on July 24. It strengthened the suspicion among the Entente Powers that Germany was not sincere in protesting that she desired to maintain the peace of Europe. It unfortunately made them doubt her sincerity, when, a little later, she genuinely tried to restrain Austria and induce her to accept mediation. As Sir Eyre Crowe noted, on hearing Jagow's negative reply to the conference proposal: "So far as we know, the German Government has up to now said not a single word at Vienna in the direction of restraint or moderation. If a word had been said, we may be certain that the German Government would claim credit for having spoken at all. The inference is not reassuring as to Germany's goodwill." [69] It was suspicion of this kind which largely contributed to the ultimate catastrophe.

France is also generally stated by Entente writers to have "sent in at once a completely favorable answer." [70] But as a matter of fact France appears to have hesitated. On the following day, July 27, the French Chargé d'Affaires in London twice called attention to the proposal, adding that it "ought, I think, to be supported." [71]

On July 26, the German Ambassador, at Paris, Baron von Schoen, had stated to Bienvenu-Martin, that "Austria has declared to Russia that she does not desire territorial acquisitions . . . but only to secure peace and quiet and

[69] Minute, July 28, on B.D., 185.

[70] Oman, *The Outbreak of the War of 1914-1918* (London, 1919), p. 48; Headlam, *The History of Twelve Days* (London, 1915), p. 106; Poincaré, *Les Origines de la guerre,* p. 223 ff.

[71] Fleuriau to Bienvenu-Martin, July 27, F.Y.B., 68, 69. *Cf.* also Mensdorff to Berchtold, July 26, 5:55 P.M. (A.R.B., II, 58): "Sir A. Nicolson to whom I spoke in Grey's absence is very much disturbed. . . . He has as yet practically no news from Paris."

exercise police supervision, and consequently it rests with Russia to prevent war. Germany is at one with France in her ardent desire to preserve peace, and she sincerely hopes that France will exercise a moderating influence at St. Petersburg." Bienvenu-Martin pointed out that Germany on her part might well act on similar lines at Vienna, especially in view of the conciliatory spirit displayed by Serbia. Schoen replied that this was not possible, owing to the decision not to intervene in the Austro-Serbian dispute. Bienvenu-Martin "then asked whether the four Powers—Great Britain, Germany, Italy and France—could not make representations at St. Petersburg and Vienna, for that the matter amounted, in effect, to a dispute between Austria and Russia. The Ambassador alleged that he had no instructions. Finally, the Minister refused to agree to the German proposal, since the Prime Minister is absent. Berthelot unfortunately was not present at this interview." Berthelot, the Director of the Political Department of the Ministry for Foreign Affairs, believed that Schoen "aims at intimidating France and at securing her intervention at St. Petersburg. All things taken together, and considering the whole attitude of Germany and Austria-Hungary, he [Berthelot] inclines to the view that these Powers are seeking a brilliant diplomatic victory, but not war at any price, although in the last instance they would not shrink from it. He regards an emphatic and energetic action by England at Berlin as useful." [72]

France in fact had no more desire to exert pressure for peace on her Russian ally, than did Germany on her Austrian ally. Such pressure might have tended to sow distrust between two allies just at the moment when they most

[72] Sevastopulo to Sazonov, July 26, tgs. nos. 187, 188; M.F.R., p. 514; Romberg, pp. 12-15; *Livre Noir,* II, p. 278; R.O.B., 28, 29, where parts are suppressed. For Schoen's account, see K.D., 200, 235, 240 and 241; and *The Memoirs of an Ambassador* (London, 1922), p. 181 ff.

M. BIENVENU-MARTIN (left) Acting-Minister for Foreign Affairs in July, 1914; M. PHILIPPE BERTHELOT (rear), Political Director of the French Foreign Office; FREIHERR VON SCHOEN (right), German Ambassador in Paris, 1910-1914.

needed to stand together, and would not have been welcome in the capital where it was exerted. In the case of France and Russia this is seen from paragraphs in despatches of Izvolski and Sazonov which were suppressed from the original *Russian Orange Book.* On July 27, immediately after his return from St. Petersburg, Izvolski telegraphed to Sazonov:

"Directly after my return to Paris, I discussed the situation with Bienvenu-Martin, in the presence of Berthelot and Abel Ferry. They confirmed the details of the steps taken by the German Ambassador, of which you have been informed by Sevastopulo's telegrams nos. 187 and 188. . . . Schoen laid especial emphasis on the expression of solidarity of Germany and France. According to the conviction of the Minister of Justice [Bienvenu-Martin], these steps on the part of Germany are taken with the evident object of disuniting Russia and France, of inducing the French Government to make representations at St. Petersburg, of thus compromising our ally in our eyes, and, finally, in case of war, of throwing the responsibility not on Germany, who is ostensibly making every effort to maintain peace, but on Russia and France. . . . Altogether, I am surprised how correctly the Minister of Justice and his colleagues understand the situation, and how firm and calm is their determination to give us the most complete support, and to avoid the slightest appearance of disunity between us." [73]

Fortunately for the French point of view, Sir Edward Grey's proposal was capable of being interpreted as including mediation between Austria and Serbia, as well as between Austria and Russia, for it spoke of "Vienna, Belgrade, and St. Petersburg." This was seen by Viviani, who informed Bienvenu-Martin from on board the *France,* "The action of the four less interested Powers cannot . . . be

[73] Izvolski to Sazonov, July 27; M.F.R., p. 516; Romberg, pp. 22-23; *Livre Noir,* II, p. 281-282; *cf.* also R.O.B., 35.

exerted only at Vienna and St. Petersburg. In proposing to exert it also at Belgrade, which means in fact between Vienna and Belgrade, Sir Edward Grey grasps the logic of the situation; and, in not excluding St. Petersburg, he offers on the other hand to Germany a method of withdrawing with perfect dignity from the *démarche* by which the German Government have caused it to be known at Paris and London that the affair was looked upon by them as purely Austro-Serbian and without any general character." [74]

Without waiting, however, for Viviani's reply, the French Foreign Office, on July 27, upon the repeated urging from London, finally accepted Grey's proposal, but did not want it acted upon until Germany had exerted pressure at Vienna: "Ministry for Foreign Affairs thinks that it would be dangerous for *Entente* Ambassadors to speak at Vienna, until it is known that the Germans have done so with some success." [75] It is, therefore, hardly true, as Professor Oman says, that "Paris sent in at once a completely favorable answer." [76]

When Grey's proposal was presented at St. Petersburg, Russia did not favor it. Sazonov had already entered upon "direct conversations" with Vienna, by which he hoped to induce Austria to accept modifications in her demands on Serbia. If Sazonov could accomplish this by conciliatory negotiations conducted at the same time that extensive military preparations were taking place in case they failed, he would have secured a great diplomatic triumph by his own efforts directly for Russia, without having to accept a solution of the crisis brought about by a conference of the Powers or by moderating counsels from France. So he at first preferred to pursue his "direct conversations," rather than have Sir Edward Grey take the initiative in calling a

[74] Viviani to Bienvenu-Martin, July 28; F.Y.B., 76.

[75] Bertie to Grey, July 27, 2:45 P.M.; B.D., 183; also 194, 211; and F.Y.B., 61, 70, 71.

[76] Oman, p. 48.

conference of Ambassadors. If the former failed, he could always fall back on the latter. This explains his negative answer to Sir Edward's proposal:

> The British Ambassador, upon instructions from his Government, asked me whether Russia would agree that England should take the initiative in convoking a conference in London of the representatives of England, France, Germany and Italy, in order that they might examine *à quatre* the possibility of a way out of the present situation.
>
> I replied to the Ambassador that I have begun direct conversations with the Austro-Hungarian Ambassador favorably; but I have not as yet received any reply as to the proposal made by me for revising the note by the two Cabinets. If our direct explanations with the Vienna Cabinet lead to no result, I should be ready to accept the English proposal, or any other, which would bring about a peaceful solution of the conflict.
>
> I wish, however, from this day forth, to put an end to a misunderstanding which slipped into the answer [of Bienvenu-Martin to Schoen]. In case it is a question of exercising a moderating influence at St. Petersburg, we reject it in advance, because we have from the beginning taken a stand which we cannot at all alter, since we have already met all the demands of Austria-Hungary which are acceptable.[77]

To this Izvolski replied reassuringly:

> According to my conversation yesterday at the Quai d'Orsay, the Acting Minister of Foreign Affairs does not for a minute admit the possibility of exercising a moderating influence in St. Petersburg, but only replied to the German Ambassador that it was not Russia, but Austria, that was

[77] Sazonov's tg. No. 1521 to Izvolski in Paris and Benckendorff in London, July 27, *Krasnyi Arkhiv*, I, p. 174; Romberg, p. 16; *Livre Noir*, II, p. 279. The first part of this telegram was also communicated to the Russian Ambassadors in Berlin, Vienna and Rome; the last paragraph, significantly enough, was suppressed from R.O.B., 32, but found its way in a curtailed form into B.B.B., 53; for an explanation of this curtailment, see B.D., 206, note.

> menacing the peace of Europe; and that, in any case, if there was a question of any moderating influence, this should be exercised not only in St. Petersburg, but first of all in Vienna. As a result of his conversation with Baron Schoen, the Minister declined to accept the German proposal.[78]

The last paragraph of Sazonov's telegram and the whole of Izvolski's reply, both of which were suppressed from the *Russian Orange Book* along with other passages which did not square with the Russian thesis that Germany was to blame and that Russia had done everything possible to avert war, throw a new light on Russian diplomacy in the July crisis. Russia and her French ally were insisting that Berlin exercise a moderating influence at Vienna, while Russia herself refused from the outset to accept any such influence, and was supported in this by France. In this respect Russia was pursuing an uncompromising attitude, threatening to the peace of Europe, exactly analogous to that of Germany from July 5 to 28, who had been insisting that France and England should exercise a moderating influence at St. Petersburg, while she herself refused to do likewise at Vienna. But there was soon a difference: by July 28 Germany had abandoned her hitherto uncompromising attitude, as we shall see later, and really began to attempt to exercise an increasingly strong moderating influence at Vienna; but France and England continued to refrain from restraining Russia, and Russia proceeded to the general mobilization, which she had been warned would make a European War inevitable.

Since none of the Powers, except Italy, gave an immediate and unconditional acceptance to his conference proposal, and since Russia and Germany decidedly preferred to await first the success of the "direct negotiations," Grey

[78] Izvolski to Sazonov, tg. no. 198, July 28; M.F.R., p. 517; Romberg, p. 30; *Livre Noir,* II, p. 283.

willingly put his own proposal aside for the moment. "I entirely agree," he telegraphed to Goschen, "that direct exchange of views between Austria and Russia is the most preferable method of all, and as long as there is a prospect of that taking place I would suspend every other suggestion. . . . It will no doubt relieve the tension and make the situation less critical." [79]

What were these "direct conversations" between Sazonov and Szápáry at St. Petersburg which originated simultaneously and moved parallel with Grey's conference proposal, and were partly responsible for its being dropped?

DIRECT CONVERSATIONS BETWEEN VIENNA AND ST. PETERSBURG, JULY 26-28

It is said by most writers that it was Sazonov who originated the attempt to find a peaceful solution of the crisis by direct negotiations between St. Petersburg and Vienna.[80] As a matter of fact, the idea had occurred to Sir Edward Grey at the outset, but had been put aside and lost to sight. It was the German Ambassador in St. Petersburg, Count Pourtalès, who was really responsible for bringing this peace proposal into practical operation.

On Sunday morning, July 26, after the break-up of the maneuvers at Krasnoe Selo and the other military decisions on the preceding afternoon,[81] Count Pourtalès and M. Sazonov happened to meet on the platform of the rail-

[79] July 28, 4:00 P.M., B.D., 218. Nicolson also, "puzzled by the fresh proposals which Sazonov makes almost daily," believed his last proposal to open up conversations direct with Vienna "seems the best procedure" (letter to Buchanan, July 28; B.D., 239); see also above, at notes, 1-9.

[80] *Cf.* Headlam, pp. 107, 117; Oman, p. 51. This is also stated by Paléologue to Bienvenu-Martin, July 27, (F.Y.B., 54) and is implied by Buchanan to Grey, July 27, (B.D., 179); but *cf.* Buchanan to Grey, July 29 (B.D., 271, suppressed from B.B.B.): Sazonov "does not wish reference to be made to the fact that it was at the suggestion of the German Ambassador that he had proposed direct conversation with Austria."

[81] See above, ch. vi, last part.

way station at Krasnoe Selo. They entered the same carriage and traveled up to St. Petersburg together.

Pourtalès, finding Sazonov much less excited than the day before, took advantage of this informal opportunity again to urge that Austria had no hostile intentions toward Russia, and was only seeking measures of safety to protect herself from the Serbian danger on her borders. Sazonov replied that Russia likewise had no desire for war; a bridge must therefore be found, on the one hand, to satisfy the demands of Austria, the legitimacy of which he recognized so far as they related directly to the instigators of the crime; and, on the other hand, to make their acceptance possible to Serbia; some of the demands would have to be toned down, and he urged joint action by all the Powers, including Germany, to bring this about. Pourtalès then urgently advised him to have a frank and friendly talk with Szápáry, the Austrian Ambassador at St. Petersburg, with whom Sazonov had had no words since the excited interview of Friday, when first confronted with the Austrian ultimatum. On arriving at St. Petersburg, Pourtalès then went to see Szápáry, told him of Sazonov's calm and conciliatory state of mind, and gave him the same good advice to seek a frank and friendly direct conversation with the Russian Minister.[82]

Acting on the German Ambassador's suggestion, Szápáry at once went to see Sazonov and had the friendly conversation for which Pourtalès had thus prepared the way. We have five accounts of the conversations: the first-hand accounts by Szápáry to Berchtold, and by Sazonov to the Russian Ambassadors at Vienna and London; and the reports by Pourtalès, Buchanan, and Paléologue as they heard it from the two principals.[83] It is worth while to

[82] Pourtalès's diary in K.D., IV, p. 161; Graf Pourtalès, *Am Scheidewege zwischen Krieg und Frieden* (Berlin, 1919) p. 19; Pourtalès to Bethmann, July 26, 3:15 P. M., arrived at Berlin 7:01 P. M., and immediately forwarded to Tschirschky at Vienna; K.D., 217.

give Szápáry's account, although it is long, partly because his narrative is more detailed than those of the others, partly because the most interesting parts of it were suppressed in the original *Austrian Red Book* of 1915, and partly because it throws very interesting light on Sazonov:

> Have just had a long conversation with M. Sazonov. The German Ambassador had already told me in the forenoon that early today, he had found the Minister [Sazonov] much calmer and more conciliatory. He had advised him to seek a conversation with me, for he knew that I was filled with the best intentions toward Russia, and how greatly I regretted that our action against Serbia met with so little understanding in St. Petersburg. Sazonov received me very cordially, in contrast to his decidedly piqued attitude on Friday. He spoke to me of his above-mentioned conversation with Count Pourtalès, and said that if I myself had not already come to him of my own accord, he would have begged me to visit him in order to have a chance to speak frankly with me. Last Friday, he had been somewhat taken by surprise and had not controlled himself so much as he had wished; besides, at that time, our conversation was a purely official one.
>
> I replied that I also had wished to have the opportunity to speak frankly with him, since I had the impression that mistaken ideas in regard to the character of our action were prevalent in Russia. We seem to be suspected of wishing to push forward into Balkan territory and to begin a march to Salonica or even to Constantinople. Others indeed went so far as to describe our action as the starting point of a preventive war against Russia, which had been planned by Germany. All these suppositions, I said, were partly erroneous and partly absolutely unreasonable. The aim of our action was self-preservation and self-defense against hostile propaganda of word, writing, and deed, which threat-

[83] A.R.B., II, 73; R.O.B., 25; K.D., 238; B.D., 170, 179, 207-209; F.Y.B., 54.

ened our existence. It would occur to no one in Austria-Hungary to threaten Russian interests, or indeed to pick a quarrel with Russia. Yet we are absolutely determined to attain the aim we have set before ourselves, and we consider the path which we have chosen the most practicable. As, however, the action under discussion was an act of self-defense, I would not conceal from him that every consequence which might arise had been considered by us. Nevertheless, I was quite clear, I said, that if a conflict between the Great Powers arose, the consequences would be most fearful, and then the religious, moral, and social order of the world would be at stake. In glaring colors I set forth, as Sir Edward Grey also has probably done here, a notion of what might follow if a European war broke out.

Sazonov agreed with me thoroughly and seemed uncommonly pleased with the purport of my explanations. He began assuring me that in Russia, not only he, but the whole Ministry, and, what is of the greatest importance, his Sovereign, were filled with similar feelings toward Austria-Hungary. He could not deny, he said, that in Russia there were old grievances against Austria; he admitted that he had had them too, but this belonged to the past and must not interfere with practical politics; and as far as the Slavs were concerned—though indeed he ought not to say this to an Austro-Hungarian Ambassador, he said—he had no sympathy at all for the Balkan Slavs. In fact, they were a heavy burden for Russia, and we could hardly imagine what Russia had already had to suffer from them.

Our aim, he said, as I had described it to him, was an entirely legitimate one, but he considered the path we were pursuing to attain it was not the safest way. He said the Note which we had presented was not happy in its form. He had been studying it meanwhile, and, if I had time, he would like to look it through once more with me. I remarked that I was at his service, but was not authorized either to discuss the text of the Note with him nor to interpret it. His remarks, however, would of course be of interest. The Minister then went through all the points of the Note, and today found seven of the ten points acceptable without great difficulty; only the two points [5 and 6] dealing with the collaboration of Austro-Hungarian officials in Serbia, and the point [4] dealing with the removal of officers and civil servants to be designated *ad libitum* by us seemed to him to be unacceptable in their present form; with regard to Point 5 I was in a position to give an authentic interpretation in the sense of your Excellency's telegram No. 172 of July 25; [84] with regard to the other two points, I said I did not know how my Government interpreted them, but that they were both necessary demands. M. Sazonov thought that one might for instance have in mind consular intervention at the legal proceedings; and concerning the dismissal of officials, proofs of the guilt of the persons accused would still have to be produced. Otherwise, King Peter would run the risk of being killed at once. I replied that this view of the case by the Minister made the best justification of our action in Serbia. M. Sazonov said that we ought to remember that the Karageorgevitch family would, without doubt, be the last dynasty in Serbia. Did we want to set up on our frontier an anarchistic witches's caldron? Surely not! I replied that we certainly had an interest in the maintenance of the monarchical form of government, but also, that the last remark of the Minister again proved how necessary firm action on our part in Serbia was.

By way of summing up what had been said, the Minister declared that in the matter of the Note, it was really merely a question of phraseology, and that perhaps a more acceptable way for us could be found, by which these difficulties could be gotten over. Would we accept, he said, the mediation of our ally, the King of Italy, or that of the

[84] Berchtold to Szápáry, telegram no. 172, July 25, 1 P.M., A.R.B., II, 38: "By point 5 we mean 'collaboration' in the creation of a secret '*bureau de sûreté* in Belgrade, which would function like the analogous Russian creations in Paris and Berlin, and would coöperate with the Serbian police and administrative boards." It must be remembered that at the time of this interview Sazonov and Szápáry were not yet aware of the text of the Serbian reply (*cf.* B.D., 207-209).

King of England? I replied that I was not in a position to express an opinion; that I did not know what dispositions my Government had already taken; that matters had already begun to move; and that certain things could not be retracted when once they had been started. Moreover, the Serbians had already mobilized yesterday [Saturday, July 25], and what else had happened since then, I did not know.

At the close of the conversation, M. Sazonov again in the warmest words expressed his pleasure at the explanations which I had given and which had materially calmed him. He would also, he said, make a report of our conversation to Tsar Nicholas, whom he would see day after to-morrow [Tuesday, July 28], which was his day for being received in audience.

Russian policy has traveled a long distance in two days —from the first rude rejection of our procedure and from the proposition for a judicial investigation of our *dossier*, making a European question out of the whole affair; and from that point on again to a recognition of the legitimacy to our claims and to a request for mediators. Nevertheless, we must not overlook the fact that along with this backing-water policy on the part of the diplomatists, there is setting in a lively activity on the part of the militarists, as a result of which Russia's military, and therefore also her diplomatic, situation threatens daily to become less favorable for us.

P.S. Incidentally in the course of the conversation, M. Sazonov asked whether I could let him see our *dossier;* upon my replying that I was not in possession of a copy, he asked whether it could not be shown to M. Shebeko [Russian Ambassador] in Vienna.[85]

[85] Szápáry to Berchtold, July 27, 2:15 P.M. [July 26, 2:15 P.M., or July 27, 2:15 A.M.]; A.R.B., II, 73. This telegram is also dated '27' instead of '26' by Gooss, p. 206, and in the *Austrian Red Book* of 1915. That 'July 27, 2:15 P.M.' is incorrect is evident from the fact that it bears the serial number '165,' and must therefore be prior to number '168,' which was dispatched on July 27 at 4:30 A.M. The other accounts make it clear that this interview took place around noon or a little later on July 26. As it is doubtful whether such a long telegram could have been put into cipher by 2:15 P.M. on Sunday,

Pourtalès' Sunday advice to Sazonov and Szápáry thus seemed likely to bear good results by opening admirably the way to "direct conversations," and for it he was warmly thanked by both when he saw them later in the day.

In the evening, after talking with both men again, he reported:

> Count Szápáry had an extended interview this afternoon with Sazonov. Both men, with whom I talked after it, were favorably impressed by it. . . . [Here follows a summary of the interview, similar to Szápáry's account.] The Minister begged me urgently to tell him whether I could not make some sort of a proposal. In reply I emphasized the fact that I was not authorized to make any proposals, and therefore could only express my personal views; but that the following way seemed to me perhaps practicable. In case the Vienna Cabinet should consent to modify somewhat the form of its demands, as the expressions of Count Szápáry seemed to indicate was not altogether out of the question, perhaps an attempt could be made, with this in view, to get into touch with Austria directly. Should an agreement result from this, then . . . [cipher group lacking] Serbia could be advised by Russia to accept the demands of Austria on the basis agreed upon between Russia and Austria, and to let the Austrian Government know this through the mediation of a third Power.
>
> Sazonov, upon whom I again strongly impressed the fact that I did not speak in the name of my Government, declared that he would at once telegraph to the Russian Ambassador in Vienna along the lines of my proposal.[86]

Accordingly on Sunday evening Sazonov telegraphed to the Russian Ambassador in Vienna informing him of the

one may conclude that it was probably dispatched on July 27 at 2:15 A. M., 'P. M.' being a misprint for 'A. M.' It arrived at Vienna at 4:30 P. M., which would be about 16 hours or the normal period of transmission between Vienna and St. Petersburg at this congested time.

[86] Pourtalès to Bethmann, July 26, 10:10 P.M., arrived July 27, 12:45 A.M.; K.D., 238.

interview with Szápáry. He instructed him to ask Berchtold to authorize Szápáry to discuss at St. Petersburg a redrafting of certain points in the ultimatum which would satisfy Austria's main demands and yet be acceptable to Serbia.[87] Thus was opened the way for "direct conversations," which Berlin preferred to Grey's conference proposal, which the British Foreign Office approved, and which Paléologue also "believed preferable to any other procedure and likely to succeed;" as he summed it up, Sazonov proposed to Austria: "Take back your ultimatum; modify its form; and I will guarantee you the result." [88]

Unfortunately, however, all these hopes were misplaced, owing to Berchtold's obstinacy and determination to proceed with his plan of military action against Serbia. Proposals for preserving peace, instead of being accepted by him, decided him to forestall them by presenting Europe with the *fait accompli* of an Austrian Declaration of War on Serbia.

SUMMARY

Such were a few of the more important proposals for preserving peace, prior to July 28; they all came to nothing.

Grey's original suggestion for "direct conversations," vetoed by Poincaré as "very dangerous," was quickly dropped and completely lost to sight.

The Entente efforts to have Austria extend the time-limit were either directly rejected by Vienna, or rendered impossible by the shortness of the time within which the Powers had to act.

Grey's proposal for mediation between Austria and Russia, accepted in principle by Germany, was not immediately accepted by France, who wanted mediation between Austria and Serbia, nor by the Russian Ambassador in Lon-

87 Sazonov to Shebeko, July 26; R.O.B., 25.

88 Paléologue to Bienvenu-Martin, July 26; F.Y.B., 54; *cf.* also Paléologue, I, 28.

don who was "very apprehensive" that it would encourage Germany in the impression that the Triple Entente was lacking in solidarity.

Grey's proposal for a conference of the Ambassadors of four Powers, rejected for various reasons by Germany, not accepted immediately by France, and put aside by Russia in favor of "direct conversations," was quickly suspended by its author, who also agreed that "the direct exchange of views between Vienna and St. Petersburg is the most preferable of all."

But these "direct conversations," suggested by the German Ambassador in St. Petersburg, and taken up by Sazonov, were thwarted by Berchtold's refusal to consent to any modification of his demands, and by his declaration of war on Serbia with the deliberate purpose of forestalling any kind of mediation which might prevent Austrian military action against Serbia.

As it took many hours for telegrams to come and go, and as the situation changed rapidly from day to day, it was essential for the success of these various peace proposals that they should be accepted immediately. But they were not so accepted. With the exception of England and Italy, the different Powers, for one reason or another, in the case of each proposal, either preferred other methods, or delayed immediate acceptance, or gave a negative reply. So the proposals for preserving peace made prior to the Austrian Declaration of War on Serbia fell to the ground. After Austria had faced Europe with the *fait accompli,* it was more difficult than ever to get satisfactory peace proposals accepted.

CHAPTER IX

GERMANY'S BELATED PEACE EFFORTS

UNTIL Monday, July 27, Bethmann and his colleagues at Berlin had adhered consistently to their policy of hoping and insisting that the Austro-Serbian conflict could and should be localized. Early on Sunday afternoon, July 26, having heard of some of the Russian military decisions at Krasnoe Selo and that "all preparations are being made for mobilization against Austria,"[1] Bethmann again stated Germany's attitude and sought to dissuade Russia from taking mobilization measures which might endanger the peace of Europe:

> Since Count Berchtold has stated to Russia that Austria wishes to make no territorial acquisitions in Serbia, but only to bring about quiet, maintenance of European peace depends on Russia alone. Confiding in Russia's love of peace and in our long-established friendly relations, we trust that she will take no step that will seriously endanger the peace of Europe.[2]

At the same time, in similar telegrams to London and Paris, Bethmann urged England and France to exercise a

[1] Pourtalès to Bethmann, July 25, received July 26, 3:28 A.M., K.D., 194.

[2] Bethmann to Pourtalès, July 26, 1:35 P.M.; K.D., 198. Later in the evening (7:15 P.M.; K.D., 219) he made a stronger appeal, indicating his willingness "to support Russia's desire not to have the integrity of the Serbian Kingdom placed in question." Both communications "made a very good impression" on Sazonov, who said "a way must be found of giving Serbia her deserved lesson while sparing her sovereign rights," as might be done if Germany would coöperate in influencing Austria, to moderate some of her demands (Pourtalès to Bethmann, July 28; K.D., 282).

moderating influence at St. Petersburg. But these failed completely of their desired effect.[3]

Similarly on Monday morning, July 27, after rejecting Grey's conference proposal in favor of "direct negotiations," Bethmann telegraphed to Paris: "We cannot mediate in the conflict between Austria and Serbia, but possibly later between Austria and Russia." This suggestion of mediation between Austria and Russia hints at the beginning of a change in his attitude—the first sign of an eventual abandonment of "localization," and the possible adoption of some mediatory rôle to secure an agreement between Vienna and St. Petersburg. Pourtalès's telegrams, with the news of "direct conversations," were at once forwarded, with slight omissions and without comment, to Tschirschky at Vienna.[4] And Jagow told the Russian Chargé d'Affaires "that he could not advise Austria to give way, but that the very fact of Pourtalès's telegram being transmitted to Vienna means that he rather recommended such a way out of the situation." [5] By Monday evening there were further signs that Bethmann was beginning to waver in his mind as to the wisdom of his "localization" policy.

GERMAN DOUBTS AS TO "LOCALIZATION"

An important factor in Germany's immediate decisions was the hurried return of the Kaiser to Potsdam on the afternoon of July 27.[6] "The Foreign Office," Jagow was

[3] K.D., 199, 200. Lichnowsky could not see Grey, who had gone out of town over Sunday; but from talks with Nicolson and Tyrrell he concluded that "localization" must be abandoned in favor of Grey's mediation proposal (K.D., 218, 236). In Paris Bienvenu-Martin at first seemed ready to exercise moderation at St. Petersburg, after Germany had shown that she was exercising it at Vienna (K.D., 235, 240, 241, 252). But Berthelot and Sazonov were emphatically opposed to any pressure being put upon Russia (see above, p. 391 f.).

[4] K.D., 217, 238, notes.

[5] Bronevski to Sazonov, July 27; *Krasnyi Arkhiv,* I, p. 172; the last clause is suppressed from R.O.B., 38.

[6] At 3:00 P.M. according to Moltke (*Erinnerungen,* p. 381,) who had a conference with him shortly afterwards.

reported to have said, "regret this step which was taken on His Majesty's own initiative. They fear that His Majesty's return may cause speculation and excitement." [7] During his northern cruise he had been furnished by Bethmann with scanty but fairly optimistic reports, calculated to keep the Kaiser calm and deter him from giving any orders to the German Fleet which might cause alarm.[8] But Bethmann had been unsuccessful. Hearing from the Admiralty that the Kaiser, on the strength of a Wolff telegram, had directed the Fleet to make preparations to return home, Bethmann "ventured most humbly to advise that Your Majesty order no premature return of the Fleet." Upon this the Kaiser made the characteristic annotation:

> Unbelievable assumption! Unheard of! It never entered my mind!!! This was done on report of my Minister about the mobilization at Belgrade! This *may* cause mobilization of Russia; *will* cause mobilization of Austria. In this case I must keep my fighting forces by land and sea *collected*. In the Baltic there is not a single ship!! Moreover, I am not accustomed to take military measures on the strength of one Wolff telegram, but on that of the general situation, and that situation the *Civilian* Chancellor does not yet grasp.[9]

The Kaiser had also been irritated while still at sea, because it was through a newspaper agency, and not officially through Bethmann, that he had first learned the terms of Austria's demands on Serbia.[10] As the Kaiser neared Berlin, Bethmann sent him another optimistic summary of the situation, and prepared a sheaf of the latest

7 Rumbold to Grey, July 26; B.D., 147.

8 K.D., 67, 116, 125, 182, 191, 197, 221.

9 July 25; K.D., 182. The Minister at Belgrade had reported on the evening of July 24: "Mobilization is already in full swing" (K.D., 158); the news was premature when sent, but true when it reached the Kaiser on July 25 at 3:45 P. M.

10 Kaiser to Foreign Office, July 26; K.D., 231.

telegrams, which had poured into the Foreign Office, to be given him upon his arrival at Potsdam.[11]

The military and naval leaders had also returned to Berlin by the afternoon of July 27. Moltke, before the crisis arose, had planned to return from his cure at Karlsbad on July 25, but delayed a day.[12] On his arrival he talked with Bethmann and agreed that an attitude of calm should prevail, but took also the precaution of sending to the Foreign Office a draft in his own hand of the ultimatum to be sent to Belgium in case of war.[13] After talking with Bethmann again next morning, the 27th, he wrote to his wife: "The situation continues to be decidedly not clear. Not very quickly will it clear up; it will be some fourteen days before one can know or say anything definite." [14]

Admiral Tirpitz had been requested by Bethmann on July 24 not to return from his summer home in Switzerland, in order to avoid arousing alarming comment which might embarrass the Foreign Office in its "localization" policy. Nevertheless, on his own responsibility, the Grand Admiral also returned to Berlin on July 27, convinced that Bethmann was pursuing a perilous path in allowing such tension to develop with Russia in the foolish hope that an Austro-Serbian conflict could be localized, and that even in case of war on the Continent England would remain neutral. "The Chancellor," he had written to a subordinate just before leaving Switzerland, "is absolutely on the wrong track, wrapped up in his idea of winning the favor of perfidious Albion. . . . We must, at all costs, come to an understanding with Russia, and play the Bear and the Whale against each other." [15]

11 Bethmann to Kaiser, July 27, 11:20 A.M.; K.D., 245.

12 K.D., 74, 197.

13 K.D., 376, note 1.

14 Moltke, *Erinnerungen*, p. 381. This indicates that he still supposed Austria would not declare war on Serbia until Conrad had completed the concentration of the Austrian forces calculated for August 12.

15 Tirpitz, *Erinnerungen* (Berlin, 1920), p. 150; *cf.* also pp. 213 f. and 236 f. Tirpitz, according to his later memoirs, would have liked to see

The Kaiser and his officials, who were now back in Berlin, were all vexed at the way in which the Chancellor had kept them absent from the capital and insufficiently informed. They were seriously alarmed at the way Bethmann had allowed Berchtold to draw so heavily upon the blank check of July 5. They had been told that, in order to secure the successful "localization" of the Austro-Serbian dispute, calm was necessary; but they were doubtless of the same mind as the Kaiser, who, while at sea, pencilled ironically on one of Bethmann's admonitions to calmness in spite of rumors of Russian mobilization: "To remain calm is the citizens' first duty! just keep calm, always keep calm!! A calm mobilization is something new, indeed!" [16]

They saw that a serious crisis was very rapidly developing for which no special military preparations had been made, and for which the diplomatic situation began to look unfavorable. Russia, drawing encouragement from France and England, was making louder objections and more wide-reaching military preparations than had been anticipated. Lichnowsky's reports from London were pessimistic: "Since the appearance of the Austrian demands, nobody here believes in localizing conflict. . . . Consider moment arrived to start mediation along lines suggested by Sir Edward Grey"; Grey's secretary "pointed out to me, repeatedly and with emphasis, the immense importance of Serbia's territory remaining unviolated until the question of the conference had been settled, as otherwise every effort would have been in vain and the world war would be inevitable. The localization of the conflict as hoped for in Berlin

Bethmann ousted from the Chancellorship, and his incompetent subordinate, Jagow, replaced by some strong and able man like Hintze, who unfortunately, however, at the moment was sitting in Mexico. But though the Kaiser was irritated at Bethmann, he declared on July 29 that "he could not part with this man, because he enjoys the confidence of Europe" (*ibid.*, p. 237)

[16] K.D., 197.

was wholly impossible, and must be dropped from the calculations of practical policies." [17]

The Italian Foreign Minister, San Giuliano, had declared that, since Austria had not consulted her ally "before entering upon a move so portentously aggressive, . . . Italy could not consider herself bound in connection with the further consequences. . . . The Austrian Note was worded so aggressively and so ineptly, that the public opinion both of Europe and of Italy would be against Austria—no Italian Government could stand against it. . . . The Triple Alliance compact was an obligation in connection with a defensive war; Austria was now proceeding aggressively; and Italy, therefore, even in the event of Russian intervention, would not be further obligated." [18]

So it began to look as if Bethmann's optimism and "localization" policy might prove a frightful blunder.[19]

At a conference at Potsdam late on Monday afternoon, July 27, between the Kaiser, Bethmann, Jagow, Moltke, and some other officials,[20] in spite of the irritation at the Chancellor, there still seems to have been substantial solidarity of opinion that he was correct in his view that a peaceful solution for the crisis could be found; and no important military orders were issued.[21] "Localization" apparently still remained the German program.

17 Lichnowsky to Bethmann, July 26; K.D., 218, 236.

18 Flotow to Bethmann, July 24; K.D., 156, 168. For other disquieting reports received by July 27 concerning Italy, arising from Berchtold's failure to respect Italy's feelings as an ally and to purchase her loyalty by satisfactory compensations, see K.D., 46, 109, 119, 136, 211, 244; and above, ch. v., at notes 119-128.

19 Lichnowsky had already realized this (*cf.* his reports *passim* and especially his letter to Bethmann of July 16, and Jagow's reply; K.D., 62, 72); Tirpitz and Helfferich, writing their recollections with the advantage of hind-sight, also claim to have quickly realized it; but Bethmann, with a less clear perception of what Bismarck used to call the "imponderabilia" has always asserted that he steered the only available course.

20 Moltke, *Erinnerungen,* p. 381; Tirpitz, *Politische Dokumente,* II, 2, says that he and the Minister of War, Falkenhayn, were not present.

21 *Investigating Commission,* II, pp. 8 f., 15; and Montgelas, in KSF, V, 1208 ff., December, 1927.

GERMAN ADVICE TO AUSTRIA

But on returning from Potsdam to Berlin, Bethmann and Jagow found a handful of new telegrams which showed that the situation was becoming more serious, and which indicated the doubtful wisdom of continuing to adhere rigidly to the policy of strict "localization." Germany must pay more heed to mediation proposals and advise Berchtold to give them consideration. She must attempt, but without giving Austria offense or doubt as to her continued support, to take back into her own hands that freedom of action in the Serbian question which she had so unwisely abandoned on July 5. Instead of saying at Vienna, as she had done three weeks earlier, that the Kaiser "naturally cannot take any stand in the questions between Austria and Serbia, for they are beyond his competence,"[22] Germany must assume the rôle of mediator, and advise Austria to consider the English and Russian peace proposals. Otherwise, there would be an increase in the suspicion which was being circulated by the French Ambassadors[23] that Germany was egging Austria on, knew the text of the ultimatum from the beginning, wanted war, and was acting *mala fide* in pretending to desire peace. Moreover, England would be dangerously antagonized and might not, in case of a continental war, preserve the neutral attitude, for which Germany hoped and which she believed had just been promised by King George to Prince Henry of Prussia.[24]

One of the telegrams which Bethmann and Jagow found was the full text of the Serbian reply which had been

[22] See above, ch. v, at note 37.

[23] F.Y.B., 15, 32, 38, 41, 43, 48, 67, 74; K.D., 215, 415, 485.

[24] "King of Great Britain said to Prince Henry of Prussia that England would maintain neutrality in case war should break out between Continental Powers" (German Naval Attaché in London to German Naval Office, July 26; K.D., 207; *cf.* also K.D., 201 and 374).

handed in at the Foreign Office by the Serbian Legation early in the afternoon.[25]

Though Bethmann had already been given to understand that it "agreed to nearly all the points," [26] the reading of the text showed him definitely how conciliatory it was, and how far Serbia had yielded to the demands. He may well have been irritated at Berchtold for not having even yet sent a copy of it to Berlin.[27]

There were four new telegrams telling of Russian military preparations along the German frontier: Kovno put in a state of war; the mouth of the Düna barred with mines; and troop movements at several points.[28]

A telegram from Vienna announced Austria's sudden decision "to issue the official declaration of war tomorrow, or the day after tomorrow at the latest, primarily in order to cut the ground from every attempt at intervention," [29] instead of adhering to the plan, already notified to Berlin, of waiting until about August 12, when the concentration of the troops would be completed.

A telegram from Lichnowsky indicated the disturbing

25 It was dispatched from Belgrade to the Serbian Legation in Berlin on July 25, 7:40 P. M.; arrived July 26, 8:58 P. M.; and was handed over in a hardly legible form by the Serbian Chargé d'Affaires to the Berlin Foreign Office next day, but at what hour is not precisely indicated (K.D., 271, note 3). Bethmann, telegraphing to the Kaiser July 27, at 11:20 A. M., speaks of "Serbia's answer to the ultimatum, the text of which we have not yet been able to get hold of" (K.D., 245); and ten minutes later he telegraphed to Vienna: "Please telegraph text of the Serbian reply immediately" (K.D., 246). It was evidently not in hand at the conference at Potsdam, since it was sent to the Kaiser by special messenger at 9:30 P. M.; but did not arrive in time for him to read it that night (K.D., 270, note 2; 293). Jules Cambon seems to be mistaken in saying that the Serbian Chargé d'Affaires gave it to Jagow "this morning" (July 27; F.Y.B., 74).

26 K.D., 245.

27 Berchtold delayed forwarding it until he had time to annotate it; see above, ch. vii, note 42.

28 K.D., 264, 274-276; see also above, ch. vi, "The Russian Danger."

29 Tschirschky to Berlin, July 27, 3:20 P. M.; arrived 4:37 P. M.; sent to the Emperor the same night, and to the Army and Navy Staffs next morning; K.D., 257, see also below, at notes 42-54.

fact that Sir Edward Grey was losing patience with Germany. Grey had just read the text of the Serbian reply, and found that "Serbia had agreed to the Austrian demands to an extent he would never have believed possible." Should Austria reject it as a foundation for negotiations, or occupy Belgrade, "Russia could not regard such action with equanimity, and would have to accept it as a direct challenge. The result would be the most frightful war Europe had ever seen, and no one could tell to what such a war would lead." Grey therefore requested Germany to use her influence to get Vienna to accept the Serbian reply, either as satisfactory or as a basis for conferences. He was convinced that it lay in Germany's hands to settle the matter by proper representations. "I found the Minister vexed for the first time," Lichnowsky added; "he spoke with great seriousness and seemed absolutely to expect that we should successfully make use of our influence to settle the matter. . . . I am convinced that if war should come after all, we should no longer be able to count on British sympathy or British support, as every evidence of ill-will would be seen in Austria's procedure." [30]

In view of all this serious news, Bethmann decided that the time had come to accede to Grey's request to act as mediator. He telegraphed to Tschirschky at Vienna the text of Lichnowsky's telegram with its warning and its proposal from Grey that the Serbian Note be accepted as a basis for a settlement, and added:

> Since we have already refused one English proposal for a conference, it is impossible for us to waive *a limine* this English suggestion also. By refusing every proposal for mediation, we should be held responsible for the conflagration by the whole world, and be set forth as the original

[30] Lichnowsky to Bethmann, July 27, 1:31 P.M., received 4:37 P.M.; forwarded to Vienna 11:50 P.M.; and to the Kaiser by messenger July 28 at 5 A.M.; K.D., 258, 277, 283.

> instigators of the war. That would also make our position impossible in our own country, where we must appear as having been forced into war. Our situation is all the more difficult, inasmuch as Serbia has apparently yielded to a very great degree. Therefore we cannot refuse the mediator's rôle, and must submit the English proposal to the consideration of the Vienna Cabinet, especially as London and Paris continue to make their influences felt in St. Petersburg. I request Count Berchtold's opinion on the English suggestion, as likewise his views on M. Sazonov's desire to negotiate directly with Vienna.[31]

But by the time Tschirschky presented this communication to Berchtold, the Austrian Minister replied that "now, since the opening of hostilities on the part of Serbia and the ensuing [Austrian] declaration of war, England's move was made too late." [32] Berchtold had faced his ally, as well as Europe, with the *fait accompli* of war with Serbia, and so "cut the ground from any attempt at intervention."

There has been much discussion as to the sincerity of Bethmann's action in this matter. On this same evening the Austrian Ambassador at Berlin, Szögyény, telegraphed to Berchtold at 9:15 P. M.:

> [1] The Foreign Secretary [Jagow] very decisively informed me in strict confidence that the German Government would shortly acquaint Your Excellency with possible English proposals of mediation.
>
> [2] The German Government give the most positive assurance that they do not identify themselves in any way with the proposals, they are even decidedly against their being considered, and they only forward them, in compliance with the English request.
>
> [3] In doing so they are guided by the view that it is of the utmost importance that England should not make

31 Bethmann to Tschirschky, July 27, 11:50 P. M.; arrived at the Embassy in Vienna at 5:30 A.M.; K.D., 277.

32 Tschirschky to Bethmann, July 28, 4:55 P.M.; K.D., 313.

common cause with Russia and France at the present moment. Consequently everything must be avoided that would break down the wire between Germany and England which has hitherto worked so well. If Germany were to tell Sir Edward Grey plainly that she would not forward the request to Austria-Hungary, which England thinks more likely to be considered if it comes through Germany, this would lead to the very state of affairs it is so essential to avoid.

[4] Moreover, the German Government at every single English request of the kind in Vienna, would declare to her [*bei jedem einzelnen derartigen Verlangen Englands in Wien demselben erklären*] most emphatically that it would in no wise endorse to Austria-Hungary such attempts at intervention, and only passed them on in compliance with England's wish.

[5] Yesterday, as he said, the English Government had approached him [Jagow], through the German Ambassador in London and directly through their representative here, to persuade him to support England's request concerning our modification of the Note to Serbia. He, Jagow, had replied that he would indeed comply with Sir Edward Grey's wish to forward England's request to Your Excellency, but he himself could not endorse it, since the Serbian conflict was a question of prestige for the Austro-Hungarian Monarchy, in which Germany also was concerned.

[6] He, the Secretary of State, had therefore forwarded Sir Edward Grey's note to Herr von Tschirschky, but without instructing him to submit it to Your Excellency; he had then been able to inform the British Cabinet that he did not directly reject the English wish, but had even passed it on to Vienna.

[7] In conclusion the Secretary of State repeated his attitude, and begged me, in order to avoid any misunderstanding, to assure Your Excellency that his having acted as intermediary in this instance does not at all mean that he is in favor of the English proposal being considered.[33]

[33] Szögyény to Berchtold, July 27, 9:15 P.M., arrived at Vienna

Several observations may be made upon this Szögyény telegram, which is somewhat confused, inaccurate, and repetitious.

(1) In the 4th paragraph it is not at all clear whether "*demselben*" means "to England" or "to Vienna." The two ablest French and German experts, Renouvin and Montgelas, interpret it to mean "to England"; but if so, Szögyény was contradicting the essential notion expressed in his first three paragraphs. If it means "to Vienna," Szögyény's statement is contradicted by the fact that the German Government never declared in Vienna "that it would in no wise endorse to Austria-Hungary such attempts at intervention."

(2) In the 5th paragraph it is not clear to what Szögyény refers. England expressed no wish for "the modification of the *Note to Serbia*" on July 26 ("Yesterday"). This may be a confusion in Szögyény's mind with Grey's request of July 25 (not "Yesterday"), received in Berlin the same day, that Germany "may feel able to influence the Austrian Government to take a favorable view of it," i.e., of the *Serbian reply;* this request, as Szögyény states in his 6th paragraph, was in fact forwarded at once to Tschirschky in Vienna, and England was so informed.[34] Szögyény can hardly have been thinking of the English proposal for a conference of Ambassadors, made at London to Lichnowsky on July 26 and at Berlin by Goschen on July 27 (both cannot be "*Yesterday*"), which Germany frankly rejected at once,[35] because he sent a report about that later.[36]

July 28, 9:00 A.M.; A.R.B., II, 68; Gooss, p. 173 ff. The American Delegation at the Versailles Peace Conference cited only the first two paragraphs of this telegram, which, taken by themselves, give a false impression. For different interpretations of this famous Szögyény despatch, see, among others, H. Delbrück, in *Preussische Jahrbücher,* vol. 176, pp. 487-490, June, 1919; Renouvin, pp. 121-126; Montgelas, *Leitfaden,* p. 176 f.

[34] B.D., 115, 149; K.D., 186, notes to 186, and 191a.

[35] See above, ch. viii, at notes 58-69.

[36] Szögyény to Berchtold, July 28, 7:40 P.M., (some *thirty hours after the event!*); A.R.B., II, 84: "The English mediation proposal according to which Germany, Italy, England and France should come together in

(3) No evidence exists that Jagow told England "the Serbian dispute was a question of prestige for the Austro-Hungarian Monarchy, in which Germany also was concerned," as Szögyény alleged at the end of the 5th paragraph.

(4) Szögyény was at this time so old a man, that his recall had already been decided upon and his successor selected. His age and the nervous strain of these days would explain the confusion and inaccuracy of this telegram, and make it doubtful whether it can be completely relied on, especially as this was not the only instance of his inaccuracy and unreliability in this crisis.[37]

(5) Finally, and most important, it has usually been assumed that when Szögyény announced in the 1st paragraph that "the German Government would shortly acquaint Your Excellency with possible English proposals of mediation," he was referring to Lichnowsky's telegram proposing mediation on the basis of the Serbian reply, and forwarded with Bethmann's comment, which has been quoted above at notes 30-31. If this was actually the case, and if Szögyény's telegram is trustworthy (which is open to doubt), it would throw a sinister light upon the sincerity of Bethmann's action. But it is quite possible that it was not Lichnowsky's telegram referred to above, but the British proposal for a Conference of the Four Powers, which Szögyény understood from Jagow might soon be passed on to Vienna. Jagow frankly and emphatically rejected the proposal, and there was nothing underhanded or deceitful in his telling Szögyény that the German Government was decisively opposed to its being considered, and only passed it on in compliance with England's wish. It may be objected that Jagow does not appear to have forwarded the

a conference in London, to find a way for the settlement of the present difficulties, has been rejected by Germany on the ground that a conference would not be the suitable means for accomplishing the aim."

[37] K.D., 324. See above, ch. v, note 43.

Conference proposal to Vienna. But this is easily explained. During the morning of July 27, Berlin had only an indefinite and informal knowledge of the Conference proposal contained in a telegram sent by Lichnowsky on Sunday evening.[38] Szögyény may have been told that Germany disapproved of this, and that if she forwarded it to Vienna it would not mean that she in any way endorsed it. Later in the day Goschen made the formal request for a Conference; this was rejected,[39] but Jagow and Bethmann, in hurrying out to Potsdam, neglected to forward it to Vienna. When they returned from Potsdam, read the text of the Serbian reply, and found Lichnowsky's telegram with a a good mediation proposal, they forwarded the latter instead of the Conference proposal. Another objection which might be raised to this view that Szögyény was thinking of a Conference proposal which Berlin might soon forward to Vienna is the fact that his telegram was sent at 9:15 P. M., and would hardly apply to a conversation around noon. But he was often many hours late in getting information at the German Foreign Office and in forwarding it to Vienna; such a delay of some nine hours would be nothing unusual for him.[40] Furthermore, it is very doubtful whether Bethmann and Jagow could have returned from Potsdam early enough to read Lichnowsky's telegram, tell Szögyény they disapproved it but were forwarding it to please the English, and

[38] In reply to this telegram of Lichnowsky's (K.D., 236; see above at note 17) Bethmann telegraphed to him at 1:00 P.M. (K.D., 248): "No knowledge here up to present of Sir Edward Grey's proposal to hold a conference *à quatre* there. We could not take part in such a conference, as we should not be able to summon Austria before a European court of justice."

[39] Goschen to Grey, July 27, 6:17 P.M.; B.D., 185.

[40] For instance, Germany requested from Vienna the text of the Serbian reply at 11:30 A.M. (K.D., 246), and Szögyény does not report the news until 5:50 P.M. Similarly, Goschen reported the rejection of the Conference proposal on Monday at 6:17 P.M. (B.D., 185), and Szögyény did not report it until more than twenty-four hours later on Tuesday at 7:40 P.M. (A.R.B., II, 84).

still leave time for Szögyény to put it all into cipher by 9:15 P. M.

It would seem, therefore, that there are good grounds for thinking that the Szögyény telegram referred to the Conference proposal, which was openly and frankly rejected, and not to the later mediation proposal forwarded by Bethmann toward midnight.

One may conclude that Bethmann was sincere, on the evening of July 27, in assuming the rôle of mediator to the extent of calling upon Berchtold to consider the proposals of Sir Edward Grey and of Sazonov for finding a settlement, in which Austria should accept the Serbian reply as a sufficiently satisfactory basis for further discussions. No doubt Bethmann was largely influenced by his desire not to antagonize England. But if this had been his only motive in forwarding the British proposal, as one school of interpreters of the Szögyény telegram believe, there was no need for him to have included Sazonov's "direct conversations" among the proposals which Berchtold was asked to consider. No doubt also Bethmann ought to have given stronger advice, if he wanted to make certain of restraining Austria, but he did not wish to offend her or raise doubts as to Germany's loyalty as an ally.[41] But even had he spoken in stronger terms, it would not have prevented the Austrian declaration of war on Serbia, because Berchtold had already decided on this step in order "to cut the ground from any attempt at intervention." When Tschirschky presented Bethmann's communication he was told that, since Austria and Serbia were already at war, "England's move was made too late."

[41] It is significant that in forwarding Lichnowsky's telegram to Vienna he omitted the last sentence which might seem to imply that Austria was under Germany's thumb: "The key to the situation is to be found in Berlin, and, if peace is seriously desired there, Austria can be restrained from prosecuting, as Sir E. Grey expresses it, a foolhardy policy" (K.D. 258, 277).

THE AUSTRIAN DECLARATION OF WAR ON SERBIA, JULY 28

There had been a general fear in Europe that Austria would quickly follow her diplomatic break with Serbia by a declaration of war or an opening of hostilities. This also had at first been the expectation and advice of Germany, in order to secure "localization" and by quick action reduce the likelihood of Russian intervention.[42] When this did not take place, there was some feeling of relief, and the prospects for the success of "direct conversations" seemed good. The reason that military action did not follow the diplomatic break at once was that the first day of Austria's partial mobilization was not to be until July 28, and the armies would not be concentrated for action until about two weeks later. Conrad did not want war until his armies were concentrated. Tschirschky was informed of this about noon on July 26. Berlin learned of it on the morning of July 27, and was therefore not expecting a declaration of war or the opening of hostilities until about August 12.[43]

But when Pashitch's advance summary of the Serbian reply began to make a favorable impression,[44] and when Berlin transmitted Grey's hope that Vienna would take a favorable view of it,[45] Berchtold began to doubt the wisdom of so long a delay. "When do you want a declaration of war?" he asked Conrad toward noon on July 26. "About August 12," the Chief of Staff replied. "The diplomatic situation will not last as long as that," said Berchtold.[46] However, no change in Conrad's plans was made at the moment. The Vienna authorities still believed that Russia would not move, and that there was no need for haste in

42 Szögyény to Berchtold, July 25, 2:12 P.M.; A.R.B., II, 32; and Tschirschky to Bethmann, July 26, 4:50 P.M.; K.D., 213.

43 Conrad, IV, 131 f. Tschirschky to Bethmann, July 26, 4:50 P.M.; K.D., 213. Dirr, p. 148. Moltke, *Erinnerungen,* p. 381. Szögyény to Berchtold, July 27, 5:50 P.M.; A.R.B., II, 67.

44 B.D., 114, 115.

45 K.D., 186; A.R.B., II, 57.

46 Conrad, IV, 131 f.

dealing with Serbia. But on July 27, when the news of the Krasnoe Selo military preparations and demonstrations came in,[47] they "decided to issue the declaration of war tomorrow, or at latest day after tomorrow, in order to cut the ground from every attempt at intervention." [48]

Such an intervention seemed even more likely, in the course of the evening, with the arrival of Szápáry's despatch proposing "direct conversations" [49] and news of Grey's proposal for a Conference.[49a] Berchtold therefore instructed Szápáry that he might converse with Sazonov, but "without entering into any kind of a binding engagement." [50] At the same time a declaration of war against Serbia was drawn up, together with a memorandum to persuade Emperor Francis Joseph to authorize its being sent "early tomorrow morning." It contained two main arguments. First, since the Serbian reply was cleverly worded and conciliatory in form but wholly worthless in substance, the Entente Powers might make an attempt to reach a peaceful settlement, "unless a clear situation is brought about by a declaration of war." And second, the Serbians had opened hostilities by firing on Austrian troops at Temes-Kubin on the Danube. Berchtold then went to Ischl. By using these two arguments he won the Emperor's assent, telephoned the news to Vienna, and the Austrian declaration of war was then dispatched to Nish a little before noon on July 28, in an uncoded telegram in French.[51]

[47] July 27, 7 and 8 A.M.; A.R.B., II, 49, 60; see also above, ch. vi, "The Russian Danger."

[48] Tschirschky to Bethmann, July 27, 3:20 P.M.; K.D., 257. *Cf.* also Berchtold to Szögyény, July 27, 11:10 P.M. (A.R.B., II, 69), where he says the declaration of war will be issued "in a few days" [*in den nächsten Tagen*], even though active military operations could not begin until a couple of weeks later, when Conrad had concentrated the troops.

[49] Received July 27, 4:30 P.M.; see above ch. viii, at note 85.

[49a] Mensdorff to Berchtold, July 27, received 6:30 P.M.; A.R.B., II, 71.

[50] Berchtold to Szápáry, July 27, 10:20 P.M.; Gooss, 210.

[51] A.R.B., II, 78; S.B.B., 45-47. B.D., 225, 233. Mr. H. F. Armstrong, to whom the present writer is indebted for the accompanying facsimile,

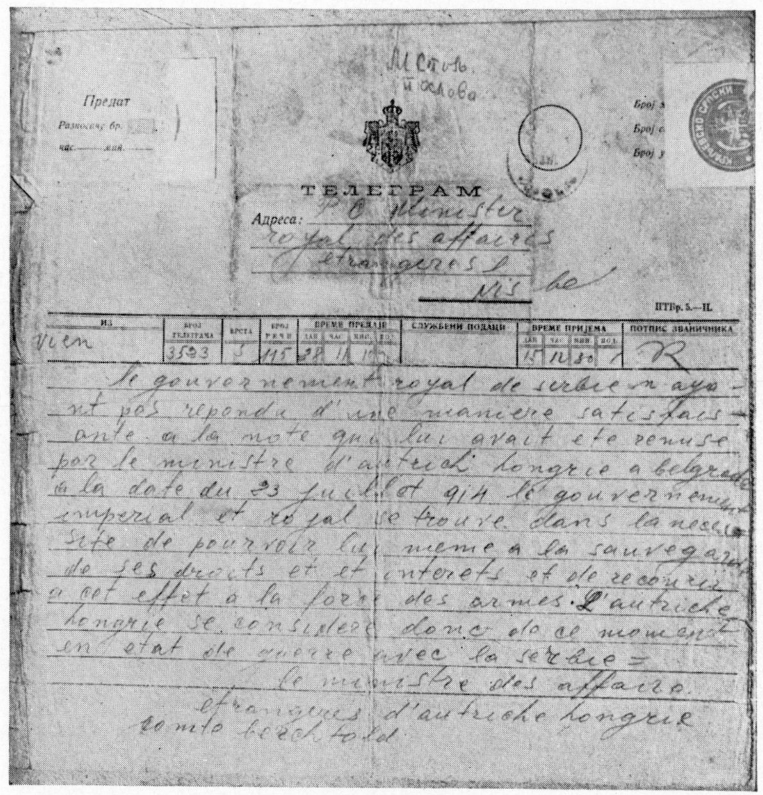

ТЕЛЕГРАМ

Адреса: P. C. Minister royal des affaires etrangeres de Nis

ИЗ	БРОЈ ТЕЛЕГРАМА	ВРСТА	БРОЈ РЕЧИ	ВРЕМЕ ПРЕДАЈЕ	СЛУЖБЕНИ ПОДАЦИ	ВРЕМЕ ПРИЈЕМА	ПОТПИС ЗВАНИЧНИКА
Vien	3593	3	115	28 11 10		15 12 30	R

le gouvernement royal de serbie n ayant pas repondu d une maniere satisfaisante a la note qui lui avait ete remise par le ministre d autriche hongrie a belgrade a la date du 23 juillet 914 le gouvernement imperial et royal se trouve dans la necessite de pourvoir lui meme a la sauvegarde de ses droits et interets et de recourir a cet effet a la force des armes. L'autriche hongrie se considere donc de ce moment en etat de guerre avec la serbie =

le ministre des affaires etrangeres d'autriche hongrie comte berchtold

FACSIMILE OF THE AUSTRO-HUNGARIAN DECLARATION OF WAR ON SERBIA

The telegram, sent from Vienna July 15/28 at 11:10 A.M. and received at Nish at 12.30 P.M., runs in translation as follows:

The Royal Serbian Government not having answered in a satisfactory manner the note of July 23, 1914, presented by the Austro-Hungarian Minister at Belgrade, the Imperial and Royal Government are themselves compelled to see to the safeguarding of their rights and interests, and, with this object, to have recourse to force of arms. Austria-Hungary consequently considers herself henceforward in a state of war with Serbia.

The Austro-Hungarian Minister for Foreign Affairs,

COUNT BERCHTOLD.

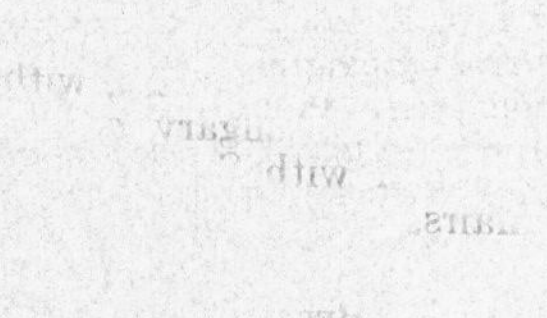

Berchtold had now "brought about a clear situation" by his *fait accompli.* When the Russian Ambassador came to propose "direct conversations," Berchtold told him that he could not accept the Serbian reply as a basis for discussion, "because war on Serbia has been declared today." [52] Similarly Berchtold informed Germany and England that Grey's proposal for a conference came "too late," and, "in view of the state of war already existing, has been outstripped by events"; [53] and also that Austria "would have to decline any suggestion of negotiations on basis of Serbian reply. Prestige of the Dual Monarchy was now engaged, and nothing could prevent conflict." [54]

The precipitate declaration of war by Austria thus forestalled the English and Russian proposals for taking the Serbian reply as a basis for negotiations. It created a new situation. To meet this new situation, several new proposals for preserving the peace of Europe, and at the same time satisfying Austria and Serbia, were quickly forthcoming from Germany and England (but no longer from Russia). One of these in fact was outlined by the Kaiser several hours before he was aware that Austria had declared war. It is commonly known as the "pledge plan" or "Halt in Belgrade" proposal.

gives an interesting history of it in *Current History,* Oct., 1927, p. 95. As telegraph connections with Belgrade were broken off, it was sent *via* Czernowitz and Bucharest.

The first draft of the declaration of war gave, as one of the grounds for war, the Serbian provocation at Temes-Kubin, but as this was not confirmed, it was omitted from the final declaration of war. Some writers believe that the Temes-Kubin rumor was invented to deceive and persuade Francis Joseph, and it is significant that Conrad makes no mention of it. Berchtold explained to the Emperor next day, July 29, that the Temes-Kubin conflict had been too insignificant to include in the Declaration to Serbia as a ground for war; Gooss, p. 218.

52 Berchtold to Szápáry, July 28, 11:40 P.M.; A.R.B., II, 95.

53 Berchtold to Szögyény, July 28, 11:00 P.M.; and to Mensdorff. July 29, 1:00 A.M.; A.R.B., II, 81, 90.

54 Bunsen to Grey, July 28, 1:10 P.M.; B.D., 227; *cf.* also 226, 230; K.D., 313; and A.R.B., II, 82.

THE KAISER'S "PLEDGE PLAN"

When the Kaiser awoke on Tuesday morning, July 28, he had before him the text of the Serbian reply and many of the other documents which had led Bethmann the night before to ask Berchtold to consider the British and Russian peace proposals. The Kaiser was greatly impressed with the conciliatory and yielding character of the Serbian reply and the diplomatic success which Austria had achieved, as appears from his annotation on it:

> "A brilliant performance for a time-limit of only 48 hours. This is more than one could have expected! A great moral success for Vienna; but with it every reason for war drops away, and Giesl ought to have remained quietly in Belgrade! After such a thing, *I* should never have ordered mobilization."[55]

He therefore wrote at once to Jagow: "I am convinced that on the whole the wishes of the Danubian Monarchy have been acceded to. The few reservations that Serbia makes could be settled by negotiation. It contains the announcement *orbi et urbi* of a capitulation of the most humiliating kind, and as a result, *every cause for war* falls to the ground. Nevertheless, the piece of paper, like its contents, is of little value so long as it is not translated into *deeds.* The Serbians are Orientals, therefore lying, deceitful, and masters in evasion. In order that these beautiful promises may be converted into reality and deeds," and "in order to give the army, now mobilized *to no purpose* for the third time, the external *satisfaction d'honneur* of an ostensible success," Austria should be given temporary military occupation of Belgrade as a pledge. "I propose that we say to Austria: Serbia has been forced to retreat in a very humiliating manner, and we offer our congratulations;

[55] K.D., 271.

naturally, as a result, *no more cause for war exists;* but a *guarantee* that the promises *will be carried out,* is probably necessary; that could probably be secured by a *temporary* military occupation of a portion of Serbia, similar to the way we left troops in France in 1871 until the billions were paid. *On this basis* I am ready to *mediate for peace* with Austria. . . . Submit a proposal to me, along the lines sketched out, to be communicated to Vienna." [56]

Thus the Kaiser was ready at last to yield to England's request that he act as a mediator and advise Vienna to abandon the idea of war with Serbia. But while Sir Edward Grey had urged that Austria be dissuaded from any military action, the Kaiser was ready to permit it to the extent of having Austria secure a tangible pledge that the Serbian promises would be really carried out. Before the Kaiser's proposal could be embodied in a despatch and communicated to Austria, the latter, as we have seen, had already declared war on Serbia. It then remained to be seen whether Austria, and especially Russia, would be willing to accept the Kaiser's mediation proposal, which was sincerely calculated to avert a European war.

Before the Kaiser's autograph letter to Jagow had been brought from Potsdam to Berlin and put in the form of a concrete proposal to Vienna, Bethmann had received irritating news concerning Berchtold's attempt to rattle the German sword, his persistent neglect of Germany's advice to satisfy Italy, and his secret intention to partition Serbia. Bethmann had understood on July 5 that he was agreeing to support Austria in her vital interest of putting an end to the dangerous Greater Serbia propaganda; that danger was now taken care of by the Serbian reply, if its promises were duly carried out. He did not understand, and he did

[56] William II to Jagow, July 28, 10:00 A.M.; and a similar note by his secretary to Moltke, "who is entirely in accord with my views;" K.D., 293, and note 6 of new edition. Italics are the Kaiser's.

not intend, that Germany should be forced to follow Berchtold in secret plans which Austria had withheld from her ally, and which might involve the rupture of the Triple Alliance by Italy's withdrawal from it, and even the rupture of the peace of Europe in such a way that Germany and Austria would seem to be responsible. He would not permit that Russia and the Pan-Slav Press should back up Serbia in a continuance of the Greater Serbia menace, but on the other hand, he thought Austria ought to satisfy the Russian desire that Serbia be not subjected to a partition.[57]

Bethmann therefore refused to allow Berchtold to rattle the German sword. Berchtold and Conrad had asked Tschirschky that Berlin warn St. Petersburg that the military preparations against Austria were so threatening that counter-measures would have to be taken.[58] Instead of acceding to this suggestion, Bethmann tried to calm and restrain the Vienna authorities by telling them: "Military reports concerning Russia, so far as known here, are only rumors, and are not yet confirmed. Even according to General Moltke's view, a categorical declaration at St. Petersburg would seem today to be premature."[59] And at the same time, in reply to Sazonov's admission that "a way must be found of giving Serbia her deserved lesson while sparing her sovereign rights,"[60] he instructed Pourtalès: "Please tell Sazonov that I am grateful for his communication and for its conciliatory spirit, and further hope that Austria's declaration of disinterestedness will satisfy Russia and serve as a basis for further agreement."[61]

Bethmann also heard that Berchtold was persisting in

[57] *Cf.* Bethmann to the Prussian Ministers at the Federated German States, July 28; K.D., 307; and also his telegrams to Vienna quoted below.

[58] Tschirschky to Bethmann, July 27 [July 28, 1:45 A.M., received 4 A.M.]; K.D., 281.

[59] Bethmann to Tschirschky, July 28, 3:20 P.M.; K.D., 299.

[60] See above, note 2.

[61] Bethmann to Pourtalès, July 28, 3:35 P.M.; K.D., 300.

his neglect to follow German advice in regard to satisfying Italy's hopes for compensation.[62] The German Ambassador in Rome had reported San Giuliano as insisting that "the existence of Serbia is an unconditional necessity for Italy. This barrier against Austria cannot be allowed to disappear." [63] Instructions had therefore been sent from Berlin to Vienna that the Kaiser "considers it absolutely necessary that Austria should come to an understanding in time with Italy about Art. VII and the compensation question"; an immediate conference between Berchtold and the Italian Ambassador is "urgently necessary." [64]

Most irritating of all was the news from London concerning Austria's doings. Though Berchtold had disclaimed any intention to annex Serbian territory [65] and had declared Austria's "territorial disinterestedness," the Austrian Ambassador in London had confided to Lichnowsky that Serbia was to be "beaten to the earth," and "it was the intention to present portions of Serbia to Bulgaria and presumably also to Albania." [66] These were secret intentions which had been expressed at the Austrian Ministerial Council of July 19,[67] but which were contrary to Bethmann's expectations and contrary to what he had been sincerely stating to the Powers. He therefore noted indignantly: "This duplicity of Austria's is intolerable. They refuse to give us information as to their program, and state expressly that Count Hoyos's statements which suggested a partition of Serbia were purely personal; at St. Petersburg they are lambs with not a wicked thought in their hearts, and in

62 See above, at note 18, and also ch. v, at notes 119-128.

63 Flotow to Bethmann, July 27, 2:40 P.M.; K.D., 261.

64 Jagow to Tschirschky, July 27, 9 P.M., and 9:30 P.M.; K.D., 267, 269.

65 In conversation with the Russian Chargé d'Affaires in Vienna on July 24 (A.R.B., II, 23), but this disclaimer had not been confirmed by Szápáry in St. Petersburg.

66 Lichnowsky to Bethmann, July 28, 12:58 P.M., received 3:45 P.M.; K.D., 301.

67 See above, ch. v, at notes 104-106.

London their Embassy talks of giving away portions of Serbian territory to Bulgaria and Albania." [68]

It was thus with some justifiable irritation at Austria that Bethmann took up the Kaiser's offer to mediate on the basis of the "pledge plan" and embodied it in the following telegram to Vienna:

> [Aside from a declaration to Russia that it intends no territorial acquisition in Serbia] the Austro-Hungarian Government, in spite of repeated questions as to its purposes, has left us in the dark. The reply now at hand of the Serbian Government to the Austrian ultimatum makes it evident that Serbia has in fact met the Austrian demands in so wide-reaching a manner that if the Austro-Hungarian Government adopted a wholly uncompromising attitude, a gradual revulsion of public opinion against it in all Europe would have to be reckoned with. . . . [Russia will presumably be satisfied] if the Vienna Cabinet repeats in St. Petersburg the definite declaration that territorial acquisitions in Serbia lie far from its purpose, and that its military measures aim solely at a temporary occupation of Belgrade and other definite points of Serbian territory in order to compel the Serbian Government to a complete fulfilment of the demands, and to serve as guarantees for future good behavior, to which Austria-Hungary unquestionably has a claim after her experiences with Serbia. The occupation could be regarded like the German occupation in France after the Peace of Frankfort, as security for the demand of the war indemnity. As soon as the Austrian demands were fulfilled, a withdrawal would follow. . . . You are immediately to express yourself emphatically in this sense to Count Berchtold and have him take the proper step in St. Petersburg. You are carefully to avoid giving the impression that we wish to hold Austria back. It is solely a question of finding a method which will make possible the accomplishment of Austria's purpose of cutting the vital nerve of Greater Serbian propaganda without at the same

[68] K.D., 301, note.

time unchaining a world war, and in the end, if this is unavoidable, of improving as far as practicable the conditions under which it is to be waged. Wire reply.[69]

This telegram of Bethmann's was a step in the right direction. It was well adapted to the new situation created by the fact that Austria was already at war with Serbia, which he had just learned. It was aimed to make the Austrian armies "halt in Belgrade." But its language was not sufficiently vigorous to compel immediate assent from Berchtold. Nor did it correspond precisely with the Kaiser's more decisive instructions that Vienna was to be told that "no more cause for war exists." Bethmann was too much afraid of offending Austria. He was too much concerned with preventing the odium of responsibility for a war from falling on Germany and Austria, rather than with preventing such a war altogether. However, he also at once informed Russia that he was striving to persuade Vienna to have a frank discussion with St. Petersburg and to make plain in an unobjectionable and satisfactory manner the purpose and extent of Austria's procedure.[70] He likewise told the British Ambassador that "he was doing his very best both at Vienna and at St. Petersburg to get the two Governments to discuss the situation directly with each other and in a friendly way. He had great hopes that such discussion would take place and lead to a satisfactory result." He reiterated his desire to coöperate with England, and his intention to do his utmost to maintain the general peace. His last words to Goschen were: "A war between the

[69] Bethmann to Tschirschky, July 28, 10:15 P.M., K.D., 323. *Cf.* A.R.B., III, 24, and Gooss, pp. 243-244. Bethmann also telegraphed to Tschirschky Pourtalès' account of Sazonov's more conciliatory attitude and his admission that a means must be found for giving Serbia her "deserved lesson" and building a bridge upon which Austria could retreat, K.D., 282, 309.

[70] Bethmann to Pourtalès and the other German Ambassadors abroad, July 28, 9 P.M.; K.D., 315.

Great Powers must be avoided."[71] But neither to Russia nor to England did he indicate the exact terms of the "pledge plan," as he wished to learn first whether it would be acceptable to Austria. On this point he was to be kept in nerve-racking suspense for sixty critical hours, and finally answered in the negative!

THE "WILLY-NICKY" TELEGRAMS

Besides informing Sazonov through the usual diplomatic channels that Germany was mediating at Vienna to bring Austria to a direct and satisfactory agreement with Russia, Bethmann decided on this same evening of July 28 to have recourse to a direct exchange of telegrams between the Kaiser and the Tsar. In times past this "Willy-Nicky" correspondence had often done much to cement the traditional friendship and good relations between Prussia and Russia. It might be a help in the present time of trouble. Accordingly, a draft telegram was drawn up in the Foreign Office, submitted to the Kaiser, who made several changes in it, and sent from Berlin at 1:45 A. M. on July 29:

> It is with the gravest concern that I hear of the impression which the action of Austria against Servia is creating in your country. The unscrupulous agitation that has been going on in Servia for years has resulted in the outrageous crime, to which archduke Franz Ferdinand fell a victim. The spirit that led Servians to murder their own king and his wife still dominates the country. You will doubtless agree with me that we both, you and me, have a common interest as well as all Sovereigns to insist that all the persons morally responsible for the dastardly murder should receive their deserved punishment. In this case politics play no part at all.
>
> On the other hand I fully understand how difficult it is

[71] Goschen to Grey, July 28, midnight; B.D., 249; this last sentence was suppressed from B.B.B., 71, in 1914. *Cf.* also Bethmann to Lichnowsky, July 28, 8:40 P.M.; K.D., 314.

for you and your Government to face the drift of your public opinion. Therefore, with regard to the hearty and tender friendship which binds us both from long ago with firm ties, I am exerting my utmost influence to induce the Austrians to deal straightly to arrive to a satisfactory understanding with you. I confidently hope you will help me in my efforts to smooth over difficulties that may still arise.

Your very sincere and devoted friend and cousin

Willy [72]

The same idea had occurred almost simultaneously to the Tsar and the little group of advisers around him who were sincerely anxious to prevent the Austro-Serbian conflict from developing into a Russo-German war. Prince Trubetzkoi told Chelius, the Kaiser's personal representative at the side of the Tsar, that Serbia's answer and readiness to submit the question to arbitration ought to make it possible to avoid a European war. "We do not love the Serbs at all," he told Chelius, "but they are our Slavic blood-brothers, and we cannot leave our brothers in the lurch when they are in trouble. Austria can annihilate them, and that we could not permit." He hoped that the Kaiser would advise Austria not to over-stretch the bow, but to recognize Serbia's conciliatory promises and accept the arbitration of the Hague Tribunal. "The return of your Kaiser has made us all feel easier, for we trust in His Majesty and want no war, nor does Tsar Nicholas. It would be a good thing if the two Monarchs should come to an understanding by telegraph." [73]

The suggestion that the Austro-Serbian conflict be submitted to arbitration at the Hague, which Pashitch had already appended to the Serbian reply, possibly at Russian

[72] K.D., 335; *Krasnyi Arkhiv,* IV, p. 18; Schilling's Diary, p. 45.

[73] Chelius to the Berlin Foreign Office, July 28, received July 29, 3:42 A.M. (K.D., 337), a couple of hours after the Kaiser had sent his first telegram to the Tsar.

suggestion,[74] was a favorite one with the Tsar. The Hague Tribunal owed its origin to him. On July 27 he had written to Sazonov:

> I will receive you tomorrow at six o'clock. An idea has come to me and, not to lose time which is golden, I am communicating it to you. Why do we not try, after coming to an understanding with France and England, and afterwards with Germany and Italy, to propose to Austria that she submit her conflict with Serbia to the examination of the Hague Tribunal? Perhaps the moment is not yet lost before irreparable events occur. Try to take this step today, before your report [to me tomorrow] in order to gain time. In me hope for peace is not yet extinct.[75]

This letter of the Tsar's is one of many evidences of his sincere desire to use every means for preserving peace. But Sazonov paid no attention to it. Instead, he was counting on bluffing Austria into a diplomatic retreat by the threat of partial mobilization, and at the same time carrying on the extensive measures of the "Period Preparatory to War" which would facilitate a more speedy general mobilization. While the Tsar was making this proposal of the Hague Tribunal, his Minister of Foreign Affairs was instructing his agents abroad to telegraph all information about troop movements, was rejecting in advance any moderating influence to be exercised at St. Petersburg, and was assuring Montenegro that Russia would not be indifferent to Serbia's fate and therefore Montenegro should coördinate her policy with that of Serbia.[76] But there is no likelihood that, even if he had taken the step requested by the Tsar, it would have had any success. Austria would certainly have rejected it, and the Kaiser's note on it in Chelius's report was: "Nonsense." A little later, "Nicky" seeing that Sazo-

[74] See above, ch. vii, at notes 30 and 45. [75] *Livre Noir,* II, 283.
[76] Sazonov's telegrams, July 27, nos. 1504, 1514, 1521, 1522, 1523; *Krasnyi Arkhiv*. IV, pp. 48-50.

nov had taken no steps in this direction, telegraphed direct to "Willy," apparently without Sazonov's knowledge: "It would be right to give over the Austro-Serbian problem to the Hague conference (*sic*)." [77] But this merely met with an exclamation point from the Kaiser and a line from Bethmann: "The idea of the Hague Conference will be naturally excluded in this case." [78] The fact is that, from the beginning of the crisis, Pashitch's offer to submit to an arbitral tribunal such a portentous political question, involving vital interests and national honor, was never taken seriously by any of the leading statesmen of Europe.

The Tsar also, like Trubetzkoi and Bethmann, pinned hopes on a direct exchange of telegrams with the Kaiser. At 1 A. M. on July 29, he sent an appeal to Potsdam. It crossed on the wires with that sent by the Kaiser. It was cordial, but it revealed his own weakness in the face of the pressure which was being put upon him by the Russian militarists to order a general mobilization:

> Am glad you are back. In this most serious moment, I appeal to you to help me. An ignoble war has been declared to a weak country. The indignation in Russia shared fully by me is enormous. I foresee that very soon I shall be overwhelmed by the pressure brought upon me and be forced to take extreme measures which will lead to war. To try and avoid such a calamity as a European war I beg you in the name of our old friendship to do what you can to stop your allies from going too far.[79]

Replying to this, the Kaiser stated that he shared the Tsar's wish to preserve peace. He pointed out, however, as Bethmann had already done, that Austria aimed at no territorial gains at Serbia's expense, but ought nevertheless

[77] Tsar to Kaiser, July 29, 8:20 P.M.; K.D., 366; Schilling's Diary, p. 54; Paléologue, I, 36.

[78] Bethmann to Pourtalès, July 30, 2:40 A.M.; K.D., 391.

[79] K.D., 332; K.A., IV, p. 19; Schilling's Diary, p. 46.

to have a guarantee that the Serbian promises would be carried out. He added:

> I think a direct understanding between your Government and Vienna possible and desirable, and as I already telegraphed to you, my Government is continuing its exertions to promote it. Of course military measures on the part of Russia which would be looked upon by Austria as threatening would precipitate a calamity we both wish to avoid and jeopardize my position as mediator which I readily accepted on your appeal to my friendship and my help.[80]

This peace effort on the Kaiser's part made a deep impression on the Tsar. It was successful, as will appear later, to the extent of causing him to suspend the order for Russian general mobilization which had been pressed from him by the Chief of Staff and which was on the point of being dispatched over the wires. The Tsar had taken new hope and telegraphed back:

> Thank you heartily for your quick answer. Am sending Tatishchev this evening with instructions. The military measures which have now come into force were decided five days ago for reasons of defence on account of Austria's preparations. I hope from all my heart that these measures won't in any way interfere with your part as mediator which I greatly value. We need your strong pressure on Austria to come to an understanding with us.[81]

But the news of Russia's wide-reaching military preparations and partial mobilization against Austria, now admitted by the Tsar to have been "decided five days ago for reasons of defence on account of Austria's preparations,"

[80] Kaiser to Tsar, July 29, 6:30 P.M., received 9:40 P.M.; K.D., 359; K.A., IV, p. 24; Schilling's Diary, p. 55.

[81] Tsar to Kaiser, July 30, 1:20 A.M., received 1:45 A.M.; K.D., 390; Schilling's Diary, p. 56. On Tatishchev's mission, and his being stopped by Sazonov, see above, ch. vi, note 54.

when Austria had carefully avoided preparations against Russia, roused the Kaiser's indignation. He had been sincerely trying to mediate and bring Austria to accept the "pledge plan" and satisfy Russia by direct negotiations; but meanwhile Russia had been getting a five days' start in military preparations. "I cannot agree to any more mediation," he noted, "since the Tsar who requested it has at the same time secretly mobilized behind my back. It is only a manoeuvre, in order to hold us back and increase the start they have already got. My work is at an end!" [82]

So the German effort to preserve peace by the old means of direct telegrams between the two monarchs came to nothing, owing to Austria's declaration of war on Serbia and to the consequent Russian partial mobilization, as well as to the other secret military measures of the "Period Preparatory to War" which the Tsar had ordered at Krasnoe Selo on July 25. Several more telegrams were exchanged between "Willy" and "Nicky," but they had no chance of success, because Russia's general mobilization, ordered about 6 P. M. on July 30, had made a general European war virtually inevitable.

BETHMANN'S PRESSURE AT VIENNA

As we have seen above, Bethmann sent off the "pledge plan" to Vienna on the evening of July 28, with instructions to Tschirschky to express himself "emphatically" to Berchtold and to "wire reply." [83] At the same time he had notified England and Russia that he was doing his best to persuade Vienna to come to a frank and friendly discussion with St. Petersburg, and that he wished to coöperate to maintain the general peace. "A war between the Great Powers must be avoided," he had told the British Ambassador. But he now began to be seriously embarrassed because he received no reply from Berchtold to the proposed

[82] K.D. 390.

[83] See above, at note 69.

"pledge plan." All the following day he waited in vain for an answer, though telegrams even at this time of crowded wires ordinarily were transmitted between Berlin and Vienna within three or four hours. He was embarrassed at Berchtold's silence for several reasons: because the German military authorities were beginning to urge that Germany ought to take precautionary military measures in view of the news from Russia, as will be indicated later; because he could give no answer at London and St. Petersburg as to the success of his mediatory efforts at Vienna; because of the bad impression which Austria's declaration of war had meanwhile made; and because of the reports which he had received from the other capitals which seemed to indicate bad faith or stupidity on the part of his ally.[84] Therefore on the evening of July 29 he sent off three more urgent telegrams to Tschirschky, partly to inform him of these reports concerning Austria's actions and partly to get an immediate answer in regard to the "pledge plan." In the first he forwarded Lichnowsky's despatch concerning the remarks of the Austrian Ambassador in London, and added in severe disapproval of Austria:

> These expressions of the Austrian diplomats must be regarded as indications of more recent wishes and aspirations. I regard the attitude of the Austrian Government and its unparalleled procedure toward the various Governments with increasing astonishment. In St. Petersburg it declares its territorial disinterestedness; us it leaves wholly in the dark as to its programme; Rome it puts off with empty phrases about the question of compensation; in London Count Mensdorff hands out part of Serbia to Bulgaria and Albania and places himself in contradiction with Vienna's solemn declaration at St. Petersburg. From these contradictions I must conclude that the telegram disavowing Hoyos [who, on July 5 or 6 at Berlin, had spoken unofficially of Austria's partitioning Serbia] was intended

[84] See above at notes 62-68.

for the gallery, and that the Austrian Government is harboring plans which it sees fit to conceal from us, in order to assure itself in all events of German support and to avoid the refusal which might result from a frank statement.[85]

The second telegram, sent uncoded, said: "Answer by wire immediately whether telegram 174 of yesterday [concerning the 'pledge plan'] has arrived"; and the third: "I await immediate carrying out of telegram 174." [86]

Tschirschky had already on the morning of July 29 promptly carried out his original instructions in telegram 174 concerning the "pledge plan," but had been met with a dilatory and evasive answer: Berchtold was ready to repeat his declaration of territorial disinterestedness, but "as to the further declaration concerning military measures, Count Berchtold says that he is not in a position to give me a reply at once. In spite of my representations as to the urgency of the matter, I have up to this evening received no further communication." [87]

On this same day, Wednesday, July 29, while still waiting in vain for a reply from Berchtold as to the "pledge plan," Bethmann had already taken up two more peace proposals which had been suggested, and supported both energetically at Vienna. One was the suggestion from Sazonov for "direct conversations" between Vienna and St. Petersburg.[88]

Bethmann had already handed this propitious suggestion on to Vienna without comment as soon as it had been

85 Bethmann to Tschirschky, July 29, 8:00 P.M.; K.D., 361. This was for Tschirschky's personal information, but he was instructed to call Berchtold's attention to the advisability of avoiding suspicion as to his declarations to the Powers with regard to the integrity of Serbia, and to his failure to satisfy Italy.

86 Bethmann to Tschirschky, July 29, 10:18 and 10:30 P.M.; K.D., 377 and note.

87 Tschirschky to Bethmann, July 29, 11:50 P.M., received July 30, 1:30 A.M.; K.D., 388.

88 K.D., 238, 282.

received by him on July 27. But it had been evaded and then rejected by Berchtold, because Sazonov had intended that the direct conversations should take up modifications of the terms of Austria's ultimatum. Berchtold was determined not to enter into any negotiations which might touch the local issues existing purely between Austria and Serbia. As an additional reason for his refusal to "converse directly" on Austro-Serbian relations, he pointed out that the time for a peaceful settlement of those relations was passed, since the declaration of war and the opening of hostilities had already taken place. Consequently, "direct conversations" between Vienna and St. Petersburg had come to a halt, with the result that Sazonov was much incensed.[89] Sazonov concluded, though mistakenly, that because Berchtold flatly refused to discuss Austro-Serbian relations, he was also unwilling to converse at all with Russia.

To reopen "direct conversations" Bethmann now sent three more telegrams to Vienna very late on Wednesday night. After mentioning the hopeful interchange of telegrams which had begun between the Kaiser and the Tsar, he passed on Sazonov's information that Russia had decided to mobilize in her four southern districts, but added, calmingly, that this was "far from meaning war"; the Russian army might be a long time under arms without crossing the frontier, and Russia wanted to avoid war if in any way possible. It had been pointed out to Sazonov that Austria would probably take counter-measures and thus start the ball rolling. Sazonov was complaining that "direct conversations" were making no headway. "Hence we must urgently request, in order to prevent a general catastrophe, or at least to put Russia in the wrong, that Vienna inaugu-

89 For this abortive result of the proposals for "direct conversations," see A.R.B., II, 73, 95; III, 16, 17, 19, 20; and above ch. viii, at notes 80-88, and below ch. x, at note 4.

rate and continue conversations according to telegram 174," —that is, according to the "pledge plan." [90] Having heard from Sazonov that Berchtold had given a "categorical refusal" to direct conversations, and fearing there had been some misunderstanding, Bethmann telegraphed still more emphatically to Vienna a couple of hours later:

> The refusal of every exchange of views with St. Petersburg would be a serious mistake, for it provokes Russia precisely to armed interference, which Austria is primarily interested in avoiding. We are ready, to be sure, to fulfill our obligations as an ally, but must refuse to allow ourselves to be drawn by Vienna into a world conflagration frivolously and in disregard of our advice. Please say this to Count Berchtold at once with all emphasis and with great seriousness.[91]

The other plan which Bethmann also cordially took up late Wednesday night was Grey's proposal for mediation between Austria and Russia, either by the four Powers, or by Germany alone, on the basis of Serbia's reply. News had come from Rome that she was now ready, "on condition of certain interpretations, to swallow even articles 5 and 6, that is, the whole Austrian ultimatum." [92] This proposal of Grey's was eagerly welcomed by Bethmann as a possible happy solution. In sending it on to Vienna, he genuinely again "pressed the button," by adding:

> "Please show this to Berchtold immediately and add that we regard such a yielding on Serbia's part as a suitable basis for negotiation along with an occupation of a part of Serbian territory as a pledge." [93]

[90] Bethmann to Tschirschky, July 30, 12:10 and 12:30 A.M.; K.D., 383, 385.

[91] Bethmann to Tschirschky, July 30, 3 A.M.; K.D., 396.

[92] Lichnowsky to Bethmann, July 29, 2:08 P.M.; K.D., 357; on this "Italian proposal," see above, ch. viii, note 10.

[93] Bethmann to Tschirschky, July 30, 12:30 A.M.; K.D., 384.

But Berchtold was still deaf to the button; he merely made the characteristic reply that, though the integral acceptance of Austria's note would have been satisfactory before hostilities had begun, "now after the state of war has begun, Austria's conditions must naturally take another tone." [94]

Grey's proposal was all the more eagerly welcomed by Bethmann, partly because Grey quickly supplemented it by embodying the two very points which Germany herself had already been urging at Vienna and St. Petersburg in her "pledge plan," viz., a new statement by Austria of her intentions in Serbia which would satisfy Russia, and a pledge in the shape of the temporary military occupation of Belgrade which would satisfy Austria; and partly because he was alarmed at Grey's first "warning" that England could not be counted upon to remain neutral in case of a general war. As Lichnowsky reported his conversation with Grey:

> To him [Grey] personally a suitable basis for such mediation seemed to be that Austria, after the occupation perhaps of Belgrade or other places, should announce her conditions. Should Your Excellency [Bethmann], however, undertake the mediation as I was able to propose to him early this morning as a possibility, this would, of course, suit him just as well. . . . [At the close of the conversation Grey] said he wanted to make me a friendly and private statement. . . . It would be possible for her [England] to stand aside so long as the conflict is limited to Austria and Russia. But if we and France should be drawn in, then the situation would immediately be a different one, and the British Government under the circumstances would be forced to rapid decisions. In this case it would be impossible to stand aside for long and to wait; "if war breaks out, it will be the greatest catastrophe that the world has ever seen." He was far from wishing to utter any kind of

[94] Tschirschky to Bethmann, July 30, 3:20 P.M.; K.D., 432.

threat; he merely wanted to save me from being misled, and himself from reproach of insincerity, and, therefore, chose the form of a private explanation.[95]

Upon hearing of this alarming possibility, so contrary to his expectations and hopes, that England might not remain neutral, Bethmann immediately transmitted the whole Grey-Lichnowsky conversation to Vienna, and proceeded to "press the button" very vigorously:

> If Austria refuses all negotiations, we are face to face with a conflagration in which England will be against us; Rumania and Italy according to all indications will not be for us, and we shall stand two against four Powers. Through England's opposition the main blow will fall on Germany. Austria's political prestige, the military honor of her army, as well as her just claims against Serbia, can be adequately satisfied by her occupation of Belgrade or other places. Through her humiliation of Serbia, she will make her position in the Balkans as well as in her relation to Russia, strong again. Under these circumstances we must urgently and emphatically urge upon the consideration of the Vienna Cabinet the adoption of mediation in accordance with the above honorable conditions. The responsibility for the consequences which would otherwise follow would be, for Austria and for us, an uncommonly heavy one.[96]

To this urgent request by Germany for Austria's acceptance of a solution, which perhaps even yet might have avoided the conflagration of Europe, Berchtold gave no definite or frank answer. Bethmann's telegram, inclosing Lichnowsky's conversation with Grey, after being deciphered was handed to Tschirschky, Thursday, July 30,

[95] Lichnowsky to Bethmann, July 29, 6:39 P.M.; arrived 9:12 P.M.; K.D., 368. *Cf.* also Grey's report to Goschen of the same conversation, in a letter which was printed in the *British Blue Book* of 1914 (no. 89) as if sent, but which now appears to have remained in the British Archives marked, "Not sent—War" (B.D., 286).

[96] Bethmann to Tschirschky, July 30, 2:55 A.M.; K.D., 395. *Cf.* also Goschen to Grey, B.D., 329; and Gooss, pp. 233-246.

while he was at lunch with Berchtold. "Berchtold listened, pale and silent, while they were read through twice; Count Forgách took notes; finally Berchtold said he would at once lay the matter before the Emperor." After Berchtold had departed to put on another suit of clothes in which to present himself before His Majesty, Tschirschky spent a good part of the afternoon setting forth long and earnestly to Forgách and Hoyos all of Bethmann's arguments. It was useless. Instead, he was cynically informed by these two intimate advisers of Berchtold that "in view of the feeling in the army and in the people, any checking of the military operations in progress was out of the question. . . . Conrad von Hötzendorf [Austrian Chief of Staff] would lay before the Emperor this evening the order for general mobilization, as a reply to the measures already taken." He was also finally told that Berchtold could not give any answer until the following morning, for the reason that Tisza, who would not be in Vienna until then, must be consulted.[97]

By this time, the evening of July 30, Russia had ordered general mobilization, though the official news of it was not known at Berlin and Vienna until next day. But Germany had repeatedly given Russia to understand that this measure, directed against Germany as well as against Austria, and generally understood by the military authorities everywhere to mean a decision for war, would necessarily lead to German mobilization and consequently to war. So Bethmann's efforts at mediation failed. They came too late, and were not sufficiently vigorous to compel his ally to come to a timely understanding with Russia. Nor were they taken very seriously by the Entente Powers, whose faith in the sincerity of Germany's desire for peace had already been shaken by her apparent support of Austrian policy hitherto, and by the failure of her belated pressure at Vienna to produce any tangible results.

97 Tschirschky to Bethmann, July 31, 1:35 A.M.; K.D., 465.

CHAPTER X

THE RUSSIAN MOBILIZATION

At the Council of Ministers, held at Krasnoe Selo on the afternoon of July 25, as we have seen above in the chapter on "The Russian Danger," the Tsar's ministers had decided on a number of preparatory military measures. They included the wide-reaching preparations of the "Period Preparatory to War" which were intended to facilitate a Russian general mobilization against Germany as well as against Austria; they had been ordered before dawn on July 26, had been going on actively ever since, and had caused increasing alarm at Berlin in spite of the beguiling assurances of Sazonov and Sukhomlinov that no mobilization measures against Germany were intended. The decisions of July 25 also included a contingent partial mobilization against Austria, to be put into operation when Sazonov should decide that the diplomatic situation required it. It was hoped that the knowledge of this decision would prove a successful diplomatic bluff in frightening Vienna out of military action against Serbia. In the meantime, from July 25 to 28, while these military preparations had been going on to enable Russia to overcome her relative slowness in mobilization in case war became inevitable, Sazonov had appeared optimistic and been ready to carry on "direct conversations" with Vienna, with a view to finding a compromise settlement between the Austrian demands and the Serbian reply.

But on Tuesday, July 28, Sazonov's optimism received several rude shocks. He was disappointed and indignant that his proposal for "direct conversations," made two days previously, had as yet met with no response from Berchtold.

He was also unfavorably impressed by the fact that Szápáry could not give him the *dossier* which Austria had promised. His optimism began to change to pessimism. He began to conclude that Austria was fully determined on war with Serbia, and was therefore unlikely to listen to mediation proposals until punishment had been inflicted on her. Finally, he was thrown into great excitement late in the afternoon of July 28 by the arrival of the news that Austria had just declared war on Serbia. His optimism evaporated completely. He became thoroughly pessimistic, jumped nervously to the conclusion that a European conflict was probably inevitable, and that Russia should order mobilization; the only question was, should it be *partial* or *general* mobilization? This somersault in his attitude is revealed in the series of interviews and conferences which he crowded into the afternoon and evening of this busy Tuesday.

Early in the afternoon Sir George Buchanan called at the Russian Foreign Office. He found that Sazonov had received disquieting news [1] from Vienna—but not yet the

[1] What this "disquieting news" was is not clear. It may possibly have been one of three things:

(1) News received in Moscow on July 28 about 1:00 P. M. that Austrian reservists living in Moscow were urgently instructed to report themselves at the Consulate (*Investig., Comm.,* II, 87, Anlage 49).

(2) A telegram from the Russian Ambassador in Vienna: "The order for general mobilization has been signed" (R.O.B., 47). Even if this telegram is genuine, the information was unquestionably false, because, as will be indicated later, it is certain that the order for Austrian general mobilization was not signed until three days later—shortly before noon on July 31. But there are reasons for thinking that this telegram is not genuine: Sazonov does not cite it, but rather the Austrian declaration of war, as the ground for Russian partial mobilization; nor is it mentioned in Schilling's Diary; nor is it cited by the Russian General Staff or by Dobrorolski or by Danilov in their summaries of the situation on July 28. Montgelas and Stieve, *Russland und der Weltkonflikt,* p. 150 f., and Renouvin, p. 147, think this R.O.B. document is a Russian forgery. Paléologue, however, claims (I, 35) to have heard a rumor of it on July 29.

(3) The news of the Austrian declaration of war against Serbia. However, as this did not reach Nish until 12:30 P. M. one may doubt whether it could have arrived from there at St. Petersburg by 3:00 P. M., which was about the time Buchanan and Sazonov had their interview. Moreover,

report of the Austrian declaration of war on Serbia—and was already taking a "pessimistic view of the situation." Buchanan asked him whether he would not be satisfied with Austrian assurances in regard to Serbia's independence and integrity; England would welcome any arrangement to avert a European war, "but it was important that we should know the real intentions of the Imperial Government"—a phrase which suggests that Buchanan did not think that Sazonov was being completely frank with him. Sazonov replied that "no engagement which Austria might take on these two points [Serbia's independence and integrity] would satisfy Russia, and that on the day Austria crossed the Serbian frontier, order for mobilization against Austria would be issued." He added that there was no need to fear internal disturbances in Russia, and that, "in the event of war, the whole nation would be behind the Government." Buchanan suggested that as a last resort the Tsar should make a personal appeal to Francis Joseph to restrict Austria's action within limits which Russia could accept. But Sazonov again insisted that the only way to avert war was for England to let it be clearly known that she would join France and Russia. Buchanan got the impression that Russia "was thoroughly in earnest," and that Russia would fight if Austria attacked Serbia.[2]

if Sazonov had been aware of it, it seems almost certain that it would have found an important place in their conversation. It was apparently still unknown to Sazonov when he talked with Szápáry later in the afternoon, for it formed no part of their discussion, and Szápáry, in his later report of their conversation, added that the declaration of war on Serbia, "which has since taken place," will perhaps disclose Russia's real intentions (A.R.B., III, 16).

2 Buchanan to Grey, July 28, 8:45 P.M.; B.D., 247. *Cf.* also Paléologue, I, 30-32. According to Paléologue, who was waiting in the ante-chamber, Buchanan reported that he "had just begged Sazonov not to consent to any military measures which Germany could interpret as a provocation. One must leave to the German Government all responsibility and all initiative in an attack. English opinion would not countenance the idea of participating in the war unless the aggression unquestionably came from Germany." Buchanan's despatch contains nothing of all this.

After talking with Buchanan, Sazonov saw Pourtalès, and tried to convince him that Serbia's reply was satisfactory, and that Germany therefore should join in urging mediation at Vienna. But he met with little encouragement from the German Ambassador, who still adhered to his Government's "localization" policy, and did not yet know of the pressure which Bethmann was about to put on Vienna to accept the "pledge plan." On the contrary, Pourtalès complained of the hostile tone of the Russian Press and of the fact that reliable reports made it clear to Germany that Russia's military preparations were extending far beyond what Sukhomlinov had stated to the German Military Attaché on the evening of July 26. He had also learned that the military authorities had put out of commission the wireless apparatus on a German merchant ship, the *Eitel Friedrich,* in the harbor of St. Petersburg in defiance of international law. He had protested against this and the matter had been set right by the direct orders of the Tsar. But the incident gave Pourtalès further reason for expressing diplomatically to Sazonov the fear that the Russian militarists "were perhaps carrying the preparations for which they were responsible further than was intended" by Sazonov. He therefore warned Sazonov of the very serious danger which might arise in the existing critical situation from wide-reaching Russian military preparations.[3]

Either he did not report fully to Sir Edward Grey, or, more probably, Paléologue is fathering upon the British Ambassador views which he alleges (I, 33 f.) he himself expressed to Sazonov a little later and which will be discussed below.

[3] Pourtalès to Bethmann, July 28, 8:12 P.M.; K.D., 338; Szápáry to Berchtold, July 28 (dispatched July 29, 1:15 A.M.), A.R.B., II, 94. Pourtalès in his later memoir (*Am Scheideweg,* pp. 32-37) indicates that he had two interviews with Sazonov on the afternoon of July 28, a stormy one before the *Eitel Friedrich* incident, and a more peaceful one after it. Paléologue (I, 33) gives the impression that Pourtalès was so overcome with emotion at the danger of war that he could scarcely speak. On the *Eitel Friedrich* incident, see Dobrorolski, p. 104 (German ed., p. 23), and Pourtalès, *Am Scheideweg,* pp. 34-37.

Sazonov then received the Austrian Ambassador, but was disappointed that Szápáry had received no answer to the proposal of two days earlier for "direct conversations." Sazonov said that boded no good, and that the situation was serious. He again requested urgently a copy of the *dossier,* which Austria had promised to lay before the Powers, but had not yet delivered at St. Petersburg; he wanted to see it, he said, before war against Serbia should begin; otherwise, it would be too late to examine it. He and Szápáry repeated their old arguments about the Austrian ultimatum and the Serbian reply in a calm and friendly way, but without coming to any satisfactory conclusion. Szápáry then took his departure, "because the Minister had an appointment with his Imperial Master at Peterhof." [4]

Sazonov, however, apparently did not go out to Peterhof at once. He first talked with Paléologue, and communicated with the Chief of Staff concerning the ordering of mobilization in Russia in view of the news of the Austrian declaration of war on Serbia which had just arrived.

PALÉOLOGUE'S DECLARATION OF FRENCH SUPPORT

Paléologue, who says he had purposely waited until Sazonov had talked with the other ambassadors, was then closeted with the Russian Minister of Foreign Affairs in an interview of which we have two very different versions. Baron Schilling, who usually noted accurately every evening

[4] Szápáry to Berchtold, July 29, 10:00 A.M.; A.R.B., III, 16. Though dated July 29, the first part of this telegram no. 173 refers to July 28. On July 28 at 11:40 P.M., Berchtold finally telegraphed Szápáry that he was unwilling to discuss the Serbian reply as a basis for "direct conversations," because it had been rejected as unsatisfactory, and, moreover, war had already been declared (A.R.B., II, 95). Szápáry did not receive this message until the following afternoon at some time roughly between 2:00 P.M. and 6:00 P.M.; for Pourtalès reported on July 29 at 1:58 P.M. (K.D., 343) that up to that time Sazonov had received no reply from Berchtold; but at 6:10 P.M., (K.D., 365) Pourtalès reported that Vienna had finally "replied with a categorical refusal."

the substance of Sazonov's most important interviews, says:

> "The French Ambassador, upon instructions of his Government, informed the Minister of Foreign Affairs of the complete readiness of France to fulfil her obligations as an ally in case of necessity." [5]

This declaration of Paléologue's was of such extreme importance to Russia just at this juncture that it evidently overshadowed everything else in Baron Schilling's mind on July 28, because it is the only entry made in his diary for that day, aside from his usual summary of telegrams.[6] That Paléologue did make such a declaration, and that it gave further encouragement to Sazonov to stand firm and presently to approve Russian mobilization is confirmed by the fact that next day, Sazonov, in notifying Izvolski of his decision "to hasten our armaments and to assume that war is probably inevitable," added:

> "Please express to the French Government our sincere gratitude for the declaration, which has been officially made to me in its name by the French Ambassador, that we can count fully upon the assistance of our ally, France. In the existing circumstances, this declaration is especially valuable to us." [7]

Paléologue, however, in his memoirs, gives an altogether different version. He says not a word of this important declaration. Instead, after an account, perhaps more picturesque than accurate, of Pourtalès' nervousness and Sazonov's coolness, he enlarged upon his own importance as

5 Schilling's *Diary,* p. 43.

6 Possibly, however, the brevity of Schilling's *Diary* for July 28 is to be explained by the fact that one or two pages for this day were misplaced or lost.

7 Sazonov to Izvolski and to the other Russian Ambassadors, tg. no. 1551, July 29; M.F.R., p. 520; L.N., II, 289; R.O.B., 58; reported to Viviani at Paris between 2 and 3 A.M. on July 30; B.D., 373; Viviani, *Réponse au Kaiser,* p. 149; Poincaré, IV, 383.

M. PALÉOLOGUE
French Ambassador in St. Petersburg, 1914-1917

COUNT POURTALÈS
German Ambassador in St. Petersburg, 1907-1914

representative of a country which was temporarily decapitated by Poincaré's absence and the very intermittent means of communicating with him. In view of the resulting great responsibility resting upon himself as the Ambassador of France, he alleges that he begged Sazonov to be very cautious about taking any military measures which might jeopardize English support; that Sazonov said he was having great difficulty in restraining the Russian General Staff; and that he, Paléologue, then got him to promise to accept all the measures which France and England should propose to preserve peace, and to authorize him to telegraph this promise to Paris.[8] It is, however, very doubtful whether Sazonov would have been willing to make any such blanket promise, and if he did, he did not keep it, for he speedily approved at least partial mobilization, which can hardly be regarded as a measure proposed by France and England to preserve peace. In the account of this Paléologue-Sazonov conversation, Baron Schilling was presumably correct, and Paléologue was probably giving a free rein to his post-War imagination.

Whether Paléologue, in making his declaration of Franco-Russian solidarity to Sazonov, was really acting "on instructions from his Government" as Schilling says, or was saying what was not true, or was incorrectly reported by Schilling and Sazonov, must remain uncertain until the French finally make a complete publication of their documents for this period.[9] Perhaps his declaration was his way

[8] Paléologue, I, 33. A brief telegram to this effect does in fact appear in F.Y.B., 86, but it may well be questioned whether it was not sent to conceal from France, and especially from England, the fact that the Russian militarists were pressing hard for a *general mobilization,* of which Paléologue's telegram says not a word.

[9] A similar doubt as to Paléologue's veracity arises in connection with his statements on July 25, as reported by Buchanan (B.D., 125), that "he had received a number of telegrams" from Bienvenu-Martin and "was in a position to give formal assurance that France placed herself unreservedly on Russia's side;" and that the "French Government would want to know at once whether our [British] fleet was prepared to play

of carrying out a telegram sent to him by Viviani on July 27, which said: "Please say to M. Sazonov that France, appreciating like Russia the high importance for both countries of affirming their perfect understanding in regard to other Powers and of not neglecting any effort with a view to a solution of the conflict, is ready to support completely, in the interests of general peace, the action of the Imperial Government." [10] In any case, Paléologue's declaration was in keeping with the assurances which President Poincaré himself had given a week before upon his visit to Russia, and also with Izvolski's telegram from Paris on July 27: "I was surprised how well the Acting Minister for Foreign Affairs and his colleagues understand the situation, and how firm and quiet is their decision to give us fullest support and to avoid even the smallest suspicion of a disagreement with us." [11]

THE NEWS OF THE AUSTRIAN DECLARATION OF WAR ON SERBIA

In the course of the afternoon of July 28, news reached Russia of the Austrian declaration of war on Serbia. It may have arrived while Sazonov was in conversation with Paléologue and been partly the reason for the latter's declaration of French support. The news dissipated any remnants of optimism in Sazonov's mind. It made him fear that Austria would soon invade Serbia, and confirmed his growing conviction that Germany was standing behind Austria and would continue to do so, unless he made it clear that Russia was determined to threaten Austria with force in order to protect Serbia. He came to the conclusion that the time had come to order the partial mobilization which had been approved "in principle" on July 25. He therefore

part assigned to it by the Anglo-French Naval Convention." There is nothing in the *French Yellow Book,* as published, to substantiate these statements.

[10] Poincaré, IV, 335, 385 ff.

[11] Tg. no. 195; M.F.R., p. 516; L.N., II, 282; suppressed from R.O.B., 35.

announced in the various European capitals: "In view of the declaration of war by Austria against Serbia, my direct conversations with the Austrian Ambassador are obviously useless!" [11a]

In other words, he abandoned "direct conversations" as a peaceful solution many hours before he heard of Austria's "categorical refusal," which he did not learn until the following afternoon.[12] He also instructed his ambassadors abroad to inform the Governments that, in consequence of Austria's declaration of war, Russia had decided to order next day partial mobilization in the four Southern Military Districts of Odessa, Kiev, Moscow and Kazan; but added: "Russia entertains no aggressive intentions against Germany." [13]

These telegrams seem to leave no doubt that Sazonov wished to give Europe the impression that he was now merely carrying out the means of pressure upon Austria which had already been decided upon at Krasnoe Selo on July 25 and several times stated to the Powers, and that the reason for it was the Austrian declaration of war on Serbia. Pourtalès is also of the opinion that Sazonov's change in attitude "took place only on the 28th, when it

[11a] Sazonov to Benckendorff and other Russian Ambassadors, tg. no. 1538, July 28; K.A., p. 52; Schilling's *Diary,* p. 44; *cf.* R.O.B., 48, where phrases are altered, omitted, and added. In this telegram he also urged immediate English mediation to prevent Austria from crushing Serbia; B.D., 258.

[12] See above, note 4. In his memoirs (*Fateful Years,* p. 185 ff.), Sazonov pretends that he was informed of Berchtold's refusal on July 28, before authorizing partial mobilization.

[13] Sazonov to Bronevski in Berlin and other Russian Ambassadors, tgs. nos. 1539, 1540; K.A., I, p. 178; L.N., II, 283; Schilling's *Diary,* p. 44. Bronevski did not inform Jagow of this until after 5:00 P.M. on July 29 at the moment Jagow learned it with consternation from Pourtalès (Schilling's *Diary,* pp. 103, 106; K.D., 343). Izvolski informed the French Foreign Office at 11:15 A.M. on July 29, just before Poincaré's arrival in Paris (Poincaré IV, 373). Benckendorff informed Nicolson some time on July 29 (B.D., 258). Sazonov did not communicate this important decision to the foreign ambassadors in St. Petersburg until the morning of July 29 (K.D., 343; B.D., 276; *cf.* Paléologue, I, 35).

became known that the threatening attitude of Russia had not sufficed to prevent Austria from declaring war on Serbia. Undoubtedly the change in Sazonov's feeling was primarily brought about by this step on the part of the Vienna Cabinet."[14]

But it is quite possible that Sazonov's change of attitude went even further than a decision to put into effect a partial mobilization—that he now reluctantly accepted the view of the military authorities that a European war had become inevitable and that a general, instead of a partial, mobilization should be adopted. This is the view of Dobrorolski, who says:

> On July 28, the day of the Austrian declaration of war on Serbia, Sazonov's optimism vanishes at a stroke. He is filled with the idea that a general war is inevitable, and informs Ianushkevich that one must no longer delay with the mobilization of our army, . . . that he was even astonished that it had not begun sooner.[15]

To be sure, Sazonov was aware that any precipitate general mobilization on Russia's part, directed against Germany as well as against Austria, might have a bad effect upon public opinion in France and England if it should become known; but, on the other hand, he had just received from Paléologue the renewed declaration of French support, and there was the encouraging news from Sir Edward Grey that the British fleet had been ordered to remain concentrated instead of dispersing to its normal peace-time positions.[16] Sazonov also knew that a Russian general mobilization would almost certainly lead to a German general

[14] Comment of Pourtalès on the German edition of Dobrorolski, p. 38.

[15] Dobrorolski, p. 104 (German ed. p. 23). In his own memoirs Sazonov says (p. 188) that the Russian Government and public opinion was now convinced on July 28 that war was "inevitable." Chelius likewise telegraphed to the Kaiser on July 29 (K.D., 344) that "in the *entourage* of the Tsar . . . since the declaration of war, they consider a general war almost inevitable."

[16] B.D., 177, 247.

mobilization, and so to a European war. A partial mobilization, on the contrary, was less likely to call forth immediate counter-measures from Germany.[17] But even this would probably lead to Austrian general mobilization and so place European peace in serious jeopardy. But whether consciousness of these facts outweighed in his mind the arguments of the military technicians as to the folly and impossibility of a partial mobilization is not clear. He decided that the time had come for some mobilization and so informed Ianushkevich. In any event the four districts of Odessa, Kiev, Moscow and Kazan were to be mobilized, in accordance with the announcement which he was making to the Powers. He left it to Ianushkevich to argue next morning with the Tsar in favor of general mobilization.[18]

[17] *Cf.* Izvolski to Sazonov tg. no. 197, July 27: "Jules Cambon telegraphs from Berlin that, in answer to his question of what attitude Germany would take towards a partial mobilization in Russia, Jagow stated that such a mobilization would not be followed by German mobilization; but that, if Russia attacked Austria, Germany would at once reply by an attack on Russia" (M.F.R., p. 516; L.N., II, 282). Similarly also Bronevski to Sazonov, July 27, quoting Jagow as saying: "We shall mobilize if Russia mobilizes on our frontier, or if Russian troops advance on Austrian soil" (*Krasnyi Arkhiv,* I, p. 173).

[18] In *Fateful Years* Sazonov says (p. 188): "The Council of Ministers, with the Tsar presiding, decided to mobilize at once the four military districts." But there is no other substantial indication of any such Council of Ministers on July 28, and it is most unlikely. He may be confusing in his mind the Councils of July 24 and July 25. Recouly to be sure, says (p. 158) that the question of partial or general mobilization was "long discussed on Wednesday, July 28" at 5:00 P. M. at a conference between Ianushkevich, Sukhomlinov, Sazonov and Neratov. But Recouly's statement is open to three objections: (1) July 28 was not "Wednesday" but Tuesday; (2) Sazonov was so occupied with the conversations noted above on the afternoon of July 28 that he would hardly have had time for a "long discussion" before going out for his audience at Peterhof; (3) Recouly says General Danilov gave him the details of this conference, but Danilov himself in his memoirs (*Russland in Weltkrieg,* Berlin, 1925, pp. 16-22), while giving the same arguments in favor of general mobilization as those repeated by Recouly, does not mention Sazonov or Neratov as being present at any such conference; he mentions beside himself only the military specialists, Ianushkevich, Dobrorolski, and Ronzhin, the head of the Department of Military Transportation. Renouvin (p. 133 ff.), however, it may be noted, accepts Recouly's account without question.

After his conversations with the Ambassadors and his decision for partial mobilization in any event, Sazonov went out to Peterhof and reported to the Tsar on the Austrian declaration of war and the general situation. Whether he advocated the view of Ianushkevich that the time had come for general mobilization, or whether he still advised the Tsar merely in favor of his own former partial mobilization plan is not certain. We have no record of what he said to the Tsar. Presumably he gave a gloomy picture of the situation. The only evident consequence of his visit was the telegram which the Tsar sent to the Kaiser late that same night: ". . . An ignoble war has been declared to a weak country. The indignation in Russia, fully shared by me, is enormous. I foresee that very soon I shall be overwhelmed by the pressure brought upon me, and be forced to take extreme measures which will lead to war. . . ."[19] Was this "pressure" which the Tsar feared would overwhelm him, exerted only by the military leaders, or by his entourage, or perhaps by Sazonov himself?

THE TSAR'S ASSENT TO RUSSIAN GENERAL MOBILIZATION

The views of Dobrorolski and the military leaders as to the folly of a partial mobilization were strengthened by the return of Quartermaster-General Danilov. He had been on a tour of inspection in the Caucasus, but had been hastily recalled to St. Petersburg on July 26. He now used all his influence to have general mobilization ordered in place of partial mobilization. In his memoirs he sets forth at length, and in as convincing a manner as Dobrorolski, all the technical and political difficulties of a partial mobilization. The latter would provide only 13 army corps, whereas 16 were calculated as necessary for the successful blow against Austria. If the Warsaw District was left untouched, it would

19 July 29, 1:00 A.M.; K.A., IV, p. 19; Schilling's *Diary*, p. 46; K.D., 332.

be impossible to concentrate for an attack on Austria in Galicia as planned, and a wholly new scheme of campaign would have to be suddenly improvised. Worst of all, if a general mobilization should eventually follow a partial mobilization, the confusion would be intolerable, inasmuch as the Warsaw District had to draw some of its reservists from the four Districts already dislocated by partial mobilization. Owing to the greater density of population in the southwestern part of the Empire, Russia had not worked out a mobilization plan by which each Military District drew its recruits exclusively from within its own borders. This technical difficulty would mean that in case a general mobilization followed a partial mobilization, Russia would not be able to fulfil the expectation of her French ally in quickly bringing satisfactory forces against Germany.[20]

For all these and other technical reasons, therefore, Danilov insisted on the holding of a military council in which the arguments against the partial mobilization plan of July 24 and 25 were again considered. It probably met on the afternoon or evening of July 28, and was attended by Ianushkevich, Dobrorolski, Danilov, and Ronzhin, the head of the Department of Military Transportation. As a result, Ianushkevich was convinced that every effort must be made to persuade the Tsar to approve general mobilization. When therefore he heard from Sazonov that mobilization ought no longer to be delayed, he prepared two imperial ukases, one for the partial, and the other for the general, mobilization. The first was to be used if the Tsar persisted in adhering to the plan of July 25; his assent to the second was to be secured if possible.[21]

With these two draft orders in his portfolio, Ianushke-

20 Danilov, *Russland im Weltkriege,* pp. 16-22. See also similarly Dobrorolski, pp. 96-103 (German ed. pp. 14-22), and above, ch. vi, at notes 40, 73.

21 Danilov, p. 16 f.; Dobrorolski, p. 104 f. (German ed. p. 23 f); Sukhomlinov, *Erinnerungen,* p. 361 f.

vich went out to Peterhof on the morning of July 29. Apparently without much difficulty, he certainly secured the Tsar's signature to the ukase for general mobilization, and probably also to that for partial mobilization; the latter to be used in case there might come a turn for the better in the diplomatic situation.

It was one of the greatest weaknesses of Nicholas II, of which all his ministers complained from time to time, that he was too apt to assent to the minister who last happened to have his ear. This weakness was all the more disastrous because of the unfortunate Russian system of lack of Cabinet solidarity, and of the practice of separate ministerial reports to the Tsar for his supreme approval or disapproval. Ianushkevich was so confident in this weak trait in his Monarch's character, and of his own ability to win him over, that even before going out to Peterhof, he sent secret word to Zhilinski, the commander of the Warsaw Military District, and presumably to all the Military Districts, stating that "general mobilization" was imminent:

> July 17 [30] will be announced as the first day of our general mobilization. The announcement will follow upon the agreed telegram. 1785. [Signed] Lieutenant-General Ianushkevich.[22]

Some hours earlier Danilov had also asked the Warsaw Military Commander about arrangements for unloading cavalry divisions which were being pushed forward toward

22 Tg. no. 1785, Ianushkevich to Zhilinski, July 29, *ca.* 7:20 A. M.; captured by the Germans later and quoted by Höniger, pp. 100 f. and by Frantz, p. 265. This is confirmed by Zhilinski's telegram next day, after the Tsar had changed his mind and suspended general, in favor of partial, mobilization: "The Chief of the General Staff telegraphed yesterday [July 29] that July 30 would be announced as the first day of mobilization, but since this has not taken place I conclude that changes have taken place in the political situation. Would it not be possible to inform me of the changes which have taken place in this matter? 1954;" Zhilinski to Sukhomlinov, July 30, 2:25 P. M.; quoted by Höniger, p. 110, and by Frantz, p. 266.

the German frontier.[23] One can imagine how the receipt of these telegrams would lead the Russian commanders at Warsaw and at other posts along the German frontier to strain every nerve toward preparing for war, short of a public announcement of mobilization. Aware of this fact, Danilov was also conscious that Russian troops, expecting at any moment the publication of the imminent general mobilization, might commit some act of hostility on the frontier which would give Germany grounds for ordering mobilization, and which also might compromise Russia with her allies, by making Russia seem to be the aggressor. He therefore quickly telegraphed explicitly that, upon the announcement of mobilization, the opening of actual hostilities was not to take place except upon a special telegram, and the frontier troops were to be warned, "in order that no irremediable mistakes shall occur."[24] These telegrams make it clear that the military authorities confidently expected general mobilization would be approved by the Tsar and ordered on July 29, but wished to avoid as far as possible having Russia seem the aggressor.

Returning from Peterhof with the ukase for general mobilization signed by the Tsar in his pocket, Ianushkevich summoned Eggeling, the German Military Attaché. He told him that he had just come from the Tsar, but that everything was just as Sukhomlinov had said it was a couple of days before.[25] "He gave me his word of honor in the most solemn manner and offered me written confirmation that up to that moment, 3:00 P.M., nowhere had there been mobilization, i.e., the calling up of a single man or horse. He could give no guarantee for the future, he said, but would assure me most emphatically that His Majesty, now as before, did not desire mobilization on the fronts along

23 Tg. no. 1746, July 28, 11:58 P.M.; Höniger, p. 105; Frantz, p. 245.
24 Tg. no. 1754, July 29, 1:10 A.M.; Höniger, p. 105; Frantz, p. 241.
25 See above, ch. vi, at notes 107, 108.

our borders." In view of the many reports concerning the calling of reservists, including the Warsaw and Vilna districts toward Germany, Eggeling said that this statement puzzled him. "Ianushkevich replied that, on the word of an officer, such reports were mistaken; it was simply a case of a false alarm here and there."[26] Eggeling was forced to conclude that Ianushkevich was attempting to mislead him, and the historian can hardly escape the same conclusion.

While Ianushkevich was perhaps within the letter of the truth in saying that the Tsar did not desire mobilization on the German front, he knew that he had in his pocket[27] the Tsar's order for a mobilization of this very kind, and that he was going to put it into effect just as soon as he could get the necessary signatures of three other ministers.

The Tsar's signature to the mobilization ukase was not sufficient to allow it to be ordered forthwith. In order to maintain a check on the military authorities, Russian law provided that the mobilization order must also be countersigned by the Ministers of War, Marine and Interior.[28] Ianushkevich therefore handed over the mobilization order to Dobrorolski who was to get the three signatures. This officer has left a vivid and essentially accurate account of his part in the events of this most important day in his life, except that he places some of the events an hour or two too early.[29] He went first to Sukhomlinov, the Minister

[26] Pourtalès to Bethmann, July 29, 7 P.M.; K.D., 370; Eggeling, pp. 27-41; Höniger, "Untersuchungen zum Suchomlinow-Prozess," in *Deutsche Rundschau,* April, 1918, pp. 32-33.

[27] At the Sukhomlinov Trial in 1917, referring to his statement to Eggeling, Ianushkevich declared, "I considered myself justified in offering him such a written declaration, because, as a matter of fact, at this moment, mobilization had not yet been announced. I still had the ukase for mobilization in my pocket" (*Novoe Vremia,* No. 14,852, Aug. 13/26, 1917).

[28] Dobrorolski, p. 105 (German ed. p. 24); Sukomlinov, p. 361; Frantz, p. 66.

[29] Dobrorolski, pp. 105 ff. (German ed. pp. 24 ff.), and his supplementary statment in KSF, II, 78-89, April, 1924. He says that he received the document from Ianushkevich "in the morning, that is

of War, whom he found tired, depressed and apparently regretful of his recent bellicose newspaper article, "Russia is ready, France must be also." Nevertheless Sukhomlinov signed the document, though with a heavy heart, realizing now too late, says Dobrorolski, that Russia was plunging into a war for which she was not fully prepared and which was beyond her strength. In these last days it was Ianushkevich, the Chief of Staff, and not Sukhomlinov, who was most active in pressing for general mobilization.

The Minister of Marine, Grigorovich, was not to be found at the Admiralty; his adjutant said he would not return home till toward seven o'clock. Going on to the Ministry of the Interior, Dobrorolski found alarm at the danger of internal revolution. "With us," said Maklakov, "the war cannot be popular deep down among the masses of the people, among whom revolutionary ideas mean more than a victory over Germany. But one cannot escape one's fate . . ."; and crossing himself, Maklakov signed the mobilization order. These visits took two or three hours, after which Dobrorolski returned to the General Staff Office, to wait for the return of the Minister of Marine. Later in the evening he finally secured his signature also, and then was able to go to the Central Telegraph Office to dispatch the order throughout the Empire. Dobrorolski has left a vivid account of it:

> The Chief Director of the Post and Telegraph had been notified beforehand that a message of extraordinary importance was to be sent out. After I had entered the cabinet of the St. Petersburg Telegraph Office, I handed him the telegram, and waited to be present personally at the transmission of the telegram to the four corners of the Russian Em-

about noon," but it was probably not until after three in the afternoon—after Ianushkevich's interview with Eggeling. He also says it was at 9:30 P.M. that he was on the point of sending out the mobilization order over the wires, when he was suddenly recalled; but it must have been a little later, since the Kaiser's telegram which occasioned the recall of the order did not arrive until 9:40 P.M.

pire. In my presence they proceeded to click off the telegram on several typewriters in order to send it at the same moment by all the wires which connected St. Petersburg with the principal centres of the Empire, from which the despatch would be transmitted to all the towns in the governments and territorial districts. There existed a special instruction for the sending of the mobilization telegram. During its transmission no other telegrams of any sort could be sent.

The imposing room of the St. Petersburg Central Telegraph Office with its telegraph keys, to the number of some dozen, was ready to receive the mobilization telegram.

But at this moment—about 9:30 P.M.—General Ianushkevich called me on the telephone and ordered me to hold back the telegram until the arrival of a Captain in the General Staff, Tugan-Baranovski. He entered and told me that he had hurried after me through the city to bring me a special order from the Tsar not to send out the telegram for general mobilization. General mobilization was to be suspended, and in its place, by order of the Tsar, partial mobilization was to be adopted in accordance with the plan previously arranged.

I at once took back the telegram for general mobilization which I had delivered to the telegraph office and all the copies of the telegram. I notified the head of the telegraph office of the withdrawal which had taken place, and rode away.[30]

Before explaining this sudden eleventh-hour change of decision, we must glance back for a moment to see what Sazonov and the ambassadors had been doing while Ianushkevich had been out at Peterhof and Dobrorolski had been getting the necessary signatures for the general mobilization order.

On the morning of July 29 about 11 o'clock Pourtalès called upon Sazonov to make an "agreeable communication" —that Austria had renewed her declaration that she did not

30 Dobrorolski, p. 107 (German ed. p. 25 f).

intend to take Serbian territory and that Germany was striving to persuade her to come to a frank discussion with Russia and satisfy her as to the purpose and extent of her procedure in Serbia. But Sazonov replied that, since he had had no answer to his proposal for "direct conversations" and Austria had declared war on Serbia, Austria's good faith was questionable. Russia therefore had decided to mobilize the military districts on the Austrian frontier and the order would be given that very day; this did not mean war; "the Russian army would doubtless remain under arms for weeks to come without crossing the frontier." Pourtalès pointed out the peril that the General Staffs of Russia's neighbors would press for counter-measures.[31]

In notifying Pourtalès that Russia was about to order partial mobilization against Austria only, Sazonov was not necessarily acting insincerely, because he did not yet know whether Ianushkevich had persuaded the Tsar to sign the ukase for general as well as partial mobilization. But, after lunch, in his interview with the British Ambassador, he can hardly be said to have been completely frank, because he gave Buchanan to understand that "the order for partial mobilization was signed today," and that "it had been decided not to order the general mobilization which the military authorities had strongly recommended."[32] Had Sazonov by this time heard from Ianushkevich the result of his visit to Peterhof? If not, how could he say "the order for partial mobilization was signed today?" If he had heard from Ianushkevich, as is probably the case, he knew that the order for general mobilization also had been signed, and it was not true that "it had been decided not to order the general mobilization." In either case he gave Buchanan an impression of definiteness about the Russian military de-

31 Pourtalès to Bethmann, July 29, 1:58 P.M.; K.D., 343; Schilling's *Diary*, p. 47 f.

32 Buchanan to Grey, July 29, 8:40 P.M.; B.D., 276.

cisions which was not in accordance with the facts. His purpose, of course, was obvious—he wished to avoid alarming and alienating British opinion. Therefore he coupled his information about partial mobilization with the statement that mobilization would take a week or more, and that Russia would not precipitate war by immediately crossing the frontier, and he hoped England could meanwhile find some satisfactory peaceful solution.

In the middle of the afternoon, Pourtalès had a second interview with Sazonov, who sent for him to tell him the news, evidently just received from the Russian Ambassador in Vienna,[33] that Berchtold had replied with a "categorical refusal" to the request for "direct conversations." Sazonov therefore, "grasping at every straw," wished now to return to Grey's proposal for a conference of ambassadors. Pourtalès, however, said he did not know his Government's attitude on this, but "could not help feeling that the order of Russian mobilization, in case it were really impending, was a great mistake. . . . Sazonov did not deny the imminence of mobilization, but stated that Russia was compelled by Austria to take this step; mobilization, however, was far from meaning war." [34]

Sazonov next received a call from the Austrian Ambassador, who came "to clear up apparent misunderstandings." Having just received Berchtold's telegram refusing to discuss the text of the Austrian ultimatum, Szápáry had to admit that Austria was unwilling to carry on direct conversations on this subject, but was quite ready to converse on the broader basis of Austro-Russian relations; that she had no wish to injure Russian interest, was seeking no territory, and did not intend to interfere with Serbia's sovereignty.

Sazonov replied that though Austria might not take Ser-

33 *Cf.* Berchtold to Szápáry, July 28, 11:40 P.M.; A.R.B., II, 95.

34 Pourtalès to Bethmann, July 29, 6:10 P.M.; K.D., 365; *Am Scheideweg*, 41 f.

bian territory, she was nevertheless attacking Serbian sovereignty by virtually reducing her to a vassal state. This would upset the balance of power in the Balkans, and consequently injure Russian interests. There followed a long fruitless discussion in a *circulus vitiosus.* Finally Sazonov said "a ukase would be signed today ordering a mobilization of a fairly wide extent; but he could assure me most officially that their troops were not meant to attack us; they would only stand ready with arms grounded in case Russia's Balkan interests were endangered; a *note explicative* would confirm this." (No such note, however, was ever issued.)

The responsibility for this order Sazonov sought to put wholly on the military authorities, according to Szápáry's report. When Szápáry mentioned that he had heard Russia was alarmed because Austria had mobilized eight corps against Serbia, "Sazonov confirmed to me that it was not he, who knew nothing of this, but Tsar Nicholas who, upon the information of the Chief of Staff, had expressed this alarm." Szápáry pointed out that even a child in military matters ought to see the mobilization of Austria toward the south could not threaten Russia, and urged that if peace were to be preserved, a quick end should be put to the machinations of the military authorities who on the basis of false news were in danger of taking matters into their own hands. "Sazonov remarked very characteristically that he could say this to the Chief of Staff, because the latter was seeing His Majesty every day. He himself, however, in a time like the present, only went for his usual Tuesday audience, and then learned for the first time from His Majesty what the militarists had been urging upon him."

"While we were thus engaged in a confidential exchange of views," Szápáry continued, "Sazonov heard by telephone that we had bombarded Belgrade. He became like a changed man [*wie ausgewechselt*]. He sought to take up again all his previous arguments in a way which flew in the face of all logic, and said he saw now that the Tsar was right. 'You only wish to gain time by negotiations, but you go ahead and bombard an unprotected city!'" He went on to denounce Austria in the most excited fashion. Whereupon Szápáry took his leave.[35] The exact hour of this interview is uncertain, but it was probably in the later part of the afternoon, after Sazonov had heard from Ianushkevich that the Tsar had signed the ukase for general mobilization. This may explain why he spoke of "a mobilization of fairly wide extent," instead of the "partial mobilization," which he had indicated to Pourtalès and Buchanan earlier in the day.

A little later, between six and seven o'clock, while Sazonov was still in a very excited state, Pourtalès called again at the Russian Foreign Office to carry out instructions just received from Berlin. Alarmed by the rumors of wide-reaching Russian military preparations—but not of the decision for Russian partial mobilization of which he did not hear until a little later[36]—Bethmann had telegraphed to Pourtalès: "Kindly call M. Sazonov's serious attention to the fact that further continuation of Russian mobilization measures would force us to mobilize, and in that case a European war could scarcely be prevented."[37]

35 Szápáry to Berchtold, July 29, 11:00 P.M.; A.R.B. III, 19. Pourtalès, in a telegram sent at 8:00 P.M. (K.D., 378), says: "Sazonov has admitted to Szápáry that mobilization is impending, and added that a *note explicative* would be published." This indicates that the Sazonov-Szápáry interview took place prior to Pourtalès's "warning," to be mentioned in a moment. Schilling's *Diary*, p. 49, is therefore inaccurate in placing the news of the bombardment of Belgrade *after* Pourtalès's warning. Curiously enough, Schilling makes no mention of this Sazonov-Szápáry interview—possibly because it was the aim of the Russians (and especially of the French) to shift the responsibility in the final days as much as possible from Austria to Germany.

36 From Sverbeiev after 5:00 P.M. (Schilling's *Diary*, pp. 103, 106); and from Pourtalès in a telegram received at 1:58 P.M. (K.D., 343).

37 Bethmann to Pourtalès, July 29, 12:50 P.M.; received at St. Petersburg at 4:35 P.M.; K.D., 342; Schilling's *Diary*, p. 48. Allowing time for decodification, and for the codification of Pourtalès' reply which was

In stating this to Sazonov, Pourtalès said "it did not imply a threat, but simply a friendly opinion." But Sazonov received it "in a state of great excitement" and said he would report it to the Tsar.[38] Sazonov, however, appears to have interpreted it as a threat, and replied sharply: "Now I have no further doubt as to the true cause of Austria's intransigence." Pourtalès jumped up from his seat in protest, and the two parted coolly.[39]

Sazonov then informed the Tsar by telephone of the communication just made by Pourtalès. The Tsar directed him to discuss with Ianushkevich and Sukhomlinov the question of general mobilization at once, while he himself telegraphed to the Kaiser: "Thanks for your telegram conciliatory and friendly, whereas official message presented today by your Ambassador to my Minister was conveyed in a very different tone. Beg you to explain this divergency. It would be right to give over the Austro-Serbian problem to the Hague Conference. Trust in your wisdom and friendship." [40]

The news of the bombardment of Belgrade, followed by Pourtalès's warning that the further continuation of Russian mobilization measures would lead to German mobilization and war, removed any last doubts which Sazonov may have had as to need of immediate general mobilization. In the discussion with Ianushkevich, he agreed that, as war with Germany was probably unavoidable, it would be a mistake to postpone longer the general mobilization

sent at 8:00 P.M. (K.D., 378), it is clear that this third Pourtalès-Sazonov interview took place between 6 and 7 P.M., as Pourtalès correctly states in his memoir (*Am Scheideweg,* p. 45 f.). Schilling's *Diary,* p. 48, is inaccurate in placing it "at 3:00 P.M."; Schilling perhaps confused it with the second Pourtalès interview, mentioned above at note 34, which did take place about 3:00 P.M.

[38] Pourtalès to Bethmann, July 29, 8:00 P.M., K.D., 378; *cf.* Schilling's *Diary,* p. 48.

[39] Schilling's *Diary,* p. 48 f.

[40] Tsar to Kaiser, 8:20 P.M.; received 8:42 P.M.; K.D., 366; Schilling's *Diary,* p. 54. On the Tsar's Hague Tribunal idea, see preceding chapter, at notes 74-78.

or to interfere with its successful execution by first ordering a partial mobilization. This decision "was telephoned to the Tsar who authorized taking steps accordingly." It was also, according to Baron Schilling, "received with enthusiasm by the small circle of those acquainted with what was in progress." [41]

Dobrorolski, who had meanwhile collected the three necessary signatures, started for the Central Telegraph Office to send out the general mobilization order. And Sazonov dispatched a telegram to the Russian Ambassadors in Paris and London, which hardly stated fully and frankly either the communication of Pourtalès or the momentous step which Russia was on the point of taking:

> The German Ambassador informed me today of the decision of the German Government to mobilize its armed forces, if Russia did not stop her military preparations. Now, in point of fact, we only began these preparations in consequence of the mobilization of eight army corps already undertaken by Austria, and owing to her evident unwillingness to accept any means of arriving at a peaceful settlement of her dispute with Serbia.
>
> As we cannot comply with the wishes of Germany, we have no alternative but to hasten on our own armaments and to assume that war is probably inevitable.[42]

If we put confidence in the complete sincerity of the telegram just quoted, and in the accuracy of Schilling's *Diary* as to the crowded events of July 29, as some writers

41 Schilling's *Diary*, p. 50.

42 Sazonov to Izvolski and Benckendorff, tg. 1551, July 30; L.N., II, 289; B.D., 300. R.O.B., 58, omits the words, "of eight army corps;" and it was not true that Russia only began her military preparations in consequence of the mobilization already undertaken by Austria; she began them on the night of July 25-26, before she had heard of the Austrian partial mobilization against Serbia. Sazonov's telegram to Izvolski goes on to thank France for Paléologue's declaration of French support, "in the existing circumstances very valuable to us," and to urge that England should at once join Russia and France (see above, at notes 5-11).

are inclined to do,[43] it would appear that it was the warning from Pourtalès which caused the Russian decision to order general mobilization instead of partial mobilization. But it was naturally Sazonov's aim, in order to secure British aid, to make it appear that it was a German menace, and not Austria's upsetting of the balance in the Balkans, which caused Russia to "hasten her armaments," as Sazonov euphemistically referred to Russia's imminent general mobilization. And as to Schilling's *Diary,* it is clearly inaccurate in several respects: in placing the warning from Pourtalès at 3:00 P.M., instead of between 6 and 7 P.M.; in putting the news of the bombardment of Belgrade *after* the warning of Pourtalès, instead of earlier during the long Szápáry-Sazonov interview; and in saying not a word of the latter. Moreover, Dobrorolski's narrative makes no mention of the warning of Pourtalès as having any decisive influence, or of there being any hesitation or delay after Ianushkevich returned from Peterhof with the signed ukase, except the delay caused by getting the signatures of the three ministers. To be sure, Dobrorolski was a military officer, more likely to be informed in regard to what was being done by the General Staff than by the Foreign Office.

From the somewhat divergent accounts of Schilling's *Diary* and Dobrorolski's narrative, and from the summary of the activities of the Russian diplomatic and military officials given above, one may conclude that the Tsar in signing the ukases for general and partial mobilization was still hesitating in his mind between the two, and expected Ianushkevich to confer with Sazonov before sending out the order for either. Ianushkevich, however, took the Tsar's assent to general mobilization as an authorization to proceed with it directly. On returning from Peterhof to St.

[43] *Cf.* M. T. Florinsky, "The Russian Mobilization of 1914", in *Political Science Quarterly,* XLII, 215 ff., June, 1927; Poincaré, IV, 397; Renouvin, p. 135 ff., however, is more cautious and critical.

Petersburg, he informed Sazonov of his success in persuading the Tsar. He did so shortly before he talked with Eggeling about 3 P.M.,[44] and before Sazonov talked with Szápáry. Ianushkevich then went ahead getting Dobrorolski to secure the signatures for the order for general mobilization, prior to the warning from Pourtalès and without being influenced by it. Meanwhile Sazonov, not having been consulted by the Tsar, made no effort to interfere in a military matter outside his province, and acquiesced in what Ianushkevich was doing. Then came his interview with Szápáry, and his third talk with Pourtalès between 6 and 7 P.M. He now believed that Berchtold had given a "categorical refusal" to direct conversations, that Belgrade had been bombarded, and that Germany had warned that she would mobilize if the Russian military preparations did not cease. This accumulation of hostile indications, on the part of both Austria and Germany, put to flight any remaining inclination on his part in favor of his earlier partial mobilization plan. Toward 8 P.M., when he told the Tsar over the telephone of the warning from Pourtalès, and the Tsar thereupon authorized him to talk with Ianushkevich concerning mobilization at once, he agreed with the Chief of Staff that it should be ordered immediately. The decision was "received with enthusiasm" by the little circle at the Foreign Office, who now "assumed that war was almost inevitable."

It was mainly the pressure of the Russian militarists, not the warning of Pourtalès, that almost started the general mobilization order over the wires. Then the Tsar changed his mind.

44 At the Sukhomlinov Trial in 1917, Ianushkevich declared that the Tsar had instructed him to assure Pourtalès that the mobilization was no hostile act against Germany. He communicated this to Sazonov. But Sazonov feared that Pourtalès would interpret this in his own way, and advised Ianushkevich instead to give the assurance to Eggeling, the German Military Attaché. Ianushkevich, accordingly acted on this advice (Ianushkevich's testimony as reported in the *Novoe Vremia;* quoted by Oman, *The Outbreak of the War,* p. 67; and by Höniger, in the *Deutsche Rundschau,* April, 1918, p. 33).

THE TSAR'S CANCELLATION OF GENERAL MOBILIZATION

At 9:40 P.M. Nicholas II received at Peterhof a second telegram from the Kaiser. In it William II insisted that "Serbian promises on paper are wholly unreliable," and, in the dominating tone which he had so often found successful in the past with the Tsar, told him warningly:

> It would be quite possible for Russia to remain a spectator of the Austro-Serbian conflict without involving Europe in the most horrible war she ever witnessed. I think a direct understanding between your Government and Vienna possible and desirable, and as I already telegraphed you, my Government is continuing its exertions to promote it. Of course, military measures on the part of Russia which would be looked upon by Austria as threatening would precipitate a calamity we both wish to avoid, and jeopardize my position as mediator which I readily accepted on your appeal to my friendship and my help.[45]

The Kaiser apparently judged correctly the effect of this tone on the weak and changeable "Nicky," for the Tsar, ruminating on the situation, began to think he had made a mistake in signing the ukase for general mobilization. He now decided immediately and on his own initiative [46] to cancel the order for general mobilization, and to substitute in its place the apparently less dangerous partial mobilization.

The Tsar therefore called up Ianushkevich, and there followed a three-cornered telephone conversation between the Tsar, Sukhomlinov, and Ianushkevich, in which the two military men tried to convince the Tsar that he was making a terrible mistake; that there was no guarantee that the Kaiser's mediation at Vienna would be successful; that it was clear from Germany's and Austria's conduct that a

[45] Kaiser to Tsar, July 29, 6:30 P.M., received 9:40 P.M.; K.D., 359; Schilling's *Diary*, p. 55.

[46] Paléologue, I, 37.

general war had become inevitable; and that to suspend the general mobilization would only give the enemy a chance to mobilize more quickly than Russia. But for once the Tsar remained firm. Ianushkevich in despair found himself compelled to recall Dobrorolski from the telegraph office where he was on the point of sending out the order for general mobilization. In its place, toward midnight of July 29, the order for partial mobilization was dispatched over the wires.[47]

At the famous Sukhomlinov Trial in 1917, the Minister of War declared that he had disobeyed the Tsar and had persisted with the general mobilization on the night of July 29.[48] But it is now clear from the accounts of Dobrorolski and other evidence that he was lying, and in his own later memoirs he no longer insisted on this version of the events of the night of July 29.

Sazonov was at once informed by Ianushkevich of the Tsar's change of mind and of the substitution of partial for general mobilization. He had already sent one of the Secretaries, M. Basili, to inform Paléologue that it had been decided to issue orders that very night for partial mobilization, but to commence general mobilization in secret. Paléologue says he was quite taken aback: "Would it not be possible, for the moment, to be content with partial mobilization?" "No," said Basili, "the question has just been thoroughly examined by our highest military authorities." [49]

Basili then suggested that, as the Germans might decipher a French telegram, it would be better for Paléologue

[47] It was received and acted upon by the Moscow military authorities before 12:01 A. M. on July 30; Frantz, p. 262.

[48] See the present writer's extracts from the Russian Press reports of the trial in *American Historical Review*, XXVI, 246-250 (Jan., 1921); the excellent arrangement of extracts by M. Renouvin in the *Revue d'Histoire de la Guerre Mondiale,* II, 49-69 (April, 1924); and the summaries by Höniger, in *Deutsche Rundschau,* XLIV, 15-80 (April, 1918).

[49] Paléologue, I, 36.

to notify his Government of this very secret information by a telegram sent in Russian cipher via the Russian Foreign Office to Izvolski. Paléologue accepted the suggestion. But before the telegram had been put into cipher he and Basili received word of the Tsar's change of mind. So Paléologue said nothing to his Government of the momentous decision for general mobilization which Russia had been about to order. He merely repeated the account of the warning from Pourtalès, and said that the tone in which it had been made "has caused the Russian Government at once to order the mobilization of thirteen army corps which are intended against Austria-Hungary." [50]

After midnight Sazonov again had a long interview with Pourtalès, in which the difference between the Russian and German point of view became more clearly defined. Sazonov wanted Germany to press Austria to drop those demands of the ultimatum which infringed the *sovereignty* of Serbia: Russia's vital interests could not allow that Serbia should sink to a vassal state of Austria—"become a Bokhara"—by the acceptance of demands which infringed her sovereign rights. Pourtalès, on the other hand, wanted Russia to accept Austria's declaration of willingness to respect the *territorial integrity* of Serbia as sufficient. Neither man would yield to the other. Pourtalès pointed out that Germany had already gone far in putting pressure on Vienna, and that the situation now had been made very much more difficult by the fact that Russia had decided to order partial mobilization. But Sazonov flatly refused to be satisfied merely with an Austrian declaration of territorial disinterestedness in regard to Serbia.[51]

[50] Paléologue to Viviani, July 30, 1 A.M.; F.Y.B., 100; and Basili's account as reported by Recouly, p. 160 ff. This is another case in which Paléologue failed to keep his government fully and promptly informed as to events in St. Petersburg.

[51] Pourtalès to Bethmann, July 30, 4:30 A.M. and 9:30 A.M.; K.D., 401, 412.

Sazonov's insistence on this question of Serbian sovereignty was further brought to the front on the forenoon of July 30, when Pourtalès finally begged him to formulate in writing a statement which would satisfy Russia and yet have at least a prospect of being a successful solution. Sazonov then wrote out the following "formula:"

> If Austria, recognizing that the Austro-Serbian question has assumed the character of a question of European interest, declares herself ready to eliminate from her ultimatum points which violate the sovereign rights of Serbia, Russia engages to stop her military preparations.[52]

This "formula," however, represented hardly any concession on Sazonov's part, except that it did not demand the immediate halt of the Austrian operations against Serbia. Nor was it likely to prove acceptable to Austria, even after it was modified at Sir Edward Grey's suggestion, so as to provide for an Austrian occupation of Belgrade, and for intervention by the Great Powers. But neither the original nor the modified formula had any serious chance of success. It was overtaken by the very rapid course of events arising from the pressure of the militarists, and especially by the fact that a few hours after proposing his formula, Sazonov secured from the Tsar a second change of mind and final consent to general mobilization.

RUSSIAN GENERAL MOBILIZATION ORDERED

It was with dismay and despair that the Russian Chief of Staff and Minister of War had been forced by the Tsar to cancel general mobilization on the night of July 29. But they were determined not to rest until they had per-

[52] Pourtalès to Bethmann, July 30, 1:01 P.M.; K.D., 421. *Cf.* also R.O.B., 60; and Paléologue, I, 37 f., who says this formula proposal was made at 2:00 P. M. on July 30; but Paléologue is mistaken; it was made earlier, either at 2:00 A. M., as Sazonov stated to Buchanan and Paléologue (B.D., 302; F.Y.B., 103), or more probably in the late forenoon, as Pourtalès insists (*Am Scheideweg,* pp. 51 ff.).

suaded him to change his mind a second time and again to consent to the general mobilization which they considered indispensable. On the morning of July 30 they conferred again with Sazonov and found that he was wholly in agreement with them. They called the Tsar on the telephone and tried to persuade him to return to his resolution of the day before, and allow general mobilization to begin. The Tsar at first resolutely rejected their request, and finally announced curtly that he was breaking off the conversation. Ianushkevich, who held the telephone, could only inform him that Sazonov was there also, and begged permission to say a word to him. A certain silence followed, after which the Tsar expressed his consent to listen. Sazonov requested His Majesty to receive him immediately for a report which could not be delayed. After another silence the Tsar asked, "Is it all the same to you if I receive you at the same time with Tatishchev at 3 o'clock, because otherwise I have not a minute of free time today?" Sazonov thanked the Tsar, and said that he would arrive at the appointed hour.[53]

Ianushkevich then adjured Sazonov not to fail to get from the Tsar a renewed assent to general mobilization. He reiterated the technical arguments of the great danger that Russia would not be ready for war with Germany, which he believed inevitable, if there was further delay; because later general mobilization would be very seriously dislocated by the partial mobilization already ordered; this dislocation could only be avoided by an immediate general mobilization. As a further means of putting pressure on the Tsar he suggested that Sazonov use a political argument: Russia's French ally would be displeased and would regard Russia as failing to live up to the obligations of her alliance; the Kaiser would coax out of the French a promise of neutrality; and he would then fall upon Russia

[53] Schilling's *Diary,* p. 63. *Cf.* also Sazonov, *Fateful Years,* p. 199 ff.

when she was entangled in the midst of her partial mobilization.[54] Finally, he begged Sazonov, the moment he was successful in persuading the Tsar, to inform him at once by telephone from Peterhof, so that he could take immediately the necessary measures, and, before it was too late, convert the partial into a general mobilization. "After this," added the Chief of Staff, "I will retire from sight, smash my telephone, and generally take all measures so that I cannot be found to give any contrary orders for a new postponement of general mobilization." [55]

Sazonov agreed completely, and Ianushkevich telephoned to Dobrorolski: "There is hope for an improvement of the situation; be ready to come to me with all the documents immediately upon my telephone call in the afternoon." [56]

Sazonov then talked with Buchanan and Paléologue, telling them of an interview with Pourtalès, at which the German Ambassador, "seeing that war was inevitable, broke down completely and appealed to Sazonov to hold out a last straw and to make some suggestion which Pourtalès could telegraph to his Government." Whereupon Sazonov had drawn up the "formula" mentioned above. Sazonov then said in substance to the two Ambassadors: "If Austria rejects this proposal, preparations for a general mobilization will be proceeded with, and European war will be inevitable. For strategical reasons Russia can hardly postpone converting partial into general mobilization, now that she knows Germany is preparing, and excitement in the country has reached such a pitch that she cannot hold back if Austria refuses to make concession." [57] Buchanan evidently made no effort to deter Sazonov from

54 Dobrorolski, p. 108 (German ed., p. 28).

55 Schilling's *Diary,* p. 64.

56 Dobrorolski, p. 108 (German ed., p. 27).

57 Buchanan to Grey, July 30, 1:15 P.M.; received 3:15 P.M.; B.D., 302; *cf.* also F.Y.B., 103; and above, at notes 51, 52.

his purpose of converting partial into general mobilization; his failure to do so must have been an encouragement to the Russian Minister.

Paléologue, at the time of this interview, had received a dispatch from Viviani, repeating that France was ready to fulfil the obligations of the Alliance, but instructing him to advise Sazonov to avoid military measures which might offer Germany a pretext for mobilization. Paléologue telegraphed back that he had carried out these instructions.[58] But in his memoirs, and very probably at the time, he placed much more emphasis on the first part of Viviani's message assuring French loyalty to the Alliance, than upon the last part suggesting caution in mobilization measures. Moreover, Izvolski had telegraphed to Sazonov that Margerie, an official in the French Foreign Office, had said that the French Government, without wishing to interfere in Russian military preparations, thought they should be carried on in the least open and provocative manner; and that the French Minister of War advised Russia to strengthen her military preparations, but to avoid as much as possible the appearance of doing so.[59]

Sazonov then lunched with Basili and Krivoshein, the Minister of Agriculture, who also besought him to wring from the Tsar a consent to general mobilization. After lunch Sazonov went out to Peterhof with Tatishchev at 2:00 P.M. He found the Tsar pale and nervous, now fully conscious of the awful seriousness of the responsibility resting upon him. "Think of the responsibility which you are advising me to take!" said the Tsar. "Think of the thousands and thousands of men who will be sent to their death!" In reply Sazonov tried to prove to him that he

58 Poincaré, IV, 399 ff.; Paléologue, I, 39 f. Perhaps misled by the fact that in F.Y.B., 102, two of his despatches have been garbled into one, Paléologue incorrectly places this interview at 6:00 P.M. instead of in the forenoon. See also below, ch. xi, at note 6.

59 Izvolski to Sazonov, July 30; M.F.R., p. 521; L.N., II, 290.

would have nothing with which to reproach his conscience, if war broke out, because it had clearly become inevitable. Diplomacy had finished its work. It was time for His Majesty to think of the safety of his Empire. To fail to order general mobilization would only dislocate the whole Russian military organization, and disconcert Russia's allies. "It only remains to do everything necessary to meet war fully armed and under the conditions most favorable for us. Therefore it is better without fear to call forth a war by our preparations for it, and to continue these preparations carefully, rather than out of fear to give an inducement for war and be taken unawares." [60]

For almost an hour the Tsar's firm desire to avoid war at all costs made him hesitate to adopt measures which, however indispensable from a military point, were calculated, as he clearly saw, to hasten the catastrophe. The tenseness of feeling which he lived through in these minutes expressed itself among other ways in the irritability, unusual for him, with which he snubbed General Tatishchev. The latter, who had taken no part in the conversation, remarked in a moment of silence: "Yes, it is hard to decide." The Tsar replied in a sharp and displeased tone: "I will decide," and gave his decision for an immediate general mobilization. Sazonov thereupon hurried to the telephone on the ground floor of the palace, notified Ianushkevich, who was waiting impatiently for the news, and added: "Now you can smash the telephone. Give your orders, General, and then—disappear for the rest of the day." [61]

Ianushkevich immediately summoned Dobrorolski, who quickly gathered again the three necessary signatures from the ministers who at the moment were gathered in extraordinary session. His mobilization order had been so

60 Schilling's *Diary,* p. 65; and Paléologue, I, 39.

61 Schilling's *Diary,* p. 65 f.; and Dobrorolski, p. 109 (German ed p. 28); Sazonov, p. 202 ff.

planned that the first day of general mobilization was set for July 31, and so made to coincide with the day on which the troops in the four Southern Districts were actually to be called up and transportation was to begin; thus was avoided all confusion which might have resulted if general mobilization had been delayed a day longer. With the new signed ukase Dobrorolski hurried again, as the night before, to the Central Telegraph Office. "Every operator was sitting by his instrument waiting for the copy of the telegram, in order to send to all the ends of the Russian Empire the momentous news of the calling up of the Russian people. A few minutes after six, while absolute stillness reigned in the room, all the instruments began at once to click. That was the beginning moment of the great epoch." [62]

Dobrorolski waited for the confirming reply telegrams. They began to come in about 7:00 P.M., and made it certain that all the places in direct telegraph connection with St. Petersburg, which comprised all the more important cities in European and Asiatic Russia, were receiving the order promptly and correctly.[63] In the Warsaw Military District, for instance, bordering on Germany, various Russian commanding officers received the mobilization telegrams at 7:55 P.M., 8:02 P.M., 8:15 P.M., and acted upon them at once.[64]

In a remote Siberian village an English traveller was awakened a few hours later, at 4:00 A.M., by a great commotion outside his window, and was asked by an excited peasant: "Have you heard the news? There is war." [65]

During the night the red mobilization placards, calling men to the colors, had been posted up everywhere on the street corners. No further change of mind on the part of the Tsar was now possible. Russia was committed to the

62 Dobrorolski, p. 109 f. (German ed., p. 28 f.).

63 Dobrorolski, p. 110.

64 Frantz, pp. 68, 265; *cf.* Höniger, pp. 114-118.

65 Stephen Graham, *Russia and the World* (New York, 1915), p. 1 f.

step which military men everywhere, just as the Siberian peasant, understood meant war.

What were the reasons for this fatal decision to order general mobilization? The Entente Powers, in their efforts to excuse and justify it, have often alleged various reasons —which are false.

One story is that the Russian decision was brought about by a telegram from Sverbeev, the Russian Ambassador in Berlin, stating: "The order for the mobilization of the German army and navy has just been issued." It was occasioned by the publication of news to this effect soon after one o'clock by an "extra" of a Berlin newspaper, the *Lokal-Anzeiger*. This, it is said, was a trick on the part of the Germans to precipitate general mobilization in Russia and so make her seem to be the aggressor. But the news had been immediately contradicted by the German Foreign Office and the "extra" had been suppressed. The Russian Ambassador had thereupon quickly sent a second telegram, unciphered, cancelling the first, and followed it by a third, ciphered, explaining the circumstances.[66] It has now been conclusively established that none of these three telegrams reached St. Petersburg until *after* the Tsar had given his decision. They could therefore have had no influence in causing it. Nor did Sazonov or any of the Russian authorities at the time, in July, 1914, allege this *Lokal-Anzeiger* episode as an excuse for the Russian general mobilization. It was a later invention, first given notoriety by Sir Edward Grey in 1916.[67]

[66] *Krasnyi Arkhiv,* I, pp. 179 f. *The Russian Orange Book,* Nos. 61, 62, published the first and third telegrams in a falsified form, and suppressed the second.

[67] For the detailed facts, see Montgelas, in the *Deutsche Rundschau,* May, 1922, pp. 113-124; and in his *Leitfaden,* 215 ff. We have not repeated them at length here, because all careful historical scholars, like M. Renouvin (pp. 183 ff.), now follow Montgelas in rejecting this *Lokal-Anzeiger* explanation of Russian general mobilization as a legend. Even M. Sazonov, shortly before his death, admitted that "it did not cause our mobilization" (Florinsky, in *Pol. Sci. Quart.,* June, 1927, p. 222 f).

Another reason, alleged by the French Ambassador at St. Petersburg in his somewhat untrustworthy memoirs, is that the decision was caused by a menacing telegram from the Kaiser. According to this legend, Sazonov, on arriving at Peterhof, found that the Tsar "had received a very bad impression from a telegram sent him the night before in an almost menacing tone: 'If Russia mobilizes against Austria, my rôle as mediator, which I accepted at your express prayer, will be endangered, if not ruined. The whole weight of the decision lies on your shoulders now, who have to bear the responsibility for peace or war.' Having read and reread this telegram, Sazonov made a gesture of despair," and proceeded to urge general mobilization upon the Tsar, on the grounds that war was already inevitable and Germany was only pretending to mediate in order to gain time to complete secretly her preparations for attack. After hesitation, continues Paléologue, the Tsar reluctantly yielded and gave his decision. "The clock marked exactly 4:00 P.M." [68] But this telegram from the Kaiser [69] was not sent until 3:30 P.M., and was not received at Peterhof until 6:30 P.M. Being received more than two hours *after* the Tsar's decision, and half an hour *after* Dobrorolski had actually begun to send the general mobilization order over the wires, it can no more have been the cause of Russia's general mobilization than the *Lokal-Anzeiger* "extra." Either Sazonov gave Paléologue an untrue account of his audience with the Tsar; or, more probably, the French Ambassador was again drawing upon his lively imagination.

Still another reason alleged for the Russian general mobilization is that it was caused by Austria's general

68 Paléologue, I, 38 f. Sazonov (p. 202 ff.) repeats the legend. Possibly the Tsar's decision was made two or three hours earlier (*cf.* Dobrorolski, in KSF, II, 87, April, 1924), but not later than 4 P.M. Schilling's *Diary*, p. 63 ff. says Sazonov's audience began at 3 P.M., and lasted nearly an hour, which would also place the Tsar's decision at 4 P.M.

69 K.D., 420; Schilling's *Diary*, p. 67.

mobilization and by mobilization measures taken secretly but continuously by Germany for the past six days. This legend was perpetuated by the falsified form in which the *French Yellow Book* published the belated telegram in which Paléologue finally notified his Government of Russia's fatal step. The original and falsified forms may be seen side by side.[70]

Original text:	Falsified text, F.Y.B., **118**:
The general mobilization of the Russian army has been ordered.	As a result of the general mobilization of Austria and of the measures for mobilization taken secretly, but continuously, by Germany for the last six days, the order for the general mobilization of the Russian army has been given, Russia not being able, without most serious danger, to allow herself to be further out-distanced; really she is only taking military measures corresponding to those taken by Germany. For imperative reasons of strategy the Russian Government, knowing that Germany was arming, could no longer delay the conversion of her partial mobilization into a general mobilization.

As the greater part of this document in the *French Yellow Book* is now admitted by the French authorities to be a pure fabrication, it is hardly necessary to note that

70 Paléologue to Viviani, via Bergen, July 31, 10:43 A. M., received 8:30 P. M.; printed in its original form by Renouvin, p. 181 f., and in its falsified form in F.Y.B., 118. *Cf.* also Poincaré, IV, 455-458, for the delay in deciphering and bringing it to his notice.

the Austrian general mobilization was not ordered until eighteen hours after that of Russia, and that there is no truth in the statement that Germany had for six days been taking secret mobilization measures.[71] That the officials of the French Foreign Office who edited the *Yellow Book* in 1914 should have thought it necessary to resort to such a deliberate distortion of the truth, suggests that they were conscious of how fatal Russia's action was, and how largely Paléologue and France were responsible for it, and therefore sought to excuse and justify it even by falsifying documents.

Was Sazonov, shortly before going out to Peterhof, strengthened in his determination to persuade the Tsar to order general mobilization by the conversation which he had with Buchanan and Paléologue, and by the telegram from Izvolski?[72] Or, as M. Renouvin ingeniously suggests,[73] did this conversation and telegram merely cause him, upon his return from Peterhof after securing the order for general mobilization, to inform Paléologue, with an economy of truth hardly usual toward one's own ally, that the Russian Government "was resolved to proceed secretly with the preliminary measures [*premières mesures*] of general mobilization."[74] One would not know with certainty from this ambiguous phrase that the Russian Government had already ordered full mobilization, and it is the claim of Renouvin and Poincaré that the Cabinet at Paris was not aware of the Russian general mobilization, so far as any information had come from Paléologue, until more than a whole day after it had been ordered, that is, until the arrival

[71] On Bethmann's restraint on Moltke and the German military authorities, and on Austrian general mobilization, see below, ch. xi.

[72] See above, at notes 57-59.

[73] Renouvin, pp. 186 ff.

[74] Paléologue to Viviani, July 30, 9:15 P. M., received 11:30 P. M.; part of this telegram is printed in F.Y.B., 102, but the passage quoted was suppressed; what appears to be the complete text is given by C. Appuhn and P. Renouvin, *Introduction aux Tableaux d'Histoire de Guillaume II*, (Paris, 1923), p. xcv.

at 8:30 P.M. on July 31 of the telegram that Paléologue sent via Bergen at 10:43 A. M.[75]

If Renouvin and Poincaré are correct, then Paléologue's telegram had deceived his Government. Who was the guilty author of the deceit? Did Sazonov mislead Paléologue, who innocently passed on the misinformation to Paris? Or did Paléologue know the truth from Sazonov or others, and conceal from Paris the plain fact that the order for general mobilization had been sent out over the wires three hours before he sent his own ambiguous message that Russia "was resolved to proceed secretly with the preliminary measures of general mobilization"? One cannot say with certainty. M. Renouvin makes Sazonov the author of the deceit. But one of Buchanan's telegrams leads one to think that it may have been Paléologue—that again the French Ambassador knew important information which he concealed from his Government. Buchanan apparently telegraphed on July 30 at 6:40 P.M. correctly and unambiguously: "It has been decided to issue orders for general mobilization." [76] Since Buchanan and Paléologue were in such close and constant touch with each other, is it not highly probable that Paléologue knew as well as Buchanan soon after 6:00 P.M. on July 30 that general mobilization had been decided upon? And if so, he should have sent a clear and unambiguous message to that effect, instead of one which misled his Government at Paris. Paléologue's rôle during the July crisis is one of the questions which most needs clearing up through complete and satisfactory edition of the French documents.

Thus it is not the *Lokal-Anzeiger* "extra," nor the Kaiser's telegram, nor Austrian mobilization which can explain or excuse the Russian general mobilization. What

[75] *Cf.* Renouvin, p. 190, note 3: "The French Government did not interpret M. Paléologue's message as the announcement of general mobilization;" and Poincaré, IV, 403 f., 408, 452 ff.

[76] B.D., 347, and explanatory note.

influence Buchanan and Paléologue had upon Sazonov on July 30 is uncertain. The Russian general mobilization was caused by the fact that Sazonov and the military officers on July 30 simply held the same views as on the evening of July 29, when they would have sent out the order for general mobilization had not the Tsar changed his mind. The situation had not changed essentially in the meantime, except that the partial mobilization, already ordered on the night of July 29, made the military authorities demand even more insistently an immediate general mobilization, because of technical military considerations.

"MOBILIZATION MEANS WAR"

By ordering general mobilization about 6:00 P.M. on July 30, Russia had now taken the step which military men everywhere clearly understood almost certainly meant war. This was also clearly understood by Sazonov and the Tsar, as appears from Schilling's account of their conversation at Peterhof and the Tsar's long hesitation to assume the terrible responsibility. Partial mobilization might be undertaken by a Great Power without leading to war, as had happened on several occasions in Russia and Austria in the preceding years. But general mobilization by a Great Power was generally understood to mean that it had only resorted to this final step of putting the great military machine in motion, with the automatic movement of the troops to the frontier with the greatest despatch, when it had finally concluded that war could no longer be avoided.

"Mobilization means war." This was a political maxim which for years had been widely accepted by military men on the Continent everywhere. It had been plainly hinted at by Pourtalès to Sazonov during the July crisis. It was stated by the French and Russian Chiefs of Staff, and accepted by the Tsar, as far back as 1892, as is seen from the records of the negotiations for the Franco-Russian Alliance:

"General Obruchev emphasized finally the necessity of the immediate and simultaneous mobilization of the Russian and French armies at the first news received by either of the two countries of a mobilization of the forces of the Triple Alliance. He understands further that this mobilization of France and Russia would be followed immediately by positive results, by acts of war, in a word would be inseparable from an 'aggression.'"[77]

Similarly, General Boisdeffre, in talking with the Tsar the day after the Military Convention had been approved, remarked:

"The mobilization is the declaration of war. To mobilize is to oblige one's neighbor to do the same. Mobilization involves the carrying out of strategic transportation and concentration. Otherwise, to leave a million men on one's frontier, without doing the same simultaneously, is to deprive oneself of all possibility of moving later; it is placing oneself in the situation of an individual who, with a pistol in his pocket, should let his neighbor put a weapon to his forehead without drawing his own." [To which Alexander III replied], "That is exactly the way I understand it."[78]

In a Russian secret order approved by the Tsar on March 12, 1912, at the moment Russia helped to secure the

[77] Report of the French Military Attaché in St. Petersburg, July 16, 1892; *L'Alliance Franco-Russe*, p. 56.

[78] Report of General Boisdeffre; *ibid.*, p. 95 f. M. Renouvin, p. 309, has argued that in these negotiations the principle that "Mobilization means war" was understood to apply only to the adversaries of France and Russia, and not to a Russian mobilization. Though no doubt, in the passage just quoted, Boisdeffre had in mind mobilization by the enemies of France, he was stating a general principle, endorsed by all military men. It would be an illogical and one-sided argument to maintain that mobilization by Germany or Austria means war, and that mobilization by Russia or France does not mean war. Moreover, Obruchev speaks expressly of the mobilization of France and Russia as involving immediate acts of war: "Il entend du reste que cette mobilisation de la France et de la Russie soit suivie immédiatement d'effets actifs, d'actes de guerre, en un mot soit inséparable d'une 'aggression;'" *ibid.*, p. 56.

signing of the Serbo-Bulgarian Treaty which was to lead to the Balkan Wars, it was expressly stated that "the telegram announcing mobilization is also at the same time to be effective as the Tsar's order for the opening of hostilities against Germany and Austria."[79] Though this order, for technical and political reasons, was later cancelled, and the telegrams for mobilization and the opening of hostilities were to be issued separately, it still represented the conception of military men that general mobilization means war. Dobrorolski, for instance, speaking of the Russian mobilization of 1914, says explicitly: "The whole plan of mobilization is worked out ahead to its end in all its details. When the moment has been chosen, one only has to press the button, and the whole state begins to function automatically with the precision of a clock's mechanism. . . . The choice of the moment is influenced by a complex of varied political causes. But once the moment has been fixed, everything is settled; there is no going back; it determines mechanically the beginning of war."[80]

[79] Quoted by Frantz, pp. 46, 234.
[80] Dobrorolski, p. 92 (German ed., p. 9 f.).

CHAPTER XI

OTHER MOBILIZATIONS AND DECLARATIONS OF WAR

In following the Russian diplomatic and military steps to the point where general mobilization was ordered on the afternoon of July 30, we have outrun the narrative of events in the other capitals of Europe. In Paris, London, and Berlin also, hopes of peace and fears of imminent war had brought into opposition the activity of the diplomats and the pressure of the military authorities. The former still worked to save the situation, or at least, if that proved impossible, to make it appear that they and their allies were not responsible for the impending catastrophe. The latter pressed for military measures which they regarded as imperative to secure strategic advantages in the war which they were increasingly convinced was inevitable.

FRANCE AND THE 10-KILOMETER WITHDRAWAL

President Poincaré and M. Viviani, who landed at Dunkirk on the morning of July 29, reached Paris about noon. They were quickly informed of the precautionary military measures in anticipation of war which the Cabinet and M. Messimy, the Minister of War, had been taking in their absence since the evening of July 25. The measures included the return to their standing quarters of troops in training, the recall of officers on leave, and provision for the transportation from Morocco of all possible troops.[1]

[1] Poincaré, IV, 360-369; Recouly, pp. 61 ff., giving Messimy's narrative; and for the detailed military measures, see the French General Staff History, *Les Armées Françaises dans la Grande Guerre* (Paris, 1923),

These were all approved. They also learned of Austria's persistently intransigent attitude and of her declaration of war; of Germany's apparent complete support of Austria; of various visits which the German Ambassador had made to the French Foreign Office which did not inspire confidence as to Germany's desire for peace; of Sir Edward Grey's unwillingness definitely to commit himself as to England's future course; and of Sazonov's announcement that Russia was about to order partial mobilization.[2] At a Cabinet meeting in the afternoon Poincaré says he found all the ministers "closely united in the resolution to do the impossible to avoid war and also to neglect no preparations for defense." [3]

Late that night, or rather between 2 and 3 A.M. on July 30, Izvolski communicated to the French Minister of Foreign Affairs and the Minister of War a most important telegram just received from St. Petersburg, indicating the imminence of war. "Not being able to accede to Germany's desire [that Russia cease her military preparations], it only remains for us to hasten our armaments and regard war as imminent," Sazonov telegraphed. After expressing gratitude for Paléologue's declaration of complete French support, "especially precious to us in the present circumstances," Sazonov added: "It would be extremely desirable that England also, without losing time, should join France and Russia, for only in this way can she prevent a dangerous rupture of the European balance of power." [4]

Viviani and Messimy at once held a conference at the Elysée with Poincaré, who had gone to bed. They ap-

passim; and the analysis of it by Montgelas in KSF, V, 1206-1220, Dec. 1927; Montgelas indicates that the French measures regularly preceded the corresponding German ones, sometimes by as much as two or three days. *Cf.* also the report of the British Military Attaché in Paris on July 29; B.D., 321.

[2] Poincaré, IV, 371-378; F.Y.B., 56-85. [3] Poincaré, IV, 371.

[4] For this tg. no. 1551 from Sazonov, see above, ch. x, at note 42.

proved a telegram from Viviani to Paléologue, which was at once communicated to Izvolski, put into cipher, and sent to St. Petersburg and London at 7 A.M. on July 30. It began with a reference to Viviani's telegram of July 27 from on board the *France*, which stated the French Government's wish to support efforts for a peaceful solution of the conflict, but which, Poincaré asserts, led Paléologue to make the declaration of French support which Sazonov found "especially precious." [5] It then continued:

> France, however, is resolved to fulfil all the obligations of the Alliance.
>
> But I think in the interests of general peace and in view of the conversation pending between the less interested Powers, that it would be opportune that, as regards the precautionary and defence measures which Russia believes it necessary to adopt, she should not take immediately any step which might offer to Germany a pretext for a total or partial mobilization of her forces." [6]

What the French Government had in mind is more clearly stated in another telegram which Izvolski hastened to send to Sazonov:

> Margerie, whom I have just seen, told me that the French Government, without wishing to interfere in our military preparations, would consider it extremely desirable, in view

[5] Poincaré, IV, 335, 385. See also above, ch. X, at notes 5-11.

[6] This wording represents the present writer's approximation of the probable true original text of this passage, which is given in three quite different forms; (a) by the editors of the F.Y.B., 101; (b) by Poincaré, IV, 385 f.; and (c) by Izvolski, L.N., II, 290; (b) and (c) make no mention of Sazonov's telegram to Izvolski nor of a visit by Schoen, which form the first and last parts of (a); (a) says nothing of Viviani's telegram of July 27 from the *France*, which is mentioned in (b) and (c). Poincaré makes the last sentence read that Russia should not take immediately any steps toward a partial or total mobilization *of her own forces;* but Poincaré has misquoted his document, as is obvious from his own paraphrases on pp. 399 and 408, and from F.Y.B., 102, which indicate that Russia should not take any step which would offer *Germany* a pretext for mobilization. This tg. no. 208, from Izvolski to Sazonov, is also printed in M.F.R., p. 520, and in Romberg, p. 50 f., but was suppressed from R.O.B.

of the negotiations still pending for the preservation of peace, that these preparations should be carried on in the least open and least provocative manner. The Minister of War, on his part, expressing the same idea, told Count Ignatiev [Russian Military Attaché in Paris] that we could declare that, in the higher interests of peace, we were willing to slow down temporarily our mobilization measures, which would not hinder us from continuing and even strengthening our military preparations, while refraining, as much as possible, from the transportation of masses of troops.[7]

From these two telegrams from Paris to St. Petersburg, it appears that the French Government was anxious that Russia should not precipitate a European war, but should still continue measures in preparation for it, since it appeared inevitable. Poincaré must also have been aware that his renewal of the promise of full French support was likely to encourage Russia to defy Germany, and so lead to war. He did not wish to seem to interfere in Russian mobilization measures. Nevertheless, for diplomatic reasons, he did not want France or her ally to take any open and provocative military measures, which might seem aggressive, or might give Germany a pretext for mobilizing or—most important of all—which might make an undesirable impression on England and Italy. Apparently convinced that war was now inevitable,[8] and remembering the French mistake of being the formal aggressor in 1870,

[7] Izvolski to Sazonov, tg. no. 210, July 30; M.F.R., p. 521; L.N., II, 290. *Cf.* also Poincaré, IV, 386 f. This idea of strengthening military preparations but avoiding the appearance of doing so by refraining from troop movements *en masse* or by special trains, was immediately adopted by Messimy himself for the French corps near the German frontier, as will be seen in a moment in connection with the "10-kilometer withdrawal."

[8] *Cf.* Bertie to Grey, July 30 (B.D., 320): "The Spanish Ambassador says that the President of the Republic told a friend this morning that he considers war inevitable." This conviction would be natural in view of Sazonov's telegram and of the reports which the highly suspicious French Ambassador in Berlin had been pouring into Paris (*cf.* F.Y.B., 30, 35, 41-43, 47, 67, 73, 74, 92; and Poincaré, IV, 319 ff., 349, 414 ff.).

he did not intend to have any similar mistake made in 1914; Russia and France should wait for Germany to take the initiative and thereby incur the odium of responsibility.[9] Events were to prove his shrewdness, for Bethmann soon made the formal mistake of declaring war, which Ollivier had made in 1870. Therefore, for the present, while diplomatic negotiations were still pending, Russia should conceal as far as possible "the precautionary and defensive measures which she considered it necessary to adopt."

If President Poincaré had expressed himself with his usual vigor and clarity—if he had said unmistakably to Russia: "Do not order general mobilization for the present while diplomatic negotiations are going on"—if he had even spoken as vigorously as Bethmann was speaking to Vienna—there is a possibility that war might still have been avoided. Russian general mobilization had not yet been ordered. Viviani's telegram reached Paléologue toward noon on July 30 before Sazonov went out to Peterhof to secure the Tsar's renewed assent to general mobilization. If Poincaré had given a vigorous warning, and if Paléologue had repeated it to Sazonov, there was still time for the Russian Minister to secure the further postponement of Russian general mobilization until the "Halt in Belgrade" proposal or some other form of mediation might have kept the Powers back from the abyss.

But Poincaré was by now more concerned in securing England's aid and in taking military precautions in France, than in holding back Russia. "It would be extremely desirable that England also, without losing time, should join France and Russia, for only in this way can she prevent a

[9] *Cf.* J. Cambon to Poincaré, tg. no. 225, July 30, 4:52 P.M., received 6:10 P.M. After mentioning the *Lokal-Anzeiger* episode, Cambon says: "It is important not to publish in France the mobilization measures until after they have certainly been decided in Berlin, in order that English public opinion which can play so great a rôle in events, shall not attribute to us any initiative tending toward war" (Poincaré, IV, 420).

dangerous rupture of the European balance of power," Sazonov had telegraphed. Poincaré agreed. Several steps which he took on July 30, and page after page of his memoirs, indicate that henceforth his great aim was to get England definitely to announce that she would give France armed support.

Early on the morning of July 30 Paul Cambon in London was informed of Sazonov's telegram indicating war as imminent and of the French reply to it. Cambon was instructed to tell Grey, and remind him of the letters exchanged in 1912, by which each had agreed, if peace was threatened, immediately to discuss with the other whether both Governments should act together, and, if so, what measures they would be prepared to take in common.[10] Cambon was also to furnish Grey with a long list of military preparations which Germany was alleged to have made, "showing that the German military preparations were more advanced and more on the offensive upon the frontier than anything France had yet done." It was to let Grey "see that though France was resolute, it was not she who was taking aggressive measures." [11]

But when M. Cambon reminded Sir Edward Grey of the 1912 exchange of letters, and "said that the peace of Europe was never more seriously threatened than now," he met with disappointment. Though he acted with extreme caution and tact, not asking Grey to say directly that England would intervene, but only what he would do in certain circumstances, such as an aggression by Germany on France, Sir Edward would only say he would see

10 Poincaré, IV, 386; Grey, I, 94-96, 328-331.

11 B.D., 319 and enclosure. This was only one of several similar documents, exaggerating German military preparations and frontier aggressions, and minimizing those of France, which Cambon furnished to Grey during these critical days when Poincaré was trying to get from England a definite promise of support; *cf.* B.D., 338, 364, 473; Poincaré, IV, 435. For doubt as to their accuracy, see the analysis of the French General Staff History of the War by Montgelas, in KSF, V, 1206-1220, Dec., 1927.

him again next day after the Cabinet had met.[12] Cambon also talked with Sir Arthur Nicolson, but found little encouragement. English public opinion, said Nicolson, was indifferent to the Austro-Russian Balkan rivalry; it was not yet time to consider British intervention; German financial interests were influential in the "City" and with some of the Cabinet; Asquith did not at present dare take a resolute attitude; but Nicolson himself was "personally a partisan of intervention." [13]

On the evening of July 30 Poincaré himself spoke more bluntly and pressingly to Sir Francis Bertie, the British Ambassador in Paris. He argued very urgently that if England would make an immediate declaration of her intention to support France, "there would be no war, for Germany would at once modify her attitude, . . . and even if it did not prevent war, British aid to France at the outbreak of hostilities would assist in the maintenance of the balance of power in Europe. Aid given later might be too late, and if England remained neutral and Germany became omnipotent on the Continent, the position of England would be entirely altered to her detriment as a Great Power." Bertie replied that the doubtful attitude of the House of Commons made it difficult to make any such declaration, and that anyway the orders to the British fleet not to disperse must be a pretty clear indication to Germany of England's attitude.[14] But in his private comment to Grey, Bertie observed: "The French, instead of putting pressure on the Russian Government to moderate their zeal, expect us to give the Germans to understand that we mean fighting if war breaks out. If we gave an assurance of armed assistance to France and Russia now, Russia would become more exacting and France would follow in her wake." [15]

[12] Grey to Bertie, July 30; B.D., 319.

[13] P. Cambon to Viviani, July 30, 8:30 P.M.; Poincaré, IV, 434.

[14] Bertie to Grey, July 30; B.D., 373; *cf.* also 318.

[15] B.D., 320.

Since Sazonov's telegram had said that he was hastening Russia's military measures and considered war imminent, Poincaré, and especially the French Minister of War, wanted to take measures for increasing the frontier troops as fully and quickly as possible, and yet avoid the appearance of making military preparations which might lead to frontier encounters or which might make an unfavorable impression on England. This conflict between efforts to satisfy strategic and diplomatic interests was the origin of the famous "10-kilometer withdrawal."

At the meeting of the French Cabinet on the morning of July 30, after the arrival of Sazonov's telegram, the French Minister of War urged that *couverture* should be adopted at once. This meant that the covering troops should take up their places on the frontier, and involved the mobilization of five army corps and all the French cavalry. But there was the diplomatic objection that this might seem to give France the rôle of aggressor and endanger the hoped-for British support and Italian neutrality. To reconcile the conflicting interests of strategy and diplomacy it was decided in principle to adopt a compromise. *Couverture* was to take place, but with restrictions. The covering troops were to move up toward the frontier, so far as was possible by moving on foot and horse; reservists were not to be summoned; horses were to be bought instead of requisitioned; and the troops were to keep back a short distance from the actual frontier. This would lessen the danger of unfortunate incidents, which at this time of excitement and suspicion might be exaggerated into "aggressions" and "acts of war." As Viviani said in the Chamber of Deputies in 1919, replying to his critics who charged that the 10-kilometer order had enabled Germany to get an initial advantage and seize the French iron-ore districts: "We realized that everything might turn on some chance incident. A patrol might get on the wrong road and run up against an enemy patrol, a sergeant or a corporal might lose his head, a soldier might think himself in danger and fire off his rifle." [16]

In the *French Yellow Book* Viviani is represented as telegraphing to Paul Cambon in London on July 30: "We have held back our troops 10 kilometers from the frontier, forbidding them to approach nearer. . . . In thus delivering a strip of territory undefended to the sudden aggression of the enemy, the Government of the Republic hopes to prove that France does not bear, any more than Russia, the responsibility for the attack." [17]

As a matter of fact, however, no limit of precisely 10 kilometers was fixed at all. Neither in the telegram which Viviani really sent to Paul Cambon on July 30, nor in the order which Messimy issued to five corps commanders at 4:45 P.M., is there any mention of "10-kilometers." Viviani's telegram to Paul Cambon instructed him to call Sir Edward Grey's attention to the French and German military preparations. "England will see from them that, though France is resolute, it is not she who is taking aggressive measures. Draw Sir Edward Grey's attention to the decision taken by the Cabinet this morning. Although Germany has taken up covering positions some hundreds of meters or some kilometers from the frontier, on the whole frontier from Luxembourg to the Vosges, and placed her covering troops in their war positions, we have not done so—although our plan of campaign, conceived for the offensive, contemplates that the war positions of our covering troops shall be as near the frontier as those of the Germans. We have thus left a strip of national territory

[16] *Débats parlementaires,* January 31, 1919.

[17] F.Y.B., 106. In this document the editors have merged two telegrams (*cf.* B.D., 319, 338) into one, and the date of the second, just quoted, is falsified from July 31 to July 30. The curious reason for this falsification is given in B.D., 319, note. Poincaré (IV, 424 f., 435), either unconsciously or deliberately, repeats the falsifications.

without defense open to sudden attack. We have not done this for any other reason than to show the British Government and public opinion that France, like Russia, will not be the first to fire." Then follows a list of German frontier and other military preparations.[18] Messimy's order to the corps commanders instructed them to carry out the order of 1909 concerning mobilization of the frontier troops; those which could march on foot were to take up their positions, and those to go by rail were to be ready to entrain. "However, for diplomatic reasons, it is indispensable that no frontier incident shall be caused by us. Consequently no troops or patrols under any pretext are to approach the frontier or go beyond the line," which was then designated by naming some fifty towns and villages near the frontier.[19]

Thus, there was no line drawn exactly ten kilometers from the frontier everywhere. At numerous points it was only four or five kilometers from the frontier, as Messimy stated to the Briey Committee in 1920.[20] General Joffre even "asked that he should not feel obliged to carry out the order in absolute strictness," and the Government granted his request.[21] Nevertheless, the fact that the French Government did hold back its covering troops a few kilometers from the frontier was a wise measure. It did tend to prevent unfortunate "incidents" which might have precipitated a war. But it would be a mistake to regard it mainly as a proof of Poincaré's love of peace. Rather it

18 Viviani to P. Cambon, July 30; communicated to Grey, B.D., 319.

19 Messimy to the Commanders of the 2nd, 6th, 7th, 20th and 21st Army Corps, July 30, 4:55 P.M.; *Les Armées Françaises,* Tome I, Vol. I, Annex No. 15. Even when France ordered general mobilization on August 1, since Grey had not yet promised military support, Messimy again telegraphed the Commanders: "With a view to assuring ourselves of the support of our English neighbors, it is still essential not to have patrols or detachments cross the general line fixed by the telegram of July 30, except in case of a clearly established attack" (*ibid.,* No. 25). This was reiterated by President Poincaré himself a few hours later at 10:30 P.M. (*ibid.,* No. 26).

20 Renouvin, p. 215.

21 Renouvin, p. 215.

was a measure primarily calculated to win British approval and military support, and to minimize the fact that France was taking an important military measure preparatory to war.

THE BRITISH FLEET AND WARNINGS TO GERMANY

In England the strategic problem was different from that of the military authorities on the Continent. By arrangements made many weeks earlier, England was fortunate in having her fleet already concentrated in the most powerful naval force which the world had ever seen. There was therefore no question of feverish haste to prepare it as quickly as possible to meet the enemy, but merely of whether orders should be given to keep it concentrated, instead of allowing it to disperse again to its normal positions as in time of peace.

On Saturday, July 25, Grey and his advisers learned from Buchanan that Sazonov "thought that Russia would at any rate have to mobilize," and that Poincaré's visit had established between France and Russia a "perfect community of views" and a "solemn affirmation of the obligations imposed by the alliance." Upon this Sir Eyre Crowe commented: "We should decide *now* to mobilize the fleet as soon as any other Great Power mobilizes, and we should announce this decision without delay to the French and Russian Governments." Even at this early date he believed: "The moment has passed when it might have been possible to enlist French support in an effort to hold back Russia." The mobilization of the fleet might also, he thought, serve as a warning to Germany. But Sir Edward Grey, who had just been told by Winston Churchill, the First Lord of the Admiralty, that the fleet could be mobilized in twenty-four hours, thought it premature to make any statement as yet to France and Russia.[22] He still pre-

[22] B.D., 101, and "Minutes" by Crowe and Grey on July 25.

ferred to keep a non-committal attitude, neither encouraging the Russians and French, nor threatening the Germans.

But next day, after the arrival of more alarming news from Austria and Serbia, Winston Churchill and the First Sea Lord, on their own authority, decided that the fleet should not disperse. Grey approved, and a public announcement of the fact that the fleet was to remain concentrated appeared in the British papers on the morning of July 27.[23] Grey intended this as a warning to dispel the current impression in Germany and Austria that England would remain neutral. The announcement did help to dispel the anxieties of the Russian Ambassador, Count Benckendorff, and was received "with great satisfaction" by his colleague, Paul Cambon.[24] But in Austria and Germany it did not make as effective an impression as the British Foreign Office appears to have expected. In mentioning it to the Austrian Ambassador, Grey himself rather minimized its significance: "I had explained that we should not have thought of calling up reserves or taking any step of a menacing character; but that, our naval force having been collected for manœuvres, we could not, when there was a possibility of a European conflagration, choose this moment for dispersing it." [25] And in Germany it was at first regarded as less important than the assurance which Prince Henry of Prussia had just brought from King George that England would remain neutral.[26]

On July 28 the feeling at the British Foreign Office became more pessimistic. The officials were puzzled by the fresh proposals which Sazonov kept making almost daily. Sir Edward Grey's own mediation proposals, as well as the "direct conversations" between Vienna and St. Petersburg,

[23] Churchill, *The World Crisis,* pp. 197 ff.

[24] B.D., 177, 238, 239.

[25] Grey to Bertie, July 28; B.D., 238; *cf.* Mensdorff to Berchtold, July 27; A.R.B., II, 72.

[26] See below, at notes, 40, 41.

which he had accepted as a substitute, seemed to be making no headway in view of the Austro-German thesis that the Serbian dispute should be "localized." As Sir Arthur Nicolson summarized the situation in a letter to Buchanan: "I can quite understand Russia not being able to permit Austria to crush Serbia. I think the talk about localizing the war merely means that all the Powers are to hold the ring while Austria quietly strangles Serbia. This to my mind is quite preposterous, not to say iniquitous. I do not understand after the very satisfactory way in which Serbia has met the Austrian requests, how Austria can with any justification proceed to hostile measures against her. If she deliberately provokes war with Serbia . . . she must know very well that such an action on her part would in all probability lead to a general European conflagration, with all its untold disastrous consequences. Germany has not played a very straight game—at least so far as we are concerned—in all this business." He noted, however, with satisfaction, the orders given to keep the British fleet together, and the change in tone of the British Press, which at first in the days immediately after Sarajevo had been sympathetic toward Austria; these two facts, he thought, had made it perfectly clear to Germany and Austria that they could not count with any certainty upon England remaining neutral.[27]

Finally on July 29, after the news of the Austrian declaration of war on Serbia, which made Sazonov regard "direct conversations" as illusory and state that partial mobilization would soon take place in Russia, officials in the inner circle in England came to regard a European war as almost inevitable. "What is the use of exchanging views at this juncture?" asked Sir Arthur Nicolson. "I am of the opinion that the resources of diplomacy are, for the present, exhausted." [28] Four of Sir Edward Grey's des-

27 Nicolson to Buchanan, July 28; B.D., 239.
28 Minute on B.D., 252.

patches, dated July 29, though published in the *British Blue Book* of 1914 as if sent, are now revealed in the archives marked, "Not sent—War."[29] Mr. Asquith stated in the House of Commons that the situation was one "of extreme gravity."

In fact, on the previous afternoon, July 28, at 5 P.M., Winston Churchill had ordered that the fleet was to proceed during the night at high speed and without lights through the Straits of Dover from Portland to its fighting base at Scapa Flow. Fearing to bring this order before the Cabinet, lest it should be considered a provocative action likely to damage the chances of peace, Mr. Churchill had only informed Mr. Asquith, who at once gave his approval. On July 29, the official "warning telegram" was dispatched from the Admiralty. The British Fleet was now ready, whatever happened, to meet and control the situation.[30]

On the morning, July 29, Sir Edward Grey at last decided to give Germany a more definite warning, as Russia and France had been continually urging. Quite characteristically he first told Cambon of what he was going to say to Lichnowsky, but at the same time reiterated that his warning to Germany would not mean that England had yet made up her mind what she would do if France and Germany became involved. England was "free from engagements," and would "have to decide what British interests required."[31] To Lichnowsky Grey then repeated Sazonov's statement that after the Austrian declaration of war Russia would no longer be in a position to negotiate with Austria direct and desired a return to the British mediation proposals. Accordingly Grey suggested it would be "a suitable basis for mediation, if Austria, after occupying Belgrade, for example, or other places, should announce

29 *Cf.* B.D., 282-286.

30 Churchill, p. 207 ff; Julian S. Corbett, *History of the Great War; Naval Operations* (London, 1920), I, 25 ff.

31 Grey to Bertie, July 29; B.D., 283.

her conditions." Grey then gave to Lichnowsky, in the form of a friendly and private communication, the warning that, as long as the conflict remained confined to Austria and Russia, England could stand aside; but if Germany and France should be involved, then the situation would be immediately altered and the British Government would be forced to rapid decisions.[32]

But before Grey's warning was deciphered and known in Berlin, Bethmann took a step which caused the British Foreign Office to believe that Germany had practically determined to go to war, violate Belgium, and crush France.

BETHMANN AND MOLTKE

In Berlin, as in Paris and London, the situation was regarded as very critical on Wednesday, July 29.

Bethmann had urged Austria to accept the "Halt in Belgrade" mediation plan, but had received no answer from Vienna. Such silence on the part of his ally was extremely irritating and embarrassing to the German Chancellor.[33] Because of it, he was unable to show the Entente Powers that his pressure at Vienna was meeting with success and would bring a satisfactory solution of the crisis.

Furthermore, the German military authorities, like the General Staffs everywhere, were pressing for early military measures to insure the safety of their country and the success of their strategic plans, in case the diplomatists could not preserve peace.

Helmuth von Moltke, who bore the name but lacked the genius of his more famous uncle, was now Chief of the German General Staff, having accepted that difficult office reluctantly in 1906 in succession to Count Schlieffen. In

[32] Lichnowsky to Bethmann, July 29, 6:39 P. M., received 9:12 P. M.; K.D., 368; *cf.* also B.D., 286.

[33] See above, ch. ix, "Germany's Belated Peace Efforts."

a long summary of the political situation on July 29, Moltke now pointed out the dangerous sequence of mobilizations which would probably take place, in case Russia carried out her announced intention of ordering partial mobilization in her southern districts if Austria advanced into Serbia. Russia, he said, had been making military preparations on the frontier against Germany, as well as against Austria, so that she would be able to move her armies forward in a very few days when she actually issued her mobilization orders. France also, according to his information, appeared to be taking measures preparatory to general mobilization. The situation thus was becoming daily more unfavorable to Germany, and might lead to fateful consequences if Germany, by a collision between Austria and Russia, should be forced to mobilize and fight on two fronts. Therefore, he concluded, "it is of the greatest importance to ascertain as soon as possible whether Russia and France intend to let it come to a war with Germany." [34]

Bethmann, however, was still hoping that the "pledge plan" of "Halt in Belgrade" might bring a satisfactory solution. He therefore insisted on waiting for a reply from Vienna. He was vigorously opposed to taking any decisive military measures which might jeopardize his diplomatic efforts.

According to the information or rumors gathered by the Bavarian Military Attaché in Berlin on this day, Moltke "is exerting all his influence in favor of taking advantage of the exceptionally favorable opportunity for striking a decisive blow," pointing out the momentary military embarrassment of France, the over-confidence of Russia, and the good time of year with the harvests mostly gathered and the annual training period of recruits completed. Bethmann, on the other hand, "is putting on the brakes with all his might, and is anxious to avoid everything which

[34] K.D., 349.

might lead to similar measures in France and England and start the ball rolling."[35]

These opposing views were set forth to the Kaiser at Potsdam on the afternoon and early evening of July 29 in separate reports by the military and civilian authorities. But there was no "Potsdam Council," nor any decision in favor of German mobilization, such as was incorrectly reported next day by the suspicious French Ambassador and has been commonly assumed by later writers.[36] Bethmann was successful in "putting on the brakes," as is seen from his summary of the situation at the Prussian Council of Ministers at noon next day: "The military authorities had expressed the desire that a 'state of threatening danger of war' be proclaimed, but he had successfully defended before His Majesty the objections." Such a proclamation meant mobilization, and mobilization meant war; mediation proposals had been made at Vienna, and the answer to these must be awaited before one abandoned hope and efforts for peace; "one could not conveniently carry on military and political activities at the same time." Accordingly, "His Majesty had consented that before any further decisions were arrived at, the move at Vienna, previously explained, should be brought to a conclusion."[37] The only precautionary military measures ordered by the evening of July 29 were the protection of railways and valuable buildings, the recall of officers and men on leave, the reinforcement of frontier fortresses, and other minor measures similar to, but less extensive than, those which had been going on in

[35] Wenninger to the Bavarian Minister of War, July 29; Dirr, p. 221. For the controversy between Hermann Lutz and Theobald von Schäfer as to the trustworthiness of Wenninger's despatch, see KSF, V, 1107-1125, Nov. 1927.

[36] *Cf.* F.Y.B., 105; Bourgeois et Pagès, pp. 95, 132; Viviani, *Réponse au Kaiser,* p. 153; Oman, p. 73. For the facts concerning the separate reports made to the Kaiser, see A. von Wegerer, "Der angebliche 'Kronrat' vom 29. Juli 1914," in KSF, I, 8-12, July, 1923; and Tirpitz. *Politische Dokumente* (Hamburg and Berlin, 1926), II, 2-5.

[37] Protocol of the Prussian Council of Ministers, July 30; K.D., 456

GENERAL MOLTKE
German Chief of Staff, 1906-1914

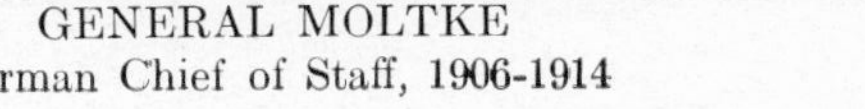

HERR VON JAGOW
German Secretary for Foreign Affairs, 1913-1916

Russia since July 26 and which had already been ordered in France.[38]

While Bethmann thus succeeded in holding back the military authorities from any decisive and irreparable step, he made a number of important diplomatic moves on July 29, some with a view to averting war, others with a view to securing advantages if war proved inevitable.

Shortly after noon he sent his warning through Pourtalès to Sazonov, that "further continuance of Russian mobilization measures would force us to mobilize." Later, at 6:30 P.M., after the arrival of the announced decision of Russian partial mobilization, the Kaiser sent the second telegram to the Tsar which led the latter to cancel the order for general mobilization which was on the point of being dispatched over the wires. These two efforts to deter Russia from the fatal step of ordering mobilization have been discussed in the preceding chapter.

On returning from Potsdam to Berlin, and finding still no answer from Vienna to his "pledge plan," Bethmann telegraphed to Tschirschky in order to secure confirmation of its arrival and an immediate reply.[39]

Then he sent for the British Ambassador to secure certainty on a question which had been very much discussed at Potsdam, and was of the greatest importance to Germany in case of a possible European War—the question of British neutrality. Bethmann had been optimistically hoping for this. He had therefore been anxious to avoid all measures which might antagonize England. On July 25 and 26 he had telegraphed to the Kaiser at sea, advising that the German fleet remain quietly away in Norwegian waters, inasmuch as reports from London indicated that the dispersal

38 *Investigating Commission,* II, 8-11; Montgelas, in KSF, V, 1206-1214, Dec., 1927; and above, ch. vi. the section on the Russian "Period Preparatory to War."

39 Bethmann to Tschirschky, July 29, 10:18 and 10:30 P.M.; K.D., 377 and note.

of the British fleet and the discharge of reservists was going on according to schedule. "For the present, at least, Sir E. Grey is not considering direct participation by England in a possible European War." [40] But the Kaiser had not followed the advice, and had ordered the German fleet to return to its base at Kiel. Bethmann's optimism had been strengthened by news that the Kaiser's brother, Prince Henry, on a visit to England, had been assured by King George on July 26: "We shall try all we can to keep out of this, and shall remain neutral." But meanwhile the announcement on the 27th that the British fleet was *not* to be dispersed made it doubtful whether King George's statement could still be relied on. Prince Henry, who came to Potsdam on the afternoon of July 29, was "convinced that this statement was made in all seriousness," and that England would remain neutral at the start, but whether she would do so permanently he doubted, "on account of her relations with France." [41]

It was about 10:30 P.M. that Bethmann sent for Goschen and "made the following strong bid for British neutrality in the event of war." Provided Great Britain remained neutral, Germany was ready to give every assurance that she aimed at no territorial acquisitions at the expense of France in Europe, though she could give no such assurance concerning the French colonies. Germany would respect the neutrality of Holland, but as regards Belgium, Bethmann "could not tell to what operations Germany might be forced by the action of France, but he could state that, provided that Belgium did not take sides against Germany, her integrity would be respected at the conclusion of the war." But he trusted that British neutrality, in case of a war which might possibly arise from the

40 K.D., 182, 221.

41 Prince Henry to the Kaiser from Kiel, July 28; K.D., 374. King George's assurance had at once been telegraphed to Berlin by the German Naval Attaché in London on July 26; K.D., 207.

present conflict, might form the basis for a future neutrality agreement between England and Germany, which had been the object of his policy ever since he had been Chancellor.[42]

Bethmann's bid for British neutrality was a most unfortunate and foolish blunder. It made the worst possible impression in London. Sir Eyre Crowe noted: "The only comment that need be made on these astounding proposals is that they reflect discredit on the statesman who makes them." He concluded that "Germany practically admits the intention to violate Belgian neutrality," and "is practically determined to go to war." [43] Sir Edward Grey, after securing the approval of Mr. Asquith, but without waiting to lay his answer before the Cabinet, replied to Goschen that the Chancellor's proposals "cannot be entertained for a moment." England's material interests made it impossible to allow France to be so crushed as to lose her position as a Great Power, even though Germany should not take territory from France as distinct from her colonies. "But apart from that, for us to make this bargain with Germany at the expense of France would be a disgrace from which the good name of this country would never recover." Nor could England bargain away her obligation and interest as regards the neutrality of Belgium. England must preserve full freedom to act as circumstances should require.[44] In his memoirs also Grey reveals the "feeling of despair" with which he read Bethmann's dishonoring proposal, which was "like a searchlight lighting up an aspect of the situation which had not yet been looked at." [45] Next day he asked the French and German Governments each for an assurance to respect the neutrality of

42 Goschen to Grey, July 30, 1:20 A.M., received 9 A.M.; B.D., 293. Bethmann had spoken from typewritten notes (*cf.* K.D., 373) and Goschen, to insure accuracy, made on the spot a draft of the Chancellor's statement and read it to him for his approval before sending it to Grey (B.D., 677).

43 Minute on B.D., 293.

44 Grey to Goschen, July 30, 3:30 P.M.; B.D., 303.

45 Grey, I, 316 ff.

Belgium, so long as no other Power violated it.[46] Bethman greatly regretted having made the bid for British neutrality. Nor would he have spoken as he did, had he known of Grey's warning to Lichnowsky [47] which reached Berlin at 9:12 P.M.[48], but which apparently had not been deciphered or handed to the Chancellor before his conversation with Goschen.

Another step taken on July 29, probably as a result of the conferences at Potsdam, was Jagow's despatch of a message in a sealed envelope to the German Minister at Brussels. It was carried by a messenger, instead of being telegraphed in cipher, because there was no immediate haste, and because it was not desirable to reveal even to the Minister himself a demand on Belgium which after all it might never be necessary to make. On opening the envelope, the Minister merely found instructions to keep safely locked up another sealed document which he would find enclosed, but which he was to open only if subsequently instructed by telegram from Berlin. The inner envelope contained an ultimatum to Belgium, based on a draft which Moltke had written with his own hand on July 26. It stated the German intention to march through Belgium, if possible with the friendly consent of Belgium; but if Belgium offered opposition, "Germany would be obliged, to her regret, to regard the Kingdom as an enemy." [49]

These two steps—the bid for British neutrality and the forwarding of the sealed ultimatum to Brussels—indicate how seriously the German authorities contemplated on the evening of July 29 the probability of war. They show that Bethmann had found himself forced to yield to Moltke's

[46] B.D., 348.

[47] So Jagow explained somewhat apologetically to Goschen next morning. Goschen says he is sure Bethmann and Jagow, or at all events Jagow, were dreadfully put out that the neutrality proposal had ever been made, and never alluded to Grey's answer to it; B.D., 677.

[48] K.D., 368.

[49] K.D., 375, 376; *cf.* also 648, 735.

view of strategic necessity and to the violation of Belgium, *if war should come.* But they do not prove that Bethmann had yet yielded to the view that war was already inevitable, or that any decision for war had been reached.

On the contrary, the Chancellor redoubled his efforts to preserve peace by putting increased pressure on Austria. After the interview with Goschen, though thoroughly tired out by his long and difficult day, Bethmann consulted with Jagow concerning the fresh telegrams which had meanwhile poured in. Among them was the Tsar's personal suggestion to the Kaiser that the Austro-Serbian problem be given over to the Hague Conference. But just as Sazonov had paid no attention to the Tsar's instructions two days earlier to take steps in this direction, so now it was decisively rejected in Berlin.[50]

A telegram from Lichnowsky told of Grey's approval of the Italian suggestion of mediation by the Great Powers on the basis of Serbia's reported willingness at last to accept even Points 5 and 6 of the Austrian ultimatum.[51] Pourtalès told of Sazonov's indignation at Vienna's "categorical refusal" to enter upon direct conversations, and of his desire to return to Grey's conference proposal; but this was coupled with the grave news that "Sazonov did not deny the imminence of mobilization," though stating that this "was far from meaning war."[52] Bethmann sent on to Vienna the substance of both of these telegrams, as well as those just exchanged between the Kaiser and the Tsar. He again "urgently requested" the acceptance of the "pledge

50 See above, ch. ix, at notes 73-78; Kaiser's marginal note, and Bethmann to Pourtalès, July 30, 2:40 A.M.; K.D., 366, 391. In *Fateful Years* (pp. 194 f., 203), M. Sazonov condemns Germany for neglecting the Tsar's "excellent suggestion" of the Hague Tribunal, but omits to mention that he himself completely neglected it two days previously. Does this indicate candor and honesty on his part?

51 Lichnowsky to Bethmann, July 29, 2:08 P.M., received 5:07 P.M.; K.D., 357.

52 Pourtalès to Bethmann, July 29, 6:10 P.M., received 8:29 P.M.; K.D., 365.

plan" of "Halt in Belgrade," and the inauguration and continuance of direct conversations between Vienna and St. Petersburg in order to satisfy Sazonov.[53]

Meanwhile Lichnowsky's later telegram had been deciphered, telling of Grey's suggestion of mediation on the basis of an Austrian occupation of Belgrade, and also of Grey's private and friendly warning that England might find it impossible to stand aside. As Grey's suggestion was very similar to Bethmann's own "Halt in Belgrade" plan, and as the warning put an end to all illusions as to the possibility of British neutrality, Bethmann welcomed Grey's suggestion as supporting his own efforts, and forwarded it to Vienna. In commenting on it, he pointed out in strong terms how dangerous it would be for Austria to refuse all negotiations, and added: "Under these circumstances we must urgently and emphatically urge upon the consideration of the Vienna Cabinet the adoption of mediation in accordance with the above honorable conditions."[54]

Then, finally, before catching a little sleep, he sent telegrams to St. Petersburg and London which he hoped would help to prevent war and secure mediation. To Pourtalès he telegraphed: "Please tell Sazonov that we are continuing to mediate; condition, however, would be the suspension for the time being of all hostilities against Austria on the part of Russia"; and to Lichnowsky: "Kindly thank Sir E. Grey for his frank explanation and tell him that we are continuing to mediate in Vienna and are urgently advising the acceptance of his proposal."[55]

On the morning of July 30 Bethmann at last received a reply from Vienna to his "Halt in Belgrade" mediation plan, but the reply was wholly unsatisfactory and non-com-

[53] Bethmann to Tschirschky, July 30, 12:10 and 12:30 A.M.; K.D., 383, 385.

[54] Bethmann to Tschirschky July 30, 2:55 A.M.; K.D., 395.

[55] Bethmann to Pourtalès and to Lichnowsky, July 30, 2:55 A.M.; K.D.. 392, 393.

mittal on one of the essential points. Berchtold was ready to repeat the declaration concerning Austria's territorial disinterestedness, but "so far as the further declaration with reference to military measures is concerned, Count Berchtold says that he is not in a position to give me a reply at once. In spite of my representations as to the urgency of the matter, I have up to this evening received no further communication."[56]

Accordingly, in his summary of the situation to the Prussian Ministry of State about noon, Bethmann gave an account of his efforts to bring about an understanding between Vienna and St. Petersburg, seconded by Grey's proposal of mediation based on the Austrian occupation of Belgrade, but had to admit that the result of his efforts was still uncertain. The Kaiser had consented, however, that no decisive steps toward mobilization should be taken until the move at Vienna had been brought to a conclusion. Nor would he himself give up his hope and efforts to maintain peace, as long as it had not been repelled.[57]

Late in the afternoon he learned that Berchtold rejected the Italian suggestion that Serbia might at last be willing to accept Points 5 and 6 of the ultimatum; such an acceptance might have sufficed, if Serbia had manifested her willingness earlier; but "now, since a state of war had supervened, Austria's conditions would naturally be different." Berchtold had, however, instructed Szápáry to begin conversations with Sazonov at St. Petersburg on Austro-Russian (but not Austro-Serbian) relations. He himself would explain to the Russian Ambassador in Vienna that Austria had no idea of making any territorial acquisitions in Serbia, and that, after the conclusion of peace, the occupation of Serbian territory would be merely temporary to

56 Tschirschky to Bethmann, July 30, 11:50 P.M., received July 30, 1:30 A.M.; K.D., 388.

57 Protocol of the Prussian Ministry of State, July 30; K.D., 456.

secure the fulfilment of Austrian demands; to the extent that Serbia fulfilled the conditions of peace, evacuation would follow. But as to accepting Grey's suggestion for a mediation by a conference of the Powers, involving the cessation of hostilities, he could not give an answer until next day after an audience with Francis Joseph.[58]

In order to find out what Vienna was intending to do, the Berlin Foreign Office resorted to the telephone,[59] but Tschirschky's reply indicated that Berchtold was not likely to yield to the mediation proposals which Bethmann had been so constantly urging; in any case Berchtold would not give a definite reply until he had consulted Tisza who would not be back in Vienna until early the following morning.[60]

Meanwhile the Kaiser, also impatient, had finally telegraphed personally to Francis Joseph: "I should be honestly obliged to you if you would favor me with your decision as soon as possible." [61]

While Bethmann had thus been trying in vain to get an answer from Vienna, Moltke had become increasingly nervous over the situation. On the morning of July 30 he was still willing to abide by the decision of Bethmann and the Kaiser, that Russia's partial mobilization did not necessitate Germany's mobilization, for he wrote out for Captain Fleischmann, whom Conrad had sent to Berlin as *liaison* officer, the following telegram for the Austrian Chief of Staff:

> Russia's mobilization is not yet a cause for mobilization. [Moltke meant for *Germany's* mobilization, but Conrad seems to have understood for *Austria's* mobilization.] Not until state of war exists between Austria and Russia. In contrast to the mobilizations and demobilizations which have been customary in Russia, Germany's mobilization

[58] Tschirschky to Bethmann, July 30, 2:30 P.M.; received 5:25 P.M.; K.D., 433.

[59] *Cf.* K.D., 441.

[60] K.D., 440.

[61] July 30, 7:15 P.M.; K.D., 437.

would unconditionally lead to war. Do not declare war on Russia, but await Russia's attack.[62]

Moltke seemed to be convinced that Russia was forcing Europe into war, and, in order to make it clear that Russia was the aggressor, he believed that the initiative in the declaration of war should come, not from Austria or from Germany, but from Russia—a point of view exactly analogous to that of Poincaré, Paléologue and Jules Cambon, who were convinced that Germany was forcing Europe into war and that the odium of the initiative must be carefully left to her.

In the afternoon, however, after hearing that Sazonov had said that it was impossible to stop the Russian mobilization, and that the Tsar admitted that the preparatory measures had been going on for five days, Moltke became much excited and believed that the danger to Germany and Austria was critical. He talked with Bienerth, the Austrian Military Attaché, who then telegraphed to Conrad:

> Moltke said that he regards the situation as critical if the Austro-Hungarian Monarchy does not mobilize immediately against Russia. Russia's announced declaration concerning mobilization she has ordered makes necessary countermeasures by Austria-Hungary, and must also be cited in the public explanation. Thereby there would arise the *casus foederis* for Germany. With Italy make some honorable agreement by promising compensations, so that Italy will remain actively in the Triple Alliance; in fact, do not leave a man on the Italian frontier. Decline the renewed

[62] Fleischmann to Conrad, July 30; Conrad, IV, 151 f. For Fleischmann's *letter* to Conrad, sent July 30 and received July 31, which gave a fuller account of Moltke's statements, see Theobald von Schäfer, "Generaloberst von Moltke in den Tagen vor der Mobilmachung und seine Einwirkung auf Oesterreich-Ungarn," in KSF, IV, 522 f., Aug., 1926; this valuable article of Schäfer's (KSF, IV, 514-549) contains important hitherto unpublished material from the Vienna War Archives, which throws new light on the documents published by Conrad, and which was unknown to Mr. Heinrich Kanner when he wrote *Der Schlüssel zur Kriegsschuldfrage* (Munich, 1927).

> advances made by England for the maintenance of peace. The standing firm in a European war [*Durchhalten des europäischen Krieges*] is the last chance of saving Austria-Hungary. Germany will go with her unconditionally."[63]

In speaking thus, Moltke exceeded his authority and improperly gave *political* advice, which belonged exclusively within the functions of the Chancellor. He exemplified one of the great evils of militarism: the danger in time of crisis of interference by the military officials in civilian affairs. Moltke had no authority to interpret the alliance, or to say that the Russian mobilization furnished the *casus foederis* for Germany. It belonged to the Chancellor alone to interpret Germany's treaty obligations; and just the night before, Bethmann had told Moltke and Falkenhayn, the Prussian Minister of War, that Russian partial mobilization did not constitute the *casus foederis,* and that there was therefore not yet any occasion for Germany to mobilize. To this Moltke had objected "mildly, very mildly."[64]

In saying that Austria ought to give satisfactory compensations to Italy, Moltke was, to be sure, merely reiterating what the Berlin Foreign Office had been urging unsuccessfully upon Berchtold for many days past. But his suggestion that Austria decline the British peace proposal ran directly counter to the very thing Bethmann had been striving for. If any excuse for Moltke's remarks is to be found, one may perhaps say that he was merely expressing his personal opinions to the Austrian Military Attaché, rather than offering Austria official advice, since nothing is

63 Bienerth to Conrad, July 30, 5:30 P.M., received and deciphered during the night at Vienna; Conrad, IV, 152; Schäfer, p. 525 f. The Austrian Ambassador, Szögyény, in two telegrams to Berchtold (5:30 P.M. and 7:40 P.M., received 7:20 P.M. and 10:20 P.M. (A.R.B., 32, 34) mentions Bienerth's conversation with Moltke, and emphasizes the importance of satisfying Italy, but says nothing of declining the British proposal.

64 Falkenhayn's notes in H. v. Zwehl, *Erich v. Falkenhayn* (Berlin. 1926), p. 57.

said of the *casus foederis* or declining the British proposal in the Austrian Ambassador's report of Moltke's remarks, nor in the following laconic telegram which Moltke himself is believed to have sent direct to Conrad later:

> Stand firm to Russian mobilization [*Russische Mobilisierung durchhalten*]. Austria-Hungary must be preserved. Mobilize at once against Russia. Germany will mobilize. Bring Italy, by compensations, to her alliance obligations.[65]

Moltke feared that, through Austria's delay in mobilizing against Russia, Germany would be left to bear the brunt of the Russian attack. In his conversations and correspondence with Conrad ever since 1909 Moltke had always urged that, in case of danger from an Austro-Serbian war developing into a general European War, Austria should send only a minimum force against Serbia, and make her maximum effort against Russia in Galicia, in order to relieve the Russian pressure against East Prussia. Germany could then deliver her crushing blow against France in the West. Conrad, on the other hand, had always argued that Moltke should send a considerable force against Russia, in order to relieve the Russian pressure against Austria in Galicia. Each Chief of Staff had thus quite naturally represented the selfish interests of his own country, and they had never reached that perfect harmony of a "military convention,"

65 The "Moltke telegram" is nowhere to be found in the German Archives, or in the Vienna War Archives, or among Conrad's papers, says Schäfer, p. 526. It is printed in Conrad, IV, 152, as being received on July 31 at 7:45 A.M. When it was sent cannot be ascertained; quite possibly late in the evening after Moltke had received two reports of the Russian general mobilization, mentioned below. He feared lest Conrad, intent on his campaign against Serbia, would not mobilize quickly against Russia.

For accounts in English giving two views of this Moltke telegram and its significance, see R. Grelling, "Moltke, the Man Who Made the War," in *Current History,* Sept., 1926, pp. 916-925; and Count Montgelas, "Justifying Germany in 1914," *ibid.*, April, 1927, pp. 77-80. *Cf.* also Kanner, *Der Schlüssel zur Kriegsschuldfrage,* p. 40 ff.; and Renouvin, p. 194 f. (Eng. trans., 213 ff.).

fixing the precise number of troops which each was to employ against Russia, which Dr. Kanner regards as the "key" to the question of war responsibility.[66] On the contrary, this Moltke telegram, and other evidence to be cited below in connection with Austrian general mobilization, betray an extraordinary, though brief, lack of confidence and understanding on the part of these two Chiefs of Staff toward each other, such as was quite lacking on the part of the Russian and French Chiefs of Staff.

In the course of the evening of July 30, probably about 11:00 P.M., Moltke talked again with Bethmann. A little later—shortly after midnight—Moltke told Major Haeften that he had received "two reliable reports from independent sources, stating that mobilization of all Russia's armed forces had already been ordered." [67] This was altogether likely, as Russian general mobilization had been ordered at 6 P.M., and the orders had been quickly transmitted to the Warsaw District on the German frontier.[68]

Whether Moltke had already heard these "two reliable reports" when he talked with Bethmann is uncertain, but quite probable. For he caused Bethmann to waver momentarily in his hope to avoid war and his determination to keep "putting the brakes" on the military authorities.

At 9:00 P.M. the Chancellor had sent an "urgent" telegram No. 200, to Tschirschky at Vienna, recalling Grey's proposal which Austria was reported as likely to reject, and informing him of Grey's promises to work for peace at Paris and St. Petersburg. He added the emphatic warning and advice:

[66] *Cf.* Dr. Heinrich Kanner, *Der Schlüssel zur Kriegsschuldfrage,* Munich, 1926, *passim;* and the present writer's review of it, with Dr. Kanner's rejoinder, in *Amer. Hist. Rev.,* XXXII, 317-319, 942-946, Jan., July, 1927.

[67] Note by Haeften, Aug. 2, 1914; printed in Schulthess, *Europäischer Geschichtskalender,* 1917, II, p. 996 ff.; and quoted by Montgelas, *Leitfaden,* p. 137.

[68] See above, ch. x, at notes 62-65.

If England's efforts succeed, while Vienna declines everything, Vienna will be giving documentary evidence that it absolutely wants a war, into which we shall be drawn, while Russia remains free from responsibility. That would place us, in the eyes of our own people, in an untenable position. Thus we can only urgently advise Austria to accept the Grey proposal, which preserves her status for her in every way. Your Excellency will at once express yourself most emphatically on this matter to Count Berchtold, perhaps also to Count Tisza.[69]

Then, after hearing what Moltke had to say, Bethmann telegraphed again to Tschirschky at 11:20 P.M.: "Please do not carry out instructions No. 200 for the present." [70] His reason appears in a draft telegram which, however, was quickly replaced by another telegram and was never sent to Tschirschky. In the unsent draft telegram Bethmann said: "I cancelled the order of instructions in No. 200, as the General Staff just informs me that the military preparations of our neighbors, especially in the East, will force us to a speedy decision, unless we do not wish to expose ourselves to the danger of surprise." [71] This indeed looks as if Bethmann had at last yielded to Moltke. But hardly had this telegram been drafted, when the Chancellor learned of the following telegram from the King of England to Prince Henry of Prussia:

> So pleased to hear of William's efforts to concert with Nicky to maintain peace. . . . My Government is doing its utmost suggesting to Russia and France to suspend further military preparations, if Austria will consent to be satisfied with occupation of Belgrade and neighboring Serbian territory as a hostage for satisfactory settlement of her demands, other countries meanwhile suspending their war preparations. Trust William will use his great influence to induce

69 Bethmann to Tschirschky, July 30, 9:00 P.M., received July 31, 3:00 A.M.; K.D., 441.

70 K.D., 450.

71 K.D., 451.

Austria to accept this proposal, thus proving that Germany and England are working together to prevent what would be an international catastrophe. Pray assure William that I am doing and shall continue to do all that lies in my power to preserve peace of Europe.[72]

This telegram gave Bethmann new hope. Instead of sending the draft telegram, with Moltke's alarming news which would have tended to make Austria decide for general mobilization, Bethmann sent on to Vienna King George's friendly message. explaining that its arrival had caused the cancellation of No. 200. He directed Tschirschky to communicate King George's telegram to Berchtold "without delay," and again added: "A definite decision in Vienna during the course of the day is urgently desired." [73]

These telegrams seem to show that Bethmann for a brief moment wavered and gave up hope. But they do *not* show, as has sometimes been maintained, that he definitely and completely changed his attitude, yielded to Moltke's pressure, and decided to send an ultimatum to Russia several hours before he learned of the Russian general mobilization.[74] On the contrary, after a brief delay he again put forward at Vienna the British proposal in the shape of King George's telegram, though he did not renew his emphatic warning in telegram No. 200.[75] His momentary wavering was caused by Moltke's news about Russian military preparations. But as this was not definite, he still refused to agree to Germany's sending an ultimatum to Russia or to ordering the "Threatening Danger of War," which was the preliminary step to German mobilization. He was determined to wait still further, until he received the answer from Vienna to the "Halt in Belgrade" proposal, or until the news

[72] George V to Prince Henry, July 30, 8:54 P. M., received 11:08 P. M.; K.D., 452.

[73] Bethmann to Tschirschky, July 31, 2:45 A. M.; received 9:00 A.M.; K.D., 464.

[74] *Cf.* Kanner, *Der Schüssel*, p. 41 f.

[75] Renouvin. (Eng. trans., p. 191) emphasizes this point.

of Russian general mobilization was definitely confirmed, as it was confirmed in a despatch from Pourtalès which arrived at 11:40 A.M. next day. He hoped soon to have certainty on these two points. As Moltke and Falkenhayn were pressing for an early decision, Bethmann consented that it should be made next day, July 31, at noon.[76] No decision therefore was taken on the night of July 30. And Moltke, shortly after his conversation with Bethmann, stated to Haeften very pessimistically that he did not know how it would all end. "Tomorrow noon comes the decision for peace or war. The Chancellor, the Minister of War, and I have an audience together with His Majesty." Though he had two reliable reports concerning Russian general mobilization, Moltke added: "Before advising His Majesty to mobilize, I wish to await a third confirmation of the news about Russian mobilization." [77]

About 7 A.M., July 31, Moltke received a telephone message from a Staff Officer at Allenstein in East Prussia, stating that the frontier had been completely closed by the Russians and that the red placards ordering mobilization had already been posted up. Moltke replied: "It is necessary that you procure one of these posted orders. I must have certainty as to whether they are really mobilizing against us. Before having that certainty, I am not able to elicit a mobilization order." [78] In other words, Moltke himself admits that Bethmann was unwilling to agree to a decision until Germany had conclusive and absolute evidence of the Russian general mobilization which was suspected and which in fact had been ordered some twelve hours earlier. This evidence was finally supplied in the telegram from Pourtalès at 11:40 A.M. Had Bethmann not received it—had the Tsar not yielded to Sazonov and the Russian militarists

[76] Zwehl, *E. v. Falkenhayn*, p. 57.
[77] Schulthess, *Europäischer Geschichtskalender*, 1917, II, p. 996.
[78] Schulthess, *Europäischer Geschichtskalender*, 1917, II, p. 1000.

—it is probable that Bethmann would still have held out against Moltke and Falkenhayn, and a further breathing-space been given for consideration of the "Halt in Belgrade" proposal, or for Sazonov's "formula," or for other negotiations toward a peaceful solution. This is not to say, however, that, in this late stage of the crisis, it is probable that a peaceful solution would have been found. But at any rate it would have given the civilian officials in St. Petersburg and Berlin further opportunity to try to find a solution, and the arguments of military necessity would have had less of a hearing in both capitals.

However, as the events actually took place, it was the precipitate Russian general mobilization, and not any "military convention" between Moltke and Conrad such as Dr. Kanner imagines, which determined Germany's decision for "Threatening Danger of War," followed by her ultimatums and mobilization, in view of the European War which even Bethmann recognized was made inevitable by Russia's step.

AUSTRIAN GENERAL MOBILIZATION, JULY 31

In Vienna Berchtold and Conrad were dominated more by a determination to carry out a campaign against Serbia than by a fear of war with Russia. Hence the Austrian ultimatum, the partial mobilization exclusively against Serbia with careful avoidance of provocative measures in Galicia, and the declaration of war on Serbia, all of which have already been described.

Even after moving against Serbia and bombarding Belgrade, Conrad had still assumed that Russia would not resort to armed intervention. He had therefore sent no troops to the Galician front. But upon Sazonov's announcement that Russia would mobilize in her southern districts if Austria crossed the Serbian frontier,[79] Conrad began to realize

[79] Szápáry to Berchtold, July 29, 4:26 P.M., received 10 P.M.; A.R.B., III, 18.

that the Galician front was in danger. He regarded as grotesque Sazonov's assurance that Russian troops once mobilized would stand idle on the frontier with arms stacked. He at once resolved that Austria ought to mobilize, both as a defensive measure of safety against superior Russian forces, and as a counter-bluff which he somewhat illogically seemed to think might frighten Russia off.[80] Early on July 30, the German Ambassador in Vienna noted: "Here they are resolved to mobilize, as soon as Germany approves; firmly resolved to permit no further Russian mobilization. Proposal: say to St. Petersburg and eventually to Paris, that if the mobilization continues, general mobilization will begin in Austria and Germany." [81] That is, Berchtold and Conrad proposed to rattle the German sword, by having Bethmann threaten Russia and France with general mobilization by the Central Powers, unless Russian mobilization measures ceased.

But when the Austrian Ambassador in Berlin tried to persuade Germany to take such a step,[82] Germany refused. She had already gone as far in this direction as she deemed prudent in the "warning" given by Pourtalès to Sazonov on July 29. Szögyény was therefore informed by Jagow that since Germany had already pointed out in a friendly spirit at St. Petersburg the dangerous consequences of Russian mobilization, she could not again take the same step. She advised Austria to make representations at St. Petersburg on her own account.[83]

But Conrad did not wait for the arrival of this discouraging answer. Nor did he and Berchtold give serious heed to Bethmann's renewed urgent advice to accept Grey's peace

80 Conrad, IV, 145-147.

81 Tschirschky's short-hand note on a telegram (K.D., 385) which he received July 30 at 6:00 A.M.; *Investigating Commission,* I, 98.

82 Memoranda of Szögyény and Jagow, July 30; K.D., 427, 429.

83 Jagow to Tschirschky, July 30, 9:00 P.M.; K.D., 442. Szögyény to Berchtold, July 31, 12:38 A.M.; A.R.B., III, 51.

proposal, which Tschirschky says he presented "most impressively" after lunch on July 30. Berchtold, "who listened pale and silent," merely said he would report to the Emperor about it at once, and went to change his clothes in order to appear in the correct garb for an audience. From Berchtold's subordinates, Hoyos and Forgach, Tschirschky learned that "the restriction of the military operations [now in progress against Serbia] was, in their opinion, out of the question, in view of the feeling in the army and among the people. Count Tisza will appear in Vienna early tomorrow. His opinion must be obtained on this far-reaching decision." Tschirschky learned also that Conrad was about to submit to Francis Joseph the order for Austrian general mobilization as the reply to the measures already taken by Russia.[84]

In spite of Bethmann's advice which had just been urged by Tschirschky, Berchtold and Conrad, at their audience with Emperor Francis Joseph later in the afternoon, persuaded the aged monarch to approve the following decisions. War against Serbia was to be carried out; Grey's proposal was to be answered very politely in form but without accepting it in substance. General mobilization in Austria was to be ordered on August 1, with August 4 as the first day of mobilization; but this question would be discussed again next day.[85]

The final reservation, providing for discussion again next day of the date of mobilization, was probably mainly owing to the necessity of getting Count Tisza's approval. It may have also been partly owing to the arrival of Fleischmann's telegram from Moltke: "Russia's mobilization is not yet a cause for mobilization," [86] and to Bethmann's continued urgent advice to accept Grey's mediation proposal. In fact,

[84] Tschirschky to Bethmann, July 30, 5:20 P.M., received 5:56 P.M.; and July 31, 1:35 A.M., received 4:35 A.M.; K.D., 434, 465.

[85] Conrad, IV, 151.

[86] Conrad, IV, 152: and see above, at note 62.

says Conrad: "While Emperor Francis Joseph, at this hardest moment of his life, was taking with deep solemnity and calm resolution the step whose heavy consequences were as clear to him as its inevitability, it seemed as if Emperor William was thinking of retreat, and as if the feeling in Berlin had changed on account of Italy's jumping out." [87] Nevertheless, in spite of Berlin's attitude, Conrad seems to have concluded after the audience that the Austrian general mobilization was a settled question as soon as it should have Tisza's approval early next morning. He was even resolved that it should be ordered *next day,* July 31, instead of August 1, as agreed at the audience with the Emperor. Therefore at 7:30 P.M., he wrote out a telegram, to be sent to Berlin at 8:00 A.M. on July 31, which stated: "According to His Majesty's decision it is resolved: to carry through the war against Serbia; to mobilize the rest of the army and to concentrate it in Galicia; first day of mobilization, August 4. Mobilization order will be issued today, July 31." [88] The telegram was, in fact, sent off as directed at 8:00 A.M. on July 31.

Meanwhile, in the course of the night, had come Bienerth's telegram, and at 7:45 A.M. Moltke's own telegram urging Austria to mobilization at once.[89] These telegrams did not cause Austrian mobilization, except in the sense that they removed any hesitation on Conrad's part concerning the order he had written the previous evening, and confirmed Berchtold in the decision taken in the audience with the Emperor the day before to reject the substance of Grey's proposal while appearing to yield to it in form.

87 Conrad, IV, 151.

88 Schäfer, p. 536. Conrad also gave Tschirschky to understand that he had resolved on Austrian mobilization, for Tschirschky noted on a telegram received July 30 at 10:00 A.M. (K.D., 396), that Conrad would discuss general mobilization with the Emperor in the afternoon and then tell the Russian Ambassador that it meant "no hostility, no conflict; precaution, no threat, still less any idea of attack" (*Investigating Commission,* I, 99).

89 See above, at notes 63, 65.

When Conrad took Moltke's telegram to Berchtold and the other Ministers, Berchtold exclaimed: "Who is in charge? Moltke or Bethmann?" After reading aloud Emperor William's telegram to Francis Joseph, urging the "Halt in Belgrade" proposal, Berchtold turned to the others and said: "I called you together because I had the impression that Germany was drawing back; now I have the most satisfactory assurances from the highest military authority."[90]

Francis Joseph's final assent was thereupon secured to an order for general mobilization, fixing August 4 as the first day of mobilization. The order reached the Ministry of War on July 31 at 12:23 P.M., and was immediately published. It did not, however, immediately remove all misunderstandings between Conrad and Moltke in the course of the afternoon. Conrad, in ordering general mobilization, did not at first expect war with Russia. He had not yet heard of Russian general mobilization and believed he could still carry through the war against Serbia, as he had telegraphed to Moltke at 8:00 A.M. on July 31. Upon receiving this, Moltke had immediately begged Conrad "not to divert strong forces from the main struggle, which in his opinion ought to be waged against Russia, by an undertaking against Serbia. The main force must be held ready against Russia, because the German rear covering-forces are inadequate against a decisive Russian advance."[91] At 6:00 P.M. he telephoned to Vienna: "Is Austria going to leave us in the lurch?"[92]

Conrad telephoned in reply at 9:30 P.M., asking for a definite statement whether he was to reckon with certainty on war with Russia taking place immediately; he did not know whether Russia was only bluffing, and therefore he did not want to be diverted from his action against Serbia.

90 Conrad, IV, 153. Berchtold was referring to Moltke.

91 Fleischmann to Conrad, July 31, 11:15 A.M., received 6:05 P.M.; Schäfer, p. 540.

92 Schäfer, p. 541.

It was not until late in the evening of July 31 that he was convinced by Moltke and by the Kaiser's next telegram to Francis Joseph that Germany expected that her ultimatums to Russia and France would be rejected, and that Austria's main effort ought therefore to be directed against Russia and not against Serbia.[93]

The Austrian general mobilization was not a decisive factor in the final chain of events causing the war. It was not ordered until eighteen hours after the Russian general mobilization had been ordered, and did not contribute to the steps which Germany took in answer to the Russian mobilization.

After securing Francis Joseph's final approval of Austrian general mobilization, Berchtold now deceived Europe by the pretense of adopting a more conciliatory attitude, which is contradicted by his real intentions as revealed in the minutes of the secret Ministerial Council held about noon. With the Russian Ambassador in Vienna he took up conversations again in a most friendly manner, and to all the Powers he pretended that Austria was ready to "approach nearer" Grey's proposal.[94] To the British Ambassador he gave the impression, as Bunsen later wrote to Grey, that

> Austria, in fact, had finally yielded, and that she herself had at this point good hopes of a peaceful issue is shown by the communication made to you on the 1st of August by Count Mensdorff to the effect that Austria had neither "banged the door" on compromise nor cut off the conversations. . . . Unfortunately these conversations at St. Petersburg and Vienna were cut short by the transfer of the dispute to the more dangerous ground of a direct conflict between Germany and Russia. Germany intervened on the 31st July by means of her double ultimatums to St. Peters-

[93] Schäfer, pp. 541-544.

[94] A.R.B., III, 62, 65, 66, 78, 94; *Krasnyi Arkhiv,* I, p. 186; Schilling's *Diary,* p. 72; B.D., 360, 412; Poincaré, IV, 465 ff.

> burg and Paris. The ultimatums were of a kind to which only one answer is possible, and Germany declared war on Russia on the 1st August, and on France on the 3rd August. A few days' delay might in all probability have saved Europe from one of the greatest calamities in history.[95]

How far Berchtold was, however, from the slightest intention of really and honestly yielding to mediation and stopping the Austrian advance in Serbia is now unmistakably revealed in the protocol of the minutes of the Ministerial Council. After stating Grey's last proposal and Bethmann's strong urging that it be accepted, Berchtold pointed out that experience showed that mediatory Powers always tried to reach a compromise by forcing one Power to pare down the conditions it had made:

> It was probable that they would attempt this now also, when in the present conjuncture France, England, and Italy also would represent the Russian standpoint, and we [Austria] should have a very doubtful support in the present German Ambassador in London. From Prince Lichnowsky everything else was to be expected except that he would represent our interests warmly. If the action should end now merely with a gain of prestige, it would in my opinion have been undertaken wholly in vain. From a mere occupation of Belgrade we should gain absolutely nothing, even if Russia should give her consent to it. All this would be mere tinsel [*Flitterwerk*]. Russia would come forward as the savior of Serbia, and especially of the Serbian army. The latter would remain intact, and in two or three years we should again have to look forward to the attack of Serbia under much more unfavorable conditions.

He had therefore had an audience with Francis Joseph. His Majesty had at once declared that there could be no check placed upon military operations, but accepted the plan "that we should carefully avoid accepting the English proposal in

[95] Bunsen to Grey, Sept. 1, 1914; B.D., 676.

actual substance, but that in the form of our answer, we should pretend to be ready to meet it. . . ." [96]

Berchtold's colleagues agreed with him or went even further. Tisza, who had now completely changed his attitude, made no opposition. To Stürgkh, "the very thought of a mediatory conference was so odious that he preferred to avoid even the pretense of accepting one." Bilinski was equally hostile to a conference, because "the course of the London Conference was so horrible to recall to memory, that all public opinion would reject the repetition of such a spectacle." [97]

There is therefore no substantial truth in the widely accepted Entente version that Austria was at last ready to yield, when Germany intervened with her ultimatum and declaration of war, and so precipitated the general European War. Germany did intervene because of the Russian general mobilization. But Austria had no genuine intention of yielding to Grey's idea, or of abandoning the campaign against Serbia and being content with the occupation of Belgrade or even neighboring territory. One reason that Austria refused to be satisfied with the occupation of Belgrade was military necessity. Her plan of campaign did not make possible an immediate occupation of Belgrade, but provided that her main attack on Serbia should come from Bosnia from the southwest, and not directly upon Belgrade from the north across the Danube.[98]

"THREATENING DANGER OF WAR" IN GERMANY, JULY 31

Bethmann had restrained Moltke from taking any irremediable military steps until a decision should be made at noon on July 31 at a meeting between themselves and the

96 A.R.B., III, 79; repeated in slightly less bald language, *ibid.*, III, 80. *Cf.* Gooss, pp. 234-243, 301-306.

97 Minutes of the Ministerial Council, July 31; A.R.B., III, 79.

98 *Cf.* R. Kiszling, "Die praktische Undurchführbarkeit eines Handstreiches auf Belgrad," in KSF, V, 231-238, March, 1927.

Kaiser.[99] By that time it was hoped that an answer would at last have come from Vienna as to the "Halt in Belgrade" plan, and that there would be definite information as to the military situation in Russia. A favorable answer from Vienna might open the way for peace. A confirmation of the reports of general mobilization in Russia would force Germany to take steps to protect herself against the danger of a war on two fronts.

In anticipation of a peaceful settlement the Kaiser at Potsdam had written out in his own hand on the morning of July 31 a long statement for the Admiralty Staff summarizing the telegrams exchanged with the Tsar, and enclosing the one to Prince Henry from George V: "His proposals are similar to mine, which I suggested to the Vienna Cabinet, which has left us for six days without an answer. . . . Diplomatic conferences have at last commenced between Vienna and Peterhof, and Peterhof has also begged London for intervention." [100] While in the midst of this, the Kaiser received a telephone message from Berlin announcing beyond the slightest doubt that general mobilization was in progress in Russia. Without waiting to consult his Foreign Office, he telegraphed to King George:

> Many thanks for your kind telegram. Your proposals coincide with my ideas and with the statements I got this night from Vienna which I have had forwarded to London. I just received news from Chancellor that official notification has reached him that this night Nicky has ordered the mobilization of his whole army and fleet. He has not even awaited the results of the mediation I am working at and left me without any news. I am off for Berlin to take measures for ensuring safety of my eastern frontiers where strong Russian troops are already posted.[101]

99 Moltke's statement to Haeften after midnight, July 30-31; Schulthess, *Europäischer Geschichtskalender,* 1917, II, 996 f.

100 K.D., 474.

101 Kaiser to George V, July 31, 12:55 P.M.; K.D., 477.

The definite news of the Russian general mobilization, ordered about 6:00 P.M. on July 30, was surprisingly late in reaching Berlin.

In St. Petersburg neither Pourtalès nor the German Military Attaché, Eggeling, knew anything of it until the morning of July 31, after the news had already been printed in the newspapers and been posted up in the streets for hours. As soon as Eggeling learned of it, he hurried to Pourtalès, who sent off a telegram at 10:20 A.M.:

> General mobilization of the army and navy ordered. First mobilization day, July 31.[102]

Bethmann telephoned the news to Potsdam. The Kaiser motored at once to Berlin. A conference took place with Bethmann, Moltke and other officials. About 1:00 P.M. it was decided to proclaim "Threatening Danger of War" [*drohende Kriegsgefahr*]. This proclamation set in motion a number of precautionary measures preparatory to actual mobilization, and was somewhat similar to the Russian "Period Preparatory to War." It did not necessarily and inevitably involve mobilization, but it meant that the German Government expected it would be followed by mobilization within at least forty-eight hours, and mobilization would mean war. As Bethmann telegraphed to Vienna, in order to persuade Austria to divert her main effort against Russia instead of against Serbia:

> After the Russian total mobilization we have proclaimed "Threatening Danger of War," which will presumably be followed within forty-eight hours by mobilization. The latter inevitably means war. We expect from Austria an immediate *active* participation in the war against Russia.[103]

102 Pourtalès to Bethmann, July 31, 10:20 A. M., received 11:40 A. M.; K.D., 473.

103 Bethmann to Tschirschky, July 31, 1:45 P. M.; received 4:20 P.M.; K.D., 479. Moltke also said the same more emphatically to Conrad in telephone conversations in the course of the afternoon and evening

It is often said that had the German Government really wanted peace, even after learning of the Russian general mobilization, it should have contented itself with declaring German mobilization and then standing on the defensive; that Sazonov would have lived up to his promises that the Russian army would make no attack but stand with arms grounded; and that this would have again given the diplomatists a chance to find a peaceful solution. It is said, in a word, that the proper answer to mobilization is counter-mobilization and not war. But this argument leaves out of view the fact that in St. Petersburg and Paris, as well as in Berlin, the maxim had long been accepted by military men, and by the highest political authorities like Tsar Alexander III,[104] that "mobilization means war." It had been clearly hinted by Pourtalès to Sazonov on the afternoon of July 29 before Russia ordered general mobilization.[105] It was obviously clear to the Tsar on July 30 in view of his hesitation to yield to Sazonov's arguments and to accept the solemn responsibility which he realized would send thousands and thousands of men to their death.[106] And it was explicitly stated by Bethmann to the Prussian Council of Ministers on July 30: "The declaration of 'Threatening Danger of War' meant mobilization, and this under our conditions—mobilization toward both sides—meant war." [107]

The argument also leaves out of view the fact that in the plans of the General Staffs everywhere on the Continent mobilization was inextricably bound up with the "plan of campaign," which provided not only for the march to the frontier but in most cases the crossing of the frontier in order to get the advantage of the offensive and the waging

(Schäfer, pp. 538-543) and Emperor William made a similar appeal to Emperor Francis Joseph at 4:40 P.M. (K.D., 503).

104 See above ch. x, at notes 77-80.

105 See above ch. x, at note 37.

106 See above, ch. x, at notes 53, 60, 61.

107 K.D., 456.

of war in the enemy's country. Mobilization started the military machine in motion, and once in motion, for technical reasons, it was virtually impossible to halt it without dislocation of the long-prepared and minutely worked out plan of campaign. Though the civilian authorities might want to stop the machine at the frontier, and might promise that they would do so, as the Tsar promised the Kaiser, it was doubtful whether they would be able to do so, owing to the insistent arguments of the military authorities that any interference with the carefully prearranged schedule would be disastrous. Even the Kaiser, whose authority in civil and military matters was not least among monarchs, on understanding from Lichnowsky that England might guarantee the neutrality of France, for a moment on August 1, thought he could halt the German army, once in motion, from crossing the frontier into Luxemburg. But even he was quickly overborne by Moltke and by the news that Lichnowsky had made a "mistake," and made to realize that it was impossible.[108] And, as a matter of fact, at this very moment, a detachment of German soldiers appeared already to have crossed the frontier and violated the neutrality of Luxemburg.[109]

Furthermore, the argument leaves out of view the fact, just suggested, that when mobilizations have taken place, "military necessity" tends to prevail over the diplomatic considerations of the civilians. This was particularly true in Germany. It was perfectly recognized in St. Petersburg and Paris, as well as in Berlin, that as Germany would have to fight a war on two fronts, and as she was threatened by the superior number of troops which Russia and France could bring against her, she would have to strike her main blow first at one and then at the other. She could not divide

108 K.D., 562, 570, 575, 578, 579, 596, 603, 612, 630, 631; B.D., 419, 453, 460; and the dramatic narrative of Moltke, *Erinnerungen,* pp. 19-23.

109 Protest of Eyschen, Minister of the Grand Duchy of Luxemburg, to Jagow, Aug. 1, 9:30 P.M.; K.D., 602.

her main forces and face both fronts at once. Taking advantage of the fact that she could mobilize more rapidly than Russia, she would have to make her first attack on France, in the West, while the Russian forces were slowly gathering in the East. She must equalize her inferiority in numbers by the greater speed of her military machine. For Germany merely to have answered mobilization by counter-mobilization, and to have stood on the defensive while diplomatic negotiations (probably futile) proceeded, would have meant that she would lose all her advantage in speed. The Russian armies would have had time gradually to mobilize and to concentrate on the East Prussian frontier, in overwhelming numbers, thus compelling Germany either to divide her forces and face superior numbers, simultaneously East and West, or to open her eastern territory to Russian invasion while she made her main effort against France in the West. These were military considerations, convincing to the German civilian as well as military authorities,[110] and recognized by the military authorities in Russia and France, which made it obviously impossible for Germany merely to answer Russian general mobilization by counter-mobilization. It was not Germany's lack of desire for peace, but her "plan of campaign," arising from her inferior numbers and her double frontier, which compelled her, after proclaiming "Threatening Danger of War," followed by mobilization, to move at once beyond her frontier.

Germany's plan of campaign also contemplated going through the relatively flat and less strongly fortified territory of Belgium, in defiance of international law and of Prussia's guarantee of Belgian neutrality. Only in so doing, the militarists believed, could Germany strike and crush

110 Bethmann, *Betrachtungen* (Berlin, 1919), I, 164 ff.; H. v. Kuhl, *Der deutsche Generalstab in Vorbereitung und Durchführung des Weltkrieges* (2nd ed., Berlin, 1920), p. 98 ff.; W. Groener, *Das Testament des Grafen Schlieffen* (Berlin, 1927), pp. 10 ff., 195 ff.; R. Kann, *Le Plan de Campagne allemand de 1914 et son Exécution* (Paris, 1923), p. 26 ff.

the French forces quickly, so that she could then turn against Russia. By going through Belgium it was calculated that a decisive victory—a "Cannae"—could be won within six weeks. On the other hand, to attempt to reach the French armies by striking straight west, without touching the neutralized territories of Luxemburg and Belgium, would take months, on account of the hilly country, the rising escarpments,[111] and the strong lines of defensive forts which France had built since 1870.

Bethmann, with his juristic training and upon the advice of a legal expert in the Foreign Office, wished to keep within the requirements of the Hague Convention of 1907, which declared that hostilities must not commence without previous warning, either in the form of a reasoned declaration of war or an ultimatum with a conditional declaration of war. Compelled to accept the German plan of campaign which provided for an ultimatum to Belgium, demanding passage across her territory, he desired to regularize it by a previous formal declaration of a state of war between Germany and Russia, in case Russia did not accede to an ultimatum to demobilize at once. Falkenhayn, and especially Tirpitz, were opposed to such a declaration of war against Russia. They thought it an unnecessary, foolish and clumsy mistake in diplomatic technique, which would make an unfortunate impression on public opinion and brand Germany before the world as the aggressor.[112] Pourtalès also was of this opinion. The course of events showed that he was right. But, at the moment, Bethmann and Jagow seemed to have believed that

[111] *Cf.* W. M. Davis, *Handbook of Northern France* (Cambridge, 1918), p. 27 ff.

[112] *Cf.* Zwehl, *Erich v. Falkenhayn*, p. 58; Tirpitz, *Politische Dokumente*, II, 11-12; and the communications of H. E. Barnes and B. E. Schmitt, in the *Amer. Hist. Review,* XXXIII, 456-459, January, 1928. Moltke appears to have been indifferent on this question; Bethmann (*Betrachtungen,* I, 156) is correct in saying that Falkenhayn opposed a declaration of war on Russia, but incorrect in saying that he himself was persuaded to it by Moltke.

a violation of Belgian neutrality prior to Germany's being formally at war with Russia would affect world opinion more adversely than a German initiative in declaring war. So Bethmann decided at once to send an ultimatum to Russia and another to Russia's ally.

Pourtalès was therefore informed that Russia's mobilization of her entire army and navy, undertaken while negotiations were still pending, and before Germany had taken any mobilization measures, had compelled Germany to proclaim "Threatening Danger of War." "Mobilization must follow in case Russia does not suspend every war measure against Austria-Hungary and ourselves within twelve hours and make us a distinct declaration to that effect. Please inform Sazonov of this, and telegraph the hour of your communication."[113]

Pourtalès received this message shortly after 11:00 P.M., deciphered it, and delivered it to Sazonov at midnight. Sazonov replied to him, as the Tsar had done, that for technical reasons it was impossible to suspend the mobilization measures.[114]

As the time-limit for Russia's final answer did not expire until noon on August 1, Pourtalès made an effort in another direction. Taking advantage of his personal friendship with Count Fredericks, the Tsar's Minister of the Household, he sent him a letter entreating him to use his influence with the Tsar to prevent the catastrophe of war before it should be too late. The Count saw the Tsar, but Nicholas II could only assure him, as he had assured the Kaiser, that Russian mobilization did not mean war and that he hoped German mobilization did not mean so either.[115]

In the ultimatum to Paris, Baron Schoen was instructed

[113] Bethmann to Pourtalès, July 31, 3:30 P.M., received 11:10 P.M.; K.D., 490.

[114] Pourtalès to Bethmann, Aug. 1, 1:00 A.M.; K.D., 536; Pourtalès, *Am Scheideweg,* pp. 74-76.

[115] K.D., 539, 546; Pourtalès, *Am Scheideweg,* pp. 76-81.

to inform France of the demands which were being made at St. Petersburg, and to say that German mobilization would inevitably mean war. He was to "ask the French Government if it intends to remain neutral in a Russo-German war. Answer must be given within eighteen hours." If, contrary to expectation, France declared its intention to remain neutral, the Ambassador was to demand the turning over of the fortresses of Toul and Verdun to be held as a pledge of neutrality and returned after the completion of the war with Russia.[116]

At 7:00 P.M., when Baron Schoen went to the Quai d'Orsay to carry out these instructions, the French Government had already learned from the French Ambassador in Berlin that Germany had declared "Threatening Danger of War" in consequence of the Russian general mobilization, and that Schoen was about to ask what France's attitude would be.[117] Viviani therefore had had time to consult with Poincaré how he should evade a direct answer. In reply to Schoen's question he simply said: "Let me hope that extreme decisions can be avoided, and permit me to take time to reflect." He promised to give an answer at the expiration of the eighteen hours, that is, on Saturday, August 1, at 1:00 P.M.[118]

Next day, when Schoen came before the expiration of the eighteen hours to repeat his question whether France would remain neutral, Viviani replied: "France will act in accordance with her interests." As he made no promise of neutrality, Schoen naturally said nothing of his secret in-

[116] Bethmann to Schoen, July 31, 3:30 P.M.; K.D., 491.

[117] Jules Cambon to Viviani, July 31, 3:50 P.M., received 4:25 P.M.; omitted from F.Y.B., but printed by Poincaré, IV, 446 f.

[118] Schoen to Bethmann, July 31, 8:17 P.M., received Aug. 1, 12:30 A.M.; K.D., 528. Viviani, *Réponse au Kaiser,* pp. 192 f. Poincaré, IV, 448-451. According to Schoen, Viviani said he had no news of any general mobilization in Russia, only of precautionary measures. According to Viviani, Schoen talked of asking for his passports. The interview was painful but courteous.

structions to ask for Toul and Verdun. The French did not learn of this German intention until they succeeded during the war in deciphering the German telegrams exchanged in July, 1914.[119]

The proclamation of "Threatening Danger of War" had been urged by Moltke and Falkenhayn since the evening of July 29. But Bethmann had held out against it until receiving definite news that Russia had ordered general mobilization. As the Russian order had been given because Sazonov and Ianushkevich had persuaded the Tsar that war was inevitable, so now the Russian mobilization was the decisive fact which at last convinced the civil as well as the military authorities in Germany that war was inevitable. News of the Russian step caused military considerations everywhere (except in England) to take precedence over political considerations, and rendered futile and illusory all the later diplomatic efforts. Some of these efforts were made sincerely but without serious expectation of success; some were only diplomatic gestures calculated to give an appearance of pacific intentions and to throw the odium of responsibility upon the opposing side. Thus, neither the Russian "formula" which Sazonov had proposed to Pourtalès,[120] nor the personal appeal which Pourtalès made in a visit on his own initiative to the Tsar at Peterhof,[121] nor the final exchange of telegrams between "Willy" and "Nicky,"[122] nor Berchtold's pretense of being at last ready to make some concessions,[123] could have any chance of success. As these last diplomatic efforts were futile and illusory, they need not be set forth in detail.

119 Schoen to Bethmann, Aug. 1, 1:05 P. M., received 6:10 P. M.; K.D., 571; *cf.* also 543, 598; Viviani, p. 204; Poincaré, IV, 478 f.

120 See above, ch. x, at note 52.

121 On the early afternoon of July 31; K.D., 535; Pourtalès, *Am Scheideweg,* pp. 64-73.

122 K.D., 480, 487, 546, 600; Schilling's *Diary,* pp. 72 ff., 81 f.

123 See above, at note 94.

MOBILIZATION IN FRANCE AND GERMANY, AUGUST 1

Shortly after Schoen had made his first communication concerning the Russian mobilization and the steps that Germany was forced to take in consequence, the French Government finally received, on July 31, at 8:30 P.M., Paléologue's belated telegram announcing it.[124] This left no doubt that the news of it, which had already come from German sources through Jules Cambon, Schoen, and a telegraph agency, was correct. This news, coupled with that of the German "Threatening Danger of War" received from Cambon, left little doubt in the minds of the French Cabinet that a European War was inevitable. General Joffre demanded the complete mobilization of the eastern army corps. "Every delay of twenty-four hours in calling up reservists and sending the telegram for *couverture* means a retardation of the concentration forces, that is, the initial abandonment of fifteen to twenty kilometers of territory for every day of delay." At 5:00 P.M., therefore, before Schoen came to ask Viviani about French neutrality, the Cabinet decided to order that *couverture,* which had been already ordered with limitations on July 30 in connection with the "10-kilometer withdrawal," should now take place in its fullest extent.[125]

A little later at 1:00 A.M., the Russian Military Attaché at Paris reported to St. Petersburg:

> The French Minister of War has declared to me in a tone of hearty enthusiasm the firm decision of the French Government for War, and begged me to confirm the hope of the French General Staff that all our efforts will be directed against Germany, and that Austria will be treated as a *quantité négligeable.*[126]

[124] See above, ch. x, at note 70.

[125] Poincaré, IV, 458.

[126] Izvolski to Sazonov, July 31 [Aug. 1], 1:00 A.M.; M.F.R., 522; L.N., II, 294.

In the evening occurred the tragic assassination of Jean Jaurès, the veteran socialist leader who had long opposed the policies of M. Poincaré which he feared would some day lead his country into war.[127] There came also the secret assurance from Rome that the Italian Government considered itself freed by Austria's conduct from its Triple Alliance obligations.[128] But Sir Edward Grey continued in a non-committal attitude which was most distressing to Paul Cambon in London and to the French Cabinet in Paris.[129]

Early next morning, Saturday, August 1, General Joffre, surmising that Germany was proceeding to full mobilization under cover of "Threatening Danger of War," declared that he could no longer assume the responsibility of command unless France ordered general mobilization. The Cabinet then authorized the Minister of War to order it before 4 P.M.[130] In view of Schoen's communication and Viviani's answer to it, and in view of a telegram from Paléologue announcing Germany's ultimatum to Russia, it seemed certain that Germany would soon mobilize, even if, as Joffre surmised, she was not already doing so. About 3:45 P.M., after the Minister of War handed over the mobilization order to an officer of the French General Staff, it was immediately telegraphed throughout France in time so that the mobilization could begin next morning.[131]

The telegram from Pourtalès reporting that Sazonov had replied that it was impossible for technical reasons to suspend Russian mobilization had been received in Berlin on August 1 at 12:30 A.M. The time-limit for any further reply expired at noon. Schoen's telegram giving Viviani's final answer, "France will act in accordance with her inter-

127 *Cf.* F. Gouttenoire de Toury, *Jaurès et le Parti de la Guerre*, Paris, 1922. Poincaré, IV, 474 f.

128 Poincaré, IV, 473.

129 *Cf.* Poincaré, IV, 475-478, 486-494.

130 Recouly, p. 81 ff.; Poincaré, IV, 479 f.

131 Recouly, p. 85. *Les Armées françaises*, Tome I, Vol. I, Annexe, No. 21.

ests," did not reach Berlin until 6:10 P.M. But his earlier telegrams made it seem almost certain, as Germany expected, that France would not remain neutral, and certainly not hand over Toul and Verdun to German occupation. Germany therefore ordered mobilization August 1 at 5:00 P.M., quarter of an hour later than France.[132] Germany was the last of the Great Powers to take this final and supreme military measure.

Expecting that Sazonov would maintain his view that Russia could not suspend mobilization and would fail to comply with the ultimatum, Bethmann forwarded to Pourtalès a declaration of war. The Ambassador, receiving it about 6:00 P.M. went at once with it to Sazonov. Three times, with increasing signs of emotion at his painful duty, he asked the Russian Minister of Foreign Affairs whether he could not give him a favorable answer to his request of the day before. Three times Sazonov answered in the negative. "In that case, Sir," said Pourtalès, drawing from his pocket a folded paper, "I am instructed to hand you this note," and gave him the declaration of war.[133] Then losing self-control, the Ambassador went to the window and wept, saying: "I never could have believed that I should quit St. Petersburg under these conditions." He then embraced Sazonov and went away, asking that he be informed at the Embassy concerning his passports and arrangements for his departure, as he was not capable at the moment of talking about anything.[134]

The German declaration of war on France was not made

[132] K.D., 554. French mobilization at 3:45 P.M., French time, was 4:45 P.M. according to German or Central European time.

[133] Bethmann to Pourtalès, August 1, 12:52 P.M.; K.D., 542. Pourtalès to Bethmann, Aug. 1, 8:00 P.M.; K.D., 588; Pourtalès, *Am Scheideweg,* pp. 81-85. The declaration had been drawn up in two alternative forms to accord with Sazonov's possible replies. By an oversight Pourtalès left both forms in the Foreign Minister's hands, as an *aide-mémoire,* but in their agitation neither of the men noticed this fact at the moment.

[134] Schilling's *Diary,* p. 76-78.

until 6:15 P.M. on August 3. It alleged several hostile French acts: French troops had crossed the frontier in the Vosges. "A French aviator, who must have flown across Belgium territory, was shot down yesterday in an attempt to wreck the railroad at Wesel. . . . Yesterday, French airmen dropped bombs on the railroads near Karlsruhe and Nuremberg. Thus France has forced us into war." Schoen was therefore instructed to communicate the foregoing to the French Government, ask for his passports, and turn over the Embassy to the charge of the American Ambassador.[135]

The alleged hostile acts were based on false information which the German Government, in its haste, had taken no care to verify. Furthermore, the despatch to Schoen reached him in a very mutilated form, so that much of it was unintelligible. Though the declaration of war and the grounds for it were such a very serious matter, Schoen did not feel justified in taking the necessary time to get from Berlin a complete and exact text of the mutilated document. He had been told to deliver the declaration at 6:00 P.M. Bethmann again wished to be formally correct in notifying a state of war before the German forces crossed the frontier into France, as they were about to do in accordance with the pre-arranged and all-important plan of campaign.

Schoen therefore put together, as best he could, a declaration of war based on his mutilated telegram, and handed it in to Viviani. It contained the untrue allegations as to the French aviators over Wesel, Karlsruhe and Nuremberg.[136]

[135] Bethmann to Schoen, Aug. 3, 1:05 P.M., received 4:15 P.M. (German time, 5:15 P.M.); K.D., 734.

[136] K.D., 734, a, b. Poincaré, IV, 520 ff. Montgelas, *Leitfaden*, p 182 f. Renouvin, pp. 237-248 (Eng. trans., pp. 264-276).

ENGLAND AND BELGIUM

In spite of Paul Cambon's appeal to Grey on July 30, recalling their exchange of notes in 1912,[137] and in spite of a personal entreaty which President Poincaré sent by special messenger to King George on the afternoon of July 31,[138] the British Foreign Secretary still remained unwilling to give any pledge to France. As Grey notified the British Ambassador in Paris:

> I went on to say to M. Cambon that though we should have to put our policy before Parliament, we could not pledge Parliament in advance. Up to the present moment, we did not feel, and public opinion did not feel, that any treaties or obligations of this country were involved. Further developments might alter this situation and cause the Government and Parliament to take the view that intervention was justified. The preservation of the neutrality of Belgium might be, I would not say a decisive, but an important factor, in determining our attitude. . . .
>
> M. Cambon expressed great disappointment at my reply. He repeated his question of whether we would help France if Germany made an attack on her.
>
> I said that I could only adhere to the answer that, as far as things had gone at present, we could not take any engagement. *The latest news was that Russia had ordered a complete mobilization of her fleet and army. This, it seemed to me, would precipitate a crisis, and would make it appear that German mobilization was being forced by Russia.*[139]

Sir Arthur Nicolson and Sir Eyre Crowe, however, were strongly urging that "the whole policy of the Entente can

137 See above, at notes 11-13.

138 *Cf.* B.D., 366; and Poincaré, IV, 437-440.

139 Grey to Bertie, July 31; B.D., 367; and Paul Cambon's reports, in Poincaré, IV, 440-442, 475-478. The words in Italics were suppressed from the *British Blue Book* of 1914 (No. 119). They show that Grey realized the truth, but allowed it to be suppressed in order to support the Franco-Russian effort to minimize the importance of Russia's step.

have no meaning if it does not signify that in a just quarrel England would stand by her friends. This honorable expectation has been raised. We cannot repudiate it without exposing our good name to grave criticism." [140]

Sir Edward Grey knew that the Cabinet was still sharply divided on the question of British participation in a European War. He was therefore taking care to be extremely cautious in avoiding any commitments to France until opinion in the Cabinet and in Parliament should be brought more decisively to the side of France by some new fact, such as a German ultimatum to France or a refusal to respect the neutrality of Belgium. This latter possibility had been revealed to him in connection with Bethmann's "bid" for British neutrality, lighting up "like a searchlight" a new aspect of the situation.[141]

On Friday, July 31, the day after receiving Bethmann's "bid," Grey decided to clarify the Belgian question by addressing to the French and German Governments a request asking each for an assurance that it would respect the neutrality of Belgium so long as no other Power violated it.[142] He also informed the Brussels Government of this step, and added: "I assume that Belgium will to the utmost of her power maintain neutrality, and desire and expect other Powers to observe and uphold it." [143]

France at once gave an unqualified assurance in the affirmative.[144] But at Berlin Jagow told the British Ambassador that he could not possibly reply without consulting Bethmann and the Kaiser. "He rather doubted whether

140 Crowe's memorandum, July 31; B.D., 369; *cf.* also 368, and Minutes on 382, 383.

141 See above, at notes 42-45.

142 Grey to Bertie and Goschen, July 31, 5:30 P.M., B.D., 348. This step was decided upon at a Cabinet meeting in the morning, before he heard of the Russian mobilization and the consequent German "Threatening Danger of War"; *cf.* Cambon to Viviani, July 31, 8:40 P.M. (Poincaré, IV, 442).

143 Grey to Villiers, July 31, 6:15 P.M.; B.D., 351.

144 Bertie to Grey, Aug. 1, 1:12 A.M., received 2:15 A.M., B.D., 382.

they could answer at all, as any reply they might give could not fail, in the event of war, to have the undesirable effect of disclosing to a certain extent part of their plan of campaign."[145]

Already, however, on this same Friday, before hearing the dubious German reply in regard to Belgium, Sir Edward Grey determined in his own mind, in agreement with Nicolson and Crowe, that England's obligation of honor to France and her own material interests made it imperative for her to intervene on the Franco-Russian side. In the morning he had told the German Ambassador that if Germany could get any reasonable proposal put forward which made it clear that Germany and Austria were striving to preserve European peace, he would support it and go to the length of saying that, if France and Russia would not accept it, he would have nothing more to do with the consequences. "But, otherwise," he warned Lichnowsky, "if France became involved, we should be drawn in." [146] He told Cambon confidentially of this statement to Lichnowsky, but carefully explained that this "was not the same thing as taking an engagement to France," and that he could not pledge Parliament in advance.[147] Cambon could only inform Paris that Grey, "who is a partizan of immediate intervention," would discuss the matter again with the Cabinet next morning.[148]

On August 1, Cambon, knowing of Germany's ultimatums and of the French intention to order mobilization,[149] renewed his appeals to Grey. He urged very strongly the British obligation to help France, both on account of the withdrawal of the French fleet to the Mediterranean, leaving the northern coast undefended except for British assis-

145 Goschen to Grey, Aug. 1, 2 A.M., received 3:30 A.M.; B.D., 383.

146 Grey to Goschen, July 31, 2:45 P.M.; B.D., 340; *cf.* K.D., 489, 496, 497.

147 Grey to Bertie, July 31; B.D., 367. Poincaré, IV, 440 f.

148 Cambon to Viviani, July 31, 8:40 P.M.; Poincaré, IV, 442.

149 Poincaré, IV, 486.

tance, and on account of British interest. "If we [English] do not help France," Cambon said, "the Entente would disappear; and, whether victory came to Germany, or to France and Russia, our situation at the end of the war would be very uncomfortable." But Grey replied there was no obligation. That if France were forced into a war against her wish, it was because of her alliance with Russia. England had purposely kept clear of alliances in order not to be involved in this way. "This did not mean that under no circumstances would we assist France, but it did mean that France must take her own decision at this moment without reckoning on an assistance that we were not now in a position to promise." Cambon answered in dismay that he could not transmit this reply to his Government, and asked to be authorized to answer that the British Cabinet had not yet come to any decision. To mitigate Cambon's disappointment, Grey then said that the appearance of a German fleet in the English Channel and an attack on the French coasts, or a violation of Belgium might alter public opinion in England, and that he would bring these questions before the Cabinet next morning. Meanwhile Cambon might report that no decision had been taken.[150]

August 2 was the "Sunday of Resolve" for England. The Cabinet sat almost continuously all day. In the morning it was still too uncertain as to British opinion and too divided against itself to come to a decision. Until luncheon-time the danger that a considerable minority would resign from the Cabinet and thereby greatly weaken the Government at a critical moment, still caused the majority to hesitate, in spite of the arrival of news that German troops had entered Luxemburg.[151] The neutrality of Belgium, as Grey

150 Grey to Bertie, Aug. 1, 8:20 P.M., and letter Aug. 1; B.D., 426, 447. Cambon to Viviani, Aug. 1; Poincaré, IV, 487.

151 Villiers to Grey, Aug. 2, 10:50 A.M., received 11:45 A.M.; B.D., 465; *cf.* also 466-468, 472. P. Cambon appears to have received the news at 8:00 A.M., but did not discuss it with Grey until 3:00 P.M. (*cf.* C. F

told Cambon in the afternoon, "was a much more important matter"[152] than the neutrality of Luxemburg. The violation of the latter did not of itself bring a decisive change in the attitude of the Cabinet. The decisive fact was that about noon a letter was brought from Mr. Bonar Law, the leader of the Unionist Party, assuring the Cabinet of support of his followers in Parliament. Such support had already been intimated unofficially to Winston Churchill in a letter three days earlier from another prominent Unionist, Mr. F. E. Smith, later Lord Birkenhead.[153] But Mr. Bonar Law's letter might be regarded as official, and represented the expressed view of a number of most important Unionist leaders, including Lord Lansdowne, who had hurried up to London to make his influence felt. Mr. Bonar Law's letter was as follows:

> 2nd August, 1914.
>
> Dear Mr. Asquith,—Lord Lansdowne and I feel it our duty to inform you that, in our opinion, as well as in that of all the colleagues whom we have been able to consult, it would be fatal to the honor and security of the United Kingdom to hesitate in supporting France and Russia at the present juncture; and we offer our unhesitating support to the Government in any measures that they may consider necessary for that object.[154]

Roux, in *Revue des Deux Mondes,* Aug. 15, 1926. The violation of Luxemburg was regarded by Sir Edward Grey as a much less important matter than that of Belgium, partly because Luxemburg did not lie on the English channel, and partly because Luxemburg's neutrality was secured by a "collective guarantee," and Belgian neutrality by an "individual guarantee." In the case of the former, a breach of the guarantee by one of the guarantors might be regarded as liberating the other guarantors from their obligations; not so, in the case of an "individual guarantee," in which each guarantor remained obligated independently of the action of the others. (*cf.* Grey, II, 3-10; and E. C. Stowell, *The Diplomacy of the War of 1914* (Boston, 1915), pp. 376 ff., 422 ff., 600 ff.).

152 Grey to Bertie, Aug. 2, 4:45 P.M.; B.D., 487.

153 Churchill, *The World Crisis,* I, p. 215 f.

154 First published in the London *Times,* Dec. 15, 1914, with some explanatory remarks by Mr. Bonar Law; *cf.* also Lord Loreburn, *How the War Came,* p. 210; and Mr. L. J. Maxse, in *The National Review,* Aug. 1918.

Upon the receipt of this promise of support Grey and the Cabinet determined to give Cambon the assurance concerning the north coast of France about which he had asked the day before. So, about 3 P.M., Grey informed the French Ambassador that "if the German fleet comes into the Channel or through the North Sea to undertake hostile operations against the French coasts or shipping, the British fleet will give all the protection in its power." [155] This assurance was still subject to approval by Parliament, Grey added, and did not mean that England would send troops to France. It was merely a promise to make war against Germany, contingent upon a hypothetical action by the German fleet. It looked, however, like war, and led Lord Morley and Mr. John Burns to resign from the Cabinet. It gave also much comfort to the French, even though it did not go as far as they had hoped. The assurance was given before Germany presented her ultimatum to Belgium, news of which did not reach London until the morning of August 3.

About 7 P.M. on August 2 the German Minister at Brussels had handed to Mr. Davignon, the Belgian Minister of Foreign Affairs, the German demands drawn up by Moltke on July 26 and forwarded from Berlin on July 29 in a sealed envelope within a sealed envelope.[156] It stated that Germany "is in receipt of reliable information relating to the proposed advance of French armed forces along the Meuse, route Givet-Namur. They leave no doubt as to France's intention to advance against Germany through Belgian territory." As it was to be feared that Belgium would be unable, unaided, to resist the French advance, and as "it is for Germany a dictate of self-preservation that she anticipate the hostile attack," Germany regretted that she would be forced to enter upon Belgian soil. She con-

[155] Grey to Bertie, Aug. 2, 4:45 P.M.; B.D., 487.

[156] See above at note 49.

templated no hostile activities against Belgium. If the Kingdom adopted "a benevolent neutrality toward Germany," the German Government promised at the conclusion of peace to guarantee Belgium's sovereign rights and independence, to evacuate the territory, to buy for cash all the necessities required by her troops, and to make good every damage which they might cause. But should Belgium oppose German troops, or destroy railroads and tunnels, "Germany would be obliged, to her regret, to regard the Kingdom as an enemy." An unequivocal reply was demanded within twelve hours.[157]

Mr. Davignon instantly notified King Albert. A Cabinet meeting was called and sat till past midnight. It was unanimous that Belgium's honor and interests demanded the rejection of the German demand. No German "strategic interest" could justify "a violation of international law." "The Belgian Government, if it were to accept the proposals submitted to it, would sacrifice the honor of the nation and at the same time betray its duty toward Europe." It was therefore "firmly resolved to repel by all means in its power every attack upon its rights." Such was the brave reply which the little Kingdom gave to the German Minister at 7 A.M. on August 3.[158]

Mr. Davignon on the morning of August 3 at once notified the Powers of Germany's ultimatum and its rejection, but did not immediately appeal to the Guaranteeing Powers for support.[159] He was not at first convinced, according to

[157] Jagow to Below, July 29 and Aug. 2; K.D., 376, 648. The German Minister at Brussels was instructed to make certain changes in the original ultimatum, omitting the clause that Germany "will even be prepared to favor with the best of good will any possible claims of the Kingdom for territorial compensation at the expense of France," shortening the time-limit for an answer from twenty-four to twelve hours, and post-dating the ultimatum to make it appear that it had just been received.

[158] B.G.B. [*Belgian Gray Book*], 22; and K.D., 779.

[159] B.G.B., 23, 24; B.D., 521, 551, 562.

the British Minister,[160] that there was real danger from Germany, and wished, in case of aggression, to show that the Belgians were able to defend themselves. Accordingly, on August 3, King Albert merely appealed to King George for "diplomatic intervention" to safeguard the neutrality of Belgium.[161]

The news of the German ultimatum to Belgium and its categorical rejection reached Sir Edward Grey toward noon on Monday, August 3,[162] shortly before he was to make his speech in Parliament announcing the British decision to oppose by force any German attack on the north coast of France. It enabled him to bring forward more effectively the question of Belgian neutrality, which he knew would be one which would strongly affect British public opinion toward the policy which he himself was already convinced in his own mind that England ought to follow. He had little time, in the midst of reading telegrams and hurried interviews with Ambassadors and others, for composing a formal speech.[163] But what he said in the House of Commons on the afternoon of August 3 is eloquent in its simplicity and in the tragic seriousness of the subject.

Sir Edward Grey began his speech with the question of Britain's obligations to France, sketching the development of the system of alliances from the time of the first Morocco Crisis, and giving the House its first knowledge of the Anglo-French military and naval conversations and the exchange of notes in 1912. He insisted that "whatever took place between the military and naval experts, they were not binding engagements upon the Government." "We do not construe anything which has previously taken place in our diplomatic relations with other Powers in this matter as

[160] Villiers to Nicolson, Aug. 12; B.D., 670.

[161] B.G.B., 25.

[162] Villiers to Grey, Aug. 3, 9:31 A.M., received 10:55 A.M.; B.D., 521.

[163] *Cf.*, Grey, II, 10-18; the speech is reprinted, *ibid.*, pp. 308-326. For trenchant criticisms, see H. Lutz, *Lord Grey and the World War*, and Count Montgelas, *British Policy under Sir Edward Grey*, N. Y., 1928.

restricting the freedom of the Government to decide what attitude they should now take, or restrict the freedom of the House of Commons to decide what their attitude should be." He then spoke of the transfer of the French fleet to the Mediterranean to take the place of the British fleet transferred to home waters, and of the assurance given to M. Cambon the day before.

Finally he came to the question of Belgian neutrality. He referred very effectively to Germany's refusal to give an unequivocal promise to respect it, to the German ultimatum to Belgium and its rejection, and to the appeal of King Albert for "diplomatic intervention." If Belgium lost her independence, then Holland and Denmark would lose theirs; and if France were beaten to her knees and lost her position as a Great Power, England would be faced by the "unmeasured aggrandizement" of Germany. Forestalling the argument that England might stand aside, husband her strength, and intervene at the end to protect her interests, he added:

> If, in a crisis like this, we run away from those obligations of honour and interest as regards the Belgian Treaty, I doubt whether, whatever material force we might have at the end, it would be of very much value in face of the respect that we should have lost. . . . I do not believe, for a moment, that at the end of this war, even if we stood aside and remained aside, we should be in a position, a material position, to use our force decisively to undo what had happened in the course of the war, to prevent the whole of the West of Europe opposite to us—if that had been the result of the war—falling under the domination of a single Power, and I am quite sure that our moral position would be such as to have lost us all respect. I can only say that I have put the question of Belgium somewhat hypothetically, because I am not yet sure of all the facts, but, if the facts turn out to be as they have reached us at present, it is quite clear that there is an obligation on this country to do its

utmost to prevent the consequences to which those facts will lead if they are undisputed.[164]

Grey did not ask the House of Commons for definite endorsement of any precise measures. He was merely skilfully informing them of what he had done so far, assuring them that his hands were still free and that it was for Parliament to decide; but at the same time he persuasively placed before them his own conviction that England ought not to stand aside. The applause with which his speech was greeted left no doubt that Parliament would support him. After the speech and the Cabinet meeting in the evening, Grey confided to Cambon that the Cabinet had decided next morning to send instructions to the British Ambassador in Berlin to demand that the German ultimatum to Belgium be withdrawn. "If they refuse," added Grey, "there will be war."[165]

The Cabinet's decision was strengthened next day, August 4, by news that the Germans had actually violated Belgian territory. At 2 P.M. Sir Edward Grey sent the ultimatum to Berlin. He mentioned Germany's ultimatum to Belgium and the report that "Belgian territory has been violated at Gemmenich." "In these circumstances, and in view of the fact that Germany declined to give the same assurance respecting Belgium as France gave last week in reply to our request," Grey repeated his request, and asked that a satisfactory reply be received in London by midnight. Otherwise, Sir Edward Goschen was to ask for his passports, and the British Embassy was to be turned over to the care of the American Ambassador.[166]

Sir Edward Goschen took the ultimatum to the German Foreign Office about 7 P.M. Jagow told him that no such assurance as requested could be given. He had already

164 Grey II, 321-322.

165 Cambon to Viviani, Aug. 4, 12:17 A.M.; Poincaré, IV, 519 f.

166 Grey to Goschen, August 4, 2 P.M. and 5 P.M.; B.D., 594, 615

explained to Goschen earlier in the day that Germany had been compelled by strategic necessity to go through Belgium to reach France in the quickest and easiest way—that it was a matter of life and death for her. Goschen then said he should like to go and see the Chancellor as it might be his last opportunity. Goschen's narrative continues:

> I found the Chancellor very agitated. His Excellency at once began a harangue which lasted for about 20 minutes. He said that the step taken by His Majesty's Government was terrible to a degree, just for a word "neutrality" a word which in war time had so often been disregarded—just for a scrap of paper, Great Britain was going to make war on a kindred nation who desired nothing better than to be friends with her. All his efforts in that direction had been rendered useless by this last terrible step, and the policy to which, as I knew, he had devoted himself since his accession to office, had tumbled down like a house of cards. . . . I said that in the same way as he and Herr von Jagow wished me to understand that for strategical reasons it was a matter of life and death to Germany to advance through Belgium and violate her neutrality, so I would wish him to understand that it was, so to speak, a matter of "life and death" for the honor of Great Britain that she should keep her solemn engagement to do her utmost to defend Belgium's neutrality if attacked. That solemn compact simply had to be kept, or what confidence could anyone have in engagements given by Great Britain in the future? The Chancellor said "But at what price will that compact have been kept. Has the British Government thought of that?" I hinted to his Excellency as plainly as I could that fear of consequences could hardly be regarded as an excuse for breaking solemn engagements, but his Excellency was so excited, so evidently overcome by the news of our action and so little disposed to hear reason, that I refrained from adding fuel to the flame by further argument. As I was leaving he said that the blow of Great Britain joining Germany's enemies was all

> the greater that almost up to the last moment he and his Government had been working with us and supporting our efforts to maintain peace between Austria and Russia. I admitted that that had been the case, and said that it was part of the tragedy which saw the two nations fall apart just at the moment when the relations between them had been more friendly and cordial than they had been for years.[167]

As the clock struck midnight and no satisfactory answer had been given to Goschen, Germany and England were at war.

The Sarajevo spark had started the fire which had now spread over Europe. Serbia and the Great Powers were involved in a life and death struggle.

167 Goschen to Grey, Aug. 6; B.D., 671; see also 666, 667.

CHAPTER XII

CONCLUSION

None of the Powers wanted a European War. Their governing rulers and ministers, with very few exceptions, all foresaw that it must be a frightful struggle, in which the political results were not absolutely certain, but in which the loss of life, suffering, and economic consequences were bound to be terrible. This is true, in a greater or less degree, of Pashitch, Berchtold, Bethmann, Sazonov, Poincaré, San Giuliano and Sir Edward Grey. Yet none of them, not even Sir Edward Grey, could have foreseen that the political results were to be so stupendous, and the other consequences so terrible, as was actually the case.

For many of the Powers, to be sure, a European War might seem to hold out the possibility of achieving various desired advantages: for Serbia, the achievement of national unity for all Serbs; for Austria, the revival of her waning prestige as a Great Power, and the checking of nationalistic tendencies which threatened her very existence; for Russia, the accomplishment of her historic mission of controlling Constantinople and the Straits; for Germany, new economic advantages and the restoration of the European balance which had changed with the weakening of the Triple Alliance and the tightening of the Triple Entente; for France, the recovery of Alsace-Lorraine and the ending of the German menace; and for England, the destruction of the German naval danger and of Prussian militarism. All these advantages, and many others, were feverishly striven and intrigued for, on all sides, the moment the War actually broke out, but this is no good proof that any of the statesmen mentioned deliberately aimed to bring about a war to secure these advantages. One cannot judge the motives which actuated men before the War, by what they did in an absolutely new situation which arose as soon as they were overtaken by a conflagration they had sought to avert. And in fact, in the case of the two Powers between whom the immediate conflict arose, the postponement or avoidance of a European War would have facilitated the accomplishment of the ultimate advantages aimed at: Pashitch knew that there was a better chance for Serbian national unity after he had consolidated Serbian gains in the Balkan Wars, and after Russia had completed her military and naval armaments as planned for 1917; and Berchtold knew that he had a better chance of crushing the Greater Serbia danger and strengthening Austria, if he could avoid Russian intervention and a general European War.

It is also true, likewise, that the moment war was declared, it was hailed with varying demonstrations of enthusiasm on the part of the people in every country—with considerable in Serbia, Austria, Russia and Germany, with less in France, and with almost none in England. But this does not mean that the peoples wanted war or exerted a decisive influence to bring it about. It is a curious psychological phenomenon that as soon as a country engages in war, there develops or is created among the masses a frenzy of patriotic excitement which is no index of their pre-war desires. And in the countries where the demonstrations of enthusiasm were greatest, the political influence of the people on the Government was least.

Nevertheless, a European War broke out. Why? Because in each country political and military leaders did certain things, which led to mobilizations and declarations of war, or failed to do certain things which might have prevented them. In this sense, all the European countries, in a greater or less degree, were responsible. One must abandon the dictum of the Versailles Treaty that Germany and her allies were solely responsible. It was a dictum exacted by victors from vanquished, under the influence of the blindness, ignorance, hatred, and the propagandist misconceptions to which war had given rise. It was based on evidence which was incomplete and not always sound.[1] It is generally recognized by the best historical scholars in all countries to be no longer tenable or defensible. They are agreed that the responsibility for the War is a divided responsibility. But they still disagree very much as to the relative part of this responsibility that falls on each country and on each individual political or military leader.

Some writers like to fix positively in some precise mathematical fashion the exact responsibility for the war. This was done in one way by the framers of Article 231 of the Treaty of Versailles. It has been done in other ways by those who would fix the responsibility in some relative fashion, as, for instance, Austria first, then Russia, France and Germany and England. But the present writer deprecates such efforts to assess by a precise formula a very complicated question, which is after all more a matter of delicate shading than of definite white and black. Oversimplification, as Napoleon once said in framing his Code, is the enemy of precision. Moreover, even supposing that a general consensus of opinion might be reached as to the relative responsibility of any individual country or man for immediate causes connected with the July crisis of 1914, it is by no means necessarily true that the same relative responsibility would hold for the underlying causes, which

[1] For a recent analysis of the evidence laid before the Commission on Responsibility for the War at the Paris Peace Conference, and the untenability of the conclusions based upon it, see A. von Wegerer, "Die Wiederlegung der Versailles Kriegsschuldthese," in *Die Kriegsschuldfrage,* VI, 1-77, Jan., 1928; also his article, with replies to it, in *Current History,* Aug., 1928, pp. 810-828.

for years had been tending toward the creation of a dangerous situation.

One may, however, sum up very briefly the most salient facts in regard to each country.

Serbia felt a natural and justifiable impulse to do what so many other countries had done in the nineteenth century—to bring under one national Government all the discontented Serb people. She had liberated those under Turkish rule; the next step was to liberate those under Hapsburg rule. She looked to Russia for assistance, and had been encouraged to expect that she would receive it. After the assassination, Mr. Pashitch took no steps to discover and bring to justice Serbians in Belgrade who had been implicated in the plot. One of them, Ciganovitch, was even assisted to disappear. Mr. Pashitch waited to see what evidence the Austrian authorities could find. When Austria demanded coöperation of Austrian officials in discovering, though not in trying, implicated Serbians, the Serbian Government made a very conciliatory but negative reply. They expected that the reply would not be regarded as satisfactory, and, even before it was given, ordered the mobilization of the Serbian army. Serbia did not want war, but believed it would be forced upon her. That Mr. Pashitch was aware of the plot three weeks before it was executed, failed to take effective steps to prevent the assassins from crossing over from Serbia to Bosnia, and then failed to give Austria any warning or information which might have averted the fatal crime, were facts unknown to Austria in July, 1914; they cannot therefore be regarded as in any way justifying Austria's conduct; but they are part of Serbia's responsibility, and a very serious part.

Austria was more responsible for the immediate origin of the war than any other Power. Yet from her own point of view she was acting in self-defence—not against an immediate military attack, but against the corroding Greater

Serbia and Jugoslav agitation which her leaders believed threatened her very existence. No State can be expected to sit with folded arms and await dismemberment at the hands of its neighbors. Russia was believed to be intriguing with Serbia and Rumania against the Dual Monarchy. The assassination of the heir to the throne, as a result of a plot prepared in Belgrade, demanded severe retribution; otherwise Austria would be regarded as incapable of action, "worm-eaten" as the Serbian Press expressed it, would sink in prestige, and hasten her own downfall. To avert this Berchtold determined to crush Serbia with war. He deliberately framed the ultimatum with the expectation and hope that it would be rejected. He hurriedly declared war against Serbia in order to forestall all efforts at mediation. He refused even to answer his own ally's urgent requests to come to an understanding with Russia, on the basis of a military occupation of Belgrade as a pledge that Serbia would carry out the promises in her reply to the ultimatum. Berchtold gambled on a "local" war with Serbia only, believing that he could rattle the German sword; but rather than abandon his war with Serbia, he was ready to drag the rest of Europe into war.

It is very questionable whether Berchtold's obstinate determination to diminish Serbia and destroy her as a Balkan factor was, after all, the right method, even if he had succeeded in keeping the war "localized" and in temporarily strengthening the Dual Monarchy. Supposing that Russia in 1914, because of military unpreparedness or lack of support, had been ready to tolerate the execution of Berchtold's designs, it is quite certain that she would have aimed within the next two or three years at wiping out this second humiliation, which was so much more damaging to her prestige than that of 1908-09. In two or three years, when her great program of military reform was finally completed, Russia would certainly have found a pretext to reverse the balance in the Balkans in her own favor again. A further consequence of Berchtold's policy, even if successful, would have been the still closer consolidation of the Triple Entente, with the possible addition of Italy. And, finally, a partially dismembered Serbia would have become a still greater source of unrest and danger to the peace of Europe than heretofore. Serbian nationalism, like Polish nationalism, would have been intensified by partition. Austrian power and prestige would not have been so greatly increased as to be able to meet these new dangers. Berchtold's plan was a mere temporary improvement, but could not be a final solution of the Austro-Serbian antagonism. Franz Ferdinand and many others recognized this, and so long as he lived, no step in this fatal direction had been taken. It was the tragic fate of Austria that the only man who might have had the power and ability to develop Austria along sound lines became the innocent victim of the crime which was the occasion of the World War and so of her ultimate disruption.

Germany did not plot a European War, did not want one, and made genuine, though too belated efforts, to avert one. She was the victim of her alliance with Austria and of her own folly. Austria was her only dependable ally, Italy and Rumania having become nothing but allies in name. She could not throw her over, as otherwise she would stand isolated between Russia, where Panslavism and armaments were growing stronger every year, and France, where Alsace-Lorraine, Delcassé's fall, and Agadir were not forgotten. Therefore, Bethmann felt bound to accede to Berchtold's request for support and gave him a free hand to deal with Serbia; he also hoped and expected to "localize" the Austro-Serbian conflict. Germany then gave grounds to the Entente for suspecting the sincerity of her peaceful intentions by her denial of any foreknowledge of the ultimatum, by her support and justification of it when it was published, and by her refusal of Sir Edward Grey's conference proposal. However, Germany by no means had Austria so completely under her thumb as the Entente Powers and many writers have assumed. It is true that Berchtold would hardly have embarked on his gambler's policy unless he had been assured that Germany would fulfil the obligations of the alliance, and to this extent Germany must share the great responsibility of Austria. But when Bethmann realized that Russia was likely to intervene, that England might not remain neutral, and that there was danger of a world war of which Germany and Austria would appear to be the instigators, he tried to call a halt on Austria, but it was too late. He pressed mediation proposals on Vienna, but Berchtold was insensible to the pressure, and the Entente Powers did not believe in the sincerity of his pressure, especially as they produced no results.

Germany's geographical position between France and Russia, and her inferiority in number of troops, had made necessary the plan of crushing the French army quickly at first and then turning against Russia. This was only possible, in the opinion of her strategists, by marching through Belgium, as it was generally anticipated by military men that she would do in case of a European War. On July 29, after Austria had declared war on Serbia, and after the Tsar had assented to general mobilization in Russia (though this was not known in Berlin and was later postponed for a day owing to the Kaiser's telegram to the Tsar), Bethmann took the precaution of sending to the German Minister in Brussels a sealed envelope. The Minister was not to open it except on further instructions. It contained the later demand for the passage of the German army through Belgium. This does not mean, however, that Germany had decided for war. In fact, Bethmann was one of the last of the statesmen to abandon hope of peace and to consent to the mobilization of his country's army. General mobilization of the continental armies took place in the following order: Serbia, Russia, Austria, France and Germany. General mobilization by a Great Power was commonly interpreted by military men in every country, though perhaps not by Sir Edward Grey, the Tsar, and some civilian officials, as meaning that the country was on the point of making war,—that the military machine had begun to move and would not be stopped. Hence, when Germany learned of the Russian general mobilization, she sent ultimatums to St. Petersburg and Paris, warning that German mobilization would follow unless Russia suspended hers within twelve hours, and asking what would be the attitude of France. The answers being unsatisfactory, Germany then mobilized and declared war. It was the hasty Russian general mobilization, assented to on July 29 and ordered on July 30, while Germany was still trying to bring Austria to accept mediation proposals, which finally rendered the European War inevitable.

Russia was partly responsible for the Austro-Serbian conflict because of the frequent encouragement which she had given at Belgrade—that Serbian national unity would be ultimately achieved with Russian assistance at Austrian expense. This had led the Belgrade Cabinet to hope for Russian support in case of a war with Austria, and the hope did not prove vain in July, 1914. Before this, to be sure, in the Bosnian Crisis and during the Balkan Wars, Russia had put restraint upon Serbia, because Russia, exhausted by the effects of the Russo-Japanese War, was not yet ready for a European struggle with the Teutonic Powers. But in 1914 her armaments, though not yet completed, had made such progress that the militarists were confident of success, if they had French and British support. In the spring of 1914, the Minister of War, Sukhomlinov, had published an article in a Russian newspaper, though without signing his name, to the effect, "Russia is ready, France must be ready also." Austria was convinced that Russia would ultimately aid Serbia, unless the Serbian danger were dealt with energetically after the Archduke's murder; she knew that Russia was growing stronger every year; but she doubted whether the Tsar's armaments had yet reached the point at which Russia would dare to intervene; she would therefore run less risk of Russian intervention and a European War if she used the Archduke's assassination as an excuse for weakening Serbia, than if she should postpone action until the future.

Russia's responsibility lay also in the secret preparatory military measures which she was making at the same time that she was carrying on diplomatic negotiations. These alarmed Germany and Austria. But it was primarily Russia's general mobilization, made when Germany was trying to bring Austria to a settlement, which precipitated the final catastrophe, causing Germany to mobilize and declare war.

The part of France is less clear than that of the other Great Powers, because she has not yet made a full publication of her documents. To be sure, M. Poincaré, in the fourth volume of his memoirs, has made a skilful and elaborate plea, to prove "*La France innocente.*" But he is not convincing. It is quite clear that on his visit to Russia he assured the Tsar's Government that France would support her as an ally in preventing Austria from humiliating or crushing Serbia. Paléologue renewed these assurances in a way to encourage Russia to take a strong hand. He did not attempt to restrain Russia from military measures which he knew would call forth German counter-measures and cause war. Nor did he keep his Government promptly and fully informed of the military steps which were being taken at St. Petersburg. President Poincaré, upon his return to France, made efforts for peace, but his great preoccupation was to minimize French and Russian preparatory measures and emphasize those of Germany, in order to secure the certainty of British support in a struggle which he now regarded as inevitable.

Sir Edward Grey made many sincere proposals for preserving peace; they all failed owing partly, but not exclusively, to Germany's attitude. Sir Edward could probably have prevented war if he had done either of two things. If, early in the crisis, he had acceded to the urging of France and Russia and given a strong warning to Germany that, in a European War, England would take the side of the Franco-Russian Alliance, this would probably have led Bethmann to exert an earlier and more effective pressure on Austria; and it would perhaps thereby have prevented the Austrian declaration of war on Serbia, and brought to a successful issue the "direct conversations" between Vienna and St. Petersburg. Or, if Sir Edward Grey had listened to German urging, and warned France and Russia early in the crisis, that if they became involved in war, England would remain neutral, probably Russia would have hesitated with her mobilizations, and France would probably have exerted a restraining influence at St. Petersburg. But Sir Edward Grey could not say that England would take the side of France and Russia, because he had a Cabinet nearly evenly divided, and he was not sure, early in the crisis, that public opinion in England would back him up in war against Germany. He could resign, and he says in his memoirs that he would have resigned, but that would have been no comfort or aid to France, who had come confidently to count upon British support He was determined to say and do nothing which might encourage her with a hope which he could not fulfil. Therefore, in spite of the pleadings of the French, he refused to give them definite assurances until the probable German determination to go through Belgium made it clear that the Cabinet, and Parliament, and British public opinion would follow his lead in war on Germany. On the other hand, he was unwilling to heed the German pleadings that he exercise restraint at Paris and St. Petersburg, because he did not wish to endanger the Anglo-Russian Entente and the solidarity of the Triple Entente, because he felt a moral obligation to France, growing out of the Anglo-French military and naval conversations of the past years, and because he suspected that Germany was backing Austria up in an unjustifiable course and that Prussian militarists had taken the direction of affairs at Berlin out of the hands of Herr von Bethmann-Hollweg and the civilian authorities.

Italy exerted relatively little influence on the crisis in either direction.

Belgium had done nothing in any way to justify the demand which Germany made upon her. With commendable prudence, at the very first news of the ominous Austrian ultimatum, she had foreseen the danger to which she might be exposed. She had accordingly instructed her representatives abroad as to the statements which they were to make in case Belgium should decide very suddenly to mobilize to protect her neutrality. On July 29, she placed her army upon "a strengthened war footing," but did not order complete mobilization until two days later, when Austria, Russia, and Germany had already done so, and war appeared inevitable. Even after being confronted with the terrible German ultimatum, at 7 P.M. on August 2, she did not at once invite the assistance of English and French troops to aid her in the defense of her soil and her neutrality against a certain German assault; it was not until German troops had actually violated her territory, on August 4, that she appealed for the assistance of the Powers which had guaranteed her neutrality. Belgium was the innocent victim of German strategic necessity. Though the German violation of Belgium was of enormous influence in forming public opinion as to the responsibility for the War after hostilities began, it was not a cause of the War, except in so far as it made it easier for Sir Edward Grey to bring England into it.

In the forty years following the Franco-Prussian War, as we have seen, there developed a system of alliances which divided Europe into two hostile groups. This hostility was accentuated by the increase of armaments, economic rivalry, nationalist ambitions and antagonisms, and newspaper incitement. But it is very doubtful whether all these dangerous tendencies would have actually led to war, had it not been for the assassination of Franz Ferdinand. That was the factor which consolidated the elements of hostility and started the rapid and complicated succession of events which culminated in a World War, and for that factor Serbian nationalism was primarily responsible.

But the verdict of the Versailles Treaty that Germany and her allies were responsible for the War, in view of the evidence now available, is historically unsound. It should therefore be revised. However, because of the popular feeling widespread in some of the Entente countries, it is doubtful whether a formal and legal revision is as yet practicable. There must first come a further revision by historical scholars, and through them of public opinion.

INDEX